GREAT B[ritain]

POSTAL HI[STORY]
and STAMPS
to 1930

Postal History from 1300 and Fine Stamps from Queen Victoria to King George V

YOUR WANTS LIST IS WELCOME!

BUYING Collections and single items of Postal History and Fine Stamps

 # Martin Townsend

Established over 40 years - clients may rely on our reputation and expertise

PO Box 1100, Camberley, Surrey, GU15 9RY

TEL: 01462 420678 MOBILE: 07801 769 117 E-mail: Martin@martintownsend.com

www.martintownsend.com

An Unrivalled Selection Of Modern British Errors

www.markbrandon.co.uk

Mark Brandon · PO Box 6382 · Milton Keynes · MK10 1EF ·
Telephone: 01908 915553 | mark@markbrandon.co.uk

Stanley Gibbons

Great Britain
CONCISE
Stamp Catalogue

2022 edition

STANLEY GIBBONS
THE HOME OF STAMP COLLECTING

By Appointment to
Her Majesty The Queen
Philatelists
Stanley Gibbons Ltd
London

Published by Stanley Gibbons Publications
Editorial, Sales Offices and Distribution Centre:
7 Parkside, Christchurch Road, Ringwood,
Hants BH24 3SH

First Edition — May 1986	21st Edition — April 2006
Second Edition — May 1987	22nd Edition — April 2007
Third Edition — May 1988	23rd Edition — April 2008
Fourth Edition — May 1989	24th Edition — April 2009
Fifth Edition — May 1990	24th Edition — reprinted June 2009
Sixth Edition — May 1991	25th Edition — May 2010
Seventh Edition — May 1992	26th Edition — April 2011
Eighth Edition — April 1993	27th Edition — April 2012
Ninth Edition — April 1994	28th Edition — April 2013
Tenth Edition — April 1995	29th Edition — April 2014
11th Edition — April 1996	30th Edition — May 2015
12th Edition — April 1997	31st Edition — May 2016
13th Edition — April 1998	32nd Edition — June 2017
14th Edition — April 1999	33rd Edition — May 2018
15th Edition — May 2000	34th Edition — May 2019
16th Edition — April 2001	35th Edition — May 2020
17th Edition — April 2002	35th Edition — reprinted Jan 2021
18th Edition — April 2003	36th Edition — May 2021
19th Edition — April 2004	37th Edition — May 2022
20th Edition — May 2005	

Copyright Notice

The contents of this catalogue, including the numbering system and illustrations, are fully protected by copyright. Except as permitted by law, no part of this publication may be reproduced, stored in a retrieval system, or transmitted in any form or by any means, electronic, mechanical, photocopying, recording or otherwise, without the prior permission of Stanley Gibbons Limited. Requests for such permission should be addressed to the Catalogue Editor at Ringwood. This catalogue is sold on condition that it is not, by way of trade or otherwise, lent, re-sold, hired out, circulated or otherwise disposed of other than in its complete, original and unaltered form and without a similar condition including this condition being imposed on the subsequent purchaser.

© Stanley Gibbons Ltd. 2022

ISBN 13: 978-1-911304-95-1

Item No. R2887-22

Printed by
Sterling, Kettering

Contents

Preface	ix
Features of this Catalogue	x
Stanley Gibbons Holdings	xi
General Information	xii
Philatelic Information	xiv
Queen Victoria Issues	1
Key to Line-engraved Issues	4
Embossed issues	8
Key to Surface-printed Issues 1855–1883	9
Key to Surface-printed Issues 1880–1900	15
Departmental Officials	17
Post Office Telegraph Stamps	19
King Edward VII Issues	25
Departmental Officials	27
King George V Issues	33
King Edward VIII Issues	40
King George VI Issues	40
Queen Elizabeth II Issues	47
Decimal Machin Definitives	327
Decimal Machin Index ('X' numbers)	334
Decimal Machin Multi-value Coil Index	337
Decimal Machin Booklet Pane Guide ('X' numbers)	338
Decimal Machins with Elliptical Perforations ('Y' numbers)	347
Decimal Machin Booklet Pane Guide ('Y' numbers)	354
Security Machins ('U' numbers)	361
Barcoded Security Machins ('V' numbers)	376
Royal Mail Postage Labels	379
Royal Mail 'Post and Go' Stamps	379
Exhibitions Simplified Checklist	393
Regional Issues	433
England	433
Northern Ireland	435
Scotland	439
Wales	443
Isle of Man	447
Channel Islands: General Issue 1948	447
Guernsey	447
Jersey	448
Postal Fiscal Stamps	450
Postage Due Stamps	453
Post Office Stamp Booklets	457
King Edward VII	457
King George V	457
King Edward VIII	460
King George VI	460
Queen Elizabeth II	463
I. £.s.d. Booklets 1953–1970	463
II. Decimal Booklets 1971 onwards	469
A. Stitched Booklets	469
B. Folded Booklets	487
Christmas Booklets	499
III. Barcode Booklets	501
C. Machin Booklets 1987 onwards	501
D. Machin NVI Booklets 1989 onwards	504
E. Machin Penny Black Anniversary Booklet, 1990	509
F. Greetings Booklets 1990–1998	510
G. Christmas Booklets 1990 onwards	512
H. Self-adhesive NVI Booklets 2001 onwards	515
I. Self-adhesive Booklets with face values 2002 onwards	520
J. Self-adhesive NVI Special and Machin Booklets 2001 onwards	520
K. Self-adhesive 'smilers' stamps in definitive size	524
L. Self-adhesive booklets with value indicator at upper left	524
M. Self-adhesive 'smilers' and definitive stamps	525
N. Self-adhesive NVI barcode booklets	526
Post Office Label Sheets	531
Royal Mail 'Commemorative Sheets'	550
Commemorative Design Index	552

Don't think You're Treated like a VIP?
Try **PHILATELIC ROUTE-FINDER** NOW!

▶ **VIPs START HERE**

COLLECTOR: ▶ GENERAL? | ADVANCED? | SPECIALIST?

BUDGET: ▶ MODEST? | MEDIUM? | SIGNIFICANT?

YES ◀ Unit Prices? Per Stamp

Learn about **Top-UpTwenty**, On-line Instant-Purchase Price-Drop Selling-System e-mail updates

NO

Consider **Approvals** but Take Auction 1st £55 Free Offer

Up to 20,000 lot NO Buyers Premium £2M **World Auctions**

Try **Approvals** Est 62 years – 1st £25 Free

Collect **Classic GB** 1840-1940 – send wants list

Take **World Mixtures** 1st 500 Free Trial

Join 2000+ Regular Bidders in 52 different Countries – Unique, All Lots Guaranteed Reducing Estimate **Auctions** + **£55 Free Trial Offer** when you win £75+ – **It's easy to Request your FREE Catalogue Now**

▶ **It's Easy to Select Yours Now at UPA**

Sometimes Collectors Get a Raw Deal
Determine how You wish to be treated Here ...

SELLING

Continuing Collecting?

YES — Cash / Part exchange/vendor options

NO

Quality Sought — naturally

Contact Andrew Now or another member of his specialist Team to discuss the market/selling options:
andrew@upastampauctions.co.uk
☎ **01451 861111**

'money spent in the wrong way soon mounts up ...'

Successful and enjoyable collecting depends upon understanding the relationship of your budget to your interest.

Offers and services can be confusing can't they, and money spent in the wrong way soon mounts up.

In philately, sometimes it is hard to decide which way to go. Your passion may exceed your resource, so just what may be best for you?

Often, it is not what you collect but how you collect

This is the reason why my team and I have devised this quick and easy philatelic route-map QUIZ which does not ask you what you collect — but helps you to determine by your answers just which type of collecting service may best suit you ...

Presently you may find few philatelic companies other than UPA which can offer you integrated philatelic selling systems, but obviously once you determine which philatelic services best suit your collecting interest — you may have a clearer idea of which way is best to go — depending upon your levels of specialism and philatelic budget, of course

Check out our Philatelic QUIZ right now and see for yourself. To select your choice, visit our website or call my team

Dedicated to De-mystifying Philately

Andrew

Andrew McGavin,
Veteran Philatelic Auctioneer
Philatelic Expert & Author
Managing Director Universal Philatelic Auctions (UPA)

▶ Visit: www.UPAstampauctions.co.uk

Fax: 01451 861297 ~ info@upastampauctions.co.uk ~ T: 01451 861111
Participate in this Philatelic Route-Map to Enjoyable Collecting.
Find UPA also on-line at www.top-uptwenty.co.uk
New Instant-Purchase Price-Drop Selling-System

GB Conc 2022

Preface

Welcome to the 37th edition of the Great Britain Concise Stamp Catalogue, again what a year! Since the last edition the Covid pandemic has continued to turn all our lives upside down. The London 2020 International Stamp Exhibition did eventually happen, albeit renamed the 'London 2022 International Stamp Exhibition'. But with a myriad of confusing travel and quarantine restrictions in the months leading up to the show, many overseas dealers and collectors unsurprisingly decided to give it a miss.

Then, as if that wasn't enough the day before the show was due to start, storm Eunice paid us a visit and disrupted just about every form of public transport. It seemed at the time that this show just wasn't destined to happen, yet despite everything the organisers delivered a fantastic show.

Editorial developments

Apart from the usual 'new issues' and the odd explanatory note that has been added to the listings, readers will not see any major editorial changes.

Behind the scenes however that could not be further from the truth, the *Concise* catalogue data has been added for the first time to our new catalogue production database. Being by far the most complicated catalogue added so far, it is only fair to say everything hasn't gone quite as smoothly as planned.

So, if feedback from readers is 'it doesn't look any different from last years catalogue', that will be music to our ears.

A couple of minor additions are the inclusion of PO pack numbers for Collector Packs and Yearpacks, and with the continued expansion and complication of the Machin definitives. To assist readers we have added a small index at the beginning of the dedicated Machin section.

At this point, I must again thank all our readers that have made contributions to the accuracy of the catalogue and offered constructive advice. I must also thank John M Deering of 'Machin Watch' fame, who has once again edited the 'U' series security Machins, 'Post & Go' sections and assisted with the introduction of a 'V' series for the new barcode Machins.

The biggest and furthest reaching news concerning GB stamps for this year, is undoubtedly the Royal Mail 'Swap Out' scheme. Many of you are probably now wondering what on earth I'm talking about, if that includes you please read on.

The key point of the scheme is that following the introduction of the new barcoded Machins, many of the older definitive stamps (see list below) will from 31 January 2023 no longer be valid for postage. Any subsequent use of these stamps will be deemed invalid and subject to surcharge.

- All standard decimal Machin definitives from 1971 onwards
- All NVI Machin definitives, including 'Signed for', 'Special delivery' and 'Worldwide Postcard' Machins
- All decimal regional/country Machin definitives from 1971-1999
- All country emblem definitives from 1999-2020
- 2012 Olympic Worldwide International definitives
- 1990 'Double head' 150th anniversary definitives
- 1993 £10 'Brittania' high value
- 1988-1997 'Castle' high values

The soon to be invalidated stamps can be exchanged for the new barcoded versions through the Royal Mail stamp 'Swap Out' scheme. The scheme opened on 31 March 2022, stamps can only be exchanged via Tallents House and must be accompanied by the correct 'Swap Out' form. See www.royalmail.com/sending/barcoded-stamps for details.

The question for dealers and collectors alike is how will this affect Machin prices? With no 'enddate' yet announced for the scheme, we won't know for quite a while how many Machins will be 'swapped out'. The more difficult issues can only remain sought after, the more common issues whose prices have been propped up by their face values will undoubtedly need some future adjustment. I guess it's a case of - watch this space.

Vince Cordell

April 2022

Features of this Catalogue

The Concise Catalogue, now in its 35th year of publication, has established itself as an essential guide for the 'one-country' collector of Great Britain. As the popularity of Great Britain stamps continues to grow — the Concise Catalogue supplies the information you need to enhance your collection.

+ All issues from the Penny Black of 1840 to 31 March 2020 including Regional, Postage Due, Official and Postal Fiscal stamps.
+ All different stamp designs are illustrated.
+ Every basic stamp listed, including those with different watermarks or perforations and those showing graphite lines or phosphor bands.
+ Unmounted mint and mounted mint prices quoted for 1887 'Jubilee' series and all King Edward VII and King George V issues, apart from the Departmental Officials.
+ Missing colours, missing embossing, watermark errors, imperforate errors and phosphor omitted varieties from those stamps normally issued with phosphor bands.
+ Booklet panes listed up to 1970, including inverted watermark varieties.
+ Gutter Pairs and 'Traffic light' Gutter Pairs listed in mint sets.
+ First Day Covers for Special Issues from 1924 and for King Edward VIII and King George VI definitives. For the present reign the coverage also extends to Prestige Booklet panes and Regionals. All British Post Office special First Day of Issue postmarks are priced on cover.
+ Post Office Picture Cards (PHQ cards) are priced as sets, both mint and used with First Day of Issue postmarks.
+ Presentation, Collector and Gift Packs, including the scarce versions with foreign inscriptions.
+ Quick-reference diagrams for listed Machin decimal booklet panes.
+ Design Index for Commemorative and Special Stamps at the back of the catalogue.
+ Machin and commemorative underprints given separate catalogue numbers.
+ Post Office Yearbooks.
+ Royal Mail Postage Labels priced in mint or used sets and on British Post Office First Day Covers.
+ Royal Mail Post & Go stamps; with notes on machine types, errors, date codes and special inscriptions.
+ Notes on Postage Due bisects based on research by Mr P. Frost.
+ Wartime issues for the Channel Islands.
+ Separate section for Post Office Stamp Booklets with dated editions of King George VI and Queen Elizabeth listed separately.
+ Post Office Label Sheets, popularly known as 'Generic Smilers'.
+ Specimen overprints up to 1970.
+ Helpful introductory section providing definitions and guidance for the collector and including all watermark illustrations shown together to assist identification.
+ Addresses for specialist philatelic societies covering Great Britain stamps.
+ Post Office Telegraph Stamps
+ The following have been added to this edition: 101Wj, 1570a and D22Wi.

We would like to thank all those who have assisted in the compilation of this catalogue. Special thanks for amendments to this edition are due to Rowan Baker, Allan Grant, Robert Oliver, John Peart, Ian Rimmer, Kevin Samuels, David Smythe, Paul Taylor and Julian Tremayne.

Great Britain Philatelic Societies

The Great Britain Philatelic Society.
Hon. Membership Secretary: Victoria Lajer,
Stanley Gibbons Ltd., 399 Strand, London WC2R 0LX

The Modern British Philatelic Circle. Hon. Membership Secretary: A J Wilkins, 3 Buttermere Close, Brierley Hill, West Midlands, DY5 3SD.

Stanley Gibbons Holdings Plc

Stanley Gibbons Limited,
Stanley Gibbons Auctions
399 Strand, London WC2R 0LX
Tel: +44 (0)207 836 8444
E-mail: support@stanleygibbons.com
Website: www.stanleygibbons.com
for all departments, Auction and
Specialist Stamp Departments.

Open Monday–Friday 9.30 a.m. to 6 p.m.
Shop. Open Monday–Saturday 9.30
a.m. to 6 p.m.

Stanley Gibbons Publications,
Mail Order, Gibbons Stamp Monthly
and Philatelic Exporter
7 Parkside, Christchurch Road,
Ringwood, Hampshire BH24 3SH.
Tel: +44 (0)1425 472363
E-mail: support@stanleygibbons.com

Monday–Friday 8.30 a.m. to 5 p.m.

Stanley Gibbons Publications
Overseas Representation
Stanley Gibbons Publications are
represented overseas by the following

Australia
Renniks Publications PTY LTD
Unit 6, 30 Perry St, Matraville,
NSW 2036, Australia
Tel: +612 9695 7055
Website: www.renniks.com

Canada
Unitrade Associates
99 Floral Parkway, Toronto,
Ontario M6L 2C4, Canada
Tel: +1 416 242 5900
Website: www.unitradeassoc.com

Canada
F.v.H. Stamps
102-340 West Cordova Street,
Vancouver, BC, V6B 1E8, Canada
Tel: +1 604 684 8408
Website: www.fvhstamps.com

Denmark
Nordfrim A/S
Kvindevadet 42,
Otterup DK-5450, Denmark
Tel: +45 64 82 1256
Website: www.nordfrim.com

Italy
Ernesto Marini S.R.L.
V. Struppa, 300, Genova, 16165, Italy
Tel: +39 010 802 186
Website: www.ernestomarini.it

Japan
Japan Philatelic
PO Box 2, Suginami-Minami,
Tokyo 168-8081, Japan
Tel: +81 3330 41641
Website: www.yushu.co.jp

Netherlands
Uitgeverij Davo BV
PO Box 411, Ak Deventer, 7400
Netherlands
Tel: +3188 0284300
Website: www.davo.nl

New Zealand
House of Stamps
PO Box 12, Paraparaumu,
New Zealand
Tel: +61 6364 8270
Website: www.houseofstamps.co.nz

New Zealand
Philatelic Distributors
PO Box 863
15 Mount Edgecumbe Street
New Plymouth 4615, New Zealand
Tel: +6 46 758 65 68
Website: www.stampcollecta.com

Singapore
C S Philatelic Agency
Peninsula Shopping Centre #04-29
3 Coleman Street, 179804, Singapore
Tel: +65 6337-1859
Website: www.cs.com.sg

USA
Vidiforms Company Inc
115 North Route 9W, Congers,
New York NY 10920, United States
Tel: +1 845 268 4005
Website: www.showgard.com

USA
Amos Media Company
1660 Campbell Road,
Suite A, Door #9,
Sidney OH 453652480,
United States
Tel: +1 937 498 2111
Website: www.amosmedia.com

General Information

> The prices quoted in this catalogue are the estimated selling prices of Stanley Gibbons Ltd at the time of publication. They are, *unless it is specifically stated otherwise*, for examples in very fine condition for the issue concerned. Superb examples are worth more; those of a lower quality considerably less.

All prices are subject to change without prior notice and Stanley Gibbons Ltd may from time to time offer stamps below catalogue price. Individual low value stamps sold at 399, Strand are liable to an additional handling charge. Purchasers of new issues are asked to note that the prices charged for them contain an element for the service rendered and so may exceed the prices shown when the stamps are subsequently catalogued.

No guarantee is given to supply all stamps priced, since it is not possible to keep every catalogued item in stock.

Quotation of prices

The prices in the left-hand column are for unused stamps and those in the right-hand column are for used.

A dagger (†) denotes that the item listed does not exist in that condition and a blank, or dash, that it exists, or may exist, but no market price can be quoted.

Prices are expressed in pounds and pence sterling. One pound comprises 100 pence (£1 = 100p).

The method of notation is as follows: pence in numerals (e.g. 5 denotes five pence); pounds and pence up to £100, in numerals (e.g. 4·25 denotes four pounds and twenty-five pence); prices above £100 expressed in whole pounds with the '£' sign shown.

Unused and Used stamps

The prices for unused stamps of Queen Victoria issued before 1887 are for lightly hinged examples. Unused stamps of the 1887 'Jubilee' issue and from the reigns of King Edward VII and King George V are priced in both unmounted and mounted condition. The only exception is the Departmental Officials, which are priced unused, used and used on cover. Unused prices for King Edward VIII to Queen Elizabeth II issues are for unmounted mint (though when not available, mounted mint stamps are often supplied at a lower price). Prices for used stamps are for fine postally used examples, usually cancelled by a clear operational circular datestamp (See 'Operational Cancellations' in Philatelic Information section).

Prices quoted for bisects on cover or on large piece are for those dated during the period officially authorised.

Minimum price

The minimum price quoted is 10 pence. For individual stamps, prices between 10 pence and 95 pence are provided as a guide for catalogue users. The lowest price *charged* for individual stamps or sets purchased from Stanley Gibbons Ltd is £1.

Set prices

Set prices are generally for one of each value, excluding shades and varieties, but including major colour changes. Where there are alternative shades, etc., the cheapest is usually included. The number of stamps in the set is always stated for clarity.

The mint and used prices for sets containing *se-tenant* pieces are based on the prices quoted for such combinations, and not on those for individual stamps which may be considerably less.

Gutter Pairs

These, and traffic light gutter pairs, are priced as complete sets.

Used on Cover prices

To assist collectors, cover prices are quoted in a third column for postage and Official stamps issued in the reign of Queen Victoria and in boxed notes for the 1887 'Jubilee' issue and for King Edward VII stamps.

The cover should be of non-philatelic origin, bearing the correct postal rate for the period and distance involved and cancelled with the markings normal to the offices concerned. Purely philatelic items have a cover value only slightly greater than the catalogue value for the corresponding used stamps. This applies generally to those high-value stamps used philatelically rather than in the normal course of commerce.

Oversized covers, difficult to accommodate on an album page, should be reckoned as worth little more than the corresponding value of the used stamps. The condition of a cover affects its value. Except for 'wreck covers', serious damage or soiling reduces the value where the postal markings and stamps are ordinary ones. Conversely, visual appeal adds to the value and this can include freshness of appearance, important addresses, old-fashioned but legible handwriting, historic town-names, etc. The prices quoted are a base on which further value would be added to take account of the cover's postal historical importance in demonstrating such things as unusual, scarce or emergency cancels, interesting routes, significant postal markings, combination usage, the development of postal rates, and so on.

However, it should also be noted that multiples of some stamps are frequently more commonly found on cover than single usages and in such cases the cover might be worth less than the price quoted.

First Day Cover prices

Prices are quoted for commemorative first day covers from 1924 British Empire Exhibition pair onwards. These prices are for special covers (from 1937) franked with complete sets and cancelled by ordinary operational postmarks to the end of 1962 or the various standard 'First Day of Issue' markings from 1963.

Prices are provided for King Edward VIII and King George VI definitives on plain covers with operational

GENERAL INFORMATION

postmarks of the first day of issue. For some values special covers also exist and these are worth more than the prices quoted.

The Philatelic Bureau and other special 'First Day of Issue' postmarks provided by the Post Office since 1963 are listed under each issue. Prices quoted are for these postmarks used on illustrated covers (from 1964 those produced by the Post Office), franked with complete sets.

The British Post Office did not introduce special First Day of Issue postmarks for definitive issues until the first instalment of the Machin £sd series, issued 5 June 1967, although 'First Day' treatment had been provided for some Regional stamps from 8 June 1964 onwards. Prices for the First Day Covers from 1952 to 1966, showing definitive stamps are for the stamps indicated, used on illustrated envelopes and postmarked with operational cancellations.

From 1967 onwards the prices quoted are for stamps as indicated, used on illustrated envelopes and postmarked with special First Day of Issue handstamps. Other definitives issued during this period were not accepted for 'First Day' treatment by the British Post Office.

Guarantee

All stamps are guaranteed genuine originals in the following terms:

If not as described, and returned by the purchaser, we undertake to refund the price paid to us in the original transaction. If any stamp is certified as genuine by the Expert Committee of the Royal Philatelic Society, London, or by BPA Expertising Ltd, the purchaser shall not be entitled to make any claim against us for any error, omission or mistake in such certificate.

Consumers' statutory rights are not affected by the above guarantee.

The recognised Expert Committees in this country are those of the Royal Philatelic Society, London, 15 Abchurch Lane, London EC4 7BW, and B.P.A. Expertising Ltd, P.O. Box 1141, Guildford, Surrey GU5 0WR. They do not undertake valuations under any circumstances and fees are payable for their services.

Contacting the Catalogue Editor

The Editor is always interested in hearing from people who have new information which will improve or correct the Catalogue. As a general rule he must see and examine the actual stamps before they can be considered for listing; photographs or scans are insufficient evidence, although an initial email to *Thecatalogueeditor@stanleygibbons.com* will determine whether or not an item is likely to be of interest.

Where information is solicited purely for the benefit of the enquirer, the editor cannot undertake to reply if the answer is already contained in these published notes. Email communications are greatly preferred to enquiries by telephone and the editor regrets that he or his staff cannot see personal callers without a prior appointment being made. Correspondence may be subject to delay during the production period of each new edition.

Please note that the following classes of material are outside the scope of this Catalogue:

(a) Non-postal revenue or fiscal stamps.
(b) Postage stamps used fiscally.
(c) Local carriage labels and private local issues.
(d) Punctured postage stamps (perfins).
(e) Bogus or phantom stamps.
(f) Railway or airline letter fee stamps, bus or road transport company labels.
(g) Postal stationery cut-outs.
(h) All types of non-postal labels and souvenirs.
(i) Documentary labels for the postal service, e.g. registration, recorded delivery, airmail etiquettes, etc.
(j) Privately applied embellishments to official issues and privately commissioned items generally.
(k) Stamps for training postal staff.

> We regret we do not give opinions as to the genuineness of stamps, nor do we identify stamps or number them by our Catalogue.

General Abbreviations

Alph	Alphabet
Anniv	Anniversary
Brt	Bright (colour)
C.	Overprinted in carmine
Des	Designer; designed
Dp	Deep (colour)
Eng	Engraver; engraved
Horiz	Horizontal; horizontally
Imp, Imperf	Imperforate
Inscr	Inscribed
L	Left
Litho	Lithographed
Lt	Light (colour)
mm	Millimetres
MS	Miniature sheet
Opt(d)	Overprint(ed)
P, Perf	Perforated
Photo	Photogravure
Pl	Plate
Pr	Pair
Ptd	Printed
Ptg	Printing
PVA	Polyvinyl alcohol (gum)
R	Right
R.	Row
Recess	Recess-printed
T	Type
Typo	Typographed (Letterpress)
Un	Unused
Us	Used
Vert	Vertical; vertically
W or wmk	Watermark
Wmk s	Watermark sideways

(†) = Does not exist.
(—) (or blank price column) = Exists, or may exist, but no market price can be quoted.
/ between colours means 'on' and the colour following is that of the paper on which the stamp is printed.

Printers

BW	Bradbury Wilkinson & Co., Ltd.
Cartor	Cartor S.A., La Loupe, France
DLR	De La Rue & Co, Ltd, London, and (from 1961) Bogota, Colombia. De La Rue Security Print (*formerly Harrison & Sons Ltd*) from 8 September 1997.
Enschedé	Joh. Enschedé en Zonen, Haarlem, Netherlands.
Harrison	Harrison & Sons, Ltd, High Wycombe.
ISP	International Security Printers (Walsall and/or Cartor
JW	John Waddington Security Print, Ltd, Leeds.
PB	Perkins Bacon Ltd, London.
Questa	Questa Colour Security Printers, Ltd.
Waterlow	Waterlow & Sons, Ltd, London.
Walsall	Walsall Security Printers, Ltd.

Philatelic information

Catalogue Numbers
The catalogue number appears in the extreme left column. The boldface Type numbers in the next column are merely cross-reference to illustrations. Catalogue numbers in the *Gibbons Stamp Monthly* Supplements are provisional only and may need to be altered when the lists are consolidated.

Our Catalogue numbers are universally recognised in specifying stamps and as a hallmark of status.

Inverted and other watermark varieties incorporate 'Wi', etc., within the number.

Catalogue Illustrations
Stamps and first day postmarks are illustrated at three-quarters linear size. Stamps not illustrated are the same size and format as the value shown, unless otherwise indicated. Overprints, surcharges and watermarks are normally actual size. Illustrations of varieties are often enlarged to show the detail. Illustrations of miniature sheets have their dimensions, in millimetres, stated with the width given first.

Designers
Designers' names are quoted where known, though space precludes naming every individual concerned in the production of a set. In particular, photographers supplying material are usually named only when they also make an active contribution in the design stage; posed photographs of reigning monarchs are, however, an exception to this rule.

Printing Errors
Errors in printing are of major interest to this Catalogue. Authenticated items meriting consideration would include: background, centre or frame inverted or omitted; centre or subject transposed; error of colour; error or omission of value; double prints and impressions; printed both sides; and so on. Designs *tête-bêche*, whether intentionally or by accident, are listable. Colours only partially omitted are not listed. However, stamps with embossing, phosphor or both omitted and stamps printed on the gummed side are included.

Printing technology has radically improved over the years, during which time gravure and lithography have become predominant. Varieties nowadays are more in the nature of flaws which are almost always outside the scope of this book.

In no catalogue, however, do we list such items as: dry prints, kiss prints, doctor-blade flaws, colour shifts or registration flaws (unless they lead to the complete omission of a colour from an individual stamp), lithographic ring flaws, and so on. Neither do we recognise fortuitous happenings like paper creases or confetti flaws.

Paper Types
All stamps listed are deemed to be on 'ordinary' paper of the wove type and white in colour; only departures from this are normally mentioned.

A coloured paper is one that is coloured right through (front and back of the stamp). In the Catalogue the colour of the paper is given in *italics*, thus:
purple/*yellow* = purple design on yellow paper.

Papers have been made specially white in recent years by, for example, a very heavy coating of chalk. We do not classify shades of whiteness of paper as distinct varieties. The availability of many postage stamps for revenue purposes made necessary some safeguard against the illegitimate re-use of stamps with removable cancellations. This was at first secured by using fugitive inks and later by printing on chalky (chalk-surfaced) paper, both of which made it difficult to remove any form of obliteration without also damaging the stamp design. Stamps which exist on both ordinary and chalk-surfaced papers are separately listed.

The 'traditional' method of indentifying chalk-surfaced papers has been that, when touched with a silver wire, a black mark is left on the paper, and the listings in this catalogue are based on that test. However, the test itself is now largely discredited, for, although the mark can be removed by a soft rubber, some damage to the stamp will result from its use.

The difference between chalk-surfaced and pre-war ordinary papers is fairly clear: chalk-surfaced papers being smoother to the touch and showing a characteristic sheen when light is reflected off their surface. Under good magnification tiny bubbles or pock marks can be seen on the surface of the stamp and at the tips of the perforations the surfacing appears 'broken'. Traces of paper fibres are evident on the surface of ordinary paper and the ink shows a degree of absorption into it.

Initial chalk-surfaced paper printings by De La Rue had a thinner coating than subsequently became the norm. The characteristics described above are less pronounced in these printings.

Perforation Measurement
The gauge of a perforation is the number of holes in a length of 2 cm.

The Gibbons *Instanta* gauge is the standard for measuring perforations. The stamp is viewed against a dark background with the transparent gauge put on top of it. Though the gauge measures to decimal accuracy, perforations read from it are generally quoted in the Catalogue to the nearest half. For example:

Just over perf 12¾ to just under 13¼ .... = perf 13
Perf 13¼ exactly, rounded up .... = perf 13½
Just over perf 13¼ to just under 13¾ .... = perf 13½
Perf 13¾ exactly, rounded up .... = perf 14

However, where classification depends on it, actual quarter-perforations are quoted. Perforations are usually abbreviated (and spoken) as follows, though sometimes they may be spelt out for clarity.

P 14: perforated alike on all sides (read: 'perf 14').

P 14×15: the first figure refers to top and bottom, the second to left and right sides (read: 'perf 14 by 15'). This is a compound perforation.

Such headings as 'P 13×14 (vert) and P 14×13 (horiz)' indicate which perforations apply to which stamp format—vertical or horizontal.

From 1992 onwards most definitive and greetings stamps from both sheets and booklets occur with a large elliptical (oval) hole inserted in each line of vertical perforations as a security measure. The £10 definitive, No. 1658, is unique in having two such holes in the horizontal perforations.

Stamps which have the elliptical perforations hole towards the top in error are normally outside the scope of this catalogue, but in 2013 a booklet was issued in which the entire print run contained Machin stamps in this format. These are listed as U3073 and U3076.

Elliptical Perforations

Perforation Errors

Authenticated errors, where a stamp normally perforated is accidentally issued imperforate, are listed provided no traces of perforations (blind holes or indentations) remain. They must be provided as pairs, both stamps wholly imperforate, and are only priced in that form.

Numerous part-perforated stamps arose from the introduction of the Jumelle Press. This had a rotary perforator with rows of pins on one drum engaging with holes on another. Engagement is only gradual when the perforating unit is started up or stopped, giving rise to perforations 'fading out', a variety mentioned above as not listed.

Stamps from the Jumelle printings sometimes occur imperforate between stamp and sheet margin. Such errors are not listed in this catalogue, but are covered by the volumes of the *Great Britain Specialised Catalogue*.

Pairs described as 'imperforate between' have the line of perforations between the two stamps omitted.

Imperf between (vertical pair)   Imperf horizontally (vertical pair)

Imperf between (horiz pair): a horizontal pair of stamps with perfs all around the edges but none between the stamps.

Imperf between (vert pair): a vertical pair of stamps with perfs all around the edges but none between the stamps.

Where several of the rows have escaped perforation the resulting varieties are listable. Thus:

Imperf vert (horiz pair): a horizontal pair of stamps perforated at top and bottom; all three vertical directions are imperf—the two outer edges and between the stamps.

Imperf horiz (vert pair): a vertical pair perforated at left and right edges; all three horizontal directions are imperf—the top, bottom and between the stamps.

Varieties of double, misplaced or partial perforation caused by error or machine malfunction are not listable, neither are freaks, such as perforations placed diagonally from paper folds, nor missing holes caused by broken pins.

Phosphor Issues

Machines which sort mail electronically were introduced progressively and the British Post Office issued the first stamps specially marked for electronic sorting in 1957. This first issue had easily visible graphite lines printed on the back beneath the gum (see Nos. 561/6). They were issued in the Southampton area where the experiment was carried out.

The graphite lines were replaced by phosphor bands, activated by ultraviolet light. The bands are printed on the front of the stamps and show as a matt surface against the usual smooth or shiny appearance of the untreated surface of the paper. The bands show clearly in the top or bottom horizontal margins of the sheet.

The first phosphor issues appeared in 1959 (see Nos. 599/609) and these stamps also had graphite lines on the back. Further details will be found in the listings above No. 599 and 619. From 1962 onwards most commemoratives were issued in versions with or without bands. From 1967 all commemorative stamps had phosphor bands, but from 1972 they were replaced by 'all-over' phosphor covering the entire area of the stamp.

After a considerable period of development a special paper was produced in which the phosphor had been incorporated into the coating. From 15 August 1979 to April 1996 phosphorised paper was accepted for use generally, replacing phosphor bands on most issues for all values except the second class letter rate. Phosphorised paper can only be identified by ultraviolet light. The Stanley Gibbons Ultraviolet Lamp is firmly recommended for use in identifying the phosphor stamps listed in this Catalogue. *Warning*. Never stare at the lighted lamp but follow the manufacturer's instructions. Phosphor bands were reintroduced for all issues from April 1996.

During the years 1967 to 1972, when all issues, except the high values, should have shown phosphor bands, a number of stamps appeared with them omitted in error. These varieties are listed in this Catalogue. Stamps with 'all-over' phosphor omitted can only be detected by the use of an ultraviolet lamp and these varieties are listed in the Stanley Gibbons *Great Britain Specialised Catalogue*. Note that prices are for unmounted mint examples only. Varieties such as double or misplaced bands are not listed in this Catalogue.

Gum Description

All stamps listed are assumed to have gum of some kind and original gum (o.g.) means that which was present on the stamp as issued to the public. Deleterious climates and the presence of certain chemicals can cause gum to crack and, with early stamps, even make the paper deteriorate. Unscrupulous fakers are adept in removing it and regumming the stamp to meet the unreasoning demand often made for 'full o.g.' 'unmounted' or 'never hinged, mint' (NHM) in cases where such a thing is virtually impossible.

The gum normally used on stamps has been gum

PHILATELIC INFORMATION

arabic until the late 1960's when synthetic adhesives were introduced. Harrison and Sons Ltd for instance used *polyvinyl alcohol*, known to philatelists as PVA (see note above SG 723).

From 1993 many stamps have been issued with self-adhesive gum. Unused prices are for such stamps with backing paper attached, as issued. Initially such stamps were issued with a water-soluble layer of gum allowing used examples to be 'soaked off', but with the 2008 Christmas issue, most self-adhesive stamps are issued without the water-soluble layer of gum, preventing their removal from paper without damage. It is recommended that used stamps from this later period be collected 'on piece'.

Colour Identification

The 200 colours most used for stamp identification are given in the Stanley Gibbons Stamp Colour Key. The Catalogue has used the Colour Key as a standard for describing new issues for some years. The names are also introduced as lists are rewritten, though exceptions are made for those early issues where traditional names have become universally established.

In compound colour names the second is the predominant one, thus:
orange-red = a red tending towards orange.
red-orange = an orange containing more red than usual.

When comparing actual stamps with colour samples in the Colour Key, view in a good north daylight (or its best substitute: fluorescent 'colour-matching' light). Sunshine is not recommended. Choose a solid portion of the stamp design; if available, marginal markings such as solid bars of colour or colour check dots are helpful. Shading lines in the design can be misleading as they appear lighter than solid colour. Furthermore, the listings refer to colours as issued: they may deteriorate into something different through the passage of time.

Shades are particularly significant when they can be linked to specific printings. In general, shades need to be quite marked to fall within the scope of this Catalogue.

Modern colour printing by lithography is prone to marked differences of shade, even within a single run, and variations can occur within the same sheet. Such shades are not listed.

Royal Mail Colour Descriptions

In recent years Royal Mail has introduced its own colour descriptions of definitive stamps, describing, for example, the £1.05 stamp (SG 2935) as 'Gooseberry green' and incorporating this in the sheet margin of the stamp. We do not use these descriptions because they are, in many cases, unfamiliar to collectors and, should a listable change in shade occur in a later printing, we would expect that the sheet margin would continue to bear the original Royal Mail colour description.

Errors of Colour

Major colour errors in stamps or overprints which qualify for listing are: wrong colours; albinos (colourless impressions), where these have Expert Committee certificates; colours completely omitted, but only on unused stamps (if found on used stamps the information is usually footnoted) and with good credentials, missing colours being frequently faked.

Colours only partially omitted are not recognised. Colour shifts, however spectacular, are not listed.

Booklet Stamps

Single stamps from booklets are listed if they are distinguishable in some way (such as watermark or phosphor bands) from similar sheet stamps. Single booklet stamps whose only distinguishing feature is that they are imperforate on one or two adjacent sides are omitted

Booklet panes are listed where they contain stamps of different denominations *se-tenant*, where stamp-size printed labels are included, or where such panes are otherwise identifiable. Booklet panes are placed in the listing under the lowest denomination present.

Booklet panes containing single values issued up to 1970 are also listed in this catalogue. Users should note that prices are for panes with the binding margin intact and full perforations on the other three sides.

In the listing of complete booklets the numbers and prefix letters are the same as used in the Stanley Gibbons *Great Britain Specialised Catalogue*.

Coil Stamps

Stamps only issued in coil form are given full listing. If stamps are issued in both sheets and coils, the coil stamps are listed separately only where there is some feature (e.g. watermark sideways or gum change) by which single stamps can be distinguished. Coil strips containing different values *se-tenant* are also listed.

Booklet Pane with Printed Labels

Se-tenant Pane of Four

PHILATELIC INFORMATION

Multi-value Coil Strip

Coil join pairs are generally too random and easily faked to permit listing; similarly ignored are coil stamps which have accidentally suffered an extra row of perforations from the claw mechanism in a malfunctioning vending machine.

Gutter pair

Gutter Pairs

In 1988 the recess-printed Castle high value definitives were issued in sheets containing four panes separated by a gutter margin. All modern Great Britain commemoratives and special stamps are produced in sheets containing two panes separated by a blank horizontal or vertical margin known as a gutter. This feature first made its appearance on some supplies of the 1972 Royal Silver Wedding 3p and marked the introduction of Harrison & Sons' new 'Jumelle' stamp-printing press. There are advantages for both the printer and the Post Office in such a layout which has been used for most commemorative issues since 1974.

Traffic Light Gutter Pair

The term 'gutter pair' is used for a pair of stamps separated by part of the blank gutter margin as illustrated above. Most printers include some form of colour check device on the sheet margins, in addition to the cylinder or plate numbers. Harrison & Sons use round 'dabs', or spots of colour, resembling traffic lights. For the period from the 1972 Royal Silver Wedding until the end of 1979 these colour dabs appeared in the gutter margin. There was always one example to every double-pane sheet of stamps. They can also be found in the high value Machin issue printed in photogravure. Gutter pairs showing these 'traffic lights' are priced in complete sets in this catalogue.

From the 2004 Entente Cordiale set, Walsall reintroduced traffic lights in the gutters of certain sets. Where these extend over more than one section of gutter margin on any value, they are priced in blocks rather than pairs.

Miniature Sheets

A miniature sheet contains a single stamp or set with wide inscribed or decorated margins. The stamps often also exist in normal sheet format. This Catalogue lists, with **MS** prefix, complete miniature sheets which have been issued by the Post Office and which are valid for postal purposes.

Stamps from miniature sheets, not also available in normal sheet format, are not individually listed or priced in this catalogue.

Where such stamps have also appeared in a booklet, and the booklet pane differs in layout or design to the miniature sheet (e.g. 'Britain Alone' (2nd issue), Nos. 3082/5) these stamps are listed separately, but if the booklet pane is the same as the miniature sheet (e.g. 'Astronomy' , Nos. **MS**2315/a) they are only listed as complete miniature sheets or booklet panes.

Miniature Sheet containing a set of stamps

Se-tenant Combinations

Se-tenant means 'joined together'. Some sets include stamps of different design arranged *se-tenant* as blocks or strips and, in mint condition, these are usually collected unsevered as issued. The set prices quoted in this catalogue refer to the unsevered combination plus singles of any other values in the set.

Presentation and Souvenir Packs

Special Packs comprising slip-in cards with printed commemorative inscriptions and notes on the back and with protective covering, were introduced in 1964 for the Shakespeare issue. Definitive issues first appeared in Presentation Packs in 1960. Notes will be found in the listings to describe souvenir books issued on special occasions.

Issues of 1968–1969 (British Paintings to the Prince of Wales Investiture) were also issued in packs with text in

PHILATELIC INFORMATION

German for sale through the Post Office's German Agency and these are also included.

Collectors packs, first called gift packs, containing commemoratives issued in the preceding 12 months, first appeared in 1967. These are listed and priced.

It should be noted that prices given for presentation packs are for items as originally sold, including any additional inserts, such as questionnaire forms and publicity material.

13 August 1975 Public Railways Presentation Pack

Yearbooks

Special Post Office Yearbooks were first available in 1984. They contain all of the commemorative issues for one year in a hardbound book, illustrated in colour complete with slip case. These are listed and priced.

Commemorative First Day Covers

Until 1963 the Post Office did not provide any special first day of issue postmark facilities for collectors. Several philatelic organisations and stamp dealers did produce pictorial covers for the various commemorative issues and collectors serviced these to receive ordinary operational postmarks. Occasionally a special handstamp was produced which coincided with a new stamp issue, or relevant slogan postmarks, like the 1953 'Long Live the Queen' type, were in general use at the time.

On 21 March 1963 the Post Office installed special posting boxes at 11 main post offices so that collectors could obtain 'uniformly high standard' impressions, from normal operational postmarks, for their first day covers. From 7 May 1963 special 'First Day of Issue' slogans (Type A) were applied to mail posted in these special boxes, whose number had, by then, risen to 30. The Philatelic Bureau accepted orders by post for such covers from the issue of 16 May 1963 onwards.

The slogan type was replaced on 23 April 1964 by 'First Day of Issue' handstamps (Type B). These were, initially, of considerable size, but were later replaced by smaller versions (Type C) which remained in use at nearly 200 principal offices until the Christmas issue of 2 November 1998. From 1970 the Bureau postmarks as Type C were inscribed 'British Philatelic Bureau'.

Since 1972 the Post Office has provided for virtually all issues an additional 'alternative' pictorial 'First Day of Issue' cancellation, at a location connected with the issue. Being available from the Bureau, these cancellations are listed in this catalogue.

From 12 January 1999 (Millennium Inventors' Tale issue) the 'alternative' pictorial postmark has been applied to all covers posted in special first day boxes throughout the country, replacing the local, non-pictorial, cancels. A bilingual version is used when the 'alternative' office is in Wales. For collectors who prefer plain postmarks a non-pictorial version of the 'alternative' postmark is available from Royal Mail Special Handstamp Centres.

'First Day of Issue' postmarks of standard or pictorial type have occasionally been provided on a 'one-off' basis for places linked to particular stamp issues, eg Weymouth for the 1975 Sailing set. Such postmarks, which are not available from the Bureau, are footnoted only.

Royal Mail established Special Handstamp Centres in 1990 where all sponsored special handstamps and many 'First Day of Issue' postmarks are now applied.

Pictorial local 'First Day of Issue' postmarks were in use between 1988 and 1998 applied to covers posted in first day boxes and sent to main offices or Special Handstamp Centres. These included Birmingham (1993–98), Durham (1988–98), City of London (1989–98), London (1993–98), Newcastle upon Tyne (1992–94), and St Albans (1995–98). Different designs were used at the Glasgow Handstamp Centre for various places, 1993–98. As these postmarks were not available from the Bureau they are not included in this catalogue.

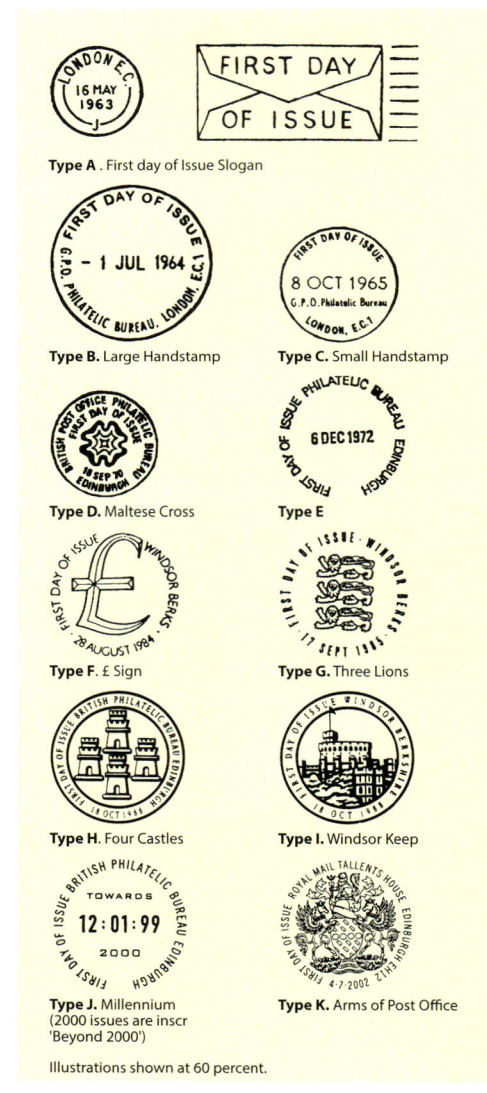

Type A. First day of Issue Slogan

Type B. Large Handstamp

Type C. Small Handstamp

Type D. Maltese Cross

Type E

Type F. £ Sign

Type G. Three Lions

Type H. Four Castles

Type I. Windsor Keep

Type J. Millennium (2000 issues are inscr 'Beyond 2000')

Type K. Arms of Post Office

Illustrations shown at 60 percent.

PHILATELIC INFORMATION

CANCELLATIONS

First day cover prices for modern issues are based on those with a Philatelic Bureau (later, 'Tallents House') postmark.

Operational Cancellations
Early cancellation devices were designed to 'obliterate' the stamp in order to prevent it being reused and this is still an important objective for today's postal administrations. Stamp collectors, on the other hand, prefer postmarks to be lightly applied, clear, and to leave as much as possible of the design visible. Dated, circular cancellations have long been 'the postmark of choice', but the definition of a 'Fine' cancellation will depend upon the types of cancellation in use at the time a stamp was current—it is clearly illogical to seek a circular datestamp on a Penny Black.

'Fine', by definition, will be superior to 'Average', so, in terms of cancellation quality, if one begins by identifying what 'Average' looks like, then one will be half way to identifying 'Fine'. The illustrations will give some guidance on mid-19th century and mid-20th century cancellations of Great Britain, but types of cancellation in general use in each country and in each period will determine the appearance of 'Fine'.

Anything less than 'Fine' will result in a downgrading of the stamp concerned, while a very fine or superb cancellation will be worth a premium.

Post Office Label Sheets
This catalogue lists complete 'Generic Smilers' sheets in a section following the booklet listings. 'Personalised' and 'Corporate' sheets are not listed, neither are identifiable single stamps from label sheets.

PHILATELIC INFORMATION

General Types of watermark *as seen through the front of the stamp*

PHILATELIC INFORMATION

No Value Indicated Stamps

From 22 August 1989 various definitive and special stamps appeared inscribed '2nd', '1st' or 'E' instead of a face value. These were sold at the current minimum rates for these services which were as follows:

Inland Postage Rate	2nd Class	1st Class
5 September 1988	14p.	19p.
2 October 1989	15p.	20p.
17 September 1990	17p.	22p.
16 September 1991	18p.	24p.
1 November 1993	19p.	25p.
8 July 1996	20p.	26p.
26 April 1999	19p.	26p.
17 April 2000	19p.	27p.
8 May 2003	20p.	28p.
1 April 2004	21p.	28p.
7 April 2005	21p.	30p.
3 April 2006	23p.	32p.
2 April 2007	24p.	34p.
7 April 2008	27p.	36p.
6 April 2009	30p.	39p.
6 April 2010	32p.	41p.
4 April 2011	36p.	46p.
30 April 2012	50p.	60p.
31 March 2014	53p.	62p.
30 March 2015	54p.	63p.
29 March 2016	55p.	64p.
27 March 2017	56p.	65p.
26 March 2018	58p.	67p.
25 March 2019	61p.	70p.
23 March 2020	65p.	76p.
1 January 2021	66p.	85p.
4 April 2022	68p.	95p.

European Airmail Rate	
26 April 1999	30p.
25 October 1999	34p.
27 April 2000	36p.
2 July 2001	37p.
27 March 2003	38p.
1 April 2004	40p.

From June 2004, European Airmail rate stamps reverted to showing a face value.

From 4 April 2022 the European Airmail rate is £1.85.

From 21 August 2006 'Large' letters were charged at a higher rate following the introduction of 'Pricing in Proportion'. Rates as follows:

Inland Postage Rate	2nd Class Large	1st Class Large
21 August 2006	37p.	44p.
2 April 2007	40p.	48p.
7 April 2008	42p.	52p.
6 April 2009	47p.	61p.
6 April 2010	51p.	66p.
4 April 2011	58p.	75p.
30 April 2012	69p.	90p.
31 March 2014	73p.	93p.
30 March 2015	74p.	95p.
29 March 2016	75p.	96p.
27 March 2017	76p.	98p.
26 March 2018	79p.	£1.01
25 March 2019	83p.	£1.06
23 March 2020	88p.	£1.15
1 January 2021	96p.	£1.29
4 April 2022	£1.05	£1.45

In 2009 special stamps were introduced for the Recorded Delivery service (renamed Royal Mail Signed For in 2013) and in 2010 for Special Delivery. Rates for these services have increased as follows:

Date	Recorded/Signed for 1st	Recorded/Signed for 1st Large	Special Delivery to 100g	Special Delivery to 500g
17 Nov 2009	£1.14	£1.36		
6 April 2010	£1.15	£1.40		
26 Oct 2010	£1.15	£1.40	£5.05	£5.50
4 April 2011	£1.23	£1.52	£5.45	£5.90
30 April 2012	£1.55	£1.85	£5.90	£6.35
2 April 2013	£1.70	£2.00	£6.22	£6.95
31 March 2014	£1.72	£2.03	£6.40	£7.15
30 March 2015	£1.73	£2.05	£6.45	£7.25
29 March 2016	£1.74	£2.06	£6.45	£7.25
27 March 2017	£1.75	£2.08	£6.45	£7.25
26 March 2018	£1.77	£2.11	£6.50	£7.30
25 March 2019	£1.90	£2.26	£6.60	£7.40
23 March 2020	£2.06	£2.45	£6.70	£7.50
1 January 2021	£2.25	£2.69	£6.85	£7.65
4 April 2022	£2.35	£2.85	£6.85	£7.65

Over the same period European and Worldwide rates have increased as follows. Note that the current rate covered by the 'E' denominated stamps is shown in the left-hand column.

	Europe 20g *	World 10g *	Europe 60/100g **	World 20g	World 40/60/100g ***
6 April 2009	56p	62p	-	90p	-
6 April 2010	70p	67p	-	97p	£1.46
4 April 2011	68p	76p	-	£1.10	£1.65
30 April 2012	87p			£1.28	£1.90
2 April 2013	88p		-	£1.25	£1.88
31 March 2014	97p		£1.47	£1.28	£2.15
30 March 2015	£1		£1.52	£1.33	£2.25
29 March 2016	£1.05		£1.52	£1.33	£2.25
27 March 2017	£1.17		£1.57	£1.40	£2.27
26 March 2018	£1.25		£1.55	£1.45	£2.25
25 March 2019	£1.35		£1.60	£1.55	£2.30
23 March 2020	£1.42		£1.68	£1.63	£2.42
1 January 2021	£1.70		£1.70	£1.70	£2.55
4 April 2022	£1.85		£1.85	£1.85	£2.55

* The Europe 20g. and Worldwide 10g. rates were combined from 30 April 2012

** The upper weight for the Europe 60g. rate, introduced on 31 March 2014, was increased to 100g. from 30 March 2015

*** The upper weight for the Worldwide 40g. rate was increased to 60g. from 31 March 2014 and 100g. from 30 March 2015

PHQ Card cancelled on First Day of Issue

PHQ Cards

From 1973 the Post Office produced sets of picture cards to accompany commemorative issues which can be sent through the post as postcards. Each card shows an enlarged colour reproduction of one stamp, initially of a single value from one set and subsequently of all values.

The Post Office gives each card a 'PHQ' serial number, hence the term. The cards are usually on sale shortly

PHILATELIC INFORMATION

before the date of issue of the stamps, but there is no officially designated 'first day'. Cards are priced in fine mint condition for complete sets as issued. Used prices are for cards franked with the stamp affixed, on the obverse, as illustrated; the stamp being cancelled with an official postmark for first day of issue.

Watermark Types

Stamps are on unwatermarked paper except where the heading to the set states otherwise.

Watermarks are detected for Catalogue description by one of four methods: (1) holding stamps to the light; (2) laying stamps face down on a dark background; (3) by use of the Morley-Bright Detector, which works by revealing the thinning of the paper at the watermark; or (4) by the more complex electric watermark detectors such as the Stanley Gibbons Detectamark Spectrum.

The diagram above shows how watermark position is described in the Catalogue. Watermarks are usually impressed so that they read normally when looked through from the printed side. However, since philatelists customarily detect watermarks by looking at the back of the stamp, the watermark diagram also makes clear what is actually seen. Note that 'G v R' is only an example and illustrations of the different watermarks employed are shown in the listings. The illustrations are actual size and shown in normal positions (from the front of the stamps).

AS DESCRIBED (Read through front of stamp)		AS SEEN DURING WATERMARK DETECTION (Stamp face down and back examined)
GvR	Normal	ЯvӘ
ЯvӘ (inverted)	Inverted	ӘvЯ
ЯvӘ (reversed)	Reversed	GvR
ӘvЯ	Inverted and reversed	ЯvӘ
GvR (sideways)	Sideways	ЯvӘ (sideways)
GvR (sideways inverted)	Sideways inverted	ЯvӘ (sideways inverted)
ЯvӘ (sideways reversed)	Sideways reversed	GvR (sideways)
ЯvӘ (sideways inverted and reversed)	Sideways inverted and reversed	GvR (sideways)

Watermark Errors and Varieties

Watermark errors are recognised as of major importance. They comprise stamps showing the wrong watermark devices or stamps printed on paper with the wrong watermark. Stamps printed on paper showing broken or deformed bits on the dandy roll, are not listable.

Underprints

From 1982 various values appeared with underprints, printed on the reverse, in blue, over the gum. These were usually from special stamp booklets, sold at a discount by the Post Office, but in 1985 surplus stocks of such underprinted paper were used for other purposes.

In this Catalogue stamps showing underprints are priced mint only. Used examples can be obtained, but care has to be taken in floating the stamps since the devices were printed on top of the gum and will be removed as the gum dissolves.

Underprint Types

1 Star with central dot   **2** Double-lined Star   **3** Double-lined 'D'

4 Multiple double lined stars

5 Multiple double-lined 'D'
(Types **4/5** are shown ¾ actual size)

Note: Types **4/5** are arranged in a random pattern so that the stamps from the same sheet or booklet pane will show the underprint in a slightly different position to the above. Stamps, when inspected, should be placed the correct way up, face down, when comparing with the illustrations.

PHILATELIC INFORMATION

Specimen Stamps

From 1847 stamps have been overprinted 'SPECIMEN' for a variety of purposes, including the provision of samples to postmasters, as a security overprint on printers' or official reference copies and, from 1859, on examples of current British stamps sent to the International Bureau of the Univeral Postal Union for distribution to member nations.

Numerous styles were employed for these 'SPECIMEN' overprints, which are now listed in this catalogue up to decimalisation in 1971. The different types are illustrated here. Note that for ease of reference type numbers are the same as those given in the *Stanley Gibbons Great Britain Specialised Catalogue* and 'missing' type numbers may have been used on stamps outside the scope of this catalogue or may refer to 'Cancelled' overprints, which are, likewise, not listed here.

SPECIMEN
1

SPECIMEN
2

SPECIMEN
3

SPECIMEN
4

SPECIMEN
5

SPECIMEN
6

SPECIMEN
7

SPECIMEN
8

SPECIMEN
9

SPECIMEN
10

SPECIMEN
11

SPECIMEN
12

SPECIMEN
13

SPECIMEN
15

SPECIMEN
16

SPECIMEN
17

SPECIMEN
22

SPECIMEN
23

SPECIMEN
26

SPECIMEN
29

SPECIMEN
30

SPECIMEN
31

SPECIMEN
32

'SPECIMEN' stamps are listed with details of the types of 'SPECIMEN' overprints found. The different types are not listed and where more than one type was used the price given is for the cheapest version. Imperforate overprints are also not listed, unless the stamp was normally issued in that form.

More detailed listings will be found in Volumes 1 and 2 of the *Great Britain Specialised Catalogue*.

GREAT BRITAIN
POSTAL HISTORY and STAMPS to 1930

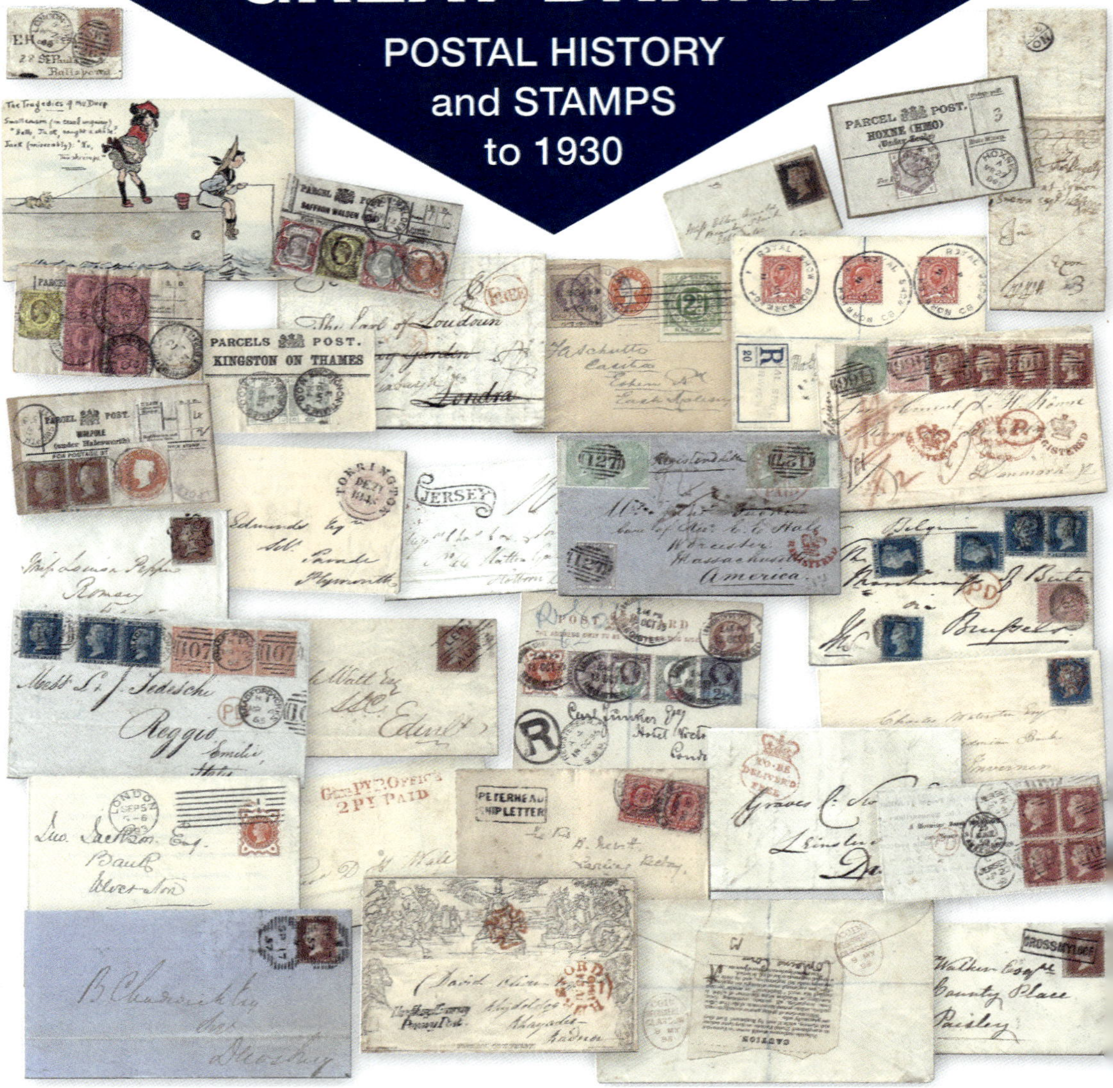

Postal History from 1300 and Fine Stamps from Queen Victoria to King George V

YOUR WANTS LIST IS WELCOME!

BUYING Collections and single items of Postal History and Fine Stamps

Martin Townsend

Established over 40 years - clients may rely on our reputation and expertise

PO Box 1100, Camberley, Surrey, GU15 9RY

TEL: 01462 420678 MOBILE: 07801 769 117 E-mail: Martin@martintownsend.com

www.martintownsend.com

Andrew G Lajer Philatelist
Great Britain
1840-1952

Fine Stamps and Postal History

Visit our website to view hundreds of fine GB items:

www.andrewglajer.co.uk

 +44(0)1189 344151

 sales@andrewglajer.co.uk

Andrew G. Lajer, The Old Post Office, Davis Way, Hurst, Reading, Berkshire, RG10 0TR, UK

 # Embassy Philatelists

RETAIL LISTS & POSTAL AUCTIONS PRODUCED MONTHLY
CATALOGUE SENT FREE ON REQUEST
1000's OF ITEMS TO VIEW AND BUY ON OUR WEBSITE

Rare GB
bought and sold daily

BUYING
From single items to major collections, for a fast professional transaction call us today.

Embassy Philatelists
P.O. BOX 1553, GUILDFORD, GU1 9YT
 Tel: 01483 811 168
Email: info@embassystamps.co.uk

www.embassystamps.co.uk

BUYING
From single items to major collections, for a fast professional transaction call us today.

Queen Victoria
20 June 1837-22 January 1901

PARLIAMENTARY ENVELOPES

When the Uniform Penny Postage was introduced on 10 January 1840 the free franking privileges of Members of Parliament were abolished. During the same month, special envelopes were introduced for mail posted from the Houses of Parliament and these remained in use until the introduction of stamps and the Mulready stationery in May 1840. Envelopes are priced in used condition only.

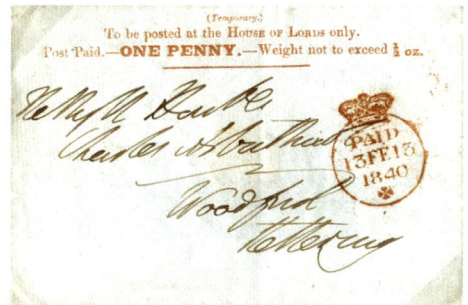

1840 (16 Jan). Inscribed 'Houses of Parliament' in black
PE2	1d. envelope	from	£8000
PE3	2d. envelope	from	£25000
PE4	4d. envelope	from	

1840 (16 Jan). Inscribed 'House of Lords' in vermilion
PE5	1d. envelope	from	£12000
PE8	2d. envelope		—

1840 (Jan). Inscribed 'House of Commons' in black
PE9	1d. envelope	from	£3000

MULREADY ENVELOPES AND LETTER SHEETS

So called from the name of the designer, William Mulready, were issued concurrently with the first British adhesive stamps.

A large number of letter sheets and much smaller quantity of envelopes were sold by businesses, advertising to promote their services.

1840 (6 May). Letter sheets
ME1	1d. black	£350	£550
	a. With advertisements printed inside from	£750	£850
	s. 'SPECIMEN', Type 2	£3750	
ME3	2d. blue	£425	£2400
	a. With advertisements printed inside from		£3500
	s. 'SPECIMEN', Type 2	£5500	

1840 (6 May). Envelopes
ME2	1d. black	£350	£550
	a. With advertisements printed inside from	£2500	£3500
	s. 'SPECIMEN', Type 2	£3750	
ME4	2d. blue	£450	£2500
	a. With advertisements printed inside from		£3500
	s. 'SPECIMEN', Type 2	£5500	

LINE-ENGRAVED ISSUES
GENERAL NOTES

Brief notes on some aspects of the line-engraved stamps follow, but for further information and a full specialist treatment of these issues collectors are recommended to consult Volume 1, Part 1 of the Stanley Gibbons *Great Britain Specialised Catalogue*.

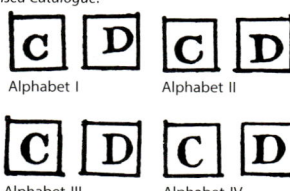

Alphabet I   Alphabet II
Alphabet III   Alphabet IV

Typical Corner Letters of the four Alphabets

Alphabets. Four different styles were used for the corner letters on stamps prior to the issue with letters in all four corners, these being known to collectors as:
Alphabet I. Used for all plates made from 1840 to the end of 1851. Letters small.
Alphabet II. Plates from 1852 to mid-1855. Letters larger, heavier and broader.
Alphabet III. Plates from mid-1855 to end of period. Letters tall and more slender.
Alphabet IV. 1861. 1d. Die II, Plates 50 and 51 only. Letters were hand-engraved instead of being punched on the plate. They are therefore inconsistent in shape and size but generally larger and outstanding.

While the general descriptions and the illustrations of typical letters given above may be of some assistance, only long experience and published aids can enable every stamp to be allocated to its particular Alphabet without hesitation, as certain letters in each are similar to those in one of the others.

Blued Paper. The blueing of the paper of the earlier issues is believed to be due to the presence of prussiate of potash in the printing ink, or in the paper, which, under certain conditions, tended to colour the paper when the sheets were damped for printing. An alternative term is *bleuté* paper.

Corner Letters. The corner letters on the early British stamps were intended as a safeguard against forgery, each stamp in the sheet having a different combination of letters. Taking the first 1d. stamp, printed in 20 horizontal rows of 12, as an example, the lettering is as follows:

Row 1.	A A, A B, A C, etc. to A L.
Row 2.	B A, B B, B C, etc. to B L.
	and so on to
Row 20	T A, T B, T C, etc. to T L.

On the stamps with four corner letters, those in the upper corners are in the reverse positions to those in the lower corners.
Thus in a sheet of 240 (12×20) the sequence is:

Row 1.	A A	B A	C A		L A
				etc. to	
	A A	A B	A C		A L
Row 2.	A B	B B	C B		L B
				etc. to	
	B A	B B	B C		B L
	and so on to				
	A T	B T	C T		L T
Row 20.				etc. to	
	T A	T B	T C		T L

Placing letters in all four corners was not only an added precaution against forgery but was meant to deter unmarked parts of used stamps being pieced together and passed off as an unused whole.

Dies. The first die of the 1d. was used for making the original die of the 2d., both the No Lines and White Lines issues. In 1855 the 1d. Die I was amended by retouching the head and deepening the lines on a transferred impression of the original. This later version, known to collectors as Die II, was used for making the dies for the 1d. and 2d. with letters in all four corners and also for the 1½d.

The two dies are illustrated above No. 17 in the catalogue.

Double letter   Guide line in corner

QUEEN VICTORIA

Guide line through value

Double Corner Letters. These are due to the workman placing his letter-punch in the wrong position at the first attempt, when lettering the plate, and then correcting the mistake; or to a slight shifting of the punch when struck. A typical example is illustrated. If a wrong letter was struck in the first instance, traces of a wrong letter may appear in a corner in addition to the correct one.

Guide Lines and Dots. When laying down the impressions of the design on the early plates, fine vertical and horizontal guide lines were marked on the plates to assist the operative. These were usually removed from the gutter margins, but could not be removed from the stamp impression without damage to the plate, so that in such cases they appear on the printed stamps, sometimes in the corners, sometimes through 'POSTAGE' or the value. Typical examples are illustrated.

Guide dots or cuts were similarly made to indicate the spacing of the guide lines. These too sometimes appear on the stamps.

Ivory Head

'Ivory Head'. The so-called 'ivory head' variety is one in which the Queen's Head shows white on the back of the stamp. It arises from the comparative absence of ink in the head portion of the design, with consequent absence of blueing. (See 'Blued Paper', above).

Line-engraving. In this context 'line-engraved' is synonymous with recess-printing, in which the engraver cuts recesses in a plate and printing (the coloured areas) is from these recesses. 'Line-engraved' is the traditional philatelic description for these stamps; other equivalent terms found are 'engraving in *taille-douce*' (French) or 'in intaglio' (Italian).

Plates. Until the introduction of the stamps with letters in all four corners, the number of the plate was not indicated in the design of the stamp, but was printed on the sheet margin. By long study of identifiable blocks and the minor variation in the design, coupled with the position of the corner letters, philatelists are now able to allot many of these stamps to their respective plates. Specialist collectors often endeavour to obtain examples of a given stamp printed from its different plates and our catalogue accordingly reflects this depth of detail.

Postmarks. The so-called Maltese Cross design was the first employed for obliterating British postage stamps and was in use from 1840 to 1844. Being hand-cut, the obliterating stamps varied greatly in detail and some distinctive types can be allotted to particular towns or offices. Local types, such as those used at Manchester, Norwich, Leeds, etc., are keenly sought. A red ink was first employed, but was superseded by black, after some earlier experiments, in February 1841. Maltese Cross obliterations in other colours are rare.

Obliteration of this type, numbered 1 to 12 in the centre, were used at the London Chief Office in 1843 and 1844.

Some straight-line cancellations were in use in 1840 at the Penny Post receiving offices, normally applied on the envelope, the adhesives then being obliterated at the Head Office. They are nevertheless known, with or without Maltese Cross, on the early postage stamps.

In 1842 some offices in south-west England used dated postmarks in place of the Maltese Cross, usually on the back of the letter since they were not originally intended as obliterators. These town postmarks have likewise been found on adhesives.

In 1844 the Maltese Cross design was superseded by numbered obliterators of varied type, one of which is illustrated. They are naturally comparatively scarce on the first 1d. and 2d. stamps.

Like the Maltese Cross they are found in various colours, some of which are rare.

Re-entry

'Union Jack' re-entry

Re-entries. Re-entries on the plate show as a doubling of part of the design of the stamp generally at top or bottom. Many re-entries are very slight while others are most marked. A typical one is illustrated.

The 'Union Jack' re-entry, so-called owing to the effect of the re-entry on the appearance of the corner stars (see illustration) occurs on stamp L K of Plate 75 of the 1d. red, Die I.

Maltese Cross   Type of Town Postmark

Type of Penny Post Cancellation

Example of 1844 type postmark

T A (T L)   M A (M L)

Varieties of Large Crown Watermark

I   II

Two states of Large Crown Watermark

QUEEN VICTORIA

Watermarks. Two watermark varieties, as illustrated, consisting of crowns of entirely different shape, are found in sheets of the Large Crown paper and fall on stamps lettered M A and T A (or M L and T L when the paper is printed on the wrong side). Both varieties are found on the 1d. rose-red of 1857, while the M A (M L) variety comes also on some plates of the 1d. of 1864 (Nos. 43, 44) up to about Plate 96. On the 2d. the T A (T L) variety is known on plates 8 and 9, and the M A (M L) on later prints of plate 9. These varieties may exist inverted, or inverted reversed on stamps lettered A A and A L and H A and H L, and some are known.

In 1861 a minor alteration was made in the Large Crown watermark by the removal of the two vertical strokes, representing *fleurs-de-lis*, which projected upwards from the uppermost of the three horizontal curves at the base of the Crown. Hence two states are distinguishable, as illustrated.

1 **1a** **2** Small Crown

(Eng Charles and Frederick Heath)

1840 (6 May). Letters in lower corners. Wmk Small Crown, W **2**. Imperf.

			Unused	Used	Used on cover
1	1	1d. intense black	£17500	£525	
2		1d. black	£12500	£375	£750
		Wi. Watermark inverted	£35000	£2500	
3		1d. grey-black (worn plate)	£16500	£500	
4	1a	2d. deep full blue	£45000	£1200	
5		2d. blue	£38000	£975	£2750
		Wi. Watermark inverted	£60000	£6000	
6		2d. pale blue	£45000	£1100	

The 1d. stamp in black was printed from Plates 1 to 11. Plate 1 exists in two states (known to collectors as 1a and 1b), the latter being the result of extensive repairs.

Repairs were also made to plates 2, 5, 6, 8, 9, 10 and 11, and certain impressions exist in two or more states.

The so-called 'Royal reprint' of the 1d. black was made in 1864, from Plate 66, Die II, on paper with Large Crown watermark, inverted. A printing was also made in carmine, on paper with the same watermark, upright.

For 1d. black with 'VR' in upper corners see No. V1.

The 2d. stamps were printed from Plates 1 and 2.

CONDITION-IMPERFORATE

LINE-ENGRAVED ISSUES

The prices quoted for the 1840 and 1841 imperforate Line engraved issues are for very 'fine' examples. As condition is most important in assessing the value of a stamp, the following definitions will assist collectors in the evaluation of individual examples.

Four main factors are relevant when considering quality.

(a) Impression. This should be clean and the surface free of any rubbing or unnatural blurring which would detract from the appearance.

(b) Margin. This is perhaps the most difficult factor to evaluate. Stamps described as 'fine', the standard adopted in this catalogue for pricing purposes, should have margins of the recognised width, defined as approximately one half of the distance between two adjoining unsevered stamps. Stamps described as 'very fine' or 'superb' should have margins which are proportionately larger than those of a 'fine' stamp. Examples with close margins should not, generally, be classified as 'fine'.

(c) Cancellation. On a 'fine' stamp this should be reasonably clear and not noticeably smudged. A stamp described as 'superb' should have a neat cancellation, preferably centrally placed or to the right.

(d) Appearance. Stamps, at the prices quoted, should always be without any tears, creases, bends or thins and should not be toned on either the front or back. Stamps with such defects are worth only a proportion of the catalogue price.

Plates of 1d. black

	Unused	Used	Used on cover
1a	£18500	£450	£1000
1b	£12500	£400	£750
2	£12500	£375	£750
3	£20000	£500	£1000
4	£13000	£425	£850
5	£12500	£400	£775
6	£13500	£400	£775
7	£13500	£450	£850
8	£16500	£525	£1000
9	£20000	£625	£1200
10	£27500	£950	£3500
11	£22000	£4600	£16000

Varieties of 1d. black

		Unused	Used
a.	On *bleuté* paper (Plates 1 to 8) ...... from	—	£775
b.	Double letter in corner .... from	£13000	£400
bb.	Re-entry .... from	£13500	£450
bc.	'PB' re-entry (Plate 5, 3rd state)	—	£8000
c.	Guide line in corner	£13000	£400
cc.	Large letters in each corner (E J, I L, J C and P A) (Plate 1b) .... from	£13500	£550
d.	Guide line through value	£13000	£450
g.	Obliterated by Maltese Cross		
	In red	†	£425
	In black	†	£375
	In blue	†	£8000
	In magenta	†	£2250
	In yellow	†	—
	In violet	†	£12000
h.	Obliterated by Maltese Cross with number in centre .... from	†	£12000
i.	Obliterated 'Penny Post' in black (without Maltese Cross) .... from	†	£3500
j.	Obliterated by town postmark (without Maltese Cross)		
	In black .... from	†	£15000
	In yellow .... from	†	£40000
	In red .... from	†	£15000
k.	Obliterated by 1844 type postmark in black .... from	†	£1800

Average

Fine

Very Fine

Superb

The actual size illustrations of 1840 1d. blacks show the various grades of quality. When comparing these illustrations it should be assumed that they are all from the same plate and that they are free of any hidden defects.

PRINTERS. Nos. 1/53a were recess-printed by Perkins Bacon & Petch, known from 1852 as Perkins Bacon & Co.

STAMPS ON COVER. Prices are quoted, for those Victorian and Edwardian issues usually found used *on cover*. In general these prices refer to single examples of the cheapest versions of each basic stamp, with other shades, plates or varieties, together with unusual frankings and postmarks, being worth more. However multiples of some stamps may be more common than single usages and in this case the covers might be worth considerably less than the price quoted.

Plates of 2d. blue (Plates 1 and 2)

Plate		Unused	Used	Used on cover
1	Shades from	£38000	£975	£2750
2	Shades from	£45000	£1000	£3000

3

QUEEN VICTORIA

Varieties of 2d. blue

		Unused	Used
a.	Double letter in corner	—	£1100
aa.	Re-entry	—	£1100
b.	Guide lines in corner	—	£1000
c.	Guide lines through value	—	£1100
e.	Obliterated by Maltese Cross		
	In red	†	£1250
	In black	†	£975
	In blue	†	£12000
	In magenta	†	£9000
f.	Obliterated by Maltese Cross with number in centre ....from	†	£14000
g.	Obliterated 'Penny Post' in black (without Maltese Cross) ....from	†	£15000
h.	Obliterated by town postmark (without Maltese Cross) in black ....from	†	£7000
i.	Obliterated by 1844 type postmark ....from		
	In black ....from	†	£2000
	In blue ....from	†	£14000

OFFICIAL STAMP

In 1840 the 1d. black (T 1), with 'V R' in the upper corners, was prepared for official use, but was never issued for postal purposes. Obliterated specimens are those which were used for experimental trials of obliterating inks, or those that passed through the post by oversight.

V1

1840. Prepared for use but not issued; 'V' 'R' in upper corners. Imperf.
V1   **V1**   1d. black £20000 £22500

1841 (10 Feb). Printed from 'black' plates. Wmk W **2**. Paper more or less blued. Imperf.

			Unused	Used	Used on cover
7	1	1d. red-brown (shades)	£2500	£130	£350
		a. 'PB' re-entry (Plate 5, 3rd state)	—	£2250	
		Wi. Watermark inverted (Plates 1b, 8 and 10) from	—	£6000	

The first printings of the 1d. in red-brown were made from Plates 1b, 2, 5 and 8 to 11 used for the 1d. black.

1d. red-brown from 'black' plates

Plate	Unused	Used	Used on Cover
1b	£23000	£375	£650
2	£25000	£325	£550
5	£9000	£180	£400
8	£11000	£275	£500
9	£5000	£190	£375
10	£2500	£200	£400
11	£8500	£130	£350

1841 (late Feb). Plate 12 onwards. Wmk W **2**. Paper more or less blued. Imperf.

		Unused	Used	Used on cover
8	1d. red-brown	£600	35·00	45·00
	s. Optd 'SPECIMEN' (1)	£2000		
	Wi. Watermark inverted	£5000	£400	
8a	1d. red-brown on very blue paper	£700	35·00	
9	1d. pale red-brown (worn plates)	£675	45·00	
10	1d. deep red-brown	£900	50·00	
11	1d. lake-red	£5250	£850	
12	1d. orange-brown	£2000	£275	

Error. No letter 'A' in right lower corner (Stamp B (A), Plate 77).
| 12a | **1** | 1d. red-brown | — | £22000 | |

The error 'No letter A in right corner' was due to the omission to insert this letter on stamp B A of Plate 77. The error was discovered some months after the plate was registered and was then corrected.

There are innumerable variations in the colour shade of the 1d. 'red' and those given in the above list represent colour groups each covering a wide range.

Varieties of 1d. red-brown, etc

		Unused	Used
b.	Major re-entry ....from	—	£100
c.	Double letter in corner ....from	£625	40·00
d.	Double Star (Plate 75) 'Union Jack' re-entry	£25000	£2500
e.	Guide line in corner	£625	38·00
f.	Guide line through value	£625	40·00
g.	Thick outer frame to stamp	£625	38·00
h.	Ivory head	£625	38·00
i.	Treasury roulette	£50000	£5000
j.	Left corner letter 'S' inverted (Plates 78, 105, 107) ....from	—	£180
k.	P converted to R (Plates 30/31, 33, 83, 86/87) ....from	—	80·00
l.	Obliterated by Maltese Cross		
	In red	†	£2500
	In black	†	60·00
	In blue	†	£650
m.	Obliterated by Maltese Cross with number in centre		
	No. 1	†	£180
	No. 2	†	£180
	No. 3	†	£225
	No. 4	†	£500
	No. 5	†	£180
	No. 6	†	£160
	No. 7	†	£160
	No. 8	†	£160
	No. 9	†	£180
	No. 10	†	£320
	No. 11	†	£350
	No. 12	†	£350
n.	Obliterated 'Penny Post' in black (without Maltese Cross)	†	£1100
o.	Obliterated by town postmark (without Maltese Cross)		
	In black ....from	†	£700
	In blue ....from	†	£1800
	In green ....from	†	£3250
	In yellow ....from	†	—
	In red ....from	†	£8000
p.	Obliterated by 1844 type postmark		
	In blue ....from	†	£250
	In red ....from	†	£5500
	In green ....from	†	£2800
	In violet ....from	†	£3500
	In black ....from	†	35·00
	In olive-yellow/brown ....from	†	£2000

Stamps with thick outer frame to the design are from plates on which the frame-lines have been straightened or recut, particularly Plates 76 and 90.

For 'Union Jack' re-entry see General Notes to Line-engraved Issues.

In 'P converted to R' the corner letter 'R' is formed from the 'P', the distinctive long tail having been hand-cut.

KEY TO LINE-ENGRAVED ISSUES

SG Nos.	Description	Date	Wmk	Perf	Die	Alphabet
THE IMPERFORATE ISSUES						
1/3	1d. black	6.5.40	SC	Imp	I	I
4/6	2d. no lines	8.5.40	SC	Imp	I	I
PAPER MORE OR LESS BLUED						
7	1d. red-brown	2.41	SC	Imp	I	I
8/12	1d. red-brown	2.41	SC	Imp	I	I
8/12	1d. red-brown	4.52	SC	Imp	I	II
13/15	2d. white lines	13.3.41	SC	Imp	I	I
THE PERFORATED ISSUES						
ONE PENNY VALUE						
16a	1d. red-brown	1848	SC	Roul	I	I
16b	1d. red-brown	1850	SC	16	I	I
17/18	1d. red-brown	2.54	SC	16	I	II
22	1d. red-brown	1.55	SC	14	I	II
24/25	1d. red-brown	27.2.55	SC	16	II	II
21	1d. red-brown	17.2.55	SC	16	II	II
26	1d. red-brown	24.7.55	LC	16	II	II
29/33	1d. red-brown	10.1.56	LC	14	II	III
37	1d. red-brown	3.1856	LC	14	II	III
NEW COLOURS ON WHITE PAPER						
38/41	1d. rose-red	3.57	LC	14	II	III
36	1d. rose-red	26.12.57	LC	16	II	III
42	1d. rose-red	9.7.61	LC	14	II	IV
TWO PENCE VALUE						
19, 20	2d. blue	1.3.54	SC	16	I	I
23	2d. blue	22.2.55	SC	14	I	I
23a	2d. blue	4.7.55	SC	14	I	II
20a	2d. blue	18.8.55	SC	16	I	II
27	2d. blue	20.7.55	LC	16	I	II

QUEEN VICTORIA

SG Nos.	Description	Date	Wmk	Perf	Die	Alphabet
34	2d. blue	20.7.55	LC	14	I	II
35	2d. blue	2.7.57	LC	14	I	III
36a	2d. blue	1.2.58	LC	16	I	III
	LETTERS IN ALL FOUR CORNERS					
48/49	½d. rose-red	1.10.70	W 9	14		—
43/44	1d. rose-red	1.4.64	LC	14		II
53a	1½d. rosy mauve	1860	LC	14		II
51/53	1½d. rose-red	1.10.70	LC	14		II
45	2d. blue	7.58	LC	14		II
46/47	2d. thinner lines	7.7.69	LC	14		II

Watermarks: SC = Small Crown, W **2**. LC = Large Crown, W **4**.

Dies: See notes above No. 17 in the catalogue.

Alphabets: See General Notes to this section.

3 White lines added   BH Spectacles variety (Plate 4)

1841 (13 Mar)–**51**. White lines added. Wmk W **2**. Paper more or less blued. Imperf.

			Unused	Used	Used on cover
13	**3**	2d. pale blue	£7500	£110	
14		2d. blue	£5000	90·00	£350
		s. Optd 'SPECIMEN' (1)	£5500		
		Wi. Watermark inverted	£18000	£875	
15		2d. deep full blue	£6500	£110	
15aa		2d. violet-blue (1851)	£22000	£1500	

The 2d. stamp with white lines was printed from Plates 3 and 4.

No. 15aa came from Plate 4 and the quoted price is for examples on thicker, lavender tinted paper.

Plates of 2d. blue

Plate		Unused	Used
3 shades	from	£5000	£100
4 shades	from	£5000	90·00

Varieties of 2d. blue

		Unused	Used
a.	Guide line in corner	£5250	£110
b.	Guide line through value	£5500	£125
bb.	Double letter in corner	£5500	£125
be	Re-entry	£6500	£225
c.	Ivory head	£5250	£100
d.	Spectacles variety: BH Plate 4 (Later printings)	£11500	£1100
e.	Obliterated by Maltese Cross		
	In red	†	—
	In black	†	£275
	In blue	†	£4000
f.	Obliterated by Maltese Cross with number in centre		
	No. 1	†	£700
	No. 2	†	£700
	No. 3	†	£700
	No. 4	†	£700
	No. 5	†	£850
	No. 6	†	£700
	No. 7	†	£1200
	No. 8	†	£1000
	No. 9	†	£1200
	No. 10	†	£1500
	No. 11	†	£850
	No. 12	†	£550
g.	Obliterated by town postmark (without Maltese Cross)		
	In black	from	†	£3000
	In blue	from	†	£4500
h.	Obliterated by 1844 type postmark		
	In black	from	†	90·00
	In blue	from	†	£875
	In red	from	†	£20000
	In green	from	†	£6000

1841 (Apr). Trial printing (unissued) on Dickinson silk-thread paper. No wmk. Imperf.

| 16 | **1** | 1d. red-brown (Plate 11) | £4750 | † |

Eight sheets were printed on this paper, six being gummed, two ungummed, but we have only seen examples without gum.

1848. Wmk W **2**. Rouletted approx 11½ by Henry Archer.

| 16a | **1** | 1d. red-brown (Plates 70, 71) | £15000 | † |

1850. Wmk W **2**. Perf 16 by Henry Archer.

			Unused	Used	Used on cover
16b	**1**	1d. red-brown (Alphabet 1) (from Plates 90–94, 96–101, 105, 107, 108, 116)	from £3000	£550	£1500
		bWi. Watermark inverted from	—	£3750	

SEPARATION TRIALS. Although the various trials of machines for rouletting and perforating were unofficial, Archer had the consent of the authorities in making his experiments, and sheets so experimented upon were afterwards used by the Post Office.

As Archer ended his experiments in 1850 and plates with corner letters of Alphabet II did not come into issue until 1852, perforated stamps with corner letters of Alphabet I may safely be assumed to be Archer productions, if genuine.

Die I   Die II   **4** Large Crown

Die I: The features of the portrait are lightly shaded and consequently lack emphasis.

Die II: (Die I retouched by William Humphrys): The lines of the features have been deepened and appear stronger. The eye is deeply shaded and made more lifelike. The nostril and lips are more clearly defined, the latter appearing much thicker. A strong downward stroke of colour marks the corner of the mouth. There is a deep indentation of colour between lower lip and chin. The band running from the back of the ear to the chignon has a bolder horizontal line below it than in Die I.

1854–57. Paper more or less blued.

*(a) Wmk Small Crown, W **2**. Perf 16.*

			Unused	Used*	Used on cover
17		1d. red-brown (Die I) (24.2.54)	£375	35·00	60·00
		a. Imperf three sides (horiz pair)	†	£6500	
		Wi. Watermark inverted	—	£350	
18		1d. yellow-brown (Die I)	£450	50·00	
19	**3**	2d. deep blue (Plate 4) (1.3.54)	£4700	£100	£200
		a. Imperf three sides (horiz pair)	†	—	
		b. Spectacles variety: BH		£550	
		s. Optd 'SPECIMEN' (2)	£2000		
		Wi. Watermark inverted	—	£325	
20		2d. pale blue (Plate 4)	£5500	£110	
20a		2d. blue (Plate 5) (18.8.55)	£10000	£350	£550
		aWi. Watermark inverted	—	£950	
21	**1**	1d. red-brown (Die II) (17.2.55)	£550	65·00	£110
		a. Imperf (Plates 2, 14)			
		Wi. Watermark inverted	£1800	£300	

*(b) Wmk Small Crown, W **2**. Perf 14.*

22	**1**	1d. red-brown (Die I) (20.1.55)	£1200	£100	£180
		Wi. Watermark inverted		£400	
23	**3**	2d. blue (Plate 4) (22.2.55)	£13000	£225	£375
		a. Spectacles variety: BH	—	£1000	
		s. Optd 'SPECIMEN' (2)	£1700		
		Wi. Watermark inverted	£18500	£675	
23a		2d. blue (Plate 5) (4.7.55)	£14000	£350	£525
		b. Imperf (Plate 5)			
		aWi. Watermark inverted	—	£950	
24	**1**	1d. red-brown (Die II) (27.2.55)	£700	70·00	£125

QUEEN VICTORIA

			Unused	Used*	Used on cover
24a		Wi. Watermark inverted	£2500	£400	
		1d. deep red-brown (very blue paper) (Die II)	£850	£110	
25		1d. orange-brown (Die II)	£1900	£225	

(c) Wmk Large Crown, W 4. Perf 16.

			Unused	Used*	Used on cover
26	1	1d. red-brown (Die II) (24.7.55)	£2500	£130	£240
		a. Imperf (Plates 6, 7, 10, 13, 14, 15) from	£4000	£3500	
		Wi. Watermark inverted	—	£1500	
27	3	2d. blue (Plate 5) (20.7.55)	£18500	£450	£575
		a. Imperf	—	£12000	
		Wi. Watermark inverted	—	£1200	

(d) Wmk Large Crown, W 4. Perf 14.

			Unused	Used*	Used on cover
29	1	1d. red-brown (Die II) (10.1.56)	£240	22·00	40·00
		a. Imperf (shades) (Plates 22, 24, 25, 32, 43) from	£3000	£3500	
		s. Optd 'SPECIMEN' (2)	£750		
		Wi. Watermark inverted	£1000	£150	
30		1d. brick-red (Die II)	£375	45·00	
31		1d. plum (Die II) (2.56)	£3500	£900	
32		1d. brown-rose (Die II)	£375	55·00	
33		1d. orange-brown (Die II) (3.57)	£725	60·00	
34	3	2d. blue (Plate 5) (20.7.55)	£2800	70·00	£200
		Wi. Watermark inverted	—	£325	
35		2d. blue (Plate 6) (2.7.57)	£3000	70·00	£200
		a. Imperf	—	£12000	
		b. Imperf between (vert pair)	†	£12500	
		Wi. Watermark inverted	—	£325	

* Nos. 17/35b **For well-centred, lightly used +125%**

1856–58. Wmk Large Crown, W **4**. Paper no longer blued.

(a) Perf 16.

			Unused	Used*	Used on cover
36	1	1d. rose-red (Die II) (26.12.57)	£2800	80·00	£160
		Wi. Watermark inverted	—	£750	
36a	3	2d. blue (Plate 6) (1.2.58)	£14500	£325	£550
		aWi. Watermark inverted	—	£1000	

(b) Die II. Perf 14.

			Unused	Used*	Used on cover
37	1	1d. red-brown (11.56)	£2750	£375	£1100
38		1d. pale red (3.57)	£425	80·00	
39		1d. pale rose-red (6.57)	£110	35·00	
40		1d. rose-red (6.57)	40·00	8·00	23·00
		a. Imperf	£4000	£2800	
		b. Imperf three sides (horiz pair)	†	—	
		s. Optd 'SPECIMEN' (6, 7, 10)	£200		
		Wi. Watermark inverted	£180	85·00	
41		1d. deep rose-red (8.57)	£140	20·00	

1861. Letters engraved on plate instead of punched (Alphabet IV).

			Unused	Used*	Used on cover
42	1	1d. rose-red (Die II) (Plates 50 and 51) (9.7.61)	£200	40·00	70·00
		a. Imperf	—	£4500	
		Wi. Watermark inverted	£700	£200	

* Nos. 36/42a **For well-centred, lightly used +125%**

The original die (Die I) was used to provide roller dies for the laying down of all the line-engraved stamps from 1840 to 1855. In that year a new master die was laid down (by means of a Die I roller die) and the impression was retouched by hand engraving by William Humphreys. This retouched die, always known to philatelists as Die II, was from that time used for preparing all new roller dies.

One Penny. The numbering of the 1d. plates recommenced at 1 on the introduction of Die II. Plates 1 to 21 were Alphabet II from which a scarce plum shade exists. Corner letters of Alphabet III appear on Plate 22 and onwards. As an experiment, the corner letters were engraved by hand on Plates 50 and 51 in 1856, instead of being punched (Alphabet IV), but punching was again resorted to from Plate 52 onwards. Plates 50 and 51 were not put into use until 1861.

Two Pence. Unlike the 1d. the old sequence of plate numbers continued. Plates 3 and 4 of the 2d. had corner letters of Alphabet I, Plate 5 Alphabet II and Plate 6 Alphabet III. In Plate 6 the white lines are thinner than before.

In both values, varieties may be found as described in the preceding issues – ivory heads, inverted watermarks, re-entries, and double letters in corners.

The change of perforation from 16 to 14 was decided upon late in 1854 since the closer holes of the former gauge tended to cause the sheets of stamps to break up when handled, but for a time both gauges were in concurrent use. Owing to faulty alignment of the impressions on the plates and to shrinkage of the paper when dampened, badly perforated stamps are plentiful in the line-engraved issues.

5 6

Showing position of the plate number on the 1d. and 2d. values (Plate 170 shown)

1864–79. Letters in all four corners. Wmk Large Crown, W **4**. Die II. Perf 14.

			Unused	Used*	Used on cover
43	5	1d. rose-red (1.4.64)	27·00	2·75	8·00
		s. Optd 'SPECIMEN' (1, 6, 8, 9) from			
44		1d. lake-red	27·00	2·75	
		a. Imperf from	£4800	£3200	
		Wi. Watermark inverted from	£110	35·00	

* Nos. 43/44a **For well-centred, lightly used +200%**

The following plate numbers are known imperf (No. 44a); 72, 79, 80, 81, 82, 83, 84, 85, 86, 87, 88, 90, 91, 92, 93, 96, 97, 98, 100, 101, 102, 103, 104, 105, 107, 108, 109, 112, 113, 114, 116, 117, 120, 121, 122, 136, 137, 142, 146, 148, 158, 162, 164, 166, 171, 174, 191 and 202.

The numbering of this series of 1d. red plates follows after that of the previous 1d. stamp, last printed from Plate 68.

Plates 69, 70, 75, 126 and 128 were prepared for this issue but rejected owing to defects, and stamps from these plates do not exist, so that specimens which appear to be from these plates (like many of those which optimistic collectors believe to be from Plate 77) bear other plate numbers. Owing to faulty engraving or printing it is not always easy to identify the plate number. Plate 77 was also rejected but some stamps printed from it were used. Seven or eight examples have been recorded, of which only three certified examples are believed to exist in private hands. Plates 226 to 228 were made but not used.

Examples of all plates except 77 are known with inverted watermark. The variety of watermark described in the General Notes to this section occurs on stamp M A (or M L) on plates up to about 96 (*Prices from £500 used*).

Re-entries in this issue are few, the best being on stamps M K and T K of Plate 71 and on S L and T L, Plate 83.

Plate	Unused	Used
71	55·00	4·00
72	60·00	5·00
73	60·00	4·00
74	60·00	2·75
76	55·00	2·75
77	—	£600000
78	£130	2·75
79	48·00	2·75
80	65·00	2·75
81	65·00	3·00
82	£130	5·00
83	£155	9·00
84	80·00	3·00
85	60·00	4·00
86	70·00	5·00
87	48·00	2·75
88	£190	9·50
89	60·00	2·75
90	60·00	2·75
91	75·00	7·00
92	55·00	2·75
93	70·00	2·75
94	65·00	6·00
95	60·00	2·75
96	65·00	2·75
97	60·00	4·50
98	70·00	7·00
99	75·00	6·00
100	80·00	3·00
101	80·00	11·00
102	65·00	2·75
103	70·00	4·50
104	£100	6·00
105	£130	9·00
106	75·00	2·75
107	80·00	9·00
108	£110	3·00
109	£120	4·50

QUEEN VICTORIA

Plate	Unused	Used
110	80·00	11·00
111	70·00	3·00
112	90·00	3·00
113	70·00	15·00
114	£325	15·00
115	£130	3·00
116	£100	11·00
117	65·00	2·75
118	70·00	2·75
119	65·00	2·75
120	27·00	2·75
121	60·00	11·00
122	27·00	2·75
123	60·00	2·75
124	42·00	2·75
125	60·00	2·75
127	75·00	3·00
129	60·00	10·00
130	75·00	3·00
131	85·00	20·00
132	£190	27·00
133	£160	11·00
134	27·00	2·75
135	£130	30·00
136	£130	24·00
137	42·00	3·00
138	32·00	2·75
139	80·00	20·00
140	32·00	2·75
141	£160	11·00
142	95·00	30·00
143	80·00	17·00
144	£130	25·00
145	48·00	3·00
146	60·00	7·00
147	70·00	4·00
148	60·00	4·00
149	60·00	7·00
150	27·00	2·75
151	80·00	11·00
152	80·00	7·50
153	£140	11·00
154	70·00	2·75
155	70·00	3·00
156	65·00	2·75
157	70·00	2·75
158	48·00	2·75
159	48·00	2·75
160	48·00	2·75
161	80·00	9·00
162	70·00	9·00
163	70·00	4·00
164	70·00	4·00
165	65·00	2·75
166	65·00	7·00
167	65·00	2·75
168	70·00	10·00
169	80·00	9·00
170	55·00	2·75
171	27·00	2·75
172	48·00	2·75
173	95·00	11·00
174	50·00	2·75
175	80·00	4·50
176	80·00	3·00
177	60·00	2·75
178	80·00	4·50
179	70·00	3·00
180	80·00	6·50
181	65·00	2·75
182	£130	6·50
183	75·00	4·00
184	48·00	3·00
185	70·00	4·00
186	90·00	3·00
187	70·00	2·75
188	95·00	12·00
189	95·00	8·50
190	70·00	7·00
191	48·00	9·00
192	70·00	2·75
193	48·00	2·75
194	70·00	10·00
195	70·00	10·00
196	70·00	6·50
197	75·00	11·00
198	60·00	7·00
199	75·00	7·00
200	80·00	2·75
201	48·00	6·00
202	80·00	10·00
203	48·00	20·00
204	75·00	3·00
205	75·00	4·00
206	75·00	11·00
207	80·00	11·00
208	75·00	18·00
209	65·00	10·00
210	90·00	15·00

Plate	Unused	Used
211	95·00	25·00
212	80·00	13·00
213	80·00	13·00
214	90·00	23·00
215	90·00	23·00
216	95·00	23·00
217	95·00	9·00
218	90·00	10·00
219	£130	85·00
220	60·00	9·00
221	95·00	20·00
222	£110	50·00
223	£130	75·00
224	£165	65·00
225	£3000	£700

1858–76 Wmk Large Crown. W **4**. Die II. Perf 14

			Unused	Used*	Used on cover
45	6	2d. blue (thick lines) (7.58)	£350	15·00	50·00
		a. Imperf (Plate 9)		£10000	
		s. Optd 'SPECIMEN' (1, 7)	£650		
		Wi. Watermark inverted	£1700	£250	
		Plate			
		7	£2000	65·00	
		8	£1850	45·00	
		9	£350	15·00	
		12	£3000	£140	
46		2d. blue (thin lines) (1.7.69)	£375	27·00	75·00
		s. Optd 'SPECIMEN' (pl. 14, 15) (6, 8, 9, 10)	£250		
		Wi. Watermark inverted	£2250	£300	
47		2d. deep blue (thin lines)	£375	30·00	
		a. Imperf (Plate 13)	£7500		
		Plate			
		13	£375	30·00	
		14	£500	38·00	
		15	£525	38·00	

* Nos. 45/47 **For well-centred, lightly used +150%**

Plates 10 and 11 of the 2d. were prepared but rejected. Plates 13 to 15 were laid down from a new roller impression on which the white lines were thinner.

There are some marked re-entries and repairs, particularly on Plates 7, 8, 9 and 12.

The T A (T L) and M A (M L) watermark varieties (described in the General Notes to this section) can be found on plates 8 and 9 (*Prices from £500 used*).

Though the paper is normally white, some printings showed blueing and stamps showing the 'ivory head' may therefore be found.

7 Showing the plate number (9)

9

(Eng Frederick Heath)

1870 (1 Oct)–**79**. Wmk W **9**, extending over three stamps. Perf 14.

			Unused	Used*	Used on cover
48	7	½d. rose-red	£110	30·00	70·00
49		½d. rose	£110	30·00	
		a. Imperf (Plates 1, 4, 5, 6, 8, 14) from	£3000	£2750	
		s. Optd 'SPECIMEN' (various plates) (2, 8, 9, 10)	£225		
		Wi. Watermark inverted	£450	£150	
		Wj. Watermark reversed	£450	£150	
		Wk. Watermark inverted and reversed	£300	£100	

QUEEN VICTORIA

Plate		
1	£325	£100
3	£240	55·00
4	£150	50·00
5	£110	30·00
6	£120	30·00
8	£600	£120
9	£5000	£700
10	£130	30·00
11	£120	30·00
12	£120	30·00
13	£120	30·00
14	£120	30·00
15	£175	50·00
19	£300	65·00
20	£350	85·00

* Nos. 48/49a **For well-centred, lightly used +200%**

The ½d. was printed in sheets of 480 (24×20) so that the check letters run from

```
     A A      A X
           to
     T A      T X
```

Plates 2, 7, 16, 17 and 18 were not completed while Plates 21 and 22, though made, were not used.

Owing to the method of perforating, the outer side of stamps in either the A or X row (ie the left or right side of the sheet) is imperf.

Stamps may be found with watermark inverted or reversed, or without watermark, the latter due to misplacement of the paper when printing.

8   Position of plate number

1870 (1 Oct)–**74**. Wmk W **4**. Perf 14.

			Unused	Used*	Used on cover
51	8	1½d. rose-red	£500	75·00	£275
		s. Optd 'SPECIMEN' (pl. 1) (2, 6)	£550		
		sa. Optd 'SPECIMEN' (pl. 3) (8, 9, 10)	£300		
52		1½d. lake-red	£600	75·00	
		a. Imperf (Plates 1 and 3) from	£7500	†	
		Wi. Watermark inverted	£3000	£500	
		Plate			
		(1)	£725	£110	
		3	£500	75·00	
		Error of lettering. OP–PC for CP–PC (Plate 1).			
53	8	1½d. rose-red	£25000	£2000	£7500
		Prepared for use in 1860, but not issued; blued paper.			
53a	8	1½d. rosy mauve (Plate 1)	£7000	—	
		b. Error of lettering, OP–PC for CP–PC	—	†	
		s. Optd 'SPECIMEN' (2, 6)	£1750		

* Nos. 51/53 **For well-centred, lightly used +125%**

Owing to a proposed change in the postal rates, 1½d. stamps were first printed in 1860, in rosy mauve, No. 53a, but the change was not approved and the greater part of the stock was destroyed, although three or four postally used examples have been recorded.

In 1870 a 1½d. stamp was required and was issued in rose-red. Plate 1 did not have the plate number in the design of the stamps, but on stamps from Plate 3 the number will be found in the frame as shown above. Plate 2 was defective and was not used.

The error of lettering OP–PC on Plate 1 was apparently not noticed by the printer, and therefore not corrected.

* Nos. 51/53 **For well-centred, lightly used +125%**

EMBOSSED ISSUES

Volume 1, Part 1 of the Stanley Gibbons *Great Britain Specialised Catalogue* gives further detailed information on the embossed issues.

> **PRICES.** The prices quoted are for cut-square stamps with average to fine embossing. Stamps with exceptionally clear embossing are worth more.

10   11

12   13

Position of die number

(Primary die engraved at the Royal Mint by William Wyon. Stamps printed at Somerset House)

1847–54. Imperf (For paper and watermark see footnote).

			Unused	Used	Used on cover
54	10	1s. pale green (11.9.47)	£24000	£1000	£1900
		s. Optd 'SPECIMEN' (red opt)	£2500		
		sa. Optd 'SPECIMEN' (black opt) (1, 2)	£2250		
55		1s. green	£24000	£1000	
56		1s. deep green	£28000	£1200	
		i. Die 1 (1847)	£24000	£1000	
		ii. Die 2 (1854)	£27000	£1100	
57	11	10d. brown (6.11.48)	£11500	£1500	£3200
		s. Optd 'SPECIMEN' (1, 2)	£3000		
		i. Die 1 (1848)	£12000	£1500	
		ii. Die 2 (1850)	£11500	£1500	
		iii. Die 3 (1853)	£11500	£1500	
		iv. Die 4 (1854)	£13000	£1750	
		v. Die 5			
58	12	6d. mauve (1.3.54)	£19500	£1000	
		s. Optd 'SPECIMEN' (1, 2)	£3500		
59		6d. dull lilac	£19500	£1000	£1900
60		6d. purple	£19500	£1000	
		Wi. Watermark inverted	£19500	£1000	
		Wj. Watermarked upright			
		Wk. Watermark inverted and reversed	£19500	£1000	
61		6d. violet	—	£4000	

The 1s. and 10d. are on 'Dickinson' paper with 'silk' threads. The 6d. is on paper watermarked V R in single-lined letters, W **13**, which may be found in four ways–upright, inverted, upright reversed, and inverted reversed. In this listing the reversed watermark is taken to be 'normal'.

> Collectors are reminded that Types **10/12** were also used to print postal stationery. 6d. stamps without watermark and 10d. and 1s. stamps without 'silk' threads come from this source and should not be confused with the adhesives, Nos. 54/61.

The die numbers are indicated on the base of the bust. Only Die 1 (1WW) of the 6d. was used for the adhesive stamps. The 10d. is from Die 1 (WW1 on stamps), and Dies 2 to 4 (2WW, 3WW and 4WW) but the number and letters on stamps from Die 1 are seldom clear and many specimens are known without any trace of them. Because of this the stamp we previously listed as 'No die number' has been deleted. That they are from Die 1 is proved by the existence of blocks showing stamps with and without the die number. The 1s. is from Dies 1 and 2 (WW1, WW2).

The normal arrangement of the 'silk' threads in the paper was in pairs running down each vertical row of the sheets, the space between the threads of each pair being approximately 5 mm and between pairs of threads 20 mm. Varieties due to misplacement of the paper in printing show a single thread on the first stamp from the sheet margin and two threads 20 mm apart on the other stamps of the row. Faulty manufacture is the cause of stamps with a single thread in the middle.

QUEEN VICTORIA

Through bad spacing of the impressions, which were handstruck, all values may be found with two impressions more or less overlapping. Owing to the small margin allowed for variation of spacing, specimens with good margins on all sides are not common.

Double impressions are known of all values.

Later printings of the 6d. had the gum tinted green to enable the printer to distinguish the gummed side of the paper.

SURFACE-PRINTED ISSUES

GENERAL NOTES

Volume 1 of the Stanley Gibbons *Great Britain Specialised Catalogue* gives further detailed information on the surface-printed issues.

'**Abnormals**'. The majority of the great rarities in the surface printed group of issues are the so-called 'abnormals', whose existence is due to the practice of printing six sheets from every plate as soon as made, one of which was kept for record purposes at Somerset House, while the others were perforated and usually issued. If such plates were not used for general production or if, before they came into full use, a change of watermark or colour took place, the six sheets originally printed would differ from the main issue in plate, colour or watermark and, if issued would be extremely rare.

The abnormal stamps of this class listed in this Catalogue and distinguished, where not priced, by an asterisk (*) are:

No.	
78	3d. Plate 3 (with white dots)
152	4d. vermilion, Plate 16
153	4d. sage-green, Plate 17
109	6d. mauve, Plate 10
124/124a	6d. pale chestnut and 6d. chestnut, Plate 12
145	6d. pale buff, Plate 13
88	9d. Plate 3 (hair lines)
98	9d. Plate 5 (see footnote to No. 98)
99	10d. Plate 1 (Wmk Emblems)
113	10d. Plate 2
91	1s. Plate 3 (Plate 2)
148/150	1s. green, Plate 14
120	2s. blue, Plate 3

Those which may have been issued, but of which no specimens are known, are 2½d. wmk Anchor, Plates 4 and 5; 3d. wmk Emblems, Plate 5; 3d. wmk Spray, Plate 21, 6d. grey, wmk Spray, Plate 18; 8d. orange, Plate 2; 1s. wmk Emblems, Plate 5; 5s. wmk Maltese Cross, Plate 4.

The 10d. Plate 1, wmk Emblems (No. 99), is sometimes reckoned among the abnormals, but was an error, due to the use of the wrong paper.

Corner Letters. With the exception of the 4d., 6d. and 1s. of 1855–1857, the ½d., 1½d., 2d. and 5d. of 1880, the 1d. lilac of 1881 and the £5 (which had letters in lower corners only, and in the reverse order to the normal), all the surface-printed stamps issued prior to 1887 had letters in all four corners, as in the later line-engraved stamps. The arrangement is the same, the letters running in sequence right across and down the sheets, whether these were divided into panes or not. The corner letters existing naturally depend on the number of stamps in the sheet and their arrangement.

Imprimaturs and Imperforate Stamps. The Post Office retained in their records (now in the National Postal Museum) one imperforate sheet from each plate, known as the Imprimatur (or officially approved) sheet. Some stamps were removed from time to time for presentation purposes and have come on to the market, but these imperforates are not listed as they were not issued. Full details can be found in Volume 1 of the *Great Britain Specialised Catalogue*.

However, other imperforate stamps are known to have been issued and these are listed where it has been possible to prove that they do not come from the Imprimatur sheets. It is therefore advisable to purchase these only when accompanied by an Expert Committee certificate of genuineness.

Plate Numbers. All stamps from No. 75 to No. 163 bear in their designs either the plate number or, in one or two earlier instances, some other indication by which one plate can be distinguished from another. With the aid of these and of the corner letters it is thus possible to 'reconstruct' a sheet of stamps from any plate of any issue or denomination.

Surface-printing. In this context the traditional designation 'surface-printing' is synonymous with letterpress—the printers' term—as meaning printing from (the surface of) raised type while philatelists often use the expression 'Typo(graphy)', although this is beginning to fall out of favour. It is also called relief printing, as the image is in relief (in French, *en épargne*), unwanted parts of the design having been cut away. Duplicate impressions can be electrotyped or stereotyped from an original die, the resulting clichés being locked together to form the printing plate.

Wing Margins. As the vertical gutters (spaces) between the panes, into which sheets of stamps of most values were divided until the introduction of the Imperial Crown watermark, were perforated through the centre with a single row of holes, instead of each vertical row of stamps on the inner side of the panes having its own line of perforation as is now usual, a proportion of the stamps in each sheet have what is called a 'wing margin' about 5 mm wide on one or other side.

The stamps with 'wing margins' are the watermark Emblems and Spray of Rose series (3d., 6d., 9d., 10d., 1s. and 2s.) with letters D, E, H or I in the south-east corner, and the watermark Garter series (4d. and 8d.) with letters F or G in the south-east corner. Knowledge of this lettering will enable collectors to guard against stamps with wing margin cut down and re-perforated, but note that wing margin stamps of Nos. 62 to 73 are also to be found re-perforated.

PRINTERS. The issues of Queen Victoria, Nos. 62/214, were typo by Thomas De La Rue & Co.

PERFORATIONS. All the surface-printed issues of Queen Victoria are perf 14, with the exception of Nos. 126/129.

KEY TO SURFACE-PRINTED ISSUES 1855–1883

SG Nos.	Description	Watermark	Date of Issue
NO CORNER LETTERS			
62	4d. carmine	Small Garter	31.7.55
63/65	4d. carmine	Medium Garter	25.2.56
66/66a	4d. carmine	Large Garter	1.57
69/70	6d. lilac	Emblems	21.10.56
71/73	1s. green	Emblems	1.11.56
SMALL WHITE CORNER LETTERS			
75/77	3d. carmine	Emblems	1.5.62
78	3d. carmine (dots)	Emblems	8.62
79/82	4d. red	Large Garter	15.1.62
83/85	6d. lilac	Emblems	1.12.62
86/88	9d. bistre	Emblems	15.1.62
89/91	1s. green	Emblems	1.12.62
LARGE WHITE CORNER LETTERS			
92	3d. rose	Emblems	1.3.65
102/103	3d. rose	Spray	7.67
93/94	4d. vermilion	Large Garter	4.7.65
96/97	6d. lilac	Emblems	7.3.65
104/107	6d. lilac	Spray	21.6.67
108/109	6d. lilac	Spray	8.3.69
122/124	6d. chestnut	Spray	12.4.72
125	6d. grey	Spray	24.4.73
98	9d. straw	Emblems	30.10.65
110/111	9d. straw	Spray	3.10.67
99	10d. brown	Emblems	11.11.67
112/114	10d. brown	Spray	1.7.67
101	1s. green	Emblems	19.1.65
115/117	1s. green	Spray	13.7.67
118/120b	2s. blue	Spray	1.7.67
121	2s. brown	Spray	27.2.80
126/127	5s. rose	Cross	1.7.67
128	10s. grey	Cross	26.9.78
129	£1 brown-lilac	Cross	26.9.78
130, 134	5s. rose	Anchor	25.11.82
131, 135	10s. grey-green	Anchor	2.83
132, 136	£1 brown-lilac	Anchor	12.82
133, 137	£5 orange	Anchor	21.3.82
LARGE COLOURED CORNER LETTERS			
138/139	2½d. rosy mauve	Anchor	1.7.75
141	2½d. rosy mauve	Orb	1.5.76
142	2½d. blue	Orb	5.2.80
157	2½d. blue	Crown	23.3.81
143/144	3d. rose	Spray	5.7.73
158	3d. rose	Crown	1.81
159	3d. on 3d. lilac	Crown	1.1.83
152	4d. vermilion	Large Garter	1.3.76
153	4d. sage-green	Large Garter	12.3.77
154	4d. brown	Large Garter	15.8.80
160	4d. brown	Crown	9.12.80
145	6d. buff	Spray	15.3.73
146/147	6d. grey	Spray	20.3.74
161	6d. grey	Crown	1.1.81
162	6d. on 6d. lilac	Crown	1.1.83
156a	8d. purple-brown	Large Garter	7.76
156	8d. orange	Large Garter	11.9.76
148/150	1s. green	Spray	1.9.73
151	1s. brown	Spray	14.10.80
163	1s. brown	Crown	24.5.81

Watermarks:		
	Anchor	W 40, W 47
	Cross	W 39
	Crown	W 49
	Emblems	W 20
	Large Garter	W 17
	Medium Garter	W 16
	Orb	W 48
	Small Garter	W 15
	Spray	W 33

Please note that all watermark illustrations are *as seen from the front of the stamp*.

QUEEN VICTORIA

14

15 Small Garter

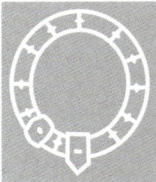

16 Medium Garter

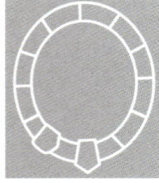

17 Large Garter

1855–57. No corner letters.

*(a) Wmk Small Garter, W **15**. Highly glazed, deeply blued paper (31 July 1855).*

			Unused	Used*	Used on cover
62	14	4d. carmine (*shades*)	£8500	£450	£780
		a. Paper slightly blued	£9000	£450	
		b. White paper	£20000	£1100	
		s. Optd 'SPECIMEN' (2, 3)	£1200		
		Wi. Watermark inverted	£11000	£1200	

*(b) Wmk Medium Garter, W **16**.*
(i) Thick, blued highly glazed paper (25 February 1856).

63	14	4d. carmine (*shades*)	£14000	£575	£1100
		a. White paper	£12000		
		s. Optd 'SPECIMEN' (2)	£1200		
		Wi. Watermark inverted	—	£1400	

(ii) Ordinary thin white paper (September 1856).

64	14	4d. pale carmine	£13000	£500	£1000
		a. Stamp printed double	†	—	
		s. Optd 'SPECIMEN' (2)	£1100		
		Wi. Watermark inverted	£17000	£1300	

(iii) Ordinary white paper, specially prepared ink (1 November 1856).

65	14	4d. rose or deep rose	£13000	£525	£1000
		s. Optd 'SPECIMEN' (4)	£1500		
		Wi. Watermark inverted	†	—	

*(c) Wmk Large Garter, W **17**. Ordinary white paper (January 1857).*

66	14	4d. rose-carmine	£2100	£150	£225
		a. Rose	£1750	£150	
		aWi. Watermark inverted	£4800	£400	
		aWj. Watermark inverted and reversed	—		
		b. Thick glazed paper	£6500	£375	
		bWi. Watermark inverted			
		s. Optd 'SPECIMEN' (2, 7)	£450		

* Nos. 62/66b **For well-centred, lightly used +125%**

18

19

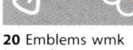

20 Emblems wmk (normal)

20a Watermark error, three roses and shamrock

20b Watermark error, three roses and thistle

1857.

*(d) Wmk Emblems, W **20**.*

			Unused	Used*	Used on cover
68	18	6d. lilac	£1350	£120	£240
69		6d. deep lilac (21.10.56)	£1800	£175	
		s. Optd 'SPECIMEN' (2, 4, 7, 8)	£600		
70		6d. pale lilac	£1350	£120	£240
		a. Azure paper	£9000	£950	
		b. Thick paper	£4000	£350	
		c. Error. Watermark W **20a**			
		Wi. Watermark inverted	£3000	£400	
		Wj. Watermark reversed		£475	
		Wk. Watermark inverted and reversed		—	
71	19	1s. deep green (1.11.56)	£5750	£550	
		s. Optd 'SPECIMEN' (2, 4, 7)	£975		
72		1s. green	£3250	£350	£425
73		1s. pale green	£3250	£350	
		a. Azure paper	—	£2000	
		b. Thick paper	—	£400	
		c. Imperf		†	—
		Wi. Watermark inverted	—	£700	
		Wj. Watermark reversed	—	£1400	
		Wk. Watermark inverted and reversed			

* Nos. 69/73b **For well-centred, lightly used +125%**

21

22

23

24

25 Plate 2

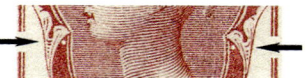

A. White dots added

B. Hair lines

1862–64. Small uncoloured corner letters. Wmk Large Garter, W **17** (4d.) or Emblems, W **20** (others).

			Unused	Used*	Used on cover
75	21	3d. deep carmine-rose (Plate 2) (1.5.62)	£4800	£575	
		s. Optd 'SPECIMEN' (2, 5, 6, 8)	£500		
76		3d. bright carmine-rose	£2700	£350	£600
		a. Error. Watermark W **20b** (stamp TF)		£5500	
		Wi. Watermark inverted	£7500	£1200	
77		3d. pale carmine-rose	£2700	£350	
		b. Thick paper	£4000	£475	
		Wj. Watermark reversed		—	
78		3d. rose (with white dots, Type A, Plate 3) (8.62)	£45000	£17000	
		a. Imperf (Plate 3)	£5500		
		s. Optd 'SPECIMEN' (2)	£2000		
79	22	4d. bright red (Plate 3) (15.1.62)	£2200	£170	
		s. Opt 'SPECIMEN' (2, 5, 6, 8)			
80		4d. pale red	£2000	£140	£300
		Wi. Watermark inverted	—	£375	

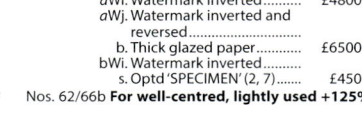

QUEEN VICTORIA

			Unused	Used*	Used on cover
81		4d. bright red (Hair lines, Type B, Plate 4) (16.10.63)	£2300	£185	
		s. Optd 'SPECIMEN' (2)	£500		
82		4d. pale red (Hair lines, Type B, Plate 4)	£2100	£150	£300
		a. Imperf (Plate 4)	£2400		
		Wi. Watermark inverted	£5500	£400	
83	23	6d. deep lilac (Plate 3) (1.12.62)	£2800	£160	
84		6d. lilac	£2250	£140	£225
		a. Azure paper	—	£1400	
		b. Thick paper	—	£375	
		c. Error. Shamrock missing from wmk (stamp TF)	—	£3000	
		d. Error. Watermark W **20b** (stamp TF)	—	£5500	
		e. Hyphen omitted (KA)**	—	£7750	
		s. Optd 'SPECIMEN' (2, 5, 8)	£600		
		Wi. Watermark inverted	£7000	£450	
		Wj. Watermark reversed	—	£550	
		Wk. Watermark inverted and reversed	£9500	—	
85		6d. lilac (Hair lines, Plate 4) (20.4.64)	£3000	£250	£350
		a. Imperf (watermark inverted)	£3250		
		b. Imperf and watermark upright	£3500		
		c. Thick paper	£3250	£280	
		d. Error. Watermark W **20b** (stamp TF)	—	—	
		s. Optd 'SPECIMEN' (2)	£600		
		Wi. Watermark inverted	£8250	£475	
		Wj. Watermark reversed	—	—	
		Wk. Watermark inverted and reversed	—	—	
86	24	9d. bistre (Plate 2) (15.1.62)	£5800	£575	£1200
		s. Optd 'SPECIMEN' (2, 6)	£750		
		Wi. Watermark inverted	£10000	£700	
		Wj. Watermark reversed	—	£850	
		Wk. Watermark inverted and reversed	—	—	
87		9d. straw	£4000	£475	£1000
		a. On azure paper	—	—	
		b. Thick paper	£6000	£550	
		c. Error. Shamrock missing from wmk (stamp TF)	†	—	
		d. Error. Watermark W **20b** (stamp TF)	†	—	
		Wi. Watermark inverted	£7000	£650	
		Wk. Watermark inverted and reversed	—	£1000	
88		9d. bistre (Hair lines, Plate 3) (5.62)	£32000	£13500	
89	25	1s. deep green (Plate No. 1 = Plate 2) (1.12.62)	£4800	£500	
90		1s. green	£3200	£300	£450
		a. 'K' in lower left corner in white circle (stamp KD)	£20000	£2750	
		awi. Watermark inverted	—	£4250	
		ab. 'K' normal (stamp KD)	—	£2200	
		b. On azure paper	—	—	
		c. Error. Watermark W **20b** (stamp TF)	—	—	
		d. Thick paper	—	£375	
		da. Thick paper, 'K' in circle as No. 90a	—	£3750	
		s. Optd 'SPECIMEN' (2, 5, 8)	£550		
		Wi. Watermark inverted	—	£450	
		Wj. Watermark reversed	—	—	
		Wk. Watermark inverted and reversed	—	£475	
91		1s. deep green (Plate No. 2 = Plate 3)	£35000		
		a. Imperf	£7250		
		s. Optd 'SPECIMEN' (2)	£4200		
		Wi. Watermark inverted	£7250		

* Nos. 75/91 **For well-centred, lightly used +125%**

The 3d. as T **21**, but with network background in the spandrels, was never issued. Optd 'SPECIMEN' *price* £800.

The plates of this issue may be distinguished as follows:

3d.	Plate 2	No white dots.
	Plate 3	White dots as illustration A.
4d.	Plate 3	No hair lines. Roman I next to lower corner letters.
	Plate 4	Hair lines in corners. (Illustration B.). Roman II.
6d.	Plate 3	No hair lines.
	Plate 4	Hair lines in corners.
9d.	Plate 2	No hair lines.
	Plate 3	Hair lines in corners. Beware of faked lines.
1s.	Plate 2	Numbered 1 on stamps.
	Plate 3	Numbered 2 on stamps and with hair lines.

** One used example of No. 84e *on piece* has been recorded, cancelled by a Glasgow Duplex postmark dated 6.1.1863.

The 9d. on azure paper (No. 87a) is very rare, only one confirmed example being known.

The variety 'K' in circle, No. 90a, is believed to be due to a damaged letter having been cut out and replaced. It is probable that the punch was driven in too deeply, causing the flange to penetrate the surface, producing an indentation showing as an uncoloured circle.

The watermark variety 'three roses and a shamrock' illustrated in W **20a** was evidently due to the substitution of an extra rose for the thistle in a faulty watermark bit. It is found on stamp TA of Plate 4 of the 3d. (No. 92a), Plates 1 (No. 70c), 5 and 6 of the 6d. (No. 97c), Plate 4 of the 9d. (No. 98b) and Plate 4 of the 1s. (No. 101a).

Similar problems occurred on stamp TF of the 6d. and 9d. Here the shamrock emblem became detached and used examples are known showing it omitted. It was replaced by a third rose (W **20b**) and this variety exists on the 6d. Plates 3, 4 and 5 (Nos. 84d/85d and 97d), 9d. Plate 4 (Nos. 87d and 98c) and 1s. green Plates 2 and 4 (Nos. 90c and 101ab).

26   **27**

28 (with hyphen)   **28a** (without hyphen)

29   **30**   **31**

1865–67. Large uncoloured corner letters. Wmk Large Garter, W **17** (4d.) or Emblems, W **20** (others).

			Unused	Used*	Used on cover
92	26	3d. rose (Plate 4) (1.3.65)	£2500	£250	£500
		a. Error. Watermark W **20a**	£7000	£1250	
		b. Thick paper	£3500	£325	
		s. Optd 'SPECIMEN' (2)	£4500		
		Wi. Watermark inverted	—	£600	
		Wj. Watermark reversed			
		Wk. Watermark inverted and reversed			
93	27	4d. dull vermilion (4.7.65)	£650	90·00	
		s. Optd 'SPECIMEN' (pl. 14) (8)	£525		
94		4d. vermilion	£575	75·00	£140
		a. Imperf (Plates 11, 12)	£7000		
		Wi. Watermark inverted	£575	75·00	
95		4d. deep vermilion	£650	90·00	
		Plate			
		7 (1865)	£650	£130	
		8 (1866)	£600	90·00	
		9 (1867)	£600	90·00	
		10 (1868)	£825	£150	
		11 (1869)	£625	90·00	
		12 (1870)	£575	75·00	
		13 (1872)	£650	75·00	
		14 (1873)	£775	£110	
96	28	6d. deep lilac (with hyphen) (7.3.65)	£1900	£200	
		s. Optd 'SPECIMEN' (pl. 5) (2)	£4750		
97		6d. lilac (with hyphen)	£1200	£140	£225
		a. Thick paper	£1600	£175	
		b. Stamp doubly printed (Plate 6)	—	£12000	
		c. Error. Watermark W **20a** (Pl 5, 6) *from*	—	£2400	
		d. Error. Watermark W **20b** (Plate 5)	—	—	
		e. Imperf (Plate 5)	—	—	
		Wi. Watermark inverted	—	£250	
		Wj. Watermark reversed	—	—	
		Wk. Watermark inverted and reversed	†	—	

QUEEN VICTORIA

			Plate		
			5 (1865)........	£1200	£140
			6 (1867)........	£3800	£250
98	29	9d. straw (Plate 4) (25.10.65)..		£4800	£600 £1400
		a. Thick paper........................		£5800	£850
		b. Error. Watermark W **20a**....		—	£2500
		c. Error. Watermark W **20b** (stamp TF)............................		—	
		s. Optd 'SPECIMEN' (2)............		£925	
		Wi. Watermark inverted.........		—	£1800
99	30	10d. red-brown (Plate 1) (11.11.67)............................			†*£55000
100	31	1s. deep green (Plate 4) (19.1.65)............................		£3000	£300
101		1s. green (Plate 4) (19.1.65)....		£2850	£275 £450
		a. Error. Watermark W **20a**....		—	£1700
		ab. Error. Watermark W **20b**....			
		b. Thick paper........................		£3500	£380
		c. Imperf between (vertical pair)...................................		—	£12000
		d. Imperf (watermark inverted).............................			—
		s. Optd 'SPECIMEN' (2)............		£650	
		Wi. Watermark inverted.........		—	£650
		Wk. Watermark inverted and reversed............................		—	£650

* Nos. 92/101c **For well-centred, lightly used +100%**

From mid-1866 to about the end of 1871 4d. stamps of this issue appeared generally with watermark inverted.

Unused examples of No. 98 from Plate 5 exist, but this was never put to press and all evidence points to such stamps originating from a portion of the Imprimatur sheet which was perforated by De La Rue in 1887 for insertion in albums to be presented to members of the Stamp Committee (*Price *£15000 unused*).

The 10d. stamps, No. 99, were printed in error on paper watermarked 'Emblems' instead of on 'Spray of Rose'.

32   **33** Spray of Rose   **34**

1867–80. Large uncoloured corner letters. Wmk Spray of Rose. W **33**.

				Unused	Used*	Used on cover
102	26	3d. deep rose (12.7.67)...........		£800	£100	
103		3d. rose.................................		£525	60·00	£110
		a. Imperf (Plates 5, 6).....*from*		£8500		
		s. Optd 'SPECIMEN' (pl. 5) (8)		£275		
		sa. Optd 'SPECIMEN' (pl. 6) (2, 8)....................................		£300		
		sb. Optd 'SPECIMEN' (pl. 7) (2, 6)....................................		£300		
		sc. Optd 'SPECIMEN' (pl. 8) (8)		£300		
		sd. Optd 'SPECIMEN' (pl. 10) (2, 8, 9)...............................		£275		
		Wi. Watermark inverted.........		£2250	£300	
			Plate			
			4 (1867)......	£1850	£300	
			5 (1868)......	£525	70·00	
			6 (1870)......	£550	70·00	
			7 (1871)......	£650	70·00	
			8 (1872)......	£625	60·00	
			9 (1872)......	£625	70·00	
			10 (1873)......	£875	£150	
104	28	6d. lilac (with hyphen) (Plate 6) (21.6.67).........................		£1900	£185	£250
		a. Imperf................................			£4800	
		Wi. Watermark inverted.........		—	£350	
105		6d. deep lilac (with hyphen) (Plate 6)............................		£1900	£185	
106		6d. purple (with hyphen) (Plate 6)............................		£1900	£210	£300
107		6d. bright violet (with hyphen) (Plate 6) (22.7.68)............................		£1900	£225	£300
108	28a	6d. dull violet (without hyphen) (Plate 8) (8.3.69)..		£1400	£190	£275
		s. Optd 'SPECIMEN' (pl. 8) (1, 8).....................................		£350		
		Wi. Watermark inverted.........		—	£275	
109		6d. mauve (without hyphen) (Plate Nos. 8 and 9)............................		£700	90·00	£140
		a. Imperf (Plate Nos. 8 and 9).....................................		£9500	£4000	
		s. Optd 'SPECIMEN' (pl. 9) (6, 8).....................................		£350		
		Wi. Watermark inverted.........		—	£250	

			Plate		
			8 (1869, mauve)..........	£800	£140
			9 (1870, mauve)..........	£700	90·00
			10 (1869, mauve)........	*	£37500
110	29	9d. straw (Plate No. 4) (3.10.67)............................		£2500	£325 £525
		s. Optd 'SPECIMEN' (2, 8, 9, 10, 11)...............................		£425	
		Wi. Watermark inverted.........		—	£650
111		9d. pale straw (Plate No. 4).....		£2400	£300
		a. Imperf (Plate 4).................		£22000	
112	30	10d. red-brown (1.7.67)............		£3600	£400 £850
		s. Optd 'SPECIMEN' (2, 5, 6, 8, 9 10, 11).........................		£500	
		Wi. Watermark inverted.........		—	£1000
113		10d. pale red-brown.................		£3600	£400
114		10d. deep red-brown.................		£5000	£600
		a. Imperf (Plate 1).................		£17000	
			Plate		
			1 (1867)........	£3600	£400
			2 (1867)........	*£50000	*£15000
115	31	1s. deep green (13.7.67)........		£1300	70·00
117		1s. green................................		£800	45·00 90·00
		a. Imperf between (horiz pair) (Plate 7).....................		—	
		b. Imperf (Plate 4).................		£7750	£5000
		s. Optd 'SPECIMEN' (pl. 4) (1, 8, 9)...................................		£400	
		sa. Optd 'SPECIMEN' (pl. 5) (2, 6, 8, 9)...............................		£425	
		sb. Optd 'SPECIMEN' (pl. 6) (8, 9).....................................		£425	
		sc. Optd 'SPECIMEN' (pl. 7) (9.		£400	
		Wi. Watermark inverted.........		£2400	£180
			Plate		
			4 (1867)........	£975	65·00
			5 (1871)........	£800	45·00
			6 (1871)........	£1200	45·00
			7 (1873)........	£1400	90·00
118	32	2s. dull blue (1.7.72).............		£4500	£225 £700
		s. Optd 'SPECIMEN' (2, 5, 8, 9 10, 11)............................		£600	
		Wi. Watermark inverted.........		—	£950
119		2s. deep blue........................		£5000	£240
		a. Imperf (Plate 1).................		£22000	
120		2s. pale blue.........................		£5000	£275
		aa. Imperf (Plate 1).................		£22000	
120a		2s. cobalt...............................		£30000	£3000
120b		2s. milky blue........................		£24000	£2000
			Plate		
			1 (1867)........	£4500	£225
			3 (1868)........	*	£16500
121		2s. brown (Plate No. 1) (27.2.80)............................		£30000	£4250
		a. Imperf................................		£30000	
		b. No watermark....................		†	—
		s. Optd 'SPECIMEN' (9)..........		£3000	
		Wi. Watermark inverted.........		—	£6000

* Nos. 102/121 **For well-centred, lightly used +75%**

Examples of the 1s. from Plates 5 and 6 without watermark are postal forgeries used at the Stock Exchange Post Office in the early 1870s. (*Prices from £850 pl.5, £2500 pl.6*)

1872–73. Large uncoloured corner letters. Wmk Spray of Rose, W **33**.

			Unused	Used*	Used on cover
122	34	6d. deep chestnut (Plate 11) (12.4.72)............................	£1300	£125	
		s. Optd 'SPECIMEN' (2, 6, 8)...	£325		
122a		6d. chestnut (Plate 11) (22.5.72)............................	£800	65·00	£150
		Wi. Watermark inverted.........	—	£325	
122b		6d. pale chestnut (Plate 11) (1872).................................	£800	65·00	
123		6d. pale buff (18.10.72)...........	£1100	£140	£250
		Wi. Watermark inverted.........	—	£375	
		Plate			
		11 (1872, pale buff)...........	£1100	£125	
		12 (1872, pale buff)...........	£3400	£350	
124		6d. chestnut (Plate 12) (1872)..		*£3800	
124a		6d. pale chestnut (Plate 12) (1872)................................		*£3500	
125		6d. grey (Plate 12) (24.4.73).....	£1900	£300	£375
		a. Imperf................................	£15000		
		s. Optd 'SPECIMEN' (6, 8, 9)...	£375		
		Wi. Watermark inverted.........	£6250	—	

* Nos. 122/125 **For well-centred, lightly used +50%**

QUEEN VICTORIA

35 **36** **37**

38

41 **42** **43**

44 **45** **46**

39 Maltese Cross **40** Large Anchor

47 Small Anchor **48** Orb

1867–83. Large uncoloured corner letters.
*(a) Wmk Maltese Cross, W **39**. Perf 15½×15.*

			Unused	Used*
126	35	5s. rose (1.7.67)	£9500	£675
		s. Optd 'SPECIMEN' (2, 6)	£1100	
127		5s. pale rose	£9500	£675
		a. Imperf (Plate 1)	£15000	
		s. Optd 'SPECIMEN' (pl. 2) (8. 9)	£1750	
		Plate		
		1 (1867)	£9500	£675
		2 (1874)	£15000	£1500
128	36	10s. greenish grey (Plate 1) (26.9.78)	£50000	£3200
		s. Optd 'SPECIMEN' (8. 9)	£4250	
129	37	£1 brown-lilac (Plate 1) (26.9.78)	£75000	£4500
		s. Optd 'SPECIMEN' (9)	£6250	

*(b) Wmk Large Anchor, W **40**. Perf 14.*
(i) Blued paper.

			Unused	Used*
130	35	5s. rose (Plate 4) (25.11.82)	£35000	£4000
		s. Optd 'SPECIMEN' (9)	£5250	
		Wi. Watermark inverted	—	£18000
131	36	10s. grey-green (Plate 1) (2.83)	£110000	£4500
		s. Optd 'SPECIMEN' (9)	£10000	
132	37	£1 brown-lilac (Plate 1) (12.82)	£140000	£7500
		s. Optd 'SPECIMEN' (9)	£12500	
133	38	£5 orange (Plate 1) (21.3.82)	£60000	£12500
		s. Optd 'SPECIMEN' (9, 11)	£3000	

(ii) White paper.

			Unused	Used*
134	35	5s. rose (Plate 4)	£28000	£3800
135	36	10s. greenish grey (Plate 1)	£130000	£4000
136	37	£1 brown-lilac (Plate 1)	£160000	£7000
		s. Optd 'SPECIMEN' (6, 9)	£11500	
137	38	£5 orange (Plate 1)	£12500	£3500
		s. Optd 'SPECIMEN' (9, 11, 16)	£3750	

* Nos. 126/137 **For well-centred, lightly used +75%**

1873–80. Large coloured corner letters.
*(a) Wmk Small Anchor, W **47**.*

			Unused	Used*	Used on cover
138	41	2½d. rosy mauve (blued paper) (1.7.75)	£900	£190	
		a. Imperf			
		Wi. Watermark inverted	£3000	£350	
		s. Optd 'SPECIMEN' (pl. 1) (8)	£350		
		Plate			
		1 (blued paper) (1875)	£900	£190	
		2 (blued paper) (1875)	£8000	£1650	
		3 (blued paper) (1875)	—	£5750	
139		2½d. rosy mauve (white paper)	£675	£120	£180
		Wi. Watermark inverted	£2750	£250	
		Plate			
		1 (white paper) (1875)	£120	£675	
		2 (white paper) (1875)	£120	£675	
		3 (white paper) (1875)	£175	£1000	
		Error of Lettering L H—F L for L H—H L (Plate 2).			
140	41	2½d. rosy mauve	£28000	£2750	

*(b) Wmk Orb, W **48**.*

			Unused	Used*	Used on cover
141	41	2½d. rosy mauve (1.5.76)	£525	85·00	£125
		s. Optd 'SPECIMEN' (pl. 3) (10)	£4200		
		sa. Optd 'SPECIMEN' (pl. 5) (9)	£220		
		sb. Optd 'SPECIMEN' (pl. 6) (8, 9)	£220		
		sc. Optd 'SPECIMEN' (pl. 7) (9)	£220		
		sd. Optd 'SPECIMEN' (pl. 10) (9)	£220		
		se. Optd 'SPECIMEN' (pl. 16) (9)	£220		
		Wi. Watermark inverted	£1900	£250	
		Plate			
		3 (1876)	£1350	£150	
		4 (1876)	£525	85·00	
		5 (1876)	£525	85·00	
		6 (1876)	£525	85·00	
		7 (1877)	£525	85·00	
		8 (1877)	£525	85·00	
		9 (1877)	£525	85·00	
		10 (1878)	£550	85·00	
		11 (1878)	£525	85·00	
		12 (1878)	£525	85·00	
		13 (1878)	£525	85·00	
		14 (1879)	£525	85·00	
		15 (1879)	£525	85·00	
		16 (1879)	£525	85·00	
		17 (1880)	£1700	£300	
142	41	2½d. blue (5.2.80)	£575	55·00	90·00
		s. Optd 'SPECIMEN' (pl. 17) (9)	£160		
		Wi. Watermark inverted	£2100	£275	
		Plate			
		17 (1880)	£575	75·00	
		18 (1880)	£575	55·00	

13

QUEEN VICTORIA

		Plate			
		19 (1880)......	£575	55·00	
		20 (1880)......	£575	55·00	
		(c) Wmk Spray of Rose, W 33.			
143	42	3d. rose (5.7.73)......................	£450	80·00	£120
		s. Optd 'SPECIMEN' (pl. 14) (2)....................................	£350		
		sa. Optd 'SPECIMEN' (pl. 17) (8, 9)......................................	£250		
		sb. Optd 'SPECIMEN' (pl. 18) (8, 9, 10)..............................	£250		
		sc. Optd 'SPECIMEN' (pl. 19) (9, 10)....................................	£250		
		Wi. Watermark inverted..........	£1650	£375	
144		3d. pale rose............................	£450	80·00	
		Plate			
		11 (1873)......	£450	80·00	
		12 (1873)......	£525	80·00	
		14 (1874)......	£525	80·00	
		15 (1874)......	£450	80·00	
		16 (1875)......	£450	80·00	
		17 (1875)......	£525	80·00	
		18 (1875)......	£525	80·00	
		19 (1876)......	£450	80·00	
		20 (1879)......	£850	£140	
145	43	6d. pale buff (Plate 13) (15.3.73)..............................	*£25000		
146		6d. deep grey (20.3.74)............	£600	£120	£150
		s. Optd 'SPECIMEN' (pl. 14) (8, 10)..................................	£300		
		sa. Optd 'SPECIMEN' (pl. 15) (8, 9)....................................	£300		
		sb. Optd 'SPECIMEN' (pl. 16) (9)..	£300		
147		6d. grey....................................	£500	90·00	
		Wi. Watermark inverted..........	£1800	£375	
		Plate			
		13 (1874)......	£500	90·00	
		14 (1875)......	£500	90·00	
		15 (1876)......	£500	90·00	
		16 (1878)......	£500	90·00	
		17 (1880)......	£950	£180	
148	44	1s. deep green (1.9.73)............	£1100	£225	
150		1s. green...................................	£650	£160	£240
		s. Optd 'SPECIMEN' (pl. 11) (8)..	£450		
		sa. Optd 'SPECIMEN' (pl. 12) (8, 9, 10)..............................	£350		
		sb. Optd 'SPECIMEN' (pl. 13) (9)..	£350		
		Wi. Watermark inverted..........	£2400	£400	
		Plate			
		8 (1873)........	£825	£175	
		9 (1874)........	£825	£175	
		10 (1874)......	£775	£200	
		11 (1875)......	£775	£175	
		12 (1875)......	£650	£160	
		13 (1876)......	£650	£160	
		14 (—)..........	*	£40000	
151		1s. orange-brown (Plate 13) (14.10.80)............................	£4750	£550	£1800
		s. Optd 'SPECIMEN' (9)...........	£550		
		Wi. Watermark inverted..........	£11000	£1800	
		(d) Wmk Large Garter, W 17.			
152	45	4d. vermilion (1.3.76)................	£3000	£475	£1100
		s. Optd 'SPECIMEN' (pl. 15) (9)..	£400		
		Wi. Watermark inverted..........	—	£1000	
		Plate			
		15 (1876)......	£3000	£475	
		16 (1877)......	*	£35000	
153		4d. sage-green (12.3.77)..........	£1400	£300	£600
		s. Optd 'SPECIMEN' (pl. 15) (9)..	£350		
		sa. Optd 'SPECIMEN' (pl. 16) (9)..	£350		
		Wi. Watermark inverted..........	£3000	£625	
		Plate			
		15 (1877)......	£1600	£325	
		16 (1877)......	£1400	£300	
		17 (1877)......	*	£20000	
154		4d. grey-brown (Plate 17) (15.8.80)..............................	£2800	£500	£1700
		a. Imperf.................................	£22000		
		s. Optd 'SPECIMEN' (9)...........	£350		
		Wi. Watermark inverted..........	—	£1200	
156	46	8d. orange (Plate 1) (11.9.76)..	£1850	£350	£625
		s. Optd 'SPECIMEN' (8, 9)......	£350		
		Wi. Watermark inverted..........	—	£900	

* Nos. 138/156 **For well-centred, lightly used +100%**
** No. 145, No. 150 plate 14, No. 152 plate 16 and No. 153 plate 17 are all 'abnormals' see Surface-printed Issues general notes.

1876 (July). Prepared for use but not issued

			Unused	
156a	46	8d. purple-brown (Plate 1)......................	£7500	
		s. Optd 'SPECIMEN' (8, 9)......................	£5500	

49 Imperial Crown

3d   6d

(50)   (51)

Surcharges in red

1880–83. Large coloured corner letters. Wmk Imperial Crown, W **49**.

			Unused	Used*	Used on cover
157	41	2½d. blue (23.3.81)......................	£450	35·00	55·00
		s. Optd 'SPECIMEN' (pl. 23) (9)..	£175		
		Wi. Watermark inverted..........	—	£550	
		Plate			
		21 (1881)......	£500	45·00	
		22 (1881)......	£450	45·00	
		23 (1881)......	£450	35·00	
158	42	3d. rose (3.81)...........................	£500	£100	£175
		s. Optd 'SPECIMEN' (pl. 21) (9)..	£250		
		Wi. Watermark inverted..........	—	£580	
		Plate			
		20 (1881)......	£900	£150	
		21 (1881)......	£500	£100	
159	42	3d. on 3d. lilac (surch Type **50**) (pl. 21) (1.1.83)..............	£650	£160	£450
		s. Optd 'SPECIMEN' (9)...........	£300		
		Wi. Watermark inverted..........		£850	
160	45	4d. grey-brown (8.12.80)..........	£450	75·00	£190
		s. Optd 'SPECIMEN' (pl. 17) (9)..	£250		
		sa. Optd 'SPECIMEN' (pl. 18) (9)..	£275		
		Wi. Watermark inverted..........	—	£650	
		Plate			
		17 (1880)......	£475	80·00	
		18 (1882)......	£450	75·00	
161	43	6d. grey (1.1.81).........................	£400	80·00	£120
		s. Optd 'SPECIMEN' (pl. 18) (9)..	£275		
		Wi. Watermark inverted..........	—	£650	
		Plate			
		17 (1881)......	£425	80·00	
		18 (1882)......	£400	80·00	
162	42	6d. on 6d. lilac (surch Type **51**) (pl. 18) (1.1.83)..............	£675	£150	£425
		a. Slanting dots (various) from..................................	£2000	£450	
		b. Optd double.........................	—	£12500	
		s. Optd 'SPECIMEN' (9)...........	£300		
		Wi. Watermark inverted..........	£3500	£850	
163	44	1s. orange-brown (24.5.81).......	£750	£170	£575
		s. Optd 'SPECIMEN' (pl. 13) (9)..	£350		
		sa. Optd 'SPECIMEN' (pl. 14) (9)..	£350		
		Wi. Watermark inverted..........	£3250	£950	
		Plate			
		13 (1881)......	£875	£170	
		14 (1881)......	£750	£170	

* Nos. 157/163 **For well-centred, lightly used +75%**
The 1s. plate 14 (line perf 14) exists in purple but was not issued in this shade (*Price* £15000 *unused*). Examples were included in a few of the Souvenir Albums prepared for members of the Stamp Committee of 1884.

QUEEN VICTORIA

KEY TO SURFACE-PRINTED ISSUES
1880–1900

SG Nos.	Description	Date of Issue
164/165	½d. green	14.10.80
187	½d. slate-blue	1.4.84
197/197e	½d. vermilion	1.1.87
213	½d. blue-green	17.4.1900
166	1d. Venetian red	1.1.80
170/171	1d. lilac, Die I	12.7.81
172/174	1d. lilac, Die II	12.12.81
167	1½d. Venetian red	14.10.80
188	1½d. lilac	1.4.84
198	1½d. purple and green	1.1.87
168/168a	2d. rose	8.12.80
189	2d. lilac	1.4.84
199/200	2d. green and red	1.1.87
190	2½d. lilac	1.4.84
201	2½d. purple on blue paper	1.1.87
191	3d. lilac	1.4.84
202/204	3d. purple on yellow paper	1.1.87
192	4d. dull green	1.4.84
205/205a	4d. green and brown	1.1.87
206	4½d. green and carmine	15.9.92
169	5d. indigo	15.3.81
193	5d. dull green	1.4.84
207	5d. purple and blue, Die I	1.1.87
207a	5d. purple and blue, Die II	1888
194	6d. dull green	1.4.84
208/208a	6d. purple on rose-red paper	1.1.87
195	9d. dull green	1.8.83
209	9d. purple and blue	1.1.87
210/210b	10d. purple and carmine	24.2.90
196	1s. dull green	1.4.84
211	1s. green	1.1.87
214	1s. green and carmine	11.7.1900
175	2s.6d. lilac on blued paper	2.7.83
178/179	2s.6d. lilac	1884
176	5s. rose on blued paper	1.4.84
180/181	5s. rose	1884
177/177a	10s. ultramarine on blued paper	1.4.84
182/183a	10s. ultramarine	1884
185	£1 brown-lilac, wmk Crowns	1.4.84
186	£1 brown-lilac, wmk Orbs	6.1.88
212	£1 green	28.1.91

Note that the £5 value used with the above series is listed as Nos. 133 and 137.

52   *53*
54   *55*   *56*

Normal   Recut tail to 'R'

1880–81. Wmk Imperial Crown, W 49.

			Unused	Used*	Used on cover
164	52	½d. deep green (14.10.80)	55·00	22·00	30·00
		a. Imperf	£5000		
		b. No watermark	£10000		
		s. Optd 'SPECIMEN' (9)	60·00		
		Wi. Watermark inverted	£2400	£575	
165		½d. pale green	55·00	22·00	
166	53	1d. Venetian red (1.1.80)	35·00	15·00	30·00
		a. Imperf	£4250		

			Unused	Used*	Used on cover
		b. Error. Wmk **48**	†	£27000	
		c. Re-cut tail to 'R'	£550	£275	
		s. Optd 'SPECIMEN' (9)	£100		
		Wi. Watermark inverted	—	£350	
167	54	1½d. Venetian red (14.10.80)	£250	60·00	£160
		s. Optd 'SPECIMEN' (9)	80·00		
		Wi. Watermark inverted	†	—	
168	55	2d. pale rose (8.12.80)	£350	£120	£300
		s. Optd 'SPECIMEN' (9)	£110		
		Wi. Watermark inverted	£3000	£850	
168a		2d. deep rose	£375	£120	
169	56	5d. indigo (15.3.81)	£725	£175	£325
		a. Imperf	£6750	£4500	
		s. Optd 'SPECIMEN' (9, 12, 13)	£160		
		Wi. Watermark inverted	—	£4800	
164/169	Set of 5		£1275	£350	

* Nos. 164/169 **For well-centred, lightly used +75%**

The re-cut tail to 'R' variety occurs on plate 12, in the top right hand corner on stamp lettered GR-RG.
Two used examples of the 1d. value have been reported on the Orb (fiscal) watermark.

57   Die I   Die II

1881. Wmk Imperial Crown, W **49**.

(a) 14 dots in each corner, Die I (12 July).

			Unused	Used*	Used on cover
170	57	1d. lilac	£225	45·00	60·00
		s. Optd 'SPECIMEN' (9)	70·00		
		Wi. Watermark inverted	—	£600	
171		1d. pale lilac	£225	45·00	

(b) 16 dots in each corner, Die II (13 December).

			Unused	Used*	Used on cover
172	57	1d. lilac	2·75	2·25	4·00
		s. Optd 'SPECIMEN' (9, 12)	60·00		
		Wi. Watermark inverted	60·00	35·00	
172a		1d. bluish lilac	£475	£150	
173		1d. deep purple	2·75	2·25	
		a. Printed both sides	£700	†	
		b. Frame broken at bottom	£750	£350	
		c. Printed on gummed side	£700	†	
		d. Imperf three sides (pair)	£7500	†	
		e. Printed both sides but impression on back inverted	£800	†	
		f. No watermark	£8000	†	
		g. Blued paper	—		
174		1d. mauve	2·75	1·75	
		a. Imperf (pair)	£6000		

* Nos. 170/174 **For well-centred, lightly used +50%**

1d. stamps with the words 'PEARS SOAP' printed on the back in orange, blue or mauve *price from* £550, *unused*.

The variety 'frame broken at bottom' (No. 173b) shows a white space just inside the bottom frame-line from between the 'N' and 'E' of 'ONE' to below the first 'N' of 'PENNY', breaking the pearls and cutting into the lower part of the oval below 'PEN'.

58   *59*   *60*

QUEEN VICTORIA

1883–84. Large coloured corner letters. Wmk Large Anchor, W **40**.
(a) Blued paper.

			Unused	Used*
175	58	2s.6d. lilac (2.7.83)	£6000	£1500
		s. Optd 'SPECIMEN' (9)	£625	
176	59	5s. rose (1.4.84)	£12500	£4000
		s. Optd 'SPECIMEN' (9, 11)	£1600	
177	60	10s. ultramarine (1.4.84)	£40000	£8250
		s. Optd 'SPECIMEN' (9)	£2850	
177a		10s. cobalt (5.84)	£55000	£12500
		s. Optd 'SPECIMEN' (9)	£5500	

(b) White paper.

			Unused	Used*
178	58	2s.6d. lilac	£600	£160
		s. Optd 'SPECIMEN' (9, 11, 12, 13)	£425	
179		2s.6d. deep lilac	£825	£225
		a. On blued paper	£8000	£3600
		Wi. Watermark inverted	—	£11500
180	59	5s. rose	£1100	£250
		Wi. Watermark inverted	†	£12500
181		5s. crimson	£975	£250
		s. Optd 'SPECIMEN' (9, 11, 12, 13)	£450	
182	60	10s. cobalt	£42000	£8250
		s. Optd 'SPECIMEN' (9)	£3400	
183		10s. ultramarine	£2250	£525
		s. Optd 'SPECIMEN' (9, 11, 13)	£550	
183a		10s. pale ultramarine	£2500	£550

* Nos. 175/183a **For well-centred, lightly used +50%**
For No. 180 perf 12 see note below No. 196.

61

Broken frames, Plate 2

1884 (1 Apr). Wmk Three Imperial Crowns, W **49**.
185	61	£1 brown-lilac	£28000	£3000
		a. Frame broken	£55000	£5000
		s. Optd 'SPECIMEN' (9, 11, 12)	£2800	
		Wi. Watermark inverted	—	£35000

1888 (Feb). Wmk Three Orbs, W **48**.
186	61	£1 brown-lilac	£60000	£4500
		a. Frame broken	£100000	£7500
		s. Optd 'SPECIMEN' (11)	£6800	

* Nos. 185/186a **For well-centred, lightly used +50%**
The broken-frame varieties, Nos. 185a and 186a, are on Plate 2 stamps JC and TA, as illustrated. See also No. 212a.

1883 (1 Aug). (9d.) or **1884** (1 Apr) (others). Wmk Imperial Crown, W **49** (sideways on horiz designs).

			Unused	Used*	Used on cover
187	52	½d. slate-blue	35·00	10·00	20·00
		a. Imperf	£3250		
		s. Optd 'SPECIMEN' (9)	50·00		
		Wi. Watermark inverted	£3000	£350	
188	62	1½d. lilac	£125	45·00	£120
		a. Imperf	£3250		
		s. Optd 'SPECIMEN' (9)	85·00		
		Wi. Watermark inverted	£3000	£280	
189	63	2d. lilac	£230	80·00	£150
		a. Imperf	£4000		
		s. Optd 'SPECIMEN' (9)	85·00		
		Wi. Watermark sideways inverted	—	—	
190	64	2½d. lilac	95·00	20·00	30·00
		a. Imperf	£4000		
		s. Optd 'SPECIMEN' (9)	85·00		
		Wi. Watermark sideways inverted	£600	—	
191	65	3d. lilac	£280	£100	£180
		a. Imperf	£4000		
		s. Optd 'SPECIMEN' (9)	85·00		
		Wi. Watermark inverted	†	£1200	
192	66	4d. dull green	£580	£210	£350
		a. Imperf	£4000		
		s. Optd 'SPECIMEN' (9)	£190		
193	62	5d. dull green	£580	£210	£350
		a. Imperf	£4500		
		s. Optd 'SPECIMEN' (9)	£190		
194	63	6d. dull green	£625	£240	£380
		a. Imperf	£4500		
		s. Optd 'SPECIMEN' (9)	£220		
		Wi. Watermark sideways inverted	£1400	—	
195	64	9d. dull green (1.8.83)	£1250	£480	£4750
		s. Optd 'SPECIMEN' (9)	£425		
		Wi. Watermark sideways inverted	£2000	£775	
196	65	1s. dull green	£1600	£325	£625
		a. Imperf	£5500		
		s. Optd 'SPECIMEN' (9)	£375		
		Wi. Watermark inverted	—	—	
187/196 *Set of 10*			£5000	£1600	

* Nos. 187/196 **For well-centred, lightly used +100%**
The normal sideways watermark shows the top of the crown pointing to the right *as seen from the back of the stamp*.
The above prices are for stamps in the true dull green colour. Stamps which have been soaked, causing the colour to run, are virtually worthless.
Stamps of the above set and No. 180 are also found perf 12; these are official perforations, but were never issued. A second variety of the 5d. is known with a line instead of a stop under the 'd' in the value; this was never issued and is therefore only known unused (*Price* £25,000).

71 **72** **73**

74 **75** **76**

77 **78** **79**

62 **63** **64**

65 **66**

16

QUEEN VICTORIA

80   **81**   **82**

Die I   Die II

Die I: Square dots to right of 'd'
Die II Thin vertical lines to right of 'd'

1½d. Deformed leaf (Duty plate 4, R. 19/1)

1887 (1 Jan)–**92. Jubilee issue.** New types. The bicoloured stamps have the value tablets, or the frames including the value tablets, in the second colour. Wmk Imperial Crown, W **49** (Three Crowns on £1).

			Unmtd mint	Mtd mint	Used*
197	71	½d. vermilion	2·50	1·75	1·25
		a. Printed on gummed side	£4000	£3000	
		b. Printed both sides			
		c. Doubly printed	—	£25000	
		d. Imperf (showing bottom margins)	£6500	£5000	
		s. Optd 'SPECIMEN' (9, 10, 12)		35·00	
		Wi. Watermark inverted	90·00	60·00	60·00
197e		½d. orange-vermilion	2·50	1·75	1·20
198	72	1½d. dull purple and pale green	25·00	18·00	8·00
		a. Purple part of design double	—	—	£9000
		b. Deformed leaf	£1100	£800	£450
		s. Optd 'SPECIMEN' (6, 9, 12)		55·00	
		Wi. Watermark inverted	£1600	£1200	£500
199	73	2d. green and scarlet	£550	£425	£260
200		2d. grey-green and carmine	50·00	35·00	15·00
		s. Optd 'SPECIMEN' (6, 9, 12, 13)		60·00	
		Wi. Watermark inverted	£1600	£1200	£525
201	74	2½d. purple/blue	45·00	25·00	5·00
		a. Printed on gummed side (Wmk. inverted)	£15000	£12000	
		b. Imperf three sides	—	£9500	
		c. Imperf	—	£10000	
		d. Missing 'd' in value	†	†	£9500
		s. Optd 'SPECIMEN' (6, 9, 12, 13)		75·00	
		Wi. Watermark inverted	£4500	£3500	£1400
202	75	3d. purple/yellow	45·00	25·00	5·00
		a. Imperf (wmk inverted)	—	£10000	
		s. Optd 'SPECIMEN' (6, 9, 12)		60·00	
		Wi. Watermark inverted	—	—	£725
203		3d. deep purple/yellow	60·00	30·00	5·00
204		3d. purple/orange (1890)	£1300	£800	
205	76	4d. green and purple-brown	60·00	40·00	18·00
		aa. Imperf	—	£12000	
		s. Optd 'SPECIMEN' (6, 9, 10, 12)		60·00	
		Wi. Watermark inverted	£1600	£1200	£650
205a		4d. green and deep brown	60·00	40·00	18·00
206	77	4½d. green and carmine (15.9.92)	17·00	11·00	45·00
		s. Optd 'SPECIMEN' (9, 13)	£500	£400	
		Wi. Watermark inverted			
206a		4½d. green and deep bright carmine	£1000	£750	£650
207	78	5d. dull purple and blue (Die I)	£1100	£800	£120
		s. Optd 'SPECIMEN' (9, 12)	90·00	65·00	
207a		5d. dull purple and blue (Die II) (1888)	60·00	42·00	15·00
		s. Optd 'SPECIMEN' (13)	—		
		Wi. Watermark inverted		£12500	£1250
208	79	6d. purple/rose-red	60·00	40·00	15·00
		s. Optd 'SPECIMEN' (9, 10, 12)		65·00	
		Wi. Watermark inverted	£10000	£7500	£2000
208a		6d. deep purple/rose-red	60·00	40·00	15·00
209	80	9d. dull purple and blue	£110	75·00	48·00
		s. Optd 'SPECIMEN' (6, 9, 12)	£100	70·00	
		Wi. Watermark inverted	£11000	£8000	£2800
210	81	10d. dull purple and carmine (shades) (24.2.90)	90·00	60·00	45·00
		aa. Imperf	—	£12500	
		s. Optd 'SPECIMEN' (9, 13, 15)	£150	£110	
		Wi. Watermark inverted	£1300	£9500	£3000
210a		10d. dull purple and deep dull carmine	£800	£625	£250
210b		10d. dull purple and scarlet	£170	95·00	65·00
211	82	1s. dull green	£375	£275	80·00
		s. Optd 'SPECIMEN' (9, 10, 12)	£100	75·00	
		Wi. Watermark inverted	£2200	£1700	£975
212	61	£1 green (28.1.91)	£5000	£3500	£800
		a. Frame broken	£10000	£7500	£2000
		s. Optd 'SPECIMEN' (9, 11, 13, 15, 16)		£1100	
		Wi. Watermark inverted	—	£85000	£13000

* Nos. 197/212a **For well-centred, lightly used +50%**

The broken-frame varieties, No. 212a, are on Plate 2 stamps JC or TA, as illustrated above No. 185.

½d. stamps with 'PEARS SOAP' printed on the back in orange, blue or mauve, *price from £525 each*.

No used price is quoted for No. 204 as it is not possible to authenticate the paper colour on stamps in used condition.

1900. Colours changed. Wmk Imperial Crown, W **49**

			Unmtd Mint	Mtd Mint	Used*
213	71	½d. blue-green (17.4)	2·00	2·25	6·50
		a. Printed on gummed side	—	†	†
		b. Imperf	£6000		
		s. Optd 'SPECIMEN' (11, 15)		£650	
		Wi. Watermark inverted	75·00	95·00	
214	82	1s. green and carmine (11.7)	65·00	£140	£1000
		s. Optd 'SPECIMEN' (15)		£950	
		Wi. Watermark inverted	£1900	£1100	
Set of 14			£950	£1900	£1100

* 213/214 **For well-centred, lightly used +50%**

The ½d. No. 213, in bright blue, is a colour changeling caused by a consituent of the ink used for some months in 1900.

USED ON COVER PRICES		
No.	197	7·00
No.	198	25·00
No.	200	28·00
No.	201	8·00
No.	202	38·00
No.	205	42·00
No.	206	£100
No.	207	£275
No.	207a	50·00
No.	208	95·00
No.	209	£275
No.	210	£300
No.	211	£190
No.	213	6·50
No.	214	£1000

DEPARTMENTAL OFFICIALS

The following Official stamps were exclusively for the use of certain government departments. Until 1882 official mail used ordinary postage stamps purchased at post offices, the cash being refunded once a quarter. Later the government departments obtained Official stamps by requisition.

Official stamps may have been on sale to the public for a short time at Somerset House but they were not sold from post offices. The system of only supplying the Government departments with stamps was open to abuse so that all official stamps were withdrawn on 13 May 1904.

OVERPRINTS, PERFORATIONS, WATERMARKS. All official stamps were overprinted by Thomas De La Rue & Co. and are perf 14. Except for the 5s., and 10s. on Anchor watermarked paper W **40**, they are on Crown watermarked paper *unless otherwise stated*.

QUEEN VICTORIA

INLAND REVENUE

These stamps were used by revenue officials in the provinces, mail to and from Head Office passing without a stamp. The London Office used these stamps only for foreign mail.

I.R. OFFICIAL (O1)   **I. R. OFFICIAL** (O2)

1882–1901. Stamps of Queen Victoria. Optd with T **O1** (½d. to 1s.) or T **O2** (others).

> **PRICES.** Please note that the price columns in this section are for *mounted mint, used* and *used on cover* examples. For Government Parcels and Board of Education stamps, they are for *mint* and *used* only.

(a) Issues of 1880–1881.

			Unused	Used*	Used on cover
O1	52	½d. deep green (1.11.82)	£135	60·00	£120
O2		½d. pale green	90·00	40·00	
		s. Optd 'SPECIMEN' (9)	£325		
O3	57	1d. lilac (Die II) (1.10.82)	10·00	7·00	30·00
		a. Optd in blue-black	£300	£125	
		b. 'OFFICIAL' omitted	—	£12500	
		c. Imperf	£4500		
		ca. Imperf, optd in blue-black	£4500		
		s. Optd 'SPECIMEN' (9, 15)	£180		
		Wi. Watermark inverted	—	£2200	
O4	43	6d. grey (Plate 18) (3.11.82)	£575	£140	
		s. Optd 'SPECIMEN' (9, 15)	£325		

No. O3 with the lines of the overprint transposed is an essay.

(b) Issues of 1884–1888.

			Unused	Used*	Used on cover
O5	52	½d. slate-blue (8.5.85)	£110	35·00	£135
		s. Optd 'SPECIMEN' (9)	£325		
O6	64	2½d. lilac (12.3.85)	£525	£180	£1400
		s. Optd 'SPECIMEN' (9)	£325		
O7	65	1s. dull green (12.3.85)	£6000	£1900	
		s. Optd 'SPECIMEN' (9)	£1250		
O8	59	5s. rose (blued paper) (Wmk Anchor) (12.3.85)	£17500	£6500	
		a. Raised stop after 'R'	£18500	£7250	
		s. Optd 'SPECIMEN' (9, 11)	£2750		
O9		5s. rose (Wmk Anchor) (3.90)	£12000	£2500	
		a. Raised stop after 'R'	£14000	£3200	
		b. Optd in blue-black	£14000	£3200	
		s. Optd 'SPECIMEN' (9, 11, 13, 16)	£1750		
O9c	60	10s. cobalt (blued paper) (Wmk Anchor) (12.3.85)	£38000	£9500	
		ca. Raised stop after 'R'			
		cb. cobalt (white paper) (Wmk Anchor)	£22000	£7750	
		cs. Optd 'SPECIMEN' (11)	£4500		
O9d		10s. ultramarine (blued paper) (Wmk Anchor) (12.3.85)	£27000	£8500	
		da. Raised stop after 'R'	£27000	£8500	
		ds. Optd 'SPECIMEN' (10)	£3750		
O10		10s. ultramarine (Wmk Anchor) (3.90)	£11500	£3750	
		a. Raised stop after 'R'	£12500	£4500	
		b. Optd in blue-black	£12500	£4500	
		s. Optd 'SPECIMEN' (9, 10, 11, 16)	£2750		
O11	61	£1 brown-lilac (Wmk Crowns) (12.3.85)	£60000	£22000	
		a. Frame broken	£85000	—	
		s. Optd 'SPECIMEN' (11)	£5000		
O12		£1 brown-lilac (Wmk Orbs) (optd in blue-black) (3.90)	£85000	£30000	
		a. Frame broken	£125000		
		s. Optd 'SPECIMEN' (9, 11)	£8500		

Nos. O3, O13, O15 and O16 may be found showing worn impressions of the overprint with thicker letters.

(c) Issues of 1887–1892.

			Unused	Used*	Used on cover
O13	71	½d. vermilion (15.5.88)	15·00	7·00	£110
		a. Without 'I.R.'	£7000		
		b. Imperf	£7000		
		c. Optd double (imperf)	£8000		
		s. Optd 'SPECIMEN' (9, 15)	£120		
O14	74	2½d. purple/blue (2.92)	£175	30·00	£450
		s. Optd 'SPECIMEN' (9, 13, 15)	£120		
O15	82	1s. dull green (9.89)	£1000	£375	£3750
		a. Optd in blue-black	£2250		
		s. Optd 'SPECIMEN' (9, 15)	£260		
O16	61	£1 green (6.92)	£12500	£2500	
		a. No stop after 'R'	—	£4000	
		b. Frame broken	£20000	£5250	
		s. Optd 'SPECIMEN' (9, 10, 15)	£2250		

(d) Issues of 1887 and 1900.

			Unused	Used*	Used on cover
O17	71	½d. blue-green (4.01)	20·00	15·00	£350
		s. Optd 'SPECIMEN' (15)	£160		
O18	79	6d. purple/rose-red (1.7.01)	£625	£150	
		s. Optd 'SPECIMEN' (15, 16)	£250		
O19	82	1s. green and carmine (12.01)	£4250	£1800	
		s. Optd 'SPECIMEN' (15)	£1100		

* Nos. O1/O19 **For well-centred, lightly used +35%**

OFFICE OF WORKS

These were issued to Head and Branch (local) offices in London and in Branch (local) offices at Birmingham, Bristol, Edinburgh, Glasgow, Leeds, Liverpool, Manchester and Southampton. The overprints on stamps of value 2d. and upwards were created later in 1902, the 2d. for registration fees and the rest for overseas mail.

O.W. OFFICIAL (O3)

1896 (24 Mar)–**02**. Stamps of Queen Victoria. Optd with T **O3**.

			Unused	Used*	Used on Cover
O31	71	½d. vermilion	£350	£150	£800
		s. Optd 'SPECIMEN' (9, 15)	£325		
O32		½d. blue-green (2.02)	£475	£225	
		s. Optd 'SPECIMEN' (15)	£450		
O33	57	1d. lilac (Die II)	£500	£150	£1000
		s. Optd 'SPECIMEN' (9, 15, 16)	£325		
O34	78	5d. dull purple and blue (Die II) (29.4.02)	£4000	£1400	
		s. Optd 'SPECIMEN' (16)	£1250		
O35	81	10d. dull purple and carmine (28.5.02)	£7250	£2250	
		s. Optd 'SPECIMEN' (16)	£2600		

ARMY

Letters to and from the War Office in London passed without postage. The overprinted stamps were distributed to District and Station Paymasters nationwide, including Cox and Co., the Army Agents, who were paymasters to the Household Division.

ARMY OFFICIAL (O4)   **ARMY OFFICIAL** (O5)

1896 (1 Sept)–**01**. Stamps of Queen Victoria optd with T **O4** (½d., 1d.) or T **O5** (2½d., 6d.).

			Unused	Used*	Used on cover
O41	71	½d. vermilion	10·00	5·00	65·00
		a. 'OFFICIAI' (R.13/7)	£300	£130	
		b. Lines of opt transposed	£4700		
		s. Optd 'SPECIMEN' (9)	£225		
		Wi. Watermark inverted	£800	£375	
O42		½d. blue-green (6.00)	10·00	15·00	
		s. Optd 'SPECIMEN' (15)	£500		
		Wi. Watermark inverted	£1000	£650	
O43	57	1d. lilac (Die II)	8·00	7·00	£110
		a. 'OFFICIAI' (R.13/7)	£240	£150	
		s. Optd 'SPECIMEN' (9)	£500		
O44	74	2½d. purple/blue	50·00	35·00	£775
		s. Optd 'SPECIMEN' (9)	£225		
O45	79	6d. purple/rose-red (20.9.01)	£110	60·00	£1700
		s. Optd 'SPECIMEN' (15)	£500		

Nos. O41a and O43a occur in sheets overprinted by Forme 1, this was replaced in February 189 by Forme 2.

QUEEN VICTORIA

GOVERNMENT PARCELS

These stamps were issued to all departments, including Head Office, for use on parcels weighing over 3lb. Below this weight government parcels were sent by letter post to avoid the 55% of the postage paid from accuring to the railway companies, as laid down by parcel-post regulations. Most government parcels stamps suffered heavy postmarks in use.

GOVT PARCELS
(O7)

1883 (1 Aug)–**86**. Stamps of Queen Victoria. Optd with T **O7**.

			Unused	Used
O61	62	1½d. lilac (1.5.86)	£400	£100
		a. No dot under 'T'	£775	£175
		b. Dot to left of 'T'	£775	£175
		s. Optd 'SPECIMEN' (9)		
O62	62	6d. dull green (1.5.86)	£3500	£1400
		s. Optd 'SPECIMEN' (9)	£300	
O63	64	9d. dull green	£2750	£1200
		Wi. Watermark sideways inverted	†	—
		s. Optd 'SPECIMEN' (9)	£300	
O64	44	1s. orange-brown (watermark Crown, pl. 13)	£1750	£300
		a. No dot under 'T'	£2750	£500
		b. Dot to left of 'T'	£2750	£500
		s. Optd 'SPECIMEN' (9)	£325	
O64c		1s. orange-brown (pl. 14)	£3500	£600
		ca. No dot under 'T'	£4500	£850
		cb. Dot to left of 'T'		

1887–**90**. Stamps of Queen Victoria. Optd with T **O7**.

			Unused	Used
O65	72	1½d. dull purple and pale green (29.10.87)	£170	30·00
		a. No dot under 'T'	£260	75·00
		b. Dot to right of 'T'	£260	75·00
		c. Dot to left of 'T'	£260	75·00
		s. Optd 'SPECIMEN' (9, 10, 13, 15)	£300	
O66	79	6d. purple/*rose-red* (19.12.87)	£275	75·00
		a. No dot under 'T'	£375	£120
		b. Dot to right of 'T'	£375	£120
		c. Dot to left of 'T'	£375	£120
		s. Optd 'SPECIMEN' (9, 13, 15)	£250	
O67	80	9d. dull purple and blue (21.8.88)	£425	£120
		a. Optd in blue-black	£675	
		s. Optd 'SPECIMEN' (9, 10, 13, 15)	£300	
		Wi. Watermark inverted		
O68	82	1s. dull green (25.3.90)	£700	£275
		a. No dot under 'T'	£1000	£500
		b. Dot to right of 'T'	£1000	£500
		c. Dot to left of 'T'	£1000	£500
		d. Optd in blue-black	£1200	
		s. Optd 'SPECIMEN' (9, 13, 15)	£300	

1891–**1900**. Stamps of Queen Victoria. Optd with T **O7**.

			Unused	Used
O69	57	1d. lilac (Die II) (18.6.97)	£100	30·00
		a. No dot under 'T'	£160	75·00
		b. Dot to left of 'T'	£160	75·00
		c. Optd inverted	£7500	£3500
		d. Optd inverted. Dot to left of 'T'	£8500	£4500
		s. Optd 'SPECIMEN' (15)	£450	
		Wi. Watermark inverted	—	£500
O70	73	2d. grey-green and carmine (24.10.91)	£250	50·00
		a. No dot under 'T'	£400	£125
		b. Dot to left of 'T'	£400	£125
		s. Optd 'SPECIMEN' (9, 11, 13, 15, 16)	£300	
O71	77	4½d. green and carmine (29.9.92)	£400	£275
		b. Dot to right of 'T'		
		Wi. Watermark inverted	—	£9000
		s. Optd 'SPECIMEN' (9, 13, 15)	£300	
O72	82	1s. green and carmine (11.00)	£650	£275
		a. Optd inverted	†	£15000
		s. Optd 'SPECIMEN' (9)	£400	

* O61/O72 **For well-centred lightly used +100%**

The 'no dot under T' variety occurred on R.12/3 and 20/2. The 'dot to left of T' comes four times in the sheet on R.2/7, 6/7, 7/9 and 12/9. The best example of the 'dot to right of T' is on R.20/1. All three varieties were corrected around 1897.

BOARD OF EDUCATION

BOARD OF EDUCATION
(O8)

1902 (19 Feb). Stamps of Queen Victoria. Optd with T **O8**.

			Unused	Used	Used on cover
O81	78	5d. dull purple and blue (II)	£5750	£1500	£4250
		s. Optd 'SPECIMEN' (15)	£1400		
O82	82	1s. green and carmine	£12000	£6000	—
		s. Optd 'SPECIMEN' (15)	£3000		

POST OFFICE TELEGRAPH STAMPS

The telegraph system in the United Kingdom was originally operated by private companies, some of which issued their own stamps.

The Post Office took over the service in 1870, producing telegraph forms with impressed 1s. stationery dies and blank forms to which postage stamps were applied.

To assist in the separate accounting of revenues from the postal and telegraph services, special Post Office Telegraph stamps were issued from 1 February 1876 and from 1 May of that year the use of postage stamps to pre-pay telegraph services was prohibited.

Telegraph stamps were in use for little over five years, when it was decided to withdraw them and postage stamps were, once again, used for telegraph services.

PLATE NUMBERS Like the postage stamps of the period, all telegraph stamps showed their plate number within the design. These are listed under their respective values.

WATERMARKS To differentiate them from postage stamps, all telegraph stamps were in horizontal format and the watermarks appear sideways. Apart from the Shamrock watermark, W **T12**, all were as used for postage stamps of the period. For the purposes of this listing, watermark sideways refers to the top of the watermark device pointing to the right of the stamp *as viewed from the gummed side of the stamp*; watermark sideways inverted refers to the top of the device pointing to the left.

T1 T2 T3

T4 T5 T6

T7

T8  T9

T10

QUEEN VICTORIA

T11

T12

1876 (1 Feb)–**81**. Wmks as listed. Perf 15×15½ (5s., 10s., £5), Perf 14 (others).

			Unused	Used
T1	T1	½d. orange (W **T12**) (Plate 5) (1.4.80)	30·00	35·00
		a. Imperf (vertical pair)	£2000	
		s. Optd 'SPECIMEN' (9)	65·00	
T2	T2	1d. red-brown (W **T12**)	30·00	28·00
		Wi. Watermark inverted	£300	£175
		s. Optd 'SPECIMEN' (9, 10)	65·00	
		Plate		
		Plate 1	30·00	28·00
		Plate 2	35·00	28·00
		Plate 3	35·00	28·00
T3	T3	3d. carmine (W **33** sideways)	£100	60·00
		Wi. Watermark sideways inverted	£300	£280
		s. Optd 'SPECIMEN' (9, 10)	80·00	
		Plate		
		Plate 1	£100	75·00
		Plate 2	£100	60·00
		Plate 3	£125	90·00
T4		3d. carmine (W **49** sideways inverted) (6.6.81)	£150	£120
		Plate		
		Plate 3	£150	£120
		Plate 4 (watermark sideways)	£475	£250
		Plate 5. (watermark sideways)	£475	£250
T5	T4	4d. sage-green (W **17** sideways inverted) (Plate 1) (1.3.77)	£150	£125
		a. Imperf (vertical pair)	—	—
		wi. Watermark sideways	75·00	
		s. Optd 'SPECIMEN' (9, 11)	£125	80·00
T6	T5	6d. grey (W **33** sideways) (1.3.77)	75·00	
		s. Optd 'SPECIMEN' (9, 11)		
		Plate		
		Plate 1	£125	80·00
		Plate 2	£300	£160
T7		6d. grey (W **49** sideways inverted) (1.81)	£240	£150
		a. Imperf (vertical pair)		
T8	T6	1s. deep green (W **33** sideways)	£120	50·00
		Wi. Watermark sideways inverted	£500	
		s. Optd 'SPECIMEN' (9, 10)	£110	
		Plate		
		Plate 1	£180	65·00
		Plate 2	£140	65·00
		Plate 3	£140	55·00
		Plate 4	£200	55·00
		Plate 5	£120	50·00
		Plate 6	£120	50·00
		Plate 7	£350	55·00
		Plate 8	£180	55·00
		Plate 9	£180	55·00
		Plate 10	£220	70·00
T9		1s. brown-orange (W **33** sideways) (10.80)	£225	£150
		s. Optd 'SPECIMEN' (9)	£120	
		Plate		
		Plate 10	£225	£150
		Plate 12	£250	£190
T10		1s. brown-orange (W **49** sideways) (2.81)	£250	£200
		a. Imperf (vertical pair)		
		Wi. Watermark sideways inverted	£250	£200
		s. Optd 'SPECIMEN' (12)	£500	
		Plate		
		Plate 11	£250	£200
		Plate 12	£550	£300
T11	T7	3s. slate-blue (W **33** sideways) (Plate 1) (1.3.77)	£175	80·00
		Wi. Watermark sideways inverted	—	£500
		s. Optd 'SPECIMEN' (8, 9, 11)	£120	
T12		3s. slate-blue (W **49** sideways inverted) (Plate 1) (8.81)	£6500	£3800
T13	T8	5s. rose (W **39**) (Perf 15×15½)	£1100	£200
		s. Optd 'SPECIMEN' (8, 9, 10)	£250	
		Plate		
		Plate 1	£1100	£200
		Plate 2	£2250	£375
T14		5s. rose (W **39**) (Perf 14) (Plate 2) (1880)	£7000	£600
T15		5s. rose (W **40**) (Perf 14) (Plate 3) (5.81)	£7000	£1100
		s. Optd 'SPECIMEN' (9, 12)	£1000	
T16	T9	10s. rey-green (W **39**) (Plate 1) (13.77)	£1750	£450
		s. Optd 'SPECIMEN' (8, 9, 11)	£400	
T17	T10	£1 brown-lilac (W **T12** sideways×3) (Plate 1) (1.3.77)	£8250	£950
		s. Optd 'SPECIMEN' (8, 9, 11)	£900	
T18	T11	£5 orange (W **T12** sideways inverted×3), (Plate 1) (1.3.77)	£45000	£3200
		s. Optd 'SPECIMEN' (8, 9, 11)	£2800	

* Nos. T1/T18 **For well-centred lightly used +75%**

catawiki

Now is the perfect time
to sell your stamps on Catawiki

Make extra money. Sign up for free to sell your stamps on Catawiki. Our secure payment system, team of in-house Experts and dedicated Customer Experience Specialists are here to help you get started.

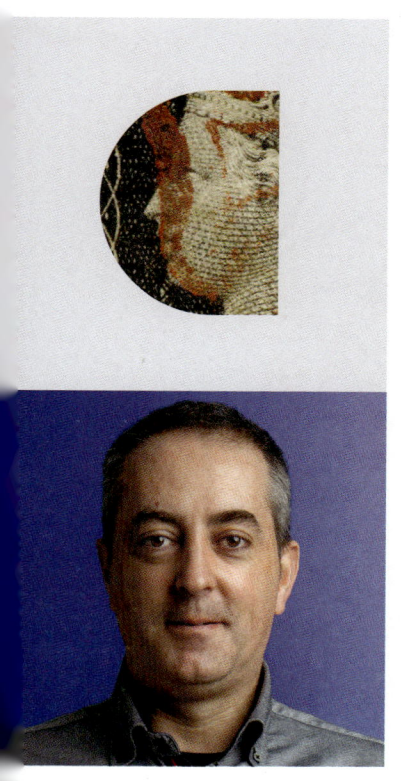

...tanasio Soriano
...uctioneer

...uy and sell on Catawiki.com

Download on the App Store

GET IT ON Google Play

We are the "Serious Buyers" of GB Stamps

Especially good quality mint or used collections of pre QEII.

Specialised collections of all GB apart from Decimal Machins.

Line-engraved Specialist collections especially "old time lots".

National & International Exhibits especially Silver medal and above.

MARK BLOXHAM
STAMPS LTD

W: www.philatelic.co.uk   T: +44 (0)1661 871953   E: mark@philatelic.co.uk

For all **Your** British Family of Nations Philatelic **Wants** please contact

COLLECTORS EXCHANGE

SERVING COLLECTORS SINCE 1980
WE ALSO STOCK W/W TOPICAL SETS

Despite being the largest British Specialty Dealers in the South Eastern U.S., we are known to be USER FRIENDLY with extensive stocks of stamps and postal history of Great Britain and the entire area of British postal influence - Aden to Zululand.

Please visit us at the various shows that we attend – say hello to Jean and John Latter and look over what we have to offer.

ALSO AVAILABLE AT
www.britishstampsamerica.com

ORLANDO STAMP SHOP, 1814A EDGEWATER DRIVE, ORLANDO, FLORIDA 32804, USA

PHONE +1 407-620-0908

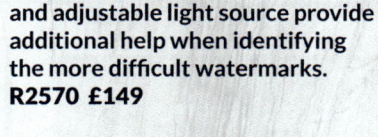

Detectamark Spectrum Watermark Detector

The Stanley Gibbons Detectamark Spectrum makes it easy to discover those hidden rarities. It's simple to use and the versatile colour settings and adjustable light source provide additional help when identifying the more difficult watermarks.
R2570 £149

KEY FEATURES
- Easy to discover hidden rarities
- Unique multiple colour settings
- It's able to detect watermarks on modern stamps printed on thick, chalk surfaced papers with full gum, which other detectors fail to identify
- No chemicals or solvents are used making this a safe, clean and highly effective
- Lightweight and battery operated

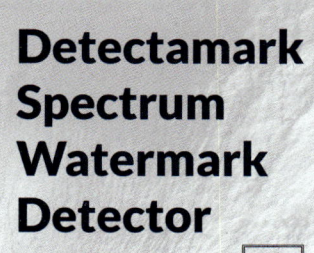

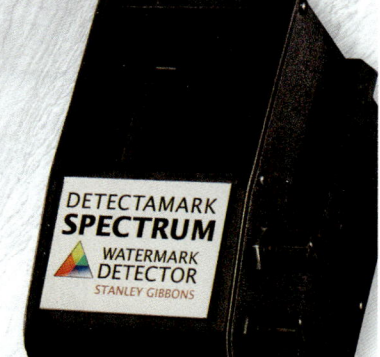

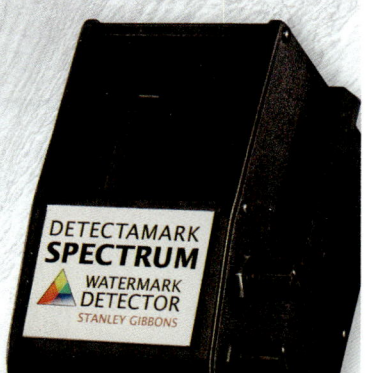

G Embassy Philatelists B

RETAIL LISTS & POSTAL AUCTIONS PRODUCED MONTHLY
CATALOGUE SENT FREE ON REQUEST
1000's OF ITEMS TO VIEW AND BUY ON OUR WEBSITE

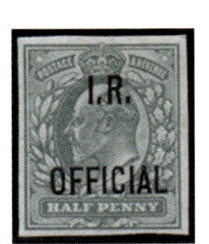

Imprimatur

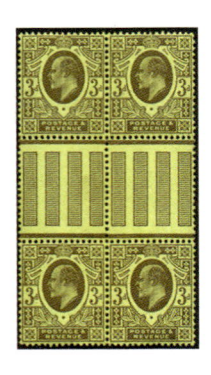

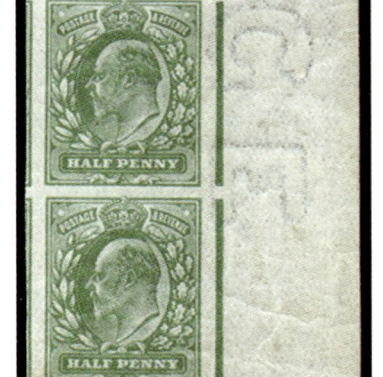

SG. 270c 'Imperf Pair'

Embassy Philatelists

P.O. BOX 1553, GUILDFORD, GU1 9YT
Tel: 01483 811 168
Email: info@embassystamps.co.uk

Est. 40 Years

www.embassystamps.co.uk

BUYING
From single items to major collections, for a fast professional transaction call us today.

BUYING
From single items to major collections, for a fast professional transaction call us today.

King Edward VII
22 January 1901-6 May 1910

PRINTINGS. Distinguishing De La Rue printings from the provisional printings of the same values made by Harrison & Sons Ltd. or at Somerset House may prove difficult in some cases. For very full guidance Volume 2 of the Stanley Gibbons *Great Britain Specialised Catalogue* should prove helpful.

Note that stamps perforated 15×14 must be Harrison; the 2½d., 3d. and 4d. in this perforation are useful reference material, their shades and appearance in most cases matching the Harrison perf 14 printings.

Except for the 6d. value, all stamps on chalk-surfaced paper were printed by De La Rue.

Of the stamps on ordinary paper, the De La Rue impressions are usually clearer and of a higher finish than those of the other printers. The shades are markedly different except in some printings of the 4d., 6d. and 7d. and in the 5s., 10s. and £1.

Used stamps in good, clean, unrubbed condition and with dated postmarks can form the basis of a useful reference collection, the dates often assisting in the assignment to the printers.

PRICES. For Nos. 215/266 prices are quoted for unmounted mint, mounted mint and used stamps.

USED STAMPS. For well-centred, lightly used examples of King Edward VII stamps, add the following percentages to the used prices quoted below:
De La Rue printings (Nos. 215/266)—3d. values+35%, 4d. orange+100%, 6d.+75%, 7d. and 1s.+25%, all other values+50%.
Harrison printings (Nos. 267/286)—all values and perforations+75%.
Somerset House printings (Nos. 287/320)—1s. values+25%, all other values+50%.

Deformed tablet (Pl. D4, R. 5/9)

(Des E. Fuchs)

1902 (1 Jan)–**10**. Printed by De La Rue & Co. Wmk Imperial Crown W **49** (½d. to 1s. Three Crowns on £1); Large Anchor, W **40** (2s.6d. to 10s.). Ordinary paper. Perf 14.

			Unmtd mint	Mtd mint	Used
215	**83**	½d. dull blue-green (1.1.02)	2·75	2·00	1·50
		s. Optd 'SPECIMEN' (15)		£350	
		Wi. Watermark inverted	£3750	£2750	£2000
216		½d. blue-green	2·75	2·00	1·50
217		½d. pale yellowish green (26.11.04)	2·75	2·00	1·50
218		½d. yellowish green	2·75	2·00	1·50
		a. Pair. No. 218 plus St Andrew's Cross label	£275	£175	£200
		aw. Pair. No. 218 Wi plus St Andrew's Cross label	£275	£175	£200
		b. Booklet pane. No. 218×5 plus St Andrew's Cross label	£975	£700	£550
		bw. Booklet pane. No. 218×5 plus St Andrew's Cross label. Wmk inverted	£975	£700	£550
		c. Booklet pane. No. 218×6 (6.06)	£375	£275	£225
		cw. Booklet pane. No. 218Wi×6	£375	£275	£225
		d. Doubly printed (bottom row on one pane) (Control H9)	£25000	£20000	
		s. Optd 'SPECIMEN' (17, 22)		£275	
219		1d. scarlet (1.1.02)	2·75	2·00	1·50
		a. Booklet pane. No. 219×6 (16.3.04)	£325	£250	£200
		aw. Booklet pane. No. 219Wi×6	£325	£250	£200
		s. Optd 'SPECIMEN' (15, 16, 17, 22)		£250	
		Wi. Watermark inverted	8·00	4·00	4·00
220		1d. bright scarlet	2·75	2·00	1·50
		a. Imperf (pair)	†	£28000	
221	**84**	1½d. dull purple and green (21.3.02)	95·00	50·00	24·00
		a. Deformed leaf		£825	£425
		s. Optd 'SPECIMEN' (15)		£275	
222		1½d. slate-purple and green	75·00	45·00	24·00
		Wi. Watermark inverted	—	—	£900
223		1½d. pale dull purple and green (chalk-surfaced paper) (7.05)	75·00	45·00	24·00
		s. Optd 'SPECIMEN' (17)		£700	
224		1½d. slate-purple and bluish green (chalk-surfaced paper)	75·00	45·00	22·00
225	**85**	2d. yellowish green and carmine-red (25.3.02)	£125	70·00	25·00
		Wi. Watermark inverted	£28000		
		s. Optd 'SPECIMEN' (16)		£550	
226		2d. grey-green and carmine-red (1904)	£150	85·00	35·00
227		2d. pale grey-green and carmine-red (chalk-surfaced paper) (4.06)	45·00	32·00	
		a. Deformed tablet		£1000	£750
		s. Optd 'SPECIMEN' (17)		£700	
		Wi. Watermark inverted		£20000	
228		2d. pale grey-green and scarlet (chalk-surfaced paper) (1909)	80·00	45·00	32·00
229		2d. dull blue-green and carmine (chalk-surfaced paper) (1907)	£180	90·00	50·00
230	**86**	2½d. ultramarine (1.1.02)	34·00	20·00	15·00
		s. Optd 'SPECIMEN' (15, 17)		£125	
231		2½d. pale ultramarine	34·00	20·00	15·00
		Wi. Watermark inverted	—	—	£4200
232	**87**	3d. dull purple/*orange-yellow* (20.3.02)	£100	50·00	18·00

KING EDWARD VII

			Unmtd mint	Mtd mint	Used
		s. Optd 'SPECIMEN' (15)		£350	
		Wi. Watermark inverted			
		a. Chalk-surfaced paper (3.06)	£450	£250	£100
232b		3d. deep purple/*orange-yellow*	90·00	45·00	18·00
232c		3d. pale reddish purple/*orange-yellow* (chalk-surfaced paper) (3.06)	£425	£225	85·00
		cs. Optd 'SPECIMEN' (17)		£700	
233		3d. dull reddish purple/*yellow* (lemon back) (chalk-surfaced paper)	£425	£225	85·00
233b		3d. pale purple/*lemon* (chalk-surfaced paper)	85·00	45·00	20·00
234		3d. purple/*lemon* (chalk-surfaced paper)	85·00	45·00	20·00
235	88	4d. green and grey-brown (27.3.02)	£125	70·00	35·00
		s. Optd 'SPECIMEN' (16)		£450	
		Wi. Watermark inverted			
236		4d. green and chocolate-brown	£125	70·00	35·00
		a. Chalk-surfaced paper (1.06)	75·00	40·00	20·00
		Wi. watermark inverted			£9500
238		4d. deep green and chocolate-brown (chalk-surfaced paper) (1.06)	75·00	40·00	20·00
239		4d. brown-orange (1.11.09)	£300	£180	£140
		s. Optd 'SPECIMEN' (17)		£700	
240		4d. pale orange (12.09)	45·00	20·00	18·00
241		4d. orange-red (12.09)	50·00	25·00	20·00
242	89	5d. dull purple and ultramarine (14.5.02)	£130	65·00	22·00
		s. Optd 'SPECIMEN' (16)		£350	
		a. Chalk-surfaced paper (5.06)	£120	60·00	22·00
		as. Optd 'SPECIMEN' (17)		£700	
243		5d. slate-purple and ultramarine (14.5.02)	65·00	22·00	50·00
		a. Chalk-surfaced paper (5.06)	60·00	22·00	
		Wi. Watermark inverted	£5500		
245	83	6d. pale dull purple (1.1.02)	85·00	45·00	22·00
		s. Optd 'SPECIMEN' (15)		£400	
		a. Chalk-surfaced paper (1.06)	85·00	45·00	22·00
246		6d. slate-purple	85·00	45·00	22·00
		a. Chalk-surfaced paper	85·00	45·00	22·00
248		6d. dull purple (chalk-surfaced paper) (1.06)	85·00	45·00	22·00
		s. Optd 'SPECIMEN' (17)		£700	
		Wi. Watermark inverted	—	—	£3500
249	90	7d. grey-black (4.5.10)	24·00	15·00	22·00
		s. Optd 'SPECIMEN' (17)		£700	
249a		7d. deep grey-black	£170	£120	£100
250	91	9d. dull purple and ultramarine (7.4.02)	£275	£140	75·00
		s. Optd 'SPECIMEN' (16)		£450	
		a. Chalk-surfaced paper (6.05)	£250	£140	75·00
		aWi. Watermark inverted	—		£3500
251		9d. slate-purple and ultramarine	£275	£140	75·00
		a. Chalk-surfaced paper (6.05)	£225	£120	75·00
		as. Optd 'SPECIMEN' (17)		£725	
254	92	10d. dull purple and carmine (3.7.02)	£300	£150	75·00
		s. Optd 'SPECIMEN' (16)		£500	
		a. No cross on crown	£775	£425	£300
		b. Chalk-surfaced paper (9.06)	£300	£140	75·00
255		10d. slate-purple and carmine (chalk-surfaced paper) (9.06)	£275	£140	75·00
		a. No cross on crown	£725	£450	£275
		s. Optd 'SPECIMEN' (17)		£700	
256		10d. dull purple and scarlet (chalk-surfaced paper) (9.10)	£260	£140	75·00
		a. No cross on crown	£725	£425	£250
257	93	1s. dull green and carmine (24.3.02)	£225	£100	40·00
		s. Optd 'SPECIMEN' (16)		£400	
		a. Chalk-surfaced paper (9.05)	£225	£100	40·00
		as. Optd 'SPECIMEN' (17)		£725	
259		1s. dull green and scarlet (chalk-surfaced paper) (9.10)	£225	£100	55·00
260	94	2s.6d. lilac (5.4.02)	£525	£275	£150
		s. Optd 'SPECIMEN' (15, 16)		£400	
		Wi. Watermark inverted	£6500	£5000	£3500
261		2s.6d. pale dull purple (chalk-surfaced paper) (7.10.05)	£675	£350	£180
		s. Optd 'SPECIMEN' (17)		£3250	
		Wi. Watermark inverted	£10000	£7500	£4250
262		2s.6d. dull purple (chalk-surfaced paper)	£650	£350	£180
263	95	5s. bright carmine (5.4.02)	£850	£450	£220
		s. Optd 'SPECIMEN' (16, 17)		£400	
		Wi. Watermark inverted	—	£65000	£5750
264		5s. deep bright carmine	£900	£450	£220
265	96	10s. ultramarine (5.4.02)	£2000	£1000	£500
		s. Optd 'SPECIMEN' (16, 17)		£500	
		Wi. Watermark inverted	—	£85000	£40000
266	97	£1 dull blue-green (16.6.02)	£3000	£2000	£825
		s. Optd 'SPECIMEN' (16, 17)		£1400	
		Wi. Watermark inverted	—	£110000	£24000

USED ON COVER PRICES		
No.	215	2·50
No.	217	2·50
No.	219	2·50
No.	221	50·00
No.	225	50·00
No.	230	£1250
No.	232	25·00
No.	236a	45·00
No.	240	40·00
No.	242	50·00
No.	245	60·00
No.	249	£200
No.	250	£250
No.	254	£225
No.	257	£175
No.	260	£1250
No.	263	£1850

97a

1910 (May). Prepared for use, by De La Rue but not issued. Wmk Imperial Crown, W **49**. Perf 14.

			Unmtd mint	Mtd mint	Used
266a	97a	2d. Tyrian plum	—	£90000	—
		s. Optd 'SPECIMEN' (17)		£50000	

One example of this stamp is known used, but it was never issued to the public.

1911. Printed by Harrison & Sons. Ordinary paper. Wmk Imperial Crown W **49**.

(a) Perf 14.

			Unmtd mint	Mtd mint	Used
267	83	½d. dull yellow-green (3.5.11)	6·00	2·75	4·00
		a. Pair. No. 267×5 plus St Andrew's Cross label	£400	£300	£300
		aw. Pair. No. 267Wi×5 plus St Andrew's Cross label	£400	£300	£300
		s. Optd 'SPECIMEN' (22)		£325	
		b. Booklet pane. Five stamps plus St Andrew's Cross label	£1250	£800	£650
		bw. Booklet pane. Five stamps plus St Andrew's Cross label. Wmk inverted	£1250	£800	£650
		c. Booklet pane. No. 267×6	£425	£325	£275
		cw. Booklet pane. No. 267Wi×6	£425	£325	£275
		d. Watermark sideways	†	†	£30000
		e. Imperf (pair)	—	£35000	†
		Wi. Watermark inverted	£100	60·00	60·00
268		½d. dull green	6·00	3·00	4·00
269		½d. deep dull green	17·00	11·00	10·00
270		½d. pale bluish green	85·00	40·00	40·00
271		½d. bright green (fine impression) (6.11)	£425	£275	£170
272		1d. rose-red (3.5.11)	18·00	8·00	15·00
		a. No watermark (*brick-red*)	75·00	50·00	—
		b. Booklet pane. No. 272×6	£325	£250	£200
		bw. Booklet pane. No. 272Wi×6	£325	£250	£200
		s. Optd 'SPECIMEN' (22)		£325	
		Wi. Watermark inverted	90·00	50·00	50·00
273		1d. deep rose-red	18·00	8·00	15·00
274		1d. rose-carmine	£100	55·00	50·00
275		1d. aniline pink (5.11)	£1250	£750	£400

KING EDWARD VII

No.			Unmtd mint	Mtd mint	Used
275a		1d. aniline rose	£300	£180	£140
276	86	2½d. bright blue (10.7.11)	£175	65·00	38·00
		Wi. Watermark inverted	£3000	£2100	£1250
277	87	3d. purple/lemon (12.9.11)	£275	£150	£250
		s. Optd 'SPECIMEN' (22)		£300	
277a		3d. grey/lemon	£7000	£4500	
278	88	4d. bright orange (12.7.11)	£225	£120	55·00
		s. Optd 'SPECIMEN' (22)		£240	
267/278 Set of 5			£575	£300	£300

(b) Perf 15×14.

No.			Unmtd mint	Mtd mint	Used
279	83	½d. dull green (30.10.11)	65·00	40·00	45·00
		Wi. Watermark inverted	†	†	£3500
279a		½d. deep dull green	90·00	45·00	45·00
280		1d. rose-red (4.10.11)	80·00	45·00	25·00
281		1d. rose-carmine (4.11.11)	35·00	15·00	15·00
		Wi. Watermark inverted	†	†	—
282		1d. pale rose-carmine	40·00	22·00	15·00
283	86	2½d. bright blue (14.10.11)	50·00	22·00	15·00
		s. Optd 'SPECIMEN' (22)			
284		2½d. dull blue	50·00	22·00	15·00
		Wi. Watermark inverted	—	—	£3000
285	87	3d. purple/lemon (22.9.11)	80·00	45·00	15·00
285a		3d. grey/lemon	£4250	£3250	
286	88	4d. bright orange (11.11.11)	60·00	30·00	15·00
279/286 Set of 5			£250	£130	90·00

No. 272a was probably a trial printing.

USED ON COVER PRICES

No.	267	6·00
No.	272	18·00
No.	276	75·00
No.	277	£550
No.	278	£175
No.	279	£100
No.	281	30·00
No.	283	35·00
No.	285	40·00
No.	286	65·00

1911–13. Printed at Somerset House. Ordinary paper. Wmk as 1902–1910. Perf 14.

No.			Unmtd mint	Mtd mint	Used
287	84	1½d. reddish purple and bright green (13.7.11)	90·00	45·00	38·00
288		1½d. dull purple and green	60·00	30·00	30·00
289		1½d. slate-purple and green (1.12)	65·00	30·00	30·00
290	85	2d. deep dull green and red (8.8.11)	60·00	28·00	22·00
		a. Deformed tablet		£925	£550
		s. Optd 'SPECIMEN' (22)		£325	
291		2d. deep dull green and carmine	70·00	30·00	25·00
292		2d. grey-green and bright carmine (carmine shows clearly on back) (11.3.12)	55·00	28·00	28·00
293	89	5d. dull reddish purple and bright blue (7.8.11)	60·00	30·00	22·00
		s. Optd 'SPECIMEN' (22)			—
294		5d. deep dull reddish purple and bright blue	55·00	30·00	22·00
295	83	6d. royal purple (31.10.11)	£110	50·00	90·00
296		6d. bright magenta (chalk-surfaced paper) (31.10.11)	£17500	£12500	†
		s. Optd 'SPECIMEN' (22)		£4750	
297		6d. dull purple	60·00	30·00	22·00
		s. Optd 'SPECIMEN' (22)		£400	
298		6d. reddish purple (11.11)	60·00	30·00	28·00
		a. No cross on crown (various shades)	£1800	£1200	
299		6d. very deep reddish purple (11.11)	£120	55·00	45·00
300		6d. dark purple (3.12)	70·00	35·00	28·00
301		6d. dull purple 'Dickinson' coated paper* (3.13)	£425	£250	£190
		s. Optd 'SPECIMEN' (26)		—	
303		6d. deep plum (chalk-surfaced paper) (7.13)	60·00	30·00	75·00
		a. No cross on crown	£1950	£1250	
		s. Optd 'SPECIMEN' (26)		—	
305	90	7d. slate-grey (1.8.12)	30·00	15·00	22·00
		s. Optd 'SPECIMEN' (26)		£350	
306	91	9d. reddish purple and light blue (24.7.11)	£200	95·00	75·00
		s. Optd 'SPECIMEN' (22)		£450	
306a		9d. deep dull reddish purple and deep bright blue (9.11)	£200	95·00	75·00
307		9d. reddish purple and blue (10.11)	£130	60·00	60·00
307a		9d. deep plum and blue (7.13)	£125	60·00	60·00
308		9d. slate-purple and cobalt-blue (3.12)	£350	£160	£110
309	92	10d. dull purple and scarlet (9.10.11)	£200	95·00	75·00
		s. Optd 'SPECIMEN' (22)		£375	
310		10d. dull reddish purple and aniline pink	£500	£275	£225
311		10d. dull reddish purple and carmine (5.12)	£150	80·00	60·00
		a. No cross on crown	£2800	£1800	
312	93	1s. dark green and scarlet (13.7.11)	£240	£120	60·00
		s. Optd 'SPECIMEN' (22, 23, 26)		£350	
313		1s. deep green and scarlet (9.10.11)	£180	80·00	40·00
		Wi. Watermark inverted	£240	£150	†
314		1s. green and carmine (15.4.12)	£140	60·00	35·00
315	94	2s.6d. dull greyish purple (15.9.11)	£1750	£950	£450
		s. Optd 'SPECIMEN' (22)		£425	
316		2s.6d. dull reddish purple	£625	£300	£180
		Wi. Watermark inverted	†	†	—
317		2s.6d. dark purple	£675	£325	£190
318	95	5s. carmine (29.2.12)	£875	£425	£200
		s. Optd 'SPECIMEN' (26)		—	
319	96	10s. blue (14.1.12)	£2100	£1100	£600
320	97	£1 deep green (3.9.11)	£3000	£2000	£750
		s. Optd 'SPECIMEN' (22)		£2200	

* No. 301 was on an experimental coated paper which does not respond to the silver test.

Following plate repairs, No. 290a was relocated to R. 5/6 for two Somerset House printings in November and December 1911.

USED ON COVER PRICES

No.	288	60·00
No.	290	55·00
No.	293	65·00
No.	297	90·00
No.	305	£200
No.	307	£190
No.	311	£225
No.	314	£200
No.	316	£1700
No.	318	£1750

DEPARTMENTAL OFFICIALS

PRICES. Please note that, with the exception of Government Parcels Stamps the price columns in this section are for mounted mint, used and used on cover examples. For Governemtn Parcels Stamps they are for mint and used only.

INLAND REVENUE

These stamps were used by revenue officials in the provinces, mail to and from Head Office passing without a stamp. The London Office used these stamps only for foreign mail.

I.R. **I. R.**

OFFICIAL **OFFICIAL**

(O1) (O2)

1902–04. Stamps of King Edward VII. Optd with T **O1** (½d. to 1s.) or T **O2** (others). Ordinary paper.

No.			Unused	Used	Used on cover
O20	83	½d. blue-green (4.2.02)	32·00	4·50	£150
		s. Optd 'SPECIMEN' (15)	£425		
O21		1d. scarlet (4.2.02)	22·00	3·00	95·00
		s. Optd 'SPECIMEN' (15)	£425		
O22	86	2½d. ultramarine (19.2.02)	£1000	£275	
		s. Optd 'SPECIMEN' (15, 16)	£575		
O23	83	6d. pale dull purple (14.3.04)	£500000	£300000	
		s. Optd 'SPECIMEN' (16)	£38000		
O24	93	1s. dull green and carmine (29.4.02)	£3750	£900	
		s. Optd 'SPECIMEN' (16)	£1200		
O25	95	5s. bright carmine (29.4.02)	£38000	£10000	
		a. Raised stop after 'R'	£42000	£12000	
		s. Optd 'SPECIMEN' (16)	£6500		
O26	96	10s. ultramarine (29.4.02)	£85000	£45000	
		a. Raised stop after 'R'	£95000	£45000	
		s. Optd 'SPECIMEN' (16)	£20000		

KING EDWARD VII

			Unused	Used	Used on cover
O27	97	£1 dull blue-green (29.4.02)..	£50000	£18000	
		s. Optd 'SPECIMEN' (16)........	£12500		

Although an issue date of 4 February has long been recorded, the 1d. is not currently brown used before 24 February and the ½d. before early March 1902.

OFFICE OF WORKS

These were issued to Head and Branch (local) offices in London and to Branch (local) offices at Birmingham, Bristol, Edinburgh, Glasgow, Leeds, Liverpool, Manchester and Southampton. The overprints on stamps of value 2d. and upwards were created later in 1902, the 2d. for registration fees and the rest for overseas mail.

O.W.

OFFICIAL
(O3)

1902 (11 Feb)–**03**. Stamps of King Edward VII. Optd with T **O3**. Ordinary paper.

			Unused	Used	Used on Cover
O36	83	½d. blue-green (2.02)...............	£575	£180	£2000
		s. Optd 'SPECIMEN' (15)........	£425		
O37		1d. scarlet.................................	£575	£180	£425
		s. Optd 'SPECIMEN' (15)........	£425		
O38	85	2d. yellowish green and carmine-red (27.4.02).......	£2000	£450	£3250
		s. Optd 'SPECIMEN' (16)........	£850		
O39	86	2½d. ultramarine (29.4.02).......	£3500	£675	£4250
		s. Optd 'SPECIMEN' (16)........	£900		
O40	92	10d. dull purple and carmine (28.5.03)............................	£40000	£7000	
		s. Optd 'SPECIMEN' (16)........	£8000		

* O31/O40 **For well-centered, lightly used +25%.**

ARMY

Letters to and from the War Office in London passed without postage. The overprinted stamps were distributed to District and Station Paymasters nationwide, including Cox and Co., the Army Agents, who were paymasters to the Household Division.

ARMY   ARMY

OFFICIAL   OFFICIAL
(O4)   (O6)

1902–03. Stamps of King Edward VII optd with T **O4** (Nos. O48/O50) or T **O6** (No. O52). Ordinary paper.

			Unused	Used	Used on cover
O48	83	½d. blue-green (11.2.02)..........	6·00	2·50	£100
		s. Optd 'SPECIMEN' (15)........	£350		
O49		1d. scarlet (11.2.02)..................	6·00	2·50	£100
		a. 'ARMY' omitted..................	†	—	
		s. Optd 'SPECIMEN' (15)........	£350		
O50		6d. pale dull purple (23.8.02)...	£175	80·00	
		s. Optd 'SPECIMEN' (16)........	£425		
O52		6d. pale dull purple (12.03).....	£2800	£1600	

GOVERNMENT PARCELS

These stamps were issued to all departments, including Head Office, for use on parcels weighing over 3 lb. Below this weight government parcels were sent by letter post to avoid the 55% of the postage paid from accruing to the railway companies, as laid down by parcel-post regulations. Most government parcels stamps suffered heavy postmarks in use.

GOVT PARCELS
(O7)

1902. Stamps of King Edward VII. Optd with T **O7**. Ordinary paper.

			Unused	Used	
O74	83	1d. scarlet (30.10.02)................	75·00	22·00	
		s. Optd 'SPECIMEN' (16)........	£350		
O75	85	2d. yellowish green and carmine-red (29.4.02)............................	£225	60·00	
		s. Optd 'SPECIMEN' (15, 16).................	£350		
O76	83	6d. pale dull purple (19.2.02).................	£275	60·00	
O77	91	9d. dull purple and ultramarine (28.8.02).................	£650	£175	
		a. Opt double, one albino....................	£25000		
		s. Optd 'SPECIMEN' (16).................	£500		
O78	93	1s. dull green and carmine (17.12.02)_	£1350	£300	
		s. Optd 'SPECIMEN' (16).................	£550		

BOARD OF EDUCATION

BOARD OF EDUCATION
(O8)

1902 (19 Feb)–**04**. Stamps of King Edward VII. Optd with T **O8**. Ordinary paper.

			Unused	Used	Used on cover
O83	83	½d. blue-green.........................	£180	45·00	£550
		s. Optd 'SPECIMEN' (15)........	£375		
O84		1d. scarlet.................................	£180	45·00	£550
		s. Optd 'SPECIMEN' (15)........	£375		
O85	86	2½d. ultramarine........................	£5000	£475	
		s. Optd 'SPECIMEN' (15)........	£1100		
O86	89	5d. dull purple and ultramarine (6.2.04)............	£30000	£8500	
		s. Optd 'SPECIMEN' (16)........	£7000		
O87	93	1s. dull green and carmine (23.12.02)............................	£160000		
		s. Optd 'SPECIMEN' (16)........	£30000		

ROYAL HOUSEHOLD

R.H.

OFFICIAL
(O9)

1902. Stamps of King Edward VII optd with T **O9**. Ordinary paper.

			Unused	Used	Used on cover
O91	83	½d. blue-green (29.4.02)..........	£375	£200	£1100
		s. Optd 'SPECIMEN' (16)........	£750		
O92		1d. scarlet (19.2.02)..................	£325	£175	£1000
		s. Optd 'SPECIMEN' (15)........	£750		

ADMIRALTY

ADMIRALTY   ADMIRALTY

OFFICIAL   OFFICIAL
(O10)   (O11) (with different 'M')

1903 (1 Apr). Stamps of King Edward VII optd with T **O10**. Ordinary paper.

			Unused	Used	Used on cover
O101	83	½d. blue-green.........................	30·00	15·00	
		s. Optd 'SPECIMEN' (16)........	£400		
O102		1d. scarlet.................................	20·00	10·00	£300
		s. Optd 'SPECIMEN' (16)........	£400		
O103	84	1½d. dull purple and green.......	£325	£150	
		s. Optd 'SPECIMEN' (16)........	£500		
O104	85	2d. yellowish green and carmine-red........................	£350	£160	
		s. Optd 'SPECIMEN' (16)........	£500		
O105	86	2½d. ultramarine........................	£475	£150	
		s. Optd 'SPECIMEN' (16)........	£500		
O106	87	3d. purple/*yellow*.....................	£425	£160	
		s. Optd 'SPECIMEN' (16)........	£500		

1903–04. Stamps of King Edward VII optd with T **O11**. Ordinary paper.

			Unused	Used	Used on cover
O107	83	½d. blue-green (9.03)...............	60·00	28·00	£500
		s. Optd 'SPECIMEN' (16)........	£400		
O108		1d. scarlet (12.03)....................	60·00	28·00	£160
		s. Optd 'SPECIMEN' (16)........	£400		
O109	84	1½d. dull purple and green (2.04)...................................	£1900	£650	

			Unused	Used	Used on cover
O110	85	2d. yellowish green and carmine red (3.04)	£2700	£900	
		s. Optd 'SPECIMEN' (16)	£750		
O111	86	2½d. ultramarine (3.04)	£2900	£950	
		s. Optd 'SPECIMEN' (16)	£950		
O112	87	3d. dull purple/*orange-yellow* (12.03)	£2600	£400	
		s. Optd 'SPECIMEN' (16)	£750		

Stamps of various issues perforated with a Crown and initials ('H.M.O.W.', 'O.W.', 'B.T.' or 'S.O.') or with initials only ('H.M.S.O.' or 'D.S.I.R.') have also been used for official purposes, but these are outside the scope of the catalogue.

BB STAMPS LTD

Est. 1988

Great Britain 1840 – Date

https://www.bbstamps.co.uk

200+ newly listed items every week.
Sign up for our newsletter to keep up to date.

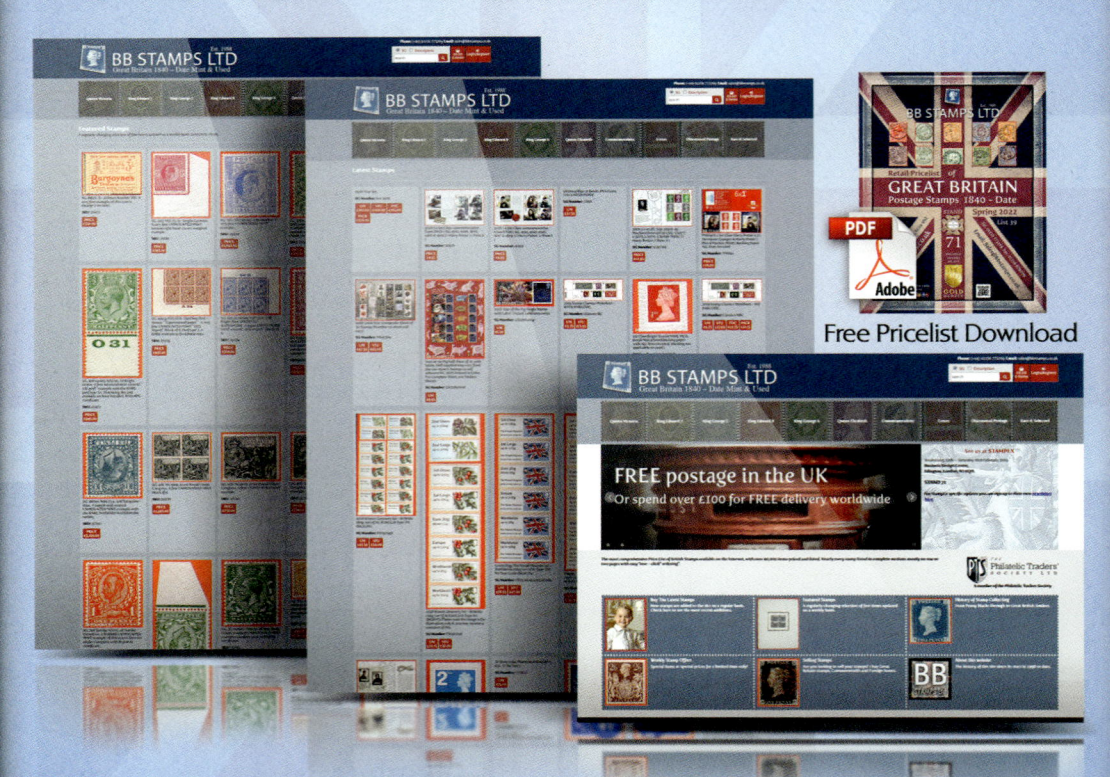

Free Pricelist Download

The most comprehensive Price List of British Stamps available on the Internet, with over 40,000 items priced and listed. Nearly every stamp listed in complete sections mostly on one or two pages with easy "one - click" ordering.

GOLD PTS MEMBER

BB Stamps Ltd, PO Box 6267, NEWBURY, Berkshire, RG 14 9NZ
Tel: 01256 773269   Fax: 01256 679009
Email: Sales@bbstamps.co.uk | www.bbstamps.co.uk

GREAT BRITAIN POSTAL AUCTIONS

AUCTIONS HELD FIVE TIMES PER YEAR.....CATALOGUES SENT FREE ON REQUEST

(Pl.225)

(SG 177a) (SG 173g)

(MAGENTA) (SG 346c)

('CHROME') ('CAMBRIDGE')

Embassy Philatelists

P.O. BOX 1553, GUILDFORD, GU1 9YT

Tel: 01483 811 168
Email: info@embassystamps.co.uk

www.embassystamps.co.uk

BUYING
From single items to major collections, for a fast professional transaction call us today.

BUYING
From single items to major collections, for a fast professional transaction call us today.

Selling your stamp collection?

Warwick and Warwick have an expanding requirement for world collections, single country collections, single items, covers, proof material and specialised collections. Our customer base is increasing dramatically and we need an ever-larger supply of quality material to keep pace with demand. The market is currently very strong for G.B. and British Commonwealth and the Far East. If you are considering the sale of your collection, now is the time to act.

FREE VALUATIONS
We will provide a free, professional valuation of your collection, without obligation on your part to proceed. Either we will make you a fair, binding private treaty offer, or we will recommend inclusion of your property in our next public auction.

FREE TRANSPORTATION
We can arrange insured transportation of your collection to our Warwick offices completely free of charge. If you decline our offer, we ask you to cover the return carriage costs only.

FREE VISITS
Visits by our valuers are possible anywhere in the country or abroad, usually within 48 hours, in order to value larger and valuable collections. Please phone for details.

ADVISORY DAYS
We have an ongoing programme of advisory days, in all regions of the United Kingdom, where you can meet us and discuss the sale of your collection. Visit our website for further details.

EXCELLENT PRICES
Because of the strength of our customer base we are in a position to offer prices that we feel sure will exceed your expectations.

ACT NOW
Telephone or email us today with details of your property.

Warwick & Warwick
Auctioneers and Valuers
www.warwickandwarwick.com

Warwick & Warwick Ltd., Chalon House, Scar Bank, Millers Road, Warwick CV34 5DB England
Tel: (01926) 499031 • Fax: (01926) 491906
Email: info@warwickandwarwick.com

Get the experts on your side!

/warwickauctions   @warwickauctions

King George V

6 May 1910-20 January 1936

Further detailed information on the issues of King George V will be found in Volume 2 of the Stanley Gibbons *Great Britain Specialised Catalogue*.

PRINTERS. Types **98** to **102** were letterpress printed by Harrison & Sons Ltd, with the exception of certain preliminary printings made at Somerset House and distinguishable by the controls 'A.11', 'B.11' or 'B.12' (the Harrison printings do not have a full stop after the letter). The booklet stamps, Nos. 334/337, and 344/345 were printed by Harrison only.

WATERMARK VARIETIES. Many British stamps to 1967 exist without watermark owing to misplacement of the paper, and with either inverted, reversed, or inverted and reversed watermarks. A proportion of the low-value stamps issued in booklets have the watermark inverted in the normal course of printing.

Low values with watermark sideways are normally from stamp rolls used on machines with sideways delivery or, from June 1940, certain booklets.

STAMPS WITHOUT WATERMARK. Stamps found without watermark, due to misplacement of the sheet in relation to the dandy roll, are not listed here but will be found in the *Great Britain Specialised Catalogue*.

The 1½d. and 5d. 1912–1922, and ½d., 2d. and 2½d., 1924–1926, listed here, are from whole sheets completely without watermark.

98   **99**   **100** Simple Cypher

For type difference with Types **101/102** see notes below the latter.

Die A   Die B

Dies of Halfpenny

Die A. The three upper scales on the body of the right hand dolphin form a triangle; the centre jewel of the cross inside the crown is suggested by a comma.

Die B. The three upper scales are incomplete; the centre jewel is suggested by a crescent.

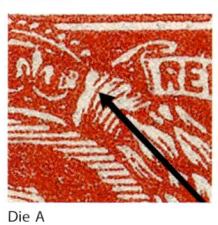

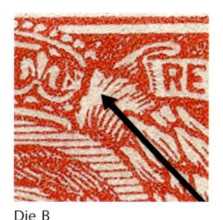

Die A   Die B

Dies of One Penny

Die A. The second line of shading on the ribbon to the right of the crown extends right across the wreath; the line nearest to the crown on the right hand ribbon shows as a short line at the bottom of the ribbon.

Die B. The second line of shading is broken in the middle; the first line is little more than a dot.

(Des Bertram Mackennal and G. W. Eve. Head from photograph by W. and D. Downey. Die eng J. A. C. Harrison)

1911–12. Wmk Imperial Crown, W **49**. Perf 15×14.

			Unmtd mint	Mtd mint	Used
321	**98**	½d. pale green (Die A) (22.6.11)	10·00	5·00	4·00
322		½d. green (Die A) (22.6.11)	8·00	4·00	4·00
		a. Error. Perf 14 (8.11)	—	£16000	£1000
		s. Optd 'SPECIMEN' (22)		£800	
		Wi. Watermark inverted	20000	—	£2200
323		½d. bluish green (Die A)	£400	£300	£180
324		½d. yellow-green (Die B)	18·00	12·00	1·50

			Unmtd mint	Mtd mint	Used
		a. booklet pane No. 324×6 (8.11)	£350	£250	
		aw. booklet pane No. 324Wi×6	£350	£250	
		s. Optd 'SPECIMEN' (22)		£350	
		Wi. Watermark inverted	35·00	20·00	7·50
325		½d. bright green (Die B)	13·00	8·00	1·50
		a. Watermark sideways	—	—	£5750
326		½d. bluish green (Die B)	£260	£160	£100
327	**99**	1d. carmine-red (Die A) (22.6.11)	10·00	4·50	2·50
		c. Watermark sideways	†	†	£17000
		s. Optd 'SPECIMEN' (22)		£550	
		Wi. Watermark inverted	£2200	£1500	£1250
328		1d. pale carmine (Die A) (22.6.11)	25·00	14·00	3·00
		a. No cross on crown	£1250	£850	£500
329		1d. carmine (Die B)	15·00	10·00	3·00
		a. Booklet pane, No. 329×6 (8.11)	£350	£250	
		aw. Booklet pane, No. 329Wi×6	£350	£250	
		s. Optd 'SPECIMEN' (22)		£350	
		Wi. Watermark inverted	35·00	20·00	7·50
330		1d. pale carmine (Die B)	15·00	10·00	4·00
		a. No cross on crown	£1100	£800	£500
331		1d. rose-pink (Die B)	£225	£125	45·00
332		1d. scarlet (Die B) (6.12)	80·00	45·00	18·00
		a. Booklet pane, No. 332×6 (8.11)	£550	£400	
		aw. Booklet pane, No. 332Wi×6	£550	£400	
		s. Optd 'SPECIMEN' (22)		£750	
		Wi. Watermark inverted	80·00	45·00	18·00
333		1d. aniline scarlet (Die B)	£375	£240	£110
		a. Booklet pane, No. 333×6	£2000	£1500	
		aw. Booklet pane, No. 333Wi×6	£2000	£1500	
		Wi. Watermark inverted	£375	£240	£110

For note on the aniline scarlet No. 333 see below No. 343.

1912 (28 Sept). Booklet stamps. Wmk Royal Cypher (Simple), W **100**. Perf 15×14.

			Unmtd mint	Mtd mint	Used
334	**98**	½d. pale green (Die B)	90·00	45·00	40·00
335		½d. green (Die B)	90·00	45·00	40·00
		a. Booklet pane, No. 334×6 (9.12)	£500	£375	
		aw. Booklet pane, No. 334Wi×6	£500	£375	
		s. Optd 'SPECIMEN' (22, 26)		£300	
		Wi. Watermark inverted	90·00	45·00	40·00
		Wj. Watermark reversed	£1750	£1100	£800
		Wk. Watermark inverted and reversed	£1750	£1100	£800
336	**99**	1d. scarlet (Die B)	40·00	30·00	30·00
		a. Booklet pane, No. 336×6 (9.12)	£400	£275	
		aw. Booklet pane, No. 336Wi×6	£400	£275	
		s. Optd 'SPECIMEN' (22, 26)		£325	
		Wi. Watermark inverted	40·00	30·00	30·00
		Wj. Watermark reversed	£1750	£1100	£800
		Wk. Watermark inverted and reversed	—	—	£850
337		1d. bright scarlet (Die B)	40·00	30·00	30·00

101   **102**   **103** Multiple Cypher

Type differences

½d. In T **98** the ornament above 'P' of 'HALFPENNY' has two thin lines of colour and the beard is undefined. In T **101** the ornament has one thick line and the beard is well defined.

1d. In T **99** the body of the Lion is unshaded and in T **102** it is shaded.

1912 (1 Jan). Wmk Imperial Crown, W **49**. Perf 15×14.

			Unmtd mint	Mtd mint	Used
338	**101**	½d. deep green	28·00	15·00	8·00
339		½d. green	15·00	8·00	4·00
		s. Optd 'SPECIMEN' (26)		£325	
340		½d. yellow-green	15·00	8·00	4·00
		a. No cross on crown	£190	£100	55·00
		Wi. Watermark inverted	£1750	£1100	£750
341	**102**	1d. bright scarlet	10·00	5·00	2·00
		a. No cross on crown	£150	£110	55·00

KING GEORGE V

			Unmtd mint	Mtd mint	Used
		b. Printed double, one albino	£375	£275	
		Wi. Watermark inverted	£650	£425	£400
342		1d. scarlet	10·00	5·00	2·00
343		1d. aniline scarlet*	£275	£175	£100
		a. No cross on crown	£1750	£1200	

* Our prices for the aniline scarlet 1d. stamps, Nos. 333 and 343, are for the example in which the colour is suffused on the surface of the stamp and shows through clearly on the back. Examples without these characteristics but which show 'aniline' reactions under the quartz lamp are relatively common.

1912 (Aug). Wmk Royal Cypher (Simple), W **100**. Perf 15×14.

			Unmtd mint	Mtd mint	Used
344	101	½d. green	14·00	7·00	3·00
		a. No cross on crown	£325	£225	£175
		s. Optd 'SPECIMEN' (26)		£550	
		Wi. Watermark inverted	£600	£375	£275
		Wj. Watermark reversed	£675	£425	£300
		Wk. Watermark inverted and reversed	20·00	12·00	20·00
345	102	1d. scarlet	15·00	8·00	4·50
		a. No cross on crown	£175	£100	50·00
		Wi. Watermark inverted	28·00	18·00	25·00
		Wj. Watermark reversed	£200	£125	£125
		Wk. Watermark inverted and reversed	20·00	12·00	20·00

1912 (Sept–Oct). Wmk Royal Cypher (Multiple), W **103**. Perf 15×14.

			Unmtd mint	Mtd mint	Used
346	101	½d. green (10.12)	20·00	12·00	8·00
		a. No cross on crown	£300	£200	£150
		b. Imperf	£250	£175	
		c. Watermark sideways	†	†	£4250
		d. Printed on gummed side	—	—	†
		Wi. Watermark inverted	20·00	12·00	20·00
		Wj. Watermark reversed	22·00	15·00	20·00
		Wk. Watermark inverted and reversed	£160	£100	£110
347		½d. yellow-green	20·00	15·00	8·00
348		½d. pale green	25·00	15·00	8·00
349	102	1d. bright scarlet	25·00	18·00	10·00
350		1d. scarlet	25·00	18·00	10·00
		a. No cross on crown	£225	£150	60·00
		b. Imperf	£225	£150	
		c. Watermark sideways	£325	£190	£220
		d. Watermark sideways. No cross on crown	£1200	£750	£750
		Wi. Watermark inverted	55·00	30·00	35·00
		Wj. Watermark reversed	55·00	30·00	35·00
		Wk. Watermark inverted and reversed	£1600	£1000	£700

Two Dies of the 2d.

Die I. Inner frame-line at top and sides close to solid of background. Four complete lines of shading between top of head and oval frame-line. These four lines do not extend to the oval itself. White line round 'TWOPENCE' thin.

Die II. Inner frame-line farther from solid of background. Three lines between top of head and extending to the oval. White line round 'TWOPENCE' thicker.

(Des Bertram Mackennal (heads) and G. W. Eve (frames). Coinage head (½d., 1½d., 2d., 3d. and 4d.); large medal head (1d., 2½d.); intermediate medal head (5d. to 1s.); small medal head used for fiscal stamps. Dies eng J. A. C. Harrison) (Letterpress by Harrison & Sons Ltd., except the 6d. printed by the Stamping Department of the Board of Inland Revenue, Somerset House. The latter also made printings of the following which can only be distinguished by the controls: ½d. B.13; 1½d. A.12; 2d. C.13; 2½d. A.12; 3d. A.12, B.13, C.13; 4d. B.13; 5d. B.13; 7d. C.13; 8d. C.13; 9d. agate B.13; 10d. C.13; 1s. C.13)

1912–24. Wmk Royal Cypher (Simple), W **100**. Chalk-surfaced paper (6d.). Perf 15×14.

			Unmtd mint	Mtd mint	Used
351	105	½d. green (16.1.13)	3·00	1·00	1·00
		a. Partial double print (half of bottom row) (Control G15)	—	£18000	
		b. Gummed both sides	£20000	—	—
		c. Booklet pane, No. 351×6 (4.13)	£140	£120	
		cw. Booklet pane, No. 351Wi×6	£140	£100	
		s. Optd 'SPECIMEN' (23, 26)		£150	
		Wi. Watermark inverted	4·00	3·00	1·50
		Wj. Watermark reversed	80·00	55·00	60·00
		Wk. Watermark inverted and reversed	6·00	4·00	3·50
352		½d. bright green	3·00	1·00	1·00
353		½d. deep green	10·00	5·00	2·00
354		½d. yellow-green	10·00	6·00	3·00
355		½d. very yellow (Cyprus) green (1914)	£11000	£8000	
356		½d. blue-green	60·00	40·00	25·00
357	104	1d. bright scarlet (8.10.12)	3·00	1·00	1·00
		a. 'Q' for 'O' (R. 1/4) (Control E14)	£250	£175	£175
		ab. 'Q' for 'O' (R. 4/11) (Control T22)	£450	£350	£190
		ac. Reversed 'Q' for 'O' (R. 15/9) (Control T22)	£400	£300	£240
		ad. Inverted 'Q' for 'O' (R. 20/3)	£550	£375	£240
		b. Tête-bêche (pair)	—	£70000	†
		c. Booklet pane, No. 357×6 (4.13)	£175	£120	
		cw. Booklet pane, No. 357Wi×6	£175	£120	
		s. Optd 'SPECIMEN' (23, 26)		£200	
		Wi. Watermark inverted	4·00	2·00	1·00
		Wj. Watermark reversed	£150	95·00	£110
		Wk. Watermark inverted and reversed	6·00	3·00	3·00
358		1d. vermilion	9·00	5·00	2·50
359		1d. pale rose-red	30·00	20·00	5·00
360		1d. carmine-red	20·00	11·00	5·00
361		1d. scarlet-vermilion	£180	£125	50·00
		a. Printed on back	£450	£300	†
362	105	1½d. red-brown (15.10.12)	10·00	6·00	1·50
		a. 'PENCF' (R. 15/12)	£400	£300	£250
		b. Booklet pane. No. 362×4 plus two printed labels (2.24)	£800	£600	
		bw. Booklet pane, No. 362Wi×4 plus two printed labels	£775	£600	
		c. Booklet pane, 1½d. (No. 362)×6 (10.18)	£200	£150	
		cw. Booklet pane, 1½d. (No. 362Wi)×6	£200	£150	

KING GEORGE V

			Unmtd mint	Mtd mint	Used
		s. Optd 'SPECIMEN' (23, 26)		£125	
		Wi. Watermark inverted	9·00	5·00	2·00
		Wj. Watermark reversed	70·00	50·00	50·00
		Wk. Watermark inverted and reversed	15·00	8·00	8·00
363		1½d. chocolate-brown	20·00	11·00	2·00
		a. No watermark	£375	£250	£240
364		1½d. chestnut	5·00	3·00	1·00
		a. 'PENCF' (R. 15/12)	£175	£125	£110
365		1½d. yellow-brown	30·00	20·00	16·00
366	106	2d. orange-yellow (Die I) (20.8.12)	14·00	8·00	3·00
367		2d. reddish orange (Die I) (11.13)	10·00	6·00	3·00
368		2d. orange (Die I)	8·00	4·00	3·00
		a. Booklet pane, No. 368×6 (7.20)	£425	£350	
		aw. Booklet pane, No. 368Wi×6	£425	£350	
		s. Optd 'SPECIMEN' (26)		£250	
		Wi. Watermark inverted	22·00	12·00	12·00
		Wj. Watermark reversed	25·00	15·00	15·00
		Wk. Watermark inverted and reversed	18·00	10·00	10·00
369		2d. bright orange (Die I)	8·00	5·00	3·00
370		2d. orange (Die II) (9.21)	8·00	5·00	3·50
		a. Booklet pane, No. 370×6 (8.21)	£500	£350	
		aw. Booklet pane, No. 370Wi×6	£500	£350	
		s. Optd 'SPECIMEN' (15, 23)		£800	
		Wi. Watermark inverted	60·00	40·00	40·00
		Wk. Watermark inverted and reversed	£200	£140	£130
371	104	2½d. cobalt-blue (18.10.12)	22·00	12·00	4·00
371a		2½d. bright blue (1914)	22·00	12·00	4·00
372		2½d. blue	22·00	12·00	4·00
		s. Optd 'SPECIMEN' (15, 23, 26)		£120	
		Wi. Watermark inverted	£120	85·00	85·00
		Wj. Watermark reversed	£100	65·00	65·00
		Wk. Watermark inverted and reversed	45·00	28·00	28·00
373		2½d. indigo-blue* (1920)	£4500	£3000	£2500
373a		2½d. dull Prussian blue* (12.20)	£1500	£1200	£850
374	106	3d. dull reddish violet (9.10.12)	22·00	12·00	3·00
375		3d. violet	15·00	8·00	3·00
		s. Optd 'SPECIMEN' (15, 23, 26)		£250	
		Wi. Watermark inverted	£160	95·00	£110
		Wj. Watermark reversed	£850	£500	£500
		Wk. Watermark inverted and reversed	40·00	30·00	30·00
376		3d. bluish violet (11.13)	20·00	9·00	3·00
377		3d. pale violet	17·00	10·00	3·00
378		4d. deep grey-green (15.1.13)	75·00	45·00	25·00
379		4d. grey-green	25·00	15·00	2·00
		s. Optd 'SPECIMEN' (15, 23, 26)		£125	
		Wi. Watermark inverted	50·00	30·00	30·00
		Wj. Watermark reversed	£550	£350	£350
		Wk. Watermark inverted and reversed	£140	90·00	£100
380		4d. pale grey-green	40·00	25·00	5·00
381	107	5d. brown (30.6.13)	25·00	15·00	5·00
		s. Optd 'SPECIMEN' (15, 23, 26)		£250	
		Wi. Watermark inverted	£1800	£1200	£1100
		Wj. Watermark reversed	†	†	—
		Wk. Watermark inverted and reversed	£500	£400	£400
382		5d. yellow-brown	25·00	15·00	5·00
		a. No watermark	£2000	£1200	
383		5d. bistre-brown	£275	£185	75·00
384		6d. dull purple (1.8.13)	45·00	25·00	10·00
		s. Optd 'SPECIMEN' (15, 23, 26)		£200	
385		6d. reddish purple (8.13)	30·00	15·00	7·00
		a. Perf 14 (9.20)	£150	90·00	£110
		Wi. Watermark inverted	85·00	50·00	60·00
		Wj. Watermark reversed	£5500	£4500	
		Wk. Watermark inverted and reversed	£150	£100	£100
386		6d. deep reddish purple	90·00	50·00	5·00
387		7d. olive (1.8.13)	35·00	20·00	10·00
		s. Optd 'SPECIMEN' (26)		£200	
		Wi. Watermark inverted	85·00	50·00	60·00
		Wj. Watermark reversed	†	†	—
		Wk. Watermark inverted and reversed	£6000	£5000	
388		7d. bronze-green (1915)	£120	70·00	25·00
389		7d. sage-green (1917)	£120	70·00	18·00
390		8d. black/yellow (1.8.13)	55·00	32·00	11·00
		s. Optd 'SPECIMEN' (26)		£250	
		Wi. Watermark inverted	£220	£150	£150
		Wj. Watermark reversed	£375	£250	£250
		Wk. Watermark inverted and reversed	£7000	£5500	
391		8d. black/yellow-buff (granite) (5.17)	60·00	40·00	15·00
392	108	9d. agate (30.6.13)	30·00	15·00	6·00
		a. Printed double, one albino	—	£1200	†
		s. Optd 'SPECIMEN' (26)		£425	
		Wi. Watermark inverted	£240	£175	£175
		Wk. Watermark inverted and reversed	£240	£175	£175
393		9d. deep agate	45·00	25·00	6·00
393a		9d. olive-green (9.22)	£225	£110	30·00
		as. Optd 'SPECIMEN' (15, 23)		£750	
		aWi. Watermark inverted	£120	£900	£825
		aWk. Watermark inverted and reversed	£1500	£1100	£1100
393b		9d. pale olive-green	£250	£120	40·00
394		10d. turquoise-blue (1.8.13)	40·00	22·00	20·00
		s. Optd 'SPECIMEN' (15, 23, 26)		£425	
		Wi. Watermark inverted	£4000	£3000	£2500
		Wk. Watermark inverted and reversed	£475	£325	£300
394a		10d. deep turquoise-blue	£150	90·00	30·00
395		1s. bistre (1.8.13)	40·00	20·00	4·00
		s. Optd 'SPECIMEN' (15, 23, 26, 31)		£375	
		Wi. Watermark inverted	£350	£250	£225
		Wk. Watermark inverted and reversed	£120	70·00	70·00
396		1s. bistre-brown	55·00	35·00	12·00
Set of 15			£475	£250	95·00

Imperf stamps of this issue exist but may be wartime colour trials.

† The impression of No. 361a is set sideways and is very pale. Nos. 362a and 364a occur on Plates 12 and 29 and are known from Controls L18, M18, M19, O19 and Q21. The flaws were corrected by 1921.

* No. 373 comes from Control O20 and also exists on toned paper.
No. 373a comes from Control R21 and also exists on toned paper, but both are unlike the rare Prussian blue shade of the 1935 2½d. Jubilee issue.

Examples of the 2d., T **106** which were in the hands of philatelists, are known bisected in Guernsey from 27 December 1940 to February 1941.
See also Nos. 418/429.

1913 (Aug.). Wmk Royal Cypher (Multiple), W **103**. Perf 15×14.

			Unmtd mint	Mtd mint	Used
397	105	½d. bright green	£250	£150	£180
		a. Watermark sideways	†	†	£18000
		Wi. Watermark inverted	£1200	£900	
398	104	1d. dull scarlet	£350	£225	£225
		Wi. Watermark inverted	£1600	£1100	

Both these stamps were originally issued in rolls only. Subsequently sheets were found, so that horizontal pairs and blocks are known but are of considerable rarity.

NOTE. All illustrations of re-entries on Nos. 399–417 are copyright GB Philatelic Publications Ltd and Bryan Kearsley and are reproduced with their permission

109

110 Single Cypher

A

KING GEORGE V

Major Re-entries on 2s.6d.

No. 400a

Nos. 406/407a

No. 415b

No. 417a

(Des Bertram Mackennal. Dies eng J. A. C. Harrison. Recess)

High values, so-called Sea Horses design T **109**. Background around portrait consists of horizontal lines, Type A. Wmk Single Cypher, W **110**. Perf 11×12.

1913 (30 June). Printed by Waterlow Bros & Layton.

			Unmtd mint	Mtd mint	Used
399	109	2s.6d. deep sepia-brown	£850	£400	£200
		s. Optd 'SPECIMEN' (23, 26)		£650	
400		2s.6d. sepia-brown	£600	£300	£150
		a. Re-entry (Plate 3, R. 2/1)	£2800	£1800	£800
		Wk. Watermark inverted and reversed	†	†	—
401		5s. rose-carmine	£1300	£625	£325
		s. Optd 'SPECIMEN' (26)		£950	
402		10s. indigo-blue (1.8)	£1800	£1000	£475
		s. Optd 'SPECIMEN' (23, 26, 29)		£1200	
403		£1 green (1.8.13)	£3750	£2800	£1400
		s. Optd 'SPECIMEN' (23, 26)		£3000	
404		£1 dull blue-green (1.8)	£3800	£2800	£1600

* 399/404 **For well-centred, lightly used +35%**

1915 (Sept–Dec). Printed by De la Rue & Co.

			Unmtd mint	Mtd mint	Used
405	109	2s.6d. deep yellow-brown (10.15)	£680	£375	£250
		Wi. Watermark inverted	£2400	£1500	
406		2s.6d. yellow-brown (inc. worn plates)	£550	£325	£225
		a. Re-entry (Plate 3, R. 2/1)	£3000	£2000	£950
		s. Optd 'SPECIMEN' (23)		£1400	
		Wi. Watermark inverted	£1800	£1250	£875
		Wj. Watermark reversed	£1800	£1250	£1000
		Wk. Watermark inverted and reversed	£4750	£4000	
407		2s.6d. grey-brown (inc. worn plates)	£700	£400	£300
		a. Re-entry (Plate 3, R. 2/1)	£3000	£2000	£950
		Wi. Watermark inverted	£1800	£1250	£1000
		Wj. Watermark reversed	£1800	£1250	£1000
408		2s.6d. sepia (seal-brown)	£550	£325	£250
		Wi. Watermark inverted	£1800	£1250	£1000
		Wj. Watermark reversed	£1800	£1250	£1000
409		5s. bright carmine	£1100	£650	£400
		s. Optd 'SPECIMEN' (23)		£1250	
		Wi. Watermark inverted	£6750	£4750	
		Wj. Watermark reversed	£6250	£4500	
		Wk. Watermark inverted and reversed	—	£18000	†
410		5s. pale carmine (worn plate)	£1400	£800	£500
411		10s. deep blue (12.15)	£5500	£3750	£1000
		s. Optd 'SPECIMEN' (26)		£2800	
412		10s. blue	£4000	£3250	£900
		Wk. Watermark inverted and reversed	—	—	†
413		10s. pale blue	£4250	£3500	£900

* 405/413 **For well-centred, lightly used +45%**

No. 406/407 were produced from the original Waterlow plates as were all De La Rue 5s. and 10s. printings. Examples of Nos. 406/407, 410 and 411 occur showing degrees of plate wear. No. 412Wk. one damaged mint example is recorded.

1918 (Dec)–**19**. Printed by Bradbury Wilkinson & Co, Ltd.

			Unmtd mint	Mtd mint	Used
413a	109	2s.6d. olive-brown	£350	£190	£100
		as. Optd 'SPECIMEN' (15, 23, 26, 31, 32)		£1000	
414		2s.6d. chocolate-brown	£325	£160	75·00
415		2s.6d. reddish brown	£325	£160	75·00
415a		2s.6d. pale brown	£340	£175	85·00
		b. Major re-entry (Plate 3/5L, R. 1/2)	£1600	£1000	£500
416		5s. rose-red (1.19)	£475	£325	£135
		s. Optd 'SPECIMEN' (15, 23, 26, 31, 32)		£1200	
417		10s. dull grey-blue (1.19)	£850	£475	£175
		a. Re-entry (Plate 1/3L, R.1/1)	£2250	£1800	£1000
		s. Optd 'SPECIMEN' (15, 23, 26, 31, 32)		£1400	
413a/417 and 403 Set of 4			£5800	£4000	£1500

* 413a/417 **For well-centred, lightly used +35%**

DISTINGUISHING PRINTINGS. Note that the £1 value was only printed by Waterlow.

Waterlow and De La Rue stamps measure exactly 22.1 mm vertically. In the De La Rue printings the gum is usually patchy and yellowish, and the colour of the stamp, particularly in the 5s., tends to show through the back. The holes of the perforation are smaller than those of the other two printers, but there is a thick perforation tooth at the top of each vertical side.

In the Bradbury Wilkinson printings the height of the stamp is 22.6–23.1 mm due to the use of curved plates. On most of the 22.6 mm high stamps a minute coloured guide dot appears in the margin just above the middle of the upper frame-line.

For (1934) re-engraved Waterlow printings see Nos. 450/452.

KING GEORGE V

UNITED KINGDOM OF GREAT BRITAIN AND NORTHERN IRELAND

111 Block Cypher   **111a**

The watermark T **111a**, as compared with T **111**, differs as follows: Closer spacing of horizontal rows (12½ mm instead of 14½ mm). Letters shorter and rounder. Watermark thicker. The dandy roll to produce watermark T **111a** was provided by Somerset House in connection with experiments in paper composition undertaken during 1924–1925. These resulted in a change from rag only paper to that made from a mixture including esparto and sulphite.

(Letterpress by Waterlow & Sons, Ltd (all values except 6d.) and later, 1934–1935, by Harrison & Sons, Ltd (all values). Until 1934 the 6d. was printed at Somerset House where a printing of the 1½d. was also made in 1926 (identifiable only by control E.26). Printings by Harrisons in 1934–1935 can be identified, when in mint condition, by the fact that the gum shows a streaky appearance vertically, the Waterlow gum being uniformly applied, but Harrisons also used up the balance of the Waterlow 'smooth gum' paper)

1924 (Feb)–26. Wmk Block Cypher, W **111**. Perf 15×14.

			Unmtd mint	Mtd mint	Used
418	105	½d. green	2·00	1·00	1·00
		a. Watermark sideways (5.24)	18·00	9·00	3·25
		aWi. Watermark sideways inverted	£650	£450	
		b. Doubly printed	£12500	£9500	†
		c. No watermark	£4000	—	
		d. Booklet pane, No. 418×6 (2.24)	£120	85·00	
		dw. Booklet pane, 418Wi×6	£120	85·00	
		s. Optd 'SPECIMEN' (15, 23, 30, 32)		90·00	
		Wi. Watermark inverted	7·00	3·50	1·00
419	104	1d. scarlet	2·00	1·00	1·00
		a. Watermark sideways	40·00	20·00	15·00
		b. Experimental paper, W **111a** (10.24)	40·00	22·00	
		c. Partial double print, one inverted	—	—	
		d. Inverted 'Q' for 'O' (R. 20/3)	£850	£500	
		e. Booklet pane, No. 419×6 (2.24)	£120	85·00	
		ew. Booklet pane, No. 419Wi×6	£120	85·00	
		s. Optd 'SPECIMEN' (15, 23, 30, 32)		90·00	
		Wi. Watermark inverted	7·00	4·00	1·50
420	105	1½d. red-brown	2·00	1·00	1·00
		a. Tête-bêche (pair)	£750	£500	£800
		b. Watermark sideways (8.24)	20·00	10·00	3·50
		bWi. Watermark sideways inverted	—	£900	
		c. Printed on the gummed side	£1000	£650	
		d. Booklet pane. No. 420×4 plus two printed labels (3.24)	£300	£225	
		dw. Booklet pane. No. 420Wi×4 plus two printed labels	£300	£225	
		e. Booklet pane, No. 420×6 (2.24)	70·00	50·00	
		ew. Booklet pane, No. 420Wi×6	70·00	50·00	
		f. Booklet pane. No. 420b×4 plus two printed labels, watermark sideways	£14000	£10000	
		g. Experimental paper, W **111a** (10.24)	£160	£120	£120
		h. Double impression	—	—	†
		s. Optd 'SPECIMEN' (15, 23, 30, 32)		90·00	
		Wi. Watermark inverted	3·50	2·00	1·00
421	106	2d. orange (Die II) (7.24)	4·00	2·50	2·50
		a. No watermark	£2250	£1800	
		b. Watermark sideways (7.26)	£210	£100	£100
		c. Partial double print	—	£25000	†
		s. Optd 'SPECIMEN' (23, 32)		£100	
		Wi. Watermark inverted	90·00	55·00	55·00
422	104	2½d. blue (10.10.24)	10·00	5·00	3·00
		a. No watermark	£3800	£2800	
		b. Watermark sideways	†	†	£18000
		s. Optd 'SPECIMEN' (23, 32)		£550	
		Wi. Watermark inverted	£140	90·00	90·00
423	106	3d. violet (10.10.24)	20·00	10·00	2·50
		s. Optd 'SPECIMEN' (23, 32)		£750	
		Wi. Watermark inverted	£140	90·00	90·00
424		4d. grey-green (10.10.24)	28·00	12·00	2·50
		a. Printed on the gummed side	£6250	£4250	†
		s. Optd 'SPECIMEN' (23, 32)		£650	
		Wi. Watermark inverted	£240	£150	£150
425	107	5d. brown (17.10.24)	40·00	20·00	3·00
		s. Optd 'SPECIMEN' (23, 26, 32)		£140	
		Wi. Watermark inverted	£225	£150	£150
426		6d. reddish purple (chalk-surfaced paper) (9.24)	20·00	12·00	2·50
		Wi. Watermark inverted	90·00	60·00	60·00
		Wk. Watermark inverted and reversed	£700	£450	£400
426a		6d. purple (6.26)	8·00	4·00	1·50
		as. Optd 'SPECIMEN' (23, 26, 32)		£425	
		aWi. Watermark inverted	£140	90·00	90·00
427	108	9d. olive-green (11.11.24)	40·00	12·00	3·50
		s. Optd 'SPECIMEN' (23, 26, 32)		£140	
		Wi. Watermark inverted	£175	£120	£120
428		10d. turquoise-blue (28.11.24)	85·00	40·00	40·00
		s. Optd 'SPECIMEN' (23, 32)		£750	
		Wi. Watermark inverted	£3750	£2750	£2400
429		1s. bistre-brown (10.24)	50·00	22·00	3·00
		s. Optd 'SPECIMEN' (23, 32)		£550	
		Wi. Watermark inverted	£600	£375	£375
418/429 Set of 12			£250	£110	60·00

The normal sideways watermark shows the top of the Crown pointing to the right, *as seen from the back of the stamp.*
There are numerous shades in this issue.
The 6d. on chalk-surfaced and ordinary papers was printed by both Somerset House and Harrisons. The Harrison printings have streaky gum, differ slightly in shade, and that on chalk-surfaced paper is printed in a highly fugitive ink. The prices quoted are for the commonest (Harrison) printing in each case.

112

Scratch across the Lion's nose (left pane, R. 1/4)    Tail to 'N' of 'EXHIBITION' (Left pane, R. 1/5)

(Des H. Nelson. Eng J. A. C. Harrison. Recess Waterlow)

1924–25. British Empire Exhibition. W **111**. Perf 14.

(a) Dated 1924 (23.4.24).

			Unmtd mint	Mtd mint	Used
430	112	1d. scarlet	12·00	10·00	11·00
		a. Scratch across the Lion's nose	£225	£150	85·00
		b. Tail to 'N' of EXHIBITION	£225	£150	85·00
		s. Optd 'SPECIMEN' (15, 23, 30)		£1100	
431		1½d. brown	20·00	15·00	15·00
		s. Optd 'SPECIMEN' (15, 23, 30)		£1100	
Set of 2			30·00	25·00	26·00
First Day Cover					£450

(b) Dated 1925 (9.5.25).

			Unmtd mint	Mtd mint	Used
432	112	1d. scarlet	25·00	15·00	30·00
		s. Optd 'SPECIMEN' (30)		£1000	
433		1½d. brown	60·00	40·00	70·00
		s. Optd 'SPECIMEN' (30)		£1000	
Set of 2			80·00	55·00	£100
First Day Cover					£1700

KING GEORGE V

113 **114** **115**

118 **119** **120**

121 **122**

116 St George and the Dragon

117

Des J. Farleigh) (Types **113** and **115**), E. Linzell (T **114**) and H. Nelson (T **116**). Eng C. G. Lewis (T **113**), T. E. Storey (T **115**), both at the Royal Mint; J. A. C. Harrison, of Waterlow (Types **114** and **116**). Letterpress by Waterlow from plates made at the Royal Mint, except (T **116**), recess by Bradbury Wilkinson from die and plate of their own manufacture

1929 (10 May). Ninth UPU Congress, London.

(a) W **111**. *Perf 15×14.*

			Unmtd mint	Mtd mint	Used
434	113	½d. green	3·00	2·25	2·25
		a. Watermark sideways	80·00	55·00	50·00
		b. Booklet pane, No. 434×6 (5.29)	£250	£200	
		bw. Booklet pane, No. 343Wi×6 (5.29)	£300	£225	
		Wi. Watermark inverted	35·00	15·00	12·00
435	114	1d. scarlet	3·00	2·25	2·25
		a. Watermark sideways	£140	90·00	90·00
		b. Booklet pane, No. 435×6 (5.29)	£250	£200	
		bw. Booklet pane, No. 435Wi×6 (5.29)	£300	£225	
		Wi. Watermark inverted	35·00	15·00	12·00
436		1½d. purple-brown	3·00	2·25	1·75
		a. Watermark sideways	90·00	60·00	55·00
		b. Booklet pane. No. 436×4 plus two printed labels	£500	£375	
		bw. Booklet pane. No. 436Wi×4 plus two printed labels	£500	£375	
		c. Booklet pane, No. 436×6 (5.29)	85·00	60·00	
		cw. Booklet pane, No. 436Wi×6	£110	80·00	
		Wi. Watermark inverted	15·00	5·00	6·00
437	115	2½d. blue	28·00	10·00	10·00
		s. Optd 'SPECIMEN' (32)		£3000	
		Wi. Watermark inverted	£3750	£2750	£1100

(b) W **117**. *Perf 12.*

438	116	£1 black	£1100	£750	£600
		s. Optd 'SPECIMEN' (32, red opt)		£3000	
Set of 4 (to 2½d.)			35·00	15·00	14·50
First Day Cover (Nos. 434/437) (4 values)					£675
First Day Cover (Nos. 434/438) (5 values)					£14000

PRINTERS. All subsequent issues were printed in photogravure by Harrison & Sons Ltd *except where otherwise stated.*

1934–36. W **111**. Perf 15×14.

			Unmtd mint	Mtd mint	Used
439	118	½d. green (17.11.34)	1·00	50	50
		a. Watermark sideways	17·00	10·00	5·00
		aWi. Watermark sideways inverted	£600	£450	£150
		b. Imperf three sides	£7750	£5250	
		c. Booklet pane, No. 439×6 (1.35)	£120	85·00	
		cw. Booklet pane, No. 439Wi×6	£130	95·00	
		s. Optd 'SPECIMEN' (23, 32)		£500	
		Wi. Watermark inverted	22·00	11·00	1·50
440	119	1d. scarlet (24.9.34)	1·00	50	50
		a. Imperf (pair)	£7000	£5000	
		b. Printed on gummed side	£1000	£750	
		c. Watermark sideways (30.4.35)	40·00	20·00	12·00
		cWi. Watermark sideways inverted	£190	£125	—
		d. Double impression	†	†	£18000
		e. Imperf between (pair)	£12500	£8500	
		f. Imperf (three sides) (pair)	£9500	£7000	
		g. Booklet pane, No. 440×6 (1.35)	£120	85·00	
		gw. Booklet pane, No. 440Wi×6	£130	95·00	
		s. Optd 'SPECIMEN' (23, 32)		£600	
		Wi. Watermark inverted	20·00	9·00	3·00
441	118	1½d. red-brown (20.8.34)	1·00	50	50
		a. Imperf (pair)	£1700	£1250	
		b. Imperf (three sides) (lower stamp in vert pair)	£6000	£4000	
		c. Imperf between (horiz pair)			
		d. Watermark sideways	15·00	10·00	5·00
		dWi. Watermark sideways inverted			
		e. Booklet pane. No. 441×4 plus two printed labels	£275	£200	
		ew. Booklet pane. No. 441Wi×4 plus two printed labels	£275	£200	
		f. Booklet pane, No. 441×6 (1.35)	42·00	30·00	
		fw. Booklet pane, No. 441Wi×6	55·00	40·00	
		s. optd 'SPECIMEN' (23, 32)		£650	
		Wi. Watermark inverted	8·00	4·00	1·00
442	120	2d. orange (19.1.35)	1·50	75	75
		a. Imperf (pair)	£6500	£5000	
		b. Watermark sideways (30.4.35)	£225	£125	90·00
		s. Optd 'SPECIMEN' (30, 32)		—	
443	119	2½d. bright blue (18.3.35)	2·50	1·50	1·25
		s. Optd 'SPECIMEN' (23)		£700	
444	120	3d. reddish violet (18.3.35)	3·00	1·50	1·25
		s. Optd 'SPECIMEN' (23, 30)		£650	
		Wi. Watermark inverted	—	—	£9000
445		4d. deep grey-green (2.12.35)	4·00	2·00	1·25
		s. Optd 'SPECIMEN' (23, 30)		£400	
		Wi. Watermark inverted	†	†	£9000
446	121	5d. yellow-brown (17.2.36)	13·00	6·50	2·75
		s. Optd 'SPECIMEN' (23)		£650	
447	122	9d. deep olive-green (2.12.35)	20·00	12·00	2·25
		s. Optd 'SPECIMEN' (23)		£650	
448		10d. turquoise-blue (24.2.36)	30·00	15·00	10·00
		s. Optd 'SPECIMEN' (23, 32)		£700	
449		1s. bistre-brown (24.2.36)	40·00	15·00	1·25
		a. Double impression	—	—	†
		s. Optd 'SPECIMEN' (23, 32)		£125	
Set of 11			95·00	50·00	20·00

The normal sideways watermark shows the top of the Crown pointing to the right, *as seen from the back of the stamp.*

The ½d. imperf three sides, No. 439b, is known in a block of four, from a sheet, to which the bottom pair is imperf at top and sides.

Owing to the need for wider space for the perforations the size of the designs of the ½d. and 2d. were once, and the 1d. and 1½d. twice reduced from that of the first printings.

The format description, size in millimetres and SG catalogue number are given but further details will be found in the *Great Britain Specialised Catalogue*, Volume 2.

Description	Size	SG Nos.	Date of Issue
½d. intermediate format	18.4×22.2	—	19.11.34
½d. small format	17.9×21.7	439	14.2.35
1d. large format	18.7×22.5	—	24.9.34
1d. intermediate format	18.4×22.2	—	1934
1d. small format	17.9×21.7	440	8.2.35
1½d. large format	18.7×22.5	—	20.8.34
1½d. intermediate format	18.4×22.2	—	1934
1½d. small format	17.9×21.7	441	7.2.35
2d. intermediate format	18.4×22.2	—	21.1.35
2d. small format	18.15×21.7	442	1935

There are also numerous minor variations, due to the photographic element in the process.

Examples of 2d., T **120**, which were in the hands of philatelists are known bisected in Guernsey from 27 December 1940 to February 1941.

B

123

(Eng. J. A. C. Harrison. Recess Waterlow)

1934 (16 Oct). T **109** (re-engraved). Background around portrait consists of horizontal and diagonal lines, Type B. W **110**. Perf 11×12.

			Unmtd mint	Mtd mint	Used
450	109	2s.6d. chocolate-brown	£150	80·00	40·00
		s. Optd 'SPECIMEN' (23, 30)		£3250	
451		5s. bright rose-red	£400	£175	85·00
		s. Optd 'SPECIMEN' (23, 30)		£3250	
452		10s. indigo	£500	£350	80·00
		s. Optd 'SPECIMEN' (23, 30)		£3250	
Set of 3			£1000	£575	£190

There are numerous other minor differences in the design of this issue.

(Des B. Freedman)

1935 (7 May). Silver Jubilee. W **111**. Perf 15×14.

			Unmtd mint	Mtd mint	Used
453	123	½d. green	1·00	1·00	1·00
		a. Booklet pane, No. 453×4 (5.35)	70·00	50·00	
		aw. Booklet pane, No. 453Wi×4	80·00	60·00	
		s. Optd 'SPECIMEN' (23)		£1400	
		Wi. Watermark inverted	15·00	8·00	3·00
454		1d. scarlet	2·00	1·50	2·00
		a. Booklet pane, No. 454×4 (5.35)	60·00	45·00	
		aw. Booklet pane, No. 454Wi×4, watermark inverted	75·00	55·00	
		s. Optd 'SPECIMEN' (23)		£1400	
		Wi. Watermark inverted	15·00	8·00	4·00
455		1½d. red-brown	1·25	1·00	1·00
		a. Booklet pane, No. 455×4 (5.35)	25·00	18·00	
		aw. Booklet pane, No. 455Wi×4	30·00	22·00	
		s. Opts 'SPECIMEN' (23)		£1400	
		Wi. Watermark inverted	5·00	3·00	1·50
456		2½d. blue	8·00	5·00	6·50
		s. Optd 'SPECIMEN' (23)		£1750	
456a		2½d. Prussian blue	£15000	£12000	£14000
Set of 4			11·00	7·50	9·50
First Day Cover					£650

The 1d., 1½d. and 2½d. values differ from T **123** in the emblem in the panel at right.

Four sheets of No. 456a, printed in the wrong shade, were issued in error by the Post Office Stores Department on 25 June 1935. It is known that three of the sheets were sold from the sub-office at 134 Fore Street, Upper Edmonton, London, between that date and 4 July.

King Edward VIII
20 January-10 December 1936

King George VI
11 December 1936-6 February 1952

Further detailed information on the stamps of King Edward VIII will be found in Volume 2 of the Stanley Gibbons *Great Britain Specialised Catalogue*.

Further detailed information on the stamps of King George VI will be found in Volume 2 of the Stanley Gibbons *Great Britain Specialised Catalogue*.

PRICES. From No. 457 prices quoted in the first column are for stamps in unmounted mint condition.

124  / **125**

126 King George VI and Queen Elizabeth **127**

Colon flaw (Cyl. 7 No dot, R. 10/1, later corrected)

(Des H. Brown, adapted Harrison using a photo by Hugh Cecil)

1936. W **125**. Perf 15×14.

457	**124**	½d. green (1.9.36)	30	30
		a. Double impression	—	
		b. Booklet pane. No. 457×6 (10.36)	30·00	
		bw. Booklet pane. No. 457×6, watermark inverted	45·00	
		Wi. Watermark inverted	10·00	5·00
		s. Optd 'SPECIMEN' (30, 32)	£775	
458		1d. scarlet (14.9.36)	60	50
		a. Booklet pane. No. 458×6 (10.36)	25·00	
		aw. Booklet pane. No. 458×6, watermark inverted	40·00	
		Wi. Watermark inverted	9·00	5·00
		s. Optd 'SPECIMEN' (30, 32)	£775	
459		1½d. red-brown (1.9.36)	30	30
		a. Booklet pane. No. 459×4 plus two printed labels (10.36)	£100	
		aw. Booklet pane. No. 459Wi×4 plus two printed labels	£100	
		b. Booklet pane. No. 459×6 (10.36)	15·00	
		bw. Booklet pane. No. 459×6, watermark inverted	15·00	
		c. Booklet pane. No. 459×2	30·00	
		cw. Booklet pane. No. 459×2, watermark inverted	30·00	
		d. Imperf (pair)	—	
		s. Optd 'SPECIMEN' (30, 32)	£775	
		Wi. Watermark inverted	1·00	1·00
460		2½d. bright blue (1.9.36)	30	85
		s. Optd 'SPECIMEN' (30)	£850	
Set of 4			1·25	1·75
457/460 Set of 4			1·25	1·75

First Day Covers

1.9.36	Nos. 457, 459/460		£175
14.9.36	No. 458		£200

(Des E. Dulac)

1937 (13 May). Coronation. W **127**. Perf 15×14.

461	**126**	1½d. maroon	30	30
		a. Colon flaw	70·00	
		s. Optd 'SPECIMEN' (32)	£750	
First Day Cover				35·00

128  / **129**  / **130**

King George VI and National Emblems

(Des Types **128/129**, E. Dulac (head) and E. Gill (frames). T **130**, E. Dulac (whole stamp))

1937–47. W **127**. Perf 15×14.

462	**128**	½d. green (10.5.37)	30	25
		a. Watermark sideways (1.38)	75	60
		ab. Booklet pane. No. 462a×4 (6.40)	£110	
		b. Booklet pane. No 462×6 (8.37)	50·00	
		bw. Booklet pane. No. 462Wi×6	80·00	
		c. Booklet pane. No. 462×2 (8.37)	£120	
		cw. Booklet pane. No. 462Wi×2	£120	
		Wi. Watermark inverted	10·00	60
463		1d. scarlet (10.5.37)	30	25
		a. Watermark sideways (2.38)	20·00	9·00
		ab. Booklet pane. No. 463a×4 (6.40)	£175	
		b. Booklet pane. No. 463×6 (2.38)	65·00	
		bw. Booklet pane. No. 463Wi×6	£275	
		c. Booklet pane. No. 463×2 (2.38)	£125	
		cw. Booklet pane. No. 463Wi×2	£125	
		s. Optd 'SPECIMEN' (32)		
		Wi. Watermark inverted	40·00	3·00
464		1½d. red-brown (30.7.37)	30	25
		a. Watermark sideways (2.38)	1·25	1·25
		b. Booklet pane. No. 464×4 plus two printed labels (8.37)	£140	
		bw. Booklet pane. No. 464Wi×4 plus two printed labels	£140	
		c. Booklet pane. No. 464×6 (8.37)	60·00	
		cw. Booklet pane. No. 464Wi×6	£100	
		d. Booklet pane. No. 464×2 (1.38)	35·00	
		dw. Booklet pane. No. 464Wi×2	50·00	
		e. Imperf three sides (pair)	£6500	
		s. Optd 'SPECIMEN' (32)		
		Wi. Watermark inverted	15·00	1·25
465		2d. orange (31.1.38)	1·25	50
		a. Watermark sideways (2.38)	75·00	40·00
		b. Bisected (*on cover*)	†	60·00
		c. Booklet pane. No. 465×6 (6.40)	£175	
		cw. Booklet pane. No. 465Wi×6	£425	
		s. Optd 'SPECIMEN' (26)	£325	

KING GEORGE VI

466		Wi. Watermark inverted	60·00	22·00
		2½d. ultramarine (10.5.37)	40	25
		a. Watermark sideways (6.40)	75·00	35·00
		b. Tête-bêche (horiz pair)	—	
		c. Booklet pane. No. 466×6 (6.40)	£150	
		cw. Booklet pane. No. 466Wi×6	£375	
		Wi. Watermark inverted	55·00	22·00
467		3d. violet (31.1.38)	5·00	1·00
		s. Optd 'SPECIMEN' (26, 30)	£300	
468	129	4d. grey-green (21.11.38)	60	75
		a. Imperf (pair)	£9000	
		b. Imperf three sides (horiz pair)	£9500	
		s. Optd 'SPECIMEN' (23)	£200	
469		5d. brown (21.11.38)	3·50	85
		a. Imperf (pair)	£8500	
		b. Imperf three sides (horiz pair)	£9000	
		s. Optd 'SPECIMEN' (23)	£250	
470		6d. purple (30.1.39)	1·50	60
		s. Optd 'SPECIMEN' (23)	£250	
471	130	7d. emerald-green (27.2.39)	5·00	60
		a. Imperf three sides (horiz pair)	£9000	
		s. Optd 'SPECIMEN' (23)	£250	
472		8d. bright carmine (27.2.39)	7·50	80
		s. Optd 'SPECIMEN' (23)	£250	
473		9d. deep olive-green (1.5.39)	6·50	80
		s. Optd 'SPECIMEN' (23)	£250	
474		10d. turquoise-blue (1.5.39)	7·00	80
		aa. Imperf (pair)	£250	
		s. Optd 'SPECIMEN' (23)	£250	
474a		11d. plum (29.12.47)	3·00	2·75
		as. Optd 'SPECIMEN' (30)	£275	
475		1s. bistre-brown (1.5.39)	9·00	75
		s. Optd 'SPECIMEN' (23, 30)	£160	
Set of 15			45·00	10·00

For later printings of the lower values in apparently lighter shades and different colours, see Nos. 485/490 and 503/508.

No. 465b was authorised for use in Guernsey from 27 December 1940 until February 1941.

Nos. 468b and 469b are perforated at foot only and each occurs in the same sheet as Nos. 468a and 469a.

No. 471a is also perforated at foot only, but occurs on the top row of a sheet.

First Day Covers

10.5.37	Nos. 462/463, 466	45·00
30.7.37	No. 464	45·00
31.1.38	Nos. 465, 467	£110
21.11.38	Nos. 468/469	70·00
30.1.39	No. 470	65·00
27.2.39	Nos. 471/472	90·00
1.5.39	Nos. 473/474, 475	£525
29.12.47	No. 474a	60·00

131 132

133

Mark in shield (R. 1/7)   Gashed diadem (R. 2/7)

Gashed crown (R. 5/5)   Broken stem (R. 1/4)

Blot on scroll (R. 2/5)   Scratch on scroll (R. 4/6)

(Des E. Dulac (T **131**) and the Honourable G. R. Bellew (T **132**). Eng J. A. C. Harrison. Recess Waterlow)

1939–48. W **133**. Perf 14.

476	131	2s.6d. brown (4.9.39)	£100	8·00
		aa. Mark in shield	£190	85·00
		ab. Gashed diadem	£190	85·00
		ac. Gashed crown	£190	85·00
		as. Optd 'SPECIMEN' (23)	£300	
476b		2s.6d. yellow-green (9.3.42)	15·00	1·50
		bs. Optd 'SPECIMEN' (9, 23, 26, 30)	£300	1·50
477		5s. red (21.8.39)	20·00	2·00
		s. Optd 'SPECIMEN' (9, 23, 26, 30)	£300	
478	132	10s. dark blue (30.10.39)	£260	22·00
		aa. Broken stem	£275	80·00
		ab. Blot on scroll	£275	80·00
		ac. Scratch on scroll	£350	£100
		s. Optd 'SPECIMEN' (23)	£500	
478b		10s. ultramarine (30.11.42)	45·00	5·00
		bs. Optd 'SPECIMEN' (9, 23, 30)	£425	
478c		£1 brown (1.10.48)	25·00	26·00
		cs. Optd 'SPECIMEN' (30)	—	
Set of 6			£425	60·00

First Day Covers

21.8.39	No. 477	£850
4.9.39	No. 475	£1800
30.10.39	No. 478	£3250
9.3.41	No. 476b	£1750
30.11.41	No. 478b	£3750
1.10.48	No. 478c	£350

The 10s. dark blue was pre-released in Northern Ireland on 3 October 1939.

134 Queen Victoria and King George VI

(Des H. L. Palmer)

1940 (6 May). Centenary of First Adhesive Postage Stamps. W **127**. Perf 14½×14.

479	134	½d. green	30	75
		s. Optd 'SPECIMEN' (23, 30)	£750	
480		1d. scarlet	1·00	75
		s. Optd 'SPECIMEN' (23, 30)	£750	
481		1½d. red-brown	50	1·50
		s. Optd 'SPECIMEN' (23, 30)	£750	
482		2d. orange	1·00	75
		a. Bisected (on cover)	†	50·00
		s. Optd 'SPECIMEN' (23, 30)	£750	
483		2½d. ultramarine	2·25	50
		s. Optd 'SPECIMEN' (23, 30)	£750	
484		3d. violet	3·00	3·50
		s. Optd 'SPECIMEN' (23, 30)	£750	
Set of 6			8·75	4·25
First Day Cover				55·00

No. 482a was authorised for use in Guernsey from 27 December 1940 until February 1941.

1941–42. Head as Nos. 462/467, but with lighter background to provide a more economic use of the printing ink. W **127**. Perf 15×14.

485	128	½d. pale green (1.9.41)	30	30
		a. Tête-bêche (horiz pair)	—	
		b. Imperf (pair)	£8500	
		c. Booklet pane. No. 485×6 (3.42)	30·00	

KING GEORGE VI

	cw. Booklet pane. No. 485Wi×6	45·00		
	d. Booklet pane. No. 485×4 (1948)	—		
	e. Booklet pane. No. 485×2 (12.47)	15·00		
	s. Optd 'SPECIMEN' (23)	£750		
	Wi. Watermark inverted	4·00	50	
486	1d. pale scarlet (11.8.41)	30	30	
	a. Watermark sideways (10.42)	5·00	4·50	
	b. Imperf (pair)	£8000		
	c. Imperf three sides (horiz pair)	£8500		
	d. Booklet pane. No. 486×4 (1948)	—		
	e. Booklet pane. No. 486×2 (12.47)	40·00		
	f. Imperf between (vert pair)	£6000		
	s. Optd 'SPECIMEN' (23)	£750		
487	1½d. pale red-brown (28.9.42)	60	80	
	a. Booklet pane. No, 487×4 (1948)	—		
	b. Booklet pane. No. 487×2 (12.47)	15·00		
	s. Optd 'SPECIMEN' (23)	£750		
488	2d. pale orange (6.10.41)	50	50	
	a. Watermark sideways (6.42)	28·00	20·00	
	b. Tête-bêche (horiz pair)	£18000		
	c. Imperf (pair)	£7500		
	d. Imperf pane*	£16000		
	e. Booklet pane. No. 488×6 (3.42)	30·00		
	ew. Booklet pane. No. 488Wi×6	30·00		
	s. Optd 'SPECIMEN' (23)	£750		
	Wi. Watermark inverted	4·00	1·00	
489	2½d. light ultramarine (21.7.41)	30	30	
	a. Watermark sideways (8.42)	15·00	12·00	
	b. Tête-bêche (horiz pair)	—		
	c. Imperf (pair)	£4800		
	d. Imperf pane*	£12000		
	e. Imperf three sides (horiz pair)	£7500		
	f. Booklet pane. No. 489×6 (3.42)	20·00		
	fw. Booklet pane. No. 489Wi×6	20·00		
	s. Optd 'SPECIMEN' (23)	£750		
	Wi. Watermark inverted	1·50	1·00	
490	3d. pale violet (3.11.41)	2·50	1·00	
	s. Optd 'SPECIMEN' (32)	£750		
Set of 6		3·50	2·75	

* Imperf panes show one row of perforations either at the top or bottom of the pane of six.

First Day Covers

21.7.41	No. 489	45·00
11.8.41	No. 486	25·00
1.9.41	No. 485	25·00
6.10.41	No. 488	60·00
3.11.41	No. 490	£110
28.9.42	No. 487	55·00

135 Symbols of Peace and Reconstruction

136 Symbols of Peace and Reconstruction

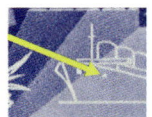

Extra porthole aft (Cyl. 11 No dot, R. 16/1)

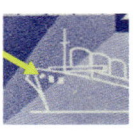

Extra porthole fore (Cyl. 8 Dot, R. 5/6)

Seven berries (Cyl. 4 No dot, R. 12/5)

(Des H. L. Palmer (T **135**) and R. Stone (T **136**))

1946 (11 June). Peace. W **127**. Perf 15×14.

491	135	2½d. ultramarine	20	20
		a. Extra porthole aft	95·00	
		b. Extra porthole fore	£160	
		s. Optd 'SPECIMEN' (30)	£600	
492	136	3d. violet	20	50
		a. Seven berries	35·00	
		s. Optd 'SPECIMEN' (30)	£600	
Set of 2			40	50
First Day Cover				65·00

137 King George VI and Queen Elizabeth

138 King George VI and Queen Elizabeth

(Des G. Knipe and Joan Hassall from photographs by Dorothy Wilding)

1948 (26 Apr). Royal Silver Wedding. W **127**. Perf 15×14 (2½d.) or 14×15 (£1).

493	137	2½d. ultramarine	35	20
		s. Optd 'SPECIMEN' (30)	£600	
494	138	£1 blue	40·00	40·00
		s. Optd 'SPECIMEN' (30)	£600	
Set of 2			40·00	40·00
First Day Cover				£425

1948 (10 May). Stamps of 1d. and 2½d. showing seaweed-gathering were on sale at eight Head Post Offices in Great Britain, but were primarily for use in the Channel Islands and are listed there (see Nos. C1/C2, after Royal Mail Post & Go Stamps).

139 Globe and Laurel Wreath

140 Speed

141 Olympic Symbol

142 Winged Victory

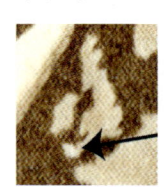

White blob on Lands End (Cyl. 3 No dot R. 7/3)

Spot below '9' (Cyl. 3 No dot R. 8/4)

Crown flaw (Cyl. 1 No dot, R. 20/2, later retouched)

(Des P. Metcalfe (T **139**), A. Games (T **140**), S. D. Scott (T **141**) and E. Dulac (T **142**))

1948 (29 July). Olympic Games. W **127**. Perf 15×14.

495	139	2½d. ultramarine	50	10
		s. Optd 'SPECIMEN' (26)	£500	
496	140	3d. violet	50	50
		a. Crown flaw	75·00	
		s. Optd 'SPECIMEN' (26)	£500	
497	141	6d. bright purple	3·25	75
		s. Optd 'SPECIMEN' (26)	£500	
498	142	1s. brown	4·50	2·00
		a. White blob on Lands End	95·00	
		b. Spot below '9'	95·00	
		s. Optd 'SPECIMEN' (26)	£500	
Set of 4			8·00	3·00
First Day Cover				50·00

KING GEORGE VI

143 Two Hemispheres 
144 UPU Monument, Bern 
145 Goddess Concordia, Globe and Points of Compass 
146 Posthorn and Globe

Lake in Asia (Cyl. 3 Dot, R. 14/1) 
Lake in India (Cyl. 2 No dot, R. 8/2)

Retouched background to '1/-' (R. 8/5)

(Des Mary Adshead (T **143**), P. Metcalfe (T **144**), H. Fleury (T **145**) and the Honourable G. R. Bellew (T **146**))

1949 (10 Oct). 75th Anniversary of Universal Postal Union. W **127**. Perf 15×14.

499	**143**	2½d. ultramarine	25	10
		a. Lake in Asia	£145	
		b. Lake in India	£100	
		s. Optd 'SPECIMEN' (30)	—	
500	**144**	3d. violet	25	50
		s. Optd 'SPECIMEN' (30)	—	
501	**145**	6d. bright purple	50	75
		s. Optd 'SPECIMEN' (30)	—	
502	**146**	1s. brown	1·00	1·25
		a. Retouched background to '1/-'	75·00	
		s. Optd 'SPECIMEN' (30)	—	
Set of 4			1·50	2·50
First Day Cover				80·00

1950–52. 4d. as No. 468 and others as Nos. 485/489, but colours changed. W **127**. Perf 15×14.

503	**128**	½d. pale orange (3.5.51)	30	30
		a. Imperf (pair)	£7000	
		b. Tête-bêche (horiz pair)	—	
		c. Imperf pane*	£13000	
		d. Booklet pane. No. 503×6 (5.51)	10·00	
		dw. Booklet pane. No. 503Wi×6	10·00	
		e. Booklet pane. No. 503×4 (5.51)	15·00	
		ew. Booklet pane. No. 503Wi×4	15·00	
		f. Booklet pane. No. 503×2 (5.51)	15·00	
		Wi. Watermark inverted	50	50
504		1d. light ultramarine (3.5.51)	30	30
		a. Watermark sideways (5.51)	1·10	1·25
		b. Imperf (pair)	£4800	
		c. Imperf three sides (horiz pair)	£6500	
		d. Booklet pane. No. 504×3 plus three printed labels (3.52)	18·00	
		dw. Booklet pane. No. 504Wi×3 plus three printed labels	18·00	
		e. Booklet pane. No. 504Wi×3 plus three printed labels. Partial tête-bêche pane	£8500	
		f. Booklet pane. No. 504×6 (1.53)	40·00	
		fw. Booklet pane. No. 504Wi×6	45·00	
		g. Booklet pane. No. 504×4 (5.51)	20·00	
		gw. Booklet pane. No. 504Wi×4	35·00	
		h. Booklet pane. No. 504×2 (5.51)	15·00	
		Wi. Watermark inverted	4·50	2·50
505		1½d. pale green (3.5.51)	65	60
		a. Watermark sideways (9.51)	3·25	5·00
		b. Booklet pane. No. 505×6 (3.52)	30·00	
		bw. Booklet pane. 505Wi×6	40·00	
		c. Booklet pane. No. 505×4 (5.51)	15·00	
		cw. Booklet pane. No. 505Wi×4	20·00	
		d. Booklet pane. No. 505×2 (5.51)	15·00	
		Wi. Watermark inverted	6·00	1·00
506		2d. pale red-brown (3.5.51)	75	40
		a. Watermark sideways (5.51)	1·75	2·00
		b. Tête-bêche (horiz pair)	—	
		c. Imperf three sides (horiz pair)	£8000	
		d. Booklet pane. No. 506×6 (5.51)	40·00	
		dw. Booklet pane. No. 506Wi×6	40·00	
		Wi. Watermark inverted	6·00	6·50
507		2½d. pale scarlet (3.5.51)	60	40
		a. Watermark sideways (5.51)	1·75	1·75
		b. Tête-bêche (horiz pair)	—	
		c. Booklet pane. No. 507×6 (5.51)	8·00	
		cw. Booklet pane. No. 507Wi×6	10·00	
		Wi. Watermark inverted	2·00	1·25
508	**129**	4d. light ultramarine (2.10.50)	2·00	1·75
		a. Double impression	†	£7000
Set of 6			4·00	3·25

* BOOKLET ERRORS. Those listed as imperf panes show one row of perforations either at the top or at the bottom of the pane of six.
No. 504c is perforated at foot only and only occurs in the same sheet as No. 504b.
No. 506c is also perforated at foot only.

First Day Covers

2.10.50	No. 508	£125
3.5.51	Nos. 503/507	55·00

147 HMS *Victory*
148 White Cliffs of Dover 
149 St George and the Dragon 
150 Royal Coat of Arms 

(Des Mary Adshead (Types **147**/**148**), P. Metcalfe (Types **149**/**150**). Recess Waterlow)

1951 (3 May). W **133**. Perf 11×12.

509	**147**	2s.6d. yellow-green	7·50	1·00
		s. Optd 'SPECIMEN' (30)	£1000	
510	**148**	5s. red	35·00	1·00
		s. Optd 'SPECIMEN' (30)	£1000	
511	**149**	10s. ultramarine	15·00	7·50
		s. Optd 'SPECIMEN' (30)	£1000	
512	**150**	£1 brown	45·00	18·00
		s. Optd 'SPECIMEN' (30)	£1000	
Set of 4			£100	25·00
First Day Cover				£950

151 Commerce and Prosperity
152 Festival Symbol 

(Des E. Dulac (T **151**), A. Games (T **152**))

1951 (3 May). Festival of Britain. W **127**. Perf 15×14.

513	**151**	2½d. scarlet	20	15
514	**152**	4d. ultramarine	30	35
Set of 2			40	40
First Day Cover				40·00

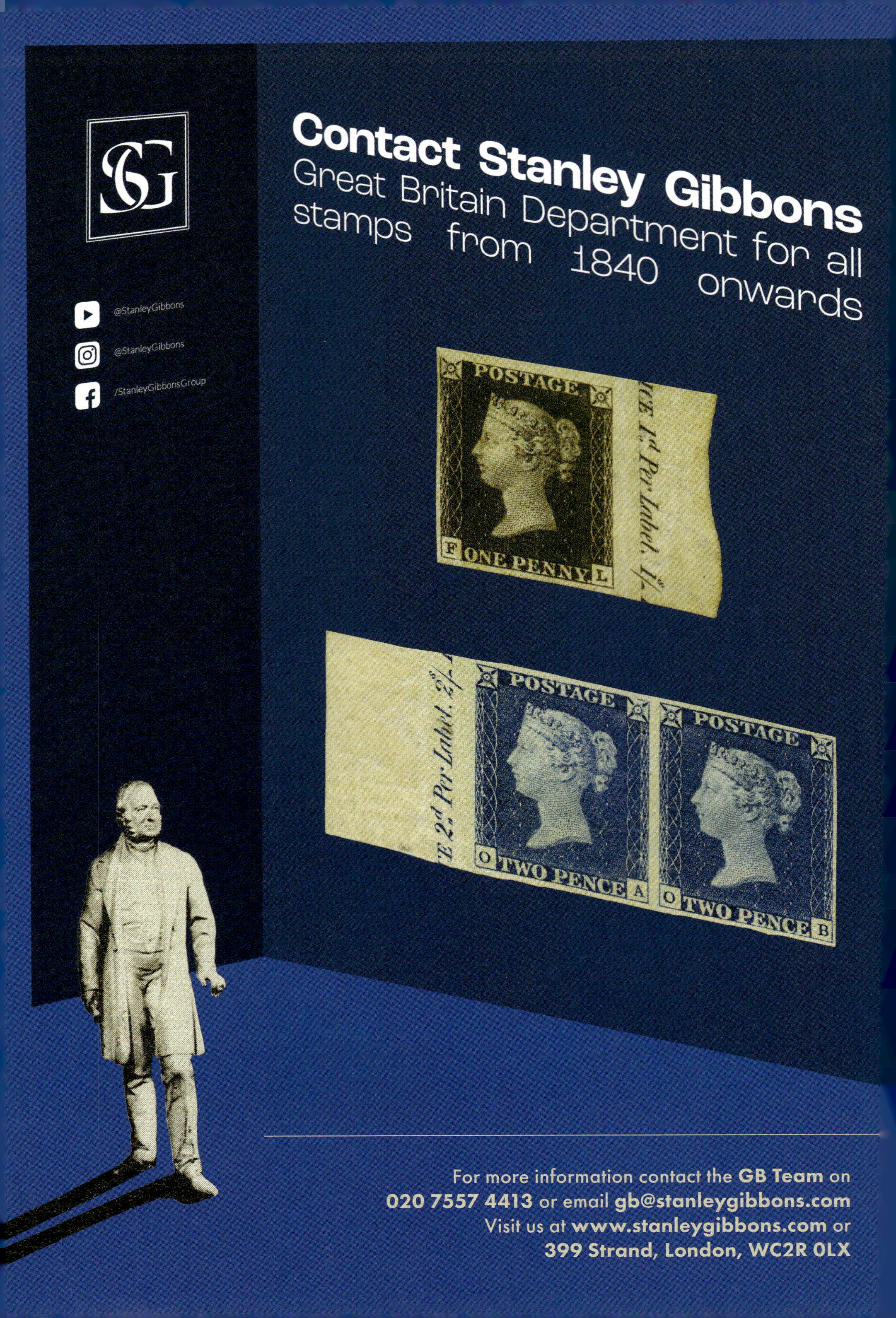

Contact Stanley Gibbons
Great Britain Department for all stamps from 1840 onwards

@StanleyGibbons
@StanleyGibbons
/StanleyGibbonsGroup

For more information contact the **GB Team** on
020 7557 4413 or email gb@stanleygibbons.com
Visit us at **www.stanleygibbons.com** or
399 Strand, London, WC2R 0LX

G Embassy Philatelists B

RETAIL LISTS & POSTAL AUCTIONS PRODUCED MONTHLY
CATALOGUE SENT FREE ON REQUEST
1000's OF ITEMS TO VIEW AND BUY ON OUR WEBSITE

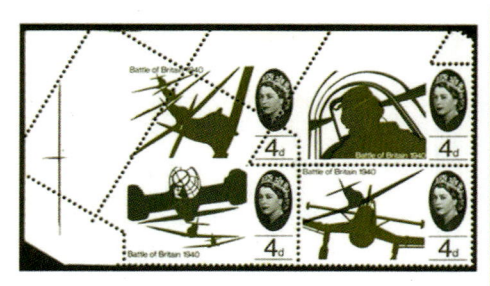

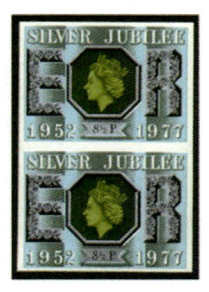

Embassy Philatelists

P.O. BOX 1553, GUILDFORD, GU1 9YT

Tel: 01483 811 168
Email: info@embassystamps.co.uk

www.embassystamps.co.uk

BUYING
From single items to major collections, for a fast professional transaction call us today.

BUYING
From single items to major collections, for a fast professional transaction call us today.

An Unrivalled Selection Of Modern British Errors

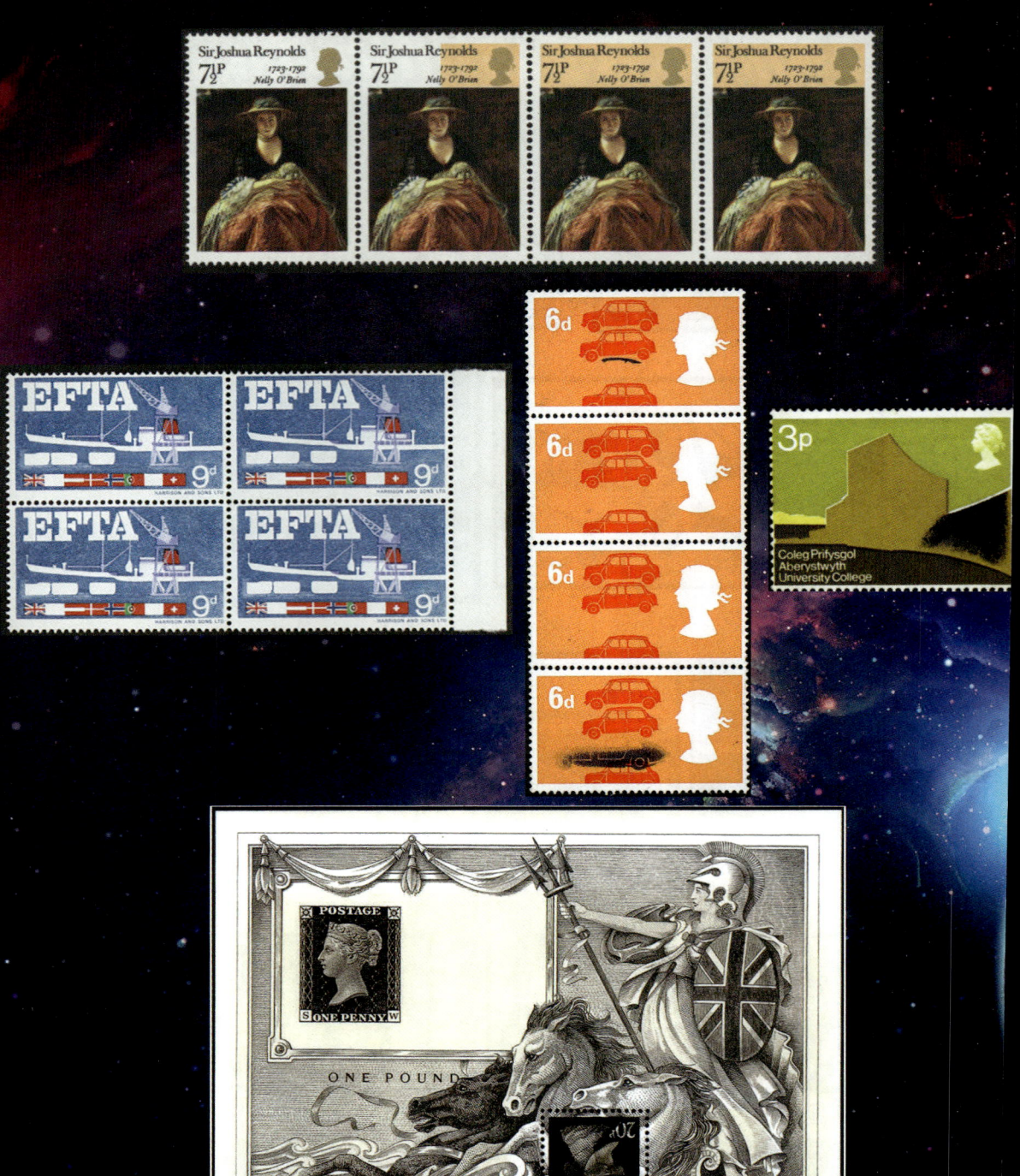

www.markbrandon.co.uk

Mark Brandon · PO Box 6382 · Milton Keynes · MK10 1EF ·
Telephone: 01908 915553 | mark@markbrandon.co.uk

Queen Elizabeth II

6 February 1952

Further detailed information on the stamps of Queen Elizabeth II will be found in Volumes 3, 4 and 5 of the Stanley Gibbons *Great Britain Specialised Catalogue*.

153 Tudor Crown **154**

155 **156** **157**

158 **159** **160**

Queen Elizabeth II and National Emblems

Extra white dot below 'd' at left (Cyl. 13 dot, R. 17/10)

Butterfly flaw (Cyl. 6 dot, R. 19/1)

I   II

Two types of the 2½d.

Type I: In the frontal cross of the diadem, the top line is only half the width of the cross.

Type II: The top line extends to the full width of the cross and there are signs of strengthening in other parts of the diadem.

(Des Enid Marx (T **154**), M. Farrar-Bell (Types **155**/**156**), G. Knipe (T **157**), Mary Adshead (T **158**), E. Dulac (Types **159**/**160**). Portrait by Dorothy Wilding)

1952–54. W **153**. Perf 15×14.

515	**154**	½d. orange-red (31.8.53)	25	15
		Wi. Watermark inverted (3.54)	2·00	2·00
		l. Booklet pane No. 515×6 (3.54)	4·00	
		lWi. Booklet pane No. 515Wi×6 (22.7.54)	4·00	
		m. Booklet pane No. 515×4 (22.7.54)	8·00	
		mWi. Booklet pane No. 515Wi×4 (22.7.54)	10·00	
		n. Booklet pane No. 515×2 (22.9.53)	5·00	
516		1d. ultramarine (31.8.53)	30	20
		Wi. Watermark inverted (3.54)	6·00	3·00
		l. Booklet pane No. 516×6 (3.54)	35·00	
		lWi. Booklet pane No. 516Wi×6 (3.54)	75·00	
		la. Booklet pane. No. 516×3 plus three printed labels	50·00	
		laWi. Booklet pane. No. 516Wi×3 plus three printed labels	50·00	
		m. Booklet pane No. 516×4 (22.7.54)	12·00	
		mWi. Booklet pane No. 516Wi×4 (22.7.54)	45·00	
		n. Booklet pane No. 516×2 (2.9.53)	5·00	
517		1½d. green (5.12.52)	25	20
		a. Watermark sideways (15.10.54)	1·25	1·25
		c. Extra dot	28·00	
		d. Butterfly flaw. Cyl. 6 dot (block of 6).	£800	
		Wi. Watermark inverted (5.53)	1·25	1·25
		l. Booklet pane No. 517×6 (5.53)	4·00	
		lWi. Booklet pane No. 517Wi×6 (5.53)	4·00	
		lbWi. Imperf pane*	12·00	
		m. Booklet pane No. 517×4 (22.7.54)	12·00	
		mWi. Booklet pane No. 517Wi×4 (22.7.54)	15·00	
		n. Booklet pane No. 517×2 (2.9.53)	9·00	
518		2d. red-brown (31.8.53)	30	20
		a. Watermark sideways (8.10.54)	2·00	2·00
		Wi. Watermark inverted (3.54)	30·00	22·00
		l. Booklet pane No. 518×6 (3.54)	60·00	
		lWi. Booklet pane No. 518Wi×6 (3.54)	£200	
519	**155**	2½d. carmine-red (Type I) (5.12.52)	30	15
		a. Watermark sideways (15.11.54)	12·00	12·00
		b. Type II (booklets) (5.53)	1·25	1·25
		bWi. Watermark inverted (5.53)	1·00	1·00
		l. Booklet pane No. 519b×6 (Type II) (5.53)	6·00	
		lWi. Booklet pane No. 519bWi×6 (Type II) (5.53)	4·50	
520		3d. deep lilac (18.1.54)	1·50	90
521	**156**	4d. ultramarine (2.11.53)	3·25	1·25
522	**157**	5d. brown (6.7.53)	1·00	3·50
523		6d. reddish purple (18.1.54)	4·00	1·00
		a. Imperf three sides (pair)	£3750	
524		7d. bright green (18.1.54)	9·50	5·50
525	**158**	8d. magenta (6.7.53)	1·25	85
526		9d. bronze-green (8.2.54)	23·00	4·75
527		10d. Prussian blue (8.2.54)	18·00	4·75
528		11d. brown-purple (8.2.54)	35·00	15·00
529	**159**	1s. bistre-brown (6.7.53)	80	50
530	**160**	1s.3d. green (2.11.53)	4·50	3·25
531	**159**	1s.6d. grey-blue (2.11.53)	14·00	3·75
Set of 17			£100	40·00

* BOOKLET ERRORS. This pane of six stamps is completely imperf.

Stamps with sideways watermark come from left-side delivery coils and stamps with inverted watermark are from booklets.

See also Nos. 540/556, 561/566, 570/594 and 599/618a. For stamps as Types **154**/**155** and **157**/**160** with face values in decimal currency see Nos. 2031/2033, 2258/2259, **MS**2326, **MS**2367, 2378/2379 and 3329.

First Day Covers

5.12.52	Nos. 517, 519	28·00
6.7.53	Nos. 522, 525, 526	60·00
31.8.53	Nos. 515/516, 518	60·00
2.11.53	Nos. 521, 530/531	£200
18.1.54	Nos. 520, 523/524	£125
8.2.54	Nos. 526/528	£250

161 **162**

163 **164**

(Des E. Fuller (2½d.), M. Goaman (4d.), E. Dulac (1s.3d.), M. Farrar-Bell (1s.6d.). Portrait (except 1s.3d.) by Dorothy Wilding)

1953 (3 June). Coronation. W **153**. Perf 15×14.

532	**161**	2½d. carmine-red	20	20
533	**162**	4d. ultramarine	80	40
534	**163**	1s.3d. deep yellow-green	3·00	1·00
535	**164**	1s.6d. deep grey-blue	6·50	2·00
Set of 4			10·00	3·50
First Day Cover				75·00

For a £1 value as T **163** see Nos. **MS**2147 and 2380.

QUEEN ELIZABETH II/1955

165 St Edward's Crown

166 Carrickfergus Castle

167 Caernarvon Castle

168 Edinburgh Castle

169 Windsor Castle

The paper of De La Rue printings is uniformly white, identical with that of Waterlow printings from February 1957 onwards, but earlier Waterlow printings are on paper which is creamy by comparison.

In this and later issues of Types **166/169** the dates of issue given for changes of watermark or paper are those on which supplies were first sent by the Supplies Department to Postmasters.

A used example of No. 538a has been reported with watermark inverted.

Two white dots extending upwards from shamrock at left appearing as rabbit's ears. Occurs in booklets in position 2 or 5 in pane of 6

Butterfly flaw (Cyl. 14 dot, R.19/1)

Butterfly flaw (Cyl. 15 dot, R. 19/1)

'Swan's head' flaw. Top of '2' is extended and curled. Occurs in booklets in positions 1 and 4 in pane of 6

(Des L. Lamb. Portrait by Dorothy Wilding. Eng Harold J. Bard and Benjamin Savinson (lettering). Recess Waterlow (until 31.12.57) and De La Rue (subsequently))

1955–58. W **165**. Perf 11×12.

536	**166**	2s.6d. black-brown (23.9.55)	15·00	2·00
		a. De La Rue printing (17.7.58)	30·00	2·50
		Wi. Watermark inverted	†	£3000
537	**167**	5s. rose-carmine (23.9.55)	40·00	4·00
		a. De La Rue printing. *Scarlet-vermilion* (30.4.58)	65·00	10·00
538	**168**	10s. ultramarine (1.9.55)	90·00	14·00
		a. De La Rue printing. *Dull ultramarine* (25.4.58)	£225	22·00
539	**169**	£1 black (1.9.55)	£140	35·00
		a. De La Rue printing (28.4.58)	£350	65·00
Set of 4 (Nos. 536/539)			£250	50·00
Set of 4 (Nos. 536a/539a)			£600	90·00
First day Cover (Nos. 538/539) (1.9.55)				£850
First Day Cover (Nos. 536/537) (23.9.55)				£650

See also Nos. 595/598a and 759/762.

For stamps inscribed in decimal currency see Nos. **MS**2530 and 3221.

On 1 January 1958, the contract for printing the high values, Types **166** to **169**, was transferred to De La Rue & Co, Ltd. The work of the two printers is very similar, but the following notes will be helpful to those attempting to identify Waterlow and De La Rue stamps of the W **165** issue.

The De La Rue sheets are printed in pairs and have a '-|' or '|-' shaped guide-mark at the centre of one side-margin, opposite the middle row of perforations, indicating left and right-hand sheets respectively.

The Waterlow sheets have a small circle (sometimes crossed) instead of a '|-' and this is present in both side-margins opposite the sixth row of stamps, though one is sometimes trimmed off. Short dashes are also present in the perforation gutter between the marginal stamps marking the middle of the four sides and a cross is at the centre of the sheet. The four corners of the sheet have two lines forming a right-angle as trimming marks, but some are usually trimmed off. All these gutter marks and sheet trimming marks are absent in the De La Rue printings. De La Rue used the Waterlow die and no alterations were made to it, so that no difference exists in the design or its size, but the making of new plates at first resulted in slight but measurable variations in the width of the gutters between stamps, particularly the horizontal, as follows:

	Waterlow	*De La Rue*
Horiz gutters, mm	3.8 to 4.0	3.4 to 3.8

Later De La Rue plates were however less distinguishable in this respect.

For a short time in 1959 the De La Rue 2s.6d. appeared with one dot in the bottom margin below the first stamp.

It is possible to sort singles with reasonable certainty by general characteristics. The individual lines of the De La Rue impression are cleaner and devoid of the whiskers of colour of Waterlow's, and the whole impression lighter and softer.

Owing to the closer setting of the horizontal rows the strokes of the perforating comb are closer; this results in the topmost tooth on each side of De La Rue stamps being narrower than the corresponding teeth in Waterlow's which were more than normally broad.

Shades also help. The 2s.6d. De La Rue is a warmer, more chocolate shade than the blackish brown of Waterlow; the 5s. a lighter red with less carmine than Waterlow's; the 10s. more blue and less ultramarine; the £1 less intense black.

1955–58. W **165**. Perf 15×14.

540	**154**	½d. orange-red (booklets 9.55, sheets 12.12.55)	20	15
		Wi. Watermark inverted (9.55)	45	40
		l. Booklet pane No. 540×6 (9.55)	2·50	
		lWi. Booklet pane No. 540Wi×6 (9.55)	4·00	
		lc. Part perf pane*	£4500	
		lcWi. Part perf pane*	£4500	
		m. Booklet pane No. 540×4 (5.7.56)	8·00	
		mWi. Booklet pane No. 540Wi×4 (5.7.56)	8·00	
		n. Booklet pane No. 540×2 (11.57)	25·00	
541		1d. ultramarine (19.9.55)	30	15
		b. *Tête-bêche* (horiz pair)		
		Wi. Watermark inverted (9.55)	65	60
		l. Booklet pane No. 541×6 (8.55)	5·00	
		lWi. Booklet pane No. 541Wi×6 (8.55)	5·00	
		la. Booklet pane. No. 541×3 plus three printed labels	18·00	
		laWi. Booklet pane. No. 541Wi×3 plus three printed labels	18·00	
		m. Booklet pane No. 541×4 (5.7.56)	10·00	
		mWi. Booklet pane No. 541Wi×4 (5.7.56)	10·00	
		n. Booklet pane No. 541×2 (11.57)	25·00	
542		1½d. green (booklet 8.55, sheets 11.10.55)	25	30
		a. Watermark sideways (7.3.56)	35	70
		b. *Tête-bêche* (horiz pair)	—	
		c. Extra dot	28·00	
		d. Rabbit's ears	42·00	
		e. Butterfly flaw (Cyl. 14 dot) block of 6	90·00	
		f. Butterfly flaw (Cyl. 15 dot) block of 6	75·00	
		Wi. Watermark inverted (8.55)	75	70
		l. Booklet pane No. 542×6 (8.55)	3·50	
		lWi. Booklet pane No. 542Wi×6 (8.55)	5·00	
		m. Booklet pane No. 542×4 (5.7.56)	12·00	
		mWi. Booklet pane No. 542Wi×4 (5.7.56)	12·00	
		n. Booklet pane No. 542×2 (11.57)	30·00	
543		2d. red-brown (6.9.55)	25	35
		aa. Imperf between (vert pair)	£4750	
		a. Watermark sideways (31.7.56)	55	70
		ab. Imperf between (horiz pair)	£4750	
		Wi. Watermark inverted (9.55)	11·00	9·00
		l. Booklet pane No. 543×6 (9.55)	30·00	
		lWi. Booklet pane No. 543Wi×6 (9.55)	90·00	
543b		2d. light red-brown (17.10.56)	30	20
		ba. *Tête-bêche* (horiz pair)	£3250	
		bWi. Watermark inverted (1.57)	9·00	7·00
		d. Watermark sideways (5.3.57)	8·00	7·00
		bl. Booklet pane No. 543b×6 (1.57)	15·00	
		blb. Imperf pane*	£5000	
		blc. Part perf pane*	£5000	
		blWi. Booklet pane No. 543bWi×6 (1.57)	40·00	
		blbWi. Imperf pane*		

1955/QUEEN ELIZABETH II

544	155	2½d. carmine-red (Type I) (28.9.55)..........	30	25
		a. Watermark sideways (Type I) (23.3.56)...	1·50	1·75
		b. Type II (booklets 9.55, sheets 1957)..	45	45
		ba. Tête-bêche (horiz pair)......................	£3250	
		bd. Swan's head flaw..............................	95·00	
		bWi. Watermark inverted (9.55)...............	55	70
		bl. Booklet pane No. 544b×6 (Type II) (9.55)...	3·50	
		blb. Imperf pane*.....................................	£5000	
		blc. Part perf pane*.................................	£4250	
		blWi. Booklet pane No. 544bWi×6 (Type II) (9.55)..	3·50	
		blbWi. Imperf pane*.................................	£5000	
		blcWi. Part perf pane*.............................	£4250	
545		3d. deep lilac (17.7.56)...........................	40	25
		aa. Tête-bêche (horiz pair)......................	£3000	
		a. Imperf three sides (pair)....................	£2750	
		b. Watermark sideways (22.11.57).......	18·00	17·00
		Wi. Watermark inverted (1.10.57)..........	1·25	1·25
		l. Booklet pane No. 545×6 (1.10.57)..	5·00	
		lWi. Booklet pane No. 545Wi×6 (1.10.57)..	10·00	
		m. Booklet pane No. 545×4 (22.4.59)..	60·00	
		mWi. Booklet pane No. 545Wi×4 (22.4.59)..	75·00	
546	156	4d. ultramarine (14.11.55).....................	1·25	45
547	157	5d. brown (21.9.55).................................	6·00	6·00
548		6d. reddish purple (20.12.55).................	4·50	1·25
		aa. Imperf three sides (pair)....................	£5250	
		a. Deep claret (8.5.58)...........................	4·50	1·40
		ab. Imperf three sides (pair)....................	£5250	
549		7d. bright green (23.4.56).......................	50·00	10·00
550	158	8d. magenta (21.12.55)..........................	7·00	1·25
551		9d. bronze-green (15.12.55)..................	20·00	2·75
552		10d. Prussian blue (22.9.55)....................	20·00	2·75
553		11d. brown-purple (28.10.55)..................	1·00	1·10
554	159	1s. bistre-brown (3.11.55).....................	22·00	65
555	160	1s.3d. green (27.3.56)...............................	30·00	1·60
556	159	1s.6d. grey-blue (27.3.56)........................	23·00	1·60
Set of 18		....	£160	27·00

* BOOKLET ERRORS. Those listed as imperf panes show one row of perforations either at top or bottom of the booklet pane; those as part perf panes have one row of three stamps imperf on three sides.

The dates given for Nos. 540/556 are those on which they were first issued by the Supplies Department to postmasters.

In December 1956 a completely imperforate sheet of No. 543b was noticed by clerks in a Kent post office, one of whom purchased it against PO regulations. In view of this irregularity we do not consider it properly issued.

Types of 2½d. In this issue, in 1957, Type II formerly only found in stamps from booklets, began to replace Type I on sheet stamps.

170 Scout Badge and 'Rolling Hitch

171 Scouts coming to Britain

172 Globe within a Compass

(Des Mary Adshead (2½d.), P. Keely (4d.), W. H. Brown (1s.3d.))

1957 (1 Aug). World Scout Jubilee Jamboree. W **165**. Perf 15×14.

557	170	2½d. carmine-red..	20	20
558	171	4d. ultramarine...	50	50
559	172	1s.3d. green..	3·00	2·00
Set of 3		....	3·50	2·50
First Day Cover		....		25·00

173

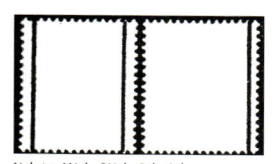

½d. to 1½d., 2½d., 3d., 2d.

Graphite line arrangements (Stamps viewed from back)

(Adapted F. Langfield)

1957 (12 Sep). 46th Inter-Parliamentary Union Conference. W **165**. Perf 15×14.

560	173	4d. ultramarine...	40	40
First Day Cover		....		£150

GRAPHITE-LINED ISSUES. These were used in connection with automatic sorting machinery, first introduced experimentally at Southampton in December 1957.

The graphite lines were printed in black on the back, beneath the gum; two lines per stamp, except for the 2d.

In November 1959 phosphor bands were introduced (see notes after No. 598).

Extra stop before '1d.' at right. Occurs in sideways delivery coils (Roll No. 2). This was retouched on No. 571.

Stop below 'd' at left missing. Occurs on sideways delivery coils (Roll No. 3). The dot was added for No. 571.

1957 (19 Nov). Graphite-lined issue. Two graphite lines on the back, except 2d. value, which has one line. W **165**. Perf 15×14.

561	154	½d. orange-red...	50	40
562		1d. ultramarine...	70	60
		a. Extra stop...	40·00	
		b. Stop omitted......................................	40·00	
563		1½d. green...	2·00	1·75
		a. Both lines at left................................	£1600	£600
564		2d. light red-brown..................................	2·50	2·50
		a. Line at left..	£700	£250
565	155	2½d. carmine-red (Type II).........................	8·50	7·00
566		3d. deep lilac...	1·40	1·25
Set of 6		....	14·00	12·00
First Day Cover		....		90·00

No. 564a results from a misplacement of the line and horizontal pairs exist showing one stamp without line. No. 563a results from a similar misplacement.

See also Nos. 587/594.

176 Welsh Dragon

177 Flag and Games Emblem

178 Welsh Dragon

QUEEN ELIZABETH II/1958

Short scale (Cyl. 2 Dot, R. 1/1)   Shoulder flaw (Cyl. 2 Dot, R. 12/2)

(Des R. Stone (3d.), W. H. Brown (6d.), P. Keely (1s.3d.))

1958 (18 July). Sixth British Empire and Commonwealth Games, Cardiff. W **165**. Perf 15×14.

567	**176**	3d. deep lilac	10	10
		a. Short scale	40·00	
		d. Shoulder flaw	40·00	
568	**177**	6d. reddish purple	30	30
569	**178**	1s.3d. green	1·00	1·00
Set of 3			1·20	1·20
First Day Cover				75·00

179 Multiple Crowns

'd' at right joined to shamrock by white line. Occurs on vertical delivery coils (Roll No. 11)

1958–65. W **179**. Perf 15×14.

570	**154**	½d. orange-red (25.11.58)	10	10
		a. Watermark sideways (26.5.61)	75	75
		d. 'd' joined to shamrock	30·00	
		Wi. Watermark inverted (11.58)	1·50	1·50
		k. Chalk-surfaced paper (15.7.63)	2·50	2·75
		kWi. Watermark inverted	2·75	3·00
		l. Booklet pane No. 570×6 (11.58)	5·50	
		lc. Part perf pane*	£4000	
		lWi. Booklet pane No. 570Wi×6 (11.58)	5·50	
		m. Booklet pane No. 570×4 (13.8.59)	6·00	
		mWi. Booklet pane No. 570Wi×4 (13.8.59)	6·00	
		mb. Booklet pane No. 570b×4	10·00	
		mk. Booklet pane. No. 570k×3 se-tenant with 574k	9·00	
		mkWi. Booklet pane No. 570kWi×3 se-tenant with No. 574Wi (15.7.63)	9·00	
		mn. Booklet pane. No. 570a×2 se-tenant with 574g×2 (1.7.64)	2·25	
571		1d. ultramarine (booklets 11.58, sheets 24.3.59)	10	10
		aa. Imperf (vert pair from coil)	£4500	
		a. Watermark sideways (26.5.61)	1·50	1·50
		d. Tête-bêche (horiz pair)	£2750	
		Wi. Watermark inverted (11.58)	50	50
		l. Booklet pane No. 571×6 (11.58)	7·00	
		lb. Imperf pane*	£6000	
		lc. Part perf pane*	£4500	
		lWi. Booklet pane No. 571Wi×6 (11.58)	8·00	
		lbWi. Imperf pane*	£6000	
		m. Booklet pane No. 571×4 (13.8.59)	8·00	
		mWi. Booklet pane No. 571Wi×4 (13.8.59)	8·00	
		mb. Booklet pane. No. 571a×4	12·00	
		mn. Booklet pane. No. 571a×2 se-tenant with 575a×2 (1d. values at left) (16.8.65)	12·00	
		mna. Booklet pane. 1d. values at right	13·00	
572		1½d. green (booklets 12.58, sheets 30.8.60)	10	15
		b. Watermark sideways (26.5.61)	9·00	9·00
		c. Tête-bêche (horiz pair)	£2750	
		Wi. Watermark inverted (11.58)	1·50	1·25
		l. Booklet pane No. 572×6 (12.58)	10·00	
		lc. Part perf pane*	£6500	
		lWi. Booklet pane No. 572Wi×6 (12.58)	12·00	
		m. Booklet pane No. 572×4 (13.8.59)	10·00	
		mWi. Booklet pane No. 572Wi×4 (13.8.59)	12·00	
		mb. Booklet pane. No. 572b×4	35·00	
573		2d. light red-brown (4.12.58)	10	10
		a. Watermark sideways (3.4.59)	1·00	1·00
		Wi. Watermark inverted (10.4.61)	£140	70·00
		l. Booklet pane No. 573×6 (10.4.61)	£100	
		lWi. Booklet pane No. 573Wi×6 (10.4.61)	£900	
574	**155**	2½d. carmine-red (Type II) (booklets 11.58, sheets 15.9.59)	10	20
		b. Tête-bêche (horiz pair)	—	
		d. Swan's head flaw	£100	
		Wi. Watermark inverted (Type II) (11.58)	4·50	3·00
		e. Watermark sideways (Type I) (10.11.60)	40	60
		ea. Imperf strip of 6	—	
		f. Type I (wmk upright) (4.10.61)	70	70
		g. Watermark sideways (Type II) (1.7.64)	70	1·25
		k. Chalk-surfaced paper (Type II) (15.7.63)	50	80
		kWi. Do. Watermark inverted (15.7.63)	75	1·25
		l. Booklet pane No. 574×6 (Type II) (11.58)	17·00	
		lb. Imperf pane*		
		lc. Part perf pane*	£4000	
		lWi. Booklet pane No. 574Wi×6 (Type II) (11.58)		
		mk. Booklet pane No. 574k×4 (Type II) (15.7.63)	2·00	
		mkWi. Booklet pane No. 574kWi×4 (Type II) (15.7.63)	2·00	
575		3d. deep lilac (booklets 11.58, sheets 8.12.58)	20	15
		a. Watermark sideways (24.10.58)	50	55
		d. Phantom 'R' (Cyl 41 no dot)	£375	
		da. Do. First retouch	30·00	
		db. Do. Second retouch	30·00	
		e. Phantom 'R' (Cyl 37 no dot)	55·00	
		ea. Do. Retouch	20·00	
		Wi. Watermark inverted (11.58)	50	55
		l. Booklet pane No. 575×6 (11.58)	3·50	
		lb. Imperf pane*	£4250	
		lc. Part perf pane*	£4000	
		lWi. Booklet pane No. 575Wi×6 (11.58)	4·00	
		lcWi. Part per pane*	£4000	
		m. Booklet pane No. 575×4 (2.11.60)	25·00	
		mWi. Booklet pane No. 575Wi×4 (2.11.60)	25·00	
		mb. Booklet pane. No. 575a×4 (26.5.61)	5·00	
576	**156**	4d. ultramarine (29.10.58)	45	35
		a. Deep ultramarine†† (28.4.65)	15	15
		ab. Watermark sideways (31.5.65)	70	55
		ae. Double impression	—	
		al. Booklet pane No. 576×6 (21.6.65)	6·00	
		alb. Imperf pane*	£5000	
		alc. Part perf pane*	£4500	
		aWi. Watermark inverted (21.6.65)	60	75
		alWi. Booklet pane No. 576aWi×4 (21.6.65)	12·00	
		am. Booklet pane. No. 576ab×4 (16.8.65)	7·00	
577		4½d. chestnut (9.2.59)	10	25
		a. Phantom frame	£100	
578	**157**	5d. brown (10.11.58)	30	40
579		6d. deep claret (23.12.58)	30	25
		a. Imperf three sides (pair)	£4000	
		b. Imperf (pair)	£4500	
580		7d. bright green (26.11.58)	50	45
581	**158**	8d. magenta (24.2.60)	60	40
582		9d. bronze-green (24.3.59)	60	40
583		10d. Prussian blue (18.11.58)	1·00	50
584	**159**	1s. bistre-brown (30.10.58)	75	30
585	**160**	1s.3d. green (17.6.59)	75	30
586	**159**	1s.6d. grey-blue (16.12.58)	5·00	40
Set of 17 (one of each value)			9·00	4·25
First Day Cover (No. 577) (9.2.59)				£250
Presentation Pack**			£275	

*   BOOKLET ERROR. See note after No. 556.
** This was issued in 1960 and comprises Nos. 542, 553, 570/571 and 573/586. It exists in two forms: (a) inscribed '10s6d' for sale in the UK and (b) inscribed '$1.80' for sale in the USA.
†† This 'shade' was brought about by making more deeply etched cylinders, resulting in apparent depth of colour in parts of the design. There is no difference in the colour of the ink.

Sideways watermark. The 2d., 2½d., 3d. and 4d. come from coils and the ½d., 1d., 1½d., 2½d., 3d. and 4d. come from booklets. In coil stamps the sideways watermark shows the top of the watermark to the left *as seen from the front of the stamp*. In the booklet stamps it comes equally to the left or right.

Nos. 570k and 574k only come from 2s. Holiday Resort experimental undated booklets issued in 1963, in which one page contained 1×2½d. se-tenant with 3×½d. (See No. 570mk).

No. 574l comes from coils, and the Holiday Resort experimental booklets dated 1964 comprising four panes each containing two of these 2½d. stamps se-tenant vertically with two ½d. No. 570a. (See No. 570mn).

No. 574b comes from a booklet.
No. 574d is from a booklet with watermark upright.
Nos. 574e and 574ea come from sideways delivery coils
No. 574f comes from sheets bearing cylinder number 42 and vertical delivery coils.

In 1964 No. 575 was printed from cylinder number 70 no dot and dot on an experimental paper which is distinguishable by an additional watermark letter 'T' lying on its side, which occurs about four times in the sheet, usually in the side margins, 48,000 sheets were issued.

No. 575 is known imperforate and tête-bêche. These came from booklet sheets which were not issued *(price £70 per pair)*.

1958/QUEEN ELIZABETH II

Phantom 'R' varieties

Nos. 575d and 615aa (Cyl 41 no dot)

No. 575da

No. 575e (Cyl 37 no dot)

Phantom Frame variety Nos. 577a and 616ba

3d. An incomplete marginal rule revealed an 'R' on cyls 37 and 41 no dot below R. 20/12. It is more noticeable on cyl 41 because of the wider marginal rule. The 'R' on cyl 41 was twice retouched, the first being as illustrated here (No. 575da) and traces of the 'R' can still be seen in the second retouch.

No. 575d is best collected in a block of four or six with full margins in order to be sure that it is not 615a with phosphor lines removed.

The retouch on cyl 37 (575ea) is not easily identified: there is no trace of the 'R' but the general appearance of that part of the marginal rule is uneven.

4½d. An incomplete marginal rule revealed a right-angled shape frame line on cyl. 8 no dot below R. 20/12. It occurs on ordinary and phosphor.

DOLLIS HILL TRIAL STAMPS. From 1957 to 1972 trials were carried out at the Post Office Research Station, Dollis Hill, London, to determine the most efficient method of applying phosphor to stamps in connection with automatic letter sorting. Stamps were frequently applied to 'live' mail to test sorting machinery.

The 2d. light red-brown and 3d. deep lilac stamps from these trials exist on unwatermarked paper, prices from £300 (2d.), £350 (3d.), mint or used.

WHITER PAPER. On 18 May 1962 the Post Office announced that a whiter paper was being used for the current issue (including Nos. 595/598). This is beyond the scope of this catalogue, but the whiter papers are listed in Vol. 3 of the *Stanley Gibbons Great Britain Specialised Catalogue*.

1958 (24 Nov)–61. Graphite-lined issue. Two graphite lines on the back, except 2d. value, which has one line. W **179**. Perf 15×14.

587	154	½d. orange-red (15.6.59)	9·00	9·00
		Wi. Watermark inverted (4.8.59)	3·25	4·00
		l. Booklet pane No. 587×6 (4.8.59)	65·00	
		lWi. Booklet pane No. 587Wi×6 (4.8.59)	25·00	
588		1d. ultramarine (18.12.58)	2·00	1·50
		a. Misplaced graphite lines (7.61)*	80	1·25
		b. Three graphite lines	65·00	60·00
		Wi. Watermark inverted (4.8.59)	1·50	2·00
		l. Booklet pane No. 588×6 (4.8.59)	30·00	
		lWi. Booklet pane No. 588Wi×6 (4.8.59)	20·00	
589		1½d. green (4.8.59)	90·00	80·00
		Wi. Watermark inverted (4.8.59)	75·00	60·00
		l. Booklet pane No. 589×6 (4.8.59)	£500	
		lWi. Booklet pane No. 589Wi×6 (4.8.59)	£250	
590		2d. light red-brown (24.11.58)	10·00	3·50
		a. One line at exteme left as seen from back	£1250	
591	155	2½d. carmine-red (Type II) (9.6.59)	12·00	10·00
		Wi. Watermark inverted (4.8.59)	65·00	50·00
		l. Booklet pane No. 591×6 (Type II) (21.8.59)	£120	
		lWi. Booklet pane No. 591Wi×6 (Type II) (21.8.59)	£400	
592		3d. deep lilac (24.11.58)	90	65
		a. Misplaced graphite lines (5.61)*	£550	£425
		b. One graphite line	£2500	£2500
		c. Three graphite lines*	£150	£120
		Wi. Watermark inverted (4.8.59)	1·00	1·25
		l. Booklet pane No. 592×6 (4.8.59)	6·00	
		lWi. Booklet pane No. 592Wi×6 (4.8.59)	7·00	
593	156	4d. ultramarine (29.4.59)	5·50	5·00
		a. Misplaced graphite lines (1961)*	£2400	
594		4½d. chestnut (3.6.59)	6·50	5·00
Set of 8 (cheapest)			£110	70·00

* No. 588a (in coils), and Nos. 592a/592c and 593a (all in sheets) result from the use of a residual stock of graphite-lined paper. As the use of graphite lines had ceased, the register of the lines in relation to the stamps was of no importance and numerous misplacements occurred – two lines close together, one line only, etc. No. 588a refers to two lines at left or right; No. 592a refers to stamps with two lines only at left and both clear of the perforations No. 592b refers to stamps with a single line and Nos. 588b, 592c and 593a to stamps with two lines at left (with left line down perforations) and traces of a third line down the opposite perforations.

Nos. 587/589 were only issued in booklets or coils.

No. 592Wi was included in 4s.6d. booklets, Nos. L15 and L16, dated April and June 1959. These represent production dates not issue dates.

166 Carrickfergus Castle

167 Caernarvon Castle

168 Edinburgh Castle

169 Windsor Castle

(Recess D.L.R. (until 31.12.62), then B.W.)

1959–68. W **179**. Perf 11×12.

595	166	2s.6d. black-brown (22.7.59)	10·00	75
		Wi. Watermark inverted	—	£3250
		a. B.W. printing (1.7.63)	35	40
		aWi. Watermark inverted	£3250	£280
		k. Chalk-surfaced paper (30.5.68)	50	1·50
596	167	5s. scarlet-vermilion (15.6.59)	45·00	2·00
		Wi. Watermark inverted	£9000	£600
		a. B.W. ptg. *Red* (shades) (3.9.63)	1·25	50
		ab. Printed on the gummed side	£1600	
		aWi. Watermark inverted	£400	£300
597	168	10s. blue (21.7.59)	55·00	5·00
		a. B.W. ptg. Bright ultramarine (16.10.63)	4·50	4·50
		aWi. Watermark inverted	—	£3250
598	169	£1 black (30.6.59)	£120	12·00
		Wi. Watermark inverted	—	£3000
		a. B.W. printing (14.11.63)	13·00	8·00
		aWi. Watermark inverted	£15000	£3750
		k. Chalk-surfaced paper	£5250	
Set of 4 (Nos. 595/598)			£195	17·00
Set of 4 (Nos. 595a/598a)			15·00	11·00
Presentation Pack (1960)* from			£1400	

* This exists in three forms: (a) inscribed '$6.50' for sale in the USA; (b) without price for sale in the UK; inscribed '£1 18s' for sale in the UK.

The B.W. printings have a marginal Plate Number. They are generally more deeply engraved than the D.L.R. showing more of the Diadem detail and heavier lines on Her Majesty's face. The vertical perf is 11.9 to 12 against D.L.R. 11.8.

See also Nos. 759/762.

PHOSPHOR BAND ISSUES. These are printed on the front and are wider than graphite lines. They are not easy to see but show as broad vertical bands at certain angles to the light.

Values representing the rate for printed papers (and when this was abolished in 1968 for second class mail) have one band and others two, three or four bands as stated, according to the size and format.

In the small size stamps the bands are on each side with the single band at left *(except where otherwise stated)*. In the large size commemorative stamps the single band may be at left, centre or right, varying in different designs. The bands are vertical on both horizontal and vertical designs *except where otherwise stated*.

The phosphor was originally applied by letterpress but later usually by photogravure and sometimes using flexography, a relief printing process using rubber cylinders.

Three different types of phosphor have been used, distinguishable by the colour emitted under an ultraviolet lamp, the first being green, then blue and then violet. Different sized bands are also known. All these are fully listed in Vol. 3 of the Stanley Gibbons *Great Britain Specialised Catalogue*.

QUEEN ELIZABETH II/1959

Varieties. Misplaced and missing phosphor bands are known but such varieties are beyond the scope of this Catalogue.

1959 (18 Nov). Phosphor-Graphite issue. Two phosphor bands on front and two graphite lines on back, except 2d. value, which has one band on front and one line on back.

(a) W 165. Perf 15×14.

599	154	½d. orange-red	4·25	4·25
600		1d. ultramarine	11·00	11·00
601		1½d. green	4·50	4·50

(b) W 179.

605	154	2d. light red-brown (1 band)	6·00	4·25
		a. Error. W 165	£200	£175
606	155	2½d. carmine-red (Type II)	22·00	18·00
607		3d. deep lilac	12·00	8·00
608	156	4d. ultramarine	20·00	16·00
609		4½d. chestnut	30·00	20·00
Set of 8			£100	80·00
Presentation Pack			£300	

Examples of the 2½d., No. 606, exist showing watermark W **165**, but this was not officially issued.

The Presentation Pack was issued in 1960 and comprises two each of Nos. 599/609. It exists in two forms: (a) inscribed '3s 8d' for sale in the UK and (b) inscribed '50c' for sale in the USA.

1960 (22 June)–**67**. Phosphor issue. Two phosphor bands on front, except where otherwise stated. W **179**. Perf 15×14.

610	154	½d. orange-red	10	15
		a. Watermark sideways (14.7.61)	15·00	15·00
		b. 'd' joined to shamrock	25·00	
		Wi. Watermark inverted (14.8.60)	1·50	1·50
		l. Booklet pane. No. 610×6 (14.8.60)	7·00	
		lWi. Booklet pane No. 610Wi×6 (14.8.60)	10·00	
		ma. Booklet pane. No. 610a×4	45·00	
611		1d. ultramarine	10	10
		a. Watermark sideways (14.7.61)	1·10	1·10
		Wi. Watermark inverted (14.8.60)	65	65
		l. Booklet pane. No. 611a×4	10·00	
		lWi. Booklet pane No. 611Wi×6 (14.8.60)	7·00	
		mb. Booklet pane. No. 611a×4 (14.7.61)	18·00	
		mm. Booklet pane. No. 611a×2 se-tenant with 615d×2†† (16.8.65)	18·00	
		mma. Booklet pane. No. 611a×2 se-tenant with 615da×2 (16.8.65)	18·00	
		mn. Booklet pane. No. 611a×2 se-tenant with 615b×2†† (11.67)	10·00	
		mna. Ditto. 1d. values at right	10·00	
612		1½d. green	15	15
		a. Watermark sideways (14.7.61)	20·00	20·00
		Wi. Watermark inverted (14.8.60)	25·00	22·00
		l. Booklet pane. No. 612×6 (14.8.60)	55·00	
		lWi. Booklet pane No. 612Wi×6 (14.8.60)	£150	
		mb. Booklet pane. No. 612a×4	80·00	
613		2d. light red-brown (1 band)	22·00	22·00
613a		2d. light red-brown (2 bands) (4.10.61)	10	15
		aa. Imperf three sides*** (pair)	£4500	
		ab. Watermark sideways (6.4.67)	1·00	1·00
614	155	2½d. carmine-red (Type II) (2 bands)**	40	30
		Wi. Watermark inverted (14.8.60)	£175	£175
		l. Booklet pane No. 614×6 (Type II) (14.8.60)	£120	
		lWi. Booklet pane No. 614Wi×6 (Type II) (14.8.60)	£1200	
614a		2½d. carmine-red (Type II) (1 band) (4.10.61)	60	75
		aWi. Watermark inverted (3.62)	50·00	42·00
		al. Booklet pane No. 614a×6 (Type II) (3.62)	£110	
		alWi. Booklet pane No. 614aWi×6 (Type II) (3.62)	£300	
614b		2½d. carmine-red (Type I) (1 band) (4.10.61)	45·00	40·00
615		3d. deep lilac (2 bands)	60	55
		aa. Phantom 'R' (Cyl 41 no dot)	55·00	
		Wi. Watermark inverted (14.8.60)	50	90
		a. Imperf three sides (horiz pair)	£2000	
		b. Watermark sideways (14.7.61)	1·75	1·75
		l. Booklet pane No. 615×6 (14.8.60)	8·00	
		lWi. Booklet pane No. 615Wi×6 (14.8.60)	8·00	
		bm. Booklet pane. No. 615b×4	30·00	
615c		3d. deep lilac (1 band at right) (29.4.65)	60	55
		ca. Band at left	60	70
		cWi. Watermark inverted (band at right) (2.67)	8·00	7·00
		cWia. Watermark inverted (band at left) (2.67)	80·00	80·00
		cl. Booklet pane No. 615c×4 and No. 615ca×2 (2.67)	35·00	
		clWi. Booklet pane No. 615cWi×4 and No. 615caWi×2 (2.67)	£120	
		d. Watermark sideways (band at right) (16.8.65)	5·50	5·00
		da. Watermark sideways (band at left)	5·50	5·00
		e. One centre band (8.12.66)	40	45
		eWi. Watermark inverted (8.67)	4·00	4·00
		ea. Wmk sideways (19.6.67)	1·00	1·00
		el. Booklet pane No. 615ce×6 (8.67)	7·00	
		elWi. Booklet pane No. 615ceWi×6 (8.67)	24·00	
		em. Booklet pane. No. 615ea×4	30·00	
616	156	4d. ultramarine	3·50	3·50
		a. Deep ultramarine (28.4.65)	25	25
		ab. Wmk sideways	1·10	1·10
		aWi. Watermark inverted (21.6.65)	75	75
		al. Booklet pane No. 616a×6 (21.6.65)	3·50	
		alc. Part perf pane*	£4750	
		alWi. Booklet pane No. 616aWi×6 (21.6.65)	3·50	
		alcWi. Part perf pane*	£4750	
		am. Booklet pane. No. 616ab×4	15·00	
616b		4½d. chestnut (13.9.61)	55	30
		ba. Phantom frame	£100	
616c	157	5d. brown (9.6.67)	55	35
617		6d. purple	55	30
617a		7d. bright green (15.2.67)	70	50
617b	158	8d. magenta (28.6.67)	70	55
617c		9d. bronze-green (29.12.66)	70	65
617d		10d. Prussian blue (30.12.66)	1·00	1·00
617e	159	1s. bistre-brown (28.6.67)	1·00	35
618	160	1s.3d. green	1·90	2·50
618a	159	1s.6d. grey-blue (12.12.66)	2·00	2·00
Set of 17 (one of each value)			10·50	8·00

** No. 614 with two bands on the creamy paper was originally from cylinder 50 dot and no dot. When the change in postal rates took place in 1965 it was re-issued from cylinder 57 dot and no dot on the whiter paper. Some of these latter were also released in error in districts of South-east London in September 1964. The shade of the re-issue is slightly more carmine.

***No. 613aa comes from the bottom row of a sheet which is imperf at bottom and both sides.

† Booklet pane No. 611mm shows the 1d. stamps at left and No. 611mna the 1d. stamps at right.

†† Booklet pane No. 611mn comes from 2s. booklets of January and March 1968. The two bands on the 3d. stamp were intentional because of the technical difficulties in producing one band and two band stamps se-tenant.

The automatic facing equipment was brought into use on 6 July 1960 but the phosphor stamps may have been released a few days earlier.

The stamps with watermark sideways are from booklets except Nos. 613ab and 615cea which are from coils. No. 616ab comes from both booklets and coils.

The Phosphor-Graphite stamps had the phosphor applied by letterpress but the Phosphor issue can be divided into those with the phosphor applied letterpress and others where it was applied by photogravure. Moreover the photogravure form can be further divided into those which phosphoresce green, blue or violet under ultraviolet light, All these are fully listed in Volume 3 of the Stanley Gibbons *Great Britain Specialised Catalogue*.

No. 615aa (Phantom 'R'), see illustration and footnote following No. 586.

Unlike previous one-banded phosphor stamps, No. 615c has a broad band extending over two stamps so that alternate stamps have the band at left or right (*same prices either way*). No. 615cWi comes from the 10s. phosphor booklet of February 1967 and No. 615ceWi comes from the 10s. phosphor booklets of August 1967 and February 1968.

180 Postboy of 1660   **181** Posthorn of 1660

Broken mane (Cyl. 1 No dot, R. 17/2)

(Des R. Stone (3d.), Faith Jaques (1s.3d.))

1960 (7 July). Tercentenary of Establishment of General Letter Office. W **179** (sideways on 1s.3d.). Perf 15×14 (3d.) or 14×15 (1s.3d.).

619	180	3d. deep lilac	20	20
		a. Broken mane	70·00	
620	181	1s.3d. green	1·60	1·75
Set of 2			1·60	1·75
First Day Cover				50·00

1960/QUEEN ELIZABETH II

182 Conference Emblem  **182a** Conference Emblem

(Des R. Stone (emblem, P. Rahikainen))

1960 (19 Sep). First Anniversary of European Postal and Telecommunications Conference. Chalk-surfaced paper. W **179**. Perf 15×14.

621	**182**	6d. bronze-green and purple	1·00	20
622	**182a**	1s.6d. brown and blue	5·50	2·25
Set of 2			6·00	2·25
First Day Cover				50·00

SCREENS. Up to this point all photogravure stamps were printed in a 200 screen (200 dots per linear inch), but all later commemorative stamps are a finer 250 screen. Exceptionally No. 622 has a 200 screen for the portrait and a 250 screen for the background.

183 Thrift Plant   **184** 'Growth of Savings'

185 Thrift Plant

(Des P. Gauld (2½d.), M. Goaman (others))

1961 (28 Aug). Centenary of Post Office Savings Bank. Chalk-surfaced paper. W **179** (sideways on 2½d.) Perf 14×15 (2½d.) or 15×14 (others).

623A	**183**	2½d. black and red	10	10
		a. Black omitted	—	
624A	**184**	3d. orange-brown and violet	10	10
		a. Orange-brown omitted	£500	
		b. Perf through side sheet margin	35·00	38·00
625A	**185**	1s.6d. red and blue	1·00	1·25
623A/625A Set of 3			1·00	1·25
First Day Cover				45·00

B. 'Thrissell' Machine.

623B	**183**	2½d. black and red	1·50	1·50
624B	**184**	3d. orange-brown and violet	30	30
		a. Orange-brown omitted	£1200	

Timson   Thrissell

Timson    Thrissell

2½d. TIMSON. Cyls 1E-1F. Deeply shaded portrait (brownish black).
2½d. THRISSELL. Cyls 1D-1B or 1D (dot)-1B (dot). Lighter portrait (grey-black).
3d. TIMSON. Cyls 3D-3E. Clear, well-defined portrait with deep shadows and bright highlights.
3d. THRISSELL. Cyls 3C-3B or 3C (dot)-3B (dot). Dull portrait, lacking in contrast.

Sheet marginal examples without single extension perf hole on the short side of the stamp are always 'Timson', as are those with large punch-hole not coincident with printed three-sided box guide mark.

The 3d. 'Timson' perforated completely through the right hand side margin comes from a relatively small part of the printing perforated on a sheet-fed machine.

Normally the 'Timsons' were perforated in the reel, with three large punch-holes in both long margins and the perforations completely through both short margins. Only one punch-hole coincides with the guide-mark.

The 'Thrissells' have one large punch-hole in one long margin, coinciding with guide-mark and one short margin imperf (except sometimes for encroachments).

186 CEPT Emblem    **187** Doves and Emblem

188 Doves and Emblem

(Des M. Goaman (Doves T. Kurpershoek))

1961 (18 Sept). European Postal and Telecommunications (CEPT) Conference, Torquay. Chalk-surfaced paper. W **179**. Perf 15×14.

626	**186**	2d. orange, pink and brown	10	10
		a. Orange omitted	£10000	
		b. Pink omitted	—	
627	**187**	4d. buff, mauve and ultramarine	10	10
628	**188**	10d. turquoise, pale green and Prussian blue	20	20
		a. Pale green omitted	£16000	
		b. Turquoise omitted	£5000	
Set of 3			30	30
First Day Cover				4·00

189 Hammer Beam Roof, Westminster Hall    **190** Palace of Westminster

53

QUEEN ELIZABETH II/1961

(Des Faith Jaques)

1961 (25 Sept). Seventh Commonwealth Parliamentary Conference. Chalk-surfaced paper. W **179** (sideways on 1s.3d.) Perf 15×14 (6d.) or 14×15 (1s.3d.).

629	**189**	6d. purple and gold............................	10	10
		a. Gold omitted................................	£1800	
630	**190**	1s.3d. green and blue........................	1·25	1·25
		a. Blue (Queen's head) omitted............	£25000	
		b. Green omitted.............................	—	
Set of 2			1·25	1·25
First Day Cover...				25·00

191 Units of Productivity

192 National Productivity

193 Unified Productivity

Lake in Scotland (Cyls. 2A-2B Dot, R. 1/3)

Kent omitted (Cyls. 2C-2B No dot, R. 18/2)

Lake in Yorkshire (Cyls. 2C-2B Dot, R. 19/1)

(Des D. Gentleman)

1962 (14 Nov). National Productivity Year. Chalk-surfaced paper. W **179** (inverted on 2½d. and 3d.). Perf 15×14.

631	**191**	2½d. myrtle-green and carmine-red (shades)...	10	10
		a. Blackish olive and carmine-red.........	25	15
		p. One phosphor band. *Blackish olive and carmine-red*..............................	60	50
632	**192**	3d. light blue and violet (shades).........	25	25
		a. Light blue (Queen's head) omitted	£4250	
		b. Lake in Scotland............................	£150	
		c. Kent omitted................................	70·00	
		p. Three phosphor bands...................	1·50	80
		d. Lake in Yorkshire..........................	35·00	
633	**193**	1s.3d. carmine, light blue and deep green...	80	80
		a. Light blue (Queen's head) omitted.	£10000	
		p. Three phosphor bands...................	35·00	22·00
Set of 3 (Ordinary)...			1·00	1·00
Set of 3 (Phosphor)..			35·00	22·00
First Day Cover (Ordinary)...................................				45·00
First Day Cover (Phosphor).................................				£125

194 Campaign Emblem and Family

195 Children of Three Races

(Des M. Goaman)

1963 (21 Mar). Freedom from Hunger. Chalk-surfaced paper. W **179** (inverted). Perf 15×14.

634	**194**	2½d. crimson and pink.......................	10	10
		p. One phosphor band......................	3·00	1·25
635	**195**	1s.3d. bistre-brown and yellow...........	1·00	1·00
		p. Three phosphor bands...................	30·00	23·00
Set of 2 (Ordinary)...			1·00	1·00
Set of 2 (Phosphor)..			30·00	23·00

First Day Cover (Ordinary)...................................				25·00
First Day Cover (Phosphor).................................				40·00

196 'Paris Conference'

(Des R. Stone)

1963 (7 May). Paris Postal Conference Centenary. Chalk-surfaced paper. W **179** (inverted). Perf 15×14.

636	**196**	6d. green and mauve.........................	20	20
		a. Green omitted..............................	£3750	
		p. Three phosphor bands...................	3·00	2·75
First Day Cover (Ordinary)...................................				7·50
First Day Cover (Phosphor).................................				30·00

197 Posy of Flowers

198 Woodland Life

'Caterpillar' flaw (Cyl. 3B Dot, R. 3/2)

(Des S. Scott (3d.), M. Goaman (4½d.))

1963 (16 May). National Nature Week. Chalk-surfaced paper. W **179**. Perf 15×14.

637	**197**	3d. yellow, green, brown and black......	10	10
		a. 'Caterpillar' flaw...........................	75·00	
		p. Three phosphor bands...................	30	30
		pa. 'Caterpillar' flaw..........................	75·00	
638	**198**	4½d. black, blue, yellow, magenta and brown-red...	15	15
		p. Three phosphor bands...................	1·40	1·40
Set of 2 (Ordinary)...			20	20
Set of 2 (Phosphor)..			1·50	1·50
First Day Cover (Ordinary)...................................				12·00
First Day Cover (Phosphor).................................				35·00

Special First Day of Issue Postmark

London EC (Type A) (*ordinary*).....	12·00
London EC (Type A) (*phosphor*)...	35·00

This postmark was used on First Day Covers serviced by the Philatelic Bureau.

199 Rescue at Sea

200 19th-century Lifeboat

201 Lifeboatmen

(Des D. Gentleman)

1963 (31 May). Ninth International Lifeboat Conference, Edinburgh. Chalk-surfaced paper. W **179**. Perf 15×14.

639	**199**	2½d. blue, black and red.....................	10	10
		p. One phosphor band......................	50	60
640	**200**	4d. red, yellow, brown, black and blue	20	20
		p. Three phosphor bands...................	50	60
641	**201**	1s.6d. sepia, yellow and grey-blue........	1·50	1·50
		p. Three phosphor bands...................	48·00	28·00
Set of 3 (Ordinary)...			1·50	1·50

1963/QUEEN ELIZABETH II

Set of 3 (Phosphor)	48·00	28·00
First Day Cover (Ordinary)		20·00
First Day Cover (Phosphor)		55·00

Special First Day of Issue Postmark

London (ordinary)	65·00
London (phosphor)	85·00

This postmark was used on First Day Covers serviced by the Philatelic Bureau.

202 Red Cross

203

204

(Des H. Bartram)

1963 (15 Aug). Red Cross Centenary Congress. Chalk-surfaced paper. W **179**. Perf 15×14.

642	**202**	3d. red and deep lilac	25	25
		a. Red omitted	£12000	
		p. Three phosphor bands	1·10	1·00
		pa. Red omitted	—	
643	**203**	1s.3d. red, blue and grey	1·25	1·25
		p. Three phosphor bands	35·00	30·00
644	**204**	1s.6d. red, blue and bistre	1·25	1·25
		p. Three phosphor bands	35·00	27·00
Set of 3 (Ordinary)			2·50	2·50
Set of 3 (Phosphor)			65·00	55·00
First Day Cover (Ordinary)				20·00
First Day Cover (Phosphor)				60·00

Special First Day of Issue Postmark

London E.C. (ordinary)	80·00
London E.C. (phosphor)	£110

This postmark was used on First Day Covers serviced by the Philatelic Bureau.

205 Commonwealth Cable

(Des P. Gauld)

1963 (3 Dec). Opening of COMPAC (Trans-Pacific Telephone Cable). Chalk-surfaced paper. W **179**. Perf 15×14.

645	**205**	1s.6d. blue and black	1·25	1·25
		a. Black omitted	£5500	
		p. Three phosphor bands	7·25	7·00
First Day Cover (Ordinary)				12·00
First Day Cover (Phosphor)				35·00

Special First Day of Issue Postmark

Philatelic Bureau, London EC 1 (Type A) (ordinary)	12·00
Philatelic Bureau, London EC 1 (Type A) (phosphor)	35·00

Special First Day of Issue Postmark

London EC 1 (Type A) (ordinary)	12·00
London EC 1 (Type A) (phosphor)	35·00

PRESENTATION PACKS. Special Packs comprising slip-in cards with printed commemorative inscriptions and descriptive notes on the back and with protective covering, were introduced in 1964 with the Shakespeare issue. These are listed and priced. Issues of 1968–1969 (British Paintings to the Prince of Wales Investiture) were also issued in packs with text in German for sale through the Post Office's German Agency and these are also quoted. Subsequently, however, the packs sold in Germany were identical with the normal English version with the addition of a separate printed insert card with German text. These, as also English packs with Japanese and Dutch printed cards for sale in Japan and the Netherlands respectively, are listed in Vols. 3 and 5 of the Stanley Gibbons *Great Britain Specialised Catalogue*.

206 Puck and Bottom (*A Midsummer Night's Dream*)

207 Feste (*Twelfth Night*)

208 Balcony Scene (*Romeo and Juliet*)

209 Eve of Agincourt (*Henry V*)

210 Hamlet contemplating Yorick's Skull (*Hamlet*) and Queen Elizabeth II

(Des D. Gentleman. Photo Harrison & Sons (3d., 6d., 1s.3d., 1s.6d.). Des C. and R. Ironside. Eng Nigel Alan Dow. Recess B.W. (2s.6d.))

1964 (23 Apr). Shakespeare Festival. Chalk-surfaced paper. W **179**. Perf 11×12 (2s.6d.) or 15×14 (others).

646	**206**	3d. yellow-bistre, black and deep violet-blue (shades)	10	10
		p. Three phosphor bands	25	25
647	**207**	6d. yellow, orange, black and yellow-olive (shades)	20	20
		p. Three phosphor bands	75	75
648	**208**	1s.3d. cerise, blue-green, black and sepia (shades)	40	40
		Wi. Watermark inverted	£1500	
		p. Three phosphor bands	2·00	2·00
		pWi. Watermark inverted	£400	
649	**209**	1s.6d. violet, turquoise, black and blue (shades)	60	60
		Wi. Watermark inverted		£1300
		p. Three phosphor bands	2·50	2·50
650	**210**	2s.6d. deep slate-purple (shades)	1·25	1·25
		Wi. Watermark inverted	£1000	
Set of 5 (Ordinary)			2·00	2·00
Set of 4 (Phosphor) (Nos. 646p/649p)			5·00	5·00
First Day Cover (Ordinary)				5·00
First Day Cover (Phosphor)				9·00
Presentation Pack (Ordinary)			12·00	

The 3d. is known with yellow-bistre missing in the top two-thirds of the figures of Puck and Bottom. This occurred in the top row only of a sheet.

Special First Day of Issue Postmarks

Stratford-upon-Avon, Warwicks (ordinary)	15·00
Stratford-upon-Avon, Warwicks (phosphor)	22·00

This postmark was used on First Day Covers serviced by the Philatelic Bureau, as well as on covers posted at Stratford PO.

211 Flats near Richmond Park (Urban Development)

212 Shipbuilding Yards, Belfast (Industrial Activity)

QUEEN ELIZABETH II/1964

213 Beddgelert Forest Park, (Snowdonia Forestry) 
214 Nuclear Reactor, Dounreay (Technological Development)

Short line under 2½d. (Cyl. 3D, various positions)

(Des D. Bailey)

1964 (1 July). 20th International Geographical Congress, London. Chalk-surfaced paper. W **179**. Perf 15×14.

651	211	2½d. black, olive-yellow, olive-grey and turquoise-blue	10	10
		p. One phosphor band	40	50
		a. Short line under 2½d.	14·00	
652	212	4d. orange-brown, red-brown, rose, black and violet	30	30
		a. Violet (face value) omitted	£225	
		c. Violet and red-brown (dock walls) omitted	£425	
		d. Red brown (dock walls) omitted	—	
		Wi. Watermark inverted	£750	
		p. Three phosphor bands	1·25	1·25
653	213	8d. yellow-brown, emerald, green and black	80	80
		a. Green (lawn) omitted	£16000	
		Wi. Watermark inverted	£2200	
		p. Three phosphor bands	2·50	3·50
654	214	1s.6d. yellow-brown, pale pink, black and brown	1·40	1·40
		Wi. Watermark inverted	55·00	
		p. Three phosphor bands	28·00	22·00
Set of 4 (Ordinary)			2·00	2·00
Set of 4 (Phosphor)			30·00	25·00
First Day Cover (Ordinary)				10·00
First Day Cover (Phosphor)				35·00
Presentation Pack (Ordinary)			£100	

A used example of the 4d. is known with the red-brown omitted.

Special First Day of Issue Postmark
GPO Philatelic Bureau, London EC 1 (Type B) (*ordinary*)	10·00
GPO Philatelic Bureau, London EC 1 (Type B) (*phosphor*)	35·00

215 Spring Gentian
216 Dog Rose 
217 Honeysuckle 
218 Fringed Water Lily

Broken petal (Cyl. 3A, Dot, R. 1/2)
Line through 'INTER' (Cyl. 2A No Dot, R. 1/1) 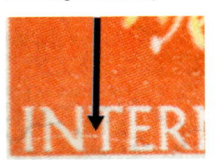

(Des M. and Sylvia Goaman)

1964 (5 Aug). Tenth International Botanical Congress, Edinburgh. Chalk-surfaced paper. W **179**. Perf 15×14.

655	215	3d. violet, blue and sage-green	25	25
		a. Blue omitted	£15000	
		b. Sage-green omitted	£18000	
		c. Broken petal	65·00	
		p. Three phosphor bands	40	40
		pc. Broken petal	65·00	
656	216	6d. apple-green, rose, scarlet and green	30	30
		p. Three phosphor bands	2·50	2·75
657	217	9d. lemon, green, lake and rose-red	80	80
		a. Green (leaves) omitted	£16000	
		b. Line through 'INTER'	65·00	
		Wi. Watermark inverted	75·00	
		p. Three phosphor bands	4·50	4·50
		pb. Line through 'INTER'	65·00	
658	218	1s.3d. yellow, emerald, reddish violet and grey-green	1·25	1·25
		a. Yellow (flowers) omitted	—	
		Wi. Watermark inverted	£2500	
		p. Three phosphor bands	25·00	20·00
Set of 4 (Ordinary)			2·00	2·00
Set of 4 (Phosphor)			30·00	25·00
First Day Cover (Ordinary)				10·00
First Day Cover (Phosphor)				35·00
Presentation Pack (Ordinary)			£125	

Unissued Goaman designs of the 3d and 9d values on perforated and gummed paper are known.

Special First Day of Issue Postmark
GPO Philatelic Bureau, London EC 1 (Type B) (*ordinary*)	10·00
GPO Philatelic Bureau, London EC 1 (Type B) (*phosphor*)	35·00

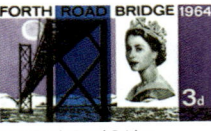

219 Forth Road Bridge
220 Forth Road and Railway Bridges 

(Des A. Restall)

1964 (4 Sept). Opening of Forth Road Bridge. Chalk-surfaced paper. W **179**. Perf 15×14.

659	219	3d. black, blue and reddish violet	10	10
		p. Three phosphor bands	50	50
660	220	6d. blackish lilac, light blue and carmine-red	20	20
		a. Light blue omitted	£5000	
		Wi. Watermark inverted	5·00	
		p. Three phosphor bands	2·25	2·25
		pWi. Watermark inverted	£800	
Set of 2 (Ordinary)			25	25
Set of 2 (Phosphor)			2·50	2·50
First Day Cover (Ordinary)				3·00
First Day Cover (Phosphor)				10·00
Presentation Pack (Ordinary)			£325	

Special First Day of Issue Postmarks
GPO Philatelic Bureau, London EC 1 (Type B) (*ordinary*)	15·00
GPO Philatelic Bureau, London EC 1 (Type B) (*phosphor*)	20·00
North Queensferry, Fife (*ordinary*)	50·00
North Queensferry, Fife (*phosphor*)	£130
South Queensferry, West Lothian (*ordinary*)	40·00
South Queensferry, West Lothian (*phosphor*)	95·00

221 Sir Winston Churchill

(Des D. Gentleman and Rosalind Dease, from photograph by Karsh)

1965 (8 Jul). Churchill Commemoration. Chalk-surfaced paper. W **179**. Perf 15×14.

I. 'REMBRANDT' Machine.

661	221	4d. black and olive-brown	15	15
		Wi. Watermark inverted	3·00	
		p. Three phosphor bands	20	20

II. 'TIMSON' Machine.

661a		4d. black and olive-brown	50	50

III. 'L. & M. 4' Machine.

662		1s.3d. black and grey	45	45
		Wi. Watermark inverted	£140	
		p. Three phosphor bands	1·00	1·00
Set of 2 (Ordinary)			60	60
Set of 2 (Phosphor)			1·10	1·10
First Day Cover (Ordinary)				4·75
First Day Cover (Phosphor)				5·00
Presentation Pack (Ordinary)			40·00	

The 1s.3d. shows a closer view of Churchill's head.

1965/QUEEN ELIZABETH II

Two examples of the 4d. value exist with the Queen's head omitted, one due to something adhering to the cylinder and the other due to a paper fold. The stamp also exists with Churchill's head omitted, also due to a paper fold.

Rembrandt

Timson

4d. REMBRANDT. Cyls 1A-1B dot and no dot. Lack of shading detail on Churchill's portrait. Queen's portrait appears dull and coarse. This is a rotary machine which is sheet-fed.

4d. TIMSON. Cyls 5A-6B no dot. More detail on Churchill's portrait, furrow on forehead, his left eyebrow fully drawn and more shading on cheek. Queen's portrait lighter and sharper. This is a reel-fed two-colour 12 in. wide rotary machine and the differences in impressions are due to the greater pressure applied by this machine.

1s.3d. Cyls 1A-1B no dot. The 'Linotype and Machinery No. 4' machine is an ordinary sheet-fed rotary press machine. Besides being used for printing the 1s.3d. stamps it was also employed for overprinting the phosphor bands on both values.

Special First Day of Issue Postmark
GPO Philatelic Bureau, London EC 1 (Type B) (*ordinary*) .... 4·75
GPO Philatelic Bureau, London EC 1 (Type B) (*phosphor*) .... 5·00

A first Day of Issue handstamp was provided at Baldon, Oxford, for this issue.

222 Simon de Montfort's Seal

223 Parliament Buildings (after engraving by Hollar, 1647)

(Des S. Black (6d.), R. Guyatt (2s.6d.))

1965 (19 July). 700th Anniversary of Simon de Montfort's Parliament. Chalk-surfaced paper. W **179**. Perf 15×14.

663	222	6d. olive-green..................................	10	10
		p. Three phosphor bands.................	50	50
664	223	2s.6d. black, grey and pale drab.........	40	40
		Wi. Watermark inverted...................	60·00	
Set of 2 (Ordinary)			40	40
First Day Cover (Ordinary)				6·00
First Day Cover (Phosphor)				20·00
Presentation Pack (Ordinary)				65·00

Special First Day of Issue Postmark
GPO Philatelic Bureau, London EC 1 (Type B) (*ordinary*) .... 6·00
A First Day of Issue handstamp was provided at Evesham, Worcs., for this issue.

224 Bandsmen and Banner   **225** Three Salvationists

(Des M. Farrar-Bell (3d.), G. Trenaman (1s.6d.))

1965 (9 Aug). Salvation Army Centenary. Chalk-surfaced paper. W **179**. Perf 15×14.

665	224	3d. indigo, grey-blue, cerise, yellow and brown...................................	10	10
		p. One phosphor band........................	20	20
666	225	1s.6d. red, blue, yellow and brown.........	60	60
		p. Three phosphor bands...................	90	90
Set of 2 (Ordinary)			60	60
Set of 2 (Phosphor)			1·00	1·00
First Day Cover (Ordinary)				10·00
First Day Cover (Phosphor)				22·00

The Philatelic Bureau did not provide First Day Cover services for Nos. 665/670.

226 Lister's Carbolic Spray   **227** Lister and Chemical Symbols

(Des P. Gauld (4d.), F. Ariss (1s.))

1965 (1 Sept). Centenary of Joseph Lister's Discovery of Antiseptic Surgery. Chalk-surfaced paper. W **179**. Perf 15×14.

667	226	4d. indigo, brown-red and grey-black..	10	10
		a. Brown-red (tube) omitted...............	£475	
		b. Indigo omitted................................	£5500	
		p. Three phosphor bands...................	25	25
		pa. Brown-red (tube) omitted..............	£5000	
668	227	1s. black, purple and new blue...........	40	40
		Wi. Watermark inverted....................	£675	
		p. Three phosphor bands...................	1·00	1·00
		pWi. Watermark inverted...................	£550	
Set of 2 (Ordinary)			45	45
Set of 2 (Phosphor)			1·10	1·10
First Day Cover (Ordinary)				5·00
First Day Cover (Phosphor)				9·00

228 Trinidad Carnival Dancers   **229** Canadian Folk Dancers

(Des D. Gentleman and Rosalind Dease)

1965 (1 Sept). Commonwealth Arts Festival. Chalk-surfaced paper. W **179**. Perf 15×14.

669	228	6d. black and orange..........................	10	10
		p. Three phosphor bands...................	40	40
670	229	1s.6d. black and light reddish violet........	40	40
		p. Three phosphor bands...................	1·25	1·25
Set of 2 (Ordinary)			45	45
Set of 2 (Phosphor)			1·50	1·50
First Day Cover (Ordinary)				7·00
First Day Cover (Phosphor)				14·00

230 Flight of Supermarine Spitfires   **231** Pilot in Hawker Hurricane Mk I

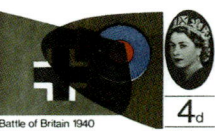

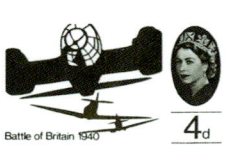

232 Wing-tips of Supermarine Spitfire and Messerschmitt Bf 109   **233** Supermarine Spitfires attacking Heinkel He-111H Bomber

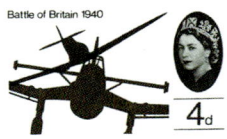

QUEEN ELIZABETH II/1965

234 Supermarine Spitfire attacking Junkers Ju 87B Stuka Dive-bomber

235 Hawker Hurricanes Mk I over Wreck of Dornier Do-17Z Bomber

236 Anti-aircraft Artillery in Action

237 Air Battle over St Paul's Cathedral

(Des D. Gentleman and Rosalind Dease (4d.×6 and 1s.3d.), A. Restall (9d.))

1965 (13 Sept). 25th Anniversary of Battle of Britain. Chalk-surfaced paper. W **179**. Perf 15×14.

671	**230**	4d. yellow-olive and black	25	25
		a. Block of 6. Nos. 671/676	2·50	2·50
		p. Three phosphor bands	40	40
		pa. Block of 6. Nos. 671p/676p	3·75	3·75
672	**231**	4d. yellow-olive, olive-grey and black	25	25
		p. Three phosphor bands	40	40
673	**232**	4d. red, new blue, yellow-olive, olive-grey and black	25	25
		p. Three phosphor bands	40	40
674	**233**	4d. olive-grey, yellow-olive and black	25	25
		p. Three phosphor bands	40	40
675	**234**	4d. olive-grey, yellow-olive and black	25	25
		p. Three phosphor bands	40	40
676	**235**	4d. olive-grey, yellow-olive, new blue and black	25	25
		a. New blue omitted	†	£4000
		p. Three phosphor bands	40	40
677	**236**	9d. bluish violet, orange and slate purple	1·75	1·75
		Wi. Watermark inverted	£100	
		p. Three phosphor bands	2·00	2·00
678	**237**	1s.3d. light grey, deep grey, black, light blue and bright blue	1·75	1·75
		a. Face value omitted*	£1100	
		Wi. Watermark inverted	£190	
		p. Three phosphor bands	2·00	2·00
		pWi. Watermark inverted	5·00	
Set of 8 (Ordinary)			5·50	5·50
Set of 8 (Phosphor)			7·00	7·00
First Day Cover (Ordinary)				10·00
First Day Cover (Phosphor)				15·00
Presentation Pack (Ordinary)			40·00	

* No. 678a is caused by a 12 mm downward shift of black which resulted in the value being omitted from the top row of one sheet.

Nos. 671/678 were issued together *se-tenant* in blocks of six (3×2) within the sheet.

No. 676a is only known commercially used *on cover* from Truro.

Special First Day of Issue Postmark
GPO Philatelic Bureau, London EC 1 (Type C) (*ordinary*) .... 10·00
GPO Philatelic Bureau, London EC 1 (Type C) (*phosphor*) .... 15·00

238 Tower and Georgian Buildings

239 Tower and Nash Terrace, Regent's Park

(Des C. Abbott)

1965 (8 Oct). Opening of Post Office Tower. Chalk-surfaced paper. W **179** (sideways on 3d.). Perf 14×15 (3d.) or 15×14 (1s.3d.).

679	**238**	3d. olive-yellow, new blue and bronze-green	10	10
		a. Olive-yellow (Tower) omitted	£4750	£1900
		p. One phosphor band at right	15	15
		pa. Band at left	15	15
		pb. Horiz pair. Nos. 679p/679pa	30	50
680	**239**	1s.3d. bronze-green, yellow-green and blue	20	20
		Wi. Watermark inverted	£175	
		p. Three phosphor bands	30	30
		pWi. Watermark inverted	£200	
Set of 2 (Ordinary)			25	25
Set of 2 (Phosphor)			40	40
First Day Cover (Ordinary)				2·50
First Day Cover (Phosphor)				4·75
Presentation Pack (Ordinary)			12·50	
Presentation Pack (Phosphor)				12·50

The one phosphor band on No. 679p was produced by printing broad phosphor bands across alternate vertical perforations. Individual stamps show the band at right or left.

Special First Day of Issue Postmark
GPO Philatelic Bureau, London E.C. 1 (Type C) (*ordinary*) .... 2·50
GPO Philatelic Bureau, London E.C. 1 (Type C) (*phosphor*) .... 4·75

The Philatelic Bureau did not provide First Day Cover services for Nos. 681/684.

240 UN Emblem

241 ICY Emblem

Broken circle (Cyl. 1A Dot, R. 11/4)

Lake in Russia (Cyl. 1A Dot, R. 19/3)

(Des J. Matthews)

1965 (25 Oct). 20th Anniversary of UNO and International Co-operation Year. Chalk-surfaced paper. W **179**. Perf 15×14.

681	**240**	3d. black, yellow-orange and light blue	10	10
		a. Broken circle	65·00	
		b. Lake in Russia	65·00	
		p. One phosphor band	25	25
		pa. Broken circle	65·00	
		pb. Lake in Russia	65·00	
682	**241**	1s.6d. black, bright purple and light blue	35	35
		Wi. Watermark inverted		£2250
		p. Three phosphor bands	1·00	1·00
Set of 2 (Ordinary)			40	40
Set of 2 (Phosphor)			1·10	1·10
First Day Cover (Ordinary)				5·00
First Day Cover (Phosphor)				9·00

242 Telecommunications Network

243 Radio Waves and Switchboard

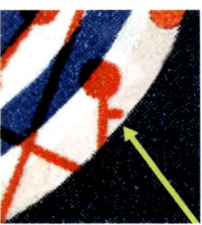

Red pin with arm (Cyl. 1D, R. 1/4)

1965 / QUEEN ELIZABETH II

(Des A. Restall)

1965 (15 Nov). International Telecommunications Union Centenary. Chalk-surfaced paper. W **179**. Perf 15×14.

683	242	9d. red, ultramarine, deep slate, violet, black and pink	20	20
		Wi. Watermark inverted	30·00	
		p. Three phosphor bands	75	75
		pWi. Watermark inverted	£110	
684	243	1s.6d. red, greenish blue, indigo, black and light pink	40	40
		a. Light pink omitted	£3000	£2000
		b. Red pin with arm	—	
		Wi. Watermark inverted	—	
		p. Three phosphor bands	2·00	2·00
		pb. Red pin with arm	35·00	
Set of 2 (Ordinary)			50	50
Set of 2 (Phosphor)			2·50	2·50
First Day Cover (Ordinary)				8·00
First Day Cover (Phosphor)				13·00

Originally scheduled for issue on 17 May 1965, supplies from the Philatelic Bureau were sent in error to reach a dealer on that date and another dealer received his supply on 27 May.

244 Robert Burns (after Skirving chalk drawing)

245 Robert Burns (after Nasmyth portrait)

(Des G. Huntly)

1966 (25 Jan). Burns Commemoration. Chalk-surfaced paper. W **179**. Perf 15×14.

685	244	4d. black, deep violet-blue and new blue	10	10
		p. Three phosphor bands	20	20
686	245	1s.3d. black, slate-blue and yellow-orange	20	20
		p. Three phosphor bands	90	90
Set of 2 (Ordinary)			25	25
Set of 2 (Phosphor)			1·00	1·00
First Day Cover (Ordinary)				1·20
First Day Cover (Phosphor)				3·50
Presentation Pack (Ordinary)			40·00	

Special First Day of Issue Postmarks

Alloway, Ayrshire (ordinary)	12·00
Alloway, Ayrshire (phosphor)	15·00
Ayr (ordinary)	12·00
Ayr (phosphor)	15·00
Dumfries (ordinary)	12·00
Dumfries (phosphor)	15·00
Edinburgh (ordinary)	12·00
Edinburgh (phosphor)	15·00
Glasgow (ordinary)	12·00
Glasgow (phosphor)	15·00

A special Philatelic Bureau was set up in Edinburgh to deal with First Day Covers of this issue. The Bureau serviced covers to receive the above postmarks, and other versions were applied locally. The locally applied handstamps were 38–39 mm in diameter, the Bureau postmarks, applied by machine 35 mm. The Ayr, Edinburgh, Glasgow and Kilmarnock postmarks are similar in design to that for Alloway. Similar handstamps were also provided at Greenock and Mauchline, but the Bureau did not provide a service for these.

246 Westminster Abbey

247 Fan Vaulting, Henry VII Chapel

(Des Sheila Robinson. Photo Harrison (3d.). Des and eng Nigel Alan Dow (portrait) and Frederick Warner of Bradbury Wilkinson. Recess (2s.6d.))

1966 (28 Feb). 900th Anniversary of Westminster Abbey. Chalk-surfaced paper (3d.). W **179**. Perf 15×14 (3d.) or 11×12 (2s.6d.).

687	246	3d. black, red-brown and new blue	10	10
		p. One phosphor band	10	10
688	247	2s.6d. black	30	30
Set of 2			30	30
First Day Cover (Ordinary)				2·50
First Day Cover (Phosphor)				8·00
Presentation Pack (Ordinary)			40·00	

Special First Day of Issue Postmark

GPO Philatelic Bureau, London EC 1 (Type B) (ordinary)	2·50

The Bureau did not provide a First Day Cover service for the 3d. phosphor stamp.

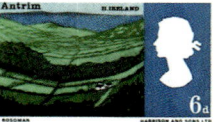

248 View near Hassocks, Sussex

249 Antrim, Northern Ireland

250 Harlech Castle, Wales

251 Cairngorm Mountains Scotland

Green flaw on tree trunk (Cyl. 1B Dot, R. 3/4)

'AN' for 'AND' (Cyl. 1A No dot, R. 10/3)

Broken 'D' (Cyl. 2B, R. 14/2)

(Des L. Rosoman. Queen's portrait, adapted by D. Gentleman from coinage)

1966 (2 May). Landscapes. Chalk-surfaced paper. W **179**. Perf 15×14.

689	248	4d. black, yellow-green and new blue	10	10
		a. Green flaw	40·00	
		p. Three phosphor bands	10	10
		pa. Green flaw	35·00	
690	249	6d. black, emerald and new blue	10	10
		a. 'AN' for 'AND'	65·00	
		Wi. Watermark inverted	6·00	
		p. Three phosphor bands	10	10
		pa. 'AN' for 'AND'	65·00	
		pWi. Watermark inverted	£170	
691	250	1s.3d. black, greenish yellow and greenish blue	15	15
		a. Broken 'D'	35·00	
		p. Three phosphor bands	15	15
		pa. Broken 'D'	35·00	
692	251	1s.6d. black, orange and Prussian blue	15	15
		Wi. Watermark inverted	22·00	
		p. Three phosphor bands	15	15
Set of 4 (Ordinary)			40	40
Set of 4 (Phosphor)			40	40
First Day Cover (Ordinary)				3·50
First Day Cover (Phosphor)				4·50

Blocks of four of Nos. 689 and 690 are known with the Queen's head and face value omitted on one stamp and a partial omission on the second, due to a paper fold (Price per block £10,000)

Special First Day of Issue Postmark

GPO Philatelic Bureau, London EC 1 (Type B) (ordinary)	3·50
GPO Philatelic Bureau, London EC 1 (Type B) (phosphor)	4·50

First Day of Issue handstamps were provided at Lewes, Sussex; Coleraine, Co. Londonderry; Harlech, Merioneth and Grantown-on-Spey, Morayshire, for this issue.

QUEEN ELIZABETH II/1966

252 Players with Ball
253 Goalmouth Mêlée 
254 Goalkeeper saving Goal 

(Des D. Gentleman (4d.), W. Kempster (6d.), D. Caplan (1s.3d.). Queen's portrait adapted by D. Gentleman from coinage)

1966 (1 June). World Cup Football Championship. Chalk-surfaced paper. W **179** (sideways on 4d.). Perf 14×15 (4d.) or 15×14 (others).

693	252	4d. red, reddish purple, bright blue, flesh and black	10	10
		p. Two phosphor bands	10	10
694	253	6d. black, sepia, red, apple green and blue	10	10
		a. Black omitted	£160	
		b. Apple-green omitted	£5000	
		c. Red omitted	£7750	
		Wi. Watermark inverted	5·00	
		p. Three phosphor bands	10	10
		pa. Black omitted	£2000	
695	254	1s.3d. black, blue, yellow, red and light yellow-olive	15	15
		a. Blue omitted	£300	
		Wi. Watermark inverted	£150	
		p. Three phosphor bands	15	15
		pWi. Watermark inverted	2·00	
Set of 3 (Ordinary)			30	30
Set of 3 (Phosphor)			30	30
First Day Cover (Ordinary)				9·00
First Day Cover (Phosphor)				11·50
Presentation Pack (Ordinary)			30·00	

Special First Day of Issue Postmark
GPO Philatelic Bureau, London EC 1 Type C) (ordinary) .... 9·00
GPO Philatelic Bureau, London EC 1 Type C) (phosphor) .... 11·50

A First Day of Issue handstamp was provided at Wembley, Middx, for this issue.

255 Black-headed Gull
256 Blue Tit  
257 European Robin 
258 Blackbird 

(Des J. Norris Wood)

1966 (8 Aug). British Birds. Chalk-surfaced paper. W **179**. Perf 15×14.

696	255	4d. grey, black, red, emerald-green, bright blue, greenish yellow and bistre	10	10
		Wi. Watermark inverted	4·00	
		a. Block of 4. Nos. 696/699	40	40
		ab. Black (value), etc. omitted* (block of four)	£12500	
		c. Black only omitted*	—	
		aWi. Watermark inverted (block of four)	18·00	
		p. Three phosphor bands	10	10
		pWi. Watermark inverted	20·00	
		pa. Block of 4. Nos. 696p/699p	40	40
		paWi. Watermark inverted (block of four)	85·00	
697	256	4d. black, greenish yellow, grey, emerald-green, bright blue and bistre	10	10
		b. Black '4d' only omitted	£2000	
		Wi. Watermark inverted	4·00	
		p. Three phosphor bands	10	10
		pWi. Watermark inverted	20·00	
698	257	4d. red, greenish yellow, black, grey, bistre, reddish brown and emerald-green	10	10
		a. Black only omitted*		
		Wi. Watermark inverted	4·00	
		p. Three phosphor bands	10	10
		pWi. Watermark inverted	20·00	
699	258	4d. black, reddish brown, greenish yellow, grey and bistre**	10	10
		b. Black '4d' only omitted***	£2000	
		Wi. Watermark inverted	4·00	
		p. Three phosphor bands	10	10
		pWi. Watermark inverted	20·00	
Set of 4 (Ordinary)			40	40
Set of 4 (Phosphor)			40	40
First Day Cover (Ordinary)				3·50
First Day Cover (Phosphor)				4·50
Presentation Pack (Ordinary)			15·00	

* In No. 696ab the blue, bistre and reddish brown are also omitted but in No. 696c and 698a only the black is omitted.
** In No. 699 the black was printed over the bistre.
*** A partial omission caused by a dry print affecting only the face value on the last column of the sheet.

Nos. 696/699 were issued together *se-tenant* in blocks of four within the sheet.

Nos. 697b and 699b are the result of a partial impression of the black, rendering the '4d' only omitted.

Other colours omitted, and the stamps affected:

d.	Greenish yellow (Nos. 696/699)	£750
pd.	Greenish yellow (Nos. 696p/699p)	£1500
e.	Red (Nos. 696 and 698)	£750
f.	Emerald-green (Nos. 696/698)	£160
pf.	Emerald-green (Nos. 696p/698p)	£160
g.	Bright blue (Nos. 696/697)	£550
pg.	Bright blue (Nos. 696p and 697p)	£3250
h.	Bistre (Nos. 696/699)	£160
ph.	Bistre (Nos. 696p/699p)	£1500
j.	Reddish brown (Nos. 698/699)	£100
pj.	Reddish brown (Nos. 698p and 699p)	£140

The prices quoted are for each stamp.

Special First Day of Issue Postmark
GPO Philatelic Bureau, London EC 1 (Type C) (ordinary) .... 3·50
GPO Philatelic Bureau, London EC 1 (Type C) (phosphor) .... 4·50

259 Cup Winners

1966 (18 Aug). England's World Cup Football Victory. Chalk-surfaced paper. W **179** (sideways). Perf 14×15.

700	259	4d. red, reddish purple, bright blue, flesh and black	10	10
First Day Cover				7·50

These stamps were only put on sale at post offices in England, the Channel Islands and the Isle of Man, and at the Philatelic Bureau in London and also, on 22 August, in Edinburgh on the occasion of the opening of the Edinburgh Festival as well as at Army post offices at home and abroad.

The Philatelic Bureau did not service First Day Covers for this stamp, but a First Day of Issue handstamp was provided inscribed 'Harrow & Wembley' to replace the 'Wembley Middx', postmark of the initial issue.

1966/QUEEN ELIZABETH II

260 Jodrell Bank Radio Telescope

261 British Motor cars

262 SRN 6 Hovercraft

263 Windscale Reactor

270 Norman Ship

271 Norman Horsemen attacking Harold's Troops

Broken 'D' (Cyl. 1C, R. 19/6)

Club flaw (Cyl. 1A No dot, R. 7/2)

(All the above are scenes from the Bayeux Tapestry)

(Des D. and A. Gillespie (4d., 6d.), A. Restall (others))

1966 (19 Sept). British Technology. Chalk-surfaced paper. W **179**. Perf 15×14.

701	**260**	4d. black and lemon	10	10
		p. Three phosphor bands	10	10
702	**261**	6d. red, deep blue and orange	10	10
		a. Red (Mini cars) omitted	£12500	
		b. Deep blue (Jaguar and inscr) omitted	£10000	
		c. Broken 'D'	35·00	
		p. Three phosphor bands	10	10
		pc. Broken 'D'	35·00	
703	**262**	1s.3d. black, orange-red, slate and light greenish blue	15	15
		p. Three phosphor bands	20	20
704	**263**	1s.6d. black, yellow-green, bronze-green, lilac and deep blue	15	15
		p. Three phosphor bands	20	20
Set of 4 (Ordinary)			40	40
Set of 4 (Phosphor)			50	50
First Day Cover (Ordinary)				2·50
First Day Cover (Phosphor)				2·50
Presentation Pack (Ordinary)			20·00	

Special First Day of Issue Postmark

GPO Philatelic Bureau, Edinburgh 1 (Type C) (*ordinary*)	2·50
GPO Philatelic Bureau, Edinburgh 1 (Type C) (*phosphor*)	2·50

(Des D. Gentleman. Photo. Queen's head die-stamped (6d., 1s.3d.))

1966 (14 Oct). 900th Anniversary of Battle of Hastings. Chalk-surfaced paper. W **179** (sideways on 1s.3d.). Perf 15×14.

705	**264**	4d. black, olive-green, bistre, deep blue, orange, magenta, green, blue and grey	10	10
		a. Strip of 6. Nos. 705/710	60	60
		ab. Imperforate strip of 6	£1800	
		aWi. Strip of 6. Watermark inverted	45·00	
		Wi. Watermark inverted	7·00	
		p. Three phosphor bands	10	10
		pa. Strip of 6. Nos. 705p/710p	60	60
		pWi. Watermark inverted	3·00	
		paWi. Strip of 6. Watermark inverted	20·00	
706	**265**	4d. black, olive-green, bistre, deep blue, orange, magenta, green, blue and grey	10	10
		Wi. Watermark inverted	7·00	
		p. Three phosphor bands	10	10
		pWi. Watermark inverted	2·00	
707	**266**	4d. black, olive-green, bistre, deep blue, orange, magenta, green, blue and grey	10	10
		Wi. Watermark inverted	7·00	
		p. Three phosphor bands	10	10
		pWi. Watermark inverted	3·00	
708	**267**	4d. black, olive-green, bistre, deep blue, magenta, green, blue and grey	10	10
		Wi. Watermark inverted	7·00	
		p. Three phosphor bands	10	10
		pWi. Watermark inverted	3·00	
709	**268**	4d. black, olive-green, bistre, deep blue, orange, magenta, green, blue and grey	10	10
		Wi. Watermark inverted	7·00	
		p. Three phosphor bands	10	10
		pWi. Watermark inverted	3·00	
710	**269**	4d. black, olive-green, bistre, deep blue, orange, magenta, green, blue and grey	10	10
		Wi. Watermark inverted	7·00	
		p. Three phosphor bands	10	10
		pWi. Watermark inverted	3·00	
711	**270**	6d. black, olive-green, violet, blue, green and gold	10	10
		Wi. Watermark inverted	42·00	
		p. Three phosphor bands	10	10
		pWi. Watermark inverted	75·00	
712	**271**	1s.3d. black, lilac, bronze-green, rosine, bistre-brown and gold	20	30
		a. Lilac omitted	£3750	
		b. Club flaw	28·00	
		Wi. Watermark sideways inverted (top of crown pointing to right)*	50·00	
		p. Four phosphor bands	20	40
		pa. Lilac omitted	£950	
		pb. Club flaw	28·00	

QUEEN ELIZABETH II/1966

pWi.	Watermark sideways inverted (top of crown pointing to right)*	50·00	
Set of 8 (Ordinary)		85	1·00
Set of 8 (Phosphor)		85	1·00
First Day Cover (Ordinary)			2·00
First Day Cover (Phosphor)			3·25
Presentation Pack (Ordinary)		8·50	

* The normal sideways watermark shows the tops of the Crowns pointing to the left, *as seen from the back of the stamp*.

Nos. 705/710 show battle scenes and they were issued together *se-tenant* in horizontal strips of six within the sheet.

Other colours omitted in the 4d. values and the stamps affected:

b.	Olive-green (Nos. 705/710)	40·00
pb.	Olive-green (Nos. 705p/710p)	40·00
c.	Bistre (Nos. 705/710)	40·00
pc.	Bistre (Nos. 705p/710p)	40·00
d.	Deep blue (Nos. 705/710)	50·00
pd.	Deep blue (Nos. 705p/710p)	50·00
e.	Orange (Nos. 705/707 and 709/710)	40·00
pe.	Orange (Nos. 705p/707p and 709p/710p)	40·00
f.	Magenta (Nos. 705/710)	40·00
pf.	Magenta (Nos. 705p/710p)	40·00
g.	Green (Nos. 705/710)	38·00
pg.	Green (Nos. 705p/710p)	38·00
h.	Blue (Nos. 705/710)	30·00
ph.	Blue (Nos. 705p/710p)	40·00
j.	Grey (Nos. 705/710)	30·00
pj.	Grey (Nos. 705p/710p)	40·00
pk.	Magenta and green (Nos. 705p/710p)	—

The prices quoted are for each stamp.

Nos. 705 and 709, with grey and blue omitted, have been seen commercially used, posted from Middleton-in-Teesdale.

The 6d. phosphor is known in a yellowish gold as well as the reddish gold as used in the 1s.3d.

Three examples of No. 712 in a right-hand top corner block of 10 (2×5) are known with the Queen's head omitted as a result of a double paper fold prior to die-stamping. The perforation is normal. Of the other seven stamps, four have the Queen's head misplaced and three are normal.

MISSING GOLD HEADS. The 6d. and 1s.3d. were also issued with the die-stamped gold head omitted but as these can also be removed by chemical means we are not prepared to list them unless a way is found of distinguishing the genuine stamps from the fakes which will satisfy the Expert Committees.

The same remarks apply to Nos. 713/714.

Special First Day of Issue Postmark
GPO Philatelic Bureau, Edinburgh 1 (Type C) (*ordinary*)	2·00
GPO Philatelic Bureau, Edinburgh 1 (Type C) (*phosphor*)	3·25

A First Day of Issue handstamp was provided at Battle, Sussex, for this issue.

272 King of the Orient

273 Snowman

Missing 'T' (Cyl. 1E No dot, R. 6/2)

(Des Tasveer Shemza (3d.), J. Berry (1s.6d.) (winners of children's design competition). Photo, Queen's head die-stamped)

1966 (1 Dec). Christmas, Children's Paintings. Chalk-surfaced paper. W **179** (sideways on 3d.). Perf 14×15.

713	**272**	3d. black, blue, green, yellow, red and gold	10	10
		a. Queen's head double	—	†
		ab. Queen's head double, one albino	£350	
		b. Green omitted		£3250
		c. Missing 'T'	25·00	
		p. One phosphor band at right	10	10
		pa. Band at left	10	10
		pb. Horiz pair. Nos. 713p/713pa	20	20
		pc. Missing 'T'	45·00	
714	**273**	1s.6d. blue, red, pink, black and gold	10	10
		a. Pink (hat) omitted	£2500	
		Wi. Watermark inverted	30·00	
		p. Two phosphor bands	10	10
		pWi. Watermark inverted	90·00	
Set of 2 (Ordinary)			20	20
Set of 2 (Phosphor)			20	20
First Day Cover (Ordinary)				70
First Day Cover (Phosphor)				70
Presentation Pack (Ordinary)			10·00	

No. 713a refers to stamps showing two impressions, one directly below the other, both with embossing. Examples showing two partial strikes on opposite sides of the stamp, caused by a colour shift are common.

The single phosphor band on No. 713p was produced by printing broad phosphor bands across alternate perforations. Individual stamps show the band at right or left.

Special First Day of Issue Postmarks
GPO Philatelic Bureau, Edinburgh 1 (Type C) (*ordinary*)	70
GPO Philatelic Bureau, Edinburgh 1 (Type C) (*phosphor*)	70
Bethlehem, Llandeilo, Carms (Type C) (*ordinary*)	2·00
Bethlehem, Llandeilo, Carms (Type C) (*phosphor*)	2·00

274 Sea Freight

275 Air Freight

Broken undercarriage leg (Cyl. 2, No dot, R. 13/6)

(Des C. Abbott)

1967 (20 Feb). European Free Trade Association (EFTA). Chalk-surfaced paper. W **179**. Perf 15×14.

715	**274**	9d. deep blue, red, lilac, green, brown, new blue, yellow and black	10	10
		a. Black (Queen's head, etc.), brown, new blue and yellow omitted	£900	
		b. Lilac omitted	£130	
		c. Green omitted	£130	
		d. Brown (rail trucks) omitted	80·00	
		e. New blue omitted	£130	
		f. Yellow omitted	£130	
		Wi. Watermark inverted	£140	
		p. Three phosphor bands	10	10
		pb. Lilac omitted	£180	
		pc. Green omitted	£130	
		pd. Brown omitted	80·00	
		pe. New blue omitted	£130	
		pf. Yellow omitted	£140	
		pWi. Watermark inverted	£1200	
716	**275**	1s.6d. violet, red, deep blue, brown, green, blue-grey, new blue, yellow and black	10	10
		a. Red omitted		
		b. Deep blue omitted	£425	
		c. Brown omitted	£130	
		d. Blue-grey omitted	£130	
		e. New blue omitted	£130	
		f. Yellow omitted	£130	

1967/QUEEN ELIZABETH II

g. Green omitted	£2500	
h. Broken undercarriage leg	40·00	
p. Three phosphor bands	10	10
pa. Red omitted	—	
pb. Deep blue omitted	£130	
pc. Brown omitted	80·00	
pd. Blue-grey omitted	£130	
pf. New blue omitted	£130	
ph. Broken undercarriage leg	40·00	
pWi. Watermark inverted	50·00	
Set of 2 (Ordinary)	20	20
Set of 2 (Phosphor)	20	20
First Day Cover (Ordinary)		5·00
First Day Cover (Phosphor)		5·00
Presentation Pack (Ordinary)	20·00	

Special First Day of Issue Postmark
GPO Philatelic Bureau, Edinburgh 1 (Type C) (*ordinary*) .... 5·00
GPO Philatelic Bureau, Edinburgh 1 (Type C) (*phosphor*) .... 5·00

276 Hawthorn and Bramble
277 Larger Bindweed and Viper's Bugloss 
278 Ox-eye Daisy, Coltsfoot and Buttercup 
279 Bluebell, Red Campion and Wood Anemone 
280 Dog Violet 
281 Primroses 

(Des Rev. W. Keble Martin (Types **276/279**), Mary Grierson (others))

1967 (24 Apr). British Wild Flowers. Chalk-surfaced paper. W **179**. Perf 15×14.

717	276	4d. grey, lemon, myrtle-green, red, agate and slate-purple	10	10
		a. Block of 4. Nos. 717/720	40	40
		aWi. Block of 4. Watermark inverted	9·00	
		b. Grey double*		
		c. Red omitted	£3250	
		f. Slate-purple omitted	£4000	
		Wi. Watermark inverted	2·00	
		p. Three phosphor bands	10	10
		pa. Block of 4. Nos. 717p/720p	40	40
		paWi. Block of 4. Watermark inverted	9·00	
		pd. Agate omitted	£2500	
		pf. Slate-purple omitted	£425	
		pWi. Watermark inverted	2·00	
718	277	4d. grey, lemon, myrtle-green, red, agate and violet	10	10
		b. Grey double*		
		Wi. Watermark inverted	2·00	
		p. Three phosphor bands	10	10
		pd. Agate omitted	£2500	
		pe. Violet omitted		
		pWi. Watermark inverted	2·00	
719	278	4d. grey, lemon, myrtle-green, red and agate	10	10
		b. Grey double*		
		Wi. Watermark inverted	2·00	
		p. Three phosphor bands	10	10
		pd. Agate omitted	£2500	
		pWi. Watermark inverted	2·00	
720	279	4d. grey, lemon, myrtle-green, reddish purple, agate and violet	10	10
		b. Grey double*		
		c. Reddish purple omitted	£1800	
		d. Value omitted†	£7250	
		Wi. Watermark inverted	2·00	
		p. Three phosphor bands	10	10
		pd. Agate omitted	£2500	
		pe. Violet omitted		
		pWi. Watermark inverted	2·00	
721	280	9d. lavender-grey, green, reddish violet and orange-yellow	15	15
		Wi. Watermark inverted	1·25	
		p. Three phosphor bands	15	15
722	281	1s.9d. lavender-grey, green, greenish yellow and orange	15	15
		p. Three phosphor bands	15	15
Set of 6 (Ordinary)			50	50
Set of 6 (Phosphor)			50	50
First Day Cover (Ordinary)				1·25
First Day Cover (Phosphor)				7·00
Presentation Pack (Ordinary)			20·00	
Presentation Pack (Phosphor)			20·00	

* The double impression of the grey printing affects the Queen's head, value and inscription.
† No. 720d was caused by something obscuring the face value on R. 14/6 during the printing of one sheet.

Nos. 717/720 were issued together *se-tenant* in blocks of four within the sheet.

Special First Day of Issue Postmark
GPO Philatelic Bureau, Edinburgh 1 (Type C) (*ordinary*) .... 1·20
GPO Philatelic Bureau, Edinburgh 1 (Type C) (*phosphor*) .... 7·00

PHOSPHOR BANDS. Issues from No. 723 are normally with phosphor bands only, except for the high values but some stamps have appeared with the phosphor bands omitted in error. Such varieties are listed under 'y' numbers and are priced unused only. See also further notes after 1971–1996 Decimal Machin issue.

PHOSPHORISED PAPER. Following the adoption of phosphor bands the Post Office started a series of experiments involving the addition of the phosphor to the paper coating before the stamps were printed. No. 743c was the first of these experiments to be issued for normal postal use. See also notes after 1971–1996 Decimal Machin issue.

PVA GUM. Polyvinyl alcohol was introduced by Harrisons in place of gum arabic in 1968. As it is almost invisible a small amount of pale yellowish colouring was introduced to make it possible to check that the stamps had been gummed. Although this can be distinguished from gum arabic in unused stamps there is, of course, no means of detecting it in used examples. Where the two forms of gum exist on the same stamps, the PVA type are listed under 'v' numbers, except in the case of the 1d. and 4d. (vermilion), both one centre band, which later appeared with gum arabic and these have 'g' numbers. 'v' and 'g' numbers are priced unused only. All stamps printed from No. 763 onwards were issued with PVA gum only *except where otherwise stated*.

It should be further noted that gum arabic is shiny in appearance, and that, normally, PVA gum has a matt appearance. However, depending upon the qualities of the paper ingredients and the resultant absorption of the gum, occasionally, PVA gum has a shiny appearance. In such cases, especially in stamps from booklets, it is sometimes impossible to be absolutely sure which gum has been used except by testing the stamps chemically which destroys them. Therefore, whilst all gum arabic is shiny it does not follow that all shiny gum is gum arabic.

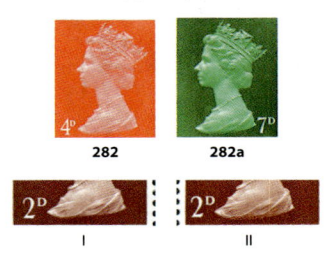

282   **282a**

Two types of the 2d.

I. Value spaced away from left side of stamp (cylinders 1 no dot and dot).

II. Value close to left side from new multipositive used for cylinders 5 no dot and dot onwards. The portrait appears in the centre, thus conforming to the other values.

Three types of the Machin head, known as Head A, B or C, are distinguished by specialists. These are illustrated in Vol. 3 of the *Great Britain Specialised Catalogue*.

(Des after plaster cast by Arnold Machin)

1967 (5 June)–**70**. Chalk-surfaced paper. Two phosphor bands *except where otherwise stated*. PVA gum except Nos. 725m, 728, 729, 731, 731a, 740, 742/742a, 743/743a and 744/744a. No wmk. Perf 15×14.

723	282	½d. orange-brown (5.2.68)	10	10
		y. Phosphor omitted	30·00	
724		1d. light olive (shades) (2 bands) (5.2.68)	10	10
		a. Imperf (coil strip)†	£3750	
		b. Part perf pane*	£5000	
		c. Imperf pane*	£5750	
		d. Uncoated paper (1970)**	£150	
		y. Phosphor omitted	4·00	
		l. Booklet pane. No. 724×2 *se-tenant* with 730×2 (6.4.68)	3·00	
		ly. Booklet pane. Phosphor omitted	90·00	

QUEEN ELIZABETH II/1967

		m. Booklet pane. No. 724×4 se-tenant with 734×2 (6.1.69)............	3·50	
		my. Booklet pane. Phosphor omitted..	£225	
		n. Booklet pane. No. 724×6, 734×3, 734b×3 and 735×3 se-tenant (1.12.69)...............................	8·50	
		na. Booklet pane. Uncoated paper**...	£3000	
		ny. Booklet pane. Phosphor omitted..	£225	
		s. Optd 'SPECIMEN' (14 mm).............	£250	
725		1d. yellowish olive (1 centre band) (16.9.68)..	45	45
		g. Gum arabic (27.8.69)........................	1·00	
		l. Booklet pane. No. 725×4 se-tenant with 732×2........................	4·00	
		ly. Booklet pane. Phosphor omitted..	35·00	
		m. Coil strip. No. 728×2 se-tenant with 729, 725g and 733g (27.8.69)	2·50	
726		2d. lake-brown (Type I) (2 bands) (5.2.68)...	10	10
		y. Phosphor omitted..........................	40·00	
727		2d. lake-brown (Type II) (2 bands) (1969)...	10	10
		y. Phosphor omitted..........................	2·00	
728		2d. lake-brown (Type II) (1 centre band) (27.8.69)................................	35	40
729		3d. violet (shades) (1 centre band) (8.8.67)...	10	10
		a. Imperf (vert pair)............................	£950	
		y. Phosphor omitted..........................	4·00	
		v. PVA gum (shades) (12.3.68).........	1·00	
		vy. Phosphor omitted.........................	4·00	
730		3d. violet (2 bands) (6.4.68)................	10	15
		a. Uncoated paper**..........................	£6000	
731		4d. deep sepia (shades) (2 bands)......	10	10
		y. Phosphor omitted..........................	4·00	
		a. Deep olive-brown..........................	1·00	1·00
		ay. Phosphor omitted.........................	6·00	
		b. Part perf pane*...............................	£4000	
		v. PVA gum (shades) (22.1.68).........	1·00	
		vy. Phosphor omitted.........................	4·00	
732		4d. deep olive-brown (shades) (1 centre band) (16.9.68)...................	10	10
		a. Part perf pane*...............................	£4250	
		l. Booklet pane. Two stamps plus two printed labels...................	1·00	
		ly. Booklet pane. Phosphor omitted..	60·00	
733		4d. bright vermilion (1 centre band) (6.1.69)...	10	10
		a. Tête-bêche (horiz pair)....................	£5000	
		b. Uncoated paper**..........................	20·00	
		y. Phosphor omitted..........................	4·00	
		l. Booklet pane. Two stamps plus two printed labels (3.3.69)......	1·00	
		ly. Booklet pane. Phosphor omitted..	75·00	
		g. Gum arabic (27.8.69)........................	1·00	
		gy. Phosphor omitted..........................	£175	
		s. Optd 'SPECIMEN' (14 mm).............	45·00	
734		4d. bright vermilion (1 band at left) (6.1.69)...	65	75
		a. Uncoated paper**..........................	£425	
		s. Optd 'SPECIMEN' (14 mm).............	£275	
		b. One band at right (1.12.69)...........	1·00	1·00
		bs. optd 'SPECIMEN' (14 mm)...........	£275	
		ba. Ditto. Uncoated paper**...............	£425	
735		5d. royal blue (shades) (1.7.68)...........	10	10
		a. Imperf pane*....................................	£3500	
		b. Part perf pane*...............................	£2500	
		c. Imperf (pair)††...............................	£350	
		d. Uncoated paper**..........................	40·00	
		y. Phosphor omitted..........................	6·00	
		e. Deep blue..	1·00	1·00
		ey. Phosphor omitted.........................	6·00	
		s. Optd 'SPECIMEN' (14 mm).............	60·00	
736		6d. bright reddish purple (shades) (5.2.68)...	10	10
		y. Phosphor omitted..........................	35·00	
		a. Bright magenta...............................	9·00	9·00
		b. Claret...	1·25	1·25
		by. Phosphor omitted.........................	45·00	
737	282a	7d. bright emerald (1.7.68).................	25	25
		y. Phosphor omitted..........................	£100	
738		8d. bright vermilion (1.7.68)................	10	15
		y. Phosphor omitted..........................	£450	
739		8d. light turquoise-blue (6.1.69)........	25	25
		y. Phosphor omitted..........................	80·00	
740		9d. myrtle-green (8.8.67).....................	25	25
		y. Phosphor omitted..........................	60·00	
		v. PVA gum (29.11.68).........................	1·00	
		vy. Phosphor omitted.........................	£120	
741	282	10d. drab (1.7.68)....................................	25	25
		a. Uncoated paper**..........................	85·00	
		y. Phosphor omitted..........................	85·00	
742		1s. light bluish violet (shades)..............	20	20
		y. Phosphor omitted..........................	£120	
		a. Pale bluish violet...........................	1·00	1·00
		av. PVA gum (26.4.68).........................	1·00	
		avy. Phosphor omitted........................	12·00	
743		1s.6d. greenish blue and deep blue (shades) (8.8.67)..............................	25	25
		a. Greenish blue omitted..................	£160	
		y. Phosphor omitted..........................	15·00	
		v. PVA gum (28.8.68)...........................	1·00	
		va. Greenish blue omitted.................	£100	
		vy. Phosphor omitted.........................	22·00	
		vb. Prussian blue and indigo..............	7·00	7·00
		vby. Phosphor omitted........................	18·00	
		c. Phosphorised paper (Prussian blue and indigo) (10.12.69).......	30	35
		ca. Prussian blue omitted...................	£450	
744		1s.9d. dull orange and black (shades)......	25	25
		y. Phosphor omitted..........................	65·00	
		a. Bright orange and black................	1·00	1·00
		av. PVA gum (16.11.70).......................	2·50	
		Set of 16 (one of each value and colour).............................	2·00	2·25
		Presentation Pack (one of each value) (1968)........................	7·00	
		Presentation Pack (German) (1969)...................................	90·00	

* BOOKLET ERRORS. See note after No. 556.

** Uncoated paper. This does not respond to the chalk test, and may be further distinguished from the normal chalk-surfaced paper by the fibres which clearly show on the surface, resulting in the printing impression being rougher, and by the screening dots which are not so evident. The 1d., 4d. and 5d. come from the £1 Stamps for Cooks Booklet (1969); the 3d. and 10d. from sheets (1969). The 20p. and 50p. high values (Nos. 830/831) exist with similar errors.

† No. 724a occurs in a vertical strip of four, top stamp perforated on three sides, bottom stamp imperf three sides and the two middle stamps completely imperf.

†† No. 735c comes from the original state of cylinder 15 which is identifiable by the screening dots which extend through the gutters of the stamps and into the margins of the sheet. This must not be confused with imperforate stamps from cylinder 10, a large quantity of which was stolen from the printers early in 1970.

The 1d. with centre band and PVA gum (No. 725) only came in the September 1968 10s. booklet. The 1d., 2d. and 4d. with centre band and gum arabic (Nos. 725g, 728 and 733g respectively) only came in the coil strip (No. 725m).

The 3d. (No. 730) appeared in booklets on 6.4.68, from coils during December 1968 and from sheets in January 1969.

The 4d. with one side band at left (No. 734) came from 10s. (band at left) and £1 (band at left or right) booklet se-tenant panes, and the 4d. with one side band at right (No. 734b) came from the £1 booklet se-tenant panes only.

Gum. The 1d. (No. 725), 3d. (No. 729), 4d. (Nos. 731 and 733), 9d., 1s., 1s.6d. and 1s.9d. exist with gum arabic as well as PVA gum; the 2d. (No. 728) and coil strip (No. 725m) exist only with gum arabic, while the remainder have PVA gum only.

The 4d. (No. 731) in shades of washed-out grey are colour changelings which we understand are caused by the concentrated solvents used in modern dry cleaning methods.

For decimal issue, see Nos. X841, etc.

First Day Covers

5.6.67	Nos. 731, 742, 744..	2·00
8.8.67	Nos. 729, 740, 743..	2·00
5.2.68	Nos. 723/724, 726, 736...	2·25
1.7.68	Nos. 735, 737/738, 741...	3·00

283 *Master Lambton* (Sir Thomas Lawrence)

284 *Mares and Foals in a Landscape* (George Stubbs)

285 *Children Coming Out of School* (L. S. Lowry)

1967/QUEEN ELIZABETH II

(Des S. Rose)

1967 (10 July). British Paintings (1st series). Chalk-surfaced paper. Two phosphor bands. No wmk. Perf 14×15 (4d.) or 15×14 (others).

748	283	4d. rose-red, lemon, brown, black, new blue and gold	10	10
		a. Gold (value and Queen's head) omitted	£200	
		b. New blue omitted	£10000	
		y. Phosphor omitted	7·00	
749	284	9d. Venetian red, ochre, grey-black, new-blue, greenish yellow and black	10	10
		a. Black (Queen's head and value) omitted	£775	
		ab. Black (Queen's head only) omitted	£1500	
		y. Phosphor omitted	£500	
750	285	1s.6d. greenish yellow, grey, rose, new blue, grey-black and gold	10	10
		a. Gold (Queen's head) omitted	£200	
		b. New blue omitted	£200	
		c. Grey (clouds and shading) omitted	£120	
		y. Phosphor omitted	£300	
Set of 3			30	30
First Day Cover				1·00
Presentation Pack			20·00	

See also Nos. 771/774.

Special First Day of Issue Postmark
GPO Philatelic Bureau, Edinburgh 1 (Type C) .... 2·00

A First Day of Issue handstamp was provided at Bishop Auckland, Co. Durham, for this issue.

286 *Gipsy Moth IV*

(Des M. and Sylvia Goaman)

1967 (24 July). Sir Francis Chichester's World Voyage. Chalk-surfaced paper. Three phosphor bands. No wmk. Perf 15×14.

751	286	1s.9d. black, brown-red, light emerald and blue	10	10
First Day Cover				40

Special First Day of Issue Postmark
GPO Philatelic Bureau, Edinburgh 1	2·50
Greenwich, London SE10	2·50
Plymouth, Devon	2·50

The Philatelic Bureau and Greenwich postmarks are similar in design to that for Plymouth. A First Day of Issue handstamp was provided at Chichester, Sussex for this date.

287 Radar Screen

288 *Penicillium notatum*

289 Vickers VC-10 Jet Engines

290 Television Equipment

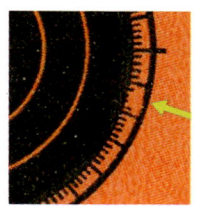

Broken scale (Cyl. 1c, R. 10/2)

(Des C. Abbott (4d., 1s.), Negus-Sharland team (others))

1967 (19 Sept). British Discovery and Invention. Chalk-surfaced paper. Three phosphor bands (4d.) or two phosphor bands (others). W **179** (sideways on 1s.9d.). Perf 14×15 (1s.9d.) or 15×14 (others).

752	287	4d. greenish yellow, black and vermilion	10	10
		a. Broken scale	45·00	
		y. Phosphor omitted	5·00	
753	288	1s. blue-green, light greenish blue, slate-purple and bluish violet	10	10
		Wi. Watermark inverted	20·00	
		y. Phosphor omitted	10·00	
754	289	1s.6d. black, grey, royal blue, ochre and turquoise-blue	10	10
		Wi. Watermark inverted	£325	
		y. Phosphor omitted	£600	
755	290	1s.9d. black, grey-blue, pale olive-grey, violet and orange	10	10
		a. Pale olive-grey omitted	—	£3500
		b. Orange (Queen's head) omitted	—	
		y. Phosphor omitted	£600	
Set of 4			40	40
First Day Cover				70
Presentation Pack			9·00	

Special First Day of Issue Postmark
GPO Philatelic Bureau, Edinburgh (Type C) 70

WATERMARK. All issues from this date are on unwatermarked paper *unless otherwise stated.*

291 *The Adoration of the Shepherds* (School of Seville)

292 *Madonna and Child* (Murillo)

293 *The Adoration of the Shepherds* (Louis le Nain)

(Des S. Rose)

1967. Christmas, Paintings. Chalk-surfaced paper. One phosphor band (3d.) or two phosphor bands (others). Perf 15×14 (1s.6d.) or 14×15 (others).

756	291	3d. olive-yellow, rose, blue, black and gold (27.11)	10	10
		a. Gold (value and Queen's head) omitted	90·00	
		ab. Gold (Queen's head only) omitted	£1500	
		ac. Gold (value only) omitted	£1500	
		b. Printed on the gummed side	£500	
		c. Rose omitted	£3250	
		d. Olive-yellow omitted	—	
		y. Phosphor omitted	1·00	
757	292	4d. bright purple, greenish yellow, new blue, grey-black and gold (18.10)	10	10

QUEEN ELIZABETH II/1967

	a. Gold (value and Queen's head) omitted		70·00	
	ab. Gold (Queen's head only) omitted		£3000	
	b. Gold ('4D' only) omitted		£1800	
	c. Greenish yellow (Child, robe and Madonna's face) omitted		£5000	
	d. Greenish yellow and gold omitted		£10000	
	y. Phosphor omitted		£175	
758	293	1s.6d. bright purple, bistre, lemon, black, orange-red, ultramarine and gold (27.11)	15	15
	a. Gold (value and Queen's head) omitted		£10000	
	ab. Gold (value only) omitted		£2000	
	ac. Gold (Queen's head only) omitted		£2000	
	b. Ultramarine omitted		£575	
	c. Lemon omitted		£12000	
	y. Phosphor omitted		12·00	
Set of 3			30	30
First Day Covers (2)				3·00

Distinct shades exist of the 3d. and 4d. values but are not listable as there are intermediate shades. For the 4d., stamps from one machine show a darker background and give the appearance of the yellow colour being omitted, but this is not so and these should not be confused with the true missing yellow No. 757c.

No. 757b comes from stamps in the first vertical row of a sheet.

The 3d. and 4d. values are known imperforate. They are of proof status.

Special First Day of Issue Postmarks

GPO Philatelic Bureau, Edinburgh 1 (4d.) (18 October) (Type C)	1·00
GPO Philatelic Bureau, Edinburgh 1 (3d., 1s.6d.) (27 November) (Type C)	2·00
Bethlehem, Llandeilo, Carms (4d.) (18 October) (Type C)	2·00
Bethlehem, Llandeilo, Carms (3d., 1s.6d.) (27 November) (Type C)	3·00

Gift Pack 1967

1967 (27 Nov). Comprises Nos. 715p/722p and 748/758
CP758c Gift Pack (PO Pack No. 1).............. 2·25

166 Carrickfergus Castle
167 Caernarvon Castle 
168 Edinburgh Castle 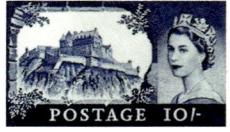
169 Windsor Castle 

(Recess Bradbury Wilkinson)

1967–68. No wmk. White paper. Perf 11×12.

759	166	2s.6d. black-brown (1.7.68)	10	20
760	167	5s. red (10.4.68)	50	50
761	168	10s. bright ultramarine (10.4.68)	4·50	2·00
762	169	£1 black (4.12.67)	6·50	2·00
Set of 4			10·00	4·25

PVA GUM. All the following issues from this date have PVA gum *except where footnotes state otherwise*.

294 Tarr Steps, Exmoor
295 Aberfeldy Bridge 
296 Menai Bridge 
297 M4 Viaduct 

(Des A. Restall (9d.), L. Rosoman (1s.6d.), J. Matthews (others))

1968 (29 Apr). British Bridges. Chalk-surfaced paper. Two phosphor bands. Perf 15×14.

763	294	4d. black, bluish violet, turquoise-blue and gold	10	10
		a. Printed on gummed side	35·00	
		y. Phosphor omitted	10·00	
764	295	9d. red-brown, myrtle-green, ultramarine, olive-brown, black and gold	10	15
		a. Gold (Queen's head) omitted	£225	
		b. Ultramarine omitted	†	£5000
		y. Phosphor omitted	15·00	
765	296	1s.6d. olive-brown, red-orange, bright green, turquoise-green and gold	15	20
		a. Gold (Queen's head) omitted	£300	
		b. Red-orange (rooftops) omitted	£300	
		y. Phosphor omitted	50·00	
766	297	1s.9d. olive-brown, greenish yellow, dull green, dp ultramarine and gold	15	25
		a. Gold (Queen's head) omitted	£275	
		y. Phosphor omitted	10·00	
		ya. Gold (Queen's head) and Phosphor omitted	£2500	
Set of 4			45	65
First Day Cover				90
Presentation Pack			5·25	

No. 764b is only known on First day covers posted from Canterbury, Kent or the Philatelic Bureau, Edinburgh.

Used examples of the 1s.6d. and 1s.9d. are known with both the gold and the phosphor omitted.

Special First Day of Issue Postmarks

GPO Philatelic Bureau, Edinburgh 1	2·25
Bridge, Canterbury, Kent	10·00
Aberfeldy, Perthshire (Type A) (9d. value only)	10·00
Menai Bridge, Anglesey (Type A) (1s.6d. value only)	10·00

The Bridge, Canterbury, postmark is similar in design to that for the Philatelic Bureau.

298 'TUC' and Trades Unionists
299 Mrs Emmeline Pankhurst (statue) 
300 Sopwith Camel and English Electric Lightning Fighters 
301 Captain Cook's *Endeavour* and Signature 

(Des D. Gentleman (4d.), C. Abbott (others))

1968 (29 May). Anniversaries (1st series). Events described on stamps. Chalk-surfaced paper. Two phosphor bands. Perf 15×14.

767	298	4d. emerald, olive, blue and black	10	10
		y. Phosphor omitted	40·00	
768	299	9d. reddish violet, bluish grey and black	10	10
		y. Phosphor omitted	10·00	
769	300	1s. olive-brown, blue, red, slate-blue and black	15	20
		y. Phosphor omitted	10·00	
770	301	1s.9d. yellow-ochre and blackish brown	20	25
		y. Phosphor omitted	£190	
Set of 4			50	60
First Day Cover				2·50
Presentation Pack			5·00	

See also Nos. 791/795 and 819/823.

Special First Day of Issue Postmarks

GPO Philatelic Bureau, Edinburgh 1 (Type C)	3·00
Manchester (4d. value only)	1·00
Aldeburgh, Suffolk (9d. value only)	2·00
Hendon, London NW 4 (1s. value only)	3·00
Whitby, Yorkshire (1s.9d. value only)	4·00

The Philatelic Bureau postmark was used on sets of four, but the other postmarks were only available on single stamps.

1968 / QUEEN ELIZABETH II

302 *Queen Elizabeth I* (unknown artist)
303 *Pinkie* (Sir Thomas Lawrence) 
304 *Ruins of St Mary le Port* (John Piper) 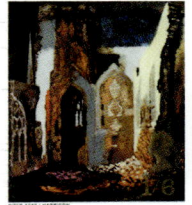
305 *The Hay Wain* (John Constable) 

(Des S. Rose)

1968 (12 Aug). British Paintings (2nd series). Queen's head embossed. Chalk-surfaced paper. Two phosphor bands. Perf 15×14 (1s.9d.) or 14×15 (others).

771	302	4d. black, vermilion, greenish yellow, grey and gold	10	10
		a. Gold (value and Queen's head) omitted	£250	
		b. Vermilion omitted*	£550	
		c. Embossing omitted	90·00	
		y. Phosphor omitted	1·50	
		ya. Gold (value and Queen's head) omitted and Phosphor omitted	£3000	
772	303	1s. mauve, new blue, greenish yellow, black, magenta and gold	10	15
		a. Gold (value and Queen's head) omitted	£6000	
		b. Gold (value and Queen's head), embossing and phosphor omitted	£500	
		c. Embossing omitted	†	
		y. Phosphor omitted	7·00	
773	304	1s.6d. slate, orange, black, mauve, greenish yellow, ultramarine and gold	15	20
		a. Gold (value and Queen's head) omitted	£250	
		b. Embossing omitted	£275	
		y. Phosphor omitted	10·00	
774	305	1s.9d. greenish yellow, black, new blue, red and gold	15	20
		a. Gold (value and Queen's head) and embossing omitted	£750	
		b. Red omitted	£6500	
		c. Embossing omitted		£140
		y. Phosphor omitted	20·00	
Set of 4			45	60
First Day Cover				1·00
Presentation Pack (PO Pack No. 1)			4·50	
Presentation Pack (German)			30·00	

* The effect of this is to leave the face and hands white and there is more yellow and olive in the costume.

No. 774a is only known with the phosphor also omitted.

The 4d. also exists with the value only omitted resulting from a colour shift.

Special First Day of Issue Postmark
GPO Philatelic Bureau, Edinburgh 1 (Type C) .... 2·00

Gift Pack 1968

1968 (16 Sept). Comprises Nos. 763/774.
CP774c	Gift Pack (PO Pack No. 2)	3·00
CP774d	Gift Pack (German)	80·00

Collectors Pack 1968

1968 (1 Sept). Comprises Nos. 752/758 and 763/774.
CP774e	Collectors Pack (PO Pack No. 3)	2·50

306 Boy and Girl with Rocking Horse

307 Girl with Doll's House
308 Boy with Train Set 

(Des Rosalind Dease. Head printed in gold and then embossed)

1968 (25 Nov). Christmas, Children's Toys. Chalk-surfaced paper. One centre phosphor band (4d.) or two phosphor bands (others). Perf 15×14 (4d.) or 14×15 (others).

775	306	4d. black, orange, vermilion, ultramarine, bistre and gold	10	10
		a. Gold omitted	£3750	
		b. Vermilion omitted*	£450	
		c. Ultramarine omitted	£425	
		d. Bistre omitted	†	—
		e. Orange omitted	†	—
		f. Embossing omitted	6·00	
		y. Phosphor omitted	5·00	
		ya. Embossing and Phosphor omitted		
776	307	9d. yellow-olive, black, brown, yellow, magenta, orange, turquoise-green and gold	15	15
		a. Yellow omitted	£150	
		b. Turquoise-green (dress) omitted	£15000	
		c. Embossing omitted	6·00	
		y. Phosphor omitted	10·00	
		ya. Embossing and Phosphor omitted	10·00	
777	308	1s.6d. ultramarine, yellow-orange, bright purple, blue-green, black and gold	15	20
		a. Embossing omitted		
		y. Phosphor omitted	15·00	
Set of 3			35	40
First Day Cover				1·00
Presentation Pack (PO Pack No. 4)			9·00	
Presentation Pack (German)			30·00	

No. 775c is only known with phosphor also omitted.

Two machines were used for printing for the 4d. value:

Stamps from cylinders 1A-1B-2C-1D-1E in combination with 1F, 2F or 3F (gold) were printed entirely on the Rembrandt sheet-fed machine. They invariably have the Queen's head level with the top of the boy's head and the sheets are perforated through the left side margin.

Stamps from cylinders 2A-2B-3C-2D-2E in combination with 1F, 2F, 3F or 4F (gold) were printed on the reel-fed Thrissell machine in five colours (its maximum colour capacity) and subsequently sheet-fed on the Rembrandt machine for the Queen's head and the embossing. The position of the Queen's head is generally lower than on the stamps printed at one operation but it varies in different parts of the sheet and is not, therefore, a sure indication for identifying single stamps. Another small difference is that the boy's grey pullover is noticeably 'moth-eaten' in the Thrissell printings and is normal on the Rembrandt. The Thrissell printings are perforated through the top margin.

Special First Day of Issue Postmarks
GPO Philatelic Bureau, Edinburgh 1 (Type C) .... 1·00
Bethlehem, Llandeilo, Carms (Type C) .... 2·50

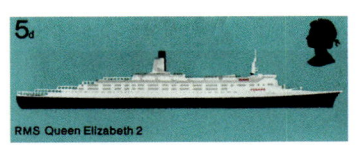

309 RMS *Queen Elizabeth 2*

QUEEN ELIZABETH II/1969

310 Elizabethan Galleon

311 East Indiaman

312 *Cutty Sark*

313 SS *Great Britain*

314 RMS *Mauretania*

(Des D. Gentleman)

1969 (15 Jan). British Ships. Chalk-surfaced paper. Two vertical phosphor bands at right (1s.), one horizontal phosphor band (5d.) or two phosphor bands (9d.). Perf 15×14.

778	**309**	5d. black, grey, red and turquoise	10	10
		a. Black (Queen's head, value, hull and inscr) omitted	£2750	
		b. Grey (decks, etc.) omitted	£180	
		c. Red (inscription) omitted	£180	
		y. Phosphor omitted	5·00	
		ya. Red and phosphor omitted	£140	
779	**310**	9d. red, blue, ochre, brown, black and grey	10	10
		a. Strip of 3. Nos. 779/781	40	50
		ab. Red and blue omitted	£2250	
		ac. Blue omitted	£2250	
		y. Phosphor omitted	12·00	
		ya. Strip of 3. Nos. 779/781. Phosphor omitted	40·00	
780	**311**	9d. ochre, brown, black and grey	10	10
		y. Phosphor omitted	12·00	
781	**312**	9d. ochre, brown, black and grey	10	10
		y. Phosphor omitted	12·00	
782	**313**	1s. brown, black, grey, green and greenish yellow	15	15
		a. Pair. Nos. 782/783	50	60
		ab. Greenish yellow omitted	£3000	
		y. Phosphor omitted	32·00	
		ya. Pair. Nos. 782/783. Phosphor omitted	65·00	
783	**314**	1s. red, black, brown, carmine and grey	15	15
		a. Carmine (hull overlay) omitted	£20000	
		b. Red (funnels) omitted	£15000	
		c. Carmine and red omitted	£15000	
		y. Phosphor omitted	32·00	
Set of 6			80	1·00
First Day Cover				1·50
Presentation Pack (PO Pack No. 5)			3·00	
Presentation Pack (German)			38·00	

The 9d. and 1s. values were arranged in horizontal strips of three and pairs respectively throughout the sheet.

No. 779ab is known only with the phosphor also omitted.

Special First Day of Issue Postmark
GPO Philatelic Bureau, Edinburgh 1 (Type C) ..... 1·75

315 Concorde in Flight

316 Plan and Elevation Views

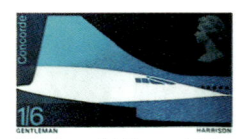

317 Concorde's Nose and Tail

(Des M. and Sylvia Goaman (4d.), D. Gentleman (9d., 1s.6d.))

1969 (3 Mar). First Flight of Concorde. Chalk-surfaced paper. Two phosphor bands. Perf 15×14.

784	**315**	4d. yellow-orange, violet, greenish blue, blue-green and pale green	10	10
		a. Violet (value etc.) omitted	£575	
		b. Yellow-orange omitted	£575	
		y. Phosphor omitted	2·00	
		ya. Yellow-orange and phosphor omitted	£575	
785	**316**	9d. ultramarine, emerald, red and grey-blue	15	15
		a. Face value and inscr omitted	—	
		y. Phosphor omitted	£140	
786	**317**	1s.6d. deep blue, silver-grey and light blue	15	15
		a. Silver-grey omitted	£575	
		y. Phosphor omitted	10·00	
Set of 3			35	35
First Day Cover				4·00
Presentation Pack (PO Pack No. 6)			7·50	
Presentation Pack (German)			75·00	

No. 785a is caused by a colour shift of the grey-blue. On the only known example the top of the Queen's head appears across the perforations at foot.

No. 786a affects the Queen's head which appears in the light blue colour.

Special First Day of Issue Postmarks
GPO Philatelic Bureau, Edinburgh (Type C) ..... 4·00
Filton, Bristol (Type C) ..... 12·00

318 Queen Elizabeth II (See also T **357**)

(Des after plaster cast by Arnold Machin. Eng Robert Goodbehear and Nigel Alan Dow (portrait) and J. G. Heymes (background and lettering). Recess Bradbury Wilkinson)

1969 (5 Mar). Perf 12.

787	**318**	2s.6d. brown	20	20
788		5s. crimson-lake	85	25
789		10s. deep ultramarine	3·00	3·75
790		£1 bluish black	1·75	75
Set of 4			5·00	4·50
First Day Cover				6·50
Presentation Pack (PO Pack No. 7)			16·00	
Presentation Pack (German)			55·00	

Special First Day of Issue Postmarks
GPO Philatelic Bureau (Type C) ..... 12·00
Windsor, Berks (Type C) ..... 18·00

For decimal issue, see Nos. 829/831b and notes after No. 831b.

319 Page from *Daily Mail*, and Vickers FB-27 Vimy Aircraft

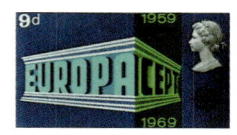

320 Europa and CEPT Emblems

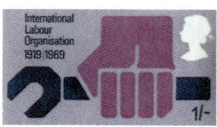

321 ILO Emblem

322 Flags of NATO Countries

1969/QUEEN ELIZABETH II

323 Vickers FB-27 Vimy Aircraft and Globe showing Flight

(Des P. Sharland (5d., 1s., 1s.6d.), M. and Sylvia Goaman (9d., 1s.9d.))

1969 (2 Apr). Anniversaries (2nd series). Events described on stamps. Chalk-surfaced paper. Two phosphor bands. Perf 15×14.

791	**319**	5d. black, pale sage-green, chestnut and new blue...............	10	10
		y. Phosphor omitted................	£180	
792	**320**	9d. pale turquoise, deep blue, light emerald-green and black............	10	15
		y. Phosphor omitted................	18·00	
		a. Uncoated paper*................	£1500	
		ay. Phosphor omitted............	—	
793	**321**	1s. bright purple, deep blue and lilac..	15	20
		y. Phosphor omitted................	15·00	
794	**322**	1s.6d. red, royal blue, yellow-green, black, lemon and new blue.............	15	20
		e. Black omitted................	£100	
		f. Yellow-green (from flags) omitted.	70·00	
		fy. Yellow-green and phosphor omitted................	70·00	
		g. Lemon (from flags) omitted............	†	£3000
		y. Phosphor omitted................	9·00	
795	**323**	1s.9d. yellow-olive, greenish yellow and pale turquoise-green.............	25	30
		a. Uncoated paper*................	£275	
		y. Phosphor omitted................	10·00	
Set of 5............			65	80
First Day Cover............				1·10
Presentation Pack (PO Pack No. 9)............			4·50	
Presentation Pack (German)............			50·00	

* Uncoated paper. The second note after No. 744 also applies here.
No. 794g is only known used on First Day Cover from Liverpool.
A trial of the 9d value in green and red is known.

Special First Day of Issue Postmarks
GPO Philatelic Bureau, Edinburgh (Type C)................ 1·10

324 Durham Cathedral
325 York Minster 
326 St Giles, Edinburgh 
327 Canterbury Cathedral 
328 St Paul's Cathedral 
329 Liverpool Metropolitan Cathedral 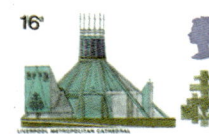

(Des P. Gauld)

1969 (28 May). British Architecture (1st series). Cathedrals. Chalk-surfaced paper. Two phosphor bands. Perf 15×14.

796	**324**	5d. grey-black, orange, pale bluish violet and black...............	10	10
		a. Block of 4. Nos. 796/799............	40	50
		ab. Block of 4. Uncoated paper†............	£850	
		b. Pale bluish violet omitted............	£7500	
797	**325**	5d. grey-black, pale bluish violet, new blue and black...............	10	10
		b. Pale bluish violet omitted............	£7500	
798	**326**	5d. grey-black, purple, green and black...............	10	10
		c. Green omitted*............	90·00	
799	**327**	5d. grey-black, green, new blue and black...............	10	10
800	**328**	9d. grey-black, ochre, pale drab, violet and black...............	15	20
		a. Black (value) omitted............	£200	
		y. Phosphor omitted............	45·00	
801	**329**	1s.6d. grey-black, pale turquoise, pale reddish violet, pale yellow-olive and black...............	20	25
		a. Black (value) omitted............	£2000	
		b. Black (value) double............	£375	
		y. Phosphor omitted............	20·00	
Set of 6............			70	85
First Day Cover............				1·00
Presentation Pack (PO Pack No. 10)............			5·50	
Presentation Pack (German)............			35·00	

* The missing green on the roof top is known on R. 2/5, R. 8/5 and R. 10/5 but all are from different sheets and it only occurred in part of the printing, being 'probably caused by a batter on the impression cylinder'. Examples are also known with the green partly omitted.
† Uncoated paper. The second note after No. 744 also applies here.

Nos. 796/799 were issued together *se-tenant* in blocks of four throughout the sheet.

Special First Day of Issue Postmark
GPO Philatelic Bureau, Edinburgh (Type C)................ 1·00

330 The King's Gate, Caernarvon Castle
331 The Eagle Tower, Caernarvon Castle 
332 Queen Eleanor's Gate, Caernarvon Castle 
333 Celtic Cross, Margam Abbey 
334 HRH The Prince of Wales (after photograph by G. Argent) 

(Des D. Gentleman)

1969 (1 July). Investiture of HRH The Prince of Wales. Chalk-surfaced paper. Two phosphor bands. Perf 14×15.

802	**330**	5d. deep olive-grey, light olive-grey, deep grey, light grey, red, pale turquoise-green, black and silver...............	10	10
		a. Strip of 3. Nos. 802/804............	30	50
		b. Black (value and inscr) omitted............	£500	
		c. Red omitted*............	£950	
		d. Deep grey omitted**............	£350	
		e. Pale turquoise-green omitted............	£950	
		f. Light grey (marks on walls, window frames etc) omitted............	£5500	
		y. Phosphor omitted............	5·00	
		ya. Strip of 3. Nos. 802/804. Phosphor omitted............	15·00	
803	**331**	5d. deep olive-grey, light olive-grey, deep grey, light grey, red, pale turquoise-green, black and silver...............	10	10
		b. Black (value and inscr) omitted............	£500	
		c. Red omitted*............	£950	

QUEEN ELIZABETH II/1969

		d. Deep grey omitted**	£350	
		e. Pale turquoise-green omitted	£950	
		f. Light grey omitted	£5500	—
		y. Phosphor omitted	5·00	
804	332	5d. deep olive-grey, light olive-grey, deep grey, light grey, red, pale turquoise-green, black and silver	10	10
		b. Black (value and inscr) omitted	£500	
		c. Red omitted*	£950	
		d. Deep grey omitted**	£350	
		e. Pale turquoise-green omitted	£950	
		f. Light grey omitted	£5500	
		y. Phosphor omitted	5·00	
805	333	9d. deep grey, light grey, black and gold	15	20
		y. Phosphor omitted	25·00	
806	334	1s. blackish yellow-olive and gold	15	20
		y. Phosphor omitted	45·00	
Set of 5			55	80
First Day Cover				1·00
Presentation Pack† (PO Pack No. 11)			3·00	
Presentation Pack (German)			35·00	
Presentation Pack (Welsh)			35·00	

* The 5d. value is also known with the red misplaced downwards and where this occurs the red printing does not take very well on the silver background and in some cases is so faint it could be mistaken for a missing red. However, the red can be seen under a magnifying glass and caution should therefore be exercised when purchasing copies of Nos. 802c/804c.

** The deep grey affects the dark portions of the windows and doors.

† In addition to the generally issued Presentation Pack a further pack in different colours and with all texts printed in both English and Welsh was made available exclusively through Education Authorities for free distribution to all schoolchildren in Wales and Monmouthshire.

Nos. 802/804 were issued together *se-tenant* in strips of three throughout the sheet.

No. 803f is also known commercially used *on cover*.

Special First Day of Issue Postmarks

GPO Philatelic Bureau, Edinburgh (Type C)	1·00
Day of Investiture, Caernarvon	1·50

335 Mahatma Gandhi

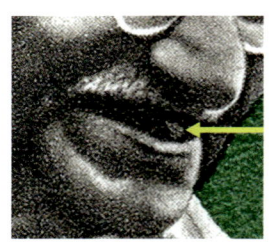

'Tooth' flaw (Cyl. 2A, R. 20/3)

(Des B. Mullick)

1969 (13 Aug). Gandhi Centenary Year. Chalk-surfaced paper. Two phosphor bands. Perf 15×14.

807	335	1s.6d. black, green, red-orange and grey	25	30
		a. Tooth flaw	40·00	
		b. Printed on the gummed side	£1200	
		y. Phosphor omitted	10·00	
First Day Cover				3·25

Special First Day of Issue Postmark

GPO Philatelic Bureau, Edinburgh (Type C)	3·25

Collectors Pack 1969

1969 (15 Sept). Comprises Nos. 775/786 and 791/807.

CP807b	Collectors Pack (PO Pack No. 12)	10·00

336 National Giro 'G' Symbol

337 Telecommunications, International Subscriber Dialling

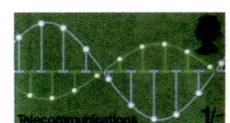

338 Telecommunications, Pulse Code Modulation

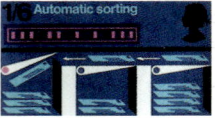

339 Postal Mechanisation, Automatic Sorting

(Des D. Gentleman. Litho De La Rue)

1969 (1 Oct). Post Office Technology Commemoration. Chalk-surfaced paper. Two phosphor bands. Perf 13½×14.

808	336	5d. new blue, greenish blue, lavender and black	10	10
		y. Phosphor omitted	8·00	
809	337	9d. emerald, violet-blue and black	10	10
810	338	1s. emerald, lavender and black	15	15
		y. Phosphor omitted	£325	
811	339	1s.6d. bright purple, light blue, grey-blue and black	20	20
Set of 4			50	50
First Day Cover				75
Presentation Pack (PO Pack No. 13)			5·00	

Special First Day of Issue Postmark

GPO Philatelic Bureau, Edinburgh (Type C)	75

340 Herald Angel

341 The Three Shepherds

342 The Three Kings

(Des F. Wegner. Queen's head (and stars 4d., 5d. and scrollwork 1s.6d.) printed in gold and then embossed)

1969 (26 Nov). Christmas, Traditional Religious Themes. Chalk-surfaced paper. Two phosphor bands (5d., 1s.6d.) or one centre band (4d.). Perf 15×14.

812	340	4d. vermilion, new blue, orange, bright purple, light green, bluish violet, blackish brown and gold	10	10
		a. Gold (Queen's head etc.) omitted	£7500	
		b. Centre band 3½ mm	30	20
813	341	5d. magenta, light blue, royal blue, olive-brown, green, greenish yellow, red and gold	10	10
		a. Light blue (sheep, etc.) omitted	£100	
		b. Red omitted*	£1800	
		c. Gold (Queen's head) omitted	£950	
		d. Green omitted	£300	
		e. Olive-brown, red and gold omitted	£10000	
		f. Embossing omitted	25·00	
		y. Phosphor omitted	5·00	
814	342	1s.6d. greenish yellow, bright purple, bluish violet, deep slate, orange, green, new blue and gold	15	15
		a. Gold (Queen's head etc.) omitted	£130	
		b. Deep slate (value) omitted	£425	
		c. Greenish yellow omitted	£400	
		e. New blue omitted	£120	
		f. Embossing omitted	12·00	
		y. Phosphor omitted	6·00	
		ya. Embossing and phosphor omitted	12·00	
Set of 3			30	30
First Day Cover				70
Presentation Pack (PO Pack No. 14)			3·00	

* The effect of the missing red is shown on the hat, leggings and purse which appear as dull orange.

No. 812 has one centre band 8 mm wide but this was of no practical use in the automatic facing machines and after about three-quarters of the stamps had been printed the remainder were printed with a 3½ mm band (No. 812b).

No. 813e was caused by a paper fold and also shows the phosphor omitted.

Used copies of the 5d. have been seen with the olive-brown or greenish yellow (tunic at left) omitted.

1970/QUEEN ELIZABETH II

Special First Day of Issue Postmarks
PO Philatelic Bureau, Edinburgh (Type C).................... 70
Bethlehem, Llandeilo, Carms (Type C)........................ 1·00

343 Fife Harling 
344 Cotswold Limestone 
345 Welsh Stucco 
346 Ulster Thatch

Lemon omitted from left chimney (Cyl. 1H, R. 12/2)

(Des D. Gentleman (5d., 9d.), Sheila Robinson (1s., 1s.6d.))

1970 (11 Feb). British Rural Architecture. Chalk-surfaced paper. Two phosphor bands. Perf 15×14.

815	343	5d. grey, grey-black, black, lemon, greenish blue, orange-brown, ultramarine and green	10	10
		a. Lemon omitted	£140	
		b. Grey (Queen's head and cottage shading) omitted	—	
		c. Greenish blue (door) omitted	†	£3000
		d. Grey black (inscription and face value) omitted	£12000	
		e. Grey black (face value only) omitted	£10000	
		f. Green omitted (cobblestones)		
		g. Lemon omitted from left chimney	35·00	
		y. Phosphor omitted	2·00	
816	344	9d. orange-brown, olive-yellow, bright green, black, grey-black and grey	15	15
		y. Phosphor omitted	30·00	
817	345	1s. deep blue, reddish lilac, drab and new blue	15	15
		a. New blue omitted	£110	
		y. Phosphor omitted	£110	
818	346	1s.6d. greenish yellow, black, turquoise-blue and lilac	20	25
		a. Turquoise-blue omitted	£11000	
		y. Phosphor omitted	5·00	
Set of 4			55	60
First Day Cover				85
Presentation Pack (PO Pack No. 15)			3·00	

Used examples of the 5d. exist, one of which is *on piece*, with the greenish blue colour omitted.

Special First Day of Issue Postmark
British Philatelic Bureau, Edinburgh (Type C)................ 85

347 Signing the Declaration of Arbroath
348 Florence Nightingale attending Patients 
349 Signing of International Co-operative Alliance 
350 Pilgrims and *Mayflower* 
351 Sir William Herschel, Francis Baily, Sir John Herschel and Telescope 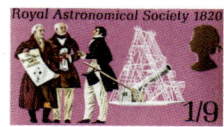

(Des F. Wegner (5d., 9d. and 1s.6d.), Marjorie Saynor (1s., 1s.9d.). Queen's head printed in gold and then embossed)

1970 (1 Apr). Anniversaries (3rd series). Events described on stamps. Chalk-surfaced paper. Two phosphor bands. Perf 15×14.

819	347	5d. black, yellow-olive, blue, emerald, greenish yellow, rose-red, gold and orange-red	10	10
		a. Gold (Queen's head) omitted	£2500	
		b. Emerald omitted	£400	
		y. Phosphor omitted	£375	
820	348	9d. ochre, deep blue, carmine, black, blue-green, yellow-olive, gold and blue	10	10
		a. Ochre omitted	£400	
		b. Embossing omitted	15·00	
		y. Phosphor omitted	7·00	
821	349	1s. green, greenish yellow, brown, black, cerise, gold and light blue	15	15
		a. Gold (Queen's head) omitted	80·00	
		b. Green and embossing omitted	£120	
		c. Green omitted	£120	
		d. Brown omitted	£250	
		e. Embossing omitted	12·00	
		y. Phosphor omitted	10·00	
		ya. Brown and phosphor missing	£250	
		yb. Embossing and phosphor missing	22·00	
822	350	1s.6d. greenish yellow, carmine, deep yellow-olive, emerald, black, blue, gold and sage-green	20	20
		a. Gold (Queen's head) omitted	£300	
		b. Emerald omitted	£150	
		c. Embossing omitted	6·00	
		y. Phosphor omitted	9·00	
823	351	1s.9d. black, slate, lemon, gold and bright purple	20	20
		a. Lemon (trousers and document) omitted	£6000	£4000
		b. Embossing omitted	75·00	
		y. Phosphor omitted	9·00	
Set of 5			70	70
First Day Cover				95
Presentation Pack (PO Pack No. 16)			4·00	

No. 823a is known mint, or used on First Day Cover postmarked London WC.

Special First Day of Issue Postmark
British Philatelic Bureau, Edinburgh (Type C)................ 95

First Day of Issue handstamps were provided at Arbroath, Angus; Billericay, Essex; Boston, Lincs and Rochdale, Lancs for this issue.

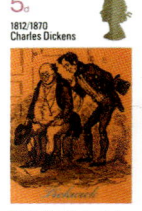

352 Mr Pickwick and Sam Weller (*Pickwick Papers*)
353 Mr and Mrs Micawber (*David Copperfield*)

QUEEN ELIZABETH II/1970

354 David Copperfield and Betsy Trotwood (*David Copperfield*)
355 Oliver Asking for More (*Oliver Twist*)
356 Grasmere (from engraving by J. Farrington, RA) 

(Des Rosalind Dease. Queen's head printed in gold and then embossed)

1970 (3 June). Literary Anniversaries (1st series). Death Centenary of Charles Dickens (novelist) (5d.×4) and Birth Bicentenary of William Wordsworth (poet) (1s.6d.). Chalk-surfaced paper. Two phosphor bands. Perf 14×15.

824	352	5d. black, orange, silver, gold and magenta	10	10
		a. Block of 4. Nos. 824/827	40	60
		ab. Imperf (block of four)	£1500	
		ac. Silver (inscr) omitted (block of four)	—	
825	353	5d. black, magenta, silver, gold and orange	10	10
826	354	5d. black, light greenish blue, silver, gold and yellow-bistre	10	10
		b. Yellow-bistre (value) omitted	£5500	
827	355	5d. black, yellow-bistre, silver, gold and light greenish blue	10	10
		b. Yellow-bistre (background) omitted	£15000	
		c. Light greenish blue (value) omitted*	£650	
		d. Light greenish blue and silver (inscr at foot) omitted	£20000	
828	356	1s.6d. yellow-olive, black, silver, gold and bright blue	15	20
		a. Gold (Queen's head) omitted	£7500	
		b. Silver ('Grasmere') omitted	£200	
		c. Bright blue (face value) omitted	£12000	
		d. Bright blue and silver omitted	£15000	
		e. Embossing omitted	6·00	
		y. Phosphor omitted	5·00	
		ya. Embossing and phosphor omitted	22·00	
Set of 5			50	70
First Day Cover				90
Presentation Pack (PO Pack No. 17)			4·00	

* No. 827c (unlike No. 826b) comes from a sheet on which the colour was only partially omitted so that, although No. 827 was completely without the light greenish blue colour, it was still partially present on No. 826.

Essays exist of Nos. 824/827 showing the Queen's head in silver and with different inscriptions. (*Price £13,000 per block of 4*).

Special First Day of Issue Postmarks
British Philatelic Bureau, Edinburgh (Type C)	90
Cockermouth, Cumberland (Type C) (No. 828 only)	90
Rochester, Kent (Type C) (Nos. 824/827)	90

A First Day of Issue handstamp was provided at Broadstairs, Kent, for this issue.

NOTE. For Nos. 829/831*b* and Types **356***a* and **357** see Decimal Machin Definitive section.

358 Runners
359 Swimmers 
360 Cyclists 

(Des A. Restall. Litho D.L.R.)

1970 (15 July). Ninth British Commonwealth Games. Chalk-surfaced paper. Two phosphor bands. Perf 13½×14.

832	358	5d. pink, emerald, greenish yellow and deep yellow-green	10	10
		a. Greenish yellow omitted	£7500	
		y. Phosphor omitted	£200	
833	359	1s.6d. light greenish blue, lilac, bistre-brown and Prussian blue	15	15
		y. Phosphor omitted	60·00	
834	360	1s.9d. yellow-orange, lilac, salmon and deep red-brown	15	15
Set of 3			45	45
First Day Cover				75
Presentation Pack (PO Pack No. 19)			3·00	

Special First Day of Issue Postmark
British Philatelic Bureau, Edinburgh (Type C) .... 1·00

Collectors Pack 1970

1970 (14 Sept). Comprises Nos. 808/828 and 832/834.
CP834*a*   Collectors Pack (PO Pack No. 20) .... 15·00

361 1d. Black (1840) — 1840 first engraved issue
362 1s. Green (1847) — 1847 first embossed issue
363 4d. Carmine (1855) — 1855 first surface printed issue

(Des D. Gentleman)

1970 (18 Sept). Philympia 70 Stamp Exhibition. Chalk-surfaced paper. Two phosphor bands. Perf 14×14½.

835	361	5d. grey-black, brownish bistre, black and dull purple	10	10
		a. Dull purple (Queen's head) omitted	—	
		y. Phosphor omitted	8·00	
836	362	9d. light drab, bluish green, stone, black and dull purple	15	15
		y. Phosphor omitted	15·00	
837	363	1s.6d. carmine, light drab, black and dull purple	20	20
		y. Phosphor omitted	5·00	
Set of 3			40	40
First Day Cover				75
Presentation Pack (PO Pack No. 21)			3·00	

Special First Day of Issue Postmark
British Post Office Philatelic Bureau, Edinburgh (Type D) .... 1·00

364 Shepherds and Apparition of the Angel
365 Mary, Joseph and Christ in the Manger 
366 The Wise Men bearing gifts

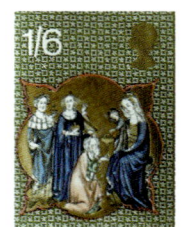

1970/QUEEN ELIZABETH II

(Des Sally Stiff after *De Lisle Psalter*. Queen's head printed in gold and then embossed)

1970 (25 Nov). Christmas, *Robert de Lisle Psalter*. Chalk-surfaced paper. One centre phosphor band (4d.) or two phosphor bands (others). Perf 14×15.

838	364	4d. brown-red, turquoise-green, pale chestnut, brown, grey-black, gold and vermilion..................................	10	10
		a. Embossing omitted........................	50·00	
		y. Phosphor omitted..........................	90·00	
839	365	5d. emerald, gold, blue, brown-red, ochre, grey-black and violet............	10	10
		a. Gold (Queen's head) omitted..........	†	£2750
		b. Emerald omitted.............................	£120	
		c. Imperf (pair)....................................	£300	
		d. Ochre omitted.................................	£3750	†
		e. Embossing omitted........................	15·00	
		y. Phosphor omitted..........................	5·00	
840	366	1s.6d. gold, grey-black, pale turquoise-green, salmon, ultramarine, ochre and yellow-green..............................	15	15
		a. Salmon omitted...............................	£190	
		b. Ochre omitted.................................	£120	
		c. Embossing omitted........................	35·00	
		y. Phosphor omitted..........................	12·00	
		ya. Embossing and phosphor omitted	60·00	
Set of 3..			30	30
First Day Cover...				40
Presentation Pack (PO Pack No. 22).......................			4·00	

Special First Day of Issue Postmark
British Post Office Philatelic Bureau, Edinburgh (Type D).............. 50
Bethlehem, Llandeilo, Carms.. 1·00

NOTE. Nos. 841/880 are no longer used. For 1971–1996 definitives in decimal currency with conventional perforations on all sides, see Nos. X841/X1058, T **367**, see Decimal Machin Definitives section.

(New Currency. 100 new pence = £1)

368 *A Mountain Road* (T. P. Flanagan)

369 *Deer's Meadow* (Tom Carr)

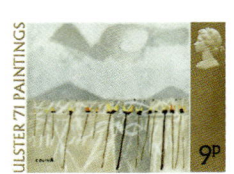

370 *Slieve na brock* (Colin Middleton)

(Des Stuart Rose)

1971 (16 June). Ulster 1971 Paintings. Multicoloured Chalk-surfaced paper. Two phosphor bands. Perf 15×14.

881	368	3p. *A Mountain Road* (T. P. Flanagan)....	10	10
		y. Phosphor omitted..........................	6·00	—
		a. Venetian red omitted.....................		
882	369	7½p. *Deer's Meadow* (Tom Carr).............	15	20
		a. Pale olive-grey omitted*.................	£350	
		y. Phosphor omitted..........................	25·00	
883	370	9p. *Slieve na brock* (Colin Middleton)....	20	20
		a. Orange (*flowers*) omitted.................	£2500	
		y. Phosphor omitted..........................	15·00	
Set of 3..			40	45
First Day Cover...				75
Presentation Pack (PO Pack No. 26a)..................			3·00	

* This only affects the boulder in the foreground, which appears whitish and it only applied to some stamps in the sheet.

Special First Day of Issue Postmarks
British Post Office Philatelic Bureau, Edinburgh (Type D, see Introduction).. 1·10
Belfast... 3·00

First Day of Issue handstamps, in the same design as that for Belfast, were provided at Armagh, Ballymena, Coleraine, Cookstown, Enniskillen, Londonderry, Newry, Omagh and Portadown for this issue.

371 John Keats (150th Death Anniversary)

372 Thomas Gray (Death Bicentenary)

373 Sir Walter Scott (Birth Bicentenary)

(Des Rosalind Dease. Queen's head printed in gold and then embossed)

1971 (28 July). Literary Anniversaries (2nd series). Multicoloured Chalk-surfaced paper. Two phosphor bands. Perf 15×14.

884	371	3p. John Keats..	10	10
		a. Gold (Queen's head) omitted..........	£225	
		y. Phosphor omitted..........................	5·00	
885	372	5p. Thomas Gray.....................................	15	20
		a. Gold (Queen's head) omitted..........	£900	
		y. Phosphor omitted..........................	35·00	
886	373	7½p. Sir Walter Scott..................................	20	20
		b. Embossing omitted........................	40·00	
		y. Phosphor omitted..........................	22·00	
Set of 3..			40	45
First Day Cover...				75
Presentation Pack (PO Pack No. 32)...................			3·00	

Special First Day of Issue Postmarks
British Post Office Philatelic Bureau, Edinburgh (Type D, see Introduction).. 1·00
London EC.. 3·00

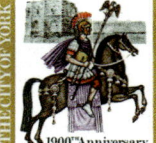

374 Servicemen and Nurse of 1921

375 Roman Centurion

376 Rugby Football, 1871

(Des F. Wegner)

1971 (25 Aug). Anniversaries (4th series). Events described on stamps. Multicoloured Chalk-surfaced paper. Two phosphor bands. Perf 15×14.

887	374	3p. Servicemen and Nurse of 1921........	10	10
		a. Deep blue omitted*........................	£875	
		b. Red-orange (nurse's cloak) omitted...	£700	
		c. Olive-brown (faces, etc.) omitted...	£600	
		d. Black omitted..................................	—	
		e. Grey omitted...................................	—	
		f. Olive-green omitted........................	—	
		y. Phosphor omitted..........................	3·00	
888	375	7½p. Roman Centurion..............................	15	20
		a. Grey omitted...................................	£280	
		b. Ochre omitted.................................	—	
		y. Phosphor omitted..........................	18·00	
889	376	9p. Rugby Football, 1871.......................	20	20
		a. Olive-brown omitted.....................	£250	
		b. New blue omitted...........................	£6000	
		c. Myrtle-green omitted.....................	—	£2750
		d. Lemon (jerseys) omitted................	£7000	£3250
		y. Phosphor omitted..........................	£350	
Set of 3..			40	45

QUEEN ELIZABETH II/1971

First Day Cover	1·00
Presentation Pack (PO Pack No. 32A)	3·00

* The effect of the missing deep blue is shown on the sailor's uniform, which appears as grey.

Special First Day of Issue Postmarks

British Post Office Philatelic Bureau, Edinburgh (Type D, see Introduction)	1·10
Maidstone	5·00
Twickenham	5·00
York	5·00

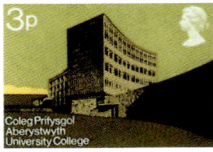

377 Physical Sciences Building, University College of Wales, Aberystwyth

378 Faraday Building, Southampton University

379 Engineering Department, Leicester University

380 Hexagon Restaurant, Essex University

(Des N. Jenkins)

1971 (22 Sept). British Architecture (2nd series). Modern University Buildings. Multicoloured Chalk-surfaced paper. Two phosphor bands. Perf 15×14.

890	377	3p. University College of Wales, Aberystwyth	10	10
		a. Lemon omitted	†	—
		b. Black (windows) omitted	£8500	
		y. Phosphor omitted	9·00	
891	378	5p. Southampton University	25	20
		y. Phosphor omitted	75·00	
892	379	7½p. Leicester University	20	30
		y. Phosphor omitted	15·00	
893	380	9p. Essex University	30	40
		a. Pale lilac omitted	—	
		y. Phosphor omitted	20·00	
Set of 4			55	75
First Day Cover				80
Presentation Pack (PO Pack No. 33)			5·00	

Mint examples of the 5p. exist with a larger 'P' following the face value.
No. 890a is only known used on commercial cover from Wantage.
No. 890b is only a partial omission with traces of black on the wall at the far right.

Special First Day of Issue Postmarks

British Post Office Philatelic Bureau, Edinburgh (Type D, see Introduction)	1·00
Aberystwyth	4·00
Colchester	4·00
Leicester	4·00
Southampton	4·00

Collectors Pack 1971

1971 (29 Sept). Comprises Nos. 835/840 and 881/893.

CP893a	Collectors Pack (PO Pack No. 34)	20·00

381 Dream of the Wise Men

382 Adoration of the Magi

383 Ride of the Magi

(Des Clarke-Clements-Hughes design team, from stained-glass windows, Canterbury Cathedral. Queen's head printed in gold and then embossed)

1971 (13 Oct). Christmas, Stained-glass Windows. Multicoloured Ordinary paper. One centre phosphor band (2½p.) or two phosphor bands (others). Perf 15×14.

894	381	2½p. Dream of the Wise Men	10	10
		a. Imperf (pair)	£500	
		b. Embossing omitted	—	
895	382	3p. Adoration of the Magi	10	10
		a. Gold (Queen's head) omitted	£1800	
		b. Carmine-rose omitted	£5000	
		c. Lemon (window panels) omitted	£225	
		d. New blue omitted	†	£3000
		e. Reddish violet (tunics etc) omitted	£6000	
		f. Carmine-rose and lemon omitted		£5000
		g. Reddish violet and embossing omitted		£4000
		h. Embossing omitted	15·00	
		y. Phosphor omitted	5·00	
		ya. Embossing and phosphor omitted	£100	
896	383	7½p. Ride of the Magi	20	20
		a. Gold (Queen's head) omitted	£175	
		b. Lilac omitted	£900	
		c. Emerald omitted	£550	
		d. Lemon omitted		£3000
		f. Embossing omitted	50·00	
		g. Embossing double	50·00	
		y. Phosphor omitted	12·00	
		ya. Embossing and phosphor omitted	35·00	
		yb. Phosphor on back but omitted on front	55·00	
Set of 3			35	35
First Day Cover				80
Presentation Pack (PO Pack No. 35)			2·25	

A used example of No. 894 has been reported with gold (Queen's head) omitted.

Special First Day of Issue Postmarks

British Post Office Philatelic Bureau, Edinburgh (Type D, see Introduction)	1·00
Bethlehem, Llandeilo, Carms	4·00
Canterbury	4·00

WHITE CHALK-SURFACED PAPER. From No. 897 all issues, with the exception of Nos. 904/908, were printed on fluorescent white paper, giving a stronger chalk reaction than the original cream paper.

384 Sir James Clark Ross

385 Sir Martin Frobisher

386 Henry Hudson

387 Robert Falcon Scott

1972/**QUEEN ELIZABETH II**

(Des Marjorie Saynor. Queen's head printed in gold and then embossed)

1972 (16 Feb). British Polar Explorers. Multicoloured Two phosphor bands. Perf 14×15.

897	384	3p. Sir James Clark Ross	10	10
		a. Gold (Queen's head) omitted	£175	
		b. Slate-black (hair, etc.) omitted	£5750	
		c. Lemon omitted	£10000	
		d. Embossing omitted	45·00	
		e. Gold (Queen's head) and embossing omitted	£250	
		y. Phosphor omitted	5·00	
		ya. Embossing and phosphor omitted	35·00	
898	385	5p. Sir Martin Frobisher	10	15
		a. Gold (Queen's head) omitted	£300	
		b. Embossing omitted	25·00	
		y. Phosphor omitted	12·00	
		ya. Gold and phosphor omitted	£325	
		yb. Embossing and phosphor omitted		
899	386	7½p. Henry Hudson	10	15
		a. Gold (Queen's head) omitted	£300	
		y. Phosphor omitted	18·00	
900	387	9p. Robert Falcon Scott	20	25
		y. Phosphor omitted	£350	
Set of 4			45	60
First Day Cover				85
Presentation Pack (PO Pack No. 39)			4·00	

An example of the 3p. is known used *on piece* with the flesh colour omitted.

Special First Day of Issue Postmarks

Philatelic Bureau, Edinburgh	85
London WC	2·00

388 Statuette of Tutankhamun    **389** 19th-century Coastguard

390 Ralph Vaughan Williams and Score

(Des Rosalind Dease (3p.), F. Wegner (7½p.), C. Abbott (9p.). Queen's head printed in gold and then embossed (7½p., 9p.))

1972 (26 Apr). Anniversaries (5th series). Events described on stamps. Multicoloured Two phosphor bands. Perf 15×14.

901	388	3p. Statuette of Tutankhamun	10	10
		a. Face value omitted	—	
902	389	7½p. 19th-century Coastguard	20	20
		a. Embossing omitted	£225	
		y. Phosphor omitted	£275	
903	390	9p. Ralph Vaughan Williams	20	25
		a. Gold (Queen's head) omitted	£2500	
		b. Brown (facial features) omitted	£3000	
		c. Deep slate omitted	—	
		d. Embossing omitted	—	
		y. Phosphor omitted	35·00	
Set of 3			45	50
First Day Cover				85
Presentation Pack (PO Pack No. 40)			2·25	

Special First Day of Issue Postmarks

Philatelic Bureau, Edinburgh	95
London EC	1·50

391 St Andrew's, Greensted-juxta-Ongar, Essex 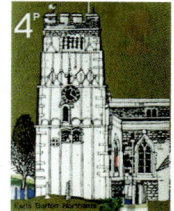   **392** All Saints, Earls Barton, Northants

393 St Andrew's, Letheringsett, Norfolk 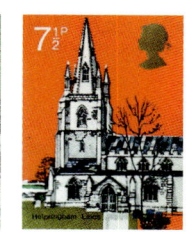   **394** St Andrew's, Helpringham, Lincs

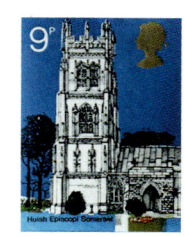

395 St Mary the Virgin, Huish Episcopi, Somerset

(Des R. Maddox. Queen's head printed in gold and then embossed)

1972 (21 June). British Architecture (3rd series). Village Churches. Multicoloured Ordinary paper. Two phosphor bands. Perf 14×15.

904	391	3p. St Andrew's, Greensted-juxta-Ongar	10	10
		a. Gold (Queen's head) omitted	£225	
		b. Orange-vermilion omitted		£2250
		c. Embossing omitted	35·00	
		y. Phosphor omitted	8·00	
		ya. Gold (Queen's head) and phosphor omitted	£325	
		yb. Embossing and phosphor omitted	22·00	
905	392	4p. All Saints, Earls Barton	10	10
		a. Gold (Queen's head) omitted	£4000	
		b. Violet-blue omitted	£250	
		c. Embossing omitted	12·00	
		ya. Phosphor omitted	20·00	
		yb. Embossing and phosphor omitted	60·00	
906	393	5p. St Andrew's, Letheringsett	10	20
		a. Gold (Queen's head) omitted	£275	
		b. Red omitted	†	£2750
		c. Embossing omitted	50·00	
		y. Phosphor omitted	25·00	
907	394	7½p. St Andrew's, Helpringham	15	20
		y. Phosphor omitted	20·00	
		ya. Embossing and phosphor omitted	50·00	
908	395	9p. St Mary the Virgin, Huish Episcopi	15	20
		a. Embossing omitted	22·00	
		y. Phosphor omitted	15·00	
Set of 5			55	80
First Day Cover				1·25
Presentation Pack (PO Pack No. 41)			4·75	

Nos. 905a and 906a only exist with the phosphor omitted.

Special First Day of Issue Postmarks

Philatelic Bureau, Edinburgh	1·40
Canterbury	2·50

QUEEN ELIZABETH II/1972

Belgica 72 Souvenir Pack

1972 (24 June). Comprises Nos. 894/896 and 904/908.
CP908*b* Souvenir Pack.. 3·75

This pack was specially produced for sale at the Belgica '72 Stamp Exhibition, held in Brussels between 24 June and 9 July. It contains information on British stamps with a religious theme with text in English, French and Flemish, and was put on sale at Philatelic Bureaux in Britain on 26 June.

396 Microphones, 1924–1969

397 Horn Loudspeaker

398 TV Camera, 1972

399 Oscillator and Spark Transmitter, 1897

(Des D. Gentleman)

1972 (13 Sept). Broadcasting Anniversaries. 75th Anniversary of Marconi and Kemp's Radio Experiments. Perf 15×14

909	396	3p. Microphones, 1924–1969	10	10
		a. Greenish yellow (terminals) omitted	£4000	
910	397	5p. Horn Loudspeaker	10	10
		y. Phosphor omitted	10·00	
		ya. Phosphor on back but omitted on front	45·00	
911	398	7½p. TV Camera, 1972	15	20
		a. Brownish slate (Queen's head) omitted	†	£2750
		y. Phosphor omitted	12·00	
912	399	9p. Oscillator and Spark Transmitter	15	20
		a. Brownish slate (Queen's head) omitted	£6000	
		y. Phosphor omitted	13·00	
		ya. Phosphor on back but omitted on front	£100	
Set of 4			45	55
First Day Cover				1·25
Presentation Pack (PO Pack No. 43)			3·25	

In addition to the generally issued Presentation Pack a further pack exists inscribed '1922–1972'. This pack of stamps commemorating the 50th Anniversary of the BBC was specially produced as a memento of the occasion for the BBC staff. It was sent with the good wishes of the Chairman and Board of Governors, the Director-General and Board of Management. The pack contains Nos. 909/911 only (*Price* £35).

No. 911a is only found in First Day Covers posted from the Philatelic Bureau in Edinburgh.

Special First Day of Issue Postmarks
Philatelic Bureau, Edinburgh.. 1·40
London W1.. 3·00

400 Angel holding Trumpet

401 Angel playing Lute

402 Angel playing Harp

(Des Sally Stiff. Photo and embossing)

1972 (18 Oct). Christmas. Angels. Multicoloured One centre phosphor band (2½p.) or two phosphor bands (others). Perf 14×15.

913	400	2½p. Angel holding Trumpet	10	10
		a. Gold omitted	£1100	
		b. Embossing omitted	15·00	
		c. Deep grey omitted	£2800	
		y. Phosphor omitted	15·00	
914	401	3p. Angel playing Lute	10	10
		a. Red-brown omitted	£950	
		b. Bright green omitted	£225	
		c. Bluish violet omitted	£225	
		d. Lavender omitted	—	
		e. Gold omitted	£1250	
		f. Embossing omitted	10·00	
		y. Phosphor omitted	8·00	
		ya. Embossing and phosphor omitted	15·00	
915	402	7½p. Angel playing Harp	20	20
		a. Ochre omitted	£200	
		b. Blackish violet (shadow) omitted	—	
		c. Embossing omitted	20·00	
		y. Phosphor omitted	15·00	
		ya. Embossing and phosphor omitted	30·00	
Set of 3			35	35
First Day Cover				85
Presentation Pack (PO Pack No. 44)			2·00	

The gold printing on the 3p. is from two cylinders: 1E and 1F. Examples have been seen with the gold of the 1F cylinder omitted, but these are difficult to detect on single stamps.

Special First Day of Issue Postmarks
Philatelic Bureau, Edinburgh.. 1·00
Bethlehem, Llandeilo, Carms... 3·00

403 Queen Elizabeth and Duke of Edinburgh

403a Queen Elizabeth and Duke of Edinburgh

I. Jumelle Machine

II. Rembrandt Machine

The 3p. JUMELLE has a lighter shade of the brownish black than the 3p. REMBRANDT. It also has the brown cylinders less deeply etched, which can be distinguished in the Duke's face which is slightly lighter, and in the Queen's hair where the highlights are sharper.
3p. REMBRANDT. Cylinders 3A-1B-11C no dot. Sheets of 100 (10×10).
3p. JUMELLE. Cylinders 1A-1B-3C dot and no dot. Sheets of 100 (two panes 5×10, separated by gutter margin).

1972/QUEEN ELIZABETH II

(Des J. Matthews from photo by N. Parkinson)

1972 (20 Nov). Royal Silver Wedding. Multicoloured 'All-over' phosphor (3p.) or without phosphor (20p.). Perf 14×15.

I. Rembrandt Machine.

916	**403**	3p. Queen Elizabeth and Duke of Edinburgh	20	20
		a. Silver omitted	£600	
917	**403a**	20p. Queen Elizabeth and Duke of Edinburgh	60	60

II. Jumelle Machine.

918	**403**	3p. Queen Elizabeth and Duke of Edinburgh	50	50
Set of 2			75	75
Gutter Pair (No. 918)			1·50	
Traffic Light Gutter Pair			20·00	
First Day Cover				60
Presentation Pack (PO Pack No. 45)			2·00	
Presentation Pack (Japanese)			3·00	
Souvenir Book			1·25	

The souvenir book is a 12 page booklet containing photographs of the Royal Wedding and other historic events of the royal family and accompanying information.

Special First Day of Issue Postmarks

Philatelic Bureau, Edinburgh	70
Windsor, Berks	2·50

Collectors Pack 1972

1972 (20 Nov). Comprises Nos. 897/917.

CP918a		Collectors Pack (PO Pack No. 47)	12·00

404 Europe   **404a**

404b

(Des P. Murdoch)

1973 (3 Jan). Britain's Entry into European Communities. Multicoloured Two phosphor bands. Perf 14×15.

919	**404**	3p. Europe (lilac background)	10	10
920	**404a**	5p. Europe (new blue jigsaw pieces)	15	20
		a. Pair. Nos. 920/921	35	45
921	**404b**	5p. Europe (light emerald-green jigsaw pieces)	15	20
Set of 3			40	45
First Day Cover				70
Presentation Pack (PO Pack No. 48)			4·00	

Nos. 920/921 were printed horizontally *se-tenant* throughout the sheet.

Special First Day of Issue Postmarks

Philatelic Bureau, Edinburgh	80

405 Oak Tree

(Des D. Gentleman)

1973 (28 Feb). Tree Planting Year. British Trees (1st issue). Multicoloured Two phosphor bands. Perf 15×14.

922	**405**	9p. Oak Tree	15	15
		a. Brownish black (value and inscr) omitted	£750	
		b. Brownish grey (Queen's head) omitted	£700	
		y. Phosphor omitted	90·00	
First Day Cover				40
Presentation Pack (PO Pack No. 49)			1·25	

See also No. 949.

Special First Day of Issue Postmarks

Philatelic Bureau, Edinburgh	50

> **CHALK-SURFACED PAPER.** The following issues are printed on chalk-surfaced paper but where 'all-over' phosphor has been applied there is no chalk reaction except in the sheet margins outside the phosphor area.

406 David Livingstone   **407** Henry M. Stanley

408 Sir Francis Drake   **409** Walter Raleigh

410 Charles Sturt

(Des Marjorie Saynor. Queen's head printed in gold and then embossed)

1973 (18 Apr). British Explorers. Multicoloured. 'All-over' phosphor. Perf 14×15.

923	**406**	3p. David Livingstone	10	10
		a. Pair. Nos. 923/924	20	20
		b. Gold (Queen's head) omitted	£125	
		c. Turquoise-blue (background and inscr) omitted	£1500	
		d. Light orange-brown omitted	£800	
		e. Embossing omitted	35·00	
924	**407**	3p. Henry M Stanley	10	10
		b. Gold (Queen's head) omitted	£125	
		c. Turquoise-blue (background and inscr) omitted	£1500	
		d. Light orange-brown omitted	£800	
		e. Embossing omitted	35·00	
925	**408**	5p. Sir Francis Drake	20	20
		a. Gold (Queen's head) omitted	£250	
		b. Grey-black omitted	£2250	
		c. Sepia omitted	£4000	
		d. Embossing omitted	9·00	
926	**409**	7½p. Walter Raleigh	20	20
		a. Gold (Queen's head) omitted	£7500	
		b. Ultramarine (eyes) omitted	—	—
927	**410**	9p. Charles Sturt	20	20

QUEEN ELIZABETH II/1973

a. Gold (Queen's head) omitted	£225	
b. Brown-grey printing double from..	£300	
c. Grey-black omitted	£3750	
d. Brown-red (rivers on map) omitted	£950	
e. Embossing omitted	40·00	
Set of 5	75	75
First Day Cover		90
Presentation Pack (PO Pack No. 50)	2·25	

Nos. 923/924 were issued horizontally *se-tenant* throughout the sheet.

Caution is needed when buying missing gold heads in this issue as they can be removed by using a hard eraser, etc., but this invariably affects the 'all-over' phosphor. Genuine examples have the phosphor intact. Used examples off cover cannot be distinguished as much of the phosphor is lost in the course of floating.

In the 5p. value the missing grey-black affects the doublet, which appears as brownish grey, and the lace ruff, which is entirely missing.

In the 5p. value the missing sepia effects only Drake's hair, which appears much lighter.

The double printing of the brown-grey (cylinder 1F) on the 9p., is a most unusual type of error to occur in a multicoloured photogravure issue. Two sheets are known and it is believed that they stuck to the cylinder and went through a second time. This would result in the following two sheets missing the colour but at the time of going to press this error has not been reported. The second print is slightly askew and more prominent in the top half of the sheets. Examples from the upper part of the sheet showing a clear double impression of the facial features are worth a substantial premium over the price quoted.

Special First Day of Issue Postmarks

Philatelic Bureau, Edinburgh .... 1·00

First Day of Issue handstamps were provided at Blantyre, Glasgow, and Denbigh for this issue.

411
412 
413 

(Types **411/413** show sketches of W. G. Grace by Harry Furniss)

(Des E. Ripley. Queen's head printed in gold and then embossed)

1973 (16 May). County Cricket 1873–1973. 'All-over' phosphor. Perf 14×15.

928	411	3p. black, ochre and gold	10	10
		a. Gold (Queen's head) omitted	£5000	
		b. Embossing omitted	25·00	
929	412	7½p. black, light sage-green and gold	30	30
		b. Embossing omitted	35·00	
930	413	9p. black, cobalt and gold	40	40
		b. Embossing omitted	85·00	
Set of 3			75	75
First Day Cover				1·25
Presentation Pack (PO Pack No. 51)			3·25	
Souvenir Book			3·50	
PHQ Card (No. 928) (1)			35·00	£150

Nos. 928/930 with two phosphor bands are known.

The souvenir book is a 24 page illustrated booklet containing a history of County Cricket with text by John Arlott.

The PHQ Card did not become available until mid-July. The used price quoted is for an example used in July or August 1973.

Special First Day of Issue Postmarks

Philatelic Bureau, Edinburgh .... 1·40
Lords, London NW .... 3·00

414 *Self-portrait* (Reynolds)
415 *Self-portrait* (Raeburn) 
416 *Nelly O'Brien* (Reynolds) 
417 *Rev. R. Walker (The Skater)* (Raeburn) 

(Des S. Rose. Queen's head printed in gold and then embossed)

1973 (4 July). British Paintings (3rd series). 250th Birth Anniversary of Sir Joshua Reynolds and 150th Death Anniversary of Sir Henry Raeburn. Multicoloured 'All-over' phosphor. Perf 14×15.

931	414	3p. *Self-portrait* (Reynolds)	10	10
		a. Gold (Queen's head) omitted	£120	
		c. Gold (Queen's head) and embossing omitted	£140	
932	415	5p. *Self-portrait* (Raeburn)	15	15
		a. Gold (Queen's head) omitted	£140	
		b. Greenish yellow omitted	£950	
		c. Embossing omitted	30·00	
933	416	7½p. *Nelly O'Brien* (Reynolds)	15	15
		a. Gold (Queen's head) omitted	£225	
		b. Cinnamon omitted	£12500	
		c. Embossing omitted	25·00	
934	417	9p. *Rev. R. Walker (The Skater)* (Raeburn)	20	20
		b. Brownish rose omitted	£175	
		c. Embossing omitted	£150	
Set of 4			50	50
First Day Cover				80
Presentation Pack (PO Pack No. 52)			1·75	

1973/QUEEN ELIZABETH II

Special First Day of Issue Postmarks
Philatelic Bureau, Edinburgh .... 1·80

418	Court Masque Costumes	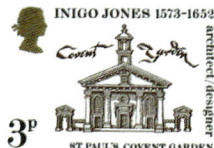	419	St Paul's Church, Covent Garden
420	Prince's Lodging, Newmarket		421	Court Masque Stage Scene

(Des Rosalind Dease. Litho and typo Bradbury Wilkinson)

1973 (15 Aug). 400th Birth Anniversary of Inigo Jones (architect and designer). Multicoloured 'All-over' phosphor. Perf 15×14.

935	**418**	3p. Court Masque Costumes	10	10
		a. Pair. Nos. 935/936	20	25
		ab. Face values omitted	—	
		ac. Deep mauve ptg double (pair)	£4750	
		c. 9 mm phosphor band*	20·00	
936	**419**	3p. St Paul's Church, Covent Garden	10	10
937	**420**	5p. Prince's Lodging, Newmarket	15	15
		a. Pair. Nos. 937/938	30	35
		c. 9 mm phosphor band*	20·00	
938	**421**	5p. Court Masque Stage Scene	15	15
Set of 4			40	50
First Day Cover				70
Presentation Pack (PO Pack No. 53)			1·60	
PHQ Card (No. 936) (2)			95·00	95·00

The 3p. and 5p. values were printed horizontally *se-tenant* within the sheet.

No. 935ab is caused by the omission of virtually all the black printing from one horizontal row.

* On part of the printings for both values the 'all-over' phosphor band missed the first vertical row and a 9 mm phosphor band was applied to correct this.

Special First Day of Issue Postmarks
Philatelic Bureau, Edinburgh 80

422	Palace of Westminster seen from Whitehall	423 Palace of Westminster seen from Millbank

(Des R. Downer. Recess and typo Bradbury Wilkinson)

1973 (12 Sept). 19th Commonwealth Parliamentary Conference. Multicoloured 'All-over' phosphor. Perf 15×14.

939	**422**	8p. Palace of Westminster seen from Whitehall	15	15
940	**423**	10p. Palace of Westminster seen from Millbank	20	20
Set of 2			30	30
First Day Cover				55
Presentation Pack (PO Pack No. 54)			1·50	
Souvenir Book			3·50	
PHQ Card (No. 939) (3)			18·00	70·00

The souvenir book is a 12 page booklet containing a history of the Palace of Westminster.

Special First Day of Issue Postmarks
Philatelic Bureau, Edinburgh .... 1·60

424 Princess Anne and Captain Mark Phillips	424a Princess Anne and Captain Mark Phillips

(Des C. Clements and E. Hughes from photo by Lord Lichfield)

1973 (14 Nov). Royal Wedding. 'All-over' phosphor. Perf 15×14.

941	**424**	3½p. Princess Anne and Captain Mark Phillips	10	10
		a. Imperf (horiz pair)	£5000	
942	**424a**	20p. deep brown and silver	35	25
		a. Silver omitted	£6000	
Set of 2			40	30
Set of 2 Gutter Pairs			80	
Set of 2 Traffic Light Gutter Pairs			65·00	
First Day Cover				40
Presentation Pack (PO Pack No. 56)			1·25	
PHQ Card (No. 941) (4)			3·75	20·00

Special First Day of Issue Postmarks
Philatelic Bureau, Edinburgh .... 1·25
Westminster Abbey, London SW1 .... 3·50
Windsor, Berks .... 3·50

425	426	
427	428	
429	430	

(Types **425**/**430** show scenes from the carol *Good King Wenceslas*)

(Des D. Gentleman)

1973 (28 Nov). Christmas, Good King Wenceslas. Multicoloured One centre phosphor band (3p.) or 'All-over' phosphor (3½p.). Perf 15×14.

943	**425**	3p. King Wenceslas sees peasant	15	15
		a. Strip of 5. Nos. 943/947	90	1·10
		ab. Rosy mauve omitted (strip of 5)	£8000	
		b. Imperf (horiz strip of 5)	£4000	
		c. Black (face value) omitted*	£6000	
		g. Gum arabic	20	
		ga. Strip of 5. Nos. 943g/947g	1·20	
		gb. Imperf (strip of 5. Nos. 943g/947g)	£4250	
944	**426**	3p. Page tells king about peasant	15	15
		g. Gum arabic	20	
945	**427**	3p. King and page set out	15	15
		g. Gum arabic	20	
946	**428**	3p. King encourages page	15	15
		g. Gum arabic	20	
947	**429**	3p. King and page give food to peasant	15	15
		g. Gum arabic	20	
948	**430**	3½p. Peasant, King and page	15	15
		a. Imperf (pair)	£350	
		b. Grey-black (value, inscr, etc.) omitted	£150	
		c. Salmon-pink omitted	£100	

	d. Blue (leg, robes) omitted	£250	
	e. Rosy mauve (robe at right) omitted	£125	
	f. Blue and rosy mauve omitted	£400	
	g. Bright rose-red (King's robe) omitted	£150	
	h. Red-brown (logs, basket, etc.) omitted		
	i. Turquoise-green (leg, robe, etc.) omitted	£3750	
	j. Gold (background) omitted	†	—
Set of 6		95	1·10
First Day Cover			1·25
Presentation Pack (PO Pack No. 57)		1·75	

The 3p. values depict the carol *Good King Wenceslas* and were printed horizontally *se-tenant* within the sheet.

Examples of No. 948j are only known used *on covers* from Gloucester. The 3½p. has also been seen with the lavender-grey omitted used *on piece*.
No. 948h is only known used. The true error shows the pile of logs at night completely omitted.

The 3p. and 3½p. are normally with PVA gum with added dextrin, but the 3½p. also exists with normal PVA gum.

* No. 943c is known in a corner marginal strip of five showing a progressive dry print of black leaving a total omission on the first stamp. Adjacent similar strips of five all show traces of black.

Special First Day of Issue Postmarks
Philatelic Bureau, Edinburgh		1·25
Bethlehem, Llandeilo, Carms		2·75

Collectors Pack 1973

1973 (28 Nov). Comprises Nos. 919/948.
CP948k		Collectors Pack (PO Pack No. 58)	11·50

431 Horse Chestnut

(Des D. Gentleman)

1974 (27 Feb). British Trees (2nd issue). Multicoloured 'All-over' phosphor. Perf 15×14.
949	**431**	10p. Horse Chestnut	20	15
Gutter Pair			40	
Traffic Light Gutter Pair			45·00	
First Day Cover				40
Presentation Pack (PO Pack No. 59)			1·10	
PHQ Card (5)			80·00	80·00

The pack number is stated to be 58 on the reverse but the correct number is 59.

Special First Day of Issue Postmarks
Philatelic Bureau, Edinburgh	50

432 First Motor Fire Engine, 1904
433 Prizewinning Fire Engine, 1863 
434 First Steam Fire Engine, 1830 
435 Fire Engine, 1766 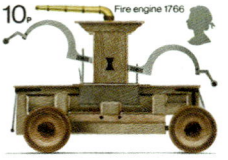

(Des D. Gentleman)

1974 (24 Apr). Bicentenary of the Fire Prevention (Metropolis) Act. Multicoloured 'All-over' phosphor. Perf 15×14.
950	**432**	3½p. First Motor Fire Engine, 1904	10	10
		a. Imperf (pair)	£650	
951	**433**	5½p. Prizewinning Fire Engine, 1863	10	10
952	**434**	8p. First Steam Fire Engine, 1830	15	20
953	**435**	10p. Fire Engine, 1766	20	20
Set of 4			50	55
Set of 4 Gutter Pairs			1·00	
Set of 4 Traffic Light Gutter Pairs			36·00	
First Day Cover				1·10
Presentation Pack (PO Pack No. 60)			1·50	
PHQ Card (No. 950) (6)			65·00	70·00

The 3½p. exists with ordinary PVA gum.

Special First Day of Issue Postmarks
Philatelic Bureau, Edinburgh	1·60

436 P & O Packet, *Peninsular*, 1888 
437 Farman HF. III Biplane, 1911 
438 Airmail-blue Van and Post Box, 1930 
439 Imperial Airways Short S.21 Flying Boat *Maia*, 1937

'Bomb burst' damage to wheels at left (Cyl. 1C, R. 6/4)

(Des Rosalind Dease)

1974 (12 June). Centenary of Universal Postal Union. Multicoloured 'All-over' phosphor. Perf 15×14.
954	**436**	3½p. P & O Packet, *Peninsular*, 1888	10	10
955	**437**	5½p. Farman HF. III Biplane, 1911	10	10
		a. 'Bomb burst'	50·00	
956	**438**	8p. Airmail-blue Van and Post box, 1930	10	10
957	**439**	10p. Imperial Airways Short S.21 Flying Boat *Maia*, 1937	15	15
Set of 4			40	40
Set of 4 Gutter Pairs			80	
Set of 4 Traffic Light Gutter Pairs			28·00	
First Day Cover				60
Presentation Pack (PO Pack No. 64)			2·00	

Special First Day of Issue Postmark
Philatelic Bureau, Edinburgh	70

440 Robert the Bruce
441 Owain Glyndwr 
442 Henry V 
443 The Black Prince

1974/QUEEN ELIZABETH II

(Des F. Wegner)

1974 (10 July). Medieval Warriors. Multicoloured 'All-over' phosphor. Perf 15×14.

958	440	4½p. Robert the Bruce	10	10
959	441	5½p. Owain Glyndwr	15	15
960	442	8p. Henry V	15	15
961	443	10p. The Black Prince	15	15
Set of 4			50	50
Set of 4 Gutter Pairs			1·00	
Set of 4 Traffic Light Gutter Pairs			40·00	
First Day Cover				1·25
Presentation Pack (PO Pack No. 65)			1·60	
PHQ Cards (set of 4) (7)			12·00	30·00

Imperforate pairs of No. 961 are known and thought to be of proof status (Price £700 per pair).

Special First Day of Issue Postmark
Philatelic Bureau, Edinburgh .... 1·75

444 Churchill in Royal Yacht Squadron Uniform

445 Prime Minister, 1940

446 Secretary for War and Air, 1919

447 War Correspondent, South Africa, 1899

(Des C. Clements and E. Hughes)

1974 (9 Oct). Birth Centenary of Sir Winston Churchill. Multicoloured 'All-over' phosphor. Perf 14×15.

962	444	4½p. Churchill in Royal Yacht Squadron Uniform	10	10
963	445	5½p. Prime Minister, 1940	20	15
964	446	8p. Secretary for War and Air, 1919	30	30
965	447	10p. War Correspondent, South Africa, 1899	30	30
Set of 4			80	75
Set of 4 Gutter Pairs			1·60	
Set of 4 Traffic Light Gutter Pairs			22·00	
First Day Cover				80
Presentation Pack (PO Pack No. 66)			1·75	
PHQ Card (No. 963) (8)			2·75	15·00
Souvenir Book			1·50	

The souvenir book consists of an illustrated folder containing a biography of Sir Winston.

Nos. 962/965 come with PVA gum containing added dextrin, but the 8p. also exists with normal PVA.

Special First Day of Issue Postmark
Philatelic Bureau, Edinburgh .... 1·75
Blenheim, Woodstock, Oxford .... 4·00
House of Commons, London SW .... 4·00

448 Adoration of the Magi (York Minster, circa 1355)

449 The Nativity (St Helen's Church, Norwich, circa 1480)

450 Virgin and Child (Ottery St Mary Church, circa 1350)

451 Virgin and Child (Worcester Cathedral, circa 1224)

(Des Peter Hatch Partnership)

1974 (27 Nov). Christmas, Church Roof Bosses. Multicoloured. One phosphor band (3½p.) or 'All-over' phosphor (others). Perf 15×14.

966	448	3½p. York Minster	10	10
		a. Light stone (background shading) omitted	—	
		y. Phosphor omitted	12·00	
967	449	4½p. St Helen's Church, Norwich	10	10
968	450	8p. Ottery St Mary Church	10	10
969	451	10p. Worcester Cathedral	15	15
Set of 4			40	40
Set of 4 Gutter Pairs			80	
Set of 4 Traffic Light Gutter Pairs			24·00	
First Day Cover				70
Presentation Pack (PO Pack No. 67)			1·50	

The phosphor band in the 3½p. was first applied down the centre of the stamp but during the printing this was deliberately placed to the right between the roof boss and the value; however, intermediate positions, due to shifts, are known.

Two used examples of the 3½p. have been reported with the light brown colour omitted.

Special First Day of Issue Postmarks
Philatelic Bureau, Edinburgh 80
Bethlehem, Llandeilo, Carms .... 1·75

Collectors Pack 1974

1974 (27 Nov). Comprises Nos. 949/969.
CP969a   Collectors Pack (PO Pack No. 68) .... 4·75

452 Invalid in Wheelchair

(Des P. Sharland)

1975 (22 Jan). Health and Handicap Funds. 'All-over' phosphor. Perf 15×14.

970	452	4½p.+1½p. Invalid in Wheelchair	15	15
Gutter Pair			30	
Traffic Light Gutter Pair			2·25	
First Day Cover				30

Special First Day of Issue Postmark
Philatelic Bureau, Edinburgh 40

453 Peace – Burial at Sea

454 Snow Storm: Steam-boat off a Harbour's Mouth

455 The Arsenal, Venice

456 St Laurent

QUEEN ELIZABETH II/1975

(Des S. Rose)

1975 (19 Feb). Birth Bicentenary of J. M. W. Turner (painter). Multicoloured 'All-over' phosphor. Perf 15×14.

971	453	4½p. *Peace – Burial at Sea*	10	10
972	454	5½p. *Snow Storm: Steam-boat off a Harbour's Mouth*	10	10
973	455	8p. *The Arsenal, Venice*	10	10
974	456	10p. *St Laurent*	15	15
Set of 4			40	40
Set of 4 Gutter Pairs			80	
Set of 4 Traffic Light Gutter Pairs			5·50	
First Day Cover				50
Presentation Pack (PO Pack No. 69)			1·50	
PHQ Card (No. 972) (9)			18·00	20·00

Special First Day of Issue Postmarks
London WC .... 1·50
Philatelic Bureau, Edinburgh 75

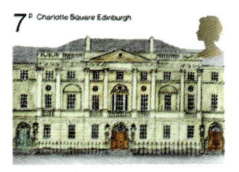

457 Charlotte Square, Edinburgh

458 The Rows, Chester

459 Royal Observatory, Greenwich

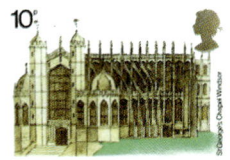

460 St George's Chapel, Windsor

461 National Theatre, London

(Des P. Gauld)

1975 (23 Apr). European Architectural Heritage Year. Multicoloured 'All-over' phosphor. Perf 15×14.

975	457	7p. Charlotte Square, Edinburgh	10	10
		a. Pair. Nos. 975/976	20	20
976	458	7p. The Rows, Chester	10	10
977	459	8p. Royal Observatory, Greenwich	10	10
978	460	10p. St George's Chapel, Windsor	15	15
979	461	12p. National Theatre, London	20	20
Set of 5			60	60
Set of 5 Gutter Pairs			1·25	
Set of 5 Traffic Light Gutter Pairs			14·00	
First Day Cover				80
Presentation Pack (PO Pack No. 70)			1·50	
PHQ Cards (Nos. 975/977) (10)			4·75	10·00

Nos. 975/976 were printed horizontally *se-tenant* within the sheet.

Special First Day of Issue Postmark
Philatelic Bureau, Edinburgh .... 1·75

462 Sailing Dinghies

463 Racing Keel Yachts

464 Cruising Yachts

465 Multihulls

(Des A. Restall. Recess and photo)

1975 (11 June). Sailing. Multicoloured 'All-over' phosphor. Perf 15×14.

980	462	7p. Sailing Dinghies	10	10
981	463	8p. Racing Keel Yachts	10	10
		a. Black omitted	£100	
982	464	10p. Cruising Yachts	15	15
983	465	12p. Multihulls	20	20
Set of 4			50	50
Set of 4 Gutter Pairs			1·00	
Set of 4 Traffic Light Gutter Pairs			18·00	
First Day Cover				70
Presentation Pack (PO Pack No. 71)			1·25	
PHQ Card (No. 981) (11)			2·75	8·00

On No. 981a the recess-printed black colour is completely omitted.

Special First Day of Issue Postmark
Philatelic Bureau, Edinburgh .... 1·25
A First Day of Issue handstamp was provided at Weymouth for this issue.

466 Stephenson's *Locomotion*, 1825

467 Abbotsford, 1876

468 Caerphilly Castle, 1923

469 High Speed Train, 1975

(Des B. Craker)

1975 (13 Aug). 150th Anniversary of Public Railways. Multicoloured 'All-over' phosphor. P 15×14.

984	466	7p. Stephenson's *Locomotion*, 1825	10	10
985	467	8p. *Abbotsford*, 1876	20	20
986	468	10p. *Caerphilly Castle*, 1923	20	20
987	469	12p. High Speed Train, 1975	30	30
Set of 4			70	70
Set of 4 Gutter Pairs			1·40	
Set of 4 Traffic Light Gutter Pairs			7·50	
First Day Cover				90
Presentation Pack (PO Pack No. 72)			2·00	
PHQ Cards (set of 4) (12)			30·00	30·00
Souvenir Book			1·60	

The souvenir book is an eight page booklet containing a history of the railways.

Special First Day of Issue Postmarks
Philatelic Bureau, Edinburgh .... 1·00
Darlington, Co. Durham .... 4·00
Shildon, Co. Durham .... 5·00
Stockton-on-Tees, Cleveland .... 4·00

470 Palace of Westminster

(Des R. Downer)

1975 (3 Sept). 62nd Inter-Parliamentary Union Conference. Multicoloured 'All-over' phosphor. Perf 15×14.

988	470	12p. Palace of Westminster	20	20
Gutter Pair			40	

1975/QUEEN ELIZABETH II

Traffic Light Gutter Pair	2·25	
First Day Cover		30
Presentation Pack (PO Pack No. 74)	85	

Special First Day of Issue Postmark
Philatelic Bureau, Edinburgh 40

471 Emma and Mr Woodhouse (*Emma*)

472 Catherine Morland (*Northanger Abbey*)

473 Mr Darcy (*Pride and Prejudice*)

474 Mary and Henry Crawford (*Mansfield Park*)

(Des Barbara Brown)

1975 (22 Oct). Birth Bicentenary of Jane Austen (novelist). Multicoloured 'All-over' phosphor. Perf 14×15.

989	471	8½p. Emma and Mr Woodhouse	10	10
990	472	10p. Catherine Morland	15	15
991	473	11p. Mr Darcy	15	15
992	474	13p. Mary and Henry Crawford	25	20
Set of 4			60	55
Set of 4 Gutter Pairs			1·25	
Set of 4 Traffic Light Gutter Pairs			7·00	
First Day Cover				75
Presentation Pack (PO Pack No. 75)			7·00	
PHQ Cards (set of 4) (13)			9·50	15·00

Special First Day of Issue Postmarks
Philatelic Bureau, Edinburgh 85
Steventon, Basingstoke, Hants .... 1·50

475 Angels with Harp and Lute

476 Angel with Mandolin

477 Angel with Horn

478 Angel with Trumpet

(Des R. Downer)

1975 (26 Nov). Christmas. Angels. Multicoloured One phosphor band (6½p.), phosphor-inked background (8½p.), 'All-over' phosphor (others). Perf 15×14.

993	475	6½p. Angels with Harp and Lute	10	10
994	476	8½p. Angel with Mandolin	10	10
995	477	11p. Angel with Horn	20	15
996	478	13p. Angel with Trumpet	20	20
Set of 4			45	50
Set of 4 Gutter Pairs			1·10	
Set of 4 Traffic Light Gutter Pairs			5·00	

First Day Cover		75
Presentation Pack (PO Pack No. 76)	1·50	

The 6½p. exists with both ordinary PVA gum and PVA containing added dextrin.

Special First Day of Issue Postmarks
Philatelic Bureau, Edinburgh 60
Bethlehem, Llandeilo, Dyfed .... 1·00

Collectors Pack 1975

1975 (26 Nov). Comprises Nos. 970/996.
CP996a   Collectors Pack (PO Pack No. 77) .... 4·25

479 Housewife

480 Policeman

481 District Nurse

482 Industrialist

(Des P. Sharland)

1976 (10 Mar). Telephone Centenary. Multicoloured 'All-over' phosphor. Perf 15×14.

997	479	8½p. Housewife	10	10
		a. Deep rose (vase and picture frame) omitted	£4750	
		b. Imperf (pair)	£1500	
998	480	10p. Policeman	15	15
999	481	11p. District Nurse	15	15
1000	482	13p. Industrialist	25	20
Set of 4			60	55
Set of 4 Gutter Pairs			1·25	
Set of 4 Traffic Light Gutter Pairs			11·00	
First Day Cover				60
Presentation Pack (PO Pack No. 78)			1·40	

Special First Day of Issue Postmark
Philatelic Bureau, Edinburgh 70

483 Hewing Coal (Thomas Hepburn)

484 Machinery (Robert Owen)

485 Chimney Cleaning (Lord Shaftesbury)

486 Hands clutching Prison Bars (Elizabeth Fry)

(Des D. Gentleman)

1976 (28 Apr). Social Reformers. Multicoloured 'All-over' phosphor. Perf 15×14.

1001	483	8½p. Hewing Coal (Thomas Hepburn)	10	10
1002	484	10p. Machinery (Robert Owen)	15	15
1003	485	11p. Chimney Cleaning (Lord Shaftesbury)	15	15
1004	486	13p. Hands clutching Prison Bars (Elizabeth Fry)	25	20
Set of 4			60	55
Set of 4 Gutter Pairs			1·25	
Set of 4 Traffic Light Gutter Pairs			5·00	
First Day Cover				60

QUEEN ELIZABETH II/1976

Presentation Pack (PO Pack No. 79)	1·25	
PHQ Card (No. 1001) (14)	2·75	9·00

Special First Day of Issue Postmark
Philatelic Bureau, Edinburgh 70

487 Benjamin Franklin (bust by Jean-Jacques Caffieri)

(Des P. Sharland)

1976 (2 June). Bicentenary of American Revolution. Multicoloured 'All-over' phosphor. Perf 14×15.

1005	487	11p. Benjamin Franklin	20	20
		Gutter Pair	40	
		Traffic Light Gutter Pair	2·25	
		First Day Cover		50
		Presentation Pack (PO Pack No. 80)	65	
		PHQ Card (15)	2·25	8·00

Special First Day of Issue Postmark
Philatelic Bureau, Edinburgh 60

488 'Elizabeth of Glamis'
489 'Grandpa Dickson'
490 'Rosa Mundi'
491 'Sweet Briar'

(Des Kristin Rosenberg)

1976 (30 June). Centenary of Royal National Rose Society. Multicoloured 'All-over' phosphor. Perf 14×15.

1006	488	8½p. 'Elizabeth of Glamis'	10	10
1007	489	10p. 'Grandpa Dickson'	15	15
1008	490	11p. 'Rosa Mundi'	15	15
1009	491	13p. 'Sweet Briar'	25	20
		a. Value omitted*	—	
		Set of 4	60	55
		Set of 4 Gutter Pairs	1·25	
		Set of 4 Traffic Light Gutter Pairs	6·00	
		First Day Cover		60
		Presentation Pack (PO Pack No. 81)	1·50	
		PHQ Cards (set of 4) (16)	14·00	15·00

* During repairs to the cylinder the face value on R.1/9 was temporarily covered with copper. This covering was inadvertently left in place during printing, but the error was discovered before issue and most examples were removed from the sheets. Two mint and one used example have so far been reported, but only one of the mint remains in private hands.

Special First Day of Issue Postmark
Philatelic Bureau, Edinburgh 70

492 Archdruid
493 Morris Dancing 
494 Scots Piper 
495 Welsh Harpist 

(Des Marjorie Saynor)

1976 (4 Aug). British Cultural Traditions. Multicoloured 'All-over' phosphor. Perf 14×15.

1010	492	8½p. Archdruid	10	10
1011	493	10p. Morris Dancing	15	15
1012	494	11p. Scots Piper	15	15
1013	495	13p. Welsh Harpist	25	20
		Set of 4	60	55
		Set of 4 Gutter Pairs	1·25	
		Set of 4 Traffic Light Gutter Pairs	6·00	
		First Day Cover		60
		Presentation Pack (PO Pack No. 82)	1·25	
		PHQ Cards (set of 4) (17)	7·50	12·00

The 8½p. and 13p. commemorate the 800th anniversary of the Royal National Eisteddfod.

Special First Day of Issue Postmarks
Philatelic Bureau, Edinburgh	70
Cardigan, Dyfed	1·25

496 Woodcut from *The Canterbury Tales*
497 Extract from *The Tretyse of Love* 
498 Woodcut from *The Game and Playe of Chesse* 
499 Early Printing Press 

(Des R. Gay. Queen's head printed in gold and then embossed)

1976 (29 Sept). 500th Anniversary of British Printing. Multicoloured 'All-over' phosphor. Perf 14×15.

1014	496	8½p. Woodcut from *The Canterbury Tales*	10	10
1015	497	10p. Extract from *The Tretyse of Love*	15	15
1016	498	11p. Woodcut from *The Game and Playe of Chesse*	15	15
1017	499	13p. Early Printing Press	25	25
		Set of 4	60	60
		Set of 4 Gutter Pairs	1·25	

1976/QUEEN ELIZABETH II

Set of 4 Traffic Light Gutter Pairs	6·00	
First Day Cover		65
Presentation Pack (PO Pack No. 83)	1·25	
PHQ Cards (set of 4) (18)	6·00	9·00

Special First Day of Issue Postmarks

Philatelic Bureau, Edinburgh	75
London SW1	1·00

500 Virgin and Child
501 Angel with Crown
502 Angel appearing to Shepherds
503 The Three Kings

(Des Enid Marx)

1976 (24 Nov). Christmas, English Medieval Embroidery. Multicoloured One phosphor band (6½p.) or 'All-over' phosphor (others). Perf 15×14.

1018	500	6½p. Virgin and Child	10	10
		a. Imperf (pair)	£550	
1019	501	8½p. Angel with Crown	15	15
1020	502	11p. Angel appearing to Shepherds	15	15
		a. Uncoated paper*	75·00	30·00
1021	503	13p. The Three Kings	20	20
Set of 4			55	55
Set of 4 Gutter Pairs			1·10	
Set of 4 Traffic Light Gutter Pairs			4·50	
First Day Cover				60
Presentation Pack (PO Pack No. 87)			1·40	
PHQ Cards (set of 4) (19)			1·80	5·00

*See footnote after No. 744.

Special First Day of Issue Postmarks

Philatelic Bureau, Edinburgh	70
Bethlehem, Llandeilo, Dyfed	1·25

Collectors Pack 1976

1976 (24 Nov). Comprises Nos. 997/1021.
CP1021a Collectors Pack (PO Pack No. 88) .... 5·50

504 Lawn Tennis
505 Table Tennis
506 Squash
507 Badminton

(Des A. Restall)

1977 (12 Jan). Racket Sports. Multicoloured Phosphorised paper. Perf 15×14.

1022	504	8½p. Lawn Tennis	10	10
		a. Imperf (horiz pair)	£1500	
1023	505	10p. Table Tennis	15	15
1024	506	11p. Squash	15	15
		a. Imperf (horiz pair)	£4500	
1025	507	13p. Badminton	20	20
Set of 4			55	55
Set of 4 Gutter Pairs			1·10	
Set of 4 Traffic Light Gutter Pairs			5·50	
First Day Cover				60
Presentation Pack (PO Pack No. 89)			1·50	
PHQ Cards (set of 4) (20)			3·50	8·00

Special First Day of Issue Postmark

Philatelic Bureau, Edinburgh	70

For Nos. 1026/1028 and T **508** see Decimal Machin Definitives section

509 Steroids, Conformational Analysis
510 Vitamin C, Synthesis
511 Starch, Chromatography
512 Salt, Crystallography

(Des J. Karo)

1977 (2 Mar). Royal Institute of Chemistry Centenary. Multicoloured 'All-over' phosphor. Perf 15×14.

1029	509	8½p. Steroids, Conformational Analysis	10	10
		a. Imperf (horiz pair)	£3750	
1030	510	10p. Vitamin C, Synthesis	15	15
1031	511	11p. Starch, Chromatography	15	15
1032	512	13p. Salt, Crystallography	20	20
Set of 4			55	55
Set of 4 Gutter Pairs			1·10	
Set of 4 Traffic Light Gutter Pairs			5·50	
First Day Cover				60
Presentation Pack (PO Pack No. 92)			1·50	
PHQ Cards (set of 4) (21)			3·50	8·00

Special First Day of Issue Postmark

Philatelic Bureau, Edinburgh	70

513 **514** **515** **516**

Types **513**/**516** differ in the decorations of 'ER'.

(Des R. Guyatt)

1977 (11 May–15 June). Silver Jubilee. Multicoloured 'All-over' phosphor. Perf 15×14.

1033	513	8½p. Pale turquoise-green background	10	10
		a. Imperf (pair)	£950	
1034		9p. Lavender background (15.6.77)	20	20
1035	514	10p. Ochre background	10	10
		a. Imperf (horiz pair)	£3000	
1036	515	11p. Rose-pink background	25	30
		a. Imperf (horiz pair)	£3000	
1037	516	13p. Bistre-yellow background	25	30
		a. Imperf (pair)	£2000	
Set of 5			80	85
Set of 5 Gutter Pairs			1·60	
Set of 5 Traffic Light Gutter Pairs			8·00	
First Day Covers (2)				90
Presentation Pack (PO Pack No. 94) (Nos. 1033, 1035/1037)			1·00	

QUEEN ELIZABETH II/1977

PHQ Cards (set of 5) (22)	5·50	10·00
Souvenir Book	1·25	

The Souvenir book is a 16 page booklet containing a history of the Queen's reign.

Special First Day of Issue Postmarks

Philatelic Bureau, Edinburgh (Nos. 1033, 1035/1037) (11.5.77)	50
Philatelic Bureau, Edinburgh (No. 1034) (15.6.77)	50
Windsor, Berks (Nos. 1033, 1035/1037) (11.5.77)	1·00
Windsor, Berks (No. 1034) (15.6.77)	50

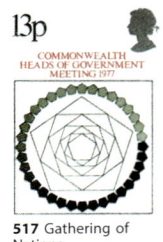

517 Gathering of Nations

(Des P. Murdoch. Recess and photo)

1977 (8 June). Commonwealth Heads of Government Meeting, London. Multicoloured 'All-over' phosphor. Perf 14×15.

1038	517	13p. Gathering of Nations	20	20
		Gutter Pair	40	
		Traffic Light Gutter Pair	1·75	
		First Day Cover		40
		Presentation Pack (PO Pack No. 95)	45	
		PHQ Card (23)	1·25	1·50

Special First Day of Issue Postmarks

Philatelic Bureau, Edinburgh	45
London SW	55

518 Hedgehog
519 Brown Hare 
520 Red Squirrel 
521 Otter 
522 Badger 

(Des P. Oxenham)

1977 (5 Oct). British Wildlife. Multicoloured 'All-over' phosphor. Perf 14×15.

1039	518	9p. Hedgehog	15	20
		a. Horiz strip of 5. Nos. 1039/1043	70	95
		b. Imperf (vert pair)	£3000	
		c. Imperf (horiz pair. Nos. 1039/1040)	£2750	
1040	519	9p. Brown Hare	15	20
1041	520	9p. Red Squirrel	15	20
1042	521	9p. Otter	15	20
1043	522	9p. Badger	15	20
		Set of 5	70	95
		Gutter Strip of 10	1·40	
		Traffic Light Gutter Strip of 10	5·00	
		First Day Cover		1·00
		Presentation Pack (PO Pack No. 96)	1·00	
		PHQ Cards (set of 5) (25)	1·50	2·50

Nos. 1039/1043 were printed horizontally se-tenant within the sheet.

Special First Day of Issue Postmark

Philatelic Bureau, Edinburgh	1·10

523 'Three French Hens, Two Turtle Doves and a Partridge in a Pear Tree'
524 'Six Geese-a-laying, Five Gold Rings, Four Colly Birds' 
525 'Eight Maids-a-milking, Seven Swans-a-swimming' 
526 'Ten Pipers piping, Nine Drummers drumming' 
527 'Twelve Lords a-leaping, Eleven Ladies dancing' 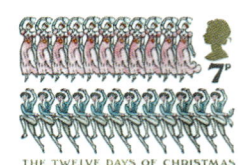
528 'A Partridge in a Pear Tree' 

(Des D. Gentleman)

1977 (23 Nov). Christmas, *The Twelve Days of Christmas*. Multicoloured One centre phosphor band (7p.) or 'All-over' phosphor (9p.). Perf 15×14.

1044	523	7p. 'Three French Hens, Two Turtle Doves and a Partridge in a Pear Tree'	10	10
		a. Horiz strip of 5. Nos. 1044/1048	50	50
		ab. Imperf (strip of 5. Nos. 1044/1048)	£2500	
1045	524	7p. 'Six Geese-a-laying, Five Gold Rings, Four Colly Birds'	10	10
1046	525	7p. 'Eight Maids-a-milking, Seven Swans-a-swimming'	10	10
1047	526	7p. 'Ten Pipers piping, Nine Drummers drumming'	10	10
1048	527	7p. 'Twelve Lords a-leaping, Eleven Ladies dancing'	10	10
1049	528	9p. 'A Partridge in a Pear Tree'	10	20
		a. Imperf (pair)	£1100	
		Set of 6	60	70
		Set of 6 Gutter Pairs	1·25	
		Traffic Light Gutter Pairs	3·75	
		First Day Cover		75
		Presentation Pack (PO Pack No. 97)	90	
		PHQ Cards (set of 6) (26)	1·50	2·50

Nos. 1044/1048 were printed horizontally se-tenant within the sheet.

Special First Day of Issue Postmarks

Philatelic Bureau, Edinburgh	75
Bethlehem, Llandeilo, Dyfed	80

Collectors Pack 1977

1977 (23 Nov). Comprises Nos. 1022/1025 and 1029/1049.

CP1049b	Collectors Pack (PO Pack No. 98)	3·75

1978/QUEEN ELIZABETH II

529 Oil. North Sea
530 Coal. Modern Pithead Production Platform 
531 Natural Gas. Flame Rising from Sea 
532 Electricity. Nuclear Power Station and Uranium Atom 

(Des P. Murdoch)

1978 (25 Jan). Energy Resources. Multicoloured 'All-over' phosphor. Perf 14×15.

1050	529	9p. Oil	10	10
1051	530	10½p. Coal	15	15
1052	531	11p. Natural Gas	15	15
1053	532	13p. Electricity	20	20
Set of 4			55	55
Set of 4 Gutter Pairs			1·10	
Set of 4 Traffic Light Gutter Pairs			4·50	
First Day Cover				60
Presentation Pack (PO Pack No. 99)			85	
PHQ Cards (set of 4) (27)			1·50	2·50

Special First Day of Issue Postmark
Philatelic Bureau, Edinburgh 70

533 The Tower of London
534 Holyroodhouse 
535 Caernarvon Castle 
536 Hampton Court Palace 

(Des R. Maddox (stamps), J. Matthews (miniature sheet))

1978 (1 Mar). British Architecture (4th series), Historic Buildings. Multicoloured 'All-over' phosphor. Perf 15×14.

1054	533	9p. The Tower of London	10	10
1055	534	10½p. Holyroodhouse	15	15
1056	535	11p. Caernarvon Castle	15	15
1057	536	13p. Hampton Court Palace	20	20
Set of 4			55	55
Set of 4 Gutter Pairs			1·10	
Set of 4 Traffic Light Gutter Pairs			4·25	
First Day Cover				60
Presentation Pack (PO Pack No. 100)			75	
PHQ Cards (set of 4) (28)			1·50	2·50
MS1058 121×89 mm. Nos. 1054/1057 (sold at 53½p.)			70	70
	a. Imperforate		£9500	
	b. Light yellow-olive (Queen's head) omitted		£14000	
	c. Rose-red (Union Jack on 9p.) omitted		£5000	
	d. Orange-yellow omitted		£6500	
	e. New blue (Union Jack on 9p.) omitted		85	
First Day Cover				85

The premium on No. **MS**1058 was used to support the London 1980 International Stamp Exhibition.

No. **MS**1058d is most noticeable on the 10½p. (spheres absent on towers) and around the roadway and arch on the 13p.

Special First Day of Issue Postmarks
Philatelic Bureau, Edinburgh (stamps)	80
Philatelic Bureau, Edinburgh (miniature sheet)	95
London EC (stamps)	90
London EC (miniature sheet)	1·00

537 State Coach
538 St Edward's Crown 
539 The Sovereign's Orb 
540 Imperial State Crown 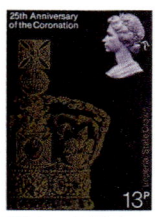

(Des J. Matthews)

1978 (31 May). 25th Anniversary of Coronation. Multicoloured 'All-over' phosphor. Perf 14×15.

1059	537	9p. State Coach	15	20
1060	538	10½p. St Edward's Crown	20	20
1061	539	11p. The Sovereign's Orb	20	20
1062	540	13p. Imperial State Crown	25	25
Set of 4			70	75
Set of 4 Gutter Pairs			1·40	
Set of 4 Traffic Light Gutter Pairs			4·25	
First Day Cover (Philatelic Bureau, Edinburgh)				80
Presentation Pack (PO Pack No. 101)			85	
PHQ Cards (set of 4) (29)			1·50	2·25
Souvenir Book			1·25	

The souvenir book is a 16 page booklet illustrated with scenes from the Coronation.

Special First Day of Issue Postmarks
Philatelic Bureau, Edinburgh	85
London SW1	95

541 Shire Horse
542 Shetland Pony 
543 Welsh Pony 
544 Thoroughbred 

(Des P. Oxenham)

1978 (5 July). Horses. Multicoloured 'All-over' phosphor. Perf 15×14.

1063	541	9p. Shire Horse	10	10
		a. Imperf (vert pair)	—	
1064	542	10½p. Shetland Pony	15	15
1065	543	11p. Welsh Pony	15	15

QUEEN ELIZABETH II/1978

1066	**544**	13p. Thoroughbred	20	20
Set of 4			55	55
Set of 4 Gutter Pairs			1·10	
Set of 4 Traffic Light Gutter Pairs			4·50	
First Day Cover (Philatelic Bureau, Edinburgh)				60
Presentation Pack (PO Pack No. 102)			75	
PHQ Cards (set of 4) (30)			1·00	1·75

Special First Day of Issue Postmarks
Philatelic Bureau, Edinburgh 65
Peterborough 75

545 Penny-farthing and 1884 Safety Bicycle
546 1920 Touring Bicycles 
547 1978 Small-wheel Bicycles 
548 1978 Road Racers 

(Des F. Wegner)

1978 (2 Aug). Centenaries of Cyclists' Touring Club and British Cycling Federation. Multicoloured 'All-over' phosphor. Perf 15×14.

1067	**545**	9p. Penny-farthing and 1884 Safety Bicycle	10	10
		a. Imperf (pair)	£350	
1068	**546**	10½p. 1920 Touring Bicycles	15	15
1069	**547**	11p. 1978 Small-wheel Bicycles	15	15
1070	**548**	13p. 1978 Road racers	20	20
		a. Imperf (pair)	£1200	
Set of 4			55	55
Set of 4 Gutter Pairs			1·10	
Set of 4 Traffic Light Gutter Pairs			4·25	
First Day Cover (Philatelic Bureau, Edinburgh)				60
Presentation Pack (PO Pack No. 103)			75	
PHQ Cards (set of 4) (31)			1·00	1·75

Special First Day of Issue Postmarks
Philatelic Bureau, Edinburgh 65
Harrogate, North Yorkshire 75

549 Singing Carols round the Christmas Tree
550 The Waits 
551 18th-century Carol Singers 
552 The Boar's Head Carol

(Des Faith Jaques)

1978 (22 Nov). Christmas, Carol singers. Multicoloured One centre phosphor band (7p.) or 'All-over' phosphor (others). Perf 15×14.

1071	**549**	7p. Singing Carols round the Christmas Tree	10	10
		a. Imperf (pair)	£400	
1072	**550**	9p. The Waits	15	15
		a. Imperf (pair)	£1000	
1073	**551**	11p. 18th-century Carol Singers	15	15
		a. Imperf (horiz pair)	£1100	
1074	**552**	13p. *The Boar's Head Carol*	20	20
Set of 4			55	55
Set of 4 Gutter Pairs			1·10	
Set of 4 Traffic Light Gutter Pairs			4·00	
First Day Cover				60
Presentation Pack (PO Pack No. 104)			75	
PHQ Cards (set of 4) (32)			1·00	1·75

Special First Day of Issue Postmarks
Philatelic Bureau, Edinburgh 65
Bethlehem, Llandeilo, Dyfed 70

Collectors Pack 1978
1978 (22 Nov). Comprises Nos. 1050/1057 and 1059/1074.
CP1074a   Collectors Pack (PO Pack No. 105) ...... 3·75

553 Old English Sheepdog
554 Welsh Springer Spaniel 
555 West Highland Terrier 
556 Irish Setter 

(Des P. Barrett)

1979 (7 Feb). Dogs. Multicoloured 'All-over' phosphor. Perf 15×14.

1075	**553**	9p. Old English Sheepdog	10	10
1076	**554**	10½p. Welsh Springer Spaniel	15	15
1077	**555**	11p. West Highland Terrier	15	15
		a. Imperf (horiz pair)	£3000	
1078	**556**	13p. Irish Setter	20	20
Set of 4			55	55
Set of 4 Gutter Pairs			1·10	
Set of 4 Traffic Light Gutter Pairs			4·00	
First Day Cover				60
Presentation Pack (PO Pack No. 106)			70	
PHQ Cards (set of 4) (33)			80	1·50

Special First Day of Issue Postmarks
Philatelic Bureau, Edinburgh 65
London 75

557 Primroses
558 Daffodils 
559 Bluebells 
560 Snowdrops 

(Des P. Newcombe)

1979 (21 Mar). Spring Wild Flowers. Multicoloured 'All-over' phosphor. Perf 14×15.

1079	**557**	9p. Primroses	10	10
		a. Imperf (vert pair)	£550	
1080	**558**	10½p. Daffodils	15	15
		a. Imperf (vert pair)	£1500	
1081	**559**	11p. Bluebells	15	15
		a. Imperf (horiz pair)	£1500	
1082	**560**	13p. Snowdrops	20	20
		a. Imperf (horiz pair)	£1200	

1979/QUEEN ELIZABETH II

Set of 4	55	55
Set of 4 Gutter Pairs	1·10	
Set of 4 Traffic Light Gutter Pairs	4·00	
First Day Cover		60
Presentation Pack (PO Pack No. 107)	70	
PHQ Cards (set of 4) (34)	80	1·25

Special First Day of Issue Postmark

Philatelic Bureau, Edinburgh		65

561 **562** **563** **564**

(Des S. Cliff)

1979 (9 May). First Direct Elections to European Assembly. Multicoloured (colours of backgrounds to flag panels given) Phosphorised paper. Perf 15×14.

1083	561	9p. dull ultramarine	10	10
1084	562	10½p. chestnut	15	15
1085	563	11p. grey-green	15	15
1086	564	13p. brown	20	20
Set of 4			55	55
Set of 4 Gutter Pairs			1·10	
Set of 4 Traffic Light Gutter Pairs			4·00	
First Day Cover				60
Presentation Pack (PO Pack No. 108)			70	
PHQ Cards (set of 4) (35)			80	1·25

Nos. 1083/1086 show Hands placing National Flags in Ballot Boxes.

Special First Day of Issue Postmarks

Philatelic Bureau, Edinburgh		65
London SW		70

565 *Saddling Mahmoud for the Derby, 1936* (Sir Alfred Munnings)

566 *The Liverpool Great National Steeple Chase, 1839* (aquatint by F. C. Turner)

567 *The First Spring Meeting, Newmarket, 1793* (J. N. Sartorius)

568 *Racing at Dorsett Ferry, Windsor, 1684* (Francis Barlow)

(Des S. Rose)

1979 (6 June). Horse Racing Paintings Bicentenary of the Derby (9p.). Multicoloured 'All-over' phosphor. Perf 15×14.

1087	565	9p. Saddling Mahmoud for the Derby, 1936	10	10
1088	566	10½p. The Liverpool Great National Steeple Chase, 1839	15	15
1089	567	11p. The First Spring Meeting, Newmarket, 1793	15	15
1090	568	13p. Racing at Dorsett Ferry, Windsor, 1684	20	20
Set of 4			55	55
Set of 4 Gutter Pairs			1·10	
Set of 4 Traffic Light Gutter Pairs			4·50	
First Day Cover				60
Presentation Pack (PO Pack No. 109)			70	
PHQ Cards (set of 4) (36)			80	1·25

Special First Day of Issue Postmarks

Philatelic Bureau, Edinburgh		65
Epsom, Surrey		70

569 *The Tale of Peter Rabbit* (Beatrix Potter)

570 *The Wind in the Willows* (Kenneth Grahame)

571 *Winnie-the-Pooh* (A. A. Milne)

572 *Alice's Adventures in Wonderland* (Lewis Carroll)

(Des E. Hughes)

1979 (11 July). International Year of the Child. Children's Book Illustrations. Multicoloured 'All-over' phosphor. Perf 14×15.

1091	569	9p. The Tale of Peter Rabbit	15	15
1092	570	10½p. The Wind in the Willows	20	20
1093	571	11p. Winnie-the-Pooh	20	20
1094	572	13p. Alice's Adventures in Wonderland	25	25
Set of 4			75	75
Set of 4 Gutter Pairs			1·50	
Set of 4 Traffic Light Gutter Pairs			3·75	
First Day Cover				80
Presentation Pack (PO Pack No. 110)			1·00	
PHQ Cards (set of 4) (37)			80	1·40

Nos. 1091/1094 depict original illustrations from four books.

Special First Day of Issue Postmark

Philatelic Bureau, Edinburgh		85

First Day of Issue handstamps were provided at Hartfield, East Sussex and Stourbridge, West Midlands for this issue.

573 Sir Rowland Hill

574 Postman, *circa* 1839

575 London Postman, *circa* 1839

576 Woman and Young Girl with Letters, 1840

QUEEN ELIZABETH II/1979

(Des E. Stemp)

1979 (22 Aug–24 Oct). Death Centenary of Sir Rowland Hill. Multicoloured 'All-over' phosphor. Perf 14×15.

1095	573	10p. Sir Rowland Hill	15	15
		a. Imperf (horiz pair)	£3500	
1096	574	11½p. Postman, circa 1839	15	15
1097	575	13p. London Postman, circa 1839	20	20
1098	576	15p. Woman and Young Girl with Letters, 1840	25	25

Set of 4 .... 70 70
Set of 4 Gutter Pairs .... 1·40
Set of 4 Traffic Light Gutter Pairs .... 3·75
First Day Cover 75
Presentation Pack (PO Pack No. 111) 80
PHQ Cards (set of 4) (38) .... 50 1·25

MS1099 89×121 mm. Nos. 1095/1098 (sold at 59½p.)
(24.10.79) 70 75
    a. Imperforate £4000
    b. Brown-ochre (15p. background, etc.) omitted £4250
    c. Gold (Queen's head) omitted £600
    d. Brown-ochre, myrtle-green and gold omitted £12000
    e. Bright blue (13p. background, etc.) omitted £4250
    f. Myrtle-green (10p. (background), 15p.) omitted £4250
    g. Pale greenish yellow omitted £700
    h. Rosine omitted £1500
    i. Bistre-brown omitted £1600
    j. Grey-black and pale greenish yellow omitted .... —

First Day Cover 80

The premium on No. **MS**1099 was used to support the London 1980 International Stamp Exhibition.

Examples of No. **MS**1099 showing face values on the stamps of 9p., 10½p., 11p. and 13p., with a sheet price of 53½p., were prepared, but not issued.

Special First Day of Issue Postmarks

Philatelic Bureau, Edinburgh (stamps) (22.8.79) 80
Philatelic Bureau, Edinburgh (miniature sheet) (24.10.79) 85
London EC (stamps) (22.8.79) 80
London EC (miniature sheet) (24.10.79) 85

First Day of Issue handstamps were provided at Kidderminster, Worcestershire on 22 August (pictorial) and 24 October (Type C) and at Sanquhar, Dumfriesshire on 22 August and 24 October (both Type C).

577 Policeman on the Beat

578 Policeman directing Traffic

579 Mounted Policewoman

580 River Patrol Boat

(Des B. Sanders)

1979 (26 Sept). 150th Anniversary of Metropolitan Police. Multicoloured Phosphorised paper. Perf 15×14.

1100	577	10p. Policeman on the Beat	15	15
1101	578	11½p. Policeman directing Traffic	15	15
1102	579	13p. Mounted Policewoman	20	20
1103	580	15p. River Patrol Boat	25	25

Set of 4 .... 70 70
Set of 4 Gutter Pairs .... 1·40
Set of 4 Traffic Light Gutter Pairs .... 3·75
First Day Cover 75
Presentation Pack (PO Pack No. 112) 80
PHQ Cards (set of 4) (39) .... 50 1·25

Special First Day of Issue Postmarks

Philatelic Bureau, Edinburgh 80
London SW 80

581 The Three Kings

582 Angel appearing to the Shepherds

583 The Nativity

584 Mary and Joseph travelling to Bethlehem

585 The Annunciation

(Des F. Wegner)

1979 (21 Nov). Christmas, Nativity Scenes. Multicoloured One centre phosphor band (8p.) or phosphorised paper (others). Perf 15×14.

1104	581	8p. The Three Kings	10	10
		a. Imperf (pair)	£500	
1105	582	10p. Angel appearing to the Shepherds	15	15
		a. Imperf between (vert pair)	—	
		b. Imperf (pair)	£600	
1106	583	11½p. The Nativity	15	15
1107	584	13p. Mary and Joseph travelling to Bethlehem	20	20
1108	585	15p. The Annunciation	20	20

Set of 5 .... 75 75
Set of 5 Gutter Pairs .... 1·50
Set of 5 Traffic Light Gutter Pairs .... 4·50
First Day Cover 80
Presentation Pack (PO Pack No. 113) 80
PHQ Cards (set of 5) (40) .... 50 1·25

Special First Day of Issue Postmarks

Philatelic Bureau, Edinburgh 85
Bethlehem, Llandeilo, Dyfed 85

Collectors Pack 1979

1979 (21 Nov). Comprises Nos. 1075/1098 and 1100/1108.
CP1108a   Collectors Pack (PO Pack No. 114) ...... 4·50

586 Common Kingfisher

587 Dipper

1980/QUEEN ELIZABETH II

588 Moorhen
589 Yellow Wagtails 

(Des M. Warren)

1980 (16 Jan). Centenary of Wild Bird Protection Act. Multicoloured Phosphorised paper. Perf 14×15.

1109	586	10p. Common Kingfisher	15	15
1110	587	11½p. Dipper	15	15
1111	588	13p. Moorhen	20	20
1112	589	15p. Yellow Wagtails	20	20
Set of 4			60	60
Set of 4 Gutter Pairs			1·25	
First Day Cover				65
Presentation Pack (PO Pack No. 115)			70	
PHQ Cards (set of 4) (41)			50	1·00

Special First Day of Issue Postmarks

Philatelic Bureau, Edinburgh	70
Sandy, Beds	75

590 *Rocket* approaching Moorish Arch, Liverpool
591 First and Second Class Carriages passing through Olive Mount Cutting 
592 Third Class Carriage and Sheep Truck crossing Chat Moss 
593 Horsebox and Carriage Truck near Bridgewater Canal 
594 Goods Truck and Mail Coach at Manchester 
593a Grey step and dot above (Cyl. 1A, R. 8/4) 

(Des D. Gentleman)

1980 (12 Mar). 150th Anniversary of Liverpool and Manchester Railway. Multicoloured Phosphorised paper. Perf 15×14.

1113	590	12p. Rocket	15	10
		a. Strip of 5. Nos. 1113/1117	75	60
		ab. Imperf (horiz strip of 5. Nos. 1113/1117)	£3250	
		ac. Lemon omitted (horiz strip of 5. Nos. 1113/1117)	£15000	
1114	591	12p. First and Second Class Carriages	15	10
1115	592	12p. Third Class Carriage and Sheep Truck	15	10
1116	593	12p. Horsebox and Carriage Truck	15	10
		a. Grey step	30·00	
1117	594	12p. Goods Truck and Mail-Coach	15	10
Set of 5			75	60
Gutter Block of 10			1·50	
First Day Cover				70
Presentation Pack (PO Pack No. 116)			85	
PHQ Cards (set of 5) (42)			50	1·25

Nos. 1113/1117 were printed together, *se-tenant*, in horizontal strips of five throughout the sheet.

Special First Day of Issue Postmarks

Philatelic Bureau, Edinburgh	75
Liverpool	80
Manchester	80

595 Montage of London Buildings

During the printing of No. 1118 the die was re-cut resulting in the following two types:

Type I (original). Top and bottom lines of shading in portrait oval broken. Hatched shading below left arm of Tower Bridge and hull of ship below right arm. Other points: Hatched shading on flag on Westminster Abbey, bottom right of Post Office Tower and archway of entrance to Westminster Abbey.

QUEEN ELIZABETH II/1980

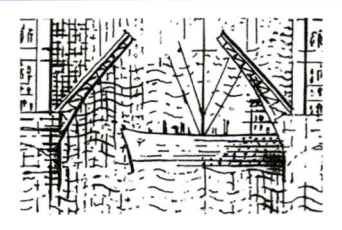

Type II (re-engraved). Lines in oval unbroken. Solid shading on bridge and ship. Also solid shading on flag, Post Office Tower and archway.

(Des J. Matthews. Eng G. Holt. Recess)

1980 (9 Apr–7 May). London 1980 International Stamp Exhibition. Phosphorised paper. Perf 14½×14.

1118	**595**	50p. agate (I)	75	70
		a. Type II	75	70
Gutter Pair			1·50	
First Day Cover				75
Presentation Pack (PO Pack No. 117)			85	
PHQ Card (43)			20	80
MS1119 90×123 mm. No. 1118a (sold at 75p.) (7.5.80)			75	95
		a. Error. Imperf	£3750	
First Day Cover				95

Examples of No. 1118 are known in various shades of green. Such shades result from problems with the drying of the printed sheets on the press, but are not listed as similar colours can be easily faked.

Special First Day of Issue Postmarks
Philatelic Bureau, Edinburgh (stamp) (9.4.80)	80
Philatelic Bureau, Edinburgh (miniature sheet) (7.5.80)	1·00
London SW (stamp) (9.4.80)	1·00
London SW (miniature sheet) (7.5.80)	1·00

596 Buckingham Palace

597 The Albert Memorial

598 Royal Opera House

599 Hampton Court

600 Kensington Palace

(Des Sir Hugh Casson)

1980 (7 May). London Landmarks. Multicoloured Phosphorised paper. Perf 14×15.

1120	**596**	10½p. Buckingham Palace	10	10
1121	**597**	12p. The Albert Memorial	15	15
		a. Imperf (vert pair)	—	
1122	**598**	13½p. Royal Opera House	20	15
		a. Imperf (pair)	£2200	
1123	**599**	15p. Hampton Court	20	20
1124	**600**	17½p. Kensington Palace	25	20
		a. Silver (Queen's head) omitted	£650	
Set of 5			85	75
Set of 5 Gutter Pairs			4·25	
First Day Cover				80
Presentation Pack (PO Pack No. 118)			90	
PHQ Cards (set of 5) (43)			60	1·10

No. 1124a shows the Queen's head in pale greenish yellow, this colour being printed beneath the silver for technical reasons.

Special First Day of Issue Postmarks
Philatelic Bureau, Edinburgh	85
Kingston-upon-Thames	85

601 Charlotte Brontë (*Jane Eyre*)

602 George Eliot (*The Mill on the Floss*)

603 Emily Brontë (*Wuthering Heights*)

604 Mrs Gaskell (*North and South*)

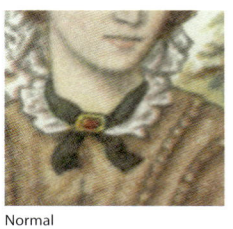

Normal   Missing jewel (R.3/3)

(Des Barbara Brown)

1980 (9 July). Famous Authoresses. Multicoloured Phosphorised paper. Perf 15×14.

1125	**601**	12p. Charlotte Brontë	15	15
		Ea. Missing 'p' in value (R. 4/6)	25·00	
		b. Missing jewel	25·00	
1126	**602**	13½p. George Eliot	15	15
		a. Pale blue omitted	£2500	
1127	**603**	15p. Emily Brontë	25	25
1128	**604**	17½p. Mrs Gaskell	30	30
		a. Imperf and slate-blue omitted (pair)	£750	
Set of 4			75	75
Set of 4 Gutter Pairs			1·50	
First Day Cover				80
Presentation Pack (PO Pack No. 119)			80	
PHQ Cards (set of 4) (44)			50	1·00

Nos. 1125/1128 show authoresses and scenes from novels.
Nos. 1125/1126 also include the Europa CEPT emblem.

Special First Day of Issue Postmarks
Philatelic Bureau, Edinburgh	85
Haworth, Keighley, W. Yorks	90

605 Queen Elizabeth the Queen Mother

1980/QUEEN ELIZABETH II

(Des J. Matthews from photograph by N. Parkinson)

1980 (4 Aug). 80th Birthday of Queen Elizabeth the Queen Mother. Multicoloured Phosphorised paper. Perf 14×15.

1129	**605**	12p. Queen Elizabeth the Queen Mother	25	25
		a. Imperf (horiz pair)	£1200	
		Gutter Pair	50	
		First Day Cover		50
		PHQ Card (45)	20	40

Special First Day of Issue Postmarks
Philatelic Bureau, Edinburgh 60
Glamis Castle, Forfar 65

606 Sir Henry Wood
607 Sir Thomas Beecham 
608 Sir Malcolm Sargent 
609 Sir John Barbirolli 

(Des P. Gauld)

1980 (10 Sept). British Conductors. Multicoloured Phosphorised paper. Perf 14×15.

1130	**606**	12p. Sir Henry Wood	15	15
1131	**607**	13½p. Sir Thomas Beecham	15	15
1132	**608**	15p. Sir Malcolm Sargent	25	25
1133	**609**	17½p. Sir John Barbirolli	30	30
		Set of 4	75	75
		Set of 4 Gutter Pairs	1·50	
		First Day Cover		80
		Presentation Pack (PO Pack No. 120)	80	
		PHQ Cards (set of 4) (46)	60	1·00

Special First Day of Issues
Postmarks Philatelic Bureau, Edinburgh 85
London SW 90

610 Running
611 Rugby 
612 Boxing 
613 Cricket 

(Des R. Goldsmith. Litho Questa)

1980 (10 Oct). Sport Centenaries. Multicoloured Phosphorised paper. Perf 14×14½.

1134	**610**	12p. Running	15	15
		a. Gold (Queen's head) omitted	—	
1135	**611**	13½p. Rugby	15	15
1136	**612**	15p. Boxing	25	25
		a. Gold (Queen's head) omitted	—	
1137	**613**	17½p. Cricket	30	30
		Set of 4	75	75
		Set of 4 Gutter Pairs	1·50	
		First Day Cover		80
		Presentation Pack (PO Pack No. 121)	80	
		PHQ Cards (set of 4) (47)	60	1·00

Centenaries: 12p. Amateur Athletics Association; 13½p. Welsh Rugby Union; 15p. Amateur Boxing Association; 17½p. First England–Australia Test Match.

Nos. 1134a and 1136a were caused by paper folds.

Special First Day of Issue Postmarks
Philatelic Bureau, Edinburgh 85
Cardiff 90

614 Christmas Tree
615 Candles 
616 Apples and Mistletoe 
617 Crown, Chains and Bell 
618 Holly 

(Des J. Matthews)

1980 (19 Nov). Christmas. Multicoloured One centre phosphor band (10p.) or phosphorised paper (others). Perf 15×14.

1138	**614**	10p. Christmas Tree	10	10
		a. Imperf (horiz pair)	£1400	
1139	**615**	12p. Candles	15	15
1140	**616**	13½p. Apples and Mistletoe	15	15
		a. Imperf (pair)	£2000	
1141	**617**	15p. Crown, Chains and Bell	25	25
1142	**618**	17½p. Holly	25	25
		Set of 5	80	80
		Set of 5 Gutter Pairs	1·60	
		First Day Cover		85
		Presentation Pack (PO Pack No. 122)	85	
		PHQ Cards (set of 5) (48)	75	1·00

Special First Day of Issue Postmarks
Philatelic Bureau, Edinburgh 90
Bethlehem, Llandeilo, Dyfed 95

Collectors Pack 1980

1980 (19 Nov). Comprises Nos. 1109/1118 and 1120/1142.
CP1142a   Collectors Pack (PO Pack No. 123) ...... 5·50

QUEEN ELIZABETH II/1981

619 St Valentine's Day

620 Morris Dancers

621 Lammastide

622 Medieval Mummers

(Des F. Wegner)

1981 (6 Feb). Folklore. Multicoloured Phosphorised paper. Perf 15×14.

1143	619	14p. St Valentine's Day	20	20
1144	620	18p. Morris Dancers	20	20
1145	621	22p. Lammastide	30	35
1146	622	25p. Medieval Mummers	40	45
Set of 4			1·00	1·10
Set of 4 Gutter Pairs			2·00	
First Day Cover				1·10
Presentation Pack (PO Pack No. 124)			1·10	
PHQ Cards (set of 4) (49)			60	1·20

Types **619/620** also include the Europa CEPT emblem.

Special First Day of Issue Postmarks

Philatelic Bureau, Edinburgh	1·25
London WC	1·25

623 Blind Man with Guide Dog

624 Hands spelling 'Deaf' in Sign Language

625 Disabled Man in Wheelchair

626 Disabled Artist with Foot painting

(Des J. Gibbs)

1981 (25 Mar). International Year of the Disabled. Multicoloured. Phosphorised paper. Perf 15×14.

1147	623	14p. Blind Man with Guide Dog	20	20
		a. Imperf (pair)	£450	
1148	624	18p. Hands spelling 'Deaf'	20	20
1149	625	22p. Disabled Man in Wheelchair	35	35
1150	626	25p. Disabled Artist with Foot painting	45	45
Set of 4			1·10	1·10
Set of 4 Gutter Pairs			2·25	
First Day Cover				1·20
Presentation Pack (PO Pack No. 125)			1·25	
PHQ Cards (set of 4) (50)			60	1·25

All known examples of No. 1147a are creased.

Special First Day of Issue Postmarks

Philatelic Bureau, Edinburgh	1·25
Windsor	1·25

627 Small tortoiseshell

628 Large Blue

629 Peacock

630 Chequered Skipper

(Des G. Beningfield)

1981 (13 May). Butterflies. Multicoloured Phosphorised paper. Perf 14×15.

1151	627	14p. Small tortoiseshell	20	20
		a. Imperf (pair)	£4250	
1152	628	18p. Large Blue	20	20
1153	629	22p. Peacock	35	35
1154	630	25p. Chequered Skipper	45	45
Set of 4			1·10	1·10
Set of 4 Gutter Pairs			2·25	
First Day Cover				1·20
Presentation Pack (PO Pack No. 126)			1·25	
PHQ Cards (set of 4) (51)			60	1·25

Special First Day of Issue Postmarks

Philatelic Bureau, Edinburgh	1·25
London SW	1·25

631 Glenfinnan, Scotland

632 Derwentwater, England

633 Stackpole Head, Wales

634 Giant's Causeway, Northern Ireland

635 St Kilda, Scotland

(Des M. Fairclough)

1981 (24 June). 50th Anniversary of National Trust for Scotland. British Landscapes. Multicoloured Phosphorised paper. Perf 15×14.

1155	631	14p. Glenfinnan, Scotland	20	20
1156	632	18p. Derwentwater, England	20	20
1157	633	20p. Stackpole Head, Wales	25	25
1158	634	22p. Giant's Causeway, Northern Ireland	35	35
1159	635	25p. St Kilda, Scotland	45	45
Set of 5			1·25	1·25

1981/QUEEN ELIZABETH II

Set of 5 Gutter Pairs	2·50	
First Day Cover		1·40
Presentation Pack (PO Pack No. 127)	1·40	
PHQ Cards (set of 5) (52)	75	1·40

Special First Day of Issue Postmarks
Philatelic Bureau, Edinburgh	1·40
Glenfinnan	1·40
Keswick	1·40

636 Prince Charles and Lady Diana Spencer

(Des J. Matthews from photograph by Lord Snowdon)

1981 (22 July). Royal Wedding. Multicoloured Phosphorised paper. Perf 14×15.

1160	636	14p. Prince Charles and Lady Diana Spencer	25	20
1161		25p. Prince Charles and Lady Diana Spencer	40	35
Set of 2			60	50
Set of 2 Gutter Pairs			1·25	
First Day Cover				1·20
Presentation Pack (PO Pack No. 127a)			1·10	
Souvenir Book			1·25	
PHQ Cards (set of 2) (53)			30	70

The souvenir book is a 12 page illustrated booklet with a set of mint stamps in a sachet attached to the front cover.

Special First Day of Issue Postmarks
Philatelic Bureau, Edinburgh	1·25
Caernarfon, Gwynedd	1·50
London EC	1·30

637 'Expeditions'
638 'Skills' 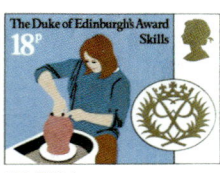
639 'Service' 
640 'Recreation' 

(Des P. Sharland. Litho J.W.)

1981 (12 Aug). 25th Anniversary of Duke of Edinburgh's Award Scheme. Multicoloured Phosphorised paper. Perf 14.

1162	637	14p. 'Expeditions'	20	20
1163	638	18p. 'Skills'	20	20
1164	639	22p. 'Service'	35	35
1165	640	25p. 'Recreation'	45	45
Set of 4			1·10	1·10
Set of 4 Gutter Pairs			2·25	
First Day Cover				1·25
Presentation Pack (PO Pack No. 128)			1·25	
PHQ Cards (set of 4) (54)			60	1·25

Special First Day of Issue Postmarks
Philatelic Bureau, Edinburgh	1·25
London W2	1·50

641 Cockle-dredging from *Linsey II*
642 Hauling in Trawl Net 
643 Lobster Potting 
644 Hoisting Seine Net 

(Des B. Sanders)

1981 (23 Sept). Fishing Industry. Multicoloured Phosphorised paper. Perf 15×14.

1166	641	14p. Cockle-dredging from *Linsey II*	20	20
1167	642	18p. Hauling in Trawl Net	20	20
1168	643	22p. Lobster Potting	35	35
1169	644	25p. Hoisting Seine Net	45	45
Set of 4			1·10	1·10
Set of 4 Gutter Pairs			2·25	
First Day Cover				1·25
Presentation Pack (PO Pack No. 129)			1·25	
PHQ Cards (set of 4) (55)			60	1·25

Nos. 1166/1169 were issued on the occasion of the centenary of the Royal National Mission to Deep Sea Fishermen.

Special First Day of Issue Postmarks
Philatelic Bureau, Edinburgh	1·25
Hull	1·50

645 Father Christmas
646 Jesus Christ 
647 Flying Angel 
648 Joseph and Mary arriving at Bethlehem 
649 Three Kings approaching Bethlehem 

(Des Samantha Brown (11½p.), Tracy Jenkins (14p.), Lucinda Blackmore (18p.), Stephen Moore (22p.), Sophie Sharp (25p.))

1981 (18 Nov). Christmas. Children's Pictures. Multicoloured One phosphor band (11½p.) or phosphorised paper (others). Perf 15×14.

1170	645	11½p. Father Christmas	20	20
1171	646	14p. Jesus Christ	20	20
1172	647	18p. Flying Angel	20	20
1173	648	22p. Joseph and Mary arriving at Bethlehem	30	30
1174	649	25p. Three Kings approaching Bethlehem	40	40
Set of 5			1·25	1·25
Set of 5 Gutter Pairs			2·50	
First Day Cover				1·40

QUEEN ELIZABETH II/1981

Presentation Pack (PO Pack No. 130)	1·25	
PHQ Cards (set of 5) (56)	75	1·40

Special First Day of Issue Postmarks
Philatelic Bureau, Edinburgh	1·50
Bethlehem, Llandeilo, Dyfed	1·50

Collectors Pack 1981

1981 (18 Nov). Comprises Nos. 1143/1174.
CP1174*a*   Collectors Pack (PO Pack No. 131)...... 7·25

650 Charles Darwin and Giant Tortoises
651 Darwin and Marine Iguanas 
652 Darwin, Cactus Ground Finch and Large Ground Finch 
653 Darwin and Prehistoric Skulls 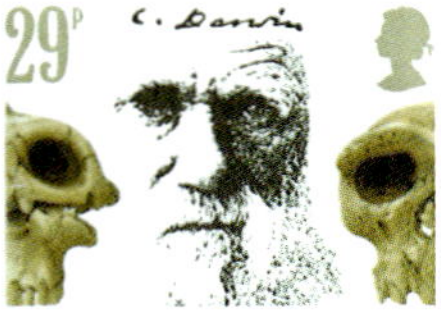

(Des D. Gentleman)

1982 (10 Feb). Death Centenary of Charles Darwin. Multicoloured Phosphorised paper. Perf 15×14.

1175	650	15½p. Charles Darwin and Giant Tortoises	20	20
1176	651	19½p. Darwin and Marine Iguanas	25	25
1177	652	26p. Darwin, Cactus Ground Finch and Large Ground Finch	35	35
1178	653	29p. Darwin and Prehistoric Skulls	50	50
Set of 4			1·25	1·25
Set of 4 Gutter Pairs			2·50	
First Day Cover				1·25
Presentation Pack (PO Pack No. 132)			1·25	
PHQ Cards (set of 4) (57)			60	1·25

Special First Day of Issue Postmarks
Philatelic Bureau, Edinburgh	1·50
Shrewsbury	1·50

654 Boys' Brigade
655 Girls' Brigade 
656 Boy Scout Movement 
657 Girl Guide Movement 

(Des B. Sanders)

1982 (24 Mar). Youth Organisations. Multicoloured Phosphorised paper. Perf 14×15.

1179	654	15½p. Boys' Brigade	20	20
1180	655	19½p. Girls' Brigade	25	25
1181	656	26p. Boy Scout Movement	35	35
1182	657	29p. Girl Guide Movement	50	50
Set of 4			1·25	1·25
Set of 4 Gutter Pairs			2·50	
First Day Cover				1·40
Presentation Pack (PO Pack No. 133)			1·40	
PHQ Cards (set of 4) (58)			60	1·40

Nos. 1179/1182 were issued on the occasion of the 75th anniversary of the Boy Scout Movement; the 125th birth anniversary of Lord Baden-Powell and the centenary of the Boys' Brigade (1983).

Special First Day of Issue Postmarks
Edinburgh Philatelic Bureau	1·50
Glasgow	1·50
London SW	1·50

658 Ballerina
659 Harlequin 
660 Hamlet 
661 Opera Singer 

(Des A. George)

1982 (28 Apr). Europa. British Theatre. Multicoloured Phosphorised paper. Perf 14×15.

1183	658	15½p. Ballerina	20	20
1184	659	19½p. Harlequin	25	25
1185	660	26p. Hamlet	35	35
1186	661	29p. Opera Singer	50	50
Set of 4			1·25	1·25
Set of 4 Gutter Pairs			2·50	
First Day Cover				1·40
Presentation Pack (PO Pack No. 134)			1·40	
PHQ Cards (set of 4) (59)			60	1·40

Special First Day of Issue Postmarks
Philatelic Bureau, Edinburgh	1·50
Stratford-upon-Avon	1·50

662 Henry VIII and *Mary Rose*
663 Admiral Blake and *Triumph* 
664 Lord Nelson and HMS *Victory* 
665 Lord Fisher and HMS *Dreadnought*

1982/QUEEN ELIZABETH II

666 Viscount Cunningham and HMS *Warspite*

(Des Marjorie Saynor. Eng Czesław Slania. Recess and photo)

1982 (16 June). Maritime Heritage. Multicoloured Phosphorised paper. Perf 15×14.

1187	662	15½p. Henry VIII and *Mary Rose*	20	20
		a. Imperf (pair)	£2000	
		b. Black (ship and waves) omitted	—	£1250
1188	663	19½p. Admiral Blake and *Triumph*	25	25
1189	664	24p. Lord Nelson and HMS *Victory*	35	35
1190	665	26p. Lord Fisher and HMS *Dreadnought*	40	40
		a. Imperf (pair)	£3750	
1191	666	29p. Viscount Cunningham and HMS *Warspite*	50	50
Set of 5			1·60	1·60
Set of 5 Gutter Pairs			3·25	
First Day Cover				1·75
Presentation Pack (PO Pack No. 136)			1·75	
PHQ Cards (set of 5) (60)			75	1·75

Nos. 1187/1191 were issued on the occasion of Maritime England Year, the Bicentenary of the Livery Grant by the City of London to the Worshipful Company of Shipwrights and the raising of the *Mary Rose* from Portsmouth Harbour.

Special First Day of Issue Postmarks
Philatelic Bureau, Edinburgh	1·90
Portsmouth	1·90

667 'Strawberry Thief' (William Morris)

668 Untitled (Steiner and Co)

669 'Cherry Orchard' (Paul Nash)

670 'Chevron' (Andrew Foster)

(Des Peter Hatch Partnership)

1982 (23 July). British Textiles. Multicoloured Phosphorised paper. Perf 14×15.

1192	667	15½p. 'Strawberry Thief' (William Morris)	20	20
		a. Imperf (horiz pair)	£1600	
1193	668	19½p. Untitled (Steiner and Co)	25	25
		a. Imperf (vert pair)	£3250	
1194	669	26p. 'Cherry Orchard' (Paul Nash)	35	35
1195	670	29p. 'Chevron' (Andrew Foster)	50	50
Set of 4			1·25	1·25
Set of 4 Gutter Pairs			2·50	
First Day Cover				1·40
Presentation Pack (PO Pack No. 137)			1·40	
PHQ Cards (set of 4) (61)			60	1·40

Nos. 1192/1195 were issued on the occasion of the 250th birth anniversary of Sir Richard Arkwright (inventor of spinning machine).

Special First Day of Issue Postmarks
Philatelic Bureau, Edinburgh	1·50
Rochdale	1·50

671 Development of Communications

672 Technological Aids

(Des Delaney and Ireland)

1982 (8 Sept). Information Technology. Multicoloured Phosphorised paper. Perf 14×15.

1196	671	15½p. Development of Communications	25	25
		a. Imperf (pair)	£275	
1197	672	26p. Technological Aids	35	35
		a. Imperf (pair)	£2000	
Set of 2			55	55
Set of 2 Gutter Pairs			1·10	
First Day Cover				60
Presentation Pack (PO Pack No. 138)			60	
PHQ Cards (set of 2) (62)			30	60

Special First Day of Issue Postmarks
Philatelic Bureau, Edinburgh	60
London WC	60

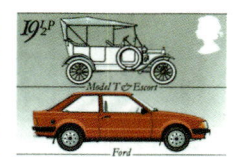

673 Austin Seven and Metro

674 Ford Model T and Escort

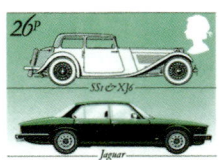

675 Jaguar SS 1 and XJ6

676 Rolls-Royce Silver Ghost and Silver Spirit

(Des S. Paine. Litho Questa)

1982 (13 Oct). British Motor Cars. Multicoloured. Phosphorised paper. Perf 14½×14.

1198	673	15½p. Austin Seven and Metro	20	20
1199	674	19½p. Ford Model T and Escort	25	25
		a. Rose-red, grey and black printings double	£900	
		b. Black printed double	£2750	
1200	675	26p. Jaguar SS 1 and XJ6	35	35
1201	676	29p. Rolls-Royce Silver Ghost and Silver Spirit	50	50
		a. Black printing quadruple	£600	
		b. Bright orange, carmine-red, grey and black printings double	£1100	
		c. Black printing quadruple grey printing triple and purple and carmine printings double	£1100	
Set of 4			1·25	1·25
Set of 4 Gutter Pairs			2·50	
First Day Cover				1·40
Presentation Pack (PO Pack No. 139)			1·40	
PHQ Cards (set of 4) (63)			60	1·40

The price for Nos. 1199b is for a complete doubling of both cars, examples showing doubling of only one car or parts of two cars are worth less.

Special First Day of Issue Postmarks
Philatelic Bureau, Edinburgh	1·40
Birmingham	1·50
Crewe	1·50

QUEEN ELIZABETH II/1982

677 *While Shepherds Watched*
678 *The Holly and the Ivy* 
679 *I Saw Three Ships* 
680 *We Three Kings* 
681 *Good King Wenceslas* 

(Des Barbara Brown)

1982 (17 Nov). Christmas. Carols. Multicoloured One phosphor band (12½p.) or phosphorised paper (others). Perf 15×14.

1202	677	12½p. *While Shepherds Watched*	20	20
1203	678	15½p. *The Holly and the Ivy*	20	20
		a. Imperf (pair)	£2200	
1204	679	19½p. *I Saw Three Ships*	25	25
		a. Imperf (pair)	£3000	
1205	680	26p. *We Three Kings*	35	30
1206	681	29p. *Good King Wenceslas*	50	50
Set of 5			1·40	1·40
Set of 5 Gutter Pairs			2·75	
First Day Cover				1·50
Presentation Pack (PO Pack No. 140)			1·50	
PHQ Cards (set of 5) (64)			75	1·50

Special Day of Issue Postmarks

Philatelic Bureau, Edinburgh .... 1·60
Bethlehem, Llandeilo, Dyfed .... 1·60

Collectors Pack 1982

1982 (17 Nov). Comprises Nos. 1175/1206.
CP1206a   Collectors Pack (PO Pack No. 141) ...... 12·00

682 Atlantic Salmon
683 Northern Pike 
684 Brown Trout 
685 Eurasian Perch 

(Des A. Jardine)

1983 (26 Jan). British River Fish. Multicoloured Phosphorised paper. Perf 15×14.

1207	682	15½p. Atlantic Salmon	20	20
		a. Imperf (pair)	£1400	
1208	683	19½p. Northern Pike	25	25
1209	684	26p. Brown Trout	35	35
		a. Imperf (pair)	£2000	
1210	685	29p. Eurasian Perch	50	50
Set of 4			1·25	1·25
Set of 4 Gutter Pairs			2·50	
First Day Cover				1·40

Presentation Pack (PO Pack No. 142) .... 1·40 1·40
PHQ Cards (set of 4) (65) .... 60 1·40
All known examples of No. 1209a are creased.

Special First Day of Issue Postmarks

Philatelic Bureau, Edinburgh .... 1·50
Peterborough .... 1·60

686 Tropical Island
687 Desert 
688 Temperate Farmland 
689 Mountain Range 

(Des D. Fraser)

1983 (9 Mar). Commonwealth Day. Geographical Regions. Multicoloured Phosphorised paper. Perf 14×15.

1211	686	15½p. Tropical Island	20	20
1212	687	19½p. Desert	25	25
1213	688	26p. Temperate Farmland	35	35
1214	689	29p. Mountain Range	50	50
Set of 4			1·25	1·25
Set of 4 Gutter Pairs			2·50	
First Day Cover				1·40
Presentation Pack (PO Pack No. 143)			1·40	
PHQ Cards (set of 4) (66)			60	1·40

Special First Day of Issue Postmarks

Philatelic Bureau, Edinburgh .... 1·50
London SW .... 1·50

690 Humber Bridge
691 Thames Flood Barrier 
692 *Iolair* (oilfield emergency support vessel) 

(Des M. Taylor)

1983 (25 May). Europa. Engineering Achievements. Multicoloured Phosphorised paper. Perf 15×14.

1215	690	16p. Humber Bridge	20	20
1216	691	20½p. Thames Flood Barrier	30	30
1217	692	28p. *Iolair*	50	50
Set of 3			90	90
Set of 3 Gutter Pairs			1·75	
First Day Cover				1·00
Presentation Pack (PO Pack No. 144)			1·00	
PHQ Cards (set of 3) (67)			40	1·00

Special First Day of Issue Postmarks

Philatelic Bureau, Edinburgh .... 1·00
Hull .... 1·10

1983/QUEEN ELIZABETH II

693 Musketeer and Pikeman, The Royal Scots (1633)

694 Fusilier and Ensign, The Royal Welch Fusiliers (mid-18th-century)

695 Riflemen, 95th Rifles (The Royal Green Jackets) (1805)

696 Sergeant (khaki service) and Guardsman (full dress), The Irish Guards (1900)

697 Paratroopers, The Parachute Regiment (1983)

(Des E. Stemp)

1983 (6 July). British Army Uniforms. Multicoloured Phosphorised paper. Perf 14×15.

1218	693	16p. The Royal Scots...............	20	20
1219	694	20½p. The Royal Welch Fusiliers......	25	25
1220	695	26p. The Royal Green Jackets.........	35	35
		a. Imperf (pair)............	£3000	
1221	696	28p. The Irish Guards............	40	40
		a. Imperf (pair)............	£2800	
1222	697	31p. The Parachute Regiment.........	50	50
Set of 5...............			1·60	1·60
Set of 5 Gutter Pairs...............			3·25	
First Day Cover...............				1·75
Presentation Pack (PO Pack No. 145)............			1·75	
PHQ Cards (set of 5) (68)............			75	1·75

Nos. 1218/1222 were issued on the occasion of the 350th anniversary of the Royal Scots, the senior line regiment of the British Army.

Special First Day of Issue Postmarks
Philatelic Bureau, Edinburgh... 1·90
Aldershot... 1·90

698 20th-century Garden, Sissinghurst

699 19th-century Garden, Biddulph Grange

700 18th-century Garden, Blenheim

701 17th-century Garden, Pitmedden

(Des Liz Butler. Litho J.W.)

1983 (24 Aug). British Gardens. Multicoloured. Phosphorised paper. Perf 14.

1223	698	16p. Sissinghurst...............	20	20
1224	699	20½p. Biddulph Grange.........	25	25
1225	700	28p. Blenheim...............	35	35
1226	701	31p. Pitmedden...............	50	50
Set of 4...............			1·25	1·25
Set of 4 Gutter Pairs...............			2·50	
First Day Cover...............				1·40
Presentation Pack (PO Pack No. 146)............			1·40	
PHQ Cards (set of 4) (69)............			60	1·40

Nos. 1223/1226 were issued on the occasion of the death bicentenary of 'Capability' Brown (landscape gardener).

Special First Day of Issue Postmarks
Philatelic Bureau, Edinburgh... 1·40
Oxford... 1·50

702 Merry-go-round

703 Big Wheel, Helter-skelter and Performing Animals

704 Side Shows

705 Early Produce Fair

(Des A. Restall)

1983 (5 Oct). British Fairs. Multicoloured phosphorised paper. Perf 15×14.

1227	702	16p. Merry-go-round...............	20	20
1228	703	20½p. Big Wheel, Helter-skelter and Performing Animals.........	25	25
1229	704	28p. Side Shows...............	35	35
1230	705	31p. Early Produce Fair.........	50	50
Set of 4...............			1·25	1·25
Set of 4 Gutter Pairs...............			2·50	
First Day Cover...............				1·40
Presentation Pack (PO Pack No. 147)............			1·40	
PHQ Cards (set of 4) (70)............			60	1·40

Nos. 1227/1230 were issued to mark the 850th anniversary of St Bartholomew's Fair, Smithfield, London.

Special First Day of Issue Postmarks
Philatelic Bureau, Edinburgh... 1·40
Nottingham.. 1·40

706 Christmas Post (pillar box)

707 The Three Kings (chimney pots)

99

QUEEN ELIZABETH II/1983

708 World at Peace (Dove and Blackbird)
709 Light of Christmas (street lamp) 
710 Christmas Dove (hedge sculpture) 

(Des T. Meeuwissen)

1983 (16 Nov). Christmas. Multicoloured. One phosphor band (12½p.) or phosphorised paper (others). Perf 15×14.

1231	706	12½p. Christmas Post (pillar box)	20	20
		a. Imperf (horiz pair)	£1400	
1232	707	16p. The Three Kings (chimney pots)	20	20
		a. Imperf (pair)	£1300	
1233	708	20½p. World at Peace (Dove and Blackbird)	25	25
1234	709	28p. Light of Christmas (street lamp)	35	35
1235	710	31p. Christmas Dove (hedge sculpture)	50	50
Set of 5			1·50	1·50
Set of 5 Gutter Pairs			3·00	
First Day Cover				1·50
Presentation Pack (PO Pack No. 148)			1·50	
PHQ Cards (set of 5) (71)			75	1·50

Special First Day of Issue Postmarks
Philatelic Bureau, Edinburgh .... 1·50
Bethlehem, Llandeilo, Dyfed .... 1·50

Collectors Pack 1983
1983 (16 Nov). Comprises Nos. 1207/1235.
CP1235a Collectors Pack (PO Pack No. 149) ...... 13·50

711 Arms of the College of Arms
712 Arms of King Richard III (founder) 
713 Arms of the Earl Marshal of England 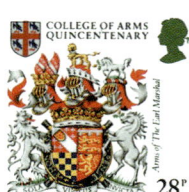
714 Arms of the City of London 

(Des J. Matthews)

1984 (17 Jan). 500th Anniversary of College of Arms. Multicoloured. Phosphorised paper. Perf 14½.

1236	711	16p. Arms of the College of Arms	25	25
1237	712	20½p. Arms of King Richard III (founder)	30	30
1238	713	28p. Arms of the Earl Marshal of England	40	40
1239	714	31p. Arms of the City of London	50	50
		a. Imperf (horiz pair)	£8000	
Set of 4			1·25	1·25
Set of 4 Gutter Pairs			2·50	
First Day Cover				1·50
Presentation Pack (PO Pack No. 150)			1·50	
PHQ Cards (set of 4) (72)			60	1·50

Special First Day of Issue Postmarks
Philatelic Bureau, Edinburgh .... 1·50
London EC .... 1·50

715 Highland Cow
716 Chillingham Wild Bull 
717 Hereford Bull 
718 Welsh Black Bull 
719 Irish Moiled Cow 

(Des B. Driscoll)

1984 (6 Mar). British Cattle. Multicoloured Phosphorised paper. Perf 15×14.

1240	715	16p. Highland Cow	25	25
		a. Imperf (vert pair)	£6750	
1241	716	20½p. Chillingham Wild Bull	30	30
1242	717	26p. Hereford Bull	35	35
1243	718	28p. Welsh Black Bull	40	40
1244	719	31p. Irish Moiled Cow	50	50
		a. Imperf (pair)	—	
Set of 5			1·60	1·60
Set of 5 Gutter Pairs			3·25	
First Day Cover				1·75
Presentation Pack (PO Pack No. 151)			1·75	
PHQ Cards (set of 5) (73)			75	1·75

Nos. 1240/1244 were issued on the occasion of the centenary of the Highland Cattle Society and the bicentenary of the Royal Highland and Agricultural Society of Scotland.

Special First Day of Issue Postmarks
Philatelic Bureau, Edinburgh .... 1·75
Oban, Argyll .... 1·90

720 Garden Festival Hall, Liverpool
721 Milburngate Centre, Durham 
722 Bush House, Bristol 
723 Commercial Street Development, Perth 

(Des R. Maddox and Trickett and Webb Ltd)

1984 (10 Apr). Urban Renewal. Multicoloured Phosphorised paper. Perf 15×14.

1245	720	16p. Garden Festival Hall, Liverpool	25	25
1246	721	20½p. Milburngate Centre, Durham	30	30
		a. Imperf (horiz pair)	£4250	
1247	722	28p. Bush House, Bristol	40	40

1984/QUEEN ELIZABETH II

1248	723	31p. Commercial Street Development, Perth		50	50
		a. Imperf (pair)		£3500	
Set of 4				1·25	1·25
Set of 4 Gutter Pairs				2·50	
First Day Cover					1·50
Presentation Pack (PO Pack No. 152)				1·50	
PHQ Cards (set of 4) (74)				60	1·50

Nos. 1245/1248 were issued on the occasion of 150th anniversaries of the Royal Institute of British Architects and the Chartered Institute of Building, and to commemorate the first International Gardens Festival, Liverpool.

Special First Day of Issue Postmarks
Philatelic Bureau, Edinburgh	1·50
Liverpool	1·50

724 CEPT 25th Anniversary Logo

725 Abduction of Europa

(Des J. Larrivière (T **724**), F. Wegner (T **725**))

1984 (15 May). 25th Anniversary of CEPT (Europa) (T **724**) and Second Elections to European Parliament (T **725**). Multicoloured Phosphorised paper. Perf 15×14.

1249	724	16p. CEPT 25th Anniversary Logo		30	30
		a. Horiz pair. Nos. 1249/1250		60	60
		ab. Imperf (horiz pair)		£3000	
1250	725	16p. Abduction of Europa		30	30
1251	724	20½p. CEPT 25th Anniversary Logo		35	35
		a. Horiz pair. Nos. 1251/1252		70	70
		ab. Imperf (horiz pair)		£3250	
1252	725	20½p. Abduction of Europa		35	35
Set of 4				1·25	1·25
Set of 2 Gutter Blocks of 4				2·50	
First Day Cover					1·40
Presentation Pack (PO Pack No. 153)				1·40	
PHQ Cards (set of 4) (75)				60	1·40

Nos. 1249/1250 and 1251/1252 were each printed together, *se-tenant*, in horizontal pairs throughout the sheets.

Special First Day of Issue Postmarks
Philatelic Bureau, Edinburgh	1·40
London SW	1·50

726 Lancaster House

(Des P. Hogarth)

1984 (5 June). London Economic Summit Conference. Multicoloured Phosphorised paper. Perf 14×15.

1253	726	31p. Lancaster House		50	50
Gutter Pair				1·00	
First Day Cover					60
PHQ Card (76)				20	60

Special First Day of Issue Postmarks
Philatelic Bureau, Edinburgh	60
London SW	60

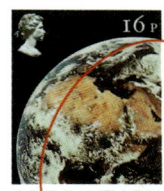

727 View of Earth from *Apollo 11*

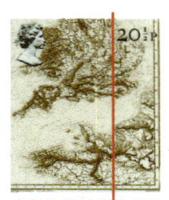

728 Navigational Chart of English Channel

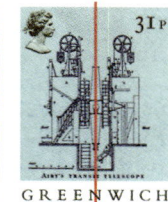

729 Greenwich Observatory

730 Sir George Airy's Transit Telescope

(Des H. Waller. Litho Questa)

1984 (26 June). Centenary of the Greenwich Meridian. Multicoloured Phosphorised paper. Perf 14×14½.

1254	727	16p. View of Earth from *Apollo 11*		25	25
		a. Black printing double		†	£975
1255	728	20½p. Navigational Chart of English Channel		30	30
1256	729	28p. Greenwich Observatory		40	40
1257	730	31p. Sir George Airy's Transit Telescope		50	50
Set of 4				1·25	1·25
Set of 4 Gutter Pairs				2·50	
First Day Cover					1·50
Presentation Pack (PO Pack No. 154)				1·50	
PHQ Cards (set of 4) (77)				60	1·50

On Nos. 1254/1257 the Meridian is represented by a scarlet line.

Special First Day of Issue Postmarks
Philatelic Bureau, Edinburgh	1·60
London SE10	1·75

731 Bath Mail Coach, 1784

732 Attack on Exeter Mail, 1816

733 Norwich Mail in Thunderstorm, 1827

734 Holyhead and Liverpool Mails leaving London, 1828

735 Edinburgh Mail Snowbound, 1831

QUEEN ELIZABETH II/1984

(Des K. Bassford and S. Paine. Eng C. Slania. Recess and photo)

1984 (31 July). Bicentenary of First Mail Coach Run, Bath and Bristol to London. Multicoloured Phosphorised paper. Perf 15×14.

1258	731	16p. Bath Mail Coach, 1784	25	25
		a. Horiz strip of 5. Nos. 1258/1262	1·25	1·25
		ab. Imperf (horiz pair. Nos. 1261/1262)	£3500	
1259	732	16p. Attack on Exeter Mail, 1816	25	25
1260	733	16p. Norwich Mail in Thunderstorm, 1827	25	25
1261	734	16p. Holyhead and Liverpool Mails leaving London, 1828	25	25
1262	735	16p. Edinburgh Mail Snowbound, 1831	25	25
Set of 5			1·25	1·25
Gutter Block of 10			2·50	
First Day Cover				1·40
Presentation Pack (PO Pack No. 155)			1·40	
Souvenir Book			3·25	
PHQ Cards (set of 5) (78)			75	1·40

Nos. 1258/1262 were printed together, *se-tenant*, in horizontal strips of five throughout the sheet.

No. 1258ab also includes No. 1260 perforated at left only.

The souvenir book is a 24 page illustrated booklet with a set of mint stamps in a sachet attached to the front cover.

Special First Day of Issue Postmarks

Philatelic Bureau, Edinburgh	1·40
Bristol	1·40

736 Nigerian Clinic

737 Violinist and Acropolis, Athens

738 Building Project, Sri Lanka

739 British Council Library, Middle East

(Des F. Newell and J. Sorrell)

1984 (25 Sept). 50th Anniversary of the British Council. Multicoloured Phosphorised paper. Perf 15×14.

1263	736	17p. Nigerian Clinic	25	25
1264	737	22p. Violinist and Acropolis, Athens	30	30
1265	738	31p. Building Project, Sri Lanka	40	40
1266	739	34p. British Council Library, Middle East	50	50
Set of 4			1·40	1·40
Set of 4 Gutter Pairs			2·75	
First Day Cover				1·50
Presentation Pack (PO Pack No. 156)			1·50	
PHQ Cards (set of 4) (79)			60	1·50

Special First Day of Issue Postmarks

Philatelic Bureau, Edinburgh	1·50
London SW	1·50

740 The Holy Family

741 Arrival in Bethlehem

742 Shepherd and Lamb

743 Virgin and Child

744 Offering of Frankincense

(Des Yvonne Gilbert)

1984 (20 Nov). Christmas. Multicoloured One phosphor band (13p.) or phosphorised paper (others). Perf 15×14.

1267	740	13p. The Holy Family	25	25
		u. Underprint Type **4**	60	
1268	741	17p. Arrival in Bethlehem	25	25
		a. Imperf (pair)	£3000	
1269	742	22p. Shepherd and Lamb	30	30
1270	743	31p. Virgin and Child	40	40
1271	744	34p. Offering of Frankincense	50	50
Set of 5			1·60	1·60
Set of 5 Gutter Pairs			3·25	
First Day Cover				1·75
Presentation Pack (PO Pack No. 157)			1·75	
PHQ Cards (set of 5) (80)			75	1·75

Examples of No. 1267u from the 1984 Christmas booklet (No. FX7) show a random pattern of blue double-lined stars printed on the reverse over the gum.

Special First Day of Issue Postmarks

Philatelic Bureau, Edinburgh	1·90
Bethlehem, Llandeilo, Dyfed	1·90

Collectors Pack 1984

1984 (20 Nov). Comprises Nos. 1236/1271.

CP1271a	Collectors Pack (PO Pack No. 158)	16·00

Post Office Yearbook

1984 Comprises Nos. 1236/1271 in 24 page hardbound book with slip case, illustrated in colour

YB1271a	Yearbook	42·00

745 'Flying Scotsman'

746 'Golden Arrow'

747 'Cheltenham Flyer'

748 'Royal Scot'

749 'Cornish Riviera'

1985/QUEEN ELIZABETH II

(Des Terrance Cuneo)

1985 (22 Jan). Famous Trains. Multicoloured Phosphorised paper. Perf 15×14.

1272	745	17p. 'Flying Scotsman'............................	25	25
		a. Imperf (pair).................................	£2000	
1273	746	22p. 'Golden Arrow'..............................	30	30
1274	747	29p. 'Cheltenham Flyer'........................	40	40
1275	748	31p. 'Royal Scot'...................................	40	40
1276	749	34p. 'Cornish Riviera'...........................	50	50
Set of 5			1·75	1·75
Set of 5 Gutter Pairs			3·50	
First Day Cover				1·90
Presentation Pack (PO Pack No. 159).................			1·90	
PHQ Cards (set of 5) (81).....................................			75	1·90

Nos. 1272/1276 were issued on the occasion of the 150th anniversary of the Great Western Railway Company.

Special First Day of Issue Postmarks
Philatelic Bureau, Edinburgh..	2·00
Bristol..	2·25

750 Buff tailed bumblebee

751 Seven spotted Ladybird

752 Wart-biter bush-cricket

753 Stag Beetle

754 Emperor dragonfly

(Des G. Beningfield)

1985 (12 Mar). Insects. Multicoloured Phosphorised paper. Perf 14×15.

1277	750	17p. Buff tailed bumblebee..................	25	25
1278	751	22p. Seven spotted Ladybird................	30	30
1279	752	29p. Wart-biter bush-cricket................	40	40
1280	753	31p. Stag beetle.....................................	40	40
1281	754	34p. Emperor dragonfly.......................	50	50
		a. Imperf (vert pair)...........................	—	
Set of 5			1·75	1·75
Set of 5 Gutter Pairs			3·50	
First Day Cover				1·90
Presentation Pack (PO Pack No. 160).................			1·90	
PHQ Cards (set of 5) (82).....................................			75	1·90

Nos. 1277/1281 were issued on the occasion of the centenaries of the Royal Entomological Society of London's Royal Charter, and of the Selborne Society.

Special First Day of Issue Postmarks
Philatelic Bureau, Edinburgh..	1·90
London SW...	2·00

755 Water Music (George Frederick Handel)

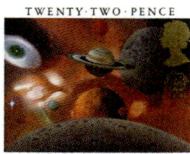

756 The Planets Suite (Gustav Holst)

757 The First Cuckoo (Frederick Delius)

758 Sea Pictures (Edward Elgar)

(Des W. McLean)

1985 (14 May). Europa. European Music Year. British Composers. Multicoloured Phosphorised paper. Perf 14×14½.

1282	755	17p. Water Music (George Frederick Handel)...................................	25	25
		a. Imperf (vert pair)...........................	£3250	
1283	756	22p. The Planets Suite (Gustav Holst)......	30	30
		a. Imperf (pair)..................................	£3000	
1284	757	31p. The First Cuckoo (Frederick Delius)	45	45
1285	758	34p. Sea Pictures (Edward Elgar).........	55	55
Set of 4			1·40	1·40
Set of 4 Gutter Pairs			2·75	
First Day Cover				1·50
Presentation Pack (PO Pack No. 161).................			1·50	
PHQ Cards (set of 4) (83).....................................			60	1·50

Nos. 1282/1285 were issued on the occasion of the 300th birth anniversary of Handel.

Special First Day of Issue Postmarks
Philatelic Bureau, Edinburgh..	1·50
Worcester...	1·75

759 RNLI Lifeboat and Signal Flags

760 Beachy Head Lighthouse and Chart

761 Marecs A Communications Satellite and Dish Aerials

762 Buoys

(Des F. Newell and J. Sorrell. Litho J.W.)

1985 (18 June). Safety at Sea. Multicoloured Phosphorised paper. Perf 14.

1286	759	17p. RNLI Lifeboat and Signal Flags........	25	25
1287	760	22p. Beachy Head Lighthouse and Chart..	30	30
1288	761	31p. Marecs A Communications Satellite and Dish Aerials...............	45	45
1289	762	34p. Buoys...	55	55
Set of 4			1·40	1·40
Set of 4 Gutter Pairs			2·75	
First Day Cover				1·50
Presentation Pack (PO Pack No. 162).................			1·50	
PHQ Cards (set of 4) (84).....................................			60	1·50

Nos. 1286/1289 were issued on the occasion of the bicentenary of the unimmersible lifeboat and the 50th anniversary of Radar.

Special First Day of Issue Postmarks
Philatelic Bureau, Edinburgh..	1·50
Eastbourne..	1·50

QUEEN ELIZABETH II/1985

763 Datapost Motorcyclist, City of London
764 Rural Postbus 
765 Parcel Delivery in Winter 
766 Town Letter Delivery 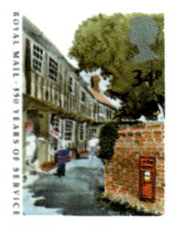

(Des P. Hogarth)

1985 (30 July). 350 Years of Royal Mail Public Postal Service. Multicoloured Phosphorised paper. Perf 14×15.

1290	**763**	17p. Datapost Motorcyclist	25	25
		a. Imperf on 3 sides (vert pair)	£1250	
		u. Underprint Type **5**	50	
1291	**764**	22p. Rural Postbus	30	30
		a. Imperf (vert pair)	—	
1292	**765**	31p. Parcel Delivery in Winter	45	45
		a. Imperf	£1800	
1293	**766**	34p. Town Letter Delivery	55	55
		a. Imperf between (vert pair)	£875	
		b. Imperf (vert pair)	—	
Set of 4			1·40	1·40
Set of 4 Gutter Pairs			2·75	
First Day Cover				1·50
Presentation Pack (PO Pack No. 163)			1·50	
PHQ Cards (set of 4) (85)			60	1·50

No. 1290a shows perforation indentations at right, but is imperforate at top, bottom and on the left-hand side.
Examples of No. 1290u from the 1985 £1·70 booklet (sold at £1·53) (No. FT4) show a blue double-lined D in a random pattern, on the reverse over the gum.

Special First Day of Issue Postmarks
Philatelic Bureau, Edinburgh .... 1·50
Bagshot, Surrey .... 1·50

767 King Arthur and Merlin
768 Lady of the Lake 
769 Queen Guinevere and Sir Lancelot 
770 Sir Galahad 

(Des Yvonne Gilbert)

1985 (3 Sept). Arthurian Legends. Multicoloured Phosphorised paper. Perf 15×14.

1294	**767**	17p. King Arthur and Merlin	25	25
		a. Imperf (pair)	£3500	
1295	**768**	22p. Lady of the Lake	30	30
1296	**769**	31p. Queen Guinevere and Sir Lancelot	45	45
1297	**770**	34p. Sir Galahad	55	55
Set of 4			1·40	1·40
Set of 4 Gutter Pairs			2·75	

First Day Cover .... 1·50
Presentation Pack (PO Pack No. 164) .... 1·50
PHQ Cards (set of 4) (86) .... 60 1·50

Nos. 1294/1297 were issued on the occasion of the 500th anniversary of the printing of Sir Thomas Malory's *Morte d'Arthur*.
Trials are known with face value and inscription in a different typeface.

Special First Day of Issue Postmarks
Philatelic Bureau, Edinburgh .... 1·50
Tintagel, Cornwall .... 1·50

771 Peter Sellers (from photo by Bill Brandt)
772 David Niven (from photo by Cornell Lucas) 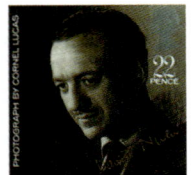
773 Charlie Chaplin (from photo by Lord Snowdon) 
774 Vivien Leigh (from photo by Angus McBean) 
775 Alfred Hitchcock (from photo by Howard Coster) 

(Des K. Bassford)

1985 (8 Oct). British Film Year. Multicoloured Phosphorised paper. Perf 14½.

1298	**771**	17p. Peter Sellers	25	25
1299	**772**	22p. David Niven	30	30
1300	**773**	29p. Charlie Chaplin	45	45
1301	**774**	31p. Vivien Leigh	50	50
1302	**775**	34p. Alfred Hitchcock	55	55
Set of 5			1·90	1·90
Set of 5 Gutter Pairs			3·75	

First Day Cover .... 2·10
Presentation Pack (PO Pack No. 165) .... 2·10
Souvenir Book .... 4·75
PHQ Cards (set of 5) (87) .... 75 2·10

The souvenir book is a 24 page illustrated booklet with a set of mint stamps in a sachet attached to the front cover.

Special First Day of Issue Postmarks
Philatelic Bureau, Edinburgh .... 2·10
London WC .... 2·10

776 Principal Boy
777 Genie

1985/QUEEN ELIZABETH II

778 Dame
779 Good Fairy 
780 Pantomime Cat 

(Des A. George)

1985 (19 Nov). Christmas. Pantomime Characters. Multicoloured One phosphor band (12p.) or phosphorised paper (others). Perf 15×14.

1303	776	12p. Principal Boy	20	20
		a. Imperf (pair)	£1400	
		u. Underprint Type **4**	50	
1304	777	17p. Genie	25	25
		a. Imperf (pair)	£3250	
1305	778	22p. Dame	30	30
1306	779	31p. Good Fairy	40	40
1307	780	34p. Pantomime Cat	50	50
Set of 5			1·40	1·40
Set of 5 Gutter Pairs			2·75	
First Day Cover				1·60
Presentation Pack (PO Pack No. 166)			1·60	
PHQ Cards (set of 5) (88)			75	1·60
Christmas Folder (contains No. 1303×50)			25·00	

Examples of No. 1303u from the 1985 Christmas booklet (No. FX8) show a random pattern of blue double-lined stars printed on the reverse over the gum.

Special First Day of Issue Postmarks
Philatelic Bureau, Edinburgh .... 1·60
Bethlehem, Llandeilo, Dyfed .... 1·75

Collectors Pack 1985

1985 (19 Nov). Comprises Nos. 1272/1307.
CP1307a   Collectors Pack (PO Pack No. 167) ...... 16·00

Post Office Yearbook

1985. Comprises Nos. 1272/1307 in 32 page hardbound book with slip case, illustrated in colour
YB1307a   Yearbook .... 30·00

781 Light Bulb and North Sea Oil Drilling Rig (Energy)
782 Thermometer and Pharmaceutical Laboratory (Health) 
783 Garden Hoe Steelworks (Steel) 
784 Loaf of Bread and Cornfield (Agriculture) 

(Des K. Bassford. Litho Questa)

1986 (14 Jan). Industry Year. Multicoloured Phosphorised paper. Perf 14½×14.

1308	781	17p. Light Bulb and North Sea Oil Drilling Rig (Energy)	25	25
1309	782	22p. Thermometer and Pharmaceutical Laboratory (Health)	30	30
1310	783	31p. Garden Hoe Steelworks (Steel)	45	45
1311	784	34p. Loaf of Bread and Cornfield (Agriculture)	55	55
Set of 4			1·40	1·40
Set of 4 Gutter Pairs			2·75	
First Day Cover				1·60
Presentation Pack (PO Pack No. 168)			1·60	
PHQ Cards (set of 4) (89)			60	1·60

Special First Day of Issue Postmarks
Philatelic Bureau, Edinburgh .... 1·60
Birmingham .... 1·60

785 Dr Edmond Halley as Comet
786 *Giotto* Spacecraft approaching Comet 
787 'Maybe Twice in a Lifetime' 
788 Comet orbiting Sun and Planets 

(Des R. Steadman)

1986 (18 Feb). Appearance of Halley's Comet. Multicoloured Phosphorised paper. Perf 15×14.

1312	785	17p. Dr Edmond Halley as Comet	25	25
		Imperf (pair)		
1313	786	22p. *Giotto* Spacecraft approaching Comet	30	30
1314	787	31p. 'Maybe Twice in a Lifetime'	45	45
		Imperf (pair)		
1315	788	34p. Comet orbiting Sun and Planets	55	55
Set of 4			1·40	1·40
Set of 4 Gutter Pairs			2·75	
First Day Cover				1·60
Presentation Pack (PO Pack No. 168*)			1·60	
PHQ Cards (set of 4) (90)			60	1·60

* The presentation pack was incorrectly numbered 168.

Special First Day of Issue Postmarks
Philaelic Bureau, Edinburgh .... 1·60
London SE10 .... 1·75

789 Queen Elizabeth in 1928, 1942 and 1952
790 Queen Elizabeth in 1958, 1973 and 1982 

(Des J. Matthews)

1986 (21 Apr). 60th Birthday of Queen Elizabeth II. Phosphorised paper. Perf 15×14.

1316	789	17p. Queen Elizabeth in 1928, 1942 and 1952. Grey-black, turquoise-green, bright green, green and dull blue	30	40
		a. Pair. Nos. 1316/1317	80	1·00
1317	790	17p. Queen Elizabeth in 1958, 1973 and 1982. Grey-black, dull blue, greenish blue and indigo	30	40
1318	789	34p. Queen Elizabeth in 1928, 1942 and 1952. Grey-black, deep dull purple, yellow-orange and red	60	75
		a. Pair. Nos. 1318/1319	1·40	1·75
1319	790	34p. Queen Elizabeth in 1958, 1973 and 1982. Grey-black, olive-brown, yellow-brown, olive-grey and red	60	75
Set of 4			2·00	2·50
Set of 2 Gutter Blocks of 4			4·00	
First Day Cover				2·60
Presentation Pack (PO Pack No. 170)			2·10	
Souvenir Book			3·75	
PHQ Cards (set of 4) (91)			60	2·60

Nos. 1316/1317 and 1318/1319 were each printed together, *se-tenant*, in horizontal pairs throughout the sheet.

QUEEN ELIZABETH II/1986

The souvenir book is a special booklet, fully illustrated and containing a mint set of stamps.

Special First Day of Issue Postmarks
Philatelic Bureau, Edinburgh .... 2·75
Windsor .... 2·75

791 Barn Owl
792 Pine Marten 
793 Wild Cat 
794 Natterjack Toad 

(Des K. Lilly)

1986 (20 May). Europa. Nature Conservation. Endangered Species. Multicoloured Phosphorised paper. Perf 14½×14.

1320	791	17p. Barn Owl	25	25
1321	792	22p. Pine Marten	30	30
1322	793	31p. Wild Cat	45	45
1323	794	34p. Natterjack Toad	55	55
Set of 4			1·50	1·50
Set of 4 Gutter Pairs			3·00	
First Day Cover				1·60
Presentation Pack (PO Pack No. 171)			1·60	
PHQ Cards (set of 4) (92)			60	1·60

Special First Day of Issue Postmarks
Philatelic Bureau, Edinburgh .... 1·60
Lincoln .... 1·75

795 Peasants working in Fields
796 Freemen working at Town Trades 
797 Knight and Retainers 
798 Lord at Banquet 

(Des Tayburn Design Consultancy)

1986 (17 June). 900th Anniversary of *Domesday Book*. Multicoloured Phosphorised paper. Perf 15×14.

1324	795	17p. Peasants working in Fields	25	25
1325	796	22p. Freemen working at Town Trades...	30	30
1326	797	31p. Knight and Retainers	45	45
1327	798	34p. Lord at Banquet	55	55
Set of 4			1·50	1·50
Set of 4 Gutter Pairs			3·00	
First Day Cover				1·60
Presentation Pack (PO Pack No. 172)			1·60	
PHQ Cards (set of 4) (93)			60	1·60

Special First Day of Issue Postmarks
Philatelic Bureau, Edinburgh .... 1·60
Gloucester .... 1·60

799 Athletics
800 Rowing 
801 Weightlifting 
802 Rifle Shooting 
803 Hockey 

(Des N. Cudworth)

1986 (15 July). 13th Commonwealth Games, Edinburgh and World Hockey Cup for Men, London (34p.). Multicoloured Phosphorised paper. Perf 15×14.

1328	799	17p. Athletics	25	25
1329	800	22p. Rowing	30	30
		a. imperf (pair)		—
1330	801	29p. Weightlifting	45	45
1331	802	31p. Rifle Shooting	45	45
1332	803	34p. Hockey	55	55
		a. Imperf (pair)	£2750	
Set of 5			1·75	1·75
Set of 5 Gutter Pairs			3·50	
First Day Cover				1·90
Presentation Pack (PO Pack No. 173)			1·90	
PHQ Cards (set of 5) (94)			75	1·90

No. 1332 also marked the centenary of the Hockey Association.

Special First Day of Issue Postmarks
Philatelic Bureau, Edinburgh .... 1·90
Head Post Office, Edinburgh .... 1·90

804 Prince Andrew and Miss Sarah Ferguson (from photo by Gene Nocon)
805 Prince Andrew and Miss Sarah Ferguson (from photo by Gene Nocon) 

(Des J. Matthews)

1986 (22 July). Royal Wedding. Multicoloured. One phosphor band (12p.) or phosphorised paper (17p.). Perf 14×15.

1333	804	12p. Prince Andrew and Miss Sarah Ferguson	25	25
1334	805	17p. Prince Andrew and Miss Sarah Ferguson	40	40
		a. Imperf (pair)	£700	
Set of 2			60	60
Set of 2 Gutter Pairs			1·25	
First Day Cover				70
Presentation Pack (PO Pack No. 174)			75	
PHQ Cards (set of 2) (95)			30	75

Special First Day of Issue Postmarks
Philatelic Bureau, Edinburgh 70
London, SW1 75

1986/QUEEN ELIZABETH II

806 Stylised Cross on Ballot Paper

(Des J. Gibbs. Litho Questa)

1986 (19 Aug). 32nd Commonwealth Parliamentary Association Conference. Multicoloured. Phosphorised paper. Perf 14×14½.

1335	806	34p. Stylised Cross on Ballot Paper	50	50
		a. Imperf between (vert pair)	—	
Gutter Pair			1·00	
First Day Cover				55
PHQ Card (96)			15	55

Special First Day of Issue Postmarks
Philatelic Bureau, Edinburgh	55
London, SW1	55

807 Lord Dowding and Hawker Hurricane Mk I
808 Lord Tedder and Hawker Typhoon IB 
809 Lord Trenchard and de Havilland DH.9A 
810 Sir Arthur Harris and Avro Type 683 Lancaster 
811 Lord Portal and de Havilland DH.98 Mosquito 

(Des B. Sanders)

1986 (16 Sept). History of the Royal Air Force. Multicoloured Phosphorised paper. Perf 14½.

1336	807	17p. Lord Dowding and Hawker Hurricane Mk I	25	25
		a. Imperf (pair)	£2200	
1337	808	22p. Lord Tedder and Hawker Typhoon IB	35	35
		a. Face value omitted*	£650	
		b. Queen's head omitted*	£650	
1338	809	29p. Lord Trenchard and de Havilland DH.9A	45	45
1339	810	31p. Sir Arthur Harris and Avro Type 683 Lancaster	50	50
1340	811	34p. Lord Portal and de Havilland DH.98 Mosquito	55	55
Set of 5			2·00	2·00
Set of 5 Gutter Pairs			4·00	
First Day Cover				2·10
Presentation Pack (PO Pack No. 175)			2·10	
PHQ Cards (set of 5) (97)			75	2·10

Nos. 1336/1340 were issued to celebrate the 50th anniversary of the first RAF Commands.

* Nos. 1337a/1337b come from three consecutive sheets on which the stamps in the first vertical row are without the face value and those in the second vertical row the Queen's head.

Special First Day of Issue Postmarks
Philatelic Bureau, Edinburgh	2·10
Farnborough	2·10

812 The Glastonbury Thorn
813 The Tanad Valley Plygain 
814 The Hebrides Tribute 
815 The Dewsbury Church Knell 
816 The Hereford Boy Bishop 

(Des Lynda Gray)

1986 (18 Nov–2 Dec). Christmas. Folk Customs. Multicoloured One phosphor band (12p., 13p.) or phosphorised paper (others). Perf 15×14.

1341	812	12p. The Glastonbury Thorn	25	25
		a. Imperf (pair)	£1800	
1342		13p. The Glastonbury Thorn	25	25
		u. Underprint Type 4 (2.12)	50	
1343	813	18p. The Tanad Valley Plygain	30	30
1344	814	22p. The Hebrides Tribute	40	40
1345	815	31p. The Dewsbury Church Knell	45	45
1346	816	34p. The Hereford Boy Bishop	50	50
Set of 6			1·90	1·90
Set of 6 Gutter Pairs			3·75	
First Day Covers (2)				2·40
Presentation Pack (PO Pack No. 176) (Nos. 1342/1346)			2·00	
PHQ Cards (set of 5) (98) (Nos. 1342/1346)			75	1·75
Christmas Folder (contains No. 1342u×36)			18·00	

No. 1341 represented a discount of 1p., available between 2 and 14 December 1986, on the current second class postage rate.

Special First Day of Issue Postmarks
Philatelic Bureau, Edinburgh (Nos. 1342/1346) (18.11.86)	1·90
Bethlehem, Llandeilo, Dyfed (Nos. 1342/1346) (18.11.86)	2·00
Philatelic Bureau, Edinburgh (No. 1341) (2.12.86)	50

Collectors Pack 1986

1986 (18 Nov). Comprises Nos. 1308/1340 and 1342/1346.
CP1346a	Collectors Pack (PO Pack No. 177)	16·00

Post Office Yearbook

1986 (18 Nov). Comprises Nos. 1308/1346 in 32 page hardbound book with slip case, illustrated in colour
YB1346a	Yearbook	23·00

817 North American Blanket Flower
818 Globe Thistle

QUEEN ELIZABETH II/1987

819 Echeveria
820 Autumn Crocus 

1987 (20 Jan). Flower Photographs by Alfred Lammer. Multicoloured Phosphorised paper. Perf 14½×14.

1347	817	18p. North American Blanket Flower	25	25
1348	818	22p. Globe Thistle	30	30
1349	819	31p. Echeveria	45	45
		a. Imperf (pair)	£4000	
1350	820	34p. Autumn Crocus	55	55
Set of 4			1·50	1·50
Set of 4 Gutter Pairs			3·00	
First Day Cover				1·60
Presentation Pack (PO Pack No. 178)			1·60	
PHQ Cards (set of 4) (99)			60	1·60

Special First Day of Issue Postmarks
Philatelic Bureau, Edinburgh ... 1·60
Richmond, Surrey ... 1·75

821 The Principia Mathematica
822 Motion of Bodies in Ellipses 
823 Optick Treatise 
824 The System of the World 

(Des Sarah Godwin)

1987 (24 Mar). 300th Anniversary of *The Principia Mathematica* by Sir Isaac Newton. Multicoloured Phosphorised paper. Perf 14×15.

1351	821	18p. The Principia Mathematica	25	25
		a. Imperf (pair)	£4000	
1352	822	22p. Motion of Bodies in Ellipses	30	30
1353	823	31p. Optick Treatise	45	45
1354	824	34p. The System of the World	55	55
Set of 4			1·50	1·50
Set of 4 Gutter Pairs			3·00	
First Day Cover				1·60
Presentation Pack (PO Pack No. 179)			1·60	
PHQ Cards (set of 4) (100)			60	1·60

Special First Day of Issue Postmarks
Philatelic Bureau, Edinburgh ... 1·60
Woolsthorpe, Lincs ... 1·75

825 Willis Faber and Dumas Building, Ipswich
826 Pompidou Centre, Paris 
827 Staatsgalerie, Stuttgart 
828 European Investment Bank, Luxembourg 

(Des B. Tattersfield)

1987 (12 May). Europa. British Architects in Europe. Multicoloured Phosphorised paper. Perf 15×14.

1355	825	18p. Willis Faber and Dumas Building, Ipswich	25	25
1356	826	22p. Pompidou Centre, Paris	30	30
1357	827	31p. Staatsgalerie, Stuttgart	45	45
		a. Imperf (horiz pair)	£4000	
1358	828	34p. European Investment Bank, Luxembourg	55	55
Set of 4			1·50	1·50
Set of 4 Gutter Pairs			3·00	
First Day Cover				1·60
Presentation Pack (PO Pack No. 180)			1·60	
PHQ Cards (set of 4) (101)			50	1·60

Special First Day of Issue Postmarks
Philatelic Bureau, Edinburgh ... 1·60
Ipswich ... 1·60

829 Brigade Members with Ashford Litter, 1887
830 Bandaging Blitz Victim, 1940 
831 Volunteer with fainting Girl, 1965 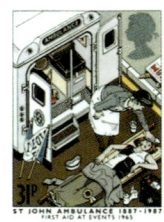
832 Transport of Transplant Organ by Air Wing, 1987 

(Des Debbie Cook. Litho Questa)

1987 (16 June). Centenary of St John Ambulance Brigade. Multicoloured Phosphorised paper. Perf 14×14½.

1359	829	18p. Brigade Members with Ashford Litter, 1887	25	25
		a. Black printing double	†	£650
		b. Black printing triple	†	£950
1360	830	22p. Bandaging Blitz Victim, 1940	30	30
1361	831	31p. Volunteer with fainting Girl, 1965	45	45
1362	832	34p. Transport of Transplant Organ by Air Wing, 1987	55	55
Set of 4			1·50	1·50
Set of 4 Gutter Pairs			3·00	
First Day Cover				1·60
Presentation Pack (PO Pack No. 181)			1·60	
PHQ Cards (set of 4) (102)			60	1·60

Special First Day of Issue Postmarks
Philatelic Bureau, Edinburgh ... 1·60
London, EC1 ... 1·60

1987/QUEEN ELIZABETH II

833 Arms of the Lord Lyon King of Arms
834 Scottish Heraldic Banner of Prince Charles
835 Arms of Royal Scottish Academy of Painting, Sculpture and Architecture 
836 Arms of Royal Society of Edinburgh 

(Des J. Matthews)

1987 (21 July). 300th Anniversary of Revival of Order of the Thistle. Multicoloured Phosphorised paper. Perf 14½.

1363	833	18p. Arms of the Lord Lyon King of Arms........	25	25
1364	834	22p. Scottish Heraldic Banner of Prince Charles............	30	30
1365	835	31p. Arms of Royal Scottish Academy of Painting, Sculpture and Architecture............	45	45
1366	836	34p. Arms of Royal Society of Edinburgh............	55	55
Set of 4............			1·50	1·50
Set of 4 Gutter Pairs............			3·00	
First Day Cover............				1·60
Presentation Pack (PO Pack No. 182)............			1·60	
PHQ Cards (set of 4) (103)............			60	1·60

Special First Day of Issue Postmarks
Philatelic Bureau, Edinburgh............ 1·60
Rothesay, Isle of Bute............ 1·75

837 Crystal Palace, *Monarch of the Glen* (Landseer) and Grace Darling
838 Great Eastern, *Beeton's Book of Household Management* and Prince Albert 
839 Albert Memorial, Ballot Box and Disraeli 
840 Diamond Jubilee Emblem, Newspaper Placard for Relief of Mafeking and Morse Key 

(Des M. Dempsey. Eng C. Slania. Recess and photo)

1987 (8 Sept). 150th Anniversary of Queen Victoria's Accession. Multicoloured Phosphorised paper. Perf 15×14.

1367	837	18p. Crystal Palace, *Monarch of the Glen* (Landseer) and Grace Darling........	25	25
1368	838	22p. *Great Eastern, Beeton's Book of Household Management* and Prince Albert............	30	30
1369	839	31p. Albert Memorial, Ballot Box and Disraeli............	45	45
1370	840	34p. Diamond Jubilee Emblem, Newspaper Placard for Relief of Mafeking and Morse Key............	55	55
Set of 4............			1·50	1·50
Set of 4 Gutter Pairs............			3·00	
First Day Cover............				1·60
Presentation Pack (PO Pack No. 183)............			1·60	
PHQ Cards (set of 4) (104)............			60	1·60

Special First Day of Issue Postmarks
Philatelic Bureau, Edinburgh............ 1·60
Newport, Isle of Wight............ 1·60

841 Pot by Bernard Leach
842 Pot by Elizabeth Fritsch 
843 Pot by Lucie Rie 
844 Pot by Hans Coper 

(Des T. Evans)

1987 (13 Oct). Studio Pottery. Multicoloured Phosphorised paper. Perf 14½×14.

1371	841	18p. Pot by Bernard Leach............	25	25
1372	842	26p. Pot by Elizabeth Fritsch............	35	35
1373	843	31p. Pot by Lucie Rie............	45	45
1374	844	34p. Pot by Hans Coper............	55	55
		a. Imperf (vert pair)............	£3000	
Set of 4............			1·50	1·50
Set of 4 Gutter Pairs............			3·00	
First Day Cover............				1·60
Presentation Pack (PO Pack No. 184)............			1·60	
PHQ Cards (set of 4) (105)............			60	1·60

Special First Day of Issue Postmarks
Philatelic Bureau, Edinburgh............ 1·60
St Ives, Cornwall............ 1·60

845 Decorating the Christmas Tree
846 Waiting for Father Christmas 
847 Sleeping Child and Father Christmas in Sleigh 
848 Child reading 
849 Child playing Recorder and Snowman 

109

QUEEN ELIZABETH II/1987

(Des M. Foreman)

1987 (17 Nov). Christmas. Multicoloured One phosphor band (13p.) or phosphorised paper (others). Perf 15×14.

1375	845	13p. Decorating the Christmas Tree	20	20
		u. Underprint Type 4	50	
1376	846	18p. Waiting for Father Christmas	25	25
1377	847	26p. Sleeping Child and Father Christmas in Sleigh	30	30
1378	848	31p. Child reading	40	40
1379	849	34p. Child playing Recorder and Snowman	50	50
Set of 5			1·50	1·50
Set of 5 Gutter Pairs			3·00	
First Day Cover				1·60
Presentation Pack (PO Pack No. 185)			1·60	
PHQ Cards (set of 5) (106)			75	1·60
Christmas Folder (contains No. 1375u×36)			18·00	

Examples of the 13p. value from special folders, containing 36 stamps and sold for £4·60, show a blue underprint of double-lined stars printed on the reverse over the gum.

Special First Day of Issue Postmarks
Philatelic Bureau, Edinburgh	1·60
Bethlehem, Llandeilo, Dyfed	1·75

Collectors Pack 1987

1987 (17 Nov). Comprises Nos. 1347/1379.
CP1379a Collectors Pack (PO Pack No. 186) ...... 16·00

Post Office Yearbook

1987 (17 Nov). Comprises Nos. 1347/1379 in 32 page hardbound book with slip case, illustrated in colour
YB1379a Yearbook .... 13·00

850 Short-spined Sea scorpion ('Bull-rout') (Jonathan Couch)

851 Yellow Water Lily (Major Joshua Swatkin)

852 Whistling ('Bewick's') Swan (Edward Lear)

853 *Morchella esculenta* (James Sowerby)

(Des. E. Hughes)

1988 (19 Jan). Bicentenary of Linnean Society. Archive Illustrations. Multicoloured Phosphorised paper. Perf 15×14.

1380	850	18p. Short-spined Sea scorpion ('Bull-rout')	25	25
1381	851	26p. Yellow Water Lily	35	35
1382	852	31p. Whistling ('Bewick's') Swan	45	45
		a. Imperf (horiz pair)	£3500	
1383	853	34p. *Morchella esculenta*	60	60
Set of 4			1·50	1·50
Set of 4 Gutter Pairs			3·00	
First Day Cover				1·60
Presentation Pack (PO Pack No. 187)			1·60	
PHQ Cards (set of 4) (107)			60	1·60

Special First Day of Issue Postmarks
Philatelic Bureau, Edinburgh	1·75
London, W1	1·75

854 Revd William Morgan (Bible translator, 1588)

855 William Salesbury (New Testament translator, 1567)

856 Bishop Richard Davies (New Testament translator, 1567)

857 Bishop Richard Parry (editor of Revised Welsh Bible, 1620)

(Des K. Bowen)

1988 (1 Mar). 400th Anniversary of Welsh Bible. Multicoloured Phosphorised paper. Perf 14½×14.

1384	854	18p. Revd William Morgan	25	25
		a. Imperf (vert pair)	£3000	
1385	855	26p. William Salesbury	35	35
1386	856	31p. Bishop Richard Davies	45	45
1387	857	34p. Bishop Richard Parry	60	60
Set of 4			1·50	1·50
Set of 4 Gutter Pairs			3·00	
First Day Cover				1·60
Presentation Pack (PO Pack No. 188)			1·60	
PHQ Cards (set of 4) (108)			60	1·60

Special First Day of Issue Postmarks
Philatelic Bureau, Edinburgh	1·75
Ty Mawr, Wybrnant, Gwynedd	1·75

858 Gymnastics (Centenary of British Amateur Gymnastics Association)

859 Downhill Skiing (Ski Club of Great Britain)

860 Tennis (Centenary of Lawn Tennis Association)

861 Football (Centenary of Football League)

(Des J. Sutton)

1988 (22 Mar). Sports Organisations. Multicoloured Phosphorised paper. Perf 14½.

1388	858	18p. Gymnastics	25	25
		a. Imperf (pair)		
1389	859	26p. Downhill Skiing	35	35
1390	860	31p. Tennis	45	45
1391	861	34p. Football	60	60
Set of 4			1·50	1·50
Set of 4 Gutter Pairs			3·00	
First Day Cover				1·60
Presentation Pack (PO Pack No. 189)			1·60	
PHQ Cards (set of 4) (109)			50	1·60

Special First Day of Issue Postmarks
Philatelic Bureau, Edinburgh	1·75
Wembley	1·75

862 *Mallard* and Mailbags on Pick-up Arms

863 Loading Transatlantic Mail on Liner *Queen Elizabeth*

1988/QUEEN ELIZABETH II

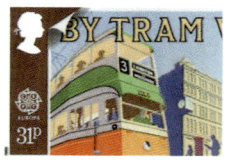

864 Glasgow Tram No. 1173 and Pillar Box

865 Imperial Airways Handley Page HP.45 *Horatius* and Airmail Van

(Des M. Dempsey)

1988 (10 May). Europa. Transport and Mail Services in 1930s.' Multicoloured Phosphorised paper. Perf 15×14.

1392	862	18p. *Mallard* and Mailbags on Pick-up Arms	25	25
1393	863	26p. Loading Transatlantic Mail on Liner *Queen Elizabeth*	35	35
1394	864	31p. Glasgow Tram No. 1173 and Pillar Box	45	45
1395	865	34p. Imperial Airways Handley Page HP.45 *Horatius* and Airmail Van	60	60
Set of 4			1·50	1·50
Set of 4 Gutter Pairs			3·00	
First Day Cover				1·60
Presentation Pack (PO Pack No. 190)			1·60	
PHQ Cards (set of 4) (110)			60	1·60

Trials exist with alternative face values; 19p, 27p, 32p and 35p.

Special First Day of Issue Postmarks
Philatelic Bureau, Edinburgh .... 1·75
Glasgow .... 1·75

866 Early Settler and Sailing Clipper

867 Queen Elizabeth II with British and Australian Parliament Buildings

868 W. G. Grace (cricketer) and Tennis Racquet

869 Shakespeare, John Lennon (entertainer) and Sydney Opera House

(Des G. Emery. Litho Questa)

1988 (21 June). Bicentenary of Australian Settlement. Multicoloured Phosphorised paper. Perf 14½.

1396	866	18p. Early Settler and Sailing Clipper	25	25
		a. Horiz pair. Nos. 1396/1397	55	55
1397	867	18p. Queen Elizabeth II with British and Australian Parliament Buildings	25	25
1398	868	34p. W. G. Grace and Tennis Racquet	50	50
		a. Horiz pair. Nos. 1398/1399	1·10	1·10
1399	869	34p. Shakespeare, John Lennon and Sydney Opera House	50	50
Set of 4			1·50	1·50
Set of 2 Gutter Blocks of 4			3·00	
First Day Cover				1·60
Presentation Pack (PO Pack No. 191)			1·60	
Souvenir Book			6·00	
PHQ Cards (set of 4) (111)			60	1·60

Nos. 1396/397 and 1398/1399 were each printed together, *se-tenant*, in horizontal pairs throughout the sheets, each pair showing a background design of the Australian flag.

The 40 page souvenir book contains the British and Australian sets which were issued on the same day in similar designs.

Special First Day of Issue Postmarks
Philatelic Bureau, Edinburgh .... 1·90
Portsmouth .... 1·90

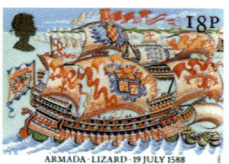

870 Spanish Galeasse off The Lizard

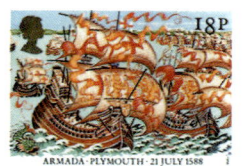

871 English Fleet leaving Plymouth

872 Engagement off Isle of Wight

873 Attack of English Fire-ships, Calais

874 Armada in Storm, North Sea

(Des G. Evernden)

1988 (19 July). 400th Anniversary of Spanish Armada. Multicoloured Phosphorised paper. Perf 15×14.

1400	870	18p. Spanish Galeasse off The Lizard	25	25
		a. Horiz strip of 5. Nos. 1400/1404	1·40	1·40
1401	871	18p. English Fleet leaving Plymouth	25	25
1402	872	18p. Engagement off Isle of Wight	25	25
1403	873	18p. Attack of English Fire-ships, Calais	25	25
		a. '88' for '1988' in imprint (strip of 5)	35·00	
1404	874	18p. Armada in Storm, North Sea	25	25
		a. '988' for '1988' in imprint (strip of 5)	35·00	
Set of 5			1·40	1·40
Gutter Block of 10			2·75	
First Day Cover				1·50
Presentation Pack (PO Pack No. 192)			1·50	
PHQ Cards (set of 5) (112)			75	1·50

Nos. 1400/1404 were printed together, *se-tenant*, in horizontal strips of five throughout the sheet, forming a composite design.

On R. 3/10 the imprint reads 88, with traces of the 9 visible, on R. 4/4 it reads 988, both on the Dot pane. Both were quickly retouched to show 1988

Special First Day of Issue Postmarks
Philatelic Bureau, Edinburgh .... 1·60
Plymouth .... 1·75

875 'The Owl and the Pussy-cat'

876 'Edward Lear as a Bird' (self-portrait)

877 'Cat' (from alphabet book)

878 'There was a Young Lady whose Bonnet...' (limerick)

111

QUEEN ELIZABETH II/1988

(Des M. Swatridge and S. Dew)

1988 (6–27 Sept). Death Centenary of Edward Lear (artist and author). Multicoloured Phosphorised paper. Perf 15×14.

1405	**875**	19p. 'The Owl and the Pussy-cat'............	25	25
1406	**876**	27p. 'Edward Lear as a Bird' (self-portrait).................	35	35
1407	**877**	32p. 'Cat' (from alphabet book).............	45	45
1408	**878**	35p. 'There was a Young Lady whose Bonnet...' (limerick)...............	60	60

Set of 4..................	1·50	1·50
Set of 4 Gutter Pairs..................	3·00	
First Day Cover..................		1·60
Presentation Pack (PO Pack No. 193)...............	1·60	
PHQ Cards (set of 4) (113)..................	60	1·60
MS1409 122×90 mm. Nos. 1405/1408 (sold at £1·35) (27.9.88)..................	3·25	3·50
First Day Cover..................		3·75

The premium on No. **MS**1409 was used to support the Stamp World London 90 International Stamp Exhibition.

Special First Day of Issue Postmarks

Philatelic Bureau, Edinburgh (stamps) (6.9.88)................	1·75
Philatelic Bureau, Edinburgh (miniature sheet) (27.9.88)............	3·75
London N7 (stamps) (6.9.88)................	1·75
London N22 (miniature sheet) (27.9.88)................	3·75

879 Carrickfergus Castle

880 Caernarfon Castle

881 Edinburgh Castle

882 Windsor Castle

(Des from photos by Prince Andrew, Duke of York. Eng C. Matthews. Recess Harrison)

1988 (18 Oct). Ordinary paper. Perf 15×14.

1410	**879**	£1 Carrickfergus Castle. Bottle green..	3·50	25
1411	**880**	£1·50 Caernarfon Castle. Maroon...........	3·75	50
1412	**881**	£2 Edinburgh Castle. Indigo...............	6·50	75
1413	**882**	£5 Windsor Castle. Deep brown..........	17·00	1·50

Set of 4..................	28·00	2·75
Set of 4 Gutter Pairs (vert or horiz)................	60·00	
First Day Cover..................		16·00
Presentation Pack (PO Pack No. 18)...............	30·00	

For similar designs, but with silhouette of Queen's head see Nos. 1611/1614 and 1993/1996.

Special First Day of Issue Postmarks

(For illustrations see Introduction)..................	
Philatelic Bureau Edinburgh (Type H)................	16·00
Windsor, Berkshire (Type 1)................	20·00

883 Journey to Bethlehem

884 Shepherds and Star

885 Three Wise Men

886 Nativity

887 The Annunciation

(Des L. Trickett)

1988 (15 Nov). Christmas. Christmas Cards. Multicoloured One phosphor band (14p.) or phosphorised paper (others). Perf 15×14.

1414	**883**	14p. Journey to Bethlehem................	25	25
		a. Error. '13p.' instead of '14p.'...........	£7500	
		b. Imperf (pair)................	£1500	
1415	**884**	19p. Shepherds and Star................	25	25
		a. Imperf (pair)................	£850	
1416	**885**	27p. Three Wise Men................	35	35
1417	**886**	32p. Nativity................	40	40
1418	**887**	35p. The Annunciation................	55	55

Set of 5..................	1·60	1·60
Set of 5 Gutter Pairs..................	3·25	
First Day Cover..................		1·75
Presentation Pack (PO Pack No. 194)...............	1·75	
PHQ Cards (set of 5) (114)..................	75	1·75

Examples of No. 1414a were found in some 1988 Post Office Yearbooks.

Special First Day of Issue Postmarks

Philatelic Bureau, Edinburgh................	1·75
Bethlehem, Llandeilo, Dyfed................	1·90

Collectors Pack 1988

1988 (15 Nov). Comprises Nos. 1380/1408, 1414/1418.

CP1418a	Collectors Pack (PO Pack No. 195)......	16·00

Post Office Yearbook

1988 (15 Nov). Comprises Nos. 1380/1404, **MS**1409, 1414/1418 in 32 page hardbound book with slip case, illustrated in colour

YB1418a	Yearbook.................................	13·00

888 Atlantic Puffin

889 Avocet

890 Oystercatcher

891 Northern Gannet

(Des D. Cordery)

1989 (17 Jan). Centenary of Royal Society for the Protection of Birds. Multicoloured Phosphorised paper. Perf 14×15.

1419	**888**	19p. Atlantic Puffin................	25	25
1420	**889**	27p. Avocet................	35	35
1421	**890**	32p. Oystercatcher................	45	45
1422	**891**	35p. Northern Gannet................	60	60

Set of 4..................	1·50	1·50
Set of 4 Gutter Pairs..................	3·00	
First Day Cover..................		1·60
Presentation Pack (PO Pack No. 196)...............	1·60	
PHQ Cards (set of 4) (115)..................	60	1·60

Special First Day of Issue Postmarks

Philatelic Bureau, Edinburgh................	1·75
Sandy, Bedfordshire................	1·75

1989/QUEEN ELIZABETH II

892 Rose
893 Cupid 
894 Yachts 
895 Fruit 
896 Teddy Bear 

(Des P. Sutton)

1989 (31 Jan). Greetings Stamps. Multicoloured Phosphorised paper. Perf 15×14.

1423	892	19p. Rose	50	60
		a. Booklet pane. Nos. 1423/1427×2 plus 12 half stamp-size labels	24·00	
		b. Horiz strip of 5. Nos. 1423/1427	10·00	12·00
1424	893	19p. Cupid	50	60
1425	894	19p. Yachts	50	60
1426	895	19p. Fruit	50	60
1427	896	19p. Teddy Bear	50	60

Set of 5 .... 10·00 12·00
First Day Cover .... 12·00

Nos. 1423/1427 were printed together, *se-tenant*, in horizontal strips of five, two such strips forming the booklet pane with 12 half stamp-size labels.

Nos. 1423/1427 were only issued in £1·90 booklet No. FY1.

Special First Day of Issue Postmarks
Philatelic Bureau, Edinburgh .... 12·00
Lover, Salisbury, Wilts .... 12·00

897 Fruit and Vegetables
898 Meat Products 
899 Dairy Products 
900 Cereal Products 

(Des Sedley Place Ltd)

1989 (7 Mar). Food and Farming Year. Multicoloured Phosphorised paper. Perf 14×14½.

1428	897	19p. Fruit and Vegetables	25	25
1429	898	27p. Meat Products	35	35
1430	899	32p. Dairy Products	45	45
1431	900	35p. Cereal Products	60	60

Set of 4 .... 1·50 1·50
Set of 4 Gutter Pairs .... 3·00
First Day Cover .... 1·60
Presentation Pack (PO Pack No. 197) .... 1·60
PHQ Cards (set of 4) (116) .... 60 1·60

Special First Day of Issue Postmarks
Philatelic Bureau, Edinburgh .... 1·60
Stoneleigh, Kenilworth, Warwicks .... 1·75

901 Mortarboard (150th Anniversary of Public Education in England)
902 Cross on Ballot Paper (Third Direct Elections to European Parliament) 
903 Posthorn (26th Postal, Telegraph and Telephone International Congress, Brighton) 
904 Globe (Inter-Parliamentary Union Centenary Conference, London) 

(Des Lewis Moberly from firework set-pieces. Litho Questa)

1989 (11 Apr). Anniversaries. Multicoloured Phosphorised paper. Perf 14×14½.

1432	901	19p. Mortarboard	25	25
		a. Horiz pair. Nos. 1432/1433	60	60
1433	902	19p. Cross on Ballot Paper	25	25
1434	903	35p. Posthorn	50	50
		a. Horiz pair. Nos. 1434/1435	1·10	1·10
1435	904	35p. Globe	50	50

Set of 4 .... 1·50 1·50
Set of 2 Gutter Strips of 4 .... 3·00
First Day Cover .... 1·60
Presentation Pack (PO Pack No. 198) .... 1·60
PHQ Cards (set of 4) (117) .... 60 1·60

Nos. 1432/1433 and 1434/1435 were each printed together, *se-tenant*, in horizontal pairs throughout the sheets.

Stamps as No. 1435, but inscribed 'ONE HUNDREDH CONFERNCE' were prepared but not issued.

Special First Day of Issue Postmarks
Philatelic Bureau, Edinburgh .... 1·60
London SW .... 1·75

905 Toy Train and Aeroplanes
906 Building Bricks

QUEEN ELIZABETH II/1989

907 Dice and Board Games
908 Toy Robot, Boat and Doll's House 

(Des D. Fern)

1989 (16 May). Europa. Games and Toys. Multicoloured Phosphorised paper. Perf 14×15.

1436	905	19p. Toy Train and Aeroplanes	25	25
1437	906	27p. Building Bricks	35	35
1438	907	32p. Dice and Board Games	45	45
1439	908	35p. Toy Robot, Boat and Doll's House	60	60
Set of 4			1·50	1·50
Set of 4 Gutter Strips			3·00	
First Day Cover				1·60
Presentation Pack (PO Pack No. 199)			1·60	
PHQ Cards (set of 4) (118)			60	1·60

Special First Day of Issue Postmarks

Philatelic Bureau, Edinburgh	1·75
Leeds	1·75

909 Ironbridge, Shropshire 
910 Tin Mine, St Agnes Head, Cornwall

911 Cotton Mills, New Lanark, Strathclyde 
912 Pontcysyllte Aqueduct, Clwyd

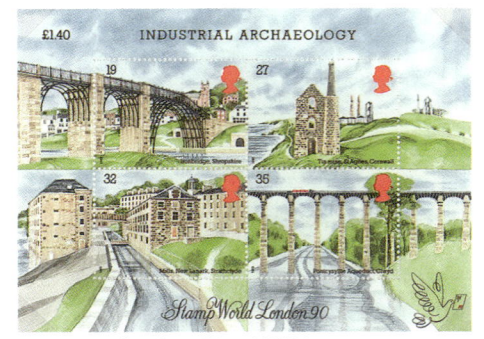

912a Horizontal versions of Types **909/912**

(Des R. Maddox)

1989 (4–25 July). Industrial Archaeology. Multicoloured Phosphorised paper. Perf 14×15.

1440	909	19p. Ironbridge, Shropshire	25	25
1441	910	27p. Tin Mine, St Agnes Head, Cornwall	35	35
1442	911	32p. Cotton Mills, New Lanark, Strathclyde	45	45
1443	912	35p. Pontcysyllte Aqueduct, Clwyd	60	60
Set of 4			1·50	1·50
Set of 4 Gutter Pairs			3·00	
First Day Cover				1·60
Presentation Pack (PO Pack No. 200)			1·60	
PHQ Cards (set of 4) (119)			50	1·60
MS1444 **912a** 122×90 mm. Horizontal versions of Types **909/912** (sold at £1·40) (25.7.89)			3·00	3·00
First Day Cover				3·00

The premium on No. **MS**1444 was used to support the Stamp World London 90 International Stamp Exhibition.

Special First Day of Issue Postmarks

Philatelic Bureau, Edinburgh (stamps) (4.7.89)	1·75
Philatelic Bureau, Edinburgh (miniature sheet) (25.7.89)	3·00
Telford (stamps) (4.7.89)	1·75
New Lanark (miniature sheet) (25.7.89)	3·25

For Nos. 1445/1452 see Decimal Machin Definitives section.

915 Snowflake (×10) 
916 *Calliphora erythrocephala* (×5) (fly)

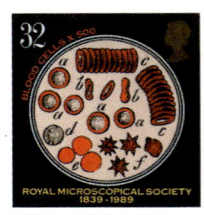

917 Blood Cells (×500)
918 Microchip (×600) 

(Des K. Bassford. Litho Questa)

1989 (5 Sept). 150th Anniversary of Royal Microscopical Society. Multicoloured Phosphorised paper. Perf 14½×14.

1453	915	19p. Snowflake	25	25
1454	916	27p. *Calliphora erythrocephala*	35	35
1455	917	32p. Blood Cells	45	45
1456	918	35p. Microchip	60	60
Set of 4			1·50	1·50
Set of 4 Gutter Pairs			3·00	
First Day Cover				1·60
Presentation Pack (PO Pack No. 201)			1·60	
PHQ Cards (set of 4) (120)			60	1·60

Special First Day of Issue Postmarks

Philatelic Bureau, Edinburgh	1·65
Oxford	1·75

919 Royal Mail Coach
920 Escort of Blues and Royals

1989/QUEEN ELIZABETH II

921 Lord Mayor's Coach
922 Passing St Paul's 
923 Blues and Royals Drum Horse 

(Des P. Cox)

1989 (17 Oct). Lord Mayor's Show, London. Multicoloured. Phosphorised paper. Perf 14×15.

1457	919	20p. Royal Mail Coach	25	25
		a. Horiz strip of 5. Nos. 1457/1461	1·40	1·40
		ab. Imperf (horiz strip of 5. Nos. 1457/1461)	£6000	
		ac. Imperf (horiz strip of 4. Nos. 1457/1460)	£5000	
		ad. Imperf (horiz strip of 3. Nos. 1457/1459)	£4000	
1458	920	20p. Escort of Blues and Royals	25	25
1459	921	20p. Lord Mayor's Coach	25	25
1460	922	20p. Passing St Paul's	25	25
1461	923	20p. Blues and Royals Drum Horse	25	25
Set of 5			1·40	1·40
Gutter Strip of 10			2·75	
First Day Cover				1·50
Presentation Pack (PO Pack No. 202)			1·50	
PHQ Cards (set of 5) (121)			75	1·50

Nos. 1457/1461 were printed together, *se-tenant*, in horizontal strips of five throughout the sheet.

This issue commemorates the 800th anniversary of the installation of the first Lord Mayor of London.

Nos. 1457ab/1457ad come from a sheet partly imperf at left.

Stamps of Types **919/923**, but each with face value of 19p., were prepared but not issued. One mint *se-tenant* strip has been recorded. See also No. 2957.

Special First Day of Issue Postmarks
Philatelic Bureau, Edinburgh ... 1·40
London, EC4 ... 1·50

924 14th-century Peasants from Stained-glass Window
925 Arches and Roundels, West Front 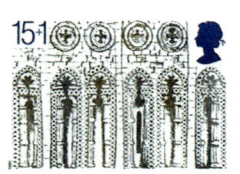
926 Octagon Tower 
927 Arcade from West Transept 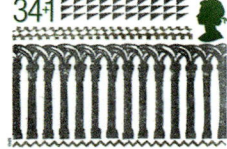
928 Triple Arch from West Front 

(Des D. Gentleman)

1989 (14 Nov). Christmas. 800th Anniversary of Ely Cathedral. Multicoloured One phosphor band (15p., 15p.+1p.) or phosphorised paper (others). Perf 15×14.

1462	924	15p. 14th-century Peasants from Stained-glass Window	25	25
1463	925	15p.+1p. Arches and Roundels, West Front	25	35
		a. Imperf (pair)	£1600	
1464	926	20p.+1p. Octagon Tower	35	35
		a. Imperf (pair)	£1600	
1465	927	34p.+1p. Arcade from West Transept	45	45
1466	928	37p.+1p. Triple Arch from West Front	60	60
Set of 5			1·75	1·75
Set of 5 Gutter Pairs			3·50	
First Day Cover				1·90
Presentation Pack (PO Pack No. 203)			1·90	
PHQ Cards (set of 5) (122)			75	1·90

Trials are known showing different values and including an additional design.

Special First Day of Issue Postmarks
Philatelic Bureau, Edinburgh ... 1·90
Bethlehem, Llandeilo, Dyfed ... 1·90
Ely ... 1·90

Collectors Pack 1989

1989 (14 Nov). Comprises Nos. 1419/1422, 1428/1443 and 1453/1466.
CP1466a   Collectors Pack (PO Pack No. 204) ... 15·50

Post Office Yearbook

1989 (14 Nov). Comprises Nos. 1419/1422, 1428/1444 and 1453/1466 in hardbound book with slip case, illustrated in colour
YB1466a   Yearbook ... 14·00

929 Queen Victoria and Queen Elizabeth II

(Des J. Matthews (after Wyon and Machin))

1990 (10 Jan–12 June). 150th Anniversary of the Penny Black.
(a) Photo Harrison. Perf 15×14.

1467	929	15p. bright blue	30	30
		a. Imperf (pair)	£1200	
		l. Booklet pane. No. 1467×10 with horizontal edges of pane imperf (30.1.90)	4·75	
1468		15p. bright blue (1 side band at left) (30.1.90)	3·75	3·75
		a. Band at right (20.3.90)	1·75	1·75
		l. Booklet pane. No. 1468×2 and 1470 plus label	9·75	
1468a			1·75	1·75
1469		20p. brownish black and cream (phosphorised paper)	40	40
		a. Imperf (pair)	£1200	
		l. Booklet pane. No. 1469×5 plus label with vertical edges of pane imperf (30.1.90)	5·00	
		m. Booklet pane. No. 1469×10 with horizontal edges of pane imperf (30.1.90)	5·25	
		n. Booklet pane. No. 1469×6 with margins all round (20.3.90)	1·50	
		r. Booklet pane. No. 1469×4 with three edges of pane imperf (17.4.90)	3·75	
1470		20p. brownish black and cream (2 bands) (30.1.90)	80	80
1471		29p. deep mauve (phosphorised paper)	55	55
1472		29p. deep mauve (2 bands) (20.3.90)	3·75	3·75

115

QUEEN ELIZABETH II/1990

1473		34p. deep bluish grey (phosphorised paper)	70	70
1474		37p. rosine (phosphorised paper)	75	75
		(b) Litho Walsall. Perf 14 (from booklets).		
1475	929	15p. bright blue (30.1.90)	50	50
		l. Booklet pane. No. 1475×4 with three edges of pane imperf	3·00	
		m. Booklet pane. No. 1475×10 with three edges of pane imperf (12.6.90)	5·50	
1476		20p. brownish black and cream (phosphorised paper) (30.1.90)	50	50
		l. Booklet pane. No. 1476×5 plus label with three edges of pane imperf	8·00	
		m. Booklet pane. No. 1476×4 with three edges of pane imperf	4·00	
		n. Booklet pane. No. 1476×10 with three edges of pane imperf (12.6.90)	8·00	
		(c) Litho Questa. Perf 15×14 (from booklets).		
1477	929	15p. bright blue (17.4.90)	85	85
1478		20p. brownish black (phosphorised paper) (17.4.90)	85	85
Set of 5 (Nos. 1467, 1469, 1471, 1473/1474)			2·50	2·50
First Day Cover (Nos. 1467, 1469, 1471, 1473/1474)				2·75
Presentation Pack (PO Pack No. 21) (Nos. 1467, 1469, 1471, 1473/1474)			2·90	

Nos. 1475/1476 do not exist perforated on all four sides, but come with either one or two adjacent sides imperforate.

Nos. 1468, 1468a, 1470, 1472 and 1475/1478 were only issued in stamp booklets, Nos. JA1 to JD3.

Nos. 1468a, 1470 and 1472 occur in the *se-tenant* pane from the 1990 London Life £5 booklet (No. DX11). This pane is listed as No. X906m.

For illustrations showing the difference between photogravure and lithography see beneath T **367**.

For No. 1469 in miniature sheet see Nos. **MS**1501 and **MS**3965.

For No. 1476 with one elliptical hole on each vertical side see Nos. 2133 and 2955.

For T **929** redrawn with '1st' face value see No. 2133*a* and 2956.

Colour trials are known denominated 19p. in several colours.

Special First Day of Issue Postmark

Philatelic Bureau, Edinburgh (in red)	2·75
Windsor, Berks (Type G, see Introduction) (in red)	2·75

930 Kitten  **931** Rabbit

932 Duckling  **933** Puppy

(Des T. Evans. Litho Questa)

1990 (23 Jan). 150th Anniversary of Royal Society for Prevention of Cruelty to Animals. Multicoloured Phosphorised paper. Perf 14×14½.

1479	930	20p. Kitten	30	30
		a. Silver (Queen's head and face value) omitted	£650	
1480	931	29p. Rabbit	45	45
		a. Imperf (horiz pair)	£2800	
1481	932	34p. Duckling	55	55
		a. Silver (Queen's head and face value) omitted	£1000	
1482	933	37p. Puppy	65	65
Set of 4			1·75	1·75
Set of 4 Gutter Pairs			3·50	
First Day Cover				1·90
Presentation Pack (PO Pack No. 205)			1·90	
PHQ Cards (set of 4) (123)			80	1·90

Special First Day of Issue Postmarks

Philatelic Bureau, Edinburgh	2·00
Horsham	2·25

934 Teddy Bear  **935** Dennis the Menace

936 Punch  **937** Cheshire Cat

938 The Man in the Moon  **939** The Laughing Policeman

940 Clown  **941** Mona Lisa

942 Queen of Hearts  **943** Stan Laurel (comedian)

(Des Michael Peters and Partners Ltd)

1990 (6 Feb). Greetings Stamps. Smiles. Multicoloured Two phosphor bands. Perf 15×14.

1483	934	20p. Teddy Bear	60	70
		a. Booklet pane. Nos. 1483/1492 with margins all round	11·50	12·50
1484	935	20p. Dennis the Menace	60	70
1485	936	20p. Punch	60	70
1486	937	20p. Cheshire Cat	60	70
1487	938	20p. The Man in the Moon	60	70
1488	939	20p. The Laughing Policeman	60	70
1489	940	20p. Clown	60	70
1490	941	20p. Mona Lisa	60	70
1491	942	20p. Queen of Hearts	60	70
1492	943	20p. Stan Laurel	60	70
Set of 10			11·50	12·50
First Day Cover				13·00

Nos. 1483/1492 were only issued in £2 booklet No. KX1.

The design of Nos. 1483, 1485/1487, 1489 and 1492 extend onto the pane margin.

For Types **934**/**943** inscribed (1st), see Nos. 1550/1559.

SET PRICES. Please note that set prices for booklet greetings stamps are for complete panes. Sets of single stamps are worth considerably less.

Special First Day of Issue Postmarks

Philatelic Bureau, Edinburgh	12·50
Giggleswick, North Yorkshire	12·50

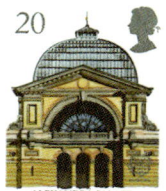

1990/QUEEN ELIZABETH II

944 Alexandra Palace (Stamp World London 90 Exhibition)
945 Glasgow School of Art 
946 British Philatelic Bureau, Edinburgh 
947 Templeton Carpet Factory, Glasgow 

(Des P. Hogarth)

1990 (6–20 Mar). Europa (Nos. 1493 and 1495) and Glasgow 1990 European City of Culture (Nos. 1494 and 1496). Multicoloured Phosphorised paper. Perf 14×15.

1493	**944**	20p. Alexandra Palace (Stamp World London 90 Exhibition)	25	25
		a. Booklet pane. No. 1493×4 with margins all round (20 Mar)	1·40	
1494	**945**	20p. Glasgow School of Art	35	35
1495	**946**	29p. British Philatelic Bureau, Edinburgh	45	45
1496	**947**	37p. Templeton Carpet Factory, Glasgow	60	60
Set of 4			1·50	1·50
Set of 4 Gutter Pairs			3·00	
First Day Cover				1·60
Presentation Pack (PO Pack No. 206)			1·60	
PHQ Cards (set of 4) (124)			80	1·60

Booklet pane No. 1493a comes from the £5 London Life booklet No. DX11.

Special First Day of Issue Postmarks
Philatelic Bureau, Edinburgh .... 1·75
Glasgow .... 1·75

948 Export Achievement Award
949 Technological Achievement Award 

(Des S. Broom. Litho Questa)

1990 (10 Apr). 25th Anniversary of Queen's Awards for Export and Technology. Multicoloured Phosphorised paper. Perf 14×14½.

1497	**948**	20p. Export Achievement Award	25	25
		a. Horiz pair. Nos. 1497/1498	60	60
1498	**949**	20p. Technological Achievement Award	25	25
1499	**948**	37p. Export Achievement Award	50	50
		a. Horiz pair. Nos. 1499/1500	1·10	1·10
1500	**949**	37p. Technological Achievement Award	50	50
Set of 4			1·50	1·50
Set of 2 Gutter Strips of 4			3·00	
First Day Cover				1·60
Presentation Pack (PO Pack No. 207)			1·60	
PHQ Cards (set of 4) (125)			80	1·60

Nos. 1497/1498 and 1499/1500 were each printed together, *se-tenant*, in horizontal pairs throughout the sheets.

Special First Day of Issue Postmarks
Philatelic Bureau, Edinburgh .... 1·75
London, SW .... 1·75

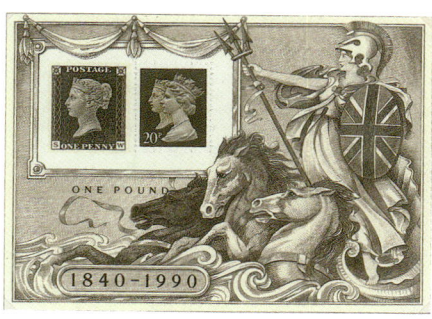

949a

(Des Sedley Place Design Ltd. Eng C. Matthews. Recess and photo Harrison)

1990 (3 May). Stamp World London '90 International Stamp Exhibition. Sheet 122×89 mm containing No. 1469. Phosphorised paper. Perf 15×14.

MS1501	**949a** 20p. brownish black and cream (*sold at* £1)	2·40	2·40
	a. Error. Imperf	—	
	b. Black (recess-printing) omitted	—	
	c. Black (recess-printing) inverted	—	
First Day Cover			2·50
Souvenir Book (Nos. 1467, 1469, 1471, 1473/1474 and **MS**1501)		8·50	

The premium on No. **MS**1501 was used to support the Stamp World London '90 International Stamp Exhibition.

In No. **MS**1501 only the example of the 20p. is perforated.

No. **MS**1501b shows an albino impression on the reverse. The 1d. black and Seahorse background are omitted due to one sheet becoming attached to the underside of another prior to recess printing.

No. **MS**1501c shows the recess part of the design inverted in relation to the photogravure of T *929*.

For the single 20p stamp, see No. 1469. For the same stamp redrawn with '1st' face value or with one elliptical hole on each vertical side see Nos. 2133 and 2955/2956.

Special First Day of Issue Postmarks
Philatelic Bureau, Edinburgh (in red) .... 2·50
City of London (in red) .... 2·50

A First Day of Issue handstamp as Type B was provided at Alexandra Palace, London N22 for this issue.

950 Cycad and Sir Joseph Banks Building
951 Stone Pine and Princess of Wales Conservatory 
952 Willow Tree and Palm House 
953 Cedar Tree and Pagoda 

117

QUEEN ELIZABETH II/1990

(Des P. Leith)

1990 (5 June). 150th Anniversary of Kew Gardens. Multicoloured Phosphorised paper. Perf 14×15.

1502	950	20p. Cycad and Sir Joseph Banks Building	25	25
1503	951	29p. Stone Pine and Princess of Wales Conservatory	35	35
1504	952	34p. Willow Tree and Palm House	45	45
1505	953	37p. Cedar Tree and Pagoda	60	60
Set of 4			1·50	1·50
Set of 4 Gutter Pairs			3·00	
First Day Cover				1·60
Presentation Pack (PO Pack No. 208)			1·60	
PHQ Cards (set of 4) (126)			80	1·60

Special First Day of Issue Postmarks
Philatelic Bureau, Edinburgh .... 1·75
Kew, Richmond .... 1·75

954 Thomas Hardy and Clyffe Clump, Dorset

(Des J. Gibbs)

1990 (10 July). 150th Birth Anniversary of Thomas Hardy (author). Multicoloured Phosphorised paper. Perf 14×15.

1506	954	20p. Thomas Hardy	30	30
		a. Imperf (pair)	£4000	
Gutter Pair			60	
First Day Cover				40
Presentation Pack (PO Pack No. 209)			55	
PHQ Card (127)			20	40

Special First Day of Issue Postmarks
Philatelic Bureau, Edinburgh 60
Dorchester 60

955 Queen Elizabeth the Queen Mother

956 Queen Elizabeth

957 Elizabeth, Duchess of York

958 Lady Elizabeth Bowes-Lyon

(Des J. Gorham from photographs by N. Parkinson (20p.), Dorothy Wilding (29p.), B. Park (34p.), Rita Martin (37p.))

1990 (2 Aug). 90th Birthday of Queen Elizabeth the Queen Mother. Multicoloured Phosphorised paper. Perf 14×15.

1507	955	20p. Queen Elizabeth the Queen Mother	40	40
1508	956	29p. Queen Elizabeth	60	60
1509	957	34p. Elizabeth, Duchess of York	90	90
1510	958	37p. Lady Elizabeth Bowes-Lyon	1·10	1·10
Set of 4			2·75	2·75
Set of 4 Gutter Pairs			5·50	
First Day Cover				2·90

Presentation Pack (PO Pack No. 210) .... 2·90
PHQ Cards (set of 4) (128) 80   2·90

For these designs with Queen's head and frame in black see Nos. 2280/2283.

Special First Day of Issue Postmarks
Philatelic Bureau, Edinburgh .... 3·00
Westminster, SW1 .... 3·00

> For Nos. 1511/1516 see Decimal Machin Definitives section.

959 Victoria Cross

960 George Cross

961 Distinguished Service Cross and Distinguished Service Medal

962 Military Cross and Military Medal

963 Distinguished Flying Cross and Distinguished Flying Medal

(Des J. Gibbs and J. Harwood)

1990 (11 Sept). Gallantry Awards. Multicoloured Phosphorised paper. Perf 14×15 (vert) or 15×14 (horiz).

1517	959	20p. Victoria Cross	35	35
1518	960	20p. George Cross	35	35
1519	961	20p. Distinguished Service Cross and Distinguished Service Medal	35	35
		a. Imperf (pair)	£1200	
1520	962	20p. Military Cross and Military Medal	35	35
1521	963	20p. Distinguished Flying Cross and Distinguished Flying Medal	35	35
Set of 5			1·50	1·50
Set of 5 Gutter Pairs			3·00	
First Day Cover				1·60
Presentation Pack (PO Pack No. 211)			1·60	
PHQ Cards (set of 5) (129)			1·00	1·60

For T **959** with 'all-over' phosphor and Perf 14×14½ see No. 2666.

Special First Day of Issue Postmarks
Philatelic Bureau, Edinburgh .... 1·75
Westminster, SW1 .... 1·75

964 Armagh Observatory, Jodrell Bank Radio Telescope and La Palma Telescope

965 Newton's Moon and Tides Diagram and Early Telescopes

1990/QUEEN ELIZABETH II

966 Greenwich Old Observatory and Early Astronomical Equipment

967 Stonehenge, Gyroscope and Navigation by Stars

(Des J. Fisher. Litho Questa)

1990 (16 Oct). Astronomy. Multicoloured Phosphorised paper. Perf 14×14½.

1522	964	22p. Armagh Observatory, Jodrell Bank Radio Telescope and La Palma Telescope	25	25
		a. Gold (Queen's head) omitted	£675	
1523	965	26p. Newton's Moon and Tides Diagram and Early Telescopes	35	35
1524	966	31p. Greenwich Old Observatory and Early Astronomical Equipment	45	45
1525	967	37p. Stonehenge, Gyroscope and Navigation by Stars	60	60
Set of 4			1·50	1·50
Set of 4 Gutter Pairs			3·00	
First Day Cover				1·60
Presentation Pack (PO Pack No. 212)			1·60	
PHQ Cards (set of 4) (130)			80	1·60

Nos. 1522/1525 marked the centenary of the British Astronomical Association and the bicentenary of the Armagh Observatory.

Special First Day of Issue Postmarks
Philatelic Bureau, Edinburgh .... 1·75
Armagh .... 1·75

968 Building a Snowman

969 Fetching the Christmas Tree

970 Carol Singing

971 Tobogganing

972 Ice Skating

(Des J. Gorham and A. Davidson)

1990 (13 Nov). Christmas. Multicoloured One phosphor band (17p.) or phosphorised paper (others). Perf 15×14.

1526	968	17p. Building a Snowman	25	25
		a. Imperf (pair)	£1600	
		b. Booklet pane of 20	5·00	
1527	969	22p. Fetching the Christmas Tree	25	25
		a. Imperf (horiz pair)	£1600	
1528	970	26p. Carol Singing	35	35
1529	971	31p. Tobogganing	45	40
1530	972	37p. Ice skating	60	60
Set of 5			1·75	1·75
Set of 5 Gutter Pairs			3·50	
First Day Cover				1·90
Presentation Pack (PO Pack No. 213)			1·90	
PHQ Cards (set of 5) (131)			1·00	1·90

Booklet pane No. 1526b has the horizontal edges of the pane imperforate.

Special First Day of Issue Postmarks
Philatelic Bureau, Edinburgh .... 1·90
Bethlehem, Llandeilo, Dyfed .... 1·90

Collectors Pack 1990

1990 (13 Nov). Comprises Nos. 1479/1482, 1493/1510 and 1517/1530.
CP1530a   Collectors Pack (PO Pack No. 214)......   18·00

Post Office Yearbook

1990 (13 Nov). Comprises Nos. 1479/1482, 1493/1500, 1502/1510, 1517/1530 in hardbound book with slip case
YB1530a   Yearbook...   18·00

973 King Charles Spaniel

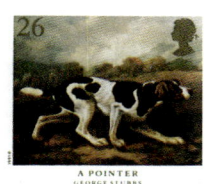

974 A Pointer

975 Two Hounds in a Landscape

976 A Rough Dog

977 Fino and Tiny

(Des Carroll, Dempsey and Thirkell Ltd)

1991 (8 Jan). Dogs. Paintings by George Stubbs. Multicoloured Phosphorised paper. Perf 14×14½.

1531	973	22p. King Charles Spaniel	25	25
		a. Imperf (pair)	£1400	
1532	974	26p. A Pointer	30	30
1533	975	31p. Two Hounds in a Landscape	40	40
		a. Imperf (pair)	£1800	
1534	976	33p. A Rough Dog	45	45
1535	977	37p. Fino and Tiny	60	60
Set of 5			1·75	1·75
Set of 5 Gutter Pairs			3·50	
First Day Cover				2·00
Presentation Pack (PO Pack No. 215)			2·00	
PHQ Cards (set of 5) (132)			1·00	2·00

Special First Day of Issue Postmarks
Philatelic Bureau, Edinburgh .... 2·25
Birmingham .... 2·25

978 Thrush's Nest

979 Shooting Star and Rainbow

QUEEN ELIZABETH II/1991

980 Magpies and Charm Bracelet

981 Black Cat

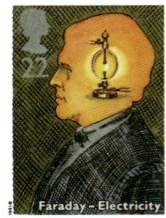

988 Michael Faraday (inventor of electric motor) (Birth Bicentenary)

989 Charles Babbage (computer science pioneer) (Birth Bicentenary)

982 Common Kingfisher with Key

983 Mallard and Frog

990 Radar Sweep of East Anglia (50th Anniversary of Operational Radar Network)

991 Gloster Whittle E28/39 over East Anglia (50th Anniversary of First Flight of Sir Frank Whittle's Jet Engine)

(Des P. Till (Nos. 1546/1547), J. Harwood (Nos. 1548/1549))

1991 (5 Mar). Scientific Achievements. Multicoloured Phosphorised paper. Perf 14×15.

1546	988	22p. Michael Faraday	35	35
		a. Imperf (pair)	£425	
1547	989	22p. Charles Babbage	35	35
1548	990	31p. Radar Sweep of East Anglia	55	55
1549	991	37p. Gloster Whittle E28/39 over East Anglia	65	65
Set of 4			1·75	1·75
Set of 4 Gutter Pairs			3·50	
First Day Cover				1·90
Presentation Pack (PO Pack No. 216)			1·90	
PHQ Cards (set of 4) (133)			50	1·90

984 Four-leaf Clover in Boot and Match Box

985 Pot of Gold at End of Rainbow

Special First Day of Issue Postmarks
Philatelic Bureau, Edinburgh .... 2·00
South Kensington, London, SW7 .... 2·00

986 Heart-shaped Butterflies

987 Wishing Well and Sixpence

992 Teddy Bear

(Des T. Meeuwissen)

(Des Michael Peters and Partners Ltd)

1991 (5 Feb). Greetings Stamps. Good Luck. Multicoloured Two phosphor bands. Perf 15×14.

1536	978	(1st) Thrush's Nest	1·20	1·00
		a. Booklet pane. Nos. 1536/1545 plus 12 half stamp-size labels with margins on 3 sides	13·50	
1537	979	(1st) Shooting Star and Rainbow	1·20	1·00
1538	980	(1st) Magpies and Charm Bracelet	1·20	1·00
1539	981	(1st) Black Cat	1·20	1·00
1540	982	(1st) Common Kingfisher with Key	1·20	1·00
1541	983	(1st) Mallard and Frog	1·20	1·00
1542	984	(1st) Four-leaf clover in Boot and Match Box	1·20	1·00
1543	985	(1st) Pot of Gold at End of Rainbow	1·20	1·00
1544	986	(1st) Heart-shaped Butterflies	1·20	1·00
1545	987	(1st) Wishing Well and Sixpence	1·20	1·00
Set of 10			10·50	9·00
First Day Cover				9·25

Nos. 1536/1545 were only issued in £2·20 booklet, No. KX2 (sold at £2·40 from 16 September 1991)
The backgrounds of the stamps form a composite design.

1991 (26 Mar). Greetings Stamps. Smiles. As Nos. 1483/1492, but inscribed '1st' as T **992**. Multicoloured Two phosphor bands. Perf 15×14.

1550	992	(1st) Teddy Bear	1·20	1·00
		a. Booklet pane. Nos. 1550/1559 plus 12 half stamp-size labels with margins on 3 sides	13·50	
1551	935	(1st) Dennis the Menace	1·20	1·00
1552	936	(1st) Punch	1·20	1·00
1553	937	(1st) Cheshire Cat	1·20	1·00
1554	938	(1st) The Man in the Moon	1·20	1·00
1555	939	(1st) The Laughing Policeman	1·20	1·00
1556	940	(1st) Clown	1·20	1·00
1557	941	(1st) Mona Lisa	1·20	1·00
1558	942	(1st) Queen of Hearts	1·20	1·00
1559	943	(1st) Stan Laurel	1·20	1·00
Set of 10			10·50	9·00
First Day Cover				9·25

Special First Day of Issue Postmarks
Philatelic Bureau, Edinburgh .... 9·50
Greetwell, Lincs .... 9·50

Nos. 1550/1559 were originally issued in £2·20 booklet, No. KX3 (sold at £2·40 from 16 September 1991 and at £2·50 from 1 November 1993).
The designs of Nos. 1550, 1552/1554, 1556 and 1559 extend onto the pane margin.

1991 / QUEEN ELIZABETH II

The stamps were re-issued in sheets of ten, printed in photogravure by Questa, each with *se-tenant* label on 22 May 2000 in connection with 'customised' stamps available at Stamp Show 2000. The labels show either a pattern of ribbons at £2.95 (No. LS1), or a personal photograph for £5.95.

A similar sheet, but printed in lithography by Questa instead of in photogravure, appeared on 3 July 2001 (No. LS5). Stamps from this sheet were perforated 14½×14 instead of the previous 15×14. Sheets showing greetings on the labels were available from the Bureau or Postshops at £2.95 each or with personal photographs at £12.95 for two.

Similar sheets each containing ten examples of Nos. 1550/1551 and 1555/1557 were only available with personal photograph. From 29 October 2001 sheets with personal photographs could also be purchased, on an experimental basis, from photo-booths situated at six post offices.

On 1 October 2002 three further sheets appeared printed in lithography by Questa. One contained Nos. 1550/1551 each×10 with greetings labels and cost £5.95 (No. LS9). Both designs were also available in sheets of 20 with personal photographs at £14.95 a sheet.

SET PRICES. Please note that set prices for booklet greetings stamps are for complete panes. Sets of single stamps are worth considerably less.

Special First Day of Issue Postmarks
Philatelic Bureau, Edinburgh .... 9·50
Laughterton, Lincs .... 9·50

993 Man Looking at Space
994 Man Looking at Space 
995 Space Looking at Man 
996 Space Looking at Man 

(Des J. M. Folon)

1991 (23 Apr). Europa. Europe in space. Multicoloured. Phosphorised paper. Perf 14½×14.

1560	993	22p. Man Looking at Space	35	35
		a. Horiz pair. Nos 1560/1561	75	75
1561	994	22p. Man Looking at Space	35	35
1562	995	37p. Space Looking at Man	65	65
		a. Horiz pair. Nos 1562/1563	1·40	1·40
1563	996	37p. Space Looking at Man	65	65
Set of 4			1·90	1·90
Set of 2 Gutter Pairs of 4			3·75	
First Day Cover				2·10
Presentation Pack (PO Pack No. 217)			2·10	
PHQ Cards (set of 4) (134)			80	2·10

Nos. 1560/1561 and 1562/1563 were each printed together, *se-tenant*, in horizontal pairs throughout the sheets, each pair forming a composite design.

Special First Day of Issue Postmarks
Philatelic Bureau, Edinburgh .... 2·10
Cambridge .... 2·25

997 Fencing
998 Hurdling 
999 Diving 
1000 Rugby 

(Des Huntley Muir Partners)

1991 (11 June). World Student Games, Sheffield (Nos.1564/1566) and World Cup Rugby Championship, London (No. 1567). Multicoloured Phosphorised paper. Perf 14½×14.

1564	997	22p. Fencing	35	35
1565	998	26p. Hurdling	45	45
1566	999	31p. Diving	55	55
1567	1000	37p. Rugby	75	75
Set of 4			1·90	1·90
Set of 4 Gutter Pairs			3·75	
First Day Cover				2·10
Presentation Pack (PO Pack No. 218)			2·10	
PHQ Cards (set of 4) (135)			80	2·10

Special First Day of Issue Postmarks
Philatelic Bureau, Edinburgh .... 2·10
Sheffield .... 2·25

1001 'Silver Jubilee'
1002 'Mme Alfred Carrière' 
1003 Rosa moyesii 
1004 'Harvest Fayre' 
1005 'Mutabilis' 

(Des Yvonne Skargon. Litho Questa)

1991 (16 July). Ninth World Congress of Roses, Belfast. Multicoloured Phosphorised paper. Perf 14½×14.

1568	1001	22p. 'Silver Jubilee'	30	30
		a. Silver (Queen's head) omitted	£2250	
		b. Black printing double	£3000	£2000
1569	1002	26p. 'Mme Alfred Carrière'	35	35
1570	1003	31p. *Rosa moyesii*	40	40
		a. Silver (Queen's head) omitted	—	£4000
1571	1004	33p. 'Harvest Fayre'	55	55
1572	1005	37p. 'Mutabilis'	65	65
Set of 5			2·00	2·00
Set of 5 Gutter Pairs			4·00	
First Day Cover				2·25
Presentation Pack (PO Pack No. 219)			2·25	
PHQ Cards (set of 5) (136)			60	2·25

Special First Day of Issue Postmarks
Philatelic Bureau, Edinburgh .... 2·25
Belfast .... 2·50

1006 Iguanodon
1007 Stegosaurus 
1008 Tyrannosaurus 
1009 Protoceratops 
1010 Triceratops 

(Des B. Kneale)

1991 (20 Aug). 150th Anniversary of Dinosaurs' Identification by Owen. Multicoloured Phosphorised paper. Perf 14½×14.

1573	**1006**	22p. Iguanodon	35	35
		a. Imperf (pair)	£1500	
1574	**1007**	26p. Stegosaurus	40	40
1575	**1008**	31p. Tyrannosaurus	45	45
1576	**1009**	33p. Protoceratops	60	60
1577	**1010**	37p. Triceratops	75	75
Set of 5			2·25	2·25
Set of 5 Gutter Pairs			4·50	
First Day Cover				2·75
Presentation Pack (PO Pack No. 220)			3·00	
PHQ Cards (set of 5) (137)			1·00	2·50

Special First Day of Issue Postmarks
Philatelic Bureau, Edinburgh... 2·75
Plymouth... 3·00

1011 Map of 1816
1012 Map of 1906 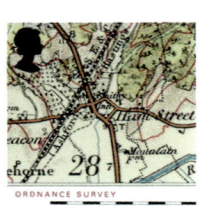
1013 Map of 1959 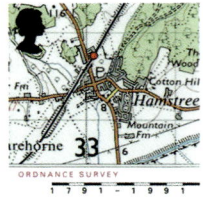
1014 Map of 1991 

(Des H. Brown. Recess (eng C. Matthews) and litho Harrison (24p.), litho Harrison (28p.), Questa (33p., 39p.))

1991 (17 Sept). Bicentenary of Ordnance Survey. Maps of Hamstreet, Kent. Multicoloured. Phosphorised paper. Perf 14½×14.

1578	**1011**	24p. Map of 1816	35	35
		a. Black (litho) printing treble and magenta printing double	£850	
		b. Black (litho) and magenta printing double	£1200	
		c. Black (litho) printing double	£1200	
1579	**1012**	28p. Map of 1906	45	45
1580	**1013**	33p. Map of 1959	55	55
1581	**1014**	39p. Map of 1991	75	75
Set of 4			1·90	1·90
Set of 4 Gutter Pairs			3·75	
First Day Cover				2·00
Presentation Pack (PO Pack No. 221)			2·25	
PHQ Cards (set of 4) (138)			80	2·00

Mint examples of T **1012** exist with a face value of 26p. (*Price* £4000).

Special First Day of Issue Postmarks
Philatelic Bureau, Edinburgh... 2·00
Southampton.. 2·25

1015 Adoration of the Magi
1016 Mary and Jesus in Stable 
1017 Holy Family and Angel 
1018 The Annunciation 
1019 The Flight into Egypt 

(Des D. Driver)

1991 (12 Nov). Christmas. Illuminated Letters from Acts of Mary and Jesus Manuscript in Bodleian Library, Oxford. Multicoloured One phosphor band (18p.) or phosphorised paper (others). Perf 15×14.

1582	**1015**	18p. Adoration of the Magi	25	25
		a. Imperf (pair)	—	
		b. Booklet pane of 20	5·00	
1583	**1016**	24p. Mary and Jesus in Stable	30	30
1584	**1017**	28p. Holy Family and Angel	40	40
1585	**1018**	33p. The Annunciation	55	55
		a. Imperf (pair)	—	
1586	**1019**	39p. The Flight into Egypt	70	70
Set of 5			1·90	1·90
Set of 5 Gutter Pairs			3·75	
First Day Cover				2·00
Presentation Pack (PO Pack No. 222)			2·10	
PHQ Cards (set of 5) (139)			60	2·00

Booklet pane No. 1582b has margins at left, top and bottom.

Special First Day of Issue Postmarks
Philatelic Bureau, Edinburgh... 2·00
Bethlehem, Landeilo, Dyfed... 2·00

Collectors Pack 1991

1991 (12 Nov). Comprises Nos. 1531/1535, 1546/5419 and 1560/1586.
CP1586a   Collectors Pack (PO Pack No. 223)...... 18·00

Post Office Yearbook

1991 (13 Nov). Comprises Nos. 1531/1535, 1546/1549 and 1560/1586 in hardbound book with slip case
YB1586a   Yearbook... 16·00

1992/QUEEN ELIZABETH II

1020 Fallow Deer in Scottish Forest

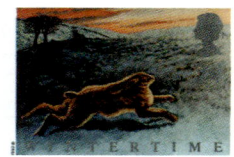

1021 Hare on North Yorkshire Moors

1022 Fox in the Fens

1023 Redwing and Home Counties Village

1024 Welsh Mountain Sheep in Snowdonia

(Des J. Gorham and K. Bowen)

1992 (14 Jan–25 Feb). The Four Seasons. Wintertime. Multicoloured One phosphor band (18p.) or phosphorised paper (others). Perf 15×14.

1587	1020	18p. Fallow Deer in Scottish Forest........	25	25
1588	1021	24p. Hare on North Yorkshire Moors......	30	30
		a. Imperf (pair)..	£325	
1589	1022	28p. Fox in the Fens.................................	45	45
1590	1023	33p. Redwing and Home Counties Village...	55	55
1591	1024	39p. Welsh Mountain Sheep in Snowdonia..	70	70
		a. Booklet pane. No. 1591a×4 with margins all round (25.2.92)............	2·75	

Set of 5.. 2·00 2·00
Set of 5 Gutter Pairs.. 4·00
First Day Cover.. 2·10
Presentation Pack (PO Pack No. 224)................................... 2·25
PHQ Cards (set of 5) (140).. 1·00 2·10

Booklet pane No. 1591a comes from the £6 Cymru-Wales booklet No. DX13.

Special First Day of Issue Postmarks
Philatelic Bureau, Edinburgh.. 2·10
Brecon.. 2·10

1025 Flower Spray

1026 Double Locket

1027 Key

1028 Model Car and Cigarette Cards

1029 Compass and Map

1030 Pocket Watch

1031 1854 1d. Red Stamp and Pen

1032 Pearl Necklace and Pen

1033 Marbles

1034 Bucket, Spade and Starfish

(Des Trickett and Webb Ltd)

1992 (28 Jan). Greetings Stamps. Memories. Multicoloured Two phosphor bands. Perf 15×14.

1592	1025	(1st) Flower Spray.....................................	1·20	1·00
		a. Booklet pane. Nos. 1592/1601 plus 12 half stamp-size labels with margins on 3 sides................	13·50	
1593	1026	(1st) Double Locket.................................	1·20	1·00
1594	1027	(1st) Key..	1·20	1·00
1595	1028	(1st) Model Car and Cigarette Cards......	1·20	1·00
1596	1029	(1st) Compass and Map..........................	1·20	1·00
1597	1030	(1st) Pocket Watch..................................	1·20	1·00
1598	1031	(1st) 1854 1d. Red Stamp and Pen.........	1·20	1·00
1599	1032	(1st) Pearl Necklace and Pen..................	1·20	1·00
1600	1033	(1st) Marbles..	1·20	1·00
1601	1034	(1st) Bucket, Spade and Starfish.............	1·20	1·00

Set of 10... 10·50 9·25
First Day Cover... 9·50
Presentation Pack (PO Pack No. G1)..................................... 13·50

Nos. 1592/1601 were only issued in £2·40 booklet, No. KX4 (sold at £2·50 from 1 November 1993 and at £2·60 from 8 July 1996)

The backgrounds of the stamps form a composite design.

Special First Day of Issue Postmarks
Philatelic Bureau, Edinburgh.. 9·50
Whimsey, Gloucestershire... 9·50

1035 Queen Elizabeth in Coronation Robes and Parliamentary Emblem

1036 Queen Elizabeth in Garter Robes and Archiepiscopal Arms

1037 Queen Elizabeth with Baby Prince Andrew and Royal Arms

1038 Queen Elizabeth at Trooping the Colour and Service Emblems

QUEEN ELIZABETH II/1992

1039 Queen Elizabeth and Commonwealth Emblem

(Des Why Not Associates. Litho Questa)

1992 (6 Feb). 40th Anniversary of Accession. Two phosphor bands. Perf 14½×14.

1602	**1035**	24p. Queen Elizabeth in Coronation Robes and Parliamentary Emblem	40	50
		a. Horiz strip of 5. Nos. 1602/1606	2·75	3·00
1603	**1036**	24p. Queen Elizabeth in Garter Robes and Archiepiscopal Arms	40	50
1604	**1037**	24p. Queen Elizabeth with Baby Prince Andrew and Royal Arms	40	50
1605	**1038**	24p. Queen Elizabeth at Trooping the Colour and Service Emblems	40	50
1606	**1039**	24p. Queen Elizabeth and Commonwealth Emblem	40	50
Set of 5			2·75	3·00
Gutter Block of 10			5·50	
First Day Cover				3·25
Presentation Pack (PO Pack No. 225)			3·25	
PHQ Cards (set of 5) (141)			1·00	3·25

Nos. 1602/1606 were printed together, *se-tenant*, in horizontal strips of five throughout the sheet.

Special First Day of Issue Postmarks
Philatelic Bureau, Edinburgh	3·25
Buckingham Palace, London SW1	3·50

1040 Tennyson in 1888 and *The Beguiling of Merlin* (Sir Edward Burne-Jones)

1041 Tennyson in 1856 and *April Love* (Arthur Hughes)

1042 Tennyson in 1864 and *I am Sick of the Shadows* (John Waterhouse)

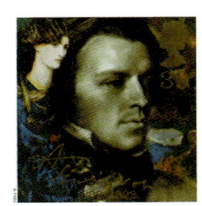

1043 Tennyson as a Young Man and *Mariana* (Dante Gabriel Rossetti)

(Des Irene von Treskow)

1992 (10 Mar). Death Centenary of Alfred, Lord Tennyson (poet). Multicoloured Phosphorised paper. Perf 14½×14.

1607	**1040**	24p. Tennyson in 1888 and *The Beguiling of Merlin*	35	35
1608	**1041**	28p. Tennyson in 1856 and *April Love*	50	50
1609	**1042**	33p. Tennyson in 1864 and *I am Sick of the Shadows*	60	60
1610	**1043**	39p. Tennyson as a Young Man and *Mariana*	75	75
Set of 4			2·00	2·00
Set of 4 Gutter Pairs			4·00	
First Day Cover				2·25
Presentation Pack (PO Pack No. 226)			2·25	
PHQ Cards (Set of 4) (142)			80	2·25

Special First Day of Issue Postmarks
Philatelic Bureau, Edinburgh	2·25
Isle of Wight	2·25

1044 Carrickfergus Castle

1044a Caernarfon Castle

1044b Edinburgh Castle

1044c Carrickfergus Castle

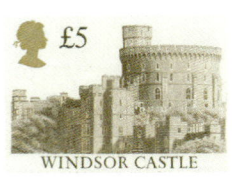

1044d Windsor Castle

Original head Re-etched head

Re-etched head

In 1994 the £1, £1·50, £2 and £5 were issued with the Queen's head re-etched, showing a pattern of diagonal lines, as opposed to the horizontal and diagonal lines of the original versions.

CASTLE
Harrison Plates (Nos. 1611/1614)

CASTLE
Enschedé Plates (Nos. 1993/1996)

(Des from photos by Prince Andrew, Duke of York. Eng C. Matthews. Recess Harrison)

1992 (24 Mar)–**95**. Designs as Nos. 1410/1413, but showing Queen's head in silhouette as T **1044d**. Perf 15×14 (with one elliptical hole in each vertical side).

1611	**1044**	£1 Carrickfergus Castle (bottle green and gold†)	5·50	50
		r. Re-etched cylinder (1994)	8·00	3·00
1612	**1044a**	£1·50 Caernarfon Castle (maroon and gold†)	6·00	75
		r. Re-etched cylinder (1994)	8·00	1·50

1992 / QUEEN ELIZABETH II

1613	**1044b**	£2 Edinburgh Castle (indigo and gold†)	8·00	1·00
		r. Re-etched cylinder (1994)	12·00	2·50
1613a	**1044c**	£3 Carrickfergus Castle (reddish violet and gold†) (22.8.95)	19·00	1·75
1614	**1044d**	£5 Windsor Castle (deep brown and gold†)	18·00	2·00
		a. Gold† (Queen's head) omitted	£575	
		r. Re-etched cylinder (1994)	22·00	4·00
Set of 5			50·00	5·50
Set of 5 Gutter Pairs (vert or horiz)			£100	
Set of 4 re-etched cylinders (1994)			50·00	8·00
Set of 4 gutter pairs re-etched cylinders (1994)			£100	
First Day Cover (Nos. 1611/1613, 1614)				20·00
First Day Cover (No. 1613a)				6·00
Presentation Pack (PO Pack No. 27) (Nos. 1611/1613, 1614)			38·00	
Presentation Pack (PO Pack No. 33) (No. 1613a)			20·00	
PHQ Cards (D2–D5)†† (Nos. 1611/1613, 1614)			80	6·00
PHQ Card (D8) (No. 1613a)			20	2·00

† The Queen's head on these stamps is printed in optically variable ink which changes colour from gold to green when viewed from different angles.

†† The PHQ Cards for this issue did not appear until 16 February 1993. The Bureau FDI cancellation is 3 March 1993 (the date of issue of the £10).

The £1.50 (5 March 1996), £2 (2 May 1996), £3 (February 1997) and £5 (17 September 1996) subsequently appeared on PVA (white gum) instead of the tinted PVAD previously used.

See also Nos. 1410/1413 and 1993/1996.

Special First Day of Issue Postmarks (for illustrations see Introduction)

Philatelic Bureau, Edinburgh (Type H) (£1, £1.50, £2, £5)	20·00
Windsor, Berkshire (Type I) (£1, £1.50, £2, £5)	20·00
Philatelic Bureau, Edinburgh (Type H) (£3)	6·00
Carrickfergus, Antrim (as Type I) (£3)	7·00

1045 British Olympic Association Logo (Olympic Games, Barcelona)

1046 British Paralympic Association Symbol (Paralympics '92, Barcelona)

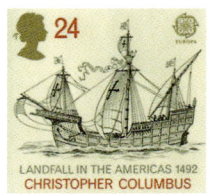

1047 *Santa Maria* 500th Anniversary of Discovery of America by Columbus)

1048 *Kaisei* (Japanese cadet brigantine) (Grand Regatta Columbus, 1992)

1049 British Pavilion, EXPO '92, Seville

(Des K. Bassford (Nos. 1615/1616, 1619), K. Bassford and S. Paine. Eng C. Matthews (Nos. 1617/1618). Litho Questa (Nos. 1615/1616, 1619) or recess and litho Harrison (Nos. 1617/1618))

1992 (7 Apr). Europa. International Events. Multicoloured Phosphorised paper. Perf 14×14½.

1615	**1045**	24p. British Olympic Association Logo	30	30
		a. Horiz pair. Nos. 1615/1616	80	80
1616	**1046**	24p. British Paralympic Association Symbol	30	30
1617	**1047**	24p. *Santa Maria*	40	40
		a. Cream omitted		
1618	**1048**	39p. *Kaisei*	65	65
1619	**1049**	39p. British Pavilion, EXPO '92, Seville	65	65
Set of 5			2·25	2·25
Set of 3 Gutter Pairs and a Gutter Strip of 4			4·50	
First Day Cover				2·50
Presentation Pack (PO Pack No. 227)			2·50	
PHQ Cards (set of 5) (143)			1·00	2·50

Nos. 1615/1616 were printed together, *se-tenant*, in horizontal pairs throughout the sheet.

Special First Day of Issue Postmarks

Philatelic Bureau, Edinburgh	2·50
Liverpool	2·50

1050 Pikeman

1051 Drummer

1052 Musketeer

1053 Standard-bearer

(Des J. Sancha)

1992 (16 June). 350th Anniversary of the Civil War. Multicoloured Phosphorised paper. Perf 14½×14.

1620	**1050**	24p. Pikeman	35	35
		a. Imperf (pair)	£300	
1621	**1051**	28p. Drummer	45	45
1622	**1052**	33p. Musketeer	55	55
1623	**1053**	39p. Standard-bearer	70	70
Set of 4			1·90	1·90
Set of 4 Gutter Pairs			3·75	
First Day Cover				2·00
Presentation Pack (PO Pack No. 228)			2·00	
PHQ Cards (set of 4) (144)			80	2·00

Special First Day of Issue Postmarks

Philatelic Bureau, Edinburgh	2·00
Banbury, Oxfordshire	2·00

1054 The Yeomen of the Guard

1055 The Gondoliers

1056 The Mikado

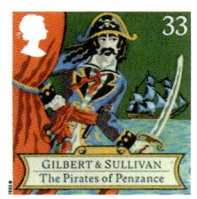

1057 The Pirates of Penzance

QUEEN ELIZABETH II/1992

1058 *Iolanthe*

(Des Lynda Gray)

1992 (21 July). 150th Birth Anniversary of Sir Arthur Sullivan (composer). Gilbert and Sullivan Operas. Multicoloured One phosphor band (18p.) or phosphorised paper (others). Perf 14½×14.

1624	1054	18p. The Yeomen of the Guard	25	25
1625	1055	24p. The Gondoliers	30	30
		a. Imperf (pair)	£375	
1626	1056	28p. The Mikado	40	40
1627	1057	33p. The Pirates of Penzance	55	55
1628	1058	39p. Iolanthe	70	70
Set of 5			2·00	2·00
Set of 5 Gutter Pairs			4·00	
First Day Cover				2·25
Presentation Pack (PO Pack No. 229)			2·25	
PHQ Cards (set of 5) (145)			1·00	2·25

Special First Day of Issue Postmarks
Philatelic Bureau, Edinburgh		2·25
Birmingham		2·25

1059 'Acid Rain Kills' 
1060 'Ozone Layer'

1061 'Greenhouse Effect'
1062 'Bird of Hope' 

(Des Christopher Hall (24p.), Lewis Fowler (28p.), Sarah Warren (33p.), Alice Newton-Mold (39p.). Adapted Trickett and Webb Ltd)

1992 (15 Sept). Protection of the Environment. Children's Paintings. Multicoloured Phosphorised paper. Perf 14×14½.

1629	1059	24p. 'Acid Rain Kills'	35	35
		a. Large full stop after '4'	20·00	
1630	1060	28p. 'Ozone Layer'	40	40
1631	1061	33p. 'Greenhouse Effect'	55	55
1632	1062	39p. 'Bird of Hope'	70	70
Set of 4			1·75	1·75
Set of 4 Gutter Pairs			3·50	
First Day Cover				1·90
Presentation Pack (PO Pack No. 230)			2·00	
PHQ Cards (set of 4) (146)			80	1·90

Special First Day of Issue Postmarks
Philatelic Bureau, Edinburgh (in green)		2·00
Torridon (in green)		2·10

1063 European Star

(Des D. Hockney)

1992 (13 Oct). Single European Market. Multicoloured Phosphorised paper. Perf 15×14.

1633	1063	24p. European Star	40	40
Gutter Pair			80	
First Day Cover				75
Presentation Pack (PO Pack No. 231)			80	
PHQ Card (147)			20	50

Special First Day of Issue Postmarks
Philatelic Bureau, Edinburgh		75
Westminster		1·00

1064 Angel Gabriel, St James's, Pangbourne 
1065 Madonna and Child, St Mary's, Bibury

1066 King with Gold, Our Lady and St Peter, Leatherhead 
1067 Shepherds, All Saints, Porthcawl

1068 Kings with Frankincense and Myrrh, Our Lady and St Peter, Leatherhead

(Des Carroll, Dempsey and Thirkell Ltd from windows by Karl Parsons (18p., 24p., 33p.) and Paul Woodroffe (28p. 39p.))

1992 (10 Nov). Christmas. Stained-glass Windows. Multicoloured One centre band (18p.) or phosphorised paper (others). Perf 15×14.

1634	1064	18p. Angel Gabriel	25	25
		a. Booklet pane of 20	5·00	
		b. Imperf (pair)	£200	
1635	1065	24p. Madonna and Child	30	30
1636	1066	28p. King with Gold	40	40
1637	1067	33p. Shepherds	55	55
1638	1068	39p. Kings with Frankincense and Myrrh	70	70
Set of 5			2·00	2·00
Set of 5 Gutter Pairs			4·00	
First Day Cover				2·10
Presentation Pack (PO Pack No. 232)			2·25	
PHQ Cards (set of 5) (148)			1·00	2·25

Booklet pane No. 1634a comes from a special £3 Christmas booklet and has margins at left, top and bottom.

Special First Day of Issue Postmarks
Philatelic Bureau, Edinburgh		2·10
Bethlehem, Llandeilo, Dyfed		2·10
Pangbourne		2·25

Collectors Pack 1992

1992 (10 Nov). Comprises Nos. 1587/1591, 1602/1610 and 1615/1638.
CP1638a	Collectors Pack (PO Pack No. 233)	19·00

Post Office Yearbook

1992 (11 Nov). Comprises Nos. 1587/1591, 1602/1610 and 1615/1638 in hardbound book with slip case, illustrated in colour
YB1638a	Yearbook	19·00

1993/QUEEN ELIZABETH II

1069 Mute Swan Cob and St Catherine's Chapel, Abbotsbury
1070 Cygnet and Decoy 
1071 Swans and Cygnet 
1072 Eggs in Nest and Tithe Barn, Abbotsbury 
1073 Young Swan and the Fleet 

(Des D. Gentleman)

1993 (19 Jan). 600th Anniversary of Abbotsbury Swannery. Multicoloured One phosphor band (18p.) or phosphorised paper (others). Perf 14×15.

1639	1069	18p. Mute Swan Cob	30	30
1640	1070	24p. Cygnet	50	50
1641	1071	28p. Swans and Cygnet	80	80
1642	1072	33p. Eggs in Nest	1·00	1·00
1643	1073	39p. Young Swan	1·40	1·40
Set of 5			3·75	3·75
Set of 5 Gutter Pairs			7·50	
First Day Cover				4·00
Presentation Pack (PO Pack No. 234)			4·00	
PHQ Cards (set of 5) (149)			1·00	4·00

Special First Day of Issue Postmarks
Philatelic Bureau, Edinburgh .... 4·00
Abbotsbury, Dorset .... 4·00

1074 Long John Silver and Parrot (*Treasure Island*)
1075 Tweedledum and Tweedledee (*Alice Through the Looking-Glass*) 
1076 William (*William* books) 
1077 Mole and Toad (*The Wind in the Willows*) 
1078 Teacher and Wilfrid (*The Bash Street Kids*) 
1079 Peter Rabbit and Mrs Rabbit (*The Tale of Peter Rabbit*) 
1080 Snowman (*The Snowman*) and Father Christmas (*Father Christmas*) 
1081 The Big Friendly Giant and Sophie (*The BFG*) 
1082 Bill Badger and Rupert Bear 
1083 Aladdin and the Genie 

(Des Newell and Sorell)

1993 (2 Feb–10 Aug). Greetings Stamps. Gift Giving. Multicoloured Two phosphor bands. Perf 15×14 (with one elliptical hole in each horizontal side).

1644	1074	(1st) Long John Silver and Parrot	1·20	1·00
		a. Booklet pane. Nos. 1644/1653	13·50	
1645	1075	(1st) Tweedledum and Tweedledee	1·20	1·00
1646	1076	(1st) William	1·20	1·00
1647	1077	(1st) Mole and Toad	1·20	1·00
1648	1078	(1st) Teacher and Wilfrid	1·20	1·00
1649	1079	(1st) Peter Rabbit and Mrs Rabbit (Mrs Rabbit in blue dress)	1·20	1·00
		a. Peter Rabbit and Mrs Rabbit (Mrs Rabbit in lilac dress) (10.8.93)	1·25	1·40
		b. Booklet pane. No. 1649a×4 with margins all round (10.8.93)	5·00	
1650	1080	(1st) Snowman and Father Christmas	1·20	1·00
1651	1081	(1st) The Big Friendly Giant and Sophie	1·20	1·00
1652	1082	(1st) Bill Badger and Rupert Bear	1·20	1·00
1653	1083	(1st) Aladdin and the Genie	1·20	1·00
Set of 10			10·50	9·25
First Day Cover				9·50
Presentation Pack (PO Pack No. G2)			13·50	
PHQ Cards (set of 10) (GS1)			2·00	9·50

Nos. 1644/1653 were issued in £2·40 booklet, No. KX5 (*sold at £2·50 from 1 November 1993*), together with a pane of 20 half stamp-sized labels. The stamps and labels were affixed to the booklet cover by a common gutter margin

No. 1649a and booklet pane 1649b come from the £6 (£5·64) Beatrix Potter booklet No. DX15.

Special First Day of Issue Postmarks
Philatelic Bureau, Edinburgh (No. 1644a) (2.2.93) .... 9·50
Greetland (No. 1644a) (2.2.93) .... 9·50
Philatelic Bureau, Edinburgh (No. 1649b) (10.8.93) .... 5·50
Keswick (No. 1649b) (10.8.93) .... 5·50

SET PRICES. Please note that set prices for booklet greetings stamps are for complete panes. Sets of single stamps are worth considerably less.

1084 Decorated Enamel Dial
1085 Escapement, Remontoire and Fusée

QUEEN ELIZABETH II/1993

1086 Balance, Spring and Temperature Compensator
1087 Back of Movement 

(Des H. Brown and D. Penny. Litho Questa)

1993 (16 Feb). 300th Birth Anniversary of John Harrison (inventor of the marine chronometer). Details of 'H4' Clock. Multicoloured Phosphorised paper. Perf 14½×14.

1654	1084	24p. Decorated Enamel Dial	30	30
1655	1085	28p. Escapement, Remontoire and Fusée	45	45
1656	1086	33p. Balance, Spring and Temperature Compensator	55	55
1657	1087	39p. Back of Movement	70	70
Set of 4			1·75	1·75
Set of 4 Gutter Pairs			3·50	
First Day Cover				2·00
Presentation Pack (PO Pack No. 235)			2·00	
PHQ Cards (set of 4) (150)			80	2·00

Special First Day of Issue Postmarks
Philatelic Bureau, Edinburgh ... 2·00
Greenwich ... 2·25

1088 Britannia

(Des B. Craddock, adapted Roundel Design Group. Litho (silver die-stamped, Braille symbol for 'TEN' embossed) Questa)

1993 (2 Mar). Granite paper. Multicoloured Perf 14×14½ (with two elliptical holes in each horizontal side).

1658	1088	£10 Britannia	40·00	12·00
		a. Silver omitted	£3000	
		b. Braille symbol for 'TEN' omitted	£1800	
		c. Fluorescent 'Ten Pounds'*	65·00	25·00
First Day Cover				18·00
Presentation Pack (PO Pack No. 28)			45·00	
PHQ Card (D1)			50	25·00

* Examples from Plate 2A also show 'Ten Pounds' at the bottom right-hand corner under UV light (No. 1658c).

The paper used for No. 1658 contains fluorescent coloured fibres which, together with the ink used on the shield, react under UV light.

Special First Day of Issue Postmarks
Philatelic Bureau, Edinburgh ... 18·00
Windsor ... 20·00

1089 Dendrobium hellwigianum
1090 Paphiopedilum Maudiae 'Magnificum' 
1091 Cymbidium lowianum 
1092 Vanda Rothschildiana 
1093 Dendrobium vexillarius var albiviride 

(Des Pandora Sellars)

1993 (16 Mar). 14th World Orchid Conference, Glasgow. Multicoloured One phosphor band (18p.) or phosphorised paper (others). Perf 15×14.

1659	1089	18p. Dendrobium hellwigianum	30	30
		a. Imperf (pair)	£3500	
1660	1090	24p. Paphiopedilum Maudiae 'Magnificum'	35	35
1661	1091	28p. Cymbidium lowianum	45	45
1662	1092	33p. Vanda Rothschildiana	50	50
		a. Copyright logo and '1993' omitted (R. 10/6, dot pane)	20·00	20·00
1663	1093	39p. Dendrobium vexillarius var albiviride	60	60
Set of 5			2·00	2·00
Set of 5 Gutter Pairs			4·00	
First Day Cover				2·25
Presentation Pack (PO Pack No. 236)			2·25	
PHQ Cards (set of 5) (151)			1·00	2·25

Special First Day of Issue Postmarks
Philatelic Bureau, Edinburgh ... 2·25
Glasgow ... 2·40

For Nos. 1664/1672 and Y1667/Y1803 see Decimal Machin Definitives section.

1094 Family Group (bronze sculpture) (Henry Moore)
1095 Kew Gardens (lithograph) (Edward Bawden) 
1096 St Francis and the Birds (Stanley Spencer) 
1097 Still Life: Odyssey I (Ben Nicholson) 

(Des. A. Dastor)

1993 (11 May). Europa. Contemporary Art. Multicoloured Phosphorised paper. Perf 14×14½.

1767	1094	24p. Family Group (bronze sculpture) (Henry Moore)	35	35
1768	1095	28p. Kew Gardens (lithograph) (Edward Bawden)	50	50
1769	1096	33p. St Francis and the Birds (Stanley Spencer)	60	60
1770	1097	39p. Still Life: Odyssey I (Ben Nicholson)	70	70
Set of 4			2·00	2·00
Set of 4 Gutter Pairs			4·00	
First Day Cover				2·25
Presentation Pack (PO Pack No. 237)			2·25	
PHQ Cards (set of 4) (152)			80	2·25

Special First Day of Issue Postmarks
British Philatelic Bureau, Edinburgh ... 2·25
London SW ... 2·40

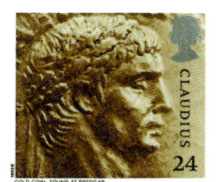

1993/QUEEN ELIZABETH II

1098 Emperor Claudius (from gold coin)
1099 Emperor Hadrian (bronze head) 
1100 Goddess Roma (from gemstone) 
1101 Christ (Hinton St Mary mosaic) 

(Des J. Gibbs)

1993 (15 June). Roman Britain. Multicoloured Phosphorised paper with two phosphor bands. Perf 14×14½.

1771	1098	24p. Emperor Claudius	35	35
1772	1099	28p. Emperor Hadrian	50	50
1773	1100	33p. Goddess Roma	60	60
1774	1101	39p. Christ	70	70
Set of 4			2·00	2·00
Set of 4 Gutter Pairs			4·00	
First Day Cover				2·25
Presentation Pack (PO Pack No. 238)			2·25	
PHQ Cards (set of 4) (153)			80	2·25

Special First Day of Issue Postmarks
Philatelic Bureau, Edinburgh ... 2·40
Caerllion ... 2·40

1102 *Midland Maid* and other Narrow Boats, Grand Junction Canal
1103 *Yorkshire Lass* and other Humber Keels, Stainforth and Keadby Canal 
1104 *Valley Princess* and other Horse-drawn Barges, Brecknock and Abergavenny Canal 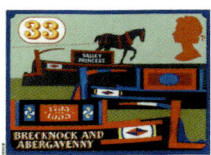
1105 Steam Barges, including *Pride of Scotland*, and Fishing Boats, Crinan Canal 

(Des T. Lewery. Litho Questa)

1993 (20 July). Inland Waterways. Multicoloured Two phosphor bands. Perf 14½×14.

1775	1102	24p. Narrow Boats, Grand Junction Canal	35	35
1776	1103	28p. Humber Keels, Stainforth and Keadby Canal	50	50
1777	1104	33p. Horse-drawn Barges, Brecknock and Abergavenny Canal	60	60
1778	1105	39p. Steam Barges and Fishing Boats, Crinan Canal	70	70
Set of 4			2·00	2·00
Set of 4 Gutter Pairs			4·00	
First Day Cover				2·25
Presentation Pack (PO Pack No. 239)			2·25	
PHQ Cards (set of 4) (154)			50	2·25

Nos. 1775/1778 commemorate the bicentenary of the Acts of Parliament authorising the canals depicted.

Special First Day of Issue Postmarks
Philatelic Bureau, Edinburgh ... 2·40
Gloucester ... 2·40

1106 Horse Chestnut
1107 Blackberry 
1108 Hazel 
1109 Rowan 
1110 Pear 

(Des Charlotte Knox)

1993 (14 Sept). The Four Seasons. Autumn. Fruits and Leaves. Multicoloured One phosphor band (18p.) or phosphorised paper (others). Perf 15×14.

1779	1106	18p. Horse Chestnut	30	30
1780	1107	24p. Blackberry	35	35
1781	1108	28p. Hazel	45	45
1782	1109	33p. Rowan	50	50
1783	1110	39p. Pear	60	60
Set of 5			2·00	2·00
Set of 5 Gutter Pairs			4·00	
First Day Cover				2·25
Presentation Pack (PO Pack No. 240)			2·25	
PHQ Cards (set of 5) (155)			1·00	2·25

Special First Day of Issue Postmarks
Philatelic Bureau, Edinburgh ... 2·40
Taunton ... 2·50

1111 The Reigate Squire
1112 The Hound of the Baskervilles 
1113 The Six Napoleons 
1114 The Greek Interpreter

QUEEN ELIZABETH II/1993

1115 *The Final Problem*

(Des A. Davidson. Litho Questa)

1993 (12 Oct). Sherlock Holmes. Centenary of the Publication of *The Final Problem*. Multicoloured Phosphorised paper. Perf 14×14½.

1784	**1111**	24p. *The Reigate Squire*	30	30
		a. Horiz strip of 5. Nos. 1784/1788	1·90	2·40
1785	**1112**	24p. *The Hound of the Baskervilles*	30	30
1786	**1113**	24p. *The Six Napoleons*	30	30
1787	**1114**	24p. *The Greek Interpreter*	30	30
1788	**1115**	24p. *The Final Problem*	30	30
Set of 5			1·90	2·40
Gutter strip of 10			3·75	
First Day Cover				2·50
Presentation Pack (PO Pack No. 241)			2·75	
PHQ Cards (set of 5) (156)			1·00	2·50

Nos. 1784/1788 were printed together, *se-tenant*, in horizontal strips of five throughout the sheet.

Special First Day of Issue Postmarks
Philatelic Bureau, Edinburgh	2·50
London NW1	2·75

A First Day of Issue handstamp was provided at Autumn Stampex, London SW1, for this issue.

For No. 1789, T **1116**, see Decimal Machin Definitives section.

1117 Bob Cratchit and Tiny Tim
1118 Mr and Mrs Fezziwig 
1119 Scrooge 
1120 The Prize Turkey 
1121 Mr Scrooge's Nephew 

(Des Q. Blake)

1993 (9 Nov). Christmas. 150th Anniversary of Publication of *A Christmas Carol* by Charles Dickens. Multicoloured. One phosphor band (19p.) or phosphorised paper (others). Perf 15×14.

1790	**1117**	19p. Bob Cratchit and Tiny Tim	30	30
		a. Imperf (pair)	£3000	
1791	**1118**	25p. Mr and Mrs Fezziwig	40	40
1792	**1119**	30p. Scrooge	50	50
1793	**1120**	35p. The Prize Turkey	55	55
1794	**1121**	41p. Mr Scrooge's Nephew	65	65
Set of 5			2·10	2·10
Set of 5 Gutter Pairs			4·25	
First Day Cover				2·50
Presentation Pack (PO Pack No. 242)			2·75	
PHQ Cards (set of 5) (157)			1·00	2·25

Special First Day of Issue Postmarks
Philatelic Bureau, Edinburgh	2·50
Bethlehem, Llandeilo	2·50

A First Day of Issue handstamp (pictorial) was provided at the City of London for this issue.

Collectors Pack 1993

1993 (9 Nov). Comprises Nos. 1639/1643, 1654/1657, 1659/1663, 1767/1788 and 1790/1794.
CP1794a	Collectors Pack (PO Pack No. 243)	22·00

Post Office Yearbook

1993 (9 Nov). Comprises Nos. 1639/1643, 1654/1657, 1659/1663, 1767/1788 and 1790/1794 in hardbound book with slip case, illustrated in colour
YB1794a	Yearbook	20·00

1122 Class 5 No. 44957 and Class B1 No. 61342 on West Highland Line
1123 Class A1 No. 60149 *Amadis* at Kings Cross 
1124 Class 4 No. 43000 on Turntable at Blyth North 
1125 Class 4 No. 42455 near Wigan Central 
1126 Class Castle No. 7002 *Devizes Castle* on Bridge crossing Worcester and Birmingham Canal 

(Des B. Delaney)

1994 (18 Jan). The Age of Steam. Railway Photographs by Colin Gifford. Multicoloured One phosphor band (19p.) or phosphorised paper with two bands (others). Perf 14½.

1795	**1122**	19p. Class 5 No. 44957 and Class B1 No. 61342	30	30
1796	**1123**	25p. Class A1 No. 60149 *Amadis*	40	40
1797	**1124**	30p. Class 4 No. 43000 on Turntable	50	50
1798	**1125**	35p. Class 4 No. 42455	60	60
1799	**1126**	41p. Class Castle No. 7002 *Devizes Castle* on Bridge	70	70
Set of 5			2·25	2·25
Set of 5 Gutter Pairs			4·50	
First Day Cover				2·50
Presentation Pack (PO Pack No. 244)			3·00	
PHQ Cards (set of 5) (158)			1·00	2·50

Nos. 1796/1799 are on phosphorised paper and also show two phosphor bands.

Special First Day of Issue Postmarks
Philatelic Bureau, Edinburgh	2·50
York	2·50

A First Day of Issue handstamp (pictorial) was provided at Bridge of Orchy for this issue.

1994/QUEEN ELIZABETH II

1127 Dan Dare and the Mekon
1128 The Three Bears 
1129 Rupert Bear 
1130 Alice (*Alice in Wonderland*) 
1131 Noggin and the Ice Dragon 
1132 Peter Rabbit posting Letter 
1133 Red Riding Hood and the Wolf 
1134 Orlando Marmalade Cat 
1135 Biggles 
1136 Paddington Bear on Station 

(Des Newell and Sorrell)

1994 (1 Feb). Greetings Stamps. Messages. Multicoloured Two phosphor bands. Perf 15×14 (with one elliptical hole in each vertical side).

1800	1127	(1st) Dan Dare and the Mekon	1·20	1·00
		a. Booklet pane. Nos. 1800/1809	13·50	
1801	1128	(1st) The Three Bears	1·20	1·00
1802	1129	(1st) Rupert Bear	1·20	1·00
1803	1130	(1st) Alice (*Alice in Wonderland*)	1·20	1·00
1804	1131	(1st) Noggin and the Ice Dragon	1·20	1·00
1805	1132	(1st) Peter Rabbit posting Letter	1·20	1·00
1806	1133	(1st) Red Riding Hood and the Wolf	1·20	1·00
1807	1134	(1st) Orlando Marmalade Cat	1·20	1·00
1808	1135	(1st) Biggles	1·20	1·00
1809	1136	(1st) Paddington Bear on Station	1·20	1·00
Set of 10			10·50	9·00
First Day Cover				9·25
Presentation Pack (PO Pack No. G3)			13·50	
PHQ Cards (set of 10) (GS2)			2·00	9·25

Nos. 1800/1809 were issued in £2·50 stamp booklet, No. KX6 (*sold at £2·60 from 8 July 1996*), together with a pane of 20 half stamp-sized labels.
The stamps and labels were attached to the booklet cover by a common gutter margin.

Special First Day of Issue Postmarks
Philatelic Bureau, Edinburgh .... 9·25
Penn, Wolverhampton .... 9·25

1137 Castell Y Waun (Chirk Castle), Clwyd, Wales
1138 Ben Arkle, Sutherland, Scotland 
1139 Mourne Mountains, County Down, Northern Ireland 
1140 Dersingham, Norfolk, England 
1141 Dolwyddelan, Gwynedd, Wales 

1994 (1 Mar–26 July). 25th Anniversary of Investiture of the Prince of Wales. Paintings by Prince Charles. Multicoloured One phosphor band (19p.) or phosphorised paper (others). Perf 15×14.

1810	1137	19p. Castell Y Waun (Chirk Castle), Clwyd, Wales	30	30
1811	1138	25p. Ben Arkle, Sutherland, Scotland	35	35
1812	1139	30p. Mourne Mountains, County Down, Northern Ireland	45	45
		a. Booklet pane. No. 1812×4 with margins all round (26.7.94)	1·75	1·75
1813	1140	35p. Dersingham, Norfolk, England	60	60
1814	1141	41p. Dolwyddelan, Gwynedd, Wales	70	70
Set of 5			2·25	2·25
Set of 5 Gutter Pairs			4·50	
First Day Cover				2·40
Presentation Pack (PO Pack No. 245)			2·50	
PHQ Cards (set of 5) (159)			1·00	2·50

Booklet pane No. 1812a comes from the £6·04 Northern Ireland booklet No. DX16.

Special First Day of Issue Postmarks
Philatelic Bureau, Edinburgh .... 2·50
Caernarfon .... 2·50

1142 Bather at Blackpool
1143 Where's my Little Lad? 
1144 Wish You were Here! 
1145 Punch and Judy Show 

131

QUEEN ELIZABETH II/1994

1146 The Tower Crane Machine

(Des M. Dempsey and B. Dare. Litho Questa)

1994 (12 Apr). Centenary of Picture Postcards. Multicoloured One side band (19p.) or two phosphor bands (others). Perf 14×14½.

1815	**1142**	19p. Bather at Blackpool	30	30
1816	**1143**	25p. Where's my Little Lad?	35	35
1817	**1144**	30p. Wish You were Here!	45	45
1818	**1145**	35p. Punch and Judy Show	60	60
1819	**1146**	41p. The Tower Crane Machine	70	70
Set of 5			2·25	2·25
Set of 5 Gutter Pairs			4·50	
First Day Cover				2·40
Presentation Pack (PO Pack No. 246)			2·40	
PHQ Cards (set of 5) (160)			1·00	2·40

Special First Day of Issue Postmarks
Philatelic Bureau, Edinburgh	2·50
Blackpool	2·50

1147 British Lion and French Cockerel over Tunnel

1148 Symbolic Hands over Train

(Des G. Hardie (T **1147**), J.-P. Cousin (T **1148**))

1994 (3 May). Opening of Channel Tunnel. Multicoloured Phosphorised paper. Perf 14×14½

1820	**1147**	25p. British Lion and French Cockerel	30	35
		a. Horiz pair. Nos. 1820/1821	1·00	1·10
1821	**1148**	25p. Symbolic Hands over Train	30	35
1822	**1147**	41p. British Lion and French Cockerel	50	60
		a. Horiz pair. Nos. 1822/1823	1·50	1·75
		ab. Imperf (horiz pair)	£2500	
1823	**1148**	41p. Symbolic Hands over Train	50	60
Set of 4			2·25	2·50
First Day Cover				2·75
First Day Covers (2) (UK and French stamps)				6·00
Presentation Pack (PO Pack No. 247)			2·75	
Presentation Pack (UK and French Stamps)			15·00	
Souvenir Book			32·00	
PHQ Cards (set of 4) (161)			60	2·50

Nos. 1820/1821 and 1822/1823 were printed together, *se-tenant*, in horizontal pairs throughout the sheets.

Stamps in similar designs were also issued by France. These are included in the joint presentation pack and souvenir book.

Special First Day of Issue Postmarks
Philatelic Bureau, Edinburgh	2·75
Folkestone	3·00

1149 Groundcrew replacing Smoke Canisters on Douglas Boston of 88 Sqn

1150 HMS *Warspite* (battleship) shelling Enemy Positions

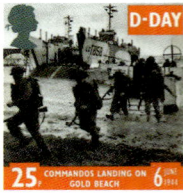

1151 Commandos landing on Gold Beach

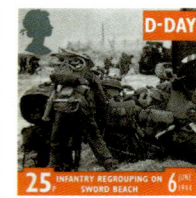

1152 Infantry regrouping on Sword Beach

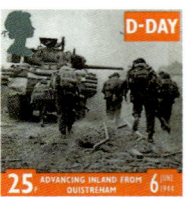

1153 Tank and Infantry advancing, Ouistreham

(Des K. Bassford from contemporary photographs. Litho Questa)

1994 (6 June). 50th Anniversary of D-Day. Multicoloured Two phosphor bands. Perf 14½×14.

1824	**1149**	25p. Groundcrew replacing Smoke Canisters on Douglas Boston	35	30
		a. Horiz strip of 5. Nos. 1824/1828	2·10	1·75
1825	**1150**	25p. HMS *Warspite* shelling Enemy Positions	35	30
1826	**1151**	25p. Commandos landing on Gold Beach	35	30
1827	**1152**	25p. Infantry regrouping on Sword Beach	35	30
1828	**1153**	25p. Tank and Infantry advancing, Ouistreham	35	30
Set of 5			2·10	1·75
Gutter block of 10			4·25	
First Day Cover				1·90
Presentation Pack (PO Pack No. 248)			2·40	
PHQ Cards (set of 5) (162)			1·00	1·90

Nos. 1824/1828 were printed together, *se-tenant*, in horizontal strips of five throughout the sheet.

Special First Day of Issue Postmarks
Philatelic Bureau, Edinburgh	2·00
Portsmouth	2·00

1154 The Old Course, St Andrews

1155 The 18th Hole, Muirfield

1994/QUEEN ELIZABETH II

1156 The 15th Hole ('Luckyslap'), Carnoustie

1157 The 8th Hole ('The Postage Stamp'), Royal Troon

1158 The 9th Hole, Turnberry

(Des P. Hogarth)

1994 (5 July). Scottish Golf Courses. Multicoloured One phosphor band (19p.) or phosphorised paper (others). Perf 14½×14.

1829	1154	19p. The Old Course, St Andrews	30	30
1830	1155	25p. The 18th Hole, Muirfield	35	35
1831	1156	30p. The 15th Hole ('Luckyslap'), Carnoustie	45	45
1832	1157	35p. The 8th Hole ('The Postage Stamp'), Royal Troon	60	60
1833	1158	41p. The 9th Hole, Turnberry	70	70
Set of 5			2·10	2·10
Set of 5 Gutter Pairs			4·25	
First Day Cover				2·25
Presentation Pack (PO Pack No. 249)			2·40	
PHQ Cards (set of 5) (163)			1·00	2·25

Nos. 1829/1833 commemorate the 250th anniversary of golf's first set of rules produced by the Honourable Company of Edinburgh Golfers.

Special First Day of Issue Postmarks
Philatelic Bureau, Edinburgh		2·25
Turnberry		2·50

1159 Royal Welsh Show, Llanelwedd

1160 All England Tennis Championships, Wimbledon

1161 Cowes Week

1162 Test Match, Lord's

1163 Braemar Gathering

(Des M. Cook)

1994 (2 Aug). The Four Seasons. Summertime. Multicoloured One phosphor band (19p.) or phosphorised paper (others). Perf 15×14.

1834	1159	19p. Royal Welsh Show, Llanelwedd	30	30
1835	1160	25p. All England Tennis Championships, Wimbledon	35	35
1836	1161	30p. Cowes Week	45	45
1837	1162	35p. Test Match, Lord's	60	60
1838	1163	41p. Braemar Gathering	70	70
Set of 5			2·10	2·10
Set of 5 Gutter Pairs			4·25	
First Day Cover				2·25
Presentation Pack (PO Pack No. 250)			2·40	
PHQ Cards (set of 5) (164)			1·00	2·25

Special First Day of Issue Postmarks
Philatelic Bureau, Edinburgh		2·25
Wimbledon		2·25

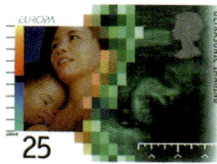

1164 Ultrasonic Imaging

1165 Scanning Electron Microscopy

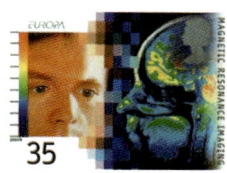

1166 Magnetic Resonance Imaging

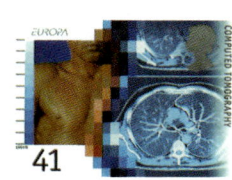

1167 Computed Tomography

(Des P. Vermier and J.-P. Tibbles. Gravure Enschedé)

1994 (27 Sept). Europa. Medical Discoveries. Multicoloured Phosphorised paper. Perf 14×14½.

1839	1164	25p. Ultrasonic Imaging	40	40
		a. Imperf (vert pair)	£3250	
1840	1165	30p. Scanning Electron Microscopy	50	50
1841	1166	35p. Magnetic Resonance Imaging	60	60
1842	1167	41p. Computed Tomography	70	70
Set of 4			2·00	2·00
Set of 4 Gutter Pairs			4·00	
First Day Cover				2·25
Presentation Pack (PO Pack No. 251)			2·40	
PHQ Cards (set of 4) (165)			80	2·25

Special First Day of Issue Postmarks
Philatelic Bureau, Edinburgh		2·25
Cambridge		2·25

1168 Mary and Joseph

1169 Three Wise Men

1170 Mary with Doll

1171 Shepherds

1172 Angels

QUEEN ELIZABETH II/1994

(Des Yvonne Gilbert)

1994 (1 Nov). Christmas. Children's Nativity Plays. Multicoloured One phosphor band (19p.) or phosphorised paper (others). Perf 15×14.

1843	1168	19p. Mary and Joseph	30	30
		a. Imperf (pair)	£125	
1844	1169	25p. Three Wise Men	35	35
1845	1170	30p. Mary with Doll	45	45
		a. Imperf (pair)	—	
1846	1171	35p. Shepherds	55	60
1847	1172	41p. Angels	65	70
Set of 5			2·00	2·10
Set of 5 Gutter Pairs			4·00	
First Day Cover				2·25
Presentation Pack (PO Pack No. 252)			2·25	
PHQ Cards (set of 5) (166)			1·00	2·25

Special First Day of Issue Postmarks
Philatelic Bureau, Edinburgh .... 2·25
Bethlehem, Llandeilo .... 2·25

Collectors Pack 1994

1994 (14 Nov). Comprises Nos. 1795/1847.
CP1847a   Collectors Pack (PO Pack No. 253) ...... 27·00

Post Office Yearbook

1994 (14 Nov). 1795/1799 and 1810/1847 in hardbound book with slip case, illustrated in colour
YB1847a   Yearbook .... 20·00

1173 Sophie (black cat)

1174 Puskas (Siamese) and Tigger (tabby)

1175 Chloe (ginger cat)

1176 Kikko (tortoiseshell) and Rosie (Abyssinian)

1177 Fred (black and white cat)

(Des Elizabeth Blackadder. Litho Questa)

1995 (17 Jan). Cats. Multicoloured One phosphor band (19p.) or two phosphor bands (others). Perf 14½×14.

1848	1173	19p. Sophie	30	30
1849	1174	25p. Puskas and Tigger	40	40
1850	1175	30p. Chloe	50	50
1851	1176	35p. Kikko and Rosie	60	60
1852	1177	41p. Fred	70	70
Set of 5			2·25	2·25
Set of 5 Gutter Pairs			4·50	
First Day Cover				2·50
Presentation Pack (PO Pack No. 254)			2·50	
PHQ Cards (set of 5) (167)			1·00	2·50

Special First Day of Issue Postmarks
Philatelic Bureau, Edinburgh .... 2·50
Kitts Green .... 2·50

1178 Dandelions

1179 Chestnut Leaves

1180 Garlic Leaves

1181 Hazel Leaves

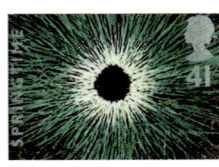

1182 Spring Grass

1995 (14 Mar). The Four Seasons. Springtime. Plant Sculptures by Andy Goldsworthy. Multicoloured One phosphor band (19p.) or two phosphor bands (others). Perf 15×14.

1853	1178	19p. Dandelions	30	30
1854	1179	25p. Chestnut Leaves	35	35
1855	1180	30p. Garlic Leaves	45	45
1856	1181	35p. Hazel Leaves	55	55
1857	1182	41p. Spring Grass	65	65
Set of 5			2·00	2·00
Set of 5 Gutter Pairs			4·00	
First Day Cover				2·25
Presentation Pack (PO Pack No. 255)			2·40	
PHQ Cards (set of 5) (168)			1·00	2·25

Special First Day of Issue Postmarks
Philatelic Bureau, Edinburgh .... 2·40
Springfield .... 2·40

1183 *La Danse à la Campagne* (Renoir)

1184 *Troilus and Criseyde* (Peter Brookes)

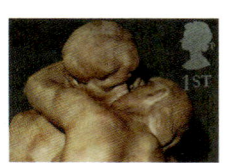

1185 *The Kiss* (Rodin)

1186 *Girls on the Town* (Beryl Cook)

1187 *Jazz* (Andrew Mockett)

1188 *Girls performing a Kathak Dance* (Aurangzeb period)

1995/QUEEN ELIZABETH II

1189 *Alice Keppel with her Daughter* (Alice Hughes)

1190 *Children Playing* (L. S. Lowry)

1191 *Circus Clowns* (Emily Firmin and Justin Mitchell)

1192 Decoration from *All the Love Poems of Shakespeare* (Eric Gill)

(Des Newell and Sorrell. Litho Walsall)

1995 (21 Mar). Greetings Stamps. Greetings in Art. Multicoloured Two phosphor bands. Perf 14½×14 (with one elliptical hole in each vertical side).

1858	1183	(1st) *La Danse à la Campagne*	1·20	1·00
		a. Booklet pane. Nos. 1858/1867	13·50	
		ab. Silver (Queen's head and '1ST') and phosphor omitted	£6000	
1859	1184	(1st) *Troilus and Criseyde*	1·20	1·00
1860	1185	(1st) *The Kiss*	1·20	1·00
1861	1186	(1st) *Girls on the Town*	1·20	1·00
1862	1187	(1st) *Jazz*	1·20	1·00
1863	1188	(1st) *Girls performing a Kathak Dance*	1·20	1·00
1864	1189	(1st) *Alice Keppel with her Daughter*	1·20	1·00
1865	1190	(1st) *Children Playing*	1·20	1·00
1866	1191	(1st) *Circus Clowns*	1·20	1·00
1867	1192	(1st) Decoration from *All the Love Poems of Shakespeare*	1·20	1·00
Set of 10			10·50	9·00
First Day Cover				9·25
Presentation Pack (PO Pack No. G4)			13·50	
PHQ Cards (set of 10) (GS3)			2·00	9·25

Nos. 1858/1867 were issued in £2·50 stamp booklet, No. KX7 (sold at £2·60 from 8 July 1996), together with a pane of 20 half stamp-sized labels. The stamps and labels were attached to the booklet cover by a common gutter margin.

No. 1858ab exists on first day covers bearing the Philatelic Bureau Edinburgh First Day of Issue postmark.

Special First Day of Issue Postmarks
Philatelic Bureau, Edinburgh .... 9·25
Lover .... 9·25

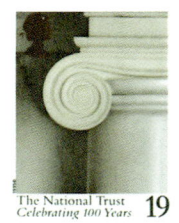

1193 Fireplace Decoration, Attingham Park, Shropshire

1194 Oak Seedling

1195 Carved Table Leg, Attingham Park

1196 St David's Head, Dyfed, Wales

1197 Elizabethan Window, Little Moreton Hall, Cheshire

(Des T. Evans)

1995 (11–25 Apr). Centenary of The National Trust. Multicoloured One phosphor band (19p.), two phosphor bands (25p., 35p.) or phosphorised paper (30p., 41p.). Perf 14×15.

1868	1193	19p. Fireplace Decoration	30	30
1869	1194	25p. Oak Seedling	35	35
		a. Booklet pane. No. 1869×6 with margins all round (25.4.96)	2·00	
1870	1195	30p. Carved Table Leg	45	45
1871	1196	35p. St David's Head	55	55
1872	1197	41p. Elizabethan Window	65	65
Set of 5			2·00	2·00
Set of 5 Gutter Pairs			4·00	
First Day Cover				2·25
Presentation Pack (PO Pack No. 256)			2·40	
PHQ Cards (set of 5) (169)			1·00	2·25

Booklet pane No. 1869a comes from the £6 National Trust booklet No. DX17.

Special First Day of Issue Postmarks
Philatelic Bureau, Edinburgh .... 2·40
Alfriston .... 2·40

1198 British Troops and French Civilians celebrating

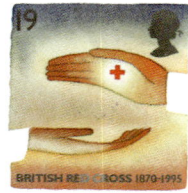

1199 Symbolic Hands and Red Cross

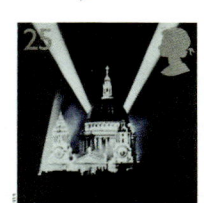

1200 St Paul's Cathedral and Searchlights

1201 Symbolic Hand releasing Peace Dove

1202 Symbolic Hands

(Des J. Gorham (Nos. 1873, 1875), J-M. Folon (others))

1995 (2 May). Europa. Peace and Freedom. Multicoloured One phosphor band (Nos. 1873/1874) or two phosphor bands (others). Perf 14½×14.

1873	1198	19p. British Troops and French Civilians celebrating	35	35
1874	1199	19p. Symbolic Hands and Red Cross	35	35
1875	1200	25p. St Paul's Cathedral and Searchlights	45	45
1876	1201	25p. Symbolic Hand releasing Peace Dove	45	45

QUEEN ELIZABETH II/1995

1877	**1202**	30p. Symbolic Hands		60	60
		a. Imperf (vert pair)		—	
Set of 5				2·00	2·00
Set of 5 Gutter Pairs				4·00	
First Day Cover					2·25
Presentation Pack (PO Pack No. 257)				2·40	
PHQ Cards (set of 5) (170)				60	2·25

Nos. 1873 and 1875 commemorate the 50th anniversary of the end of the Second World War.

No. 1874 commemorate the 125th anniversary of the British Red Cross Society.

For No. 1875 with the face value expressed as '1st' see No. **MS**2547.

Nos. 1876/1877 commemorate the 50th anniversary of the United Nations.

Nos. 1876/1877 include the EUROPA emblem.

Special First Day of Issue Postmarks
Philatelic Bureau, Edinburgh	2·40
London SW	2·40

A First Day of Issue handstamp (pictorial) was provided at London EC4 for this issue.

1203 *The Time Machine*
1204 *The First Men in the Moon* 
1205 *The War of the Worlds* 
1206 *The Shape of Things to Come* 

(Des Siobhan Keaney. Litho Questa)

1995 (6 June). Science Fiction. Novels by H. G. Wells. Multicoloured Two phosphor bands. Perf 14½×14.

1878	**1203**	25p. The Time Machine		40	40
1879	**1204**	30p. The First Men in the Moon		50	50
1880	**1205**	35p. The War of the Worlds		60	60
1881	**1206**	41p. The Shape of Things to Come		70	70
Set of 4				2·00	2·00
Set of 4 Gutter Pairs				4·00	
First Day Cover					2·25
Presentation Pack (PO Pack No. 258)				2·40	
PHQ Cards (set of 4) (171)				50	2·25

Nos. 1878/1881 commemorate the centenary of publication of Wells's *The Time Machine*.

Special First Day of Issue Postmarks
Philatelic Bureau, Edinburgh	2·40
Wells	2·40

1207 *The Swan, 1595*
1208 *The Rose, 1592* 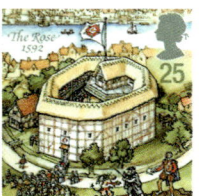
1209 *The Globe, 1599* 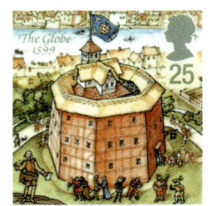
1210 *The Hope, 1613* 
1211 *The Globe, 1614* 

(Des C. Hodges. Litho Walsall)

1995 (8 Aug). Reconstruction of Shakespeare's Globe Theatre. Multicoloured Two phosphor bands. Perf 14½.

1882	**1207**	25p. The Swan, 1595		40	30
		a. Horiz strip of 5. Nos. 1882/1886		2·00	2·25
1883	**1208**	25p. The Rose, 1592		40	30
1884	**1209**	25p. The Globe, 1599		40	30
1885	**1210**	25p. The Hope, 1613		40	30
1886	**1211**	25p. The Globe, 1614		40	30
Set of 5				2·00	2·25
Gutter Strip of 10				4·00	
First Day Cover					2·40
Presentation Pack (PO Pack No. 259)				2·40	
PHQ Cards (set of 5) (172)				1·00	2·40

Nos. 1882/1886 were issued together, *se-tenant*, in horizontal strips of five throughout the sheet with the backgrounds forming a composite design.

Special First Day of Issue Postmarks
Philatelic Bureau, Edinburgh	2·50
Stratford-upon-Avon	2·50

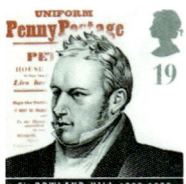

1212 Sir Rowland Hill and Uniform Penny Postage Petition
1213 Hill and Penny Black 
1214 Guglielmo Marconi and Early Wireless 
1215 Marconi and Sinking of *Titanic* (liner) 

(Des The Four Hundred, Eng C. Slania. Recess and litho Harrison)

1995 (5 Sept). Pioneers of Communications. Multicoloured One phosphor band (19p.) or phosphorised paper (others). Perf 14½×14.

1887	**1212**	19p. Sir Rowland Hill and Uniform Penny Postage Petition		40	40
1888	**1213**	25p. Hill and Penny Black		50	50
		a. Silver (Queen's head and face value) omitted		£800	
1889	**1214**	41p. Guglielmo Marconi and Early Wireless		65	65
1890	**1215**	60p. Marconi and Sinking of *Titanic* (liner)		75	75
Set of 4				2·10	2·10
Set of 4 Gutter Pairs				4·25	

1995/QUEEN ELIZABETH II

First Day Cover		2·25
Presentation Pack (PO Pack No. 260)	2·50	
PHQ Cards (set of 4) (173)	80	2·25

Nos. 1887/1888 mark the birth bicentenary of Sir Rowland Hill. Nos. 1889/1890 the centenary of the first radio transmissions.

Special First Day of Issue Postmarks
Philatelic Bureau, Edinburgh	2·25
London EC	2·25

1216 Harold Wagstaff
1217 Gus Risman 
1218 Jim Sullivan 
1219 Billy Batten 
1220 Brian Bevan 

(Des C. Birmingham)

1995 (3 Oct). Centenary of Rugby League. Multicoloured One phosphor band (19p.) or two phosphor bands (others). Perf 14½×14.

1891	1216	19p. Harold Wagstaff	30	30
1892	1217	25p. Gus Risman	35	35
1893	1218	30p. Jim Sullivan	45	45
1894	1219	35p. Billy Batten	55	55
1895	1220	41p. Brian Bevan	65	65
Set of 5			2·10	2·10
Set of 5 Gutter Pairs			4·25	
First Day Cover				2·25
Presentation Pack (PO Pack No. 261)			2·40	
PHQ Cards (set of 5) (174)			1·00	2·25

Special First Day of Issue Postmarks
Philatelic Bureau, Edinburgh	2·25
Huddersfield	2·25

A First Day of Issue handstamp (pictorial) was provided at Headingly, Leeds for this issue.

1221 European Robin in Mouth of Pillar Box
1222 European Robin on Railings and Holly 
1223 European Robin on Snow-covered Milk Bottles 
1224 European Robin on Road Sign 
1225 European Robin on Door Knob and Christmas Wreath 

(Des K. Lilly)

1995 (30 Oct). Christmas. Christmas Robins. Multicoloured One phosphor band (19p.) or two phosphor bands (others). Perf 15×14.

1896	1221	19p. Robin in Mouth of Pillar Box	30	30
1897	1222	25p. Robin on Railings	35	40
1898	1223	30p. Robin on Milk Bottles	50	55
1899	1224	41p. Robin on Road Sign	60	65
1900	1225	60p. Robin on Door Knob	75	80
Set of 5			2·25	2·50
Set of 5 Gutter Pairs			4·50	
First Day Cover				2·75
Presentation Pack (PO Pack No. 262)			2·50	
PHQ Cards (set of 5) (175)			1·00	2·75

The 19p. value was re-issued on 3 October 2000 in sheets of 20, each with a *se-tenant* label showing Christmas greetings (*sold for* £3·99) (No. LS2) or a personal photograph (*sold for* £7·99). These sheets were printed in gravure by Questa and were sold by the Philatelic Bureau and selected philatelic outlets.

Similar sheets were available from 9 October 2001 when the price for a personalised version was increased to £8·75. These could also be purchased, on an experimental basis, from photo-booths at six post offices.

Special First Day of Issue Postmarks
Philatelic Bureau, Edinburgh	2·90
Bethlehem, Llandeilo	2·90

Year Pack 1995

1995 (30 Oct). Comprises Nos. 1848/1900.
CP1900a	Year Pack (PO Pack No. 263)	25·00

Post Office Yearbook

1995 (30 Oct). Comprises Nos. 1848/1857 and 1868/1900 in hardback book with slip case, illustrated in colour
YB1900a	Yearbook	20·00

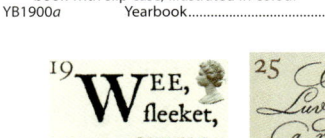

1226 Opening Lines of *To a Mouse* and Fieldmouse
1227 *O my Luve's like a red, red rose* and Wild Rose 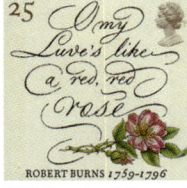
1228 *Scots, wha hae wi Wallace bled* and Sir William Wallace 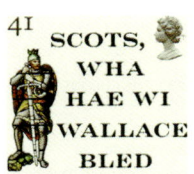
1229 *Auld Lang Syne* and Highland Dancers 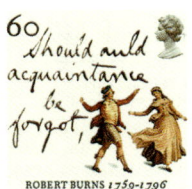

(Des Tayburn Design Consultancy. Litho Questa)

1996 (25 Jan). Death Bicentenary of Robert Burns (Scottish poet). Multicoloured One phosphor band (19p.) or two phosphor bands (others). Perf 14½.

1901	1226	19p. Opening Lines of *To a Mouse* and Fieldmouse	40	40
1902	1227	25p. *O my Luve's like a red, red rose* and Wild Rose	50	50
1903	1228	41p. *Scots, wha hae wi Wallace bled* and Sir William Wallace	65	70
1904	1229	60p. *Auld Lang Syne* and Highland Dancers	75	80
Set of 4			2·00	2·25
Set of 4 Gutter Pairs			4·00	
First Day Cover				2·40

QUEEN ELIZABETH II / 1996

Presentation Pack (PO Pack No. 264)			2·40	
PHQ Cards (set of 4) (176)			80	2·40

Special First Day of Issue Postmarks

Philatelic Bureau, Edinburgh		2·50
Dumfries		2·50

1230 'MORE! LOVE' (Mel Calman)
1231 'Sincerely' (Charles Barsotti) 
1232 'Do you have something for the HUMAN CONDITION?' (Leo Cullum) 
1233 'MENTAL FLOSS' (Mel Calman) 
1234 '4.55 P.M.' (Charles Barsotti) 
1235 'Dear lottery prize winner' (Larry) 
1236 'I'm writing to you because....' (Mel Calman) 
1237 'FETCH THIS, FETCH THAT' (Charles Barsotti) 
1238 'My day starts before I'm ready for it' (Mel Calman) 
1239 'THE CHEQUE IN THE POST' (Jack Ziegler) 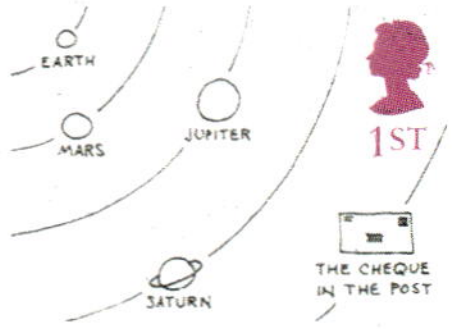

(Des M. Wolff. Litho Walsall)

1996 (26 Feb–11 Nov). Greetings Stamps. Cartoons. Multicoloured 'All over' phosphor. Perf 14½×14 (with one elliptical hole in each vertical side).

1905	1230	(1st) 'MORE! LOVE'	1·20	1·00
		a. Booklet pane. Nos. 1905/1914	13·50	
		p. Two phosphor bands (11.11.96)	2·50	2·50
		pa. Booklet pane. Nos. 1905p/1914p	24·00	24·00
1906	1231	(1st) 'Sincerely'	1·20	1·00
		p. Two phosphor bands (11.11.96)	2·50	2·50
1907	1232	(1st) 'Do you have something for the HUMAN CONDITION?'	1·20	1·00
		p. Two phosphor bands (11.11.96)	2·50	2·50
1908	1233	(1st) 'MENTAL FLOSS'	1·20	1·00
		p. Two phosphor bands (11.11.96)	2·50	2·50
1909	1234	(1st) '4.55 P.M.'	1·20	1·00
		p. Two phosphor bands (11.11.96)	2·50	2·50
1910	1235	(1st) 'Dear lottery prize winner'	1·20	1·00
		p. Two phosphor bands (11.11.96)	2·50	2·50
1911	1236	(1st) 'I'm writing to you because....'	1·20	1·00
		p. Two phosphor bands (11.11.96)	2·50	2·50
1912	1237	(1st) 'FETCH THIS, FETCH THAT'	1·20	1·00
		p. Two phosphor bands (11.11.96)	2·50	2·50
1913	1238	(1st) 'My day starts before I'm ready for it' (Mel Calman)	1·20	1·00
		p. Two phosphor bands (11.11.96)	2·50	2·50
1914	1239	(1st) 'THE CHEQUE IN THE POST' (Jack Ziegler)	1·20	1·00
		p. Two phosphor bands (11.11.96)	2·50	2·50
Set of 10 (Nos. 1905/1914)			10·50	9·00
Set of 10 (Nos. 1905p/1914p)			24·00	24·00
First Day Cover (Nos. 1905/1914)				9·50
Presentation Pack (PO Pack No. G5) (Nos. 1905/1914)			13·50	
PHQ Cards (set of 10) (GS4)			2·00	9·50

Nos. 1905/1914 were issued in £2·50 stamp booklets, Nos. KX8/KX8a (sold at £2·60 *from 8 July 1996*), together with a pane of 20 half stamp-sized labels. The stamps and labels were attached to the booklet cover by a common gutter margin.

These designs were re-issued on 18 December 2001 in sheets of ten, each with a *se-tenant* label showing cartoon comments (*sold for £2·95*) (No. LS6). They were re-issued again on 29 July 2003 in sheets of 20 (*sold for £6·15*) containing two of each design, each stamp accompanied by a half stamp-size label showing a crossword grid (clues printed on the bottom sheet margin) (No. LS13). Sheets of 20 with personal photographs on the labels and a crossword puzzle in the bottom sheet margin were also available, at £14·95 a sheet from Royal Mail, Edinburgh and Post Office philatelic outlets, or £15 a sheet from photo-booths.

All these sheets were printed in lithography by Questa with two phosphor bands and perforated 14½×14 (without elliptical holes), and were available from the philatelic bureau and other selected philatelic outlets.

Special First Day of Issue Postmarks

Philatelic Bureau, Edinburgh	9·50
Titterhill, Haytons Bent, Ludlow	9·50

1240 'Muscovy Duck'
1241 'Lapwing' 
1242 'White-fronted Goose' 
1243 'Bittern' 
1244 'Whooper Swan' 

(Des Moseley Webb)

1996 (12 Mar). 50th Anniversary of the Wildfowl and Wetlands Trust. Bird Paintings by C. F. Tunnicliffe. Multicoloured One phosphor band (19p.) or phosphorised paper (others). Perf 14×14½.

1915	1240	19p. 'Muscovy Duck'	30	30
1916	1241	25p. 'Lapwing'	35	35
1917	1242	30p. 'White-fronted Goose'	45	45
1918	1243	35p. 'Bittern'	55	55
1919	1244	41p. 'Whooper Swan'	65	65
Set of 5			2·10	2·10
Set of 5 Gutter Pairs			4·25	
First Day Cover				2·40
Presentation Pack (PO Pack No. 265)			2·50	
PHQ Cards (set of 5) (177)			1·00	2·40

Special First Day of Issue Postmarks

Philatelic Bureau, Edinburgh	2·50
Slimbridge, Gloucester	2·75

1996 / QUEEN ELIZABETH II

1245 The Odeon, Harrogate
1246 Laurence Olivier and Vivien Leigh in *Lady Hamilton* (film) 
1247 Old Cinema Ticket 
1248 Pathé News Still 
1249 Cinema Sign, The Odeon, Manchester 

(Des The Chase, Gravure Harrison)

1996 (16 Apr). Centenary of Cinema. Multicoloured One phosphor band (19p.) or two phosphor bands (others). Perf 14×14½.

1920	1245	19p. The Odeon, Harrogate	30	30
1921	1246	25p. Laurence Olivier and Vivien Leigh in *Lady Hamilton*	35	35
1922	1247	30p. Old Cinema Ticket	45	45
1923	1248	35p. Pathé News Still	60	60
1924	1249	41p. Cinema Sign, The Odeon, Manchester	70	70
		Set of 5	2·25	2·25
		Set of 5 Gutter Pairs	4·50	
		First Day Cover		2·40
		Presentation Pack (PO Pack No. 266)	2·50	
		PHQ Cards (set of 5) (178)	1·00	2·40

Special First Day of Issue Postmarks
Philatelic Bureau, Edinburgh .... 2·50
London, WC2 .... 2·50

1250 Dixie Dean
1251 Bobby Moore 
1252 Duncan Edwards 
1253 Billy Wright 
1254 Danny Blanchflower 

(Des H. Brown. Litho Questa)

1996 (14 May). European Football Championship. Multicoloured One phosphor band (19p.) or two phosphor bands (others). Perf 14½×14.

1925	1250	19p. Dixie Dean	30	30
		a. Booklet pane. No. 1925×4 with margins all round	1·50	
1926	1251	25p. Bobby Moore	40	40
		a. Booklet pane. No. 1926×4 with margins all round	2·00	
1927	1252	35p. Duncan Edwards	50	50
		a. Booklet pane. Nos. 1927/1929, each×2, with margins all round	3·50	
1928	1253	41p. Billy Wright	60	60
1929	1254	60p. Danny Blanchflower	90	90
		Set of 5	2·50	2·50
		Set of 5 Gutter Pairs	5·00	
		First Day Cover		2·75
		Presentation Pack (PO Pack No. 267)	2·75	
		PHQ Cards (set of 5) (179)	1·00	2·75

Booklet panes Nos. 1925a, 1926a and 1927a come from the £6·48 European Football Championship booklet, No. DX18.

Special First Day of Issue Postmarks
Philatelic Bureau, Edinburgh .... 2·75
Wembley .... 2·75

1255 Athlete on Starting Blocks
1256 Javelin 
1257 Basketball 
1258 Swimming 
1259 Athlete celebrating and Olympic Rings 

(Des N. Knight. Litho Questa)

1996 (9 July). Olympic and Paralympic Games, Atlanta. Multicoloured Two phosphor bands. Perf 14½×14.

1930	1255	26p. Athlete on Starting Blocks	30	30
		a. Horiz strip of 5. Nos. 1930/1934	2·00	2·10
1931	1256	26p. Javelin	30	30
1932	1257	26p. Basketball	30	30
1933	1258	26p. Swimming	30	30
1934	1259	26p. Athlete celebrating and Olympic Rings	30	30
		Set of 5	2·00	2·10
		Gutter Strip of 10	4·00	
		First Day Cover		2·50
		Presentation Pack (PO Pack No. 268)	2·50	
		PHQ Cards (set of 5) (180)	1·00	2·50

Nos. 1930/1934 were printed together, *se-tenant*, in horizontal strips of five throughout the sheet.

For these designs with face value expressed as '1st' see No. **MS**2554.

139

QUEEN ELIZABETH II/1996

Special First Day of Issue Postmarks
Philatelic Bureau, Edinburgh	2·50
Much Wenlock	2·75

1260 Professor Dorothy Hodgkin (scientist)
1261 Dame Margot Fonteyn (ballerina) 
1262 Dame Elisabeth Frink (sculptress) 
1263 Dame Daphne du Maurier (novelist) 
1264 Dame Marea Hartman (sports administrator) 

(Des Stephanie Nash Gravure Harrison)

1996 (6 Aug). Europa. Famous Women. Multicoloured One phosphor band (20p.) or two phosphor bands (others). Perf 14½.

1935	**1260**	20p. Professor Dorothy Hodgkin	30	30
1936	**1261**	26p. Dame Margot Fonteyn	35	35
		a. Imperf (horiz pair)	£475	
1937	**1262**	31p. Dame Elisabeth Frink	50	50
1938	**1263**	37p. Dame Daphne du Maurier	60	60
1939	**1264**	43p. Dame Marea Hartman	70	70
Set of 5			2·25	2·25
Set of 5 Gutter Pairs			4·50	
First Day Cover				2·50
Presentation Pack (PO Pack No. 269)			2·75	
PHQ Cards (set of 5) (181)			1·00	2·50

Nos. 1936/1937 include the EUROPA emblem.

Special First Day of Issue Postmarks
Philatelic Bureau, Edinburgh	2·50
Fowey	2·75

1265 *Muffin the Mule*
1266 *Sooty* 
1267 *Stingray* 
1268 *The Clangers* 
1269 *Dangermouse* 

(Des Tutssels. Gravure Harrison (No. 1940a) or Enschedé (others))

1996 (3 Sept)–**97**. 50th Anniversary of Children's Television. Multicoloured One phosphor band (20p.) or two phosphor bands (others). Perf 14½×14.

1940	**1265**	20p. Muffin the Mule	30	30
		a. Perf 15×14 (23.9.97)	65	65
		ab. Booklet pane. No. 1940a×4 with margins all round	2·75	
1941	**1266**	26p. Sooty	35	35
1942	**1267**	31p. Stingray	50	50
1943	**1268**	37p. The Clangers	60	60
1944	**1269**	43p. Dangermouse	70	70
Set of 5			2·25	2·25
Set of 5 Gutter Pairs			4·50	
First Day Cover				2·75
Presentation Pack (PO Pack No. 270)			3·00	
PHQ Cards (set of 5) (182)			1·00	2·75

Booklet pane No. 1940ab comes from the 1997 £6·15 BBC stamp booklet, No. DX19.

Special First Day of Issue Postmarks
Philatelic Bureau, Edinburgh	2·75
Alexandra Palace, London	2·75

1270 Triumph TR3
1271 MG TD 
1272 Austin-Healey 100 
1273 Jaguar XK120 
1274 Morgan Plus 4 

(Des S. Clay. Gravure Harrison)

1996 (1 Oct). Classic Sports Cars. Multicoloured One phosphor band (20p.) or two phosphor bands (others). Perf 14½.

1945	**1270**	20p. Triumph TR3	30	30
1946	**1271**	26p. MG TD	50	50
		a. Imperf (pair)	£2800	
1947	**1272**	37p. Austin-Healey 100	60	65
		a. Imperf (pair)	£1000	
1948	**1273**	43p. Jaguar XK120	70	75
		a. Imperf (horiz pair)	£1600	
1949	**1274**	63p. Morgan Plus 4	90	95
Set of 5			2·75	3·00
Set of 5 Gutter Pairs			5·50	
First Day Cover				3·25
Presentation Pack (PO Pack No. 271)			3·00	
PHQ Cards (set of 5) (183)			1·00	3·25

On Nos. 1946/1949 the right-hand phosphor band on each stamp is three times the width of that on the left.

1996/QUEEN ELIZABETH II

Special First Day of Issue Postmarks
Philatelic Bureau, Edinburgh .... 3·25
Beaulieu, Brockenhurst .... 3·25
A pictorial First Day of Issue handstamp was provided at London E1 for this issue.

1275 The Three Kings
1276 The Annunciation 
1277 The Journey to Bethlehem 
1278 The Nativity 
1279 The Shepherds 

(Des Laura Stoddart, Gravure Harrison)

1996 (28 Oct). Christmas. Multicoloured One phosphor band (2nd) or two phosphor bands (others). Perf 15×14.

1950	1275	(2nd) The Three Kings	60	35
1951	1276	(1st) The Annunciation	70	55
1952	1277	31p. The Journey to Bethlehem	50	65
1953	1278	43p. The Nativity	50	75
1954	1279	63p. The Shepherds	70	95

Set of 5 .... 2·75 3·00
Set of 5 Gutter Pairs .... 5·50
First Day Cover .... 3·25
Presentation Pack (PO Pack No. 272) .... 3·25
PHQ Cards (set of 5) (184) .... 1·00 3·25

Special First Day of Issue Postmarks
Philatelic Bureau, Edinburgh .... 3·00
Bethlehem, Llandeilo .... 3·00

Year Pack 1996
1996 (28 Oct). Comprises Nos. 1901/1954.
CP1954a   Year Pack (PO Pack No. 273) .... 27·50

Post Office Yearbook
1996 (28 Oct). Comprises Nos. 1901/1904 and 1915/1954 in hardback book with slip case, illustrated in colour
YB1954a   Yearbook .... 21·00

1280 Gentiana acaulis (Georg Ehret)
1281 Magnolia grandiflora (Ehret) 
1282 Camellia japonica (Alfred Chandler) 
1283 Tulipa (Ehret) 
1284 Fuchsia, Princess of Wales (Augusta Withers) 
1285 Tulipa gesneriana (Ehret) 
1286 Gazania splendens (Charlotte Sowerby) 
1287 Iris latifolia (Ehret) 
1288 Hippeastrum rutilum (Pierre-Joseph Redouté) 
1289 Passiflora caerulea (Ehret)

(Des Tutssels. Litho Walsall)

1997 (6 Jan). Greeting Stamps. 19th-century Flower Paintings. Multicoloured Two phosphor bands. Perf 14½×14 (with one elliptical hole in each vertical side).

1955	1280	(1st) Gentiana acaulis	1·20	1·00
		a. Booklet pane. Nos. 1955/1964	13·50	
		ab. Gold, blue-green and phosphor omitted	—	
1956	1281	(1st) Magnolia grandiflora	1·20	1·00
1957	1282	(1st) Camellia japonica	1·20	1·00
1958	1283	(1st) Tulipa	1·20	1·00
1959	1284	(1st) Fuchsia, Princess of Wales	1·20	1·00
1960	1285	(1st) Tulipa gesneriana	1·20	1·00
1961	1286	(1st) Gazania splendens	1·20	1·00
1962	1287	(1st) Iris latifolia	1·20	1·00
1963	1288	(1st) Hippeastrum rutilum	1·20	1·00
1964	1289	(1st) Passiflora caerulea	1·20	1·00

Set of 10 .... 10·50 9·00
First Day Cover .... 9·50
Presentation Pack (PO Pack No. G6) .... 13·50
PHQ Cards (set of 10) (GS5) .... 2·00 9·50

Nos. 1955/1964 were issued in £2·60 stamp booklets Nos. KX9/KX12 together with a pane of 20 half-sized labels. The stamps and labels were attached to the booklet cover by a common gutter margin.

Nos. 1955/1964 were re-issued on 21 January 2003 in se-tenant sheets of 20, each accompanied by a label showing further flowers (sold at £5·95) (No. LS11) or personal photographs (sold at £14·95). These stamps were printed in lithography by Questa and are without elliptical holes in the perforations.

For booklet stamps in designs as Nos. 1955, 1958 and 1962 and perforated 15×14, printed by Enschedé see Nos. 2463/2465.

See also Nos. 2942/2943.

Special First Day of Issue Postmarks
Philatelic Bureau, Edinburgh .... 9·50
Kew, Richmond, Surrey .... 9·50

1290 King Henry VIII
1291 Catherine of Aragon

QUEEN ELIZABETH II/1997

1292 Anne Boleyn
1293 Jane Seymour 
1294 Anne of Cleves 
1295 Catherine Howard 
1296 Catherine Parr 

(Des Kate Stephens from contemporary paintings. Gravure Harrison)

1997 (21 Jan). 450th Death Anniversary of King Henry VIII. Multicoloured Two phosphor bands. Perf 15 (No. 1965) or 14×15 (others).

1965	1290	26p. King Henry VIII	50	50
		a. Imperf (vert pair)	£3500	
1966	1291	26p. Catherine of Aragon	50	50
		a. Horiz strip of 6. Nos. 1966/1971	3·00	3·00
1967	1292	26p. Anne Boleyn	50	50
1968	1293	26p. Jane Seymour	50	50
1969	1294	26p. Anne of Cleves	50	50
1970	1295	26p. Catherine Howard	50	50
1971	1296	26p. Catherine Parr	50	50
Set of 7			3·25	3·25
Set of 1 Gutter Pair and a Gutter Strip of 12			6·50	
First Day Cover				3·75
Presentation Pack (PO Pack No. 274)			4·75	
PHQ Cards (set of 7) (185)			1·40	3·75

Nos. 1966/1971 were printed together, *se-tenant*, in horizontal strips of six throughout the sheet.

Special First Day of Issue Postmarks
Philatelic Bureau, Edinburgh	3·75
Hampton Court, East Molesey	4·00

1297 St Columba in Boat
1298 St Columba on Iona 
1299 St Augustine with King Ethelbert 
1300 St Augustine with Model of Cathedral 

(Des Claire Melinsky. Gravure Enschedé)

1997 (11 Mar). Religious Anniversaries. Multicoloured Two phosphor bands. Perf 14½.

1972	1297	26p. St Columba in Boat	40	40
		a. Imperf (pair)	£1100	
1973	1298	37p. St Columba on Iona	60	60
1974	1299	43p. St Augustine with King Ethelbert	80	85
1975	1300	63p. St Augustine with Model of Cathedral	90	95
Set of 4			2·50	2·50
Set of 4 Gutter Pairs			5·00	
First Day Cover				3·00
Presentation Pack (PO Pack No. 275)			3·25	
PHQ Cards (set of 4) (186)			80	3·00

Nos. 1972/1973 commemorate the 1400th death anniversary of St Columba.

Nos. 1974/1975 the 1400th anniversary of the arrival of St Augustine of Canterbury in Kent.

Special First Day of Issue Postmarks
Philatelic Bureau, Edinburgh	3·00
Isle of Iona	3·00

For Nos. 1976/1977, Types **1301/1302**, see Decimal Machin Definitives section.

Nos. 1978/1979 are vacant.

1303 Dracula
1304 Frankenstein 
1305 Dr Jekyll and Mr Hyde 
1306 The Hound of the Baskervilles 

(Des I. Pollock. Gravure Walsall)

1997 (13 May). Europa. Tales and Legends. Horror Stories. Multicoloured Two phosphor bands. Perf 14×15.

1980	1303	26p. *Dracula*	40	40
1981	1304	31p. *Frankenstein*	55	60
1982	1305	37p. *Dr Jekyll and Mr Hyde*	70	75
1983	1306	43p. *The Hound of the Baskervilles*	80	85
Set of 4			2·25	2·40
Set of 4 Gutter Pairs			4·50	
First Day Cover				2·75
Presentation Pack (PO Pack No. 276)			3·00	
PHQ Cards (set of 4) (187)			80	2·75

Nos. 1980/1983 commemorate the birth bicentenary of Mary Shelley (creator of Frankenstein) with the 26p. and 31p. values incorporating the EUROPA emblem.

Each value has features printed in fluorescent ink which are visible under ultraviolet light.

Special First Day of Issue Postmarks
Philatelic Bureau, Edinburgh	2·75
Whitby	2·75

1997/QUEEN ELIZABETH II

1307 Reginald Mitchell and Supermarine Spitfire MkIIA

1308 Roy Chadwick and Avro Lancaster MkI

1309 Ronald Bishop and de Havilland Mosquito B MkXVI

1310 George Carter and Gloster Meteor T Mk7

1311 Sir Sydney Camm and Hawker Hunter FGA Mk9

(Des Turner Duckworth, Gravure Harrison)

1997 (10 June). British Aircraft Designers. Multicoloured One phosphor band (20p.) or two phosphor bands (others). Perf 15×14.

1984	1307	20p. Reginald Mitchell and Supermarine Spitfire MkIIA	40	40
1985	1308	26p. Roy Chadwick and Avro Lancaster MkI	50	50
1986	1309	37p. Ronald Bishop and de Havilland Mosquito B MkXVI	60	60
1987	1310	43p. George Carter and Gloster Meteor T Mk7	80	80
1988	1311	63p. Sir Sydney Camm and Hawker Hunter FGA Mk9	90	90
Set of 5			3·00	3·00
Set of 5 Gutter Pairs			6·00	
First Day Cover				3·25
Presentation Pack (PO Pack No. 277)			3·50	
PHQ Cards (set of 5) (188)			1·00	3·25

See also No. 2868.

Special First Day of Issue Postmarks

Philatelic Bureau, Edinburgh	3·50
Duxford, Cambridge	3·50

1312 Carriage Horse and Coachman

1313 Lifeguards Horse and Trooper

1314 Blues and Royals Drum Horse and Drummer

1315 Duke of Edinburgh's Horse and Groom

(Des J.-L. Benard. Litho Walsall)

1997 (8 July). All the Queen's Horses. 50th Anniversary of the British Horse Society. Multicoloured One phosphor band (20p.) or two phosphor bands (others). Perf 14½.

1989	1312	20p. Carriage Horse and Coachman	40	40
1990	1313	26p. Lifeguards Horse and Trooper	55	60
1991	1314	43p. Blues and Royals Drum Horse and Drummer	70	75
1992	1315	63p. Duke of Edinburgh's Horse and Groom	85	85
Set of 4			2·25	2·50
Set of 4 Gutter Pairs			4·50	
First Day Cover				2·75
Presentation Pack (PO Pack No. 278)			3·00	
PHQ Cards (set of 4) (189)			50	2·75

Special First Day of Issue Postmarks

Philatelic Bureau, Edinburgh	2·75
Windsor, Berks	2·75

1315a Caernarfon Castle

1315b Edinburgh Castle

1315c Carrickfergus Castle

1315d Windsor Castle

CASTLE

Harrison plates (Nos. 1611/1614)

CASTLE

Enschedé plates (Nos. 1993/1996)

Differences between Harrison and Enschedé printings:

Harrison: 'C' has top serif and tail of letter points to right. 'A' has flat top. 'S' has top and bottom serifs.

Enschedé: 'C' has no top serif and tail of letter points upwards. 'A' has pointed top. 'S' has no serifs.

There are numerous other differences between the work of the two printers, but as the word 'CASTLE' is common to all values we have confined the comparison to that area of the stamps.

(Des from photos by Prince Andrew, Duke of York. Eng Inge Madle Recess (Queen's head by silk screen process) Enschedé)

1997 (29 July). Designs as Nos. 1611/1614 with Queen's head in silhouette as T **1044**, but re-engraved with differences in inscription as shown above. Perf 15×14 (with one elliptical hole in each vertical side).

1993	1315a	£1·50 Caernarfon Castle (maroon and gold†)	12·00	6·00
		a. Gold (Queen's head) omitted	—	£950
1994	1315b	£2 Edinburgh Castle (indigo and gold†)	14·00	2·25
		a. Gold (Queen's head) omitted	£550	
1995	1315c	£3 Carrickfergus Castle (violet and gold†)	30·00	3·50
		a. Gold (Queen's head) omitted	£2800	
1996	1315d	£5 Windsor Castle (deep brown and gold†)	35·00	10·00
		a. Gold (Queen's head) omitted	£4000	
Set of 4			80·00	18·00
Set of 4 Gutter Pairs (vert or horiz)			£175	
Presentation Pack (PO Pack No. 40)			£150	

† The Queen's head on these stamps is printed in optically variable ink which changes colour from gold to green when viewed from different angles.

No. 1996a occurs on R. 5/8 and 6/8 from some sheets.

QUEEN ELIZABETH II/1997

There was no official Royal Mail first day cover service provided for Nos. 1993/1996.
See also Nos. 1410/1413 and 1611/1614.

1316 Haroldswick, Shetland
1317 Painswick, Gloucestershire 
1318 Beddgelert, Gwynedd 
1319 Ballyroney, County Down 

(Des T. Millington. Gravure Enschedé)

1997 (12 Aug). Sub-Post Offices. Multicoloured One phosphor band (20p.) or two phosphor bands (others). Perf 14½.

1997	1316	20p. Haroldswick, Shetland	40	40
1998	1317	26p. Painswick, Gloucestershire	55	60
1999	1318	43p. Beddgelert, Gwynedd	70	75
2000	1319	63p. Ballyroney, County Down	85	85
Set of 4			2·25	2·40
Set of 4 Gutter Pairs			4·50	
First Day Cover				2·75
Presentation Pack (PO Pack No. 279)			3·00	
PHQ Cards (set of 4) (190)			80	2·75

Nos. 1997/2000 were issued on the occasion of the Centenary of the National Federation of Sub-Postmasters.

Special First Day of Issue Postmarks
Philatelic Bureau, Edinburgh	2·75
Wakefield	2·75

PRINTERS. Harrison and Sons Ltd became De La Rue Security Print on 8 September 1997. This was not reflected in the sheet imprints until mid-1998.

1320 Noddy
1321 Famous Five
1322 Secret Seven
1323 Faraway Tree
1324 Malory Towers

(Des C. Birmingham. Gravure Enschedé)

1997 (9 Sept). Birth Centenary of Enid Blyton (children's author). Multicoloured One phosphor band (20p.) or two phosphor bands (others). Perf 14×14½.

2001	1320	20p. Noddy	30	30
2002	1321	26p. Famous Five	50	50
2003	1322	37p. Secret Seven	55	60
2004	1323	43p. Faraway Tree	65	70
2005	1324	63p. Malory Towers	75	80
Set of 5			2·50	2·75
Set of 5 Gutter Pairs			5·00	
First Day Cover				3·00
Presentation Pack (PO Pack No. 280)			3·00	
PHQ Cards (set of 5) (191)			1·00	3·00

Special First Day of Issue Postmarks
Philatelic Bureau, Edinburgh	3·25
Beaconsfield	3·25

1325 Children and Father Christmas pulling Cracker
1326 Father Christmas with Traditional Cracker 
1327 Father Christmas riding Cracker 
1328 Father Christmas on Snowball 
1329 Father Christmas and Chimney 

(Des J. Gorham and M. Thomas (1st), J. Gorham (others) Gravure Harrison)

1997 (27 Oct). Christmas. 150th Anniversary of the Christmas Cracker. Multicoloured One phosphor band (2nd) or two phosphor bands (others). Perf 15×14.

2006	1325	(2nd) Children and Father Christmas pulling Cracker	90	35
		a. Imperf (pair)	£900	
2007	1326	(1st) Father Christmas with Traditional Cracker	1·20	55
2008	1327	31p. Father Christmas riding Cracker	50	60
		a. Imperf (pair)	£1500	
2009	1328	43p. Father Christmas on Snowball	50	70
2010	1329	63p. Father Christmas and Chimney	70	80
Set of 5			3·25	2·75
Set of 5 Gutter Pairs			6·50	
First Day Cover				3·00
Presentation Pack (PO Pack No. 282)			4·00	
PHQ Cards (set of 5) (192)			1·00	3·00

1997/QUEEN ELIZABETH II

The 1st value was re-issued on 3 October 2000 in sheets of ten, each with a *se-tenant* label showing Christmas greetings (*sold for £2·95*) (No. LS3) or a personal photograph (*sold for £5·95*). These sheets were printed in gravure by Questa and were sold by the Philatelic Bureau and selected philatelic outlets.

Similar sheets were available from 9 October 2001 when the price for the personalised version was increased to £12·95 for two sheets. These could also be purchased, on an experimental basis, from photo-booths situated at six post offices.

From 1 October 2002 the size of the sheet was increased to 20 either with greetings labels (*sold for £5·95*) (No. LS10) or personal photographs (*sold for £14·95*). These stamps were printed by Questa in lithography and perforated 14½×14.

Special First Day of Issue Postmarks	
Philatelic Bureau, Edinburgh	3·00
Bethlehem, Llandeilo	3·00

1330 Wedding Photograph, 1947
1331 Queen Elizabeth II and Prince Philip, 1997 

(Des D. Driver (20p., 43p.), Lord Snowdon (26p., 63p.) Gravure Harrison)

1997 (13 Nov). Royal Golden Wedding. One phosphor band (20p.) or two phosphor bands (others). Perf 15.

2011	**1330**	20p. Wedding Photograph, 1947. Gold, yellow-brown and grey-black	40	40
		a. Imperf (pair)	£3500	
		b. Face value omitted	£6000	
2012	**1331**	26p. Queen Elizabeth II and Prince Philip, 1997. Multicoloured	60	60
		a. Imperf (vert pair)	£3000	
2013	**1330**	43p. Wedding Photograph, 1947. Gold, bluish green and grey-black	1·10	1·10
2014	**1331**	63p. Queen Elizabeth II and Prince Philip, 1997. Multicoloured	1·50	1·50
Set of 4			3·25	3·25
Set of 4 Gutter Pairs			6·50	
First Day Cover				3·50
Presentation Pack (PO Pack No. 281)			3·75	
PHQ Cards (set of 4) (193)			80	3·50

For 26p. and (1st) Machin printed in gold, see Nos. 1672, Y1692, 2295, U2942, U2948/U2952, U2958, U2964/U2968, U3002 and U3015.

Special First Day of Issue Postmarks	
Philatelic Bureau, Edinburgh	3·50
London, SW1	3·75

Year Pack 1997

1997 (13 Nov). Comprises Nos. 1965/1975, 1980/1992 and 1997/2014.
CP2014*a*   Year Pack (PO Pack No. 283) .... 32·00

Post Office Yearbook

1997 (13 Nov). Comprises Nos. 1965/1975, 1980/1992 and 1997/2014 in hardback book with slip case
YB2014*a*   Yearbook .... 26·00

1332 Common Dormouse
1333 Lady's Slipper Orchid 
1334 Song Thrush 
1335 Shining Ram's-horn Snail 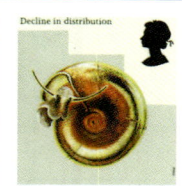
1336 Mole Cricket 
1337 Devil's Bolete 

(Des R. Maude. Litho Questa)

1998 (20 Jan). Endangered Species. Multicoloured One side phosphor band (20p.) or two phosphor bands (others). Perf 14×14½.

2015	**1332**	20p. Common Dormouse	40	40
2016	**1333**	26p. Lady's Slipper Orchid	50	50
2017	**1334**	31p. Song Thrush	60	60
2018	**1335**	37p. Shining Ram's-horn Snail	70	70
2019	**1336**	43p. Mole Cricket	85	85
2020	**1337**	63p. Devil's Bolete	1·00	1·00
Set of 6			3·75	3·75
Set of 6 Gutter Pairs			7·50	
First Day Cover				4·00
Presentation Pack (PO Pack No. 284)			4·25	
PHQ Cards (set of 6) (194)			1·25	4·00

Special First Day of Issue Postmarks	
Philatelic Bureau, Edinburgh	4·25
Selborne, Alton	4·25

1338 Diana, Princess of Wales (photo by Lord Snowdon) 
1339 At British Lung Foundation Function, April 1997 (photo by John Stillwell)

1340 Wearing Tiara, 1991 (photo by Lord Snowdon)
1341 On Visit to Birmingham, October 1995 (photo by Tim Graham) 

145

QUEEN ELIZABETH II/1998

1342 In Evening Dress, 1987 (photo by Terence Donavan)

(Des B. Robinson. Gravure Harrison)

1998 (3 Feb). Diana, Princess of Wales Commemoration. Multicoloured Two phosphor bands. Perf 14×15.

2021	1338	26p. Diana, Princess of Wales	50	30
		a. Horiz strip of 5. Nos. 2021/2025	2·00	2·00
		ab. Imperf (horiz strip of 5. Nos. 2021/2025)	£12000	
		ac. Imperf (horiz strip of 4. Nos. 2021/2024)	£7500	
		ad. Imperf (horiz strip of 3. Nos. 2021/2023)	£4500	
2022	1339	26p. At British Lung Foundation Function, April 1997	50	30
2023	1340	26p. Wearing Tiara, 1991	50	30
2024	1341	26p. On Visit to Birmingham, October 1995	50	30
2025	1342	26p. In Evening Dress, 1987	50	30
Set of 5			2·00	2·00
Gutter Strip of 10			4·00	
First Day Cover				3·00
Presentation Pack (unnumbered)			8·00	
Presentation Pack (Welsh)			60·00	

Nos. 2021/2025 were printed together, *se-tenant*, in horizontal strips of five throughout the sheet.

No. 2021ac shows No. 2025 perforated at right only.

In addition to the generally issued Presentation Pack a further pack with all text printed in English and Welsh was available.

Special First Day of Issue Postmarks
Philatelic Bureau, Edinburgh	3·00
Kensington, London	3·00

1343 Lion of England and Griffin of Edward III
1344 Falcon of Plantagenet and Bull of Clarence 
1345 Lion of Mortimer and Yale of Beaufort 
1346 Greyhound of Richmond and Dragon of Wales 
1347 Unicorn of Scotland and Horse of Hanover 

(Des J. Matthews. Recess and litho Harrison)

1998 (24 Feb). 650th Anniversary of the Order of the Garter. The Queen's Beasts. Multicoloured Two phosphor bands. Perf 15×14.

2026	1343	26p. Lion of England and Griffin of Edward III	50	30
		a. Horiz strip of 5. Nos. 2026/2030	2·25	2·25
		ab. Missing green (on Nos. 2026, 2028/2029) (horiz strip of 5)	—	
		Eay. Horiz strip of 5. Phosphor omitted	25·00	
2027	1344	26p. Falcon of Plantagenet and Bull of Clarence	50	30
2028	1345	26p. Lion of Mortimer and Yale of Beaufort	50	30
2029	1346	26p. Greyhound of Richmond and Dragon of Wales	50	30
2030	1347	26p. Unicorn of Scotland and Horse of Hanover	50	30
Set of 5			2·25	2·25
Gutter Block of 10			4·50	
First Day Cover				2·75
Presentation Pack (PO Pack No. 285)			2·50	
PHQ Cards (set of 5) (195)			1·00	2·75

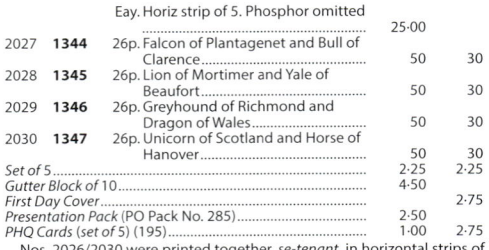

Nos. 2026/2030 were printed together, *se-tenant*, in horizontal strips of five throughout the sheet.

The phosphor bands on Nos. 2026/2030 are only half the height of the stamps and do not cover the silver parts of the designs.

Special First Day of Issue Postmarks
Philatelic Bureau, Edinburgh	2·75
London SW1	2·75

1348  **1348a**

1348b

(Des G. Knipe, adapted Dew Gibbons Design Group. Gravure Walsall)

1998 (10 Mar). As T **157** (Wilding Definitive of 1952–1954) but with face values in decimal currency as T **1348**. One side phosphor band (20p.) or two phosphor bands (others). Perf 14 (with one elliptical hole in each vertical side).

2031	1348	20p. light green (1 band at right)	40	40
		a. Band at left	40	40
		b. Booklet pane. Nos. 2031/2031a each×3 with margins all round	2·50	
		c. Booklet pane. Nos. 2031/2031a and 2032/2033, all×2, and central label with margins all round	4·50	
2032	1348a	26p. red-brown	50	50
		a. Booklet pane. No. 2032×9 with margins all round	3·25	
		b. Booklet pane. Nos. 2032/2033, each×3 with margins all round	4·25	
2033	1348b	37p. light purple	1·10	1·10
Set of 3 (*cheapest*)			1·90	1·90
First Day Cover (No. 2031c)				4·75

Nos. 2031/2033 were only issued in the 1998 £7·49 Wilding Definitives stamp booklet No. DX20.

For further Wilding designs with decimal face values and on paper watermarked W **1565** see Nos. 2258/2259, **MS**2326, **MS**2367, 2378/2379, and 3329.

Special First Day of Issue Postmarks
Philatelic Bureau, Edinburgh	4·75
London SW1	4·75

1349 St John's Point Lighthouse, County Down
1350 Smalls Lighthouse, Pembrokeshire

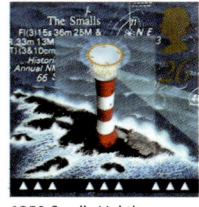

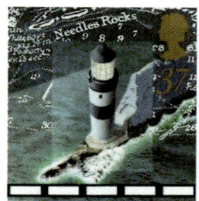

1998/QUEEN ELIZABETH II

1351 Needles Rock Lighthouse, Isle of Wight, c 1900

1352 Bell Rock Lighthouse, Arbroath, mid-19th-century

1353 Original Eddystone Lighthouse, Plymouth, 1698

(Des D. Davis and J. Boon. Litho Questa)

1998 (24 Mar). Lighthouses. Multicoloured One side phosphor band (20p.) or two phosphor bands (others). Perf 14½×14.

2034	1349	20p. St John's Point Lighthouse	40	40
2035	1350	26p. Smalls Lighthouse	50	50
2036	1351	37p. Needles Rock Lighthouse	60	60
2037	1352	43p. Bell Rock Lighthouse	80	80
2038	1353	63p. Original Eddystone Lighthouse	90	90
Set of 5			3·00	3·00
Set of 5 Gutter Pairs			6·00	
First Day Cover				3·25
Presentation Pack (PO Pack No. 286)			3·50	
PHQ Cards (set of 5) (196)			1·00	3·25

Nos. 2034/2038 commemorate the 300th anniversary of the first Eddystone Lighthouse and the final year of manned lighthouses.

Special First Day of Issue Postmarks
Philatelic Bureau, Edinburgh .... 3·50
Plymouth .... 3·50

For Nos. 2039/2040 see Decimal Machin Definitives section.

1354 Tommy Cooper

1355 Eric Morecambe

1356 Joyce Grenfell

1357 Les Dawson

1358 Peter Cook

(Des G. Scarfe. Litho Walsall)

1998 (23 Apr). Comedians. Multicoloured One side phosphor band (20p.) or two phosphor bands (others). Perf 14½×14.

2041	1354	20p. Tommy Cooper	40	40
		a. Vermilion printed double		£850
		b. Vermilion and black both printed quadruple with rose-pink and new blue both printed double	†	£1300
		c. Vermilion and black both printed double	†	£1100
2042	1355	26p. Eric Morecambe	50	50
		a. Vermilion printed double	£450	
		b. Vermilion printed triple	£675	
		c. Black printed double, vermilion printed triple	£1200	
		d. Black and vermilion printed triple	£1200	
		e. Vermilion and black both printed quadruple		
2043	1356	37p. Joyce Grenfell	60	60
2044	1357	43p. Les Dawson	80	80
2045	1358	63p. Peter Cook	90	90
		a. Vermilion printed triple	†	—
Set of 5			3·00	3·00
Set of 5 Gutter Pairs			6·00	
First Day Cover				3·25
Presentation Pack (PO Pack No. 287)			3·50	
PHQ Cards (set of 5) (197)			1·00	3·25

Stamps as T **1356**, but with a face value of 30p., were prepared but not issued. Mint examples and a first day cover have been reported (Price £1800).

On No. 2045a the red can appear double and the black also shows slight doubling. It is only known on the first day cover.

Special First Day of Issue Postmarks
Philatelic Bureau, Edinburgh .... 3·50
Morecambe .... 3·50

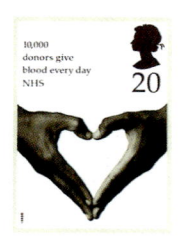

1359 Hands forming Heart

1360 Adult and Child holding Hands

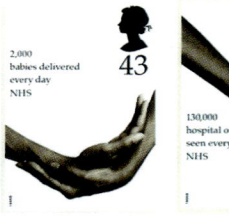

1361 Hands forming Cradle

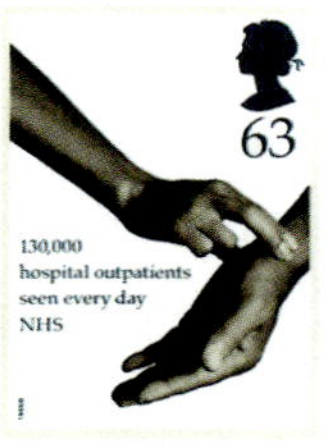

1362 Hand taking Pulse

(Des V. Frost from photos by A. Wilson. Litho Questa)

1998 (23 June). 50th Anniversary of the National Health Service. Multicoloured One side phosphor band (20p.) or two phosphor bands (others). Perf 14×14½.

2046	1359	20p. Hands forming Heart	40	40
2047	1360	26p. Adult and Child holding Hands	50	50
2048	1361	43p. Hands forming Cradle	80	80
2049	1362	63p. Hand taking Pulse	90	90
Set of 4			2·25	2·25
Set of 4 Gutter Pairs			4·50	
First Day Cover				2·75
Presentation Pack (PO Pack No. 288)			2·75	
PHQ Cards (set of 4) (198)			50	2·50

Special First Day of Issue Postmarks
Philatelic Bureau, Edinburgh .... 2·75
Tredegar, Wales .... 2·75

QUEEN ELIZABETH II/1998

1363 *The Hobbit* (J. R. R. Tolkien)
1364 *The Lion, The Witch and the Wardrobe* (C. S. Lewis) 
1365 *The Phoenix and the Carpet* (E. Nesbit) 
1366 *The Borrowers* (Mary Norton) 
1367 *Through the Looking Glass* (Lewis Carroll) 

(Des P. Malone. Gravure D.L.R.)

1998 (21 July). Famous Children's Fantasy Novels. Multicoloured One centre phosphor band (20p.) or two phosphor bands (others). Perf 15×14.

2050	**1363**	20p. *The Hobbit*	35	35
2051	**1364**	26p. *The Lion, The Witch and the Wardrobe*	45	45
		a. Imperf (pair)	£1500	
2052	**1365**	37p. *The Phoenix and the Carpet*	60	60
2053	**1366**	43p. *The Borrowers*	80	80
2054	**1367**	63p. *Through the Looking Glass*	90	90
Set of 5			3·00	3·00
Set of 5 Gutter Pairs			6·00	
First Day Cover				3·25
Presentation Pack (PO Pack No. 289)			3·25	
PHQ Cards (set of 5) (199)			1·00	3·25

Nos. 2050/2054 commemorate the birth centenary of C. S. Lewis and the death centenary of Lewis Carroll.

The PHQ card showing the T **1363** design is known incorrectly inscribed 'Tolkein'.

Special First Day of Issue Postmarks
Philatelic Bureau, Edinburgh .... 3·50
Oxford .... 3·50

1368 Woman in Yellow Feathered Costume
1369 Woman in Blue Costume and Headdress 
1370 Group of Children in White and Gold Robes 
1371 Child in Tree Costume 

(Des T. Hazael. Gravure Walsall)

1998 (25 Aug). Europa. Festivals. Notting Hill Carnival. Multicoloured One centre phosphor band (20p.) or two phosphor bands (others). Perf 14×14½.

2055	**1368**	20p. Woman in Yellow Feathered Costume	40	40
		a. Imperf (pair)	£500	
2056	**1369**	26p. Woman in Blue Costume and Headdress	60	60
2057	**1370**	43p. Group of Children in White and Gold Robes	75	75
2058	**1371**	63p. Child in Tree Costume	1·00	1·00
Set of 4			2·50	2·50
Set of 4 Gutter Pairs			5·00	
First Day Cover				3·00
Presentation Pack (PO Pack No. 290)			2·75	
PHQ Cards (set of 4) (200)			80	3·00

The 20p. and 26p. incorporate the EUROPA emblem.

Special First Day of Issue Postmarks
Philatelic Bureau, Edinburgh .... 3·00
London W11 .... 3·00

1372 Sir Malcolm Campbell's *Bluebird*, 1925
1373 Sir Henry Segrave's *Sunbeam*, 1926 
1374 John G. Parry Thomas's *Babs*, 1926 
1375 John R. Cobb's *Railton Mobil Special*, 1947 
1376 Donald Campbell's *Bluebird CN7*, 1964 

(Des Roundel Design Group. Gravure Walsall (Nos. 2059a/2059ac) or De La Rue (others)

1998 (29 Sept–13 Oct). British Land Speed Record Holders. Multicoloured One phosphor band (20p.) or two phosphor bands (others). Perf 15×14.

2059	**1372**	20p. Sir Malcolm Campbell's *Bluebird*	30	30
		a. Perf 14½×13½ (1 side band at right) (13.10.98)	75	75
		ab. Band at left	75	75
		ac. Booklet pane. Nos. 2059a and 2059ab, each×2, with margins all round	3·25	
2060	**1373**	26p. Sir Henry Segrave's *Sunbeam*	40	40
		a. Rosine (face value) omitted	£2500	
		b. '2' from face value omitted	£1500	
		c. '6' from face value omitted	£1500	
2061	**1374**	30p. John G. Parry Thomas's *Babs*	60	60
2062	**1375**	43p. John R. Cobb's *Railton Mobil Special*	80	80
2063	**1376**	63p. Donald Campbell's *Bluebird CN7*	90	90
Set of 5			2·75	2·75
Set of 5 Gutter Pairs			5·50	
First Day Cover				3·00
Presentation Pack (PO Pack No. 291)			3·25	
PHQ Cards (set of 5) (201)			1·00	3·00

Nos. 2059/2063 commemorate the 50th death anniversary of Sir Malcolm Campbell.

Nos. 2060a/2060c occur on the fourth vertical row of several sheets. Other examples show one or other of the figures partially omitted.

Nos. 2059a/2059ac come from the £6·16 British Land Speed Record Holders stamp booklet, No. DX21, and were printed by Walsall.

1998/QUEEN ELIZABETH II

There are minor differences of design between No. 2059 (sheet stamp printed by De La Rue) and Nos. 2059a/2059ab (booklet stamps printed by Walsall), which omit the date and copyright symbol.

Trials with different face values, and an alternative photograph of the *Railton Mobil Special* are known.

Each stamp also has in large yellow or silver numerals the record speed attained. (*Prices From £500 Each*)

Special First Day of Issue Postmarks
Philatelic Bureau, Edinburgh.. 3·00
Pendine.. 3·00

The mis-spelling 'PHILALETIC' in the Bureau datestamp was later corrected; same price, either spelling.

1377 Angel with Hands raised in Blessing

1378 Angel praying

1379 Angel playing Flute

1380 Angel playing Lute

1381 Angel praying

(Des Irene von Treskow. Gravure De La Rue)

1998 (2 Nov). Christmas. Angels. Multicoloured One centre phosphor band (20p.) or two phosphor bands (others). Perf 15×14.

2064	1377	20p. Angel with Hands raised in Blessing.............	35	35
		a. Imperf (pair).................	£450	
2065	1378	26p. Angel praying.............	45	45
		a. Imperf (pair).................	£1600	
2066	1379	30p. Angel playing Flute....	60	60
		a. Imperf (pair).................	£500	
2067	1380	43p. Angel playing Lute.....	80	80
		a. Imperf (pair).................	£2500	
2068	1381	63p. Angel praying.............	90	90

Set of 5.. 2·75 2·75
Set of 5 Gutter Pairs... 5·50
First Day Cover... 3·00
Presentation Pack (PO Pack No. 292)................... 3·25
PHQ Cards (set of 5) (202)...................................... 60 3·00

Special First Day of Issue Postmarks
Philatelic Bureau, Edinburgh.. 3·00
Bethlehem... 3·00

Year Pack 1998

1998 (2 Nov). Comprises Nos. 2015/2030, 2034/2038 and 2041/2068.
CP2068a   Year Pack (PO Pack No. 293)................ 40·00

Post Office Yearbook

1998 (2 Nov). Comprises Nos. 2015/2030, 2034/2038 and 2041/2068 in hardback book with slip case
YB2068a   Yearbook... 35·00

MILLENNIUM SERIES: Consecutive 1999 designs are numbered downwards from 1999/1948 to 1999/1991. 2000 designs are numbered upwards from 2000/2001 to 2000/2048.

1382 Greenwich Meridian and Clock (John Harrison's chronometer)

1383 Industrial Worker and Blast Furnace (James Watt's discovery of steam power)

1384 Early Photos of Leaves (Henry Fox-Talbot's photographic experiments)

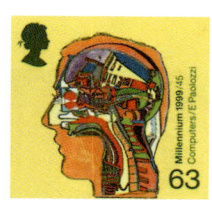

1385 Computer inside Human Head (Alan Turing's work on computers)

(Des D. Gentleman (20p.), P. Howson (26p.), Z. and Barbara Baran (43p.), E. Paolozzi (63p.), gravure, Questa (63p. No. 2072a), Enschedé (20p.) or De La Rue (others))

1999 (12 Jan–21 Sept). Millennium Series. The Inventors' Tale. Multicoloured One centre phosphor band (20p.) or two phosphor bands (others). P 14×14½.

2069	1382	20p. Greenwich Meridian and Clock......	40	40
		a. Imperf (horiz pair)...........................	£1800	
2070	1383	26p. Industrial Worker and Blast Furnace...	60	60
2071	1384	43p. Early Photographs of Leaves.........	80	80
2072	1385	63p. Computer inside Human Head.....	1·00	1·00
		a. Perf 13½×14 (21.9.99).................	1·75	1·75
		ab. Booklet pane. No. 2072a×4 with margins all round............................	7·50	

Set of 4... 2·50 2·50
Set of 4 Gutter Pairs.. 5·00
First Day Cover (Philatelic Bureau) (Type J, see Introduction)... 4·25
First Day Cover (Greenwich, London SE)............................ 4·25
Presentation Pack (PO Pack No. 294).................. 3·25
PHQ Cards (set of 4) (203)..................................... 80 2·75

No. 2072a comes from the £6·99 World Changers booklet, No. DX23.

1386 Airliner hugging Globe (International air travel)

1387 Woman on Bicycle (Development of the bicycle)

1388 Victorian Railway Station (Growth of public transport)

1389 Captain Cook and Maori (Captain James Cook's voyages)

(Des G. Hardie (20p.), Sara Fanelli (26p.), J. Lawrence (43p.), A. Klimowski (63p.). Gravure Enschedé (20p., 63p.) or De La Rue (26p.). Litho Enschedé (43p.))

1999 (2 Feb). Millennium Series. The Travellers' Tale. Multicoloured One centre phosphor band (20p.) or two phosphor bands (others). Perf 14×14½.

2073	1386	20p. Airliner hugging Globe..................	40	40
2074	1387	26p. Woman on Bicycle.........................	60	60

QUEEN ELIZABETH II/1999

2075	**1388**	43p. Victorian Railway Station................	80	80
2076	**1389**	63p. Captain Cook and Maori................	1·00	1·00
Set of 4			2·50	2·50
Set of 4 Gutter Pairs			5·00	
First Day Cover (Philatelic Bureau) (Type J, see Introduction)..				3·25
First Day Cover (Coventry)..				3·25
Presentation Pack (PO Pack No. 295)...................			3·25	
PHQ Cards (set of 4) (204)...			80	3·25

For Nos. 2077/2079, T **1390**, see Decimal Machins Definitive section

1391 Vaccinating Child (pattern in cow markings) (Jenner's development of smallpox vaccine)

1392 Patient on Trolley (nursing care)

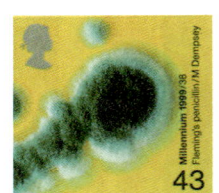

1393 Penicillin Mould (Fleming's discovery of penicillin)

1394 Sculpture of Test Tube Baby (development of in-vitro fertilisation)

(Des P. Brookes (20p.), Susan Macfarlane (26p.), M. Dempsey (43p.), A. Gormley (63p.). Gravure Questa)

1999 (2 Mar–21 Sept). Millennium Series. The Patients' Tale. Multicoloured One centre phosphor band (20p.) or two phosphor bands (others). Perf 13½×14.

2080	**1391**	20p. Vaccinating Child.............................	40	40
		a. Booklet pane. No. 2080×4 with margins all round (21.9.99)............	1·60	
2081	**1392**	26p. Patient on Trolley............................	60	60
		a. Imperf (pair)..	£3000	
2082	**1393**	43p. Penicillin Mould..............................	80	80
2083	**1394**	63p. Sculpture of Test-tube Baby...........	1·00	1·00
Set of 4			2·50	2·50
Set of 4 Gutter Pairs			5·00	
First Day Cover (Philatelic Bureau) (Type J, see Introduction)..				3·25
First Day Cover (Oldham)				3·25
Presentation Pack (PO Pack No. 296)...................			3·25	
PHQ Cards (set of 4) (205)...			80	3·25

No. 2080a comes from the £6·99 World Changers booklet, No. DX23.

1395 Dove and Norman Settler (medieval migration to Scotland)

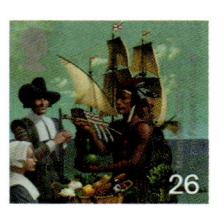

1396 Pilgrim Fathers and Native American (17th-century migration to America)

1397 Sailing Ship and Aspects of Settlement (19th-century migration to Australia)

1398 Hummingbird and Superimposed Stylised Face (20th-century migration to Great Britain)

(Des J. Byrne (20p.), W. McLean (26p.), J. Fisher (43p.), G. Powell (63p.). Litho (20p.) or gravure (others) Walsall)

1999 (6 Apr–12 May). Millennium Series. The Settlers' Tale. Multicoloured One centre phosphor band (20p.) or two phosphor bands (others). Perf 14×14½.

2084	**1395**	20p. Dove and Norman Settler...............	40	40
2085	**1396**	26p. Pilgrim Fathers and Native Amercian...	60	60
		a. Booklet pane. Nos. 2085 and 2089 with margins all round (12.5.99)....	3·00	
2086	**1397**	43p. Sailing Ship and Aspects of Settlement..	80	80
2087	**1398**	63p. Hummingbird and Superimposed Stylised Face.......................................	1·00	1·00
Set of 4			2·50	2·50
Set of 4 Gutter Pairs			5·00	
First Day Cover (Philatelic Bureau) (Type J, see Introduction)..				3·25
First Day Cover (Plymouth)...				3·25
Presentation Pack (PO Pack No. 297)...................			3·25	
PHQ Cards (set of 4) (206)...			80	3·25

No. 2085a comes from the £2·60 booklet, No. HBA1.

Imperf pairs of Nos. 2085 and 2089 are known and believed to be of proof status (Price £750).

Imperf pairs of No. 2085 with silver and phosphor omitted are known and believed to be of proof status (Price £350).

Imperf pairs of No. 2086 are known with gold, chocolate and phosphor omitted and believed to be of proof status (Price £350).

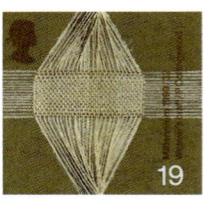

1399 Woven Threads (woollen industry)

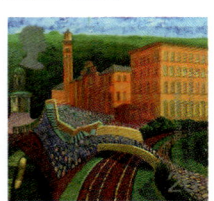

1400 Salts Mill, Saltaire (worsted cloth industry)

1401 Hull on Slipway (shipbuilding)

1402 Lloyd's Building (City of London finance centre)

(Des P. Collingwood (19p.), D. Hockney (26p.), B. Sanderson (44p.), B. Neiland (64p.). Litho (19p.) or gravure (others) De La Rue)

1999 (4 May). Millennium Series. The Workers' Tale. Multicoloured One centre phosphor band (19p.) or two phosphor bands (others). Perf 14×14½.

2088	**1399**	19p. Woven Threads.................................	40	40
		a. Bronze (Queen's head) omitted......	£500	
		ay. Bronze and phosphor omitted.......	£500	
2089	**1400**	26p. Salts Mill, Saltaire.............................	60	60
2090	**1401**	44p. Hull on Slipway................................	80	80
2091	**1402**	64p. Lloyd's Building...............................	1·00	1·00
Set of 4			2·50	2·50
Set of 4 Gutter Pairs			5·00	
First Day Cover (Philatelic Bureau) (Type J, see Introduction)..				3·25
First Day Cover (Belfast)...				3·25
Presentation Pack (PO Pack No. 298)...................			3·25	
PHQ Cards (set of 4) (207)...			80	3·25

For No. 2089, printed by Walsall in photogravure, see booklet pane No. 2085a.

1999 / QUEEN ELIZABETH II

1403 Freddie Mercury (lead singer of Queen) (Popular Music)
1404 Bobby Moore with World Cup, 1966 (Sport) 
1405 Dalek from *Dr Who* (science-fiction series) (Television) 
1406 Charlie Chaplin (film star) (Cinema) 

(Des P. Blake (19p.), M. White (26p.), Lord Snowdon (44p.), R. Steadman (64p.). Gravure Enschedé)

1999 (1 June). Millennium Series. The Entertainers' Tale. Multicoloured One centre phosphor band (19p.) or two phosphor bands (others). Perf 14×14½.

2092	1403	19p. Freddie Mercury	40	40
2093	1404	26p. Bobby Moore with World Cup	60	60
2094	1405	44p. Dalek from *Dr Who*	80	80
2095	1406	64p. Charlie Chaplin	1·00	1·00
Set of 4			2·50	2·50
Set of 4 Gutter Pairs			5·00	
First Day Cover (Philatelic Bureau) (Type J, see Introduction)				3·25
First Day Cover (Wembley)				3·25
Presentation Pack (PO Pack No. 299)			3·25	
PHQ Cards (set of 4) (208)			80	3·25

1407
1408 

Prince Edward and Miss Sophie Rhys-Jones (from photos by John Swannell)

(Adapted J. Gibbs. Gravure De La Rue)

1999 (15 June). Royal Wedding. Multicoloured Two phosphor bands. Perf 15×14.

2096	1407	26p. Prince Edward and Miss Sophie Rhys-Jones	40	40
		a. Imperf (pair)	£1800	
2097	1408	64p. Prince Edward and Miss Sophie Rhys-Jones	1·00	1·00
Set of 2			1·25	1·25
Set of 2 Gutter Pairs			2·50	
First Day Cover (Philatelic Bureau)				2·00
First Day Cover (Windsor)				2·00
Presentation Pack (PO Pack No. M01)			2·00	
PHQ Cards (set of 2) (PSM1)			40	2·00

1409 Suffragette behind Prison Window (Equal Rights for Women)
1410 Water Tap (Right to Health) 
1411 Generations of School Children (Right to Education) 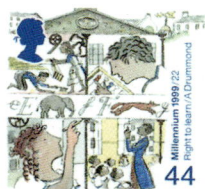
1412 'MAGNA CARTA' (Human Rights) 

(Des Natasha Kerr (19p.), M. Craig-Martin (26p.), A. Drummond (44p.), A. Kitching (64p.). Gravure De La Rue)

1999 (6 July). Millennium Series. The Citizens' Tale. Multicoloured One centre phosphor band (19p.) or two phosphor bands (others). Perf 14×14½.

2098	1409	19p. Suffragette behind Prison Window	40	40
2099	1410	26p. Water Tap	60	60
2100	1411	44p. Generations of School Children	80	80
2101	1412	64p. 'MAGNA CARTA'	1·00	1·00
Set of 4			2·50	2·50
Set of 4 Gutter Pairs			5·00	
First Day Cover (Philatelic Bureau) (Type J, see Introduction)				3·25
First Day Cover (Newtown, Powis)				3·25
Presentation Pack (PO Pack No. 300)			3·25	
PHQ Cards (set of 4) (209)			80	3·25

1413 Molecular Structures (DNA Decoding)
1414 Galapagos Finch and Fossilised Skeleton (Darwin's Theory of Evolution) 
1415 Rotation of Polarised Light by Magnetism (Faraday's work on Electricity) 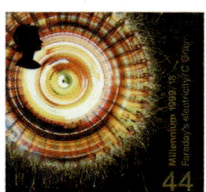
1416 Saturn (development of astronomical telescopes) 

(Des M. Curtis (19p.), R. Harris Ching (26p.), C. Gray (44p.), from Hubble Space Telescope photograph (64p.). Gravure (19p., 64p.) or litho (26p., 44p.) Questa)

1999 (3 Aug–21 Sept). Millennium Series. The Scientists' Tale. Multicoloured One centre phosphor band (19p.) or two phosphor bands (others). Perf 13½×14 (19p., 64p.) or 14×14½ (26p., 44p.).

2102	1413	19p. Molecular Structures	40	40
2103	1414	26p. Galapagos Finch and Fossilised Skeleton	60	60
		a. Imperf (pair)	£650	
		b. Perf 14½×14 (21.9.99)	1·50	1·50
		ba. Booklet pane. No. 2103b×4 with margins all round	6·50	
2104	1415	44p. Rotation of Polarised Light by Magnetism	80	80
		a. Perf 14½×14 (21.9.99)	1·50	1·50
		ab. Booklet pane. No. 2104a×4 with margins all round	6·50	
2105	1416	64p. Saturn	1·00	1·00
Set of 4			2·50	2·50
Set of 4 Gutter Pairs			5·00	
First Day Cover (Philatelic Bureau) (Type J, see Introduction)				3·25
First Day Cover (Cambridge)				3·25
Presentation Pack (PO Pack No. 301)			3·25	
PHQ Cards (set of 4) (210)			80	3·25

Nos. 2103b and 2104a come from the £6·99 World Changers booklet, No. DX23.

QUEEN ELIZABETH II/1999

1416a Solar Eclipse (*Illustration reduced. Actual size 89×121 mm*)

1999 (11 Aug). Solar Eclipse. Sheet 89×121 mm. Multicoloured. Two phosphor bands. Perf 14×14½.

MS2106	Type **1416a**×4 (*sold at £2·56*)	11·00	11·00
	a. Imperf	£5000	
First Day Cover (Philatelic Bureau)			11·50
First Day Cover (Falmouth)			11·50

1417 Upland Landscape (Strip Farming)

1418 Horse-drawn Rotary Seed Drill (Mechanical Farming)

1419 Man peeling Potato (Food Imports)

1420 Aerial View of Combine-harvester (Satellite Agriculture)

(Des D. Tress (19p.), C. Wormell (26p.), Tessa Traeger (44p.), R. Cooke (64p.). Gravure Walsall (No. 2108a) or De La Rue (others))

1999 (7–21 Sept). Millennium Series. The Farmers' Tale. Multicoloured One centre phosphor band (19p.) or two phosphor bands (others). Perf 14×14½.

2107	**1417**	19p. Upland Landscape	40	40
2108	**1418**	26p. Horse-drawn Rotary Seed Drill	60	60
		a. Booklet pane. No. 2108a×2 with margins all round (21.9.99)	3·00	
2109	**1419**	44p. Man peeling Potato	80	80
2110	**1420**	64p. Aerial View of Combine-harvester	1·00	1·00
Set of 4			2·50	2·50
Set of 4 Gutter Pairs			5·00	
First Day Cover (Philatelic Bureau) (Type J, see Introduction)				3·25
First Day Cover (Laxton, Newark)				3·25
Presentation Pack (PO Pack No. 302)			3·25	
PHQ Cards (set of 4) (211)			80	3·25

The 19p. includes the EUROPA emblem.
No. 2108a comes from the £2·60 booklet, No. HBA2.

1421 Robert the Bruce (Battle of Bannockburn, 1314)

1422 Cavalier and Horse (English Civil War)

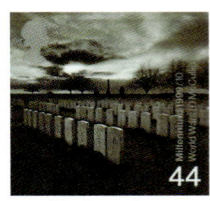

1423 War Graves Cemetery, The Somme (World Wars)

1424 Soldiers with Boy (Peacekeeping)

(Des A. Davidson (19p.), R. Kelly (26p.), D. McCullin (44p.), C. Corr (64p.). Litho (19p.) or gravure (others) Walsall)

1999 (5 Oct). Millennium Series. The Soldiers' Tale. Multicoloured. One centre phosphor band (19p.) or two phosphor bands (others). Perf 14×14½.

2111	**1421**	19p. Robert the Bruce	40	40
2112	**1422**	26p. Cavalier and Horse	60	60
2113	**1423**	44p. War Graves Cemetery, The Somme	80	80
2114	**1424**	64p. Soldiers with Boy	1·00	1·00
Set of 4			2·50	2·50
Set of 4 Gutter Pairs			5·00	
First Day Cover (Philatelic Bureau) (Type J, see Introduction)				3·25
First Day Cover (London SW)				3·25
Presentation Pack (PO Pack No. 303*)			3·25	
PHQ Cards (set of 4) (212)			80	3·25

* The presentation pack was numbered 302 in error.

1425 'Hark the herald angels sing' and Hymn book (John Wesley)

1426 King James I and Bible (Authorised Version of Bible)

1427 St Andrews Cathedral, Fife (Pilgrimage)

1428 Nativity (First Christmas)

(Des B. Neuenschwander (19p.), Clare Melinsky (26p.), Catherine Yass (44p.), C. Aitchison (64p.). Gravure De La Rue)

1999 (2 Nov). Millennium Series. The Christians' Tale. Multicoloured One centre phosphor band (19p.) or two phosphor bands (others). Perf 14×14½.

2115	**1425**	19p. 'Hark the herald angels sing' and Hymn book	40	40
		a. Imperf (pair)	£350	
2116	**1426**	26p. King James I and Bible	60	60
2117	**1427**	44p. St Andrews Cathedral, Fife	80	80
2118	**1428**	64p. Nativity	1·00	1·00
Set of 4			2·50	2·50
Set of 4 Gutter Pairs			5·00	
First Day Cover (Philatelic Bureau) (Type J, see Introduction)				3·25

1999/QUEEN ELIZABETH II

First Day Cover (St Andrews, Fife)		3·25
Presentation Pack (PO Pack No. 304)	3·25	
PHQ Cards (set of 4) (213)	80	3·25

1429 'World of the Stage' (Allen Jones)
1430 'World of Music' (Bridget Riley) 
1431 'World of Literature' (Lisa Milroy) 
1432 'New Worlds' (Sir Howard Hodgkin) 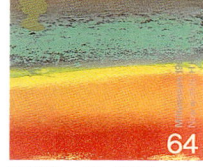

(Gravure Walsall)

1999 (7 Dec). Millennium Series. The Artists' Tale. Multicoloured. One centre phosphor band (19p.) or two phosphor bands (others). Perf 14×14½.

2119	**1429**	19p. 'World of the Stage'	40	40
2120	**1430**	26p. 'World of Music'	60	60
2121	**1431**	44p. 'World of Literature'	80	80
2122	**1432**	64p. 'New Worlds'	1·00	1·00
Set of 4			2·50	2·50
Set of 4 Gutter Pairs			5·00	
First Day Cover (Philatelic Bureau) (Type J, see Introduction)				3·25
First Day Cover (Stratford-upon-Avon)				3·25
Presentation Pack (PO Pack No. 305)			3·25	
PHQ Cards (set of 4) (214)			80	3·25

Year Pack 1999

1999 (7 Dec). Comprises Nos. 2069/2076, 2080/2105 and 2107/2122.
CP2122a   Year Pack (PO Pack No. 306)................ 65·00

Post Office Yearbook

1999 (7 Dec). Comprises Nos. 2069/2076, 2080/2105 and 2107/2122 in hardback book with slip case
YB2122a   Yearbook.............. 50·00

1433a (Illustration reduced. Actual Size 121×90 mm)

(Des D. Gentleman. Gravure De La Rue)

1999 (14 Dec). Millennium Series. Millennium Timekeeper. Sheet 120×89 mm. Multicoloured Two phosphor bands. Perf 14×14½.
MS2123 **1433a** 64p. Clock face and map of North America; 64p. Clock face and map of Asia; 64p. Clock face and map of Middle East; 64p. Clock face and map of Europe............ 11·00 11·00
First Day Cover (Philatelic Bureau)................ 11·00
First Day Cover (Greenwich SE)................ 11·00
Presentation Pack (PO Pack No. M02)................ 11·00
PHQ Cards (set of 5) (PSM02)................ 1·00 11·00

No. **MS**2123 also exists overprinted 'EARLS COURT, LONDON 22-28 MAY 2000 THE STAMP SHOW 2000' from Exhibition Premium Passes, costing £10, available from 1 March 2000 (Price £17).

The five PHQ cards show the four individual stamps and the complete miniature sheet.

> For No. 2124, T **1437**, see Decimal Machin Definitives section.

1438 Barn Owl (World Owl Trust, Muncaster) 
1439 Night Sky (National Space Science Centre, Leicester)

1440 River Goyt and Textile Mills (Torrs Walkway, New Mills)
1441 Gannets (Seabird Centre, North Berwick) 

(Litho (44p.), gravure (others) Walsall (No. 2126a/2126ab) or Questa (others))

2000 (18 Jan)–**02**. Millennium Projects (1st series). Above and Beyond. Multicoloured One centre phosphor band (19p.) or two phosphor bands (others). Perf 14×14½ (1st, 44p.) or 13½×14 (others).

2125	**1438**	19p. Barn Owl (World Owl Trust, Muncaster)	40	40
		a. Imperf (pair)	£450	
2126	**1439**	26p. Night Sky (National Space Science Centre, Leicester)	70	70
		aa. Imperf (pair)	£450	
2126a		(1st) greenish yellow, magenta, pale new blue, black and silver (26.5.2000)	2·25	2·25
		ab. Booklet pane. Nos. 2126a and 2139 with margins all round	3·00	
		ac. Booklet pane. No. 2126a×4 with margins all round (24.9.02)	9·00	
2127	**1440**	44p. River Goyt and Textile Mills (Torrs Walkway, New Mills)	1·00	1·00
2128	**1441**	64p. Gannets (Seabird Centre, North Berwick)	1·25	1·25
Set of 4 (ex No. 2126a)			3·00	3·00
Set of 4 Gutter Pairs			6·00	
First Day Cover (Philatelic Bureau) (Type J, see Introduction) (Nos. 2125/2128)				4·00
First Day Cover (Muncaster, Ravenglass) (Nos. 2125/2128)				4·00
First Day Cover (Philatelic Bureau) (No. 2126ab)				4·00
First Day Cover (Leicester) (No. 2126ab)				4·00
Presentation Pack (PO Pack No. 307)			3·75	
PHQ Cards (set of 4) (215)			80	3·50

No. 2126ab comes from the £2·70 Millennium booklet, No. HBA3.
No. 2162ac comes from the Across the Universe stamp booklet, No. DX29.
Imperforate pairs of No. 2125 with Queen's head in gold, Nos. 2126 and 2139 with inscriptions in an alternative typeface and No. 2128 with inscriptions in silver are all of proof status (*Prices from £200*).

1442 Millennium Beacon (Beacons across The Land)
1443 Garratt Steam Locomotive No. 143 pulling Train (Rheilffordd Eryri, Welsh Highland Railway) 

153

QUEEN ELIZABETH II/2000

1444 Lightning (Dynamic Earth Centre, Edinburgh)
1445 Multicoloured Lights (Lighting Croydon's Skyline) 

(Gravure De La Rue)

2000 (1 Feb). Millennium Projects (2nd series). Fire and Light. Multicoloured One centre phosphor band (19p.) or two phosphor bands (others). Perf 14×14½.

2129	**1442**	19p. Millennium Beacon (Beacons across The Land)	40	40
2130	**1443**	26p. Garratt Steam Locomotive No. 143 pulling Train (Rheilffordd Eryri, Welsh Highland Railway)	70	70
2131	**1444**	44p. Lightning (Dynamic Earth Centre, Edinburgh)	1·00	1·00
2132	**1445**	64p. Multicoloured Lights (Lighting Croydon's Skyline)	1·25	1·25

Set of 4 .... 3·00 3·00
Set of 4 Gutter Pairs .... 6·00
First Day Cover (Philatelic Bureau) (Type J, see Introduction) .... 3·50
First Day Cover (Edinburgh 3°10'W) .... 3·50
Presentation Pack (PO Pack No. 308) .... 3·75
PHQ Cards (set of 4) (216) .... 1·25 3·50

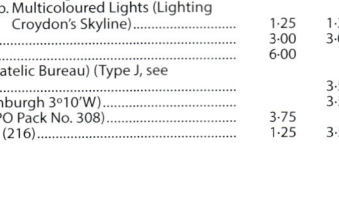

1449 Cliff Boardwalk (Parc Arfordirol, Llanelli Coast)
1450 Reflections in Water (Portsmouth Harbour Development) 

(Litho (44p.), gravure (others) Walsall)

2000 (7 Mar). Millennium Projects (3rd series). Water and Coast. Multicoloured One centre phosphor band (19p.) or two phosphor bands (others). Perf 14×14½.

2134	**1447**	19p. Beach Pebbles (Turning the Tide, Durham Coast)	40	40
2135	**1448**	26p. Frog's Legs and Water Lilies (National Pondlife Centre, Merseyside)	70	70
2136	**1449**	44p. Cliff Boardwalk (Parc Arfordirol, Llanelli Coast)	1·00	1·00
2137	**1450**	64p. Reflections in Water (Portsmouth Harbour Development)	1·25	1·25
		a. Phosphor omitted	£175	

Set of 4 .... 3·00 3·00
Set of 4 Gutter Pairs .... 6·00
First Day Cover (Philatelic Bureau) (Type J, see Introduction) .... 4·00
First Day Cover (Llanelli) .... 4·00
Presentation Pack (PO Pack No. 309) .... 3·75
PHQ Cards (set of 4) (217) .... 1·25 4·50

929 Queen Victoria and Queen Elizabeth II
1446 Queen Victoria and Queen Elizabeth II

(Des J. Matthews. Gravure Walsall)

2000 (15 Feb)–**2017**. T **929** redrawn as T **1446** (No.2133*a*). Two phosphor bands. Perf 14 (No. 2133*a*) or perf 14½×14 (both with one elliptical hole in each vertical side).

2133	**929**	20p brownish black and cream (5.6.17)	1·10	1·10
2133*a*	**1446**	(1st) brownish black and cream	1·10	1·10
		al. Booklet pane. No. 2133*a*×6 with margins all round	8·50	

First Day Cover (Philatelic Bureau) (No. 2133*al*) .... 9·50
First Day Cover (London SW5) (No. 2133*al*) .... 9·50

No. 2133 comes from the £15·14 50th Anniversary of the Machin booklet, No. DY21.

No. 2133*a* was only issued in the £7·50 Special by Design booklet, No. DX24.

For Nos. 2133/2133*a* but printed Litho see Nos. 2955/2956.

See also Nos. 1478, **MS**1501 and **MS**3965.

1451 Reed Beds, River Braid (ECOS, Ballymena) 
1452 South American Leafcutter Ants (Web of Life Exhibition, London Zoo)

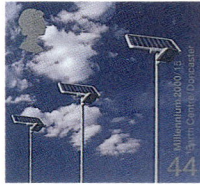

1453 Solar Sensors (Earth Centre, Doncaster)
1454 Hydroponic Leaves (Project SUZY, Teesside) 

(Gravure De La Rue)

2000 (4 Apr). Millennium Projects (4th series). Life and Earth. Multicoloured One centre phosphor band (2nd) or two phosphor bands (others). Perf 14×14½.

2138	**1451**	(2nd) Reed Beds, River Braid	90	90
2139	**1452**	(1st) South American Leafcutter Ants	1·00	1·00
		a. Imperf (pair)		
2140	**1453**	44p. Solar Sensors	1·00	1·00
2141	**1454**	64p. Hydroponic Leaves	1·25	1·25

Set of 4 .... 3·75 3·75
Set of 4 Gutter Pairs .... 7·50
First Day Cover (Philatelic Bureau) (Type J, see Introduction) .... 4·00
First Day Cover (Doncaster) .... 4·00
Presentation Pack (PO Pack No. 310) .... 4·25
PHQ Cards (set of 4) (218) .... 1·25 4·50

For No. 2139 printed by Walsall in gravure, see booklet pane No. 2126ab.

Types **1453**/**1454** with face values of 45p. and 65p. were prepared, but not issued.

1447 Beach Pebbles (Turning the Tide, Durham Coast)
1448 Frog's Legs and Water Lilies (National Pondlife Centre, Merseyside)

2000/QUEEN ELIZABETH II

1455 Pottery Glaze (Ceramica Museum, Stoke-on-Trent)
1456 Bankside Galleries (Tate Modern, London) 
1457 Road Marking (Cycle Network Artworks) 
1458 People of Salford (Lowry Centre, Salford) 

(Gravure Enschedé)

2000 (2 May). Millennium Projects (5th series). Art and Craft. Multicoloured. One centre phosphor band (2nd) or two phosphor bands (others). Perf 14×14½.

2142	1455	(2nd) Pottery Glaze	90	90
2143	1456	(1st) Bankside Galleries	1·00	1·00
2144	1457	45p. Road Marking	1·00	1·00
2145	1458	65p. People of Salford	1·25	1·25
Set of 4			3·75	3·75
Set of 4 Gutter Pairs			7·50	
First Day Cover (Philatelic Bureau) (Type J, see Introduction)				4·00
First Day Cover (Salford)				4·00
Presentation Pack (PO Pack No. 311)			4·25	
PHQ Cards (set of 4) (219)			1·25	4·00

For Nos. **MS**2146/**MS**2147, Types **1459**/**1459a**, see Decimal Machin Definitives section.

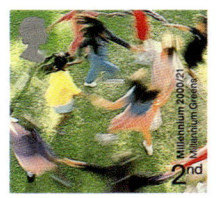

1460 Children playing (Millennium Greens Project)
1461 Millennium Bridge, Gateshead 
1462 Daisies (Mile End Park, London) 
1463 African Hut and Thatched Cottage (On the Meridian Line Project) 

(Gravure (2nd, 45p.) or litho (1st, 65p.) Walsall)

2000 (6 June). Millennium Projects (6th series). People and Places. Multicoloured One centre phosphor band (2nd) or two phosphor bands (others). Perf 14×14½.

2148	1460	(2nd) Children playing	90	90
2149	1461	(1st) Millennium Bridge, Gateshead	1·00	1·00
2150	1462	45p. Daisies	1·00	1·00
2151	1463	65p. African Hut and Thatched Cottage	1·25	1·25
Set of 4			3·75	3·75
Set of 4 Gutter Pairs			7·50	
First Day Cover (Philatelic Bureau) (Type J, see Introduction)				4·00
First Day Cover (Gateshead)				4·00
Presentation Pack (PO Pack No. 312)			4·25	
PHQ Cards (set of 4) (220)			1·25	4·50

1464 Raising the Stone (Strangford Stone, Killyleagh)
1465 Horse's Hooves (Trans Pennine Trail, Derbyshire) 
1466 Cyclist (Kingdom of Fife Cycleways, Scotland) 
1467 Bluebell Wood (Groundwork's Changing Places Project) 

(Gravure Walsall (Nos. 2153a, 2155a) or Enschedé (others))

2000 (4 July–18 Sept). Millennium Projects (7th series). Stone and Soil. Multicoloured One centre phosphor band (2nd) or two phosphor bands (others). Perf 14×14½

2152	1464	(2nd) Raising the Stone	90	90
2153	1465	(1st) Horse's Hooves	1·00	1·00
		a. Booklet pane. Nos. 2153 and 2157 with margins all round (18.9.2000)	2·40	
2154	1466	45p. Cyclist	90	90
2155	1467	65p. Bluebell Wood	1·10	1·10
		a. Booklet pane. No. 2155×2 with margins all round (18.9.2000)	2·25	
Set of 4			3·50	3·50
Set of 4 Gutter Pairs			7·00	
First Day Cover (Philatelic Bureau) (Type J, see Introduction)				4·00
First Day Cover (Killyleagh)				4·00
Presentation Pack (PO Pack No. 313)			4·00	
PHQ Cards (set of 4) (221)			1·25	4·25

No. 2153a comes from the £2·70 Millennium booklet, No. HBA4.
No. 2155a comes from the £7 Treasury of Trees booklet, No. DX26.

1468 Tree Roots (Yews for the Millennium Project)
1469 Sunflower (Eden Project, St Austell) 
1470 Sycamore Seeds (Millennium Seed Bank, Wakehurst Place, West Sussex) 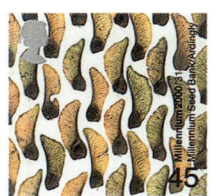
1471 Forest, Doire Dach (Forest for Scotland) 

(Gravure Walsall (Nos. 2156a, 2158a, 2159a) or De La Rue (others))

2000 (1 Aug–18 Sept). Millennium Projects (8th series). Tree and Leaf. Multicoloured One centre phosphor band (2nd) or two phosphor bands (others). Perf 14×14½.

2156	1468	(2nd) Tree Roots	90	90
		a. Booklet pane. No. 2156×4 with margins all round (18.9.2000)	4·00	

155

QUEEN ELIZABETH II/2000

2157	**1469**	(1st) Sunflower	1·00	1·00
2158	**1470**	45p. Sycamore Seeds	90	90
		a. Booklet pane. No. 2158×4 with margins all round (18.9.2000)	3·75	
2159	**1471**	65p. Forest, Doire Dach	1·10	1·10
		a. Booklet pane. No. 2159×2 with margins all round (18.9.2000)	2·40	
Set of 4			3·50	3·50
Set of 4 Gutter Pairs			7·00	
First Day Cover (Philatelic Bureau) (Type J, see Introduction)				4·00
First Day Cover (St Austell)				4·00
Presentation Pack (PO Pack No. 314)			4·00	
PHQ Cards (set of 4) (222)			1·25	4·25

Nos. 2156a, 2158a and 2159a come from the £7 Treasury of Trees booklet, No. DX26.

For No. 2157 printed by Walsall in gravure, see booklet pane No. 2153a.

1472 Queen Elizabeth the Queen Mother

1472a Royal Family on Queen Mother's 100th Birthday

(Des J. Gibbs from photo by J. Swannell. Gravure Questa (Nos. 2160, **MS**2161a) or De La Rue (No. **MS**2161))

2000 (4 Aug). Queen Elizabeth the Queen Mother's 100th Birthday. Multicoloured Phosphorised paper plus two phosphor bands. Perf 14½.

2160	**1472**	27p. Queen Elizabeth the Queen Mother	1·25	1·25
		a. Booklet pane. No. 2160×4 with margins all round	5·00	
MS2161 121×89mm. **1472a** 27p.×4, Royal Family on Queen Mother's 100th Birthday			5·00	5·00
		a. Booklet pane. As No. **MS**2161, but larger, 150×95 mm, and with additional silver frame	5·00	5·25
First Day Cover (Philatelic Bureau) (No. 2160a)				5·25
First Day Cover (London SW1) (No. 2160a)				5·25
First Day Cover (Philatelic Bureau) (No. **MS**2161)				5·25
First Day Cover (London SW1) (No. **MS**2161)				5·25
Presentation Pack (PO Pack No. M04) (No. **MS**2161)			11·00	
PHQ Cards (set of 5) (PSM04)			1·50	5·50

No. 2160 was only issued in the £7·03 The Life of the Century booklet, No. DX25 and as part of Nos. **MS**2161/**MS**2161a.

The complete miniature sheet is shown on one of the PHQ cards with the others depicting individual stamps.

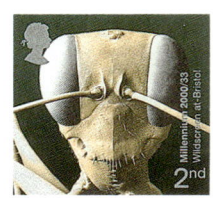

1473 Head of *Gigantiops destructor* (Ant) (Wildscreen at Bristol)

1474 Gathering Water Lilies on Broads (Norfolk and Norwich Project)

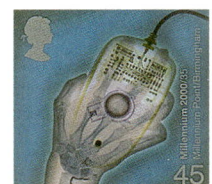

1475 X-ray of Hand holding Computer Mouse (Millennium Point, Birmingham)

1476 Tartan Wool Holder (Scottish Cultural Resources Access Network)

(Litho Walsall)

2000 (5 Sept). Millennium Projects (9th series). Mind and Matter. Multicoloured One centre phosphor band (2nd) or two phosphor bands (others). Perf 14×14½.

2162	**1473**	(2nd) Head of *Gigantiops destructor* (Ant)	90	90
2163	**1474**	(1st) Gathering Water Lilies on Broads	1·00	1·00
2164	**1475**	45p. X-ray of Hand holding Computer Mouse	90	90
2165	**1476**	65p. Tartan Wool Holder	1·10	1·10
Set of 4			3·50	3·50
Set of 4 Gutter Pairs			7·00	
First Day Cover (Philatelic Bureau) (Type J, see Introduction)				4·00
First Day Cover (Norwich)				4·00
Presentation Pack (PO Pack No. 315)			4·00	
PHQ Cards (set of 4) (223)			1·25	4·25

1477 Acrobatic Performers (Millennium Dome)

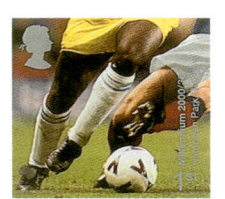

1478 Football Players (Hampden Park, Glasgow)

1479 Bather (Bath Spa Project)

1480 Hen's Egg under Magnification (Centre for Life, Newcastle)

(Litho (2nd) or gravure (others) Questa)

2000 (3 Oct). Millennium Projects (10th series). Body and Bone. Multicoloured One centre phosphor band (2nd) or two phosphor bands (others). Perf 14×14½ (2nd) or 13½×14 (others).

2166	**1477**	(2nd) Acrobatic Performers	90	90
2167	**1478**	(1st) Football Players	1·00	1·00
2168	**1479**	45p. Bather	90	90
2169	**1480**	65p. Hen's Egg under Magnification	1·10	1·10
Set of 4			3·50	3·50
Set of 4 Gutter Pairs			7·00	
First Day Cover (Philatelic Bureau) (Type J, see Introduction)				4·00
First Day Cover (Glasgow)				4·50
Presentation Pack (PO Pack No. 316)			4·00	
PHQ Cards (set of 4) (224)			1·25	4·25

2000/QUEEN ELIZABETH II

1481 Virgin and Child Stained-glass Window, St Edmundsbury Cathedral (Suffolk Cathedral Millennium Project)

1482 Floodlit Church of St Peter and St Paul, Overstowey (Church Floodlighting Trust)

1483 12th-century Latin Gradual (St Patrick Centre, Downpatrick)

1484 Chapter House Ceiling, York Minster (York Millennium Mystery Plays)

(Gravure De La Rue)

2000 (7 Nov). Millennium Projects (11th series). Spirit and Faith. Multicoloured One centre phosphor band (2nd) or two phosphor bands (others). Perf 14×14½.

2170	1481	(2nd) Virgin and Child Stained-glass Window, St Edmundsbury Cathedral............................	90	90
		a. Imperf pair............................	£400	
2171	1482	(1st) Floodlit Church of St Peter and St Paul, Overstowey............................	1·00	1·00
		a. Imperf (pair)............................	£450	
2172	1483	45p. 12th-century Latin Gradual............	90	90
2173	1484	65p. Chapter House Ceiling, York Minster............................	1·10	1·10
Set of 4............................			3·50	3·50
Set of 4 Gutter Pairs............................			7·00	
First Day Cover (Philatelic Bureau) (Type J, see Introduction)............................				4·00
First Day Cover (Downpatrick)............................				4·00
Presentation Pack (PO Pack No. 317)............................			4·00	
PHQ Cards (set of 4) (225)............................			1·25	4·25

No. 2173 has been reported with the gold omitted, leaving the Queen's head in yellow. It is only known used.

Post Office Yearbook

2000 (7 Nov). Comprises Nos. 2125/2126, 2127/2132, 2134/2145, 2148/2159 and **MS**2161/2177 in hardback book with slip case
YB2173a Yearbook............................ 48·00

The last two issues in the Millennium Projects Series were supplied for insertion into the above at a later date.

1485 Church Bells (Ringing in the Millennium)

1486 Eye (Year of the Artist)

1487 Top of Harp (Canolfan Mileniwm, Cardiff)

1488 Silhouetted Figure within Latticework (TS2K Creative Enterprise Centres, London)

(Gravure De La Rue)

2000 (5 Dec). Millennium Projects (12th series). Sound and Vision. Multicoloured. One centre phosphor band (2nd) or two phosphor bands (others). Perf 14×14½.

2174	1485	(2nd) Church Bells............................	90	90
2175	1486	(1st) Eye	1·00	1·00
2176	1487	45p. Top of Harp............................	90	90
2177	1488	65p. Silhouetted Figure within Latticework............................	1·10	1·10
Set of 4............................			3·50	3·50
Set of 4 Gutter Pairs............................			7·00	
First Day Cover (Philatelic Bureau) (Type J, see Introduction)............................				4·00
First Day Cover (Cardiff)............................				4·00
Presentation Pack (PO Pack No. 318)............................			4·00	
PHQ Cards (set of 4) (226)............................			1·25	4·25

Collectors Pack 2000

2000 (5 Dec) Comprises Nos. 2125/216, 2127/2132, 2134/2145, 2148/2159 and **MS**2161/2177.
CP2177a Collectors Pack (PO Pack No. 319)...... 65·00

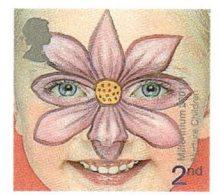

1489 Flower (Nurture Children)

1490 Tiger (Listen to Children)

1491 Owl (Teach Children)

1492 Butterfly (Ensure Children's Freedom)

(Des Why Not Associates. Gravure De La Rue)

2001 (16 Jan). New Millennium. Rights of the Child. Face Paintings. Multicoloured One centre phosphor band (2nd) or two phosphor bands (others). Perf 14×14½.

2178	1489	(2nd) Flower (Nurture Children)............	90	90
2179	1490	(1st) Tiger (Listen to Children)............	1·00	1·00
2180	1491	45p. Owl (Teach Children)............	1·00	1·00
2181	1492	65p. Butterfly (Ensure Children's Freedom)............	1·25	1·25
Set of 4............................			3·75	3·75
Set of 4 Gutter Pairs............................			7·50	
First Day Cover (Philatelic Bureau)............................				4·00
First Day Cover (Hope, Hope Valley)............................				4·00
Presentation Pack (PO Pack No. 319)............................			4·25	
PHQ Cards (set of 4) (227)............................			1·25	4·25

1493 Love

1494 THANKS

1495 abc (New Baby)

1496 WELCOME

QUEEN ELIZABETH II/2001

1497 Cheers

(Des Springpoint Design. Gravure Enschedé)

2001 (6–13 Feb). Greetings Stamps. Occasions. Multicoloured Two phosphor bands. Perf 14×14½.

2182	1493	(1st) Love	1·20	1·00
2183	1494	(1st) THANKS	1·20	1·00
2184	1495	(1st) abc (New Baby)	1·20	1·00
2185	1496	(1st) WELCOME	1·20	1·00
2186	1497	(1st) Cheers	1·20	1·00
Set of 5			5·50	4·50
Set of 5 Gutter Pairs			11·00	
First Day Cover (Philatelic Bureau)				4·75
First Day Cover (Merry Hill, Wolverhampton)				4·75
Presentation Pack (PO Pack No. M05) (13.2.01)			7·25	
PHQ Cards (set of 5) (PSM05)			1·50	5·00

The silver-grey backgrounds are printed in Iriodin ink which gives a shiny effect.

Further packs of Nos. 2182/2186 were sold from 3 July 2001. These comprised the listed stamps in blocks of ten (from sheets) with an insert describing the occasion (*Price £10 per pack*).

Nos. 2182/2186 were re-issued on 1 May 2001 in sheets of 20 printed by Questa in lithography instead of gravure, in connection with the 'customised' stamps scheme. Such sheets contained 20 examples of either Nos. 2182, 2184 or 2185, or ten each of Nos. 2183 and 2186.

Sheets with personal photographs printed on the labels were available from Royal Mail in Edinburgh at £12 each.

From 5 June 2001 a similar sheet (No. LS4) containing four of each design in horizontal strips, with postal symbols on the labels, was sold at £5·95.

1498 Dog and Owner on Bench

1499 Dog in Bath

1500 Boxer at Dog Show

1501 Cat in Handbag

1502 Cat on Gate

1503 Dog in Car

1504 Cat at Window

1505 Dog Behind Fence

1506 Cat watching Bird

1507 Cat in Washbasin

(Des johnson banks. Gravure Walsall)

2001 (13 Feb). Cats and Dogs. Multicoloured Self-adhesive. Two phosphor bands. Perf 15×14 die-cut.

2187	1498	(1st) Dog and Owner on Bench	1·20	1·00
		a. Sheetlet of 10. Nos. 2187/2196	11·00	9·00
		aa. Imperf (sheetlet)	—	
		b. Booklet pane. Nos. 2187/2196 plus No. 2040×2	25·00	
		ba. Imperf (pane)		
2188	1499	(1st) Dog in Bath	1·20	1·00
2189	1500	(1st) Boxer at Dog Show	1·20	1·00
2190	1501	(1st) Cat in Handbag	1·20	1·00
2191	1502	(1st) Cat on Gate	1·20	1·00
2192	1503	(1st) Dog in Car	1·20	1·00
2193	1504	(1st) Cat at Window	1·20	1·00
2194	1505	(1st) Dog Behind Fence	1·20	1·00
2195	1506	(1st) Cat watching Bird	1·20	1·00
2196	1507	(1st) Cat in Washbasin	1·20	1·00
Set of 10			11·00	9·00
First Day Cover (Philatelic Bureau)				9·75
First Day Cover (Petts Wood, Orpington)				9·75
Presentation Pack (PO Pack No. 320)			12·00	
PHQ Cards (set of 10) (228)			3·00	12·00

Nos. 2187/2196 were printed together in sheetlets of ten (5×2), with the surplus self-adhesive paper around each stamp retained. The pane has vertical roulettes between rows 2/3 and 4/5 with the design on the reverse of the backing paper similar to Booklet No. PM1.

1508 'RAIN'

1509 'FAIR'

1510 'STORMY'

1511 'VERY DRY'

1511a The Weather (*Illustration reduced. Actual size 105×105 mm*)

(Des H. Brown and T. Meeuwissen. Gravure De La Rue)

2001 (13 Mar). The Weather. Multicoloured One side phosphor band (19p.) or two phosphor bands (others). Perf 14½.

2197	1508	19p. 'RAIN'	70	70
2198	1509	27p. 'FAIR'	80	80
2199	1510	45p. 'STORMY'	95	95
2200	1511	65p. 'VERY DRY'	1·10	1·10
Set of 4			3·25	3·25

2001/QUEEN ELIZABETH II

Set of 4 Gutter Pairs	6·50
First Day Cover (Philatelic Bureau)	3·50
First Day Cover (Fraserburgh)	3·50
Presentation Pack (PO Pack No. 321)	9·00
MS2201 **1511**a 105×105 mm. Nos. 2197/2200	9·25 9·25
First Day Cover (Philatelic Bureau)	10·00
First Day Cover (Fraserburgh)	10·00
PHQ Cards (set of 5) (229)	1·50 14·00

Nos. 2197/2200 show the four quadrants of a barometer dial which are combined on the miniature sheet.

The reddish violet on both the 27p. and the miniature sheet is printed in thermochromic ink which changes from reddish violet to light blue when exposed to heat.

The PHQ cards depict the four values and the miniature sheet.

1512 Vanguard Class Submarine, 1992

1513 Swiftsure Class Submarine, 1973

1514 Unity Class Submarine, 1939

1515 Holland Type Submarine, 1901

1516 White Ensign

1517 Union Jack

1518 Jolly Roger flown by HMS Proteus (submarine)

1519 Flag of Chief of Defence Staff

1519a (Illustration reduced. Actual size 92×97 mm)

(Des D. Davis. Gravure Questa)

2001 (10 Apr–22 Oct). Centenary of Royal Navy Submarine Service. Multicoloured One centre phosphor band (2nd) or two phosphor bands (others). Perf 15×14.

(a) Submarines. Ordinary gum.

2202	**1512**	(2nd) Vanguard Class Submarine, 1992	90	90
		a. Perf 15½×15 (22.10.01)	2·00	2·00
		ab. Booklet pane. Nos. 2202a and 2204a, each×2, with margins all round	7·00	
2203	**1513**	(1st) Swiftsure Class Submarine, 1973	1·00	1·00
		a. Perf 15½×15 (22.10.01)	1·95	1·95
		b. Imperf (pair)	£950	
		ab. Booklet pane. Nos. 2203a and 2205a, each×2, with margins all round	8·00	
2204	**1514**	45p. Unity Class Submarine, 1939	90	90
		a. Perf 15½×15 (22.10.01)	2·00	2·00
2205	**1515**	65p. Holland Type Submarine, 1901	1·10	1·10
		a. Perf 15½×15 (22.10.01)	2·00	2·00
Set of 4			3·50	3·50
Set of 4 Gutter Pairs			7·00	
First Day Cover (Philatelic Bureau)				3·75
First Day Cover (Portsmouth)				3·75
Presentation Pack (PO Pack No. 322)			16·00	
PHQ Cards (set of 4) (230)			1·25	4·00

(b) Flags. Ordinary gum. Perf 14½.

MS2206 92×97 mm. **1519**a (1st) White Ensign; (1st) Union Jack; (1st) Jolly Roger flown by HMS *Proteus* (submarine); (1st) Flag of Chief of Defence Staff (22.10.01) .... 5·25 5·25

a. Booklet pane. As No. **MS**2206 but larger, 152×96 mm	5·25
First Day Cover (Tallents House)	4·75
First Day Cover (Rosyth, Dunfermline)	5·25
Presentation Pack (PO Pack No. M06)	15·00
PHQ Cards (set of 5) (PSM07)	1·50 6·00

(c) Self-adhesive. Die-cut Perf 15½×14 (No. 2207) or 14½ (others).

2207	**1513**	(1st) Swiftsure Class Submarine, 1973 (17.4.01)	30·00	30·00
		a. Booklet pane. No. 2207×2 plus No. 2040×4	70·00	
		ab. Booklet pane. Imperf	£3750	
2208	**1516**	(1st) White Ensign (22.10.01)	7·00	7·00
		a. Booklet pane. Nos. 2208/2209 plus No. 2040×4	15·00	
		ab. Booklet pane. Imperf		
2209	**1518**	(1st) Jolly Roger flown by HMS *Proteus* (submarine) (22.10.01)	7·00	7·00

Nos. 2202a/2205a were only issued in the £6·76 Unseen and Unheard booklet, No. DX27.

Nos. 2207/2209 only come from two different £1·62 self-adhesive booklets, Nos. PM2 and PM4.

T **1516** was re-issued on 21 June 2005 in sheets of 20, printed in lithography by Cartor and sold at £6·55, containing four vertical rows of five stamps alternated with half stamp-size printed labels showing signal flags (No. LS25). These sheets with personalised photographs were available at £14·95 from the Royal Mail.

It was subsequently issued, printed in lithography, perf 14½, in booklets Nos. DX35 and DX41 (see No. 2581).

T **1517** was re-issued on 27 July 2004 in sheets of 20, printed in lithography by Walsall and sold at £6·15 containing vertical strips of five stamps alternated with half stamp-size printed labels (No. LS20) These sheets with personalised photographs were available at £14·95 from the Royal Mail in Edinburgh.

It was subsequently issued, printed in lithography, perf 14½, in booklet No. DX41 (see No. 2805).

T **1518** was subsequently issued, printed in lithography, perf 14½, in booklet No. DX47 (see No. 2970).

The five PHQ cards depict the four designs and the complete miniature sheet, No. **MS**2206.

1520 Leyland X2 Open-top, London General B Type, Leyland Titan TD1 and AEC Regent 1

1521 AEC Regent 1, Daimler COG5, Utility Guy Arab Mk II and AEC Regent III RT Type

QUEEN ELIZABETH II/2001

1522 AEC Regent III RT Type, Bristol KSW5G Open-top, AEC Routemaster and Bristol Lodekka FSF6G

1523 Bristol Lodekka FSF6G, Leyland Titan PD3/4, Leyland Atlantean PDR1/1 and Daimler Fleetline CRG6LX-33

1527 Top Hat by Stephen Jones

1528 Spiral Hat by Philip Treacy

(Des Rose Design from photos by N. Knight. Litho Enschedé)

2001 (19 June). Fashion Hats. Multicoloured 'All-over' phosphor. Perf 14½.

2216	1525	(1st) Toque Hat by Pip Hackett	1·20	1·00
2217	1526	(E) Butterfly Hat by Dai Rees	2·25	1·50
2218	1527	45p. Top Hat by Stephen Jones	90	90
2219	1528	65p. Spiral Hat by Philip Treacy	1·10	1·10
Set of 4			4·75	4·00
Set of 4 Gutter Pairs			9·50	
First Day Cover (Tallents House)				4·25
First Day Cover (Ascot)				4·25
Presentation Pack (PO Pack No. 324)			5·25	
PHQ Cards (set of 4) (232)			1·50	4·50

1524 Daimler Fleetline CRG6LX-33, MCW Metrobus DR102/43, Leyland Olympian ONLXB/1R and Dennis Trident

(Des M. English. Litho Questa)

2001 (15 May). 150th Anniversary of First Double-decker Bus. Multicoloured 'All-over' phosphor. Perf 14½×14.

2210	1520	(1st) Leyland X2 Open-top, London General B Type, Leyland Titan TD1 and AEC Regent 1	1·20	1·00
		a. Horiz strip of 5. Nos. 2210/2214	5·50	4·50
		ab. Imperf (horiz strip of 5)	£3500	
		b. Grey omitted	—	
2211	1521	(1st) AEC Regent 1, Daimler COG5, Utility Guy Arab Mk II and AEC Regent III RT Type	1·20	1·00
2212	1522	(1st) AEC Regent III RT Type, Bristol KSW5G Open-top, AEC Routemaster and Bristol Lodekka FSF6G	1·20	1·00
		a. Grey omitted	—	
2213	1523	(1st) Bristol Lodekka FSF6G, Leyland Titan PD3/4, Leyland Atlantean PDR1/1 and Daimler Fleetline CRG6LX-33	1·20	1·00
		a. Grey omitted	—	
2214	1524	(1st) Daimler Fleetline CRG6LX-33, MCW Metrobus DR102/43, Leyland Olympian ONLXB/1R and Dennis Trident	1·20	1·00
		a. Grey omitted	—	
Set of 5			5·50	4·50
Gutter Strip of 10			11·00	
First Day Cover (Philatelic Bureau)				4·75
First Day Cover (Covent Garden, London WC2)				4·75
Presentation Pack (PO Pack No. 323)			9·00	
PHQ Cards (set of 6) (231)			1·75	5·50
MS2215 120×105 mm. Nos. 2210/2214			6·00	6·00
First Day Cover (Philatelic Bureau)				7·50
First Day Cover (Covent Garden, London WC2)				7·50

Nos. 2210/2214 were printed together, *se-tenant*, in horizontal strips of five throughout the sheet. The illustrations of the first bus on No. 2210 and the last bus on No. 2214 continue onto the sheet margins.

In No. **MS**2215 the illustrations of the AEC Regent III RT Type and the Daimler Fleetline CRG6LX-33 appear twice.

The six PHQ cards show the six stamps and No. **MS**2215.

1529 Common Frog

1530 Great Diving Beetle

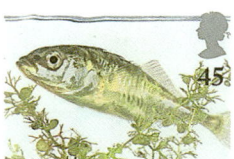

1531 Three-Spined Stickleback

1532 Southern Hawker Dragonfly

(Des J. Gibbs. Gravure De La Rue)

2001 (10 July). Europa. Pond Life. Multicoloured Two phosphor bands. Perf 15×14.

2220	1529	(1st) Common Frog	1·00	1·00
2221	1530	(E) Great Diving Beetle	1·75	1·50
2222	1531	45p. Three-Spined Stickleback	90	1·00
2223	1532	65p. Southern Hawker Dragonfly	1·10	1·20
Set of 4			4·25	4·00
Set of 4 Gutter Pairs			8·50	
First Day Cover (Tallents House)				4·75
First Day Cover (Oundle, Peterborough)				5·00
Presentation Pack (PO Pack No. 325)			5·00	
PHQ Cards (set of 4) (233)			1·50	4·75

The 1st and E values incorporate the EUROPA emblem.

The bluish silver on all four values is in Iriodin ink and was used as a background for those parts of the design below the water line.

1525 Toque Hat by Pip Hackett

1526 Butterfly Hat by Dai Rees

1533 Policeman

1534 Clown

1535 Mr Punch
1536 Judy 
1537 Beadle 
1538 Crocodile 

(Des K. Bernstein from puppets by Bryan Clarkez)

2001 (4 Sept). Punch and Judy Show Puppets. Multicoloured Two phosphor bands. Perf 14×15.

(a) Gravure Walsall. Ordinary gum.

2224	1533	(1st) Policeman	1·20	1·00
		a. Horiz strip of 6. Nos. 2224/2229	6·50	5·50
2225	1534	(1st) Clown	1·20	1·00
2226	1535	(1st) Mr Punch	1·20	1·00
2227	1536	(1st) Judy	1·20	1·00
2228	1537	(1st) Beadle	1·20	1·00
2229	1538	(1st) Crocodile	1·20	1·00
Set of 6			6·50	5·50
Gutter Block of 12			13·00	
First Day Cover (Tallents House)				6·25
First Day Cover (Blackpool)				6·50
Presentation Pack (PO Pack No. 326)			7·00	
PHQ Cards (set of 6) (234)			1·75	6·25

(b) Gravure Questa. Self-adhesive. Die-cut Perf 14×15½.

2230	1535	(1st) Mr Punch	7·00	7·00
		a. Booklet pane. Nos. 2230/2231 plus No. 2040×4	15·00	
2231	1536	(1st) Judy	7·00	7·00

Nos. 2224/2229 were printed together, *se-tenant*, as horizontal strips of six in sheets of 60 (6×10).

Nos. 2230/2231 were only issued in £1·62 stamp booklet, No. PM3.

Imperforate strips of 6 with alternative background colours to Nos. 2224, 2228 and 2229 are of proof status (*Price £3000*).

1539 Carbon 60 Molecule (Chemistry)
1540 Globe (Economic Sciences) 
1541 Embossed Dove (Peace)
1542 Crosses (Physiology or Medicine)
1543 Poem *The Addressing of Cats* by T. S. Eliot in Open Book (Literature) 
1544 Hologram of Boron Molecule (Physics) 

(Des P. Vermier. Eng Inge Madlé (1st). Printed Litho and silk-screen (2nd), litho and recess (1st), litho and embossed (E), litho (45p.), litho and hologram (65p.) Enschedé)

2001 (2 Oct). Centenary of Nobel Prizes. Multicoloured One side phosphor band (2nd) or phosphor frame (others). Perf 14½.

2232	1539	(2nd) Carbon 60 Molecule (Chemistry)	90	90
2233	1540	(1st) Globe (Economic Sciences)	1·20	1·00
2234	1541	(E) Embossed Dove (Peace)	2·25	1·50
2235	1542	40p. Crosses (Physiology or Medicine)	1·50	1·50
2236	1543	45p. Poem *The Addressing of Cats* by T. S. Eliot in Open Book (Literature)	2·00	2·00
2237	1544	65p. Hologram of Boron Molecule (Physics)	2·50	2·50
Set of 6			8·75	8·50
Set of 6 Gutter Pairs			17·00	
First Day Cover (Tallents House)				9·00
First Day Cover (Cambridge)				9·00
Presentation Pack (PO Pack No. 327)			15·00	
PHQ Cards (set of 6) (235)			1·75	9·75

The grey-black on No. 2232 is printed in thermochromic ink which temporarily changes to pale grey when exposed to heat.

The centre of No. 2235 is coated with a eucalyptus scent.

Trials, differing slightly from the issued stamps, are known for all values.

No. 2237 has been reported completely imperforate, its status is unknown.

1545 Robins with Snowman
1546 Robins on Bird Table 
1547 Robins skating on Bird Bath 
1548 Robins with Christmas Pudding 
1549 Robins in Paper Chain Nest 

(Des A. Robins and H. Brown. Gravure De La Rue)

2001 (6 Nov). Christmas. Robins. Self-adhesive. Multicoloured One centre phosphor band (2nd) or two phosphor bands (others). Die-cut perf 14½.

2238	1545	(2nd) Robins with Snowman	90	90
		a. Booklet pane. No. 2238×24	22·00	
		b. Imperf (pair)	£450	
2239	1546	(1st) Robins on Bird Table	1·20	1·00
		a. Booklet pane. No. 2239×12	16·00	
		b. Imperf (pair)	—	

QUEEN ELIZABETH II/2001

2240	**1547**	(E) Robins skating on Bird Bath	2·25	1·50
2241	**1548**	45p. Robins with Christmas Pudding	1·00	1·10
2242	**1549**	65p. Robins in Paper Chain Nest	1·10	1·25
		a. Imperf (pair) (die-cut perforations and roulettes omitted)	£600	
		ab. Imperf (pair) (die-cut perforations only omitted)	£275	
		b. Imperf backing paper (pair) (roulettes omitted)	£125	
Set of 5			6·00	5·00
First Day Cover (Tallents House)				5·50
First Day Cover (Bethlehem, Llandeilo)				5·50
Presentation Pack (PO Pack No. 328)			6·25	
PHQ Cards (set of 5) (236)			1·50	5·50

Nos. 2238/2242 were each printed in sheets of 50 with the surplus backing paper around each stamp retained and separated by gauge 9 roulettes.

The 1st value was re-issued on 30 September 2003 in sheets of 20 (*sold at £6·15*) printed in lithography instead of gravure, each stamp accompanied by a stamp-size label showing a snowman (No. LS14). Sheets with personal photographs printed on the labels were available from Royal Mail, Edinburgh for £14·95 or photo-booths at selected post offices and Safeway stores for £15.

The 2nd and 1st values were re-issued together on 1 November 2005 in sheets of 20, printed in lithography by Cartor (*sold at £5·60*), containing ten 2nd class and ten 1st class stamps, each stamp accompanied by a label showing a snowman (No. LS27). Separate sheets of 20 2nd class and 20 1st class were available with personalised photographs at £9·95 (2nd) or £14·95 (1st) from Royal Mail.

No. 2238b shows both the die-cut perforations and the roulettes omitted.

Stamps from booklet panes Nos. 2238a and 2239a differ from those in sheets by omitting the roulettes in the backing paper between each stamp. Instead there are roulettes after the first and then every alternate horizontal row to assist with the folding of the booklets.

Trials of (2nd) and (1st) stamps in alternative designs are known.

Year Pack 2001

2001 (6 Nov). Comprises Nos. 2178/2200, 2202/2206, 2210/2214, 2216/2229 and 2232/2242.
CP2242a   Year Pack (PO Pack No. 329) .... 70·00

Post Office Yearbook

2001 (6 Nov) Comprises Nos. 2178/2196, **MS**2201/2206, 2210/2214, 2216/2229 and 2232/2242 in hardback book with slip case
YB2242a   Yearbook .... 48·00

1550 How the Whale got his Throat
1551 How the Camel got his Hump 
1552 How the Rhinoceros got his Skin 
1553 How the Leopard got his Spots 
1554 The Elephant's Child 
1555 The Sing-Song of Old Man Kangaroo 
1556 The Beginning of the Armadillos 
1557 The Crab that played with the Sea 
1558 The Cat that walked by Himself 
1559 The Butterfly that stamped 

(Des I. Cohen. Gravure Walsall)

2002 (15 Jan). Centenary of Publication of Rudyard Kipling's Just So Stories. Self-adhesive. Multicoloured Two phosphor bands. Die-cut Perf 15×14.

2243	**1550**	(1st) How the Whale got his Throat	1·20	1·00
		a. Sheetlet of 10. Nos. 2243/2252	11·00	9·00
2244	**1551**	(1st) How the Camel got his Hump	1·20	1·00
2245	**1552**	(1st) How the Rhinoceros got his Skin	1·20	1·00
2246	**1553**	(1st) How the Leopard got his Spots	1·20	1·00
2247	**1554**	(1st) The Elephant's Child	1·20	1·00
2248	**1555**	(1st) The Sing-Song of Old Man Kangaroo	1·20	1·00
2249	**1556**	(1st) The Beginning of the Armadillos	1·20	1·00
2250	**1557**	(1st) The Crab that played with the Sea	1·20	1·00
2251	**1558**	(1st) The Cat that walked by Himself	1·20	1·00
2252	**1559**	(1st) The Butterfly that stamped	1·20	1·00
Set of 10			11·00	9·00
First Day Cover (Tallents House)				9·25
First Day Cover (Burwash, Etchingham)				9·25
Presentation Pack (PO Pack No. 330)			12·00	
PHQ Cards (set of 10) (237)			3·00	11·00

Nos. 2243/2252 were printed together in sheetlets of ten (5×2), with the surplus self-adhesive paper around each stamp retained.

No. 2243a was in the form of an unfolded booklet with vertical roulettes between columns 2/3 and 4/5 and the backing design being an illustrated booklet cover. However, since it was sold unfolded, we treat it as a sheetlet rather than a booklet.

1560 Queen Elizabeth II, 1952 (Dorothy Wilding)
1561 Queen Elizabeth II, 1968 (Cecil Beaton) 
1562 Queen Elizabeth II, 1978 (Lord Snowdon) 
1563 Queen Elizabeth II, 1984 (Yousef Karsh)

2002/QUEEN ELIZABETH II

1564 Queen Elizabeth II, 1996 (Tim Graham)  **1565**

1567 Rabbits ('a new baby') **1568** 'LOVE'

1569 Aircraft Skywriting 'hello' **1570** Bear pulling Potted Topiary Tree (Moving Home)

(Des Kate Stephens. Gravure De La Rue)

2002 (6 Feb). Golden Jubilee. Studio portraits of Queen Elizabeth II by photographers named. Multicoloured One centre phosphor band (2nd) or two phosphor bands (others). W **1565** (sideways). Perf 14½×14.

2253	1560	(2nd) Queen Elizabeth II, 1952 (Dorothy Wilding)	90	90
		a. Watermark upright	3·00	3·00
		b. Booklet pane. Nos. 2253a/2256a with margins all round	7·50	
2254	1561	(1st) Queen Elizabeth II, 1968 (Cecil Beaton)	1·20	1·00
		a. Watermark upright	1·40	1·40
		b. Booklet pane. Nos. 2254a/2257a with margins all round	8·00	
2255	1562	(E) Queen Elizabeth II, 1978 (Lord Snowdon)	2·25	1·50
		a. Watermark upright. No DX28	2·00	1·40
2256	1563	45p. Queen Elizabeth II, 1984 (Yousef Karsh)	1·00	1·10
		a. Watermark upright	1·40	1·40
2257	1564	65p. Queen Elizabeth II, 1996 (Tim Graham)	1·10	1·25
		a. Watermark upright	3·00	3·00
Set of 5			5·75	5·00
Set of 5 Gutter Pairs			11·50	
First Day Cover (Tallents House)				5·25
First Day Cover (Windsor)				5·50
Presentation Pack (PO Pack No. 331)			7·00	
PHQ Cards (set of 5) (238)			1·50	5·75

The turquoise-green is used as an underlay for the black colour on all five values.

Nos. 2253a/2257a were only issued in the £7·29 A Glorious Accession booklet, No DX28.

Trials, including dates and with values in a different typeface, are known for all values.

1571 Flowers ('best wishes')

(Des I. Bilbey (Nos. 2260, 2264), A. Kitching (No. 2261), Hoop Associates (No. 2262) and G. Percy (No. 2263))

2002 (5 Mar)–**2003**. Greetings Stamps. Occasions. Multicoloured Two phosphor bands.

(a) Litho Questa. Ordinary gum. Perf 15×14.

2260	1567	(1st) Rabbits 'a new baby'	1·20	1·10
2261	1568	(1st) 'LOVE'	1·20	1·10
2262	1569	(1st) Aircraft Skywriting 'hello'	1·20	1·10
2263	1570	(1st) Bear pulling Potted Topiary Tree (Moving Home)	1·20	1·10
2264	1571	(1st) 'best wishes'	1·20	1·10
Set of 5			5·50	5·00
Set of 5 Gutter Pairs			11·00	
First Day Cover (Tallents House)				5·25
First Day Cover (Merry Hill, Wolverhampton)				5·50
Presentation Pack (PO Pack No. M07)			5·75	
PHQ Cards (set of 5) (PSM08)			1·50	6·00

(b) Gravure Questa. Self-adhesive. Die-cut Perf 15×14.

2264a	1569	(1st) Aircraft Skywriting 'hello' (4.3.03)	3·00	3·00
		ab. Booklet pane. No. 2264a×2 plus No. 2295×4	7·50	

Nos. 2260/2264 were re-issued on 23 April 2002 in sheets of 20 with half stamp-size labels, with either the five designs *se-tenant* with greetings on the labels (No. LS7, *sold at* £5·95) or in sheets of one design with personal photographs on the labels (*sold at* £12·95). These sheets, printed by Questa in lithography, were perforated 14 instead of 15×14.

T **1569** was re-issued in sheets of 20 with half stamp-size *se-tenant* labels all printed in lithography as follows: on 30 January 2004 for Hong Kong Stamp Expo (No. LS17, Walsall), on 21 April 2005 for Pacific Explorer 2005 World Stamp Expo (No. LS24, Walsall, Perf 14), on 25 May 2006 for Washington 2006 International Stamp Exhibition (No. LS30, Cartor, Perf 14) on 14 November 2006 for Belgica 2006 International Stamp Exhibition (No. LS36, Cartor, Perf 14), on 5 August 2008 for Beijing 2008 Olympic Expo (No. LS48, Cartor, Perf 14), on 3 August 2009 for Thaipex 09 Stamp Exhibition (No. LS64, Cartor, Perf 14), on 21 October 2009 for Italia 2009 International Stamp Exhibition (No. LS66, Cartor, Perf 14) and on 4 December 2009 for MonacoPhil International Stamp Exhibition (No. LS69, Cartor, Perf 14).

No. 2264a was only issued in £1·62 stamp booklet, No. PM8, in which the surplus self-adhesive paper around each stamp was removed.

1566 **1566a**

(Des M. Farrar-Bell (2nd), Enid Marx (1st). Gravure Enschedé)

2002 (6 Feb). As Types **154/155** (Wilding definitive of 1952–1954), but with service indicator as Types **1566/1566a**. One centre phosphor band (2nd) or two phosphor bands (1st). W **1565**. Uncoated paper. Perf 15×14 (with one elliptical hole in each vertical side).

2258	1566	(2nd) carmine-red	1·20	1·20
		a. Watermark diagonal	2·00	2·00
		b. Booklet pane. Nos. 2258b×2, 2258a×4 and 2259×4 with centre blank label and margins all round. This is a pane of 12 stamps four of each type	8·00	
2259	1566a	(1st) green	1·25	1·25
Set of 2			2·12	2·20
First Day Cover (Tallents House) (No. 2258b)				8·00
First Day Cover (Windsor) (No. 2258b)				8·00

Nos. 2258/2259 were only issued in the £7·29 A Gracious Accession booklet, No. DX28.

No. 2258b contains a block of eight, four of each value, with a blank central label, plus an additional 2nd value shown to the left at such an angle so as to produce a diagonal watermark.

First day cover postmarks were as Nos. 2253/2257.

For other Wilding designs with decimal values see Nos. 2031/2033, **MS**2326, **MS**2367, 2378/2380 and 3329.

1572 Studland Bay, Dorset  **1573** Luskentyre, South Harris

QUEEN ELIZABETH II/2002

1574 Cliffs, Dover, Kent
1575 Padstow Harbour, Cornwall 
1576 Broadstairs, Kent 
1577 St Abb's Head, Scottish Borders 
1578 Dunster Beach, Somerset 
1579 Newquay Beach, Cornwall 
1580 Portrush, County Antrim 
1581 Sand-spit, Conwy 

(Des R. Cooke. Litho Walsall)

2002 (19 Mar). British Coastlines. Multicoloured Two phosphor bands. Perf 14½.

2265	1572	27p. Studland Bay, Dorset	50	50
		a. Block of 10. Nos. 2265/2274	4·50	4·50
		b. Silver omitted (block of 10)	£3750	
2266	1573	27p. Luskentyre, South Harris	50	50
2267	1574	27p. Cliffs, Dover, Kent	50	50
2268	1575	27p. Padstow Harbour, Cornwall	50	50
2269	1576	27p. Broadstairs, Kent	50	50
2270	1577	27p. St Abb's Head, Scottish Borders	50	50
2271	1578	27p. Dunster Beach, Somerset	50	50
2272	1579	27p. Newquay Beach, Cornwall	50	50
2273	1580	27p. Portrush, County Antrim	50	50
2274	1581	27p. Sand-spit, Conwy	50	50
Set of 10			4·50	4·50
Gutter Block of 20			9·00	
First Day Cover (Tallents House)				4·75
First Day Cover (Poolewe, Achnasheen)				5·00
Presentation Pack (PO Pack No. 332)			5·00	
PHQ Cards (set of 10) (239)			3·00	6·00

Nos. 2265/2274 were printed together, *se-tenant*, in blocks of ten (5×2) throughout the sheet.

1582 Slack Wire Act
1583 Lion Tamer 
1584 Trick Tri-cyclists 
1585 Krazy Kar 
1586 Equestrienne 

(Des R. Fuller. Gravure Questa)

2002 (10 Apr*). Europa. Circus. Multicoloured One centre phosphor band (2nd) or two phosphor bands (others). Perf 14½.

2275	1582	(2nd) Slack Wire Act	90	90
2276	1583	(1st) Lion Tamer	1·20	1·00
		a. Imperf (vert pair)	£1250	
2277	1584	(E) Trick Tri-cyclists	2·25	1·50
		a. Imperf (pair)	£1500	
2278	1585	45p. Krazy Kar	1·00	1·10
2279	1586	65p. Equestrienne	1·10	1·25
Set of 5			5·25	5·00
Set of 5 Gutter Pairs			11·00	
First Day Cover (Tallents House)				5·25
First Day Cover (Clowne, Chesterfield)				5·50
Presentation Pack (PO Pack No. 333)			5·75	
PHQ Cards (set of 5) (240)			1·50	5·75

* Due to the funeral of the Queen Mother, the issue of Nos. 2275/2279 was delayed from 9 April, the date which appears on first day covers. The 1st and E values incorporate the EUROPA emblem.

1587 Queen Elizabeth the Queen Mother
1587a Queen Elizabeth 
1587b Elizabeth, Duchess of York 
1587c Lady Elizabeth Bowes-Lyon

2002/QUEEN ELIZABETH II

(Des J. Gorham from photographs by N. Parkinson (1st), Dorothy Wilding (E), B. Park (45p.), Rita Martin (65p.). Gravure De La Rue)

2002 (25 Apr). Queen Elizabeth the Queen Mother Commemoration. Multicoloured Two phosphor bands. Perf 14×15.

2280	**1587**	(1st) Queen Elizabeth the Queen Mother	1·20	1·00
2281	**1587a**	(E) Queen Elizabeth	2·25	1·50
2282	**1587b**	45p. Elizabeth, Duchess of York	1·00	1·10
2283	**1587c**	65p. Lady Elizabeth Bowes-Lyon	1·10	1·25
Set of 4			4·75	4·25
Set of 4 Gutter Pairs			9·50	
First Day Cover (Tallents House)				4·50
First Day Cover (London SW1)				4·75
Presentation Pack (PO Pack No. M08)			5·00	

1588 Airbus A340-600 (2002)
1589 Concorde (1976) 
1590 Trident (1964) 
1591 VC10 (1964) 
1592 Comet (1952) 

(Des Roundel)

2002 (2 May). 50th Anniversary of Passenger Jet Aviation. Airliners. Multicoloured One centre phosphor band (2nd) or two phosphor bands (others). Perf 14½.

(a) Gravure De La Rue. Ordinary gum.

2284	**1588**	(2nd) Airbus A340-600 (2002)	90	90
2285	**1589**	(1st) Concorde (1976)	1·20	1·00
2286	**1590**	(E) Trident (1964)	2·25	1·50
2287	**1591**	45p. VC10 (1964)	1·20	1·20
2288	**1592**	65p. Comet (1952)	1·40	1·40
Set of 5			6·25	6·00
Set of 5 Gutter Pairs			12·50	
First Day Cover (Tallents House)				6·50
First Day Cover (Heathrow Airport, London)				7·00
Presentation Pack (PO Pack No. 334)			7·00	
MS2289 120×105 mm. Nos. 2284/2288			7·00	7·00
First Day Cover (Tallents House)				7·50
First Day Cover (Heathrow Airport, London)				7·50
PHQ Cards (set of 6) (241)			1·75	12·00

(b) Gravure Questa. Self-adhesive. Die-cut Perf 14½.

2290	**1589**	(1st) Concorde (1976)	3·00	3·00
		a. Booklet pane. No. 2040×4 and No. 2290×2	7·50	

No. 2290 was only issued in £1·62 stamp booklet, No. PM5.
The complete miniature sheet is shown on one of the PHQ cards with the others depicting individual stamps.
See also No. 2897.

1593 Crowned Lion with Shield of St George

1594 Top Left Quarter of English Flag, and Football
1595 Top Right Quarter of English Flag, and Football 
1596 Bottom Left Quarter of English Flag, and Football 
1597 Bottom Right Quarter of English Flag, and Football 

(Des Sedley Place (No. 2291), H. Brown (No. **MS**2292). Gravure Walsall)

2002 (21 May). World Cup Football Championship, Japan and Korea. Multicoloured Two phosphor bands. Perf 14½×14.

(a) Ordinary gum.

2291	**1593**	(1st) Crowned Lion with Shield of St George	1·25	1·25
Gutter Pair			2·50	
MS2292 145×74 mm. No. 2291; Type **1594** (1st) Top Left Quarter of English Flag, and Football; Type **1595** (1st) Top Right Quarter of English Flag, and Football; Type **1596** (1st) Bottom Left Quarter of English Flag, and Football; Type **1597** (1st) Bottom Right Quarter of English Flag, and Football. Perf 14½ (square) or 15×14 (horiz)			5·00	5·00
First Day Cover (Tallents House) (No. **MS**2292)				5·50
First Day Cover (Wembley) (No. **MS**2292)				5·50
Presentation Pack (PO Pack No. 335) (No. **MS**2292)			5·75	
PHQ Cards (set of 6) (242)			1·75	7·50

(b) Self-adhesive. Die-cut Perf 15×14.

2293	**1594**	(1st) Top Left Quarter of English Flag, and Football	3·00	3·00
		a. Booklet pane. Nos. 2293/2294 plus No. 2040×4	7·50	
2294	**1595**	(1st) Top Right Quarter of English Flag, and Football	3·00	3·00

Stamps as T **1593** but with 'WORLD CUP 2002' inscription omitted were issued on 17 May 2007 in sheets of 20 with *se-tenant* labels showing scenes from Wembley Stadium, printed in lithography by Cartor (No. LS39).

Stamps as T **1597** also exist in sheets of 20 with *se-tenant* half stamp-sized labels, printed in lithography by Questa (No. LS8). Such sheets, with the labels showing match scenes or supporters, were available at £5·95 from philatelic outlets, or with personal photographs at £12·95 from Royal Mail in Edinburgh.

Nos. 2293/2294 were only issued in £1·62 stamp booklet, No. PM6.
The complete miniature sheet is shown on one of the PHQ cards with the others depicting individual stamps from No. **MS**2292 and No. 2291.

For Nos. 2295/2298 see Decimal Machin Definitives section.

1598 Swimming

QUEEN ELIZABETH II/2002

1599 Running

1600 Cycling

1601 Long Jump

1602 Wheelchair Racing

(Des Madeleine Bennett. Gravure Enschedé)

2002 (16 July). 17th Commonwealth Games, Manchester. Multicoloured One side phosphor band (2nd) or two phosphor bands (others). Perf 14½.

2299	**1598**	(2nd) Swimming	90	90
2300	**1599**	(1st) Running	1·20	1·00
2301	**1600**	(E) Cycling	2·25	1·50
2302	**1601**	47p. Long Jump	1·10	1·25
2303	**1602**	68p. Wheelchair Racing	1·20	1·50
Set of 5			5·75	5·50
Set of 5 Gutter Pairs			11·50	
First Day Cover (Tallents House)				6·00
First Day Cover (Manchester)				6·00
Presentation Pack (PO Pack No. 336)			6·00	
PHQ Cards (set of 5) (243)			1·50	6·75

On Nos. 2300/2303 the phosphor bands appear at the right and the centre of each stamp.

1603 Tinkerbell

1604 Wendy, John and Michael Darling in front of Big Ben

1605 Crocodile and Alarm Clock

1606 Captain Hook

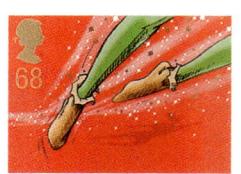

1607 Peter Pan

(Des Tutssels. Gravure De La Rue)

2002 (20 Aug). 150th Anniversary of Great Ormond Street Children's Hospital. *Peter Pan* by Sir James Barrie. Multicoloured One centre phosphor band (2nd) or two phosphor bands (others). Perf 15×14.

2304	**1603**	(2nd) Tinkerbell	90	90
2305	**1604**	(1st) Wendy, John and Michael Darling in front of Big Ben	1·20	1·00
2306	**1605**	(E) Crocodile and Alarm Clock	2·25	1·50
2307	**1606**	47p. Captain Hook	1·10	1·25
2308	**1607**	68p. Peter Pan	1·20	1·50
Set of 5			5·75	5·50
Set of 5 Gutter Pairs			11·50	
First Day Cover (Tallents House)				6·00
First Day Cover (Hook)				6·00
Presentation Pack (PO Pack No. 337)			6·00	
PHQ Cards (set of 5) (244)			1·50	6·75

1608 Millennium Bridge, 2001

1609 Tower Bridge, 1894

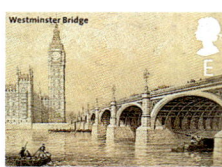

1610 Westminster Bridge, 1864

1611 Blackfriars Bridge, *c* 1800 (William Marlow)

1612 London Bridge, *c* 1670 (Wenceslaus Hollar)

(Des Sarah Davies and R. Maude)

2002 (10 Sept). Bridges of London. Multicoloured One centre phosphor band (2nd) or two phosphor bands (others).

(a) Litho Questa. Ordinary gum. Perf 15×14.

2309	**1608**	(2nd) Millennium Bridge, 2001	90	90
2310	**1609**	(1st) Tower Bridge, 1894	1·20	1·00
2311	**1610**	(E) Westminster Bridge, 1864	2·25	1·50
2312	**1611**	47p. *Blackfriars Bridge, c* 1800	1·20	1·60
2313	**1612**	68p. *London Bridge, c* 1670	1·40	1·75
Set of 5			6·25	6·00
Set of 5 Gutter Pairs			12·50	
First Day Cover (Tallents House)				6·25
First Day Cover (London SE1)				6·25
Presentation Pack (PO Pack No. 338)			30·00	
PHQ Cards (set of 5) (245)			1·50	7·00

(b) Gravure Questa. Self-adhesive. Die-cut Perf 15×14.

2314	**1609**	(1st) Tower Bridge, 1894	3·00	3·00
		a. Booklet pane. No. 2314×2, and No. 2295×4	7·50	

No. 2314 was only issued in £1·62 stamp booklets in which the surplus self-adhesive paper around each stamp was removed, No. PM7.

2002/QUEEN ELIZABETH II

1613a Galaxies and Nebulae *(Illustration reduced. Actual size 120×89 mm)*

(Des Rose Design. Gravure Questa)

2002 (24 Sept). Astronomy. Sheet 120×89 mm. Multicoloured Two phosphor bands. Perf 14½×14.

MS2315	**1613a**	Galaxies and Nebulae (1st) Planetary nebula in Aquila; (1st) Seyfert 2 galaxy in Pegasus; (1st) Planetary nebula in Norma; (1st) Seyfert 2 galaxy in Circinus	4·80	4·80
		a. Booklet pane. As No. **MS**2315, but larger, 150×95 mm	5·75	
First Day Cover (Tallents House)				5·00
First Day Cover (Star, Glenrothes)				5·00
Presentation Pack (PO Pack No. 339)			11·00	
PHQ Cards (set of 5) (246)			1·50	5·00

Booklet pane No. **MS**2315a comes from the £6·83 Across the Universe booklet No. DX29.

The five PHQ cards depict the four designs and the complete miniature sheet.

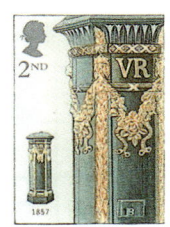

1614 Green Pillar Box, 1857

1615 Horizontal Aperture Box, 1874

1616 Air Mail Box, 1934

1617 Double Aperture Box, 1939

1618 Modern Style Box, 1980

(Des Silk Pearce. Eng C. Slania. Recess and litho Enschedé)

2002 (8 Oct). 150th Anniversary of the First Pillar Box. Multicoloured One centre phosphor band (2nd) or two phosphor bands (others). Perf 14×14½.

2316	**1614**	(2nd) Green Pillar Box, 1857	90	90
2317	**1615**	(1st) Horizontal Aperture Box, 1874	1·20	1·00
2318	**1616**	(E) Air Mail Box, 1934	2·25	1·50
2319	**1617**	47p. Double Aperture Box, 1939	1·20	1·10
2320	**1618**	68p. Modern Style Box, 1980	1·40	1·25
Set of 5			6·25	5·00
Set of 5 Gutter Pairs			12·50	
First Day Cover (Tallents House)				5·25
First Day Cover (Bishops Caundle, Sherborne)				5·25
Presentation Pack (PO Pack No. 340)			6·75	
PHQ Cards (set of 5) (247)			1·50	5·50

1619 Blue Spruce Star

1620 Holly

1621 Ivy

1622 Mistletoe

1623 Pine Cone

(Des Rose Design. Gravure De La Rue)

2002 (5 Nov). Christmas. Self-adhesive. Multicoloured One centre phosphor band (2nd) or two phosphor bands (others). Die-cut Perf 14½×14.

2321	**1619**	(2nd) Blue Spruce Star	90	90
		a. Booklet pane. No. 2321×24	22·00	
		b. Imperf (pair)	45·00	
2322	**1620**	(1st) Holly	1·20	1·00
		a. Booklet pane. No. 2322×12	16·00	
		b. Imperf (pair)	£125	
2323	**1621**	(E) Ivy	2·25	1·50
2324	**1622**	47p. Mistletoe	1·25	1·25
2325	**1623**	68p. Pine Cone	1·40	1·40
Set of 5			6·00	5·00
First Day Cover (Tallents House)				5·25
First Day Cover (Bethlehem, Llandeilo)				5·25
Presentation Pack (PO Pack No. 341)			6·00	
PHQ Cards (set of 5) (248)			1·50	5·75

Nos. 2321/2325 were each printed in sheets of 50, with the surplus backing paper around each stamp retained, separated by gauge 9 roulettes.

Nos. 2321b and 2322b show both the die-cut perforations and the roulettes omitted.

Year Pack 2002

2002 (5 Nov). Comprises Nos. 2243/2257, 2260/2264, 2265/2288, **MS**2292, 2299/2313 and **MS**2315/2325.

CP2325a	Year Pack (PO Pack No. 342)	65·00

Post Office Yearbook

2002 (5 Nov). Comprises Nos. 2243/2257, 2260/2264, 2265/2288, 2291/2292, 2299/2313 and **MS**2315/2325 in hardback book with slip case

YB2325a	Yearbook	48·00

QUEEN ELIZABETH II/2002

1623a

(Des Rose Design. Gravure De La Rue)

2002 (5 Dec). 50th Anniversary of Wilding Definitives (1st issue). Sheet 124×70 mm, printed on pale cream. One centre phosphor band (2nd) or two phosphor bands (others). W **1565**. Perf 15×14 (with one elliptical hole in each vertical side).

MS2326	**1623a**	1p. orange-red; 2p. ultramarine; 5p. red-brown; (2nd) carmine-red; (1st) green; 33p. brown; 37p. magenta; 47p. bistre-brown; 50p. green and label showing National Emblems	5·00	5·00
		a. Imperf		£8000
First Day Cover (Tallents House)				5·25
First Day Cover (Windsor)				5·25
Presentation Pack (PO Pack No. 59)			25·00	
PHQ Cards (set of 5) (D21)			1·50	5·00

The five PHQ cards depict the 1st, 2nd, 33p, 37p. and 47p. stamps.

For further Wilding designs with decimal face values, see Nos. 2031/2033, 2258/2259, **MS**2367 and 2378/2380

1624 Barn Owl landing

1625 Barn Owl with folded Wings and Legs down

1626 Barn Owl with extended Wings and Legs down

1627 Barn Owl in Flight with Wings lowered

1628 Barn Owl in Flight with Wings raised

1629 Kestrel with Wings folded

1630 Kestrel with Wings fully extended upwards

1631 Kestrel with Wings horizontal

1632 Kestrel with wings partly extended downwards

1633 Kestrel with wings fully extended downwards

(Des J. Gibbs from photographs by S. Dalton. Litho Walsall)

2003 (14 Jan). Birds of Prey. Multicoloured Phosphor background. Perf 14½.

2327	**1624**	(1st) Barn Owl landing	1·20	1·00
		a. Block of 10. Nos. 2327/2336	10·50	9·00
		ab. Brownish grey and phosphor omitted	£1600	
2328	**1625**	(1st) Barn Owl with folded Wings and Legs down	1·20	1·00
2329	**1626**	(1st) Barn Owl with extended Wings and Legs down	1·20	1·00
2330	**1627**	(1st) Barn Owl in Flight with Wings lowered	1·20	1·00
2331	**1628**	(1st) Barn Owl in Flight with Wings raised	1·20	1·00
2332	**1629**	(1st) Kestrel with Wings folded	1·20	1·00
2333	**1630**	(1st) Kestrel with Wings fully extended upwards	1·20	1·00
2334	**1631**	(1st) Kestrel with Wings horizontal	1·20	1·00
2335	**1632**	(1st) Kestrel with wings partly extended downwards	1·20	1·00
2336	**1633**	(1st) Kestrel with wings fully extended downwards	1·20	1·00
Set of 10			10·50	9·00
Gutter Block of 20			21·00	
First Day Cover (Tallents House)				9·25
First Day Cover (Hawkshead Ambleside)				9·25
Presentation Pack (PO Pack No. 343)			11·00	
PHQ Cards (set of 10) (249)			3·00	11·00

Nos. 2327/2336 were printed together, *se-tenant*, in blocks of ten (5×2) throughout the sheet.

No. 2327ab shows the owl white on Nos. 2327/2331, and the face value with Queen's head omitted on Nos. 2332/2336.

1634 'Gold star, See me, Playtime'

1635 'IU, XXXX, S.W.A.L.K.'

1636 'Angel, Poppet, Little terror'

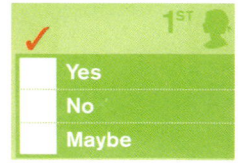

1637 'Yes, No, Maybe'

2003/QUEEN ELIZABETH II

1638 'Oops!, Sorry, Will try harder'

1639 'I did it!, You did it!, We did it!'

(Des UNA, Sara Wiegand and M. Exon. Litho Questa)

2003 (4 Feb). Greetings Stamps. Occasions. Multicoloured Two phosphor bands. Perf 14½×14.

2337	1634	(1st) 'Gold star, See me, Playtime'	1·20	1·00
		a. Block of 6. Nos. 2337/2342	6·25	5·50
		b. Imperf (block of 6)	£2250	
2338	1635	(1st) 'IU, XXXX, S.W.A.L.K.'	1·20	1·00
2339	1636	(1st) 'Angel, Poppet, Little terror'	1·20	1·00
2340	1637	(1st) 'Yes, No, Maybe'	1·20	1·00
2341	1638	(1st) 'Oops!, Sorry, Will try harder'	1·20	1·00
2342	1639	(1st) 'I did it!, You did it!, We did it!'	1·20	1·00
Set of 6			6·25	5·50
Gutter Block of 12			12·50	
First Day Cover (Tallents House)				5·75
First Day Cover (Merry Hill, Wolverhampton)				5·75
Presentation Pack (PO Pack No. M09)			6·00	
PHQ Cards (set of 6) (PSM09)			1·75	6·25

Nos. 2337/2342 were printed together, *se-tenant*, in blocks of six (3×2) throughout the sheet.

Nos. 2337/2342 were also issued in sheets of 20 (containing four of Nos. 2338 and 2340 and three each of the others) with *se-tenant* labels (No. LS12). Such sheets with the labels showing printed faces were available at £5·95 from philatelic outlets, or with personalised photographs at £14·95 from Royal Mail in Edinburgh.

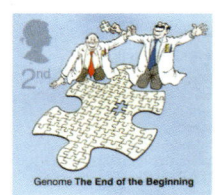

1640 Completing the Genome Jigsaw

1641 Ape with Moustache and Scientist

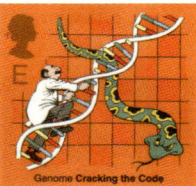

1642 DNA Snakes and Ladders

1643 Animal Scientists

1644 Genome Crystal Ball

(Des Williams Murray Hamm and P. Brookes. Litho Enschedé)

2003 (25 Feb). 50th Anniversary of Discovery of DNA. Multicoloured One centre phosphor band (2nd) or two phosphor bands (others). Perf 14½.

2343	1640	(2nd) Completing the Genome Jigsaw	90	90
		a. Booklet pane. Nos. 2343/2344, each×2, with margins all round	3·50	
2344	1641	(1st) Ape with Moustache and Scientist	1·20	1·00
2345	1642	(E) DNA Snakes and Ladders	2·25	1·50
		a. Booklet pane. No. 2345/2×4 with margins all round	5·25	
2346	1643	47p. Animal Scientists	1·10	1·40
2347	1644	68p. Genome Crystal Ball	1·25	1·60
Set of 5			6·00	5·75
Set of 5 Gutter Pairs			12·00	
First Day Cover (Tallents House)				6·25
First Day Cover (Cambridge)				6·50
Presentation Pack (PO Pack No. 344)			6·00	
PHQ Cards (set of 5) (250)			1·50	6·25

Booklet panes Nos. 2343a and 2345a come from the £6·99 Microcosmos booklet, No. DX30.

1645 Strawberry

1646 Potato

1647 Apple

1648 Red Pepper

1649 Pear

1650 Orange

1651 Tomato

1652 Lemon

1653 Brussels Sprout

1654 Aubergine

(Des johnson banks. Gravure Walsall)

2003 (25 Mar). Fruit and Vegetables. Self-adhesive. Multicoloured Two phosphor bands. Perf 14½×14 die-cut (without teeth around protruding tops or bottoms of the designs).

2348	1645	(1st) Strawberry	1·20	1·00
		a. Sheet*let* of 10. Nos. 2348/2357 and pane of decorative labels	10·50	
		ab. Imperf (block of 10)	£1800	
2349	1646	(1st) Potato	1·20	1·00
2350	1647	(1st) Apple	1·20	1·00
2351	1648	(1st) Red Pepper	1·20	1·00
2352	1649	(1st) Pear	1·20	1·00

QUEEN ELIZABETH II/2003

2353	**1650**	(1st) Orange	1·20	1·00
2354	**1651**	(1st) Tomato	1·20	1·00
2355	**1652**	(1st) Lemon	1·20	1·00
2356	**1653**	(1st) Brussels Sprout	1·20	1·00
2357	**1654**	(1st) Aubergine	1·20	1·00

Set of 10 .... 10·50 9·00
First Day Cover (Tallents House) .... 9·25
First Day Cover (Pear Tree, Derby) .... 9·25
Presentation Pack (PO Pack No. 345) .... 12·00
PHQ Cards (set of 10) (251) .... 3·00 10·50

Nos. 2348/2357 were printed together in sheets of ten with the surplus self-adhesive paper around each stamp retained.

The stamp pane is accompanied by a similar-sized pane of self-adhesive labels showing ears, eyes, mouths, hats, etc which are intended for the adornment of fruit and vegetables depicted. This pane is separated from the stamps by a line of roulettes.

Nos. 2348/2357 were re-issued on 7 March 2006 in sheets of 20, containing two of each of the ten designs accompanied by *se-tenant* labels with speech bubbles and stickers showing eyes, hats, etc. in the sheet margin (No. LS29). These sheets were printed in lithography by Cartor and sold for £6·55.

No. 2355 was also available in sheets of 20 with personal photographs on the labels at £14·95 per sheet from Royal Mail Edinbugh.

> For Nos. 2357a/2359 (Overseas Booklet Stamps), T **1655**, see Decimal Machin Definitives sections

1656 Amy Johnson (pilot) and Biplane

1657 Members of 1953 Everest Team

1658 Freya Stark (traveller and writer) and Desert

1659 Ernest Shackleton (Antarctic explorer) and Wreck of *Endurance*

1660 Francis Chichester (yachtsman) and *Gipsy Moth IV*

1661 Robert Falcon Scott (Antarctic explorer) and Norwegian Expedition at the Pole

(Des H. Brown)

2003 (29 Apr). Extreme Endeavours (British Explorers). Multicoloured One centre phosphor band (2nd) or two phosphor bands (others). Perf 15×14½.

(a) Gravure Questa. Ordinary gum.

2360	**1656**	(2nd) Amy Johnson	90	90
2361	**1657**	(1st) Members of 1953 Everest Team	1·20	1·00
2362	**1658**	(E) Freya Stark	2·25	1·50
2363	**1659**	42p. Ernest Shackleton	1·00	1·00
2364	**1660**	47p. Francis Chichester	1·10	1·25
2365	**1661**	68p. Robert Falcon Scott	1·25	1·40

Set of 6 .... 6·75 6·25
Set of 6 Gutter Pairs .... 13·50
First Day Cover (Tallents House) .... 7·00
First Day Cover (Plymouth) .... 7·00
Presentation Pack (PO Pack No. 346) .... 7·25
PHQ Cards (set of 6) (252) .... 1·75 6·50

(b) Gravure De La Rue. Self-adhesive. Die-cut Perf 14½.

2366	**1657**	(1st) Members of 1953 Everest Team	3·00	3·00
		a. Booklet pane. No. 2366×2 plus No. 2295×4	7·50	

The phosphor bands on Nos. 2361/2365 are at the centre and right of each stamp.

No. 2366 was only issued in £1·62 stamp booklet, No. PM9, in which the surplus self-adhesive paper around each stamp was removed.

Gummed perforated trials with alternative face values and/or designs are known.

1661a

(Des Rose Design. Gravure De La Rue)

2003 (20 May). 50th Anniversary of Wilding Definitives (2nd issue). Sheet 124×70 mm, printed on pale cream. One centre phosphor band (20p.) or two phosphor bands (others). W **1565**. Perf 15×14 (with one elliptical hole in each vertical side).

MS2367 **1661a** 4p. deep lilac; 8p. ultramarine; 10p. reddish purple; 20p. bright green; 28p. bronze-green; 34p. brown-purple; (E) chestnut; 42p. Prussian blue; 68p. grey-blue and label showing National Emblems .... 4·50 4·75
  a. Imperf
First Day Cover (Tallents House) .... 5·50
First Day Cover (Windsor) .... 5·50
Presentation Pack (PO Pack No. 61) .... 9·00

1662 Guardsmen in Coronation Procession

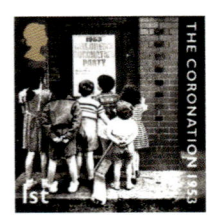

1663 East End Children reading Coronation Party Poster

1664 Queen Elizabeth II in Coronation Chair with Bishops of Durham and Bath and Wells

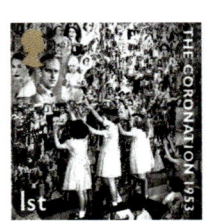

1665 Children in Plymouth working on Royal Montage

2003/QUEEN ELIZABETH II

1666 Queen Elizabeth II in Coronation Robes (photograph by Cecil Beaton)

1667 Children's Race at East End Street Party

1668 Coronation Coach passing through Marble Arch

1669 Children in Fancy Dress

1670 Coronation Coach outside Buckingham Palace

1671 Children eating at London Street Party

(Des Kate Stephens. Gravure De La Rue (sheets) or Walsall (booklets))

2003 (2 June). 50th Anniversary of Coronation. W **1565**. Multicoloured Two phosphor bands. Perf 14½×14.

2368	**1662**	(1st) Guardsmen in Coronation Procession..........................	1·20	1·00
		a. Block of 10. Nos. 2368/2377............	10·50	9·00
		b. Booklet pane. Nos. 2368, 2370, 2373 and 2375 with margins all round............................	4·25	
2369	**1663**	(1st) East End Children......................	1·20	1·00
		b. Booklet pane. Nos. 2369, 2372, 2374 and 2377 with margins all round............................	4·25	
2370	**1664**	(1st) Queen Elizabeth II in Coronation Chair................................	1·20	1·00
2371	**1665**	(1st) Children in Plymouth......................	1·20	1·00
2372	**1666**	(1st) Queen Elizabeth II in Coronation Robes................................	1·20	1·00
2373	**1667**	(1st) Children's Race................................	1·20	1·00
2374	**1668**	(1st) Coronation Coach passing through Marble Arch......................	1·20	1·00
2375	**1669**	(1st) Children in Fancy Dress...................	1·20	1·00
2376	**1670**	(1st) Coronation Coach outside Buckingham Palace.........................	1·20	1·00
2377	**1671**	(1st) Children eating at London Street Party.....................................	1·20	1·00
Set of 10..			10·50	9·00
Gutter Block of 20...			21·00	
First Day Cover (Tallents House)...................................				9·50
First Day Cover (London SW1).......................................				9·50
Presentation Pack (PO Pack No. 347)..................................			11·00	
PHQ Cards (set of 10) (253)..			3·00	10·00

Nos. 2368/2377 were printed together, *se-tenant*, as blocks of ten (5×2) in sheets of 60 (2 panes of 30).

No. 2372 does not show a silhouette of the Queen's head in gold as do the other nine designs.

Booklet pane Nos. 2368b/2369b come from the £7·46 A perfect Coronation booklet, No. DX31.

QUEEN ELIZABETH II/2003

1671a

1671b

1671c

(Gravure Walsall)

2003 (2 June). 50th Anniversary of Coronation. Booklet stamps. W **1565**. Two phosphor bands. Perf 15×14 (with one elliptical hole in each vertical side for Nos. 2378/2379).

2378	**1671a**	47p. bistre-brown	2·00	2·00
		a. Booklet pane. Nos. 2378/2379, each×2, and 2380 with margins all round	32·00	
2379	**1671b**	68p. grey-blue	2·50	2·50
2380	**1671c**	£1 deep yellow-green	26·00	26·00
Set of 3			30·00	30·00

Nos. 2378/2380 were only issued in the £7·46 A Perfect Coronation booklet, No. DX31.

Stamps as Nos. 2378/2379, but on pale cream, were also included in the Wilding miniature sheets, No. **MS**2326 or No. **MS**2367.

A £1 design as No. 2380, but on phosphorised paper, was previously included in the Stamp Show 2000 miniature sheet, No. **MS**2147.

1672 Prince William in September 2001 (Brendan Beirne)

1673 Prince William in September 2000 (Tim Graham)

1674 Prince William in September 2001 (Camera Press)

1675 Prince William in September 2001 (Tim Graham)

(Des Madeleine Bennett. Gravure Walsall)

2003 (17 June). 21st Birthday of Prince William of Wales. Multicoloured Phosphor backgrounds. Perf 14½.

2381	**1672**	28p. Prince William in September 2001	95	95
2382	**1673**	(E) Prince William in September 2000	2·25	1·50
2383	**1674**	47p. Prince William in September 2001	1·70	1·90
2384	**1675**	68p. Prince William in September 2001	2·10	2·25
Set of 4			6·25	6·00
Set of 4 Gutter Pairs			12·50	
First Day Cover (Tallents House)				6·25
First Day Cover (Cardiff)				6·25
Presentation Pack (PO Pack No. 348)			8·00	
PHQ Cards (set of 4) (254)			1·25	6·75

1676 Loch Assynt, Sutherland

1677 Ben More, Isle of Mull

1678 Rothiemurchus, Cairngorms

1679 Dalveen Pass, Lowther Hills

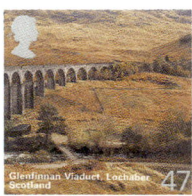

1680 Glenfinnan Viaduct, Lochaber

1681 Papa Little, Shetland Islands

(Des Phelan Barker. Gravure De La Rue)

2003 (15 July). A British Journey. Scotland. Multicoloured One centre phosphor band (2nd) or two phosphor bands (others). Perf 14½.

(a) Ordinary gum.

2385	**1676**	(2nd) Loch Assynt, Sutherland	90	90
2386	**1677**	(1st) Ben More, Isle of Mull	1·20	1·00
2387	**1678**	(E) Rothiemurchus, Cairngorms	2·25	1·50
2388	**1679**	42p. Dalveen Pass, Lowther Hills	1·00	1·00
2389	**1680**	47p. Glenfinnan Viaduct, Lochaber	1·10	1·25
2390	**1681**	68p. Papa Little, Shetland Islands	1·25	1·40
Set of 6			7·00	6·25
Set of 6 Gutter Pairs			14·00	
First Day Cover (Tallents House)				6·75
First Day Cover (Baltasound, Unst, Shetland)				6·75
Presentation Pack (PO Pack No. 349)			7·00	
PHQ Cards (set of 6) (255)			1·75	6·75

(b) Self-adhesive. Die-cut Perf 14½.

2391	**1677**	(1st) Ben More, Isle of Mull	3·00	3·00
		a. Booklet pane. No. 2391×2, and No. 2295×4	7·50	

No. 2391 was only issued in £1·68 stamp booklet, No. PM10, in which the surplus self-adhesive paper around each stamp was removed.

Perforated trials of this set with alternative face values or designs are known.

1682 'The Station' (Andrew Davidson)

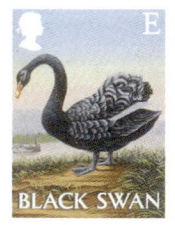

1683 'Black Swan' (Stanley Chew)

2003/QUEEN ELIZABETH II

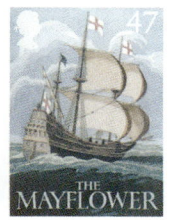

1684 'The Cross Keys' (George Mackenney)

1685 'The Mayflower' (Ralph Ellis)

1686 'The Barley Sheaf' (Joy Cooper)

(Des Elmwood. Gravure De La Rue)

2003 (12 Aug.). Europa. British Pub Signs. Multicoloured Two phosphor bands. Perf 14×14½.

2392	1682	(1st) 'The Station'	1·20	1·00
		a. Booklet pane. No. 2392×4 with margins all round (16.3.04)	4·25	
2393	1683	(E) 'Black Swan'	2·25	1·50
2394	1684	42p. 'The Cross Keys'	1·00	1·00
2395	1685	47p. 'The Mayflower'	1·25	1·25
2396	1686	68p. 'The Barley Sheaf'	1·40	1·40
Set of 5			6·25	5·50
Set of 5 Gutter Pairs			12·50	
First Day Cover (Tallents House)				5·75
First Day Cover (Cross Keys, Hereford)				5·75
Presentation Pack (PO Pack No. 350)			6·75	
PHQ Cards (set of 5) (256)			1·50	6·00

The 1st and E values include the EUROPA emblem.
No. 2392a comes from the £7·44 Letters by Night booklet, No. DX32.

1687 Meccano Constructor Biplane, c 1931

1688 Wells-Brimtoy Clockwork Double-decker Omnibus, c 1938

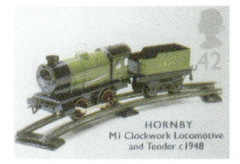

1689 Hornby M1 Clockwork Locomotive and Tender, c 1948

1690 Dinky Toys Ford Zephyr, c 1956

1691 Mettoy Friction Drive Space Ship Eagle, c 1960

(Des Trickett and Webb)

2003 (18 Sept). Classic Transport Toys. Multicoloured Two phosphor bands.

(a) Gravure Enschedé. Ordinary gum. Perf 14½×14.

2397	1687	(1st) Meccano Constructor Biplane	1·20	1·00
2398	1688	(E) Wells-Brimtoy Clockwork Double-decker Omnibus	2·25	1·50
2399	1689	42p. Hornby M1 Clockwork Locomotive and Tender	95	1·00
2400	1690	47p. Dinky Toys Ford Zephyr	1·25	1·25
2401	1691	68p. Mettoy Friction Drive Space Ship Eagle	1·40	1·50
Set of 5			6·25	5·50
Set of 5 Gutter Pairs			12·50	
First Day Cover (Tallents House)				5·75
First Day Cover (Toye, Downpatrick)				5·75
Presentation Pack (PO Pack No. 351)			6·75	
PHQ Cards (set of 6) (257)			1·75	6·00
MS2402 115×105mm. Nos. 2397/2401			6·50	5·50
First Day Cover (Philatelic Bureau, Edinburgh)				6·75

(b) Gravure De La Rue. Self-adhesive. Die-cut Perf 14½×14.

2403	1687	(1st) Meccano Constructor Biplane	3·00	3·00
		a. Booklet pane. No. 2403×2 and No. 2295×4	7·50	

No. 2403 was only issued in £1·68 stamp booklet, No. PM11, in which the surplus self-adhesive paper around each stamp was removed.
The complete miniature sheet is shown on one of the PHQ cards with the others depicting individual stamps.

1692 Coffin of Denytenamun, Egyptian, c 900BC

1693 Alexander the Great, Greek, c 200BC

1694 Sutton Hoo Helmet, Anglo-Saxon, c AD600

1695 Sculpture of Parvati, South Indian, c AD1550

1696 Mask of Xiuhtecuhtli, Mixtec-Aztec, c AD1500

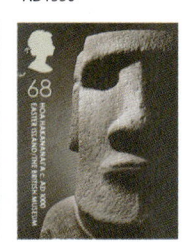

1697 Hoa Hakananai'a, Easter Island, c AD1000

(Des Rose Design. Gravure Walsall)

2003 (7 Oct). 250th Anniversary of the British Museum. Multicoloured One side phosphor band (2nd), two phosphor bands ((1st), (E), 47p.) or phosphor background at left and band at right (42p., 68p.). Perf 14×14½.

2404	1692	(2nd) Coffin of Denytenamun	90	90
2405	1693	(1st) Alexander the Great	1·20	1·00
2406	1694	(E) Sutton Hoo Helmet	2·25	1·50
2407	1695	42p. Sculpture of Parvati	90	1·00
2408	1696	47p. Mask of Xiuhtecuhtli	1·00	1·00
2409	1697	68p. Hoa Hakananai'a	1·10	1·25
Set of 6			6·25	6·00
Set of 6 Gutter Pairs			12·50	

QUEEN ELIZABETH II/2003

First Day Cover (Tallents House)..		6·50
First Day Cover (London WC1)..		6·50
Presentation Pack (PO Pack No. 352).....................................	7·00	
PHQ Cards (set of 6) (258)...	1·75	6·00

1698 Ice Spiral

1699 Icicle Star

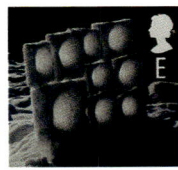

1700 Wall of Ice Blocks

1701 Ice Ball

1702 Ice Hole

1703 Snow Pyramids

(Des D. Davis. Gravure De La Rue)

2003 (4 Nov). Christmas. Ice Sculptures by Andy Goldsworthy. Self-adhesive. Multicoloured One side phosphor band (2nd), 'all-over' phosphor (1st) or two bands (others). Die-cut Perf 14½×14.

2410	**1698**	(2nd) Ice Spiral...	90	90
		a. Booklet pane. No. 2410×24............	22·00	
2411	**1699**	(1st) Icicle Star...	1·20	1·00
		a. Booklet pane. No. 2411×12............	16·00	
2412	**1700**	(E) Wall of Ice Blocks................................	2·25	1·50
2413	**1701**	53p. Ice Ball..	1·25	1·25
2414	**1702**	68p. Ice Hole...	1·40	1·50
2415	**1703**	£1·12 Snow Pyramids...............................	1·50	1·60
Set of 6..			7·50	6·75
First Day Cover (Tallents House)..				7·50
First Day Cover (Bethlehem, Llandeilo).................................				7·50
Presentation Pack (PO Pack No. 353)....................................			7·25	
PHQ Cards (set of 6) (259)...			1·75	7·00

Nos. 2410/2415 were each printed in sheets of 50 with the surplus backing paper around each stamp removed.

The 2nd and 1st class were also issued in separate sheets of 20 printed in lithography instead of gravure, each stamp accompanied by a half stamp-size *se-tenant* label showing either ice sculptures (2nd) or animals (1st) (Nos. LS15/LS16). Both sheets have the backing paper around each stamp retained.

The 2nd class sheet was sold for £4·20 and the 1st class for £6·15. These sheets were also available with personal photographs instead of labels at £9·95 (2nd) or £14·95 (1st) from Royal Mail, Edinburgh or £15 from photo-booths at selected post offices and Safeway stores.

Year Pack 2003

2003 (4 Nov). Comprises Nos. 2327/2357, 2360/2365, 2368/2377, 2381/2390, 2392/2401 and 2404/2415
CP2415*a*   Year Pack (PO Pack No. 354)................   70·00

Post Office Yearbook

2003 (4 Nov). Comprises Nos. 2327/2357, 2360/2365, 2368/2377, 2381/2390, 2392/2401 and 2404/2415 in hardback book with slipcase
YB2415*a*   Yearbook...   55·00

1704 Rugby Scenes (*Illustration reduced. Actual size 115×88 mm*)

(Des Why Not Associates. Litho Walsall)

2003 (19 Dec). England's Victory in Rugby World Cup Championship, Australia. Sheet 115×85 mm. Multicoloured Two phosphor bands. Perf 14.

MS2416 **1704** (1st) England flags and fans; (1st) England team standing in circle before match; 68p. World Cup trophy; 68p. Victorious England players after match..	9·00	9·00
First Day Cover (Tallents House)..		9·25
First Day Cover (Twickenham)...		9·25
Presentation Pack (PO Pack No. M9B)...................................	20·00	

1705 *Dolgoch*, Rheilffordd Talyllyn Railway, Gwynedd

1706 CR Class 439, Bo'ness and Kinneil Railway, West Lothian

1707 GCR Class 8K, Leicestershire

1708 GWR Manor Class *Bradley Manor*, Severn Valley Railway, Worcestershire

1709 SR West Country Class *Blackmoor Vale*, Bluebell Railway, East Sussex

1710 BR Standard Class, Keighley and Worth Valley Railway, Yorkshire

2004/QUEEN ELIZABETH II

(Des Roundel. Litho De La Rue)

2004 (13 Jan–16 Mar). Classic Locomotives. Multicoloured One side phosphor band (20p.) or two phosphor bands (others). Perf 14½.

2417	1705	20p. *Dolgoch*, Rheilffordd Talyllyn Railway	65	65
2418	1706	28p. CR Class 439, Bo'ness and Kinneil Railway	75	75
		a. Booklet pane. Nos. 2418/2420 with margins all round (16.3.04)	2·25	
2419	1707	(E) GCR Class 8K	2·25	1·50
2420	1708	42p. GWR Manor Class *Bradley Manor*, Severn Valley Railway	1·00	1·10
2421	1709	47p. SR West Country Class *Blackmoor Vale*, Bluebell Railway	1·10	1·25
		a. Imperf (pair)	£1600	
2422	1710	68p. BR Standard Class, Keighley and Worth Valley Railway	1·25	1·25
Set of 6			5·75	5·50
Set of 6 Gutter Pairs			12·50	
First Day Cover (Tallents House)				6·00
First Day Cover (York)				6·00
Presentation Pack (PO Pack No. 355)			10·00	
PHQ Cards (set of 7) (260)			2·00	6·25
MS2423 190×67 mm. Nos. 2417/2422			14·50	14·50
First Day (Tallents House)				15·00
First Day Cover (York)				15·00

No. 2418a comes from the £7·44 Letters by Night booklet, No. DX32.

The seven PHQ cards depict the six individual stamps and the miniature sheet.

1711 Postman

1712 Face

1713 Duck

1714 Baby

1715 Aircraft

(Des S. Kambayashi. Litho De La Rue)

2004 (3 Feb). Occasions. Multicoloured Two phosphor bands. Perf 14½×14.

2424	1711	(1st) Postman	1·20	1·00
		a. Horiz strip of 5. Nos. 2424/2428	5·50	4·50
		ab. Imperf strip of 5		
2425	1712	(1st) Face	1·20	1·00
2426	1713	(1st) Duck	1·20	1·00
2427	1714	(1st) Baby	1·20	1·00
2428	1715	(1st) Aircraft	1·20	1·00
Set of 5			5·50	4·50
Gutter Block of 10			11·00	
First Day Cover (Tallents House)				5·00
First Day Cover (Merry Hill, Wolverhampton)				5·00
Presentation Pack (PO Pack No. M10)			5·75	
PHQ Cards (set of 5) (PSM10)			1·50	6·00

Nos. 2424/2428 were printed together, *se-tenant*, as horizontal strips of five in sheets of 25 (5×5).

Nos. 2424/2428 were also issued in sheets of 20 containing vertical strips of the five designs alternated with half stamp-size labels (No. LS18). These sheets with printed labels were available at £6·15 from philatelic outlets, or with personalised photographs at £14·95 from Royal Mail in Edinburgh.

1716 Map showing Middle Earth

1717 Forest of Lothlórien in Spring

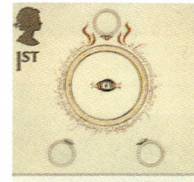

1718 Dust Jacket for The Fellowship of the Ring

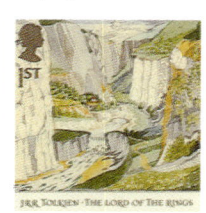

1719 Rivendell

1720 The Hall at Bag End

1721 Orthanc

1722 Doors of Durin

1723 Barad-dûr

1724 Minas Tirith

1725 Fangorn Forest

(Des HGV Design. Litho Walsall)

2004 (26 Feb). 50th Anniversary of Publication of *The Fellowship of the Ring* and *The Two Towers* by J. R. R. Tolkien. Multicoloured Two phosphor bands. Perf 14½.

2429	1716	(1st) Map showing Middle Earth	1·20	1·00
		a. Block of 10. Nos. 2429/2438	11·00	9·00
2430	1717	(1st) Forest of Lothlórien in Spring	1·20	1·00
2431	1718	(1st) Dust Jacket for *The Fellowship of the Ring*	1·20	1·00
2432	1719	(1st) Rivendell	1·20	1·00
2433	1720	(1st) The Hall at Bag End	1·20	1·00
2434	1721	(1st) Orthanc	1·20	1·00
2435	1722	(1st) Doors of Durin	1·20	1·00
2436	1723	(1st) Barad-dûr	1·20	1·00
2437	1724	(1st) Minas Tirith	1·20	1·00
2438	1725	(1st) Fangorn Forest	1·20	1·00
Set of 10			11·00	9·00
Gutter Block of 20			22·00	
First Day Cover (Tallents House)				9·25
First Day Cover (Oxford)				9·25

QUEEN ELIZABETH II/2004

Presentation Pack (PO Pack No. 356)	11·50	
PHQ Cards (set of 10) (261)	3·00	10·50

Nos. 2429/2438 were printed together, *se-tenant*, in blocks of ten (5×2) throughout the sheet.

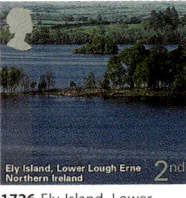

1726 Ely Island, Lower Lough Erne

1727 Giant's Causeway, Antrim Coast

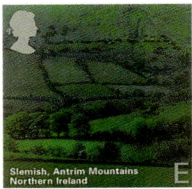

1728 Slemish, Antrim Mountains

1729 Banns Road, Mourne Mountains

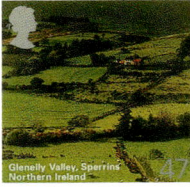

1730 Glenelly Valley, Sperrins

1731 Islandmore, Strangford Lough

(Des Phelan Barker. Gravure Enschedé (sheets) or De La Rue (booklet))

2004 (16 Mar). A British Journey. Northern Ireland. Multicoloured One side phosphor band (2nd) or two phosphor bands (others). Perf 14½.

(a) Ordinary gum.

2439	**1726**	(2nd) Ely Island, Lower Lough Erne	90	90
2440	**1727**	(1st) Giant's Causeway, Antrim Coast	1·20	1·00
2441	**1728**	(E) Slemish, Antrim Mountains	2·25	1·50
2442	**1729**	42p. Banns Road, Mourne Mountains	85	85
2443	**1730**	47p. Glenelly Valley, Sperrins	85	95
2444	**1731**	68p. Islandmore, Strangford Lough	1·00	1·10
Set of 6			6·25	5·50
Set of 6 Gutter Pairs			12·50	
First Day Cover (Tallents House)				5·75
First Day Cover (Garrison, Enniskillen)				5·75
Presentation Pack (PO Pack No. 357)			6·75	
PHQ Cards (set of 6) (262)			1·75	5·75

(b) Self-adhesive. Die-cut Perf 14½.

2445	**1727**	(1st) Giant's Causeway, Antrim Coast	3·25	3·25
		a. Booklet pane. No. 2445×2 and No. 2295×4	6·75	
		ab. Imperf (pane)	£950	

No. 2445 was only issued in £1·68 stamp booklet, No. PM12, in which the surplus self-adhesive paper around each stamp was removed.

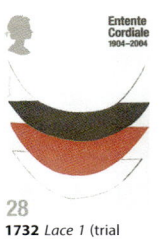

1732 *Lace 1* (trial proof) 1968 (Sir Terry Frost)

1733 *Coccinelle* (Sonia Delaunay)

(Des Rose Design. Gravure Walsall)

2004 (6 Apr). Contemporary Paintings. Centenary of the Entente Cordiale. Multicoloured Two phosphor bands. Perf 14×14½.

2446	**1732**	28p. *Lace 1* (trial proof) 1968	80	80
2447	**1733**	57p. *Coccinelle*	1·25	1·25
Set of 2			1·75	1·75
Set of 2 Gutter Pairs			3·50	
Set of 2 Traffic Light Gutter Blocks of 4			10·00	
First Day Cover (Tallents House)				1·90
First Day Cover (London SW1)				1·90
First Day Cover (UK and French stamps)				5·00
Presentation Pack (PO Pack No. 358)			8·00	
Presentation Pack (UK and French stamps)			8·00	
PHQ Cards (set of 2) (263)			60	2·00

Stamps in similar designs were issued by France and these are included in the joint Presentation Pack.

1734 *RMS Queen Mary 2, 2004* (Edward D. Walker)

1735 *SS Canberra, 1961* (David Cobb)

1736 *RMS Queen Mary, 1936* (Charles Pears)

1737 *RMS Mauretania, 1907* (Thomas Henry)

1738 *SS City of New York, 1888* (Raphael Monleaon y Torres)

1739 *PS Great Western, 1838* (Joseph Walter)

MS2454 (Illustration reduced. Actual size 114×104mm)

(Des J. Gibbs. Gravure De La Rue)

2004 (13 Apr). Ocean Liners. Multicoloured Two phosphor bands. Perf 14½×14.

(a) Ordinary gum.

2448	**1734**	(1st) RMS *Queen Mary 2*, 2004	1·20	1·00
2449	**1735**	(E) SS *Canberra*, 1961	2·25	1·50
		a. Imperf (pair)	£375	
2450	**1736**	42p. RMS *Queen Mary*, 1936	70	80
2451	**1737**	47p. RMS *Mauretania*, 1907	75	85

2452	**1738**	57p. SS *City of New York*, 1888		80	90
2453	**1739**	68p. PS *Great Western*, 1838		85	95
Set of 6				5·75	5·00
Set of 6 Gutter Pairs				11·50	
First Day Cover (Tallents House)					5·50
First Day Cover (Southampton)					5·50
Presentation Pack (PO Pack No. 359)				6·00	
PHQ Cards (set of 7) (264)				2·00	5·25
MS2454 114×104mm. Nos. 2448/2453				7·25	7·25
First Day Cover (Tallents House)					7·50
First Day Cover (Southampton)					7·50
		(b) *Self-adhesive. Die-cut Perf 14½×14.*			
2455	**1734**	(1st) RMS *Queen Mary 2*, 2004		3·00	3·00
		a. Booklet pane. No. 2455×2 and			
			No. 2295×4		7·50

Nos. 2448/2455 commemorate the introduction to service of the *Queen Mary 2*.

No. 2455 was only issued in £1·68 stamp booklet, No. PM13, in which the surplus self-adhesive paper around each stamp was removed.

No. **MS**2454 is known to exist with a face value of '53' on No. 2452. It is known perforated and imperforate.

The complete miniature sheet is shown on one of the PHQ cards with the others depicting individual stamps.

See also No. 2614.

1740 *Dianthus Allwoodii*, Group

1741 Dahlia, Garden Princess

1742 Clematis, Arabella

1743 Miltonia, French Lake

1744 Lilium, Lemon Pixie

1745 Delphinium, Clifford Sky

(Des Rose Design. Gravure Enschedé)

2004 (25 May). Bicentenary of the Royal Horticultural Society (1st issue). Multicoloured One side phosphor band (2nd) or 'all-over' phosphor (others). Perf 14½.

2456	**1740**	(2nd) *Dianthus Allwoodii* Group		90	90
		a. Booklet pane. Nos. 2456,			
		2458/2459 and 2461 with			
		margins all round		6·75	
2457	**1741**	(1st) Dahlia, Garden Princess		1·20	1·00
		a. Booklet pane. Nos. 2457 and			
		2460, each×2, with margins all			
		round		5·75	
2458	**1742**	(E) Clematis, Arabella		2·25	1·50
2459	**1743**	42p. Miltonia, French Lake		80	85
2460	**1744**	47p. Lilium, Lemon Pixie		85	90
2461	**1745**	68p. Delphinium, Clifford Sky		90	1·00
Set of 6				6·00	5·50
Set of 6 Gutter Pairs				12·00	
First Day Cover (Tallents House)					5·75
First Day Cover (Wisley, Woking)					5·75
Presentation Pack (PO Pack No. 360)				6·50	
PHQ Cards (set of 7) (265)				2·00	6·50
MS2462 115×105 mm. Nos. 2456/2461				6·50	6·50
First Day Cover (Tallents House)					7·25
First Day Cover (Wisley, Woking)					7·25

Booklet panes Nos. 2456a/2457a come from the £7·23 Glory of the Garden booklet, No. DX33.

The 1st class stamp was also issued in sheets of 20, printed in lithography by Walsall and sold at £6·15, containing vertical strips of five stamps alternated with printed labels giving information about dahlias (No. LS19). These sheets with personalised photographs were available at £14·95 from the Royal Mail in Edinburgh.

The complete miniature sheet is shown on one of the PHQ cards with the others depicting individual stamps.

1280 *Gentiana acaulis* (Georg Ehret)

1283 *Tulipa* (Ehret)

1287 *Iris latifolia* (Ehret)

(Litho Enschedé)

2004 (25 May). Bicentenary of the Royal Horticultural Society (2nd issue). Booklet stamps. Designs as Nos. 1955, 1958 and 1962 (1997 Greetings Stamps 19th-century Flower Paintings). Multicoloured Two phosphor bands. Perf 15×14 (with one elliptical hole in each vert side.)

2463	**1280**	(1st) *Gentiana acaulis* (Georg Ehret)	2·75	2·75
		a. Booklet pane. Nos. 2463, 2464×2		
		and 2465 with margins all round	7·00	
2464	**1283**	(1st) *Tulipa* (Ehret)	1·40	1·40
2465	**1287**	(1st) *Iris latifolia* (Ehret)	2·75	2·75
Set of 3			6·50	6·50

On Nos. 2463/2465 the phosphor bands appear at the left and the centre of each stamp.

Nos. 2463/2465 were only issued in the £7·23 Glory of the Garden booklet, No. DX33.

1746 Barmouth Bridge

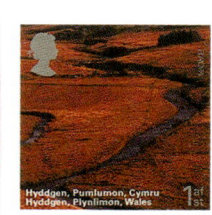

1747 Hyddgen, Plynlimon

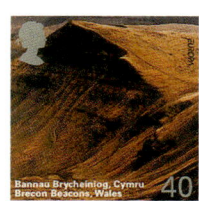

1748 Brecon Beacons

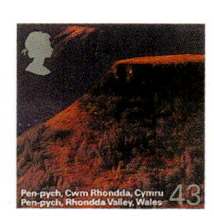

1749 Pen-pych, Rhondda Valley

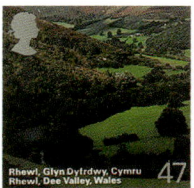

1750 Rhewl, Dee Valley

1751 Marloes Sands

QUEEN ELIZABETH II/2004

(Des Phelan Barker. Gravure De La Rue)

2004 (15 June). A British Journey. Wales. Multicoloured One centre phosphor band (2nd), 'all-over' phosphor (1st) or two phosphor bands (others). Perf 14½.

(a) Ordinary gum.

2466	1746	(2nd) Barmouth Bridge	90	90
		a. Imperf (pair)	£350	
2467	1747	(1st) Hyddgen, Plynlimon	1·20	1·00
		a. Imperf (pair)	£350	
2468	1748	40p. Brecon Beacons	70	70
2469	1749	43p. Pen-pych, Rhondda Valley	75	75
2470	1750	47p. Rhewl, Dee Valley	80	85
		a. Imperf (pair)	£250	
2471	1751	68p. Marloes Sands	90	95
		a. Imperf (pair)	£350	
Set of 6			4·50	4·50
Set of 6 Gutter Pairs			9·00	
First Day Cover (Tallents House)				4·75
First Day Cover (Llanfair)				4·75
Presentation Pack (PO Pack No. 361)			4·75	
PHQ Cards (set of 6) (266)			1·75	5·25

(b) Self-adhesive. Die-cut perf 14½.

2472	1747	(1st) Hyddgen, Plynlimon	3·00	3·00
		a. Booklet pane. No. 2472×2 and No. 2295×4	7·50	

The 1st and 40p. values include the EUROPA emblem.

Imperf pairs of Types **1748** and **1749** with alternative face values are of proof status. (*Price* £1000 *per pair*).

No. 2472 was only issued in £1·68 stamp booklet, No. PM14, in which the surplus self-adhesive paper around each stamp was removed.

1752 Sir Rowland Hill Award

1753 William Shipley (Founder of Royal Society of Arts)

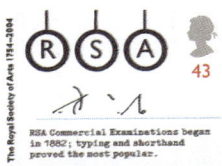

1754 'RSA' as Typewriter Keys and Shorthand

1755 Chimney Sweep

1756 Gill Typeface

1757 'Zero Waste'

(Des D. Birdsall. Litho Walsall)

2004 (10 Aug). 250th Anniversary of the Royal Society of Arts. Multicoloured Two phosphor bands. Perf 14.

2473	1752	(1st) Sir Rowland Hill Award	1·20	1·00
2474	1753	40p. William Shipley	75	75
2475	1754	43p. 'RSA' as Typewriter Keys and Shorthand	80	80
2476	1755	47p. Chimney Sweep	1·00	1·00
2477	1756	57p. Gill Typeface	1·25	1·25
2478	1757	68p. 'Zero Waste'	1·50	1·50
Set of 6			5·50	5·50
Set of 6 Gutter Pairs			11·00	
First Day Cover (Tallents House)				5·75
First Day Cover (London WC2)				5·75
Presentation Pack (PO Pack No. 362)			6·00	
PHQ Cards (set of 6) (267)			1·75	6·50

1758 Pine Marten

1759 Roe Deer

1760 Badger

1761 Yellow-necked Mouse

1762 Wild Cat

1763 Red Squirrel

1764 Stoat

1765 Natterer's Bat

1766 Mole

1767 Fox

(Des Kate Stephens. Gravure Enschedé)

2004 (16 Sept). Woodland Animals. Multicoloured Two phosphor bands. Perf 14½.

2479	1758	(1st) Pine Marten	1·20	1·00
		a. Block of 10. Nos. 2479/2488	10·50	9·00
2480	1759	(1st) Roe Deer	1·20	1·00
2481	1760	(1st) Badger	1·20	1·00
2482	1761	(1st) Yellow-necked Mouse	1·20	1·00
2483	1762	(1st) Wild Cat	1·20	1·00
2484	1763	(1st) Red Squirrel	1·20	1·00
2485	1764	(1st) Stoat	1·20	1·00
2486	1765	(1st) Natterer's Bat	1·20	1·00
2487	1766	(1st) Mole	1·20	1·00
2488	1767	(1st) Fox	1·20	1·00
Set of 10			10·50	9·00
Gutter Block of 20			21·00	
Traffic Light Gutter Block of 20			40·00	
First Day Cover (Tallents House)				9·25
First Day Cover (Woodland, Bishop Auckland)				9·25
Presentation Pack (PO Pack No. 363)			11·00	
PHQ Cards (set of 10) (268)			3·00	10·00

Nos. 2479/2488 were printed together, *se-tenant*, in blocks of ten (5×2) throughout sheets of 30.

2004/QUEEN ELIZABETH II

For the miniature sheet celebrating the opening of the new Scottish Parliament Building, Edinburgh, issued 5 October 2004, see Regionals Section.

1768 Private McNamara, 5th Dragoon Guards, Heavy Brigade charge, Battle of Balaklava

1769 Piper Muir, 42nd Regt of Foot, amphibious assault on Kerch

1770 Sergeant Major Edwards, Scots Fusilier Guards, gallant action, Battle of Inkerman

1771 Sergeant Powell, 1st Regt of Foot Guards, Battles of Alma and Inkerman

1772 Sergeant.Major Poole, Royal Sappers and Miners, defensive line, Battle of Inkerman

1773 Sergeant Glasgow, Royal Artillery, gun battery besieged Sevastopol

(Des Atelier Works. Litho Walsall)

2004 (12 Oct). 150th Anniversary of the Crimean War. One centre phosphor band (2nd) or two phosphor bands (others). Perf 14.

2489	1768	(2nd) Private McNamara	90	90
		a. Greyish silver and phosphor omitted	£700	
2490	1769	(1st) Piper Muir	1·20	1·00
2491	1770	40p. Sergeant Major Edwards	1·00	1·00
2492	1771	57p. Sergeant Powell	1·10	1·10
		a. Imperf	£400	
2493	1772	68p. Sergeant Major Poole	1·25	1·25
		a. Imperf	£1000	
2494	1773	£1·12 Sergeant Glasgow	1·60	1·60
Set of 6			6·00	6·00
Set of 6 Gutter Pairs			12·00	
Set of 6 Traffic Light Gutter Pairs			38·00	
First Day Cover (Tallents House)				6·25
First Day Cover (London SW3)				6·50
Presentation Pack (PO Pack No. 364)			6·25	
PHQ Cards (set of 6) (269)			1·75	7·00

Nos. 2489/2494 show Crimean Heroes photographs taken in 1856.

1774 Father Christmas on Snowy Roof

1775 Celebrating the Sunrise

1776 On Roof in Gale

1777 With Umbrella in Rain

1778 On Edge of Roof with Torch

1779 Sheltering behind Chimney

(Des R. Briggs. Gravure De La Rue)

2004 (2 Nov). Christmas. Multicoloured One centre phosphor band (2nd) or two phosphor bands (others). Perf 14½×14.

(a) Self-adhesive.

2495	1774	(2nd) Father Christmas on Snowy Roof..	90	90
		a. Booklet pane. No. 2495×24	22·00	
2496	1775	(1st) Celebrating the Sunrise	1·20	1·00
		a. Booklet pane. No. 2496×12	16·00	
2497	1776	40p. On Roof in Gale	80	80
2498	1777	57p. With Umbrella in Rain	1·00	1·00
2499	1778	68p. On Edge of Roof with Torch	1·10	1·10
2500	1779	£1·12 Sheltering behind Chimney	1·25	1·25
Set of 6			5·50	5·50
First Day Cover (Tallents House)				5·75
First Day Cover (Bethlehem, Llandeilo)				6·00
Presentation Pack (PO Pack No. 365)			5·75	
PHQ Cards (set of 7) (270)			2·00	6·25

(b) Ordinary gum.

MS2501	115×105 mm. As Nos. 2495/2500		6·00	6·00
First Day Cover (Tallents House)				6·25
First Day Cover (Bethlehem, Llandeilo)				6·50

Nos. 2495/2500 were each printed in sheets of 50 with the surplus backing paper around each stamp removed.

The 2nd and 1st class were also issued together in sheets of 20, sold at £5·40, containing ten 2nd class and ten 1st class, each value arranged in vertical rows of five alternated with rows of half stamp-size labels showing Father Christmas (No. LS21).

Separate sheets of 20 2nd class and 20 1st class were available with personalised photographs at £9·95 (2nd class) or £14·95 (1st class) from Royal Mail, Edinburgh. These sheets were printed in lithography instead of photogravure and had the backing paper around the stamps retained.

Trials are known showing alternative face values.

The seven PHQ cards depict the six individual stamps and the miniature sheet.

Year Pack 2004

2004 (2 Nov). Comprises Nos. 2417/22422, 2424/2444, 2446/2453, 2456/2461, 2466/2471 and 2473/2500.

CP2500a	Year Pack (PO Pack No. 366)	65·00

Post Office Yearbook

2004 (2 Nov). Comprises Nos. 2417/2422, 2424/2444, 2446/2453, 2456/2461, 2466/2471 and 2473/2500 in hardback book with slipcase

YB2500a	Yearbook	60·00

QUEEN ELIZABETH II/2005

1780 British Saddleback Pigs
1781 Khaki Campbell Ducks 
1782 Clydesdale Mare and Foal 
1783 Dairy Shorthorn Cattle 
1784 Border Collie Dog 
1785 Light Sussex Chicks 
1786 Suffolk Sheep 
1787 Bagot Goat 
1788 Norfolk Black Turkeys 
1789 Embden Geese 

(Des C. Wormell. Gravure Enschedé)

2005 (11 Jan). Farm Animals. Multicoloured Two phosphor bands. Perf 14½.

2502	1780	(1st) British Saddleback Pigs	1·20	1·00
		a. Block of 10. Nos. 2502/2511	10·50	9·00
2503	1781	(1st) Khaki Campbell Ducks	1·20	1·00
2504	1782	(1st) Clydesdale Mare and Foal	1·20	1·00
2505	1783	(1st) Dairy Shorthorn Cattle	1·20	1·00
2506	1784	(1st) Border Collie Dog	1·20	1·00
2507	1785	(1st) Light Sussex Chicks	1·20	1·00
2508	1786	(1st) Suffolk Sheep	1·20	1·00
2509	1787	(1st) Bagot Goat	1·20	1·00
2510	1788	(1st) Norfolk Black Turkeys	1·20	1·00
2511	1789	(1st) Embden Geese	1·20	1·00
Set of 10			10·50	9·00
Gutter Block of 20			21·00	
Traffic Light Gutter Block of 20			65·00	
First Day Cover (Tallents House)				9·25
First Day Cover (Paddock, Huddersfield)				9·50
Presentation Pack (PO Pack No. 367)			11·00	
PHQ Cards (set of 10) (271)			3·00	10·50

Nos. 2502/2511 were printed together, *se-tenant*, in blocks of ten (5×2) throughout sheets of 30.

Nos. 2502/2511 were also issued in sheets of 20, containing two of each of the ten designs, arranged in vertical strips of five alternated with printed labels showing black and white illustrations of farm scenes (No. LS22). These sheets were printed in lithography by Walsall and sold for £6·15.

They were also available with personal photographs on the labels at £14·95 per sheet from Royal Mail, Edinburgh.

1790 Old Harry Rocks, Studland Bay
1791 Wheal Coates, St Agnes 
1792 Start Point, Start Bay 
1793 Horton Down, Wiltshire 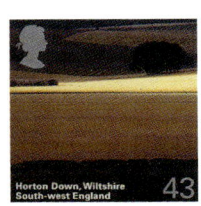
1794 Chiselcombe, Exmoor 
1795 St James's Stone, Lundy 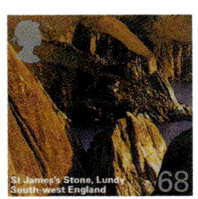

(Des J. Phelan and Lissa Barker. Gravure De La Rue)

2005 (8 Feb). A British Journey. South West England. Multicoloured One centre phosphor band (2nd) or two phosphor bands (others). Perf 14½.

2512	1790	(2nd) Old Harry Rocks, Studland Bay	90	90
2513	1791	(1st) Wheal Coates, St Agnes	1·20	1·00
2514	1792	40p. Start Point, Start Bay	75	75
2515	1793	43p. Horton Down, Wiltshire	85	85
2516	1794	57p. Chiselcombe, Exmoor	1·00	1·00
2517	1795	68p. St James's Stone, Lundy	1·25	1·25
Set of 6			5·25	5·25
Set of 6 Gutter Pairs			10·50	
First Day Cover (Tallents House)				5·50
First Day Cover (The Lizard, Helston)				5·75
Presentation Pack (PO Pack No. 368)			5·50	
PHQ Cards (set of 6) (262)			1·75	5·75

Perforated examples of T **1794** are known with face value of 47p are known (*price* £1250).

1796 Mr Rochester
1797 Come to Me 
1798 In the Comfort of her Bonnet

2005/QUEEN ELIZABETH II

1799 La Ligne des Rats
1800 Refectory 
1801 Inspection 

(Des P. Willberg. Litho Walsall)

2005 (24 Feb). 150th Anniversary of Charlotte Brontë. Illustrations of scenes from *Jane Eyre* by Paula Rego. Multicoloured One centre phosphor band (2nd), or two phosphor bands (others). Perf 14×14½.

2518	**1796**	(2nd) Mr Rochester	90	90
		a. Booklet pane. Nos. 2518/2519, both×2, with margins all round	3·50	
2519	**1797**	(1st) Come to Me	1·20	1·00
2520	**1798**	40p. In the Comfort of her Bonnet	1·00	1·00
		a. Booklet pane. Nos. 2520/2523 with margins all round	4·50	
2521	**1799**	57p. La Ligne des Rats	1·25	1·25
2522	**1800**	68p. Refectory	1·40	1·40
2523	**1801**	£1·12 Inspection	1·60	1·60
Set of 6			6·50	6·50
Set of 6 Gutter Pairs			13·00	
Set of 6 Traffic Light Gutter Blocks of 4			48·00	
First Day Cover (Tallents House)				6·75
First Day Cover (Haworth, Keighley)				7·00
Presentation Pack (PO Pack No. 369)			6·75	
PHQ Cards (set of 7) (273)			2·00	7·00
MS2524 114×105 mm. Nos. 2518/2523			6·50	6·50
First Day Cover (Tallents House)				6·75
First Day Cover (Haworth, Keighley)				7·00

Booklet panes Nos. 2518a and 2520a come from the £7·43 The Brontë Sisters booklet, No. DX34.

The complete miniature sheet is shown on one of the PHQ cards with the others depicting individual stamps.

1802 Spinning Coin
1803 Rabbit out of Hat Trick 
1804 Knotted Scarf Trick 
1805 Card Trick 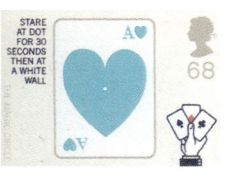
1806 Pyramid under Fez Trick 

(Des G. Hardie and Tatham Design. Gravure Walsall)

2005 (15 Mar). Centenary of the Magic Circle. Multicoloured Two phosphor bands. Perf 14½×14.

2525	**1802**	(1st) Spinning Coin	1·20	1·00
2526	**1803**	40p. Rabbit out of Hat Trick	1·00	1·00
2527	**1804**	47p. Knotted Scarf Trick	1·25	1·25
2528	**1805**	68p. Card Trick	1·40	1·40
2529	**1806**	£1·12 Pyramid under Fez Trick	5·50	5·50
Set of 5			5·75	5·75
Set of 5 Gutter Pairs			11·50	
First Day Cover (Philatelic Bureau, Edinburgh)				6·00
First Day Cover (London NW1)				6·00
Presentation Pack (PO Pack No. 370)			6·00	
PHQ Cards (set of 5) (274)			1·50	6·00

Nos. 2525/2529 are each printed with instructions for the illusion or trick on the stamp.

No. 2525 can be rubbed with a coin to reveal the 'head' or 'tail' of a coin. The two versions, which appear identical before rubbing, are printed in alternate rows of the sheet, indicated by the letters H and T in the side margins of the sheet.

No. 2525 was also issued in sheets of 20, printed in lithography instead of gravure and sold at £6·15, containing vertical rows of five stamps alternated with half stamp-size printed labels illustrating magic tricks (No. LS23). These sheets were also available with personal photographs on the labels at £14·95 per sheet from Royal Mail, Edinburgh.

Nos. 2526 and 2528 each show optical illusions.

The bright mauve on No. 2527 and the bright mauve, new blue, and lilac on No. 2529 are printed in thermochromic inks which fade temporarily when exposed to heat, making the pyramid under the centre fez visible.

1806a First Castles Definitives (*Illustration reduced. Actual size 127×73 mm*)

(Des Sedley Place. Recess and litho Enschedé)

2005 (22 Mar). 50th Anniversary of First Castles Definitives. Printed on pale cream paper. 'All-over' phosphor. Perf 11×11½.

MS2530 127×73 mm. **1806a** First Castles Definitives 50p. brownish-black; 50p. black; £1 dull vermilion; £1 royal blue	4·50	4·50
First Day Cover (Tallents House)		5·75
First Day Cover (Windsor)		5·75
Presentation Pack (PO Pack No. 69)	5·75	
PHQ Cards (set of 5) (D28)	1·50	5·75

The five PHQ cards depict the whole miniature sheet and the four stamps it contains.

See also No. 3221.

1807 Royal Wedding (*Illustration reduced. Actual size 85×115 mm*)

(Des Rose Design. Litho Enschedé)

2005 (9 Apr). Royal Wedding. Sheet 85×115 mm. Multicoloured 'All-over' phosphor. Perf 13½×14.

MS2531 **1807** Royal Wedding 30p.×2 Prince Charles and Mrs Camilla Parker Bowles laughing; 68p.×2 Prince Charles and Mrs Camilla Parker Bowles smiling into camera	4·50	4·50
First Day Cover (Tallents House)		5·00
First Day Cover (Windsor)		5·00
Presentation Pack (PO Pack No. M10)	8·00	

No. **MS**2531 was officially issued on 9 April. It was originally intended for issue on 8 April, and many post offices put it on sale on that day. Royal Mail first day covers were dated 8 April, but could be ordered with a 9 April Windsor handstamp. Our prices cover either date.

QUEEN ELIZABETH II/2005

1808 Hadrian's Wall, England 
1809 Uluru-Kata Tjuta National Park, Australia
1816 Ensign of the Scots Guards, 2002
1817 Queen taking the salute as Colonel-in-Chief of the Grenadier Guards, 1983

1810 Stonehenge, England 
1811 Wet Tropics of Queensland, Australia

1812 Blenheim Palace, England 
1813 Greater Blue Mountains Area, Australia
1818 Trumpeter of the Household Cavalry, 2004
1819 Welsh Guardsman, 1990s

1814 Heart of Neolithic Orkney, Scotland
1815 Purnululu National Park, Australia 

(Des J. Godfrey. Litho Enschedé)

2005 (21 Apr). World Heritage Sites. Multicoloured One side phosphor band (2nd) or two phosphor bands (others). Perf 14½.

2532	1808	2nd Hadrian's Wall, England	90	90
		a. Horiz pair. Nos. 2532/2533	1·75	1·75
2533	1809	2nd Uluru-Kata Tjuta National Park, Australia	90	90
2534	1810	1st Stonehenge, England	1·20	1·00
		a. Horiz pair. Nos. 2534/2535	2·40	2·40
2535	1811	1st Wet Tropics of Queensland, Australia	1·20	1·00
2536	1812	47p. Blenheim Palace, England	80	80
		a. Horiz pair. Nos. 2536/2537	1·60	1·60
2537	1813	47p. Greater Blue Mountains Area, Australia	80	80
2538	1814	68p. Heart of Neolithic Orkney, Scotland	1·00	1·00
		a. Horiz pair. Nos. 2538/2539	2·00	2·00
2539	1815	68p. Purnululu National Park, Australia	1·00	1·00
Set of 8			6·50	6·50
Set of 4 Gutter Strips of 4			14·00	
Set of 4 Traffic Light Gutter Blocks of 8			32·00	
First Day Cover (Tallents House)				7·75
First Day Cover (Blenheim Palace, Woodstock)				7·75
First Day Covers (UK and Australian stamps) (2)				12·50
Presentation Pack (PO Pack No. 371)			7·50	
Presentation Pack (UK and Australian stamps)			11·00	
PHQ Cards (set of 8) (275)			2·50	7·50

The two designs of each value were printed together, *se-tenant*, in horizontal pairs in sheets of 30 (6×5).

Stamps in these designs were also issued by Australia and these are included in the joint Presentation Pack.

1820 Queen riding side-saddle, 1972
1821 Queen and Duke of Edinburgh in carriage, 2004 

(Des A. Altmann. Litho Walsall)

2005 (7 June). Trooping the Colour. Multicoloured One phosphor band (2nd), two phosphor bands (others). Perf 14½.

2540	1816	(2nd) Ensign of the Scots Guards, 2002	90	90
2541	1817	(1st) Queen taking the salute as Colonel-in-Chief of the Grenadier Guards, 1983	1·20	1·00
2542	1818	42p. Trumpeter of the Household Cavalry, 2004	85	85
2543	1819	60p. Welsh Guardsman, 1990s	1·00	1·00
2544	1820	68p. Queen riding side-saddle, 1972	1·10	1·10
2545	1821	£1·12 Queen and Duke of Edinburgh in carriage, 2004	1·60	1·60
Set of 6			5·75	5·75
Set of 6 Gutter Pairs			11·50	
First Day Cover (Tallents House)				6·00
First Day Cover (London SW1)				6·00
Presentation Pack (PO Pack No. 372)			5·75	
PHQ Cards (set of 7) (276)			2·00	11·00
MS2546 115×105 mm. Nos. 2540/2545			5·50	5·50
First Day Cover (Tallents House)				5·75
First Day Cover (London SW1)				5·75

The seven PHQ cards show the six stamps and No. **MS**2546.

2005 / QUEEN ELIZABETH II

1822 End of the War (*Illustration reduced. Actual size 115×105 mm*)

(Des J. Matthews. Gravure Enschedé)

2005 (5 July). 60th Anniversary of End of the Second World War. Sheet 115×105 mm containing design as T **1200** (1995 Peace and Freedom) but with service indicator and No. 1668×5. Two phosphor bands. Perf 15×14 (with one elliptical hole in each vert side) (No. 1668) or 14½×14 (other).

MS2547	**1822**	End of the War (1st) gold×5; (1st) silver, blue and grey-black	6·25	5·25
First Day Cover (Tallents House)			5·50
First Day Cover (Peacehaven, Newhaven)			5·50

1823 Norton F.1, Road Version of Race Winner (1991)

1824 BSA Rocket 3, Early Three Cylinder 'Superbike' (1969)

1825 Vincent Black Shadow, Fastest Standard Motorcycle (1949)

1826 Triumph Speed Twin, Two Cylinder Innovation (1938)

1827 Brough Superior, Bespoke Luxury Motorcycle (1930)

1828 Royal Enfield, Small Engined Motor Bicycle (1914)

(Des I. Chilvers and M. English. Litho Walsall)

2005 (19 July). Motorcycles. Multicoloured Two phosphor bands. Perf 14×14½.

2548	1823	(1st) Norton F.1	1·20	90
2549	1824	40p. BSA Rocket 3	60	60
2550	1825	42p. Vincent Black Shadow	65	65
2551	1826	47p. Triumph Speed Twin	80	80
2552	1827	60p. Brough Superior	1·00	1·00
2553	1828	68p. Royal Enfield	1·25	1·25
Set of 6			4·50	4·50
Set of 6 Gutter Pairs			9·50	
First Day Cover (Tallents House)				5·75
First Day Cover (Solihull)				5·75
Presentation Pack (PO Pack No. 373)			5·25	
PHQ Cards (set of 6) (277)			1·75	5·75

1829 London 2012 Host City (*Illustration reduced. Actual size 115×105 mm*)

(Des CDT Design. Litho Walsall)

2005 (5 Aug). London's Successful Bid for Olympic Games, 2012. Sheet 115×105 mm containing designs as Types **1255**/**1259**, but with service indicator. Multicoloured Two phosphor bands. Perf 14½.

MS2554	**1829**	London 2012 Host City (1st) Athlete celebrating×2; (1st) Javelin; (1st) Swimming; (1st) Athlete on starting blocks; (1st) Basketball	6·00	5·00
First Day Cover (Tallents House)			5·75
First Day Cover (London E15)			5·75
Presentation Pack (PO Pack No. M11)			6·25

Stamps from No. **MS**2554 are all inscribed 'London 2012–Host City' and have imprint date 2005.

The design as T **1259** omits the Olympic rings.

1830 African Woman eating Rice

1831 Indian Woman drinking Tea

1832 Boy eating Sushi

1833 Woman eating Pasta

1834 Woman eating Chips

1835 Teenage Boy eating Apple

(Des Catell Ronca and Rose Design. Gravure Enschedé)

2005 (23 Aug). Europa. Gastronomy. Changing Tastes in Britain. Multicoloured. One side phosphor band (2nd) or two phosphor bands (others). Perf 14½.

2555	1830	(2nd) African Woman eating Rice	90	90
2556	1831	(1st) Indian Woman drinking Tea	1·20	1·00
2557	1832	42p. Boy eating Sushi	60	60
2558	1833	47p. Woman eating Pasta	75	75
2559	1834	60p. Woman eating Chips	90	1·00
2560	1835	68p. Teenage Boy eating Apple	1·10	1·25

183

QUEEN ELIZABETH II/2005

Set of 6	4·75	4·75
Set of 6 Gutter Pairs	9·50	
First Day Cover (Tallents House)		5·00
First Day Cover (Cookstown)		5·00
Presentation Pack (PO Pack No. 374)	5·00	
PHQ Cards (set of 6) (278)	1·75	5·75

The 1st and 42p. values include the EUROPA emblem.

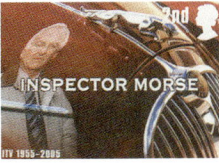

1836 *Inspector Morse*

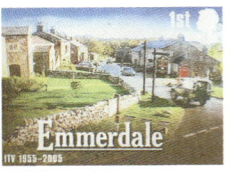

1837 *Emmerdale*

1838 *Rising Damp*

1839 *The Avengers*

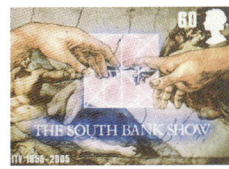

1840 *The South Bank Show*

1841 *Who Wants to be a Millionaire*

(Des Kate Stephens. Litho D.L.R.)

2005 (15 Sept). 50th Anniversary of Independent Television. Classic ITV Programmes. Multicoloured One side phosphor band (2nd) or two phosphor bands (others). Perf 14½×14.

2561	1836	(2nd) *Inspector Morse*	90	90
2562	1837	(1st) *Emmerdale*	1·20	1·00
2563	1838	42p. *Rising Damp*	60	60
2564	1839	47p. *The Avengers*	75	75
2565	1840	60p. *The South Bank Show*	90	90
2566	1841	68p. *Who Wants to be a Millionaire*	1·10	1·10
Set of 6			4·75	4·75
Set of 6 Gutter Pairs			9·50	
First Day Cover (Tallents House)				5·25
First Day Cover (London SE19)				5·25
Presentation Pack (PO Pack No. 375)			5·00	
PHQ Cards (set of 6) (279)			1·75	5·75

The 1st class stamps were also issued in sheets of 20 sold at £6·55, printed in lithography by Walsall, containing four vertical rows of five stamps alternated with half stamp-size labels (No. LS26). These sheets with personalised photographs were available at £14·95 from the Royal Mail.

1842 *Gazania splendens* (Charlotte Sowerby)

1842a Aircraft Skywriting 'hello'

1842b 'LOVE'

1842c Union Flag

1842d Teddy Bear

1842e European Robin in Mouth of Pillar Box

(Gravure Walsall)

2005 (4 Oct). Smilers Booklet stamps (1st series). Self-adhesive. Multicoloured Two phosphor bands. Die-cut Perf 15×14.

2567	1842	(1st) *Gazania splendens*	1·20	1·25
		a. Booklet pane. Nos. 2567/2572	9·00	
2568	1842a	(1st) Aircraft Skywriting 'hello'	1·20	1·25
2569	1842b	(1st) 'LOVE'	1·20	1·25
2570	1842c	(1st) Union Jack	1·20	1·25
2571	1842d	(1st) Teddy Bear	1·20	1·25
2572	1842e	(1st) European Robin in Mouth of Pillar Box	1·20	1·25
Set of 6			9·00	9·00
First Day Cover (Tallents House) (Type K, see Introduction)				9·25
First Day Cover (Windsor) (Type K)				9·25

Nos. 2567/2572 were only issued in stamp booklets, Nos. QA1 and QA2, in which the surplus backing paper around each stamp was removed.

Stamps in these designs in separate sheets printed in lithography by Cartor were available with personal photographs on the labels at £14·95 per sheet from Royal Mail, Edinburgh.

Nos. 2567/2572 were re-issued on 4 July 2006 in sheets of 20 with *se-tenant* greetings labels (No. LS32), printed by Cartor in lithography instead of gravure and sold at £6·95 per sheet.

Nos. 2568/2570 were re-issued on 15 January 2008 in sheets of 20 with circular *se-tenant* labels printed in lithography by Cartor and sold at £7·35 (No. LS45). These sheets were perforated with one elliptical hole on each vert side.

These three designs were available in separate sheets of ten (*sold at £8·95*) or 20 (*sold at £14·95*) with personal photographs on the labels from Royal Mail, Edinburgh.

No. 2572 was re-issued on 8 May 2010 with other greetings stamps in sheets of 20 with *se-tenant* greetings labels, printed in lithography by Cartor (No. LS73), and sold for £10 per sheet. These sheets were printed with one elliptical hole in each vertical side.

For stamp as No. 2569 with one elliptical hole in each vertical side see No. 2693.

For stamps as Nos. 2567/2568 and 2570 with one elliptical hole in each vertical side see Nos. 2819/2821.

1843 Cricket Scenes (*Illustration reduced. Actual size 115×90 mm*)

(Des Why Not Associates. Litho Cartor)

2005 (6 Oct). England's Ashes Victory. Sheet 115×90 mm. Multicoloured Two phosphor bands. Perf 14½×14.

MS2573	**1843**	Cricket Scenes (1st) England team with Ashes trophy; (1st) Kevin Pietersen, Michael Vaughan and Andrew Flintoff on opening day of First Test, Lord's; 68p. Michael Vaughan, Third Test, Old Trafford; 68p. Second Test cricket, Edgbaston	4·00	4·00
First Day Cover (Tallents House)				5·00
First Day Cover (London SE11)				5·00
Presentation Pack (PO Pack No. M12)			4·25	

1844 *Entrepreante* with dismasted British *Belle Isle*

1845 Nelson wounded on Deck of HMS *Victory*

2005 / QUEEN ELIZABETH II

1846 British Cutter *Entrepreante* attempting to rescue Crew of burning French *Achille*

1847 Cutter and HMS *Pickle* (schooner)

1848 British Fleet attacking in Two Columns

1849 Franco/Spanish Fleet putting to Sea from Cadiz

(Des D. Davis. Litho Cartor)

2005 (18 Oct). Bicentenary of the Battle of Trafalgar (1st issue). Scenes from *Panorama of the Battle of Trafalgar* by William Heath. Multicoloured Two phosphor bands. Perf 15×14½.

2574	1844	(1st) *Entrepreante* with dismasted British *Belle Isle*	1·20	1·00
		a. Horiz pair. Nos. 2574/2575	2·40	2·00
		b. Booklet pane. Nos. 2574, 2576 and 2578	2·75	
2575	1845	(1st) Nelson wounded on Deck of HMS *Victory*	1·20	1·00
		b. Booklet pane. Nos. 2575, 2577 and 2579	2·75	
2576	1846	42p. British Cutter *Entrepreante* attempting to rescue Crew of burning French *Achille*	70	80
		a. Horiz pair. Nos. 2576/2577	1·60	1·60
2577	1847	42p. Cutter and HMS *Pickle* (schooner)	70	80
2578	1848	68p. British Fleet attacking in Two Columns	1·00	1·10
		a. Horiz pair. Nos. 2578/2579	2·00	2·00
2579	1849	68p. Franco/Spanish Fleet putting to Sea from Cadiz	1·00	1·10
Set of 6			5·00	5·00
Set of 3 Gutter Strips of 4			10·50	
First Day Cover (Tallents House)				5·50
First Day Cover (Portsmouth)				5·50
Presentation Pack (PO Pack No. 376)			5·75	
PHQ Cards (set of 7) (280)			2·00	11·50
MS2580 190×68 mm. Nos. 2574/2579			5·25	5·50
First Day Cover (Tallents House)				5·75
First Day Cover (Portsmouth)				5·75

Nos. 2574/2575, 2576/2577 and 2578/2579 were each printed together, *se-tenant*, in horizontal pairs throughout the sheets, each pair forming a composite design.

Booklet panes Nos. 2574b/2575b come from the £7·26 Battle of Trafalgar booklet, No. DX35.

The phosphor bands are at just left of centre and at right of each stamp.

The seven PHQ cards depict the six individual stamps and the miniature sheet.

1516 White Ensign

(Litho Cartor or De La Rue)

2005 (18 Oct). Bicentenary of the Battle of Trafalgar (2nd issue). Booklet stamp. Design as T **1516** (2001 White Ensign from Submarine Centenary). Multicoloured Two phosphor bands. Perf 14½.

2581	1516	(1st) White Ensign. Multicoloured	1·50	1·50
		a. Booklet pane. No. 2581×3 with margins all round	7·00	

No. 2581 was issued in the £7·26 Bicentenary of the Battle of Trafalgar booklet, No. DX35, printed by Cartor, the £7·40 Ian Fleming's James Bond booklet, No. DX41, which was printed by De La Rue (see booklet pane No. 2805a) and the £7·93 Royal Navy Uniforms booklet, No. DX47.

1850 Black Madonna and Child from Haiti

1851 *Madonna and Child* (Marianne Stokes)

1852 The Virgin Mary with the Infant Christ

1853 *Choctaw Virgin Mother and Child* (Fr. John Giuliani)

1854 Madonna and the Infant Jesus (from India)

1855 *Come let us adore Him* (Dianne Tchumut)

(Des Irene von Treskow. Gravure De La Rue)

2005 (1 Nov). Christmas. Madonna and Child Paintings. Multicoloured One side phosphor band (2nd) or two phosphor bands (others). Perf 14½×14.

(a) Self-adhesive.

2582	1850	(2nd) Black Madonna and Child from Haiti	90	90
		a. Booklet pane. No. 2582×24	22·00	
2583	1851	(1st) *Madonna and Child*	1·20	1·00
		a. Booklet pane. No. 2583×12	16·00	
2584	1852	42p. The Virgin Mary with the Infant Christ	90	90
2585	1853	60p. *Choctaw Virgin Mother and Child*	1·00	1·00
2586	1854	68p. Madonna and the Infant Jesus	1·25	1·25
2587	1855	£1·12 *Come let us adore Him*	1·40	1·40
Set of 6			5·75	5·75
First Day Cover (Tallents House)				6·00
First Day Cover (Bethlehem, Llandeilo)				6·00
Presentation Pack (PO Pack No. 377)			6·00	
PHQ Cards (set of 7) (281)			2·00	12·00

The seven PHQ cards depict the six individual stamps and the miniature sheet.

(b) Ordinary gum.

MS2588 115×102 mm. As Nos. 2582/2587		5·75	5·75
First Day Cover (Tallents House)			6·00
First Day Cover (Bethlehem, Llandeilo)			6·00

Year Pack

2005 (1 Nov). Comprises Nos. 2502/2523, 2525/2529, **MS**2531/2545, 2548/2553, 2555/2566, 2574/2579 and 2582/2587.

CP2587a	Year Pack (PO Pack No. 378)	65·00

Post Office Yearbook

2005 (1 Nov). Comprises Nos. 2502/2523, 2525/2529, **MS**2531/2545, 2548/2553, 2555/2566, 2574/2579 and 2582/2587.

YB2587a	Yearbook	60·00

Miniature Sheet Collection

2005 (1 Nov). Comprises Nos. **MS**2524, **MS**2530/**MS**2531, **MS**2546/ **MS**2547, **MS**2554, **MS**2573, **MS**2580 and **MS**2588.
MS2588a Miniature Sheet Collection .... 45·00

1856 *The Tale of Mr Jeremy Fisher* (Beatrix Potter)
1857 *Kipper* (Mick Inkpen) 
1858 *The Enormous Crocodile* (Roald Dahl) 
1859 *More About Paddington* (Michael Bond) 
1860 *Comic Adventures of Boots* (Satoshi Kitamura) 
1861 *Alice's Adventures in Wonderland* (Lewis Carroll) 
1862 *The Very Hungry Caterpillar* (Eric Carle) 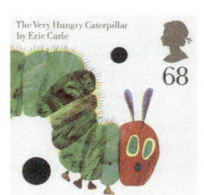
1863 *Maisy's ABC* (Lucy Cousins) 

(Des Rose Design. Litho D.L.R.)

2006 (10 Jan). Animal Tales. Multicoloured One side phosphor band (2nd) or two phosphor bands (others). Perf 14½.

2589	1856	(2nd) *The Tale of Mr Jeremy Fisher* (Beatrix Potter).........	90	90
		a. Horiz pair. Nos. 2589/2590.......	1·75	1·75
2590	1857	(2nd) *Kipper* (Mick Inkpen)	90	90
2591	1858	(1st) *The Enormous Crocodile* (Roald Dahl)	1·20	1·00
		a. Horiz pair. Nos. 2591/2592.......	2·40	2·40
2592	1859	(1st) *More About Paddington* (Michael Bond)	1·20	1·00
2593	1860	42p. *Comic Adventures of Boots* (Satoshi Kitamura)	80	80
		a. Horiz pair. Nos. 2593/2594.......	1·60	1·60
2594	1861	42p. *Alice's Adventures in Wonderland* (Lewis Carroll)	80	80
2595	1862	68p. *The Very Hungry Caterpillar* (Eric Carle)	1·00	1·00
		a. Horiz pair. Nos. 2595/2596.......	2·00	2·00
2596	1863	68p. *Maisy's ABC* (Lucy Cousins)	1·00	1·00
Set of 8			7·00	6·75
Set of 4 Gutter Blocks of 4			14·00	
Set of 4 Traffic Light Gutter Blocks of 8			50·00	
First Day Cover (Tallents House)				7·75
First Day Cover (Mousehole, Penzance, Cornwall)				7·75
First Day Cover (Nos. 2595/2596 UK and US stamps)				4·00
Presentation Pack (PO Pack No. 379)			8·75	
PHQ Cards (set of 8) (282)			2·50	7·75

Nos. 2589/2590, 2591/2592, 2593/2594 and 2595/2596 were printed together, *se-tenant*, in horizontal pairs in sheets of 60 (2 panes 6×5).

A design as No. 2592 but self-adhesive was issued in sheets of 20, printed in lithography by Cartor sold at £6·55, containing four vertical rows of five stamps alternated with printed labels (No. LS28). This sheet was also available with personal photographs on the labels at £14·95 from Royal Mail.

No. 2595 contains two die-cut holes.

1864 Carding Mill Valley, Shropshire
1865 Beachy Head, Sussex 
1866 St Paul's Cathedral, London 
1867 Brancaster, Norfolk 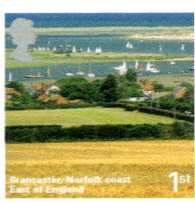
1868 Derwent Edge, Peak District 
1869 Robin Hood's Bay, Yorkshire 
1870 Buttermere, Lake District 
1871 Chipping Campden, Cotswolds 
1872 St Boniface Down, Isle of Wight 
1873 Chamberlain Square, Birmingham 

(Des Phelan Barker Design Consultants. Gravure D.L.R.)

2006 (7 Feb). A British Journey. England. Multicoloured Two phosphor bands. Perf 14½.

2597	1864	(1st) Carding Mill Valley, Shropshire.......	1·20	1·00
		a. Block of 10. Nos. 2597/2606...........	10·50	9·00
2598	1865	(1st) Beachy Head, Sussex..............	1·20	1·00
2599	1866	(1st) St Paul's Cathedral, London............	1·20	1·00
2600	1867	(1st) Brancaster, Norfolk................	1·20	1·00
2601	1868	(1st) Derwent Edge, Peak District...........	1·20	1·00
2602	1869	(1st) Robin Hood's Bay, Yorkshire...........	1·20	1·00
2603	1870	(1st) Buttermere, Lake District.............	1·20	1·00
2604	1871	(1st) Chipping Campden, Cotswolds.....	1·20	1·00
2605	1872	(1st) St Boniface Down, Isle of Wight.....	1·20	1·00

2006/QUEEN ELIZABETH II

2606	**1873**	(1st) Chamberlain Square, Birmingham	1·20	1·00

Set of 10	10·50	9·00
Gutter Block of 20	21·00	
First Day Cover (Tallents House)		9·50
First Day Cover (Tea Green, Luton)		9·75
Presentation Pack (PO Pack No. 380)	11·00	
PHQ Cards (set of 10) (283)	3·00	9·75

Nos. 2597/2606 were printed together, *se-tenant*, as blocks of ten (5×2) in sheets of 60 (2 panes of 30).

1874 Royal Albert Bridge

1875 Box Tunnel

1876 Paddington Station

1877 PSS *Great Eastern* (paddle-steamer)

1878 Clifton Suspension Bridge Design

1879 Maidenhead Bridge

(Des Hat-trick Design. Litho Enschedé)

2006 (23 Feb). Birth Bicentenary of Isambard Kingdom Brunel (engineer) (1st issue). Multicoloured Phosphor-coated paper (42p.) or two phosphor bands (others). Perf 14×13½.

2607	**1874**	(1st) Royal Albert Bridge	1·20	1·00
		a. Booklet pane. Nos. 2607, 2609 and 2612	2·50	
2608	**1875**	40p. Box Tunnel	60	60
		a. Booklet pane. Nos. 2608 and 2610/2611	2·50	
2609	**1876**	42p. Paddington Station	65	65
2610	**1877**	47p. PSS *Great Eastern*	80	80
		a. Booklet pane. No. 2610 and No. 2614×2	7·00	
2611	**1878**	60p. Clifton Suspension Bridge	1·00	1·00
2612	**1879**	68p. Maidenhead Bridge	1·25	1·25
Set of 6			4·75	4·75
Set of 6 Gutter Pairs			9·50	
First Day Cover (Tallents House)				5·25
First Day Cover (Bristol)				5·25
Presentation Pack (PO Pack No. 381)			5·75	
PHQ Cards (set of 7) (284)			2·00	11·00
MS2613 190×65 mm. Nos. 2607/2612			5·00	5·00
		a. Imperforate	—	
First Day Cover (Philatelic Bureau, Edinburgh)				5·50
First Day Cover (Bristol)				5·50

The phosphor bands on Nos. 2607/2608 and 2610/2612 are at just left of centre and at right of each stamp.

Booklet panes Nos. 2607a/2608a and 2610a come from the £7·40 Isambard Kingdom Brunel booklet, No. DX36.

The complete miniature sheet is shown on one of the PHQ Cards with the others depicting individual stamps.

1739 PS *Great Western, 1838* (Joseph Walter)

(Litho Enschedé)

2006 (23 Feb). Birth Bicentenary of Isambard Kingdom Brunel (2nd issue). Booklet stamp. Design as T **1739** (PSS *Great Western* from 2004 Ocean Liners). Multicoloured Two phosphor bands. Perf 14½×14.

2614	**1739**	68p. PSS *Great Western, 1838* (Joseph Walter)	2·50	2·50

No. 2614 was only issued in the £7·40 Isambard Kingdom Brunel booklet, No. DX36.

> For the miniature sheet celebrating the opening of the New Welsh Assembly, Cardiff, issued 1 March 2006, see the Regional Section.

1880 Sabre-tooth Cat

1881 Giant Deer

1882 Woolly Rhino

1883 Woolly Mammoth

1884 Cave Bear

(Des A. Davidson and H. Brown. Litho Enschedé)

2006 (21 Mar). Ice Age Animals. Black and silver. Two phosphor bands. Perf 14½.

2615	**1880**	(1st) Sabre-tooth Cat	1·20	1·00
2616	**1881**	42p. Giant Deer	90	90
2617	**1882**	47p. Woolly Rhino	1·00	1·00
2618	**1883**	68p. Woolly Mammoth	1·10	1·10
2619	**1884**	£1·12 Cave Bear	1·50	1·50
Set of 5			5·00	5·00
Set of 5 Gutter Pairs			10·00	
First Day Cover (Tallents House)				5·50
First Day Cover (Freezywater, Enfield)				5·50
Presentation Pack (PO Pack No. 382)			5·50	
PHQ Cards (set of 5) (285)			1·50	5·75

187

QUEEN ELIZABETH II/2006

1885 On *Britannia*, 1972
1886 At Royal Windsor Horse Show, 1985 
1887 At Heathrow Airport, 2001 
1888 As Young Princess Elizabeth with Duchess of York, 1931 
1889 At State Banquet, Ottawa, 1951 
1890 Queen in 1960 
1891 As Princess Elizabeth, 1940 
1892 With Duke of Edinburgh, 1951 

(Des Sedley Place. Gravure Enschedé)

2006 (18 Apr). 80th Birthday of Queen Elizabeth II. Black, turquoise-green and grey. One side phosphor band (No. 2620), one centre phosphor band (No. 2621) or two phosphor bands (others). Perf 14½.

2620	**1885**	(2nd) On *Britannia*, 1972	90	90
		a. Horiz pair. Nos. 2620/2621	1·75	1·75
2621	**1886**	(2nd) At Royal Windsor Horse Show, 1985	90	90
2622	**1887**	(1st) At Heathrow Airport, 2001	1·20	1·00
		a. Horiz pair. Nos. 2622/2623	2·40	2·00
2623	**1888**	(1st) As Young Princess Elizabeth with Duchess of York, 1931	1·20	1·00
2624	**1889**	44p. At State Banquet, Ottawa, 1951	75	75
		a. Horiz pair. Nos. 2624/2625	1·50	1·50
2625	**1890**	44p. Queen in 1960	75	75
2626	**1891**	72p. As Princess Elizabeth, 1940	1·00	1·00
		a. Horiz pair. Nos. 2626/2627	2·00	2·00
2627	**1892**	72p. With Duke of Edinburgh, 1951	1·00	1·00
Set of 8			6·75	6·50
Set of 4 Gutter Strips of 4			13·50	
First Day Cover (Tallents House)				6·75
First Day Cover (Windsor)				6·75
Presentation Pack (PO Pack No. 383)			7·00	
PHQ Cards (set of 8) (286)			2·50	7·50

Nos. 2620/2621, 2622/2623, 2624/2625 and 2626/2627 were each printed together, *se-tenant*, as horizontal pairs in sheets of 60 (2 panes 6×5).

1893 England (1966)
1894 Italy (1934, 1938, 1982) 
1895 Argentina (1978, 1986) 
1896 Germany (1954, 1974, 1990) 
1897 France (1998) 
1898 Brazil (1958, 1962, 1970, 1994, 2002) 

(Des Madeleine Bennett. Litho Walsall)

2006 (6 June). World Cup Football Championship, Germany. World Cup Winners. Multicoloured Two phosphor bands. Perf 14½.

2628	**1893**	(1st) England	1·20	1·00
2629	**1894**	42p. Italy	80	80
2630	**1895**	44p. Argentina	85	85
2631	**1896**	50p. Germany	1·00	1·00
2632	**1897**	64p. France	1·25	1·25
2633	**1898**	72p. Brazil	1·40	1·40
Set of 6			5·50	5·50
Set of 6 Gutter Pairs			11·00	
First Day Cover (Tallents House)				5·75
First Day Cover (Balls Park, Hertford)				5·75
Presentation Pack (PO Pack No. 384)			6·00	
PHQ Cards (set of 6) (287)			1·75	6·50

The 1st class stamp was also issued in sheets of 20, sold for £6·95, printed in lithography by Cartor, containing four vertical rows of five stamps alternated with labels showing scenes from the 1966 World Cup final (No. LS31).

1899 30 St Mary Axe, London
1900 Maggie's Centre, Dundee 
1901 Selfridges, Birmingham 
1902 Downland Gridshell, Chichester 
1903 An Turas, Isle of Tiree 
1904 The Deep, Hull

2006 / QUEEN ELIZABETH II

(Des Roundel. Gravure Walsall)

2006 (20 June). Modern Architecture. Multicoloured Two phosphor bands. Perf 14½.

2634	**1899**	(1st) 30 St Mary Axe, London	1·20	1·00
2635	**1900**	42p. Maggie's Centre, Dundee	65	65
2636	**1901**	44p. Selfridges, Birmingham	70	70
2637	**1902**	50p. Downland Gridshell, Chichester	85	85
2638	**1903**	64p. An Turas, Isle of Tiree	1·00	1·00
2639	**1904**	72p. The Deep, Hull	1·25	1·25

Set of 6	5·00	5·00
Set of 6 Gutter Pairs	10·00	
First Day Cover (Tallents House)		5·50
First Day Cover (London EC3)		5·50
Presentation Pack (PO Pack No. 385)	5·50	
PHQ Cards (set of 6) (288)	1·75	5·75

1905 Sir Winston Churchill (Walter Sickert) 
1906 Sir Joshua Reynolds (self-portrait) 
1907 T. S. Eliot (Patrick Heron)

1908 Emmeline Pankhurst (Georgina Agnes Brackenbury) 
1909 Virginia Woolf (photo by George Charles Beresford) 
1910 Bust of Sir Walter Scott (Sir Francis Leggatt Chantry)

1913 1911 Mary Seacole (Albert Charles Challen)
1914 Charles Darwin (John Collier) 

(Des P. Willberg. Gravure De La Rue)

2006 (18 July). 150th Anniversary of National Portrait Gallery, London. Multicoloured Two phosphor bands. Perf 14½.

2640	**1905**	(1st) Sir Winston Churchill	1·20	1·00
		a. Block of 10. Nos. 2640/2649	10·50	9·00
2641	**1906**	(1st) Sir Joshua Reynolds	1·20	1·00
2642	**1907**	(1st) T. S. Eliot	1·20	1·00
2643	**1908**	(1st) Emmeline Pankhurst	1·20	1·00
2644	**1909**	(1st) Virginia Woolf	1·20	1·00
2645	**1910**	(1st) Bust of Sir Walter Scott	1·20	1·00
2646	**1911**	(1st) Mary Seacole	1·20	1·00
2647	**1912**	(1st) William Shakespeare	1·20	1·00
2648	**1913**	(1st) Dame Cicely Saunders	1·20	1·00
2649	**1914**	(1st) Charles Darwin	1·20	1·00

Set of 10	10·50	9·00
Gutter Block of 20	21·00	
Traffic Light Gutter Block of 20	40·00	
First Day Cover (Tallents House)		9·50
First Day Cover (London WC2)		9·50
Presentation Pack (PO Pack No. 386)	11·00	
PHQ Cards (set of 10) (289)	3·00	10·00

Nos. 2640/2649 were printed together, *se-tenant*, as blocks of ten (5×2) in sheets of 60 (2 panes of 30).

For Nos. 2650/2657, **MS**2658, Types **1915/1917** see Decimal Machin Definitives section.

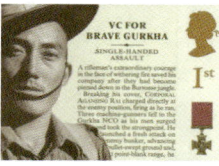

1918 Corporal Agansing Rai 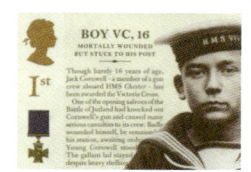
1919 Boy Seaman Jack Cornwell

1920 Midshipman Charles Lucas 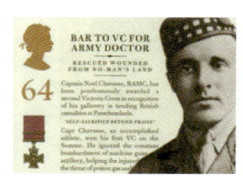
1921 Captain Noel Chavasse

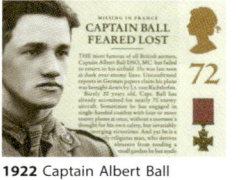

1922 Captain Albert Ball
1923 Captain Charles Upham 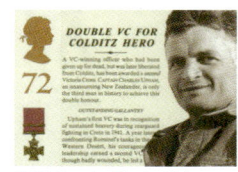

(Des Atelier Works. Litho Enschedé)

2006 (21 Sept). 150th Anniversary of the Victoria Cross (1st issue). Multicoloured One side phosphor band. Perf 14½×14.

2659	**1918**	(1st) Corporal Agansing Rai	1·20	1·00
		a. Horiz pair. Nos. 2659/2660	2·40	2·00
		b. Booklet pane. Nos. 2659, 2661 and 2663	3·60	
		ba. Booklet pane. Bronze and phosphor omitted	£7500	
2660	**1919**	(1st) Boy Seaman Jack Cornwell	1·20	1·00
		b. Booklet pane. Nos. 2660, 2662 and 2664	3·60	
		ba. Booklet pane. Bronze and phosphor omitted	£7500	
2661	**1920**	64p. Midshipman Charles Lucas	90	90
		a. Horiz pair. Nos. 2661/2662	1·75	1·75
2662	**1921**	64p. Captain Noel Chavasse	90	90
2663	**1922**	72p. Captain Albert Ball	1·25	1·25
		a. Horiz pair. Nos. 2663/2664	2·40	2·40
2664	**1923**	72p. Captain Charles Upham	1·25	1·25

Set of 6	6·25	6·00
Set of 3 Gutter Strips of 4	12·20	
First Day Cover (Tallents House)		6·25
First Day Cover (Cuffley, Potters Bar, Herts)		6·25
Presentation Pack (PO Pack No. 387)	6·50	
PHQ Cards (set of 7) (290)	2·00	13·50
MS2665 190×67 mm. Nos. 2659/2664 and 2666	6·50	6·50
a. Imperforate		
First Day Cover (Tallents House)		6·50
First Day Cover (Cuffley, Potters Bar, Herts)		6·50

Nos. 2659/2660, 2661/2662 and 2663/2664 were each printed together, *se-tenant*, as horizontal pairs in sheets of 60 (2 panes 6×5).

Booklet panes Nos. 2659b/2660b come from the £7·44 Victoria Cross booklet No. DX37.

The seven PHQ Cards depict the six individual stamps and the miniature sheet.

(Litho Enschedé)

2006 (21 Sept). 150th Anniversary of the Victoria Cross (2nd issue). Booklet stamp. Design as No. 1517 (1990 Gallantry Awards). Multicoloured 'All-over' phosphor. Perf 14×14½.

2666	**959**	20p. Victoria Cross	1·50	1·50
		a. Booklet pane. Nos. 2666×4	6·50	6·50

No. 2666 was only issued in No. **MS**2665 and in the £7·44 Victoria Cross booklet, No. DX37.

1924 Sitar Player and Dancer
1925 Reggae Bass Guitarist and African Drummer 
1926 Fiddler and Harpist 
1927 Sax Player and Blues Guitarist 
1928 Maraca Player and Salsa Dancers 

(Des CDT Design. Litho Cartor)

2006 (3 Oct). Europa. Integration. Sounds of Britain. Multicoloured 'All-over' phosphor. Perf 14½.

2667	1924	(1st) Sitar Player and Dancer	1·20	1·00
2668	1925	42p. Reggae Bass Guitarist and African Drummer	1·00	1·00
2669	1926	50p. Fiddler and Harpist	1·10	1·10
2670	1927	72p. Sax Player and Blues Guitarist	1·25	1·25
2671	1928	£1·19 Maraca Player and Salsa Dancers	1·75	1·75
Set of 5			5·50	5·50
Set of 5 Gutter Pairs			11·00	
Set of 5 Traffic Light Gutter Blocks of 4			26·00	
First Day Cover (Tallents House)				6·00
First Day Cover (Rock, Kidderminster, Worcs)				6·00
Presentation Pack (PO Pack No. 388)			6·00	
PHQ Cards (set of 5) (291)			1·50	6·25

The 1st class and 50p. values include the EUROPA emblem.

1929 'New Baby' (Alison Carmichael) 
1930 'Best Wishes' (Alan Kitching) 
1931 'THANK YOU' (Alan Kitching) 
1932 Balloons (Ivan Chermayeff) 
1933 Firework (Kam Tang) 
1934 Champagne, Flowers and Butterflies (Olaf Hajek)

(Des NB Studio. Gravure Walsall)

2006 (17 Oct). Smilers Booklet stamps (2nd series). Occasions. Self-adhesive. Multicoloured Two phosphor bands. Die-cut Perf 15×14.

2672	1929	(1st) 'New Baby'	1·20	1·00
		a. Booklet pane. Nos. 2672/2677	7·50	
2673	1930	(1st) 'Best Wishes'	1·20	1·00
2674	1931	(1st) 'THANK YOU'	1·20	1·00
2675	1932	(1st) Balloons	1·20	1·00
2676	1933	(1st) Firework	1·20	1·00
2677	1934	(1st) Champagne, Flowers and Butterflies	1·20	1·00
Set of 6			7·00	6·00
First Day Cover (Tallents House)				6·25
First Day Cover (Grinshill, Shrewsbury)				6·25
Presentation Pack (PO Pack No. M13)			10·00	
PHQ Cards (set of 6) (D29)			1·75	7·00

Nos. 2672/2677 were issued in £1·92 stamp booklet, No. QA3, in which the surplus backing paper around each stamp was removed.

Nos. 2672/2677 were also issued in sheets of 20 (No. LS33), containing four of Nos. 2672 and 2677 and three of each of the other designs, each stamp accompanied by a *se-tenant* greetings label. These sheets were printed by Cartor in lithography instead of gravure and sold at £6·95 each.

These designs were available in separate sheets with personal photographs printed on the labels from Royal Mail in Edinburgh at £14·95 each.

Stamps as No. 2672 but perforated with one elliptical hole on each vertical side were issued on 28 October 2008 in sheets of 20 with circular *se-tenant* Peter Rabbit labels (No. LS50). These sheets were printed by Cartor in lithography instead of gravure and sold for £7·95 each.

Similar sheets of ten stamps and ten *se-tenant* labels were sold in £7·95 packs.

No. 2674 was issued on 8 May 2010 with other greetings stamps in sheets of 20 with *se-tenant* greetings labels printed in lithography by Cartor (No. LS73), sold for £10 per sheet. These sheets were printed with one elliptical hole in each vertical side.

1935 Snowman
1936 Father Christmas 
1937 Snowman 
1938 Father Christmas 
1939 Reindeer 
1940 Christmas Tree 

(Des T. Kiuchi, Rose Design and CDT Design. Gravure De La Rue)

2006 (7 Nov). Christmas. Multicoloured One centre phosphor band (No. 2678) or two phosphor bands (others). Perf 15×14.

(a) Self-adhesive.

2678	1935	(2nd) Snowman	90	90
		a. Booklet pane. No. 2678×12	13·50	
2679	1936	(1st) Father Christmas	1·20	1·00
		a. Booklet pane. No. 2679×12	16·00	
2680	1937	(2nd Snowman Large)	1·25	1·00
2681	1938	(1st Father Christmas Large)	1·70	1·25
2682	1939	72p. Reindeer	1·10	1·10
2683	1940	£1·19 Christmas Tree	1·50	1·50
Set of 6			6·75	6·00
First Day Cover (Tallents House)				7·00
First Day Cover (Bethlehem, Llandeilo)				7·00
Presentation Pack (PO Pack No. 389)			7·25	
PHQ Cards (set of 7) (292)			2·00	13·50

(b) Ordinary gum.

MS2684	115×102 mm. As Nos. 2678/2683		6·75	6·75
First Day Cover (Tallents House)				7·00
First Day Cover (Bethlehem, Llandeilo)				7·00

The 2nd and 1st class stamps were also issued together in sheets of 20 sold at £6, printed in lithography by Cartor, containing ten 1st class and ten 2nd class stamps, each value arranged in vertical rows of five alternating with rows of printed labels (No. LS34).

The phosphor bands have the date (2006) reversed out at the bottom (2nd) or bottom left (others).

Separate sheets of 20 1st or 20 2nd class were available with personalised photographs at £9·95 (2nd class) or £14·95 (1st class) and in 2010 the same designs with one elliptical hole on each vertical side were available from Royal Mail, Edinburgh. All these sheets had the backing paper around the stamps retained.

The seven PHQ Cards depict the six individual stamps and the miniature sheet.

1941 Lest We Forget (*Illustration reduced. Actual size 124×71 mm*)

(Des Hat-trick Design. Gravure De La Rue)

2006 (9 Nov). Lest We Forget (1st issue). 90th Anniversary of the Battle of the Somme. Sheet 124×71 mm containing new stamp as No. 2883 and designs as Nos. EN17a, NI102, S120 and W109. Multicoloured Two phosphor bands. Perf 14½ (1st) or 15×14 (with one elliptical hole in each vertical side) (72p.).

MS2685	**1941**	(1st) Poppies on barbed wire stems; 72p.×4 As Nos. EN17 (Type I), NI102, S120 and W109	5·50	5·50
		First Day Cover (Tallents House)		6·00
		First Day Cover (London SW1)		6·00
		Presentation Pack (PO Pack No. 390)	7·25	

The 1st class stamp was also issued in sheets of 20 with *se-tenant* labels showing war memorials, printed in lithography by Cartor (No. LS35).

No. **MS**2685 (including the Northern Ireland stamp) is printed in gravure. See also Nos. **MS**2796 and **MS**2886.

Year Pack

2006 (9 Nov). Comprises Nos. 2589/2612, 2615/2649, 2659/2664, 2667/2671, 2678/2683 and **MS**2685.

CP2685a	Year Pack (PO Pack No. 391)	65·00

Post Office Yearbook

2006 (9 Nov). Comprises Nos. 2589/2612, 2615/2649, 2659/2664, 2667/2671, 2678/2683 and **MS**2685.

YB2685a	Yearbook	75·00

Miniature Sheet Collection

2006 (30 Nov). Comprises Nos. **MS**2613, **MS**2658, **MS**2665, **MS**2684/**MS**2685, **MS**S153 and **MS**W143.

MS2685a	Miniature Sheet Collection	38·00

1942 *with the beatles*

1943 *Sgt Pepper's Lonely Hearts Club Band*

1944 *Help!*

1945 *Abbey Road*

1946 *Revolver*

1947 *Let It Be*

1948 Beatles Memorabilia (*Illustration reduced. Actual size 115×89 mm*)

(Des johnson banks)

2007 (9 Jan). The Beatles. Album Covers. Multicoloured Two phosphor bands.

(*a*) *Self-adhesive. Gravure Walsall. Die-cut irregular Perf 13½–14½.*

2686	**1942**	(1st) *with the beatles*	1·20	1·00
		a. Horiz pair. Nos. 2686/2687	2·40	
2687	**1943**	(1st) *Sgt Pepper's Lonely Hearts Club Band*	1·20	1·00
2688	**1944**	64p. *Help!*	90	90
		a. Horiz pair. Nos. 2688/2689	1·80	
2689	**1945**	64p. *Abbey Road*	90	90
2690	**1946**	72p. *Revolver*	1·25	1·25
		a. Horiz pair. Nos. 2690/2691	2·50	
2691	**1947**	72p. *Let It Be*	1·25	1·25
		Set of 6	6·25	6·00
		First Day Cover (Tallents House)		6·25
		First Day Cover (Liverpool)		6·50
		Presentation Pack (PO Pack No. 392) (Nos. 2686/**MS**2692)	10·00	
		PHQ Cards (set of 11) (293)	3·25	15·50

(*b*) *Ordinary gum. Litho Walsall. Perf 14.*

MS2692	115×89 mm. **1948** Beatles Memorabilia (1st) Guitar; (1st) Yellow Submarine lunch box and keyrings; (1st) Record *Love Me Do*; (1st) Beatles tea tray and badges		3·75	3·75
	First Day Cover (Tallents House)			6·25
	First Day Cover (Liverpool)			6·50

Nos. 2686/2691 are all die-cut in the shape of a pile of records.

Nos. 2686/2687, 2688/2689 and 2690/2691 were each printed together in sheets of 60 (2 panes of 30), with the two designs alternating horizontally and the surplus backing paper around each stamp removed.

Nos. 2686/**MS**2692 commemorate the 50th anniversary of the first meeting of Paul McCartney and John Lennon.

The complete miniature sheet is on one of the 11 PHQ cards, with the others depicting individual stamps, including those from No. **MS**2692.

1842b

(Gravure Walsall)

2007 (16 Jan)–**2008**. Smilers Booklet stamp (3rd series). 'LOVE' design as No. 2569. Self-adhesive. Multicoloured. Two phosphor bands. Die-cut Perf 15×14 (with one elliptical hole in each vertical side).

2693	**1842b**	(1st) multicoloured	5·50	5·50
		a. Booklet pane. No. 2655×5 and No. 2693	18·00	
		b. Booklet pane. No. 2693×2 with two attached labels and No. 2295×4 (15.1.08)	16·00	

No. 2693 was issued in stamp booklets, Nos. SA1 and SA2, in which the surplus backing paper around each stamp was removed.

No. 2693 was re-issued on 8 May 2010 with other greetings stamps in sheets of 20 with *se-tenant* greetings labels printed in lithography by Cartor (No. LS73), sold for £10 per sheet.

Nos. 2694/698 are left vacant.

1949 Moon Jellyfish  **1950** Common Starfish

1951 Beadlet Anemone  **1952** Bass

1953 Thornback Ray  **1954** Lesser Octopus

1955 Common Mussels  **1956** Grey Seal

1957 Shore Crab  **1958** Common Sun Star

(Des A. Ross. Litho Walsall)

2007 (1 Feb). Sea Life. Multicoloured Two phosphor bands. Perf 14½.

2699	1949	(1st) Moon Jellyfish	1·20	1·00
		a. Block of 10. Nos. 2699/2708	10·50	9·00
2700	1950	(1st) Common Starfish	1·20	1·00
2701	1951	(1st) Beadlet Anemone	1·20	1·00
2702	1952	(1st) Bass	1·20	1·00
2703	1953	(1st) Thornback Ray	1·20	1·00
2704	1954	(1st) Lesser Octopus	1·20	1·00
2705	1955	(1st) Common Mussels	1·20	1·00
2706	1956	(1st) Grey Seal	1·20	1·00
2707	1957	(1st) Shore Crab	1·20	1·00
2708	1958	(1st) Common Sun Star	1·20	1·00
Set of 10			10·50	9·00
Gutter Block of 20			21·00	
First Day Cover (Tallents House)				9·25
First Day Cover (Seal Sands, Middlesbrough, Cleveland)				9·50
Presentation Pack (PO Pack No. 393)			11·00	
PHQ Cards (set of 10) (294)			3·00	10·50

Nos. 2699/2708 were printed together, *se-tenant*, as blocks of ten (5×2) in sheets of 60 (2 panes of 30).

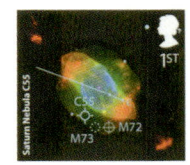

1959 Saturn Nebula C55 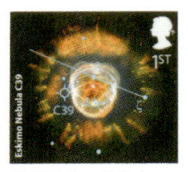 **1960** Eskimo Nebula C39

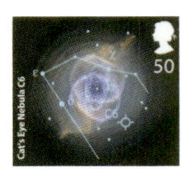

1961 Cat's Eye Nebula C6 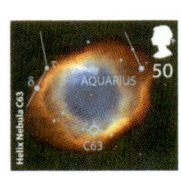 **1962** Helix Nebula C63

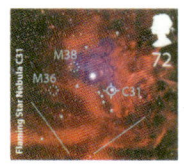

1963 Flaming Star Nebula C31 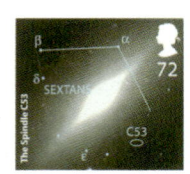 **1964** The Spindle C53

(Des D. Davis. Gravure Walsall)

2007 (13 Feb). 50th Anniversary of *The Sky at Night* (TV programme). Nebulae. Self-adhesive. Multicoloured Two phosphor bands. Die-cut Perf 14½×14.

2709	1959	(1st) Saturn Nebula C55	1·20	1·00
		a. Horiz pair. Nos. 2709/2710	2·40	
2710	1960	(1st) Eskimo Nebula C39	1·20	1·00
2711	1961	50p. Cat's Eye Nebula C6	1·00	1·00
		a. Horiz pair. Nos. 2711/2712	2·00	
2712	1962	50p. Helix Nebula C63	1·00	1·00
2713	1963	72p. Flaming Star Nebula C31	1·25	1·25
		a. Horiz pair. Nos. 2713/2714	2·40	
2714	1964	72p. The Spindle C53	1·25	1·25
Set of 6			6·00	5·75
First Day Cover (Tallents House)				6·25
First Day Cover (Star, Glenrothes, Fife)				6·25
Presentation Pack (PO Pack No. 394)			7·00	
PHQ Cards (set of 6) (295)			1·75	7·00

Nos. 2709/2710, 2711/2712 and 2713/2714 were each printed together in sheets of 60 (2 panes of 30), with the two designs alternating horizontally and the surplus backing paper around each stamp removed.

1965 Iron Bridge (Thomas Telford)  **1966** Steam Locomotive and Railway Tracks

1967 Map of British Isles and Australia (telephone)  **1968** Camera and Television (John Logie Baird)

2007/QUEEN ELIZABETH II

1969 Globe as Web (email and internet)

1970 Couple with Suitcases on Moon (space travel)

(Des P. Willberg. Gravure De La Rue)

2007 (1 Mar). World of Invention (1st issue). Self-adhesive. Multicoloured Two phosphor bands. Die-cut Perf 14½×14.

2715	1965	(1st) Iron Bridge	1·20	1·00
		a. Horiz pair. Nos. 2715/2716	2·40	
2716	1966	(1st) Steam Locomotive and Railway Tracks	1·20	1·00
2717	1967	64p. Map of British Isles and Australia	90	90
		a. Horiz pair. Nos. 2717/2718	1·75	
2718	1968	64p. Camera and Television	90	90
2719	1969	72p. Globe as Web	1·25	1·25
		a. Horiz pair. Nos. 2719/2720	2·50	
2720	1970	72p. Couple with Suitcases on Moon	1·25	1·25
Set of 6			6·25	6·00
First Day Cover (Tallents House)				6·25
First Day Cover (Pont Menai, Menai Bridge, Gwynedd)				6·25
Presentation Pack (PO Pack No. 395)			6·50	
PHQ Cards (set of 7) (296)			2·00	7·25

Nos. 2715/2716, 2717/2718 and 2719/2720 were each printed together in sheets of 60 (2 panes of 30), with the two designs alternating horizontally and the surplus backing paper around each stamp removed.

The seven PHQ Cards depict the six individual stamps and No. **MS**2727.

(Gravure De La Rue)

2007 (1 Mar). World of Invention (2nd issue). Ordinary gum. Multicoloured Two phosphor bands. Perf 14½×14.

2721	1965	(1st) Iron Bridge	1·20	1·00
		a. Booklet pane. Nos. 2721/2724	7·00	
		b. Booklet pane. Nos. 2721/2722 and 2725/2726	7·00	
2722	1966	(1st) Steam Locomotive and Railway Tracks	1·20	1·00
2723	1967	64p. Map of British Isles and Australia	2·50	2·50
2724	1968	64p. Camera and Television	2·50	2·50
2725	1969	72p. Globe as Web	2·50	2·50
2726	1970	72p. Couple with Suitcases on Moon	2·50	2·50
Set of 6			11·00	11·00
MS2727 115×104 mm. Nos. 2721/2726			12·00	12·00
First Day Cover (Tallents House)				12·50
First Day Cover (Pont Menai, Menai Bridge, Gwynedd)				12·50

Nos. 2721/2726 were only issued in the £7·49 World of Invention booklet, No. DX38 and in No. **MS**2727.

1971 William Wilberforce and Anti-slavery Poster

1972 Olaudah Equiano and Map of Slave Trade Routes

1973 Granville Sharp and Slave Ship

1974 Thomas Clarkson and Diagram of Slave Ship

1975 Hannah More and Title Page of *The Sorrows of Yamba*

1976 Ignatius Sancho and Trade/Business Card

(Des Howard Brown. Litho Cartor)

2007 (22 Mar). Bicentenary of the Abolition of the Slave Trade. Multicoloured Two phosphor bands. Perf 14½.

2728	1971	(1st) William Wilberforce	1·00	1·00
		a. Horiz pair. Nos. 2728/2729	2·00	
		ab. Gold and phosphor omitted	£3500	
2729	1972	(1st) Olaudah Equiano	1·00	1·00
2730	1973	50p. Granville Sharp	80	80
		a. Horiz pair. Nos. 2730/2731	1·60	
2731	1974	50p. Thomas Clarkson	80	80
2732	1975	72p. Hannah More	90	90
		a. Horiz pair. Nos. 2732/2733	1·75	
2733	1976	72p. Ignatius Sancho	90	90
Set of 6			5·00	5·00
Set of 3 Gutter Strips of 4			11·00	
Set of 3 Traffic Light Gutter Strips of 4			42·00	
First Day Cover (Tallents House)				5·75
First Day Cover (Hull)				5·75
Presentation Pack (PO Pack No. 396)			6·00	
PHQ Cards (set of 6) (297)			1·75	6·00

Nos. 2728/2729, 2730/2731 and 2732/2733 were each printed together, se-tenant, in horizontal pairs throughout the sheets.

For miniature sheet entitled Celebrating England, issued 23 April 2007, see Regionals Section

1977 Ice Cream Cone

1978 Sandcastle

1979 Carousel Horse

1980 Beach Huts

1981 Deckchairs

1982 Beach Donkeys

(Des Phelan Barker. Gravure De La Rue)

2007 (15 May). Beside the Seaside. Multicoloured Two phosphor bands. Perf 14½.

2734	1977	1st Ice Cream Cone	1·20	1·00
2735	1978	46p. Sandcastle	80	80
2736	1979	48p. Carousel Horse	90	90
2737	1980	54p. Beach Huts	1·00	1·00
2738	1981	69p. Deckchairs	1·10	1·10
2739	1982	78p. Beach Donkeys	1·25	1·25
Set of 6			5·50	5·50
Set of 6 Gutter Pairs			11·00	
First Day Cover (Tallents House)				5·75
First Day Cover (Blackpool)				5·75
Presentation Pack (PO Pack No. 397)			6·00	
PHQ Cards (set of 6) (298)			1·75	6·25

For T **1977**, but self-adhesive, see No. 2848

193

1983 Wembley Stadium *(Illustration reduced. Actual size 113×103 mm)*

(Des Roundel. Gravure De La Rue)

2007 (17 May). New Wembley Stadium, London. Sheet 113×103 mm containing design as T **1593** but with 'WORLD CUP 2002' inscription omitted, and Nos. EN6b and EN18, each×2. Multicoloured One centre phosphor band (2nd) or two phosphor bands (others). Perf 14½×14 (1st) or 15×14 (with one elliptical hole in each vertical side) (2nd, 78p.).

MS2740	**1983**	Wembley Stadium (1st) As Type **1593**; (2nd) No. EN6b×2; 78p. No. EN18×2 and one central stamp-size label	4·75	4·75
		First Day Cover (Tallents House)		5·00
		First Day Cover (Wembley)		5·00

The design as T **1593** omits the 'WORLD CUP 2002' inscription at the left of the stamp. T **1593** (without 'WORLD CUP' inscription) was issued in sheets of 20 with *se-tenant* labels (No. LS39). These sheets were sold for £7·35.

1984 Arnold Machin **1985** 1967 4d. Machin

1986 The Machin Definitives *(Illustration reduced. Actual size 127×73 mm)*

(Des Jeffery Matthews and Together Design. Gravure and embossed De La Rue)

2007 (5 June). 40th Anniversary of the First Machin Definitives. 'All-over' phosphor (1st) or two phosphor bands (others). Perf 14½ (1st) or 15×14 (with one elliptical hole in each vertical side) (£1).

2741	**1984**	(1st) Arnold Machin	1·75	1·75
		a. Booklet pane. Nos. 2741/2742, each×2, with margins all round	7·50	
2742	**1985**	(1st) 1967 4d. Machin	1·75	1·75
MS2743	127×73mm **1986** The Machin Definitives Nos. 2741/2742, Y1743 and Y1744		4·75	4·75
		a. Imperf	£4500	
First Day Cover (Tallents House) (No. **MS**2743)				5·00
First Day Cover (Windsor) (No. **MS**2743)				5·00
First Day Cover (Stoke-on-Trent) (No. **MS**2743)				5·00
Presentation Pack (PO Pack No. 398) (No. **MS**2743)			5·50	
PHQ Cards (set of 3) (299) (Nos. 2741/**MS**2743)			1·00	7·50

Nos. 2741/2742 were only issued in the £7·66 The Machin, The Making of a Masterpiece booklet, No. DX39 and in No. **MS**2743.

Stamps as T **1984** but with phosphor frames were issued in sheets of 20 with *se-tenant* labels showing the 1967–1969 Machin definitives (No. LS40). These sheets were sold for £7·35.

1987 Stirling Moss in Vanwall 2.5L, 1957  **1988** Graham Hill in BRM P57, 1962

1989 Jim Clark in Lotus 25 Climax, 1963  **1990** Jackie Stewart in Tyrrell 006/2, 1973

1991 James Hunt in McLaren M23, 1976  **1992** Nigel Mansell in Williams FW11, 1986

(Des True North. Litho Cartor)

2007 (3 July). Grand Prix. Racing Cars. Multicoloured Two phosphor bands. Perf 14½.

2744	**1987**	(1st) Stirling Moss in Vanwall 2.5L	1·20	1·00
2745	**1988**	(1st) Graham Hill in BRM P57	1·20	1·00
2746	**1989**	54p. Jim Clark in Lotus 25 Climax	90	90
2747	**1990**	54p. Jackie Stewart in Tyrrell 006/2	90	90
2748	**1991**	78p. James Hunt in McLaren M23	1·25	1·25
2749	**1992**	78p. Nigel Mansell in Williams FW11	1·25	1·25
Set of 6			5·75	5·50
Set of 6 Gutter Pairs			11·00	
First Day Cover (Tallents House)				6·00
First Day Cover (Silverstone, Towcester, Northants)				6·00
Presentation Pack (PO Pack No. 399)			6·00	
PHQ Cards (set of 6) (300)			1·75	6·25

Nos. 2744/2749 commemorate the 50th anniversary of Stirling Moss's Victory in the British Grand Prix and the centenary of the opening of Brooklands race track.

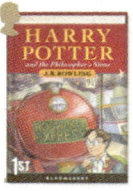

1993 Harry Potter and the Philosopher's Stone 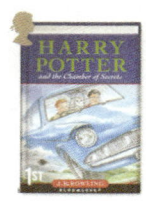 **1994** Harry Potter and the Chamber of Secrets 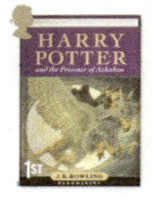 **1995** Harry Potter and the Prisoner of Azkaban

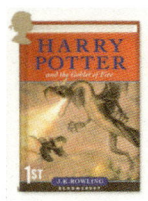

2007/QUEEN ELIZABETH II

1996 Harry Potter and the Goblet of Fire
1997 Harry Potter and the Order of the Phoenix 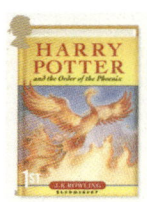
1998 Harry Potter and the Half-Blood Prince 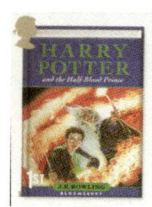
1999 Harry Potter and the Deathly Hallows 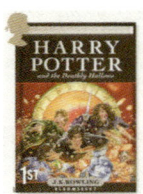
2000 Crests of Hogwarts School and its Four Houses (*illustration reduced. Actual size 123×70 mm*) 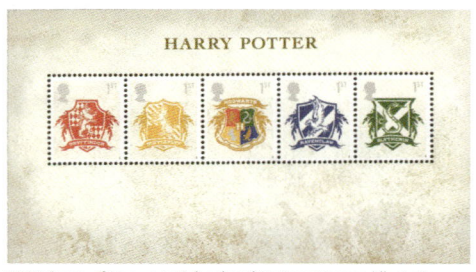

(True North. Litho Walsall)

2007 (17 July). Publication of Final Book in the Harry Potter Series. Multicoloured

(a) Book Covers. 'All-over' phosphor. Perf 14½.

2750	1993	(1st) Harry Potter and the Philosopher's Stone	1·20	1·00
		a. Horiz strip of 7. Nos. 2750/2756	7·25	6·25
2751	1994	(1st) Harry Potter and the Chamber of Secrets	1·20	1·00
2752	1995	(1st) Harry Potter and the Prisoner of Azkaban	1·20	1·00
2753	1996	(1st) Harry Potter and the Goblet of Fire	1·20	1·00
2754	1997	(1st) Harry Potter and the Order of the Phoenix	1·20	1·00
2755	1998	(1st) Harry Potter and the Half-Blood Prince	1·20	1·00
2756	1999	(1st) Harry Potter and the Deathly Hallows	1·20	1·00
Set of 7			7·25	6·25
Gutter Block of 14			14·50	
Traffic Light Gutter Block of 14			32·00	
First Day Cover (Tallents House)				6·50
First Day Cover (Broom, Alcester, Warwickshire)				6·50
Presentation Pack (Nos. 2750/2757) (PO Pack No. M16)			12·00	
PHQ Cards (set of 13) (HP)			4·00	19·50

(b) Crests of Hogwarts School and its Four Houses. Multicoloured Two phosphor bands. Perf 15×14.

MS2757 123×70 mm. **2000** Crests of Hogwarts School and its Four Houses (1st) Gryffindor; (1st) Hufflepuff; (1st) Hogwarts; (1st) Ravenclaw; (1st) Slytherin	5·50 54·50
First Day Cover (Tallents House)	5·75
First Day Cover (Broom, Alcester, Warwickshire)	5·75

Nos. 2750/2756 were printed together, *se-tenant*, as horizontal strips of seven stamps in sheets of 56 (2 panes 7×4).

Stamps as those within No. **MS**2757 but self-adhesive were issued in sheets of 20 containing the five designs *se-tenant* with labels depicting either magic spells (No. LS41), sold for £7·35 or personal photographs (sold for £14·95). The magic spells labels are printed in thermochromic ink which fades temporarily when exposed to heat, revealing the meaning of the spells.

The complete miniature sheet is shown on one of the 13 PHQ cards with the others depicting individual stamps including those from No. **MS**2757.

2001 Scout and Campfire
2002 Scouts Rock Climbing 
2003 Scout Planting Tree 
2004 Adult Volunteer Teaching Scout Archery 
2005 Scouts Learning Gliding 
2006 Scouts From Many Nations 

(Des Gez Fry and The Work Room. Litho Enschedé)

2007 (26 July). Europa. Centenary of Scouting and 21st World Scout Jamboree, Chelmsford, Essex. Multicoloured Two phosphor bands. Perf 14½×14.

2758	2001	(1st) Scout and Campfire	1·20	1·00
2759	2002	46p. Scouts Rock climbing	80	80
2760	2003	48p. Scout planting Tree	85	85
2761	2004	54p. Adult Volunteer teaching Scout Archery	95	95
2762	2005	69p. Scouts learning gliding	1·10	1·10
2763	2006	78p. Scouts from Many Nations	1·25	1·25
Set of 6			5·50	5·50
Set of 6 Gutter Pairs			11·00	
First Day Cover (Tallents House)				6·00
First Day Cover (Brownsea Island, Poole, Dorset)				6·00
Presentation Pack (PO Pack No. 400)			6·00	
PHQ Cards (set of 6) (301)			1·75	6·25

The 1st class and 48p. values include the EUROPA emblem.

2007 White-tailed Eagle
2008 Bearded Tit 
2009 Red Kite 
2010 Cirl Bunting 
2011 Marsh Harrier 
2012 Avocet 

195

QUEEN ELIZABETH II / 2007

2013 Bittern
2014 Dartford Warbler 
2015 Corncrake 
2016 Peregrine Falcon 

(Des Kate Stephens. Litho Da La Rue)

2007 (4 Sept). Action for Species (1st series). Birds. Multicoloured Two phosphor bands. Perf 14½.

2764	**2007**	(1st) White-tailed Eagle	1·20	1·00
		a. Block of 10. Nos. 2764/2773	10·50	9·00
2765	**2008**	(1st) Bearded Tit	1·20	1·00
2766	**2009**	(1st) Red Kite	1·20	1·00
2767	**2010**	(1st) Cirl Bunting	1·20	1·00
2768	**2011**	(1st) Marsh Harrier	1·20	1·00
2769	**2012**	(1st) Avocet	1·20	1·00
2770	**2013**	(1st) Bittern	1·20	1·00
2771	**2014**	(1st) Dartford Warbler	1·20	1·00
2772	**2015**	(1st) Corncrake	1·20	1·00
2773	**2016**	(1st) Peregrine Falcon	1·20	1·00
Set of 10			10·50	9·00
Gutter Block of 20			21·00	
First Day Cover (Tallents House)				9·50
First Day Cover (Dartford)				9·50
Presentation Pack (PO Pack No. 401)			11·00	
PHQ Cards (set of 10) (302)			3·00	9·75

Nos. 2764/2773 were printed together, *se-tenant*, as blocks of ten (5×2) in sheets of 60 (2 panes of 30).

2017 NCO, Royal Military Police, 1999
2018 Tank Commander, 5th Royal Tank Regiment, 1944 
2019 Observer, Royal Field Artillery, 1917 
2020 Rifleman, 95th Rifles, 1813 
2021 Grenadier, Royal Regiment of Foot of Ireland, 1704 
2022 Trooper, Earl of Oxford's Horse, 1661 

(Des Graham Turner and Atelier Works. Litho Enschedé)

2007 (20 Sept)-**2015**. Military Uniforms (1st series). British Army Uniforms. Multicoloured Two phosphor bands. Perf 14½.

2774	**2017**	(1st) NCO, Royal Military Police	1·20	1·00
		a. Horiz strip of 3. Nos. 2774/2776	3·60	3·00
		b. Booklet pane. Nos. 2774/2776 with margins all round (14.5.15)	3·60	
2775	**2018**	(1st) Tank Commander, 5th Royal Tank Regiment	1·00	1·00
2776	**2019**	(1st) Observer, Royal Field Artillery	1·00	1·00
		a. Booklet pane. No. 2776×4 with margins all round	1·00	1·00
		b. Booklet pane No. 2776×4 with margins all round	4·00	
2777	**2020**	78p. Rifleman, 95th Rifles	1·25	1·25
		a. Horiz strip of 3. Nos. 2777/2779	3·75	3·75
		b. Booklet pane. Nos. 2777/2779 with margins all round	3·75	3·75
2778	**2021**	78p. Grenadier, Royal Regiment of Foot of Ireland	1·25	1·25
2779	**2022**	78p. Trooper, Earl of Oxford's Horse	1·25	1·25
Set of 6			7·00	6·50
Set of 2 Gutter blocks of 6			14·00	
Set of 2 Traffic Light Gutter blocks of 6			30·00	
First Day Cover (Tallents House)				7·00
First Day Cover (Boot, Holmrook, Cumbria)				7·00
Presentation Pack (PO Pack No. 402)			7·25	
PHQ Cards (set of 6) (303)			1·75	7·00

Nos. 2774/2776 and 2777/2779 were each printed together, *se-tenant*, in horizontal strips of three stamps in sheets of 60 (2 panes 6×5).

Booklet panes Nos. 2774b and 2777b come from the £7·66 British Army Uniforms booklet, No., DX40.

Booklet pane 2776b comes from the £13·96 Centenary of First World War (2nd issue) booklet, No DY13.

See also Nos. 2862/2867 and 2964/2969.

2023 Leaving St Paul's Cathedral after Thanksgiving Service, 2006 
2024 Inspecting King's Troop Royal Horse Artillery, Regents Park, 1997 
2025 At Garter Ceremony, Windsor, 1980 
2026 At Royal Ascot, 1969 
2027 At Premiere of *The Guns of Navarone*, 1961 
2028 At Clydebank, 1947

2029 Photographs of the Royal Family (*illustration reduced. Actual size 115×89 mm*)

(Des Studio David Hillman)

2007 (16 Oct). Diamond Wedding of Queen Elizabeth II and Duke of Edinburgh. Blackish brown and black.

(a) *Ordinary gum. Litho Cartor. 'All-over' phosphor. Perf 14½×14.*

2780	**2023**	(1st) Leaving St Paul's Cathedral	1·20	1·00
		a. Horiz pair. Nos. 2780/2781	2·40	2·00

2781	**2024**	(1st) Inspecting King's Troop Royal Horse Artillery	1·20	1·00
2782	**2025**	54p. At Garter Ceremony	85	85
		a. Horiz pair. Nos. 2782/2783	1·75	1·75
2783	**2026**	54p. At Royal Ascot	85	85
2784	**2027**	78p. At Premiere of *The Guns of Navarone*	1·25	1·25
		a. Horiz pair. Nos. 2784/2785	2·50	2·50
2785	**2028**	78p. At Clydebank	1·25	1·25

Set of 6 .... 5·75 5·50
Set of 3 Gutter blocks of 4 .... 11·50
First Day Cover (Tallents House) .... 7·25
First Day Cover (Windsor, Berks) .... 7·25
Presentation Pack (PO Pack No. 403) (Nos. 2780/
MS2786) .... 11·50
PHQ Cards (set of 11) (304) .... 3·25 15·50

(b) Self-adhesive. Gravure Walsall. Multicoloured Two phosphor bands. Perf 14½.

MS2786 115×89 mm. **2029** Photographs of the Royal Family (1st) Royal family, Balmoral, 1972; (1st) Queen and Prince Philip, Buckingham Palace, 2007; 69p. Royal family, Windsor Castle, 1965; 78p. Princess Elizabeth, Prince Philip, Prince Charles and Princess Anne, Clarence House, 1951 .... 4·25 4·25
First Day Cover (Tallents House) .... 5·75
First Day Cover (Windsor, Berks) .... 5·75

Nos. 2780/2781, 2782/2783 and 2784/2785 were each printed together, *se-tenant*, in horizontal pairs throughout the sheets.

The complete miniature sheet is shown on one of the 11 PHQ cards with the others depicting individual stamps including those from No. **MS**2786.

2030 *Madonna and Child* (William Dyce), *c* 1827

2031 *The Madonna of Humility* (Lippo di Dalmasio), *c* 1390–1400)

(Des Peter Willberg. Gravure De La Rue)

2007 (6 Nov). Christmas (1st issue). Paintings of the Madonna and Child. Self-adhesive. Multicoloured One centre phosphor band (2nd) or two phosphor bands (1st). Die-cut Perf 15×14 (with one elliptical hole in each vertical side).

2787	**2030**	(2nd) *Madonna and Child*	90	90
2788	**2031**	(1st) *The Madonna of Humility*	1·20	1·10

First Day Cover (Tallents House) .... 2·75
First Day Cover (Bethlehem, Llandeilo) .... 2·75

2032 Angel playing Trumpet ('PEACE')  
2033 Angel playing Lute ('GOODWILL') 
2034 Angel playing Trumpet ('PEACE')

2035 Angel playing Lute ('GOODWILL')
2036 Angel playing Flute ('JOY') 
2037 Angel playing Tambourine ('GLORY') 

(Des Marco Ventura and Rose Design. Gravure De La Rue)

2007 (6 Nov). Christmas (2nd issue). Angels. Multicoloured One centre phosphor band (No. 2789) or two phosphor bands (others). Perf 15×14.

(a) Self-adhesive.

2789	**2032**	(2nd) Angel playing Trumpet	90	90
		a. Booklet pane. No. 2789×12	13·50	
2790	**2033**	(1st) Angel playing Lute	1·20	1·00
		a. Booklet pane. No. 2790×12	16·00	
2791	**2034**	(2nd Large) Angel playing Trumpet	1·25	1·25
2792	**2035**	(1st Large) Angel playing Lute	1·70	1·50
2793	**2036**	78p. Angel playing Flute	1·50	1·50
2794	**2037**	£1·24 Angel playing Tambourine	2·25	2·25

Set of 6 .... 7·75 7·50
First Day Cover (Tallents House) .... 7·75
First Day Cover (Bethlehem, Llandeilo) .... 8·00
Presentation Pack (Nos. 2787/2794) (PO Pack No. 404) .... 9·75
PHQ Cards (set of 9) (305) .... 2·75 17·50

(b) Ordinary gum.

MS2795 115×102 mm. As Nos. 2789/2794 .... 7·75 7·50
First Day Cover (Tallents House) .... 7·75
First Day Cover (Bethlehem, Llandeilo) .... 8·00

The phosphor bands on Nos. 2791/2792 are at the centre and right of each stamp.

The 2nd class, 1st class and 78p. stamps were also issued together in sheets of 20 sold at £8·30 containing eight 1st class, eight 2nd class and four 78p. stamps, arranged in vertical strips of five stamps alternated with printed labels (No. LS42).

Separate sheets of 20 1st, 20 2nd or ten 78p. were available with personalised photographs from Royal Mail, Edinburgh. These were sold at £9·95 for 20 2nd or £14·95 for 20 1st or ten 78p.

All these sheets were printed in lithography by Cartor and had the backing paper around the stamps retained.

The PHQ cards depict Nos. 2787/2794 and **MS**2795.

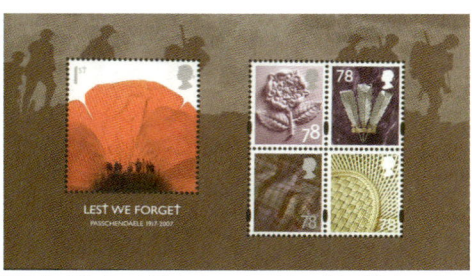

2038 Lest We Forget (*Illustration reduced. Actual size 124×70 mm*)

(Des Hat-trick design. Litho De La Rue)

2007 (8 Nov). Lest We Forget (2nd issue). 90th Anniversary of the Battle of Passchendaele. Sheet 124×70 mm containing new stamp as No. 2884 and designs as Nos. EN18, NI128, S121 and W110. Multicoloured Two phosphor bands. Perf 14½ (1st) or 15×14 (with one elliptical hole in each vertical side) (78p.).

MS2796 **2038** Lest We Forget (1st) Soldiers in poppy flower; 78p.×4 As Nos. EN18, NI128, S121 and W110 .... 6·00 6·00
First Day Cover (Tallents House) .... 6·25
First Day Cover (London SW1) .... 6·25
Presentation Pack (PO Pack No. 405) .... 6·50

No. **MS**2796 (including the England, Northern Ireland, Scotland and Wales stamps) is printed in lithography. A single example of the Soldiers in Poppy stamp from No. **MS**2796 is known with the silver (Queen's head and value) omitted.

The 1st class stamp was also issued in sheets of 20 with *se-tenant* labels showing soldiers and their letters home, printed in lithography by Cartor and sold at £7·35 (No. LS43).

Year Pack

2007 (8 Nov). Comprises Nos. 2686/2692, 2699/2720, 2728/2739, **MS**2743/2794 and **MS**2796.
CP2796a   Year Pack (PO Pack No. 406) £120

Post Office Yearbook

2007 (8 Nov). Comprises Nos. 2686/2692, 2699/2720, 2728/2739, **MS**2743/2794 and **MS**2796.
YB2796a   Yearbook .... 80·00

Miniature Sheet Collection

2007 (8 Nov). Comprises Nos. **MS**2692, **MS**2727, **MS**2740, **MS**2743, **MS**2757, **MS**2786 and **MS**2795/**MS**2796.
MS2796a Miniature Sheet Collection .... 48·00

2039 *Casino Royale*

2040 *Dr No*

QUEEN ELIZABETH II/2008

2041 Goldfinger

2042 Diamonds are Forever

2043 For Your Eyes Only

2044 From Russia with Love

(Des A2. Litho De La Rue)

2008 (8 Jan). Birth Centenary of Ian Fleming (author of James Bond books). Book Covers. Multicoloured Two phosphor bands. Perf 14½×14.

2797	**2039**	(1st) Casino Royale	1·20	1·00
		a. Booklet pane. Nos. 2797, 2799 and 2801 with margins all round	3·00	
2798	**2040**	(1st) Dr No	1·20	1·00
		a. Booklet pane. Nos. 2798, 2800 and 2802 with margins all round	3·00	
		aa. Phosphor omitted	£850	
2799	**2041**	54p. Goldfinger	90	90
2800	**2042**	54p. Diamonds are Forever	90	90
2801	**2043**	78p. For Your Eyes Only	1·25	1·25
2802	**2044**	78p. From Russia with Love	1·25	1·25
Set of 6			5·50	5·50
Set of 6 Gutter Pairs			11·00	
First Day Cover (Tallents House)				6·75
First Day Cover (London SE1)				6·75
Presentation Pack (PO Pack No. 407)			6·50	
PHQ Cards (set of 7) (306)			2·00	15·00
MS2803 189×68 mm. Nos. 2797/2802			9·25	9·25
First Day Cover (Tallents House)				9·50
First Day Cover (London SE1)				9·50

Booklet panes Nos. 2797a/2798a come from the £7·40 Ian Fleming's James Bond booklet, No. DX41.

The seven PHQ cards depict the individual stamps and No. **MS**2803.

No. 2804 is vacant.

1517 Union Jack

(Litho De La Rue)

2008 (8 Jan). Ian Fleming's James Bond. Booklet stamp. Design as T **1517** (2001 Union Jack from Submarine Centenary). Multicoloured Two phosphor bands. Perf 14½.

2805	**1517**	(1st) multicoloured	2·00	2·00
		a. Booklet pane. Nos. 2581 and 2805, each×2, with margins all round	7·00	

No. 2805 was issued in the £7·40 Ian Fleming's James Bond booklet, No. DX41. It had previously been issued in Post Office Label sheet No. LS20. For White Ensign stamp from booklet No. DX41 see No. 2581.

2045 Assistance Dog carrying Letter (Retriever, Rowan)

2046 Mountain Rescue Dog (Cross-bred, Merrick)

2047 Police Dog (German Shepherd, Max)

2048 Customs Dog (Springer Spaniel, Max)

2049 Sheepdog (Border Collie, Bob)

2050 Guide Dog (Labrador, Warwick)

(Des Redpath Design. Litho Cartor)

2008 (5 Feb). Working Dogs. Multicoloured Two phosphor bands. Perf 14½.

2806	**2045**	(1st) Assistance Dog carrying Letter	1·20	1·00
2807	**2046**	46p. Mountain Rescue Dog	80	80
2808	**2047**	48p. Police Dog	80	80
2809	**2048**	54p. Customs Dog	1·00	1·00
2810	**2049**	69p. Sheepdog	1·10	1·10
2811	**2050**	78p. Guide Dog	1·25	1·25
Set of 6			5·25	5·25
Set of 6 Gutter Pairs			10·50	
First Day Cover (Tallents House)				6·75
First Day Cover (Hound Green, Basingstoke, Hants)				6·75
Presentation Pack (PO Pack No. 408)			6·50	
PHQ Cards (set of 6) (307)			1·75	6·25

The 1st class value includes the EUROPA emblem.

2051 Henry IV (1399–1413)

2052 Henry V (1413–1422)

2053 Henry VI (1422–1461 and 1470–1471)

2054 Edward IV (1461–1470 and 1471–1483)

2055 Edward V (1483)

2056 Richard III (1483–1485)

2008/QUEEN ELIZABETH II

2057 The Age of Lancaster and York

(Des Atelier Works. Litho Cartor)

2008 (28 Feb). Kings and Queens (1st issue). Houses of Lancaster and York. Multicoloured Two phosphor bands. Perf 14½.

2812	**2051**	(1st) Henry IV	1·20	1·00
2813	**2052**	(1st) Henry V	1·20	1·00
2814	**2053**	54p. Henry VI	90	1·00
2815	**2054**	54p. Edward IV	90	1·00
2816	**2055**	69p. Edward V	1·10	1·10
2817	**2056**	69p. Richard III	1·10	1·10

Set of 6 .... 5·25 5·25
Set of 6 Gutter Pairs .... 10·50
Set of 6 Traffic Light Gutter Blocks of 4 .... 35·00
First Day Cover (Tallents House) .... 6·75
First Day Cover (Tewkesbury) .... 6·75
Presentation Pack (PO Pack No. 409) (Nos. 2812/
MS2818) .... 11·00
PHQ Cards (set of 11) (308) .... 3·25 15·00
MS2818 123×70 mm. **2057** The Age of Lancaster and York (1st) Owain Glyn Dwr (Parliament), 1404; (1st) Henry V's triumph at Battle of Agincourt, 1415; 78p. Yorkist victory at Battle of Tewkesbury, 1471; 78p. William Caxton, first English printer, 1477 .... 4·00 4·25
First Day Cover (Tallents House) .... 5·00
First Day Cover (Tewkesbury) .... 5·00

The complete miniature sheet is shown on one of the 11 PHQ cards with the others depicting individual stamps including those from No. **MS**2818.

1842 *Gazania splendens* (Charlotte Sowerby) 
1842a Aircraft Skywriting 'hello' 
1842c Union Flag

1932 Balloons (Ivan Chermayeff)
1933 Firework (Kam Tang) 
1934 Champagne, Flowers and Butterflies (Olaf Hajek) 

(Gravure Walsall)

2008 (28 Feb). Smilers Booklet stamps (4th series). Self-adhesive. Multicoloured Two phosphor bands. Die-cut Perf 15×14 (with one elliptical hole in each vertical side).

2819	**1842a**	(1st) Aircraft Skywriting 'hello'	5·50	5·50
		a. Booklet pane. Nos. 2819/2824	30·00	
2820	**1842**	(1st) *Gazania splendens*	5·50	5·50
2821	**1842c**	(1st) Union Jack	5·50	5·50
2822	**1932**	(1st) Balloons	5·50	5·50
2823	**1933**	(1st) Firework	5·50	5·50
2824	**1934**	(1st) Champagne, Flowers and Butterflies	5·50	5·50

Set of 6 .... 30·00 30·00

Nos. 2819/2824 were issued in £2·04 booklet, No. QA4, in which the surplus backing paper around each stamp was removed.

Similar sheets of ten stamps and ten *se-tenant* labels were only sold in packs for £7·95 each.

No. 2819 was re-issued again on 8 May 2010 for London 2010 Festival of Stamps in sheets of 20 *se-tenant* (No. LS72) printed in lithography by Cartor and originally sold for £8·50 per sheet.

No. 2819 is also present on label sheets (Nos. LS92 and LS100) and No. 2823 on label sheet (No. LS91).

No. 2819 was issued in sheets of 20 with *se-tenant* labels on 8 May 2010 for London 2010 Festival of Stamps (No. LS72), 28 July 2011 for Philanippon '11 World Stamp Exhibition, Yokohama (No. LS77), on 18 June 2012 for Indonesia 2012 International Stamp Exhibition, Jakarta (No. LS81), on 10 May 2013 for Australia 2013 World Stamp Exhibition, Melbourne (No. LS86), on 2 August 2013 for Bangkok 2013 World Stamp Exhibition, Thailand (No. LS87), on 1 December 2014 for Kuala Lumpur 2014 FIF Exhibition (No. LS92), on 13 May 2015 for Europhilex London 2015 Exhibition (No. LS95), on 28 May 2016 for New York World Stamp Show (No. LS100), on 28 May 2017 for Finlandia 2017 FIP Exhibition, Tampere (No. LS105), on 29 May 2019 for Stockholmia 2019 International Stamp Exhibition (No. LS116) and on 19 February 2022 for London International Stamp Exhibition (No. LS140).

Nos. 2819, 2820 and 2822 were issued again on 30 April 2009 in separate sheets of 20, (Nos. LS60/LS63) with circular *se-tenant* labels showing Jeremy Fisher (No. 2819), Wild Cherry fairy (No. 2820), Little Miss Sunshine or Big Ears (No. 2822), sold for £8·50 per sheet.

Similar sheets of ten stamps and ten *se-tenant* labels were sold in £7·95 packs.

Nos. 2820 and 2822 were each issued on 28 October 2008 in separate sheets of 20, (Nos. LS51/LS53) with circular *se-tenant* labels showing the Almond Blossom fairy (No. 2820), Mr Men or Noddy (No. 2822). These sheets were printed in lithography by Cartor and originally sold for £9·95 per sheet.

Nos. 2821/2823 were issued on 8 May 2010 with other greetings stamps in sheets of 20 with *se-tenant* greetings labels, (No. LS73) sold for £10 per sheet.

No. 2821 was issued on 12 February 2011 in sheets of 20 with *se-tenant* labels for Indipex International Stamp Exhibition, (No. LS76) sold at £8·50 per sheet.

No. 2823 was issued in sheets of 20 with *se-tenant* labels on 20 January 2012 for Lunar New Year, Year of the Dragon (No. LS80), on 7 February 2013 for Year of the Snake (No. LS84), 10 December 2013 for Year of the Horse (No. LS89), on 19 November 2014 for Year of the Sheep (No. LS91), on 9 November 2015 for Year of the Monkey (No. LS98), on 15 November 2016 for Year of the Rooster (No. LS104), on 16 November 2017 for Year of the Dog (No. LS109), on 15 November 2018 for Year of the Pig (No. LS114), on 18 November 2019 for Year of the Rat (No. LS119) on 8 December 2020 for Year of the Ox (No. LS130) and on 8 December 2021 for Year of the Tiger (No. LS137).

All the above sheets were printed by Cartor (known from late 2013 onwards as International Security Printers) in lithography instead of photogravure.

> For the miniature sheet entitled Celebrating Northern Ireland, issued 11 March 2008, see Regionals Section.

2058 Lifeboat, Barra 
2059 Lifeboat approaching Dinghy, Appledore

2060 Helicopter Winchman, Portland 
2061 Inshore lifeboat, St Ives

2062 Rescue Helicopter, Lee-on-Solent
2063 Launch of Lifeboat, Dinbych-y-Pysgod, Tenby 

(Des Hat-trick Design. Litho Walsall)

2008 (13 Mar). Rescue at Sea. Multicoloured 'All-over' phosphor. Perf 14½×14*.

2825	**2058**	(1st) Lifeboat, Barra	1·20	1·00
2826	**2059**	46p. Lifeboat approaching Dinghy, Appledore	80	80
2827	**2060**	48p. Helicopter Winchman, Portland	90	90
2828	**2061**	54p. Inshore lifeboat, St Ives	1·00	1·00

QUEEN ELIZABETH II/2008

2829	**2062**	69p. Rescue Helicopter, Lee-on- Solent	1·10	1·10
2830	**2063**	78p. Launch of Lifeboat, Dinbych-y-Pysgod, Tenby	1·25	1·25
		Set of 6	5·25	5·25
		Set of 6 Gutter Pairs	10·50	
		First Day Cover (Tallents House)		6·50
		First Day Cover (Poole, Dorset)		6·50
		Presentation Pack (PO Pack No. 411)	6·00	
		PHQ Cards (set of 6) (309)	1·50	6·25

* Nos. 2825/2830 have interrupted perforations along the top and bottom edges of the stamps, the gaps in the perforations forming the three dots and three dashes that spell out 'SOS' in morse code.

2064 *Lysandra bellargus* (Adonis Blue)

2065 *Coenagrion mercuriale* (Southern Damselfly)

2066 *Formica rufibarbis* (Red-barbed Ant)

2067 *Pareulype berberata* (Barberry Carpet Moth)

2068 *Lucanus cervus* (Stag Beetle)

2069 *Cryptocephalus coryli* (Hazel Pot Beetle)

2070 *Gryllus campestris* (Field Cricket)

2071 *Hesperia comma* (Silver-spotted Skipper)

2072 *Pseudepipona herrichii* (Purbeck Mason Wasp)

2073 *Gnorimus nobilis* (Noble Chafer)

(Des Andrew Ross. Litho De La Rue)

2008 (15 Apr). Action for Species (2nd series). Insects. Multicoloured Phosphor background. Perf 14½.

2831	**2064**	(1st) *Lysandra bellargus* (Adonis blue)	1·20	1·00
		a. Block of 10. Nos. 2831/2840	10·50	9·00
2832	**2065**	(1st) *Coenagrion mercuriale* (southern damselfly)	1·20	1·00
2833	**2066**	(1st) *Formica rufibarbis* (red-barbed ant)	1·20	1·00
2834	**2067**	(1st) *Pareulype berberata* (barberry carpet moth)	1·20	1·00
2835	**2068**	(1st) *Lucanus cervus* (stag beetle)	1·20	1·00
2836	**2069**	(1st) *Cryptocephalus coryli* (hazel pot beetle)	1·20	1·00
2837	**2070**	(1st) *Gryllus campestris* (field cricket)	1·20	1·00
2838	**2071**	(1st) *Hesperia comma* (silver-spotted skipper)	1·20	1·00
2839	**2072**	(1st) *Pseudepipona herrichii* (Purbeck mason wasp)	1·20	1·00
2840	**2073**	(1st) *Gnorimus nobilis* (noble chafer)	1·20	1·00
		Set of 10	10·50	9·00
		Gutter Block of 20	21·00	
		First Day Cover (Tallents House)		9·25
		First Day Cover (Crawley, W. Sussex)		9·50
		Presentation Pack (PO Pack No. 412)	11·00	
		PHQ Cards (set of 10) (310)	3·00	9·75

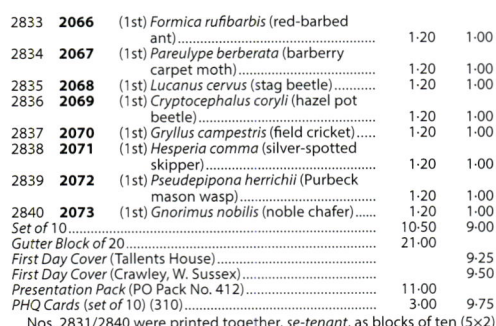

Nos. 2831/2840 were printed together, *se-tenant*, as blocks of ten (5×2) in sheets of 60 (2 panes of 30).

2074 Lichfield Cathedral

2075 Belfast Cathedral

2076 Gloucester Cathedral

2077 St David's Cathedral

2078 Westminster Cathedral

2079 St Magnus Cathedral, Kirkwall, Orkney

2080 St Paul's Cathedral

(Des Howard Brown. Litho Enschedé)

2008 (13 May). Cathedrals. Multicoloured 'All-over' phosphor. Perf 14½.

2841	**2074**	(1st) Lichfield Cathedral	1·20	1·00
2842	**2075**	48p. Belfast Cathedral	85	85
2843	**2076**	50p. Gloucester Cathedral	1·00	1·00
2844	**2077**	56p. St David's Cathedral	1·10	1·10
2845	**2078**	72p. Westminster Cathedral	1·25	1·25
2846	**2079**	81p. St Magnus Cathedral, Kirkwall, Orkney	1·40	1·40
		Set of 6	6·00	6·00
		Set of 6 Gutter Pairs	12·00	
		Set of 6 Traffic Light Gutter Pairs	32·00	
		First Day Cover (Tallents House)		6·75
		First Day Cover (London EC4)		6·75
		Presentation Pack (PO Pack No. 413) (Nos. 2841/**MS**2847)	11·00	
		PHQ Cards (set of 11) (311)	3·25	16·00

2008/QUEEN ELIZABETH II

MS2847 115×89 mm. **2080** St Paul's Cathedral (1st) multicoloured; (1st) multicoloured; 81p. multicoloured; 81p. multicoloured. Perf 14½×14 .... 4·00 4·00
First Day Cover (Tallents House) .... 4·50
First Day Cover (London EC4) .... 4·50

No. **MS**2847 commemorates the 300th anniversary of St Paul's Cathedral. The complete miniature sheet is shown on one of the 11 PHQ cards with the others depicting individual stamps including those from No. **MS**2847.

1977 Ice Cream Cone

(Gravure Walsall)

2008 (13 May). Beside the Seaside (2nd series). As T **1977** but self-adhesive. Multicoloured Two phosphor bands. Die-cut Perf 14½.
2848 **1977** (1st) Ice Cream Cone. Multicoloured ..... 3·00 3·00
    a. Booklet pane. No. 2848×2 and No. 2295×4 .... 7·50

No. 2848 was only issued in £2·16 booklet, No. PM15, in which the surplus self-adhesive paper was removed from around the 1st class gold stamps (No. 2295), but retained from around No. 2848.

2081 Carry on Sergeant    **2082** Dracula

2083 Carry on Cleo    **2084** The Curse of Frankenstein

2085 Carry on Screaming    **2086** The Mummy

(Des Elmwood. Litho Walsall)

2008 (10 June). Posters for Carry On and Hammer Horror Films. Multicoloured Two phosphor bands. Perf 14.
2849 **2081** (1st) *Carry on Sergeant* .... 1·20 1·00
2850 **2082** 48p. *Dracula* 80 80
2851 **2083** 50p. *Carry on Cleo* 90 90
2852 **2084** 56p. *The Curse of Frankenstein* .... 1·00 1·00
2853 **2085** 72p. *Carry on Screaming* .... 1·10 1·10
2854 **2086** 81p. *The Mummy* .... 1·25 1·25
Set of 6 .... 5·50 5·50
Set of 6 Gutter Pairs .... 11·00
First Day Cover (Tallents House) .... 6·25
First Day Cover (Bray, Maidenhead, Berks) .... 6·25
Presentation Pack (PO Pack No. 414) .... 6·25
PHQ Cards (set of 6) (312) .... 1·50 7·00
PHQ Cards (brick wall background) and Stamps Set .... 7·00

Nos. 2849/2854 commemorate the 50th anniversary of *Dracula* and the first Carry On film (*Carry on Sergeant*).

2087 Red Arrows, Dartmouth Regatta Airshow, 2006    **2088** RAF Falcons Parachute Team, Biggin Hill, 2006

2089 Spectator watching Red Arrows, Farnborough, 2006 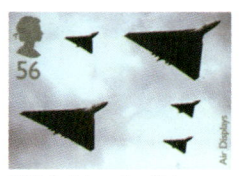   **2090** Prototype Avro Vulcan Bombers and Avro 707s, Farnborough, 1953

2091 Parachutist Robert Wyndham on Wing of Avro 504, 1933   **2092** Air Race rounding the Beacon, Hendon, c 1912

(Des Roundel. Gravure De La Rue)

2008 (17 July). Air Displays. Multicoloured Two phosphor bands. Perf 14½×14.
2855 **2087** (1st) Red Arrows .... 1·20 1·00
2856 **2088** 48p. RAF Falcons Parachute Team 80 80
2857 **2089** 50p. Spectator watching Red Arrows 90 90
2858 **2090** 56p. Prototype Avro Vulcan Bombers and Avro 707s .... 1·00 1·00
2859 **2091** 72p. Parachutist Robert Wyndham on Wing of Avro 504 .... 1·10 1·10
2860 **2092** 81p. Air Race rounding the Beacon .... 1·25 1·25
Set of 6 .... 5·50 5·50
Set of 6 Gutter Pairs .... 11·00
First Day Cover (Tallents House) .... 6·25
First Day Cover (Farnborough, Hants) .... 6·25
Presentation Pack (PO Pack No. 415) .... 6·25
PHQ Cards (set of 6) (313) .... 1·75 6·25

The 1st class stamp was also issued in sheets of 20 with *se-tenant* labels, printed in lithography by Cartor, and sold for £7·75 per sheet (No. LS47). See also No. 2869.

2093 Landmarks of Beijing and London

(Des Why Not Associates. Litho Walsall)

2008 (22 Aug). Handover of Olympic Flag from Beijing to London. Sheet 115×76 mm. Multicoloured Phosphorised paper. Perf 14½.
MS2861 **2093** Landmarks of Beijing and London (1st) National Stadium, Beijing; (1st) London Eye; (1st) Tower of London; (1st) Corner Tower of the Forbidden City, Beijing .... 5·00 5·00
    a. UV varnish (Olympic Rings) omitted £4500
First Day Cover (Tallents House) .... 5·25
First Day Cover (London E15) .... 5·25
Presentation Pack (PO Pack No. M17) .... 30·00
PHQ Cards (set of 5) (OGH) .... 60 5·00

The Olympic rings overprinted on No. **MS**2861 are in silk-screen varnish.

QUEEN ELIZABETH II/2008

The five PHQ cards show the four individual stamps and the complete miniature sheet.

2094 Drum Major, RAF Central Band, 2007
2095 Helicopter Rescue Winchman, 1984 
2096 Hawker Hunter Pilot, 1951 
2097 Lancaster Air Gunner, 1944 
2098 WAAF Plotter, 1940 
2099 Pilot, 1918 

(Des Graham Turner and Atelier Works. Litho Walsall)

2008 (18 Sept). Military Uniforms (2nd series). RAF Uniforms. Multicoloured Two phosphor bands. Perf 14.

2862	2094	(1st) Drum Major, RAF Central Band......	1·20	1·00
		a. Horiz strip of 3. Nos. 2862/2864.....	3·50	3·00
		b. Booklet pane. Nos. 2862/2864 with margins all round................	3·50	
2863	2095	(1st) Helicopter Rescue Winchman........	1·20	1·00
2864	2096	(1st) Hawker Hunter Pilot......................	1·20	1·00
2865	2097	81p. Lancaster Air Gunner......................	1·40	1·40
		a. Horiz strip of 3. Nos. 2865/2867.....	4·25	4·25
		b. Booklet pane. Nos. 2865/2867 with margins all round................	4·25	
2866	2098	81p. WAAF Plotter....................................	1·40	1·40
2867	2099	81p. Pilot...	1·40	1·40
Set of 6...			7·00	6·75
Set of 2 Gutter Strips of 6..			14·00	
Set of 2 Traffic Light Gutter Blocks of 12........................			28·00	
First Day Cover (Tallents House).......................................				7·00
First Day Cover (Hendon, London NW9)..........................				7·00
Presentation Pack (PO Pack No. 416)..............................			7·00	
PHQ Cards (set of 6) (314)..			1·75	7·75

Nos. 2862/2864 and 2865/2867 were each printed together, *se-tenant*, as horizontal strips of three stamps in sheets of 60 (2 panes 6×5).

Booklet panes Nos. 2862b and 2865b come from the £7·15 Pilot to Plane, RAF Uniforms booklet No. DX42.

See also Nos. 2774/2779 and 2964/2969.

1307 Reginald Mitchell and Supermarine Spitfire MkIIA
2087 Red Arrows, Dartmouth Regatta Airshow, 2006 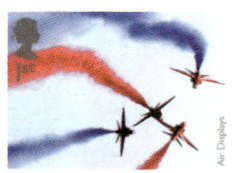

(Litho Walsall)

2008 (18 Sept). Pilot to Plane. RAF Uniforms. Booklet stamps. Designs as T **1307** (Spitfire from 1997 British Aircraft Designers) and T **2087** (Red Arrows from 2008 Air Displays). Multicoloured Two phosphor bands. Perf 14.

2868	1307	20p. Reginald Mitchell and Supermarine Spitfire MkIIA............	1·25	1·25
		a. Booklet pane. Nos. 2868/2869, each×2, with margins all round.....	6·00	
2869	2087	(1st) Red Arrows.....................................	1·25	1·25

Nos. 2868/2869 were only issued in the £7·15 Pilot to Plane, RAF Uniforms booklet, No. DX42.

2100 Millicent Garrett Fawcett (suffragist)
2101 Elizabeth Garrett Anderson (physician, women's health) 
2102 Marie Stopes (family planning pioneer) 
2103 Eleanor Rathbone (family allowance campaigner) 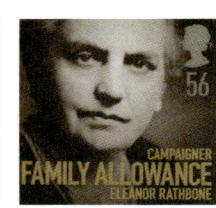
2104 Claudia Jones (civil rights activist) 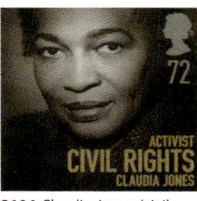
2105 Barbara Castle (politician, Equal Pay Act) 

(Des Together Design. Gravure Walsall)

2008 (14 Oct). Women of Distinction. Multicoloured 'All-over' phosphor. Perf 14×14½.

2870	2100	(1st) Millicent Garrett Fawcett................	1·20	1·00
2871	2101	48p. Elizabeth Garrett Anderson............	80	80
2872	2102	50p. Marie Stopes.....................................	90	90
2873	2103	56p. Eleanor Rathbone............................	1·00	1·00
2874	2104	72p. Claudia Jones....................................	1·10	1·10
2875	2105	81p. Barbara Castle..................................	1·25	1·25
Set of 6...			5·25	5·25
Set of 6 Gutter Pairs..			10·50	
First Day Cover (Tallents House).......................................				6·25
First Day Cover (Aldeburgh, Suffolk)................................				6·25
Presentation Pack (PO Pack No. 417)..............................			6·00	
PHQ Cards (set of 6) (315)..			1·75	6·25

SELF-ADHESIVE STAMPS. Collectors are reminded that from November 2008, self-adhesive stamps no longer incorporated a layer of water-soluble gum and will not 'soak-off'. It is advised that, from this point, all used self-adhesive stamps are collected with a neat margin of backing paper.

2106 Ugly Sisters from *Cinderella*
2107 Genie from *Aladdin* 
2108 Ugly Sisters from *Cinderella* 
2109 Captain Hook from *Peter Pan* 
2110 Genie from *Aladdin* 
2111 Wicked Queen from *Snow White*

2008/QUEEN ELIZABETH II

(Des Steve Haskins. Gravure De La Rue)

2008 (4 Nov). Christmas. Multicoloured One centre band (No. 2876) or two phosphor bands (others). Perf 15×14.

(a) Self-adhesive.

2876	2106	(2nd) Ugly Sisters.........................	90	90
		a. Booklet pane. No. 2876×12............	13·50	
2877	2107	(1st) Genie.................................	1·20	1·00
		a. Booklet pane. No. 2877×12............	16·00	
2878	2108	(2nd Ugly Sisters, Large)............	1·25	1·25
2879	2109	50p. Captain Hook.....................	1·00	1·00
2880	2110	(1st Genie, Large)......................	1·70	1·50
2881	2111	81p. Wicked Queen....................	1·75	1·75
Set of 6			6·25	6·25
First Day Cover (Tallents House)................				6·50
First Day Cover (Bethlehem, Llandeilo).......				6·50
Presentation Pack (PO Pack No. 418).........			7·00	
PHQ Cards (set of 7) (316).........................			2·00	12·00

(b) Ordinary gum.

MS2882 114×102 mm. As Nos. 2876/2881		6·50	6·50
First Day Cover (Tallents House)................			6·75
First Day Cover (Bethlehem, Llandeilo).......			7·00

The phosphor bands on Nos. 2878 and 2880 are at the centre and right of each stamp.

The 2nd class, 1st class and 81p. stamps were also issued together in sheets of 20, sold for £8·85, containing eight 1st class, eight 2nd class and four 81p. stamps, arranged in vertical strips of five stamps alternated with printed labels (No. LS54).

Separate sheets of ten 1st, 20 1st, 20 2nd or ten 81p. stamps were available with personalised photographs from Royal Mail, Edinburgh. These were sold at £7·50 for ten 1st, £8·50 for 20 2nd or £13·50 for 20 1st or 81p.

Separate sheets of ten 1st, 20 1st, 20 2nd or ten 81p. stamps were available with personalised photographs.

All these sheets were printed in lithography by Cartor and had the backing paper around the stamps retained.

The seven PHQ cards depict the six stamps and No. **MS**2882.

2112 Seven Poppies on Barbed Wire Stems

2113 Soldiers in Poppy Flower

2114 Soldier's Face in Poppy Flower

2115 Lest We Forget

(Des hat-trick design. Litho Cartor ISP (No. 2883b) or De La Rue (others))

2008 (6 Nov)–**2017**. Lest We Forget (3rd issue). 90th Anniversary of the Armistice. Multicoloured Two phosphor bands. Perf 14½ (1st) or 15×14 (with one elliptical hole in each vertical side) (81p.).

2883	2112	(1st) Seven Poppies on Barbed Wire Stems...............................	1·20	1·00
		a. Horiz strip of 3. Nos. 2883/2885...	3·50	4·50
		b. Booklet pane No. 2883, 2884×2 and 2885 se-tenant (31.7.17).....	5·00	
2884	2113	(1st) Soldiers in Poppy Flower.............	1·20	1·00
2885	2114	(1st) Soldier's Face in Poppy Flower....	1·20	1·00
Set of 3			3·50	4·50
Gutter Strip of 6			7·00	
Traffic Light Gutter Block of 12...................			25·00	
MS2886 124×70 mm. **2115** Lest We Forget No. 2885 and as Nos. EN19, NI129, S122 and W111.......			5·75	5·75
First Day Cover (Tallents House)................				6·75
First Day Cover (London SW1)....................				6·75
Presentation Pack (PO Pack No. 419).........			7·25	
PHQ Cards (set of 6) (317).........................			1·80	9·50

Nos. 2883/2885 were printed together, *se-tenant*, in horizontal strips of three stamps in sheets of 30.

No. **MS**2886 (including the England, Northern Ireland, Scotland and Wales stamps) is printed in lithography.

The 1st class stamp, T **2114**, was also issued in sheets of 20 with *se-tenant* labels showing artefacts from the trenches, printed in lithography by Cartor and sold at £7·75 (No. LS55).

No. 2885 has the two phosphor bands shaped around each side of the poppy.

A Miniature Sheet Collection containing Nos. **MS**2685, **MS**2796, **MS**2886 and a replica embroidered postcard in a folder was sold for £26·95.

Booklet pane 2883b is from the £15·41 premium booklet No. DY22.

The six PHQ cards depict Nos. **MS**2685, **MS**2796 and 2883/**MS**2886.

Year Pack

2008 (6 Nov). Comprises Nos. 2797/2802, 2806/**MS**2818, 2825/**MS**2847, 2849/2867, 2870/2881, **MS**2886 and **MS**NI152

| CP2886a | Year Pack (PO Pack No. 420)................ | 85·00 |

Post Office Yearbook

2008 (6 Nov). Comprises Nos. 2797/2802, 2806/**MS**2818, 2825/**MS**2847, 2849/2867, 2870/2881, **MS**2886 and **MS**NI152/**MS**NI153

| YB2886a | Yearbook.. | 85·00 |

Miniature Sheet Collection

2008 (6 Nov). Comprises Nos. **MS**2803, **MS**2818, **MS**2847, **MS**2861, **MS**2882, **MS**2886 and **MS**NI152/**MS**NI153

| **MS**2886a | Miniature Sheet Collection.............................. | 45·00 |

2116 Supermarine Spitfire (R. J. Mitchell)

2117 Mini Skirt (Mary Quant)

2118 Mini (Sir Alec Issigonis)

2119 Anglepoise Lamp (George Carwardine)

2120 Concorde (Aérospatiale-BAC)

2121 K2 Telephone Kiosk (Sir Giles Gilbert Scott)

QUEEN ELIZABETH II/2009

2122 Polypropylene Chair (Robin Day)
2123 Penguin Books (Edward Young) 
2124 London Underground Map (based on original design by Harry Beck) 
2125 Routemaster Bus (design team led by AAM Durrant) 

(Des HGV Design. Litho Cartor)

2009 (13 Jan). British Design Classics (1st series). Multicoloured Phosphor background. Perf 14½.

2887	2116	(1st) Supermarine Spitfire	1·20	1·00
		a. Block of 10. Nos. 2887/2896	10·50	9·00
		ab. Black printed treble	—	
		b. Booklet pane. Nos. 2887, 2889 and 2896×2	4·75	
2888	2117	(1st) Mini Skirt	1·20	1·00
		a. Booklet pane. Nos. 2888, 2890, 2892 and 2893/2895	6·00	
2889	2118	(1st) Mini	1·20	1·00
2890	2119	(1st) Anglepoise Lamp	1·20	1·00
2891	2120	(1st) Concorde	1·20	1·00
		a. Booklet pane. Nos. 2891 and 2897, each×2	4·75	
2892	2121	(1st) K2 Telephone Kiosk	1·20	1·00
2893	2122	(1st) Polypropylene Chair	1·20	1·00
2894	2123	(1st) Penguin Books	1·20	1·00
2895	2124	(1st) London Underground Map	1·20	1·00
2896	2125	(1st) Routemaster Bus	1·20	1·00
Set of 10			10·50	9·00
Gutter Block of 20			21·00	
First Day Cover (Tallents House)				9·00
First Day Cover (Longbridge, Birmingham)				9·00
Presentation Pack (PO Pack No. 421)			11·00	
PHQ Cards (set of 10) (318)			3·00	9·75

No. 2887 was also issued on 15 September 2010 in sheets of 20 with *se-tenant* labels, (No. LS74), sold at £8·50 per sheet.

Nos. 2887/2896 were printed together, *se-tenant*, in blocks of ten (2×5) throughout sheets of 30 stamps.

Booklet panes Nos. 2887b, 2888a and 2891a come from the £7·68 British Design Classics booklet, No. DX44.

No. 2889 was also issued in sheets of 20 with *se-tenant* labels, on 13 January 2009. (No. LS56), sold at £7·75 per sheet.

No. 2891 was also issued on 2 March 2009 in sheets of 20 with *se-tenant* labels, (No. LS57), and sold at £7·75 per sheet.

The above sheets were all printed in lithography by Cartor and perforated 14×14½.

For self-adhesive versions of these stamps see Nos. 2911/2915b.

1589 Concorde (1976)

(Litho Cartor)

2009 (13 Jan). British Design Classics (2nd series). Booklet stamp. Design as No. 2285 (Concorde from 2002 Passenger Jet Aviation). Multicoloured Two phosphor bands. Perf 14½.

2897	1589	(1st) Concorde (1976). Multicoloured	4·50	4·50

No. 2897 was only issued in the £7·68 British Design Classics booklet, No. DX44.

For the miniature sheet entitled Robert Burns 250th Anniversary, issued on 22 January, see the Regional Section.

2126 Charles Darwin 
2127 Marine Iguana 
2128 Finches 
2129 Atoll 
2130 Bee Orchid 
2131 Orangutan

2132 Fauna and Map of the Galapagos Islands

(Des Hat-trick design (Nos. 2898/2903) or Howard Brown (No. **MS**2904))

2009 (12 Feb). Birth Bicentenary of Charles Darwin (naturalist and evolutionary theorist) (1st issue). Multicoloured

(a) Self-adhesive. Gravure De La Rue. 'All-over' phosphor. Perf 14.

2898	2126	(1st) Charles Darwin	1·20	1·00
2899	2127	48p. Marine Iguana	1·10	1·10
2900	2128	50p. Finches	1·25	1·25
2901	2129	56p. Atoll	1·40	1·40
2902	2130	72p. Bee Orchid	1·75	1·75
2903	2131	81p. Orangutan	2·00	2·00
Set of 6			7·50	7·50
First Day Cover (Tallents House)				8·25
First Day Cover (Shrewsbury)				8·25
Presentation Pack (PO Pack No. 423) (Nos. 2898/**MS**2904)			10·50	
PHQ Cards (set of 11) (320)			3·25	16·50

(b) Ordinary gum. Litho De La Rue. Two phosphor bands. Perf 14.

MS2904 115×89 mm. **2132** Fauna and Map of the Galapagos Islands (1st) Flightless Cormorant; (1st) Giant Tortoise and Cactus Finch; 81p. Marine Iguana; 81p. Floreana Mockingbird ... 5·00 5·00
    a. Booklet pane. No. **MS**2904 150×96 mm. ... 5·00
First Day Cover (Tallents House) ... 6·00
First Day Cover (Shrewsbury) ... 6·00

Nos. 2898/2903 have jigsaw perforations on the two vertical sides.

Booklet pane No. 2904a comes from the £7·75 Charles Darwin booklet No. DX45.

The complete miniature sheet is shown on one of the 11 PHQ cards with the others depicting individual stamps, including those from No. **MS**2904.

2009/QUEEN ELIZABETH II

(Gravure De La Rue)

2009 (12 Feb). Birth Bicentenary of Charles Darwin (naturalist and evolutionary theorist) (2nd issue). Multicoloured Phosphorised paper. Perf 14.

2905	2126	(1st) Charles Darwin	6·00	6·00
		a. Booklet pane. Nos. 2905 and 2909/2910	13·50	
2906	2127	48p. Marine Iguana	6·00	6·00
		a. Booklet pane. Nos. 2906/2908	13·50	
2907	2128	50p. Finches	6·00	6·00
2908	2129	56p. Atoll	6·00	6·00
2909	2130	72p. Bee Orchid	6·00	6·00
2910	2131	81p. Orangutan	6·00	6·00
Set of 6			32·00	32·00

Nos. 2905/2910 were only issued in the £7·75 Charles Darwin booklet, No. DX45.

Nos. 2905/2910 have Jigsaw perforations on both vertical sides.

For Nos. U2911/U2954, U2975/U3037, U3045/U3052 U3055/U3059 and U3060/U3157 and Types **2132a/2132d** see Decimal Machin Definitives section.

(Gravure Walsall)

2009 (10 Mar)–**2010**. British Design Classics (3rd series). Booklet stamps. Designs as Nos. 2887/2889, 2891/2892 and 2896. Self-adhesive. Multicoloured. Phosphor background. Die-cut perf 14½.

2911	2121	(1st) K2 Telephone Kiosk	2·00	2·00
		a. Booklet pane. Nos. 2911/2912 and U2983×4	7·50	
2912	2125	(1st) Routemaster Bus	2·00	2·00
2913	2118	(1st) Mini (21.4.09)	2·00	2·00
		a. Booklet pane. No. 2913×2 and U2983×4	7·50	
2914	2120	(1st) Concorde (18.8.09)	2·00	2·00
		a. Booklet pane. No. 2914×2 and U2983×4	7·50	
2915	2117	(1st) Mini Skirt (17.9.09)	2·00	2·00
		a. Booklet pane. No. 2915×2 and U2983×4	5·75	
2915b	2116	(1st) Supermarine Spitfire (15.9.10)	2·00	2·00
		ba. Booklet pane. No. 2915b×2 and U3016×4	7·50	
Set of 6			10·00	10·00

Nos. 2911/2915b were only issued in booklets, Nos. PM16/PM17, PM19/PM20 and PM25, initially sold for £2·16 (No. PM16), £2·34 (Nos. PM17, PM19/PM20) or £2·46 (No. PM25).

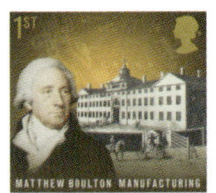

2133 Matthew Boulton and Factory (manufacturing)

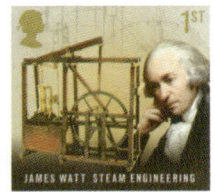

2134 James Watt and Boulton & Watt Condensing Engine (steam engineering)

2135 Richard Arkwright and Spinning Machine (textiles)

2136 Josiah Wedgwood and Black Basalt Teapot and Vase (ceramics)

2137 George Stephenson and Locomotion (railways)

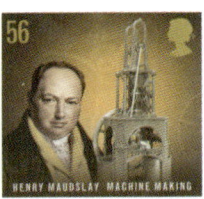

2138 Henry Maudslay and Table Engine (machine making)

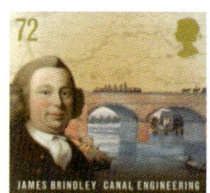

2139 James Brindley and Bridgewater Canal Aqueduct (canal engineering)

2140 John McAdam (road building)

(Des Webb and Webb. Litho Enschedé)

2009 (10 Mar). Pioneers of the Industrial Revolution. Multicoloured 'All-over' phosphor. Perf 14×14½.

2916	2133	(1st) Matthew Boulton	1·20	1·00
		a. Horiz pair. Nos. 2916/2917	2·40	2·00
2917	2134	(1st) James Watt	1·20	1·00
2918	2135	50p. Richard Arkwright	70	70
		a. Horiz pair. Nos. 2918/2919	1·40	1·40
2919	2136	50p. Josiah Wedgwood	70	70
2920	2137	56p. George Stephenson	85	85
		a. Horiz pair. Nos. 2920/2921	1·75	1·75
2921	2138	56p. Henry Maudslay	85	85
2922	2139	72p. James Brindley	1·00	1·00
		a. Horiz pair. Nos. 2922/2923	2·00	2·00
2923	2140	72p. John McAdam	1·00	1·00
Set of 8			6·75	6·50
Set of 4 Gutter Strips of 4			13·50	
First Day Cover (Tallents House)				7·50
First Day Cover (Steam Mills, Cinderford)				7·50
Presentation Pack (PO Pack No. 425)			7·25	
PHQ Cards (set of 8) (321)			2·40	8·00

Nos. 2916/2917, 2918/2919, 2920/2921 and 2922/2923 were each printed together, *se-tenant*, as horizontal pairs in sheets of 60 (2 panes 6×5).

2141 Henry VII (1485–1509)

2142 Henry VIII (1509–1547)

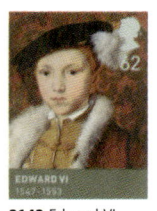

2143 Edward VI (1547–1553)

2144 Lady Jane Grey (1553)

2145 Mary I (1553–1558)

2146 Elizabeth I (1558–1603)

2147 The Age of the Tudors

(Des Atelier Works. Litho Cartor)

2009 (21 Apr). Kings and Queens (2nd issue). House of Tudor. Multicoloured Two phosphor bands. Perf 14.

2924	2141	(1st) Henry VII	1·20	1·00
2925	2142	(1st) Henry VIII	1·20	1·00
2926	2143	62p. Edward VI	90	90

205

QUEEN ELIZABETH II/2009

2927	2144	62p. Lady Jane Grey		90	90
		a. Imperf (pair)		£4250	
2928	2145	81p. Mary I		1·25	1·25
2929	2146	81p. Elizabeth I		1·25	1·25

Set of 6 .... 5·75 5·50
Set of 6 Gutter Pairs .... 11·50
Set of 6 Traffic Light Gutter Blocks of 4 .... 30·00
First Day Cover (Tallents House) .... 7·50
First Day Cover (London SE10) .... 7·50
Presentation Pack (PO Pack No. 426) (Nos. 2924/MS2930) .... 7·25
PHQ Cards (set of 11) (322) .... 3·25 16·00

MS2930 123×70 mm. **2147** The Age of the Tudors (1st) Mary Rose (galleon), 1510; (1st) Field of Cloth of Gold Royal Conference, 1520; 90p. Royal Exchange (centre of commerce), 1565; 90p. Francis Drake (circumnavigation), 1580 .... 4·25 4·25
First Day Cover (Tallents House) .... 5·00
First Day Cover (London SE10) .... 5·00

The complete miniature sheet is shown on one of the 11 PHQ cards with the others depicting individual stamps including those from No. **MS**2930.

The PHQ Card for the Royal Exchange design has the inscription for Sir Francis Drake and vice versa.

2148 *Allium sphaerocephalon* (Round-headed Leek)

2149 *Luronium natans* (Floating Water-plantain)

2150 *Cypripedium calceolus* (Lady's Slipper Orchid)

2151 *Polygala amarella* (Dwarf Milkwort)

2152 *Saxifraga hirculus* (Marsh Saxifrage)

2153 *Stachys germanica* (Downy Woundwort)

2154 *Euphorbia serrulata* (Upright Spurge)

2155 *Pyrus cordata* (Plymouth Pear)

2156 *Polygonum maritimum* (Sea Knotgrass)

2157 *Dianthus armeria* (Deptford Pink)

2158 Royal Botanic Gardens, Kew

(Des Studio Dempsey. Litho Cartor)

2009 (19 May). Action for Species (3rd series). Plants. Multicoloured

(a) Phosphor background. Perf 14½.

2931	2148	(1st) *Allium sphaerocephalon* (Round-headed Leek)	1·20	1·00
		a. Block of 10. Nos. 2931/2940	10·50	9·00
2932	2149	(1st) *Luronium natans* (Floating Water-plantain)	1·20	1·00
2933	2150	(1st) *Cypripedium calceolus* (Lady's Slipper Orchid)	1·20	1·00
2934	2151	(1st) *Polygala amarella* (Dwarf Milkwort)	1·20	1·00
2935	2152	(1st) *Saxifraga hirculus* (Marsh Saxifrage)	1·20	1·00
2936	2153	(1st) *Stachys germanica* (Downy Woundwort)	1·20	1·00
2937	2154	(1st) *Euphorbia serrulata* (Upright Spurge)	1·20	1·00
2938	2155	(1st) *Pyrus cordata* (Plymouth Pear)	1·20	1·00
2939	2156	(1st) *Polygonum maritimum* (Sea Knotgrass)	1·20	1·00
2940	2157	(1st) *Dianthus armeria* (Deptford Pink)	1·20	1·00

Set of 10 .... 10·50 9·00
Gutter Block of 10 .... 21·00
First Day Cover (Tallents House) .... 11·00
First Day Cover (Kew, Richmond) .... 11·00
Presentation Pack (PO Pack No. 427) (Nos. 2931/MS2941) .... 15·00
PHQ Cards (set of 15) (323) .... 4·50 13·50

(b) 250th Anniversary of Royal Botanic Gardens, Kew. Two phosphor bands. Perf 14×14½.

MS2941 115×89 mm. 2158 Royal Botanic Gardens, Kew (1st) Palm House, Kew Gardens; (1st) Millennium Seed Bank, Wakehurst Place; 90p. Pagoda, Kew Gardens; 90p. Sackler Crossing, Kew Gardens .... 4·25 4·25
First Day Cover (Tallents House) .... 5·00
First Day Cover (Kew, Richmond) .... 5·00

Nos. 2931/2940 were printed together, *se-tenant*, as blocks of ten (5×2) in sheets of 60 (2 panes of 30).

The complete miniature sheet is shown on one of the 15 PHQ cards with the others depicting individual stamps including those from No. **MS**2941.

1287 *Iris latifolia* (Ehret)

1283 *Tulipa gesneriana* (Ehret)

2009/QUEEN ELIZABETH II

(Gravure Walsall)

2009 (21 May). 50th Anniversary of NAFAS (National Association of Flower Arrangement Societies). Booklet stamps. Designs as Nos. 1958 and 1962 (1997 Greetings Stamps, 19th-century Flower Paintings). Self-adhesive. Multicoloured Two phosphor bands. Die-cut Perf 14 (with one elliptical hole in each vert side).

2942	**1287**	(1st) *Iris latifolia*.................................	4·25	4·25
		a. Booklet pane. Nos. 2942/2943 and U2983×4.....................	10·00	
2943	**1283**	(1st) *Tulipa gesneriana*..............................	4·25	4·25

Nos. 2942/2943 were only issued in stamp booklet, No. PM18.

2159 Dragon
2160 Unicorn 
2161 Giant 
2162 Pixie 
2163 Mermaid 
2164 Fairy 

(Des Dave McKean and Morgan Radcliffe. Gravure De La Rue)

2009 (16 June). Mythical Creatures. Multicoloured 'All-over' phosphor. Perf 14½.

2944	**2159**	(1st) Dragon..	1·20	1·00
2945	**2160**	(1st) Unicorn...	1·20	1·00
2946	**2161**	62p. Giant...	1·00	1·00
2947	**2162**	62p. Pixie..	1·00	1·00
2948	**2163**	90p. Mermaid..	1·50	1·50
2949	**2164**	90p. Fairy...	1·50	1·50
Set of 6...			6·50	6·25
Set of 6 Gutter Pairs...			13·00	
First Day Cover (Tallents House).................................				8·00
First Day Cover (Dragonby, Scunthorpe).....................				8·00
Presentation Pack (PO Pack No. 428)........................			7·00	
PHQ Cards (set of 6) (324)..			1·75	8·00

2165 George V Type B Wall Letter Box, 1933–1936 
2166 Edward VII Ludlow Letter Box, 1901–1910 
2167 Victorian Lamp Letter Box, 1896 
2168 Elizabeth II Type A Wall Letter Box, 1962–1963

2169 Post Boxes

(Des Elmwood. Litho Cartor)

2009 (18 Aug). Post Boxes. Multicoloured 'All-over' phosphor. Perf 14.

2950	**2165**	(1st) George V Type B Wall Letter Box.....	1·20	1·00
		a. Booklet pane. Nos. 2950/2953 with margins all round..................	4·25	
2951	**2166**	56p. Edward VII Ludlow Letter Box.........	1·10	1·10
2952	**2167**	81p. Victorian Lamp Letter Box...............	1·25	1·25
2953	**2168**	90p. Elizabeth II Type A Wall Letter Box	1·25	1·25
Set of 4...			4·25	4·25
MS2954 145×74 mm **2169** Post Boxes Nos. 2950/2953...			4·25	4·25
First Day Cover (Tallents House).................................				5·00
First Day Cover (Wakefield, West Yorkshire)................				5·00
Presentation Pack (PO Pack No. 430)........................			4·75	
PHQ Cards (set of 5) (326)..			1·50	9·25

Nos. 2950/2953 were only issued in the £8·18 Treasures of the Archive booklet, No. DX46 and in No. **MS**2954.

T **2165** was also issued in sheets of 20 with *se-tenant* labels showing post boxes (No. LS65), sold for £8·35 per sheet.

The five PHQ cards show the four individual stamps and the miniature sheet.

929 Queen Victoria and Queen Elizabeth II
1446 Queen Victoria and Queen Elizabeth II 

(Litho Cartor)

2009 (18 Aug). Treasures of the Archive (1st series). Booklet stamps. Designs as T **929** (1990 150th anniversary of the Penny Black) and T **1446** (with redrawn 1st face value). Printed in lithography. Two phosphor bands. Perf 14½×14 (with one elliptical hole in each vert side).

2955	**929**	20p. brownish-black and grey-brown...	80	80
		a. Booklet pane. Nos. 2955/2956, each×4 with central label and margins all round............................	7·00	
2956	**1446**	(1st) brownish-black and grey-brown...	1·25	1·25

Nos. 2955/2956 were only issued in the £8·18 Treasures of the Archive booklet, No. DX46.

For Nos. 2955/2956 printed gravure see Nos. 2133/2133a.
Also see Nos. 1478, **MS**1501 and **MS**3695.

QUEEN ELIZABETH II/2009

919 Royal Mail Coach

(Litho Cartor)

2009 (18 Aug). Treasures of the Archive (2nd series). Booklet stamps. Design as T **919** (1989 Lord Mayor's Show). Multicoloured 'All-over' phosphor. Perf 14.

2957	919	20p. Royal Mail Coach. Multicoloured....	1·50	1·50
		a. Booklet pane. No. 2957×4 with margins all round..............	6·00	

No. 2957 was only issued in the £8·18 Treasures of the Archive booklet, No. DX46.

2170 Firefighting    **2171** Chemical Fire

2172 Emergency Rescue    **2173** Flood Rescue

2174 Search and Rescue    **2175** Fire Safety

(Des Rose Design. Gravure De La Rue)

2009 (1 Sept). Fire and Rescue Service. Multicoloured 'All-over' phosphor. Perf 14×14½.

2958	2170	(1st) Firefighting..............................	1·20	1·00
2959	2171	54p. Chemical Fire........................	90	90
2960	2172	56p. Emergency Rescue...............	1·10	1·10
2961	2173	62p. Flood Rescue........................	1·25	1·25
2962	2174	81p. Search and Rescue...............	1·25	1·40
2963	2175	90p. Fire Safety............................	1·40	1·40
Set of 6...			6·25	6·25
Set of 6 Gutter Pairs...			12·50	
First Day Cover (Tallents House)............................				7·50
First Day Cover (Hose, Melton Mowbray)............				7·50
Presentation Pack (PO Pack No. 429)...................			6·75	
PHQ Cards (set of 6) (325)......................................			1·75	7·50

2176 Flight Deck Officer, 2009    **2177** Captain, 1941    **2178** Second Officer WRNS, 1918

2179 Able Seaman, 1880    **2180** Royal Marine, 1805    **2181** Admiral, 1795

(Des Graham Turner and Atelier Works. Litho Cartor)

2009 (17 Sept). Military Uniforms (3rd series). Royal Navy Uniforms. Multicoloured Phosphor background. Perf 14.

2964	2176	(1st) Flight Deck Officer........................	1·20	1·00
		a. Horiz strip of 3. Nos. 2964/2966.....	3·50	3·00
		b. Booklet pane. Nos. 2964/2966 with margins all round..............	3·50	
2965	2177	(1st) Captain..	1·20	1·00
2966	2178	(1st) Second Officer WRNS....................	1·20	1·00
2967	2179	90p. Able Seaman.................................	1·40	1·40
		a. Horiz strip of 3. Nos. 2967/2969.....	4·00	4·00
		b. Booklet pane. Nos. 2967/2969 with margins all round..............	4·00	
2968	2180	90p. Royal Marine.................................	1·40	1·40
2969	2181	90p. Admiral..	1·40	1·40
Set of 6...			7·00	6·50
Set of 2 Gutter Strips of 6.......................................			14·00	
Set of 2 Traffic Light Gutter Blocks of 12.............			30·00	
First Day Cover (Tallents House)............................				7·75
First Day Cover (Portsmouth)................................				7·75
Presentation Pack (PO Pack No. 431)....................			7·50	
PHQ Cards (set of 6) (327)......................................			21·00	13·00

Nos. 2964/2966 and 2967/2969 were each printed together, *se-tenant*, as horizontal strips of three in sheets of 60 (2 panes 6×5).

Booklet panes Nos. 2964b and 2967b were from the £7·93 Royal Navy Uniforms booklet, No. DX47.

1518 Jolly Roger flown by HMS *Proteus* (submarine)

(Litho Cartor)

2009 (17 Sept). Royal Navy Uniforms. Booklet stamp. Design as T **1518** (Jolly Roger flag from 2001 Submarine Centenary). Multicoloured Two phosphor bands. Perf 14½.

2970	1518	(1st) Jolly Roger flown by HMS *Proteus* (submarine)..............................	4·75	6·00
		a. Booklet pane. Nos. 2970 and 2581, each×2 with margins all round....................................	7·00	

No. 2970 was only issued in the £7·93 Royal Navy Uniforms booklet, No. DX47.

2009/QUEEN ELIZABETH II

2182 Fred Perry 1909–1995 (lawn tennis champion)

2183 Henry Purcell 1659–1695 (composer and musician)

2184 Sir Matt Busby 1909–1994 (footballer and football manager)

2185 William Gladstone 1809–1898 (statesman and Prime Minister)

2186 Mary Wollstonecraft 1759–1797 (pioneering feminist)

2187 Sir Arthur Conan Doyle 1859–1930 (writer and creator of Sherlock Holmes)

2188 Donald Campbell 1921–1967 (water speed record broken 1959)

2189 Judy Fryd 1909–2000 (campaigner and founder of MENCAP)

2190 Samuel Johnson 1709–1784 (lexicographer, critic and poet)

2191 Sir Martin Ryle 1918–1984 (radio survey of the Universe 1959)

(Des Together Design. Litho Cartor)

2009 (8 Oct). Eminent Britons. Multicoloured Phosphor background. Perf 14½.

2971	2182	(1st) Fred Perry	1·20	1·00
		a. Horiz strip of 5. Nos. 2971/2975	5·25	4·50
2972	2183	(1st) Henry Purcell	1·20	1·00
2973	2184	(1st) Sir Matt Busby	1·20	1·00
2974	2185	(1st) William Gladstone	1·20	1·00
2975	2186	(1st) Mary Wollstonecraft	1·20	1·00
2976	2187	(1st) Sir Arthur Conan Doyle	1·20	1·00
		a. Horiz strip of 5. Nos. 2976/2980	5·25	4·50
2977	2188	(1st) Donald Campbell	1·20	1·00
2978	2189	(1st) Judy Fryd	1·20	1·00
2979	2190	(1st) Samuel Johnson	1·20	1·00
2980	2191	(1st) Sir Martin Ryle	1·20	1·00
Set of 10			10·50	9·00

Set of 2 Gutter Strips of 10	21·00	
First Day Cover (Tallents House)		9·25
First Day Cover (Britannia, Bacup, Lancashire)		9·25
Presentation Pack (PO Pack No. 432)	11·00	
PHQ Cards (set of 10) (328)	3·00	9·75

Nos. 2971/2975 and 2976/2980 were each printed together, se-tenant, as horizontal strips of five stamps in sheets of 50 (2 panes 5×5).
No. 2980 includes the EUROPA emblem.

2192 Canoe Slalom

2193 Paralympic Games Archery

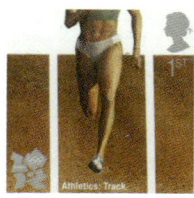

2194 Athletics, Track

2195 Diving

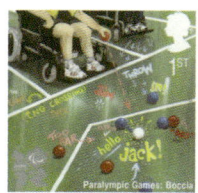

2196 Paralympic Games, Boccia

2197 Judo

2198 Paralympic Games, Dressage

2199 Badminton

2200 Weightlifting

2201 Basketball

(Des John Royle (No. 2981), George Hardie (No. 2982), Nathalie Guinamard (No. 2983), Julian Opie (No. 2984), David Doyle (No. 2985), Paul Slater (No. 2986), Andrew Davidson (No. 2987), David Holmes (No. 2988), Guy Billout (No. 2989), Huntley Muir (No. 2990) and Studio David Hillman (all). Litho Cartor)

2009 (22 Oct)–**2012**. Olympic and Paralympic Games, London (2012) (1st issue). Multicoloured 'All-over' phosphor. Perf 14½.

2981	2192	(1st) Canoe Slalom	1·20	1·00
		a. Horiz strip of 5. Nos. 2981/2985	5·25	4·50
2982	2193	(1st) Paralympic Games Archery	1·20	1·00
		b. Booklet pane. Nos. 2982 and 2987 with margins all round (27.7.12)	3·75	
2983	2194	(1st) Athletics, Track	1·20	1·00

QUEEN ELIZABETH II/2009

		b. Booklet pane. Nos. 2983 and 3104 with margins all round (27.7.12)	3·75	
2984	2195	(1st) Diving	1·20	1·00
		b. Booklet pane. Nos. 2984 and 3196 with margins all round (27.7.12)	3·75	
2985	2196	(1st) Paralympic Games Boccia	1·20	1·00
2986	2197	(1st) Judo	1·20	1·00
		a. Horiz strip of 5. Nos. 2986/2990	5·25	4·50
2987	2198	(1st) Paralympic Games Dressage	1·20	1·00
2988	2199	(1st) Badminton	1·20	1·00
2989	2200	(1st) Weightlifting	1·20	1·00
2990	2201	(1st) Basketball	1·20	1·00
Set of 10			10·50	9·00
Set of 2 Gutter Strips of 5			21·00	
First Day Cover (Tallents House)				9·25
First Day Cover (Badminton, Glos)				9·25
Presentation Pack (PO Pack No. M18)			11·00	
PHQ Cards (set of 10) (OXPG1)			3·00	10·00

Nos. 2981/2985 and 2986/2990 were each printed together, *se-tenant*, as horizontal strips of five stamps in sheets of 50 (2 panes 5×5).
See also Nos. 3020/3023.

2202 Angel playing Lute 
2203 Madonna and Child 
2204 Angel playing Lute

2205 Joseph 
2206 Madonna and Child 
2207 Wise Man

2208 Shepherd

(Des Andrew Ross. Gravure De La Rue)

2009 (3 Nov). Christmas. Stained-glass Windows. Multicoloured. One centre band (No. 2202) or two phosphor bands (others). Perf 14½×14 (with one elliptical hole in each vert side).

(a) Self-adhesive.

2991	2202	(2nd) Angel playing Lute	90	90
		a. Booklet pane. No. 2991×12	13·50	
2992	2203	(1st) Madonna and Child	1·20	1·00
		a. Booklet pane. No. 2992×12	16·00	
2993	2204	(2nd Angel playing Lute Large)	1·25	1·10
2994	2205	56p. Joseph	1·10	1·10
2995	2206	(1st Madonna and Child Large)	1·70	1·40
2996	2207	90p. Wise Man	1·75	1·75
2997	2208	£1·35 Shepherd	2·40	2·40
Set of 7			9·25	8·75
First Day Cover (Tallents House)				9·00
First Day Cover (Bethlehem, Llandeilo)				9·00
Presentation Pack (PO Pack No. 433)			9·50	
PHQ Cards (set of 8) (328)			2·40	17·50

(b) Ordinary gum.

MS2998 115×102 mm. As Nos. 2991/2997			9·25	8·75
First Day Cover (Tallents House)				9·00
First Day Cover (Bethlehem, Llandeilo)				9·00

The 2nd class, 1st class, 56p and 90p stamps were also issued together in sheets of 20 (No. LS67), sold for £9, containing eight 2nd class, eight 1st class, two 56p and two 90p stamps, each stamp accompanied by a *se-tenant* label.

Separate sheets of 20 2nd, 20 1st, ten 1st, ten 56p and ten 90p were available with personal photographs from Royal Mail, Edinburgh. These were sold at £7·50 for ten 1st, £9·50 for 20 2nd or ten 56p or £13·50 for 20 1st or ten 90p.

All these sheets were printed in lithography by Cartor and had the backing paper around the stamps retained.

For the 2nd class stamp printed in lithography with ordinary gum see No. 3186*a*.

The eight PHQ cards show the seven stamps and No. **MS**2998.

For Nos. U3045/U3052 see Decimal Machin Definitives section.

Year Pack

2009 (3 Nov). Comprises Nos. 2887/2896, 2898/**MS**2904, 2916/**MS**2941, 2944/2949, **MS**2954, 2958/2969, 2971/2997, **MS**S157 and **MS**W147.
CP2998*a*   Year Pack (PO Pack No. 434) (*sold for £60*) .... 95·00

Post Office Yearbook

2009 (3 Nov). Comprises Nos. 2887/2896, 2898/**MS**2904, 2916/**MS**2941, 2944/2949, **MS**2954, 2958/2969, 2971/2997, **MS**S157 and **MS**W147.
YB2998*a*   Yearbook (*sold for £65*) .... 95·00

Miniature Sheet Collection

2009 (3 Nov). Comprises Nos. **MS**2904, **MS**2930, **MS**2941, **MS**2954, **MS**2998, **MS**S157 and **MS**W147.
MS2998*a* Miniature Sheet Collection (*sold for £21·30*) .... 32·00

2209 *The Division Bell* (Pink Floyd) 
2210 *A Rush of Blood to the Head* (Coldplay)

2211 *Parklife* (Blur) 
2212 *Power Corruption and Lies* (New Order)

2213 *Let It Bleed* (Rolling Stones) 
2214 *London Calling* (The Clash)

2215 *Tubular Bells* (Mike Oldfield) 
2216 *Led Zeppelin IV* (Led Zeppelin)

2217 *Screamadelica* (Primal Scream)
2218 *The Rise and Fall of Ziggy Stardust and the Spiders from Mars* (David Bowie)

(Des Studio Dempsey)

2010 (7 Jan). Classic Album Covers (1st issue). Multicoloured 'All-over' phosphor.

(a) Self-adhesive. Gravure De La Rue. Die-cut Perf 14½ (interrupted).

2999	2209	(1st) *The Division Bell* (Pink Floyd)	1·20	1·00
		a. Horiz strip of 5. Nos. 2999/3003	5·25	—
3000	2210	(1st) *A Rush of Blood to the Head* (Coldplay)	1·20	1·00
3001	2211	(1st) *Parklife* (Blur)	1·20	1·00
3002	2212	(1st) *Power Corruption and Lies* (New Order)	1·20	1·00
3003	2213	(1st) *Let It Bleed* (Rolling Stones)	1·20	1·00

2010/QUEEN ELIZABETH II

3004	2214	(1st) *London Calling* (The Clash)...............	1·20	1·00
		a. Horiz strip of 5. Nos. 3004/3008......	5·25	—
3005	2215	(1st) *Tubular Bells* (Mike Oldfield)............	1·20	1·00
3006	2216	(1st) *IV* (Led Zeppelin)............................	1·20	1·00
3007	2217	(1st) *Screamadelica* (Primal Scream).......	1·20	1·00
3008	2218	(1st) *The Rise and Fall of Ziggy Stardust and the Spiders from Mars* (David Bowie)..	1·20	1·00
Set of 10...			10·50	9·00
First Day Cover (Tallents House)...				9·25
First Day Cover (Oldfield, Keighley)....................................				9·25
Presentation Pack (PO Pack No. 435)..................................			11·00	
PHQ Cards (set of 10) (330)..			4·00	12·00

Nos. 2999/3003 and 3004/3008 were each printed together, as horizontal strips of five stamps in sheets of 50 (2 panes of 25).

The right-hand edges of Nos. 2999/3008 are all cut around to show the vinyl disc protruding from the open edge of the album cover.

MS3019

2010 (7 Jan). Classic Album Covers (2nd issue). Multicoloured 'All-over' phosphor. Litho Cartor. Perf 14½ (interrupted).

3009	2213	(1st) *Let It Bleed* (Rolling Stones).............	1·25	1·25
		a. Booklet pane. Nos. 3009/3014......	7·75	
3010	2216	(1st) *Led Zeppelin IV* (Led Zeppelin).........	1·25	1·25
3011	2218	(1st) *The Rise and Fall of Ziggy Stardust and the Spiders from Mars* (David Bowie)..	1·25	1·25
3012	2212	(1st) *Power Corruption and Lies* (New Order)...	1·25	1·25
3013	2217	(1st) *Screamadelica* (Primal Scream).......	1·25	1·25
3014	2209	(1st) *The Division Bell* (Pink Floyd)..........	1·25	1·25
3015	2215	(1st) *Tubular Bells* (Mike Oldfield)............	1·25	1·25
		a. Booklet pane. Nos. 3015/3018......	5·25	
3016	2214	(1st) *London Calling* (The Clash)...............	1·25	1·25
3017	2211	(1st) *Parklife* (Blur)...................................	1·25	1·25
3018	2210	(1st) *A Rush of Blood to the Head* (Coldplay)..	1·25	1·25
Set of 10...			13·00	13·00
MS3019 223×189 mm. Nos. 3009/3018............................			25·00	25·00
First Day Cover (Tallents House)...				25·00
First Day Cover (Oldfield, Keighley)....................................				25·00

Nos. 3009/3018 were only issued in the £8·06 Classic Album Covers booklet, No. DX48 and in No. **MS**3019.

The right-hand edges of Nos. 3009/3018 and the miniature sheet No. **MS**3019 are all cut around in an imperforate section to show the vinyl disc protruding from the open edge of the album cover.

A miniature sheet containing No. 3014×10 *The Division Bell* (Pink Floyd) was issued on 6 March 2010 and sold for £4·75 per sheet.

2194 Athletics, Track  **2201** Basketball

(Gravure Walsall)

2010 (7 Jan–25 Feb). Olympic and Paralympic Games, London (2012) (2nd issue). Booklet stamps. Designs as Nos. 2982/2983, 2986 and 2990. Self-adhesive. Multicoloured 'All-over' phosphor. Die-cut Perf 14½.

3020	2197	(1st) Judo...	2·00	2·00
		a. Booklet pane. Nos. 3020/3021 and U2983×4........................	7·50	
3021	2193	(1st) Paralympic Games Archery............	2·00	2·00
3022	2194	(1st) Athletics, Track (25.2.10)................	2·00	2·00
		a. Booklet pane. Nos. 3022/3023 and U3016×4........................	7·50	
3023	2201	(1st) Basketball (25.2.10)........................	2·00	2·00
Set of 4...			5·50	5·50

Nos. 3020/3021 and 3022/3023 were only issued in separate booklets, Nos. PM21/PM22, each sold for £2·34.

2219 Smilers

(Des Hat-trick Design. Litho Cartor)

2010 (26 Jan). Business and Consumer Smilers. Sheet 124×71 mm. Multicoloured Two phosphor bands. Perf 14½×14 (with one elliptical hole in each vertical side).

MS3024 **2219** Smilers (1st) Propellor driven aircraft (Andrew Davidson); (1st) Vintage sports roadster (Andrew Davidson); (1st) Recreation of crown seal (Neil Oliver); (1st) Birthday cake (Annabel Wright); (1st) Steam locomotive (Andrew Davidson); (1st) Ocean liner (Andrew Davidson); (1st) Six poppies on barbed wire stems; (1st) Birthday present (Annabel Wright); (Europe up to 20 grams) Bird carrying envelope (Lucy Davey); (Worldwide up to 20 grams) 'hello' in aeroplane vapour trail (Lucy Davey)...			12·50	10·00
First Day Cover (Tallents House)...				10·50
Presentation Pack (PO Pack No. M19)..................................			13·00	
PHQ Cards (set of 11) (D31)..			4·25	20·00

No. **MS**3024 was sold for £4·58.

Stamps in designs as within No. **MS**3024 but self-adhesive were available printed together, *se-tenant*, in sheets of 20 containing two of each design with greetings labels (No. LS70), sold for £9·70 per sheet.

The (1st) birthday cake, (1st) birthday present, Europe and Worldwide designs were also available in separate sheets with personal photographs.

A stamp as the crown seal design in No. **MS**3024 but self-adhesive was issued on 15 September 2011 in sheets of 20 with postmark labels for the 350th Anniversary of the Postmark, No. LS78 sold for £9·50.

The other 1st class designs were for the business customised service.

Stamps as the (1st) birthday cake (×4), (1st) birthday present (×4), Europe bird carrying envelope (×2) and Worldwide 'hello' in aeroplane vapour trail (×2) designs but self-adhesive were issued together with Nos. 2572, 2674, 2693 and 2821/2823 on 8 May 2010 in sheets of 20 stamps with *se-tenant* greetings labels printed in lithography by Cartor, (No. LS73), and sold for £10 per sheet.

The 11 PHQ cards show the ten individual stamps and the complete miniature sheet.

2197 Judo   **2193** Paralympic Games Archery

2220 Girlguiding UK

QUEEN ELIZABETH II/2010

(Des Together Design. Litho Cartor)

2010 (2 Feb). Centenary of Girlguiding. Sheet 190×67 mm. Multicoloured Phosphor background. Perf 14×14½.

MS3025	**2220**	Girlguiding UK (1st) Rainbows; 56p. Brownies; 81p. Guides; 90p. Senior Section members	4·25	4·50
		First Day Cover (Tallents House)		5·25
		First Day Cover (Guide, Blackburn)		5·25
		Presentation Pack (PO Pack No. 436)	5·50	
		PHQ Cards (set of 5) (331)	2·00	9·00

The five PHQ cards show the four individual stamps and the complete miniature sheet.

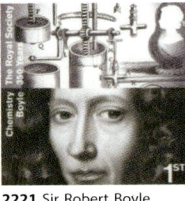

2221 Sir Robert Boyle (chemistry)

2222 Sir Isaac Newton (optics)

2223 Benjamin Franklin (electricity)

2224 Edward Jenner (pioneer of smallpox vaccination)

2225 Charles Babbage (computing)

2226 Alfred Russel Wallace (theory of evolution)

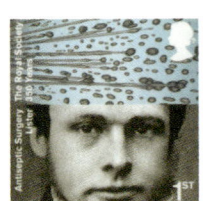

2227 Joseph Lister (antiseptic surgery)

2228 Ernest Rutherford (atomic structure)

2229 Dorothy Hodgkin (crystallography)

2230 Sir Nicholas Shackleton (earth sciences)

(Des Hat-trick Design. Litho Cartor)

2010 (25 Feb). 350th Anniversary of the Royal Society. Multicoloured 'All-over' phosphor. Perf 14½.

3026	**2221**	(1st) Sir Robert Boyle	1·20	1·00
		a. Block of 10. Nos. 3026/3035	10·50	9·00
		b. Booklet pane. Nos. 3026, 3030/3031 and 3035 with margins all round	4·25	
3027	**2222**	(1st) Sir Isaac Newton	1·20	1·00
		a. Booklet pane. Nos. 3027/3028 and 3033×2 with margins all round	4·25	
3028	**2223**	(1st) Benjamin Franklin	1·20	1·00
3029	**2224**	(1st) Edward Jenner	1·20	1·00
		a. Booklet pane. Nos. 3029×2, 3032 and 3034 with margins all round	4·25	
3030	**2225**	(1st) Charles Babbage	1·20	1·00
3031	**2226**	(1st) Alfred Russell Wallace	1·20	1·00
3032	**2227**	(1st) Joseph Lister	1·20	1·00
3033	**2228**	(1st) Ernest Rutherford	1·20	1·00
3034	**2229**	(1st) Dorothy Hodgkin	1·20	1·00
3035	**2230**	(1st) Sir Nicholas Shackleton	1·20	1·00
		Set of 10	10·50	9·00
		Gutter Block of 20	21·00	
		First Day Cover (Tallents House)		10·00
		First Day Cover (London SW1)		10·00
		Presentation Pack (PO Pack No. 437)	11·00	
		PHQ Cards (set of 10) (332)	4·00	11·50

Nos. 3026/3035 were printed together, *se-tenant*, as blocks of ten (5×2) in sheets of 60 (2 panes of 30).

Booklet panes Nos. 3026b, 3027a and 3029a come from the £7·72 350th Anniversary of The Royal Society booklet, No. DX49.

2231 Pixie (mastiff cross)

2232 Button

2233 Herbie (mongrel)

2234 Mr Tumnus

2235 Tafka (border collie)

2236 Boris (bulldog cross)

2237 Casey (lurcher)

2238 Tigger

2010/**QUEEN ELIZABETH II**

2239 Leonard (Jack Russell cross)
2240 Tia (terrier cross) 

(Des CDT Design. Litho Cartor)

2010 (11 Mar). 150th Anniversary of Battersea Dogs and Cats Home. Multicoloured. Phosphor background. Perf 14½.

3036	2231	(1st) Pixie (mastiff cross)	1·20	1·00
		a. Block of 10. Nos. 3036/3045	10·50	9·00
3037	2232	(1st) Button	1·20	1·00
3038	2233	(1st) Herbie (mongrel)	1·20	1·00
3039	2234	(1st) Mr Tumnus	1·20	1·00
3040	2235	(1st) Tafka (border collie)	1·20	1·00
3041	2236	(1st) Boris (bulldog cross)	1·20	1·00
3042	2237	(1st) Casey (lurcher)	1·20	1·00
3043	2238	(1st) Tigger	1·20	1·00
3044	2239	(1st) Leonard (Jack Russell cross)	1·20	1·00
3045	2240	(1st) Tia (terrier cross)	1·20	1·00
Set of 10			10·50	9·00
Gutter Block of 20			21·00	
First Day Cover (Tallents House)				9·50
First Day Cover (London SW8)				9·50
Presentation Pack (PO Pack No. 438)			11·00	
PHQ Cards (set of 10) (333)			4·00	11·50

Nos. 3036/3045 were printed together, *se-tenant*, as blocks of ten (5×2) in sheets of 60 (2 panes of 30).

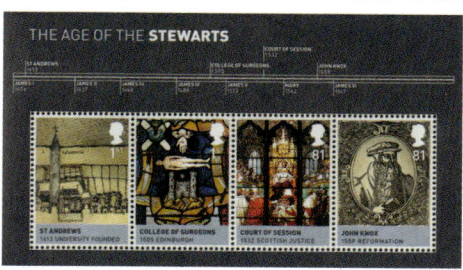

2248 The Age of the Stewarts

(Des Atelier Works. Litho Cartor)

2010 (23 Mar). Kings and Queens (3rd issue). House of Stewart. Multicoloured Two phosphor bands. Perf 14.

3046	2241	(1st) James I	1·20	1·00
3047	2242	(1st) James II	1·20	1·00
3048	2243	(1st) James III	1·20	1·00
3049	2244	62p. James IV	1·00	1·00
3050	2245	62p. James V	1·00	1·00
3051	2246	81p. Mary	1·25	1·25
3052	2247	81p. James VI	1·25	1·25
Set of 7			7·25	6·75
Set of 7 Gutter Pairs			14·50	
Set of 7 Traffic Light Gutter Blocks of 4			32·00	
First Day Cover (Tallents House)				8·00
First Day Cover (Linlithgow, West Lothian)				8·00
Presentation Pack (PO Pack No. 439) (Nos. 3046/ MS3053)			12·00	
PHQ Cards (set of 12) (334)			4·75	11·50
MS3053 123×70 mm. **2248** The Age of the Stewarts (1st) Foundation of the University of St Andrews, 1413; (1st) Foundation of the College of Surgeons, Edinburgh, 1505; 81p. Foundation of Court of Session, 1532; 81p. John Knox (Reformation, 1559)			4·25	4·25
First Day Cover (Tallents House)				4·75
First Day Cover (Linlithgow, West Lothian)				4·75

The complete miniature sheet is shown on one of the 12 PHQ cards with the others depicting individual stamps including those from No. **MS**3053.

2241 James I (1406–1437)
2242 James II (1437–1460)
2243 James III (1460–1488)

2244 James IV (1488–1513)
2245 James V (1513–1542)
2246 Mary (1542–1567)

2247 James VI (1567–1625)

2249 Humpback Whale (*Megaptera novaeangliae*) 
2250 Wildcat (*Felis silvestris*)

2251 Brown Long-eared Bat (*Plecotus auritus*) 
2252 Polecat (*Mustela putorius*)

2253 Sperm Whale (*Physeter macrocephalus*)
2254 Water Vole (*Arvicola terrestris*) 

213

QUEEN ELIZABETH II/2010

2255 Greater Horseshoe Bat (*Rhinolophus ferrumequinum*)
2256 Otter (*Lutra lutra*) 
2257 Dormouse (*Muscardinus avellanarius*) 
2258 Hedgehog (*Erinaceus europaeus*) 

2261 King George V and Queen Elizabeth II
2262 1924 British Empire Exhibition 1½d. Brown Stamp
2263 1924 British Empire Exhibition 1d. Scarlet Stamp
2264 Two Portraits of King George V
2265 1913 £1 Green Sea Horses Design Stamp
2266 1913 10s. Blue Sea Horses Design Stamp

(Des Jason Godfrey. Litho Cartor)

2010 (13 Apr). Action for Species (4th series). Mammals. Multicoloured 'All-over' phosphor. Perf 14½.

3054	**2249**	(1st) Humpback Whale	1·20	1·00
		a. Block of 10. Nos. 3054/3063	10·50	9·00
3055	**2250**	(1st) Wildcat	1·20	1·00
3056	**2251**	(1st) Brown Long-eared Bat	1·20	1·00
3057	**2252**	(1st) Polecat	1·20	1·00
3058	**2253**	(1st) Sperm Whale	1·20	1·00
3059	**2254**	(1st) Water Vole	1·20	1·00
3060	**2255**	(1st) Greater Horseshoe Bat	1·20	1·00
3061	**2256**	(1st) Otter	1·20	1·00
3062	**2257**	(1st) Dormouse	1·20	1·00
3063	**2258**	(1st) Hedgehog	1·20	1·00
Set of 10			10·50	9·00
Gutter Block of 20			21·00	
First Day Cover (Tallents House)				9·50
First Day Cover (Batts Corner, Farnham)				9·50
Presentation Pack (PO Pack No. 440)			11·00	
PHQ Cards (set of 10) (335)			4·00	11·00

Nos. 3054/3063 were printed together, *se-tenant*, as blocks of ten (5×2) in sheets of 60 (2 panes of 30).
See also Nos. 3095/3096.

No. 3064, T **2259** is vacant.

2260 King George V and Queen Elizabeth II (1st); Two portraits of King George V (£1)

(Des Sedley Place. Litho Cartor)

2010 (6 May). London 2010 Festival of Stamps and Centenary of Accession of King George V (1st issue). 'All-over' phosphor. Perf 14½×14.
MS3065 141×74 mm **2260** (1st) rosine; £1 blackish brown, grey-brown and silver .... 3·75 4·00
First Day Cover (Tallents House) .... 12·00
First Day Cover (Sandringham, Norfolk) .... 12·00

A miniature sheet as No. **MS**3065 but inscr 'BUSINESS DESIGN CENTRE, LONDON 8–15 MAY 2010' along the top right margin was only available at London 2010 Festival of Stamps (*Price* £9·75).

The eight PHQ cards depict the individual stamps from Nos. **MS**3065 and **MS**3072 and the complete miniature sheets.

2267

(Des Sedley Place. Litho Cartor (Nos. 3066 and 3069) or recess and litho Enschedé (others))

2010 (6–8 May). London 2010 Festival of Stamps and Centenary of Accession of King George V (2nd issue). (except Nos. 3066, 3069) 'All-over' phosphor. Perf 14½×14.

3066	**2261**	(1st) rosine (6.5.10)	1·25	1·25
		a. Booklet pane. Nos. 3066 and 3069, each×3 with margins all round (8.5.10)	9·50	
3067	**2262**	(1st) 1924 British Empire Exhibition 1½d. Brown Stamp (8.5.10)	1·50	1·50
		a. Booklet pane. Nos. 3067/3068, each×2	6·00	
3068	**2263**	(1st) 1924 British Empire Exhibition 1d. Scarlet Stamp (8.5.10)	1·50	1·50
3069	**2264**	£1 blackish brown, grey-brown and silver (8.5.10)	2·50	2·50

3070	**2265**	£1 1913 £1 Green Sea Horses Design Stamp (8.5.10)	2·25	2·25
		a. Booklet pane. Nos. 3070/3071 with margins all round	4·50	
3071	**2266**	£1 1913 10s. Blue Sea Horses Design Stamp (8.5.10)	2·25	2·25
Set of 6			11·00	11·00
Gutter Pair (No. 3066)			2·50	
MS3072 115×90 mm **2267** Nos. 3067/3068 and 3070/3071 (8.5.10)			4·50	4·75
First Day Cover (Tallents House) (No. **MS**3072)				12·00
First Day Cover (London N1) (No. **MS**3072)				12·00
Presentation Pack (PO Pack No. 441) (Nos. **MS**3065 and **MS**3072)			8·50	
PHQ Cards (set of 8) (336)			3·25	13·00

No. 3066 was also issued as a sheet stamp on 6 May 2010.

Nos. 3066/3071 come from the £11·15 1910–1936, King George V booklet, No. DX50.

Nos. 3066 and 3069 also come from No. **MS**3065, issued on 6 May 2010.

Nos. 3067/3068 and 3070/3071 also come from No. **MS**3072, issued on 8 May 2010.

For presentation pack and PHQ cards for No. **MS**3072 see under **MS**3065. The eight PHQ cards depict the individual stamps from Nos. **MS**3065 and **MS**3072 and the complete miniature sheets.

For No. **MS**3073, T **2268**, see Decimal Machin Definitives section.

2269 Winston Churchill

2270 Land Girl

2271 Home Guard

2272 Evacuees

2273 Air Raid Wardens

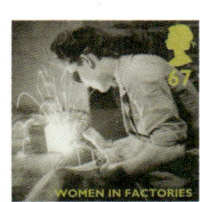

2274 Woman working in Factory

2275 Royal Broadcast by Princess Elizabeth and Princess Margaret

2276 Fire Service

(Des Why Not Associates. Litho Cartor)

2010 (13 May). Britain Alone (1st issue). Pale stone, pale bistre and black. 'All-over' phosphor. Perf 14½.

3074	**2269**	(1st) Winston Churchill	1·20	1·00
		a. Booklet pane. Nos. 3074/3075 and 3079/3080 with margins all round	4·50	
3075	**2270**	(1st) Land Girl	1·20	1·00
3076	**2271**	60p. Home Guard	90	90
		a. Booklet pane. Nos. 3076/3078 and 3081	4·50	
3077	**2272**	60p. Evacuees	90	90
3078	**2273**	67p. Air Raid Wardens	1·00	1·00
3079	**2274**	67p. Woman working in Factory	1·00	1·00
3080	**2275**	97p. Royal Broadcast by Princess Elizabeth and Princess Margaret	1·40	1·40
3081	**2276**	97p. Fire Service	1·40	1·40
Set of 8			7·75	7·50
Set of 8 Gutter Pairs			15·50	
First Day Cover (Tallents House)				8·50
First Day Cover (Dover, Kent)				8·50
Presentation Pack (PO Pack No. 442) (Nos. 3074/3081 and **MS**3086)			13·00	
PHQ Cards (set of 13) (337)			5·25	11·00

Booklet panes Nos. 3074a and 3076a come from the £9·76 Britain Alone booklet, No. DX51.

The 13 PHQ cards depict Nos. 3074/3085 and the complete miniature sheet No. **MS**3086.

2277 Evacuation of British Soldiers from Dunkirk

2278 Vessels from Upper Thames Patrol in Operation Little Ships

2279 Rescued Soldiers on Board Royal Navy Destroyer, Dover

2280 Steamship and Other Boat loaded with Troops

2281 Evacuation of British Troops from Dunkirk, 1940

(Des Why Not Associates. Litho Cartor)

2010 (13 May). Britain Alone (2nd issue). Pale stone, pale bistre and black. 'All-over' phosphor. Perf 14½.

3082	**2277**	(1st) Evacuation of British Soldiers	1·40	1·40
		a. Booklet pane. Nos. 3082/3085 with margins all round	5·00	
3083	**2278**	60p. Vessels from Upper Thames Patrol	1·40	1·40
3084	**2279**	88p. Rescued Soldiers	1·40	1·40
3085	**2280**	97p. Steamship and Other Boat loaded with Troops	1·40	1·40
Set of 4			5·00	5·00
MS3086 115×89 mm. **2281** Evacuation of British Troops from Dunkirk, 1940 Nos. 3082/3085			5·00	5·00
First Day Cover (Tallents House) (No. **MS**3086)				5·50
First Day Cover (Dover, Kent) (No. **MS**3086)				5·50

Nos. 3082/3085 were only issued in the £9·76 Britain Alone booklet, No. DX51, and in No. **MS**3086.

QUEEN ELIZABETH II/2010

2282 James I (1603–1625) 
2283 Charles I (1625–1649) 
2284 Charles II (1660–1685) 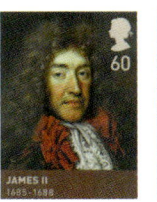
2285 James II (1685–1688) 
2286 William III (1689–1702) 
2287 Mary II (1689–1694) 
2288 Anne (1702–1714)

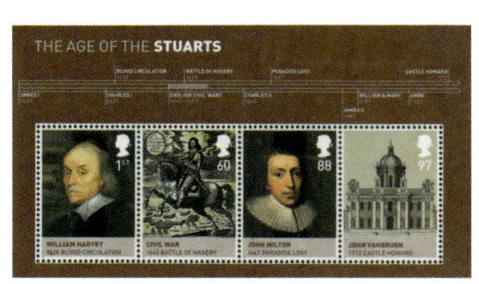

2289 The Age of the Stuarts

(Des Atelier Works. Litho Cartor)

2010 (15 June). Kings and Queens (4th issue). House of Stuart. Multicoloured Two phosphor bands. Perf 14.

3087	**2282**	(1st) James I	1·20	1·00
3088	**2283**	(1st) Charles I	1·20	1·00
3089	**2284**	60p. Charles II	90	90
3090	**2285**	60p. James II	90	90
3091	**2286**	67p. William III	1·10	1·10
3092	**2287**	67p. Mary II	1·10	1·10
3093	**2288**	88p. Anne	1·40	1·40
Set of 7			6·75	6·50
Set of 7 Gutter Pairs			13·50	
Set of 7 Traffic Light Gutter Blocks of 4			30·00	
First Day Cover (Tallents House)				8·50
First Day Cover (Royal Oak, Filey)				8·50
Presentation Pack (PO Pack No. 443) (Nos. 3087/3093 and **MS**3094)			12·00	
PHQ Cards (set of 12) (338)			4·75	16·00

MS3094 123×70 mm. **2289** The Age of the Stuarts (1st) William Harvey (discovery of blood circulation, 1628); 60p. Civil War Battle of Naseby, 1645; 88p. John Milton (*Paradise Lost*, 1667); 97p. Castle Howard (John Vanbrugh, 1712) .... 4·75 4·75
First Day Cover (Tallents House) .... 5·00
First Day Cover (Royal Oak, Filey) .... 5·00

The complete miniature sheet is shown on one of the 12 PHQ cards with the others depicting individual stamps including those from No. **MS**3094.

2256 Otter (*Lutra lutra*)
2258 Hedgehog (*Erinaceus europaeus*) 

(Gravure Walsall)

2010 (15 June). Mammals. Booklet stamps. Designs as Nos. 3061 and 3063. Self-adhesive. Multicoloured Die-cut Perf 14½.

3095	**2256**	(1st) Otter	3·00	3·00
		a. Booklet pane. Nos. 3095/3096 and No. U3016×4	11·00	
3096	**2258**	(1st) Hedgehog	3·00	3·00

Nos. 3095/3096 were only issued in booklet, No. PM23.

2290 Paralympic Games, Rowing
2291 Shooting 
2292 Modern Pentathlon 
2293 Taekwondo 
2294 Cycling 
2295 Paralympic Games, Table Tennis 
2296 Hockey 
2297 Football 
2298 Paralympic Games, Goalball 
2299 Boxing

2010 / QUEEN ELIZABETH II

(Des Marion Hill (No. 3097), David Hillman (No. 3098), Katherine Baxter (No. 3099), James Fryer (No. 3100), Matthew Dennis (No. 3101), Michael Craig Martin (No. 3102), Darren Hopes (No. 3103), Alex Williamson (No. 3104), Tobatron (No. 3105), Stephen Ledwidge (No. 3106), Studio David Hillman (all). Litho Cartor)

2010 (27 July). Olympic and Paralympic Games, London (2012) (3rd issue). Multicoloured 'All-over' phosphor. Perf 14½.

3097	2290	(1st) Paralympic Games, Rowing	1·20	1·00
		a. Horiz strip of 5. Nos. 3097/3101	5·25	4·50
3098	2291	(1st) Shooting	1·20	1·00
3099	2292	(1st) Modern Pentathlon	1·20	1·00
3100	2293	(1st) Taekwondo	1·20	1·00
3101	2294	(1st) Cycling	1·20	1·00
3102	2295	(1st) Paralympic Games, Table Tennis	1·20	1·00
		a. Horiz strip of 5. Nos. 3102/3106	5·25	4·50
3103	2296	(1st) Hockey	1·20	1·00
3104	2297	(1st) Football	1·20	1·00
3105	2298	(1st) Paralympic Games, Goalball	1·20	1·00
3106	2299	(1st) Boxing	1·20	1·00
Set of 10			10·50	9·00
Set of 2 Gutter Strips of 10			21·00	
First Day Cover (Tallents House)				9·25
First Day Cover (Rowington, Warwick)				9·25
Presentation Pack (PO Pack No. 444)			11·00	
PHQ Cards (set of 10) (339)			4·00	11·00

Nos. 3097/3101 and 3102/3106 were each printed together, *se-tenant*, in horizontal strips of five stamps in sheets of 50 (2 panes 5×5).

(Gravure Walsall)

2010 (27 July–12 Oct). Olympic and Paralympic Games, London (2012) (4th issue). Booklet stamps. Designs as Nos. 3097, 3101/3102 and 3104. Self-adhesive. Multicoloured 'All-over' phosphor. Die-cut perf 14½.

3107	2290	(1st) Paralympic Games, Rowing	2·00	2·00
		a. Booklet pane. Nos. 3107/3108 and Nos. U3016×4	7·50	
3108	2295	(1st) Paralympic Games, Table Tennis	2·00	2·00
3108a	2297	(1st) Football (12.10.10)	2·00	2·00
		ab. Booklet pane. Nos. 3108a/3108b and U2932×4	7·50	
3108b	2294	(1st) Cycling (12.10.10)	2·00	2·00
Set of 4			7·50	7·50

Nos. 3107/3108 and 3108a/3108b were only issued in two separate stamp booklets, Nos. PM24 and PM26, each originally sold for £2·46.

(Des Delaney Design Consultants. Gravure De La Rue)

2010 (19 Aug). Great British Railways. Gold, bluish grey and black. 'All-over' phosphor. Perf 14.

3109	2300	(1st) LMS Coronation Class Locomotive	1·20	1·00
3110	2301	(1st) BR Class 9F Locomotive *Evening Star*	1·20	1·00
3111	2302	67p. GWR King Class Locomotive *King William IV*	90	90
3112	2303	67p. LNER Class A1 Locomotive *Royal Lancer*	90	90
3113	2304	97p. SR King Arthur Class Locomotive *Sir Mador de la Porte*	1·25	1·25
3114	2305	97p. LMS NCC Class WT No. 2	1·25	1·25
Set of 6			6·00	5·75
Set of 6 Gutter Pairs			12·00	
First Day Cover (Tallents House)				7·00
First Day Cover (Swindon)				7·00
Presentation Pack (PO Pack No. 445)			7·00	
PHQ Cards (set of 6) (340)			2·50	7·50

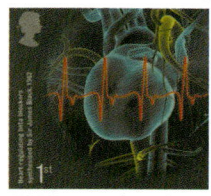

2300 LMS Coronation Class Locomotive, Euston Station, 1938

2301 BR Class 9F Locomotive *Evening Star*, Midsomer Norton, 1962

2302 GWR King Class Locomotive *King William IV*, near Teignmouth, 1935

2303 LNER Class A1 Locomotive *Royal Lancer*, 1929

2304 SR King Arthur Class Locomotive *Sir Mador de la Porte*, Bournemouth Central Station, 1935–1939

2305 LMS NCC Class WT No. 2, Larne Harbour, c 1947

2306 Heart-regulating Beta Blockers (Sir James Black, 1962)

2307 Antibiotic Properties of Penicillin (Sir Alexander Fleming, 1928)

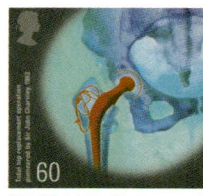

2308 Total Hip Replacement Operation (Sir John Charnley, 1962)

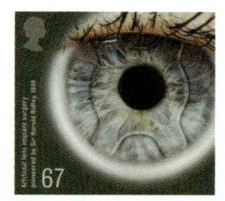

2309 Artificial Lens Implant Surgery (Sir Harold Ridley, 1949)

2310 Malaria Parasite transmitted by Mosquitoes (proved by Sir Ronald Ross, 1897)

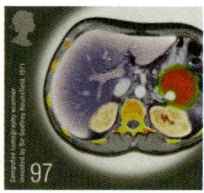

2311 Computed Tomography Scanner (Sir Godfrey Hounsfield, 1971)

(Des Howard Brown. Litho Cartor)

2010 (16 Sept). Medical Breakthroughs. Multicoloured 'All-over' phosphor. Perf 14×14½.

3115	2306	(1st) Heart-regulating Beta Blockers	1·20	1·00
3116	2307	58p. Antibiotic Properties of Penicillin	90	90
3117	2308	60p. Total Hip Replacement Operation	1·00	1·00
3118	2309	67p. Artificial Lens Implant Surgery	1·10	1·10
3119	2310	88p. Malaria Parasite transmitted by Mosquitoes	1·25	1·25
3120	2311	97p. Computed Tomography Scanner	1·40	1·40
Set of 6			6·00	6·00
Set of 6 Gutter Pairs			12·00	
First Day Cover (Tallents House)				8·00
First Day Cover (Paddington, London W2)				8·00
Presentation Pack (PO Pack No. 446)			7·25	
PHQ Cards (set of 6) (341)			2·50	7·50

See also No. 3153.

217

QUEEN ELIZABETH II/2010

2312 Winnie-the-Pooh and Christopher Robin (*Now we are Six*)

2313 Winnie-the-Pooh and Piglet (*The House at Pooh Corner*)

2314 Winnie-the-Pooh and Rabbit (*Winnie-the-Pooh*)

2315 Winnie-the-Pooh and Eeyore (*Winnie-the-Pooh*)

2316 Winnie-the-Pooh and Friends (*Winnie-the-Pooh*)

2317 Winnie-the-Pooh and Tigger (*The House at Pooh Corner*)

MS3127 115×89 mm. **2318** Winnie-the-Pooh (1st) Winnie-the-Pooh and Christopher Robin (from *Now we are Six*); 60p. Christopher Robin reads to Winnie-the-Pooh (from *Winnie-the-Pooh*); 88p. Winnie-the-Pooh and Christopher Robin sailing in umbrella (from *Winnie-the-Pooh*); 97p. Christopher Robin (putting on wellingtons) and Pooh (from *Winnie-the-Pooh*). Perf 14½... 4·75 4·75
First Day Cover (Tallents House)... 6·25
First Day Cover (Hartfield, East Sussex).................................... 6·25

The 1st class value includes the EUROPA emblem.
Stamps from No. **MS**3127 show lines from poem *We Too* by A. A. Milne. 'Wherever I am, there's always Pooh' (1st); 'There's always Pooh and Me. Whatever I do, he wants to do' (60p.); 'Where are you going to-day?' says Pooh: 'Well that's very odd 'cos I was too' (88p.); 'Let's go together,' says Pooh, says he. 'Let's go together,' says Pooh (97p.).

The 11 PHQ cards show the six stamps, the four individual stamps within No. **MS**3127 and the complete miniature sheet.

SELF-ADHESIVE STAMPS. Collectors are reminded that used self-adhesive stamps will no longer 'soak-off'. They should be collected with a neat margin of backing paper.

2319 Wallace and Gromit Carol singing

2320 Gromit posting Christmas Cards

2321 Wallace and Gromit Carol singing

2322 Wallace and Gromit decorating Christmas Tree

2323 Gromit posting Christmas Cards

2324 Gromit carrying Christmas Pudding

2325 Gromit wearing Oversized Sweater

2318 Winnie-the-Pooh

(Des Magpie Studio. Litho Cartor.)

2010 (12 Oct). Europa. Children's Books. Winnie-the-Pooh by A. A. Milne. Book Illustrations by E. H. Shepard. Yellow-brown, pale stone and black. 'All-over' phosphor. Perf 14×14½.

3121	2312	(1st) Winnie-the-Pooh and Christopher Robin..................................	1·20	1·00
3122	2313	58p. Winnie-the-Pooh and Piglet............	90	90
3123	2314	60p. Winnie-the-Pooh and Rabbit..........	1·00	1·00
3124	2315	67p. Winnie-the-Pooh and Eeyore..........	1·10	1·10
3125	2316	88p. Winnie-the-Pooh and Friends........	1·25	1·25
3126	2317	97p. Winnie-the-Pooh and Tigger...........	1·40	1·40

Set of 6.. 6·00 6·00
Set of 6 Gutter Pairs... 12·00
First Day Cover (Tallents House)... 8·00
First Day Cover (Hartfield, East Sussex).................................. 8·00
Presentation Pack (PO Pack No. 447) (Nos. 3121/3126 and **MS**3127).. 11·50
PHQ Cards (set of 11) (342).. 4·25 15·00

MS3135

2010/QUEEN ELIZABETH II

(Gravure De La Rue)

2010 (2 Nov). Christmas with Wallace and Gromit. Multicoloured One centre band (No. 3128) or two bands (others). Perf 14½×14 (with one elliptical hole in each vert side).

(a) Self-adhesive.

3128	2319	(2nd) Wallace and Gromit Carol singing.	90	90
		a. Booklet pane. No. 3128×12............	13·50	
3129	2320	(1st) Gromit posting Christmas Cards....	1·20	1·00
		a. Booklet pane. No. 3129×12............	16·00	
3130	2321	(2nd Wallace and Gromit Carol singing. Large)	1·25	1·00
3131	2322	60p. Wallace and Gromit decorating Christmas Tree..................	1·10	1·10
3132	2323	(1st Gromit posting Christmas Cards.... Large)	1·70	1·40
3133	2324	97p. Gromit carrying Christmas Pudding...........................	1·40	1·40
3134	2325	£1·46 Gromit wearing Oversized Sweater..........................	2·00	2·00
Set of 7			8·25	8·00
First Day Cover (Tallents House)..................................				9·50
First Day Cover (Bethlehem, Llandeilo)........................				9·50
Presentation Pack (PO Pack No. 448).............................			10·00	
PHQ Cards (set of 8) (343)...........................			3·25	16·50

(b) Ordinary gum.

MS3135 115×102 mm. Nos. 3128/3134......................	8·25	8·00
First Day Cover (Tallents House)..................................		9·50
First Day Cover (Bethlehem, Llandeilo)........................		9·50

The 2nd class, 1st class, 60p and 97p stamps were also issued together in sheets of 20 (No. LS75), sold for £9·30, containing eight 2nd class, eight 1st class, two 60p and two 97p stamps, each stamp accompanied by a *se-tenant* label.

Separate sheets of 20 2nd, 20 1st, ten 1st, ten 60p and ten 97p were available with personal photographs on the labels from Royal Mail, Edinburgh. These were sold at £7·80 for ten 1st, £9·95 for 20 2nd or ten 60p, £13·95 for 20 1st and £14·50 for ten 97p.

All these sheets were printed in lithography by Cartor and had the backing paper around the stamps retained.

The eight PHQ cards show the seven individual stamps and the miniature sheet.

Year Pack

2010 (2 Nov). Comprises Nos. 2999/3008, **MS**3025/3063, **MS**3065, **MS**3072, 3074/3081, **MS**3086/**MS**3094, 3097/3106 and 3109/3134.

CP3135a	Year Pack (PO Pack No. 449) (sold for £80)..	£125

Post Office Yearbook

2010 (2 Nov). Comprises Nos. 2999/3008, **MS**3025/3063, **MS**3065, **MS**3072, 3074/3081, **MS**3086/**MS**3094, 3097/3106 and 3109/3134.

YB3135a	Yearbook (sold for £85).........................	£110

Miniature Sheet Collection

2010 (2 Nov). Comprises Nos. **MS**3024, **MS**3025, **MS**3053, **MS**3065, **MS**3072, **MS**3086, **MS**3094, **MS**3127 and **MS**3135.

MS3135a	Miniature Sheet Collection (sold for £32)..........	50·00

2326 *Joe 90*

2327 *Captain Scarlet*

2328 Thunderbird 2 (*Thunderbirds*)

2329 *Stingray*

2330 *Fireball XL5*

2331 *Supercar*

2332 Thunderbird 4; Thunderbird 3; Thunderbird 2; Thunderbird 1

(Des GBH)

2011 (11 Jan). F.A.B. The Genius of Gerry Anderson (producer of TV programmes). Multicoloured 'All-over' phosphor.

(a) Ordinary gum. Litho Cartor. Perf 14.

3136	2326	(1st) *Joe 90*...........................	1·20	1·00
		a. Horiz strip of 3. Nos. 3136/3138......	3·50	3·00
3137	2327	(1st) *Captain Scarlet*................	1·20	1·00
3138	2328	(1st) Thunderbird 2 (*Thunderbirds*)........	1·20	1·00
3139	2329	97p. *Stingray*.........................	1·50	1·50
		a. Horiz strip of 3. Nos. 3139/3141......	4·50	4·50
3140	2330	97p. *Fireball XL5*....................	1·50	1·50
3141	2331	97p. *Supercar*........................	1·50	1·50
Set of 6			7·25	6·75
Set of 2 Gutter Strips of 6.................................			14·50	
First Day Cover (Tallents House)................................				7·75
First Day Cover (Slough)...				7·75
Presentation Pack (PO Pack No. 450) (Nos. 3136/3141 and **MS**3142)..			12·50	
PHQ Cards (set of 11) (344)..................................			4·25	17·00

(b) Microlenticular Cartor and Outer Aspect Ltd, New Zealand. Perf 14.

MS3142 116×89 mm. **2332** 41p. Thunderbird 4; 60p. Thunderbird 3; 88p. Thunderbird 2; 97p. Thunderbird 1............................ 5·25 5·50
    a. Error imperforate.................................. —
First Day Cover (Tallents House)....................................... 6·00
First Day Cover (Slough).. 6·00

(c) Self-adhesive. Gravure Walsall. Die-cut Perf 14.

3143	2328	(1st) Thunderbird 2 (*Thunderbirds*)........	2·00	2·00
		a. Booklet pane. No. 3143×2 and U3016×4.............................	7·50	

Nos. 3136/3138 and 3139/3141 were each printed together, *se-tenant*, as horizontal strips of three stamps in sheets of 60 (2 panes 6×5).

The stamps within No. **MS**3142 use microlenticular technology to show each vehicle's launch sequences when the miniature sheet is tilted. One example of No. **MS**3142a is known on a first day cover.

No. 3143 was only issued in booklet, No. PM27, sold for £2·46.

The complete miniature sheet is shown on one of the 11 PHQ cards with the others depicting individual stamps including those from No. **MS**3142.

2333 Classic Locomotives of England

(Des Delaney Design Consultants. Litho Cartor)

2011 (1 Feb). Classic Locomotives (1st series). England. Sheet 180×74 mm. Multicoloured 'All-over' phosphor. Perf 14.

MS3144 **2333** Classic Locomotives of England (1st) BR Dean Goods No. 2532; 60p. Peckett R2 *Thor*; 88p. Lancashire and Yorkshire Railway 1093 No. 1100; 97p. BR WD No. 90662.................................. 4·25 4·50
First Day Cover (Tallents House)............................ 5·00
First Day Cover (Liverpool)....................................... 5·00
Presentation Pack (PO Pack No. 451)..................... 5·25
PHQ Cards (set of 5) (345)....................................... 2·00 9·00

The five PHQ cards show the four individual stamps and the complete miniature sheet.

See also No. 3215.

219

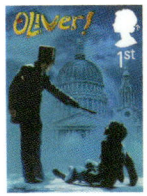

QUEEN ELIZABETH II/2011

2334 Oliver 
2335 Blood Brothers 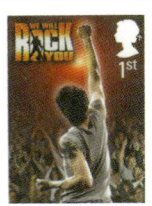
2336 We Will Rock You
2344 Michael Gambon as Dumbledore (J. K. Rowling's Harry Potter)
2345 Ralph Fiennes as Lord Voldemort (J. K. Rowling's Harry Potter)

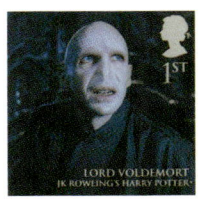

2337 Spamalot 
2338 Rocky Horror Show 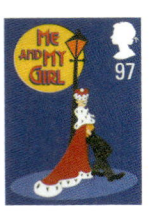
2339 Me and My Girl
2346 Merlin (Arthurian Legend)
2347 Morgan Le Fay (Arthurian Legend)

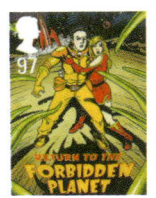

2340 Return to the Forbidden Planet
2341 Billy Elliot 
2348 Aslan (C. S. Lewis's Narnia)
2349 Tilda Swinton as The White Witch (C. S. Lewis's Narnia)

(Des Webb and Webb. Litho Cartor)

2011 (24 Feb). Musicals. Multicoloured 'All-over' phosphor. Perf 14.

3145	2334	(1st) Oliver	1·20	1·00
3146	2335	(1st) Blood Brothers	1·20	1·00
3147	2336	(1st) We Will Rock You	1·20	1·00
3148	2337	(1st) Spamalot	1·20	1·00
3149	2338	97p. Rocky Horror Show	1·30	1·30
3150	2339	97p. Me and My Girl	1·30	1·30
3151	2340	97p. Return to the Forbidden Planet	1·30	1·30
3152	2341	97p. Billy Elliot	1·30	1·30
Set of 8			8·75	8·25
Set of 8 Gutter Pairs			17·50	
Set of 8 Traffic Light Gutter Pairs			25·00	
First Day Cover (Tallents House)				9·25
First Day Cover (Dancers End, Tring)				9·25
Presentation Pack (PO Pack No. 452)			9·75	
PHQ Cards (set of 8) (346)			3·25	11·00

(Gravure Walsall)

2011 (24 Feb). 50th Anniversary of the British Heart Foundation. Booklet stamp. Design as No. 3115. Self-adhesive. Multicoloured 'All-over' phosphor. Die-cut Perf 14×14½.

3153	2306	(1st) Heart-regulating Beta Blockers	2·00	2·00
		a. Booklet pane. No. 3153×2 and U3016×4	7·50	

No. 3153 was only issued in booklet, No. PM28, sold for £2·46.

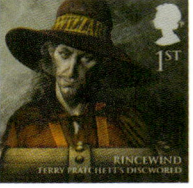

2342 Rincewind (Terry Pratchett's *Discworld*) 
2343 Nanny Ogg (Terry Pratchett's *Discworld*)
2350 African Elephant
2351 Mountain Gorilla

(Des So Design Consultants. Gravure De La Rue)

2011 (8 Mar). Magical Realms. Multicoloured 'All-over' phosphor. Perf 14½.

3154	2342	(1st) Rincewind	1·20	1·00
		a. Vert pair. Nos. 3154/3155	2·40	2·00
3155	2343	(1st) Nanny Ogg	1·20	1·00
3156	2344	(1st) Michael Gambon as Dumbledore	1·20	1·00
		a. Vert pair. Nos. 3156/3157	2·40	2·00
3157	2345	(1st) Ralph Fiennes as Lord Voldemort	1·20	1·00
3158	2346	60p. Merlin	95	95
		a. Vert pair. Nos. 3158/3159	1·90	1·90
3159	2347	60p. Morgan Le Fay	95	95
3160	2348	97p. Aslan	1·25	1·25
		a. Vert pair. Nos. 3160/3161	2·50	2·50
3161	2349	97p. Tilda Swinton as The White Witch	1·25	1·25
Set of 8			8·00	7·50
Set of 4 Gutter Strips of 4			16·00	
First Day Cover (Tallents House)				7·75
First Day Cover (Merlins Bridge, Haverfordwest)				7·75
Presentation Pack (PO Pack No. 453)			8·50	
Presentation Pack (Heroes and Villains containing Nos. 3156/3157, each×5) (2.12.11)			14·00	
PHQ Cards (set of 8) (347)			3·25	9·25

Nos. 3154/3155, 3156/3157, 3158/3159 and 3160/3161 were each printed together, *se-tenant*, as vertical pairs in sheets of 60 (2 panes 5×6).

For Nos. U3055/U3059 see Decimal Machin Definitives section

2011/QUEEN ELIZABETH II

2352 Siberian Tiger
2353 Polar Bear
2354 Amur Leopard
2355 Iberian Lynx
2356 Red Panda
2357 Black Rhinoceros
2358 African Wild Dog
2359 Golden Lion Tamarin

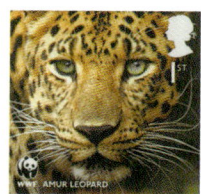

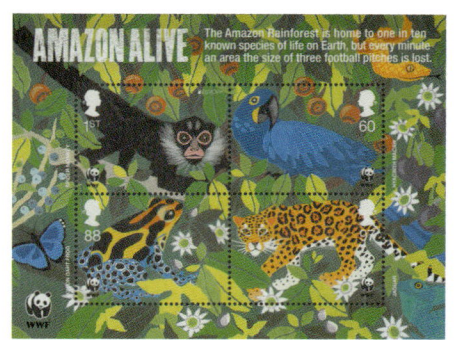

3169	2357	(1st) Black Rhinoceros	1·20	1·00
3170	2358	(1st) African Wild Dog	1·20	1·00
3171	2359	(1st) Golden Lion Tamarin	1·20	1·00
		Set of 10	10·50	9·00
		Set of 2 Gutter Strips of 10	21·00	
		First Day Cover (Tallents House)		9·50
		First Day Cover (Godalming, Surrey)		9·50
		Presentation Pack (PO Pack No. 454) (Nos. 3162/3171 and MS3172)	16·00	
		PHQ Cards (set of 15) (348)	6·00	21·00

MS3172 115×89 mm. 2360 Wildlife of the Amazon Rainforest (1st) Spider monkey; 60p. Hyacinth macaw; 88p. Poison dart frog; 97p. Jaguar ... 4·50 4·50
  a. Booklet pane. No. MS3172 but 125×96 mm with line of roulettes at left .... 4·50 4·50
First Day Cover (Tallents House) .... 5·25
First Day Cover (Godalming, Surrey) .... 5·25

Nos. 3162/3166 and 3167/3171 were each printed together, *se-tenant*, as horizontal strips of five stamps in sheets of 50 (2 panes 5×5).

Booklet panes Nos. 3162b, 3164b and MS3172a come from the £9·05 50th Anniversary of the WWF booklet, No. DX52.

The 1st class value from No. MS3172 includes the EUROPA emblem.

The complete miniature sheet is shown on one of the 15 PHQ cards with the others depicting individual stamps including those from No. MS3172.

2361 David Tennant as Hamlet, 2008
2362 Antony Sher as Prospero, *The Tempest*, 2009
2363 Chuk Iwuji as Henry VI, 2006
2364 Paul Schofield as King Lear, 1962
2365 Sara Kestelman as Titania, *A Midsummer Night's Dream*, 1970
2366 Ian McKellen and Francesca Annis as Romeo and Juliet, 1976

2360 Wildlife of the Amazon Rainforest

(Des Janice Nicholson and Rose Design (No. MS3172) or Rose Design Consultants (others). Litho Cartor).

2011 (22 Mar). 50th Anniversary of the WWF. Multicoloured 'All-over' phosphor. Perf 14 (Nos. MS3172/MS3172a) or 14½ (others).

3162	2350	(1st) African Elephant	1·20	1·00
		a. Horiz strip of 5. Nos. 3162/3166	5·25	4·50
		b. Booklet pane. Nos. 3162/3163 and 3170/3171 with margins all round	4·25	
3163	2351	(1st) Mountain Gorilla	1·20	1·00
3164	2352	(1st) Siberian Tiger	1·20	1·00
		b. Booklet pane. Nos. 3164/3169 with margins all round	6·50	
3165	2353	(1st) Polar Bear	1·20	1·00
3166	2354	(1st) Amur Leopard	1·20	1·00
3167	2355	(1st) Iberian Lynx	1·20	1·00
		a. Horiz strip of 5. Nos. 3167/3171	5·25	4·50
3168	2356	(1st) Red Panda	1·20	1·00

2367 The Four Theatres of the Royal Shakespeare Company, Stratford-upon-Avon

221

QUEEN ELIZABETH II/2011

(Des Hat-trick. Gravure (Nos. 3173/3178) or litho (No. **MS**3179) Walsall (Nos. 3173/3178) or Cartor (No. **MS**3179))

2011 (21 Apr). 50th Anniversary of the Royal Shakespeare Company. Black, brownish black and bright scarlet. 'All-over' phosphor. Perf 14½ (Nos. 3173/3178) or 14 (No. **MS**3179).

3173	**2361**	(1st) David Tennant as Hamlet................	1·20	1·00
3174	**2362**	66p. Antony Sher as Prospero, *The Tempest*..	1·00	1·00
3175	**2363**	68p. Chuk Iwuji as Henry VI.....................	1·10	1·10
3176	**2364**	76p. Paul Schofield as King Lear.............	1·25	1·25
3177	**2365**	£1 Sara Kestelman as Titania, *A Midsummer Night's Dream*.............	1·50	1·50
3178	**2366**	£1·10 Ian McKellen and Francesca Annis as Romeo and Juliet........................	1·75	1·75
Set of 6...			6·75	6·75
Set of 6 Gutter Pairs...			13·50	
First Day Cover (Tallents House)....................................				8·00
First Day Cover (Stratford-upon-Avon).........................				8·00
Presentation Pack (PO Pack No. 455) (Nos. 3173/3178 and **MS**3179)..			13·00	
PHQ Cards (set of 11) (349)...			4·50	18·00

MS3179 115×89 mm. 2367 The Four Theatres of the Royal Shakespeare Company, Stratford-upon-Avon (1st) Janet Suzman as Ophelia, *Hamlet*, 1965, Royal Shakespeare Theatre; 68p. Patrick Stewart in *Antony and Cleopatra*, 2006, Swan Theatre; 76p. Geoffrey Streatfield in *Henry V*, 2007, The Courtyard Theatre; £1·10 Judy Dench as Lady Macbeth, 1976, The Other Place... 4·25 4·25
First Day Cover (Tallents House).................................... 5·00
First Day Cover (Stratford-upon-Avon)......................... 5·00

The 11 PHQ cards show the six stamps, the four individual stamps within No. **MS**3179 and the complete miniature sheet.

2368 Prince William and Miss Catherine Middleton

(Litho Walsall)

2011 (21 Apr). Royal Wedding. Official Engagement Portraits by Mario Testino. Sheet 115×89 mm. Multicoloured 'All-over' phosphor. Perf 14½×14.

MS3180 **2368** Prince William and Miss Catherine Middleton (1st)×2 Prince William and Miss Catherine Middleton embracing; £1·10×2 Formal portrait of Prince William and Miss Catherine Middleton in Council Chamber, St James's Palace........................... 5·50 5·50
First Day Cover (Tallents House).................................... 7·00
First Day Cover (London SW1)....................................... 7·00
Presentation Pack (PO Pack No. M20)............................ 13·00
Commemorative Document... 15·00

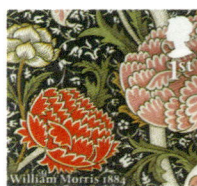

2369 Cray (fabric print by William Morris), 1884

2370 Cherries (detail from panel by Philip Webb), 1867

2371 Seaweed (wallpaper pattern by John Henry Dearle), 1901

2372 Peony (ceramic tile design by Kate Faulkner), 1877

2373 Acanthus (tile by William Morris and William de Morgan), 1876

2374 The Merchant's Daughter (detail of stained-glass window by Edward Burne-Jones), 1864

(Des Kate Stephens. Litho Cartor or Walsall (booklet stamps))

2011 (5 May). 150th Anniversary of Morris and Company (designers and manufacturers of textiles, wallpaper and furniture) (1st issue). Multicoloured 'All-over' phosphor. Perf 14×14½.

3181	**2369**	(1st) Cray..	1·20	1·00
		a. Booklet pane. Nos. 3181 and 3183/3185 with margins all round..	5·25	
3182	**2370**	(1st) Cherries...	1·20	1·00
		a. Booklet pane. Nos. 3182 and 3186, each×2, with margins all round..	5·25	
3183	**2371**	76p. Seaweed...	1·25	1·25
3184	**2372**	76p. Peony..	1·25	1·25
3185	**2373**	£1·10 Acanthus...	1·75	1·75
3186	**2374**	£1·10 The Merchant's Daughter.............	1·75	1·75
Set of 6...			7·25	7·00
Set of 6 Gutter Pairs...			14·50	
First Day Cover (Tallents House)....................................				8·00
First Day Cover (Walthamstow).....................................				8·00
Presentation Pack (PO Pack No. 456).............................			7·75	
PHQ Cards (set of 6) (350)...			2·50	8·25

Nos. 3181/3186 were also issued in premium booklet, No. DY1, sold for £9·99.

2202 Angel playing Lute

2011 (5 May). 150th Anniversary of Morris and Company (2nd issue). Design as T **2202** (2009 Christmas. Stained-glass Windows). Multicoloured One centre band. Perf 14½×14 (with one elliptical hole in each vert side).

3186a **2202** (2nd) Angel playing Lute (William Morris), Church of St James, Staveley, Kendal, Cumbria.............. 1·50 1·50
ab. Booklet pane. No. 3186a×4 with central label and margins all round.. 6·00

No. 3186a was only issued in premium booklet, No. DY1, sold for £9·99.

2375 Thomas the Tank Engine

2011/QUEEN ELIZABETH II

2376 James the Red Engine

2377 Percy the Small Engine

2378 Daisy (diesel railcar)

2379 Toby the Tram Engine

2380 Gordon the Big Engine

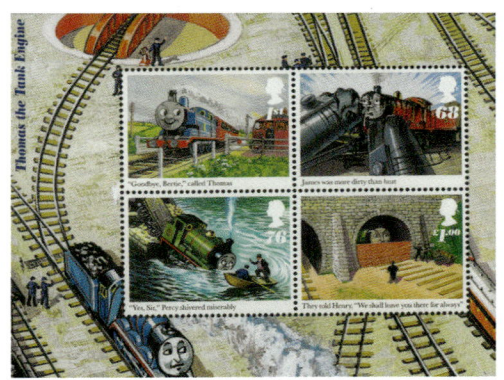

2381 Book Illustrations by John T. Kenny (76p.) or C. Reginald Dalby (others)

2382 "Goodbye, Bertie," called Thomas (from *Tank Engine Thomas Again*)

(Des Elmwood. Litho Cartor)

2011 (14 June). Thomas the Tank Engine. Multicoloured 'All-over' phosphor.

(a) Ordinary gum. Perf 14 (No. MS3193) or 14½×14 (others).

3187	2375	(1st) Thomas the Tank Engine	1·20	1·00
3188	2376	66p. James the Red Engine	1·00	1·00
3189	2377	68p. Percy the Small Engine	1·10	1·10
3190	2378	76p. Daisy (diesel railcar)	1·25	1·25
3191	2379	£1 Toby the Tram Engine	1·50	1·50
3192	2380	£1·10 Gordon the Big Engine	1·75	1·75

Set of 6 .... 6·75 6·75
Set of 6 Gutter Pairs .... 13·50
First Day Cover (Tallents House) .... 8·00
First Day Cover (Box, Corsham, Wiltshire) .... 8·00
Presentation Pack (PO Pack No. 457) (Nos. 3187/3192 and **MS**3193) .... 13·00
PHQ Cards (set of 11) (351) .... 4·50 18·00

MS3193 115×89 mm. 2381 (1st) "Goodbye, Bertie", called Thomas (from *Tank Engine Thomas Again*); 68p. James was more dirty than hurt (from *Toby the Tram Engine*); 76p. "Yes, Sir", Percy shivered miserably (from *The Eight Famous Engines*); £1. They told Henry, "We shall leave you there for always" (from *The Three Railway Engines*) .... 4·25 4·25
First Day Cover (Tallents House) .... 5·00
First Day Cover (Box, Corsham, Wiltshire) .... 5·00

(b) Self-adhesive. Die-cut perf 14 (Gravure Walsall).

3194 **2382** (1st) "Goodbye, Bertie", called Thomas (from *Tank Engine Thomas Again*).. 2·00 2·00
a. Booklet pane. Nos. 3194×2 and U3016×4 .... 7·50

Nos. 3187/3192 show scenes from TV series *Thomas and Friends*, and Nos. **MS**3193/3194 book illustrations from *The Railway Series*.

No. 3194 was only issued in stamp booklet, No. PM29, originally sold for £2·76.

The 11 PHQ cards show the six stamps, the four individual stamps within No. **MS**3193 and the complete miniature sheet.

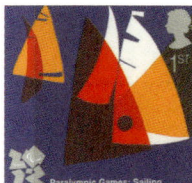

2383 Paralympic Games, Sailing

2384 Athletics, Field

2385 Volleyball

2386 Wheelchair Rugby

2387 Wrestling

2388 Wheelchair Tennis

2389 Fencing

2390 Gymnastics

223

QUEEN ELIZABETH II/2011

2391 Triathlon 
2392 Handball

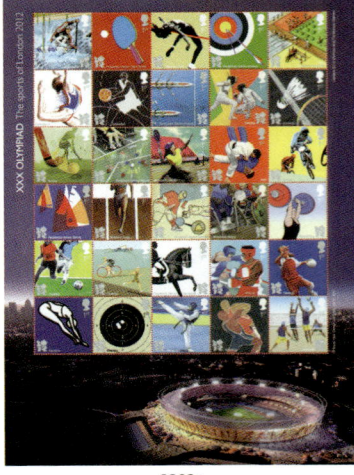

2393 The Sovereign's Sceptre with Cross
2394 St Edward's Crown

2395 Rod and Sceptre with Doves
2396 Queen Mary's Crown

2397 The Sovereign's Orb
2398 Jewelled Sword of Offering

2399 Imperial State Crown
2400 Coronation Spoon

2392a

(Des Lara Harwood and Heart (No. 3195), Anthony Pike and The Art Market (No. 3196), Ben Dalling (No. 3197), Matthew Hollings and Illustration Ltd (No. 3198), Daniel Stolle and Anna Goodson Management (No. 3199), David McConochie and The Art Market (No. 3200), Lyndon Hayes and Dutch Uncle Agency (No. 3201), Kathy Wyatt (No. 3202), Adam Simpson and Heart (No. 3203), David Cutter and Folio (No. 3204). Litho Cartor)

2011 (27 July). Olympic and Paralympic Games, London (2012) (5th issue). Multicoloured 'All-over' phosphor. Perf 14½.

3195	**2383**	(1st) Paralympic Games, Sailing	1·20	1·00
		a. Horiz strip of 5. Nos. 3195/3199	5·25	4·50
3196	**2384**	(1st) Athletics, Field	1·20	1·00
3197	**2385**	(1st) Volleyball	1·20	1·00
3198	**2386**	(1st) Wheelchair Rugby	1·20	1·00
3199	**2387**	(1st) Wrestling	1·20	1·00
3200	**2388**	(1st) Wheelchair Tennis	1·20	1·00
		a. Horiz strip of 5. Nos. 3200/3204	5·25	4·50
3201	**2389**	(1st) Fencing	1·20	1·00
3202	**2390**	(1st) Gymnastics	1·20	1·00
3203	**2391**	(1st) Triathlon	1·20	1·00
3204	**2392**	(1st) Handball	1·20	1·00
Set of 10			10·50	9·00
Set of 2 Gutter Strips of 10			21·00	
First Day Cover (Tallents House)				9·50
First Day Cover (Rugby, Warks)				9·50
Presentation Pack (PO Pack No. 458)			11·00	
PHQ Cards (set of 10) (352)			4·00	12·00

MS3204a 210×300 mm. **2392a** Nos. 2981/2990, 3097/3106 and 3195/3204 .... 35·00 35·00

Nos. 3195/3199 and 3200/3204 were each printed together, *se-tenant*, in horizontal strips of five stamps in sheets of 50 (2 panes 5×5) and in No. **MS**3204a.

(Gravure Walsall)

2011 (27 July–15 Sept). Olympic and Paralympic Games (2012) (6th issue). Booklet stamps. Designs as Nos. 3195, 3198 and 3201/32022 . Self-adhesive. Multicoloured 'All-over' phosphor. Die-cut Perf 14½×14.

3205	**2386**	(1st) Wheelchair Rugby	2·00	2·00
		a. Booklet pane. Nos. 3205/3206 and U3016×4	7·50	
3206	**2383**	(1st) Paralympic Games, Sailing	2·00	2·00
3206a	**2390**	(1st) Gymnastics (15.9.11)	2·00	2·00
		ab. Booklet pane. Nos. 3206a/3206b and U3016×4	7·50	
3206b	**2389**	(1st) Fencing (15.9.11)	2·00	2·00
Set of 4			7·50	7·50

Nos. 3205/3206 and 3206a/3206b were only issued in two separate stamp booklets, Nos. PM30 and PM32, each originally sold for £2·76.

(Des Purpose. Litho Cartor)

2011 (23 Aug). Crown Jewels. Multicoloured Phosphor background. Perf 14×14½.

3207	**2393**	(1st) The Sovereign's Sceptre with Cross	1·20	1·00
3208	**2394**	(1st) St Edward's Crown	1·20	1·00
3209	**2395**	68p. Rod and Sceptre with Doves	1·10	1·10
3210	**2396**	68p. Queen Mary's Crown	1·10	1·10
3211	**2397**	76p. The Sovereign's Orb	1·25	1·25
3212	**2398**	76p. Jewelled Sword of Offering	1·25	1·25
3213	**2399**	£1·10 Imperial State Crown	1·60	1·60
3214	**2400**	£1·10 Coronation Spoon	1·60	1·60
Set of 8			9·00	8·75
Set of 8 Gutter Pairs			£118	
First Day Cover (Tallents House)				10·00
First Day Cover (London EC3)				10·00
Presentation Pack (PO Pack No. 459)			10·00	
PHQ Cards (set of 8) (353)			3·25	11·00

2401 BR Dean Goods No. 2532

(Gravure Walsall)

2011 (23 Aug). Classic Locomotives. Black and gold. Booklet stamp. Design as 1st class stamp within No. **MS**3144. Self-adhesive. Die-cut Perf 14.

3215	**2401**	(1st) BR Dean Goods No. 2532	2·00	2·00
		a. Booklet pane. No. 3215×2 and U3016×4	7·50	

No. 3215 was only issued in booklet, No. PM31, originally sold for £2·76.

2011/QUEEN ELIZABETH II

2402 Pilot Gustav Hamel receiving Mailbag

2403 Gustav Hamel in Cockpit

2404 Pilot Clement Greswell and Blériot Monoplane

2405 Delivery of First Airmail to Postmaster General at Windsor

2406 First United Kingdom Aerial Post, 9 September 1911

(Des Robert Maude and Sarah Davies. Litho Cartor)

2011 (9 Sept). Centenary of First United Kingdom Aerial Post (1st issue). Multicoloured 'All-over' phosphor. Perf 14.

3216	2402	(1st) Pilot Gustav Hamel receiving Mailbag	1·75	1·75
		a. Booklet pane. Nos. 3216×2 and 3219, with margins all round	8·50	
3217	2403	68p. Pilot Gustav Hamel receiving Mailbag	1·75	1·75
		a. Booklet pane. Nos. 3217×2 and 3218	8·50	
3218	2404	£1 Pilot Clement Greswell and Blériot Monoplane	5·00	5·00
3219	2405	£1·10 Delivery of First Airmail to Postmaster General at Windsor	5·00	5·00
Set of 4			13·50	13·50
MS3220 146×74 mm. **2406** First United Kingdom Aerial Post, 9 September 1911 Nos. 3216/3219			8·50	8·50
First Day Cover (Tallents House)				9·50
First Day Cover (Hendon, London NW4)				9·50
Presentation Pack (PO Pack No. 460)			9·50	
PHQ Cards (set of 5) (354)			2·00	21·00

Nos. 3216/3219 were only issued in £9.99 First United Kingdom Aerial Post stamp booklet, No. DY2, and in No. **MS**3220.

The five PHQ cards show the four individual stamps and the complete miniature sheet.

2407 Windsor Castle

(Recess Phil@poste of France and litho Cartor)

2011 (9 Sept). Centenary of First United Kingdom Aerial Post (2nd issue). Black and cream. Perf 11×11½.

3221	2407	50p. Windsor Castle	2·00	2·00
		a. Booklet pane. No. 3221×4, with margins all round	8·25	

No. 3221 was only issued in £9.97 First United Kingdom Aerial Post stamp booklet, No. DY2.

For No. **MS**3222, T **2408**, see Decimal Machin Definitives section

2409 George I (1714–1727)

2410 George II (1727–1760)

2411 George III (1760–1820)

2412 George IV (1820–1830)

2413 William IV (1830–1837)

2414 Victoria (1837–1901)

2415 The Age of the Hanoverians

(Des Atelier Works. Litho Cartor)

2011 (15 Sept). Kings and Queens (5th issue). House of Hanover. Multicoloured Two phosphor bands. Perf 14.

3223	2409	(1st) George I	1·20	1·00
3224	2410	(1st) George II	1·20	1·00
3225	2411	76p. George III	1·25	1·25
3226	2412	76p. George IV	1·25	1·25
3227	2413	£1·10 William IV	1·75	1·75
3228	2414	£1·10 Victoria	1·75	1·75
Set of 6			7·25	7·00
Set of 6 Gutter Pairs			14·50	
Set of 6 Traffic Light Gutter Blocks of 4			50·00	
First Day Cover (Tallents House)				8·00
First Day Cover (London SW1)				8·00
Presentation Pack (PO Pack No. 461) (Nos. 3223/3228 and **MS**3229)			13·00	
PHQ Cards (set of 11) (355)			4·50	18·00
MS3229 123×70 mm. **2415** The Age of the Hanoverians (1st) Robert Walpole (first Prime Minister), 1721; 68p. Ceiling by Robert Adam, Kedleston Hall, 1763; 76p. Penny Black (uniform postage), 1840; £1 Queen Victoria (Diamond Jubilee), 1897			4·25	4·25
First Day Cover (Tallents House)				5·00
First Day Cover (London SW1)				5·00

The photograph of Queen Victoria in No. **MS**2415 actually shows her at the time of her Golden Jubilee in 1887.

The complete miniature sheet is shown on one of the 11 PHQ cards with the others depicting individual stamps including those from No. **MS**3229.

2416 Angel of the North

2417 Blackpool Tower

225

QUEEN ELIZABETH II/2011

2418 Carrick-a-Rede, Co. Antrim
2419 Downing Street 
2420 Edinburgh Castle 
2421 Forth Railway Bridge 
2422 Glastonbury Tor 
2423 Harlech Castle 
2424 Ironbridge 
2425 Jodrell Bank 
2426 Kursaal, Southend, Essex 
2427 Lindisfarne Priory 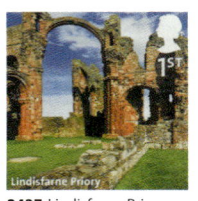

(Des Robert Maude and Sarah Davies. Litho Cartor)

2011 (13 Oct). UK A–Z (1st series). Multicoloured 'All-over' phosphor. Perf 14½.

3230	2416	(1st) Angel of the North	1·20	1·00
		a. Horiz strip of 6. Nos. 3230/3235	5·25	4·50
3231	2417	(1st) Blackpool Tower	1·20	1·00
3232	2418	(1st) Carrick-a-Rede, Co. Antrim	1·20	1·00
3233	2419	(1st) Downing Street	1·20	1·00
3234	2420	(1st) Edinburgh Castle	1·20	1·00
3235	2421	(1st) Forth Railway Bridge	1·20	1·00
3236	2422	(1st) Glastonbury Tor	1·20	1·00
		a. Horiz strip of 6. Nos. 3236/3241	5·25	4·50
3237	2423	(1st) Harlech Castle	1·20	1·00
3238	2424	(1st) Ironbridge	1·20	1·00
3239	2425	(1st) Jodrell Bank	1·20	1·00
3240	2426	(1st) Kursaal, Southend, Essex	1·20	1·00
3241	2427	(1st) Lindisfarne Priory	1·20	1·00
Set of 12			10·50	9·00
Set of 2 Gutter Strips of 12			21·00	
Set of 2 Traffic Light Gutter Strips of 24			48·00	
First Day Covers (Tallents House) (2)				11·00
First Day Covers (Blackpool) (2)				11·00
Presentation Pack (PO Pack No. 462)			12·00	
PHQ Cards (set of 12) (356)			4·75	13·00

Nos. 3230/3235 and 3236/3241 were each printed together, se-tenant, as horizontal strips of six stamps in sheets of 60 (2 panes of 30) and were also issued on 10 April 2012 in a sheet containing all 26 UK A–Z stamps.

See No. **MS**3308.

2428 Joseph visited by the Angel (Matthew 1:21) 
2429 Madonna and Child (Matthew 1:23) 
2430 Joseph visited by the Angel (Matthew 1:21) 
2431 Madonna and Child (Matthew 1:23) 
2432 Baby Jesus in the Manger (Luke 2:7) 
2433 Shepherds visited by the Angel (Luke 2:10)

2434 Wise Men and Star (Matthew 2:10)

MS3249

(Des Peter Malone/The Artworks and Together Design. Gravure De La Rue)

2011 (8 Nov). Christmas. 400th Anniversary of the *King James Bible*. Multicoloured One centre band (No. 3242) or two phosphor bands (others). Perf 14½×14 (with one elliptical hole in each vert side).

(a) Self-adhesive.

3242	2428	(2nd) Joseph visited by the Angel	90	90
		a. Booklet pane. No. 3242×12	13·50	
3243	2429	(1st) Madonna and Child	1·20	1·00
		a. Booklet pane. No. 3243×12	16·00	
3244	2430	(2nd Joseph visited by the Angel Large)	1·25	1·10
3245	2431	(1st Madonna and Child Large)	1·70	1·40
3246	2432	68p. Baby Jesus in the Manger	1·25	1·25
3247	2433	£1·10 Shepherds visited by the Angel	1·90	1·90
3248	2434	£1·65 Wise Men and Star	2·50	2·50
Set of 7			9·25	9·00
First Day Cover (Tallents House)				11·00
First Day Cover (Bethlehem, Llandeilo)				11·00
Presentation Pack (PO Pack No. 463)			10·00	
PHQ Cards (set of 8) (357)			3·25	19·50

(b) Ordinary gum.

MS3249	116×102 mm. As Nos. 3242/3248	9·25	9·00
First Day Cover (Tallents House)			10·00
First Day Cover (Bethlehem, Llandeilo)			10·00

The 2nd class, 1st class, 68p, and £1·10 stamps were also issued in sheets of 20 (No. LS79) printed in lithography and sold for £10·45, containing eight 2nd class, eight 1st class, two 68p. and two £1·10 stamps, each stamp accompanied by a *se-tenant* label with a verse from the *King James Bible*.

Separate sheets of 20 2nd, ten 1st, ten 68p. and ten £1·10 were available with personal photographs on the labels from Royal Mail, Edinburgh. These were sold at £8·30 for ten 1st, £10·95 for 20 2nd, £10·75 for ten 68p. or £15·80 for ten £1·10.

The eight PHQ cards show the seven individual stamps and the miniature sheet.

Year Pack

2011 (8 Nov). Comprises Nos. 3136/3142, **MS**3144/3152, 3154/3193, 3195/3204, 3207/3214, **MS**3220 and 3223/3248.

CP3244*a*	Year Pack (PO Pack No. 464) (*sold for £94*)	£130

Post Office Yearbook

2011 (8 Nov). Comprises Nos. 3136/3142, **MS**3144/3152, 3154/3193, 3195/3204, 3207/3214, **MS**3220 and 3223/3248.

YB3244*a*	Yearbook (*sold for £99*)	£130

Miniature Sheet Collection

2011 (8 Nov). Comprises Nos. **MS**3142, **MS**3144, **MS**3172, **MS**3179/ **MS**3180, **MS**3193, **MS**3220, **MS**3229 and **MS**3249.

MS3244*a*	Miniature Sheet Collection	45·00

2435 Paralympic Games Emblem

2436 Olympic Games Emblem

(Gravure Walsall (booklets) or De La Rue (others))

2012 (5 Jan). Olympic and Paralympic Games (7th issue). Self-adhesive. Two phosphor bands. Die-cut Perf 14½×14 (with one elliptical hole on each vert side).

3250	2435	(1st) Paralympic Games Emblem. Black and orange-red	1·25	1·25
		a. Booklet pane. Nos. 3250/3251, each×3	7·00	
3251	2436	(1st) Olympic Games Emblem. Black and orange-red	1·25	1·25
3252	2435	(Worldwide up to 20 g) Paralympic Games Emblem. Black, bright scarlet and greenish blue	2·25	2·25
3253	2436	(Worldwide up to 20 g) Olympic Games Emblem. Black, bright scarlet and greenish blue	2·25	2·25
Set of 4			7·00	7·00
First Day Cover (Tallents House)				8·00
First Day Cover (Sennen, Penzance, Cornwall)				8·00
Presentation Pack (PO Pack No. D92)			9·00	
PHQ Cards (set of 4) (D32)			1·50	8·00

Nos. 3250/3251 were printed together in sheets of 50 (2 panes 5×5), with the two designs alternating horizontally and vertically. The upper pane had No. 3250 at top left and contained 13 of No. 3250 and 12 of No. 3251. The lower pane had No. 3251 at top left and contained 13 of No. 3251 and 12 of No. 3250.

Nos. 3250/3251 were also issued in stamp booklets, No. MB9/MB10, originally sold for £2·76.

Booklet pane 3250a exists in two versions which differ in the order of the stamps within the block of six.

Nos. 3252/3253 were printed together in sheets of 25 (5×5) with the two designs alternating horizontally and vertically. There were two versions of the sheets of 25, one having No. 3252 at top left and containing 13 of No. 3252 and 12 of No. 3253, and the other having No. 3253 at top left and containing 13 of No. 3253 and 12 of No. 3252.

Nos. 3250/3253 were also issued on 27 June 2012 in sheets of 20 containing Nos. 3250/3251, each×8, and Nos. 3252/3253, each×2, all with *se-tenant* labels showing Games venues (No. LS82). These sheets were printed in lithography by Cartor.

See also Nos. 3337/3340.

2437 Charlie and the Chocolate Factory

2438 Fantastic Mr Fox

2439 James and the Giant Peach

2440 Matilda

2441 The Twits

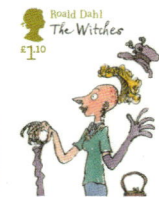

2442 The Witches

(Des Magpie Studio. Litho Cartor)

2012 (10 Jan). Roald Dahl's Children's Stories (1st issue). Book Illustrations by Quentin Blake. Multicoloured 'All-over' phosphor. Perf 14.

3254	2437	(1st) *Charlie and the Chocolate Factory*..	1·20	1·00
		a. Booklet pane. Nos. 3254 and 3256/3257 with margins all round	3·50	
3255	2438	66p. *Fantastic Mr Fox*	1·00	1·00
		a. Booklet pane. Nos. 3255 and 3258/3259 with margins all round	4·50	
3256	2439	68p. *James and the Giant Peach*	1·10	1·10
3257	2440	76p. *Matilda*	1·25	1·25
3258	2441	£1 *The Twits*	1·50	1·50
3259	2442	£1·10 *The Witches*	1·75	1·75
Set of 6			6·75	6·75
Set of 6 Gutter Pairs			13·50	
Set of 6 Traffic Light Gutter Blocks of 4			30·00	
First Day Cover (Tallents House)				9·00
First Day Cover (Great Missenden, Bucks)				9·00
Presentation Pack (PO Pack No. 465) (Nos. 3254/3259 and **MS**3264)			16·00	
PHQ Cards (set of 11) (358)			4·25	25·00

2443 The BFG Carrying Sophie in his Hand

2444 The BFG Wakes up the Giants

2445 Sophie Sitting on Buckingham Palace Window Sill

2446 The BFG and Sophie at Writing Desk

QUEEN ELIZABETH II/2012

2447 Roald Dahl's The BFG

(Des Magpie Studio. Litho Cartor)

2012 (10 Jan). Roald Dahl's Children's Stories (2nd issue). Book Illustrations by Quentin Blake. Multicoloured 'All-over' phosphor. Perf 14×14½.

3260	**2443**	(1st) The BFG carrying Sophie in his Hand	2·40	2·40
		a. Booklet pane. Nos. 3260/3263	9·00	
3261	**2444**	68p. The BFG wakes up the Giants	2·40	2·40
3262	**2445**	76p. Sophie sitting on Buckingham Palace Window sill	2·40	2·40
3263	**2446**	£1 The BFG and Sophie at Writing Desk	2·40	2·40
Set of 4			9·00	9·00
MS3264 115×89 mm. **2447** Roald Dahl's *The BFG* Nos. 3260/3263			9·00	9·00
First Day Cover (Tallents House)				9·50
First Day Cover (Great Missenden, Bucks)				9·50

Nos. 3260/3263 were only issued in £11·47 Roald Dahl, Master Storyteller premium booklet, No. DY3, and in No. **MS**3264.

No. **MS**3264 commemorates the 30th anniversary of the publication of *The BFG*.

The complete miniature sheet is shown on one of the 11 PHQ cards with the others showing individual stamps including those from No. **MS**3264.

2453 The Age of the Windsors

(Des Atelier Works. Litho Cartor)

2012 (2 Feb). Kings and Queens (6th issue). House of Windsor. Multicoloured Two phosphor bands. Perf 14.

3265	**2448**	(1st) Edward VII	1·20	1·00
3266	**2449**	68p. George V	1·00	1·00
3267	**2450**	76p. Edward VIII	1·40	1·40
3268	**2451**	£1 George VI	1·90	1·90
3269	**2452**	£1·10 Elizabeth II	2·25	2·25
Set of 5			6·75	6·75
Set of 5 Gutter Pairs			13·50	
Set of 5 Traffic Light Gutter Blocks of 4			25·00	
First Day Cover (Tallents House)				7·50
First Day Cover (Windsor, Berkshire)				7·50
Presentation Pack (PO Pack No. 466) (Nos. 3265/3269 and **MS**3270)			11·50	
PHQ Cards (set of 10) (359)			4·00	16·50
MS3270 123×70 mm. **2453** The Age of the Windsors (1st) Scott Expedition to South Pole, 1912; 68p. Queen Elizabeth the Queen Mother and King George VI in bomb damaged street, c 1940; 76p. England's winning World Cup football team, 1966; £1 Channel Tunnel, 1996			4·25	4·25
First Day Cover (Tallents House)				5·50
First Day Cover (Windsor, Berkshire)				5·50

The complete miniature sheet is shown on one of the ten PHQ cards with the others depicting individual stamps including those from No. **MS**3270.

No. 3271 is vacant.

For Nos. U3271/U3278 see Decimal Machin Definitives section

2448 Edward VII (1901–1910)

2449 George V (1910–1936)

2450 Edward VIII (1936)

2454 Diamond Jubilee *(Illustration reduced. Actual size 146×74 mm)*

(Des Sedley Place. Gravure Walsall)

2012 (6 Feb). Diamond Jubilee. (2nd issue). Multicoloured Two phosphor bands. Perf 14½×14 (with one elliptical hole in each vertical side).

MS3272 146×74 mm. **2454** Diamond Jubilee (1st)×6 Portrait from photograph by Dorothy Wilding; 1960 £1 Banknote portrait by Robert Austin; 1971 £5 Banknote portrait by Harry Eccleston; 1953 Coinage portrait by Mary Gillick; 1971 decimal coin portrait by Arnold Machin; As No. U3279	7·25	7·25
First Day Cover (Tallents House)		7·75
First Day Cover (London SW1)		7·75
Presentation Pack (PO Pack No. 93)	7·25	
PHQ Cards (set of 7) (D33)	2·75	14·50
Commemorative Document	12·00	

The 1st class slate-blue Machin stamp from No. **MS**3272 has an iridescent overprint reading 'DIAMOND JUBILEE' and the source code 'MMND'.

The seven PHQ cards show the six individual stamps and the complete miniature sheet.

2451 George VI (1936–1952)

2452 Elizabeth II (1952–)

2012 / QUEEN ELIZABETH II

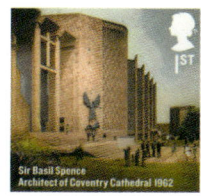

2455 Coventry Cathedral, 1962 (Sir Basil Spence, architect)

2456 Frederick Delius (1862–1934, composer)

2457 Orange Tree, Embroidery (Mary 'May' Morris 1862–1938, designer and textile artist)

2458 Odette Hallowes (1912–1995, SOE agent in occupied France)

2459 Steam Engine, 1712 (Thomas Newcomen, inventor of atmospheric steam engine)

2460 Kathleen Ferrier (1912–1953, contralto)

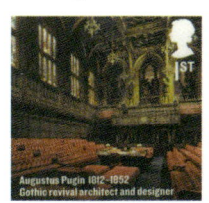

2461 Interior of Palace of Westminster (Augustus Pugin 1812–1852, Gothic revival architect and designer)

2462 Montagu Rhodes James (1862–1936 scholar and author)

2463 Bombe Code Breaking Machine (Alan Turing 1912–1954, mathematician and World War II code breaker)

2464 Joan Mary Fry (1862–1955 relief worker and social reformer)

(Des Purpose. Litho Cartor)

2012 (23 Feb). Britons of Distinction. Multicoloured 'All-over' phosphor. Perf 14½.

3273	2455	(1st) Coventry Cathedral	1·20	1·00
		a. Horiz strip of 5. Nos. 3273/3277	5·25	4·50
3274	2456	(1st) Frederick Delius	1·20	1·00
3275	2457	(1st) Orange Tree, Embroidery	1·20	1·00
3276	2458	(1st) Odette Hallowes	1·20	1·00
3277	2459	(1st) Steam Engine, 1712	1·20	1·00
3278	2460	(1st) Kathleen Ferrier	1·20	1·00
		a. Horiz strip of 5. Nos. 3278/3282	5·25	4·50
3279	2461	(1st) Interior of Palace of Westminster	1·20	1·00
3280	2462	(1st) Montagu Rhodes James	1·20	1·00
3281	2463	(1st) Bombe Code Breaking Machine	1·20	1·00
3282	2464	(1st) Joan Mary Fry	1·20	1·00
Set of 10			10·50	9·00
Set of 2 Gutter Strips of 10			21·00	
First Day Cover (Tallents House)				9·25
First Day Cover (Coventry)				9·25
Presentation Pack (PO Pack No. 467)			11·00	
PHQ Cards (set of 10) (360)			4·00	11·50

Nos. 3273/3277 and 3278/3282 were each printed together, se-tenant, as horizontal strips of five stamps in sheets of 50 (2 panes 5×5).

No. 3281 also comes from booklet pane No. 3679b in £14·60 Inventive Britain booklet, No. DY12.

2465 Classic Locomotives of Scotland

(Des Delaney Design Consultants. Litho Cartor)

2012 (8 Mar). Classic Locomotives (2nd series). Scotland. Sheet 180×74 mm. Multicoloured 'All-over' phosphor. Perf 14.

MS3283 **2465** Classic Locomotives of Scotland (1st) BR Class D34 Nos. 62471 *Glen Falloch* and 62496 *Glen Loy* at Ardlui, 9 May 1959; 68p. BR Class D40 No. 62276 *Andrew Bain* at Macduff, July 1950; £1 Andrew Barclay No. 807 *Bon Accord* propelling wagons along Miller Street, Aberdeen, June 1962; £1·10 BR Class 4P No. 54767 *Clan Mackinnon* pulling fish train, Kyle of Lochalsh, October 1948 .... 4·75 4·75

First Day Cover (Tallents House) .... 6·00
First Day Cover (Glasgow) .... 6·00
Presentation Pack (PO Pack No. 468) .... 5·50
PHQ Cards (set of 5) (361) .... 2·00 9·00

The five PHQ cards show the four individual stamps and the complete miniature sheet.

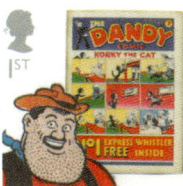

2466 *The Dandy* and Desperate Dan

2467 *The Beano* and Dennis the Menace

2468 *Eagle* and Dan Dare

2469 *The Topper* and Beryl the Peril

2470 *Tiger* and Roy of the Rovers

2471 *Bunty* and the Four Marys

229

QUEEN ELIZABETH II/2012

2472 *Buster* and Cartoon Character Buster

2473 *Valiant* and the Steel Claw

2474 *Twinkle* and Nurse Nancy

2475 *2000 AD* and Judge Dredd

(Des The Chase. Litho Cartor)

2012 (20 Mar). Comics. Multicoloured 'All-over' phosphor. Perf 14½.

3284	**2466**	(1st) *The Dandy* and Desperate Dan......	1·20	1·00
		a. Horiz strip of 5. Nos. 3284/3288......	5·25	4·50
3285	**2467**	(1st) *The Beano* and Dennis the Menace....................................	1·20	1·00
3286	**2468**	(1st) *Eagle* and Dan Dare...................	1·20	1·00
3287	**2469**	(1st) *The Topper* and Beryl the Peril.....	1·20	1·00
3288	**2470**	(1st) *Tiger* and Roy of the Rovers..........	1·20	1·00
3289	**2471**	(1st) *Bunty* and the Four Marys............	1·20	1·00
		a. Horiz strip of 5. Nos. 3289/3293......	5·25	4·50
3290	**2472**	(1st) *Buster* and Cartoon Character Buster....................................	1·20	1·00
3291	**2473**	(1st) *Valiant* and the Steel Claw............	1·20	1·00
3292	**2474**	(1st) *Twinkle* and Nurse Nancy............	1·20	1·00
3293	**2475**	(1st) *2000 AD* and Judge Dredd............	1·20	1·00
Set of 10..			10·50	9·00
Set of 2 Gutter Strips of 5.......................................			21·00	
First Day Cover (Tallents House)............................				15·00
First Day Cover (Dundee)......................................				15·00
Presentation Pack (PO Pack No. 469).....................			11·00	
PHQ Cards (set of 10)..			4·00	11·50

2476 Manchester Town Hall

2477 Narrow Water Castle, Co. Down

2478 Old Bailey, London

2479 Portmeirion, Wales

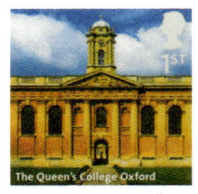

2480 The Queen's College, Oxford

2481 Roman Baths, Bath

2482 Stirling Castle, Scotland

2483 Tyne Bridge, Newcastle

2484 Urquhart Castle, Scotland

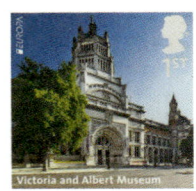

2485 Victoria and Albert Museum, London

2486 White Cliffs of Dover

2487 Station X, Bletchley Park, Buckinghamshire

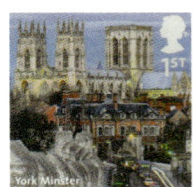

2488 York Minster

2489 London Zoo

(Des Robert Maude and Sarah Davies. Litho Cartor)

2012 (10 Apr). UK A–Z (2nd series). Multicoloured 'All-over' phosphor. Perf 14½.

3294	**2476**	(1st) Manchester Town Hall................	1·20	1·00
		a. Horiz strip of 6. Nos. 3294/3299.....	6·50	5·50
3295	**2477**	(1st) Narrow Water Castle, Co. Down......	1·20	1·00
3296	**2478**	(1st) Old Bailey, London......................	1·20	1·00
3297	**2479**	(1st) Portmeirion, Wales.....................	1·20	1·00
3298	**2480**	(1st) The Queen's College, Oxford.........	1·20	1·00
3299	**2481**	(1st) Roman Baths, Bath.....................	1·20	1·00
3300	**2482**	(1st) Stirling Castle, Scotland...............	1·20	1·00
		a. Horiz strip of 6. Nos. 3300/3305.....	6·50	5·50
3301	**2483**	(1st) Tyne Bridge, Newcastle................	1·20	1·00
3302	**2484**	(1st) Urquhart Castle, Scotland............	1·20	1·00
3303	**2485**	(1st) Victoria and Albert Museum, London....................................	1·20	1·00
3304	**2486**	(1st) White Cliffs of Dover....................	1·20	1·00
3305	**2487**	(1st) Station X, Bletchley Park, Buckinghamshire........................	1·20	1·00
3306	**2488**	(1st) York Minster................................	1·20	1·00
		a. Horiz pair. Nos. 3306/3307............	2·25	2·00
3307	**2489**	(1st) London Zoo................................	1·20	1·00
Set of 14..			15·00	12·50
Set of 2 Gutter Strips of 12 and 1 Gutter Strip of 4........			30·00	
Set of 2 Traffic Light Gutter Strips of 24 and 1 Gutter Block of 8...			50·00	
First Day Covers (Tallents House) (2)......................				15·00
First Day Covers (Dover, Kent) (2).........................				15·00
Presentation Pack (PO Pack No. 470).....................			16·00	
PHQ Cards (set of 14) (363)..................................			5·50	15·00

2012/QUEEN ELIZABETH II

2489a
MS3308 297×210 mm. **2489a**. Nos. 3230/3241 and
3294/3307 .... £100 £110

Nos. 3294/3299 and 3300/3305 were each printed together, *se-tenant*, as horizontal strips of six stamps in sheets of 60 (2 panes 6×5).

Nos. 3306/3307 were printed together, *se-tenant*, as horizontal pairs in sheets of 60 (2 panes 6×5).

No. 3303 includes the EUROPA emblem.

No. 3305 also comes from booklet pane No. 3679b in £14·60 Inventive Britain booklet No. DY12.

2490 Skirt Suit by Hardy Amies, late 1940s
2491 Outfit by Norman Hartnell, 1950s 
2492 Jacket designed by John Pearce for Granny Takes a Trip Boutique, 1960s 
2493 Print by Celia Birtwell for Outfit by Ossie Clark, late 1960s 
2494 Suit designed for Ringo Starr by Tommy Nutter 
2495 Outfit by Jean Muir, late 1970s/early 1980s 
2496 'Royal' Dress by Zandra Rhodes, 1981 
2497 Harlequin dress by Vivienne Westwood, 1993 
2498 Suit by Paul Smith, 2003 
2499 'Black Raven' by Alexander McQueen, 2009 

(Des Johnson banks. Litho Cartor)

2012 (15 May). Great British Fashion. Multicoloured Phosphor background. Perf 14½×14.

3309	2490	(1st) Skirt Suit by Hardy Amies	1·20	1·00
		a. Horiz strip of 5. Nos. 3309/3313	5·25	4·50
3310	2491	(1st) Outfit by Norman Hartnell	1·20	1·00
3311	2492	(1st) Jacket designed by John Pearce	1·20	1·00
3312	2493	(1st) Print by Celia Birtwell for Outfit by Ossie Clark	1·20	1·00
3313	2494	(1st) Suit designed	1·20	1·00
3314	2495	(1st) Outfit by Jean Muir	1·20	1·00
		a. Horiz strip of 5. Nos. 3314/3318	5·25	4·50
3315	2496	(1st) 'Royal' Dress by Zandra Rhodes	1·20	1·00
3316	2497	(1st) Harlequin dress by Vivienne Westwood	1·20	1·00
3317	2498	(1st) Suit by Paul Smith	1·20	1·00
3318	2499	(1st) 'Black Raven' by Alexander McQueen	1·20	1·00
Set of 10			10·50	9·00
Set of 2 Gutter Strips of 10			21·00	
Set of 2 Traffic Light Gutter Strips of 20			40·00	
First Day Cover (Tallents House)				11·00
First Day Cover (London W1)				11·00
Presentation Pack (PO Pack No. 471)			11·00	
PHQ Cards (set of 10) (364)			4·00	12·00

Nos. 3309/3313 and 3314/3318 were each printed together, *se-tenant*, as horizontal strips of five stamps in sheets of 50 (2 panes 5×5).

2500 Queen Elizabeth II at Golden Jubilee Thanksgiving Service, St Paul's Cathedral, London, 2002
2501 Queen Elizabeth II Trooping the Colour, 1967 
2502 Queen Elizabeth II inspecting 2nd Battalion Royal Welsh, Tidworth, 1 March 2007 
2503 First Christmas Television Broadcast, 1957 
2504 Silver Jubilee Walkabout, 1977 
2505 Queen Elizabeth II in Garter Ceremony Procession, 1997 

231

QUEEN ELIZABETH II/2012

2506 Queen Elizabeth II addressing the UN General Assembly, 1957

2507 Queen Elizabeth II at Commonwealth Games, Brisbane, Australia, 1982

(Des Kate Stephens. Photo De La Rue (3319A/3320A, 3323A/3326A), Enschedé (3321A/3322A), Litho Walsall (3319B/3326B) or Photo Walsall (3327B))

2012 (31 May)–**22**. Diamond Jubilee. Multicoloured. 'All-over' phosphor.

(a) Sheet stamps. Ordinary gum. Perf 14×14½.

3319A	**2500**	(1st) Queen Elizabeth II at Golden Jubilee Service, St Paul's Cathedral, London, 2002	1·20	1·00
		a. Horiz pair. Nos. 3319A/3320A	2·40	2·00
3320A	**2501**	(1st) Queen Elizabeth II Trooping the Colour, 1967	1·20	1·00
3321A	**2502**	77p. Queen Elizabeth II inspecting 2nd Battalion Royal Welsh, Tidworth, 1 March 2007	1·00	1·00
		a. Horiz pair. Nos. 3321A/3322A	2·00	2·00
3322A	**2503**	77p. First Christmas Television Broadcast, 1957	1·00	1·00
3323A	**2504**	87p. Silver Jubilee Walkabout, 1977	1·25	1·25
		a. Horiz pair. Nos. 3323A/3324A	2·50	2·50
3324A	**2505**	87p. Queen Elizabeth II in Garter Ceremony Procession, 1997	1·25	1·25
3325A	**2506**	£1·28 Queen Elizabeth II addressing the UN General Assembly, 1957	1·75	1·75
		a. Horiz pair. Nos. 3325A/3326A	2·50	3·50
3326A	**2507**	£1·28 Queen Elizabeth II at Commonwealth Games, Brisbane, Australia, 1982	1·75	1·75
Set of 8			1·75	1·75
Set of 4 Gutter Strips of 4			18·50	
First Day Cover (Tallents House)				11·00
Presentation Pack (PO Pack No. 72)			19·00	
PHQ Cards (Set of 8) (365)			3·25	12·00

(b) Booklet stamps. Ordinary gum. Perf 14×14½.

3319B	**2500**	(1st) Queen Elizabeth II at Golden Jubilee Service, St Paul's Cathedral, London, 2002	1·40	1·40
		b. Booklet pane. Nos. 3319B and 3323B/3325B with margins all round		
		c. Booklet pane. Nos. 3319B/3320B and 3827/3828 with margins all round (4.2.22)	5·25	
3320B	**2501**	(1st) Queen Elizabeth II Trooping the Colour, 1967	1·40	1·40
		b. Booklet pane. Nos. 3320B/3321B with margins all round		
3321B	**2502**	77p. Queen Elizabeth II inspecting 2nd Battalion Royal Welsh, Tidworth, 1 March 2007	1·40	1·40
3322B	**2503**	77p. First Christmas Television Broadcast, 1957	1·40	1·40
		b. Booklet pane. Nos. 3322B and 3326B with margins all round		
3323B	**2504**	87p. Silver Jubilee Walkabout, 1977	1·40	1·40
3324B	**2505**	87p. Queen Elizabeth II in Garter Ceremony Procession, 1997	1·40	1·40
3325B	**2506**	£1·28 Queen Elizabeth II addressing the UN General Assembly, 1957	1·75	1·75
3326B	**2507**	£1·28 Queen Elizabeth II at Commonwealth Games, Brisbane, Australia, 1982	1·75	1·75
Set of 8			11·00	11·00

(c) Self-adhesive booklet stamp. Die-cut perf 14.

3327	**2500**	(1st) Queen Elizabeth II at Golden Jubilee Service, St Paul's Cathedral, London, 2002	2·00	2·00
		a. Booklet pane. Nos. 3327×2 and No. U3274×4	7·50	

No. 3328 is vacant.

Nos. 3319A/3320A, 3321A/3322A, 3323A/3324A and 3325A/3326A were printed together, *se-tenant*, as horizontal pairs in sheets of 60 (2 panes 6×5).

Nos. 3319B/3326B come from £12·77 booklets, No. DY4.

No. 3319c comes from £19·50 premium booklets, No. DY42.

No. 3327 was only issued in stamp booklets, No. PM33, originally sold for £3·60.

2507a Queen Elizabeth II

(Des Sedley Place. Gravure Walsall)

2012 (31 May). Diamond Jubilee (4th issue). As T **2507a** but redrawn with 1st value indicator. Multicoloured Two phosphor bands. Perf 14½×14 (with one elliptical hole in each vert side).

3329		(1st) light brown	1·25	1·25

A similar stamp was issued in No. **MS**3272.

> The stamp and pane, formerly listed as Nos. 3328/3328a have been renumbered as U3279/U3279l and will be found in the Machins section of this catalogue.

2508 Mr Bumble (*Oliver Twist*)

2509 Mr Pickwick (*The Pickwick Papers*)

2510 The Marchioness (*The Old Curiosity Shop*)

2511 Mrs Gamp (*Martin Chuzzlewit*)

2512 Captain Cuttle (*Dombey and Son*)

2513 Mr Micawber (*David Copperfield*)

2514 Scenes from *Nicholas Nickleby, Bleak House, Little Dorrit* and *A Tale of Two Cities* (Illustration reduced. Actual size 190×67 mm)

(Des Howard Brown. Litho Cartor)

2012 (19 June). Birth Bicentenary of Charles Dickens. Illustrations from Character Sketches from Charles Dickens, c 1890 by Joseph Clayton Clarke ('Kyd') (Nos. 3330/3335) or Book Illustrations by Hablot Knight Browne ('Phiz') (No. **MS**3336). Multicoloured One centre band (2nd) or 'all-over' phosphor (others). Perf 14 (Nos. 3330/3335) or 14×14½ (No. **MS**3336).

3330	**2508**	(2nd) Mr Bumble (*Oliver Twist*)	90	90
3331	**2509**	(1st) Mr Pickwick (*The Pickwick Papers*)	1·20	1·00
3332	**2510**	77p. The Marchioness (*The Old Curiosity Shop*)	1·00	1·00
3333	**2511**	87p. Mrs Gamp (*Martin Chuzzlewit*)	1·40	1·40
3334	**2512**	£1·28 Captain Cuttle (*Dombey and Son*)	2·00	2·00
3335	**2513**	£1·90 Mr Micawber (*David Copperfield*)	3·00	3·00
Set of 6			8·50	8·50
Set of 6 Gutter Pairs			17·00	
Set of 6 Traffic Light Gutter Blocks of 4			38·00	
First Day Cover (Tallents House)				11·00
First Day Cover (Portsmouth)				11·00
Presentation Pack (PO Pack No. 473) (Nos. 3330/3335 and **MS**3336)			14·00	
PHQ Cards (set of 11) (366)			4·50	17·00

MS3336 190×67 mm. **2514** Scenes from *Nicholas Nickleby*, *Bleak House*, *Little Dorrit* and *A Tale of Two Cities* (1st)×4 Nicholas Nickleby caning headmaster Wackford Squeers (*Nicholas Nickleby*); Mrs Bagnet is charmed with Mr Bucket (*Bleak House*); Amy Dorrit introduces Maggy to Arthur Clennam (*Little Dorrit*); Charles Darnay arrested by French revolutionaries (*A Tale of Two Cities*)............ 3·75 3·75
First Day Cover (Tallents House).............................. 4·50
First Day Cover (Portsmouth).................................. 4·50

The complete miniature sheet is shown on one of the 11 PHQ cards with the others depicting individual stamps including those from No. **MS**3336.

2435 Paralympic Games Emblem **2436** Olympic Games Emblem

(Litho Cartor)

2012 (27 July). Olympic and Paralympic Games (8th issue). Designs as Nos. 3250/3253. Multicoloured Two phosphor bands. Perf 14½×14 (with one elliptical hole in each vert side).

3337	2436	(1st) Olympic Games Emblem. Black and orange-red............	4·00	4·00
		a. Booklet pane. Nos. 3337/3338, each×3, and 3339/3340 with central label and margins all round............		32·00
3338	2435	(1st) Paralympic Games Emblem. Black and orange-red............	4·00	4·00
3339	2436	(Worldwide up to 20 g) Olympic Games Emblem. Black, bright scarlet and greenish blue...........	6·00	6·00
3340	2435	(Worldwide up to 20g) Paralympic Games Emblem. Black, bright scarlet and greenish blue...........	6·00	6·00

Set of 4.. 18·00 18·00
First Day Cover (Philatelic Bureau Edinburgh) (No. 3337a).. 20·00
First Day Cover (London E20) (No. 3337a)............ 20·00

Nos. 3339/3340 were for use on Worldwide Mail up to 20 grams.
Nos. 3337/3340 were only issued in the £10·71 Olympic and Paralympic Games stamp booklet, No. DY5.

2515 Sports and London Landmarks (*Illustration reduced. Actual size 192×75 mm*)

(Des Hat-trick design. Litho Cartor)

2012 (27 July). Welcome to London, Olympic Games. Sheet 192×75 mm. Multicoloured 'All-over' phosphor. Perf 14½.
MS3341 **2515** Sports and London Landmarks (1st) Fencer and Tower Bridge; (1st) Athletes in race and Olympic Stadium; £1·28 Diver and Tate Modern; £1·28 Cyclist and London Eye........................... 5·50 5·50
First Day Cover (Tallents House)................................ 10·00
First Day Cover (London E20).................................... 10·00
Presentation Pack (PO Pack No. 474)................ 20·00
PHQ Cards (set of 5) (367)...................................... 2·00 9·00

The five PHQ Cards show the four individual stamps and the complete miniature sheet.

2516 Helen Glover and Heather Stanning (rowing, women's pairs)

2517 Bradley Wiggins (cycling, road, men's time trial)

2518 Tim Baillie and Etienne Stott (canoe slalom, men's canoe double (C2))

2519 Peter Wilson (shooting, shotgun men's double trap)

2520 Philip Hindes, Chris Hoy and Jason Kenny (cycling, track men's team sprint)

2521 Katherine Grainger and Anna Watkins (rowing, women's double sculls)

2522 Steven Burke, Ed Clancy, Peter Kennaugh and Geraint Thomas (cycling, track men's team pursuit)

2523 Victoria Pendleton (cycling, track women's keirin)

QUEEN ELIZABETH II/2012

2524 Alex Gregory, Tom James, Pete Reed and Andrew Triggs Hodge (rowing, men's fours)

2525 Katherine Copeland and Sophie Hosking (rowing, lightweight women's double sculls)

2526 Dani King, Joanna Rowsell and Laura Trott (cycling, track women's team pursuit)

2527 Jessica Ennis (athletics, combined women's heptathlon)

2528 Greg Rutherford (athletics, field men's long jump)

2529 Mo Farah (athletics, track men's 10,000 m)

2530 Ben Ainslie (sailing, Finn men's heavyweight dinghy)

2531 Andy Murray (tennis, men's singles)

2532 Scott Brash, Peter Charles, Ben Maher and Nick Skelton (equestrian, jumping team)

2533 Jason Kenny (cycling, track men's sprint)

2534 Alistair Brownlee (men's triathlon)

2535 Carl Hester, Laura Bechtolsheimer and Charlotte Dujardin (equestrian, dressage team)

2536 Laura Trott (cycling, track women's omnium)

2537 Chris Hoy (cycling, track men's keirin)

2012 / QUEEN ELIZABETH II

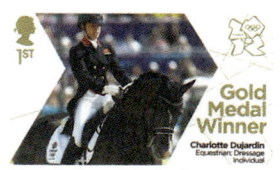

2538 Charlotte Dujardin (equestrian, dressage individual)

2539 Nicola Adams (boxing, women's fly weight)

2540 Jade Jones (taekwondo, women's under 57 kg)

2541 Ed McKeever (canoe sprint, men's kayak single (K1) 200 m)

2542 Mo Farah (athletics, track men's 5000 m)

2543 Luke Campbell (boxing, men's bantam weight)

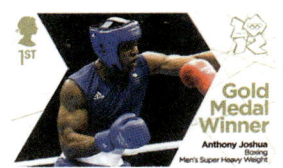

2544 Anthony Joshua (boxing, men's super heavy weight)

(Des True North and Royal Mail. Litho with digital overprint Walsall and six regional printers)

2012 (2 Aug–1 Sept). British Gold Medal Winners at London Olympic Games. Self-adhesive. Multicoloured Two phosphor panels. Die-cut perf 15×14½.

3342	2516	(1st) Helen Glover and Heather Stanning	1·25	1·25
		a. Sheetlet. No. 3342×6	6·75	6·75
3343	2517	(1st) Bradley Wiggins (1.9.12)	1·25	1·25
		a. Sheetlet. No. 3343×6	6·75	6·75
3344	2518	(1st) Tim Baillie and Etienne Stott (3.8.12)	1·25	1·25
		a. Sheetlet. No. 3344×6	6·75	6·75
3345	2519	(1st) Peter Wilson (3.8.12)	1·25	1·25
		a. Sheetlet. No. 3345×6	6·75	6·75
3346	2520	(1st) Philip Hindes, Chris Hoy and Jason Kenny (3.8.12)	1·25	1·25
		a. Sheetlet. No. 3346×6	6·75	6·75
3347	2521	(1st) Katherine Grainger and Anna Watkins (4.8.12)	1·25	1·25
		a. Sheetlet. No. 3347×6	6·75	6·75
3348	2522	(1st) Steven Burke, Ed Clancy, Peter Kennaugh and Geraint Thomas (4.8.12)	1·25	1·25
		a. Sheetlet. No. 3348×6	6·75	6·75
		b. Phosphor omitted	35·00	
3349	2523	(1st) Victoria Pendleton (4.8.12)	1·25	1·25
		a. Sheetlet. No. 3349×6	6·75	6·75
		b. Phosphor omitted	35·00	
3350	2524	(1st) Alex Gregory, Tom James, Pete Reed and Andrew Triggs Hodge (5.8.12)	1·25	1·25
		a. Sheetlet. No. 3350×6	6·75	6·75
		b. Phosphor omitted	35·00	
3351	2525	(1st) Katherine Copeland and Sophie Hosking (5.8.12)	1·25	1·25
		a. Sheetlet. No. 3351×6	6·75	6·75
		ab. Black ptg double		
		b. Phosphor omitted	35·00	
3352	2526	(1st) Dani King, Joanna Rowsell and Laura Trott (5.8.12)	1·25	1·25
		a. Sheetlet. No. 3352×6	6·75	6·75
		b. Phosphor omitted	35·00	
3353	2527	(1st) Jessica Ennis (5.8.12)	1·25	1·25
		a. Sheetlet. No. 3353×6	6·75	6·75
		b. Phosphor omitted	35·00	
3354	2528	(1st) Greg Rutherford (5.8.12)	1·25	1·25
		a. Sheetlet. No. 3354×6	6·75	6·75
3355	2529	(1st) Mo Farah (5.8.12)	1·25	1·25
		a. Sheetlet. No. 3355×6	6·75	6·75
3356	2530	(1st) Ben Ainslie (6.8.12)	1·25	1·25
		a. Sheetlet. No. 3356×6	6·75	6·75
3357	2531	(1st) Andy Murray (6.8.12)	1·25	1·25
		a. Sheetlet. No. 3357×6	6·75	6·75
3358	2532	(1st) Scott Brash, Peter Charles, Ben Maher and Nick Skelton (7.8.12)	1·25	1·25
		a. Sheetlet. No. 3358×6	6·75	6·75
3359	2533	(1st) Jason Kenny (7.8.12)	1·25	1·25
		a. Sheetlet. No. 3359×6	6·75	6·75
3360	2534	(1st) Alistair Brownlee (8.8.12)	1·25	1·25
		a. Sheetlet. No. 3360×6	6·75	6·75
3361	2535	(1st) Carl Hester, Laura Bechtolsheimer and Charlotte Dujardin (8.8.12)	1·25	1·25
		a. Sheetlet. No. 3361×6	6·75	6·75
3362	2536	(1st) Laura Trott (8.8.12)	1·25	1·25
		a. Sheetlet. No. 3362×6	6·75	6·75
3363	2537	(1st) Chris Hoy (8.8.12)	1·25	1·25
		a. Sheetlet. No. 3363×6	6·75	6·75
3364	2538	(1st) Charlotte Dujardin (10.8.12)	1·25	1·25
		a. Sheetlet. No. 3364×6	6·75	6·75
3365	2539	(1st) Nicola Adams (10.8.12)	1·25	1·25
		a. Sheetlet. No. 3365×6	6·75	6·75
3366	2540	(1st) Jade Jones (10.8.12)	1·25	1·25
		a. Sheetlet. No. 3366×6	6·75	6·75
3367	2541	(1st) Ed McKeever (12.8.12)	1·25	1·25
		a. Sheetlet. No. 3367×6	6·75	6·75
		ab. Black printed double		
		ac. Types **2541** and **2542** printed together on the same stamps		
3368	2542	(1st) Mo Farah (12.8.12)	1·25	1·25
		a. Sheetlet. No. 3368×6	6·75	6·75
		ab. Black printed double		
3369	2543	(1st) Luke Campbell (12.8.12)	1·25	1·25
		a. Sheetlet. No. 3369×6	6·75	6·75
3370	2544	(1st) Anthony Joshua (13.8.12)	1·25	1·25
		a. Sheetlet. No. 3370×6	6·75	6·75
		Set of 29 Single Stamps	35·00	35·00
		3342a/3370a Set of 29 sheetlets	£175	£175

First Day Covers (Tallents House) or (London E20) (Sheetlets, Nos. 3342a/3370a) (29) £250
First Day Cover (Tallents House) (any single gold medal stamp) .... 4·25
First Day Cover (London E20) (any single gold medal stamp) .... 4·25

The self-adhesive base sheetlets for Nos. 3342/3370 were produced by Walsall with the image, name and event of the winning athletes digitally printed by regional printers in six different locations: Attleborough, Edinburgh, London, Preston, Solihull and Swindon.

235

Nos. 3368/3370 were not produced by the Preston printer due to machinery breakdown.

Post office sheets comprised four sheetlets of six stamps (3×2), the sheetlets being separated by roulettes. The four sheetlets had one of the following inscriptions on the left margin: emblem 'TEAM GB' and Olympic rings; 'The XXX Olympiad'; barcode; Sheet number, Issue date and Printer location.

Individual stamps had to be cut from the sheetlets using scissors.

Stamps for Royal Mail first day covers came from special coil printings on non-phosphor paper, so all stamps exist, phosphor omitted, used, from this source.

Nos. 3348b/3353b were subsequently released to the trade in unused coils.

2545 Paralympic Sports and London Landmarks (*Illustration reduced. Actual size 193×75 mm*)

(Des Pearce Marchbank. Litho Cartor)

2012 (29 Aug). Welcome to London, Paralympic Games. Sheet 193×75 mm. Multicoloured 'All-over' phosphor. Perf 14½.

MS3371 **2545** Paralympic Sports and London Landmarks (1st) Athlete wearing running blades and Olympic Stadium; (1st) Wheelchair basketball player and Palace of Westminster; £1·28 Powerlifter, Millennium Bridge and St Paul's Cathedral; £1·28 Cyclist and London Eye .... 5·50   5·50
First Day Cover (Tallents House) ....   10·00
First Day Cover (London E20) ....   10·00
Presentation Pack (PO Pack No. 475) .... 9·00
PHQ Cards (set of 5) (368) .... 2·00   9·00

The five PHQ Cards show the four individual stamps and the complete miniature sheet.

2546 Sarah Storey (cycling, track women's C5 pursuit)

2547 Jonathan Fox (swimming, men's 100 m backstroke, S7)

2548 Mark Colbourne (cycling, track men's C1 pursuit)

2549 Hannah Cockroft (athletics, track women's 100 m, T34)

2550 Neil Fachie and Barney Storey (cycling, men's B 1 km time trial)

2551 Richard Whitehead (athletics, track men's 200 m, T42)

2552 Natasha Baker (equestrian, individual championship test, grade II)

2553 Sarah Storey (cycling : track women's C4-5 500 m time trial)

2554 Ellie Simmonds (swimming, women's 400 m freestyle, S6)

2555 Pamela Relph, Naomi Riches, James Roe, David Smith and Lily van den Broecke (rowing, mixed coxed four, LTAmix4+)

2556 Aled Davies (athletics, field men's discus, F42)

2557 Anthony Kappes and Craig MacLean (cycling, track men's B sprint)

2558 Jessica-Jane Applegate (swimming, women's 200 m freestyle, S14)

2559 Sophie Christiansen (equestrian, individual championship test, grade 1a)

2560 David Weir (athletics, track men's 5000 m, T54)

2561 Natasha Baker (equestrian, individual freestyle test, grade II)

2562 Ellie Simmonds (swimming, women's 200 m individual medley, SM6)

2563 Mickey Bushell (athletics, track men's 100 m, T53)

2564 Danielle Brown (archery, women's individual compound, open)

2565 Heather Frederiksen (swimming, women's 100 m backstroke, S8)

2566 Sophie Christiansen (equestrian, individual freestyle test, grade 1a)

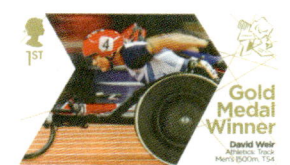

2567 David Weir (athletics, track men's 1500 m, T54)

2568 Sarah Storey (cycling, road women's C5 time trial)

2569 Ollie Hynd (swimming, men's 200 m individual medley, SM8)

2570 Sophie Christiansen, Deb Criddle, Lee Pearson and Sophie Wells (equestrian team, open)

QUEEN ELIZABETH II/2012

2571 Helena Lucas (sailing, single-person keelboat, 2·4mR)

2572 Sarah Storey (cycling, road women's C4-5 road race)

2573 Josef Craig (swimming, men's 400 m freestyle, S7)

2574 Hannah Cockroft (athletics, track women's 200 m, T34)

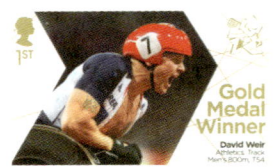

2575 David Weir (athletics, track men's 800 m, T54)

2576 Jonnie Peacock (athletics, track men's 100 m, T44)

2577 Josie Pearson (athletics, field women's discus, F51/52/53)

2578 David Stone (cycling, road mixed T1-2 road race)

2579 David Weir (athletics, road men's marathon, T54)

(Des True North and Royal Mail. Litho with digital overprint Walsall and six regional printers)

2012 (31 Aug–10 Sept). British Gold Medal Winners at London Paralympic Games. Self-adhesive. Multicoloured Two phosphor panels. Die-cut Perf 15×14½.

3372	2546	(1st) Sarah Storey	1·25	1·25
		a. Sheetlet. No. 3372×2	2·50	2·50
3373	2547	(1st) Jonathan Fox (1.9.12)	1·25	1·25
		a. Sheetlet. No. 3373×2	2·50	2·50
3374	2548	(1st) Mark Colbourne (3.9.12)	1·25	1·25
		a. Sheetlet. No. 3374×2	2·50	2·50
3375	2549	(1st) Hannah Cockroft (3.9.12)	1·25	1·25
		a. Sheetlet. No. 3375×2	2·50	2·50
3376	2550	(1st) Neil Fachie and Barney Storey (3.9.12)	1·25	1·25
		a. Sheetlet. No. 3376×2	2·50	2·50
3377	2551	(1st) Richard Whitehead (3.9.12)	1·25	1·25
		a. Sheetlet. No. 3377×2	2·50	2·50
3378	2552	(1st) Natasha Baker (3.9.12)	1·25	1·25
		a. Sheetlet. No. 3378×2	2·50	2·50
3379	2553	(1st) Sarah Storey (3.9.12)	1·25	1·25
		a. Sheetlet. No. 3379×2	2·50	2·50
3380	2554	(1st) Ellie Simmonds (3.9.12)	1·25	1·25
		a. Sheetlet. No. 3380×2	2·50	2·50
3381	2555	(1st) Pamela Relph, Naomi Riches, James Roe, David Smith and Lily van den Broecke (4.9.12)	1·25	1·25
		a. Sheetlet. No. 3381×2	2·50	2·50
3382	2556	(1st) Aled Davies (4.9.12)	1·25	1·25
		a. Sheetlet. No. 3382×2	2·50	2·50
3383	2557	(1st) Anthony Kappes and Craig MacLean (4.9.12)	1·25	1·25
		a. Sheetlet. No. 3383×2	2·50	2·50
3384	2558	(1st) Jessica-Jane Applegate (4.9.12)	1·25	1·25
		a. Sheetlet. No. 3384×2	2·50	2·50
3385	2559	(1st) Sophie Christiansen (4.9.12)	1·25	1·25
		a. Sheetlet. No. 3385×2	2·50	2·50
3386	2560	(1st) David Weir (4.9.12)	1·25	1·25
		a. Sheetlet. No. 3386×2	2·50	2·50
3387	2561	(1st) Natasha Baker (4.9.12)	1·25	1·25
		a. Sheetlet. No. 3387×2	2·50	2·50
3388	2562	(1st) Ellie Simmonds (4.9.12)	1·25	1·25
		a. Sheetlet. No. 3388×2	2·50	2·50
3389	2563	(1st) Mickey Bushell (5.9.12)	1·25	1·25
		a. Sheetlet. No. 3389×2	2·50	2·50
3390	2564	(1st) Danielle Brown (5.9.12)	1·25	1·25
		a. Sheetlet. No. 3390×2	2·50	2·50
3391	2565	(1st) Heather Frederiksen (5.9.12)	1·25	1·25
		a. Sheetlet. No. 3391×2	2·50	2·50
3392	2566	(1st) Sophie Christiansen (5.9.12)	1·25	1·25
		a. Sheetlet. No. 3392×2	2·50	2·50
3393	2567	(1st) David Weir (7.9.12)	1·25	1·25
		a. Sheetlet. No. 3393×2	2·50	2·50
3394	2568	(1st) Sarah Storey (7.9.12)	1·25	1·25
		a. Sheetlet. No. 3394×2	2·50	2·50
3395	2569	(1st) Ollie Hynd (7.9.12)	1·25	1·25
		a. Sheetlet. No. 3395×2	2·50	2·50
3396	2570	(1st) Sophie Christiansen, Deb Criddle, Lee Pearson and Sophie Wells (7.9.12)	1·25	1·25
		a. Sheetlet. No. 3396×2	2·50	2·50
3397	2571	(1st) Helena Lucas (8.9.12)	1·25	1·25
		a. Sheetlet No. 3397×2	2·50	2·50
3398	2572	(1st) Sarah Storey (8.9.12)	1·25	1·25
		a. Sheetlet. No. 3398×2	2·50	2·50
3399	2573	(1st) Josef Craig (8.9.12)	1·25	1·25
		a. Sheetlet. No. 3399×2	2·50	2·50
3400	2574	(1st) Hannah Cockroft (8.9.12)	1·25	1·25
		a. Sheetlet. No. 3400×2	2·50	2·50
3401	2575	(1st) David Weir (10.9.12)	1·25	1·25
		a. Sheetlet. No. 3401×2	2·50	2·50
3402	2576	(1st) Jonnie Peacock (10.9.12)	1·25	1·25

3403	**2577**	a. Sheetlet. No. 3402×2	2·50	2·50
		(1st) Josie Pearson (10.9.12)	1·25	1·25
3404	**2578**	a. Sheetlet. No. 3403×2	2·50	2·50
		(1st) David Stone (10.9.12)	1·25	1·25
3405	**2579**	a. Sheetlet. No. 3404×2	2·50	2·50
		(1st) David Weir (10.9.12)	1·25	1·25
		a. Sheetlet. No. 3405×2	2·50	2·50
Set of 34			40·00	40·00
3372a/3405a Set of 34 sheetlets			78·00	78·00
First Day Covers (Tallents House) (Sheetlets Nos. 3372a/3405a) (34)				£125
First Day Covers (London E20) (Sheetlets Nos. 3372a/3405a) (34)				£125
First Day Covers (Tallents House) (any single gold medal stamp)				4·25
First Day Covers (London E20) (any single gold medal stamp)				4·25

The self-adhesive base sheetlets for Nos. 3372/3405 were produced by Walsall with the image, name and event of the winning athletes digitally printed by regional printers in six different locations: Attleborough, Edinburgh, London, Preston, Solihull and Swindon.

These sheetlets of 16 stamps were divided by roulettes into eight panes of two stamps (1×2). The left margins were inscribed as follows (reading downwards): emblem and 'ParalympicsGB'; 'London 2012 Paralympic Games'; barcode; Sheet number, Issue date and Printer location.

Nos. 3372, 3373 and 3405 were each printed in separate sheetlets of 16 stamps.

Nos. 3374/3377, 3381/3384, 3385/3388, 3389/3392, 3393/3396, 3397/3400 and 3401/3404 were printed in sheetlets of 16 containing four stamps of each design.

The sheetlets of 16 containing Nos. 3378/3380 contained four each of Nos. 3378/3379 and eight of No. 3380.

2580 Scenes from Olympic and Paralympic Games (*Illustration reduced. Actual size 192×75 mm*)

(Des The Chase. Litho Walsall)

2012 (27 Sept). Memories of London 2012 Olympic and Paralympic Games. Sheet 192×75 mm. Multicoloured 'All-over' phosphor. Perf 14½.

MS3406	**2580**	Scenes from Olympic and Paralympic Games (1st) Procession of athletes, Paralympic Games; (1st) Games makers and Olympic Stadium; £1·28 Opening ceremony of Paralympic Games; £1·28 Olympic Games closing ceremony and handover to Rio	9·00	9·00
First Day Cover (Tallents House)				13·00
First Day Cover (London E20)				13·00
Presentation Pack (PO Pack No. 476)			17·50	
PHQ Cards (set of 5) (369)			2·00	16·50

The five PHQ Cards show the four individual stamps and the complete miniature sheet.

2581 BR Class D34 Nos. 62471 Glen Falloch and 62496 Glen Loy at Ardlui, 9 May 1959

(Gravure Walsall)

2012 (27 Sept). Classic Locomotives of Scotland. Booklet stamp. Design as 1st class stamp within No. **MS**3283. Self-adhesive. Multicoloured 'All-over' phosphor. Die-cut perf 14.

3407	**2581**	(1st) BR Class D34 Nos. 62471 Glen Falloch and 62496 Glen Loy	2·00	2·00
		a. Booklet pane. No. 3407×2 and U3274×4	7·50	

No. 3407 was only issued in booklet, No. PM34, originally sold for £3·60.

2582 Sun and Particles ejected from Solar Surface seen from SOHO Observatory

2583 Venus with Clouds in Southern Hemisphere seen from *Venus Express*

2584 Ice in Martian Impact Crater seen from *Mars Express*

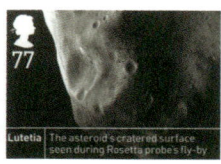

2585 Surface of Asteroid Lutetia seen from *Rosetta* Probe

2586 Saturn and its Rings seen from *Cassini* Satellite

2587 Titan (Saturn's largest moon) seen from *Huygens* Probe

(Des Osborne Ross Design. Litho Cartor)

2012 (16 Oct). Space Science. Multicoloured 'All-over' phosphor. Perf 14.

3408	**2582**	(1st) Sun	1·20	1·00
3409	**2583**	(1st) Venus	1·20	1·00
3410	**2584**	77p. Ice in Martian Impact Crater	1·25	1·25
3411	**2585**	77p. Surface of Asteroid Lutetia	1·25	1·25
3412	**2586**	£1·28 Saturn and its Rings	2·00	2·00
3413	**2587**	£1·28 Titan (Saturn's largest moon)	2·00	2·00
Set of 6			8·00	7·50
Set of 6 Gutter Pairs			16·00	
First Day Cover (Tallents House)				9·75
First Day Cover (Star, Gaerwen Gwynnedd)				9·75
Presentation Pack (PO Pack No. 477)			8·75	
PHQ Cards (set of 6) (370)			2·40	9·00

2588 Six Poppies on Barbed Wire Stems

(Des Hat-trick Design. Gravure Walsall)

2012 (23 Oct). Lest We Forget (4th issue). Self-adhesive. Multicoloured Two phosphor bands. Perf 14½×14 (with one elliptical hole in each vert side).

3414	**2588**	(1st) Six Poppies on Barbed Wire Stems	1·25	1·25

For T **2588** with ordinary gum, see No. 3717.

SELF-ADHESIVE STAMPS. Collectors are reminded that used self-adhesive stamps will no longer 'soak-off'. They should be collected with a neat margin of backing paper.

2589 Reindeer with Decorated Antlers

2590 Santa with Robin

2591 Reindeer with Decorated Antlers

QUEEN ELIZABETH II/2012

2592 Snowman and Penguin
2593 Santa with Robin 
2594 Robin with Star Decoration in Beak 
2595 Cat and Mouse decorating Christmas Tree 
2596 Steam Locomotive on Metropolitan Railway, 1863
2597 Navvies excavating 'Deep Cut' Tube Tunnel, 1898
2598 Commuters in Carriage, 1911
2599 Boston Manor Art Deco Station, 1934
2600 Train on 'Deep Cut' Line, 1938
2601 Canary Wharf Station, 1999

(Des Axel Scheffler and Webb and Webb Design. Gravure Walsall (Nos. 3415a, 3416a) or De La Rue (others))

2012 (6 Nov). Christmas. Illustrations by Axel Scheffler. Multicoloured One centre band (No. 3415) or two phosphor bands (others). Perf 14½×14 (with one elliptical hole in each vert side).

(a) Self-adhesive.

3415	2589	(2nd) Reindeer with Decorated Antlers	90	90
		a. Booklet pane. No. 3415×12	13·50	
3416	2590	(1st) Santa with Robin	1·20	1·00
		a. Booklet pane. No. 3416×12	16·00	
3417	2591	(2nd) Reindeer with Decorated Antlers.. Large)	1·25	1·10
3418	2592	87p. Snowman and Penguin	1·40	1·40
3419	2593	(1st Santa with Robin Large)	1·70	1·40
3420	2594	£1·28 Robin with Star Decoration in Beak	2·00	2·00
3421	2595	£1·90 Cat and Mouse decorating Christmas Tree	3·00	3·00
Set of 7			10·00	9·75
First Day Cover (Tallents House)				12·50
First Day Cover (Bethlehem, Llandeilo)				12·50
Presentation Pack (PO Pack No. 478)			11·00	
PHQ Cards (set of 8) (371)			3·25	21·00

(b) Ordinary gum.

MS3422	115×102 mm. As Nos. 3415/3421	10·00	9·75
First Day Cover (Tallents House)			10·00
First Day Cover (Bethlehem, Llandeilo)			10·00

The 2nd class, 1st class, 87p. and £1·28 stamps were also issued in sheets of 20 (No. LS83) containing eight 2nd class, eight 1st class, two 87p. and two £1·28 stamps, each with a *se-tenant* label. These sheets were printed in lithography and sold for £13·10 each.

Separate sheets of 20 2nd, 20 1st, ten 1st, ten 87p. and ten £1·28 were available with personal photographs on the labels from Royal Mail, Edinburgh. These were sold at £13·99 for 20 2nd, £18·25 for 20 1st, £9·99 for ten 1st, £13·55 for ten 87p. and £18·50 for ten £1·28.

The 1st class stamp printed in lithography, from either Post Office label sheets or Personalised Smilers sheets is known with the black printing double.

The eight PHQ cards depict the seven individual stamps and the miniature sheet.

Year Pack

2012 (6 Nov). Comprises Nos. 3254/3259, **MS**3264/**MS**3270, **MS**3272/3307, 3309/3318, 3319A/3326A, 3330/3336, **MS**3341, **MS**3371, **MS**3406, 3408/3413 and 3415/3421
CP3422a Year Pack (PO Pack No. 479) (sold for £80)........................... £175

Post Office Yearbook

2012 (6 Nov). Comprises Nos. 3254/3259, **MS**3264/**MS**3270, **MS**3272/3307, 3309/3318, 3319A/3326A, 3330/3336, **MS**3341, **MS**3371, **MS**3406, 3408/3413 and 3415/3421
YB3422a Yearbook (sold for £90)........................ £300

Miniature Sheet Collection

2012 (6 Nov). Comprises Nos. **MS**3264, **MS**3270, **MS**3272, **MS**3283, **MS**3336, **MS**3341, **MS**3371, **MS**3406 and **MS**3422
MS3422a Miniature Sheet Collection (sold for £35).......... 55·00

2602 Classic London Underground Posters (*Illustration reduced. Actual size 184×74 mm*)

(Des NB Studios (No. **MS**3429) or Hat-trick Design (others). Litho Cartor (Nos. 3423/3429) or gravure Walsall (No. 3430))

2013 (9 Jan). 150th Anniversary of the London Underground. Multicoloured One centre band (2nd) or 'all-over' phosphor (others).

(a) Ordinary gum. Perf 14½.

3423	2596	(2nd) Steam Locomotive on Metropolitan Railway	90	90
3424	2597	(2nd) Navvies excavating Deep Cut Tube Tunnel	90	90
3425	2598	(1st) Commuters in Carriage	1·20	1·00
3426	2599	(1st) Boston Manor Art Deco Station	1·20	1·00
3427	2600	£1·28 Train on Deep Cut Line	2·00	2·00
3428	2601	£1·28 Canary Wharf Station	2·00	2·00
Set of 6			7·25	7·00
Set of 6 Gutter Pairs			14·50	
First Day Cover (Tallents House)				8·75
First Day Cover (London W2)				8·75
Presentation Pack (PO Pack No. 480) (Nos. 3423/3428 and **MS**3429)			15·00	
PHQ Cards (set of 11) (372)			4·50	18·00
MS3429 184×74 mm. **2602** Classic London Underground Posters (1st) Golders Green, 1908, By Underground to fresh air (Maxwell Armfield), 1915 and Summer Sales (Mary Koop), 1925; 77p. For the Zoo (Charles Paine), 1921, Power (Edward McKnight-Kauffer), 1931 and The Seen (James Fitton), 1948; 87p. A train every 90 seconds (Abram Games), 1937, Thanks to the Underground (Zero Hans Schleger)), 1935 and Cut travelling time, Victoria Line (Tom Eckersley), 1969; £1·28 The London Transport Collection (Tom Eckersley), 1975, London Zoo (Abram Games), 1976 and The Tate Gallery by Tube (David Booth), 1987			5·00	5·25
First Day Cover (Tallents House)				6·50
First Day Cover (London W2)				6·50

2013/**QUEEN ELIZABETH II**

(b) Self-adhesive. Die-cut perf 14½. Die-cut perf 14½.

3430	**2599**	(1st) Boston Manor Art Deco Station, 1934....................	2·00	2·00
		a. Booklet pane. Nos. 3430×2 and U3022×4............................	7·50	
		a. Booklet pane. Nos. 3430×2 and U2968b×4..........................	6·50	1·35

No. 3430 was issued in stamp booklet, No. PM35, originally sold for £3·60.

The complete miniature sheet is shown on one of the 11 PHQ cards with the others depicting individual stamps, including those from No. **MS**3429.

2603 Elinor and Marianne Dashwood *(Sense and Sensibility)*

2604 Elizabeth Bennet and Portrait of Mr Darcy *(Pride and Prejudice)*

2605 Fanny Price *(Mansfield Park)*

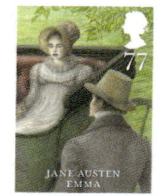

2606 Emma Woodhouse and Mr Knightley *(Emma)*

2607 Catherine Morland *(Northanger Abbey)*

2608 Anne Elliot and Captain Wentworth *(Persuasion)*

(Des Angela Barrett and Webb and Webb. Litho Cartor)

2013 (21 Feb). Bicentenary of the Publication of Jane Austen's *Pride and Prejudice*. Multicoloured 'All-over' phosphor. Perf 14.

3431	**2603**	(1st) Elinor and Marianne Dashwood....	1·20	1·00
3432	**2604**	(1st) Elizabeth Bennet and Portrait of Mr Darcy.............................	1·20	1·00
3433	**2605**	77p. Fanny Price.............................	1·25	1·25
3434	**2606**	77p. Emma Woodhouse and Mr Knightley....................................	1·25	1·25
3435	**2607**	£1·28 Catherine Morland...........................	2·00	2·00
3436	**2608**	£1·28 Anne Elliot and Captain Wentworth..................................	2·00	2·00
Set of 6...			7·75	7·50
Set of 6 Gutter Pairs...			15·50	
Set of 6 Traffic Light Gutter Pairs...			32·00	
First Day Cover (Tallents House)..				10·00
First Day Cover (Steventon, Basingstoke).............................				10·00
Presentation Pack (PO Pack No. 481)...................................			9·00	
PHQ Cards (set of 6) (373)..			2·50	9·25

2604 Elizabeth Bennet and Portrait of Mr Darcy *(Pride and Prejudice)*

2609 The Eleventh Doctor (Matt Smith, 2010–2014)

2610 The Tenth Doctor (David Tennant, 2005–2010)

2611 The Ninth Doctor (Christopher Eccleston, 2005)

2612 The Eighth Doctor (Paul McGann, 1996)

2613 The Seventh Doctor (Sylvester McCoy, 1987–1989)

2614 The Sixth Doctor (Colin Baker, 1984–1986)

2615 The Fifth Doctor (Peter Davison, 1982–1984)

2616 The Fourth Doctor (Tom Baker, 1974–1981)

2617 The Third Doctor (Jon Pertwee, 1970–1974)

2618 The Second Doctor (Patrick Troughton, 1966–1969)

2619 The First Doctor (William Hartnell, 1963–1966)

2620 Tardis

2621 Dr Who 1963–2013 (Illustration reduced. Actual size 115×89 mm)

(Des GBH. Litho Cartor (Nos. 3437/3447 and **MS**3451a) or gravure Walsall (Nos. 3448/3450) or Enschedé (No. **MS**3451))

2013 (26 Mar). 50th Anniversary of *Doctor Who* (TV programme) (1st issue). Multicoloured 'All-over' phosphor.

(a) Ordinary gum. 'All-over' phosphor. Perf 14.

3437	**2609**	(1st) Matt Smith...	1·20	1·00
		a. Horiz strip of 3. Nos. 3437/3439......	3·50	3·00
		b. Booklet pane. Nos. 3437/3439........	3·50	
3438	**2610**	(1st) David Tennant..................................	1·20	1·00
3439	**2611**	(1st) Christopher Eccleston......................	1·20	1·00
3440	**2612**	(1st) Paul McGann....................................	1·20	1·00
		a. Horiz strip of 4. Nos. 3440/3443......	4·25	4·00
		b. Booklet pane. Nos. 3440/3443.......	4·25	
3441	**2613**	(1st) Sylvester McCoy...............................	1·20	1·00
3442	**2614**	(1st) Colin Baker.......................................	1·20	1·00
3443	**2615**	(1st) Peter Davison...................................	1·20	1·00
3444	**2616**	(1st) Tom Baker..	1·20	1·00
		a. Horiz strip of 4. Nos. 3444/3447......	4·25	4·00
		b. Booklet pane. Nos. 3444/3447.......	4·25	

QUEEN ELIZABETH II/2013

3445	2617	(1st) Jon Pertwee	1·20	1·00
3446	2618	(1st) Patrick Troughton	1·20	1·00
3447	2619	(1st) William Hartnell	1·20	1·00

Set of 11 .... 12·00 10·00
Set of 1 Gutter Strip of 3 and 2 Gutter Strips of 8 ...... 24·00
First Day Covers (Tallents House) (2) .... 12·00
First Day Covers (Cardiff) (2) .... 12·00
Presentation Pack (PO Pack No. 482) (Nos. 3437/3447
 and **MS**3451) .... 18·00
PHQ Cards (set of 17) .... 6·75 18·50

(b) Self-adhesive. One centre band (2nd) or two bands. Die-cut perf 14½ (2nd) or 14½×14 (with one elliptical hole in each vert side) (1st).

3448	2609	(1st) Matt Smith	4·50	4·50
		a. Booklet pane. No. 3448, 3449×4 and 3450	14·00	
3449	2620	(1st) Tardis	1·25	1·25
3450	2619	(1st) William Hartnell	4·50	4·50

MS3451 115×89 mm. **2621** Dr Who 1963–2013 (2nd) Dalek; (2nd) The Ood; (2nd) Weeping Angel; (2nd) Cyberman; (1st) TARDIS .... 5·00 4·75
 a. Booklet pane. As No. **MS**3451 but 119×96 mm, with line of roulettes at left .... 8·00
First Day Cover (Tallents House) .... 5·00
First Day Cover (Cardiff) .... 5·00

Nos. 3437/3439 were printed together, se-tenant, as horizontal strips of three stamps in sheets of 48 (2 panes 6×4).

Nos. 3440/3443 and 3444/3447 were each printed together, se-tenant, as horizontal strips of four stamps in sheets of 48 (2 panes 4×6).

Nos. 3448/3450 were issued in stamp booklet, No. PM36, sold for £3·60.

The 1st class TARDIS stamp from booklet pane No. **MS**3451a differs from the same design in the miniature sheet by being perforated 15 all round.

The design area of No. 3449 measures 17½×21½ mm, slightly larger than the same TARDIS design (T **2620**) from the miniature sheet and premium booklet pane (Nos. **MS**3451/**MS**3451a) which measures 17×21mm. (All are 20×24 mm measured perf to perf edge).

The 1st class TARDIS stamp was also issued in sheets of 20, each stamp accompanied by a se-tenant label (No. LS85). These sheets were printed in lithography.

The complete miniature sheet is shown on one of the 17 PHQ cards with the others depicting individual stamps including those from the miniature sheet.

(Des GBH. Litho Cartor)

2013 (26 Mar). 50th Anniversary of Doctor Who (TV programme) (2nd issue). As No. 3449 but ordinary gum. Multicoloured Two phosphor bands. Perf 14½×14 with one elliptical hole in each vertical side

3452	2620	(1st) Tardis	1·25	1·25

No. 3452 only comes from pane No. U3072l in the £13·37 Dr Who premium booklet, No. DY6.

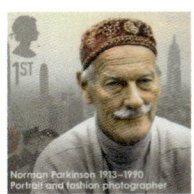

2622 Norman Parkinson (1913–1990, portrait and fashion photographer)

2623 Vivien Leigh (1913–1967, actress)

2624 Peter Cushing (1913–1994, actor)

2625 David Lloyd George (1863–1945, Prime Minister 1916–1922)

2626 Elizabeth David (1913–1992, cookery writer)

2627 John Archer (1863–1932, politician and civil rights campaigner)

2628 Benjamin Britten (1913–1976, composer and pianist)

2629 Mary Leakey (1913–1996, archaeologist and anthropologist)

2630 Bill Shankly (1913–1981, football player and manager)

2631 Richard Dimbleby (1913–1965, journalist and broadcaster)

(Des Together Design. Litho Cartor)

2013 (16 Apr). Great Britons. Multicoloured 'All-over' phosphor. Perf 14½.

3453	2622	(1st) Norman Parkinson	1·20	1·00
		a. Horiz strip of 5. Nos. 3453/3457	5·25	4·50
3454	2623	(1st) Vivien Leigh	1·20	1·00
3455	2624	(1st) Peter Cushing	1·20	1·00
3456	2625	(1st) David Lloyd George	1·20	1·00
3457	2626	(1st) Elizabeth David	1·20	1·00
3458	2627	(1st) John Archer	1·20	1·00
		a. Horiz strip of 5. Nos. 3458/3462	5·25	4·50
3459	2628	(1st) Benjamin Britten	1·20	1·00
3460	2629	(1st) Mary Leakey	1·20	1·00
3461	2630	(1st) Bill Shankly	1·20	1·00
3462	2631	(1st) Richard Dimbleby	1·20	1·00

Set of 10 .... 10·50 9·00
Set of 2 Gutter Strips of 10 .... 21·00
First Day Cover (Tallents House) .... 11·00
First Day Cover (Great Ness, Shrewsbury) .... 11·00
Presentation Pack (PO Pack No. 483) .... 11·00
PHQ Cards (set of 10) (375) .... 4·00 12·00

Nos. 3453/3457 and 3458/3462 were each printed together, se-tenant, as horizontal strips of five stamps in sheets of 50 (2 panes 5×5).

2632 Jimmy Greaves (England)

2633 John Charles (Wales)

2013/QUEEN ELIZABETH II

2634 Gordon Banks (England)
2635 George Best (Northern Ireland) 
2636 John Barnes (England) 
2637 Kevin Keegan (England) 
2638 Denis Law (Scotland) 
2639 Bobby Moore (England) 
2640 Bryan Robson (England) 
2641 Dave Mackay (Scotland) 
2642 Bobby Charlton (England) 

(Des Andrew Kinsman and True North. Litho Cartor (Nos. 3463/3474) or gravure Walsall (Nos. 3475/3476))

2013 (9 May)–**2014**. Football Heroes (1st issue). Multicoloured 'All-over' phosphor.

(a) Ordinary gum. Perf 14½.

3463	2632	(1st) Jimmy Greaves	1·20	1·00
		a. Horiz strip of 5. Nos. 3463/3467	5·50	4·50
3464	2633	(1st) John Charles	1·20	1·00
3465	2634	(1st) Gordon Banks	1·20	1·00
3466	2635	(1st) George Best	1·20	1·00
3467	2636	(1st) John Barnes	1·20	1·00
3468	2637	(1st) Kevin Keegan	1·20	1·00
		a. Horiz strip of 6. Nos. 3468/3473	6·50	5·50
3469	2638	(1st) Denis Law	1·20	1·00
3470	2639	(1st) Bobby Moore	1·20	1·00
3471	2640	(1st) Bryan Robson	1·20	1·00
3472	2641	(1st) Dave Mackay	1·20	1·00
3473	2642	(1st) Bobby Charlton	1·20	1·00
Set of 11			12·00	10·00
Set of 1 Gutter Strip of 12 and 1 Gutter Strip of 10			24·00	
First Day Cover (Tallents House)				11·00
First Day Cover (Wembley, Middlesex)				11·00
Presentation Pack (PO Pack 484)			13·00	
PHQ Cards (set of 12) (376)			4·75	11·00
MS3474 192×74 mm. Nos. 3463/3473			12·00	10·00
First Day Cover				12·00

(b) Self-adhesive. Die-cut perf 14½.

3475	2635	(1st) George Best	4·50	4·50
		a. Booklet pane. Nos. 3475/3476 and U3022×4	11·00	
3476	2639	(1st) Bobby Moore	4·50	4·50
3477	2633	(1st) John Charles (20.2.14)	4·50	4·50
		a. Booklet pane. Nos. 3477/3478 and U3022×4	11·00	
3478	2641	(1st) Dave Mackay (20.2.14)	4·50	4·50
Set of 4			16·00	16·00

Nos. 3463/3489 commemorate the 150th anniversary of the Football Association and the 140th Anniversary of the Scottish Football Association.

Nos. 3463/3467 were printed together, *se-tenant*, as horizontal strips of five stamps in sheets of 30 (5×6).

Nos. 3468/3473 were printed together, *se-tenant*, as horizontal strips of six stamps in sheets of 30 (6×5).

Nos. 3475/3476 and 3477/3478 were issued in separate booklets, Nos. PM37 and PM41, both sold for £3·60.

The 12 PHQ cards depict the 11 individual stamps and the complete miniature sheet.

(Litho Cartor)

2013 (9 May). Football Heroes (2nd issue). Self-adhesive. Multicoloured 'All-over'. phosphor. Die-cut perf 14½×14.

3479	2632	(1st) Jimmy Greaves	1·60	1·60
		a. Booklet pane. Nos. 3479/3483	7·25	7·25
3480	2633	(1st) John Charles	1·60	1·60
3481	2637	(1st) Kevin Keegan	1·60	1·60
3482	2638	(1st) Denis Law	1·60	1·60
3483	2639	(1st) Bobby Moore	1·60	1·60
3484	2634	(1st) Gordon Banks	1·60	1·60
		a. Booklet pane. Nos. 3484/3489	8·75	8·75
3485	2635	(1st) George Best	1·60	1·60
3486	2636	(1st) John Barnes	1·60	1·60
3487	2640	(1st) Bryan Robson	1·60	1·60
3488	2641	(1st) Dave Mackay	1·60	1·60
3489	2642	(1st) Bobby Charlton	1·60	1·60
Set of 11			16·00	16·00

Nos. 3479/3489 were issued in £11·11 Football Heroes premium booklet, No. DY7.

No. 3490 is vacant.

2646 Preliminary Oil Sketch for The Coronation of Queen Elizabeth II (Terence Cuneo), 1953
2647 Queen Elizabeth II in Garter Robes (Nicky Philipps), 2012 
2648 Portrait by Andrew Festing, 1999 
2649 Portrait by Pietro Annigoni, 1955 
2650 Portrait by Sergei Pavlenko, 2000 
2651 Her Majesty Queen Elizabeth II (Richard Stone), 1992 

(Gravure Walsall)

2013 (30 May). 60th Anniversary of the Coronation. Six Decades of Royal Portraits. Multicoloured. Phosphor band at left (2nd) or 'all-over' phosphor (others). Perf 14.

3491	2646	(2nd) Preliminary Oil Sketch for The Coronation of Queen Elizabeth II (Terence Cuneo), 1953	90	90
3492	2647	(1st) Queen Elizabeth II in Garter Robes (Nicky Philipps), 2012	1·20	1·00
3493	2648	78p. Portrait by Andrew Festing, 1999	1·10	1·10
3494	2649	88p. Portrait by Pietro Annigoni, 1955	1·50	1·50
3495	2650	£1·28 Portrait by Sergei Pavlenko, 2000	2·10	2·10
3496	2651	£1·88 Her Majesty Queen Elizabeth II (Richard Stone), 1992	3·00	3·00
Set of 6			8·50	8·50
Set of 6 Gutter Pairs			17·00	

243

QUEEN ELIZABETH II/2013

Set of 6 Traffic Light Gutter Blocks of 4	36·00	
First Day Cover (Tallents House)		11·00
First Day Cover (London SW1)		11·00
Presentation Pack (PO Pack No. 485)	10·00	
PHQ Cards (set of 6) (377)	12·50	10·50
Commemorative Document (Nos. 3491/3492) (2.6.13)	12·50	

2652 UTA Class W No. 103 *Thomas Somerset* with Belfast Express, Downhill, near Castlerock, c 1950

2653 Classic Locomotives of Northern Ireland

(Des Delaney Design Consultants. Gravure Walsall (No. 3497) or litho Cartor (No. **MS**3498))

2013 (18 June). Classic Locomotives (3rd series). Northern Ireland. Black, grey and gold. 'All-over' phosphor.

(a) Self-adhesive. Die-cut perf 14.

3497	**2652**	(1st) UTA Class W No. 103 *Thomas Somerset* with Belfast Express	2·00	2·00
		a. Booklet pane. No. 3497×2 and U3022×4	7·50	

(b) Ordinary gum. Sheet 180×74 mm. Perf 14.

MS3498 Classic Locomotives of Northern Ireland. As T **2652**; 78p. UTA SG3 No. 35; 88p. Peckett No. 2; £1·28 CDRJC Class 5 No. 4	5·00	5·25
First Day Cover (Tallents House)		6·50
First Day Cover (Belfast)		6·50
Presentation Pack (PO Pack No. 486)	6·25	
PHQ Cards (set of 5) (378)	2·00	6·50

No. 3497 was issued in booklet, No. PM38, sold for £3·60.

The five PHQ cards show the four individual stamps and the complete miniature sheet.

2654 Comma (*Polygonia c-album*)

2655 Orange-tip (*Anthocharis cardamines*)

2656 Small Copper (*Lycaena phlaeas*)

2657 Chalkhill Blue (*Polyommatus coridon*)

2658 Swallowtail (*Papilio machaon*)

2659 Purple Emperor (*Apatura iris*)

2660 Marsh Fritillary (*Euphydryas aurinia*)

2661 Brimstone (*Gonepteryx rhamni*)

2662 Red Admiral (*Vanessa atalanta*)

2663 Marbled White (*Melanargia galathea*)

(Des Richard Lewington and Marc & Anna. Litho Cartor (Nos. 3499/3508) or gravure (Nos. 3509/3510) Walsall)

2013 (11 July). Butterflies. Multicoloured 'All-over' phosphor.

(a) Ordinary paper. Perf 14×14½.

3499	**2654**	(1st) Comma	1·20	1·00
		a. Horiz strip of 5. Nos. 3499/3503	5·25	4·50
3500	**2655**	(1st) Orange-tip	1·20	1·00
3501	**2656**	(1st) Small Copper	1·20	1·00
3502	**2657**	(1st) Chalkhill Blue	1·20	1·00
3503	**2658**	(1st) Swallowtail	1·20	1·00
3504	**2659**	(1st) Purple Emperor	1·20	1·00
		a. Horiz strip of 5. Nos. 3504/3508	5·25	4·50
3505	**2660**	(1st) Marsh Fritillary	1·20	1·00
3506	**2661**	(1st) Brimstone	1·20	1·00
3507	**2662**	(1st) Red Admiral	1·20	1·00
3508	**2663**	(1st) Marbled White	1·20	1·00
Set of 10			10·50	9·00
Set of 2 Gutter Strips of 10			21·00	
First Day Cover (Tallents House)				12·00
First Day Cover (Lulworth Camp, Wareham, Dorset)				12·00
Presentation Pack (PO Pack No. 487)			11·00	
PHQ Cards (set of 10) (379)			4·00	11·00

(b) Self-adhesive. Die-cut perf 14×14½.

3509	**2657**	(1st) Chalkhill Blue	2·00	2·00
		a. Booklet pane. Nos. 3509/3510 and U3022×4	7·50	
3510	**2654**	(1st) Comma	2·00	2·00

Nos. 3499/3503 and 3504/3508 were each printed together, *se-tenant*, as horizontal strips of five stamps in sheets of 50 (2 panes 5×5).

Nos. 3509/3510 were issued in stamp booklet, No. PM39, sold for £3·60.

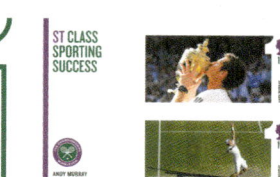

2664 Andy Murray's Wimbledon Victory

2013 / QUEEN ELIZABETH II

(Litho Walsall)

2013 (8 Aug). Andy Murray, Men's Singles Champion, Wimbledon. Sheet 192×75 mm. Multicoloured 'All-over' phosphor. Perf 14½.

MS3511 **2664** Andy Murray's Wimbledon Victory
(1st) Andy Murray kissing Wimbledon Trophy;
(1st) Andy Murray serving; £1·28 In action; £1·28
Holding Trophy... 5·25 5·50
First Day Cover (Tallents House)... 7·00
First Day Cover (Wimbledon, SW19)................................... 7·00
Presentation Pack (PO Pack No. M21).................. 6·50

2665 Jaguar E-Type, 1961

2666 Rolls-Royce Silver Shadow, 1965

2667 Aston Martin DB5, 1963

2668 MG MGB, 1962

2669 Morgan Plus 8, 1968

2670 Lotus Esprit, 1976

2671 The Workhorses

(Des Why Not Associates (Nos. 3512/3517) or Robert Maude and Sarah Davies (No. **MS**3518). Litho Cartor)

2013 (13 Aug). British Auto Legends. Multicoloured 'All-over' phosphor. Perf 13½ (Nos. 3512/3517) or 14 (No. **MS**3518).

3512	2665	(1st) Jaguar E-Type, 1961..................	1·20	1·00
		a. Horiz strip of 3. Nos. 3512/3514.....	3·25	2·75
3513	2666	(1st) Rolls-Royce Silver Shadow, 1965....	1·20	1·00
3514	2667	(1st) Aston Martin DB5, 1963.................	1·20	1·00
3515	2668	£1·28 MG MGB, 1962...............................	1·60	1·60
		a. Horiz strip of 3. Nos. 3515/3517.......	4·25	4·25
3516	2669	£1·28 Morgan Plus 8, 1968......................	1·60	1·60
3517	2670	£1·28 Lotus Esprit, 1976..........................	1·60	1·60

Set of 6... 7·50 7·00
Set of 2 Gutter Strips of 6.................................. 15·00
First Day Cover (Tallents House)..................................... 9·00

First Day Cover (Alwalton, Peterborough)................................. 9·00
Presentation Pack (PO Pack No. 488) (Nos. 3512/3517 and **MS**3518)... 13·50
PHQ Cards (set of 11) (380)............................... 4·50 17·00

MS3518 180×74 mm. **2671** The Workhorses (1st)×4
Morris Minor Royal Mail van (1953–1971); Austin
FX4 (1958–1997) London taxi; Ford Anglia 105E
(1959–1967) police car; Coastguard Land Rover
Defender 110 (from 1990) (all 40×30 mm)............ 4·50 4·00
First Day Cover (Tallents House)... 4·50
First Day Cover (Alwalton, Peterborough)....................... 4·50

Nos. 3512/3514 and 3515/3517 were each printed together, *se-tenant*, as horizontal strips of three stamps in sheets of 60 (2 panes 6×5).

The 1st value from No. **MS**3518 is inscr EUROPA.

The complete miniature sheet is shown on one of the 11 PHQ cards with the others depicting individual stamps including those from the miniature sheet.

2672 East Indiaman *Atlas*, 1813

2673 Royal Mail Ship *Britannia*, 1840

2674 Tea Clipper *Cutty Sark*, 1870

2675 Cargo Liner *Clan Matheson*, 1919

2676 Royal Mail Ship *Queen Elizabeth*, 1940

2677 Bulk Carrier *Lord Hinton*, 1986

(Des Silk Pearce. Litho Enschedé (booklet panes) or Cartor (others))

2013 (19 Sept). Merchant Navy (1st issue). Multicoloured 'All-over' phosphor. Perf 14.

3519	2672	(1st) East Indiaman *Atlas*, 1813..............	1·20	1·00
		a. Booklet pane. Nos. 3519/3521 with margins all round....................	4·00	
3520	2673	(1st) Royal Mail Ship *Britannia*, 1840......	1·20	1·00
3521	2674	(1st) Tea Clipper *Cutty Sark*, 1870...........	1·20	1·00
3522	2675	£1·28 Cargo Liner *Clan Matheson*, 1919..	1·60	1·60
		a. Booklet pane. Nos. 3522/3524 with margins all round....................	5·00	
3523	2676	£1·28 Royal Mail Ship *Queen Elizabeth*, 1940...	1·60	1·60
3524	2677	£1·28 Bulk Carrier *Lord Hinton*, 1986.......	1·60	1·60

Set of 6... 7·50 7·00
Set of 6 Gutter Pairs... 15·00
First Day Cover (Tallents House)..................................... 9·00
First Day Cover (Clydebank)... 9·00
Presentation Pack (PO Pack No. 489) (Nos. 3519/3524 and **MS**3529)... 14·50
PHQ Cards (set of 11) (381)............................... 4·50 17·00

Nos. 3519a and 3522a were only issued in the £11·19 Merchant Navy booklet, No DY8.

The complete miniature sheet is shown on one of the 11 PHQ cards with the others depicting individual stamps including those from No. **MS**3529.

2678 Destroyer HMS *Vanoc* escorting Atlantic Convoy

2679 Merchant Ship passing the Naval Control Base in the Thames Estuary

245

QUEEN ELIZABETH II/2013

2680 Sailors clearing Ice from the Decks of HMS *King George V* in Arctic Waters

2681 Naval Convoy of 24 Merchant Ships in the North Sea

2684 Polacanthus

2685 Ichthyosaurus

2686 Iguanodon

2687 Ornithocheirus

2688 Baryonyx

2689 Dimorphodon

2682 Second World War Atlantic and Arctic Convoys

2690 Hypsilophodon

2691 Cetiosaurus

(Des Silk Pearce. Litho Enschedé)

2013 (19 Sept). Merchant Navy. Multicoloured 'All-over' phosphor. Perf 14.

3525	2678	(1st) Destroyer HMS *Vanoc* escorting Atlantic Convoy	2·25	2·25
		a. Booklet pane. Nos. 3525/3528	8·00	
3526	2679	(1st) Merchant Ship passing the Naval Control Base in the Thames Estuary	2·25	2·25
3527	2680	(1st) Sailors clearing Ice from the Decks of HMS *King George V* in Arctic Waters	2·25	2·25
3528	2681	(1st) Naval Convoy of 24 Merchant Ships in the North Sea	2·25	2·25
Set of 4			8·00	8·00
MS3529	2682	Second World War Atlantic and Arctic Convoys 115×89 mm. Nos. 3525/3528	6·00	6·00
First Day Cover (Tallents House)				6·75
First Day Cover (Clydebank)				6·75

Nos. 3525/3528 were only issued in the £11·19 Merchant Navy premium booklet, No. DY8, and in No. **MS**3529.

2692 Megalosaurus

2693 Plesiosaurus

(Des John Sibbick (illustrator) and Why Not Associates. Gravure Walsall)

2013 (10 Oct). Dinosaurs. Multicoloured 'All-over' phosphor. Die-cut perf 13½×14 (with no teeth around protruding parts at top or foot of the designs).

3532	2684	(1st) Polacanthus	1·20	1·00
		a. Horiz strip of 5. Nos. 3532/3536	5·25	
3533	2685	(1st) Ichthyosaurus	1·20	1·00
3534	2686	(1st) Iguanodon	1·20	1·00
3535	2687	(1st) Ornithocheirus	1·20	1·00
3536	2688	(1st) Baryonyx	1·20	1·00
3537	2689	(1st) Dimorphodon	1·20	1·00
		a. Horiz strip of 5. Nos. 3537/3541	5·25	
3538	2690	(1st) Hypsilophodon	1·20	1·00
3539	2691	(1st) Cetiosaurus	1·20	1·00
3540	2692	(1st) Megalosaurus	1·20	1·00
3541	2693	(1st) Plesiosaurus	1·20	1·00
Set of 10			10·50	9·00
First Day Cover (Tallents House)				11·00
First Day Cover (Lyme Regis, Dorset)				11·00
Presentation Pack (PO Pack 490)			11·00	
PHQ Cards (set of 10) (382)			4·00	11·00

2683 Royal Mail Van

2673 Royal Mail Ship *Britannia*, 1840

(Gravure Walsall)

2013 (19 Sept). Royal Mail Transport By Land and Sea. Multicoloured Die-cut perf 14.

3530	2683	(1st) Royal Mail Van	5·50	5·50
		a. Booklet pane Nos. 3530/3531 and No. U3022×4	14·00	
3531	2673	(1st) Royal Mail Ship *Britannia*, 1840	5·50	5·50

The design of No. 3530 is as the Royal Mail van stamp within No. **MS**3518.

Nos. 3530/3531 were only issued in booklet, No. PM40, originally sold for £3·60.

No. 3530 includes the EUROPA emblem.

Nos. 3532/3536 and 3537/3541 were each printed together as horizontal strips of five stamps in sheets of 50 (2 panes 5×5).

2013/QUEEN ELIZABETH II

2694 Madonna and Child

2695 Virgin and Child with the Young St John the Baptist

2696 Madonna and Child

2697 St Roch Praying to the Virgin for an End to the Plague

2698 Virgin and Child with the Young St John the Baptist

2699 La Vierge au Lys

2700 Theotokos, Mother of God

MS3549 (Illustration reduced. Actual size 146×74 mm).

(Des Robert Maude and Sarah Davies. Gravure Walsall (Nos. 3542a, 3543a) or De La Rue (others))

2013 (5 Nov). Christmas. Madonna and Child Paintings. Multicoloured One centre band (No. 3542) or two bands (others). Perf 14½×15.

(a) Self-adhesive.

3542	2694	(2nd) Madonna and Child	90	90
		a. Booklet pane. No. 3542×12	13·50	
3543	2695	(1st) Virgin and Child with the Young St Johnn the Baptist (detail)	1·20	1·00
		a. Booklet pane. No. 3543×12	16·00	
3544	2696	(2nd) Madonna and Child Large)	1·25	1·10
3545	2697	88p. St Roch Praying to the Virgin for an End to the Plague (detail)	1·40	1·40
3546	2698	(1st Virgin and Child with the Young St Large) John the Baptist (detail)	1·70	1·40
3547	2699	£1·28 La Vierge au Lys	2·00	2·00
3548	2700	£1·88 Theotokos, Mother of God	3·00	3·00
Set of 7			9·75	9·50
First Day Cover (Tallents House)				12·50
First Day Cover (Bethlehem, Llandeilo)				12·50
Presentation Pack (PO Pack No. 491)			11·50	
PHQ Cards (set of 8) (383)			3·25	19·00

(b) Ordinary gum.

MS3549 146×74 mm. As Nos. 3542/3548			9·75	9·50
First Day Cover				12·50

The 2nd class, 1st class, 88p., £1·28 and £1·88 stamps were also issued in sheets of 20 containing eight 2nd class, eight 1st class, two 88p., one £1·28 and one £1·88 stamps, each stamp accompanied by a *se-tenant* label. These sheets were printed in lithography and sold for £13·62 each (No. LS88).

Separate sheets of 20 2nd, ten 1st, ten 88p. and ten £1·28 were available with personal photographs on the labels from Royal Mail, Edinburgh. These were sold at £14·50 for 20 2nd, £10·20 for ten 1st, £14·45 for ten 88p. and £18·50 for ten £1·28.

The eight PHQ cards show the seven individual stamps and the complete miniature sheet.

2701 Angels (Rosie Hargreaves)

2702 Santa (Molly Robson)

(Gravure Walsall)

2013 (5 Nov). Children's Christmas. Self-adhesive. Multicoloured One phosphor band at right (2nd) or two phosphor bands (1st). Die-cut perf 14½.

3550	2701	(2nd) Angels	1·00	1·00
3551	2702	(1st) Santa	1·25	1·25
First Day Cover (Tallents House)				4·25
First Day Cover (Bethlehem, Llandeilo)				4·25
Presentation Pack (PO Pack No. M22)			4·25	

Year Pack

2013 (5 Nov). Comprises Nos. 3423/3429, 3431/3447, **MS**3451, 3453/3473, 3491/3496, **MS**3498/3508, **MS**3511/3524, **MS**3529 and 3532/3548

CP3551a	Year Pack (PO Pack No. 492) (sold for £85)		£140

Post Office Yearbook

2013 (5 Nov). Comprises Nos. 3423/3429, 3431/3447, **MS**3451, 3453/3473, 3491/3496, **MS**3498/3508, **MS**3511/3524, **MS**3529, 3532/3548 and 3550/3551

YB3551a	Yearbook (sold for £90)		£150

Miniature Sheet Collection

2013 (5 Nov). Comprises Nos. **MS**3429, **MS**3451, **MS**3474, **MS**3498, **MS**3511, **MS**3518, **MS**3529 and **MS**3549

MS3551a Miniature Sheet Collection (sold for £33)		45·00

2703 Andy Pandy

2704 Ivor the Engine

2705 Dougal (The Magic Roundabout)

2706 Windy Miller (Camberwick Green)

2707 Mr. Benn

2708 Great Uncle Bulgaria (The Wombles)

2709 Bagpuss

2710 Paddington Bear

247

QUEEN ELIZABETH II/2014

2711 Postman Pat  **2712** Bob the Builder  **2713** Peppa Pig

2714 Shaun the Sheep

(Des Interabang. Gravure Walsall)

2014 (7 Jan). Classic Children's TV. Self-adhesive. Multicoloured 'All-over' phosphor. Die-cut perf 15.

3552	2703	(1st) Andy Pandy.................................	1·20	1·00
		a. Horiz strip of 6. Nos. 3552/3557.....	6·50	
3553	2704	(1st) Ivor the Engine............................	1·20	1·00
3554	2705	(1st) Dougal (The Magic Roundabout)....	1·20	1·00
3555	2706	(1st) Windy Miller (Camberwick Green)..	1·20	1·00
3556	2707	(1st) Mr Benn......................................	1·20	1·00
3557	2708	(1st) Great Uncle Bulgaria (The Wombles)..	1·00	1·00
3558	2709	(1st) Bagpuss......................................	1·20	1·00
		a. Horiz strip of 6. Nos. 3558/3563.....	6·50	
3559	2710	(1st) Paddington Bear........................	1·20	1·00
3560	2711	(1st) Postman Pat...............................	1·20	1·00
3561	2712	(1st) Bob the Builder...........................	1·20	1·00
3562	2713	(1st) Peppa Pig....................................	1·20	1·00
3563	2714	(1st) Shaun the Sheep........................	1·20	1·00
Set of 12...			13·00	11·00
Set of 2 Gutter Strips of 12......................................			26·00	
First Day Cover (Tallents House)...............................				13·50
First Day Cover (Wimbledon, London SW19)..........				13·50
Presentation Pack (PO Pack No. 493).......................			14·00	
PHQ Cards (set of 12) (384).....................................			4·75	12·50

Nos. 3552/3557 and 3558/3563 were each printed together, se-tenant, in horizontal strips of six stamps in sheets of 60 (6×10).

2715 Riding for the Disabled Association  **2716** The King's Troop Ceremonial Horses

2717 Dray Horses  **2718** Royal Mews Carriage Horses

2719 Police Horses  **2720** Forestry Horse

(Des Michael Denny and Harold Batten. Litho Cartor)

2014 (4 Feb). Working Horses. Multicoloured 'All-over' phosphor. Perf 14.

3564	2715	(1st) Riding for the Disabled Association.........................	1·20	1·00
3565	2716	(1st) The King's Troop Ceremonial Horses...............................	1·20	1·00
3566	2717	88p. Dray Horses........................	1·40	1·40
3567	2718	88p. Royal Mews Carriage Horses.........	1·40	1·40
3568	2719	£1·28 Police Horses................................	2·10	2·10
3569	2720	£1·28 Forestry Horse...............................	2·10	2·10
Set of 6..			8·25	8·00
Set of 6 Gutter Pairs..			16·50	
First Day Cover (Tallents House)............................				10·00
First Day Cover (Horseheath, Cambridge)............				10·00
Presentation Pack (PO Pack No. 494)....................			9·50	
PHQ Cards (set of 6) (385).....................................			2·50	9·50

2721 BR Dean Goods No. 2532  **2722** BR D34 Nos. 62471 and 62496

2723 UTA Class W No. 103 Thomas Somerset  **2724** LMS No. 7720

2725 Peckett R2 Thor  **2726** BR D40 No. 62276

2727 UTA SG3 No. 35  **2728** Hunslet No. 589 Blanche

2729 Classic Locomotives of Wales

(Des Delaney Design Consultants. Litho Enschedé (booklet))

2014 (20 Feb). Classic Locomotives (4th and 5th series). Wales (No. **MS**3578) and United Kingdom. Multicoloured 'All-over' phosphor. Perf 14.

3570	2721	(1st) BR Dean Goods No. 2532................	2·75	2·75
		a. Booklet pane. Nos. 3570 and 3574, each×2 with margins all round...	7·50	
3571	2722	(1st) BR D34 Nos. 62471 and 62496.......	2·75	2·75
		a. Booklet pane. Nos. 3571 and 3575, each×2 with margins all round...	7·50	
3572	2723	(1st) UTA Class W No. 103......................	2·75	2·75
		a. Booklet pane. Nos. 3572 and 3576, each×2 with margins all round...	7·50	
3573	2724	(1st) LMS No. 7720.................................	2·75	2·75

248

2014/QUEEN ELIZABETH II

		a. Booklet pane. Nos. 3573 and 3577, each×2 with margins all round..	7·50	
3574	**2725**	60p. Peckett R2 *Thor*...............................	2·75	2·75
3575	**2726**	68p. BR D40 No. 62276............................	2·75	2·75
3576	**2727**	78p. UTA SG3 No. 35...............................	2·75	2·75
3577	**2728**	78p. Hunslet No. 589 *Blanche*.................	2·75	2·75
Set of 8...			15·00	15·00
MS3578 180×74 mm. **2729** Classic Locomotives of Wales No. 3573; No. 3577; 88p. W&LLR No. 822 *The Earl*; £1·28 BR 5600 No. 5652...			5·00	5·25
First Day Cover (Tallents House)...				6·50
First Day Cover (Porthmadog)...				6·50
Presentation Pack (PO Pack No. 495)....................................			6·00	
PHQ Cards (set of 5) (386)...			2·00	10·00

Nos. 3570/3577 were issued only in £13·97 Classic Locomotives booklet, No. DY9, or also in No. **MS**3578 (Nos. 3573 and 3577).

For the self-adhesive version of No. 3573, see No. 3634

The five PHQ cards show the four individual stamps and the complete miniature sheet.

2730 Roy Plomley (1914–1985, broadcaster and writer)

2731 Barbara Ward (1914–1981, economist and broadcaster)

2732 Joe Mercer (1914–1990, football player and manager)

2733 Kenneth More (1914–1982, stage and screen actor)

2734 Dylan Thomas (1914–1953, poet and writer)

2735 Sir Alec Guinness (1914–2000, stage and screen actor)

2736 Noorunissa Inayat Khan (1914–1944, SOE agent in occupied France)

2737 Max Perutz (1914–2002, molecular biologist and Nobel laureate)

2738 Joan Littlewood (1914–2002, theatre director and writer)

2739 Abram Games (1914–1996, graphic designer)

(Des Purpose. Litho Cartor)

2014 (25 Mar). Remarkable Lives. Multicoloured 'All-over' phosphor. Perf 14½.

3579	**2730**	(1st) Roy Plomley......................................	1·20	1·00
		a. Horiz strip of 5. Nos. 3579/3583.....	5·25	4·50
3580	**2731**	(1st) Barbara Ward...................................	1·20	1·00
3581	**2732**	(1st) Joe Mercer..	1·20	1·00
3582	**2733**	(1st) Kenneth More..................................	1·20	1·00
3583	**2734**	(1st) Dylan Thomas..................................	1·20	1·00
3584	**2735**	(1st) Sir Alec Guinness.............................	1·20	1·00
		a. Horiz strip of 5. Nos. 3584/3588.....	5·25	4·50
3585	**2736**	(1st) Noorunissa Inayat Khan.................	1·20	1·00
3586	**2737**	(1st) Max Perutz..	1·20	1·00
3587	**2738**	(1st) Joan Littlewood...............................	1·20	1·00
3588	**2739**	(1st) Abram Games..................................	1·20	1·00
Set of 10...			10·50	9·00
Set of 2 *Gutter Strips of 10*..			21·00	
First Day Cover (Tallents House)..				11·00
First Day Cover (Swansea)..				11·00
Presentation Pack (PO Pack No. 496)................................			11·00	
PHQ Cards (set of 10) (387)..			4·00	11·00

Nos. 3579/3583 and 3584/3588 were each printed together, *se-tenant*, as horizontal strips of five stamps in sheets of 50 (2 panes 5×5).

2740 Buckingham Palace, 2014

2741 Buckingham Palace, *c* 1862

2742 Buckingham Palace, 1846

2743 Buckingham House, 1819

249

2744 Buckingham House, 1714

2745 Buckingham House, c 1700

2746 The Grand Staircase   **2747** The Throne Room

(Des Howard Brown (sheet stamps). Litho ISP Cartor (No. 3589/3594) or Enschedé (booklet panes Nos. 3589b/3594b) or gravure ISP Walsall (Nos. 3595/3596))

2014 (15 Apr). Buckingham Palace, London (1st issue). Multicoloured 'All-over phosphor'.

(a) Ordinary gum. Perf 14½.

3589	**2740**	(1st) Buckingham Palace, 2014	1·20	1·00
		a. Horiz strip of 3. Nos. 3589/3591	3·25	2·75
		b. Perf 14×13½	1·25	1·25
		ba. Booklet pane. Nos. 3589b and 3590b, each×2 with margins all round	5·00	
3590	**2741**	(1st) Buckingham Palace, c 1862	1·20	1·00
		b. Perf 14×13½	1·25	1·25
3591	**2742**	(1st) Buckingham Palace, 1846	1·20	1·00
		b. Perf 14×13½	1·25	1·25
		ba. Booklet pane. Nos. 3591b/3594b with margins all round	5·00	
3592	**2743**	(1st) Buckingham House, 1819	1·20	1·00
		a. Horiz strip of 3. Nos. 3592/3594	3·25	2·75
		b. Perf 14×13½	1·25	1·25
3593	**2744**	(1st) Buckingham House, 1714	1·20	1·00
		b. Perf 14×13½	1·25	1·25
3594	**2745**	(1st) Buckingham House, c 1700	1·20	1·00
		b. Perf 14×13½	1·25	1·25
Set of 6 (Nos. 3589/3594)			6·50	5·50
Set of 6 (Nos. 3589b/3594b)			7·50	7·50
Set of 2 Gutter Strips of 6			13·00	
First Day Cover (Tallents House)				6·75
First Day Cover (London SW1)				6·75
Presentation Pack (PO Pack No. 497) (Nos. 3589/3594 and **MS**3601)			11·50	
PHQ Cards (set of 11) (388)			4·50	13·00

(b) Self-adhesive. Die-cut perf 14.

3595	**2746**	(1st) The Grand Staircase	2·25	2·25
		a. Booklet pane. Nos. 3595/3596 and U3022×4	7·50	
3596	**2747**	(1st) The Throne Room	2·25	2·25

Nos. 3589/3591 and 3592/3594 were each printed together, *se-tenant*, as horizontal strips of three stamps in sheets of 36 (2 panes 3×6).

Nos. 3589ba and 3591ba come from £11·39 premium booklet, No. DY10.

Nos. 3595/3596 were issued in stamp booklet, No. PM42, originally sold for £3·72.

The complete miniature sheet is shown on one of the 11 PHQ cards with the others depicting individual stamps including those from No. **MS**3601.

2748 The Blue Drawing Room   **2749** The Green Drawing Room

2750 Buckingham Palace

(Des Robert Maude and Sarah Davies (No. **MS**3601). Litho Enschedé)

2014 (15 Apr). Buckingham Palace, London (2nd issue). Multicoloured 'All-over' phosphor. Perf 14.

3597	**2747**	(1st) The Throne Room	1·20	1·00
		a. Booklet pane. Nos. 3597/3600 with margins all round and roulettes at left	4·25	
3598	**2746**	(1st) The Grand Staircase	1·20	1·00
3599	**2748**	(1st) The Blue Drawing Room	1·20	1·00
3600	**2749**	(1st) The Green Drawing Room	1·20	1·00
Set of 4			4·25	3·50
MS3601 146×74 mm. **2750** Buckingham Palace Nos. 3597/3600			4·25	3·50
a. Imperf			—	
First Day Cover (Tallents House)				4·50
First Day Cover (London SW1)				4·50

Nos. 3597/3600 were only issued in the £11·39 premium booklet, No. DY10 and No. **MS**3601.

2751 *A Matter of Life and Death* (1946)

2752 *Lawrence of Arabia* (1962)

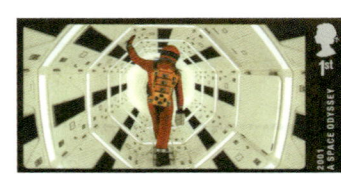

2753 *2001 A Space Odyssey* (1968)

2754 *Chariots of Fire* (1981)

2755 *Secrets and Lies* (1996)

2014 / QUEEN ELIZABETH II

2756 *Bend It Like Beckham* (2002)

2757 Films by GPO Film Unit

(Des Johnson banks (Nos. 3602/3607) or Magpie Studio (No. **MS**3608). Litho ISP Cartor (Nos. 3602/3607) or Enschedé (No. **MS**3608))

2014 (13 May). Great British Films. Multicoloured 'All-over' phosphor. Perf 14½ (Nos. 3602/3607) or 14 (No. **MS**3608).

3602	**2751**	(1st) *A Matter of Life and Death*	1·20	1·00
		a. Horiz strip of 3. Nos. 3602/3604	3·25	2·75
3603	**2752**	(1st) *Lawrence of Arabia*	1·20	1·00
3604	**2753**	(1st) *2001 A Space Odyssey*	1·20	1·00
3605	**2754**	£1·28 *Chariots of Fire*	1·60	1·60
		a. Horiz strip of 3. Nos. 3605/3607	4·25	4·25
3606	**2755**	£1·28 *Secrets and Lies*	1·60	1·60
3607	**2756**	£1·28 *Bend It Like Beckham*	1·60	1·60
Set of 6			7·50	7·00
Set of 2 Gutter Strips of 6			15·00	
First Day Cover (Tallents House)				10·00
First Day Cover (Blackheath London SE3)				10·00
Presentation Pack (PO Pack No. 498) (Nos. 3602/3607 and **MS**3608)			15·00	
PHQ Cards (set of 11) (389)			4·50	18·00
MS3608 115×89 mm. **2757** Films by GPO Film Unit (1st)×4 *Night Mail* (1936) directed by Harry Watt and Basil Wright; *Love on the Wing* (1938) directed by Norman McLaren; *A Colour Box* (1935) directed by Len Lye; *Spare Time* (1939) directed by Humphrey Jennings			5·00	4·75
First Day Cover (Tallents House)				5·00
First Day Cover (Blackheath London SE3)				5·00

Nos. 3602/3604 and 3605/3607 were each printed together, *se-tenant*, as horizontal strips of three stamps in sheets of 36 (2 panes 3×6).

The complete miniature sheet is shown on one of the 11 PHQ cards with the others depicting individual stamps including those from No. **MS**3608.

2758 Herring

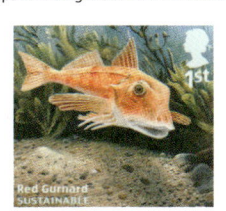

2759 Red Gurnard

2760 Dab

2761 Pouting

2762 Cornish Sardine

2763 Common Skate

2764 Spiny Dogfish

2765 Wolffish

2766 Sturgeon

2767 Conger Eel

(Des Kate Stephens. Litho ISP Cartor)

2014 (5 June). Sustainable Fish (Nos. 3609/3613) and Threatened Fish (Nos. 3614/3618). Multicoloured 'All-over' phosphor. Perf 14×14½.

3609	**2758**	(1st) Herring	1·20	1·00
		a. Horiz strip of 5. Nos. 3609/3613	5·25	4·50
3610	**2759**	(1st) Red Gurnard	1·20	1·00
3611	**2760**	(1st) Dab	1·00	1·00
3612	**2761**	(1st) Pouting	1·20	1·00
3613	**2762**	(1st) Cornish Sardine	1·20	1·00
3614	**2763**	(1st) Common Skate	1·20	1·00
		a. Horiz strip of 5. Nos. 3614/3618	5·25	4·50
3615	**2764**	(1st) Spiny Dogfish	1·20	1·00
3616	**2765**	(1st) Wolffish	1·20	1·00
3617	**2766**	(1st) Sturgeon	1·20	1·00
3618	**2767**	(1st) Conger Eel	1·20	1·00
Set of 10			10·50	9·00
Set of 2 Gutter Strips of 10			21·00	
First Day Cover (Tallents House)				11·50
First Day Cover (Fishguard)				11·50
Presentation Pack (PO Pack No. 499)			11·00	
PHQ Cards (set of 10) (390)			4·00	11·00

Nos. 3609/3613 and 3614/3618 were each printed together, *se-tenant*, as horizontal strips of five in sheets of 50 (2 panes 5×5).

2768 Judo

2769 Swimming

2770 Marathon

2771 Squash

QUEEN ELIZABETH II/2014

2772 Netball
2773 Para-athlete Cycling 

(Des Nanette Hoogslag (illustration) and Howard Brown. Litho ISP Cartor (Nos. 3619/3624) or gravure ISP Walsall (No. 3625))

2014 (17 July). Commonwealth Games, Glasgow. Multicoloured One phosphor band (No. 3619) or two bands (others).

(a) Ordinary gum. Perf 14×14½.

3619	2768	(2nd) Judo	90	90
3620	2769	(1st) Swimming	1·00	1·00
3621	2770	97p. Marathon	1·40	1·40
3622	2771	£1·28 Squash	1·75	1·75
3623	2772	£1·47 Netball	2·50	2·50
3624	2773	£2·15 Para-athlete Cycling	3·50	3·50
Set of 6			10·00	10·00
Set of 6 Gutter Pairs			20·00	
First Day Cover (Tallents House)				11·50
First Day Cover (Glasgow)				11·50
Presentation Pack (PO Pack No. 500)			10·50	
PHQ Cards (set of 6) (391)			2·50	11·50

(b) Self-adhesive. Die-cut perf 14×14½.

3625	2769	(1st) Swimming	2·00	2·00
		a. Booklet pane. Nos. 3625×2 and U3022×4	7·50	

The phosphor band on No. 3619 is at centre right of the stamps.
No. 3625 was issued in stamp booklet, No. PM43, originally sold for £3·72.

2774 Poppy (Fiona Strickland) 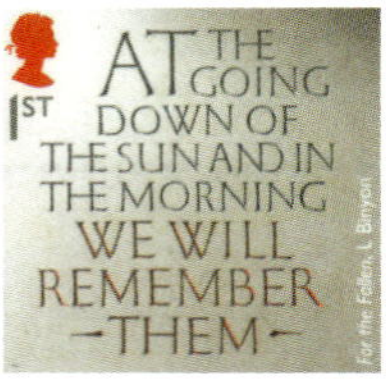
2775 Lines from *For the Fallen* (Laurence Binyon)

2776 Private William Cecil Tickle 
2777 *A Star Shell* (C. R. W. Nevinson)

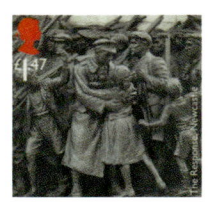

2778 *The Response* (sculpture by William Goscombe John)
2779 Princess Mary's Gift Box Fund 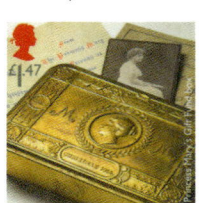

(Des Hat-trick Design. Litho ISP Cartor (Nos. 3626/3631) or Enschedé (booklet panes Nos. 3626b, 3629b))

2014 (28 July)–**2018**. Centenary of the First World War (1st issue). Multicoloured 'All-over' phosphor (Nos. 3627, 3629) or two bands (others). Perf 14½.

3626	2774	(1st) Poppy	1·20	1·00
		a. 'All-over' phosphor	1·25	1·50
		b. Booklet pane. Nos. 3626a, 3627, 3628a with margins all round	3·75	
3627	2775	(1st) Lines from *For the Fallen*	1·20	1·00
		b. Booklet pane. Nos. 3627, 3712, 3839 and 3984 with margins all round (13.9.18)	4·75	
3628	2776	(1st) Private William Cecil Tickle	1·20	1·00
		a. 'All-over' phosphor	1·25	1·50
3629	2777	£1·47 *A Star Shell*	2·50	2·50
		b. Booklet pane. Nos. 3629, 3630a, 3631a with margins all round	9·00	
3630	2778	£1·47 *The Response*	2·50	2·50
		a. 'All-over' phosphor	3·25	3·50
3631	2779	£1·47 Princess Mary's Gift Box Fund	2·50	2·50
		a. 'All-over' phosphor	3·25	3·50
Set of 6			10·00	9·25
Set of 6 Gutter Pairs			20·00	
First Day Cover (Tallents House)				11·50
First Day Cover (Newcastle upon Tyne)				11·50
Presentation Pack (PO Pack No. 501)			11·50	
PHQ Cards (set of 6) (392)			2·50	10·50

Nos. 3626a/3626b, 3628a, 3629b, 3630a and 3631a only come from £11·30 premium booklet, No. DY11.
No. 3627b comes from £15.65 premium booklet, No. DY26.

(Gravure ISP Walsall)

2014 (18 Aug). Sustainable Fish and Threatened Fish (2nd issue). Designs as Nos. 3613/3614. Self-adhesive. Multicoloured Die-cut perf 14×14½.

3632	2763	(1st) Common Skate	2·00	2·00
		a. Booklet pane. Nos. 3632/3633 and U3022×4	7·50	
3633	2762	(1st) Cornish Sardine	2·00	2·00

Nos. 3632/3633 were issued in stamp booklet, No. PM44, originally sold for £3·72.

2724 LMS No. 7720

(Gravure ISP Walsall)

2014 (18 Sept). Classic Locomotives of Wales. Booklet stamp as T **2724**. 'All-over' phosphor. Self-adhesive. Multicoloured Die-cut perf 14.

3634	2724	(1st) LMS No. 7720	2·00	2·00
		a. Booklet pane. No. 3634×2 and U3022×4	7·50	

No. 3634 was only issued in booklets, No. PM45, originally sold for £3·72.

2780 Eastbourne Bandstand 
2781 Tinside Lido, Plymouth

2782 Bangor Pier 
2783 Southwold Lighthouse

2784 Blackpool Pleasure Beach
2785 Bexhill-on-Sea Shelter

2014/QUEEN ELIZABETH II

2786 British Piers

(Des Why Not Associates. Litho ISP Cartor (Nos. 3635/3640) or Enschedé (No. **MS**3641))

2014 (18 Sept). Seaside Architecture. Multicoloured Two bands (Nos. 3635/3640) or 'All-over' phosphor (No. **MS**3641). Perf 14.

3635	**2780**	(1st) Eastbourne Bandstand	1·20	1·00
3636	**2781**	(1st) Tinside Lido, Plymouth	1·20	1·00
3637	**2782**	97p. Bangor Pier	1·40	1·40
3638	**2783**	97p. Southwold Lighthouse	1·40	1·40
3639	**2784**	£1·28 Blackpool Pleasure Beach	2·10	2·10
3640	**2785**	£1·28 Bexhill-on-Sea Shelter	2·10	2·10
Set of 6			8·50	8·00
Set of 6 Gutter Pairs			17·00	
First Day Cover (Tallents House)				10·00
First Day Cover (Eastbourne)				10·00
Presentation Pack (PO Pack No. 502) (Nos. 3635/3640 and **MS**3641)			16·00	
PHQ Cards (set of 11) (393)			4·50	19·00
MS3641 125×89 mm. **2786** British Piers (1st) Llandudno Pier; (1st) Worthing Pier; £1·28 Dunoon Pier; £1·28 Brighton Pier			5·50	5·50
First Day Cover (Tallents House)				7·00

No. 3635 includes the EUROPA emblem.

The complete miniature sheet is shown on one of the 11 PHQ cards with the others depicting individual stamps including those from the miniature sheet.

2787 Margaret Thatcher
2788 Harold Wilson 
2789 Clement Attlee 
2790 Winston Churchill 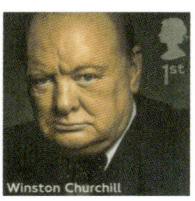
2791 William Gladstone 
2792 Robert Peel 
2793 Charles Grey 
2794 William Pitt the Younger 

(Des Together. Litho ISP Cartor)

2014 (14 Oct). Prime Ministers. Multicoloured. 'All-over' phosphor. Perf 14½.

3642	**2787**	(1st) Margaret Thatcher	1·20	1·00
		a. Horiz strip of 4. Nos. 3642/3645	4·25	3·75
3643	**2788**	(1st) Harold Wilson	1·20	1·00
3644	**2789**	(1st) Clement Attlee	1·20	1·00
3645	**2790**	(1st) Winston Churchill	1·20	1·00
3646	**2791**	97p. William Gladstone	1·60	1·60
		a. Horiz strip of 4. Nos. 3646/3649	5·75	5·75
3647	**2792**	97p. Robert Peel	1·60	1·60
3648	**2793**	97p. Charles Grey	1·60	1·60
3649	**2794**	97p. William Pitt the Younger	1·60	1·60
Set of 8			10·00	9·50
Set of 2 Gutter strips of 4			20·00	
First Day Cover (Tallents House)				11·00
First Day Cover (London SW1)				11·00
Presentation Pack (PO Pack No. 503)			11·00	
PHQ Cards (set of 8) (394)			3·25	11·50

Nos. 3642/3645 and 3646/3649 were each printed together, *se-tenant*, as horizontal strips of four stamps in sheets of 48 (2 panes 4×6).

SELF-ADHESIVE STAMPS. Collectors are reminded that used self-adhesive stamps will no longer 'soak-off'. They should be collected with a neat margin of backing paper.

2795 Collecting the Christmas Tree 
2796 Posting Christmas Cards 
2797 Collecting the Christmas Tree 
2798 Posting Christmas Cards 
2799 Building a Snowman 
2800 Carol Singing

2801 Ice Skating

(Des True North. Gravure Walsall (Nos. 3650a, 3651a) or De La Rue (others))

2014 (4 Nov). Christmas. Illustrations by Andrew Bannecker. Multicoloured One centre band (No. 3650) or two bands (others). Perf 14½×15.

(a) Self-adhesive.

3650	**2795**	(2nd) Collecting the Christmas Tree	90	90
		a. Booklet pane. No. 3650×12	13·50	
3651	**2796**	(1st) Posting Christmas Cards	1·20	1·00
		a. Booklet pane. No. 3651×12	16·00	
3652	**2797**	(2nd Collecting the Christmas Tree Large)	1·25	1·10
3653	**2798**	(1st Posting Christmas Cards Large)	1·70	1·40
3654	**2799**	£1·28 Building a Snowman	2·00	2·00
3655	**2800**	£1·47 Carol Singing	2·50	2·50
3656	**2801**	£2·15 Ice Skating	3·25	3·25
Set of 7			11·50	11·00

253

QUEEN ELIZABETH II/2014

First Day Cover (Tallents House)		14·00
First Day Cover (Bethlehem, Llandeilo)		14·00
Presentation Pack (PO Pack No. 504)	13·00	
PHQ Cards (set of 8) (395)	3·25	20·00

(b) Ordinary gum.

MS3657 156×74 mm. Nos. 3650/3656	11·50	11·00
First Day Cover (Tallents House)		14·00
First Day Cover (Bethlehem, Llandeilo)		14·00

The 2nd class, 1st class, £1·28 and £1·47 stamps were also issued in sheets of 20 containing eight 2nd class, eight 1st class, two £1·28 and two £1·47 stamps, each stamp accompanied by a *se-tenant* label. These sheets were printed in lithography and sold for £15·20 per sheet (No. LS90).

Separate sheets of 20 2nd, 20 1st, ten 1st, ten £1·28 and ten £1·47 were available with personal photographs on the labels from Royal Mail, Edinburgh. These were sold at £14·50 for 20 2nd, £18·65 for 20 1st, £10·20 for ten 1st, £18·50 for ten £1·28 and £21·85 for ten £1·47.

The eight PHQ cards show the seven individual stamps and the complete miniature sheet.

Year Pack

2014 (4 Nov). Comprises Nos. 3552/3569, **MS**3578/3594, **MS**3601/3624, 3626/3631, 3635/3656.

CP3657a	Year Pack (PO Pack No. 505) (*sold for £86*)	£140

Post Office Yearbook

2014 (4 Nov). Comprises Nos. 3552/3569, **MS**3578/3594, **MS**3601/3624, 3626/3631, 3635/3656.

YB3657a	Yearbook (*sold for £106*)	£160

Miniature Sheet Collection

2014 (4 Nov). Comprises Nos. **MS**3578, **MS**3601, **MS**3608, **MS**3641 and **MS**3657.

MS3657a	Miniature Sheet Collection (*sold for £23*)	30·00

2802 The White Rabbit
2803 Down the Rabbit Hole 
2804 Drink Me 
2805 The White Rabbit's House 
2806 The Cheshire Cat 
2807 A Mad Tea Party 
2808 The Queen of Hearts 
2809 The Game of Croquet 
2810 Alice's Evidence 
2811 A Pack of Cards 

(Grahame Baker-Smith (illustration) and Godfrey Design. Litho ISP Cartor (Nos. 3658/3667) or gravure ISP Walsall (Nos. 3668/3669))

2015 (6 Jan). Alice in Wonderland. Multicoloured One phosphor band at right (2nd) or two phosphor bands (others).

(a) Ordinary gum. Perf 14½.

3658	2802	(2nd) The White Rabbit	90	90
		a. Vert pair. Nos. 3658/3659	1·75	1·75
3659	2803	(2nd) Down the Rabbit Hole	90	90
3660	2804	(1st) Drink Me	1·20	1·00
		a. Vert pair. Nos. 3660/3661	2·40	2·00
3661	2805	(1st) The White Rabbit's House	1·20	1·00
3662	2806	81p. The Cheshire Cat	1·50	1·50
		a. Vert pair. Nos. 3662/3663	3·00	3·00
3663	2807	81p. A Mad Tea Party	1·50	1·50
3664	2808	£1·28 The Queen of Hearts	2·50	2·50
		a. Vert pair. Nos. 3664/3665	5·00	5·00
3665	2809	£1·28 The Game of Croquet	2·50	2·50
3666	2810	£1·47 Alice's Evidence	3·25	3·25
		a. Vert pair. Nos. 3666/3667	6·50	6·50
3667	2811	£1·47 A Pack of Cards	3·25	3·25
Set of 10			16·75	16·50
Set of 5 Gutter Strips of 4			35·00	
First Day Cover (Tallents House)				17·50
First Day Cover (Oxford)				17·50
Presentation Pack (PO Pack No. 506)			25·00	
PHQ Cards (Set of 10) (396)			5·00	18·00

(b) Self-adhesive. Die-cut perf 14½.

3668	2804	(1st) Drink Me	5·00	5·00
		a. Booklet pane. Nos. 3668/3669 and U3022×4	12·00	
3669	2805	(1st) The White Rabbit's House	5·00	5·00

Nos. 3658/3659, 3660/3661, 3662/3663, 3664/3665 and 3666/3667 were each printed together, *se-tenant*, as vertical pairs in sheets of 60 (2 panes 5×6).

Nos. 3658/3667 commemorate the 150th anniversary of the Publication of *Alice's Adventures in Wonderland* by Lewis Carroll.

Nos. 3668/3669 were only issued in stamp booklet, No. PM46, originally sold for £3·72

2812 Happy Birthday (NB Studio)
2813 Well Done (Webb & Webb Design Ltd) 
2814 Wedding (Caroline Gardner Ltd) 
2815 Love (Rebecca Sutherland) 
2816 Mum (The Chase) 
2817 New Baby (NB Studio) 
2818 Grandparent (NB Studio) 
2819 Dad (Webb & Webb Design Ltd)

2015/QUEEN ELIZABETH II

(Des Jenny Bowers and NB Studio. Gravure ISP Walsall (Nos. 3670/3677) or litho ISP Cartor (No. **MS**3678))

2015 (20 Jan). Smilers (5th series). Multicoloured Two phosphor bands.
(a) Self-adhesive booklet stamps. Die-cut perf 14½×14 (with one elliptical hole in each vert side).

3670	2812	(1st) Happy Birthday	1·90	1·90
		a. Booklet pane. Nos. 3670×2, 3671, 3672/3673 each×2, 3674, 3675×2 and 3676/3677	18·00	
3671	2813	(1st) Well Done	2·75	2·75
3672	2814	(1st) Wedding	1·90	1·90
3673	2815	(1st) Love	1·90	1·90
3674	2816	(1st) Mum	2·75	2·75
3675	2817	(1st) New Baby	1·90	1·90
3676	2818	(1st) Grandparent	2·75	2·75
3677	2819	(1st) Dad	2·75	2·75
Set of 8			15·00	15·00

(b) Ordinary gum. Perf 14½×14 (with one elliptical hole in each vert side).

MS3678	134×70 mm. As Nos. 3670/3677	10·00	10·00
First Day Cover (Tallents House)			10·00
First Day Cover (Greetwell, Lincoln)			10·00
Presentation Pack (PO Pack No. M23)		12·00	
PHQ Cards (set of 9) (D34)		6·75	25·00

Nos. 3670/3677 were issued in booklets of 12, No. QB1, originally sold for £7·44.

Nos. 3670/3677 were also issued in sheets of 20 with *se-tenant* greetings labels (No. LS93), printed by Cartor in lithography and originally sold at £12·90 per sheet.

Sheets of 20 stamps of the same design were available with personal photographs on the labels from Royal mail, Edinburgh.

The complete miniature sheet is shown on one of the nine PHQ cards with the others depicting individual stamps.

2820 Colossus, World's First Electronic Digital Computer

2821 World Wide Web, Revolutionary Global Communications System

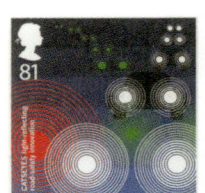

2822 Cats Eyes, Light-reflecting Road Safety Innovation

2823 Fibre Optics, Pioneering Rapid-data-transfer Technology

2824 Stainless Steel, Non-corrosive, Versatile, 100% Recyclable Alloy

2825 Carbon Fibre, High-strength, Lightweight, Composite Material

2826 DNA Sequencing, Revolution in Understanding the Genome

2827 i-LIMB, Bionic Hand with Individually Powered Digits

(Des GBH. Litho ISP Cartor)

2015 (19 Feb). Inventive Britain. Multicoloured Two phosphor bands. Perf 14½.

3679	2820	(1st) Colossus	1·20	1·00
		a. Horiz pair. Nos. 3679/3680	2·40	2·00
		b. Booklet pane. Nos. 3305, 3281×2 and 3679 with margins all round ...	4·00	
		c. Booklet pane. Nos. 3679/3680, 3683 and 3686	5·50	
3680	2821	(1st) World Wide Web	1·20	1·00
3681	2822	81p. Cats eyes	1·10	1·10
		a. Horiz pair. Nos. 3681/3682	2·25	2·25
		b. Booklet pane. Nos. 3681/3682 and 3684/3685 with margins all round	6·00	
3682	2823	81p. Fibre Optics	1·10	1·10
3683	2824	£1·28 Stainless Steel	1·75	1·75
		a. Horiz pair. Nos. 3683/3684	3·75	3·75
3684	2825	£1·28 Carbon Fibre	1·75	1·75
		a. Horiz pair. Nos. 3685/3686	4·50	4·50
3685	2826	£1·47 DNA Sequencing	2·25	2·25
3686	2827	£1·47 i-LIMB	2·25	2·25
Set of 8			11·50	11·25
Set of 4 Gutter Blocks of 4			23·00	
First Day Cover (Tallents House)				15·50
First Day Cover (Harlow)				15·50
Presentation Pack (PO Pack No. 507)			13·50	
PHQ Cards (set of 8) (397)			4·00	17·00

Nos. 3679/3680, 3681/3682, 3683/3684 and 3685/3686 were each printed together, *se-tenant*, as horizontal pairs in sheets of 60 (2 panes 6×5).

Nos. 3679b/3679c and 3681b were only issued in the £14·60 Inventive Britain booklet, No. DY12.

2828 Tarr Steps, River Barle

2829 Row Bridge, Mosedale Beck

2830 Pulteney Bridge, River Avon

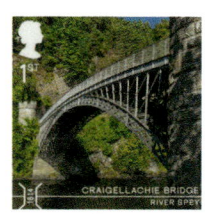

2831 Craigellachie Bridge, River Spey

2832 Menai Suspension Bridge, Menai Strait

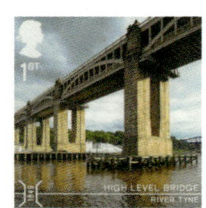

2833 High Level Bridge, River Tyne

255

QUEEN ELIZABETH II/2015

2834 Royal Border Bridge, River Tweed
2835 Tees Transporter Bridge, River Tees 
2836 Humber Bridge, River Humber 
2837 Peace Bridge, River Foyle 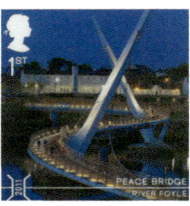

(Des GBH. Litho ISP Cartor)

2015 (5 Mar). Bridges. Multicoloured Two phosphor bands. Perf 14½×14.

3687	**2828**	(1st) Tarr Steps, River Barle	1·20	1·00
		a. Horiz strip of 5. Nos. 3687/3691	5·25	4·50
3688	**2829**	(1st) Row Bridge, Mosedale Beck	1·20	1·00
3689	**2830**	(1st) Pulteney Bridge, River Avon	1·20	1·00
3690	**2831**	(1st) Craigellachie Bridge, River Spey	1·20	1·00
3691	**2832**	(1st) Menai Suspension Bridge, Menai Strait	1·20	1·00
3692	**2833**	(1st) High Level Bridge, River Tyne	1·20	1·00
		a. Horiz strip of 5. Nos. 3692/3696	5·25	4·50
3693	**2834**	(1st) Royal Border Bridge, River Tweed	1·20	1·00
3694	**2835**	(1st) Tees Transporter Bridge, River Tees	1·20	1·00
3695	**2836**	(1st) Humber Bridge, River Humber	1·20	1·00
3696	**2837**	(1st) Peace Bridge, River Foyle	1·20	1·00
Set of 10			10·50	9·00
Set of 2 Gutter Strips of 10			21·00	
Set of 2 Traffic Light Gutter Strips of 10			26·00	
First Day Cover (Tallents House)				11·50
First Day Cover (Bridge, Canterbury)				11·50
Presentation Pack (PO Pack No. 508)			11·50	
PHQ Cards (set of 10) (398)			5·00	12·50

Nos. 3687/3691 and 3692/3696 were each printed together, *se-tenant*, as horizontal strips of five stamps in sheets of 50 (2 panes 5×5).

2838 Spike Milligan
2839 The Two Ronnies 
2840 Billy Connolly 
2841 Morecambe and Wise 
2842 Norman Wisdom 
2843 Lenny Henry 
2844 Peter Cook and Dudley Moore 
2845 Monty Python 
2846 French and Saunders  
2847 Victoria Wood 

(Des The Chase. Litho ISP Cartor (Nos. 3697/3706) or gravure ISP Walsall (Nos. 3707/3708))

2015 (1 Apr). Comedy Greats. Multicoloured Two phosphor bands.

(a) Ordinary gum. Perf 14.

3697	**2838**	(1st) Spike Milligan	1·20	1·00
		a. Horiz strip of 5. Nos. 3697/3701	5·25	4·50
3698	**2839**	(1st) The Two Ronnies	1·20	1·00
3699	**2840**	(1st) Billy Connolly	1·20	1·00
3700	**2841**	(1st) Morecambe and Wise	1·20	1·00
3701	**2842**	(1st) Norman Wisdom	1·20	1·00
3702	**2843**	(1st) Lenny Henry	1·20	1·00
		a. Horiz strip of 5. Nos. 3702/3706	5·25	4·50
3703	**2844**	(1st) Peter Cook and Dudley Moore	1·20	1·00
3704	**2845**	(1st) Monty Python	1·20	1·00
3705	**2846**	(1st) French and Saunders	1·20	1·00
3706	**2847**	(1st) Victoria Wood	1·20	1·00
Set of 10			10·50	9·00
Set of 2 Gutter Strips of 10			21·00	
First Day Cover (Tallents House)				11·50
First Day Cover (Laughterton, Lincoln)				11·50
Presentation Pack (PO Pack No. 509)			11·50	
PHQ Cards (set of 10) (399)			5·00	12·50

(b) Self-adhesive. Die-cut perf 14.

3707	**2842**	(1st) Norman Wisdom	5·50	5·50
		a. Booklet pane. Nos. 3707/3708 and U3022×4	15·00	
3708	**2841**	(1st) Morecambe and Wise	5·50	5·50

Nos. 3697/3701 and 3702/3706 were each printed together, *se-tenant*, as horizontal strips of five stamps in sheets of 50 (2 panes 5×5).

Nos. 3707/3708 were issued in stamp booklet, No. PM47, sold for £3·72.

2848 Penny Black

2849 Penny Black and 1840 2d. blue

(Des Sedley Place. Gravure ISP Walsall (No. 3709) or litho ISP Cartor (No. **MS**3710))

2015 (6 May). 175th Anniversary of the Penny Black. Multicoloured Two phosphor bands.

(a) Self-adhesive booklet stamps. Die-cut perf 14½×14 (with one elliptical hole in each vert side).

3709	**2848**	(1st) Penny Black	2·00	2·00

(b) Ordinary gum. Perf 14½×14 (with one elliptical hole in each vert side).
MS3710 156×74 mm. **2849** (1st) Penny Black×2; (1st) 1840 2d. blue×2 .... 3·50 3·75
First Day Cover (Tallents House) .... 4·75

First Day Cover (Bath)		4·75
Presentation Pack (PO Pack No. 510)	4·25	
PHQ Cards (set of 3) (400)	1·50	4·00

No. 3709 was issued in booklets of six, Nos. MB13 and MB21.

Designs as No. 3709 and (1st) Twopenny Blue as within No. **MS**3710 were also issued in sheets of 20 (No. LS94) containing ten 1st class Penny Black and ten 1st class Twopenny Blue, each stamp accompanied by a *se-tenant* label. These sheets were printed in lithography by ISP Cartor and originally sold for £12·90.

Sheets of ten or 20 1st Penny Black were available with personal photographs on the labels from Royal Mail Edinburgh, sold for £10·20 (ten) or £18·65 (20).

Miniature sheets as No. **MS**3710 with a special inscription were available only at Europhilex 2015 (*Price* £30).

The three PHQ cards show the two individual stamps and the complete miniature sheet.

See also Nos. 3806/3809.

2850 *Poppies* (Howard Hodgkin)

2851 *All the Hills and Vales Along* (Charles Hamilton Sorley)

2852 2853 *Rifleman Kulbir Thapa*

2853 *The Kensingtons at Laventie* (Eric Kennington)

2854 A British Soldier visits his Comrade's Grave

2855 London Irish Rifles' Football from Loos

(Des Hat-trick design. Litho ISP Cartor)

2015 (14 May). Centenary of the First World War (2nd issue). Multicoloured. Two phosphor bands. Perf 14½.

3711	2850	(1st) *Poppies*	1·20	1·00
		a. Booklet pane. Nos. 3711/3713 with margins all round	3·50	
3712	2851	(1st) *All the Hills and Vales Along*	1·20	1·00
3713	2852	(1st) *Rifleman Kulbir Thapa*	1·20	1·00
3714	2853	£1·52 *The Kensingtons at Laventie*	2·40	2·40
		a. Booklet pane. Nos. 3714/3716 with margins all round	7·50	
3715	2854	£1·52 A British Soldier visits his Comrade's Grave on the Cliffs	2·40	2·40
3716	2855	£1·52 London Irish Rifles' Football from Loos	2·40	2·40
Set of 6			9·50	9·00
Set of 6 Gutter Pairs			19·00	
First Day Cover (Tallents House)				12·00
First Day Cover (Winchester)				12·00
Presentation Pack (PO Pack No. 511)			11·00	
PHQ Cards (set of 6) (401)			3·00	11·50

Nos. 3711a and 3714a were only issued in £13·96 premium booklet, No DY13.

2588 Six Poppies on Barbed Wire Fence

(Des Hat-trick Design. Litho ISP Cartor)

2015 (14 May)–**2017**. Centenary of the First World War. Premium Booklet stamp. As No. 3414 but ordinary gum. Multicoloured Two phosphor bands. Perf 14½×14 (with one elliptical hole in each vertical side).

3717	**2588**	(1st) Six Poppies on Barbed Wire Stems	1·50	1·50
		a. Booklet pane. Nos. 3717×4, EN51, NI95, S158a and W148 with central label and margins all round (21·6·16)	21·00	
		b. Booklet pane. No. 3717×8 with central label and margins all round (31.7.17)	12·00	
		c. Booklet pane. Nos. 3717 and U3097, each ×4, with margins all round (13.9.18)	1·50	1·50
First Day Cover (Tallents House) (No. 3717a)				23·00
First Day Cover (Lyness, Stromness) (No. 3717a)				23·00
First Day Cover (Tallents House) (No. 3717b)				13·00
First Day Cover (Blaenannerch, Aberteifi, Cardigan) (No. 3717b)				13·00

No. 3717 comes from pane No. U3070n in the £13·96 premium booklet, No. DY13, pane No. 3717a from the £16·49 premium booklet, No. DY18, pane No. 3717b from the £15·41 premium booklet, No. DY22.

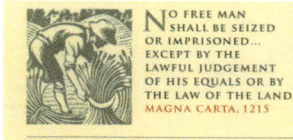

2856 2556 Magna Carta 1215

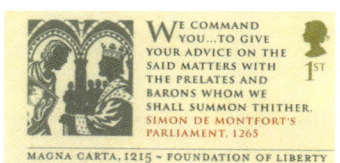

2857 Simon de Montfort's Parliament, 1265

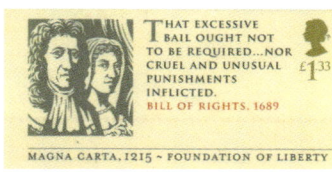

2858 Bill of Rights, 1689

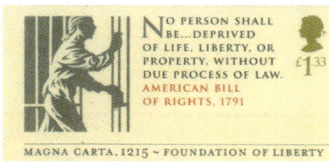

2859 American Bill of Rights, 1791

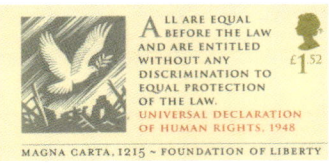

2860 Universal Declaration of Human Rights, 1948

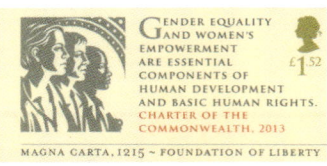

2861 Charter of the Commonwealth, 2013

(Des Howard Brown. Litho ISP Cartor)

2015 (2 June). 800th Anniversary of the *Magna Carta*. Multicoloured Two phosphor bands. Perf 14½.

3718	2856	(1st) Magna Carta	1·20	1·00
3719	2857	(1st) Simon de Montfort's Parliament	1·20	1·00
3720	2858	£1·33 Bill of Rights	1·60	1·60
3721	2859	£1·33 American Bill of Rights	1·60	1·60
3722	2860	£1·52 Universal Declaration of Human Rights	3·00	3·00
3723	2861	£1·52 Charter of the Commonwealth	3·00	3·00
Set of 6			10·00	10·00
Set of 6 Gutter pairs			20·00	
First Day Cover (Tallents House)				12·00
First Day Cover (London NW1)				12·00
Presentation Pack (PO Pack No. 512)			13·00	
PHQ Cards (set of 6) (402)			3·00	12·50

2862 The Defence of Hougoumont

2863 The Scots Greys during the Charge of the Union Brigade

2864 The French Cavalry's Assault on Allied Defensive Squares

2865 The Defence of La Haye Sainte by the King's German Legion

2866 The Capture of Plancenoit by the Prussians

2867 The French Imperial Guard's Final Assault

(Des Silk Pearce. Litho ISP Cartor)

2015 (18 June). Bicentenary of the Battle of Waterloo (1st issue). Multicoloured Two phosphor bands. Perf 14½.

3724	2862	(1st) The Defence of Hougoumont	1·20	1·00
		a. Booklet pane. Nos. 3724 and 3729 with margins all round	4·00	
3725	2863	(1st) The Scots Greys during the charge of the Union Brigade	1·20	1·00
		a. Booklet pane. Nos. 3725/3728 with margins all round	6·25	
3726	2864	£1 The French Cavalry's assault on Allied defensive Squares	1·40	1·40
3727	2865	£1 The Defence of La Haye Sainte by the King's German Legion	1·40	1·40
3728	2866	£1·52 The Capture of Plancenoit by the Prussians	2·50	2·50
3729	2867	£1·52 The French Imperial Guard's Final Assault	2·50	2·50
Set of 6			9·00	8·75
Set of 6 Gutter Pairs			18·00	
First Day Cover (Tallents House)				11·50
First Day Cover (Waterloo, Liverpool)				11·50
Presentation Pack (PO Pack No. 513) (Nos. 3724/3729 and **MS**3734)			17·00	
PHQ Cards (set of 11) (403)			5·50	22·00

Nos. 3724a and 3725a were only issued in the £14·47 premium booklet, No. DY14.

The 11 PHQ cards depict the individual stamps, including those from No. **MS**3734, and the complete miniature sheet.

2868 15th Infantry Regiment, IV Corps, Prussian Army

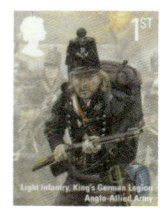

2869 Light Infantry, King's German Legion, Anglo-Allied Army

2870 92nd Gordon Highlanders, Anglo-Allied Army

2871 Grenadiers, Imperial Guard, French Army

2015/QUEEN ELIZABETH II

2872 Soldiers and Battle of Waterloo Map

(Des Chris Collingwood (illustrations) and Webb and Webb Design Ltd. Litho ISP Cartor)

2015 (18 June). Bicentenary of the Battle of Waterloo (2nd issue). Multicoloured Two phosphor bands. Perf 14.

3730	2868	(1st) 15th Infantry Regiment, IV Corps..	1·50	1·50
		a. Booklet pane. Nos. 3730/3733 with margins all round and roulettes at left..................	6·00	
3731	2869	(1st) Light Infantry, King's German Legion...	1·50	1·50
3732	2870	£1·33 92nd Gordon Highlanders..............	1·75	1·75
3733	2871	£1·33 Grenadiers, Imperial Guard............	1·75	1·75
Set of 4			6·00	6·00
MS3734 156×74 mm. **2872** Soldiers and Battle of Waterloo Map Nos. 3730/3733...................			6·00	6·00
First Day Cover (Tallents House)...				7·50
First Day Cover (Waterloo, Liverpool)....................................				7·50

Nos. 3730/3733 come from £14·47 Bicentenary of the Battle of Waterloo premium booklet, No. DY14, and No. **MS**3734.

2876 Northern Colletes Bee (*Colletes floralis*) on Wild Carrot (*Daucus carota*)

2877 Bilberry Bumblebee (*Bombus monticola*) on Bilberry (*Vaccinium myrtillus*)

2878 Large Mason Bee (*Osmia xanthomelana*) on Horseshoe Vetch (*Hippocrepis comosa*)

2879 Potter Flower Bee (*Anthophora retusa*) on Ground Ivy (*Glechoma hederacea*)

2873 Battle of Britain

(Des Supple Studio (stamps) and The Team (miniature sheet). Litho ISP Cartor)

2015 (16 July). 75th Anniversary of the Battle of Britain. Multicoloured 'All-over' phosphor. Perf 14½×14.

MS3735 190×74 mm. **2873** (1st) Pilots scramble to their Hurricanes; (1st) Supermarine Spitfires of 610 Squadron, Biggin Hill, on patrol; (1st) Armourer Fred Roberts replaces ammunition boxes on Supermarine Spitfire; £1·33 Spotters of the Auxiliary Territorial Service looking for enemy aircraft; £1·33 Operations Room at Bentley Priory; £1·33 Pilots of 32 Squadron await orders, RAF Hawkinge, Kent.. 8·25 8·25

First Day Cover (Tallents House)...		11·00
First Day Cover (London NW9)...		11·00
Presentation Pack (PO Pack No. 514)...................................	10·00	
PHQ Cards (set of 7) (404)...	3·50	13·50

The seven PHQ cards show the six individual stamps and the complete miniature sheet.
See also Nos. 4071/4073.

2880 The Honey Bee

(Des Richard Lewington (illustration) and Anna Ekelund (Nos. 3736/371) or Andy English (illustration) and Interabang (No. **MS**3742). Litho ISP Cartor (Nos. 3736/3742) or gravure ISP Walsall (No. 3743))

2015 (18 Aug). Bees. Multicoloured
(a) Ordinary gum. One centre band (No. 3736), two phosphor bands (Nos. 3737/3741) or phosphor background (No. **MS**3742). Perf 14×14½.

3736	2874	(2nd) Scabious Bee on Field Scabious......	90	90
3737	2875	(1st) Great Yellow Bumblebee on Bird's-foot Trefoil..............................	1·20	1·20
3738	2876	£1 Northern Colletes Bee on Wild Carrot...	1·50	1·50
3739	2877	£1·33 Bilberry Bumblebee on Bilberry.....	1·75	1·75
3740	2878	£1·52 Large Mason Bee on Horseshoe Vetch...	2·25	2·25
3741	2879	£2·25 Potter Flower Bee on Ground Ivy...	3·75	3·75
Set of 6			10·00	10·00
Set of 6 Gutter Pairs...			20·00	
First Day Cover (Tallents House)..				13·50
First Day Cover (St Bees)...				13·50
Presentation Pack (PO Pack No. 515) (Nos. 3736/3741 and **MS**3743)..			19·00	
PHQ Cards (set of 7) (405)...			3·50	18·00
MS3742 191×74 mm. **2880** (1st) Waggle dance; (1st) Pollination; £1·33 Making honey; £1·33 Tending young..			5·50	5·75
First Day Cover (Tallents House)...				6·00
First Day Cover (St Bees)..				6·00

(b) Self-adhesive. Two phosphor bands. Die-cut perf 14×14½.

3743	2875	(1st) Great Yellow Bumblebee (*Bombus distinguendus*) on Bird's-foot Trefoil (*Lotus corniculatus*)..............	2·00	2·00
		a. Booklet pane. Nos. 3743×2 and U3022×4...............................	7·50	

No. 3743 was issued in stamp booklet, No. PM48, originally sold for £3·78.
The seven PHQ cards depict the six individual stamps and the complete miniature sheet.

Nos. 3744/3746 are vacant.

2874 Scabious Bee (*Andrena hattorfiana*) on Field Scabious (*Knautia arvensis*)

2875 Great Yellow Bumblebee (*Bombus distinguendus*) on Bird's-foot Trefoil (*Lotus corniculatus*)

259

QUEEN ELIZABETH II/2015

2881 'Long to Reign Over Us'

(Des Sedley Place. Eng C Matthews. Recess and gravure FNMT (Spain))

2015 (9 Sept) Long to Reign Over Us (2nd issue). Multicoloured Two phosphor bands. Perf 14½×14 (with one elliptical hole in each vertical side) (Machin) or 14 (others).

MS3747 194×75 mm. **2881** Long to Reign Over Us (1st) William Wyon's City Medal depicting Queen Victoria; (1st) Portrait of Queen Elizabeth II from photograph by Dorothy Wilding; As No. U3747 (but printed gravure); £1·52 Badge of the House of Windsor depicting Round Tower of Windsor Castle; £1·52 Device from The Queen's Personal Flag............ 8·00 8·00
First Day Cover (Tallents House)... 10·00
First Day Cover (Windsor)... 10·00
Presentation Pack (PO Pack No. 516)............................. 3·00
PHQ Cards (set of 6) (406)... 3·00 12·00

Stamps from No. **MS**3747 all have an iridescent overprint reading LONG TO REIGN OVER US.

The 1st class bright lilac stamp from No. **MS**3747 has a source code 'REIGM' and year code 'O15R' within this iridescent overprint.

The PHQ cards depict the five individual stamps and the complete miniature sheet.

2882 Tackle
2883 Scrum 
2884 Try 
2885 Conversion 
2886 Pass 
2887 Drop Goal 
2888 Ruck 
2889 Line-Out 

(Des Hat-trick design and Geoff Appleton (illustrations). Litho ISP Cartor (Nos. 3748/3755) or gravure ISP Walsall (Nos. 3756/3757))

2015 (18 Sept). Rugby World Cup. Multicoloured One centre band (Nos. 3748/3749) or two bands (others)

(a) Ordinary gum. Perf 14.

3748	2882	(2nd) Tackle...	90	90
		a. Horiz pair. Nos. 3748/3749...............	1·75	1·75
3749	2883	(2nd) Scrum...	90	90
3750	2884	(1st) Try..	1·20	1·00
		a. Horiz pair. Nos. 3750/3751...............	2·40	2·00
3751	2885	(1st) Conversion...................................	1·20	1·00
3752	2886	£1 Pass...	1·50	1·50
		a. Horiz pair. Nos. 3752/3753...............	3·00	3·00
3753	2887	£1 Drop Goal...	1·50	1·50
3754	2888	£1·52 Ruck...	2·00	2·00
		a. Horiz pair. Nos. 3754/3755...............	4·00	4·00
3755	2889	£1·52 Line-Out.....................................	2·00	2·00
Set of 8..			10·00	9·75
Set of 4 Gutter Blocks of 4..			20·00	
First Day Cover (Tallents House)......................................				12·50
First Day Cover (Rugby)..				12·50
Presentation Pack (PO Pack No. 517)...........................			12·50	
PHQ Cards (set of 8) (407)..			4·00	13·00

(b) Self-adhesive. Die-cut perf 14.

3756	2884	(1st) Try..	4·00	4·00
		a. Booklet pane. Nos. 3756/3757 and U3746×4..............................	12·00	
3757	2885	(1st) Conversion...................................	4·00	4·00

Nos. 3748/3749, 3750/3751, 3752/3753 and 3754/3755 were each printed together, *se-tenant*, as horizontal pairs in sheets of 60 (2 panes 6×5).

Nos. 3756/3757 were issued in stamp booklet, No. PM49, originally sold for £3·78.

2890 Darth Vader
2891 Yoda 
2892 Obi-Wan Kenobi 
2893 Stormtrooper 
2894 Han Solo 
2895 Rey 
2896 Princess Leia 
2897 The Emperor 
2898 Luke Skywalker 
2899 Boba Fett

2015/QUEEN ELIZABETH II

2900 Finn  **2901** Kylo Ren

2902 Star Wars

(Des Malcolm Tween (illustrations) and Interabang (Nos. 3758/3769) or GBH (No. **MS**3770). Litho ISP Cartor)

2015 (20 Oct)–**2017**. Star Wars (1st issue). Multicoloured Two phosphor bands and fluorescent emblems (Nos. 3758/3769) or 'All-over' phosphor (No. **MS**3770).

(a) Ordinary gum. Perf 14½.

3758	2890	(1st) Darth Vader................................	1·20	1·00
		a. Horiz strip of 6. Nos. 3758/3763.....	6·50	5·50
		b. Booklet pane. Nos. 3758, 3760, 3763 and 3767/3769 with margins all round (17.12.15)...........	6·50	
3759	2891	(1st) Yoda..	1·20	1·00
		b. Booklet pane. Nos. 3759, 3761/3762 and 3764/3766 with margins all round (17.12.15)...........	6·50	
		c. Booklet pane. Nos. 3759, 3763, 4007 and 4009 with margins all round (14.12.17).....................	4·25	
3760	2892	(1st) Obi-Wan Kenobi.............................	1·20	1·00
3761	2893	(1st) Stormtrooper............................	1·20	1·00
3762	2894	(1st) Han Solo................................	1·20	1·00
		b. Booklet pane. Nos. 3762, 3764 and 4012/4013 with margins all round (14.12.17)......................	4·25	
3763	2895	(1st) Rey..	1·20	1·00
3764	2896	(1st) Princess Leia.............................	1·20	1·00
		a. Horiz strip of 6. Nos. 3764/3769.....	6·50	5·50
3765	2897	(1st) The Emperor............................	1·20	1·00
3766	2898	(1st) Luke Skywalker.........................	1·20	1·00
3767	2899	(1st) Boba Fett...............................	1·20	1·00
3768	2900	(1st) Finn......................................	1·20	1·00
3769	2901	(1st) Kylo Ren................................	1·20	1·00
Set of 12..			13·00	11·00
Set of 2 Gutter Strips of 12......................................			26·00	
First Day Cover (Tallents House)............................				14·00
First Day Cover (Elstree, Borehamwood)...............				14·00
Presentation Pack (PO Pack No. 518) (Nos. 3758/3769 and **MS**3770)...			21·00	
PHQ Cards (set of 19) (408)....................................			9·50	28·00

(b) Self-adhesive.

MS3770 204×75 mm. **2902** (1st) X-wing Starfighter (60×21 mm, perf 14½×14); (1st) TIE fighters (35×36 mm, perf 14); (1st) X-wing Starfighters (60×21 mm, perf 14½×14); (1st) AT-AT Walkers (41×30 mm, Perf 14); (1st) TIE fighters (27×37 mm, perf 14); (1st) Millennium Falcon (60×30 mm, perf 14½)................................. 7·00 6·50
First Day Cover (Tallents House)............................ 7·00
First Day Cover (Elstree, Borehamwood)............... 7·00

Nos. 3758/3763 and 3764/3769 were each printed together, se-tenant, as horizontal strips of six stamps in sheets of 60 (2 panes 6×5).

Nos. 3758/3769 all show fluorescent emblems under UV light. Nos. 3758, 3761 and 3765 show the symbol of the Galactic Empire, Nos. 3759/3760 show the Jedi Order symbol, Nos. 3762, 3764 and 3766 show the Rebel Alliance symbol, Nos. 3763 and 3768/3769 show the logo for the new film *Star Wars The Force Awakens* and No. 3767 shows the Mandalorian Crest.

Nos. 3758b and 3759b were only issued in £16·99 premium booklet, No. DY15.

Nos. 3759c and 3762b were issued in £15·99 premium booklet, No. DY23.

Nos. 3758/3769 were re-issued on 12 October 2017 with Nos. 4007/4014 in a sheet entitled *Star Wars. The Ultimate Collectors' Sheet* (No. **MS**4014a).

Designs as Nos. 3758/3759 and 3761/3762 but self-adhesive were issued in sheets of ten with se-tenant labels showing film stills (No. LS96), each sheet containing Nos. 3758/3759, each×3, and Nos. 3761/3762, each×2. These sheets were originally sold for £6·80 each.

The four designs were also available from Royal Mail, Edinburgh in separate sheets of ten with personal photographs on the labels, originally sold for £10·20 per sheet.

The 19 PHQ cards depict the individual stamps including those from No. **MS**3770 and the complete miniature sheet.

2903 The Journey to Bethlehem  **2904** The Nativity   **2905** The Journey to Bethlehem

2906 The Nativity  **2907** The Animals of the Nativity  **2908** The Shepherds

2909 The Three Wise Men  **2910** The Annunciation

(Des David Holmes (illustrations) and Studio David Hillman. Gravure ISP Walsall (Nos. 3771a, 3772a) or De La Rue (others))

2015 (3 Nov). Christmas. Multicoloured One centre band (No. 3771) or two bands (others). Perf 14½×15.

(a) Self-adhesive.

3771	2903	(2nd) The Journey to Bethlehem.............	90	90
		a. Booklet pane. No. 3771×12............	13·50	
3772	2904	(1st) The Nativity..............................	1·20	1·00
		a. Booklet pane. No. 3772×12............	16·00	
3773	2905	(2nd The Journey to Bethlehem Large)...	1·25	1·10
3774	2906	(1st The Nativity Large).....................................	1·70	1·40
3775	2907	£1·00 The Animals of the Nativity......	1·75	1·75
3776	2908	£1·33 The Shepherds........................	2·10	2·10
3777	2909	£1·52 The Three Wise Men................	2·50	2·50
3778	2910	£2·25 The Annunciation....................	3·50	3·50
Set of 8...			13·25	12·75
First Day Cover (Tallents House)............................				16·75
First Day Cover (Bethlehem, Llandeilo)..................				16·75
Presentation Pack (PO Pack No. 519).....................			15·00	
PHQ Cards (set of 9) (409)......................................			4·50	26·00

(b) Ordinary gum.

MS3779 190×74 mm. As Nos. 3771/3778....................... 13·25 12·75
First Day Cover (Tallents House)........................... 16·75
First Day Cover (Bethlehem, Llandeilo).................. 16·75

The 2nd class, 1st class, £1, £1·33, £1·52 and £2·25 stamps were also issued in sheets of 20 (No. LS97), containing eight 2nd class, eight 1st class and one each of £1, £1·33, £1·52 and £2·25 stamps, each stamp accompanied by a se-tenant label with a verse from the *King James Bible*. These sheets were printed in lithography by ISP Cartor and originally sold for £15·96.

The design of the 1st class stamps in the Post office Label Sheet is enlarged compared with those from counter sheets and booklets, resulting in a much diminished grey foreground at lower left.

The nine PHQ cards show the eight individual stamps and the complete miniature sheet.

Year Pack

2015 (3 Nov). Comprises Nos. 3658/3667, **MS**3678/3706, **MS**3710/3716, 3718/3729. **MS**3734, **MS**3735/**MS**3742, **MS**3747/3755 and 3758/3778
CP3779a   Year Pack (PO Pack No. 520) (sold for £117)... £150

Post Office Yearbook

2015 (3 Nov). Comprises Nos. 3658/3667, **MS**3678/3706, **MS**3710/3729, **MS**3734, **MS**3735/**MS**3742, **MS**3747/3755 and 3758/3778
YB3779a   Yearbook (sold for £137)...................... £180

Miniature Sheet Collection

2015 (3 Nov). Comprises Nos. **MS**3678, **MS**3710, **MS**3734, **MS**3735, **MS**3742, **MS**3747, **MS**3770 and **MS**3779
MS3779a Minature Sheet Collection (sold for £41)........... 55·00

QUEEN ELIZABETH II/2015

2911 X-wing Starfighter

2912 AT-AT Walkers

2913 TIE Fighters

2914 TIE Fighters

2915 X-wing Starfighters

2916 *Millennium Falcon*

(Des GBH. Litho ISP Cartor)

2015 (17 Dec). *Star Wars* (2nd issue). Self-adhesive. Multicoloured 'All-over' phosphor. Die-cut perf 14½×14 (Nos. 3780, 3784), 14 (Nos. 3781/3783) or 14½ (No. 3785).

3780	**2911**	(1st) X-wing Starfighter	1·25	1·25
		a. Booklet pane. Nos. 3780/3782	3·50	
3781	**2912**	(1st) AT-AT Walkers	1·25	1·25
3782	**2913**	(1st) TIE fighters	1·25	1·25
3783	**2914**	(1st) TIE fighters	1·25	1·25
		a. Booklet pane. Nos. 3783/3785	3·50	
3784	**2915**	(1st) X-wing Starfighters	1·25	1·25
3785	**2916**	(1st) *Millennium Falcon*	1·25	1·25
Set of 6			6·75	6·75

Nos. 3780/3785 were only issued in £16·99 *Star Wars* premium booklet, No. DY15, or No. **MS**3770.

2917 Union Flag

(Litho ISP Cartor)

2015 (17 Dec). *Star Wars* (3rd issue). As No. 2570 but ordinary gum. Multicoloured Two phosphor bands. Perf 14½×14 (with one elliptical hole in each vert side).

3786	**2917**	(1st) Union Flag	1·50	1·50

No. 3786 comes from booklet pane No. U3150l from £16·99 *Star Wars* booklet, No. DY15 and booklet pane No. U3071q from £16·99 James Bond booklet, No. DY33.

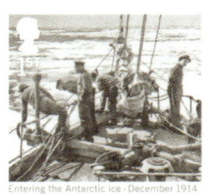

2918 Entering the Antarctic Ice, December 1914

2919 *Endurance* Frozen in Pack Ice, January 1915

2920 Striving to Free *Endurance*, February 1915

2921 Trapped in a Pressure Crack, October 1915

2922 Patience Camp, December 1915–April 1916

2923 Safe Arrival at Elephant Island, April 1916

2924 Setting out for South Georgia, April 1916

2925 Rescue of *Endurance* Crew, August 1916

(Des Robert Maude and Sarah Davies. Litho ISP Cartor)

2016 (7 Jan). Shackleton and the *Endurance* Expedition. Multicoloured. Two phosphor bands. Perf 14×14½.

3787	**2918**	(1st) Entering the Antarctic Ice	1·20	1·00
		a. Horiz pair. Nos. 3787/3788	2·40	2·00
3788	**2919**	(1st) *Endurance* Frozen in Pack Ice	1·20	1·00
3789	**2920**	£1 Striving to Free *Endurance*	1·50	1·50
		a. Horiz pair. Nos. 3789/3790	3·00	3·00
3790	**2921**	£1 Trapped in a Pressure Crack	1·50	1·50
3791	**2922**	£1·33 Patience Camp	1·75	1·75
		a. Horiz pair. Nos. 3791/3792	3·75	3·75
3792	**2923**	£1·33 Safe Arrival at Elephant Island	1·75	1·75
3793	**2924**	£1·52 Setting out for South Georgia	2·25	2·25
		a. Horiz pair. Nos. 3793/3794	4·50	4·50
3794	**2925**	£1·52 Rescue of *Endurance* Crew	2·25	2·25
Set of 8			12·25	12·00
Set of 4 Gutter blocks of 4			24·50	
First Day Cover (Tallents House)				16·00
First Day Cover (Plymouth)				16·00
Presentation Pack (PO Pack No. 521)			15·00	
PHQ Cards (set of 8) (410)			4·00	15·00

Nos. 3787/3788, 3789/3790, 3791/3792 and 3793/3794 were each printed together, *se-tenant*, as horizontal pairs in sheets of 60 (2 panes 6×5).

2016/QUEEN ELIZABETH II

2926 Sir Brian Tuke, Master of the Posts

2927 *Mail Packet off Eastbourne* (Captain Victor Howes)

2928 Penfold Pillar Box

2929 River Post

2930 Mail Coach

2931 Medway Mail Centre

(Des Atelier Works (No. 3795/3800) or Purpose (No. **MS**3801). Litho ISP Cartor)

2016 (17-18 Feb). Royal Mail 500 (1st issue). Multicoloured. Two phosphor bands. Perf 14½×14 (Nos.3795/3800) or 14 (No. **MS**3801)

3795	2926	(1st) Sir Brian Tuke	1·20	1·00
		a. Booklet pane. Nos. 3795 and 3797/3798 with margins all round (18.2.16)	6·00	
3796	2927	(1st) *Mail Packet off Eastbourne*	1·20	1·00
		a. Booklet pane. Nos. 3796 and 3799/3800 with margins all round (18.2.16)	6·00	
3797	2928	(1st) Penfold Pillar Box	1·20	1·00
3798	2929	£1·52 River Post	2·50	2·50
3799	2930	£1·52 Mail Coach	2·50	2·50
3800	2931	£1·52 Medway Mail Centre	2·50	2·50
Set of 6			10·00	9·50
Set of 6 Gutter Pairs			20·00	
Set of 6 Traffic light Gutter pairs (two stamps only in each pair)			21·00	
First Day Cover (Tallents House)				12·00
First Day Cover (London WC1)				12·00
Presentation Pack (PO Pack No. 522) (Nos. 3795/3800 and **MS**3801)			18·00	
PHQ Cards (set of 11) (411)			5·50	24·00

2932 Classic GPO Posters

MS3801 125×89 mm. **2932** Classic GPO Posters (1st) 'QUICKEST WAY BY AIR MAIL' (Edward McKnight Kauffer, 1935); (1st) 'ADDRESS your letters PLAINLY' (Hans Schleger, 1942); £1·33 'pack your parcels carefully' (Hans Unger, 1950); £1·33 'STAMPS IN BOOKS SAVE TIME' (Harry Stevens, 1960) .... 7·00 7·25
First Day Cover (Tallents House).. 7·50
First Day Cover (London WC1).. 7·50

Nos. 3795/**MS**3801 commemorate 500 years of a regular, organised postal service.

Nos. 3795a and 3796a come from £16·36 500 Years of Royal mail premium booklet No. DY16.

No. **MS**3801 additionally inscribed 'Spring Stampex, 17-20 February 2016' was only available at that exhibition (*Price* £22).

The complete miniature sheet is shown on one of the 11 PHQ cards with the others depicting individual stamps including those from the miniature sheet.

2933 'QUICKEST WAY BY AIR MAIL' (Edward McKnight Kauffer, 1935)

2934 'ADDRESS your letters PLAINLY' (Hans Schleger, 1942)

2935 'STAMPS IN BOOKS SAVE TIME' (Harry Stevens, 1960)

2936 'pack your parcels carefully' (Hans Unger, 1950)

(Litho ISP Cartor)

2016 (17–18 Feb). Royal Mail 500 (2nd issue). Multicoloured Perf 14.

3802	2933	(1st) 'QUICKEST WAY BY AIR MAIL'	1·75	1·75
		a. Booklet pane. Nos. 3802/3805 with margins all round and roulettes at left (18.2.16)	6·25	
3803	2934	(1st) 'ADDRESS your letters PLAINLY'	1·75	1·75
3804	2935	£1·33 'STAMPS IN BOOKS SAVE TIME'	1·75	1·75
3805	2936	£1·33 'pack your parcels carefully'	1·75	1·75
Set of 4			6·25	6·25

Nos. 3802/3805 come from No. **MS**3801 and £16·36 500 years of Royal Mail premium booklet, No. DY16.

2937 Penny Red

(Gravure ISP Walsall)

2016 (18 Feb). 175th Anniversary of the Penny Red. Self-adhesive. Multicoloured Two phosphor bands. Die-cut perf 14½×14 (with one elliptical hole in each vert side).

3806	2937	(1st) Penny Red	1·50	1·50

No. 3806 comes from booklets of six, No. MB16 and MB21.

No. 3806 was also issued in sheets of 20 with attached labels showing the Rainbow Trials from which the Penny Red evolved (No. LS99). These sheets were printed in lithography by ISP Cartor and originally sold for £13·10 each.

Sheets of ten or 20 of these Penny Red stamps were available from Royal Mail with personal photographs on the labels for £10·20 (ten) or £18·65 (20).

QUEEN ELIZABETH II/2016

2848 Penny Black
2938 Two Pence Blue 

(Des Atelier Works. Litho ISP Cartor)

2016 (18 Feb). Royal Mail 500 (3rd issue). Multicoloured Two phosphor bands. 14½×14 (with one elliptical hole in each vert side).

3807	2848	(1st) Penny Black	1·75	1·75
		a. Booklet pane. No. 3807×2 and Nos. 3808/3809 each×3 with central label and margins all round	14·00	
3808	2937	(1st) Penny Red	1·50	1·50
3809	2938	(1st) 2d. Blue	1·50	1·50
First Day Cover (Tallents House) (No. 3807a)				15·00
First Day Cover (London W1) (No. 3807a)				15·00

Nos. 3807/3809 come from £16·36 500 Years of Royal Mail premium booklet, No. DY16 and £17·20 Queen Victoria premium booklet, No. DY30.

2939 Nicholas Winton (1909–2015)
2940 Sue Ryder (1924–2000) 
2941 John Boyd Orr (1880–1971) 
2942 Eglantyne Jebb (1876–1928) 
2943 Joseph Rowntree (1836–1925) 
2944 Josephine Butler (1828–1906) 

(Des Hat-trick Design. Litho ISP Cartor)

2016 (15 Mar). British Humanitarians. Multicoloured Two phosphor bands. Perf 14½.

3810	2939	(1st) Nicholas Winton	1·20	1·00
		a. Horiz strip of 3. Nos. 3810/3812	3·50	3·00
3811	2940	(1st) Sue Ryder	1·20	1·00
3812	2941	(1st) John Boyd Orr	1·20	1·00
3813	2942	£1·33 Eglantyne Jebb	2·00	2·00
		a. Horiz strip of 3. Nos. 3813/3815	6·00	6·00
3814	2943	£1·33 Joseph Rowntree	2·00	2·00
3815	2944	£1·33 Josephine Butler	2·00	2·00
Set of 6			8·75	8·25
Set of 2 Gutter Strips of 6			17·50	
First Day Cover (Tallents House)				11·00
First Day Cover (Winton, Northallerton)				11·00
Presentation Pack (PO Pack No. 523)			10·00	
PHQ Cards (set of 6) (412)			3·00	11·00

Nos. 3810/3812 and 3813/3815 were each printed together, se-tenant, as horizontal strips of three stamps in sheets of 60 (2 panes 6×5).

2945 'to thine own self be true' (Hamlet)
2946 'cowards die many times before their deaths. The valiant never taste of death but once.' (Julius Caesar) 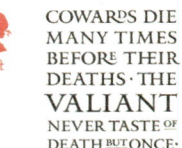
2947 'Love is a smoke made with the fume of sighs' (Romeo and Juliet) 
2948 'The fool doth think he is wise, but the wise man knows himself to be a fool.' (As You Like It) 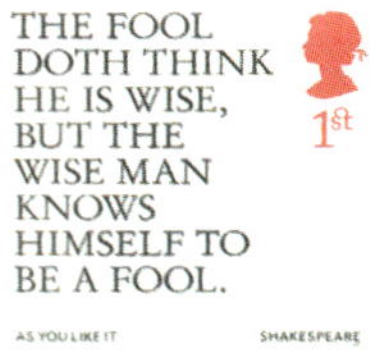
2949 'There was a star danced, and under that was I born. (Much Ado About Nothing) 
2950 'But if the while I think on thee, dear friend, all losses are restored and sorrows end.' (Sonnet 30) 
2951 'LOVE comforteth like sunshine after rain' (Venus and Adonis) 
2952 'We are such stuff as dreams are made on; and our little life is rounded with a sleep.' (The Tempest) 
2953 'Life's but a walking shadow, a poor player That struts and frets his hour upon the stage' (Macbeth) 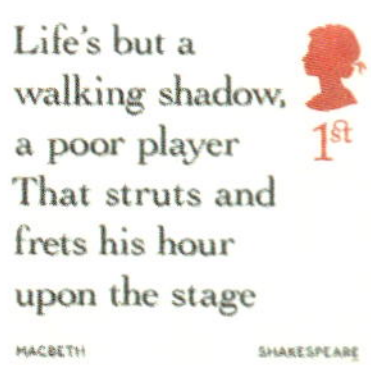
2954 'I wasted time, and now doth time waste me' (Richard II) 

(Des The Chase. Litho ISP Cartor)

2016 (5 Apr). 400th Death Anniversary of William Shakespeare. Multicoloured Two phosphor bands. Perf 14½.

3816	2945	(1st) 'to thine own self be true'	1·20	1·00
		a. Horiz strip of 5. Nos. 3816/3820	5·25	4·50
3817	2946	(1st) 'cowards die many times before their deaths. The valiant never taste of death but once.'	1·20	1·00

2016/QUEEN ELIZABETH II

3818	**2947**	(1st) 'Love is a smoke made with the fume of sighs'.................................	1·20	1·00
3819	**2948**	(1st) 'The fool doth think he is wise, but the wise man knows himself to be a fool'....................................	1·20	1·00
3820	**2949**	(1st) 'There was a star danced, and under that was I born'.....................	1·20	1·00
3821	**2950**	(1st) 'But if the while I think on thee, dear friend, all losses are restored and sorrows end.'.............................	1·20	1·00
		a. Horiz strip of 5. Nos. 3821/3825.....	5·25	4·50
3822	**2951**	(1st) 'LOVE comforteth like sunshine after rain'...	1·20	1·00
3823	**2952**	(1st) 'We are such stuff as dreams are made on; and our little life is rounded with a sleep.'.......................	1·20	1·00
3824	**2953**	(1st) 'Life's but a walking shadow, a poor player That struts and frets his hour upon the stage'.................	1·20	1·00
3825	**2954**	(1st) 'I wasted time, and now doth time waste me' (Richard II)..............	1·20	1·00
Set of 10..			10·50	9·00
Set of 2 Gutter Strips of 10..			21·00	
First Day Cover (Tallents House).....................................				12·00
First Day Cover (Stratford-upon-Avon)...........................				12·00
Presentation Pack (PO Pack No. 524)..............................			11·50	
PHQ Cards (set of 10) (413)..			5·00	12·00

Nos. 3816/3820 and 3821/3825 were each printed together, *se-tenant*, as horizontal strips of five stamps in sheets of 50 (2 panes 5×5).

2955 Princess Elizabeth and her Father the Duke of York (later King George VI), c 1930

2956 Queen Elizabeth II at State Opening of Parliament, 2012

2957 Queen Elizabeth II with Prince Charles and Princess Anne, 1952

2958 Queen Elizabeth II on Visit to New Zealand, 1977

2959 Queen Elizabeth II and Duke of Edinburgh, 1957

2960 Queen Elizabeth II with Nelson Mandela, 1996

2961 Prince Charles, Queen Elizabeth II, Prince George and Prince William

2962 Prince Charles

2963 Queen Elizabeth II

2964 Prince George

2965 Prince William

(Des Kate Stephens (Nos. 3826/3831). Litho ISP Cartor (Nos. 3826/**MS**3832) or Gravure ISP Walsall (Nos. 3833/38336))

2016 (21 Apr–9 June). 90th Birthday of Queen Elizabeth II. Multicoloured Two phosphor bands (Nos. 3826/3831) or 'all-over' phosphor (Nos. **MS**3832/**MS**3832b, 3833/38336).

*(a) Ordinary gum. Perf 14×14½ (Nos. 3826/3831) or 14 (No. **MS**3832).*

3826	**2955**	(1st) Princess Elizabeth and her Father the Duke of York................................	1·20	1·00
		a. Horiz strip of 3. Nos. 3826/3828.....	3·50	3·00
		b. Booklet pane. Nos. 3826/3828 and 3831 with margins all round...	5·75	
3827	**2956**	(1st) Queen Elizabeth II at State Opening of Parliament.....................	1·20	1·00
3828	**2957**	(1st) Queen Elizabeth II with Prince Charles and Princess Anne..............	1·20	1·00
3829	**2958**	£1·52 Queen Elizabeth II on Visit to New Zealand..	2·25	2·25
		a. Horiz strip of 3. Nos. 3829/38231...	6·75	6·75
		b. Booklet pane. Nos. 3829/3830 with margins all round.....................	4·25	
3830	**2959**	£1·52 Queen Elizabeth II and Duke of Edinburgh...	2·25	2·25
3831	**2960**	£1·52 Queen Elizabeth II with Nelson Mandela...	2·25	2·25
Set of 6..			9·25	8·75
Set of 2 Gutter Strips of 6..			18·50	
First Day Cover (Tallents House).....................................				11·50
First Day Cover (Windsor)..				11·50
Presentation Pack (PO Pack No. 525) (Nos. 3826/3831 and **MS**3832)..			14·50	
PHQ Cards (set of 11) (414)..			5·50	19·00
MS3832 189×75 mm. **2961** (1st×4) Prince Charles, Queen Elizabeth II, Prince George and Prince William...			4·50	4·25
		b. Booklet pane. No. **MS**3832 but 150×95 mm with roulettes at left.........	5·00	
First Day Cover (Tallents House).....................................				4·75
First Day Cover (Windsor)..				4·75

(b) Self-adhesive. Die-cut perf 14.

3833	**2962**	(1st) Prince Charles......................................	5·75	5·75
		a. Booklet pane. Nos. 3833/3834 and U3746×4...................................	15·00	
3834	**2963**	(1st) Queen Elizabeth II...............................	5·75	5·75
3835	**2964**	(1st) Prince George (9.6.16)......................	5·75	5·75
		a. Booklet pane. Nos. 3835/3836 and U3746×4...................................	7·50	
3836	**2965**	(1st) Prince William (9.6.16)......................	2·00	2·00
Set of 4..			14·00	14·00

Nos. 3826/3828 and 3829/3831 were each printed together, *se-tenant*, as horizontal strips of three stamps in sheets of 60 (2 panes 6×5).

Nos. 3826b, 3829b and **MS**3832b were issued in £15·11 90th Birthday of Queen Elizabeth II premium booklet, DY17.

Nos. 3833/3836 were issued in stamp booklets, Nos. PM50/PM51, originally sold for £3·84 each.

Miniature sheets as No. **MS**3832 are also available with a special inscription 'Stampex 60 Years'.

QUEEN ELIZABETH II/2016

2966 Animail

(Des Osborne Ross. Litho ISP Cartor)

2016 (17 May). Animail. Sheet 203×74 mm. Multicoloured 'All-over' phosphor. Die-cut and die-cut perf 14.

MS3837	**2966**	Animail (1st) Woodpecker; (1st) Snake; £1·05 Chimpanzee; £1·05 Bat; £1·33 Orangutan; £1·33 Koala	8·50	8·75
First Day Cover (Tallents House)				11·00
First Day Cover (Playing Place, Truro)				11·00
Presentation Pack (PO Pack No. 526)			10·00	
PHQ Cards (set of 7) (415)			3·50	15·00

The seven PHQ cards show the six individual stamps and the complete miniature sheet.

2967 *Battlefield Poppy* (Giles Revell)

2968 'Your battle wounds are scars upon my heart' (poem *To My Brother*, Vera Brittain)

2969 Munitions Worker Lottie Meade

2970 *Travoys Arriving with Wounded at a Dressing-Station at Smol, Macedonia, September 1916* (Stanley Spencer)

2971 Thiepval Memorial, Somme, France

2972 Captain A. C. Green's Battle of Jutland Commemorative Medal

(Des Hat-trick design. Litho ISP Cartor)

2016 (21 June). Centenary of the First World War (3rd issue). Multicoloured Two phosphor bands. Perf 14½.

3838	**2967**	(1st) *Battlefield Poppy*	1·20	1·00
		a. Booklet pane. Nos. 3838/3840 with margins all round	3·50	
3839	**2968**	(1st) 'Your battle wounds are scars upon my heart'	1·20	1·00
3840	**2969**	(1st) Munitions Worker Lottie Meade	1·20	1·00
3841	**2970**	£1·52 Travoys Arriving with Wounded at a Dressing-Station at Smol, Macedonia, September 1916	2·50	2·50
		a. Booklet pane. Nos. 3841/3843, with margins all round	7·50	
3842	**2971**	£1·52 Thiepval Memorial, Somme, France	2·50	2·50
3843	**2972**	£1·52 Captain A. C. Green's Battle of Jutland Commemorative Medal	2·50	2·50
Set of 6			10·00	9·50
Set of 6 Gutter Pairs			20·00	
First Day Cover (Tallents House)				12·00
First Day Cover (Lyness, Stromness)				12·00
Presentation Pack (PO Pack No. 527) (Nos. 3838/3843 and **MS**3848)			18·00	
PHQ Cards (set of 11) (416)			5·50	26·00

Nos. 3838a and 3841a were issued in £16·49 premium booklet, No. DY18.

2973 The Post Office Rifles

2974 Writing a Letter from the Western Front

2975 Delivering the Mail on the Home Front

2976 Home Depot at Regent's Park, London

2977 The Post Office at War, 1914–1918

(Des Hat-trick design. Litho ISP Cartor)

2016 (21 June). Centenary of the First World War (3rd issue). Multicoloured Two phosphor bands Perf 14.

3844	**2973**	(1st) The Post Office Rifles	1·60	1·60
		a. Booklet pane. Nos. 3844/3847 with margins all round	7·25	
3845	**2974**	(1st) Writing a Letter from the Western Front	1·60	1·60
3846	**2975**	£1·33 Delivering the Mail on the Home Front	2·50	2·50
3847	**2976**	£1·33 Home Depot at Regent's Park, London	2·50	2·50
Set of 4			7·25	7·25
MS3848 156×74 mm. **2977** The Post Office at War, 1914–1918 Nos. 3844/3847			7·25	7·25
First Day Cover (Tallents House)				8·25
First Day Cover (Lyness, Stromness)				8·25

Nos. 3844/3847 were issued in £16·49 Centenary of the First Wold War (3rd issue) premium booklet, No. DY18, and in No. **MS**3848.

2978 *The Piper at the Gates of Dawn* (1967)

2979 *Atom Heart Mother* (1970)

2980 The Dark Side of the Moon (1973)

2981 Animals (1977)

2982 Wish You Were Here (1975)

2983 The Endless River (2014)

2984 Pink Floyd on Stage

(Gravure ISP Walsall (Nos. 3849/3854) or litho ISP Cartor (No. **MS**3855))

2016 (7 July). Pink Floyd. Multicoloured
(a) Album Covers. Self-adhesive. Two phosphor bands. Die-cut perf 14½.

3849	**2978**	(1st) The Piper at the Gates of Dawn (1967)..................................	1·20	1·00
3850	**2979**	(1st) Atom Heart Mother (1970)...............	1·20	1·00
3851	**2980**	(1st) The Dark Side of the Moon (1973)...	1·20	1·00
3852	**2981**	£1·52 Animals (1977)..................................	2·50	2·50
3853	**2982**	£1·52 Wish You Were Here (1975)..............	2·50	2·50
3854	**2983**	£1·52 The Endless River (2014)..................	2·50	2·50
Set of 6...			10·00	9·50
First Day Cover (Tallents House)..				12·00
First Day Cover (Grantchester, Cambridge)........................				12·00
Presentation Pack (PO Pack No. 528) (Nos. 3849/3854 and **MS**3855)..			18·00	
PHQ Cards (set of 11) (417)...			5·50	24·00

(b) Pink Floyd on Stage. Ordinary gum. Phosphor frame. Perf 14½.
MS3855 202×74 mm. **2984** Pink Floyd on Stage (1st) UFO Club, 1966; (1st) The Dark Side of the Moon Tour, 1973; £1·52 The Wall Tour, 1981; £1·52 The Division Bell Tour, 1994.................................. 6·25 6·25
First Day Cover (Tallents House).. 8·00
First Day Cover (Grantchester, Cambridge)........................ 8·00

The right-hand edges of Nos. 3849/3854 are all cut around to show the vinyl disc protruding from the open edge of the album cover.

A *Dark Side of the Moon* maxi sheet containing No. 3851×10 was sold at £12·95, a premium of £6·55 over face value.

The 11 PHQ cards depicts the individual stamps including those from No. **MS**3855 and the complete miniature sheet.

MAGNIFIERS

LEFT TO RIGHT

2x Dome LED Magnifier
RDLM2X
£32.95

10x Jewellers Loupe
RJLM10X
£17.45

8x LED Inspection Stand Magnifier
RISM8X
£34.95

6x Linen Tester
RLTM6X
£17.45

QUEEN ELIZABETH II/2016

2985 Peter Rabbit   **2986** Mrs Tiggy-Winkle

2991 Now run along, and don't get into mischief.   **2992** And then, feeling rather sick, he went to look for some parsley.

2987 Squirrel Nutkin   **2988** Jemima Puddle-Duck

2993 But Peter, who was very naughty, ran straight away to Mr McGregor's garden, and squeezed under the gate!   **2994** He slipped underneath the gate, and was safe at last.

2989 Tom Kitten   **2990** Benjamin Bunny

(Des Charlie Smith Design. Litho ISP Cartor (Nos. 3856/3861) or gravure ISP Walsall (Nos. 3862/3863))

2016 (28 July). 150th Birth Anniversary of Beatrix Potter (writer, illustrator and conservationist) (1st issue). Multicoloured Two phosphor bands.

(a) Ordinary gum. Perf 14½×14.

3856	**2985**	(1st) Peter Rabbit	1·20	1·00
		a. Horiz pair. Nos. 3856/3857	2·40	2·00
		b. Booklet pane. Nos. 3856, 3858 and 3861 with margins all round	5·00	
3857	**2986**	(1st) Mrs Tiggy-Winkle	1·20	1·00
		b. Booklet pane. Nos. 3857 and 3859/3860 with margins all round	5·00	
3858	**2987**	£1·33 Squirrel Nutkin	2·00	2·00
		a. Horiz pair. Nos. 3858/3859	4·00	4·00
3859	**2988**	£1·33 Jemima Puddle-Duck	2·00	2·00
3860	**2989**	£1·52 Tom Kitten	2·25	2·25
		a. Horiz pair. Nos. 3860/3861	4·50	4·50
3861	**2990**	£1·52 Benjamin Bunny	2·25	2·25
Set of 6			9·75	9·50
Set of 3 *Gutter Pairs* (two stamps only in each pair)			19·50	
Set of 3 *Traffic Light Gutter Pairs* (two stamps only in each pair)			21·00	
First Day Cover (Tallents House)				12·00
First Day Cover (Near Sawrey, Ambleside)				12·00
Presentation Pack (PO Pack No. 529) (Nos. 3856/3856 and **MS**3868)			18·50	
PHQ Cards (set of 11) (418)			5·50	24·00

(b) Self-adhesive. Die-cut perf 14½×14.

3862	**2985**	(1st) Peter Rabbit	4·00	4·00
		a. Booklet pane. Nos. 3862/3863 and U3746×4	11·00	
3863	**2986**	(1st) Mrs Tiggy-Winkle	4·00	4·00

Nos. 3856/3857, 3858/3859 and 3860/3861 were printed together, *se-tenant*, as horizontal pairs in sheets of 60 (2 panes 6×5).

Nos. 3862/3863 were issued in stamp booklet, No. PM52, originally sold for £3·84.

The 11 PHQ cards depict the ten individual stamps including those from No. **MS**3868 and the complete miniature sheet.

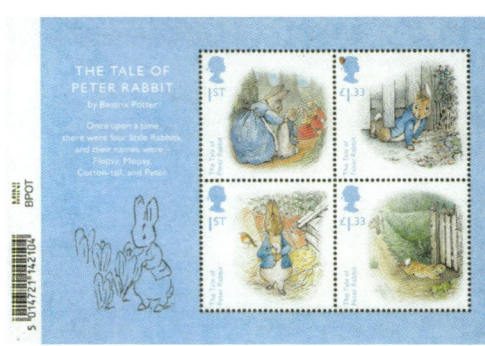

2995 Illustrations from *The Tale of Peter Rabbit*

(Des Magpie Studio (No. **MS**3868). Litho ISP Cartor)

2016 (28 July). 150th Birth Anniversary of Beatrix Potter (writer, illustrator and conservationist) (2nd issue). Multicoloured Two phosphor bands. Perf 14½.

3864	**2991**	(1st) Now run along, and don't get into mischief	2·25	2·25
		a. Booklet pane. Nos. 3864/3867 with margins all round and roulettes at left	8·00	
3865	**2992**	(1st) And then, feeling rather sick, he went to look for some parsley	2·25	2·25
3866	**2993**	£1·33 But Peter, who was very naughty, ran straight away to Mr McGregor's garden, and squeezed under the gate!	2·25	2·25
3867	**2994**	£1·33 He slipped underneath the gate, and was safe at last	2·25	2·25
Set of 4			8·25	8·25
MS3868 125×89 mm. **2995** Nos. 3864/3867 (*The Tale of Peter Rabbit*)			5·50	5·75
First Day Cover (Tallents House)				7·50
First Day Cover (Near Sawrey, Ambleside)				7·50

Nos. 3864/3867 were issued in £15·37 The Tale of Beatrix Potter premium booklet, DY19, and in No. **MS**3868.

2996 Blenheim Palace    **2997** Longleat

2998 Compton Verney

2999 Highclere Castle

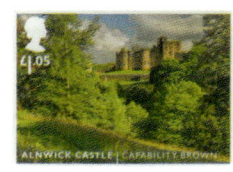

3000 Alnwick Castle

3001 Berrington Hall

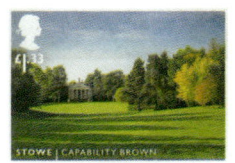

3002 Stowe

3003 Croome Park

(Des Robert Maude and Sarah Davies. Litho ISP Cartor (Nos. 3869/3876) or gravure ISP Walsall (Nos. 3877/3878))

2016 (16 Aug). Landscape Gardens. Multicoloured One centre band (2nd) or two phosphor bands (others).

(a) Ordinary gum. Perf 14.

3869	2996	(2nd) Blenheim Palace	90	90
		a. Horiz pair. Nos. 3869/3870	1·80	1·80
3870	2997	(2nd) Longleat	90	90
3871	2998	(1st) Compton Verney	1·20	1·00
		a. Horiz pair. Nos. 3871/3872	2·40	2·00
3872	2999	(1st) Highclere Castle	1·20	1·00
3873	3000	£1·05 Alnwick Castle	1·50	1·50
		a. Horiz pair. Nos. 3873/3874	3·00	3·00
3874	3001	£1·05 Berrington Hall	1·50	1·50
3875	3002	£1·33 Stowe	2·00	2·00
		a. Horiz pair. Nos. 3875/3876	4·00	4·00
3876	3003	£1·33 Croome Park	2·00	2·00
Set of 8			10·00	10·00
Set of 4 Gutter Blocks of 4			20·00	
First Day Cover (Tallents House)				13·00
First Day Cover (Kirkharle, Newcastle)				13·00
Presentation Pack (PO Pack No. 530)			13·00	
PHQ Cards (set of 8) (419)			4·00	12·00

(b) Self-adhesive. Die-cut perf 14.

3877	2998	(1st) Compton Verney	3·50	3·50
		a. Booklet pane. Nos. 3877/3878 and U3746×4	10·00	
3878	2999	(1st) Highclere Castle	3·50	3·50

Nos. 3869/3878 commemorate the 300th birth Anniversary of Capability Brown and show his landscape gardens.

Nos. 3869/3870, 3871/3872, 3873/3874 and 3875/3876 were each printed together, *se-tenant*, as horizontal pairs in sheets of 60 (2 panes 6×5).

Nos. 3877/3878 were issued in stamp booklet, No. PM53, originally sold for £3·84.

3004 Fire Breaks Out in Bakery on Pudding Lane, Sunday 2nd September 1666

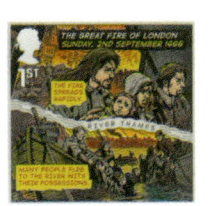

3005 The Fire Spreads Rapidly, Sunday 2nd September 1666

3006 Houses are Pulled, Monday 3rd September 1666

3007 As the Fire reaches St Paul's Citizens witness the Cathedral's Destruction, Tuesday 4th September 1666

3008 The Fire Dies Out, Wednesday 5th September 1666

3009 Christopher Wren develops Plans for the Regeneration of the City, Tuesday 11th September 1666

(Des John Higgins (artwork) and The Chase. Litho ISP Cartor)

2016 (2 Sept). 350th Anniversary of the Great Fire of London. Multicoloured Two phosphor bands. Perf 14½.

3879	3004	(1st) Fire Breaks Out in Bakery on Pudding Lane	1·20	1·00
		a. Horiz pair. Nos. 3879/3880	2·40	2·00
3880	3005	(1st) The Fire Spreads Rapidly	1·20	1·00
3881	3006	£1·05 Houses are Pulled Down to Create Breaks	1·60	1·60
		a. Horiz pair. Nos. 3881/3882	3·25	3·25
3882	3007	£1·05 As the Fire reaches St Paul's Citizens witness the Cathedral's Destruction	1·60	1·60
3883	3008	£1·52 The Fire Dies Out	2·25	2·35
		a. Horiz pair. Nos. 3883/3884	4·50	4·50
3884	3009	£1·52 Christopher Wren develops Plans for the Regeneration of the City	2·25	2·35
Set of 6			9·25	9·25
Set of 3 Gutter Blocks of 4			18·50	
First Day Cover (Tallents House)				12·00
First Day Cover (London EC3)				12·00
Presentation Pack (PO Pack No. 531)			11·00	
PHQ Cards (set of 6) (420)			3·00	11·00

Nos. 3879/3880, 3881/3882 and 3883/3884 were each printed together, *se-tenant*, as horizontal pairs in sheets of 60 (2 panes 6×5).

3010 *Murder on the Orient Express*

3011 *And Then There Were None*

3012 *The Mysterious Affair at Styles*

3013 *The Murder of Roger Ackroyd*

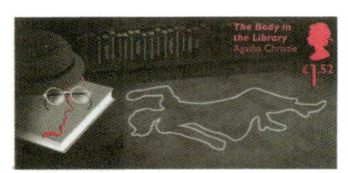

3014 *The Body in the Library*

3015 *A Murder is Announced*

3018 *Mr Bump* **3019** *Little Miss Sunshine*

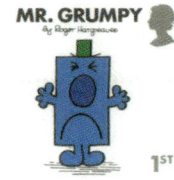

3020 *Mr Tickle* **3021** *Mr Grumpy*

3022 *Little Miss Princess* **3023** *Mr Strong*

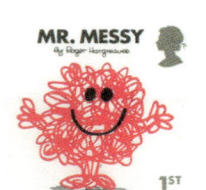

3024 *Little Miss Christmas* **3025** *Mr Messy*

(Des Studio Sutherland. Litho ISP Cartor)

2016 (15 Sept). 40th Death Anniversary of Agatha Christie (writer). Multicoloured Two phosphor bands. Perf 14½.

3885	3010	(1st) *Murder on the Orient Express*	1·20	1·00
		a. Vert pair. Nos. 3885/3886	2·40	2·00
3886	3011	(1st) *And Then There Were None*	1·20	1·00
3887	3012	£1·33 *The Mysterious Affair at Styles*	2·00	2·00
		a. Vert pair. Nos. 3887/3888	4·00	4·00
3888	3013	£1·33 *The Murder of Roger Ackroyd*	2·00	2·00
3889	3014	£1·52 *The Body in the Library*	2·25	2·25
		a. Vert pair. Nos. 3889/3890	4·50	4·50
3890	3015	£1·52 *A Murder is Announced*	2·25	2·25
Set of 6			9·75	9·50
Set of 3 Gutter Pairs (two stamps in each gutter pair)			10·25	
First Day Cover (Tallents House)				13·00
First Day Cover (Torquay)				13·00
Presentation Pack (PO Pack No. 532)			12·00	
PHQ Cards (set of 6) (421)			3·00	11·00

Nos. 3885/3886, 3887/3888 and 3889/3890 were each printed together, *se-tenant*, as vertical pairs in sheets of 48 (2 panes 4×6).

They all feature hidden secrets in the form of microtext, uv ink or thermochronic ink.

3016 *Mr Happy* **3017** *Little Miss Naughty*

(Des Supple Studio. Litho ISP Cartor (Nos. 3891/3900) or gravure ISP Walsall (Nos. 3901/3902))

2016 (20 Oct). Mr Men and Little Miss (children's books by Roger Hargreaves). Multicoloured Two phosphor bands.

(a) Ordinary gum. Perf 14½.

3891	3016	(1st) *Mr Happy*	1·20	1·00
		a. Horiz strip of 5. Nos. 3891/3895	5·25	4·50
3892	3017	(1st) *Little Miss Naughty*	1·20	1·00
3893	3018	(1st) *Mr Bump*	1·20	1·00
3894	3019	(1st) *Little Miss Sunshine*	1·20	1·00
3895	3020	(1st) *Mr Tickle*	1·20	1·00
3896	3021	(1st) *Mr Grumpy*	1·20	1·00
		a. Horiz strip of 5. Nos. 3896/3900	5·25	4·50
3897	3022	(1st) *Little Miss Princess*	1·20	1·00
3898	3023	(1st) *Mr Strong*	1·20	1·00
3899	3024	(1st) *Little Miss Christmas*	1·20	1·00
3900	3025	(1st) *Mr Messy*	1·20	1·00
Set of 10			10·50	9·00
Set of 2 Gutter Strips of 5			21·00	
First Day Cover (Tallents House)				11·50
First Day Cover (Cleckheaton)				11·50
Presentation Pack (PO Pack No. 533)			12·00	
PHQ Cards (set of 10) (422)			5·00	12·50

(b) Self-adhesive. Die-cut perf 14½.

3901	3016	(1st) *Mr Happy*	1·50	1·50
		a. Booklet pane. Nos. 3901/3902 and U3027×4	7·50	
3902	3020	(1st) *Mr Tickle*	1·50	1·50

Nos. 3891/3895 and 3896/3900 were each printed together, *se-tenant*, as horizontal strips of five stamps in sheets of 50 stamps (2 panes 5×5).

Nos. 3901/3902 were issued in stamp booklet, No. PM54, originally sold for £3·84.

Designs as Nos. 3891/3900 but self-adhesive were issued in sheets of ten with *se-tenant* labels, (No. LS101), originally sold for £6·90.

Designs as Nos. 3891, 3893/3894, 3896/3897 and 3900 were also available in sheets of ten with personal photographs on the labels, originally sold for £10·20.

SELF-ADHESIVE STAMPS. Collectors are reminded that used self-adhesive stamps will no longer 'soak-off'. They should be collected with a neat margin of backing paper.

3026 Snowman 
3027 Robin 
3028 Snowman 
3029 Robin 
3030 Christmas Tree 
3031 Lantern 
3032 Stocking 
3033 Christmas Pudding

3033a

(Des Helen Musselwhite (illustrations) and The Chase. Gravure ISP Walsall (Nos. 3903a, 3904a) or De La Rue (others))

2016 (8 Nov). Christmas. Multicoloured One centre band (No. 3903) or two bands (others). Perf 14½×15.

(a) Self-adhesive.

3903	3026	(2nd) Snowman...............................	90	90
		a. Booklet pane. No. 3903×12............	13·50	
3904	3027	(1st) Robin.......................................	1·00	1·00
		a. Booklet pane. No. 3904×12............	16·00	
3905	3028	(2nd Snowman Large).......................	1·25	1·10
3906	3029	(1st Robin Large)..............................	1·70	1·40
3907	3030	£1·05 Christmas Tree........................	1·75	1·75
3908	3031	£1·33 Lantern....................................	2·00	2·00
3909	3032	£1·52 Stocking..................................	2·50	2·50
3910	3033	£2·25 Christmas Pudding..................	3·50	3·50
Set of 8			13·25	13·00
First Day Cover (Tallents House)................................				16·50
First Day Cover (Bethlehem, Llandeilo)......................				16·50
Presentation Pack (PO Pack No. 534)........................			16·50	
PHQ Cards (set of 9) (423)..			4·50	28·00

(b) Ordinary gum.

MS3911	3033a	189×74 mm. As Nos. 3903/3910...........	13·25	13·00
First Day Cover (Tallents House)................................				16·50
First Day Cover (Bethlehem, Llandeilo)......................				16·50

The 2nd class, 1st class, £1·05, £1·33, £1·52 and £2·25 values were also issued in sheets of 20, (No. LS102), containing eight 2nd class, eight 1st class and one each of the £1·05, £1·33, £1·52 and £2·25 stamps, each stamp accompanied by a *se-tenant* label showing paper cut out work by Helen Musselwhite forming a snowy landscape. These sheets were sold for £16·21.

Separate sheets of 20 2nd, 20 1st, ten 1st, ten £1·05, ten £1·33 and ten £1·52 were available with personal photographs on the labels. These were sold at £14·60 for 20 2nd, £18·65 for 20 1st, £10·20 for ten 1st, £14·45 for ten £1·05, £18·50 for ten £1·33 and £21·85 for ten £1·52.

The 2nd class and 1st class values were also issued in sheets of 20, Celebrating 50 Years of Christmas Stamps, each stamp accompanied by a greetings label.

The 2nd class and 1st class values were also issued in sheets of 20, (No. LS103), Celebrating 50 Years of Christmas Stamps containing ten 2nd class and ten 1st class stamps, each stamp accompanied by a greetings label. These sheets were sold at £12·40.

The nine PHQ cards show the eight individual stamps and the complete miniature sheet.

Year Pack

2016 (8 Nov). Comprises Nos. 3787/**MS**3801, 3810/**MS**3832, **MS**3837/3843, **MS**3848/3861, **MS**3868/3876, 3879/3900 and 3903/3910

CP3911a	Year Pack (PO Pack No. 535) (sold for £120)..................	£160

Post Office Yearbook

2016 (8 Nov). Comprises Nos. 3787/**MS**3801, 3810/**MS**3832, **MS**3837/3843, **MS**3848/3861, **MS**3868/3876, 3879/3900 and 3903/3910

YB3911a	Yearbook (sold for £140).......................	£180

Miniature Sheet Collection

2016 (8 Nov). Comprises Nos. **MS**3801, **MS**3832, **MS**3837, **MS**3848, **MS**3855, **MS**3868 and **MS**3911

MS3911a	Miniature Sheet Collection (sold for £36)..........	50·00

3034 Battersea Shield, London, 350–50 BC
3035 Skara Brae Village, Orkney Islands, 3100–2500 BC 
3036 Star Carr Headdress, Yorkshire, 9000 BC 
3037 Maiden Castle Hill Fort, Dorset, 400 BC 
3038 Avebury Stone Circles, Wiltshire, 2500 BC 
3039 Drumbest Horns, County Antrim, 800 BC 
3040 Grime's Graves Flint Mines, Norfolk, 2500 BC 
3041 Mold Cape, Flintshire, 1900–1600 BC 

(Des Rebecca Strickson (illustrations) and True North. Litho ISP Cartor)

2017 (17 Jan). Ancient Britain. Multicoloured Two phosphor bands. Perf 14.

3912	3034	(1st) Battersea Shield.......................	1·20	1·00
		a. Horiz pair. Nos. 3912/3913............	2·40	2·00
3913	3035	(1st) Skara Brae Village....................	1·20	1·00
3914	3036	£1·05 Star Carr Headdress...............	1·75	1·75
		a. Horiz pair. Nos. 3914/3915............	3·50	3·50
3915	3037	£1·05 Maiden Castle Hill Fort...........	1·75	1·75
3916	3038	£1·33 Avebury Stone Circles............	2·00	2·00
		a. Horiz pair. Nos. 3916/3917............	4·00	4·00
3917	3039	£1·33 Drumbest Horns......................	2·00	2·00
3918	3040	£1·52 Grime's Graves Flint Mines.....	2·25	2·25
		a. Horiz pair. Nos. 3918/3919............	4·50	4·50
3919	3041	£1·52 Mold Cape...............................	2·25	2·25
Set of 8			13·00	13·00
Set of 4 Gutter Blocks of 4...			26·00	
First Day Cover (Tallents House).................................				17·00
First Day Cover (Avebury, Marlborough).....................				17·00

QUEEN ELIZABETH II/2017

Presentation Pack (PO Pack No. 536)	15·50	
PHQ Cards (set of 8) (424)	4·00	15·00

Nos. 3912/3913, 3914/3915, 3916/3917 and 3918/3919 were each printed together, *se-tenant*, as horizontal pairs in sheets of 60 (2 panes 6×5).

For No. U3920, T **3041a**, See Decimal Machin section.

3042 The Long Walk

3043 The Round Tower

3044 The Norman Gate

3045 St George's Hall

3046 The Queen's Ballroom

3047 The Waterloo Chamber

(Des Up. Litho ISP Cartor (Nos. 3920/3925) or gravure ISP Walsall (Nos. 3926/3927))

2017 (15 Feb). Windsor Castle (1st issue). Multicoloured Two phosphor bands.

(a) Ordinary gum. Perf 14½.

3920	**3042**	(1st) The Long Walk	1·20	1·00
		a. Horiz strip of 3. Nos. 3920/3922	3·50	3·00
		b. Booklet pane. Nos. 3920 and 3923 with margins all round	4·00	
3921	**3043**	(1st) The Round Tower	1·20	1·00
		b. Booklet pane. Nos. 3921/3922 and 3924/3925 with margins all round	5·50	
3922	**3044**	(1st) The Norman Gate	1·00	1·00
3923	**3045**	£1·52 St George's Hall	2·00	2·00
		a. Horiz strip of 3. Nos. 3923/3925	6·00	6·00
3924	**3046**	£1·52 The Queen's Ballroom	2·00	2·00
3925	**3047**	£1·52 The Waterloo Chamber	2·00	2·00
Set of 6			8·75	8·25
Set of 2 Gutter Strips of 3			17·00	
First Day Cover (Tallents House)				11·00
First Day Cover (Windsor)				11·00
Presentation Pack (PO Pack No. 537) (Nos. 3920/3925 and **MS**3932)			18·00	
PHQ Cards (set of 11) (425)			5·50	23·00

(b) Self-adhesive. Die-cut perf 14½.

3926	**3048**	(1st) Sir Reginald Bray Roof Boss	2·00	2·00
		a. Booklet pane. Nos. 3926/3927 and U3027×4	7·50	
3927	**3049**	(1st) Fan-vaulted Roof	2·00	2·00

Nos. 3920/3922 and 3923/3925 were each printed together, *se-tenant*, as horizontal strips of three stamps in sheets of 60 (2 panes 6×5).

Nos. 3926/3927 were issued in stamp booklet, No. PM55, originally sold for £3·84.

The 11 PHQ cards show the individual stamps including those from No. **MS**3932 and the complete miniature sheet.

3048 St George's Chapel Nave: Sir Reginald Bray Roof Bass

3049 St George's Chapel Nave: Fan-vaulted Roof

3050 St George's Chapel Quire, Garter Banners

3051 St George's Chapel Quire, St George's Cross Roof Boss

3052 St George's Chapel

(Des Up. Litho ISP Cartor)

2017 (15 Feb). Windsor Castle (2nd issue). Multicoloured Two phosphor bands. Perf 14½.

3928	**3048**	(1st) Sir Reginald Bray Roof Boss	1·60	1·60
		a. Booklet pane. Nos. 3928/3931 with margins all round and roulettes at left	7·25	
3929	**3049**	(1st) Fan-vaulted Roof	1·60	1·60
3930	**3050**	£1·33 Garter Banners	2·50	2·50
3931	**3051**	£1·33 St George's Cross Roof Boss	2·50	2·50
Set of 4			7·25	7·25

2017/QUEEN ELIZABETH II

MS3932 125×89 mm. **3052** Nos. 3928/3931		7·25	7·25
First Day Cover (Tallents House)			8·00
First Day Cover (Windsor)			8·00

Nos. 3928/3931 come from No. **MS**3932 and £14·58 Windsor Castle premium booklet, No. DY20.

No. **MS**3932 additionally inscribed 'Spring Stampex 2017' was available only at the exhibition (*Price* £50).

3053 *Hunky Dory* 
3054 *Aladdin Sane*  
3055 *Heroes* 
3056 *Let's Dance* 
3057 *Earthling* 
3058 *Blackstar*

3059 David Bowie Live

(Gravure ISP Walsall (Nos. 3933/3938) or litho ISP Cartor (No. **MS**3939))

2017 (14 Mar). David Bowie (1947–2016, singer, songwriter and actor) Commemoration. Multicoloured Two phosphor bands.

(a) Self-adhesive. Die-cut perf 14½.

3933	**3053**	(1st) *Hunky Dory*	1·20	1·00
3934	**3054**	(1st) *Aladdin Sane*	1·20	1·00
		a. Booklet pane. Nos. 3934/3935 and U3027×4	7·50	
3935	**3055**	(1st) *Heroes*	1·20	1·00
3936	**3056**	£1·52 *Let's Dance*	2·25	2·25
3937	**3057**	£1·52 *Earthling*	2·25	2·25
3938	**3058**	£1·52 *Blackstar*	2·25	2·25
Set of 6			9·25	8·75
First Day Cover (Tallents House)				11·50
First Day Cover (London SW9)				11·50
Presentation Pack (PO Pack No. 538) (Nos. 3933/3938 and **MS**3939)			17·00	
PHQ Cards (set of 11) (426)			5·50	24·00

(b) Ordinary gum. Perf 14½.

MS3939 126×89 mm. **3059** David Bowie Live (1st) The Ziggy Stardust Tour, 1973; (1st) The Serious Moonlight Tour, 1983; £1·52 The Isolar II Tour, 1978; £1·52 A Reality Tour, 2004	6·25	6·25
First Day Cover (Tallents House)		8·25
First Day Cover (London SW9)		8·25

Nos. 3933/3938 were printed in separate sheets of 50 (2 panes 5×5).

Nos. 3934/3935 were also issued in booklet, No. PM56, originally sold for £3·84.

The right-hand edges of Nos. 3933/3938 are all cut around to show the vinyl disc protruding from the open edge of the album cover.

Four Fan sheets, printed on ordinary gummed paper, were available from Royal Mail at premium prices. The Album Fan Sheet contains the complete set. Types **3053**/**3058**, and was originally sold for £12·95. The *Hunky Dory* (T **3053**×5), *Aladdin Sane* (T **3054**×5) and *Heroes* (T **3055**×5) were originally sold for £7·50 each.

The 11 PHQ cards show the individual stamps including those from No. **MS**3939 and the complete miniature sheet all printed on ordinary gummed paper, were available from Royal Mail at premium prices.

3060 Frankel
3061 Red Rum 
3062 Shergar 
3063 Kauto Star 
3064 Desert Orchid 
3065 Brigadier Gerard 
3066 Arkle 
3067 Estimate 

(Des Michael Heslop (illustrations) and Together Design. Litho ISP Cartor)

2017 (6 Apr). Racehorse Legends. Multicoloured Two phosphor bands. Perf 14.

3940	**3060**	(1st) Frankel	1·20	1·00
3941	**3061**	(1st) Red Rum	1·20	1·00
3942	**3062**	£1·17 Shergar	1·75	1·75
3943	**3063**	£1·17 Kauto Star	1·75	1·75
3944	**3064**	£1·40 Desert Orchid	2·25	2·25
3945	**3065**	£1·40 Brigadier Gerard	2·25	2·25
3946	**3066**	£1·57 Arkle	2·50	2·50
3947	**3067**	£1·57 Estimate	2·50	2·50
Set of 8			13·75	13·50
Set of 8 Gutter Pairs			27·50	
First Day Cover (Tallents House)				17·00
First Day Cover (Newmarket)				17·00
Presentation Pack (PO Pack No. 539)			16·00	
PHQ Cards (set of 8) (427)			4·00	17·00

3068 Great Tit (*Parus major*)
3069 Wren (*Troglodytes troglodytes*) 
3070 Willow Warbler (*Phylloscopus trochilus*) 
3071 Goldcrest (*Regulus regulus*) 
3072 Skylark (*Alauda arvensis*) 
3073 Blackcap (*Sylvia atricapilla*) 
3074 Song Thrush (*Turdus philomelos*) 
3075 Nightingale (*Luscinia megarhynchos*) 
3076 Cuckoo (*Cuculus canorus*) 
3077 Yellowhammer (*Emberiza citrinella*) 

(Des Federico Gemma (illustrations) and Osborne Ross. Litho ISP Cartor)

2017 (4 May). Songbirds. Multicoloured Two phosphor bands. Perf 14½.

3948	3068	(1st) Great Tit	1·20	1·00
		a. Horiz strip of 5. Nos. 3948/3952	5·25	4·50
3949	3069	(1st) Wren	1·20	1·00
3950	3070	(1st) Willow Warbler	1·20	1·00
3951	3071	(1st) Goldcrest	1·20	1·00
3952	3072	(1st) Skylark	1·20	1·00
3953	3073	(1st) Blackcap	1·20	1·00
		a. Horiz strip of 5. Nos. 3953/3957	5·25	4·50
3954	3074	(1st) Song Thrush	1·20	1·00
3955	3075	(1st) Nightingale	1·20	1·00
3956	3076	(1st) Cuckoo	1·20	1·00
3957	3077	(1st) Yellowhammer	1·20	1·00
Set of 10			10·50	9·00
Set of 2 Gutter Strips of 10			21·00	
First Day Cover (Tallents House)				12·00
First Day Cover (Warbleton, Heathfield)				12·00
Presentation Pack (PO Pack No. 540)			12·00	
PHQ Cards (set of 10) (428)			5·00	12·50

Nos. 3948/3952 and 3953/3957 were each printed together, *se-tenant*, as horizontal strips of five in sheets of 50 (2 panes 5×5).

3078 Preliminary sketch by Arnold Machin based on the Penny Black, January 1966

3079 Preparatory work by Arnold Machin using photograph of his coin mould, February 1966

3080 Essay with coinage head surrounded by Country symbols, April/May 1966

3081 Essay of Coinage head cropped and simplified, with only the denomination, October 1966

3082 Photo by John Hedgecoe with Queen Elizabeth II wearing the diadem, August 1966

3083 Essay of the first plaster cast of the Diadem Head, without corsage, October 1966

3084 The Machin definitive 50 Years of a design icon

3085 The Machin definitive Golden Anniversary celebration

3086 £1 gold foil Machin

3079 Preparatory work by Arnold Machin using photograph of his coin mould, February 1966

2017 (5 June). 50th Anniversary of the Machin Definitive. Multicoloured Two phosphor bands. Perf 14×15

3958	3078	(1st) Preliminary sketch based on the Penny Black	1·25	1·25
		a. Booklet pane. Nos. 3958/3960 with margins all round	3·75	
3959	3079	(1st) Preparatory work using photograph of his coin mould	1·25	1·25

3960	**3080**	(1st) Essay with coinage head surrounded by Country symbols, April/May 1966	1·25	1·25
3961	**3081**	(1st) Essay of coinage head, with only the denomination	1·25	1·25
		a. Booklet pane. Nos. 3961/3963 with margins all round	3·75	
3962	**3082**	(1st) Photograph by John Hedgecoe	1·25	1·25
3963	**3083**	(1st) Essay of the first plaster cast of the Diadem Head	1·25	1·25
Set of 6			6·75	6·75

MS3964 202×74 mm. **3084** 6×(1st) Types **3078**/**3083**... 11·00 11·00
MS3965 202×74 mm. **3085** No. X866; No. 1470; as Type **1116**; No. 2124; No. 2651; as No. U3067 (but MMIL code); as No. U3966 (but gravure) (Type **3086**)
.... 11·00 11·00
First Day Cover (Tallents House) (No. **MS**3964)............. 12·00
First Day Cover (High Wycombe) (No. **MS**3964)........... 12·00
First Day Cover (Tallents House) (No. **MS**3965)............. 12·00
First Day Cover (High Wycombe) (No. **MS**3965)........... 12·00
Presentation Pack (PO Pack No. 541) (Nos. **MS**3964/
MS3965)... 18·00
PHQ Cards (Set of 11) (429)... 5·50 21·00

Nos. 3958/3963 were issued in £15·14 50th Anniversary of the Machin Definitive premium booklet, DY21, and in No. **MS**3964.

The 5p, 20p and £1 stamps in No. **MS**3965 do not have an elliptical perforation hole in each vertical side.

On No. **MS**3965 only the £1 gold foil stamp is embossed.

3087 Nutley Windmill, East Sussex

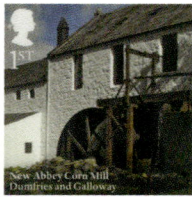

3088 New Abbey Corn Mill, Dumfries and Galloway

3089 Ballycopeland Windmill, County Down

3090 Cheddleton Flint Mill, Staffordshire

3091 Woodchurch Windmill, Kent

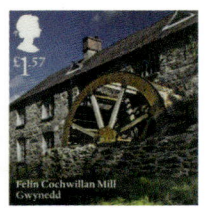

3092 Felin Cochwillan Mill, Gwynedd

(Des Atelier Works. Litho ISP Cartor)

2017 (20 June). Windmills and Watermills. Multicoloured Two phosphor bands. Perf 14½×14

3967	**3087**	(1st) Nutley Windmill, East Sussex	1·20	1·00
		a. Vert pair. Nos. 3967/3968	2·40	2·00
3968	**3088**	(1st) New Abbey Corn Mill, Dumfries and Galloway	1·20	1·00
3969	**3089**	£1·40 Ballycopeland Windmill, County Down	2·25	2·25
		a. Vert pair. Nos. 3969/3970	4·50	4·50
3970	**3090**	£1·40 Cheddleton Flint Mill, Staffordshire	2·25	2·25
3971	**3091**	£1·57 Woodchurch Windmill, Kent	2·50	2·50
		a. Vert pair. Nos. 3971/72	5·00	5·00
3972	**3092**	£1·57 Felin Cochwillan Mill, Gwynedd	2·50	2·50
Set of 6			10·75	10·50
Set of 3 Gutter Blocks of 4			21·50	
First Day Cover (Tallents House)				12·00
First Day Cover (Old Mill, Callington)				12·00

Presentation Pack (PO Pack No. 542)................................... 12·00
PHQ Cards (set of 6) (430)... 3·00 12·00

Nos. 3967/3968, 3969/3970 and 3971/3972 were each printed together, *se-tenant*, as vertical pairs in sheets of 60 (2 panes 5×6).

3093 Aquatics Centre, Queen Elizabeth Olympic Park, London

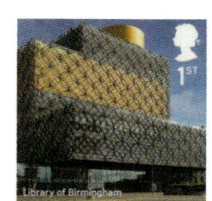

3094 Library of Birmingham

3095 SEC Armadillo (formerly Clyde Auditorium), Glasgow

3096 Scottish Parliament, Edinburgh

3097 Giant's Causeway Visitor Centre, Co. Antrim

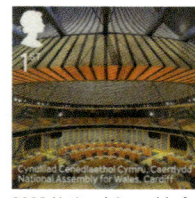

3098 National Assembly for Wales, Cardiff

3099 Eden Project, St Austell

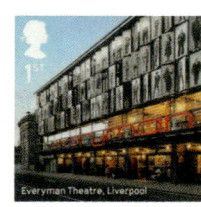

3100 Everyman Theatre, Liverpool

3101 IWM (Imperial War Museum) North, Manchester

3102 Switch House, Tate Modern, London

(Des GBH. Litho ISP Cartor)

2017 (13 July). Landmark Buildings. Multicoloured Two phosphor bands. Perf 14½

3973	**3093**	(1st) Aquatics Centre, Queen Elizabeth Olympic Park, London	1·20	1·00
		a. Horiz strip of 5. Nos. 3973/3977	5·25	5·00
3974	**3094**	(1st) Library of Birmingham	1·20	1·00
3975	**3095**	(1st) SEC Armadillo (formerly Clyde Auditorium), Glasgow	1·20	1·00
3976	**3096**	(1st) Scottish Parliament, Edinburgh	1·20	1·00
3977	**3097**	(1st) Giant's Causeway Visitor Centre, Co. Antrim	1·20	1·00

QUEEN ELIZABETH II/2017

3978	3098	(1st) National Assembly for Wales, Cardiff	1·20	1·00
		a. Horiz strip of 5. Nos. 3978/3982	5·25	5·00
3979	3099	(1st) Eden Project, St Austell	1·20	1·00
3980	3100	(1st) Everyman Theatre, Liverpool	1·20	1·00
3981	3101	(1st) IWM (Imperial War Museum) North, Manchester	1·20	1·00
3982	3102	(1st) Switch House, Tate Modern, London	1·20	1·00
Set of 10			10·50	9·00
Set of 2 Gutter Strips of 5			21·00	
First Day Cover (Tallents House)				10·50
First Day Cover (St Austell)				10·50
Presentation Pack (PO Pack No. 543)			12·00	
PHQ Cards (set of 10) (431)			5·00	10·00

Nos. 3973/3977 and 3978/3982 were each printed together, *se-tenant*, as horizontal strips of five stamps in sheets of 50 (2 panes 5×5).

3103 *Shattered Poppy* (John Ross)

3104 *Dead Man's Dump* (Isaac Rosenberg)

3105 Nurses Elsie Knocker and Mairi Chisholm

3106 *Dry Docked for Sealing and Painting* (Edward Wadsworth)

3107 Tyne Cot Cemetery, Zonnebeke, Ypres Salient Battlefields, Belgium

3108 Private Lemuel Thomas Rees's Life-saving Bible

(Des Hat-trick design. Litho ISP Cartor)

2017 (31 July). Centenary of the First World War (4th issue). Multicoloured Two phosphor bands. Perf 14½

3983	3103	(1st) *Shattered Poppy* (John Ross)	1·20	1·00
		a. Booklet pane. Nos. 3983/3985 with margins all round	4·00	
3984	3104	(1st) *Dead Man's Dump*	1·20	1·00
3985	3105	(1st) Nurses Elsie Knocker and Mairi Chisholm	1·20	1·00
3986	3106	£1·57 *Dry Docked for Sealing and Painting*	2·50	2·50
		a. Booklet pane. Nos. 3986/3988 with margins all round	7·50	
3987	3107	£1·57 Tyne Cot Cemetery, Belgium	2·50	2·50
3988	3108	£1·57 Private Lemuel Thomas Rees's Life-saving Bible	2·50	2·50
Set of 6			10·00	9·50
Set of 6 Gutter Pairs			20·00	
First Day Cover (Tallents House)				11·00
First Day Cover (Blaenannerch, Aberteifi-Cardigan)				11·00
Presentation Pack (PO Pack No. 544)			11·50	
PHQ Cards (set of 6) (432)			3·00	11·00

Nos. 3983a and 3786a were only issued in £15·41 Centenary of the First World War (4th issue). premium booklet, No DY22.

3109 The Merrythought Bear

3110 Sindy Weekender Doll

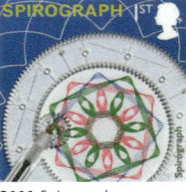

3111 Spirograph

3112 Stickle Bricks Super Set House

3113 Herald Trojan Warriors

3114 Spacehopper

3115 Fuzzy-Felt Farm Set

3116 Meccano Ferris Wheel

3117 Action Man Red Devil Parachutist

3118 Hornby Dublo Electric Train and TPO Mail Van

(Des Interabang. Litho ISP Cartor)

2017 (22 Aug). Classic Toys. Multicoloured Two phosphor bands. Perf 14½

3989	3109	(1st) The Merrythought Bear	1·20	1·00
		a. Horiz strip of 5. Nos. 3989/3993	5·25	5·00
3990	3110	(1st) Sindy Weekender Doll	1·20	1·00
3991	3111	(1st) Spirograph	1·20	1·00
3992	3112	(1st) Stickle Bricks Super Set House	1·20	1·00
3993	3113	(1st) Herald Trojan Warriors	1·20	1·00
3994	3114	(1st) Spacehopper	1·20	1·00
		a. Horiz strip of 5. Nos. 3994/3998	5·25	5·00
3995	3115	(1st) Fuzzy-Felt Farm Set	1·20	1·00
3996	3116	(1st) Meccano Ferris Wheel	1·20	1·00
3997	3117	(1st) Action Man Red Devil Parachutist	1·20	1·00
3998	3118	(1st) Hornby Dublo Electric Train and TPO Mail Van	1·20	1·00
Set of 10			10·50	9·00
Set of 2 Gutter Strips of 5			21·00	
First Day Cover (Tallents House)				10·50
First Day Cover (Toys Hill, Edenbridge)				10·50
Presentation Pack (PO Pack No. 545)			12·00	
PHQ Cards (set of 10) (433)			5·00	10·00

Nos. 3989/3993 and 3994/3998 were each printed together, *se-tenant*, as horizontal strips of five stamps in sheets of 50 (2 panes 5×5).

2017/QUEEN ELIZABETH II

3119 *The Story of Nelson*, *The Story of the First Queen Elizabeth* and *Florence Nightingale* (Adventures from History)

3120 *The Gingerbread Boy*, *Cinderella* and *The Elves and the Shoemaker* (Well-loved Tales)

3127 Maz Kanata

3128 Chewbacca

3121 *We have fun*, *Look at this* and *Things we do* (Key Words Reading Scheme)

3122 *Piggly Plays Truant*, *Tootles the Taxi and Other Rhymes* and *Smoke and Fluff* (Early Tales and Rhymes)

3129 Supreme Leader Snoke

3130 Porg

3123 *Things to Make, How it works: The Telephone* and *Tricks and Magic* (Hobbies and How it Works)

3124 *The Nurse, The Postman* and *The Fireman* (People at Work)

3131 BB-8

3132 R2-D2

3133 C-3PO

3134 K-2SO

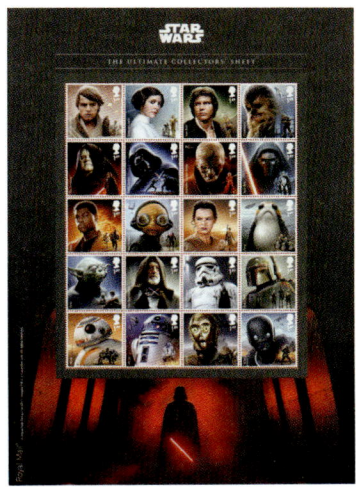

3125 *British Wild Flowers, Wild Life in Britain* and *Garden Flowers* (Nature and Conservation)

3126 *The Story of Ships, The Story of the Motor Car* and *The Story of Metals* (Achievements)

(Des True North. Litho ISP Cartor)

2017 (14 Sept). Ladybird Books. Multicoloured One centre band (Nos. 3999/4000) or two bands (others). Perf 14

3999	3119	(2nd) Adventures from History	90	90
		a. Horiz pair. Nos. 3999/4000	1·75	1·75
4000	3120	(2nd) Well-loved Tales	90	90
4001	3121	(1st) Key Words Reading Scheme	1·20	1·00
		a. Horiz pair. Nos. 4001/4002	2·40	2·00
4002	3122	(1st) Early Tales and Rhymes	1·20	1·00
4003	3123	£1·40 Hobbies and How it Works	2·25	2·25
		a. Horiz pair. Nos. 4003/4004	4·50	4·50
4004	3124	£1·40 People at Work	2·25	2·25
4005	3125	£1·57 Nature and Conservation	2·50	2·50
		a. Horiz pair. Nos. 4005/4006	5·00	5·00
4006	3126	£1·57 Achievements	2·50	2·50
Set of 8			12·25	12·00
Set of 4 Gutter Blocks of 4			24·50	
First Day Cover (Tallents House)				13·50
First Day Cover (Loughborough)				13·50
Presentation Pack (PO Pack No. 546)			14·00	
PHQ Cards (Set of 8) (434)			4·00	12·50

Nos. 3999/4000, 4001/4002, 4003/4004 and 4005/4006 were each printed together, *se-tenant*, as horizontal pairs in sheets of 60 (2 panes 6×5).

3134a Star Wars composite sheet

277

QUEEN ELIZABETH II/2017

(Des Malcolm Tween (illustrations) and Interabang. Litho ISP Cartor (Nos. 4007/4014) or gravure Walsall (Nos. 4015/4018))

2017 (12 Oct–14 Dec). *Star Wars* (4th issue). Aliens and Droids. Multicoloured Two phosphor bands.

(a) Ordinary gum. Perf 14½.

4007	3127	(1st) Maz Kanata	1·20	1·00
		a. Horiz strip of 4. Nos. 4007/4010	4·25	4·00
4008	3128	(1st) Chewbacca	1·20	1·00
		a. Booklet pane. Nos. 4008, 4010/4011 and 4014 with margins all round (14.12.17)	4·25	
		b. Booklet pane. Nos. 4008, 4010/11 and 4014 with margins all round (14 Dec)	1·00	1·00
4009	3129	(1st) Supreme Leader Snoke	1·20	1·00
4010	3130	(1st) Porg	1·20	1·00
4011	3131	(1st) BB-8	1·20	1·00
		a. Horiz strip of 4. Nos. 4011/4014	4·25	4·00
4012	3132	(1st) R2-D2	1·20	1·00
4013	3133	(1st) C-3PO	1·20	1·00
4014	3134	(1st) K-2SO	1·20	1·00
Set of 8			8·50	7·25
Set of 2 Gutter Strips of 4			17·00	
First Day Cover (Tallents House)				9·00
First Day Cover (Wookey, Wells)				9·00
Presentation Pack (PO Pack No. 547)			10·00	
PHQ Cards (Set of 8) (435)			4·00	9·00
MS4014a 297×212 mm. **3134a** Nos. 3758/3769 and 4007/4014			30·00	45·00

(b) Self-adhesive. Die-cut perf 14½.

4015	3127	(1st) Maz Kanata	1·75	1·75
		a. Booklet pane. Nos. 4015/4016 and U3027×4	7·50	
4016	3128	(1st) Chewbacca	1·75	1·75
4017	3131	(1st) BB-8	1·75	1·75
		a. Booklet pane. Nos. 4017/4018 and U3027×4	7·50	
4018	3132	(1st) R2-D2	1·75	1·75

Nos. 4007/4010 and 4011/4014 were each printed together, *se-tenant*, as horizontal strips of four stamps in sheets of 48 (2 panes 4×6).

Nos. 4011/4014 (Droid stamps) are enhanced by UV ink features.

No. 4008a was only issued in £14·32 *Star Wars*: The Making of the Droids, Aliens and Creatures premium booklet, No DY23.

Nos. 4015/4016 and 4017/4018 were each issued in stamp booklets with 1st bright scarlet stamp×4 stamps, Nos. PM57/PM58, originally sold for £3·90 each.

Designs as Nos. 4007/4014 but self-adhesive were issued in sheets of ten with *se-tenant* labels (No. LS106). These sheets originally sold for £7·20.

3135 *Virgin and Child* (attributed to Gerard David)

3136 *The Madonna and Child* (William Dyce)

3137 *Virgin and Child* (attributed to Gerard David)

3138 *The Madonna and Child* (William Dyce)

3139 *Virgin Mary with Child* (attributed to Quinten Massys)

3140 *The Small Cowper Madonna* (Raphael)

3141 *The Sleep of the Infant Jesus* (Giovanni Battista Sassoferrato)

3142 *St Luke painting the Virgin* (detail) (Eduard Jakob von Steinle)

3142a

(Gravure De La Rue or ISP Walsall (Nos. 4019a/4019b, 4020a/4020b), Litho by ISP Cartor (No. **MS**4027))

2017 (7 Nov). Christmas. Madonna and Child. Multicoloured One centre phosphor band (No. 4019) or two bands

(a) Self-adhesive. Die-cut perf 14½×15.

4019	3135	(2nd) *Virgin and Child* (attributed to Gerard David)	90	90
		a. Booklet pane. Nos. 4019 and 4028, each×6	13·50	
		b. Booklet pane. No. 4019×12	13·50	
4020	3136	(1st) *The Madonna and Child* (William Dyce)	1·20	1·00
		a. Booklet pane. Nos. 4020 and 4029, each×6	16·00	
		b. Booklet pane. No. 4020×12	16·00	
4021	3137	(2nd) *Virgin and Child* (attributed to Large) Gerard David)	1·25	1·10
4022	3138	(1st) *The Madonna and Child* (William Large) Dyce)	1·70	1·40
4023	3139	£1·17 *Virgin Mary with Child* (attributed to Quinten Massys)	1·80	1·80
4024	3140	£1·40 *The Small Cowper Madonna* (Raphael)	2·25	2·25
4025	3141	£1·57 *The Sleep of the Infant Jesus* (Giovanni Battista Sassoferrato)	2·50	2·50
4026	3142	£2·27 *St Luke painting the Virgin* (detail) (Eduard Jakob von Steinle)	3·50	3·50
Set of 8			13·50	13·00
First Day Cover (Tallents House) (Nos. 4019/4026 and 4028/4031)				18·00
First Day Cover (Bethlehem, Llandeilo) (Nos. 4019/4026 and 4028/4031)				18·00
Presentation Pack (PO Pack No. 548) (Nos. 4019/4026 and 4028/4031)			19·00	
PHQ Cards (set of 13) (436)			6·50	30·00

(b) Ordinary gum. Perf 14½×15.

MS4027		13·50	13·00
First Day Cover (Tallents House)			17·00
First Day Cover (Bethlehem, Llandeilo)			17·00

Nos. 4019 and 4028, 4020 and 4029, 4021 and 4030 and 4022 and 4031 were printed together in sheets of 50 (5×10), the upper 25 stamps being Nos. 4019, 4020, 4021 or 4022 and the lower 25 stamps Nos. 4028, 4029, 4030 or 4031. Nos. 4023/4026 were printed individually in sheets of 50 (5×10).

Nos. 4019/4020 were reprinted for Christmas 2018 by ISP Walsall in composite sheets with the 2018 1st and 2nd class Christmas stamps.

The presentation pack (No. 548) contains Nos. 4019/4026 and 4028/4031.

The 2nd class (No. 4019), 1st class (No. 4020), £1·17, £1·40, £1·57 and £2·27 values were also issued in sheets of 20 containing eight 2nd class, eight 1st class and one each of the £1·17, £1·40, £1·57 and £2·27 values, each stamp accompanied by a *se-tenant* label (No. LS107).

The 13 PHQ cards show the 12 individual stamps and No. **MS**4027.

3143 Snow Family (Arwen Wilson)

3144 Santa Claus on his sleigh on a starry night (Ted Lewis-Clark)

3145 Snow Family (Arwen Wilson)

3146 Santa Claus on his sleigh on a starry night (Ted Lewis-Clark)

2017/QUEEN ELIZABETH II

(Gravure De La Rue)

2017 (7 Nov). Children's Christmas. Multicoloured One centre phosphor band (No. 4028) or two bands. Self-adhesive. Die-cut perf 14½×15

4028	3143	(2nd) Snow Family (Arwen Wilson)............	90	90
4029	3144	(1st) Santa Claus on his sleigh on a starry night (Ted Lewis-Clark)........	1·20	1·00
4030	3145	(2nd) Snow Family (Arwen Wilson) Large)..	1·25	1·10
4031	3146	(1st Santa Claus on his sleigh on a Large) starry night (Ted Lewis-Clark)........	1·70	1·40
Set of 4			4·00	4·00

An example of No. 4029 has been reported used in West Yorkshire in late September 2017.

The 2nd class (No. 4028) and 1st class (No. 4029) values were also issued in sheets of 20 containing ten 2nd class and ten 1st class, each stamp accompanied by a *se-tenant* label (No. LS108).

Collectors Pack

2017 (20 Nov). Comprises Nos. 3912/3925, **MS**3932/3957, **MS**3964/**MS**3965, 3967/4014, 4019/4029 and **MS**4032

CP4031a	Collectors Pack (PO Pack No. 550) (sold for £119)..........................	£250

Post Office Yearbook

2017 (20 Nov). Comprises Nos. 3912/3925, **MS**3932/3957, **MS**3964/**MS**3965, 3967/4014, 4019/4031 and **MS**4032

YB4031a	Yearbook (sold for £139)......................	£325

Miniature Sheet Collection

2017 (20 Nov). Comprises Nos. **MS**3932, **MS**3939, **MS**3964/**MS**3965, **MS**4027 and **MS**4032

MS4031a	Miniature Sheet Collection (sold for £35)..........	85·00

3147 Platinum Anniversary

(Des Mytton Williams. Litho ISP. Cartor)

2017 (20 Nov). Royal Platinum Wedding Anniversary of Queen Elizabeth II and Duke of Edinburgh. Multicoloured Two phosphor bands. Perf 14

MS4032 200×67 mm **3147** (1st) Engagement of Princess Elizabeth and Lieutenant Philip Mountbatten; (1st) Princess Elizabeth and Duke of Edinburgh after their wedding at Westminster Abbey; (1st) Princess Elizabeth and Duke of Edinburgh looking at wedding photographs during their honeymoon; £1·57 Engagement photograph; £1·57 Princess Elizabeth and Duke of Edinburgh on their wedding day; £1·57 Princess Elizabeth and Duke of Edinburgh on honeymoon at Broadlands................ 10·00 10·00
First Day Cover (Tallents House).. 12·00
First Day Cover (London SW1)... 12·00
Presentation Pack (PO Pack No. 549).................................. 12·00
PHQ Cards (set of 7) (437)....................................... 3·50 18·00
Souvenir Pack... 15·00

A Limited Edition Pack of 5000 was available at £14·99.

3148 Sansa Stark (Sophie Tucker)

3149 Jon Snow (Kit Harington)

3150 Eddard Stark (Sean Bean)

3151 Olenna Tyrell (Dianna Rigg)

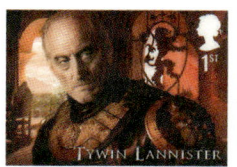

3152 Tywin Lannister (Charles Dance)

3153 Tyrion Lannister (Peter Dinklage)

3154 Cersei Lannister (Lena Headey)

3155 Arya Stark (Maisie Williams)

3156 Jaime Lannister (Nicolaj Coster-Waldau)

3157 Daenerys Targaryen (Emilia Clarke)

3158 *Game of Thrones* non-human characters

3159 The Iron Throne

(Des GBH, Litho ISP Cartor (Nos. 4033/4042) or gravure Walsall (No. 4044))

2018 (23 Jan) *Game of Thrones* (1st issue). Multicoloured Two phosphor bands.

(a) Ordinary gum. Perf 14.

4033	3148	(1st) Sansa Stark (Sophie Tucker)............	1·20	1·00
		a. Horiz strip of 5. Nos. 4033/4037.....	5·25	4·50
		b. Booklet pane Nos. 4033/4035, 4038/4040..	6·00	
4034	3149	(1st) Jon Snow (Kit Harington)................	1·20	1·00
4035	3150	(1st) Eddard Stark (Sean Bean)................	1·20	1·00
4036	3151	(1st) Olenna Tyrell (Dianna Rigg)............	1·20	1·00
		b. Booklet pane Nos. 4036/4037, 4041/4042..	6·00	
4037	3152	(1st) Tywin Lannister (Charles Dance)...	1·20	1·00
4038	3153	(1st) Tyrion Lannister (Peter Dinklage)..	1·20	1·00
		a. Horiz strip of 5. Nos. 4038/4042.....	5·25	4·50
4039	3154	(1st) Cersei Lannister (Lena Headey)......	1·20	1·00
4040	3155	(1st) Arya Stark (Maisie Williams)............	1·20	1·00
4041	3156	(1st) Jaime Lannister (Nicolaj Coster-Waldau).................................	1·20	1·00
4042	3157	(1st) Daenerys Targaryen (Emilia Clarke).................................	1·20	1·00
Set of 10			10·50	9·00
Set of 2 Gutter Strips of 10.................			21·00	
First Day Cover (Tallents House)..				10·50
First Day Cover (Belfast)...				10·50
Presentation Pack (PO Pack No. 551)..................................			12·00	
PHQ Cards (set of 16) (438).......................................			8·00	23·00

279

(b) Self-adhesive. Die-cut perf 14½×14 (with one elliptical hole on each vert side) (Iron throne) or 14½ (others).
MS4043 202×75 mm **3158** (1st) The Night King and
 White Walkers; (1st) Giants, (1st) The Iron Throne
 (18×22 mm); 1st Direwolves; (1st) Dragons.............. 7·50 7·50
First Day Cover (Tallents House).. 8·50
First Day Cover (Belfast).. 8·50
8·50

(c) Self-adhesive booklet stamp. Die-cut perf 14½×14 with one elliptical hole in each vert side.
4044 **3159** (1st) The Iron Throne................................ 1·50 1·50
 a. Booklet pane. Nos. 4044×6............. 9·00

Nos. 4033/4037 and 4038/4042 were each printed together, *se-tenant*, as horizontal strips of five stamps in sheets of 60 (2 panes 5×6).
Nos. 4033b and 4036b were only issued in £13·95 *Game of Thrones* premium booklet, No DY24.
No. 4044 was issued in stamp booklet No. MB20, sold for £3·90
Designs as Nos. 4033/4042 but self-adhesive were issued in sheets of ten with *se-tenant* labels (No. LS110), originally sold for £7·50.
The presentation pack (No. 549) contains Nos. 4033/4042 and **MS**4043.
The 16 PHQ cards show the 15 individual stamps and No. **MS**4043.

3160 The Night King and White Walkers

3161 Giants

3162 Direwolves

3163 Dragons

(Des GBH, Litho ISP Cartor)

2018 (23 Jan) *Game of Thrones* (2nd issue). Multicoloured Two phosphor bands. P.14
4045 **3160** (1st) The Night King and White Walkers
 .... 1·50 1·50
 a. Booklet pane Nos. 4045/4048......... 6·00
4046 **3161** (1st) Giants.. 1·50 1·50
4047 **3162** (1st) Direwolves... 1·50 1·50
4048 **3163** (1st) Dragons... 1·50 1·50
Set of 4 .... 5·50 5·50

Nos. 4045/4048 were issued in £13·95 *Game of Thrones* premium booklet, No. DY24.
Self-adhesive stamps as Nos. 4045/4048 were additionally available from No. **MS**4043.

(Des GBH, litho ISP Cartor)

2018 (23 Jan) *Game of Thrones* (3rd issue). Multicoloured Two phosphor bands. Perf 14½×14 (with one elliptical hole in each vert side)
4049 **3159** (1st) The Iron Throne................................ 1·50 1·50

No. 4049 was issued in the Machin booklet pane from the £13·95 *Game of Thrones* premium booklet, No DY24.

3164 The Lone Suffragette in Whitehall, c 1908

3165 The Great Pilgrimage of Suffragists, 1913

3166 Suffragette Leaders at Earl's Court, 1908

3167 Women's Freedom League poster parade, c 1907

3168 Welsh Suffragettes, Coronation Procession, 1911

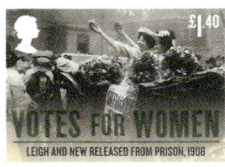

3169 Leigh and New Released from Prison, 1908

3170 Sophia Duleep Singh sells *The Suffragette*, 1913

3171 Suffragette Prisoners' Pageant, 1911

(Des Supple Studio, Litho ISP)

2018 (15 Feb) Votes for Women. Multicoloured One phosphor band (Nos. 4050/4051) or two bands. Perf 14½×14.
4050 **3164** (2nd) The Lone Suffragette in Whitehall 90 90
 a. Horiz pair. Nos. 4050/4051.............. 1·75 1·75
4051 **3165** (2nd) The Great Pilgrimage of
 Suffragists.. 90 90
4052 **3166** (1st) Suffragette Leaders at Earl's Court
 .... 1·20 1·00
 a. Horiz pair. Nos. 4052/4053.............. 2·40 2·00
4053 **3167** (1st) Women's Freedom League poster
 parade... 1·20 1·00
4054 **3168** £1·40 Welsh Suffragettes, Coronation
 Procession... 2·25 2·25
 a. Horiz pair. Nos. 4054/4055.............. 4·50 4·50
4055 **3169** £1·40 Leigh and New Released from
 Prison.. 2·25 2·25
4056 **3170** £1·57 Sophia Duleep Singh sells *The
 Suffragette*.. 2·50 2·50
 a. Horiz pair. Nos. 4056/4057.............. 5·00 5·00
4057 **3171** £1·57 Suffragette Prisoners' Pageant....... 2·50 2·50
Set of 8.. 12·25 12·00
Set of 4 Gutter Blocks of 4.. 24·50
First Day Cover (Tallents House).. 14·00
First Day Cover (London SW1).. 14·00
Presentation Pack (PO Pack No. 552).................................... 15·00
PHQ Cards (set of 8) (439)... 4·00 13·00

Nos. 4050/4051, 4052/4053, 4054/4055 and 4056/4057 were each printed together, *se-tenant*, as horizontal pairs in sheets of 60 (2 panes 6×5).

3172 Lightning F6

3173 Hawker Hurricane Mk.I

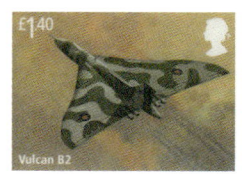

2018/QUEEN ELIZABETH II

3174 Vulcan B2
3175 Typhoon FGR4 
3176 Sopwith Camel F.1 
3177 Nimrod MR2 
3178 Royal Air Force Red Arrows 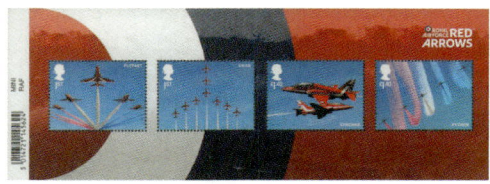

(Des Royal Mail Group Ltd with illustrations by Michael Turner, Litho ISP Cartor (4058/63, **MS**4064) or gravure ISP Walsall (4065/66))

2018 (20 Mar) RAF Centenary (1st issue). Multicoloured Two phosphor bands.

(a) Ordinary gum. Perf 14½×14.

4058	3172	(1st) Lightning F6	1·50	1·40
		a. Horiz pair. Nos. 4058/4059	3·00	3·00
		b. Booklet Pane Nos. 4058×2, 4061×2	6·00	
4059	3173	(1st) Hurricane Mk.I	1·50	1·40
		b. Booklet pane Nos. 4059/4060, 4062/4063	8·00	
4060	3174	£1·40 Vulcan B2	3·25	3·25
		a. Horiz pair. Nos. 4060/4061	6·50	6·50
4061	3175	£1·40 Typhoon FGR4	3·25	3·25
4062	3176	£1·57 Sopwith Camel F.1	3·75	3·75
		a. Horiz pair. Nos. 4062/4063	7·50	7·50
4063	3177	£1·57 Nimrod MR2	3·75	3·75
Set of 6			15·00	15·00
Set of 3 Gutter Blocks of 4			30·00	
First Day Cover (Tallents House)				16·00
First Day Cover (Cranwell, Sleaford)				16·00
Presentation Pack (PO Pack No. 553) (Nos. 4058/4063 and **MS**4064)			25·00	
PHQ Cards (set of 11) (440)			10·00	32·00
MS4064 192×74 mm **3178** Nos. 4067/4070			9·50	9·50
First Day Cover (Tallents House)				10·50
First Day Cover (Cranwell, Sleaford)				10·50

(b) Self-adhesive. Die-cut perf 14½.

4065	3172	(1st) Lightning F6	1·75	1·75
		a. Booklet pane. Nos. 4065/4066 and U3027×4	7·50	
4066	3173	(1st) Hurricane Mk.I	1·75	1·75

Nos. 4058/4059, 4060/4061 and 4062/4063 were each printed together, se-tenant, as horizontal pairs in sheets of 60 (2 panes 6×5).

Nos 4058b and 4059b were issued in £18·69 RAF Centenary premium booklet, No. DY25.

Nos. 4065/4066 were issued in stamp booklet, No. PM59, originally sold for £3·90.

The 11 PHQ cards show the individual stamps including those from No. **MS**4064 and the complete miniature sheet.

3179 Red Arrows, Flypast
3180 Red Arrows, Swan 
3181 Red Arrows, Syncro pair 
3182 Red Arrows, Python 

(Des Turner Duckworth, Litho ISP Cartor)

2018 (20 Mar) RAF Centenary (2nd issue). Red Arrows. Multicoloured Two phosphor bands. Perf 14½×14.

4067	3179	(1st) Red Arrows, Flypast	1·50	1·50
		a. Booklet pane Nos. 4067/4070	7·00	
4068	3180	(1st) Red Arrows, Swan	1·50	1·50
4069	3181	£1·40 Red Arrows, Syncro pair	3·25	3·25
4070	3182	£1·40 Red Arrows, Python	3·25	3·25
Set of 4			7·00	7·00

Nos. 4067/4070 come from No. **MS**4064 and £18·69 RAF Centenary premium booklet, No. DY25.

3183 Pilots scramble to their Hurricanes
3184 Supermarine Spitfires of 610 Squadron, Biggin Hill, on patrol 
3185 Armourer Fred Roberts replaces ammunition boxes on Supermarine Spitfire 

(Des Supple Studio (stamps) and Royal Mail Group, Supple Studio. Litho ISP Cartor)

2018 (20 Mar) RAF Centenary (3rd issue). Battle of Britain. Multicoloured Two phosphor bands. Perf 14½×14.

4071	3183	(1st) Pilots scramble	1·50	1·50
		a. Booklet pane Nos. 4071, 4072×2, 4073	5·00	
4072	3184	(1st) Spitfires	1·50	1·50
4073	3185	(1st) Armourer replaces ammunition boxes	1·50	1·50
Set of 3			4·00	4·00

Nos. 4071/4073 come from £18·69 premium booklet, No. DY25.
The images on these three stamps were previously used in No. **MS**3735 issued on 16 July 2015 to commemorate the 75th Anniversary of the Battle of Britain; those stamps were 'all-over' phosphor.

3186 Osprey (*Pandion haliaetus*)
3187 Large Blue Butterfly (*Maculinea arion*)

QUEEN ELIZABETH II/2018

3188 Eurasian Beaver (*Castor fiber*)

3189 Pool Frog (*Pelophylax lessonae*)

3190 Stinking Hawk's-beard (*Crepis foetida*)

3191 Sand Lizard (*Lacerta agilis*)

(Des Tanya Lock (illustration) and Godfrey Design. Litho ISP Cartor)

2018 (17 Apr). Reintroduced Species. Multicoloured Two phosphor bands. Perf 14½.

4074	**3186**	(1st) Osprey (*Pandion haliaetus*)...............	1·20	1·00
		a. Horiz pair. Nos. 4074/4075.............	2·40	2·00
4075	**3187**	(1st) Large Blue Butterfly (*Maculinea arion*)..	1·20	1·00
4076	**3188**	£1·45 Eurasian Beaver (*Castor fiber*).........	2·25	2·25
		a. Horiz pair. Nos. 4076/4077.............	4·50	4·50
4077	**3189**	£1·45 Pool Frog (*Pelophylax lessonae*)......	2·25	2·25
4078	**3190**	£1·55 Stinking Hawk's-beard (*Crepis foetida*)...	2·50	2·50
		a. Horiz pair. Nos. 4078/4079.............	5·00	5·00
4079	**3191**	£1·55 Sand Lizard (*Lacerta agilis*).............	2·50	2·50
Set of 6...			10·75	10·50
Set of 3 Gutter Blocks of 4..			21·50	
First Day Cover (Tallents House)...................................				13·50
First Day Cover (Frogpool, Truro)................................				13·50
Presentation Pack (PO Pack No. 554).........................			13·50	
PHQ Cards (set of 6) (441)..			4·00	12·00

Nos. 4074/4075, 4076/4077 and 4078/4079 were each printed together, *se-tenant*, as horizontal pairs in sheets of 60 (2 panes 6×5).

(Gravure ISP Walsall)

2018 (11 May). Centenary of the RAF (Royal Air Force) (4th issue). Multicoloured. Self-adhesive. Two phosphor bands. Die-cut perf 14

4080	**3179**	(1st) Red Arrows, Flypast........................	3·25	3·25
		a. Booklet pane. Nos. 4080/4081 and U3027×4..................................	12·50	
4081	**3180**	(1st) Red Arrows, Swan...........................	3·25	3·25

Nos. 4080/4081 were issued in stamp booklet, No. PM60, originally sold for £4·02.

3192 Barn Owl (*Tyto alba*)

3193 Little Owl (*Athene noctua*)

3194 Tawny Owl (*Strix aluco*)

3195 Short-eared Owl (*Asio flammeus*)

3196 Long-eared Owl (*Asio otus*)

3197 Two Young Barn Owls (*Tyto alba*)

3198 Little Owl Chicks (*Athene noctua*)

3199 Tawny Owl Chick (*Strix aluco*)

3200 Short-eared Owl Chick (*Asio flammeus*)

3201 Long-eared Owl Chick (*Asio otus*)

(Des Atelier Works. Litho ISP Cartor)

2018 (11 May). Owls. Multicoloured Two phosphor bands. Perf 14½×14.

4082	**3192**	(1st) Barn Owl (*Tyto alba*)........................	1·20	1·00
		a. Horiz strip of 5. Nos. 4082/4086.....	5·25	4·50
4083	**3193**	(1st) Little Owl (*Athene noctua*)..............	1·20	1·00
4084	**3194**	(1st) Tawny Owl (*Strix aluco*)..................	1·20	1·00
4085	**3195**	(1st) Short-eared Owl (*Asio flammeus*)..	1·20	1·00
4086	**3196**	(1st) Long-eared Owl (*Asio otus*)............	1·20	1·00
4087	**3197**	(1st) Two Young Barn Owls (*Tyto alba*)..	1·20	1·00
		a. Horiz strip of 5. Nos. 4087/4091.....	5·25	4·50
4088	**3198**	(1st) Little Owl Chicks (*Athene noctua*)..	1·20	1·00
4089	**3199**	(1st) Tawny Owl Chick (*Strix aluco*)........	1·20	1·00
4090	**3200**	(1st) Short-eared Owl Chick (*Asio flammeus*)...	1·20	1·00
4091	**3201**	(1st) Long-eared Owl Chick (*Asio otus*)..	1·20	1·00
Set of 10...			10·50	9·00
Set of 2 Gutter Strips of 10..			21·00	
Set of 2 Traffic Light Gutter Strips of 20....................			40·00	
First Day Cover (Tallents House)...................................				12·50
First Day Cover (Hooton, Ellesmere Port)..................				12·50
Presentation Pack (PO Pack No. 555).........................			12·50	
PHQ Cards (set of 10) (442)...			6·75	11·00

Nos. 4082/406 and 4087/4091 were each printed together, *se-tenant*, as horizontal strips of five stamps in sheets of 50 (2 panes 5×5).

3202 Royal Wedding

2018/QUEEN ELIZABETH II

(Des The Chase. Litho ISP Cartor)

2018 (19 May). Royal Wedding. Multicoloured. 'All-over' phosphor. Perf 14½×14.
MS4092 116×89 mm. **3202** (1st) Prince Harry and Ms Meghan Markle×2; £1·55 Prince Harry and Ms Meghan Markle (black and white photograph)×2... 7·00 7·00
First Day Cover (Tallents House)... 8·50
First Day Cover (Windsor).. 8·50
Presentation Pack (PO Pack No. M24)................................. 7·50

A souvenir pack containing Nos. **MS**3932 and **MS**4092 with silver foil cachet postmarks and imagery from the Royal Wedding was available from Royal Mail from 29 June 2018 for £24·99.

3203 Summer Exhibition (Grayson Perry)
3204 Queen of the Sky (Fiona Rae) 
3205 St. Kilda. The Great Sea Stacs (Norman Ackroyd) 
3206 Inverleith Allotments and Edinburgh Castle (Barbara Rae) 
3207 Queuing at the RA (Yinka Shonibare) 
3208 Saying Goodbye (Tracey Emin) 

(Litho ISP Cartor)

2018 (5 June). 250th Anniversary of the Royal Academy of Arts, London. Multicoloured. Two phosphor bands. Perf 14×14½.

4093	3203	(1st) Summer Exhibition (Grayson Perry)..	1·20	1·00
		a. Vert pair. Nos. 4093/4094..............	2·40	2·00
4094	3204	(1st) Queen of the Sky (Fiona Rae)...........	1·20	1·00
4095	3205	£1·25 St Kilda. The Great Sea Stacs (Norman Ackroyd)...................	1·90	1·90
		a. Vert pair. Nos. 4095/4096.............	3·75	3·75
4096	3206	£1·25 Inverleith Allotments and Edinburgh Castle (Barbara Rae)..	1·90	1·90
4097	3207	£1·55 Queuing at the RA (Yinka Shonibare)..	2·40	2·40
		a. Vert pair. Nos. 4097/4098..............	4·75	4·75
4098	3208	£1·55 Saying Goodbye (Tracey Emin).......	2·40	2·40
Set of 6...			9·75	9·50
Set of 3 Gutter Pairs (only 2 stamps in each gutter pair)...			11·50	
First Day Cover (Tallents House)..				13·00
First Day Cover (London W1)..				13·00
Presentation Pack (PO Pack No. 556).......................................			11·50	
PHQ Cards (set of 6) (443)...			4·00	11·50

Nos. 4093/4094, 4095/4096 and 4097/4098 were each printed together, se-tenant, as vertical pairs in sheets of 60 (2 panes 5×6).

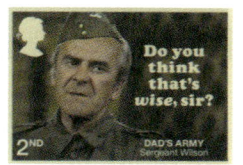

3209 Sergeant Wilson (John Le Mesurier) 'Do you think that's wise, sir?'
3210 Private Pike (Ian Lavender) 'I'll tell Mum!' 
3211 Captain Mainwaring (Arthur Lowe) 'You stupid boy!' 
3212 Lance Corporal Jones (Clive Dunn) 'Don't panic! Don't panic!' 
3213 Private Walker (James Beck) 'It won't cost you much...' 
3214 Private Frazer (John Laurie) 'We're doomed. Doomed!' 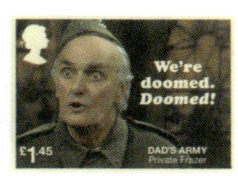
3215 Private Godfrey (Arnold Ridley) 'Do you think I might be excused?' 
3216 Chief Warden Hodges (Bill Pertwee) 'Put that light out!' 

(Des Up Design. Litho ISP Cartor (Nos. 4099/4106) or gravure ISP Walsall (Nos. 4107/4108))

2018 (26 June). 50th Anniversary of Dad's Army (BBC television sitcom 1968–1977). Multicoloured. One centre band (2nd) or two phosphor bands (others).

(a) Ordinary gum. Perf 14½×14.

4099	3209	(2nd) Sergeant Wilson (John Le Mesurier) 'Do you think that's wise, sir?'..	90	90
		a. Horiz pair. Nos. 4099/4100..............	1·75	1·75
4100	3210	(2nd) Private Pike (Ian Lavender) 'I'll tell Mum!'..	90	90
4101	3211	(1st) Captain Mainwaring (Arthur Lowe) 'You stupid boy!'.................	1·20	1·00
		a. Horiz pair. Nos. 4101/4102..............	2·40	2·00
4102	3212	(1st) Lance Corporal Jones (Clive Dunn) 'Don't panic! Don't panic!'...	1·20	1·00
4103	3213	£1·45 Private Walker (James Beck) 'It won't cost you much...'...............	2·25	2·25
		a. Horiz pair. Nos. 4103/4104.............	4·50	4·50
4104	3214	£1·45 Private Frazer (John Laurie) 'We're doomed. Doomed!'........................	2·25	2·25
4105	3215	£1·55 Private Godfrey (Arnold Ridley) 'Do you think I might be excused?'...	2·40	2·40
		a. Horiz pair. Nos. 4105/4106..............	4·75	4·75
4106	3216	£1·55 Chief Warden Hodges (Bill Pertwee) 'Put that light out!'...........	2·40	2·40
Set of 8..			12·25	12·00
Set of 4 Gutter Blocks of 4...			24·50	
First Day Cover (Tallents House)...				16·00
First Day Cover (Thetford)...				16·00
Presentation Pack (PO Pack No. 557)...			14·00	
PHQ Cards (set of 8) (444)..			5·50	14·00

QUEEN ELIZABETH II/2018

(b) Self-adhesive. Die-cut perf 14½×14.

4107	**3211**	(1st) Captain Mainwaring (Arthur Lowe) 'You stupid boy!'......................	1·75	1·75
		a. Booklet pane. Nos. 4107/4108 and U3027×4...................................	7·50	
4108	**3212**	(1st) Lance Corporal Jones (Clive Dunn) 'Don't panic! Don't panic!'...	1·75	1·75

Nos. 4099/4100, 4101/4102, 4103/4104 and 4105/4106 were each printed, *se-tenant*, as horizontal pairs in sheets of 60 (2 pairs 6×5)

Nos. 4107/4108 were issued in stamp booklet, No. PM61, originally sold for £4·02.

Stamps as Nos. 4101/4102 but self-adhesive and perforated 14×14½ were issued in sheets of ten (No. LS111) containing five stamps of each design with labels showing stills from the television series. These sheets were printed in lithography by ISP Cartor and originally sold for £7·50 each.

3217 South Front

3218 West Front

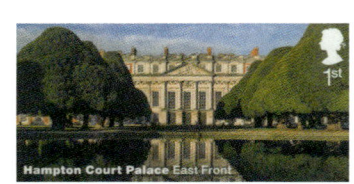

3219 East Front

3220 Pond Gardens

3221 Maze

3222 Great Fountain Garden

3223 Hampton Court Palace

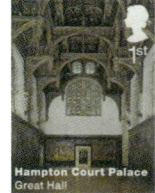

3224 Great Hall

3225 King's Great Bedchamber

(Des Osborne Ross. Litho ISP Cartor (Nos. 4109/**MS**4115) or gravure ISP Walsall (Nos. 4116/4117))

2018 (31 July). Hampton Court Palace. Multicoloured Two phosphor bands.

(a) Ordinary gum. Perf 14½.

4109	**3217**	(1st) South Front..	1·20	1·00
		a. Horiz strip of 3. Nos. 4109/4111.....	3·50	3·00
4110	**3218**	(1st) West Front..	1·20	1·00
4111	**3219**	(1st) East Front...	1·20	1·00
4112	**3220**	£1·55 Pond Gardens...................................	2·40	2·40
		a. Horiz strip of 3. Nos. 4112/4114.....	7·25	7·25
4113	**3221**	£1·55 Maze..	2·40	2·40
4114	**3222**	£1·55 Great Fountain Garden....................	2·40	2·40
Set of 6..			9·50	9·00
Set of 2 Gutter Strips of 6..			19·00	
First Day Cover (Tallents House)...				12·50
First Day Cover (East Molesey)..				12·50
Presentation Pack (PO Pack No. 558) (Nos. 4104/4114 and **MS**4115)...			17·50	
PHQ Cards (set of 11) (445)..			7·50	22·00
MS4115 156×74 mm. **3223** (1st) Great Hall; (1st) King's Great Bedchamber; £1·45 Chapel Royal; £1·45 King's Staircase...			6·50	6·50
First Day Cover (Tallents House)...				8·25
First Day Cover (East Molesey)..				8·25

(b) Self-adhesive. Die-cut perf 14.

4116	**3224**	(1st) Great Hall..	1·75	1·75
		a. Booklet pane. Nos. 4116/4117 and U3027×4...................................	7·50	
4117	**3225**	(1st) King's Great Bedchamber..............	1·75	1·75

Nos. 4109/4111 and 4112/4114 were each printed together, *se-tenant*, as horizontal strips of three stamps in sheets of 60 (2 panes 6×5).

Nos. 4116/4117 were issued in stamp booklet, No. PM62, originally sold for £4·02.

The 11 PHQ cards show the individual stamps including those from No. **MS**4115 and the complete miniature sheet.

3226 Joseph Banks, Red-tailed Tropicbird and Red Passion Flower

3227 Chief Mourner of Tahiti and a Scene with a Canoe

2018/QUEEN ELIZABETH II

3228 Captain James Cook and *Triumph of the Navigators*

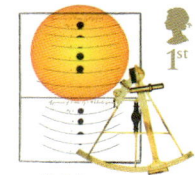

3229 Drawings of the Observations of a Transit of Venus

3230 Scarlet Clianthus and Portrait of a Maori Chief

3231 Blue-Black Grassquit and Self-Portrait of Sydney Parkinson

3232 The *Endeavour* Voyage

(Des Howard Brown (Nos. 4118/4123) or Webb & Webb Design Ltd (No. **MS**4124). Litho ISP Cartor)

2018 (16 Aug). Captain Cook and the *Endeavour* Voyage (1768–1771). Multicoloured One centre band (2nd) or two phosphor bands (others). Perf 14×14½ (Nos. 4118/4123) or 14 (No. **MS**4124).

4118	3226	(2nd) Joseph Banks, Red-tailed Tropicbird and Red Passion Flower	90	90
		a. Horiz pair. Nos. 4118/4119	1·75	1·75
4119	3227	(2nd) Chief Mourner of Tahiti and a Scene with a Canoe	90	90
4120	3228	(1st) Captain James Cook and *Triumph of the Navigators*	1·20	1·00
		a. Horiz pair. Nos. 4120/4121	2·40	2·00
4121	3229	(1st) Drawings of the Observations of a Transit of Venus	1·20	1·00
4122	3230	£1·45 Scarlet Clianthus and Portrait of a Maori Chief	2·25	2·25
		a. Horiz pair. Nos. 4122/4123	4·50	4·50
4123	3231	£1·45 Blue-Black Grassquit and Self-Portrait of Sydney Parkinson	2·25	2·25
Set of 6			7·75	7·50
Set of 3 Gutter Blocks of 4			15·50	
First Day Cover (Tallents House)				10·50
First Day Cover (Plymouth)				10·50
Presentation Pack (PO Pack No.559) (Nos. 4118/4123 and **MS**4124)			15·00	
PHQ Cards (set of 11) (446)			7·50	20·00
MS4124 125×89 mm. **3232** (1st) Chart of the discoveries made by Captain Cook (Lieutenant Roberts) ('Charting a new course: New Zealand and Australia'); (1st) Boathouse and canoes on Raiatea, Society Islands (after Sydney Parkinson); £1·45 Arched rock with Maori clifftop fort, New Zealand ('Mapping New Zealand: a Maori clifftop fort'); £1·45 Repairing the *Endeavour* on the Endeavour River, Australia (after Sydney Parkinson)			6·50	6·50
First Day Cover (Tallents House)				8·25
First Day Cover (Plymouth)				8·25

Nos. 4118/4119, 4120/4121 and 4122/4123 were each printed together, *se-tenant*, as horizontal pairs in sheets of 60 (2 panes 6×5).

Nos. 4118/**MS**4124 commemorate the 250th Anniversary of the Departure of the *Endeavour*.

The 11 PHQ cards show the ten individual stamps including those from No. **MS**4124 and the complete miniature sheet.

3233 Laurence Olivier in *The Dance of Death*

3234 Glenda Jackson in *King Lear*

3235 Albert Finney in *Hamlet*

3236 Maggie Smith in *Hedda Gabler*

3237 John Gielgud and Ralph Richardson in *No Man's Land*

3238 Sharon Benson in *Carmen Jones*

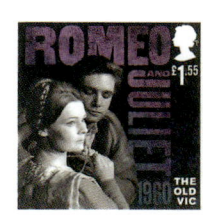

3239 Judi Dench and John Stride in *Romeo and Juliet*

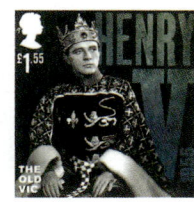

3240 Richard Burton in *Henry V*

(Des Hat-trick Design and Kelvyn Laurence Smith (typography). Litho ISP Cartor)

2018 (30 Aug). Bicentenary of The Old Vic, London. Multicoloured . Two phosphor bands. Perf 14½×14

4125	3233	(1st) Laurence Olivier in *The Dance of Death*	1·20	1·00
		a. Horiz pair. Nos. 4125/4126	2·40	2·00
4126	3234	(1st) Glenda Jackson in *King Lear*	1·20	1·00
4127	3235	£1·25 Albert Finney in *Hamlet*	1·90	1·90
		a. Horiz pair. Nos. 4127/4128	3·75	3·75
4128	3236	£1·25 Maggie Smith in *Hedda Gabler*	1·90	1·90
4129	3237	£1·45 John Gielgud and Ralph Richardson in *No Man's Land*	2·25	2·25
		a. Horiz pair. Nos. 4129/4130	4·50	4·50
4130	3238	£1·45 Sharon Benson in *Carmen Jones*	2·25	2·25
4131	3239	£1·55 Judi Dench and John Stride in *Romeo and Juliet*	2·40	2·40
		a. Horiz pair. Nos. 4131/4132	4·75	4·75
4132	3240	£1·55 Richard Burton in *Henry V*	2·40	2·40
Set of 8			13·75	13·50
Set of 4 Gutter Pairs (only 2 stamps in each gutter pair)			14·50	
Set of 4 Traffic Light Gutter Blocks (4 stamps per block)			29·00	
First Day Cover (Tallents House)				18·50
First Day Cover (London SE1)				18·50
Presentation Pack (PO Pack No. 560)			16·00	
PHQ Cards (set of 8) (447)			5·50	15·00

QUEEN ELIZABETH II/2018

Nos. 4125/416, 4127/4128, 4129/4130 and 4131/4132 were each printed together, *se-tenant*, as horizontal pairs in sheets of 60 (2 panes 6×5).

3241 *100 Poppies* (Zafer and Barbara Baran)

3242 *Anthem for Doomed Youth* (poem by Wilfred Owen) (woodblock print by Andrew Davidson)

3243 Second Lieutenant Walter Tull (1888–1918)

3244 *We Are Making a New World* (Paul Nash)

3245 The Grave of the Unknown Warrior, Westminster Abbey, London

3246 Lieutenant Francis Hopgood's Goggles

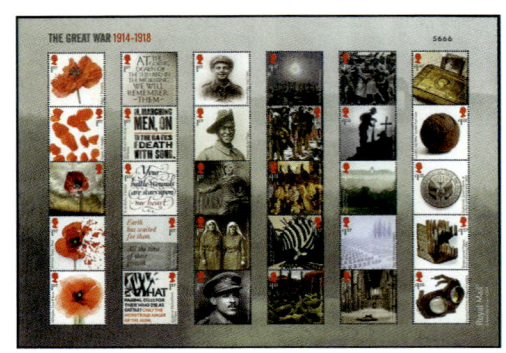

3246a The Great War composite sheet

(Des Hat-trick Design. Litho ISP Cartor (Nos. 4133/41338, **MS**4138a) or gravure ISP Walsall (Nos. 4139/4140))

2018 (13 Sept). Centenary of the First World War (5th issue). Multicoloured.
(a) Ordinary gum. Two phosphor bands. Perf 14½.

4133	3241	(1st) *100 Poppies* (Zafer and Barbara Baran)............	1·20	1·00
		a. Booklet pane. Nos. 4133/4135 with margins all round........	3·50	
4134	3242	(1st) *Anthem for Doomed Youth* (poem by Wilfred Owen) (woodblock print by Andrew Davidson)........	1·20	1·00
4135	3243	(1st) Second Lieutenant Walter Tull (1888–1918)........	1·20	1·00
4136	3244	£1·55 *We Are Making a New World* (Paul Nash)........	2·40	2·40
		a. Booklet pane. Nos. 4136/4138 with margins all round........	7·00	
4137	3245	£1·55 The Grave of the Unknown Warrior, Westminster Abbey, London........	2·40	2·40
4138	3246	£1·55 Lieutenant Francis Hopgood's Goggles........	2·40	2·40
Set of 6			9·50	9·00
Set of 6 Gutter Pairs			19·00	
First Day Cover (Tallents House)........				12·50
First Day Cover (London SW1)........				12·50
Presentation Pack (PO Pack No. 561)........			12·00	
PHQ Cards (set of 6) (448)........			4·00	11·00
MS4138a 296×210 mm. **3246a** Nos. 3626/3631, 3711/3716, 3838/3843, 3983/398 and 4133/4138....			50·00	65·00

(b) Self-adhesive. Die-cut perf 14½.

4139	2774	(1st) *Poppy* (Fiona Strickland)........	1·75	1·75
		a. Booklet pane. Nos. 4139/4140 and U3027×4........	7·50	
4140	3241	(1st) *100 Poppies* (Zafer and Barbara Baran)........	1·75	1·75

Nos. 4133a and 4136a come from £15·65 premium booklet, No. DY26.
Nos. 4139/4140 were issued in stamp booklet, No. PM63, originally sold for £4·02.
No. **MS**4138a was a special composite sheet sold for £32·94.
No. 4139 was as T **2774**, the poppy stamp issued in 2014 for the first Centenary of the First World War series, but self-adhesive and printed in gravure.
A souvenir pack containing the poppy stamps Nos. 3626, 3711, 3838, 3983 and 4133 each affixed to a poem print was sold by Royal Mail for £24·99.

3247 Hermione Granger (Emma Watson)

3248 *Hogwarts Express*

3249 Harry Potter (Daniel Radcliffe)

3250 *Flying Ford Anglia*

3251 Ron Weasley (Rupert Grint)

3252 *Hagrid's Motorbike*

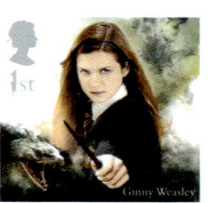

3253 Ginny Weasley (Bonnie Wright)

3254 *Triwizard Cup*

2018/QUEEN ELIZABETH II

3255 Neville Longbottom (Matthew Lewis)
3256 Knight Bus 
3257 Hogwarts Professors and The Marauders Map 

(Des True North with digital image enhancement by Smoke & Mirrors (Nos. 4141/4150, 4152/4153) or The Chase (No. **MS**4151). Litho ISP Cartor (Nos. 4141/4150, **MS**4151) or gravure ISP Walsall (Nos. 4152/4153))

2018 (16 Oct–4 Dec). Harry Potter (1st issue) Multicolour. 'All-over' phosphor (No. **MS**4151 stamps only) or two phosphor bands (others).

(a) Ordinary gum. Perf 14×14½.

4141	3247	(1st) Hermione Granger (Emma Watson).............................	1·20	1·00
		a. Horiz strip of 5. Nos. 4141/4145.....	5·25	5·00
		b. Booklet pane. Nos. 4141, 4143, 4145, 4147 and 4149 with margins all round (4.12.18).............	5·25	
4142	3248	(1st) Hogwarts Express.............................	1·20	1·00
		b. Booklet pane. Nos. 4142, 4144, 4146, 4148 and 4150 with margins all round (4.12.18).............	5·25	
4143	3249	(1st) Harry Potter (Daniel Radcliffe).......	1·20	1·00
4144	3250	(1st) Flying Ford Anglia.............................	1·20	1·00
4145	3251	(1st) Ron Weasley (Rupert Grint)............	1·20	1·00
4146	3252	(1st) Hagrid's Motorbike.............................	1·20	1·00
		a. Horiz strip of 5. Nos. 4146/4150.....	5·25	5·00
4147	3253	(1st) Ginny Weasley (Bonnie Wright).....	1·20	1·00
4148	3254	(1st) Triwizard Cup.............................	1·20	1·00
4149	3255	(1st) Neville Longbottom (Matthew Lewis).............................	1·20	1·00
4150	3256	(1st) Knight Bus.............................	1·20	1·00
Set of 10			10·50	9·00
Set of 2 Gutter Strips of 10			21·00	
First Day Cover (Tallents House)				13·00
First Day Cover (Muggleswick, Consett)				13·00
Presentation Pack (PO Pack No. 562) (Nos. 4141/4150 and **MS**4151)			19·00	
PHQ Cards (set of 16) (449)			11·00	23·00

(b) Self-adhesive. Die-cut perf 14.

MS4151 202×74 mm. **3257** (1st) Pomona Sprout (Miriam Margolyes); (1st) Horace Slughorn (Jim Broadbent); (1st) Sybill Trelawney (Emma Thompson); (1st) Remus Lupin (David Thewlis); (1st) Severus Snape (Alan Rickman)......................... 6·25 6·25
b. No. **MS**4151 with margins all round (4.12.18).. 5·00 5·00
First Day Cover (Tallents House).. 8·50
First Day Cover (Muggleswick, Consett)........................ 8·50

(c) Self-adhesive. Die-cut perf 14×14½.

4152	3247	(1st) Hermione Granger (Emma Watson).............................	1·75	1·75
		a. Booklet pane. Nos. 4152/4153 and U3027×4.............................	7·50	
4153	3249	(1st) Harry Potter (Daniel Radcliffe)........	1·75	1·75

Nos. 4141/4145 and 4146/4150 were each printed together, *se-tenant*, as horizontal strips of five stamps in sheets of 50 (2 panes 5×5).

Nos. 4141b and 4142b come from £15·50 premium booklet, No. DY27.

Nos. 4152/4153 were issued in stamp booklets, Nos. PM64/PM64a, originally sold for £4·02.

When placed under a UV light parts of the designs of Nos. 4141/4150 and 4152/4153 light up green, and No. **MS**4151 reveals additional inscriptions.

A collectors sheet (No. LS112) containing stamps as Nos. 4141/4150 but self-adhesive with labels showing Harry Potter film stills was sold for £7·70, a £1 premium over face value.

A Souvenir Stamp Art Folder containing pages of enlarged images of Nos. 4141/4150 with the stamps attached, cancelled with a special cachet postmark, and also a poster of the miniature sheet, were sold by Royal Mail for £24·99.

The 16 PHQ cards show the individual stamps including those from No. **MS**4151 and the complete miniature sheet.

3258 Man and Girl posting Letters in Wall-mounted Post Box
3259 Postal Worker emptying Post Box 
3260 Man and Girl posting Letters in Wall-mounted Post Box 
3261 Postal Worker emptying Post Box 
3262 Man and Boy approaching Rural Pillar Box 
3263 Man approaching Post Box 
3264 Woman with Dog posting Letter 
3265 Pillar Box near Church 

(Des Andrew Davidson. Gravure ISP Walsall (No. 4154/4161) or litho ISP Cartor (No. **MS**4162))

2018 (1 Nov). Christmas. Post Boxes. Multicoloured One centre band (No. 4154) or two bands (others). Perf 14½×15

(a) Self-adhesive.

4154	3258	(2nd) Man and Girl posting Letters in Wall mounted Post box..................	90	90
		a. Booklet pane. No. 4154×12............	17·00	
4155	3259	(1st) Postal Worker emptying Post box..	1·20	1·00
		a. Booklet pane. No. 4155×12............	20·00	
4156	3260	(2nd Man and Girl posting Letters in Large) Wall-mounted Post box...................	1·25	1·10
4157	3261	(1st Postal Worker emptying Post box. Large)	1·70	1·40
4158	3262	£1·25 Man and Boy approaching Rural Pillar Box.............................	1·90	1·90
4159	3263	£1·45 Man approaching Post Box............	2·25	2·25
4160	3264	£1·55 Woman with Dog posting Letter....	2·40	2·40
4161	3265	£2·25 Pillar Box near Church...................	3·50	3·50
Set of 8			13·50	13·00
First Day Cover (Tallents House)				18·00
First Day Cover (Bethlehem, Llandeilo)				18·00
Presentation Pack (PO Pack No. 563)			15·00	
PHQ Cards (set of 9) (450)			6·00	25·00

(b) Ordinary gum.

MS4162 190×74 mm. As Nos. 4154/4161......................... 13·50 13·00
First Day Cover (Tallents House).. 18·00
First Day Cover (Bethlehem, Llandeilo)..................................... 18·00

Nos. 4154 and 4155 also occur together with Nos. 4019 and 4120 respectively as vertical *se-tenant* pairs across the middle of counter sheets, due to the top and bottom halves of each sheet comprising the different stamps. Note that the original printings of Nos. 4019/4020 were by De La Rue, the 2018 reprints were by ISP (Walsall).

The 2nd class, 1st class, £1·25, £1·45, £1·55 and £2·25 values were also issued in sheets of 20 (No. LS113) containing eight 2nd class, eight 1st class and one each of the £1·25, £1·45, £1·55 and £2·25 values, each stamp accompanied by a *se-tenant* label. These sheets were printed in lithography by ISP Cartor and were originally sold for £17·50.

The nine PHQ cards show the individual stamps and the complete miniature sheet.

3266 70th Birthday of Prince of Wales

QUEEN ELIZABETH II/2018

(Des Royal Mail Group Ltd/Davies Maude. Litho ISP Cartor)

2018 (14 Nov). 70th Birthday of the Prince of Wales. Multicolour. 'All-over' phosphor. Self-adhesive. Die-cut perf 14½×15

MS4163 203×74 mm. **3266** (1st) Prince Charles; (1st) Prince Charles with Camilla, Duchess of Cornwall; (1st) Prince Charles with Prince William and Prince Harry; £1·55 Prince Charles, Prince William and Prince Harry at Cirencester Park Polo Club; £1·55 Prince Charles at Castle of Mey; £1·55 Prince Charles with schoolchildren at Llancaiach Fawr Manor...		10·50	10·50
First Day Cover (Tallents House)			13·00
First Day Cover (London SW1)			13·00
Presentation Pack (PO Pack No. 564)		12·00	
PHQ Cards (set of 7) (451)		4·75	12·00

Collectors Pack

2018 (14 Nov). Comprises Nos. 4033/**MS**4043, 4050/**MS**4064, 4074/4079, 4082/4106, 4109/**MS**4115, 4118/4138, 4141/**MS**4151, 4154/4161 and **MS**4163

CP4163*a*	Collectors Pack (PO Pack No. 565) (*sold for £133*)	£275

Post Office Yearbook

2018 (14 Nov). Comprises Nos. 4033/**MS**4043, 4050/**MS**4064, 4074/4079, 4082/4106, 4109/**MS**4115, 4118/38, 4141/**MS**4151, 4154/4061 and **MS**4163

YB4163*a*	Yearbook (*sold for £153*)	£300

Miniature Sheet Collection

2018 (14 Nov). Comprises Nos. **MS**4043, **MS**4064, **MS**4092, **MS**4115, **MS**4124, **MS**4151, **MS**4162 and **MS**4163

MS4163*a*	Miniature Sheet Collection (*sold for £42*)	85·00

3267 Pomona Sprout (Miriam Margolyes)

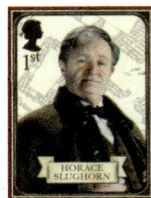

3268 Horace Slughorn (Jim Broadbent)

3269 Sybill Trelawney (Emma Thompson)

3270 Remus Lupin (David Thewlis)

3271 Severus Snape (Alan Rickman)

(The Chase. Litho ISP Cartor)

2018 (4 Dec). Harry Potter (2nd issue). Multicoloured. Self-adhesive. 'All-over' phosphor (stamps only). Die-cut perf 14.

4164	**3267**	(1st) Pomona Sprout (Miriam Margolyes)..	1·40	1·40
		a. Booklet pane. Nos. 4164/4166.......	4·00	
4165	**3268**	(1st) Horace Slughorn (Jim Broadbent)	1·40	1·40
4166	**3269**	(1st) Sybill Trelawney (Emma Thompson).......................................	1·40	1·40
4167	**3270**	(1st) Remus Lupin (David Thewlis)..........	1·40	1·40
		a. Booklet pane. Nos. 4167/4168.......	2·75	
4168	**3271**	(1st) Severus Snape (Alan Rickman).......	1·40	1·40
Set of 5			6·25	6·25

Nos. 4164/4168 were issued in No. **MS**4151 and in booklet panes 4164*a* and 4167*a* from the £15·50 Harry Potter booklet DY27.

Booklet panes Nos. 4164*a* and 4167*a* are as No. **MS**4151 but in two panes with Marauder's Map margins.

When placed under UV light, Nos. 4164*a* and 4167*a* reveal additional inscriptions.

3272 Stamp Classics

(Des Hat-trick design. Litho ISP)

2019 (15 Jan). Stamp Classics Multicoloured. Phosphor frame. Perf 14×13½.

MS4169 203×74 mm. **3272** (1st) Queen Victoria 1891 £1 green; (1st) King Edward VII 1910 2d. Tyrian plum; (1st) King George V 1913 Sea horse 2s.6d. brown; £1·55 King Edward VIII 1936 1½d. red-brown; £1·55 King George VI (and Queen Victoria) 1940 Penny Black Centenary ½d. green; £1·55 Queen Elizabeth II 1953 Coronation 2½d. carmine-red...		13·50	13·50
First Day Cover (Tallents House)			16·00
First Day Cover (London WC1)			16·00
Presentation Pack (PO Pack No. 566)		14·50	
PHQ Cards (set of 7) (452)		4·75	22·00

No. **MS**4169 commemorates the 150th Anniversary of the Royal Philatelic Society and the 50th Anniversary of Queen Elizabeth II opening the National Postal Museum, London.

No. **MS**4169 additionally inscribed 'Stampex International The Bristish National Stamp Exhibition' 13–16 February 2019' was only available at that exhibition (*Price £18*)

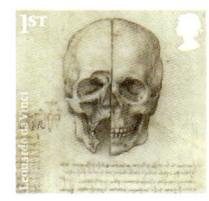

3273 The Skull Sectioned

3274 A Sprig of Guelder-rose

3275 Studies of Cats

3276 Star-of-Bethlehem and Other Plants

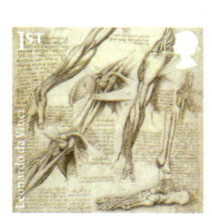

3277 The Anatomy of the Shoulder and Foot

3278 The Head of Leda

3279 The Head of a Bearded Man

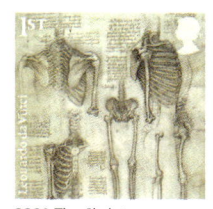

3280 The Skeleton

2019/QUEEN ELIZABETH II

3281 The Head of St Philip
3282 A Woman in a Landscape 
3283 A Design for an Equestrian Monument 
3284 The Fall of Light on a Face 

(Des Kate Stephens. Litho ISP Cartor)

2019 (13 Feb). 500th Death Anniversary of Leonardo da Vinci (1452–1519, artist) Multicoloured. Two phosphor bands. Perf 14½.

4170	3273	(1st) The Skull Sectioned	1·20	1·00
		a. Horiz strip of 6. Nos. 4170/4175	6·50	5·50
		b. Booklet pane. Nos. 4170, 4174, 4177 and 4181 with margins all round	5·25	
4171	3274	(1st) A Sprig of Guelder-rose	1·20	1·00
		b. Booklet pane. Nos. 4171/4173 and 4180 with margins all round	5·25	
4172	3275	(1st) Studies of Cats	1·20	1·00
4173	3276	(1st) A Star-of-Bethlehem and Other Plants	1·20	1·00
4174	3277	(1st) The Anatomy of the Shoulder and Foot	1·20	1·00
4175	3278	(1st) The Head of Leda	1·20	1·00
		b. Booklet pane. Nos. 4175/4176 and 4178/4179 with margins all round	5·25	
4176	3279	(1st) The Head of a Bearded Man	1·20	1·00
		a. Horiz strip of 6. Nos. 4176/4181	6·50	5·50
4177	3280	(1st) The Skeleton	1·20	1·00
4178	3281	(1st) The Head of St Philip	1·20	1·00
4179	3282	(1st) A Woman in a Landscape	1·20	1·00
4180	3283	(1st) A Design for an Equestrian Monument	1·20	1·00
4181	3284	(1st) The Fall of Light on a Face	1·20	1·00
		Set of 12	13·00	11·00
		Set of 2 Gutter Strips of 12	26·00	
		First Day Cover (Tallents House)		14·00
		First Day Cover (Windsor)		14·00
		Presentation Pack (PO Pack No. 567)	17·00	
		PHQ Cards (set of 12) (453)	7·00	12·00

Nos. 4170/4175 and 4176/4181 were each printed together, *se-tenant*, as horizontal strips of six stamps in sheets of 60 (2 panes 6×5).

Nos. 4170b, 4171b and 4175b are from the £13·10 Leonardo da Vinci booklet, No. DY28.

3285 Spider-Man 
3286 Captain Marvel 
3287 Hulk 
3288 Doctor Strange 
3289 Captain Britain 
3290 Peggy Carter 
3291 Iron Man 
3292 Union Jack 
3293 Black Panther 
3294 Thor

3295 Marvel Heroes UK

(Des Alan Davis (illustrations) and Interabang. Litho ISP Cartor (Nos. 4182/4191) or gravure ISP Walsall (Nos. 4193/4194))

2019 (14 Mar). Marvel (1st issue) Multicoloured. Two phosphor bands.

(a) Ordinary gum. Perf 14½.

4182	3285	(1st) Spider-Man	1·20	1·00
		a. Horiz strip of 5. Nos. 4182/4186	5·25	4·50
		b. Booklet pane. Nos. 4182/4184 and 4186/4188 with margins all round	5·25	
4183	3286	(1st) Captain Marvel	1·20	1·00
4184	3287	(1st) Hulk	1·20	1·00
4185	3288	(1st) Doctor Strange	1·20	1·00
		b. Booklet pane. Nos. 4185 and 4189/4191 with margins all round	5·25	
4186	3289	(1st) Captain Britain	1·20	1·00
4187	3290	(1st) Peggy Carter	1·20	1·00
		a. Horiz strip of 5. Nos. 4187/4191	5·25	4·50
4188	3291	(1st) Iron Man	1·20	1·00
4189	3292	(1st) Union Jack	1·20	1·00
4190	3293	(1st) Black Panther	1·20	1·00
4191	3294	(1st) Thor	1·20	1·00
		Set of 10	10·50	9·00
		Set of 2 Gutter Strips of 10	21·00	
		First Day Cover (Tallents House)		17·00
		First Day Cover (Shield Row, Stanley)		17·00
		Presentation Pack (PO Pack No. 568) (Nos. 4182/4191 and **MS**4192)	20·00	
		PHQ Cards (set of 16) (454)	9·00	24·00

(b) Self-adhesive.

MS4192 203×74 mm. **3295** (1st) Thanos (Perf 14); (1st) Thor, Doctor Strange and Iron Man ('He's strong.') (Perf 14½×14); (1st) Hulk, Iron Man, Black Panther and Spider-Man ('but we're stronger...') (Perf 14); £1·25 Captain Britain, Spider-Man, Iron Man, Hulk, Thor and Black Panther ('...together!') (Perf 14); £1·45 Captain Britain ('Fury, a portal is opening.') (Perf 14½×14) ... 7·25 7·25
First Day Cover (Tallents House) ... 10·00
First Day Cover (Shield Row, Stanley) ... 10·00

QUEEN ELIZABETH II/2019

(c) Self-adhesive booklet stamps. Die-cut perf 14½.

4193	3285	(1st) Spider-Man	3·50	3·50
		a. Booklet pane. Nos. 4193/4194 and U3027×4	10·00	
4194	3287	(1st) Hulk	3·50	3·50

Nos. 4182/4186 and 4187/4191 were each printed together, *se-tenant*, as horizontal strips of five stamps in sheets of 50 (2 panes 5×5).

Nos. 4193/4194 were issued in stamp booklet, No. PM65, originally sold for £4·02.

Nos. 4182/4194 commemorate the 80th Anniversary of Marvel Comics. A collector's sheet (No. LS115) containing stamps as Nos. 4182/4191 but self-adhesive was sold for £7·70, a £1 premium above face value.

The 16 PHQ cards show the 15 individual stamps, including those from No. **MS**4192, and the complete sheet.

3296 'Thanos'

3297 Thor, Doctor Strange and Iron Man ('He's strong.')

3298 Hulk, Iron Man, Black Panther and Spider-Man ('but we're stronger...')

3299 Captain Britain, Spider-Man, Iron Man, Hulk, Thor and Black Panther ('...together!')

3300 Captain Britain ('Fury, a portal is opening.')

(Des Alan Davis (illustrations) and Interabang. Litho ISP Cartor)

2019 (14 Mar). Marvel (2nd issue) Multicoloured. Self-adhesive. Two phosphor bands. Die-cut perf 14½×14 (Nos. 4196, 4199) or 14 (others).

4195	3296	(1st) Thanos	1·25	1·25
		a. Booklet pane. Nos. 4195 and 4199	4·00	
4196	3297	(1st) Thor, Doctor Strange and Iron Man ('He's strong.')	1·25	1·25
		a. Booklet pane. Nos. 4196/4198	5·00	
4197	3298	(1st) Hulk, Iron Man, Black Panther and Spider-Man ('but we're stronger...')	1·25	1·25
4198	3299	£1·25 Captain Britain, Spider-Man, Iron Man, Hulk, Thor and Black Panther ('...together!')	2·50	2·50
4199	3300	£1·45 Captain Britain ('Fury, a portal is opening.')	2·75	2·75
Set of 5			8·00	8·00

Nos. 4195/4199 were issued in No. **MS**4192 and in booklet panes 4195a and 4196a from the £17·45 Marvel booklet, No. DY29.

Booklet panes Nos. 4195a and 4196a are as No. **MS**4192 but in two panes with enlarged margins.

3301 White-tailed Eagle

3302 Merlin

3303 Hobby

3304 Buzzard

3305 Golden Eagle

3306 Kestrel

3307 Goshawk

3308 Sparrowhawk

3309 Red Kite

3310 Peregrine Falcon

(Des GBH. Litho ISP Cartor (Nos. 4200/4209) or gravure ISP Walsall (Nos. 4210/4211))

2019 (4 Apr). Birds of Prey. Multicoloured. Phosphor background.
(a) Ordinary gum. Perf 14½×14½.

4200	3301	(1st) White-tailed Eagle (*Haliaeetus albicilla*)	1·20	1·00
		a. Horiz strip of 5. Nos. 4200/4204	5·25	4·50
4201	3302	(1st) Merlin (*Falco columbarius*)	1·20	1·00
4202	3303	(1st) Hobby (*Falco subbuteo*)	1·20	1·00
4203	3304	(1st) Buzzard (*Buteo buteo*)	1·20	1·00
4204	3305	(1st) Golden Eagle (*Aquila chrysaetos*)	1·20	1·00
4205	3306	(1st) Kestrel (*Falco tinnunculus*)	1·20	1·00
		a. Horiz strip of 5. Nos. 4205/4209	5·25	4·50
4206	3307	(1st) Goshawk (*Accipiter gentilis*)	1·20	1·00
4207	3308	(1st) Sparrowhawk (*Accipiter nisus*)	1·20	1·00
4208	3309	(1st) Red Kite (*Milvus milvus*)	1·20	1·00
4209	3310	(1st) Peregrine Falcon (*Falco peregrinus*)	1·20	1·00
Set of 10			10·50	9·00
Set of 2 Gutter Strips of 10			21·00	
First Day Cover (Tallents House)				13·00
First Day Cover (Eagle, Lincoln)				13·00
Presentation Pack (PO Pack No. 569)			13·00	
PHQ Cards (set of 10) (455)			6·00	12·00

2019/QUEEN ELIZABETH II

5(b) Self-adhesive. Die-cut perf 14×14½.

4210	3304	(1st) Buzzard (*Buteo buteo*)............	15·00	15·00
		a. Booklet pane. Nos. 4210/4211 and U3027×4........................	35·00	
4211	3303	(1st) Hobby (*Falco subbuteo*)...........	15·00	15·00

Nos. 4200/4204 and 4205/4209 were each printed together, *se-tenant*, as horizontal strips of five stamps in sheets of 50 (2 panes 5×5).

Nos. 4210/4211 were issued in stamp booklet, No. PM66, originally sold for £4·02.

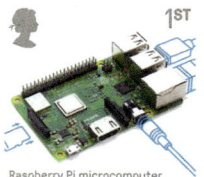

3311 Raspberry Pi Microcomputer

3312 The Falkirk Wheel Rotating Boat Lift

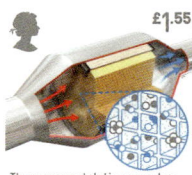

3313 Three-way Catalytic Converter

3314 Crossrail

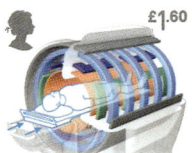

3315 Superconducting Magnet in MRI Scanner

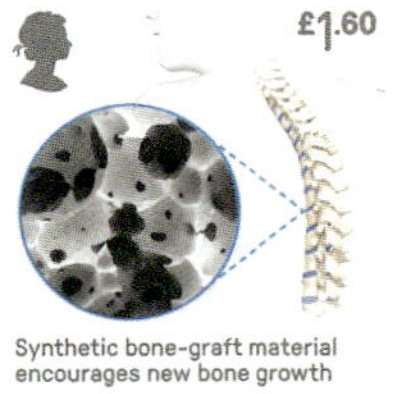

3316 Synthetic Bone-graft

3317 Harrier GR3

(Des Martin Woodward and Common Curiosity (Nos. 4212/4217) or Turner Duckworth (No. **MS**4218). Litho ISP Cartor)

2019 (2 May). British Engineering. Multicoloured. Two phosphor bands. Perf 14½×14 (Nos. 4212/4217) or 14 (No. **MS**4218)

4212	3311	(1st) Raspberry Pi Microcomputer........	1·20	1·00
		a. Horiz pair. Nos. 4212/4213............	2·40	2·00
4213	3312	(1st) The Falkirk Wheel.......................	1·20	1·00
4214	3313	£1·55 Three-way catalytic converter.......	2·40	2·40
		a. Horiz pair. Nos. 4214/4215............	4·75	4·75
4215	3314	£1·55 Crossrail......................................	2·40	2·40
4216	3315	£1·60 Superconducting Magnet.............	2·50	2·50
		a. Horiz pair. Nos. 4216/4217............	5·00	5·00
4217	3316	£1·60 Synthetic Bone-graft material.......	2·50	2·50
Set of 6...			10·75	10·50
Set of 3 *Gutter Pairs* (only 2 stamps in each *Gutter Pair*)...			11·50	
Set of 3 *Traffic Light Gutter Blocks of 4*..................			23·00	
First Day Cover (Tallents House)................................				14·50
First Day Cover (London SW1)...................................				14·50
Presentation Pack (PO Pack No. 570) (Nos. 4212/4217 and **MS**4218)...			20·00	
PHQ Cards (set of 11) (456).......................................			6·50	20·00

MS4218 203×75 mm. **3317** (1st) Harrier GR3 Short Take-off; (1st) Harrier GR3 Conventional Flight; £1·55 Harrier GR3 Transition to Landing; £1·55 Harrier GR3 Vertical Landing.................... 6·75 6·75
First Day Cover (Tallents House)............................... 8·50
First Day Cover (London SW1)................................. 8·50

Nos. 4212/4213, 4214/4215 and 4216/4217 were each printed together, *se-tenant*, as horizontal pairs in sheets of 60 (2 panes 6×5).

The 11 PHQ cards show the ten individual stamps, including those from No. **MS**4218, and the complete sheet.

3318 Queen Victoria (Heinrich von Angeli), 1890

3319 Queen Victoria and Benjamin Disraeli, 1878

3320 Queen Victoria with servant John Brown, 1876

3321 Queen Victoria wearing her Robes of State, 1859

3322 Marriage of Queen Victoria and Prince Albert, 1840

3323 Princess Victoria aged 11, 1830

3324 The Legacy of Prince Albert

(Des Webb & Webb Design. Litho ISP Cartor)

2019 (24 May). Birth Bicentenary of Queen Victoria (1st issue). Multicoloured. Two phosphor bands. Perf 14×14½ (Nos. 4219/4224) or 14 (No. **MS**4225).

4219	3318	(1st) Queen Victoria (Heinrich von Angeli), 1890.................................	1·20	1·00
		a. Horiz pair. Nos. 4219/4220............	2·40	2·00
		b. Booklet pane. Nos. 4219/4221 with margins all round....................	4·25	
4220	3319	(1st) Queen Victoria and Benjamin Disraeli, 1878..................................	1·20	1·00
4221	3320	£1·35 Queen Victoria with Servant John Brown, 1876......................................	2·00	2·00
		a. Horiz pair. Nos. 4221/4222............	4·00	4·00
4222	3321	£1·35 Queen Victoria wearing her Robes of State, 1859.............................	2·00	2·00
		b. Booklet pane. Nos. 4222/4224 with margins all round....................	7·00	
4223	3322	£1·60 Marriage of Queen Victoria and Prince Albert, 1840..............................	2·50	2·50
		a. Horiz pair. Nos. 4223/4224............	5·00	5·00
4224	3323	£1·60 Princess Victoria aged 11, 1830......	2·50	2·50

QUEEN ELIZABETH II/2019

Set of 6	10·50	10·00
Set of 3 Gutter Pairs	21·00	
First Day Cover (Tallents House)		13·50
First Day Cover (East Cowes)		13·50
Presentation Pack (PO Pack No. 571)	20·00	
PHQ Cards (set of 11) (457)	6·50	22·00

MS4225 156×74 mm. **3324** (1st) Model Lodge, Kennington; (1st) Balmoral Castle, Scotland; £1·55 The New Crystal Palace, Sydenham; £1·55 Royal Albert Hall, London ... 18·00 18·00
First Day Cover (Tallents House) ... 20·00
First Day Cover (East Cowes) ... 20·00

Nos. 4219/4220, 4221/4222 and 4223/4224 were each printed together, se-tenant, as horizontal pairs in sheets of 60 (2 panes 6×5).

The 11 PHQ cards show the individual stamps including those from No. **MS**4225 and the complete miniature sheet.

3325 Model Lodge, Kennington
3326 Balmoral Castle, Scotland 
3327 The New Crystal Palace, Sydenham 
3328 Royal Albert Hall, London 

(Des Webb & Webb Design. Litho ISP Cartor)

2019 (24 May). Birth Bicentenary of Queen Victoria (2nd issue). Multicoloured. Two phosphor bands. Perf 14

4226	3325	(1st) Model Lodge, Kennington	3·00	3·00
		a. Booklet pane. Nos. 4226/4229 with margins all round and roulettes at left	28·00	
4227	3326	(1st) Balmoral Castle, Scotland	3·00	3·00
4228	3327	£1·55 The New Crystal Palace, Sydenham	6·00	6·00
4229	3328	£1·55 Royal Albert Hall, London	6·00	6·00
		Set of 4	18·00	18·00

Nos. 4226/4229 come from No. **MS**4225 and £17·20 Queen Victoria premium booklet, No. DY30.

3329 British soldiers are briefed before embarkation

3330 HMS *Warspite* shelling in support of beach landings

3331 Paratroopers synchronising watches

3332 Soldiers wade ashore on Juno Beach

3333 An American light bomber provides air support

3334 British troops take cover as they advance inland

3335 The Normandy Landings

3336 Gold Beach
3337 Sword Beach 

(Des Baxter and Bailey. Litho ISP Cartor (Nos. 4230/**MS**4236) or gravure ISP Walsall (Nos. 4237/4238)

2019 (6 June). 75th Anniversary of D-Day. Multicoloured. Two phosphor bands.

(a) Ordinary gum. Perf 14½.

4230	3329	(1st) No. 4 Commando, 1st Special Service Brigade briefed by Commanding Officer Lieutenant-Colonel R. Dawson before Embarkation	1·20	1·00
		a. Vert pair. Nos. 4230/4231	2·40	2·00
4231	3330	(1st) HMS *Warspite* shelling German Gun Batteries	1·20	1·00
4232	3331	£1·35 Paratroopers	2·00	2·00
		a. Vert pair. Nos. 4232/4233	4·00	4·00
4233	3332	£1·35 Commandos wade ashore on Juno Beach	2·00	2·00
4234	3333	£1·60 American A-20 Havoc Light Bomber	2·50	2·50
		a. Vert pair. Nos. 4234/4235	5·00	5·00
4235	3334	£1·60 Troops take cover from enemy shell	2·50	2·50
		Set of 6	10·25	10·00
		Set of 3 Gutter Pairs (only 2 stamps in each gutter pair)	11·50	
		First Day Cover (Tallents House)		13·00
		First Day Cover (Southwick, Fareham)		13·00
		Presentation Pack (PO Pack No. 572) (Nos. 4230/4235 and **MS**4236)	18·00	
		PHQ Cards (set of 12) (458)	7·00	22·00

292

2019/QUEEN ELIZABETH II

	MS4236 203×75 mm. 3335 (1st)×5 US 4th Infantry Division, Utah Beach; US troops going ashore at Omaha Beach; British 50th Division landing on Gold Beach; Canadian 3rd Division landing at Juno Beach; British 3rd Division landing at Sword Beach.		6·25	6·25
	First Day Cover (Tallents House)			7·50
	First Day Cover (Southwick, Fareham)			7·50
	(b) Self-adhesive. Die-cut perf 14½.			
4237	3336	(1st) British 50th Division landing on Gold Beach	3·25	3·25
		a. Booklet pane. Nos. 4237/4238 and U3027×4	10·00	
4238	3337	(1st) British 3rd Division landing at Sword Beach	3·25	3·25

Nos. 4230/4231, 4232/4233 and 4234/4235 were each printed together, *se-tenant*, as vertical pairs in sheets of 60 (5×6).

Nos. 4237/4238 were issued in stamp booklet, No. PM67, originally sold for £4·20.

The 12 PHQ cards show each of the individual stamps including those from No. **MS**4236 and the complete miniature sheet.

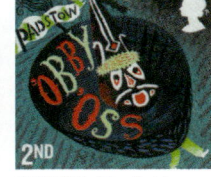

3338 Burning the Clocks, Brighton

3339 'Obby 'Oss, Padstow

3340 World Gurning Championships, Egremont

3341 Up Helly Aa, Lerwick

3342 Halloween, Londonderry

3343 Cheese Rolling, Cooper's Hill

3344 Horn Dance, Abbots Bromley

3345 Bog Snorkelling, Llanwrtyd Wells

(Des Jonny Hannah (illustrations) and NB Studio. Litho ISP Cartor)

2019 (19 July). Curious Customs. Multicoloured. One centre bank (2nd) or two bands (others). Perf 14×14½.

4239	3338	(2nd) Burning the Clocks, Brighton	90	90
		a. Horiz pair. Nos. 4239/4240	1·75	1·75
4240	3339	(2nd) 'Obby 'Oss, Padstow, Cornwall	90	90
4241	3340	(1st) World Gurning Championships, Egremont, Cumbria	1·20	1·00
		a. Horiz pair. Nos. 4241/4242	2·40	2·00
4242	3341	(1st) Up Helly Aa, Lerwick, Shetland	1·20	1·00
4243	3342	£1·55 Halloween, Londonderry	2·40	2·40
		a. Horiz pair. Nos. 4243/4244	4·75	4·75
4244	3343	£1·55 Cheese Rolling, Cooper's Hill, Brockworth, Gloucestershire	2·40	2·40
4245	3344	£1·60 Horn Dance, Abbots Bromley, Staffordshire	2·50	2·50
		a. Horiz pair. Nos. 4245/4246	5·00	5·00
4246	3345	£1·60 Bog Snorkelling, Llanwrtyd Wells, Wales	2·50	2·50
	Set of 8		12·75	12·50
	Set of 4 Gutter Pairs		25·50	
	First Day Cover (Tallents House)			14·00
	First Day Cover (Maypole, Monmouth)			14·00
	Presentation Pack (PO Pack No. 573)		15·00	
	PHQ Cards (set of 8) (459)		5·00	13·00

Nos. 4239/4240, 4241/4242, 4243/4244 and 4245/4246 were each printed together, *se-tenant*, as horizontal pairs in sheets of 60 (2 panes 6×5).

3346 Glen Affric

3347 The National Arboretum, Westonbirt

3348 Sherwood Forest

3349 Coed y Brenin

3350 Glenariff Forest

3351 Kielder Forest

(Des Up. Litho ISP Cartor)

2019 (13 Aug). Forests. Multicoloured. Two phosphor bands. Perf 14½.

4247	3346	(1st) Glen Affric	1·20	1·00
		a. Vert pair. Nos. 4247/4248	2·40	2·00
4248	3347	(1st) The National Arboretum, Westonbirt, Gloucestershire	1·20	1·00

4249	3348	£1·55 Sherwood Forest, Nottinghamshire	2·40	2·40
		a. Vert pair. Nos. 4249/4250	4·75	4·75
4250	3349	£1·55 Coed y Brenin, Gwynedd, Wales	2·40	2·40
4251	3350	£1·60 Glenariff Forest, County Antrim,	2·50	2·50
		a. Vert pair. Nos. 4251/4252	5·00	5·00
4252	3351	£1·60 Kielder Forest	2·50	2·50
Set of 6			10·75	10·50
Set of 3 Gutter Pairs (only 2 stamps in each gutter pair)			12·00	
First Day Cover (Tallents House)				13·50
First Day Cover (Westonbirt, Tetbury)				13·50
Presentation Pack (PO Pack No. 574)			13·00	
PHQ Cards (set of 6) (460)			4·00	12·50

Nos. 4247/4248, 4249/4250 and 4251/4252 were each printed together, *se-tenant*, as vertical pairs in sheets of 60 (2 panes 5×6).

Nos. 4247/4252 commemorate the Centenary of the Forestry Commission.

3352 *Honky Château*

3353 *Goodbye Yellow Brick Road*

3354 *Caribou*

3355 *Captain Fantastic and The Brown Dirt Cowboy*

3356 *Sleeping with The Past*

3357 *The One*

3358 *Made in England*

3359 *Songs from The West Coast*

3360 *Elton John Live*

(Des Royal Mail Group Ltd from original design by Studio Dempsey. Litho ISP Cartor (Nos. 4253/**MS**4261) or gravure ISP Walsall (Nos. 4262/4263)

2019 (3 Sept). Elton John. Multicoloured. Two phosphor bands.

(a) Ordinary gum. Perf 14.

4253	3352	(1st) Honky Château	1·20	1·00
		a. Horiz strip of 4. Nos. 4253/4256	4·25	3·75
4254	3353	(1st) Goodbye Yellow Brick Road	1·20	1·00
4255	3354	(1st) Caribou	1·20	1·00
4256	3355	(1st) Captain Fantastic and The Brown Dirt Cowboy	1·20	1·00
4257	3356	£1·55 Sleeping with The Past	2·40	2·40
		a. Horiz strip of 4. Nos. 4257/4260	9·25	9·25
4258	3357	£1·55 The One	2·40	2·40
4259	3358	£1·55 Made in England	2·40	2·40
4260	3359	£1·55 Songs from The West Coast	2·40	2·40
Set of 8			13·00	12·50
Set of 2 Gutter Strips of 8			26·00	
First Day Cover (Tallents House)				15·50
First Day Cover (Pinner)				15·50
Presentation Pack (PO Pack No. 575) (Nos. 4253/4260 and **MS**4261)			24·00	
Goodbye Yellow Brick Road Character Pack (containing No. 4254×10)			13·00	
Captain Fantastic and The Brown Dirt Cowboy Character Pack (containing No. 4256×10)			13·00	
PHQ Cards (set of 13) (461)			7·50	25·00
MS4261 156×74 mm. **3360** Elton John Live (1st) Madison Square Garden, 2018; (1st) Dodger Stadium, 1975; £1·55 Hammersmith Odeon, 1973; £1·55 Buckingham Palace, 2012			6·75	6·75
First day cover				8·50

(b) Self-adhesive. Die-cut perf 14.

4262	3353	(1st) Goodbye Yellow Brick Road	5·00	5·00
		a. Booklet pane. Nos. 4262/4263 and U3027×4	13·00	
4263	3355	(1st) Captain Fantastic and The Brown Dirt Cowboy	5·00	5·00

Nos. 4253/4256 and 4257/4260 were each printed together, *se-tenant*, as horizontal strips of four stamps in sheets of 48 (2 panes 4×6).

Nos. 4262/4263 were issued in stamp booklet, No. PM68, originally sold for £4·20.

A *Goodbye Yellow Brick Road* fan sheet containing No. 4254×4 was sold for £7·50.

A *Captain Fantastic and The Brown Dirt Cowboy* fan sheet containing No. 4256×4 was sold for £7·50.

The 13 PHQ cards show the individual stamps, including those from No. **MS**4261, and the complete miniature sheet.

3361 *Mary Rose*, 1511

3362 HMS *Queen Elizabeth*, 2014

3363 HMS *Victory*, 1765

3364 HMS *Dreadnought*, 1906

3365 HMS *Warrior*, 1860

3366 *Sovereign of the Seas*, 1637

3367 HMS *King George V*, 1939

3368 HMS *Beagle*, 1820

2019/QUEEN ELIZABETH II

(Des Hat-trick design. Litho ISP Cartor (Nos. 4264/4271) or gravure ISP Walsall (Nos. 4272/4273)

2019 (19 Sept). Royal Navy Ships. Multicoloured. Two phosphor bands.

(a) Ordinary gum. Perf 14.

4264	3361	(1st) *Mary Rose*, 1511 (Geoff Hunt)..........	1·20	1·00
		a. Horiz pair. Nos. 4264/4265..............	2·40	2·00
4265	3362	(1st) HMS *Queen Elizabeth*, 2014 (Robert G. Lloyd)................................	1·20	1·00
4266	3363	£1·35 HMS *Victory*, 1765 (Monamy Swaine)...	2·00	2·00
		a. Horiz pair. Nos. 4266/4267..............	4·00	4·00
4267	3364	£1·35 HMS *Dreadnought*, 1906 (H. J. Morgan)...	2·00	2·00
4268	3365	£1·55 HMS *Warrior*, 1860 (Thomas Goldsworth Dutton)........................	2·40	2·40
		a. Horiz pair. Nos. 4268/4269..............	4·75	4·75
4269	3366	£1·55 *Sovereign of the Seas*, 1637 (Paul Garnett)..	2·40	2·40
4270	3367	£1·60 HMS *King George V*, 1939 (Robert G. Lloyd)..	2·50	2·50
		a. Horiz pair. Nos. 4270/4271..............	5·00	5·00
4271	3368	£1·60 HMS *Beagle*, 1820 (John Chancellor)..	2·50	2·50
		Set of 8...	14·25	14·00
		Set of 4 Gutter Blocks of 4........................	28·50	
		First Day Cover (Tallents House).................		17·00
		First Day Cover (Portsmouth)....................		17·00
		Presentation Pack (PO Pack No. 576).......	17·00	
		PHQ Cards (set of 8) (462)...........................	5·00	16·00

(b) Self-adhesive. Die-cut perf 14.

4272	3361	(1st) *Mary Rose*, 1511 (Geoff Hunt)..........	15·00	15·00
		a. Booklet pane. Nos. 4272/4273 and U3027×4......................................	35·00	
4273	3362	(1st) HMS *Queen Elizabeth*, 2014 (Robert G. Lloyd)................................	15·00	15·00

Nos. 4264/4265, 4266/4267, 4268/4269 and 4270/4271 were each printed together, *se-tenant*, as horizontal pairs in sheets of 60 (2 panes 6×5).

Nos. 4272/4273 were issued in stamp booklet, No. PM69, originally sold for £4·20.

3369 Men's Cricket World Cup Winners

3370 Women's Cricket World Cup Winners

(Litho ISP Cartor)

2019 (26 Sept). ICC Cricket World Cup Winners. Multicoloured. All over phosphor. Perf 14½.

MS4274	203×74 mm. **3369** (1st) England Captain Eoin Morgan lifting Cricket World Cup Trophy; (1st) Eoin Morgan (with trophy) and England team; £1·60 England players celebrating; £1·60 England players congratulating Ben Stokes............................	6·75	6·75
MS4275	203×74 mm. **3370** (1st) England team after their victory ('CHAMPIONS'); (1st) England players congratulating Anya Shrubsole; £1·60 England Captain Heather Knight and teammates celebrating; £1·60 England team celebrating on balcony at Lord's Cricket Ground (2017)................................	6·75	6·75
	First Day Cover (Tallents House) (2)................................		16·00
	First Day Covers (London NW8) (2)...............................		16·00
	Presentation Pack (PO Pack No. M25)..........................	16·00	

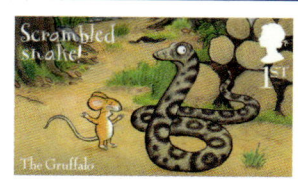

3371 'Scrambled snake!'

3372 'Gruffalo crumble!'

3373 'All was quiet in the deep dark wood.'

3374 'A mouse took a stroll'

3375 'Roasted fox!'

3376 'Owl ice cream?'

295

QUEEN ELIZABETH II/2019

3377 The Gruffalo

(Des Rose Design. Litho ISP Cartor)

2019 (10 Oct). *The Gruffalo* (by Julia Donaldson, Illustrated by Axel Scheffler). Multicoloured. Two phosphor bands. Perf 14 (No. 4276/4281) or 14½ (No. **MS**4282).

4276	**3371**	(1st) 'Scrambled snake!'...............................	1·20	1·00
		a. Horiz strip of 3. Nos. 4276/4278......	3·50	3·00
4277	**3372**	(1st) 'Gruffalo crumble!'...............................	1·20	1·00
4278	**3373**	(1st) 'All was quiet in the deep dark wood.'..	1·20	1·00
4279	**3374**	£1·60 'A mouse took a stroll'.....................	2·50	2·50
		a. Horiz strip of 3. Nos. 4279/4281.....	7·50	7·50
4280	**3375**	£1·60 'Roasted fox!'.....................................	2·50	2·50
4281	**3376**	£1·60 'Owl ice cream?'...............................	2·50	2·50

Set of 6... 10·00 9·50
Set of 2 Gutter Strips of 6.. 11·50
First Day Cover (Tallents House)....................................... 12·50
First Day Cover (Mousehole, Penzance).......................... 12·50
Presentation Pack (PO Pack No. 577) (Nos. 4276/4278 and **MS**4282).. 19·00
PHQ Cards (set of 11) (463).. 7·50 22·00
MS4282 126×89 mm. **3377** (1st) Owl; (1st) Mouse; £1·55 Snake; £1·55 Fox.. 6·75 6·75
First Day Cover (Tallents House)....................................... 8·50
First Day Cover (Mousehole, Penzance).......................... 8·50

Nos. 4276/4278 and 4279/4281 were each printed together, *se-tenant*, as horizontal strips of three stamps in sheets of 60 (2 panes 6×5).

Stamps as within No. **MS**4282 but self-adhesive were issued in sheets of ten (No. LS117) sold for £11·50, containing three of each of the two 1st class designs and two of each of the two £1·55 designs, with attached labels.

The 11 PHQ cards show the individual stamps, including those from No. **MS**4282, and the complete miniature sheet.

3378 Angel and Shepherd

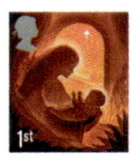

3379 Mary and Baby Jesus

3380 Angel and Shepherd

3381 Mary and Baby Jesus

3382 Joseph

3383 Baby Jesus in Manger

3384 Shepherds and Star

3385 Three Wise Men

(Des Hari & Deepti (illustrations) and Charlie Smith Design. Gravure ISP Walsall (No. 4283/4290) or litho ISP Cartor (No. **MS**4291).

2019 (5 Nov). Christmas. Nativity. Multicoloured. One central band (No. 4283) or two (others). Perf 14½×15.

(a) Self-adhesive. Gravure.

4283	**3378**	(2nd) Angel and Shepherd......................	90	90
		a. Booklet pane. No. 4283×12............	17·00	
4284	**3379**	(1st) Mary and Baby Jesus......................	1·20	1·00
		a. Booklet pane. No. 4284×12............	16·00	
4285	**3380**	(2nd Angel and Shepherd Large)...	1·25	1·25
4286	**3381**	(1st Mary and Baby Jesus Large)...	1·70	1·60
4287	**3382**	£1·35 Joseph..	2·00	2·00
4288	**3383**	£1·55 Baby Jesus in Manger....................	2·40	2·40
4289	**3384**	£1·60 Shepherds and Star.......................	2·50	2·50
4290	**3385**	£2·30 Three Wise Men..............................	3·50	3·50

Set of 8... 13·75 13·50
First Day Cover (Tallents House)....................................... 17·00
First Day Cover (Bethlehem, Llandeilo).......................... 17·00
Presentation Pack (PO Pack No. 578)............................. 17·00
PHQ Cards (set of 9) (464).. 6·00 28·00

(b) Ordinary gum. Litho.

MS4291 179×74 mm. Nos. 4283/4290................................ 13·75 13·50
First Day Cover (Tallents House)....................................... 17·00
First Day Cover (Bethlehem, Llandeilo).......................... 17·00

The 2nd class, 1st class, £1·35, £1·55, £1·60 and £2·30 values were also issued in sheets of 20 (No. LS118) containing eight 2nd class, eight 1st class and one each of the £1·35, £1·55, £1·60 and £2·30 values, each stamp accompanied by a *se-tenant* label. These sheets were printed in lithography and originally sold for £18·40.

The nine PHQ cards show the individual stamps and the complete miniature sheet.

3386 Count Dooku

3387 Lando Calrissian

3388 Sith Trooper

3389 Jannah

3390 Grand Moff Tarkin

3391 Darth Maul

2019/QUEEN ELIZABETH II

3392 Zorii
3393 Wicket W. Warrick 
3394 Poe Dameron 
3395 Queen Amidala 
3395a *Star Wars* Composite Sheet 
3396 *Star Wars* Vehicles 

(Des Malcolm Tween (illustrations) and Interabang. Litho ISP Cartor (Nos. 4292/**MS**4303) or gravure ISP Walsall (Nos. 4304/4305).

2019 (26 Nov). *Star Wars*. (5th issue). Multicoloured. 'All-over' phosphor (No. **MS**4303 stamp only) or two phosphor bands (others).

(a) Ordinary gum. Perf 14½.

4292	3386	(1st) Count Dooku (Christopher Lee)......	1·20	1·00
		a. Horiz strip of 5. Nos. 4292/4296......	5·25	5·00
		b. Booklet pane. Nos. 4292, 4294/4296, 4299 and 4300 with margins all round.............	6·50	
4293	3387	(1st) Lando Calrissian (Billy Dee Williams)..	1·20	1·00
		b. Booklet pane. Nos. 4293, 4297/4298 and 4301 with margins all round............	4·25	
4294	3388	(1st) Sith Trooper.............................	1·20	1·00
4295	3389	(1st) Jannah (Naomi Ackie)..............	1·20	1·00
4296	3390	(1st) Grand Moff Tarkin (Peter Cushing)	1·20	1·00
4297	3391	(1st) Darth Maul (Ray Park).............	1·20	1·00
		a. Horiz strip of 5. Nos. 4297/4301......	5·25	5·00
4298	3392	(1st) Zorii (Kerri Russell)...................	1·20	1·00
4299	3393	(1st) Wicket W. Warrick (Warwick Davis)...	1·20	1·00
4300	3394	(1st) Poe Dameron (Oscar Isaac).....	1·20	1·00
4301	3395	(1st) Queen Amidala (Natalie Portman)	1·20	1·00
Set of 10..			£911	9·00
Set of 2 Gutter Strips of 10...........................			21·00	
First Day Cover (Tallents House)..................				12·00
First Day Cover (Maulden, Bedford).............				12·00

Presentation Pack (PO Pack No. 579) (Nos. 4292/4301 and **MS**4303)...		20·00	
PHQ Cards (set of 16)..		11·50	20·00
MS4302 210×297 mm. Nos. 3758/3769, 4007/4014 and 4292/4301		35·00	50·00

(b) Self-adhesive.

MS4303 192×74 mm. **3396** (1st) Poe's X-wing fighter (41×30 mm) (Perf 14); (1st) Jedi starfighter (27×37 mm) (Perf 14); (1st) Slave 1 (27×37 mm) (Perf 14); (1st) TIE silencer (41×30 mm) (Perf 14); (1st) Podracers (60×21 mm) (Perf 14½×14); (1st) Speeder bikes (60×21 mm) (Perf 14½×14)........................ 7·00 7·00
First Day Cover (Tallents House)... 8·75
First Day Cover (Maulden, Bedford)... 8·75

(c) Self-adhesive. Die-cut perf 14½.

4304	3394	(1st) Poe Dameron (Oscar Isaac).............	1·75	1·75
		a. Booklet pane. Nos. 4304/4305 and U3027×4.................................	6·75	
4305	3388	(1st) Sith Trooper................................	1·75	1·75

Nos. 4292/4296 and 4297/4301 were each printed together, *se-tenant*, as horizontal strips of five stamps in sheets of 50 (2 panes 5×5).

Nos. 4304/4305 were issued in stamp booklet, No. PM70, originally sold for £4·20.

A collectors sheet (No. LS120) containing stamps as Nos. 4292/4301 but self-adhesive with labels showing film scenes was sold for £8·10, a £1·10 premium over face value.

The three *Star Wars* presentation packs from 2015, 2017 and 2019, containing Nos. 3758/3769 and **MS**3770 (PO Pack No. 518), Nos. 4007/4014 (PO Pack No. 547) and Nos. 4292/4301 and **MS**4303 (PO Pack No. 579) were issued in a trilogy by Royal Mail for £29·99.

3397 Poe's X-wing Fighter
3398 Jedi Starfighter 
3399 Podracers 
3400 Slave 1 
3401 TIE Silencer 
3402 Speeder Bikes 

2019 (26 Nov). *Star Wars* (6th issue). Multicoloured. 'All-over' phosphor (stamps only). Self-adhesive. Die-cut perf 14 (Nos. 4306/4307, 4309/4310) or 14½×14 (Nos. 4308, 4311).

4306	3397	(1st) Poe's X-wing Fighter........................	1·30	1·30
		a. Booklet pane. Nos. 4306/4308........	3·50	
4307	3398	(1st) Jedi Starfighter................................	1·30	1·30
4308	3399	(1st) Podracers...	1·30	1·30
4309	3400	(1st) Slave 1..	1·30	1·30
		a. Booklet pane. Nos. 4309/4311........	3·50	
4310	3401	(1st) TIE Silencer.......................................	1·30	1·30
4311	3402	(1st) Speeder Bikes...................................	1·30	1·30
Set of 6...			7·00	7·00

Nos. 4306/4311 were issued in No. **MS**4303 and in booklet panes 4306a and 4309a from the £17·65 *Star Wars* The Making of the Vehicles booklet, No. DY31.

QUEEN ELIZABETH II/2019

2019 (26 Nov). Collectors Pack 2019.
CP4311a   Collectors Pack (PO Pack No. 580)
          (sold for £156) £300

2019 (26 Nov). Post Office Yearbook 2019.
YB4311a   Yearbook (sold for £176) £350

2019 (26 Nov). Miniature Sheet Collection.
MS4311a Miniature Sheet Collection (sold for £58) .... 85·00

3403 *Elite*, 1984

3404 *Worms*, 1995

3405 *Sensible Soccer*, 1992

3406 *Lemmings*, 1991

3407 *Wipeout*, 1995

3408 *Micro Machines*, 1991

3409 *Dizzy*, 1987

3410 *Populous*, 1989

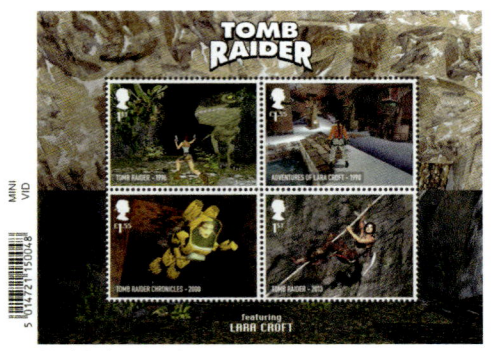

3411 *Tomb Raider*

3412 *Tomb Raider*, 1996    **3413** *Tomb Raider*, 2013

(Des Supple Studio and Bitmap Books. Litho ISP Cartor (Nos. 4312/4320) or gravure Walsall (Nos. 4321/4322))

2020 (21 Jan). Video Games. Multicoloured.
(a) Ordinary gum. Band at right (No. 4312), centre band (No. 4313) or two bands (others). Perf 14.

4312	3403	(2nd) *Elite*, 1984	90	90
		a. Vert pair. Nos. 4312/4313	1·75	1·75
4313	3404	(2nd) *Worms*, 1995	90	90
4314	3405	(1st) *Sensible Soccer*, 1992	1·20	1·00
		a. Vert pair. Nos. 4314/4315	2·40	2·00
4315	3406	(1st) *Lemmings*, 1991	1·20	1·00
4316	3407	£1·55 *Wipeout*, 1995	2·40	2·40
		a. Vert pair. Nos. 4316/4317	4·75	4·75
4317	3408	£1·55 *Micro Machines*, 1991	2·40	2·40
4318	3409	£1·60 *Dizzy*, 1987	2·50	2·50
		a. Vert pair. Nos. 4318/4319	5·00	5·00
4319	3410	£1·60 *Populous*, 1989	2·50	2·50
Set of 8			12·75	12·50
Set of 4 Gutter Blocks of 4			25·50	
First Day Cover (Tallents House)				17·00
First Day Cover (Sheffield)				17·00
Presentation Pack (PO Pack No. 581) (Nos. 4312/4319 and **MS**4320)			20·00	
PHQ Cards (set of 13)			8·75	25·00
MS4320 126×90 mm. **3411** (1st) *Tomb Raider*, 1996; (1st) *Tomb Raider*, 2013; £1·55 *Adventures of Lara Croft*, 1998; £1·55 *Tomb Raider Chronicles*, 2000			6·75	6·75
First Day Cover (Tallents House)				9·25
First Day Cover (Sheffield)				9·25

(b) Self-adhesive. Two phosphor bands. Die-cut perf 14.

4321	3412	(1st) *Tomb Raider*, 1996	5·25	5·25
		a. Booklet pane. Nos. 4321/4322 and U3027×4	14·00	
4322	3413	(1st) *Tomb Raider*, 2013	5·25	5·25

Nos. 4312/4313, 4314/4315, 4316/4317 and 4318/4319 were printed together, *se-tenant*, as vertical pairs in sheets of 60 (2 panes 5×6).

Nos. 4312/4322 have hidden features in UV ink.

Nos. 4321/4322 were issued in stamp booklet, No. PM71, originally sold for £4·20.

Stamps as within No. **MS**4320 but self-adhesive were issued in sheets of ten (No. LS121) containing three of each of the 1st class designs and two of each of the £1·55 designs, with *se-tenant* labels. These sheets were printed in lithography and originally sold for £11·40.

A Gamer Collectors Pack with eight postcards, each with stamp affixed, and certificate of authenticity all packed inside silver case, was originally sold for £14·95. It was a limited edition of 2,500 units.

The 13 PHQ cards show the 12 individual stamps, including those from No. **MS**4320, and the complete miniature sheet.

2020/QUEEN ELIZABETH II

3414 Cat's Eye Nebula

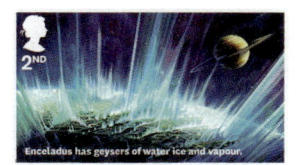

3415 Enceladus

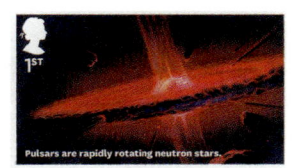

3416 Pulsars

3417 Black Holes

3418 Jupiter's Auroras

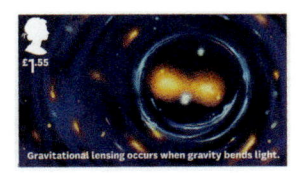

3419 Gravitational Lensing

3420 Comet 67P

3421 Cygnus A Galaxy

(Des True North. Litho ISP Cartor)

2020 (11 Feb). Visions of the Universe. Multicoloured. One centre band (2nd) or two bands (others). Perf 14.

4323	3414	(2nd) Cat's Eye Nebula	90	90
		a. Horiz pair. Nos. 4323/4324	1·75	1·75
		b. Booklet pane. Nos. 4323, 4325, 4327 and 4329 with margins all round	7·00	
4324	3415	(2nd) Enceladus (Saturn's moon)	90	90
		b. Booklet pane. Nos. 4324, 4326, 4328 and 4330 with margins all round	7·00	
4325	3416	(1st) Pulsars	1·25	1·25
		a. Horiz pair. Nos. 4325/4326	2·50	2·50
4326	3417	(1st) Black holes	1·25	1·25
4327	3418	£1·55 Jupiter's auroras	2·40	2·40
		a. Horiz pair. Nos. 4327/4328	4·75	4·75
4328	3419	£1·55 Gravitational lensing	2·40	2·40
4329	3420	£1·60 Comet 67P	2·50	2·50
		a. Horiz pair. Nos. 4329/4330	5·00	5·00
4330	3421	£1·60 Cygnus A	2·50	2·50
Set of 8			12·50	12·50
Set of 4 Gutter Pairs			25·00	
First Day Cover (Tallents House)				17·00
First Day Cover (London W1)				17·00
Presentation Pack (PO Pack No. 582)			15·00	
PHQ Cards (set of 8)			5·50	15·00

Nos. 4323/4324, 4325/4326, 4327/4328 and 4329/4330 were each printed together, *se-tenant*, as horizontal pairs in sheets of 60 (2 panes 6×5).

Booklet panes Nos. 4323b and 4324b are from the £16·55 Visions of the Universe prestige booklet, No. DY32.

(Des Sedley Place. Gravure ISP Walsall)

2020 (10 Mar). London 2020 International Stamp Exhibition. Multicoloured. Self-adhesive. Two phosphor bands. Die-cut perf 14½×14 (with one elliptical hole in each vert side).

4331	2938	(1st) Two Pence Blue	1·25	1·25
		a. Booklet pane. Nos. 3709, 3806 and 4331, each×2	7·50	

Booklet pane 4331a comes from booklet No. MB21, originally sold for £4·20.

3422 James Bond in *Casino Royale*

3423 James Bond in *Goldeneye*

3424 James Bond in *The Living Daylights*

3425 James Bond in *Live and Let Die*

3426 James Bond in *On Her Majesty's Secret Service*

3427 James Bond in *Goldfinger*

3428 Q Branch

3429 Bell-Textron Jet Pack, *Thunderball*

3430 Aston Martin DB5, *Skyfall*

(Des Interabang. Litho ISP Cartor (Nos. 4332/4337) or gravure ISP Walsall (Nos. 4339/4340))

2020 (17 Mar). James Bond. Multicoloured. (a) Ordinary gum. Two phosphor bands or 'all-over' phosphor (No. **MS**4338). Perf 14½ (No. 4332/4337) or 14×14½ (£1·55) or 14 (1st) (No. **MS**4338).

4332	3422	(1st) James Bond (Daniel Craig) in Casino Royale	1·25	1·25
		a. Horiz strip of 3. Nos. 4332/4334	3·75	3·75
		b. Booklet pane. Nos. 4332/4335 with margins all round	6·25	
4333	3423	(1st) James Bond (Pierce Brosnan) in Goldeneye	1·25	1·25
4334	3424	(1st) James Bond (Timothy Dalton) in The Living Daylights	1·25	1·25
4335	3425	£1·60 James Bond (Roger Moore) in Live and Let Die	2·50	2·50
4336	3426	£1·60 James Bond (George Lazenby) in On Her Majesty's Secret Service	2·50	2·50
		b. Booklet pane. Nos. 4336/4337 with margins all round	5·00	
4337	3427	£1·60 James Bond (Sean Connery) in Goldfinger	2·50	2·50
Set of 6			10·50	10·50
Set of 2 Gutter Strips of 6			21·00	
First Day Cover (Tallents House)				13·50
First Day Cover (Spy Post, Wellington)				13·50
Presentation Pack (PO Pack No. 583)			19·00	
PHQ Cards (set of 11)			7·50	22·00

MS4338		202×74 mm. **3428** (1st) Bell-Textron Jet Pack, *Thunderball*; (1st) Aston Martin DB5, *Skyfall*; £1·55 Lotus Esprit Submarine, *The Spy Who Loved Me*; £1·55 Little Nellie, *You Only Live Twice*	6·75	6·75
First Day Cover (Tallents House)				9·25
First Day Cover (Spy Post, Wellington)				9·25

(b) Self-adhesive. 'All-over' phosphor. Die-cut perf 14.

4339	3429	(1st) Bell-Textron Jet Pack, *Thunderball*.	5·25	5·25
		a. Booklet pane. Nos. 4339/4340 and U3027×4	14·00	
4340	3430	(1st) Aston Martin DB5, *Skyfall*	5·25	5·25

Nos. 4332/4334 and 4335/4337 were each printed together, *se-tenant*, as horizontal strips of three in sheets of 36 (2 panes 3×6).

Stamps from No. **MS**4338 have '007' perforations at top right, top left, bottom right or bottom left.

Nos. 4339/4340 were issued in stamp booklet, No. PM72, originally sold for £4·20.

Booklet panes Nos. 4332b and 4336b were issued in the £16·99 James Bond prestige booklet, No. DY33.

A collector's sheet (No. LS122) with stamps as Nos 4332/4337 but perforated 14 with attached labels showing film scenes was originally sold for £12·60. It contained Nos. 4332×2, 4333/4336 and 4337×3.

A *No Time to Die* collector's sheet (No. LS128) containing ten self-adhesive stamps as T **3430** perforated 14×14½ with attached labels showing film scenes was issued on 3 November 2020 and sold for £8·80.

The 11 PHQ cards show the ten individual stamps, including those from No. **MS**4338, and the complete miniature sheet.

3431 Little Nellie, *You Only Live Twice*

3432 Lotus Esprit Submarine, *The Spy Who Loved Me*

(Litho ISP Cartor)

2020 (17 Mar). James Bond (2nd issue). Multicoloured. 'All-over' phosphor. Perf 14 (1st) or 14×14½ (£1·55), all with '007' perforations at top right, top left, bottom right or bottom left.

4341	3429	(1st) Bell-Textron Jet Pack, *Thunderball*	1·25	1·25
		a. Booklet pane. Nos. 4341/4344 with margins all round	7·25	
4342	3430	(1st) Aston Martin DB5, *Skyfall*	1·25	1·25
4343	3431	£1·55 Little Nellie, *You Only Live Twice*	2·40	2·40
4344	3432	£1·55 Lotus Esprit Submarine, *The Spy Who Loved Me*	2·40	2·40
Set of 4			7·25	7·25

Nos. 4341/4344 were issued in No. **MS**4338 and in booklet pane No. 4341a from £16·99 James Bond booklet, No. DY33.

3433 *The Progress of Rhyme* (John Clare)

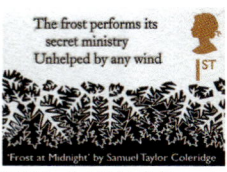

3434 *Frost at Midnight* (Samuel Taylor Coleridge)

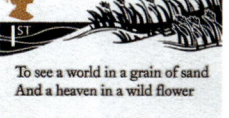

3435 *Auguries of Innocence* (William Blake)

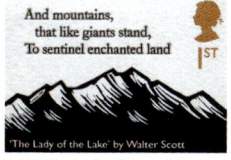

3436 *The Lady of the Lake* (Walter Scott)

3437 *To a Skylark* (Percy Bysshe Shelley)

3438 *The Rainbow* (William Wordsworth)

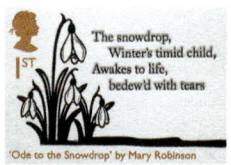

3439 *Ode to the Snowdrop* (Mary Robinson)

3440 *The Fate of Adelaide* (Letitia Elizabeth Landon)

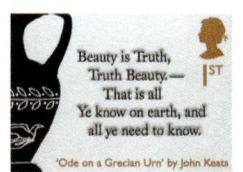

3441 *Ode to a Grecian Urn* (John Keats)

3442 *She Walks in Beauty* (Lord Byron)

(Des The Chase. Litho ISP Cartor)

2020 (7 Apr). Romantic Poets. Black and orange-brown. Two phosphor bands. Perf 14.

4345	**3433**	(1st) *The Progress of Rhyme* (John Clare)	1·25	1·25
		a. Horiz strip of 5. Nos. 4345/4349	6·25	6·25
4346	**3434**	(1st) *Frost at Midnight* (Samuel Taylor Coleridge)	1·25	1·25
4347	**3435**	(1st) *Auguries of Innocence* (William Blake)	1·25	1·25
4348	**3436**	(1st) *The Lady of the Lake* (Walter Scott)	1·25	1·25
4349	**3437**	(1st) *To a Skylark* (Percy Bysshe Shelley)	1·25	1·25
4350	**3438**	(1st) *The Rainbow* (William Wordsworth)	1·25	1·25
		a. Horiz strip of 5. Nos. 4350/4354	6·25	6·25
4351	**3439**	(1st) *Ode to the Snowdrop* (Mary Robinson)	1·25	1·25
4352	**3440**	(1st) *The Fate of Adelaide* (Letitia Elizabeth Landon)	1·25	1·25
4353	**3441**	(1st) *Ode on a Grecian Urn* (John Keats)	1·25	1·25
4354	**3442**	(1st) *She Walks in Beauty* (Lord Byron)	1·25	1·25
Set of 10			11·50	11·50
Set of 2 Gutter Strips of 10			23·00	
First Day Cover (Tallents House)				13·50
First Day Cover (Grasmere, Ambleside)				13·50
Presentation Packs (PO Pack No. 584)			13·50	
PHQ Cards (set of 10) (469)			5·75	13·00

Nos. 4345/4349 and 4350/4354 were printed together, *se-tenant*, as horizontal strips of five in sheets of 50 (2 panes 5×5).

3442a

(Litho ISP Cartor)

2020 (6 May). 180th Anniversary of the Penny Black. As T **2848** but ordinary gum. Litho. Perf 14½×14 (with one elliptical hole in each vert side).

MS4355 122×141 mm. **3442a** (1st) Penny Black×25 .... 40·00 40·00

No. **MS**4355 was issued in sheets of 25 stamps and originally sold for £19.

3443 Servicemen returning home

3444 Nurses Celebrating

3445 Crowd Celebrating

3446 Evacuees Returning

3447 Marching Troops

3448 Demobilised Servicemen

3449 Liberated Prisoners

3450 Navy Personnel Celebrating

QUEEN ELIZABETH II/2020

3451 Memorials

(Des Hat-trick design (photo colourisation (Nos. 4356/4363) Royston Leonard). Litho ISP Cartor)

2020 (8 May). 75th Anniversary of the End of the Second World War (1st issue). Multicoloured. One centre band (2nd) or two phosphor bands (others). Perf 14 (Nos. 4356/4363) or 14½ (No. **MS**4364).

4356	3443	(2nd) Serviceman Returning Home........	90	90
		a. Vert pair. Nos. 4356/4357................	1·75	1·75
		b. Booklet pane. Nos. 4356/4359 with margins all round.....................	4·25	
4357	3444	(2nd) Nurses celebrating VE Day, Liverpool, 1945...............................	90	90
4358	3445	(1st) Crowds celebrating VE Day, Piccadilly, London, 1945.................	1·25	1·25
		a. Vert pair. Nos. 4358/4359................	2·50	2·50
4359	3446	(1st) Evacuee children returning home, London, 1945..................................	1·25	1·25
4360	3447	£1·42 Troops march along Oxford Street, London, 1945.......................	2·00	2·00
		a. Vert pair. Nos. 4360/4361................	4·00	4·00
		b. Booklet pane. Nos. 4360/4363 with margins all round.....................	8·50	
4361	3448	£1·42 Soldiers and sailors leaving demobilisation centre with boxes of civilian clothes...............................	2·00	2·00
4362	3449	£1·63 Liberated Allied prisoners of war, Aomori Camp, near Yokohama, Japan..	2·25	2·25
		a. Vert pair. Nos. 4362/4363................	4·50	4·50
4363	3450	£1·63 Navy personnel in VE Day celebrations, Glasgow, 1945............	2·25	2·25
Set of 8..			11·50	11·50
Set of 4 Gutter Strips of 4..			23·00	
First Day Cover (Tallents House)..				14·00
First Day Cover (London SW1)...				14·00
Presentation Pack (PO Pack No. 585) (Nos. 4356/4363 and **MS**4364)..			20·00	
PHQ Cards (set of 13) (470)...			7·75	20·00
MS4364 202×74 mm. **3451** (1st) Hall of Names, Holocaust History Museum, Yad Vashem, Jerusalem; (1st) Runnymede Memorial; £1·63 Plymouth Naval Memorial; £1·63 Rangoon Memorial, Myanmar (all 60×30 mm)..			6·75	6·75
First Day Cover (Tallents House)..				9·00
First Day Cover (London SW1)...				9·00

Nos. 4356/4357, 4358/4359, 4360/4361 and 4362/4363 were printed together, *se-tenant*, as vertical pairs in sheets of 60 (2 panes 5×6).

The 13 PHQ cards show the ten individual stamps, including those from No. **MS**4364 and the complete miniature sheet.

3452 Hall of Names, Holocaust History Museum, Yad Vashem, Jerusalem

3453 Runnymede Memorial

3454 Plymouth Naval Memorial

3455 Rangoon Memorial, Myanmar

(Des Hat-trick design. Litho ISP Cartor)

2020 (8 May). 75th Anniversary of the End of the Second World War (2nd issue). Multicoloured. Two phosphor bands. Perf 14½.

4365	3452	(1st) Hall of Names, Holocaust History Museum, Yad Vashem, Jerusalem..	1·75	1·75
		a. Booklet pane. Nos. 4365/4368 with margins all round.....................	9·50	
4366	3453	(1st) Runnymede Memorial.....................	1·75	1·75
4367	3454	£1·63 Plymouth Naval Memorial..............	3·00	3·00
4368	3455	£1·63 Rangoon Memorial, Myanmar.......	3·00	3·00
Set of 4..			9·50	9·50

Nos. 4365/4368 were issued in No. **MS**4364 and in booklet pane No. 4365a from the £19·80 75th Anniversary of the End of the Second World War booklet, No. DY34.

3456 'That woman's tongue...' (Edna Sharples and Elsie Tanner)

3457 'Woman, Stanley, Woman' (Stan and Hilda Ogden)

3458 'Vera my little swamp duck' (Jack and Vera Duckworth)

3459 'Ken! do something!' (Deirdre and Ken Barlow)

3460 'I can't abide to see...' (Rita Sullivan and Norris Cole)

3461 'Be nice if everyday...' (Hayley and Roy Cropper)

3462 'I love you...' (Dev and Sunita Alahan)

3463 'I always thought...' (Tracy Barlow and Steve McDonald)

2020/QUEEN ELIZABETH II

3464 *Rovers Return* Barmaids

(Des The Chase. ISP Cartor (Nos. 4369/4376) or gravure ISP Walsall (Nos. 4378/4379))

2020 (28 May). *Coronation Street*. Multicoloured. One centre band (2nd) or two phosphor bands (others)

(a) Ordinary gum. Perf 14.

4369	3456	(2nd) 'That woman's tongue... (Ena Sharples and Elsie Tanner)..............	90	90
		a. Horiz pair. Nos. 4369/4370............	1·75	1·75
4370	3457	(2nd) 'Woman, Stanley, woman.' Stan and Hilda Ogden.....................	90	90
4371	3458	(1st) 'Vera, my little swamp duck.' (Jack and Vera Duckworth)......................	1·25	1·25
		a. Horiz pair. Nos. 4371/4372............	2·50	2·50
4372	3459	(1st) 'Ken! Do something!' (Deirdre and Ken Barlow)........................	1·25	1·25
4373	3460	£1·42 'I can't abide to see people gossiping.' (Rita Sullivan and Norris Cole).....................	2·00	2·00
		a. Horiz pair. Nos. 4373/4374............	4·00	4·00
4374	3461	£1·42 'Be nice if every day...'(Hayley and Roy Cropper).......................	2·00	2·00
4375	3462	£1·63 'I love you...' (Dev and Sunita Alahan).............................	2·25	2·25
		a. Horiz pair. Nos. 4375/4376............	4·50	4·50
4376	3463	£1·63 'I always thought...' (Tracy Barlow and Steve McDonald)..................	2·25	2·25
Set of 8........................			11·50	11·50
Set of 8 Gutter Pairs..................			23·00	
First Day Cover (Tallents House)........................				14·00
First Day Cover (Salford)........................				14·00
Presentation Pack (PO Pack No. 586) (Nos. 4369/4376 and **MS**4377)........................			20·00	
PHQ Card (set of 13) (471)..................			7·50	22·00

MS4377 156×74 mm. **3464** (1st) Bet Lynch; (1st) Raquel Watts; £1·42 Liz McDonald; £1·42 Gemma Winter (all 27×36 mm)................... 6·50 6·50

First Day Cover (Tallents House)........................		9·00
First Day Cover (Salford)........................		9·00

(b) Self-adhesive. Die-cut perf 14.

4378	3458	(1st) 'Vera, my little swamp duck.' (Vera and Jack Duckworth)...................	1·75	1·75
		a. Booklet pane. Nos. 4378/4379 and U3027×4.........................	7·50	
4379	3457	(1st) 'Ken! Do something!' (Deirdre and Ken Barlow)........................	1·75	1·75

Nos. 4369/4370, 4371/4372, 4373/4374 and 4375/4376 were printed together, *se-tenant*, as horizontal pairs in sheets of 60 (2 panes 6×5).

Nos. 4378/4379 were issued in stamp booklet, No. PM73, originally sold for £4·56.

Stamps as Nos. 4371/4372 but self-adhesive and perf 14×14½ were issued in collector's sheets containing five of each design, (No. LS123), sold for £8·80.

The 13 PHQ cards show the 12 individual stamps, including those from No. **MS**4377, and the complete miniature sheet.

3467 Amphitheatre at Isca Fortress, Caerleon

3468 Ribchester Helmet

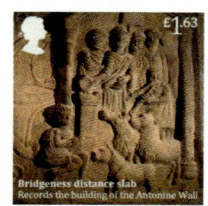

3469 Bridgeness Distance Slab at Eastern end of Antonine Wall

3470 Copper-alloy Figurine of Warrior God, Cambridgeshire

3471 Gorgon's Head from Temple to Sulis Minerva, Bath

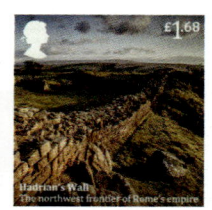

3472 Hadrian's Wall

(Des Up. Litho ISP Cartor)

2020 (18 June). Roman Britain. Multicoloured. One centre band (2nd) or two bands (others). Perf 14½×14.

4380	3465	(2nd) Dover Lighthouse........................	90	90
		a. Horiz pair. Nos. 4380/4381...............	1·75	1·75
4381	3466	(2nd) Bignor Mosaic........................	90	90
4382	3467	(1st) Amphitheatre, Caerleon........	1·25	1·25
		a. Horiz pair. Nos. 4382/4383...............	2·50	2·50
4383	3468	(1st) Ribchester Helmet........................	1·25	1·25
4384	3469	£1·63 Bridgeness distance slab, Antonine Wall........................	2·25	2·25
		a. Horiz pair. Nos. 4384/4385...............	4·50	4·50
4385	3470	£1·63 Copper-alloy figurine of Warrior God, Cambridgeshire.................	2·25	2·25
4386	3471	£1·68 Gorgon's head, Bath................	2·40	2·40
		a. Horiz pair. Nos. 4386/4387...............	4·75	4·75
4387	3472	£1·68 Hadrian's Wall........................	2·40	2·40
Set of 8........................			12·00	12·00
Set of 4 Gutter Pairs (only 2 stamps in each gutter pair)..			14·00	
Set of 4 Traffic Light Gutter Blocks (4 stamps in each gutter block)........................			28·00	
First Day Cover (Tallents House)........................				14·50
First Day Cover (Colchester)........................				14·50
Presentation Pack (PO Pack No. 587).................			14·00	
PHQ Cards (set of 8) (472)........................			4·75	13·00

Nos. 4380/4381, 4382/4383, 4384/4385 and 4386/4387 were each printed together, *se-tenant*, as horizontal pairs in sheets of 60 (2 panes 6×5).

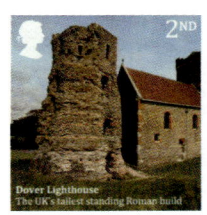

3465 Dover Lighthouse

3466 Bignor Mosaic

3473 *Queen II*, 1974

3474 *Sheer Heart Attack*, 1974

3475 *A Night At The Opera*, 1975

3476 *News of the World*, 1977

3477 *The Game*, 1980

3478 *Greatest Hits*, 1981

3479 *The Works*, 1984

3480 *Innuendo*, 1991

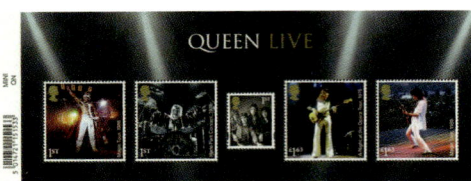

3481 Queen Live

3482 Freddie Mercury, Magic Tour, Wembley Stadium, 1986

3483 Roger Taylor, Hyde Park Concert, 1976

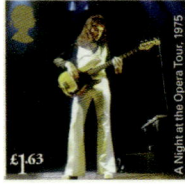

3484 John Deacon, A Night at the Opera Tour, Hammersmith Odeon, 1975

3485 Brian May, Magic Tour, Nepstadion, Budapest, 1986

Nos. 4388/4395 were printed together, *se-tenant*, as horizontal strips of four stamps in sheets of 24 (2 panes 4×6).

Nos. 4397/4398 were issued in stamp booklet, No. PM74, originally sold for £4·56.

Stamps as Nos. 4388×2, 4389, 4390×2 and 4391/4395 but self-adhesive and perf 13 with one elliptical hole in each vert side were issued with labels in a Queen Album Cover collector's sheet, (No. LS124), originally sold for £13·15.

An Album Cover Collection fan sheet containing Nos. 4388/4395 was originally sold for £10·20.

A Night at the Opera fan sheet containing No. 4390×4 was originally sold for £7·50.

The 15 PHQ cards show the 14 individual stamps including those from No. **MS**4396 and the complete miniature sheet.

(Litho ISP Cartor (Nos. 4388/4395) or gravure ISP Walsall (Nos. 4397/4398))

2020 (9 July). Queen (rock band) (1st issue). Multicoloured. Two phosphor bands.

*(a) Ordinary gum. Perf 14 (Nos. 4388/4395), 14½×14 (Queen machin size stamp from No. **MS**4396) or 14½ (other stamps from No. **MS**4396).*

4388	**3473**	(1st) *Queen II*, 1974	1·25	1·25
		a. Horiz strip of 4. Nos. 4388/4391	5·00	5·00
		b. Booklet pane. Nos. 4388/4391 with margins all round	5·00	
4389	**3474**	(1st) *Sheer Heart Attack*, 1974	1·25	1·25
4390	**3475**	(1st) *A Night At The Opera*, 1975	1·25	1·25
4391	**3476**	(1st) *News of the World*, 1977	1·25	1·25
4392	**3477**	£1·63 *The Game*, 1980	2·25	2·25
		a. Horiz strip of 4. Nos. 4392/4395	9·00	9·00
		b. Booklet pane. Nos. 4392/4395 with margins all round	9·00	
4393	**3478**	£1·63 *Greatest Hits*, 1981	2·25	2·25
4394	**3479**	£1·63 *The Works*, 1984	2·25	2·25
4395	**3480**	£1·63 *Innuendo*, 1991	2·25	2·25
Set of 8			12·50	12·50
Set of 2 Gutter Strips of 8			25·00	
First Day Cover (Tallents House)				15·00
First Day Cover (Knebworth)				15·00
Presentation Pack (PO Pack No. 588) (Nos. 4388/4395 and **MS**4396)			22·00	
PHQ Cards (set of 15) (473)			8·25	23·00
MS4396 202×74 mm. **3481** (1st) Freddie Mercury, Magic Tour, Wembley Stadium, 1986; (1st) Roger Taylor, Hyde Park Concert, 1976; (1st) Queen, Primrose Hill, London, 1974; £1·63 John Deacon, A Night at the Opera Tour, Hammersmith Odeon, 1975; £1·63 Brian May, Magic Tour, Nepstadion, Budapest, 1986			7·75	7·75
First Day Cover (Tallents House)				10·00
First Day Cover (Knebworth)				10·00

(b) Self-adhesive. Die-cut perf 14.

4397	**3473**	(1st) *Queen II*, 1974	1·75	1·75
		a. Booklet pane. Nos. 4397/4398 and U3027×4	7·50	
4398	**3475**	(1st) *A Night At The Opera*, 1975	1·75	1·75

(Litho ISP Cartor)

2020 (9 July). Queen (rock band) (2nd issue). Multicoloured. Two phosphor bands. Perf 14½.

4399	**3482**	(1st) Freddie Mercury	1·75	1·75
		a. Booklet pane. Nos. 4399/4402 with margins all round	9·50	
4400	**3483**	(1st) Roger Taylor	1·75	1·75
4401	**3484**	£1·63 John Deacon	3·00	3·00
4402	**3485**	£1·63 Brian May	3·00	3·00
Set of 4			9·50	9·50

Nos. 4399/4402 were issued in No. **MS**4396 and booklet pane No. 4399a from the £19·10 Queen premium booklet, No. DY35.

3486 Queen, Primrose Hill, London, 1974

(Litho ISP Cartor)

2020 (9 July). Queen (rock band) (3rd issue). Multicoloured. Two phosphor bands. Perf 14½×14 (with one elliptical hole in each vert side).

4403	**3486**	(1st) Queen, 1974	1·75	1·75

No. 4403 was issued in No. **MS**4396 and the machin booklet pane No. U3070r from the £19·10 Queen premium booklet, No. DY35.

A stamp as No. 4403 but self-adhesive was issued in a Queen Live Collector's Sheet containing ten stamps with labels, (No. LS125), originally sold for £8·80 and in booklets of six, No. MB22, originally sold for £5·10. See also No. 4502.

2020 / QUEEN ELIZABETH II

3487 Palace of Westminster from Old Palace Yard

3488 Palace of Westminster from River Thames

3489 Elizabeth Tower

3490 Commons Chamber

3491 Central Lobby

3492 Lords Chamber

3493 Palace of Westminster

(Des Steers McGillan Eves. Litho ISP Cartor)

2020 (30 July). Palace of Westminster. Multicoloured. Two phosphor bands. Perf 14½.

4404	**3487**	(1st) Palace of Westminster from Old Palace Yard	1·25	1·25
		a. Horiz strip of 3. Nos. 4404/4406	3·75	3·75
4405	**3488**	(1st) Palace of Westminster from River Thames	1·25	1·25
4406	**3489**	(1st) Elizabeth Tower	1·25	1·25
4407	**3490**	£1·68 Commons Chamber	2·40	2·40
		a. Horiz strip of 3. Nos. 4407/4409	7·00	7·00
4408	**3491**	£1·68 Central Lobby	2·40	2·40
4409	**3492**	£1·68 Lords Chamber	2·40	2·40
Set of 6			9·75	9·75
Set of 2 Gutter Strips of 6			20·00	
First Day Cover (Tallents House)				12·00
First Day Cover (London SW1)				12·00
Presentation Pack (PO Pack No. 589) (Nos. 4404/4409, **MS**4410)			18·00	
PHQ Cards (set of 11) (474)			6·50	20·00

MS4410 203×74 mm. **3493** (1st) Norman Porch; (1st) Chapel of St Mary Undercroft; £1·63 St Stephen's Hall; £1·63 Royal Gallery ... 6·75 6·75
First Day Cover (Tallents House) ... 9·00
First Day Cover (London SW1) ... 9·00

Nos. 4404/4406 and 4407/4409 were each printed together, *se-tenant*, as horizontal strips of three in sheets of 36 (2 panes 3×6).

The 11 PHQ cards show the ten individual stamps, including those from No. **MS**4410, and the complete miniature sheet.

3494 The Reichenbach Fall

3495 A Study in Pink

3496 The Great Game

3497 The Empty Hearse

3498 A Scandal in Belgravia

3499 The Final Problem

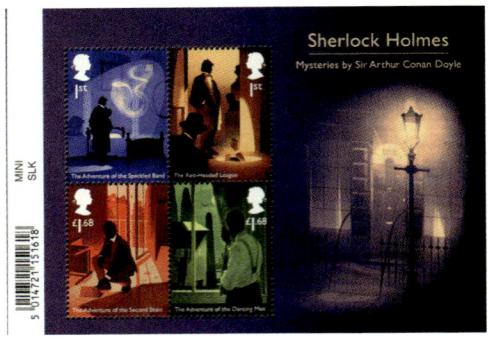

QUEEN ELIZABETH II/2020

3500 Sherlock Holmes Mysteries by Sir Arthur Conan Doyle

3501 The Red-Headed League
3502 The Adventure of the Speckled band 

(Des So Design Consultants (Nos. 4411/4416) or Karolis Strautniekas (illustrations) and NB Studio (No. **MS**4417). Litho ISP Cartor (Nos. 4411/**MS**4417) or gravure (Nos. 4418/4419))

2020 (18 Aug). Sherlock. Multicoloured. Two phosphor bands.

(a) Ordinary gum. Perf 14½ (Nos. 4411/4416) or 14 (No. **MS***4417).*

4411	3494	(1st) The Reichenbach Fall	1·25	1·25
		a. Vert pair. Nos. 4411/4412	2·50	2·50
4412	3495	(1st) A Study in Pink	1·25	1·25
4413	3496	£1·42 The Great Game	2·00	2·00
		a. Vert pair. Nos. 4413/4414	4·00	4·00
4414	3497	£1·42 The Empty Hearse	2·00	2·00
4415	3498	£1·68 A Scandal in Belgravia	2·40	2·40
		a. Vert pair. Nos. 4415/4416	4·75	4·75
4416	3499	£1·68 The Final Problem	2·40	2·40
Set of 6			10·00	10·00
Set of 3 Gutter Pairs (only 2 stamps in each gutter pair)			12·00	
First Day Cover (Tallents House)				12·00
First Day Cover (London NW1)				12·00
Presentation Pack (PO Pack No. 590) (Nos. 4411/4416 and **MS**4417)			19·00	
PHQ Cards (set of 11) (475)			6·50	19·00
MS4417 126×89 mm. **3500** (1st) The Adventure of the Speckled Band; (1st) The Red-Headed League; £1·68 The Adventure of the Second Stain; £1·68 The Adventure of the Dancing Men			6·75	6·75
First Day Cover (Tallents House)				9·00
First Day Cover (London NW1)				9·00

(b) Self-adhesive. Die-cut perf 14.

4418	3501	(1st) The Red-Headed League	2·50	2·50
		a. Booklet pane. Nos. 4418/4419 and U3027×4	10·00	
4419	3502	(1st) The Adventure of the Speckled Band	2·50	2·50

Nos. 4411/4412, 4413/4414 and 4415/4416 were each printed together, se-tenant, as vertical pairs in sheets of 36 (2 panes 3×6).

Nos. 4411/4416 show scenes from the *Sherlock* television series, and show additional inscriptions when UV light is shone over the stamps.

Stamps as Nos. 4411/4416 but self-adhesive and perf 14 were issued in collector's sheets, (No. LS126), with labels containing Nos. 4411×4, 4412×2 and one each of Nos. 4413/4416, originally sold for £11·95.

Nos. 4411 and 4413 have the two phosphor bands at left and right of the stamps as usual.

Nos. 4412 and 4414 have the two phosphor bands at left and centre of the stamp.

No. 4415 has the two phosphor bands at left and just right of centre.

No. 4416 has the two phosphor bands at left and centre of the stamp.

Nos. 4418/4419 were issued in stamp booklet, No. PM75, originally sold for £4·56.

The 11 PHQ cards show the ten individual stamps, including those from No. **MS**4417, and the complete miniature sheet.

3503 Then with a terrifying roar (*Rupert's Rainy Adventure*)
3504 The bath is rocked from side to side (*Rupert's Rainy Adventure*) 
3505 Then Algy looks a trifle glum (*Rupert and the Mare's Nest*) 
3506 The large bird says (*Rupert and the Mare's Nest*) 
3507 'There's something puzzling all of you,' Says Rupert (*Rupert and the Lost Cuckoo*) 
3508 'My cuckoo's back again' (*Rupert and the Lost Cuckoo*) 
3509 Though Rupert searches all around (*Rupert's Christmas Tree*)  
3510 The tree is such a lovely sight (*Rupert's Christmas Tree*) 

(Des Rose (from illustrations by Alfred Bestall). Litho ISP Cartor)

2020 (3 Sept). Rupert Bear. Multicoloured. Centre band (2nd) or two bands (others). Perf 14½×14

4420	3503	(2nd) Then with a terrifying roar... (*Rupert's Rainy Adventure*)	90	90
		a. Horiz pair. Nos. 4420/4421	1·75	1·75
4421	3504	(2nd) The bath is rocked... (*Rupert's Rainy Adventure*)	90	90
4422	3505	(1st) Then Algy looks a trifle glum... (*Rupert and the Mare's Nest*)	1·25	1·25
		a. Horiz pair. Nos. 4422/4423	2·50	2·50
4423	3506	(1st) The large bird says... (*Rupert and the Mare's Nest*)	1·25	1·25
4424	3507	£1·45 'There's something puzzling...' (*Rupert and the Lost Cuckoo*)	2·00	2·00
		a. Horiz pair. Nos. 4424/4425	4·00	4·00
4425	3508	£1·45 'My cuckoo's back again...' (*Rupert and the Lost Cuckoo*)	2·00	2·00
4426	3509	£1·70 Though Rupert searches... (*Rupert's Christmas Tree*)	2·40	2·40
		a. Horiz pair. Nos. 4426/4427	4·75	4·75
4427	3510	£1·70 The tree is such a lovely sight... (*Rupert's Christmas Tree*)	2·40	2·40
Set of 8			11·50	11·50
Set of 4 Gutter Pairs (only 2 stamps in each gutter pair)			13·00	
Set of 4 Traffic Light Blocks of 4			30·00	
First Day Cover (Tallents House)				14·00
First Day Cover (Canterbury)				14·00

Presentation Pack (PO Pack No. 591)..................................	14·00	
PHQ Cards (set of 8) (476)..	7·50	13·00

Nos. 4420/4421, 4422/4423, 4424/4425 and 4426/4427 were each printed together, se-tenant, as horizontal pairs in sheets of 60 (2 panes 6×5).

3511 Common Carder Bee (*Bombus pascuorum*)

3512 Painted Lady Butterfly (*Vanessa cardui*)

3513 Longhorn Beetle (*Rutpela maculata*)

3514 Elephant Hawk-moth (*Deilephila elpenor*)

3515 Marmalade Hoverfly (*Episyrphus balteatus*)

3516 Ruby-tailed Wasp (*Chrysis ignita* agg)

(Des Richard Lewington. Litho ISP Cartor).

2020 (1 Oct). Brilliant Bugs. Multicoloured. Two phosphor bands. Perf 14×14½.

4428	3511	(1st) Common Carder Bee (*Bombus pascuorum*)...	1·25	1·25
		a. Vert pair. Nos. 4428/4429	2·50	2·50
4429	3512	(1st) Painted Lady Butterfly (*Vanessa cardui*)...	1·25	1·25
4430	3513	£1·45 Longhorn Beetle (*Rutpela maculata*)...	2·00	2·00
		a. Vert pair. Nos. 4430/4431	4·00	4·00
4431	3514	£1·45 Elephant Hawk-moth (*Deilephila elpenor*)..	2·00	2·00
4432	3515	£1·70 Marmalade Hoverfly (*Episyrphus balteatus*)...	2·40	2·40
		a. Vert pair. Nos. 4432/4433	4·75	4·75
4433	3516	£1·70 Ruby-tailed Wasp (*Chrysis ignita* agg)...	2·40	2·40
Set of 6...			10·00	10·00
Set of 3 Gutter Pairs (only 2 stamps in each gutter pair)...			12·00	
First Day Cover (Tallents House)..				12·50
First Day Cover (Bugford Dartmouth)...................................				12·50
Presentation Pack (PO Pack No. 592)..................................			12·00	
PHQ Cards (set of 8) (477)..			3·50	12·00

Nos. 4428/4429, 4430/4431 and 4432/4433 were each printed together, se-tenant, as vertical pairs in sheets of 60 (2 panes 5×6).

3517 Adoration of the Magi (detail), St Andrew's Church, East Lexham

3518 Virgin and Child, St Andrew's Church, Coln Rogers

3519 Adoration of the Magi, St Andrew's Church, Lexham

3520 Virgin and Child, St Andrew's Church, Coln Rogers

3521 Virgin and Child, Church of St James, Hollowell

3522 Virgin and Child, All Saints' Church, Otley

3523 The Holy Family (detail), St Columba's Church, Topcliffe

3524 Virgin and Child, Christ Church, Coalville

(Des Up. Gravure ISP Walsall (Nos. 4434/4441) or litho ISP Cartor (No. MS4442)).

2020 (3 Nov). Christmas. Stained-glass Windows. Multicoloured. One centre band (No. 4434) or two bands (others). Perf 14½×15.
(a) Self-adhesive.

4434	3517	(2nd) Adoration of the Magi (detail), St Andrew's Church, East Lexham......	90	90
		a. Booklet pane. No. 4434×12............	12·50	
4435	3518	(1st) Virgin and Child, St Andrew's Church, Coln Rogers........................	1·00	1·00
		a. Booklet pane. No. 4435×12............	15·00	
4436	3519	(2nd Adoration of the Magi, St Large) Andrew's Church, Lexham...............	1·25	1·25
4437	3520	(1st Virgin and Child, St Andrew's Large) Church, Coln Rogers............................	1·60	1·60
4438	3521	£1·45 Virgin and Child, Church of St James, Hollowell.....................................	2·00	2·00
4439	3522	£1·70 Virgin and Child, All Saints' Church, Otley...	2·40	2·40
4440	3523	£2·50 The Holy Family (detail), St Columba's Church, Topcliffe...........	3·50	3·50
4441	3524	£2·55 Virgin and Child, Christ Church, Coalville...	3·50	3·50
Set of 8..			14·50	14·50
First Day Cover (Tallents House)..				17·00
First Day Cover (Bethlehem Llandeilo)................................				17·00
Presentation Pack (PO Pack No. 593)..................................			17·00	
PHQ Cards (set of 9) (478)..			5·25	20·00

(b) Ordinary gum.

MS4442 189×74 mm. As Nos. 4434/4441..........................	16·00	16·00
First Day Cover (Tallents House)..		17·00
First Day Cover (Bethlehem Llandeilo)................................		17·00

The 2nd class, 1st class, £1·45, £1·70, £2·50 and £2·55 values were also issued in sheets of 20, (No. LS127), containing eight 2nd class, eight 1st class and one each of the £1·45, £1·70, £2·50 and £2·55 values, each stamp accompanied by a se-tenant label.

The nine PHQ cards show the individual stamps and the complete miniature sheet.

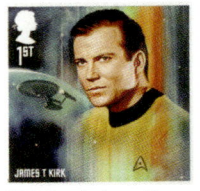

QUEEN ELIZABETH II/2020

3525 Captain James T. Kirk (William Shatner), *The Original Series*

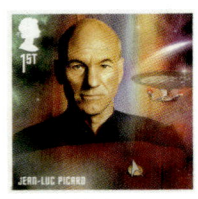

3526 Captain Jean-Luc Picard (Patrick Stewart), *The Next Generation*

3527 Captain Benjamin Sisko (Avery Brooks), *Deep Space Nine*

3528 Captain Kathryn Janeway (Kate Mulgrew), *Voyager*

3529 Captain Jonathan Archer (Scott Bakula), *Enterprise*

3530 Captain Gabriel Lorca (Jason Isaacs), *Discovery*

3531 Spock (Leonard Nimoy), *The Original Series*

3532 Deanna Troi (Marina Sirtis), *The Next Generation*

3533 Julian Bashir (Alexander Siddig), *Deep Space Nine*

3534 Malcolm Reed (Dominic Keating), *Enterprise*

3535 Michael Burnham (Sonequa Martin-Greene), *Discovery*

3536 Ash Tyler/Voq (Shazad Latif), *Discovery*

3537 *Star Trek*. The Movies

(Des Freya Betts (illustrations Nos. 4443/4454) and Interabang. Litho ISP Cartor (Nos. 4443/**MS**4455) or gravure ISP Walsall Nos. 4456/4457))

2020 (13 Nov). *Star Trek* (1st issue). Multicoloured. Two phosphor bands.

(a) Ordinary gum. Perf 14½.

4443		(1st) Captain James T. Kirk....................	1·25	1·25
		a. Horiz strip of 6. Nos. 4443/4448.....	7·50	7·50
		b. Booklet pane. Nos. 4443/4448 with margins all round...................	7·50	
4444	3526	(1st) Captain Jean-Luc Picard.................	1·25	1·25
4445	3527	(1st) Captain Benjamin Sisko.................	1·25	1·25
4446	3528	(1st) Captain Kathryn Janeway...............	1·25	1·25
4447	3529	(1st) Captain Jonathan Archer...............	1·25	1·25
4448	3530	(1st) Captain Gabriel Lorca....................	1·25	1·25
4449	3531	(1st) Spock..	1·25	1·25
		a. Horiz strip of 6. Nos. 4449/4454.....	7·50	7·50
		b. Booklet pane. Nos. 4449/4454 with margins all round...................	7·50	
4450	3532	(1st) Deanna Troi..................................	1·25	1·25
4451	3533	(1st) Julian Bashir.................................	1·25	1·25
4453	3535	(1st) Michael Burnham..........................	1·25	1·25
4454	3536	(1st) Ash Tyler/Voq...............................	1·25	1·25
Set of 12..			13·50	13·50
Set of 2 Gutter Strips of 12..........................			27·00	
First Day Cover (Tallents House)...................				15·00
First Day Cover (Beambridge Craven Arms)......				15·00
Presentation Pack (PO Pack No. 594) (Nos. 4443/4454 and **MS**4455)...................................			22·00	
PHQ Cards (set of 19) (479).........................			11·00	22·00

(b) Self-adhesive.

MS4455 146×74 mm. **3537** (1st) Montgomery Scott (Simon Pegg), new Movie Series (60×21 mm) (Perf 14½); (1st) Praetor Shinzon (Tom Hardy), Next Generation Movie, *Nemesis* (60×21 mm) (Perf 14½); (1st) Tolian Soran (Malcolm McDowell), Original Movie Series, *Generations* (27×37 mm) (Perf 14); (1st) Klingon Chancellor Gorkon (David Warner), Original Movie Series (27×37 mm) (Perf 14); (1st) Dr Carol Marcus (Alice Eve), new Movie Series, *Star Trek Into Darkness* (27×37 mm) (Perf 14); (1st) Krall (Idris Elba), new Movie Series (27×37 mm) (Perf 14)

.... 7·50 7·50

First Day Cover (Tallents House).......................... 8·50
First Day Cover (Beambridge, Craven Arms)........... 8·50

(c) Self-adhesive. Die-cut perf 14½.

4456	3525	(1st) Captain James T. Kirk....................	1·75	1·75
		a. Booklet pane. Nos. 4456/4457 and U3027×4................................	7·50	
4457	3526	(1st) Captain Jean-Luc Picard.................	1·75	1·75

Nos. 4443/4448 and 4449/4454 were printed together, *se-tenant*, as horizontal strips of five stamps in sheets of 60 (2 panes 6×5).

Nos. 4456/4457 were issued in stamp booklet, No. PM76, originally sold for £4·56.

A collector's sheet containing stamps as Nos. 4443/4454 but self-adhesive, (No. LS129), was originally sold for £8·70.

The 19 PHQ cards show the 18 individual stamps, including those from No. **MS**4455, and the complete miniature sheet.

3538 Montgomery Scott (Simon Pegg), New Movie Series

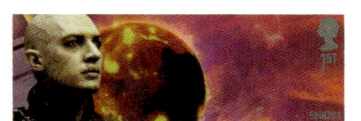

3539 Praetor Shinzon (Tom Hardy), Next Generation Movie. *Nemesis*

2020/QUEEN ELIZABETH II

3540 Tolian Soran (Malcolm McDowell), Original Movie Series. *Generations*

3541 Klingon Chancellor Gorkon (David Warner), Original Movie Series. *The Undiscovered Country*

3546 Lake District

3547 Loch Lomond and The Trossachs

3542 Dr Carol Marcus (Alice Eve), New Movie Series. *Star Trek Into Darkness*

3543 Krall (Idris Elba), *Star Trek Beyond*

3548 Snowdonia

3549 North York Moors

3550 South Downs

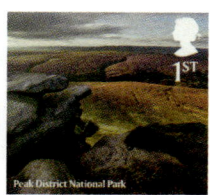

3551 Peak District

(Des Interabang. Litho ISP Cartor)

2020 (13 Nov). *Star Trek* (2nd issue). Multicoloured. Self-adhesive. Two phosphor bands. Perf 14½ (Nos. 4458/4459) or 14 (Nos. 4460/4463).

4458	3538	(1st) Montgomery Scott	1·50	1·50
		a. Booklet pane. Nos. 4458/4463	8·00	
4459	3539	(1st) Praetor Shinzon	1·50	1·50
4460	3540	(1st) Tolian Soran	1·50	1·50
4461	3541	(1st) Klingon Chancellor Gorkon	1·50	1·50
4462	3542	(1st) Dr Carol Marcus	1·50	1·50
4463	3543	(1st) Krall	1·50	1·50
Set of 6			8·00	8·00

Nos. 4458/4463 were issued in No. **MS**4455 and in booklet pane No. 4458a from the £18·35 *Star Trek* booklet, No. DY36.

Collectors Pack

2020 (13 Nov). Comprises Nos. 4312/**MS**4320, 4323/4330, 4332/**MS**4338, 4345/4354, 4356/**MS**4364, 4369/**MS**4377, 4380/**MS**4396, 4404/**MS**4417, 4420/4441 and 4433/**MS**4455

CP4463a	Collectors Pack (*sold for* £186) (PO Pack No. 595)	£325

Post Office Yearbook

2020 (13 Nov). Comprises Nos. 4312/**MS**4320, 4323/4330, 4332/**MS**4338, 4345/4354, 4356/**MS**4364, 4369/**MS**4377, 4380/**MS**4396, 4404/**MS**4417, 4420/4441 and 4433/**MS**4455

YB4463a	Yearbook (*sold for* £186)	£375

Miniature Sheet Collection

2020 (13 Nov). Comprises Nos. **MS**4320, **MS**4338, **MS**4364, **MS**4377, **MS**4396, **MS**4410, **MS**4417, **MS**4442 **MS**4455 and **MS**S180

MS4463a	Miniature Sheet Collection (*sold for* £57)	£110

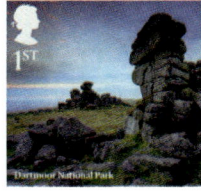

3552 Pembrokeshire Coast

3553 Broads

(Des Studio Mean. Litho ISP Cartor (Nos. 4464/4473) or gravure ISP Walsall (Nos. 4474/4475))

2021 (14 Jan). National Parks. Multicoloured. Two phosphor bands.

(a) Ordinary gum. Perf 14×14½.

4464	3544	(1st) Dartmoor	1·25	1·25
		a. Horiz strip of 5. Nos. 4464/4468	6·25	6·25
4465	3545	(1st) New Forest	1·25	1·25
4466	3546	(1st) Lake District	1·25	1·25
4467	3547	(1st) Loch Lomond and The Trossachs	1·25	1·25
4468	3548	(1st) Snowdonia	1·25	1·25
4469	3549	(1st) North York Moors	1·25	1·25
		a. Horiz strip of 5. Nos. 4469/4473	6·25	6·25
4470	3550	(1st) South Downs	1·25	1·25
4471	3551	(1st) Peak District	1·25	1·25
4472	3552	(1st) Pembrokeshire Coast	1·25	1·25
4473	3553	(1st) Broads	1·25	1·25
Set of 10			11·50	11·50
Set of 2 Gutter Strips of 10			23·00	
First Day Cover (Tallents House)				14·00
First Day Cover (Bakewell)				14·00
Presentation Pack (PO Pack No. 596)			13·50	
PHQ Cards (set of 10) (480)			5·75	13·00

(b) Self-adhesive. Die-cut perf 14×14½.

4474	3551	(1st) Peak District	1·75	1·75
		a. Booklet pane. Nos. 4474/4475 and U3027×4	7·50	
4475	3548	(1st) Snowdonia	1·75	1·75

Nos. 4464/4468 and 4469/4473 were each printed together, *se-tenant*, as horizontal strips of five stamps in sheets of 50 (2 panes 5×5).

Nos. 4474/4475 were issued in stamp booklet, No. PM77, originally sold for £4·56.

3544 Dartmoor

3545 New Forest

QUEEN ELIZABETH II/2021

3554 United Kingdom. A Celebration

(Des Hat-trick design. Litho ISP Cartor)

2021 (26 Jan). United Kingdom, A Celebration. Multicoloured. 'All-over' phosphor. Perf 15×14½.
MS4476 203×74 mm. **3554** (1st) Wheelchair athlete, cricket ball, football and racing car (Great Sport); (1st) Glass façade of office building, microphone stand silhouette, book pages and television studio (Great Creativity); £1.70 Hands making heart-shape, London Marathon, 2011, nurse reassuring patient and rainbow (Great Community); £1.70 3D illustration of binary code, London skyline, carbon fibre material and DNA (Great Industry and Innovation).. 7·25 7·25
First Day Cover (Tallents House)... 9·50
First Day Cover (London EC1)... 9·50
Presentation Pack (PO Pack No. M26).................................. 9·50
PHQ Cards (*set of* 5) (481)... 3·00 8·00

3555 'I Knew you was cheating...' (Del Boy and Boycie)

3556 'Don't worry he's house trained...' (Marlene, Del Boy and Rodney)

3557 'Play it nice and cool...' (Del Boy and Trigger)

3558 'Now brace yourself...' (Rodney and Del Boy)

3559 'Our coach has just blown up!' (Rodney and Denzel)

3560 'What have you been doing...' (Rodney and Cassandra)

3561 'It's a baby, Raquel...' (Del Boy and Raquel)

3562 'That's just over...' (Del Boy and Rodney)

3563 Del Boy, Rodney, Uncle Albert and Grandad

3564 Del Boy   **3565** Rodney

(Des Interabang. Litho ISP Cartor (Nos. 4477/**MS**4485) or gravure Walsall (Nos. 4486/4487))

2021 (16 Feb). *Only Fools and Horses* (TV sitcom, 1981–2003) (1st issue). Multicoloured. Two phosphor bands.

(a) Ordinary gum. Perf 14.

4477	3555	(1st) Type **3555**...........................	1·25	1·25
		a. Vert pair. Nos. 4477/4478........	2·50	2·50
		b. Booklet pane. Nos. 4477/4480 with margins all round........	5·00	
4478	3556	(1st) 'Don't worry he's house trained...' (Marlene, Del Boy and Rodney).....	1·25	1·25
4479	3557	(1st) 'Play it nice and cool...' (Del Boy and Trigger).............................	1·25	1·25
		a. Vert pair. Nos. 4479/4480........	2·50	2·50
4480	3558	(1st) 'Now brace yourself...' (Rodney and Del Boy)...............................	1·25	1·25

2021 / QUEEN ELIZABETH II

4481	3559	£1·70 'Our coach has just blown up!' (Rodney and Denzel)	2·40	2·40
		a. Vert pair. Nos. 4481/4482	4·75	4·75
		b. Booklet pane. Nos. 4481/4484 with margins all round	9·50	
4482	3560	£1·70 'What have you been doing...' (Rodney and Cassandra)	2·40	2·40
4483	3561	£1·70 'It's a baby, Raquel...' (Del Boy and Raquel)	2·40	2·40
		a. Vert pair. Nos. 4483/4484	4·75	4·75
4484	3562	£1·70 'That's just over...' (Del Boy and Rodney)	2·40	2·40
Set of 8			13·00	13·00
Set of 4 Gutter Pairs (only 2 stamps in each pair)			15·00	
First Day Cover (Tallents House)				15·00
First Day Cover (London SE15)				15·00
Presentation Pack (PO Pack No. 597) (Nos. 4471/4478 and MS4479)			23·00	
PHQ Cards (set of 13) (482)			7·50	22·00

MS4485 203×74 mm. **3563** (1st) Del Boy (David Jason); (1st) Rodney (Nicholas Lyndhurst); £1·70 Uncle Albert (Buster Merryfield); £1·70 Grandad (Lennard Pearce) .... 7·25 7·25
First Day Cover (Tallents House) .... 9·50
First Day Cover (London SE15) .... 9·50

(b) Self-adhesive. Die-cut perf 14.

4486	3564	(1st) Del Boy	1·75	1·75
		a. Booklet pane. Nos. 4486/4487 and U3027×4	7·25	
4487	3565	(1st) Rodney	1·75	1·75

Nos. 4477/4478, 4479/4480, 4481/4482 and 4483/4484 were each printed together, *se-tenant*, as vertical pairs in sheets of 60 (2 panes 5×6).
Nos. 4486/4487 were issued in stamp booklet, No. PM78, originally sold for £5·10.
A fan souvenir folder containing excerpts from writer John Sullivan's personal *Only Fools and Horses* scripts along with first day covers for Nos. 4477/4484 and MS4485 was sold by Royal Mail for £19·99.
Self-adhesive designs as Types **3564/3565** perforated 14×14½ were issued in sheets of ten, (No. LS131), containing five stamps of each design with labels. These sheets were printed in Lithography by ISP Cartor and originally sold for £9·60.
The 13 PHQ cards show the 12 individual stamps, including those from No. MS4485, and the complete miniature sheet.

3566 Uncle Albert
3567 Grandad 

(Des Interabang. Litho ISP Cartor.)

2021 (16 Feb). *Only Fools and Horses* (2nd issue). Multicoloured. Two phosphor bands. Perf 14.

4488	3564	(1st) Del Boy (David Jason)	1·50	1·50
		a. Booklet pane. Nos. 4488/4491 with margins all round	7·50	
4489	3565	(1st) Rodney (Nicholas Lyndhurst)	1·50	1·50
4490	3566	£1·70 Uncle Albert (Buster Merryfield)	2·75	2·75
4491	3567	£1·70 Grandad (Lennard Pearce)	2·75	2·75
Set of 4			7·50	7·50

Nos. 4488/4491 were issued in No. MS4485 and in booklet pane 4488a from £21·70 *Only Fools and Horses* booklet, No. DY37.

3568 Merlin and the Baby Arthur
3569 Arthur Draws the Sword from the Stone 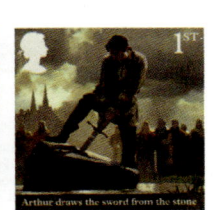
3570 Arthur takes Excalibur 
3571 Arthur Marries Guinevere 
3572 Sir Gawain and the Green Knight 
3573 Knights of the Round Table 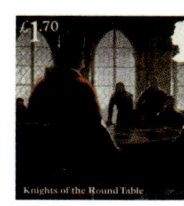
3574 Sir Lancelot Defeats the Dragon 
3575 Sir Galahad and the Holy Grail 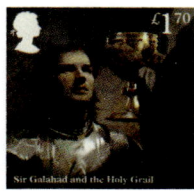
3576 Arthur Battles Mordred 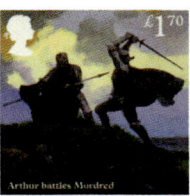
3577 The Death of King Arthur 

(Des Jaime Jones Stamp Design. Litho ISP Cartor.)

2021 (16 Mar). The Legend of King Arthur. Multicoloured. Two phosphor bands. Perf 14½.

4492	3568	(1st) Merlin and the Baby Arthur	1·25	1·25
		a. Horiz strip of 5. Nos. 4492/4496	6·25	6·25
4493	3569	(1st) Arthur draws the Sword from the Stone	1·25	1·25
4494	3570	(1st) Arthur takes Excalibur	1·25	1·25
4495	3571	(1st) Arthur marries Guinevere	1·25	1·25
4496	3572	(1st) Sir Gawain and the Green Knight	1·25	1·25
4497	3573	£1·70 Knights of the Round Table	2·40	2·40
		a. Horiz strip of 5. Nos. 4497/4501	12·00	12·00
4498	3574	£1·70 Sir Lancelot defeats the Dragon	2·40	2·40
4499	3575	£1·70 Sir Galahad and the Holy Grail	2·40	2·40
4500	3576	£1·70 Arthur battles Mordred	2·40	2·40
4501	3577	£1·70 The Death of King Arthur	2·40	2·40
Set of 10			16·00	16·00
Set of 2 Gutter Strips of 10			32·00	
First Day Cover (Tallents House)				18·00
First Day Cover (Winchester)				18·00
Presentation Pack (PO Pack No. 598)			18·00	
PHQ Cards (set of 10) (483)			5·75	16·00

Nos. 4492/4496 and 4497/4501 were each printed together, *se-tenant*, as horizontal strips of five in sheets of 50 (2 panes 5×5).

3486 Queen, 1974

QUEEN ELIZABETH II/2021

(Gravure ISP Walsall)

2021 (29 Mar). Queen (Rock Band) (4th issue). As T **3486** but self-adhesive. Two phosphor bands. Die-cut perf 14½×14 (with one elliptical hole in each vert side).

| 4502 | 3486 | (1st) Queen, 1974 | 1·75 | 1·75 |

No. 4502 was issued in booklets of six, No. MB22, originally sold for £5·10.

3580 *The Time Machine* (H. G. Wells)

3581 *Brave New World* (Aldous Huxley)

3582 *The Day of the Triffids* (John Wyndham)

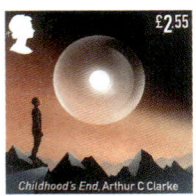

3583 *Childhood's End* (Arthur C. Clarke)

3584 *Shikasta* (Doris Lessing)

(Des Webb & Webb Design Ltd (illustrations Sabina Šinko (No. 4503), Francisco Rodriguez (No. 4504), Thomas Danthony (No. 4505), Mick Brownfield (No. 4506), Matt Murphy (No. 4507), Sarah Jones (No. 4508). Litho ISP Cantor)

2021 (15 Apr). Classic Science Fiction. Multicoloured. Two phosphor bands. Perf 14½.

4503	3579	(1st) Frankenstein (Mary Shelley)	1·25	1·25
		a. Horiz pair. Nos. 4503/4504	2·50	2·50
4504	3580	(1st) The Time Machine (H. G. Wells)	1·25	1·25
4505	3581	£1·70 Brave New World (Aldous Huxley)	2·50	2·50
		a. Horiz pair. Nos. 4505/4506	5·00	5·00
4506	3582	£1·70 The Day of the Triffids (John Wyndham)	2·50	2·50
4507	3583	£2·55 Childhood's End (Arthur C. Clarke)	3·50	3·50
		a. Horiz pair. Nos. 4507/4508	7·00	7·00
4508	3584	£2·55 Shikasta (Doris Lessing)	3·50	3·50
Set of 6			13·00	13·00
Set of 3 Gutter Pairs			26·00	
First Day Cover (Tallents House)				16·00
First Day Cover (London NW1)				16·00
Presentation Pack (PO Pack No. 599)			15·00	
PHQ Cards (set of 6) (484)			3·75	14·50

Nos. 4503/4504, 4505/4506 and 4507/4508 were printed together, *se-tenant*, as horizontal pairs in sheets of 60 (2 panes 6×5).

3585 Battle of Bosworth, 1485

3586 Battle of Tewkesbury, 1471

3587 Battle of Barnet, 1471

3588 Battle of Edgecote Moor, 1469

3589 Battle of Towton, 1461

3590 Battle of Wakefield, 1460

3591 Battle of Northampton, 1460

3592 First Battle of St. Albans, 1455

(Des Graham Turner. Litho ISP Cantor)

2021 (4 May). Wars of the Roses. Multicoloured. One centre band (2nd) or two phosphor bands (others). Perf 14.

4509	3585	(2nd) Battle of Bosworth, 1485	90	90
		a. Horiz pair. Nos. 4509/4510	1·75	1·75
4510	3586	(2nd) Battle of Tewkesbury, 1471	90	90
4511	3587	(1st) Battle of Barnet, 1471	1·25	1·25
		a. Horiz pair. Nos. 4511/4512	2·50	2·50

4512	3588	(1st) Battle of Edgecote Moor, 1469	1·25	1·25
4513	3589	£1·70 Battle of Towton, 1461	2·50	2·50
		a. Horiz pair. Nos. 4513/4514	5·00	5·00
4514	3590	£1·70 Battle of Wakefield, 1460	2·50	2·50
4515	3591	£2·55 Battle of Northampton, 1460	3·50	3·50
		a. Horiz pair. Nos. 4515/4516	7·00	7·00
4516	3592	£2·55 First Battle of St Albans, 1455	3·50	3·50
Set of 8			14·50	14·50
Set of 4 Gutter Pairs			29·00	
First Day Cover (Tallents House)				17·00
First Day Cover (Tewkesbury)				17·00
Presentation Pack (PO Pack No. 600)			15·00	
PHQ Pack (set of 8) (485)			5·00	9·75

Nos. 4509/4510, 4511/4512, 4513/4514 and 4515/4516 were each printed together, *se-tenant*, as horizontal pairs in sheets of 60 (2 panes 6×5).

3593 McCartney

3594 RAM

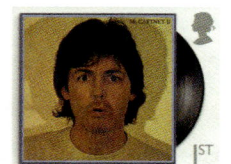

3595 Venus and Mars

3596 McCartney II

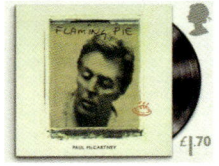

3597 Tug of War

3598 Flaming Pie

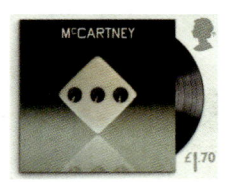

3599 Egypt Station

3600 McCartney III

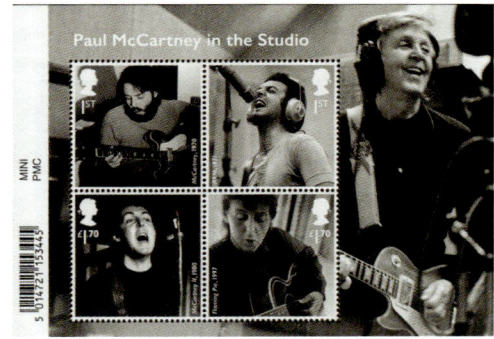

3601 Paul McCartney in the Studio

(Des Baxter & Bailey. Litho ISP Cartor (Nos. 4517/4224) or gravure ISP Walsall (Nos. 4226/4227))

2021 (28 May). Paul McCartney (1st issue). Multicoloured. Two phosphor bands.

*(a) Ordinary gum. Perf 14 (Nos. 4517/4524, 4526/4527) or 14½ (No. **MS**4525).*

4517	3593	(1st) McCartney	1·25	1·25
		a. Horiz strip of 4. Nos. 4517/4520	5·00	5·00
		b. Booklet pane. Nos. 4517/4520 with margins all round	13·50	
4518	3594	(1st) RAM	1·25	1·25
4519	3595	(1st) Venus and Mars	1·25	1·25
4520	3596	(1st) McCartney II	1·25	1·25
4521	3597	£1·70 Tug of War	2·50	2·50
4522	3598	£1·70 Flaming Pie	2·50	2·50
4523	3599	£1·70 Egypt Station	2·50	2·50
4524	3600	£1·70 McCartney III	2·50	2·50
Set of 8			13·50	13·50
Set of 2 Gutter Strips of 8			27·00	
First Day Cover (Tallents House)				16·00
First Day Cover (Liverpool)				16·00
Presentation Pack (PO Pack No. 601) (Nos. 4517/4524 and **MS**4525)			23·00	
PHQ Cards (set of 13) (486)			8·25	24·00
Souvenir Folder (containing Nos. 4517/4524 and **MS**4525 plus prints of the stamps at record cover size)			38·00	
MS4525 126×89 mm. **3601** (1st) McCartney, 1970; (1st) RAM, 1971; £1·70 McCartney II, 1980; £1·70 Flaming Pie, 1997			7·50	7·50
First Day Cover (Tallents House)				10·00
First Day Cover (Liverpool)				10·00

(b) Self-adhesive. Die-cut perf 14.

4526	3593	(1st) McCartney	1·75	1·75
		a. Booklet pane. Nos. 4526/4527 and U3027×4	7·50	
4527	3596	(1st) McCartney II	1·75	1·75

Nos. 4517/4520 and 4521/4524 were each printed together, *se-tenant*, as horizontal strips of four stamps in sheets of 48 (2 panes 4×6).

Nos. 4626/4627 were issued in stamp booklet, No. PM79, originally sold for £5·10.

A Paul McCartney Album Covers Collector's Sheet containing Nos. 4517/4518×2 and 4519/4524 with labels was originally sold for £13.

An Album cover collection fan sheet containing Nos. 4517/4524 was originally sold for £10·90.

A *RAM* fan sheet containing No. 4518×4 was originally sold for £7·50.

A *McCartney III* album fan sheet containing No. 4524×4 was originally sold for £7·50.

The 13 PHQ Cards show the 12 individual stamps, including those from No. **MS**4525 and the complete miniature sheet.

3602 McCartney, 1970

3603 RAM, 1971

3604 McCartney II, 1980

3605 Flaming Pie, 1997

2021 (28 May). Paul McCartney (2nd issue). Multicoloured. Two phosphor bands. Perf 14½.

4528	3602	(1st) McCartney, 1970	1·50	1·50
		a. Booklet pane. Nos. 4528/4531 with margins all round	8·50	
4529	3603	(1st) RAM, 1971	1·50	1·50
4530	3604	£1·70 McCartney II, 1980	2·75	2·75
4531	3605	£1·70 Flaming Pie, 1997	2·75	2·75
Set of 4			8·50	8·50

Nos. 4528/4531 were issued in No. **MS**4525 and in booklet pane 4528a from the £20·25 Paul McCartney booklet, No. DY38.

QUEEN ELIZABETH II/2021

3606 Prince Philip, Duke of Edinburgh

(Des Kate Stephens. Litho ISP Cartor)

2021 (24 June). Prince Philip, Duke of Edinburgh (1921–2021) Commemoration. Multicoloured. Phosphor band at left (2nd) or 'all-over' phosphor (others). Perf 14½×14.

MS4532	200×67 mm. **3606** (2nd) Prince Philip, Duke of Edinburgh, *circa* 1952; (1st) Prince Philip at passing out parade of Prince Andrew, Dartmouth Naval College, 1980; £1·70 Prince Philip at Royal Windsor Horse Show; £2·55 Prince Philip, *circa* 1992		8·25	8·25
First Day Cover (Tallents House)				11·00
First Day Cover (Windsor)				11·00
Presentation Pack (PO Pack No. 602)			10·50	
PHQ Cards (set of 5) (487)			3·25	9·75

3607 Dennis's First Comic Strip, 1951

3608 Dennis Adopts Gnasher, 1968

3609 Dennis's Front Cover Debut, 1974

3610 Dennis Adopts Rasher the Pig, 1979

3611 Dennis Meets his Sister Bea, 1998

3612 Dennis Reveals Dad was Dennis, 2015

(Litho ISP Cartor or gravure ISP Walsall)

2021 (1 July). Dennis and Gnasher. Multicoloured. Two phosphor bands.
(a) Ordinary gum. Perf 14.

4533	**3607**	(1st) Dennis's First Comic Strip, 1951	1·25	1·25
		a. Horiz strip of 3. Nos. 4533/4535	3·75	3·75
4534	**3608**	(1st) Dennis adopts Gnasher, 1968	1·25	1·25
4535	**3609**	(1st) Dennis's Front Cover Debut, 1974	1·25	1·25
4536	**3610**	£1·70 Dennis adopts Rasher the Pig, 1979	2·50	2·50
		a. Horiz strip of 3. Nos. 4536/4538	7·50	7·50
4537	**3611**	£1·70 Dennis meets his Sister Bea, 1998	2·50	2·50
4538	**3612**	£1·70 Dennis reveals Dad was Dennis, 2015	2·50	2·50
Set of 6			10·00	10·00
Set of 2 Gutter Strips of 6			20·00	
First Day Cover (Tallents House)				12·50
First Day Cover (Dundee)				12·50
Presentation Pack (PO Pack No. 603) (Nos. 4533/4538 and **MS**4539)			20·00	
PHQ Cards (set of 11) (488)			7·00	20·00

3613 Happy Birthday Dennis

(b) Self-adhesive. Die-cut perf 14 (Minnie the Minx) or 14½ (others).
MS4539 203×74 mm. **3613** (1st) Dennis; (1st) Gnasher; £1·70 Minnie the Minx (26×31 mm); £1·70 Dennis, his baby sister Bea and parents ... 7·25 7·25
First Day Cover (Tallents House) ... 9·75
First Day Cover (Dundee) ... 9·75

3614 Dennis    **3615** Gnasher

(c) Self-adhesive booklet stamps. Die-cut perf 14½.

4540	**3614**	(1st) Dennis	1·75	1·75
		a. Booklet pane. Nos. 4540/4541 and U3027×4	7·50	
4541	**3615**	(1st) Gnasher	1·75	1·75

Nos. 4533/4535 and 4536/4538 were each printed together, *se-tenant*, as horizontal strips of three in sheets of 60 (2 panes 6×5).

Nos. 4540/4541 were issued in stamp booklet, No. PM80, originally sold for £5·10.

A Collector's Sheet containing 1st self-adhesive Dennis and Gnasher stamps×10 as Types **3614/3615** each×5 was originally sold for £9·70.

The 11 PHQ cards show the ten individual stamps, including those from No. **MS**4539, and the complete miniature sheet.

3616 Northern Gannet    **3617** Common Cuttlefish

2021/QUEEN ELIZABETH II

3618 Grey Seal 
3619 Bottlenose Dolphin 
3620 Spiny Spider Crab 
3621 Long-snouted Sea Horse 
3622 Orca 
3623 Fried-egg Anemone 
3624 Cuckoo Wrasse 
3625 Cold-water Coral Reef

3626 Marine Food Chain

(Des Steers McGillan Eves (Nos. 4542/4551) or Maite Franchi (No. **MS**4552). Litho ISP Cartor (Nos. 4542/4551) or gravure ISP Walsall (Nos. 4553/4554))

2021 (22 July). Wild Coasts. Multicoloured. Two phosphor bands.

(a) Ordinary gum. Perf 14½ (Nos. 4542/4551) or 14 (No. MS4552).

4542	3616	(1st) Northern Gannet.................	1·25	1·25
		a. Horiz strip of 5. Nos. 4542/4546.....	6·25	6·25
4543	3617	(1st) Common Cuttlefish.................	1·25	1·25
4544	3618	(1st) Grey Seal.................	1·25	1·25
4545	3619	(1st) Bottlenose Dolphin.................	1·25	1·25
4546	3620	(1st) Spiny Spider Crab.................	1·25	1·25
4547	3621	(1st) Long-snouted Sea horse.................	1·25	1·25
		a. Horiz strip of 5. Nos. 4547/4551.....	6·25	6·25
4548	3622	(1st) Orca.................	1·25	1·25
4549	3623	(1st) Fried-egg Anemone.................	1·25	1·25
4550	3624	(1st) Cuckoo Wrasse.................	1·25	1·25
4551	3625	(1st) Cold-water Coral Reef.................	1·25	1·25
Set of 10...			11·00	11·00
Set of 2 Gutter Strips of 10...			22·00	
First Day Cover (Tallents House)...				13·00
First Day Cover (Achnasheen)...				13·00
Presentation Pack (PO Pack No. 604) (Nos. 4542/4551 and **MS**4552)...			21·00	
PHQ Cards (set of 15) (489)...			9·50	21·00
MS4552 202×74 mm. **3626** (1st) Phytoplankton; (1st) Zooplankton; £1·70 Atlantic Herring; £1·70 Harbour Porpoise...			7·25	7·25
First Day Cover (Tallents House)...				9·25
First Day Cover (Achnasheen)...				9·25

(b) Self-adhesive. Die-cut perf 14½×14.

4553	3622	(1st) Orca.................	1·75	1·75
		a. Booklet pane. Nos. 4553/4554 and U3027×4.................	7·50	
4554	3618	(1st) Grey Seal.................	1·75	1·75

Nos. 4542/4546 and 4547/4551 were each printed together, *se-tenant*, as horizontal strips of five in sheets of 50 (2 panes 5×5).

Nos. 4553/4554 were issued in stamp booklets, No. PM81, originally sold for £5·10.

A Collector's Sheet containing designs as Nos. 4542/4551 but self-adhesive was originally sold for £9·70.

The 15 PHQ cards show the 14 individual stamps, including those from No. **MS**4552, and the complete miniature sheet.

3627 Bessemer Process, Henry Bessemer, 1856

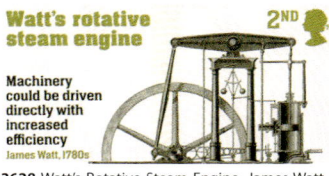

3628 Watt's Rotative Steam Engine, James Watt, 1780s

3629 Penydarren Locomotive, Richard Trevithick, 1804

3630 Spinning Jenny, James Hargreaves, *c* 1764

3631 Lombe's Silk Mill, Lombe Brothers, 1721

3632 Portland Cement, Joseph Aspdin, 1824

QUEEN ELIZABETH II/2021

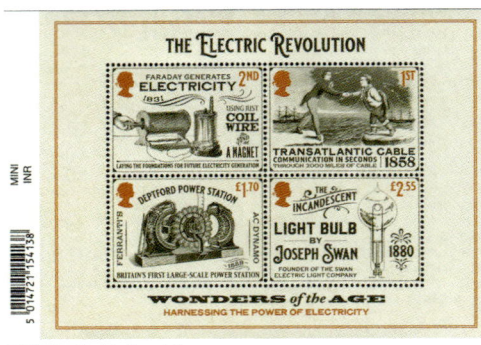

3633 The Electric Revolution

(Des Common Curiosity. Litho ISP Cartor)

2021 (12 Aug). Industrial Revolutions (1st issue). Multicoloured. One centre band (2nd) or two bands (others). Perf 14½ (Nos. 4555/4560) or 14 (No. **MS**4561).

4555	3627	(2nd) Bessemer process, Henry Bessemer, 1856....................	90	90
		a. Vert pair. Nos. 4555/4556...........	1·75	1·75
		b. Booklet pane. Nos. 4555/4558 with margins all round.........	4·25	
4556	3628	(2nd) Watt's rotative steam engine, James Watt, 1780s................	90	90
4557	3629	(1st) Penydarren locomotive, Richard Trevithick, 1804................	1·25	1·25
		a. Vert pair. Nos. 4557/4558...........	2·50	2·50
		b. Booklet pane. Nos. 4557/4560 with margins all round.........	7·50	
4558	3630	(1st) Spinning Jenny, James Hargreaves, c 1764................	1·25	1·25
4559	3631	£1·70 Lombe's Silk Mill, Lombe Brothers, 1721..............	2·50	2·50
		a. Vert pair. Nos. 4559/4560...........	5·00	5·00
4560	3632	£1·70 Portland Cement, Joseph Aspdin, 1824...........	2·50	2·50
Set of 6................			8·25	8·25
Set of 3 Gutter Strips of 4................			17·00	
First Day Cover (Tallents House)............				11·00
First Day Cover (Derby)............				11·00
Presentation Pack (PO Pack No. 605) (Nos. 4555/4560 and **MS**4561).............			19·00	
PHQ Cards (set of 11) (490)............			7·00	19·00

MS4561 126×89 mm. **3633** (2nd) Michael Faraday generates electricity, 1831; (1st) First transatlantic cable, communication, 1858; £1·70 Deptford Power Station, 1889; £2·55 The incandescent light bulb by Joseph Swan, 1880.......... 8·25 8·25
First Day Cover (Tallents House)............ 10·50
First Day Cover (Derby)............ 10·50

Nos. 4555/4556, 4557/4558 and 4559/4560 were each printed together, *se-tenant*, as vertical pairs in sheets of 60 (2 panes 5×6).

The 11 PHQ cards show the ten individual stamps, including those from No. **MS**4561, and the complete miniature sheet.

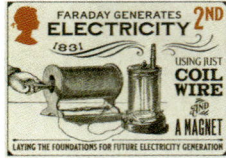

3634 Michael Faraday Generates Electricity using just Coil Wire and a Magnet, 1831

3635 First Transatlantic Cable, Communication in Seconds Through 2000 Miles of Cable, 1858

3636 AC Dynamo, Sebastian de Ferranti's Deptford Power Station, Britain's First Large-scale Power Station, 1889

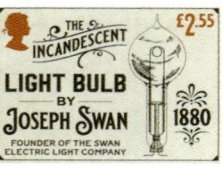

3637 The Incandescent Light Bulb by Joseph Swan, Founder of the Swan Electric Light Company, 1880

(Des Common Curiosity. Litho ISP Cartor)

2021 (12 Aug). Industrial Revolutions (2nd issue). Multicoloured. One centre band (2nd) or two bands (others). Perf 14.

4562	3634	(2nd) Michael Faraday generates electricity, 1831................	1·25	1·25
		a. Booklet pane. Nos. 4562/4565 with margins all round...........	10·00	
4563	3635	(1st) First transatlantic cable communication, 1858............	1·75	1·75
4564	3636	£1·70 Deptford Power Station, 1889........	3·00	3·00
4565	3637	£2·55 The incandescent light bulb by Joseph Swan, 1880............	4·00	4·00
Set of 4............			10·00	10·00

Nos. 4562/4565 were issued in £18·03 premium booklet, No. DY39.

3638 Mk IV Tank

3639 Matilda Mk II (A12 Infantry Tank)

3640 Churchill AVRE (Armoured Vehicles Royal Engineers) Tank

3641 Centurion Mk 9 Tank

3642 Scorpion Tank

3643 Chieftain Mk 5 Tank

3644 Challenger 2 Tank

3645 Ajax (turreted, reconnaissance and strike vehicle)

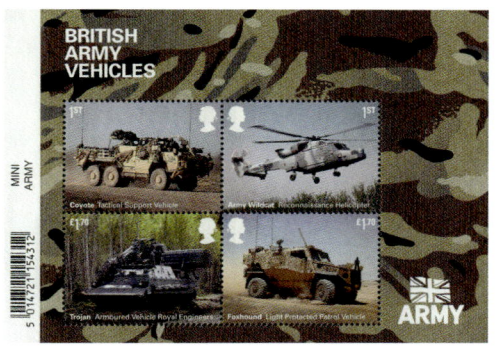

3646 British Army Vehicles

(Des Mike Graham. Litho ISP Cartor)

2021 (2 Sept). British Army Vehicles. Multicoloured. Two phosphor bands. Perf 14.

4566	3638	(1st) Mk IV Tank................................	1·25	1·25
		a. Horiz strip of 4. Nos. 4566/4569.....	5·00	5·00
4567	3639	(1st) Matilda Mk II................................	1·25	1·25
4568	3640	(1st) Churchill AVRE Tank...................	1·25	1·25
4569	3641	(1st) Centurion Mk 9 Tank...................	1·25	1·25
4570	3642	£1·70 Scorpion Tank.............................	2·50	2·50
		a. Horiz strip of 4. Nos. 4570/4573.....	10·00	10·00
4571	3643	£1·70 Chieftain Mk 5 Tank...................	2·50	2·50
4572	3644	£1·70 Challenger 2 Tank......................	2·50	2·50
4573	3645	£1·70 Ajax...	2·50	2·50
Set of 8..			13·50	13·50
Set of 8 Gutter Pairs...			27·00	
First Day Cover (Tallents House)...........................				16·00
First Day Cover (Bovington, Wareham).................				16·00
Presentation Pack (PO Pack No. 606) (Nos. 4566/4573 and **MS**4574)..			23·00	
PHQ Cards (set of 13) (491)..................................			8·25	23·00
MS4574 125×89 mm. **3646** (1st) Coyote Tactical Support Vehicle; (1st) Army Wildcat Mk 1 Reconnaissance Helicopter; £1·70 Trojan Armoured Vehicle Royal Engineers; £1·70 Foxhound Light Protected Patrol Vehicle..			7·25	7·25
First Day Cover (Tallents House)...........................				9·75
First Day Cover (Bovington, Wareham).................				9·75

the 13 PHQ cards show the 12 individual stamps, including those from No. **MS**4574, and the complete miniature sheet.

3647 Batman

3648 Batwoman

3649 Robin

3650 Batgirl

3651 Alfred

3652 Nightwing

3653 The Joker

3654 Harley Quinn

3655 The Penguin

3656 Poison Ivy

3657 Catwoman

3658 The Riddler

3659 Justice League

3660 Wonder Woman

QUEEN ELIZABETH II/2021

(Des Interabang, illustration Jim Cheung, colourist Laura Martin. Litho ISP Cartor (Nos. 4575/4580 and **MS**4587) or gravure Walsall (Nos. 4588/4589))

2021 (17 Sept). DC Collection (1st issue). Multicoloured. Two phosphor bands.

(a) Ordinary gum. Perf 14½.

4575	**3647**	(1st) Batman............................	1·25	1·25
		a. Horiz strip of 6. Nos. 4575/4580.....	7·50	7·50
		b. Booklet pane. Nos. 4575/4580 with margins all round................	7·25	
4576	**3648**	(1st) Batwoman........................	1·25	1·25
4577	**3649**	(1st) Robin..............................	1·25	1·25
4578	**3650**	(1st) Batgirl.............................	1·25	1·25
4579	**3651**	(1st) Alfred..............................	1·25	1·25
4580	**3652**	(1st) Nightwing........................	1·25	1·25
4581	**3653**	(1st) The Joker........................	1·25	1·25
		a. Horiz strip of 6. Nos. 4581/4586.....	7·50	7·50
		b. Booklet pane. Nos. 4581/4586 with margins all round................	7·25	
4582	**3654**	(1st) Harley Quinn....................	1·25	1·25
4583	**3655**	(1st) The Penguin....................	1·25	1·25
4584	**3656**	(1st) Poison Ivy.......................	1·25	1·25
4585	**3657**	(1st) Catwoman......................	1·25	1·25
4586	**3658**	(1st) The Riddler.....................	1·25	1·25
Set of 12..			15·00	15·00
Set of 2 Gutter Strips of 12..................................			30·00	
First Day Cover (Tallents House)...........................				17·00
First Day Cover (Gotham, Nottingham)...................				17·00
Presentation Pack (PO Pack No. 607) (Nos. 4575/4586 and **MS**4587).......................................			24·00	
PHQ Cards (set of 19) (492)................................			12·00	24·00

(b) Self-adhesive.

MS4587 202×74 mm. **3659** (1st) Batman (50×30 mm) (perf 14); (1st) Wonder Woman (35×30 mm) (perf 14); (1st) Superman (60×23 mm) (perf 14½×14); (1st) Green Lantern and The Flash (50×30 mm) (perf 14); (1st) Cyborg and Aquaman (35×36 mm) (perf 14); (1st) Supergirl and Shazam! (27×36 mm) (perf 14).. 7·50 7·50
First Day Cover (Tallents House)........................... 10·00
First Day Cover (Gotham, Nottingham)................... 10·00

(c) Self-adhesive booklet stamps. Die-cut perf 14½×14.

4588	**3647**	(1st) Batman............................	1·75	1·75
		a. Booklet pane. Nos. 4588/4589 and U3027×4................	7·50	
4589	**3649**	(1st) Robin..............................	1·75	1·75
4590	**3660**	(1st) Wonder Woman...............	1·75	1·75
		a. Booklet pane. No. 4590×2 and U3027×4................	7·50	
Set of 3...			5·00	5·00

Nos. 4575/4580 and 4581/4586 were each printed together, *se-tenant*, as horizontal strips of six in sheets of 60 (2 panes 6×5).

Nos. 4588/4589 were issued in stamp booklet, No. PM82, originally sold for £5·10.

No. 4590 was issued in stamp booklet, No. PM83, originally sold for £5·10.

A Batman Collector's Sheet containing designs as Nos. 4575/4586 but self-adhesive was originally sold for £11·40.

The 19 PHQ cards show the 18 individual stamps, including those from No. **MS**4587, and the complete miniature sheet.

3661 Batman

3662 Green Lantern and The Flash

3663 Superman

3664 Cyborg and Aquaman

3665 Supergirl and Shazam!

(Des Interabang illustration Jim Cheung colourist Laura Martin. Litho ISP Cartor)

2021 (17 Sept). DC Collection (2nd issue). Multicoloured. Two phosphor bands. Perf 14½×14 (No. 4594) or 14 (others).

4591	**3661**	(1st) Batman............................	1·50	1·50
		a. Booklet pane. Nos. 4591/4592.......	3·00	
4592	**3662**	(1st) Green Lantern and The Flash.........	1·50	1·50
4593	**3660**	(1st) Wonder Woman...............	1·50	1·50
		a. Booklet pane. Nos. 4593/4596.......	6·00	
4594	**3663**	(1st) Superman........................	1·50	1·50
4595	**3664**	(1st) Cyborg and Aquaman.......	1·50	1·50
4596	**3665**	(1st) Supergirl and Shazam!.....	1·50	1·50
Set of 6...			9·00	9·00

Nos. 4591/4596 were issued in booklet panes Nos. 4591a and 4593a from the £21·20 DC Collection booklet No. DY40.

Booklet panes Nos. 4591a and 4593a contain stamps in the same designs as No. **MS**4587 but are in two panes with pale blue margins.

3666 Women's Rugby World Cup Final, 2014

3667 Five Nations Championship, 1970

3668 Women's Six Nations Championship, 2015

3669 Women's Six Nations Championship, 2015

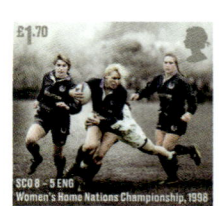

3670 Women's Home Nations Championship, 1998

3671 Five Nations Championship, 1994

3672 Women's Six Nations Championship, 2009

3673 Rugby World Cup Final, 2003

2021 / QUEEN ELIZABETH II

(Des True North. Litho ISP Cartor)

2021 (19 Oct). Rugby Union. Multicoloured. One phosphor band, slightly right of centre (2nd) or two bands (others). Perf 14×14½.

4597	3666	(2nd) Women's Rugby World Cup Final, 2014	90	90
		a. Horiz pair. Nos. 4597/4598	1·75	1·75
4598	3667	(2nd) Five Nations Championship, 1970	90	90
4599	3668	(1st) Women's Six Nations Championship, 2015	1·25	1·25
		a. Horiz pair. Nos. 4599/4600	2·50	2·50
4600	3669	(1st) Five Nations Championship, 1984	1·25	1·25
4601	3670	£1·70 Women's Home Nations Championship, 1998	2·50	2·50
		a. Horiz pair. Nos. 4601/4602	3·00	3·00
4602	3671	£1·70 Five Nations Championship, 1994	2·50	2·50
4603	3672	£2·55 Women's Six Nations Championship, 2009	3·50	3·50
		a. Horiz pair. Nos. 4603/4604	7·00	7·00
4604	3673	£2·55 Rugby World Cup Final, 2003	3·50	3·50
Set of 8			13·00	13·00
Set of 4 Gutter Strips of 4			26·00	
First Day Cover (Tallents House)				16·00
First Day Cover (Twickenham)				16·00
Presentation Pack (PO Pack No. 608)			15·00	
PHQ Cards (set of 8) (493)			5·00	14·50

Nos. 4597/4598, 4599/4600, 4601/4602 and 4603/4604 were each printed together, *se-tenant*, as horizontal pairs in sheets of 60 (2 panes 6×5).

3674 Angels
3675 Angels 
3676 Mary and Baby Jesus 
3677 Mary and Baby Jesus 
3678 Joseph and Mary on Road to Bethlehem 
3679 Shepherds see Angels 
3680 Wise Men Following Star of Bethlehem 
3681 Mary and Baby Jesus Visited by the Shepherds 

(Des Supple Studio. Gravure ISP Walsall (Nos. 4605/4612) or litho (No. MS4613))

2021 (2 Nov). Christmas. Nativity Illustrations by Joseph Cocco. Multicoloured. One centre phosphor band (Nos. 4605/4606) or two bands (others). Die-cut perf 14½×15 (Nos. 4606, 4608) or 15×14½ (others).

(a) Gravure.

4605	3674	(2nd) Angels	90	90
4606	3675	(2nd) Angels	90	90
		a. Booklet pane. No. 4606×12	12·50	
4607	3676	(1st) Mary and Baby Jesus	1·00	1·00
4608	3677	(1st) Mary and Baby Jesus	1·00	1·00
		a. Booklet pane. No. 4608×12	17·50	
4609	3678	(2nd Joseph and Mary on road to Large) Bethlehem	1·10	1·10
4610	3679	(1st Shepherds see Angels Large)	1·40	1·40
4611	3680	£1·70 Wise Men following Star of Bethlehem	2·75	2·75
4612	3681	£2·55 Mary and baby Jesus visited by the Shepherds	4·00	4·00
Set of 8			12·00	12·00
First Day Cover (Tallents House)				14·50
First Day Cover (Bethleham, Llandeilo)				14·50
Presentation Pack (PO Pack No. 609)			14·00	
PHQ Cards (set of 9) (494)				5·50

(b) Litho.

MS4613 189×74 mm. As Nos. 4605/4612		13·00	13·00
First Day Cover (Tallents House)			14·50
First Day Cover (Bethleham, Llandeilo)			14·50

The 2nd class and 1st class stamps with barcodes, Nos. 4605 and 4607, were each issued in counter sheets of 50.

The 2nd class with no barcode, No. 4606, was issued in booklets of 12 originally sold for £7·92

The 1st class with no barcode, No. 4608, was issued in booklets of 12 originally sold for £10·20.

The 2nd class with no barcode, 1st class with no barcode, £1·70 and £2·55 values were also issued in sheets of 20 containing eight 2nd class, eight 1st class, and two each of the £1·70 and £2·55 values, each stamp accompanied by a *se-tenant* label. These sheets were printed in lithography instead of gravure.

The nine PHQ cards show the individual stamps and the complete miniature sheet.

Collectors Pack

2021 (21 Nov). Comprises Nos. 4464/4473, **MS**4476/**MS**4485, 4492/4501, 4503/**MS**4525, **MS**4532/**MS**4539, 4542/**MS**4552, 4555/**MS**4561, 4566/**MS**4587 and 4597/4612

CP4613*a*	Collectors Pack (PO Pack No. 610) (sold for £180)	£350

Post Office Yearbook

2021 (2 Nov). Comprises Nos. 4464/4473, **MS**4476/**MS**4485, 4492/4501, 4503/**MS**4525, **MS**4532/**MS**4539, 4543/**MS**4552, 4555/**MS**4561, 4566/**MS**4587 and 4597/4612

YB4613*a*	Yearbook (sold for £199)	£400

Miniature Sheet Collection

2021 (2 Nov). Comprises Nos. **MS**4476, **MS**4485, **MS**4525, **MS**4532, **MS**4539, **MS**4552, **MS**4561, **MS**4574 and **MS**4587

MS4613*a* Miniature Sheet Collection (sold for £59)	£120

3682 London, July 1969

3683 East Rutherford, New Jersey, USA, August 2019

3684 Rotterdam, Netherlands, August 1995

3685 Tokyo, Japan, March 1995

3686 New York, July 1972

3687 Oslo, Norway, May 2014

3688 Hertfordshire, August 1976

3689 Dusseldorf, Germany, October 2017

3690 Rolling Stones and Tour Posters

(Des Baxter & Bailey. Litho ISP Cartor)

2022 (20 Jan). The Rolling Stones (1st issue). Multicoloured. Two phosphor bands. Perf 14 (No. 4614/4621) or 14½ (No. **MS**4622).

4614	**3682**	(1st) London, July 1969.........	1·25	1·25
		a. Horiz strip of 4. Nos. 4614/4617.....	5·00	5·00
		b. Booklet pane. Nos. 4614/4615 and 4618/4619 with margins all round..........	7·25	
4615	**3683**	(1st) East Rutherford, New Jersey, USA, August 2019..........	1·25	1·25
4616	**3684**	(1st) Rotterdam, Netherlands, August 1995..........	1·25	1·25
		b. Booklet pane. Nos. 4616/4617 and 4620/4621 with margins all round..........	7·25	
4617	**3685**	(1st) Tokyo, Japan, March 1995........	1·25	1·25
4618	**3686**	£1·70 New York, July 1972..........	2·50	2·50
		a. Horiz strip of 4. Nos. 4618/4621.....	10·00	10·00
4619	**3687**	£1·70 Oslo, Norway, May 2014..........	2·50	2·50
4620	**3688**	£1·70 Hertfordshire, August 1976.........	2·50	2·50
4621	**3689**	£1·70 Dusseldorf, Germany, October 2017..........	2·50	2·50
Set of 8..........			13·50	13·50
Set of 2 Gutter Strips of 8..........			27·00	
First Day Cover (Tallents House)..........				16·00
First Day Cover (Dartford)..........				16·00
Presentation Pack (Nos. 4614/4621 and **MS**4622) (PO Pack No. 611)..........			23·00	
PHQ Cards (set of 13)..........			8·25	24·00
Souvenir Folder (Nos. 4617/4621 and **MS**4622) (originally sold for £24·99)..........			35·00	
MS4622 202×74 mm. **3690** (1st) Rolling Stones; (1st) Rolling Stones; £1·70 Posters for Tour of Europe, 1974 and Tour of the Americas, 1975; £1·70 Posters for UK Tour, 1971 and American Tour, 1981..........			7·25	7·25
First Day Cover (Tallents House)..........				9·50
First Day Cover (Dartford)..........				9·50

Nos. 4614/4617 and 4618/4621 were each printed together, *se-tenant*, as horizontal strips of four in sheets of 60 (2 panes 4×6).

A Hyde Park fan sheet containing No. 4614×3 was originally sold for £7.

A Voodoo Lounge fan sheet containing No. 4617×3 was originally sold for £7.

The 13 PHQ cards show the 12 individual stamps, including those from No. **MS**4622, and the complete miniature sheet.

3691 Rolling Stones

3692 Rolling Stones

3693 Posters for Tour of Europe, 1974 and Tour of the Americas, 1975

3694 Posters for UK Tour, 1971 and American Tour, 1981

(Des Baxter & Bailey. Litho ISP Cartor)

2022 (20 Jan). The Rolling Stones (2nd issue). Two phosphor bands. Perf 14½.

4623	**3691**	(1st) Rolling Stones..........	1·50	1·50
		a. Booklet pane. Nos. 4623/4626 with margins all round..........	9·00	9·00
4624	**3692**	(1st) Rolling Stones..........	1·50	1·50
4625	**3693**	£1·70 Posters for Tour of Europe, 1974 and Tour of the Americas, 1975.....	3·00	3·00
4626	**3694**	£1·70 Posters for UK Tour, 1971 and American Tour, 1981..........	3·00	3·00
Set of 4..........			9·00	9·00

Nos. 4623/4626 come from No. **MS**4622 and the £20·85 premium booklet, No. DY41.

2022 / QUEEN ELIZABETH II

3695 Queen Elizabeth II at Headquarters of MI5, London, February 2020

3696 Queen Elizabeth II and Duke of Edinburgh, Washington, USA, October 1957

3697 Queen Elizabeth II on Walkabout in Worcester, April 1980

3698 Trooping the Colour, London, June 1978

3699 Leaving Provincial Museum of Alberta, Edmonton, Canada, May 2005

3700 During Silver Jubilee celebrations, Camberwell, June 1977

3701 At Victoria Park, St Vincent, February 1966

3702 Order of the Garter Ceremony, Windsor, June 1999

(Des Kate Stephens. Litho ISP Walsall)

2022 (4 Feb). Platinum Jubilee. Multicoloured. Two phosphor bands. Perf 14½.

4627	3695	(1st) Queen Elizabeth II at headquarters of MI5, London, February 2020	1·25	1·25
		a. Horiz strip of 4. Nos. 4627/4630	5·00	5·00
		b. Booklet pane. Nos. 4627, 4630/4631 and 4634 with margins all round	7·25	
4628	3696	(1st) Queen Elizabeth II and Duke of Edinburgh, Washington, USA, October 1957	1·25	1·25
		b. Booklet pane. Nos. 4628/4629 and 4632/4633 with margins all round	7·25	
4629	3697	(1st) Queen Elizabeth II on walkabout in Worcester, April 1980	1·25	1·25
4630	3698	(1st) Trooping the Colour, London, June 1978	1·25	1·25
4631	3699	£1·70 Leaving Provincial Museum of Alberta, Edmonton, Canada, May 2005	2·50	2·50
		a. Horiz strip of 4. Nos. 4631/4634	10·00	10·00
4632	3700	£1·70 During Silver Jubilee celebrations, Camberwell, June 1977	2·50	2·50
4633	3701	£1·70 At Victoria Park, St Vincent, February 1966	2·50	2·50
4634	3702	£1·70 Order of the Garter ceremony, Windsor, June 1999	2·50	2·50

Set of 8	13·50	13·50
Set of 2 Gutter Strips of 8	27·00	
First Day Cover (Tallents House)		15·00
First Day Cover (London SW1)		15·00
Presentation Pack (PO Pack No. 612)	15·00	
PHQ Cards (set of 8)	5·00	14·00

Nos. 4627/4630 and 4631/4634 were each printed together, *se-tenant*, as horizontal strips of four in sheets of 48 (2 panes 4×6).

3703 The Stamp Designs of David Gentleman

(Des hat-trick design. Litho ISP)

2022 (18 Feb). The Stamp Designs of David Gentleman. Multicoloured. One centre band (2nd) or two bands (others). Perf 14½.
MS4635 202×74 mm. **3703** (2nd) 1962 3d. National Productivity Year; (2nd) 1969 9d. British Ships; (1st) 1973 9p. British Trees; (1st) 1976 8½p. Social Reformers; £1·70 1966 6d. 900th Anniversary of the Battle of Hastings; £1·70 4d. 1965 25th Anniversary of the Battle of Britain .... 9·25 9·25

First Day Cover (Tallents House)		10·50
First Day Cover (London NW1)		10·50
Presentation Pack (PO Pack No. 613)	9·50	
PHQ Cards (set of 7)	4·50	9·50

3704 Arsenal Players Charlie George and Frank McLintock parading FA Cup, 1971

3705 Crowds on pitch at Wembley Stadium during 1923 Cup Final

3706 West Bromwich Albion Supporters at 1968 Cup Final

3707 Keith Houchen equalises for Coventry City against Tottenham Hotspur, 1987 Final

321

QUEEN ELIZABETH II/2022

3708 Lincoln City reach Quarter Finals, 2017 (FA Cup Upsets)

3709 King George VI and Queen Elizabeth present FA Cup to Sunderland Captain Raich Carter, 1937

3710 The FA Cup

(Des The Chase. Litho ISP Cartor)

2022 (8 Mar). The FA Cup. Multicoloured. Two phosphor bands. Perf 14½ (Nos. 4636/4641) or 14 (No. **MS**4642).

4636	**3704**	(1st) Arsenal Players Charlie George and Frank McLintock parading FA Cup, 1971	1·25	1·25
		a. Vert pair. Nos. 4636/4637	2·50	2·50
4637	**3705**	(1st) Crowds on pitch at Wembley Stadium during 1923 Cup Final	1·25	1·25
4638	**3706**	£1·70 West Bromwich Albion Supporters at 1968 Cup Final	2·50	2·50
		a. Vert pair. Nos. 4638/4639	5·00	5·00
4639	**3707**	£1·70 Keith Houchen equalises for Coventry City against Tottenham Hotspur, 1987 Final	2·50	2·50
4640	**3708**	£2·55 Lincoln City reach Quarter Finals, 2017 (FA Cup Upsets)	3·50	3·50
		a. Vert pair. Nos. 4640/4641	7·00	7·00
4641	**3709**	£2·55 King George VI and Queen Elizabeth present FA Cup to Sunderland Captain Raich Carter, 1937	3·50	3·50
Set of 6			13·00	13·00
Set of 3 Gutter Pairs (only 2 stamps in each pair)			15·00	
First Day Cover (Tallents House)				15·00
First Day Cover (Wembley)				15·00
Presentation Pack (Nos. 4636/4641 and **MS**4642) (PO Pack No. 614)			22·00	
PHQ Cards (set of 11)			6·00	22·00

MS4642 202×74 mm. **3710** (1st) Supporter's memorabilia; (1st) Winners' medal and trophy; £1·70 Official match-day items; £1·70 Cup Final souvenirs ...... 7·25 7·25
First Day Cover (Tallents House) .... 9·00
First Day Cover (Wembley) .... 9·00

Nos. 4636/4637, 4638/4639 and 4640/4641 were each printed together, *se-tenant*, in vertical pairs in sheets of 36 (2 panes 3×6).

3711 NHS Workers (Jessica Roberts)

3712 Captain Sir Tom Moore (Shachow Ali)

3713 NHS Hospital Cleaners (Raphael Valle Martin)

3714 NHS/My Mum (Alfie Craddock)

3715 Lab Technician (Logan Pearson)

3716 Delivery Driver (Isabella Grover)

3717 The NHS (Connie Stuart)

3718 Doctors, Nurses (Ishan Bains)

(Des Children's Competition/Royal Mail Design Team. Litho Cartor)

2022 (23 Mar). Heroes of the Covid Pandemic. Winning Entries from Schoolchildren's Stamp Design Competition. Multicoloured. Two phosphor bands. Perf 14×14½.

4643	**3711**	(1st) NHS Workers (Jessica Roberts)	1·25	1·25
		a. Horiz strip of 4. Nos. 4643/4646	5·00	5·00
4644	**3712**	(1st) Captain Sir Tom Moore (Shachow Ali)	1·25	1·25
4645	**3713**	(1st) NHS Hospital Cleaners (Raphael Valle Martin)	1·25	1·25
4646	**3714**	(1st) NHS/My Mum (Alfie Craddock)	1·25	1·25
4647	**3715**	(1st) Lab Technician (Logan Pearson)	1·25	1·25
		a. Horiz strip of 4. Nos. 4647/4650	5·00	5·00
4648	**3716**	(1st) Delivery Driver (Isabella Grover)	1·25	1·25
4649	**3717**	(1st) The NHS (Connie Stuart)	1·25	1·25
4650	**3718**	(1st) Doctors, Nurses (Ishan Bains)	1·25	1·25
Set of 8			9·00	9·00
Set of 2 Gutter Strips of 8			18·00	
First Day Cover (Tallents House)				11·00
First Day Cover (London EC1)				11·00
Presentation Pack (PO Pack No. 615)			10·00	
PHQ Cards (set of 8)			5·00	10·00

Nos. 4243/4246 and 4247/4250 were printed together, *se-tenant*, as horizontal strips of four in sheets of 48 (2 panes 4×6).

3722 Nightjar (*Caprimulgus europaeus*)

3723 Pied Flycatcher (*Ficedula hypoleuca*)

3724 Swift (*Apus apus*)

3725 Yellow Wagtail (*Motacilla flava*)

3726 Arctic Skua (*Stercorarius parasiticus*)

3727 Stone-curlew (*Burhinus oedicnemus*)

3728 Arctic Tern (*Sterna paradisaea*)

3729 Swallow (*Hirundo rustica*)

3730 Turtle Dove (*Streptopelia turtur*)

3731 Montagu's Harrier (*Circus pygargus*)

(Des Killian Mullarney (illustration) and hat-trick design. Litho Cartor)

2022 (7 Apr). Migratory Birds. Multicoloured. Two phosphor bands. Perf 14.

4651	**3722**	(1st) Nightjar (*Caprimulgus europaeus*)	1·25	1·25
		a. Horiz strip of 5. Nos. 4651/4655	6·25	6·25
4653	**3724**	(1st) Swift (*Apus apus*)	1·25	1·25
4654	**3725**	(1st) Yellow Wagtail (*Motacilla flava*)	1·25	1·25
4655	**3726**	(1st) Arctic Skua (*Stercorarius parasiticus*)	1·25	1·25
4656	**3727**	(1st) Stone-curlew (*Burhinus oedicnemus*)	1·25	1·25
		a. Horiz strip of 5. Nos. 4656/4660	6·25	6·25
4657	**3728**	(1st) Arctic Tern (*Sterna paradisaea*)	1·25	1·25
4658	**3729**	(1st) Swallow (*Hirundo rustica*)	1·25	1·25
4659	**3730**	(1st) Turtle Dove (*Streptopelia turtur*)	1·25	1·25
4660	**3731**	(1st) Montagu's Harrier (*Circus pygargus*)	1·25	1·25
Set of 10			12·50	12·50
Set of 2 Gutter Strips of 10			24·00	
First Day Cover (Tallents House)				15·00
First Day Cover (Swallownest, Sheffield)				15·00
Presentation Pack (PO Pack No. 616)			14·00	
PHQ Cards (set of 10)			6·25	14·00

Nos. 4651/4655 and 4656/4660 were each printed together, *se-tenant*, as horizontal strips of five in sheets of 50 (2 panes 5×5).

Subscribe & Save Money
on the cover price*

12-Month Print Subscription
UK £53
Europe (airmail) £90

ROW (airmail) £95

*UK print subscriptions only

Visit stanleygibbons.com/gsm
or call +44 (0)1425 472 363

PUBLIC AUCTIONS
IN THE NORTH OF ENGLAND

Our Public Sales include interesting and unusual material, with individual collections offered intact, specialised ranges, better singles or sets and Postal History.

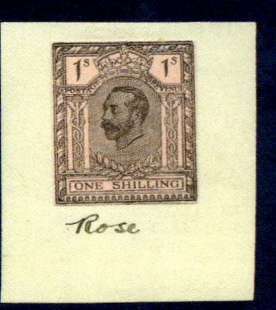

Visit our website for Great Britain Direct Sales & Private Treaty offers, regularly updated

www.corbitts.com

CORBITTS

Established 50 Years

5 Mosley Street, Newcastle upon Tyne, NE1 1YE
Tel: 0191 232 7268 Fax: 0191 261 4130
Email: info@corbitts.com

Members of: Philatelic Traders Society • American Stamp Dealers Association • American Philatelic Society

IG STAMPS

At IG Stamps we specialise in GB philatelic material. We have all the new issues right up to date including all the awkward stamps from booklets and the U number Machin stamps with security overlay.

With a no quibble refund policy and a secure checkout you know you can buy with confidence.

www.gbstampsonline.co.uk

PO BOX 3330, NORWICH, NR7 7FU
TELEPHONE 01603 419307
info@gbstampsonline.co.uk

Great Britain 1840-2015

Our latest lists cover all the periods of G.B. from Penny Blacks to modern Machins

Free Lists on Request

Definitive issues • Commemorative issues • Booklets
• Booklet panes • Commemorative FDC's
• Coils • Presentation packs • Miniature sheets
• Definitive FDC's • PHQ cards
• Specialised Wildings • Specialised Machins and more ...

For a friendly personal service, why not request your free copy today, or send us a list of your requirements.

Whether buying or selling we look forward to your enquiries

ArunStamps

P.O. BOX 15 FAKENHAM NORFOLK NR21 0EU
TELEPHONE 01328 829318 • MOBILE 07881812523
Email *info@arunstamps.co.uk* • Website *www.arunstamps.co.uk*

Subscribe & Save Money
on the cover price*

12-Month Print Subscription

UK £53
Europe (airmail) £90

ROW (airmail) £95

GIBBONS Stamp MONTHLY

Decimal Machin Definitives

Page		Date	Cat. Numbers
327	High values 'standard' perforations	1970–1972	829–831b
328–333	Denominated stamps 'standard' perforations, ordinary gum	1971–1996	X841–X1058
333	High values 'standard' perforations	1977–1987	1026–1028
334–337	Denominated stamps 'standard' perforations index		
337	Multi-value coil index		
338–341	'X' numbers booklet pane guide		
342	NVI stamps 'standard' perforations	1989–1993	1445–1516
342-344	NVI stamps 'elliptical' perforations	1993-2017	1664–1672
344	NVI stamps 'standard' perforations (Large format)	1999	2077-2079
345–346	NVI stamps booklet pane guide		
347–349	Denominated stamps 'elliptical' perforations	1993–2017	Y1667–Y1803
350–353	Stamps with 'elliptical' perforations index		
354–355	'Y' numbers booklet pane guide		
356	Self-adhesive stamps, elliptical perforations	1993–1998	1789, 1976/1977, 2039/2040, 2295–2298
356–357	'Millenium Machins'	2000	2124, MS2146, MS2147
357	NVI Overseas booklet machins	2003	2357a–2359
358	NVI 'Pricing in Proportion' Machins	2006	2650–2655
361–363	Denominated Security Machins, self-adhesive	2009–2020	U2911–U2974, U3055–U3059
362	NVI Security Machins, self-adhesive	2009–2017	U2975–U3039
3632-363	Special Service Security Machins, self-adhesive	2009–2013	U3045–U3052
363–365	Denominated Security Machins, ordinary gum	2010–2022	U3060–U3061, U3070–U3157, MS3073
363–365	NVI Security Machins, ordinary gum	2010–2021	U3065–U3067, MS3222
365	NVI 'Diamond Jubilee' Machins	2012	U3271–U3279
366	NVI 'Long to reign Over Us' Machins	2015–2016	U3744–U3747
366	'65th Anniversary of Accession' Machin	2017	U3966
366	'50th Anniversary of the Machin' Machin	2017	MS3965, U3966
367–368	'U' numbers booklet pane guide		
369–375	Security Machins (Source and year code tables)		
376	NVI Barcode Machin, self-adhesive	2021–2022	V4500–V4510
376	Denominated Barcode Machins, ordinary gum	2022	V4700–V4780
378	Barcode Machins (Source and year code tables)		

DENOMINATED STAMPS, PVA, PVAD OR GUM ARABIC, 'STANDARD' PERFORATIONS

356a

357 (Value redrawn)

(Des after plaster cast by Arnold Machin. Recess B.W.)

1970 (17 June)–**72**. Decimal Currency. Chalk-surfaced paper or phosphorised paper (10p.). Perf 12.

829	**356a**	10p. cerise	50	50
830		20p. olive-green	60	20
		a. Thinner uncoated paper*		
831		50p. deep ultramarine	1·25	25
		a. Thinner uncoated paper*	60·00	
831b	**357**	£1 bluish black (6.12.72)	2·25	40
Set of 4			3·25	1·20
First Day Cover (Nos. 829/831)				2·00
First Day Cover (No. 831b)				2·50
Presentation Pack No. 18 (Nos. 829/831)			8·00	
Presentation Pack No. 38 (Nos. 790 (or 831b), 830/831)			12·50	

* These are not as apparent as uncoated photogravure issues where there is normally a higher degree of chalk-surfacing. The 20p. is known only as a block of four with Plate No. 5. The 50p. comes from Plate No. 9.

The 10p. on phosphorised paper continued the experiments which started with the Machin 1s.6d. When the experiment had ended a quantity of the 50p. value was printed on the phosphorised paper to use up the stock. These stamps were issued on 1 February 1973, but they cannot be distinguished from No. 831 by the naked eye. (*Price £2*).

A £1 was also issued in 1970, but it is difficult to distinguish it from the earlier No. 790. In common with the other 1970 values it was issued in sheets of 100.

A whiter paper was introduced in 1973. The £1 appeared on 27 September 1973, the 20p. on 30 November 1973 and the 50p. on 20 February 1974.

Imperforate examples of No. 831b are believed to be printer's waste.

Special First Day of Issue Postmarks

British Philatelic Bureau, Edinburgh (Type C) (Nos. 829/831)	3·00
Windsor, Berks (Type C) (Nos. 829/831)	6·50
Philatelic Bureau, Edinburgh (Type E) (No. 831b)	3·00
Windsor, Berks (Type E) (No. 831b)	8·00

'X' NUMBERS. The following definitive series has been allocated 'X' prefixes to the catalogue numbers to avoid renumbering all subsequent issues

NO VALUE INDICATED. Stamps as Types **367/367a** inscribed '2nd' or '1st' are listed as Nos. 1445/1452, 1511/1516, 1664/1672, 2039/2040 and 2295.

ELLIPTICAL PERFORATIONS. These were introduced in 1993 and stamps showing them will be found listed as Nos. Y1667 etc.

367 **367a**

Printing differences

Litho   Gravure

(Illustrations enlarged ×6)

Litho. Clear outlines to value and frame formed by edges of screen.
Gravure. Uneven lines to value and frame formed by edges of screen.

Two types of the 3p., 10p. and 26p.
(Nos. X930/X930c, X886/X886b and X971/971b)

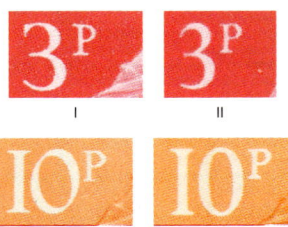

I   II

I   II

MACHINS *Denominated stamps, PVA, PVAD or gum arabic, 'standard' perforations*

	I	II

Figures of face values as I (all ptgs of 3p. bright magenta except the multi-value coil No. 930cl and sheets from 21.1.92 onwards, 10p. orange-brown except 1984 Christian Heritage £4 booklet and 26p. rosine except 1987 (£1·04 barcode booklet).

Figures of face value narrower as in II (from coil No. X930cl and in sheets from 21.2.92 (3p.), 1984 Christian Heritage £4 booklet (10p.) or 1987 £1·04 barcode booklet (26p.)). This catalogue includes changes of figure styles on these stamps where there is no other listable difference. Similar changes have also taken place on other values, but only in conjunction with listed colour, paper or perforation changes.

1971 (15 Feb)–**96**. Decimal Currency. T **367**. Chalk-surfaced paper.
(a) Photo Harrison (except for some printings of Nos. X879 and X913 in sheets produced by Enschedé and issued on 12 December 1979 (8p.) and 19 November 1991 (18p.)). With phosphor bands. Perf 15×14.

X841	½p. turquoise-blue (2 bands)	10	10
	a. Imperf (pair)†	£2500	
	y. Phosphor omitted	4·00	
	l. Booklet pane. No. X841×2 se-tenant vert with X849×2	6·00	
	ly. Booklet pane. Phosphor omitted	£225	
	la. Booklet pane. No. X841×2 se-tenant horiz with X849×2 (14.7.71)	1·00	
	lay. Booklet pane. Phosphor omitted	£375	
	m. Booklet pane. No. X841×5 plus label	2·75	
	my. Booklet pane. Phosphor omitted	£120	
	n. Coil strip. No. X849g, X841g×2 and X844g×2	3·50	
	ny. Coil strip. Phosphor omitted	£500	
	nv. Coil strip. PVA gum. No. X849, X841×2 and X844×2 (4.74)	80	
	nvy. Coil strip. Phosphor omitted	18·00	
	o. Booklet pane. No. X841, X851, X852, X852a, each×3 (24.5.72)	6·00	
	oy. Booklet pane. Phosphor omitted	£1200	
	p. Booklet pane. No. X841×3, X842 and X852×2 (24.5.72)	60·00	
	py. Booklet pane. Phosphor omitted		
	q. Coil strip. No. X870, X849, X844 and X841×2 (3.12.75)	80	
	r. Booklet pane. No. X841×2, X844×3 and X870 (10.3.76)	40	
	s. Booklet pane. No. X841×2, X844×2, X873×2 and X881×4 (8½p. values at right) (26.1.77)	1·50	
	sa. Ditto, but No. X873a and 8½p. values at left	1·50	
	t. Booklet pane. No. X841, X844, X894×3 and X902 (14p. value at right) (26.1.81)	1·50	
	ty. Booklet pane. Phosphor omitted	65·00	
	ta. Booklet pane. No. X841, X844, X894a×3 and X902 (14p. value at left)	1·50	
	tay. Booklet pane. Phosphor omitted	65·00	
	u. Booklet pane. No. X841, X857×4 and X899×3 (12½p. values at left) (1.2.82)	1·00	
	ua. Ditto, but No. X899a and 12½p. values at right	1·75	
	g. Gum arabic (from coil strip, and on 22.9.72 from sheets)	40	
	gy. Phosphor omitted	70·00	
X842	½p. turquoise-blue (1 side band at left) (24.5.72)	55·00	25·00
X843	½p. turquoise-blue (1 centre band) (14.12.77)	20	20
	l. Coil strip. No. X843×2, X875 and X845×2 (14.12.77)	85	
	m. Booklet pane. No. X843×2, X845×2 and X875 plus label (8.2.78)	35	
	my. Booklet pane. Phosphor omitted	45·00	
X844	1p. crimson (2 bands)	10	10
	a. Imperf (vert coil)	£750	
	b. Pair, one imperf 3 sides (vert coil)	£750	
	c. Imperf (pair)	5·00	
	y. Phosphor omitted		
	l. Booklet pane. No. X844×2 se-tenant vert with X848×2	4·75	
	m. Ditto, but se-tenant horiz (14.7.71)	1·00	
	my. Booklet pane. Phosphor omitted	£300	
	n. Booklet pane. No. X844×2, X876×3 and X883×3 (9p. values at right) (13.6.77)	2·50	
	na. Ditto, but No. X876a and 9p. values at left	1·50	
	g. Gum arabic (from coil strip)	50	
	gy. Phosphor omitted	70·00	
X845	1p. crimson (1 centre band) (14.12.77)	20	20
	l. Booklet pane. No. X879 and X845×2 plus label (17.10.79)	30	
	m. Coil strip. No. X879 and X845×2 plus 2 labels (16.1.80)	85	
	n. Booklet pane. No. X845×2, X860 and X898 each×3 (5.4.83)	3·50	
	ny. Booklet pane. Phosphor omitted	22·00	
	p. Booklet pane. No. X845×3, X863×2 and X900×3 (3.9.84)	2·50	
	py. Booklet pane. Phosphor omitted	£250	
	q. Booklet pane. No. X845×2 and X896×4 (29.7.86)	6·50	
	s. Booklet pane. No. X845, X867×2 and X900×3 (20.10.86)	3·25	
	sa. Ditto, but with vertical edges of pane imperf (29.9.87)	1·75	
	say. Booklet pane. Phosphor omitted	£225	
X846	1p. crimson ('all-over') (10.10.79)	20	20
X847	1p. crimson (1 side band at left) (20.10.86)	80	80
	a. Band at right (3.3.87)	4·50	4·50
	l. Booklet pane. No. X847, X901 and X912×2 (20.10.86)	1·75	
	ly. Booklet pane. Phosphor omitted	£110	
	m. Booklet pane. No. X847a, X901×2, X912×5 and X918 with margins all round (3.3.87)	7·00	
X848	1½p. black (2 bands)	20	20
	a. Uncoated paper*	£130	
	b. Imperf (pair)		
	c. Imperf 3 sides (horiz pair)	60·00	
	y. Phosphor omitted		
X849	2p. myrtle-green (2 bands)	15	15
	a. Imperf (horiz pair)	£2000	
	y. Phosphor omitted	12·00	
	l. Booklet pane. No. X849×2, X880×2 and X886×3 plus label (10p. values at right) (28.8.79)	1·50	
	la. Ditto, but No. X880a and 10p. values at left	1·50	
	m. Booklet pane. No. X849×3, X889×2 and X895×2 plus label (12p. values at right) (4.2.80)	1·50	
	my. Booklet pane. Phosphor omitted	55·00	
	ma. Booklet pane. No. X849×3, X889a×2 and X895×2 plus label (12p. values at left)	1·50	
	may. Booklet pane. Phosphor omitted	55·00	
	n. Booklet pane. No. X849, X888×3, X889a and X895×4 with margins all round (16.4.80)	2·25	
	ny. Booklet pane. Phosphor omitted	55·00	
	o. Booklet pane. No. X849×6 with margins all round (16.4.80)	80	
	oy. Booklet pane. Phosphor omitted	60·00	
	p. Booklet pane. No. X849, X857, X898, X899×3 and X899a×3 with margins all round (19.5.82)	3·50	
	py. Booklet pane. Phosphor omitted	£150	
	g. Gum arabic (from coil strip)	1·60	
	gy. Phosphor omitted	£225	
X850	2p. myrtle-green ('all-over' phosphor) (10.10.79)	25	25
X851	2½p. magenta (1 centre band)	15	15
	a. Imperf (pair)†	£225	
	y. Phosphor omitted	10·00	
	l. Booklet pane. No. X851×5 plus label	3·50	
	ly. Booklet pane. Phosphor omitted	55·00	
	m. Booklet pane. No. X851×4 plus two labels	4·00	
	my. Booklet pane. Phosphor omitted	£425	
	n. Booklet pane. No. X851×3, X852a×3 and X855×6 (24.5.72)	4·75	
	ny. Booklet pane. Phosphor omitted		
	g. Gum arabic (13.9.72)	1·00	
X852	2½p. magenta (1 band at left)	80	80
	l. Booklet pane. No. X852×2 and X855×4	4·25	
	ly. Booklet pane. Phosphor omitted	£160	
	a. Band at right (24.5.72)	80	80
X853	2½p. magenta (2 bands) (21.5.75)	20	20
X854	2½p. rose-red (2 bands) (26.8.81)	30	30
	l. Booklet pane. No. X854×3, X862×2 and X894×3 (11½p. values at left)	4·25	
	la. Ditto, but No. X894a and 11½p. values at right	4·25	
X855	3p. ultramarine (2 bands)	20	20
	a. Imperf (coil strip of 5)	£2000	
	b. Imperf (pair)†	£300	
	c. Uncoated paper*	45·00	
	y. Phosphor omitted	5·00	
	l. Booklet pane. No. X855×5 plus label	2·00	
	ly. Booklet pane. Phosphor omitted	£375	
	n. Booklet pane. No. X855×12 (24.5.72)	3·00	
	ny. Booklet pane. Phosphor omitted	£250	
	g. Gum arabic (23.8.72)	1·40	
	gy. Phosphor omitted	10·00	
X856	3p. ultramarine (1 centre band) (10.9.73)	15	15
	a. Imperf (pair)†	£275	
	b. Imperf between (vert pair)†	£475	
	c. Imperf horiz (vert pair)†	£250	
	g. Gum arabic	60	
X857	3p. bright magenta (Type I) (2 bands) (1.2.82)	25	25

Denominated stamps, PVA, PVAD or gum arabic, 'standard' perforations MACHINS

X858	3½p. olive-grey (2 bands) (shades)	£160	
	a. Imperf (pair)	40	40
	y. Phosphor omitted	£375	
	b. Bronze-green (18.7.73)	12·00	
	by. Phosphor omitted	1·25	1·25
		12·00	
X859	3½p. olive-grey (1 centre band) (24.6.74)	30	30
X860	3½p. purple-brown (1 centre band) (5.4.83)	1·75	1·75
	y. Phosphor omitted	10·00	
X861	4p. ochre-brown (2 bands)	20	20
	a. Imperf (pair)†	£1300	
	y. Phosphor omitted	38·00	
	g. Gum arabic (1.11.72)	50	
X862	4p. greenish blue (2 bands) (26.8.81)	2·25	2·25
X863	4p. greenish blue (1 centre band) (3.9.84)	1·25	1·25
	y. Phosphor omitted	90·00	
X864	4p. greenish blue (1 side band) (8.1.85)	4·50	4·50
	a. Band at left	4·50	4·50
	l. Booklet pane. No. X864, X864a, X901×2, X901a×2, X909×2 and X920 with margins all round (8.1.85)	10·00	
	ly. Booklet pane. Phosphor omitted	£2250	
X865	4½p. grey-blue (2 bands) (24.10.73)	20	20
	a. Imperf (pair)	£375	
	y. Phosphor omitted	11·00	
X866	5p. pale violet (2 bands)	20	20
	y. Phosphor omitted	£250	
X867	5p. claret (1 centre band) (20.10.86)	1·00	1·00
	y. Phosphor omitted	85·00	
X868	5½p. violet (2 bands) (24.10.73)	25	25
X869	5½p. violet (1 centre band) (17.3.75)	25	25
	a. Uncoated paper*	£250	
	y. Phosphor omitted	22·00	
X870	6p. light emerald (2 bands)	25	25
	a. Uncoated paper*	20·00	
	y. Phosphor omitted	75·00	
	g. Gum arabic (6.6.73)	2·00	
X871	6½p. greenish blue (2 bands) (4.9.74)	30	30
X872	6½p. greenish blue (1 centre band) (24.9.75)	25	25
	a. Imperf (vert pair)	£250	
	b. Uncoated paper*	£150	
	y. Phosphor omitted	15·00	
X873	6½p. greenish blue (1 band at right) (26.1.77)	80	80
	a. Band at left	80	80
X874	7p. purple-brown (2 bands) (15.1.75)	25	25
	a. Imperf (pair)	£800	
	y. Phosphor omitted	4·00	
X875	7p. purple-brown (1 centre band) (13.6.77)	25	25
	a. Imperf (pair)	£125	
	l. Booklet pane. No. X875 and X883, each×10 (15.11.78)	2·50	
X876	7p. purple-brown (1 band at right) (13.6.77)	35	35
	a. Band at left	35	35
X877	7½p. pale chestnut (2 bands)	25	25
	y. Phosphor omitted	22·00	
X878	8p. rosine (2 bands) (24.10.73)	25	25
	a. Uncoated paper*	15·00	
X879	8p. rosine (1 centre band) (20.8.79)	25	25
	a. Uncoated paper*	£550	
	b. Imperf (pair)	—	
	y. Phosphor omitted	£275	
	l. Booklet pane. No. X879 and X886, each×10 (14.11.79)	3·00	
X880	8p. rosine (1 band at right) (28.8.79)	50	50
	a. Band at left	50	50
X881	8½p. light yellowish green (2 bands) (shades) (24.9.75)	25	25
	a. Imperf (pair)	—	
	b. Yellowish green (24.3.76)	1·00	50
	y. Phosphor omitted	6·00	
X882	9p. yellow-orange and black (2 bands)	40	40
	y. Phosphor omitted	80·00	
X883	9p. deep violet (2 bands) (25.2.76)	25	25
	a. Imperf (pair)	£180	
	y. Phosphor omitted	4·50	
X884	9½p. purple (2 bands) (25.2.76)	30	30
	y. Phosphor omitted	24·00	
X885	10p. orange-brown and chestnut (2 bands) (11.8.71)	30	30
	a. Orange-brown omitted	£140	
	b. Imperf (horiz pair)	£3000	
	y. Phosphor omitted	12·00	
X886	10p. orange-brown (Type I) (2 bands) (25.2.76)	30	30
	a. Imperf (pair)	£350	
	y. Phosphor omitted	3·00	
	b. Type II (4.9.84)	14·00	14·00
	by. Phosphor omitted	£1400	
	bl. Booklet pane. No. X886b, X901a and X909×7 with margins all round	15·00	
	bly. Booklet pane. Phosphor omitted	£2000	
X887	10p. orange-brown (Type I) ('all-over') (3.10.79)	25	25
X888	10p. orange-brown (Type I) (1 centre band) (4.2.80)	25	25
	a. Imperf (pair)	£275	
	l. Booklet pane. No. X888×9 with margins all round (16.4.80)	2·25	
	ly. Booklet pane. Phosphor omitted	55·00	
	m. Booklet pane. No. X888 and X895, each×10 (12.11.80)	3·25	
X889	10p. orange-brown (Type I) (1 band at right) (4.2.80)	1·10	1·10
	a. Band at left	1·00	1·00
X890	10½p. yellow (2 bands) (25.2.76)	35	35
X891	10½p. deep dull blue (2 bands) (26.4.78)	40	40
X892	11p. brown-red (2 bands) (25.2.76)	30	30
	a. Imperf (pair)	£2500	
	y. Phosphor omitted	5·00	
X893	11½p. drab (1 centre band) (14.1.81)	30	30
	a. Imperf	£300	
	y. Phosphor omitted	7·00	
	l. Booklet pane. No. X893 and X902, each×10 (11.11.81)	4·25	
X894	11½p. drab (1 band at right) (26.1.81)	35	35
	a. Band at left	35	35
	l. Booklet pane. No. X894/X894a, each×2 and X902×6 (6.5.81)	3·75	
X895	12p. yellowish green (2 bands) (4.2.80)	40	40
	y. Phosphor omitted	8·00	
	l. Booklet pane. No. X895×9 with margins all round (16.4.80)	2·25	
	ly. Booklet pane. Phosphor omitted	65·00	
X896	12p. bright emerald (1 centre band) (29.10.85)	40	40
	a. Imperf (pair)	£2000	
	y. Phosphor omitted	12·00	
	l. Booklet pane. No. X896×9 with margins all round (18.3.86)	2·50	
	ly. Booklet pane. Phosphor omitted	£225	
	u. Underprint Type 4 (29.10.85)	80	
X897	12p. bright emerald (1 band at right) (14.1.86)	55	55
	a. Band at left	55	55
	l. Booklet pane. No. X897/X897a, each×2 and X909×6 (12p. values at left) (14.1.86)	3·50	
	la. Ditto, but 12p. values at right	3·50	
	m. Booklet pane. No. X897/X897a, each×3, X909×2 and X919 with margins all round (18.3.86)	15·00	
	my. Booklet pane. Phosphor omitted	£800	
X898	12½p. light emerald (1 centre band) (27.1.82)	30	30
	a. Imperf (pair)	£100	
	y. Phosphor omitted	6·50	
	u. Underprint Type 1 (10.11.82)	40	
	uy. Phosphor omitted	75·00	
	v. Underprint Type 2 (9.11.83)	40	
	l. Booklet pane. No. X898u and X907u, each×10 (10.11.82)	5·00	
X899	12½p. light emerald (1 band at right) (1.2.82)	30	30
	a. Band at left	30	30
	l. Booklet pane. No. X899/X899a, each×2 and X907×6 (1.2.82)††	3·00	
	ly. Booklet pane. Phosphor omitted	£3600	
	m. Booklet pane. No. X899/X899a, each×3 with margins all round (19.5.82)	2·00	
	my. Booklet pane. Phosphor omitted	45·00	
	n. Booklet pane. No. X899/X899a, each×2, and X908×6 (12½p. values at left) (5.4.83)	4·75	
	na. Ditto, but 12½p. values at right	4·75	
X900	13p. pale chestnut (1 centre band) (28.8.84)	30	30
	a. Imperf (pair)	£450	
	u. Underprint Type 2 (2.12.86)	40	
	y. Phosphor omitted	6·50	
	l. Booklet pane. No. X900×9 with margins all round (8.1.85)	2·50	
	ly. Booklet pane. Phosphor omitted	£425	
	m. Booklet pane. No. X900×6 with margins all round (3.3.87)	2·00	
	n. Booklet pane. No. X900×4 with margins all round (4.8.87)	2·25	
	o. Booklet pane. No. X900×10 with margins all round (4.8.87)	3·50	
X901	13p. pale chestnut (1 band at right) (3.9.84)	40	40
	a. Band at left	40	40
	l. Booklet pane. No. X901/X901a, each×2, and X909×6 (13p. values at left)††	3·00	
	la. Ditto, but 13p. values at right	3·00	
	m. Booklet pane. No. X901/X901a, each×3 with margins all round (4.9.84)	2·25	
	my. Booklet pane. Phosphor omitted	£325	
	n. Booklet pane. No. X901a and X912×5 (20.10.86)	3·00	
	na. Ditto, but with vertical edges of pane imperf (29.9.87)	3·00	
X902	14p. grey-blue (2 bands) (26.1.81)	90	90
	y. Phosphor omitted	30·00	
X903	14p. deep blue (1 centre band) (23.8.88)	45	45
	a. Imperf (pair)	£325	
	y. Phosphor omitted	9·00	

MACHINS *Denominated stamps, PVA, PVAD or gum arabic, 'standard' perforations*

		l. Booklet pane. No. X903×4 with margins all round	3·50		X927	a. Imperf (pair)	£2250	
		ly. Booklet pane. Phosphor omitted	£110			2p. deep green (face value as Type **367a**) (26.7.88)	75	75
		m. Booklet pane. No. X903×10 with margins all round	8·50			a. Imperf (pair)	£2250	
		n. Booklet pane. No. X903×4 with horizontal edges of pane imperf (11.10.88)	4·00			l. Booklet pane. No. X927×2 and X969×4 plus 2 labels with vert edges of pane imperf (10.9.91)	2·00	
		p. Booklet pane. No. X903×10 with horizontal edges of pane imperf (11.10.88)	5·50		X928	2p. myrtle-green (face value as Type **367a**) (5.9.88)	10·00	10·00
		py. Booklet pane. Phosphor omitted	£160			l. Coil strip. No. X928 and X932a×3	10·50	
		q. Booklet pane. No. X903×4 with three edges of pane imperf (24.1.89)	20·00		X929	2½p. rose-red (14.1.81)	20	20
		qy. Booklet pane. Phosphor omitted	35·00			l. Coil strip. No. X929 and X930×3 (6.81)	1·00	
X904		14p. deep blue (1 band at right) (5.9.88)	4·00	4·00	X930	3p. bright magenta (Type I) (22.10.80)	20	20
		l. Booklet pane. No. X904 and X914×2 plus label	5·00			a. Imperf (horiz pair)	£1400	
		ly. Booklet pane. Phosphor omitted	15·00			l. Booklet pane. No. X930, X931×2 and X949×6 with margins all round (14.9.83)	3·75	
		m. Booklet pane. No. X904×2 and X914×4 with vertical edges of pane imperf	3·75			c. Type II (10.10.89)	2·00	2·00
		my. Booklet pane. Phosphor omitted	£850			cl. Coil strip. No. X930c and X933×3	2·50	
X905		15p. bright blue (1 centre band) (26.9.89)	50	50	X931	3½p. purple-brown (30.3.83)	30	30
		a. Imperf (pair)	£500		X932	4p. greenish blue (30.12.81)	25	25
		y. Phosphor omitted	14·00			a. Pale greenish blue (14.8.84)	25	25
X906		15p. bright blue (1 band at left) (2.10.89)	3·00	3·00	X933	4p. new blue (26.7.88)	35	35
		a. Band at right (20.3.90)	2·50	2·50		a. Imperf (pair)	£2500	
		l. Booklet pane. No. X906×2 and X916 plus label	7·50			l. Coil strip. No. X933×3 and X935 (27.11.90)	1·40	
		ly. Booklet pane. Phosphor omitted	£550			m. Coil strip. No. X933 and X935, each×2 (1.10.91)	1·00	
		m. Booklet pane. No. X906a, X916, X922, 1446, 1448, 1468a, 1470 and 1472 plus label with margins all round (20.3.90)	13·00			n. Coil strip. No. X933 and X935×3 (31.1.95)	1·25	
X907		15½p. pale violet (2 bands) (1.2.82)	30	30	X934	5p. pale violet (10.10.79)	30	30
		y. Phosphor omitted	7·00		X935	5p. dull red-brown (26.7.88)	25	25
		u. Underprint Type 1 (10.11.82)	40			a. Imperf (pair)	£3750	
		l. Booklet pane. No. X907×6 with margins all round (19.5.82)	2·50		X936	6p. yellow-olive (10.9.91)	25	25
		ly. Booklet pane. Phosphor omitted	85·00		X937	7p. brownish red (29.10.85)	1·50	1·50
		m. Booklet pane. No. X907×9 with margins all round (19.5.82)	3·25		X938	8½p. yellowish green (24.3.76)	65	50
		my. Booklet pane. Phosphor omitted	50·00		X939	10p. orange-brown (Type I) (11.79)	35	35
X908		16p. olive-drab (2 bands) (5.4.83)	90	90	X940	10p. dull orange (Type II) (4.9.90)	35	35
		y. Phosphor omitted	£110		X941	11p. brown-red (27.8.80)	1·00	1·00
X909		17p. grey-blue (2 bands) (3.9.84)	50	50	X942	11½p. ochre-brown (15.8.79)	40	40
		y. Phosphor omitted	£250		X943	12p. yellowish green (30.1.80)	40	40
		u. Underprint Type 4 (4.11.85)	60		X944	13p. olive-grey (15.8.79)	55	55
		uy. Phosphor omitted	22·00		X945	13½p. purple-brown (30.1.80)	80	80
		l. Booklet pane. No. X909u×3 plus label (4.11.85)	2·25		X946	14p. grey-blue (14.1.81)	50	50
		ly. Booklet pane. Phosphor omitted	65·00		X947	15p. ultramarine (15.8.79)	60	60
		la. Booklet pane. No. X909×3 plus label (12.8.86)	3·00		X948	15½p. pale violet (14.1.81)	45	45
X910		17p. deep blue (1 centre band) (4.9.90)	70	70		a. Imperf (pair)	£200	
		a. Imperf (pair)	£1700		X949	16p. olive-drab (30.3.83)	40	40
X911		17p. deep blue (1 band at right) (4.9.90)	12·00	12·00		a. Imperf (pair)	£125	
		a. Band at left	1·50	1·50		u. Underprint Type 3 (10.8.83)	50	
		y. Phosphor omitted	12·00			l. Booklet pane. No. X949×9 with margins all round (14.9.83)	3·00	
		l. Booklet pane. No. X911 and X911a×2 plus label	10·00		X950	16½p. pale chestnut (27.1.82)	80	80
		ly. Booklet pane. Phosphor omitted	55·00		X951	17p. light emerald (30.1.80)	60	60
		m. Booklet pane. No. X911×2 and X917×3 plus three labels with vertical edges of pane imperf	3·00		X952	17p. grey-blue (30.3.83)	55	55
		my. Booklet pane. Phosphor omitted	75·00			a. Imperf (pair)	£225	
X912		18p. deep olive-grey (2 bands) (20.10.86)	60	60		u. Underprint Type 3 (5.3.85)	60	
		y. Phosphor omitted	30·00			l. Booklet pane. No. X952×6 with margins all round (4.9.84)	2·25	
X913		18p. bright green (1 centre band) (10.9.91)	50	50		m. Booklet pane. No. X952×9 with margins all round (8.1.85)	3·25	
		a. Imperf (pair)	£450		X953	17½p. pale chestnut (30.1.80)	60	60
		y. Phosphor omitted	28·00		X954	18p. deep violet (14.1.81)	60	60
X914		19p. bright orange-red (2 bands) (5.9.88)	1·00	1·00	X955	18p. deep olive-grey (28.8.84)	60	60
		y. Phosphor omitted	4·00			a. Imperf (pair)	£100	
X915		20p. dull purple (2 bands) (25.2.76)	80	80		l. Booklet pane. No. X955×9 with margins all round (3.3.87)	3·50	
X916		20p. brownish black (2 bands) (2.10.89)	2·00	2·00		m. Booklet pane. No. X955×4 with margins all round (4.8.87)	2·25	
		y. Phosphor omitted	£550			n. Booklet pane. No. X955×10 with margins all round (4.8.87)	4·75	
X917		22p. bright orange-red (2 bands) (4.9.90)	90	90	X956	19p. bright orange-red (23.8.88)	80	60
		y. Phosphor omitted	22·00			a. Imperf (pair)	£325	
X917a		25p. rose-red (2 bands) (6.2.96)	9·00	9·00		l. Booklet pane. No. X956×4 with margins all round	4·00	
X918		26p. rosine (Type I) (2 bands) (3.3.87)	8·00	8·00		m. Booklet pane. No. X956×10 with margins all round	6·50	
X919		31p. purple (2 bands) (18.3.86)	10·00	10·00		n. Booklet pane. No. X956×4 with horizontal edges of pane imperf (11.10.88)	5·00	
		y. Phosphor omitted	£800			o. Booklet pane. No. X956×10 with horizontal edges of pane imperf (11.10.88)	6·50	
X920		34p. ochre-brown (2 bands) (8.1.85)	6·00	6·00		q. Booklet pane. No. X956×4 with three edges of pane imperf (24.1.89)	20·00	
		y. Phosphor omitted	£800		X957	19½p. olive-grey (27.1.82)	1·90	1·90
X921		50p. ochre-brown (2 bands) (2.2.77)	1·75	1·75	X958	20p. dull purple (10.10.79)	1·00	1·00
X922		50p. ochre (2 bands) (20.3.90)	3·75	3·75	X959	20p. turquoise-green (23.8.88)	75	75
					X960	20p. brownish black (26.9.89)	65	65
		(b) Photo Harrison. On phosphorised paper. Perf 15×14.				a. Imperf (pair)	£825	
X924		½p. turquoise-blue (10.12.80)	20	20		l. Booklet pane. No. X960×5 plus label with vertical edges of pane imperf (2.10.89)	4·00	
		a. Imperf (pair)	£120		X961	20½p. ultramarine (30.3.83)	1·10	1·10
		l. Coil strip. No. X924 and X932×3 (30.12.81)	75			a. Imperf (pair)	£1600	
X925		1p. crimson (12.12.79)	20	20	X962	22p. blue (22.10.80)	70	70
		a. Imperf (pair)	£500			a. Imperf (pair)	£325	
		l. Coil strip. No. X925 and X932a×3 (14.8.84)	90		X963	22p. yellow-green (28.8.84)	70	70
		m. Booklet pane. No. X925 and X969, each×2 (10.9.91)	1·50			a. Imperf (horiz pair)	£2000	
X926		2p. myrtle-green (face value as Type **367**) (12.12.79)	20	20				

X964	22p. bright orange-red (4.9.90)	80	80
	a. Imperf (pair)	£875	
X965	23p. brown-red (30.3.83)	1·50	1·50
	a. Imperf (horiz pair)	£1500	
X966	23p. bright green (23.8.88)	1·25	1·25
X967	24p. violet (28.8.84)	1·60	1·60
X968	24p. Indian red (26.9.89)	2·00	2·00
	a. Imperf (horiz pair)	£3000	
X969	24p. chestnut (10.9.91)	80	80
	a. Imperf (pair)	£225	
X970	25p. purple (14.1.81)	90	90
X971	26p. rosine (Type I) (27.1.82)	90	90
	a. Imperf (horiz pair)	£800	
	b. Type II (4.8.87)	6·00	6·00
	bl. Booklet pane. No. X971b×4 with margins all round	24·00	
X972	26p. drab (4.9.90)	1·50	1·50
X973	27p. chestnut (23.8.88)	1·00	1·00
	l. Booklet pane. No. X973×4 with margins all round	8·00	
	m. Booklet pane. No. X973×4 with horizontal edges of pane imperf (11.10.88)	20·00	
X974	27p. violet (4.9.90)	1·00	1·00
X975	28p. deep violet (30.3.83)	1·00	1·00
	a. Imperf (pair)	£2000	
X976	28p. ochre (23.8.88)	1·00	1·00
X977	28p. deep bluish grey (10.9.91)	1·00	1·00
	a. Imperf (pair)	£2500	
X978	29p. ochre-brown (27.1.82)	1·10	1·10
X979	29p. deep mauve (26.9.89)	2·50	2·50
X980	30p. deep olive-grey (26.9.89)	1·25	1·25
X981	31p. purple (30.3.83)	2·00	2·00
	a. Imperf (pair)	£1250	
X982	31p. ultramarine (4.9.90)	1·50	1·50
X983	32p. greenish blue (23.8.88)	1·70	1·70
	a. Imperf (pair)	£2500	
X984	33p. light emerald (4.9.90)	1·25	1·25
X985	34p. ochre-brown (28.8.84)	1·50	1·50
X986	34p. deep bluish grey (26.9.89)	1·50	1·50
X987	34p. deep mauve (10.9.91)	1·75	1·75
X988	35p. sepia (23.8.88)	1·50	1·50
	a. Imperf (pair)	£2000	
X989	35p. yellow (10.9.91)	1·50	1·50
X990	37p. rosine (26.9.89)	1·75	1·75
X991	39p. bright mauve (10.9.91)	1·50	1·50
X991a	50p. ochre (21.1.92)	15·00	15·00
	ab. Imperf (pair)	£1800	

(c) Photo Harrison. On ordinary paper. Perf 15×14.

X992	50p. ochre-brown (21.5.80)	2·00	2·00
	a. Imperf (pair)	£1200	
X993	50p. ochre (13.3.90)	4·00	4·00
X994	75p. grey-black (face value as Type 367a) (26.7.88)	4·75	4·75

(d) Litho J.W. Perf 14.

X996	4p. greenish blue (2 bands) (30.1.80)	20	20
	y. Phosphor omitted	£1600	
X997	4p. greenish blue (phosphorised paper) (11.81)	30	30
X998	20p. dull purple (2 bands) (21.5.80)	1·50	1·50
X999	20p. dull purple (phosphorised paper) (11.81)	1·50	1·50

(e) Litho Questa. Perf 14 (Nos. X1000, X1003/X1004 and X1023) or 15×14 (others).

X1000	2p. emerald-green (face value as Type 367) (phosphorised paper) (21.5.80)	20	20
	a. Perf 15×14 (10.7.84)	25	25
X1001	2p. bright green and deep green (face value as Type 367a) (phosphorised paper) (23.2.88)	55	55
X1002	4p. greenish blue (phosphorised paper) (13.5.86)	55	55
X1003	5p. light violet (phosphorised paper) (21.5.80)	25	25
X1004	5p. claret (phosphorised paper) (27.1.82)	40	40
	a. Perf 15×14 (21.2.84)	45	45
X1005	13p. pale chestnut (1 centre band) (9.2.88)	50	50
	l. Booklet pane. No. X1005×6 with margins all round	3·00	
X1006	13p. pale chestnut (1 side band at right) (9.2.88)	50	50
	a. Band at left	50	50
	l. Booklet pane. No. X1006/X1006a each×3, X1010, X1015 and X1021 with margins all round	18·00	
	la. Grey-green (on 18p.) ptg double	£2800	
X1007	14p. deep blue (1 centre band) (11.10.88)	2·00	2·00
X1008	17p. deep blue (1 centre band) (19.3.91)	55	55
	y. Phosphor omitted	£240	
	l. Booklet pane. No. X1008×6 with margins all round	3·50	
	ly. Booklet pane. Phosphor omitted	£950	
X1009	18p. deep olive-grey (phosphorised paper) (9.2.88)	55	55
	l. Booklet pane. No. X1009×9 with margins all round	4·50	
	m. Booklet pane. No. X1009×6 with margins all round	3·00	
X1010	18p. deep olive-grey (2 bands) (9.2.88)	7·50	7·50
X1011	18p. bright green (1 centre band) (27.10.92)	55	55
	l. Booklet pane. No. X1011×6 with margins all round	3·00	
X1012	18p. bright green (1 side band at right) (27.10.92)	90	90
	a. Band at left (10.8.93)	1·50	1·50
	y. Phosphor omitted	£450	
	l. Booklet pane. No. X1012×2, X1018×2, X1022×2, 1451a, 1514a and centre label with margins all round	10·00	
	la. Bright blue (on 2nd) ptg treble		
	ly. Phosphor omitted	£4250	
	m. Booklet pane. No. X1012a, X1020, X1022 and 1451ab, each×2, with central label and margins all round (10.8.93)	7·50	
	my. Booklet pane. Phosphor omitted	£3500	
X1013	19p. bright orange-red (phosphorised paper) (11.10.88)	1·50	1·50
X1014	20p. dull purple (phosphorised paper) (13.5.86)	1·25	1·25
X1015	22p. yellow-green (2 bands) (9.2.88)	8·00	8·00
X1016	22p. bright orange-red (phosphorised paper) (19.3.91)	75	75
	l. Booklet pane. No. X1016×9 with margins all round	7·00	
	m. Booklet pane. No. X1016×6, X1019×2 and central label with margins all round	10·00	
X1017	24p. chestnut (phosphorised paper) (27.10.92)	70	70
	l. Booklet pane. No. X1017×6 with margins all round	4·50	
X1018	24p. chestnut (2 bands) (27.10.92)	1·75	1·75
	y. Phosphor omitted	£600	
X1019	33p. light emerald (phosphorised paper) (19.3.91)	2·00	2·00
X1020	33p. light emerald (2 bands) (25.2.92)	1·25	1·25
	y. Phosphor omitted	£450	
X1021	34p. bistre-brown (2 bands) (9.2.88)	8·00	8·00
X1022	39p. bright mauve (2 bands) (27.10.92)	2·00	2·00
	y. Phosphor omitted	£450	
X1023	75p. black (face value as Type 367) (ordinary paper) (30.1.80)	2·25	2·25
	a. Perf 15×14 (21.2.84)	2·75	2·75
X1024	75p. brownish grey and black (face value as Type 367a) (ordinary paper) (23.2.88)	9·00	9·00

(f) Litho Walsall. Perf 14.

X1050	2p. deep green (face value as T 367) (phosphorised paper) (9.2.93)	1·50	1·50
	l. Booklet pane. No. X1050×2 and X1053×4 plus 2 labels with vert edges of pane imperf	4·00	
X1051	14p. deep blue (1 side band at right) (25.4.89)	3·25	3·25
	y. Phosphor omitted	£225	
	l. Booklet pane. No. X1051×2 and X1052×4 with vertical edges of pane imperf	8·50	
	ly. Booklet pane. Phosphor omitted	£900	
X1052	19p. bright orange-red (2 bands) (25.4.89)	90	90
	y. Phosphor omitted	£125	
X1053	24p. chestnut (phosphorised paper) (9.2.93)	90	90
X1054	29p. deep mauve (2 bands) (2.10.89)	3·00	3·00
	l. Booklet pane. No. X1054×4 with three edges of pane imperf	12·00	
X1055	29p. deep mauve (phosphorised paper) (17.4.90)	3·00	3·00
	l. Booklet pane. No. X1055×4 with three edges of pane imperf	12·00	
X1056	31p. ultramarine (phosphorised paper) (17.9.90)	1·75	1·75
	l. Booklet pane. No. X1056×4 with horizontal edges of pane imperf	4·00	
X1057	33p. light emerald (phosphorised paper) (16.9.91)	1·75	1·75
	l. Booklet pane. No. X1057×4 with horiz edges of pane imperf	3·50	
X1058	39p. bright mauve (phosphorised paper) (16.9.91)	2·00	2·00
	l. Booklet pane. No. X1058×4 with horiz edges of pane imperf	5·75	

* See footnote after No. 744.
† These come from sheets with gum arabic.
†† Examples of Booklet panes Nos. X899l, X901l and X901la are known on which the phosphor bands were printed on the wrong values in error with the result that the side bands appear on the 15½p. or 17p. and the two bands on the 12½p. or 13p. Similarly examples of the 1p. with phosphor band at right instead of left and of the 13p. with band at left instead of right, exist from 50p. booklet pane No. X847l. Nos. X844a/X844b come from a strip of eight of the vertical coil. It comprises two normals, one imperforate at sides and bottom, one completely imperforate, one imperforate at top, left and bottom and partly perforated at right due to the bottom three stamps being perforated twice.

No. X844b is also known from another strip having one stamp imperforate at sides and bottom.

Nos. X848b/X848c come from the same sheet, the latter having perforations at the foot of the stamps only.

Multi-value coil strips Nos. X924l, X925l, X928l, X929l, X930cl and X933l/X933n were produced by the Post Office for use by a large direct mail marketing firm. From 2 September 1981 No. X929l was available from the Philatelic Bureau, Edinburgh, and, subsequently from a number of other Post Office counters. Later multi-value coil strips were sold at the Philatelic Bureau and Post Office philatelic counters.

In addition to booklet pane No. X1012m No. X1020 also comes from the *se-tenant* pane in the Wales £6 booklet. This pane is listed under No. W49l in the Wales Regional section.

PANES OF SIX FROM STITCHED BOOKLETS. Nos. X841m, X851l/X851m and X855l include one or two printed labels showing commercial advertisements. These were originally perforated on all four sides, but from the August 1971 editions of the 25p. and 30p. booklets (Nos. DH42, DQ59) and December 1971 edition of the 50p. (No. DT4) the line of perforations between the label and the binding margin was omitted. Similar panes, with the line of perforations omitted, exist for the 3p., 3½p. and 4½p. values (Nos. X856, X858 and X865), but these are outside the scope of this listing as the labels are blank.

PART-PERFORATED SHEETS. Since the introduction of the Jumelle press in 1972 a number of part perforated sheets, both definitives and commemoratives, have been discovered. It is believed that these occur when the operation of the press is interrupted. Such sheets invariably show a number of 'blind' perforations, where the pins have failed to cut the paper. Our listings of imperforate errors from these sheets are for pairs showing no traces whatsoever of the perforations. Examples showing 'blind' perforations are outside the scope of this catalogue.

In cases where perforation varieties affect *se-tenant* stamps, fuller descriptions will be found in Volumes 4 and 5 of the *GB Specialised Catalogue*.

WHITE PAPER. From 1972 printings appeared on fluorescent white paper giving a stronger chalk reaction than the original ordinary cream paper.

PHOSPHOR OMITTED ERRORS. It should be noted that several values listed with phosphor omitted errors also exist on phosphorised paper. These errors can only be identified with certainty by checking for an 'afterglow', using a short-wave ultraviolet lamp.

'ALL-OVER' PHOSPHOR. To improve mechanised handling most commemoratives from the 1972 Royal Silver Wedding 3p. value to the 1979 Rowland Hill Death Centenary set had the phosphor applied by printing cylinder across the entire surface of the stamp, giving a matt effect. Printings of the 1p., 2p. and 10p. definitives, released in October 1979, also had 'all-over' phosphor, but these were purely a temporary expedient pending the adoption of phosphorised paper. Nos. X883, X890 and X921 have been discovered with 'all-over' phosphor in addition to the normal phosphor bands. These errors are outside the scope of this catalogue.

PHOSPHORISED PAPER. Following the experiments on Nos. 743c and 829 a printing of the 4½p. definitive was issued on 13 November 1974, which had, in addition to the normal phosphor bands, phosphor included in the paper coating. Because of difficulties in identifying this phosphorised paper with the naked eye this printing is not listed separately in this catalogue.

No. X938 was the first value printed on phosphorised paper without phosphor bands and was a further experimental issue to test the efficacy of this system. From 15 August 1979 phosphorised paper was accepted for use generally, this paper replacing phosphor bands on values other than those required for the second-class rate.

Stamps on phosphorised paper show a shiny surface instead of the matt areas of those printed with phosphor bands or the overall matt appearance of 'All-over' phosphor.

DEXTRIN GUM. From 1973 printings in photogravure appeared with PVA gum to which dextrin had been added. Because this is virtually colourless a bluish green colouring matter was added to distinguish it from the earlier pure PVA.

The 4p., 5p. (light violet), 20p. and 75p. printed in lithography exist with PVA and PVAD gum. From 1988 Questa printings were with PVAD gum, but did not show the bluish green additive.

VARNISH COATING. Nos. X841 and X883 exist with and without a varnish coating. This cannot easily be detected without the use of an ultraviolet lamp as it merely reduces the fluorescent paper reaction.

POSTAL FORGERIES. In mid-1993 a number of postal forgeries of the 24p. chestnut were detected in the London area. These forgeries, produced by lithography, can be identified by the lack of phosphor in the paper, screening dots across the face value and by the perforations which were applied by a line machine gauging 11.

First Day Covers

15.2.71	½p., 1p., 1½p., 2p., 2½p., 3p., 3½p., 4p., 5p., 6p., 7½p., 9p. (Nos. X841, X844, X848/X849, X851, X855, X858, X861, X866, X870, X877, X882) (Covers carry 'POSTING DELAYED BY THE POST OFFICE STRIKE 1971' cachet)	2·50
11.8.71	10p. (No. X885)	1·00
24.5.72	Wedgwood *se-tenant* pane ½p., 2½p. (No. X841p)	25·00
24.10.73	4½p., 5½p., 8p. (Nos. X865, X868, X878)	1·00
4.9.74	6½p. (No. X871)	1·00
15.1.75	7p. (No. X874)	1·00
24.9.75	8½p. (No. X881)	1·00
25.2.76	9p., 9½p., 10p., 10½p., 11p., 20p. (Nos. X883/X884, X886, X890, X892, X915)	2·50
2.2.77	50p. (No. X921)	1·00
26.4.78	10½p. (No. X891)	1·00
15.8.79	11½p., 13p., 15p. (Nos. X942, X944, X947)	1·00
30.1.80	4p., 12p., 13½p., 17p., 17½p., 75p. (Nos. X996, X943, X945, X951, X953, X1023)	2·00
16.4.80	Wedgwood *se-tenant* pane 2p., 10p., 12p. (No. X849n)	1·25
22.10.80	3p., 22p. (Nos. X930, X962)	1·00
14.1.81	2½p., 11½p., 14p., 15½p., 18p., 25p. (Nos. X929, X893, X946, X948, X954, X970)	1·25
27.1.82	5p., 12½p., 16½p., 19½p., 26p., 29p. (Nos. X1004, X898, X950, X957, X971, X978)	2·00
19.5.82	Stanley Gibbons *se-tenant* pane 2p., 3p., 12½p. (No. X849p)	2·00
30.3.83	3½p., 16p., 17p., 20½p., 23p., 28p., 31p. (Nos. X931, X949, X952, X961, X965, X975, X981)	2·75
14.9.83	Royal Mint *se-tenant* pane 3p., 3½p., 16p. (No. X930l)	2·50
28.8.84	13p., 18p., 22p., 24p., 34p. (Nos. X900, X955, X963, X967, X985)	2·00
4.9.84	Christian Heritage *se-tenant* pane 10p., 13p., 17p. (No. X886bl)	12·00
8.1.85	*The Times se-tenant* pane 4p., 13p., 17p., 34p. (No. X864l)	8·50
29.10.85	7p., 12p. (Nos. X937, X896)	2·00
18.3.86	British Rail *se-tenant* pane 12p., 17p., 31p. (No. X897m)	9·00
3.3.87	P&O *se-tenant* pane 1p., 13p., 18p., 26p. (No. X847m)	6·00
9.2.88	*Financial Times se-tenant* pane 13p., 18p., 22p., 34p. (No. X1006l)	12·50
23.8.88	14p., 19p., 20p., 23p., 27p., 28p., 32p., 35p. (Nos. X903, X956, X959, X966, X973, X976, X983, X988)	3·50
26.9.89	15p., 20p., 24p., 29p., 30p., 34p., 37p. (Nos. X905, X960, X968, X979/X980, X986, X990)	3·00
20.3.90	London Life *se-tenant* pane 15p., (2nd), 20p., (1st), 15p., 20p., 29p. (No. X906m)	10·00
4.9.90	10p., 17p., 22p., 26p., 27p., 31p., 33p. (Nos. X910, X940, X964, X972, X974, X982, X984)	3·00
19.3.91	Alias Agatha Christie *se-tenant* pane 22p., 33p. (No. X1016m)	6·00
10.9.91	6p., 18p., 24p., 28p., 34p., 35p., 39p. (Nos. X936, X913, X969, X977, X987, X989, X991)	3·25
27.10.92	Tolkien *se-tenant* pane 18p., (2nd), 24p., (1st), 39p. (No. X1012l)	6·00
10.8.93	Beatrix Potter *se-tenant* pane 18p., (2nd), 33p., 39p. (No. X1012m)	5·50

Post Office Presentation Packs

15.2.71	PO Pack No. 26. ½p. (2 bands), 1p. (2 bands), 1½p. (2 bands), 2p. (2 bands), 2½p. magenta (1 centre band), 3p. ultramarine (2 bands), 3½p. olive-grey (2 bands), 4p. ochre-brown (2 bands), 5p. pale violet (2 bands), 6p. light emerald (2 bands), 7½p. (2 bands), 9p. yellow-orange and black (2 bands). (Nos. X841, X844, X848/X849, X851, X855, X858, X861, X866, X870, X877, X882)	9·00
15.4.71**	Scandinavia 71. Contents as above	25·00
25.11.71	PO Pack No. 37. ½p. (2 bands), 1p. (2 bands), 1½p. (2 bands), 2p. (2 bands), 2½p. magenta (1 centre band), 3p. ultramarine (2 bands) or (1 centre band), 3½p. olive-grey (2 bands) or (1 centre band), 4p. ochre-brown (2 bands), 4½p. (2 bands), 5p. pale violet (2 bands), 5½p. (2 bands) or (1 centre band), 6p. (2 bands), 6½p. (2 bands) or (1 centre band), 7p. (2 bands), 7½p. (2 bands), 8p (2 bands), 9p. yellow-orange and black (2 bands), 10p. orange-brown and chestnut (2 bands). (Nos. X841, X844, X848/X849, X851, X855 or X856, X858 or X859, X861, X865/X866, X868 or X869, X870, X871 or X872, X874, X877/X878, X882, X885)	30·00
	Later issues of this Pack contained the alternatives	
2.2.77	PO Pack No. 90. ½p. (2 bands), 1p. (2 bands), 1½p. (2 bands), 2p. (2 bands), 2½p. magenta (1 centre band), 3p. ultramarine (1 centre band), 5p. pale violet (2 bands), 6½p. (1 centre band), 7p. (2 bands) or (1 centre band), 7½p. (2 bands), 8p. (2 bands), 8½p. (2 bands), 9p. deep violet (2 bands), 9½p. (2 bands), 10p. orange-brown (2 bands), 10½p. yellow (2 bands), 11p. (2 bands), 20p. dull purple (2 bands), 50p. ochre-brown (2 bands). (Nos. X841, X844, X848/X849, X851, X856, X866, X872, X874 or X875, X877/X878, X881, X883/X884, X886, X890, X892, X915, X921)	5·00

Date	Description	Price
28.10.81	PO Pack No. 129a. 10½p. deep dull blue (2 bands), 11½p. (1 centre band), 2½p. (phosphor paper), 3p. (phosphor paper), 11½p. (phosphor paper), 12p. (phosphor paper), 13p. (phosphor paper), 13½p. (phosphor paper), 14p. (phosphor paper), 15p. (phosphor paper), 15½p. (phosphor paper), 17p. light emerald (phosphor paper), 17½p. (phosphor paper), 18p. deep violet (phosphor paper), 22p. blue (phosphor paper), 25p. (phosphor paper), 4p. greenish blue (litho, 2 bands), 75p. (litho) (Nos. X891, X893, X929/X9230, X942/X948, X951, X953/X954, X962, X970, X996, X1023)	15·00
3.8.83	PO Pack No. 1. 10p. orange-brown (1 centre band), 12½p. (1 centre band), ½p. (phosphor paper), 1p. (phosphor paper), 3p. (phosphor paper), 3½p. (phosphor paper), 16p. (phosphor paper), 16½p. (phosphor paper), 17p. grey-blue (phosphor paper), 20½p. (phosphor paper), 23p. brown-red (phosphor paper), 26p. rosine (phosphor paper), 28p. deep violet (phosphor paper), 31p. purple (phosphor paper), 50p. (ordinary paper), 2p. (litho phosphor paper), 4p. (litho phosphor paper), 5p. claret (litho phosphor paper), 20p. (litho phosphor paper), 75p. (litho) (Nos. X888, X898, X924/X925, X930/X931, X949/X950, X952, X961, X965, X971, X975, X981, X992, X997, X999, X1000, X1004, X1023)	32·00
23.10.84	PO Pack No. 5. 13p. (1 centre band), ½p. (phosphor paper), 1p. (phosphor paper), 3p. (phosphor paper), 10p. orange-brown (phosphor paper), 16p. (phosphor paper), 17p. grey-blue (phosphor paper), 18p. deep olive-grey (phosphor paper), 22p. yellow-green (phosphor paper), 24p. violet (phosphor paper), 26p. rosine (phosphor paper), 28p. deep violet (phosphor paper), 31p. purple (phosphor paper), 34p. ochre-brown (phosphor paper), 50p. (ordinary phosphor paper), 2p. (litho phosphor paper), 4p. (litho phosphor paper), 5p. claret (litho phosphor paper), 20p. (litho phosphor paper), 75p. (litho) (Nos. X900, X924/X925, X930, X939, X949, X952, X955, X963, X967, X971, X975, X981, X985, X992, X1000a, X997, X1004a, X999, X1023a)	25·00
3.3.87	PO Pack No. 9. 12p. (1 centre band), 13p. (1 centre band), 1p. (phosphor paper), 3p. (phosphor paper), 7p. (phosphor paper), 10p. orange-brown (phosphor paper), 17p. grey-blue (phosphor paper), 18p. deep olive-grey (phosphor paper), 22p. yellow-green (phosphor paper), 24p. violet (phosphor paper), 26p. rosine (phosphor paper), 28p. deep violet (phosphor paper), 31p. purple (phosphor paper), 34p. ochre-brown (phosphor paper), 50p. (ordinary paper), 2p. (litho phosphor paper), 4p. (litho phosphor paper), 5p. claret (litho phosphor paper), 20p. (litho phosphor paper), 75p. (litho) (Nos. X896, X900, X925, X930, X937, X939, X952, X955, X963, X967, X971, X975, X981, X985, X992, X1000a, X997, X1004a, X999, X1023a)	30·00
23.8.88	PO Pack No. 15. 14p. (1 centre band), 19p. (phosphor paper), 20p. turquoise-green (phosphor paper), 23p. bright green (phosphor paper), 27p. chestnut (phosphor paper), 28p. ochre (phosphor paper), 32p. (phosphor paper), 35p. sepia (phosphor paper) (Nos. X903, X956, X959, X966, X973, X976, X983, X988)	9·00
26.9.89	PO Pack No. 19. 15p. (centre band), 20p. brownish black (phosphor paper), 24p. Indian red (phosphor paper), 29p. deep mauve (phosphor paper), 30p. (phosphor paper), 34p. deep bluish grey (phosphor paper), 37p. (phosphor paper) (Nos. X905, X960, X968, X979/X980, X986, X990)	7·00
4.9.90	PO Pack No. 22. 10p. dull orange (phosphor paper), 17p. (centre band), 22p. bright orange-red (phosphor paper), 26p. drab (phosphor paper), 27p. violet (phosphor paper), 31p. ultramarine (phosphor paper), 33p. (phosphor paper) (Nos. X940, X910, X964, X972, X974, X982, X984)	7·00
14.5.91	PO Pack No. 24. 1p. (phosphor paper), 2p. (phosphor paper), 3p. (phosphor paper), 4p. new blue (phosphor paper), 5p. dull red-brown (phosphor paper), 10p. dull orange (phosphor paper), 17p. (centre band), 20p. turquoise-green (phosphor paper), 22p. bright orange-red (phosphor paper), 26p. drab (phosphor paper), 27p. violet (phosphor paper), 30p. (phosphor paper), 31p. ultramarine (phosphor paper), 32p. (phosphor paper), 33p. (phosphor paper), 37p. (phosphor paper), 50p. (ordinary paper), 75p. (ordinary paper). (Nos. X925, X927, X930, X933, X935, X940, X910, X959, X964, X972, X974, X980, X982/X984, X990, X993/4)	30·00
10.9.91	PO Pack No. 25. 6p (phosphor paper), 18p. (centre band), 24p. chestnut (phosphor paper), 28p. deep bluish grey (phosphor paper), 34p. deep mauve (phosphor paper), 35p. yellow (phosphor paper), 39p. (phosphor paper) (Nos. X913, X936, X969, X977, X987, X989, X991)	7·00

** The Scandinavia 71 was a special pack produced for sale during a visit to six cities in Denmark, Sweden and Norway by a mobile display unit between 15 April and 20 May 1971. The pack gives details of this tour and also lists the other stamps which were due to be issued in 1971, the text being in English. A separate insert gives translations in Danish, Swedish and Norwegian. The pack was also available at the Philatelic Bureau, Edinburgh.

> For stamps of this design inscribed '2nd' and '1st' see Nos. 1445/1452 and 1511/1516, and for stamps with one elliptical perforation hole on each vertical side see Nos. 1664/1672, Y1667/Y1803, 2039/2040, 2295/2298, 2650/2657, U2941/U2974 and 3271/3278.

508

1977 (2 Feb)–**87**. Perf 14×15.

1026	508	£1 bright yellow-green and blackish olive	3·00	25
		a. Imperf (pair)	£1700	
1026b		£1·30 pale drab and deep greenish blue (3.8.83)	5·50	6·00
1026c		£1·33 pale mauve and grey-black (28.8.84)	7·50	8·00
1026d		£1·41 pale drab and deep greenish blue (17.9.85)	8·50	8·50
1026e		£1·50 pale mauve and grey-black (2.9.86)	6·00	5·00
1026f		£1·60 pale drab and deep greenish blue (15.9.87)	6·50	7·00
1027		£2 light emerald and purple-brown	9·00	50
		a. Imperf (pair)	£2250	
1028		£5 salmon and chalky blue	22·00	3·00
		a. Imperf (vert pair)	£8000	
Set of 8			60·00	32·00
Set of 8 Gutter Pairs			£125	
Set of 8 Traffic Light Gutter Pairs			£150	
Presentation Pack (PO Pack No. 91 (small size)) (Nos. 1026, 1027/1028)			38·00	
Presentation Pack (PO Pack No. 13 (large size)) (Nos. 1026, 1027/1028)			£170	
Presentation Pack (PO Pack No. 14) (large size) (No. 1026f)			22·00	

Gutter pairs	Plain	Traffic Light
1026, 1027/1028	70·00	75·00
1026b	13·00	20·00
1026c	16·00	22·00
1026d	18·00	25·00
1026e	13·00	17·00
1026f	14·00	18·00

Special First Day of Issue Postmarks (for illustrations see Introduction)

Philatelic Bureau, Edinburgh (Type F) (£1, £2, £5)	10·00
Windsor, Berks (Type F) (£1, £2, £5)	12·00
Philatelic Bureau, Edinburgh (Type F) (£1·30)	6·50
Windsor, Berks (Type F) (£1·30)	6·50
British Philatelic Bureau, Edinburgh (Type F) (£1·33)	8·50
Windsor, Berks (Type F) (£1·33)	8·50
British Philatelic Bureau, Edinburgh (Type G) (£1·41)	9·00
Windsor, Berks (Type G) (£1·41)	9·00
British Philatelic Bureau, Edinburgh (Type G) (£1·50)	5·50
Windsor, Berks (Type G) (£1·50)	5·50
British Philatelic Bureau, Edinburgh (Type G) (£1·60)	7·50
Windsor, Berks (Type G) (£1·60)	7·50

MACHINS *Denominated stamps with 'standard' perforations*

Decimal Machin Index

(Denominated stamps with 'standard' perforations)

Those booklet stamps shown below with an * after the catalogue number do not exist with perforations on all four sides, but show one or two sides imperforate.

Value.	Process	Colour	Phosphor	Cat. No.	Source
½p.	photo	turquoise-blue	2 bands	X841/g	(a) with P.V.A. gum–sheets, 5p. m/v coil (X841nEv), 10p.m/v coil (X841q), 10p. booklets (DN46/75, FA1/3), 25p. booklets (DH39/52), 50p. booklets (DT1/12, FB1, FB14/16, FB19/23), £1 Wedgwood booklet (DX1) (b) with gum arabic—sheets, 5p. m/v coil (X841n)
½p.	photo	turquoise-blue	1 band at left	X842	£1 Wedgwood booklet (DX1)
½p.	photo	turquoise-blue	1 centre band	X843	10p. m/v coil (X843l), 10p. booklets (FA4/9)
½p.	photo	turquoise-blue	phos paper	X924	sheets, 12½p. m/v coil (X924l)
1p.	photo	crimson	2 bands	X844/g	(a) with P.V.A. gum—sheets, vertical coils, 5p. m/v coil (X841nEv), 10p. m/v coil (X841q), 10p. booklets (DN46/75, FA1/3), 50p. booklets (FB1/8, FB14/16) (b) with gum arabic—vertical coils, 5p. m/v coil (X841n)
1p.	photo	crimson	1 centre band	X845	10p. m/v coils (X843l, X845m), 10p. booklets (FA4/11), 50p. booklets (FB24/30, 34/36, 43/6, 48, 50)
1p.	photo	crimson	'all-over'	X846	sheets
1p.	photo	crimson	phos paper	X925	sheets, horizontal and vertical coils, 13p. m/v coil (X925l), 50p. booklet (FB59/66)
1p.	photo	crimson	1 band at left	X847	50p. booklets (FB37/42, 47, 49)
1p.	photo	crimson	1 band at right	X847a	£5 P. & O. booklet (DX8)
1½p.	photo	black	2 bands	X848	sheets, 10p. booklets (DN46/75)
2p.	photo	myrtle-green	2 bands	X849/g	(a) with P.V.A. gum—sheets, 5p. m/v coil (X841nEv), 10p. m/v coil (X841q), 10p. booklets (DN46/75), 50p. booklets (FB9/13), £3 Wedgwood booklet (DX2), £4 SG booklet (DX3) (b) with gum arabic—5p. m/v coil (X841n)
2p.	photo	myrtle-green	'all-over'	X850	sheets
2p.	photo	myrtle-green	phos paper	X926	sheets
2p.	photo	myrtle-green	phos paper	X928	14p. m/v coil (X928l)
2p.	litho	emerald-green	phos paper	X1000/a	sheets
2p.	litho	brt grn and dp grn	phos paper	X1001	sheets
2p.	photo	dp green	phos paper	X927	sheets, £1 booklets (FH23/7)
2p.	litho	dp green	phos paper	X1050*	£1 booklets (FH28/30)
2½p.	photo	magenta	1 centre band	X851/g	(a) with P.V.A. gum—sheets, horizontal and vertical coils, 25p. booklets (DH39/52), 50p. booklets (DT1/12), £1 Wedgwood booklet (DX1) (b) with gum arabic—sheets, horizontal coils
2½p.	photo	magenta	1 side band	X852/a	(a) band at left—50p. booklets (DT1/12), £1 Wedgwood booklet (DX1) (b) band at right—£1 Wedgwood booklet (DX1)
2½p.	photo	magenta	2 bands	X853	sheets
2½p.	photo	rose-red	phos paper	X929	sheets, 11½p. m/v coil (X929l)
2½p.	photo	rose-red	2 bands	X854	50p. booklets (FB17/18)
3p.	photo	ultramarine	2 bands	X855/g	(a) with P.V.A. gum—sheets, horizontal and vertical coils, 30p. booklets (DQ56/72), 50p. booklets (DT1/12), £1 Wedgwood booklet (DX1) (b) with gum arabic—sheets, horizontal coils
3p.	photo	ultramarine	1 centre band	X856/g	(a) with P.V.A. gum—sheets, horizontal and vertical coils, 30p. booklets (DQ73/4), 50p. booklets (DT13/14) (b) with gum arabic—sheets
3p.	photo	brt magenta	phos paper	X930	Type I. sheets, 11½p. m/v coil (X929l), £4 Royal Mint booklet (DX4)
3p.	photo	brt magenta	phos paper	X930c	Type II. sheets (from 21.1.92), 15p. m/v coil (X930cl)
3p.	photo	brt magenta	2 bands	X857	Type I. 50p. booklets (FB19/23), £4 SG booklet (DX3)
3½p.	photo	olive-grey	2 bands	X858/b	sheets, horizontal and vertical coils, 35p. booklets (DP1/3), 50p. booklets (DT13/14)
3½p.	photo	olive-grey	1 centre band	X859	sheet, horizontal coils, 35p. booklet (DP4), 85p. booklet (DW1)
3½p.	photo	purple-brown	phos paper	X931	sheets, £4 Royal Mint booklet (DX4)
3½p.	photo	purple-brown	1 centre band	X860	50p. booklets (FB24/6)
4p.	photo	ochre-brown	2 bands	X861/g	(a) with P.V.A. gum—sheets. (b) with gum arabic—sheets
4p.	litho	greenish blue	2 bands	X996	sheets
4p.	photo	greenish blue	2 bands	X862	50p. booklets (FB17/18)
4p.	litho	greenish blue	phos paper	X997	sheets J.W. ptg.
				X1002	sheets Questa ptg.
4p.	photo	greenish blue	phos paper	X932	12½p. m/v coil (X924l)
				X932a	13p. m/v coil (X925l), 14p. m/v coil (X928l)
4p.	photo	greenish blue	1 centre band	X863	50p. booklets (FB27/30)
4p.	photo	greenish blue	1 side band	X864/a	(a) band at right—£5*The Times* booklet (DX6) (b) band at left—£5*The Times* booklet (DX6)
4p.	photo	new blue	phos paper	X933	sheets, 15p. m/v coil (X930cl), 17p. m/v coil (X933l), 18p. m/v coil (X933m), 19p m/v coil (X933n)
4½p.	photo	grey-blue	2 bands	X865	sheets, horizontal coils, 45p. booklets (DS1/2), 85p. booklet (DW1)
5p.	photo	pale violet	2 bands	X866	sheets
5p.	photo	pale violet	phos paper	X934	sheets
5p.	litho	lt violet	phos paper	X1003	sheets
5p.	litho	claret	phos paper	X1004/a	sheets

Denominated stamps with 'standard' perforations MACHINS

Value.	Process	Colour	Phosphor	Cat. No.	Source
5p.	photo	claret	1 centre band	X867	50p. booklets (FB35/36, 43/6, 48, 50)
5p.	photo	dull red-brown	phos paper	X935	sheets, 17p. m/v coil (X933l), 18p. m/v coil (X933m), 19p m/v coil (X933n)
5½p.	photo	violet	2 bands	X868	sheets
5½p.	photo	violet	1 centre band	X869	sheets
6p.	photo	lt emerald	2 bands	X870/g	(a) with P.V.A. gum—sheets, 10p. m/v coil (X841q), 10p. booklets (FA1/3) (b) with gum arabic—sheets
6p.	photo	yellow-olive	phos paper	X936	sheets
6½p.	photo	greenish blue	2 bands	X871	sheets
6½p.	photo	greenish blue	1 centre band	X872	sheets, horizontal and vertical coils, 65p. booklet (FC1)
6½p.	photo	greenish blue	1 side band	X873/a	(a) band at right—50p. booklet (FB1A). (b) band at left—50p. booklet (FB1B)
7p.	photo	purple-brown	2 bands	X874	sheets
7p.	photo	purple-brown	1 centre band	X875	sheets, horizontal and vertical coils, 10p. m/v coil (X843l), 10p. booklets (FA4/9), 70p. booklets (FD1/8), £1.60 Christmas booklet (FX1)
7p.	photo	purple-brown	1 side band	X876/a	(a) band at right—50p. booklets (FB2A/8A) (b) band at left—50p. booklets (FB2B/8B)
7p.	photo	brownish red	phos paper	X937	sheets
7½p.	photo	pale chestnut	2 bands	X877	sheets
8p.	photo	rosine	2 bands	X878	sheets
8p.	photo	rosine	1 centre band	X879	sheets, vertical coils, 10p. m/v coil (X845m), 10p. booklets (FA10/11), 80p. booklet (FE1), £1.80 Christmas booklet (FX2)
8p.	photo	rosine	1 side band	X880/a	(a) band at right—50p. booklets (FB9A/10A) (b) band at left—50p. booklets (FB9B/10B)
8½p	photo	lt yellowish green	2 bands	X881/b	sheets, horizontal and vertical coils, 50p. booklet (FB1), 85p. booklet (FF1)
8½p.	photo	yellowish green	phos paper	X938	sheets
9p.	photo	yellow-orange and black	2 bands	X882	sheets
9p.	photo	dp violet	2 bands	X883	sheets, horizontal and vertical coils, 50p. booklets (FB2/8), 90p. booklets (FG1/8), £1.60 Christmas booklet (FX1)
9½p	photo	purple	2 bands	X884	sheets
10p.	recess	cerise	phos paper	829	sheets
10p.	photo	orange-brown and chestnut	2 bands	X885	sheets
10p.	photo	orange-brown	2 bands	X886	Type I. sheets, 50p. booklets (FB9/10), £1·80 Christmas booklet (FX2)
10p.	photo	orange-brown	2 bands	X886b	Type II. £4 Christian Heritage booklet (DX5)
10p.	photo	orange-brown	'all-over'	X887	Type I. sheets, vertical coils, £1 booklet (FH1)
10p.	photo	orange-brown	phos paper	X939	Type I. sheets
10p.	photo	orange-brown	1 centre band	X888	Type I. sheets, vertical coils, £1 booklets (FH2/4), £2·20 Christmas booklet (FX3), £3 Wedgwood booklet (DX2)
10p.	photo	orange-brown	1 side band	X889/a	Type I. (a) band at right—50p. booklets (FB11A/13A) (b) band at left—50p. booklets (FB11B/13B), £3 Wedgwood booklet (DX2)
10p.	photo	dull orange	phos paper	X940	sheets
10½p.	photo	yellow	2 bands	X890	sheets
10½p.	photo	dp dull blue	2 bands	X891	sheets
11p.	photo	brown-red	2 bands	X892	sheets
11p.	photo	brown-red	phos paper	X941	sheets
11½p	photo	ochre-brown	phos paper	X942	sheets
11½p	photo	drab	1 centre band	X893	sheets, vertical coils, £1·15 booklets (FI1/4), £2·55 Christmas booklet (FX4)
11½p.	photo	drab	1 side band	X894/a	(a) band at right—50p. booklets (FB14A/18A), £1.30 booklets (FL1/2) (b) band at left—50p. booklets FB14B/18B), £1.30 booklets (FL1/2)
12p.	photo	yellowish green	phos paper	X943	sheets, vertical coils, £1·20 booklets (FJ1/3)
12p.	photo	yellowish green	2 bands	X895	50p. booklets (FB11/13), £2·20 Christmas booklet (FX3), £3 Wedgwood booklet (DX2)
12p.	photo	brt emerald	1 centre band	X896	sheets, horizontal and vertical coils, 50p. booklet (FB34), £1·20 booklets (FJ4/6), £5 British Rail booklet (DX7)
12p.	photo	brt emerald	1 side band	X897/a	(a) band at right—£1·50 booklets (FP1/3), £5 British Rail booklet (DX7) (b) band at left—£1·50 booklets (FP1/3), £5 British Rail booklet (DX7)
12p.	photo	brt emerald	1 centre band Underprint T.4	X896u	sheets
12½p.	photo	lt emerald	1 centre band	X898	sheets, vertical coils, 50p. booklets (FB24/6), £1·25 booklets (FK1/8), £4 SG booklet (DX3)
12½p.	photo	lt emerald	1 centre band Underprint T.1	X898u	£2·80 Christmas booklet (FX5)
12½p.	photo	lt emerald	1 centre band Underprint T.2	X898v	£2·50 Christmas booklet (FX6)
12½p.	photo	lt emerald	1 side band	X899/a	(a) band at right—50p. booklets (FB19A/23A), £1·43 booklets (FN1/6), £1·46 booklets (FO1/3), £4 SG booklet (DX3), £4 Royal Mint booklet (DX4) (b) band at left—50p. booklets (FB19B/23B), £1·43 booklets (FN1/6), £1·46 booklets (FO1/3), £4 SG booklet (DX3), £4 Royal Mint booklet (DX4)
13p.	photo	olive-grey	phos paper	X944	sheets
13p.	photo	pale chestnut	1 centre band	X900	sheets, horizontal and vertical coils, 50p. booklets (FB27/30, 35/6, 43/6, 48, 50), 52p. booklet (GA1), £1·30 booklets (FL3/14, GI1), £5 *The Times* booklet (DX6), £5 P & O booklet (DX8)
13p.	photo	pale chestnut	1 centre band Underprint T.2	X900u	£1·30 Christmas booklet (FX9)
13p.	photo	pale chestnut	1 side band	X901/a	(a) band at right—50p. booklets (FB37/42, 47, 49), £1·54 booklets (FQ1/4), £4 Christian Heritage booklet (DX5), £5 *The Times* booklet (DX6), £5 P & O booklet (DX8) (b) band at left—£1 booklets (FH6/13), £1.54 booklets (FQ1/4), £4 Christian Heritage booklet (DX5), £5 *The Times* booklet (DX6)
13p.	litho	pale chestnut	1 centre band	X1005	£5 *Financial Times* booklet (DX9)
13p.	litho	pale chestnut	1 side band	X1006/a	£5 *Financial Times* booklet (DX9)
13½p.	photo	purple-brown	phos paper	X945	sheets
14p.	photo	grey-blue	phos paper	X946	sheets, vertical coils, £1·40 booklets (FM1/4)
14p.	photo	grey-blue	2 bands	X902	50p. booklets (FB14/16), £1·30 booklets (FL1/2), £2·55 Christmas booklet (FX4)

335

MACHINS Denominated stamps with 'standard' perforations

Value.	Process	Colour	Phosphor	Cat. No.	Source
14p.	photo	dp blue	1 centre band	X903	sheets, horizontal and vertical coils, 56p. booklets (GB1/4), £1·40 booklets (FM5/6, GK1, 3)
14p.	photo	dp blue	1 band at right	X904	50p. booklets (FB51/4), £1 booklets (FH14/15 and 17)
14p.	litho	dp blue	1 centre band	X1007	£1·40 booklets (GK2, 4)
14p.	litho	dp blue	1 band at right	X1051*	£1 booklet (FH16)
15p.	photo	ultramarine	phos paper	X947	sheets
15p.	photo	brt blue	1 centre band	X905	sheets, horizontal and vertical coils
15p.	photo	brt blue	1 side band	X906/a	(a) band at left—50p. booklet (FB55) (b) band at right—£5 London Life booklet (DX11)
15½p.	photo	pale violet	phos paper	X948	sheets, vertical coils, £1·55 booklets (FR1/4)
15½p.	photo	pale violet	2 bands	X907	£1·43 booklets (FN1/6), £4 SG booklet (DX3)
15½p.	photo	pale violet	2 bands Underprint T.1	X907u	£2·80 Christmas booklet (FX5)
16p.	photo	olive-drab	phos paper	X949	sheets, vertical coils, £1·60 booklets (FS1, 3/4), £4 Royal Mint booklet (DX4)
16p.	photo	olive-drab	phos paper Underprint T.3	X949u	£1·60 booklet (FS2)
16p.	photo	olive-drab	2 bands	X908	£1·46 booklets (FO1/3)
16½p.	photo	pale chestnut	phos paper	X950	sheets
17p.	photo	lt emerald	phos paper	X951	sheets
17p.	photo	grey-blue	phos paper	X952	sheets, vertical coils, £1 booklet (FH5), £1·70 booklets (FT1, 3 & 5/7), £4 Christian Heritage booklet (DX5), £5 The Times booklet (DX6), £5 British Rail booklet (DX7)
17p.	photo	grey-blue	phos paper Underprint T.3	X952u	£1·70 booklet (FT2)
17p.	photo	grey-blue	2 bands	X909	50p. booklet (FB33a), £1·50 booklets (FP1/3), £1·54 booklets (FQ1/4), £4 Christian Heritage booklet (DX5), £5 The Times booklet (DX6), £5 British Rail booklet (DX7)
17p.	photo	grey-blue	2 bands Underprint T.4	X909u	50p. booklets (FB31/3)
17p.	photo	dp blue	1 centre band	X910	sheets, vertical coils
17p.	photo	dp blue	1 side band	X911/a	(a) band at right—50p. booklet (FB57/8), £1 booklet (FH21/2) (b) band at left—50p. booklet (FB57/8)
17p.	litho	dp blue	1 centre band	X1008	£6 Alias Agatha Christie booklet (DX12)
17½p	photo	pale chestnut	phos paper	X953	sheets
18p.	photo	dp violet	phos paper	X954	sheets
18p.	photo	dp olive-grey	phos paper	X955	sheets, vertical coils, 72p. booklet (GC1), £1·80 booklets (FU1/8, GO1), £5 P & O booklet (DX8)
18p.	photo	dp olive-grey	2 bands	X912	50p. booklets (FB37/42, 47, 49), £1 booklet (FH6/13), £5 P & O booklet (DX8)
18p.	litho	dp olive-grey	phos paper	X1009	£5 Financial Times booklet (DX9)
18p.	litho	dp olive-grey	2 bands	X1010	£5 Financial Times booklet (DX9)
18p.	photo/gravure	brt green	1 centre band	X913	sheets, vertical coils
18p.	litho	brt green	1 centre band	X1011	£6 Tolkien booklet (DX14)
18p.	litho	brt green	1 side band	X1012/a	(a) band at right—£6 Tolkien booklet (DX14). (b) band at left—£6 (£5·64) Beatrix Potter booklet (DX15).
19p.	photo	brt orange-red	phos paper	X956	sheets, vertical coils, 76p. booklets (GD1/4), £1·90 booklets (FV1/2, GP1, 3)
19p.	photo	brt orange-red	2 bands	X914	50p. booklets (FB51/4), £1 booklets (FH14/15, 17)
19p.	litho	brt orange-red	phos paper	X1013	£1·90 booklets (GP2, 4)
19p.	litho	brt orange-red	2 bands	X1052*	£1 booklet (FH16)
19½p	photo	olive-grey	phos paper	X957	sheets
20p.	recess	olive-green	none	830	sheets
20p.	photo	dull purple	2 bands	X915	sheets
20p.	photo	dull purple	phos paper	X958	sheets
20p.	litho	dull purple	2 bands	X998	sheets
20p.	litho	dull purple	phos paper	X999	sheets J.W. ptg.
				X1014	sheets Questa ptg.
20p.	photo	turquoise-green	phos paper	X959	sheets
20p.	photo	brownish black	phos paper	X960	sheets, horizontal and vertical coils, £1 booklet (FH18)
20p.	photo	brownish black	2 bands	X916	50p. booklet (FB55), £5 London Life booklet (DX11)
20½p.	photo	ultramarine	phos paper	X961	sheets
22p.	photo	blue	phos paper	X962	sheets
22p.	photo	yellow-green	phos paper	X963	sheets
22p.	litho	yellow-green	2 bands	X1015	£5 Financial Times booklet (DX9)
22p.	photo	brt orange-red	2 bands	X917*	£1 booklet (FH21/2)
22p.	photo	brt orange-red	phos paper	X964	sheets, vertical coils
22p.	litho	brt orange-red	phos paper	X1016	£6 Alias Agatha Christie booklet (DX12)
23p.	photo	brown-red	phos paper	X965	sheets
23p.	photo	brt green	phos paper	X966	sheets
24p.	photo	violet	phos paper	X967	sheets
24p.	photo	Indian red	phos paper	X968	sheets
24p.	photo	chestnut	phos paper	X969	sheets, vertical coils, 50p. booklets (FB59/66), £1 booklets (FH23/7)
24p.	litho	chestnut	phos paper	X1017	£6 Tolkien booklet (DX14) (Questa ptg)
				X1053*	£1 booklet (FH28/30) Walsall ptg
24p.	litho	chestnut	2 bands	X1018	£6 Tolkien booklet (DX14)
25p.	photo	purple	phos paper	X970	sheets
25p.	photo	rose-red	2 bands	X917a	horizontal coils
26p.	photo	rosine	phos paper	X971	Type I. sheets
26p.	photo	rosine	2 bands	X918	Type I. £5 P & O booklet (DX8)
26p.	photo	rosine	phos paper	X971b	Type II. £1·04 booklet (GE1)
26p.	photo	drab	phos paper	X972	sheets
27p.	photo	chestnut	phos paper	X973	sheets, £1·08 booklets (GF1/2)
27p.	photo	violet	phos paper	X974	sheets
28p.	photo	dp violet	phos paper	X975	sheets
28p.	photo	ochre	phos paper	X976	sheets
28p.	photo	dp bluish grey	phos paper	X977	sheets
29p.	photo	ochre-brown	phos paper	X978	sheets

Denominated stamps with 'standard' perforations / Decimal Machin Multi-value coil index **MACHINS**

Value.	Process	Colour	Phosphor	Cat. No.	Source
29p.	photo	dp mauve	phos paper	X979	sheets
29p.	litho	dp mauve	2 bands	X1054*	£1·16 booklet (GG1)
29p.	litho	dp mauve	phos paper	X1055*	£1·16 booklet (GG2)
30p.	photo	dp olive-grey	phos paper	X980	sheets
31p.	photo	purple	phos paper	X981	sheets
31p.	photo	purple	2 bands	X919	£5 British Rail booklet (DX7)
31p.	photo	ultramarine	phos paper	X982	sheets
31p.	litho	ultramarine	phos paper	X1056*	£1·24 booklet (GH1)
32p.	photo	greenish blue	phos paper	X983	sheets
33p.	photo	lt emerald	phos paper	X984	sheets, vertical coils
33p.	litho	lt emerald	phos paper	X1019	£6 Alias Agatha Christie booklet (DX12)
33p.	litho	lt emerald	phos paper	X1057*	£1·32 booklet (GJ1)
33p.	litho	lt emerald	2 bands	X1020	£6 Wales booklet (DX13), £6 (£5·64) Beatrix Potter booklet (DX15)
34p.	photo	ochre-brown	phos paper	X985	sheets
34p.	photo	ochre-brown	2 bands	X920	£5 *The Times* booklet (DX6)
34p.	litho	bistre-brown	2 bands	X1021	£5 *Financial Times* booklet (DX9)
34p.	photo	dp bluish grey	phos paper	X986	sheets
34p.	photo	dp mauve	phos paper	X987	sheets
35p.	photo	sepia	phos paper	X988	sheets
35p.	photo	yellow	phos paper	X989	sheets
37p.	photo	rosine	phos paper	X990	sheets
39p.	photo	brt mauve	phos paper	X991	sheets, vertical coils
39p.	litho	brt mauve	phos paper	X1058*	78p. booklet (GD4a), £1·56 booklet (GM1)
39p.	litho	brt mauve	2 bands	X1022	£6 Tolkien booklet (DX14), £6 (£5·64) Beatrix Potter booklet (DX15)
50p.	recess	dp ultramarine	none or phos paper	831/a	sheets
50p.	photo	ochre-brown	2 bands	X921	sheets
50p.	photo	ochre-brown	none	X992	sheets
50p.	photo	ochre	2 bands	X922	£5 London Life (DX11)
50p.	photo	ochre	none	X993	sheets
50p.	photo	ochre	phos paper	X991a	sheets
75p.	litho	black	none	X1023/a	sheets
75p.	litho	brownish grey and black	none	X1024	sheets
75p.	photo	grey-black	none	X994	sheets
£1	recess	bluish black	none	831b	sheets
£1	photo	brt yellow-green and blackish olive	none	1026	sheets
£1.30	photo	drab and dp greenish blue	none	1026b	sheets
£1.33	photo	pale mauve and grey-black	none	1026c	sheets
£1.41	photo	drab and dp greenish blue	none	1026d	sheets
£1.50	photo	pale mauve and grey-black	none	1026e	sheets
£1.60	photo	pale drab and dp greenish blue	none	1026f	sheets
£2	photo	lt emerald and purple-brown	none	1027	sheets
£5	photo	salmon and chalky blue	none	1028	sheets

For 1st and 2nd class no value indicated (NVI) stamps, see Nos. 1445/52, 1511/16 and 1664/71.
For table covering Machin stamps with elliptical perforations see after Nos. Y1667, etc, in 1993.
Photo/Gravure stamps were printed from both photogravure and computer engraved (Gravure) cylinders.

DECIMAL MACHIN MULTI-VALUE COIL INDEX

The following is a simplified checklist of horizontal multi-value coils, to be used in conjunction with the main listing as details of stamps listed there are not repeated.

Strip Value	Date	Contents	Cat No.
5p.	15.2.71	½p.×2, 1p.×2, 2p.	X841n
10p.	3.12.75	½p.×2, 1p., 2p., 6p.	X841q
10p.	14.12.77	½p.×2, 1p.×2, 7p.	X843l
10p.	16.1.80	1p.×2, 8p. plus 2 labels	X845m
11½p.	6.81	2½p., 3p.×3	X929l
12½p.	30.12.81	½p., 4p.×3	X924l
13p.	14.8.84	1p., 4p.×3	X925l
14p.	5.9.88	2p., 4p.×3	X928l
15p.	10.10.89	3p., 4p.×3	X930cl
17p.	27.11.90	4p.×3, 5p.	X933l
18p.	1.10.91	4p.×2, 5p.×2	X933m
19p.	31.1.95	4p., 5p.×3	X933n

MACHINS Booklet Pane Diagrams (X numbers)

Decimal Machin Booklet Pane Guide ('X' numbers) the shaded sqaure represent printed labels.

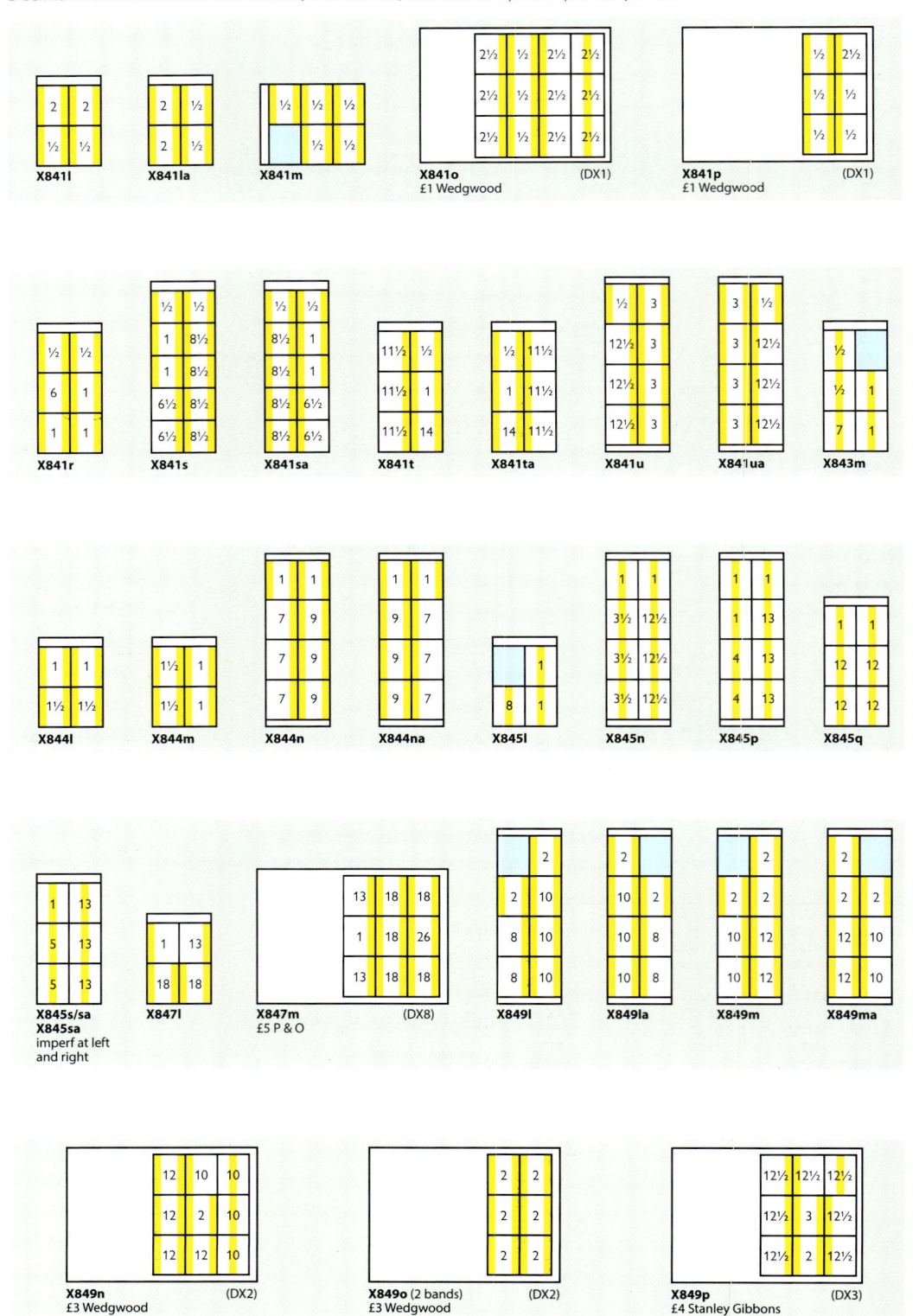

X841l	
X841la	
X841m	
X841o	£1 Wedgwood (DX1)
X841p	£1 Wedgwood (DX1)
X841r	
X841s	
X841sa	
X841t	
X841ta	
X841u	
X841ua	
X843m	
X844l	
X844m	
X844n	
X844na	
X845l	
X845n	
X845p	
X845q	
X845s/sa, X845sa	imperf at left and right
X847l	
X847m	£5 P & O (DX8)
X849l	
X849la	
X849m	
X849ma	
X849n	£3 Wedgwood (DX2)
X849o	(2 bands) £3 Wedgwood (DX2)
X849p	£4 Stanley Gibbons (DX3)

338

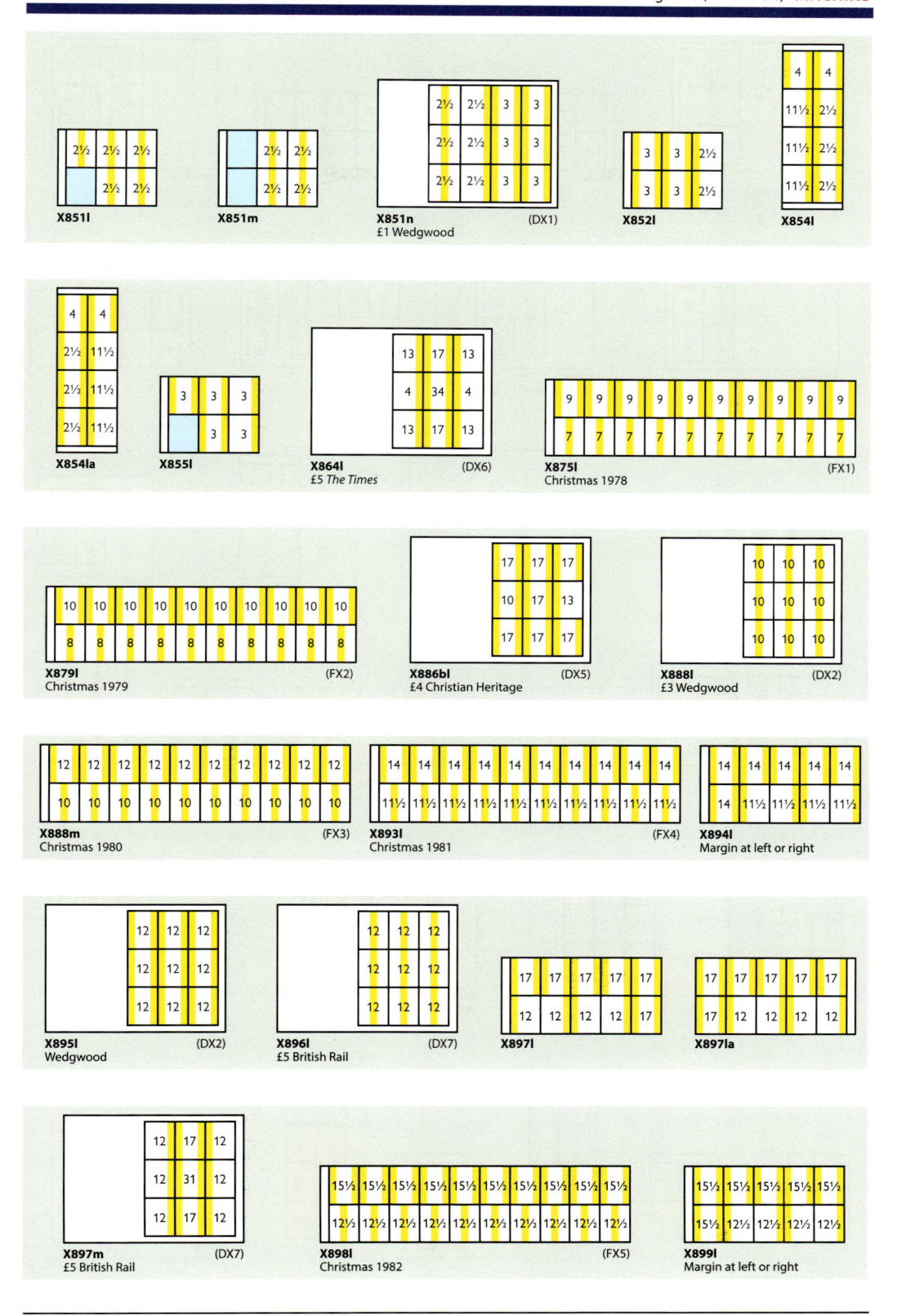

Booklet Pane Diagrams (X numbers) **MACHINS**

- **X851l**
- **X851m**
- **X851n** — £1 Wedgwood (DX1)
- **X852l**
- **X854l**
- **X854la**
- **X855l**
- **X864l** — £5 The Times (DX6)
- **X875l** — Christmas 1978 (FX1)
- **X879l** — Christmas 1979 (FX2)
- **X886bl** — £4 Christian Heritage (DX5)
- **X888l** — £3 Wedgwood (DX2)
- **X888m** — Christmas 1980 (FX3)
- **X893l** — Christmas 1981 (FX4)
- **X894l** — Margin at left or right
- **X895l** — Wedgwood (DX2)
- **X896l** — £5 British Rail (DX7)
- **X897l**
- **X897la**
- **X897m** — £5 British Rail (DX7)
- **X898l** — Christmas 1982 (FX5)
- **X899l** — Margin at left or right

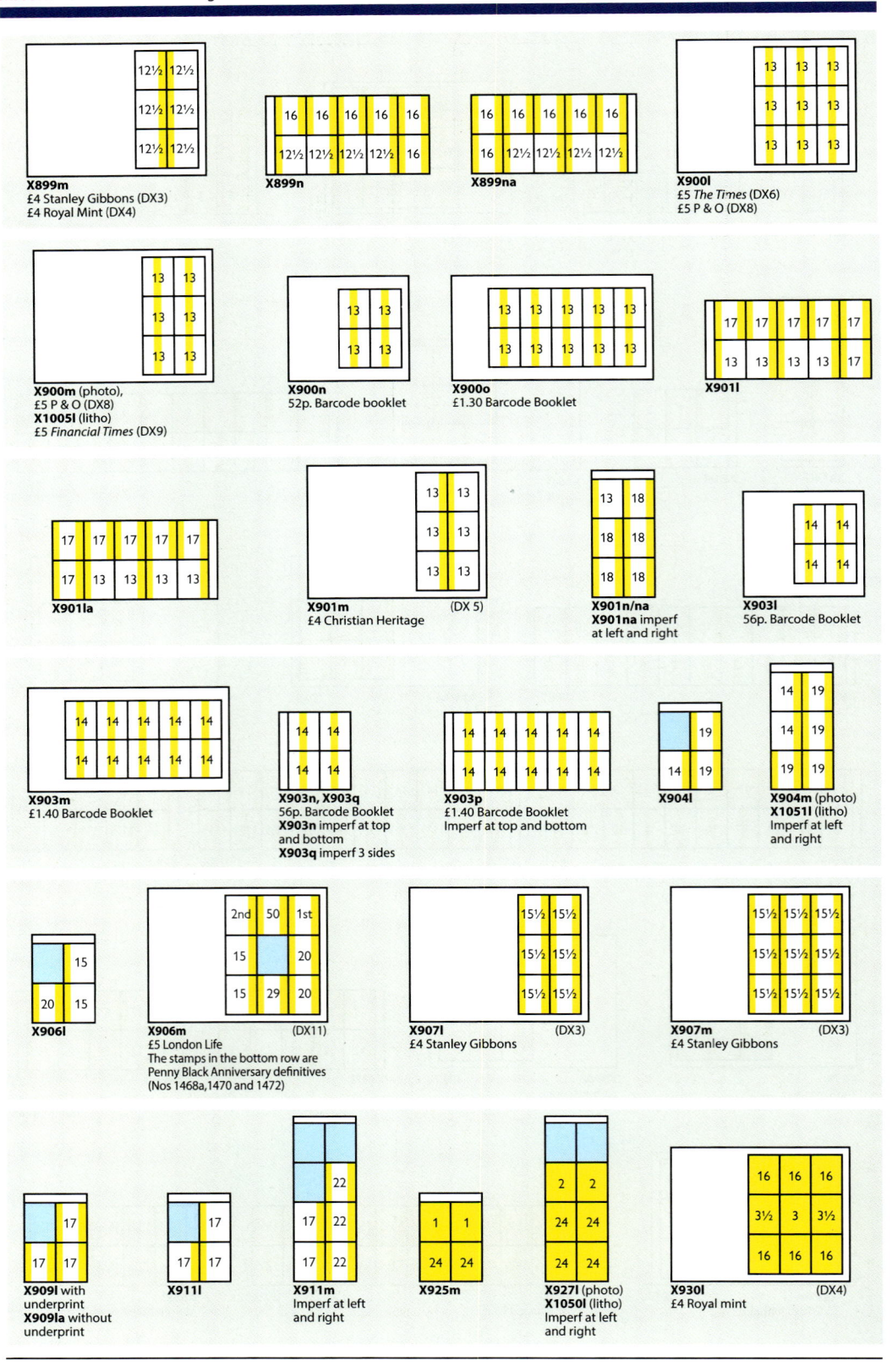

MACHINS Booklet Pane Diagrams (X numbers)

X899m
£4 Stanley Gibbons (DX3)
£4 Royal Mint (DX4)

X899n

X899na

X900l
£5 The Times (DX6)
£5 P & O (DX8)

X900m (photo),
£5 P & O (DX8)
X1005l (litho)
£5 Financial Times (DX9)

X900n
52p. Barcode booklet

X900o
£1.30 Barcode Booklet

X901l

X901la

X901m
£4 Christian Heritage (DX 5)

X901n/na
X901na imperf
at left and right

X903l
56p. Barcode Booklet

X903m
£1.40 Barcode Booklet

X903n, X903q
56p. Barcode Booklet
X903n imperf at top and bottom
X903q imperf 3 sides

X903p
£1.40 Barcode Booklet
Imperf at top and bottom

X904l

X904m (photo)
X1051l (litho)
Imperf at left and right

X906l

X906m (DX11)
£5 London Life
The stamps in the bottom row are Penny Black Anniversary definitives (Nos 1468a, 1470 and 1472)

X907l (DX3)
£4 Stanley Gibbons

X907m (DX3)
£4 Stanley Gibbons

X909l with underprint
X909la without underprint

X911l

X911m
Imperf at left and right

X925m

X927l (photo)
X1050l (litho)
Imperf at left and right

X930l (DX4)
£4 Royal mint

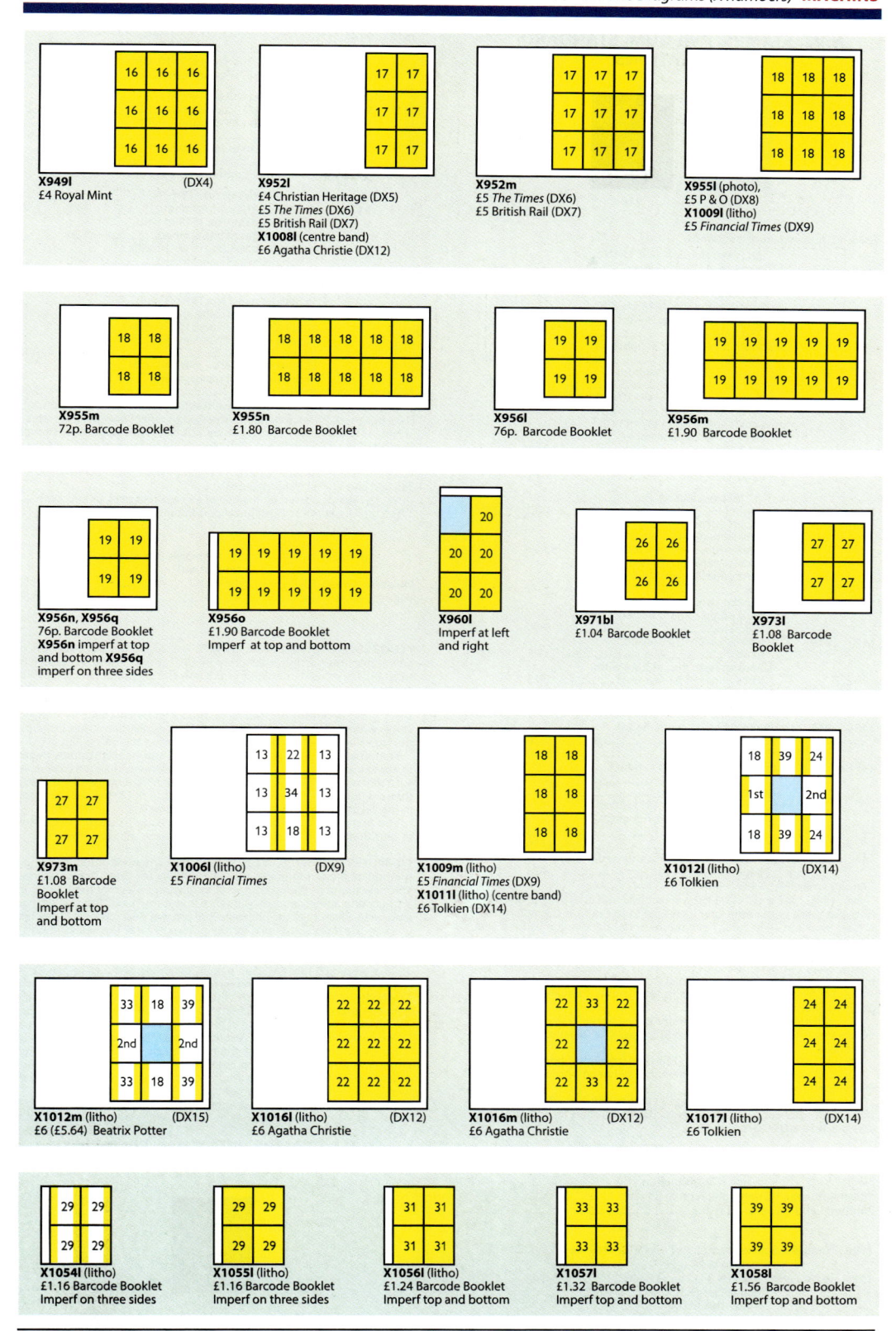

Booklet Pane Diagrams (X numbers) **MACHINS**

X949l (DX4)
£4 Royal Mint

X952l
£4 Christian Heritage (DX5)
£5 *The Times* (DX6)
£5 British Rail (DX7)
X1008l (centre band)
£6 Agatha Christie (DX12)

X952m
£5 *The Times* (DX6)
£5 British Rail (DX7)

X955l (photo),
£5 P & O (DX8)
X1009l (litho)
£5 *Financial Times* (DX9)

X955m
72p. Barcode Booklet

X955n
£1.80 Barcode Booklet

X956l
76p. Barcode Booklet

X956m
£1.90 Barcode Booklet

X956n, X956q
76p. Barcode Booklet
X956n imperf at top and bottom **X956q** imperf on three sides

X956o
£1.90 Barcode Booklet
Imperf at top and bottom

X960l
Imperf at left and right

X971bl
£1.04 Barcode Booklet

X973l
£1.08 Barcode Booklet

X973m
£1.08 Barcode Booklet
Imperf at top and bottom

X1006l (litho) (DX9)
£5 *Financial Times*

X1009m (litho)
£5 *Financial Times* (DX9)
X1011l (litho) (centre band)
£6 Tolkien (DX14)

X1012l (litho) (DX14)
£6 Tolkien

X1012m (litho) (DX15)
£6 (£5.64) Beatrix Potter

X1016l (litho) (DX12)
£6 Agatha Christie

X1016m (litho) (DX12)
£6 Agatha Christie

X1017l (litho) (DX14)
£6 Tolkien

X1054l (litho)
£1.16 Barcode Booklet
Imperf on three sides

X1055l (litho)
£1.16 Barcode Booklet
Imperf on three sides

X1056l (litho)
£1.24 Barcode Booklet
Imperf top and bottom

X1057l
£1.32 Barcode Booklet
Imperf top and bottom

X1058l
£1.56 Barcode Booklet
Imperf top and bottom

N.V.I. STAMPS, PVA GUM, STANDARD PERFORATIONS

913   914

1989 (22 Aug)–**93**. Booklet Stamps.
(a) Photo Harrison. Perf 15×14.

1445	913	(2nd) bright blue (1 centre band)	1·00	1·00
		l. Booklet pane. No. 1445×10 with horizontal edges of pane imperf	9·50	
		m. Booklet pane. No. 1445×4 with three edges of pane imperf (28.11.89)	22·00	
1446		(2nd) bright blue (1 band at right) (20.3.90)	1·60	1·60
1447	914	(1st) brownish black (phosphorised paper)	1·20	1·20
		l. Booklet pane. No. 1447×10 with horizontal edges of pane imperf	12·00	
		m. Booklet pane. No. 1447×4 with three edges of pane imperf (5.12.89)	22·00	
1448		(1st) brownish black (2 phosphor bands) (20.3.90)	1·75	1·75

(b) Litho Walsall. Perf 14.

1449	913	(2nd) bright blue (1 centre band)	1·00	1·00
		a. Imperf between (vert pair)		
		l. Booklet pane. No. 1449×4 with three edges of pane imperf	5·50	
		m. Booklet pane. No. 1449×4 with horiz edges of pane imperf (6.8.91)	5·00	
		n. Booklet pane. No. 1449×10 with horiz edges of pane imperf (6.8.91)	9·50	
1450	914	(1st) blackish brown (2 phosphor bands)	1·25	1·25
		l. Booklet pane. No. 1450×4 with three edges of pane imperf	7·75	
		y. Phosphor omitted	£400	

(c) Litho Questa. Perf 15×14.

1451	913	(2nd) bright blue (1 centre band) (19.9.89)	1·00	1·00
		y. Phosphor omitted	£160	
1451a		(2nd) bright blue (1 band at right) (25.2.92)	1·25	1·25
		ab. Band at left (10.8.93)	1·25	1·25
		al. Booklet pane. Nos. 1451aab and 1514a, each×3, with margins all round (10.8.93)	8·25	
		ay. Phosphor omitted	£450	
1452	914	(1st) brownish black (phosphorised paper) (19.9.89)	1·25	1·25

First Day Cover (Nos. 1445, 1447) .... 3·00

Nos. 1445, 1447 and 1449/1452 were initially sold at 14p. (2nd) and 19p. (1st), but these prices were later increased to reflect new postage rates.

Nos. 1446 and 1448 come from the *se-tenant* pane in the London Life £5 Booklet. This pane is listed under No. X906m in the Decimal Machin section.

Nos. 1445, 1447 and 1449/1450 do not exist perforated on all four sides, but come with either one or two adjacent sides imperforate.

No. 1450y comes from a pane in which one stamp was without phosphor bands due to a dry print.

No. 1451a comes from the *se-tenant* panes in the Wales and Tolkien £6 booklet. These panes are listed under Nos. X1012al and W49l (Wales Regionals).

No. 1451aab comes from the £6 (£5·64) Beatrix Potter booklet.

For illustrations showing the differences between photogravure and lithography see above T **367**.

For similar designs, but in changed colours, see Nos. 1511/1516, for those with elliptical perforations, Nos. 1664/1671, and for self-adhesive versions Nos. 2039/2040 and 2295.

Special First Day of Issue Postmarks (for illustrations see Introduction)

Philatelic Bureau Edingburgh (Type G) (in red)	4·50
Windsor, Berks (Type G) (in red)	4·50

1990 (7 Aug)–**92**. Booklet stamps. As Types **913**/**914**, but colours changed.
(a) Photo Harrison. Perf 15×14.

1511	913	(2nd) deep blue (1 centre band)	1·10	1·10
		l. Booklet pane. No. 1511×10 with horiz edges of pane imperf	10·00	
1512	914	(1st) bright orange-red (phosphorised paper)	1·40	1·40
		l. Booklet pane. No. 1512×10 with horiz edges of pane imperf	12·00	

(b) Litho Questa. Perf 15×14.

1513	913	(2nd) deep blue (1 centre band)	1·25	1·25
1514	914	(1st) bright orange-red (phosphorised paper)	1·50	1·80
1514a		(1st) bright orange-red (2 bands) (25.2.92)	1·50	1·50
		ay. Phosphor omitted	£700	

(c) Litho Walsall. Perf 14.

1515	913	(2nd) deep blue (1 centre band)	1·25	1·50
		l. Booklet pane. No. 1515×4 with horiz edges of pane imperf	5·00	
		m. Booklet pane. No. 1515×10 with horiz edges of pane imperf	9·50	
1516	914	(1st) bright orange-red (phosphorised paper)	1·50	1·80
		l. Booklet pane. No. 1516×4 with horiz edges of pane imperf	6·00	
		m. Booklet pane. No. 1516×10 with horiz edges of pane imperf	12·00	
		c. Perf 13	3·00	3·00
		cl. Booklet pane. No. 1516c×4 with horiz edges of pane imperf	12·00	

First Day Cover (Nos. 1515/1516) .... 3·00

Nos. 1511/1514 and 1515/1516 were initially sold at 15p. (2nd) and 20p. (1st), but these prices were later increased to reflect new postage rates.

Nos. 1511/1512 and 1515/1516 do not exist with perforations on all four sides, but come with either the top or the bottom edge imperforate.

No. 1514a comes from the *se-tenant* panes in the £6 Wales, £6 Tolkien and £5·64 Beatrix Potter booklets. These panes are listed under Nos. X1012l, 1451aal and W49a (Wales Regionals).

No. 1516c was caused by the use of an incorrect perforation comb.

For similar stamps with elliptical perforations see Nos. 1664/1672.

Special First Day of Issue Postmarks (for illustration see Introduction)

Philatelic Bureau, Edinburgh (Type G)	3·00
Windsor, Berks (Type G)	3·50

FLUORESCENT PHOSPHOR BANDS. Following the introduction of new automatic sorting machinery in 1991 it was found necessary to substantially increase the signal emitted by the phosphor bands. This was achieved by adding a fluorescent element to the phosphor which appears yellow under UV light. This combination was first used on an experimental sheet printing of the 18p., No. X913, produced by Enschedé in 1991. All values with phosphor bands from the elliptical perforations issue, including the No Value Indicated design, originally showed this yellow fluor.

From mid-1995 printings of current sheet and booklet stamps began to appear with the colour of the fluorescent element changed to blue. As such differences in fluor colour can only be identified by use of a UV lamp they are outside the scope of this catalogue, but full details will be found in the *Great Britain Specialised Catalogue Volume 4.*

The first commemorative/special stamp issue to show the change to blue fluor was the Centenary of Rugby League set, Nos. 1891/1895.

COMPUTER-ENGRAVED CYLINDERS. In 1991 Enschedé introduced a new method of preparing photogravure cylinders for Great Britain stamps. This new method utilised computer-engraving instead of the traditional acid-etching and produced cylinders without the minor flaws which had long been a feature of the photogravure process. Such cylinders were first used on Great Britain stamps for the printing of the 18p. released on 19 November 1991 (see No. X913).

Harrison and Sons continued to use the acid-etching method until mid-1996 after which most Machin values, including NVI's, were produced from computer-engraved cylinders using a very similar process to that of Enschedé. Some values exist in versions from both cylinder production methods and can often be identified by minor differences. Such stamps are, however, outside the scope of this listing, but full details can be found in the current edition of the *Great Britain Specialised Catalogue Volume 4.*

For commemorative stamps the first Harrison issue to use computer-engraved cylinders was the Centenary of Cinema set (Nos. 1920/1924).

When Walsall introduced photogravure printing in 1997 their cylinders were produced using a similar computer-engraved process.

N.V.I. STAMPS, PVA GUM, ELLIPTICAL PERFORATIONS

1093a

1993 (6 Apr)–2017. As Types 913/914, and 1093a. Perf 14 (No. 1665) or 15×14 (others) (both with one elliptical hole in each vertical side).

(a) Photo/gravure
Harrison No. 1666
Questa Nos. 1664a, 1667a
Walsall/ISP Walsall Nos. 1665, 1668s
Harrison/De La Rue, Questa or Walsall No. 1667
Harrison/De La Rue, Enschedé, Questa or Walsall/ISP Walsall Nos. 1664, 1668, 1669.

1664	913	(2nd) bright blue (1 centre band) (7.9.93)	1·00	1·00
		a. Perf 14 (1.12.98)	1·10	1·10
		b. Imperf (pair)	£950	
		l. Booklet pane. Nos. 1664 and 1667×3 plus 4 labels ('postcode' on top right label) (27.4.00)	6·75	
		la. As No. 1664l, but inscr 'postcodes' on top right label (17.4.01)	7·00	
		m. Booklet pane. Nos. 1664×2 and 1667×6 (27.4.00)	8·50	
		n. Booklet pane. Nos. 1664 and 1669, each×4, with central label and margins all round (6.2.02)	9·50	
		o. Booklet pane. Nos. 1664 and 1668, each×4, with central label and margins all round (2.6.03)	8·50	
		p. Booklet pane. Nos. 1664×4, Y1709×2 and Y1715×2, with central label and margins all round (24.2.05)	7·50	
1665		(2nd) bright blue (1 band at right) (13.10.98)	1·10	1·10
		c. Band at left	1·10	1·00
		l. Booklet pane. Nos. 1665×3 and NI81b, S91a and W80a with margins all round	7·50	
1666	914	(1st) bright orange-red (phosphorised paper)	1·20	1·20
1667		(1st) bright orange-red (2 phosphor bands) (4.4.95)	1·20	1·20
		y. Phosphor omitted	£225	
		a. Perf 14 (1.12.98)	1·25	1·25
		l. Booklet pane. No. 1667×8 with central label and margins all round (16.2.99)	9·50	
		m. Booklet pane. No. 1667×4 plus commemorative label at right (12.5.99)	5·00	
1668		(1st) gold (2 phosphor bands) (21.4.97)	1·20	1·20
		a. Imperf (pair)	£175	
		l. Booklet pane. Nos. 1668 and Y1692, each×4, and central label with margins all round (23.9.97)	6·50	
		m. Booklet pane. Nos. 1668/1669, each×4, with central label and margins all round (24.9.02)	9·00	
		o. Booklet pane. Nos. 1668 and Y1704, each×4, with central label and margins all round (16.3.04)	7·50	
		p. Booklet pane. Nos. 1668×4, Y1715×2 and Y1723×2, with central label and margins all round (25.5.04)	9·75	
		q. Booklet pane. Nos. 1668×4, Y1726×2 and Y1736×2, with central label and margins all round (18.10.05)	8·50	
		r. Booklet pane. Nos. 1668×4, Y1701×2 and Y1711×2, with central label and margins all round (23.2.06)	8·50	
1668s		(1st) brownish black (2 phosphor bands) (5.6.17)	3·00	3·00
		sl. Booklet pane. Nos. 1668s, 2133×2, 1667/1668, 2124, 2651 and U3067 with central label and margins all round (5.6.17)	10·00	
1669	1093a	(E) deep blue (2 phosphor bands) (19.1.99)	2·25	2·25

(b) Litho Questa or Walsall (No. 1670), Enschedé, Questa or Walsall (No. 1671) or De La Rue or Walsall (No. 1672).

1670	913	(2nd) bright blue (1 centre band)	1·00	90
		y. Phosphor omitted	£175	
		l. Booklet pane. Nos. 1670 and 1672, each×4, with central label and margins all round (18.9.08)	5·00	
1671	914	(1st) bright orange-red (2 phosphor bands)	1·20	1·00
		y. Phosphor omitted	£200	
		l. Booklet pane. No. 1671×4 plus commemorative label at left (27.7.94)	6·00	
		la. Ditto, but with commemorative label at right (16.5.95)	6·00	
		ly. Phosphor omitted	£400	
		m. Pane. No. 1671 with margins all round (roul 8 across top corners of pane) (Boots logo on margin) (17.8.94)	1·50	
		my. Phosphor omitted	£1500	
		ma. Without Boots logo above stamp (11.9.95)	1·50	
		mb. Ditto, but roul 10 across top corners of pane (20.2.97)	3·25	
		n. Booklet pane. No. 1671×9 with margins all round (16.2.99)	7·50	
1672		(1st) gold (2 phosphor bands) (8.1.08)	1·20	1·20
		y. Phosphor omitted	£1250	
		l. Booklet pane. No. 1672×8 with central label and margins all round (8.1.08)	11·00	

For details of sheets, booklets, etc containing these stamps see Decimal Machin Index following the 'Y' numbers.

Nos. 1664/1671 were issued in booklet panes showing perforations on all four edges.

On 6 September 1993 Nos. 1670/1671 printed in lithography by Questa were made available in sheets from post offices in Birmingham, Coventry, Falkirk and Milton Keynes. These sheet stamps became available nationally on 5 October 1993. On 29 April 1997 No. 1664 printed in photogravure by Walsall became available in sheets. On the same date Nos. 1664 and 1667 were issued in coils printed by Harrison. Sheets of No. 1667 were printed by Walsall from 18 November 1997.

No. 1665 exists with the phosphor band at the left or right of the stamp from separate panes of the £6·16 Speed stamp booklet No. DX21.

For pane containing No. 1665c see No. Y1676al.

No. 1668 was originally printed by Harrisons in booklets and Walsall in sheets and booklets for The Queen's Golden Wedding and issued on 21 April 1997. It was printed in coils by Enschedé (5.10.02), when gold became the accepted colour for 1st class definitives, and later in sheets and coils by De La Rue.

Booklet pane No. 1668m was issued on 24 September 2002 in the £6·83 Across the Universe booklet (No. DX29). It was issued again with a different central label on 25 February 2003 in the £6·99 Microcosmos booklet (No. DX30).

No. 1669 was intended for the basic European airmail rate, initially 30p., and was at first only available from Barcode booklet No. HF1, printed by Walsall. It appeared in sheets printed by De La Rue on 5 October 1999.

No. 1671m, printed by Questa, was provided by the Royal Mail for inclusion in single pre-packed greetings cards. The pane shows large margins at top and sides with lines of roulette gauging 8 stretching from the bottom corners to the mid point of the top edge. Examples included with greetings cards show the top two corners of the pane folded over. Unfolded examples were available from the British Philatelic Bureau and from other Post Office philatelic outlets. The scheme was originally limited to Boots and their logo appeared on the pane margin. Other card retailers subsequently participated and later supplies omitted the logo.

A further printing by Enschedé in 1997 showed the roulettes gauging 10 (No. 1671mb). Blank pieces of gummed paper have been found showing the perforation and rouletting of No. 1671mb, but no printing.

No. 1672 was only issued in the following booklets: £7·40 Ian Fleming's James Bond (No. DX41), Pilot to Plane (No. DX42) and Charles Darwin (No. DX45).

For illustration of differences between lithography and gravure see below Types **367** and **367a**.

For self-adhesive stamps in these colours see Nos. 2039/2040 and 2295/2298.

POSTAL FORGERIES. In mid-1994 a number of postal forgeries of the 2nd bright blue printed in lithography were detected after having been rejected by the sorting equipment. These show the Queen's head in bright greenish blue, have a fluorescent, rather than a phosphor, band and show matt, colourless gum on the reverse. These forgeries come from booklets of ten which also have forged covers.

COMMEMORATIVE BOOKLET PANES. Booklets of four 1st Class stamps with *se-tenant* commemorative label were issued for the following anniversaries or events:

300th Anniversary of the Bank of England (No. 1671l)
Birth Centenary of R. J. Mitchell (No. 1671la)
70th Birthday of Queen Elizabeth II (No. 1671la)
Hong Kong '97 International Stamp Exhibition (No. 1671la)
Commonwealth Heads of Government Meeting, Edinburgh (No. 1671la)
50th Birthday of Prince of Wales (No. 1671la)
50th Anniversary of Berlin Airlift (No. 1667m)
Rugby World Cup (No. 1667m)

First Day Covers

21.4.97	1st (No. 1668), 26p. (No. Y1692) (Type G) (Philatelic Bureau or Windsor)	3·25
23.9.97	BBC label pane 1st×4, 26p.×4 (No. 1668l), (Philatelic Bureau or London W1)	6·50
19.1.99	E (No. 1669) (Type G) (Philatelic Bureau or Windsor)	2·75
16.2.99	Profile on Print label pane 1st×8 (No. 1671n) (see Nos. 2077/2079) (Philatelic Bureau or London SW1)	5·50
6.2.02	A Gracious Accession label pane 2nd×4 and E×4 (No. 1664n) (see Nos. 2253/2257) (Tallents House or Windsor)	7·00

Date	Description	Price
24.9.02	Across the Universe label pane 1st×4, E×4 (No. 1668m) (Tallents House or Star, Glenrothes)	5·00
25.2.03	Microcosmos label pane 1st×4, E×4 (No. 1668m) (Tallents House or Cambridge)	5·00
2.6.03	A Perfect Coronation label pane 2nd×4, 1st×4 (No. 1664o) (Tallents House or London SW)	6·50
16.3.04	Letters by Night. A Tribute to the Travelling Post Office label pane 1st×4, 37p.×4 (No. 1668o) (Tallents House or London NW10)	7·50
25.5.04	The Glory of the Garden label pane 1st×4, 42p.×2, 47p.×2 (No. 1668p) (Tallents House or Wisley, Woking)	8·00
24.2.05	The Brontë Sisters label pane 2nd×4, 39p.×2, 42p.×2 (No. 1664p) (Tallents House or Haworth, Keighley)	5·00
18.10.05	Bicentenary of the Battle of Trafalgar label pane 1st×4, 50p.×2 and 68p.×2 (No. 1668q) (Tallents House and Portsmouth)	7·00
23.2.06	Birth Bicentenary of Isambard Kingdom Brunel label pane 1st×4, 35p.×2 and 40p.×2 (No. 1668r) (Tallents House or Bristol)	7·00
8.1.08	James Bond label pane 1st×8 (No. 1672l) (Tallents House or London SE1)	11·00
18.9.08	Pilot to Plane RAF Uniforms label pane 2nd×4 and 1st×4 (No.1670l) (Tallents House or Hendon, London NW9)	5·00
5.6.17	50th Anniversary of the Machin Definitive label pane 1st×6 and 20p.×2 (No. 1668sl). (Tallents House or High Wycombe)	12·00

1390   1390a

1390b

1999 (16 Feb).

(a) Embossed and litho Walsall. Self-adhesive. Die-cut perf 14×15.

2077	1390	(1st) grey (face value) (Queen's head in colourless relief) (phosphor background around head)	1·50	1·50
		l. Booklet pane. No. 2077×4 with margins all round	6·00	

(b) Eng C. Slania. Recess Enschedé. Perf 14×14½.

2078	1390a	(1st) grey-black (2 phosphor bands)	1·50	1·50
		l. Booklet pane. No. 2078×4 with margins all round	6·00	

(c) Typo Harrison. Perf 14×15.

2079	1390b	(1st) black (2 phosphor bands)	1·50	1·50
		y. Phosphor omitted	£1200	
		l. Booklet pane. No. 2079×4 with margins all round	6·00	
		ly. Booklet pane. Phosphor omitted		

Set of 3 .... 4·00 4·00
First Day Covers (Philatelic Bureau) (3 covers with Nos. 2077l, 2078l, 2079l) .... 7·00
First Day Covers (London SW1) (3 covers with Nos. 2077l, 2078l, 2079l) .... 7·00

Nos. 2077/2079 were only issued in the £7·54 Profile on Print booklet (No. DX22).

NVI Stamps. Panes with 'standard' perforations

1445l (bright blue, photo)
Imperf at top and bottom

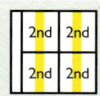

1445m (bright blue, photo)
Imperf at top and bottom

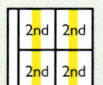

1449l (bright blue, litho)
Imperf at top, bottom and right

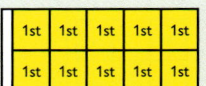

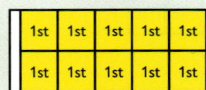

1449m (bright blue, litho)
Imperf at top and bottom

1449n (bright blue, litho)
Imperf at top and bottom

1511l (deep blue, photo)
Imperf at top and bottom

1515l (deep blue, litho)
Imperf at top and bottom

1515m (deep blue, litho)
Imperf at top, bottom and right

1447l (black, photo)
Imperf at top and bottom

1447m (black, litho)
Imperf at top and bottom

1450l (black, litho)
Imperf at top, bottom and right

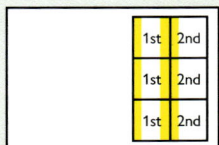

1451al (litho)   (DX15)
£6 (£5.64) Beatrix Potter

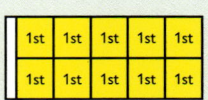

1512l (orange, photo)
Imperf at top and bottom

1516l (orange, litho P 14)
Imperf at top and bottom

1516cl (orange, litho, P 13)
Imperf at top and bottom

1516m (orange, litho)
Imperf at top and bottom

NVI Stamps. Panes with **elliptical perforations** the shaded squares represent printed labels.

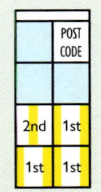

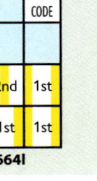

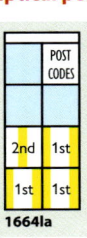

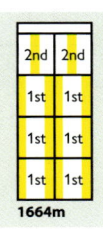

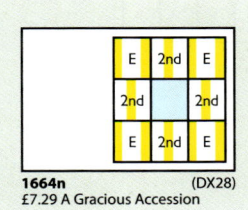

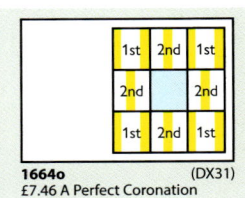

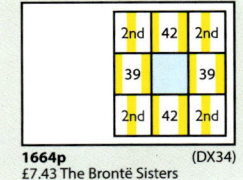

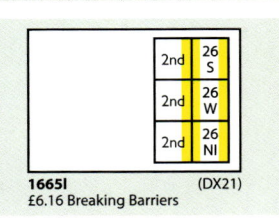

1664l

1664la

1664m

1664n   (DX28)
£7.29 A Gracious Accession

1664o   (DX31)
£7.46 A Perfect Coronation

1664p   (DX34)
£7.43 The Brontë Sisters

1665l   (DX21)
£6.16 Breaking Barriers

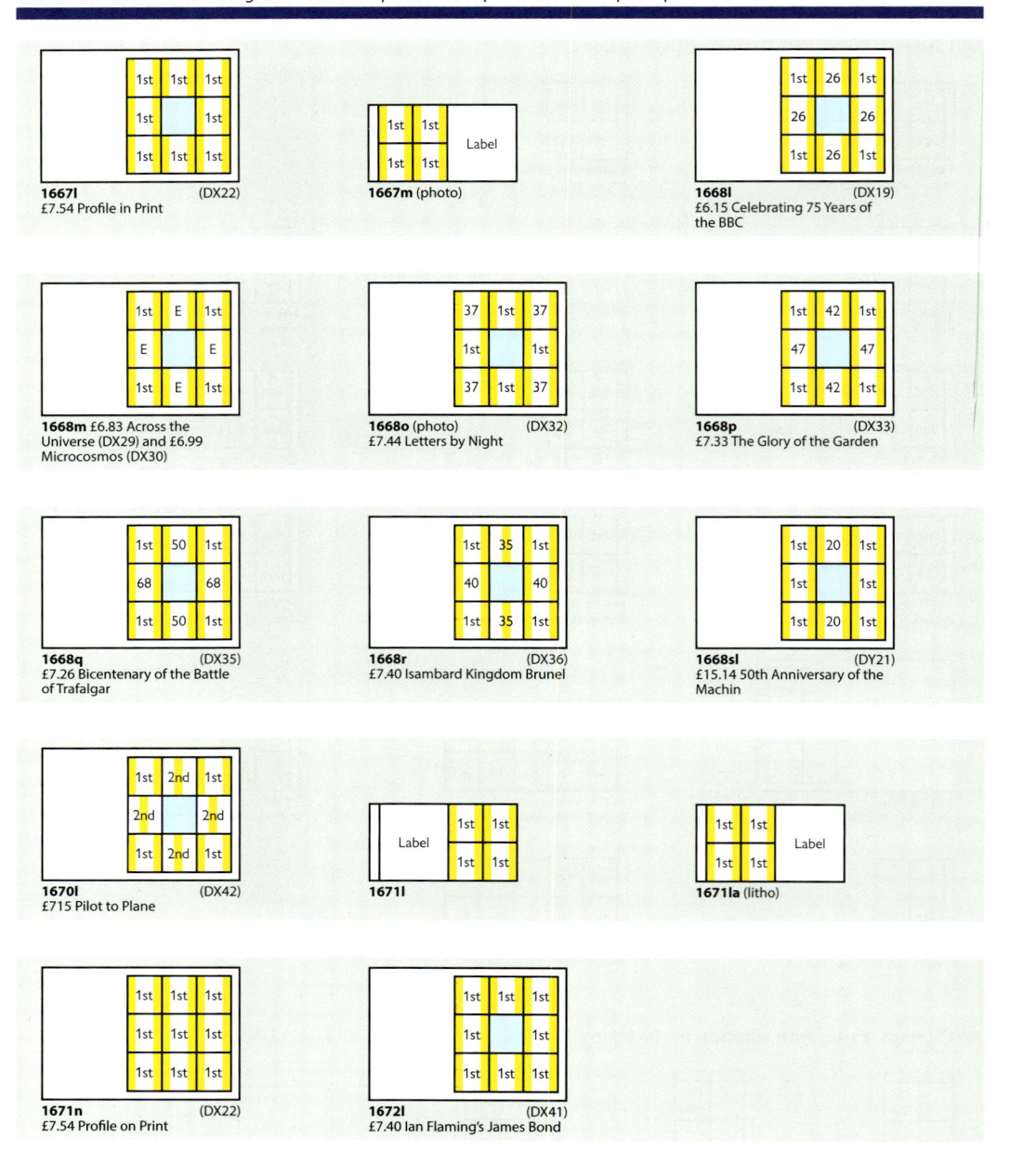

MACHINS Booklet Pane Diagrams / NVI Stamps. Standard perforations / elliptical perforations

1667l (DX22)
£7.54 Profile in Print

1667m (photo)

1668l (DX19)
£6.15 Celebrating 75 Years of the BBC

1668m £6.83 Across the Universe (DX29) and £6.99 Microcosmos (DX30)

1668o (photo) (DX32)
£7.44 Letters by Night

1668p (DX33)
£7.33 The Glory of the Garden

1668q (DX35)
£7.26 Bicentenary of the Battle of Trafalgar

1668r (DX36)
£7.40 Isambard Kingdom Brunel

1668sl (DY21)
£15.14 50th Anniversary of the Machin

1670l (DX42)
£715 Pilot to Plane

1671l

1671la (litho)

1671n (DX22)
£7.54 Profile on Print

1672l (DX41)
£7.40 Ian Flaming's James Bond

346

DENOMINATED STAMPS, PVA GUM, ELLIPTICAL PERFORATIONS

Two types of the 54p. (Nos. Y1728/Y1783)

II Normal figures of face value

III Open '4' and open lower curve of '5'

1993 (27 Apr)–**2017**. As Nos. X841, etc, but Perf 15×14 (with one elliptical hole in each vertical side).

Enschedé: 20p. (No. Y1684), 29p., 35p. (No. Y1698), 36p., 38p. (No. Y1706), 41p. (No. Y1712), 43p. (No. Y1716)

Harrison: 20p. (No. Y1686), 25p. (No. Y1689), 26p. (No. Y1692), 35p. (No. Y1699), 41p. (No. Y1713), 43p. (No. Y1717)

Walsall: 10p. (No. Y1676a), 19p. (No. Y1683), 38p. (No. Y1707a), 43p. (No. Y1717a).

Enschedé or Harrison/De La Rue: 4p., 5p., 6p., 25p. (No. Y1690), 31p., 39p. (No. Y1708), £1 (No. Y1743)

Enschedé, Harrison/De La Rue, Questa or ISP Walsall: 1p.

Enschedé, Harrison/De La Rue, Questa or Walsall: 2p.

Enschedé, Harrison/De La Rue or Walsall: 10p. (No. Y1676), 30p., 37p. (No. Y1703), 42p., 50p. (No. Y1726), 63p.

Harrison/De La Rue or Questa: 19p. (No. Y1682), 20p. (No. Y1685), 26p. (No. Y1691)

De La Rue or Walsall: 8p. (No. Y1707), 39p. (No. Y1709), 40p. (No. Y1710), 64p., 65p., 68p.

De La Rue: 7p., 8p., 9p., 12p., 14p., 15p., 16p., 17p., 20p. (No. Y1687), 22p., 33p., 34p., 35p. (No. Y1700), 37p. (Nos. Y1704/Y1705), 41p. (No. Y1714), 43p. (No. Y1718), 44p., 45p., 48p., 49p., 50p., (No. Y1727), 56p., 60p., 62p., 67p., 72p., 78p., 81p., 88p., 90p., 97p., £1 (No. Y1744), £1·46, £1·50, £2, £3, £5

Enschedé or De La Rue: 35p. (No. Y1701), 40p. (No. Y1711), 46p., 47p., 54p.

(a) Photo/gravure.

Y1667	367	1p. crimson (2 bands) (8.6.93)	20	20
		l. Booklet pane. Nos. Y1667×2, Y1685 and Y1691×3 plus 2 labels (1.12.98)	20·00	
		m. Booklet pane. Nos. Y1667/Y668, Y1682 and Y1691×3 plus 2 labels (26.4.99)	6·00	
		n. Booklet pane. Nos. Y1667×4, Y1682×3 and Y1691 with central label and margins all round (21.9.99)	2·50	
		o. Booklet pane. Nos. Y1667×2, Y1722×4 and Y1728×2 with central label and margins all round (20.9.07)	5·00	
		p. Booklet pane. Nos. Y1667, Y1668, Y1670, Y1676, Y1687, Y1727, 1664 and U3061, with central label and margins all round (5.6.17)	6·00	
Y1668		2p. deep green (2 bands) (11.4.95)	20	20
		a. Imperf (pair)	£900	
		l. Booklet pane. Nos. Y1668×4 and Nos. Y1722 and Y1724, each×2 with centre label and margins all round (5.6.07)	7·00	
		m. Booklet pane. Nos. Y1668×2, Y1676×2 and U3060×4 with central label and margins all round (10.1.12)	16·00	
Y1669		4p. new blue (2 bands) (14.12.93)	20	20
		a. Imperf	£1100	
Y1670		5p. dull red-brown (Type II) (2 bands) (8.6.93)	25	25
		l. Booklet pane. Nos. Y1670 and 2651, each×4, with centre label and margins all round (1.3.07)	4·75	
Y1671		6p. yellow-olive (2 bands)	30	30
		y. Phosphor omitted	£180	
Y1672		7p. grey (2 bands) (20.4.99)	2·75	2·75
		a. Imperf (pair)	£325	
Y1673		7p. bright magenta (2 bands) (1.4.04)	30	30
		a. Imperf (pair)	£100	
Y1674		8p. yellow (2 bands) (25.4.00)	35	35
Y1675		9p. yellow-orange (2 bands) (5.4.05)	30	30
Y1676		10p. dull orange (2 bands) (8.6.93)	35	35
		aa. Imperf pair	£1100	
		a. Perf 14 (13.10.98)	1·75	1·75
		al. Booklet pane. Nos. Y1676a×2, 1665c and Y1717a, each×3, with centre label and margins all round	8·50	
Y1677		12p. greenish blue (2 bands) (1.8.06)	70	70
Y1678		14p. rose-red (2 bands) (1.8.06)	70	70
Y1679		15p. bright magenta (2 bands) (1.4.08)	65	65
Y1680		16p. pale cerise (2 bands) (27.3.07)	65	65
Y1681		17p. brown-olive (2 bands) (31.3.09)	75	75
		a. Imperf (pair)	£1700	
Y1682		19p. bistre (1 centre band) (26.10.93)	50	50
		a. Imperf (pair)	£550	
		y. Phosphor omitted	80·00	
		l. Booklet pane. Nos. Y1682 and Y1691×7 (26.4.99)	6·50	
		ly. Phosphor omitted	£150	
Y1683		19p. bistre (1 band at right) (perf 14) (15.2.00)	90	90
		l. Booklet pane. Nos. Y1683×4 and Y1707a×2 with margins all round	12·00	
Y1684		20p. turquoise-green (2 bands) (14.12.93)	80	80
Y1685		20p. bright green (1 centre band) (25.6.96)	60	60
		a. Imperf (horiz pair)	£175	
		l. Booklet pane. Nos. Y1685 and Y1691×7 (1.12.98)	20·00	
Y1686		20p. bright green (1 band at right) (23.9.97)	1·10	1·10
		l. Booklet pane. Nos. Y1686 and Y1691, each×3 with margins all round	4·50	
Y1687		20p. bright green (2 bands) (20.4.99)	60	60
		a. Imperf (pair)	£175	
Y1688		22p. drab (2 bands) (31.3.09)	80	80
Y1689		25p. rose-red (phosphorised paper) (26.10.93)	70	70
		a. Imperf (pair)	£800	
		l. Booklet pane. No. Y1689×2 plus 2 labels (1.11.93)	1·50	
Y1690		25p. rose-red (2 bands) (20.12.94)	70	70
		y. Phosphor omitted	24·00	
		l. Booklet pane. No. Y1690×2 plus 2 labels (6.6.95)	2·00	
Y1691		26p. red-brown (2 bands) (25.6.96)	70	70
		a. Imperf (pair)	£650	
		y. Phosphor omitted	10·00	
Y1692		26p. gold (2 bands) (21.4.97)	90	90
		a. Imperf (horiz pair)	—	
Y1693		29p. grey (2 bands) (26.10.93)	90	90
Y1694		30p. deep olive-grey (2 bands) (27.7.93)	90	90
		a. Imperf (pair)	£1100	
Y1695		31p. deep mauve (2 bands) (25.6.96)	1·00	1·00
Y1696		33p. grey-green (2 bands) (25.4.00)	1·25	1·25
Y1697		34p. yellow-olive (2 bands) (6.5.03)	4·75	4·75
Y1698		35p. yellow (2 bands) (17.8.93)	1·25	1·25
Y1699		35p. yellow (phosphorised paper) (1.11.93)	7·50	7·50
Y1700		35p. sepia (2 bands) (1.4.04)	1·25	1·25
		a. Imperf (pair)	£200	
Y1701		35p. yellow-olive (5.4.05) (1 centre band)	1·25	1·25
Y1702		36p. bright ultramarine (2 bands) (26.10.93)	1·25	1·25
Y1703		37p. bright mauve (2 bands) (25.6.96)	1·00	1·00
Y1704		37p. grey-black (2 bands) (4.7.02)	1·50	1·50
Y1705		37p. brown-olive (1 centre band) (28.3.06)	1·50	1·50
Y1706		38p. rosine (2 bands) (26.10.93)	1·50	1·50
		a. Imperf (pair)	£375	
Y1707		38p. ultramarine (2 bands) (20.4.99)	1·50	1·50
		a. Perf 14 (15.2.00)	5·50	5·50
Y1708		39p. bright magenta (2 bands) (25.6.96)	1·25	1·25
		a. Imperf (pair)	£1100	
Y1709		39p. grey (2 bands) (1.4.04)	1·50	1·50
		a. Imperf (pair)	£200	
Y1710		40p. deep azure (2 bands) (25.4.00)	1·25	1·25
Y1711		40p. turquoise-blue (2 bands) (1.4.04)	1·25	1·25
		a. Imperf (pair)	£200	
Y1712		41p. grey-brown (2 bands) (26.10.93)	1·50	1·50
Y1713		41p. drab (phosphorised paper) (1.11.93)	7·50	7·50
Y1714		41p. rosine (2 bands) (25.4.00)	1·50	1·50
Y1715		42p. deep olive-grey (2 bands) (4.7.02)	1·25	1·25
Y1716		43p. deep olive-brown (2 bands) (25.6.96)	1·40	1·40
Y1717		43p. sepia (2 bands) (8.7.96)	4·75	4·75
		a. Perf 14 (13.10.98)	1·50	1·50
Y1718		43p. emerald (2 bands) (1.4.04)	1·75	1·75
		a. Imperf (pair)	£200	
Y1719		44p. grey-brown (2 bands) (20.4.99)	4·00	4·00
Y1720		44p. deep bright blue (2 bands) (28.3.06)	1·50	1·50
Y1721		45p. bright mauve (2 bands) (25.4.00)	1·50	1·50
Y1722		46p. yellow (2 bands) (5.4.05)	1·50	1·50
Y1723		47p. turquoise-green (2 bands) (4.7.02)	1·75	1·75
Y1724		48p. bright mauve (2 bands) (27.3.07)	1·75	1·75
Y1725		49p. red-brown (2 bands) (28.3.06)	2·00	2·00
Y1726		50p. ochre (2 bands) (14.12.93)	1·50	1·50
		a. Imperf (pair)	£2000	
Y1727		50p. grey (2 bands) (27.3.07)	1·50	1·50

MACHINS *Denominated stamps, PVA gum, elliptical perforations*

Y1728	54p. red-brown (Type II) (2 bands) (27.3.07)	1·50	1·50
Y1729	56p. yellow-olive (2 bands) (1.4.08)	1·75	1·75
Y1730	60p. light emerald (2 bands) (30.3.10)	1·75	1·75
Y1731	62p. rosine (2 bands) (31.3.09)	1·75	1·75
Y1732	63p. light emerald (2 bands) (25.6.96)	1·50	1·50
Y1733	64p. turquoise-green (2 bands) (20.4.99)	1·75	1·75
Y1734	65p. greenish blue (2 bands) (25.4.00)	1·75	1·75
Y1735	67p. bright mauve (2 bands) (30.3.10)	1·75	1·75
Y1736	68p. grey-brown (2 bands) (4.7.02)	2·00	2·00
Y1737	72p. rosine (2 bands) (28.3.06)	2·25	2·25
Y1738	78p. emerald (2 bands) (27.3.07)	2·25	2·25
Y1739	81p. turquoise-green (2 bands) (1.4.08)	2·00	2·00
Y1740	88p. bright magenta (2 bands) (30.3.10)	2·00	2·00
Y1741	90p. ultramarine (2 bands) (31.3.09)	2·25	2·25
Y1742	97p. violet (2 bands) (30.3.10)	2·50	2·50
Y1743	£1 bluish violet (2 bands) (22.8.95)	2·50	2·50
	a. Imperf (horiz pair)	£1100	
Y1744	£1 magenta (2 bands) (5.6.07)	2·00	2·00
	l. Booklet pane. No. Y1744×2 with centre label and margins all round	4·00	
Y1745	£1·46 greenish blue (2 bands) (30.3.10)	3·25	3·25
Y1746	£1·50 brown-red (2 bands) (1.7.03)	3·50	3·50
Y1747	£2 deep blue-green (2 bands) (1.7.03)	5·00	5·00
	a. Missing '£' in value (R. 18/1, Cyl D1 no dot)	£250	
Y1748	£3 deep mauve (2 bands) (1.7.03)	7·00	7·00
Y1749	£5 azure (2 bands) (1.7.03)	12·00	12·00

(b) Litho Cartor (1p. (No. Y1761)), 5p. (Nos. Y1763/Y1765), 10p. (No. Y1768), 16p., 17p., 20p., (No., Y1773), 22p., 50p., 54p., 60p. (No. Y1785), 62p., 67p., 90p., 97p.)
De La Rue (5p. (No. Y1762))
Questa, De La Rue or Cartor (10p. (No. Y1767))
Questa or Walsall (25p., 35p.,)
Walsall (37p., 41p. (No. Y1780) 60p. (No. Y1784), 63p.),
De La Rue (48p.)
Questa (others).

Y1760	**367**	1p. lake (2 bands) (8.7.96)	35	35
		y. Phosphor omitted	£500	
		l. Booklet pane. Nos. Y1760×2, Y1772 and Y1776×3 plus 2 labels	3·50	
		ly. Booklet pane. Phosphor omitted	£1200	
Y1761		1p. reddish purple (2 bands) (17.9.09)	2·50	2·50
		l. Booklet pane. Nos. Y1761×2, Y1770×4 and Y1789×2 with central label and margins all round	15·00	
Y1762		5p. chocolate (2 bands)(Type II) (12.2.09)	3·50	3·50
		y. Phosphor omitted	£1800	
		l. Booklet pane. Nos. 1672, Y1762, Y1767 and Y1781, each×2 with central label	15·00	
Y1763		5p. red-brown (*shades*) (13.5.10)	2·75	2·75
		l. Booklet pane. Nos. Y1763×4, Y1767×2 and Y1785×2, with central label and margins all round	18·00	
		m. Booklet pane. Nos. Y1763×4, U3155×2 and U3078×2 with central label and margins all round (9.9.11)	25·00	
Y1764		5p. lake-brown (22.3.11)	2·50	2·50
		l. Booklet pane. Nos. Y1764×3, Y1767×3, Y1788 and Y1790, with central label and margins all round	22·00	
Y1765		5p. red-brown (2 bands) (Type III) (7.1.10)	4·00	4·00
		l. Booklet pane. Nos. Y1765×2, Y1768×5 and Y1774×2 with margins all round	14·00	
Y1766		6p. yellow-olive (2 bands) (26.7.94)	8·00	8·00
		l. Booklet pane. Nos. Y1766, Y1771 and Y1775×4 with margins all round	7·50	
		la. 6p. value misplaced	£4000	
Y1767		10p. dull orange (*shades*) (2 bands) (25.4.95)	2·00	2·00
		y. Phosphor omitted	£1800	
		l. Booklet pane. Nos. Y1767, Y1771/Y1771a, Y1775×2, Y1777/Y1778, Y1780a and centre label with margins all round	10·00	
Y1768		10p. pale brownish orange (7.1.10)	2·50	2·50
Y1769		16p. pale cerise (2 bands) (13.1.09)	2·50	2·50
		l. Booklet pane. Nos. Y1769 and Y1782, each×4, with central label	16·00	
Y1770		17p. bistre (2 bands) (18.8.09)	2·50	2·50
		l. Booklet pane. Nos. Y1770×4, Y1774×2 and Y1786×2 with central label and margins all round	16·00	
Y1771		19p. bistre (1 band at left) (26.7.94)	1·25	1·25
		a. Band at right (25.4.95)	1·50	1·50
		l. Booklet pane. Nos. Y1771/Y1771a, each×3 with margins all round (25.4.95)	5·00	
Y1772		20p. bright yellow-green (1 centre band) (8.7.96)	2·00	2·00
		y. Phosphor omitted	£125	
		l. Booklet pane. Nos. Y1772 and Y1776×7	3·75	
		ly. Booklet pane. Phosphor omitted	£200	
Y1773		20p. light green (2 bands) (7.1.10)	3·00	3·00
		l. Booklet pane. Nos. Y1773×4, Y1783×2 and Y1786×2 with central label and margins all round	15·00	
Y1774		22p. olive-brown (2 bands) (18.8.09)	3·50	3·50
		l. Booklet pane. Nos. Y1774 and Y1783, each×4 with central label and margins all round (25.2.10)	15·00	
Y1775		25p. red (2 bands) (1.11.93)	85	85
		l. Booklet pane. Nos. Y1775, NI72, S84 and W73, each×2, with centre label and margins all round (14.5.96)	5·00	
Y1776		26p. chestnut (2 bands) (8.7.96)	65	65
		y. Phosphor omitted	10·00	
Y1777		30p. olive-grey (2 bands) (25.4.95)	2·50	2·50
Y1778		35p. yellow (2 bands) (1.11.93)	90	90
Y1779		37p. bright mauve (2 bands) (8.7.96)	2·50	2·50
Y1780		41p. drab (2 bands) (1.11.93)	1·40	1·40
		a. Grey-brown (25.4.95)	1·75	1·75
		y. Phosphor omitted	£800	
Y1781		48p. bright mauve (2 bands) (12.2.09)	2·75	2·75
		y. Phosphor omitted	£1800	
Y1782		50p. grey (2 bands) (13.1.09)	3·50	3·50
Y1783		54p. chestnut (2 bands) (Type III) (7.1.10)	3·50	3·50
Y1784		60p. dull blue-grey (2 bands) (9.8.94)	1·50	1·50
Y1785		60p. emerald (2 bands) (13.5.10)	6·00	6·00
Y1786		62p. rosine (2 bands) (18.8.09)	3·75	3·75
Y1787		63p. light emerald (2 bands) (8.7.96)	3·25	3·25
		y. Phosphor omitted	£525	
Y1788		67p. bright mauve (2 bands) (22.3.11)	10·00	10·00
Y1789		90p. bright blue (2 bands) (22.3.11)	4·75	4·75
Y1790		97p. bluish violet (2 bands) (22.3.11)	10·00	10·00

(c) Eng C. Slania. Recess Enschedé (until March 2000) or De La Rue (from 11 April 2000).

Y1800	**367**	£1·50 red (9.3.99)	4·50	2·00
Y1801		£2 dull blue (9.3.99)	5·00	2·25
Y1802		£3 dull violet (9.3.99)	7·00	3·00
Y1803		£5 brown (9.3.99)	12·00	5·00
		a. Imperf (pair)	£600	

PHQ Card (D7) (No. Y1725)	50	8·00
PHQ Cards (D30) (Nos. 1664, 1668, Y1667/Y1668, Y1670, Y1675/Y1676, Y1679/Y1680, Y1687, Y1724, Y1727, Y1729, Y1739, Y1744, Y1746/Y1749, 2357a, 2652/2653, 2358/2359)		7·00

Nos. Y1743/Y1749 are printed in Iriodin ink which gives a shiny effect to the solid part of the background behind the Queen's head.

A gravure-printed £5 stamp, as No. Y1749 but in sepia is believed to have come from stock stolen from the printer. Both unused and used examples are known.

No. Y1766la shows the 6p. value printed 22 mm to the left so that its position on the booklet pane is completely blank except for the phosphor bands. Other more minor misplacements exist.

The De La Rue printings of the high values, Nos. Y1800/Y1803 cannot easily be identified from the original Enschedé issue as single stamps.

For self-adhesive versions of the 42p. and 68p. see Nos. 2297/2298.

First Day Covers

26.10.93	19p., 25p., 29p., 36p., 38p., 41p. (Nos. Y1682, Y1689, Y1693, Y1702, Y1706, Y1712)	6·00
9.8.94	60p. (No. Y1784)	2·00
25.4.95	National Trust *se-tenant* pane 10p., 19p., 25p., 30p., 35p., 41p. (No. Y1767l)	10·00
22.8.95	£1 (No. Y1743)	3·00
14.5.96	European Football Championship *se-tenant* pane 25p.×8 (No. Y1775l)	5·00
25.6.96	20p., 26p., 31p., 37p., 39p., 43p., 63p. (Nos. Y1685, Y1691, Y1695, Y1703, Y1708, Y1716, Y1732)	8·00
13.10.98	Speed *se-tenant* pane 10p., 2nd, 43p. (No. Y1676al)	8·00
9.3.99	£1·50, £2, £3, £5 (Nos. Y1800/Y1803) (Type G) (Philatelic Bureau or Windsor)	15·00
20.4.99	7p., 38p., 44p., 64p. (Nos. Y1672, Y1707, Y1719, Y1733) (Type G) (Philatelic Bureau or Windsor)	5·00
21.9.99	World Changers *se-tenant* pane 1p., 19p., 26p. (No. Y1667n) (Philatelic Bureau or Downe, Orpington)	2·50
25.4.00	8p., 33p., 40p., 41p., 45p., 65p. (Nos. Y1674, Y1696, Y1710, Y1714, Y1721, Y1734) (Type G) (Philatelic Bureau or Windsor)	5·00
4.7.02	37p., 42p., 47p., 68p. (Nos. Y1704, Y1715, Y1723, Y1736) (Type K) (Tallents House or Windsor)	5·00
6.5.03	34p., (No. Y1697) (Type K) (Tallents House or Windsor)	4·50
1.7.03	£1·50, £2, £3, £5 (Nos. Y1746/Y1749) (Type K) (Tallents House or Windsor)	25·00

Date	Description	Price
1.4.04	7p., 35p., 39p., 40p., 43p. Worldwide postcard (Nos. Y1673, Y1700, Y1709, Y1711, Y1718, 2357a) (Type K) (Tallents House or Windsor)	9·00
5.4.05	9p., 35p., 46p. (Nos. Y1675, Y1701, Y1722) (Type K) (Tallents House or Windsor)	2·25
28.3.06	37p., 44p., 49p., 72p. (Nos. Y1703, Y1720, Y1725, Y1737) (Type K) (Tallents House or Windsor)	4·25
1.3.07	World of Invention label pane 5p., 1st (No. Y1670l) (Tallents House or Menai Bridge, Gwynedd)	5·00
27.3.07	16p., 48p., 50p., 54p., 78p. (Nos. Y1680, Y1724, Y1727/Y1728, Y1738) (Type K) (Tallents House or Windsor)	6·00
5.6.07	Machin Anniversary se-tenant pane 2p., 46p., 48p. (No. Y1668l) (Tallents House, Windsor or Stoke-on-Trent)	6·50
20.9.07	Army Uniforms se-tenant pane 1p., 46p., 54p. (No. Y1667o) (Tallents House or Boot, Holmrook, Cumbria)	5·00
1.4.08	15p., 56p., 81p. (Nos. Y1679, Y1727, Y1739) (Type K) (Tallents House or Windsor)	4·50
13.1.09	British Design Classics se-tenant pane 16p., 50p. (No. Y1769l) (Tallents House or Longbridge, Birmingham)	16·00
12.2.09	Charles Darwin se-tenant pane 5p., 10p., 1st, 48p. (No. Y1762l) (Tallents House or Shrewsbury)	15·00
31.3.09	17p., 22p., 62p., 90p. (Nos. Y1681, Y1688, Y1731, Y1741) (Type K) (Tallents House or Windsor)	6·00
18.8.09	Treasures of the Archive se-tenant pane 17p., 22p., 62p., (No. Y1770l) (Tallents House or London EC1)	16·00
17.9.09	Royal Navy Uniforms se-tenant pane 1p., 17p., 90p. (No. Y1761l) (Tallents House or Portsmouth)	15·00
7.1.10	Classic Album Covers se-tenant pane 20p., 54p., 52p. (No. Y1773l) (Tallents House or Oldfield, Keighley)	15·00
25.2.10	Royal Society se-tenant pane 22p., 54p. (No. Y1774l) (Tallents House or London SW1)	15·00
30.3.10	60p., 67p., 88p., 97p., £1·46, Europe up to 20 grams, Worldwide up to 20 grams (Nos. Y1730, Y1735, Y1740, Y1742, Y1745, 2357b, 2358a) (Type K) (Tallents House or Windsor)	20·00
13.5.10	Britain Alone se-tenant pane 5p., 10p., 60p., (No. Y1763l) (Tallents House or Dover, Kent)	15·00
22.3.11	WWF se-tenant pane 5p., 10p., 67p., 97p. (No. Y1764l) (Tallents House or Godalming, Surrey)	20·00
9.9.11	Aerial Post Centenary se-tenant pane 5p., 1st, 76p. (No. Y1763m) (Tallents House or Hendon, London NW4)	25·00
10.1.12	Roald Dahl se-tenant pane 2p., 10p., 68p. (No. Y1668m) (Tallents House or Great Missenden, Bucks)	15·00
5.6.17	50th Anniversary of the Machin Definitive se-tenant pane 1p., 2p., 5p., 10p., 20p., 50p. 2nd £1 (No. Y1667p) (Tallents House or High Wycombe)	8·00

For first day covers for Nos. Y1677/Y1678 see under Nos. 2650/2657.

Post Office Presentation Packs

Date	Description	Price
26.10.93	PO Pack No. 30. 19p. (1 centre band), 25p. (phosphor paper), 29p., 36p., 38p. rosine, 41p. grey-brown (Nos. Y1682, Y1689, Y1693, Y1702, Y1706, Y1712)	6·00
21.11.95	PO Pack No. 34. 1p. (photo), 2p., 4p., 5p., 6p. (photo), 10p. (photo), 19p. (1 centre band), 20p. turquoise-green, 25p. (photo) (2 bands), 29p., 30p. (photo), 35p. (photo) (2 bands), 36p., 38p. rosine, 41p. grey-brown, 50p., 60p., £1 (Nos. Y1667/Y1671, Y1676, Y1682, Y1684, Y1690, Y1693/Y1694, Y1698, Y1702, Y1706, Y1712, Y1726, Y1743, Y1784)	35·00
25.6.96	PO Pack No. 35. 20p. bright green (1 centre band), 26p. (photo), 31p., 37p. (photo), 39p., 43p. deep olive brown, 63p. (photo) (Nos. Y1685, Y1691, Y1695, Y1703, Y1708, Y1716, Y1732)	8·00
21.4.97	PO Pack No. 38. 1st, 26p. gold (Nos. 1668, Y1692)	6·00
20.10.98	PO Pack No. 41. 2nd bright blue (1 centre band), 1st bright orange-red (2 phosphor bands), 1p., 2p., 4p., 5p., 6p., 10p., 20p. bright green (1 centre band), 26p., 30p., 31p., 37p., 39p., 43p. sepia, 50p., 63p., £1 (Nos. 1664, 1667, Y1667/Y1671, Y1676, Y1685, Y1691, Y1694/Y1695, Y1703, Y1708, Y1717, Y1726, Y1732)	18·00
9.3.99	PO Pack No. 43 or 43a. £1·50, £2, £3, £5 (Nos. Y1800/Y1803)	38·00
20.4.99	PO Pack No. 44. 7p., 19p., 38p. ultramarine, 44p., 64p. (Nos. Y1672, Y1682, Y1707, Y1719, Y1733)	9·50
25.4.00	PO Pack No. 49. 8p., 33p., 40p., 41p. rosine, 45p., 65p. (Nos. Y1674, Y1696, Y1710, Y1714, Y1721, Y1734)	8·50
12.3.02	PO Pack No. 57. 2nd, 1st, E, 1p., 2p., 4p., 5p., 8p., 10p., 20p., 33p., 40p., 41p., 45p., 50p., 65p., £1 (Nos. 1664, 1667, 1669, Y1667/Y1670, Y1674, Y1676, Y1687, Y1696, Y1710, Y1714, Y1721, Y1726, Y1734, Y1743)	16·00
4.7.02	PO Pack No. 58. 37p., 42p., 47p., 68p. (Nos. Y1704, Y1715, Y1723, Y1736)	6·50
1.7.03	PO Pack No. 62. £1·50, £2, £3, £5 (Nos. Y1746/Y1749)	25·00
1.4.04	PO Pack No. 67. 1st gold (D.L.R. printing), 7p., 35p., 39p., 40p., 43p. Worldwide postcard (Nos. 1668, Y1673, Y1700, Y1709, Y1711, Y1718, 2357a)	10·00
6.9.05	PO Pack No. 71. 1p., 2p., 5p., 9p., 10p., 20p., 35p., 40p., 42p., 46p., 47p., 50p., 68p., £1., 2nd, 1st, Worldwide postcard, Europe up to 40 grams, Worldwide up to 40 grams (Nos. Y1667/Y1668, Y1670, Y1675/Y1676, Y1687, Y1701, Y1711, Y1715, Y1722/Y1723, Y1726, Y1736, Y1743, 2039, 2295, 2357a, 2358, 2359)	50·00
28.3.06	PO Pack No. 72. 37p., 44p., 49p., 72p. (Nos. Y1705, Y1720, Y1725, Y1737)	11·00
27.3.07	PO Pack No. 75. 16p., 48p., 50p., 54p., 78p. (Nos. Y1680, Y1724, Y1727, Y1728, Y1738)	10·00
5.6.07	PO Pack No. 77. 2nd, 1st, 1p., 2p., 5p., 10p., 14p., 16p., 20p., 46p., 48p., 50p., 54p., 78p., £1, Worldwide postcard, Europe up to 40 grams, Worldwide up to 40 grams, 2nd Large, 1st Large (Nos. 1664, 1668, Y1667/Y1668, Y1670, Y1676, Y1678/Y1679, Y1687, Y1722, Y1724, Y1727/Y1728, Y1738, Y1744, 2357a, 2358, 2359, 2652/2653)	45·00
1.4.08	PO Pack. No. 78. 15p., 56p., 81p. (Nos. Y1679, Y1729, Y1739)	5·00
31.3.09	PO Pack No. 84 17p., 22p., 62p., 90p. (Nos. Y1681, Y1688, Y1731, Y1741)	8·50
30.3.10	PO Pack No. 86. 60p. 67p., 88p., 97p., £1·46, Europe up to 20 grams, Worldwide up to 20 grams, 1st Recorded Signed For, 1st Large Recorded Signed For (Nos. Y1730, Y1735, Y1740, Y1742, Y1745, 2357b, 2358a, U3045/U3046)	28·00
8.5.10	PO Pack No. 88. 2nd, 1st, 1p., 2p., 5p., 9p., 10p., 20p., 50p., 60p., 67p., 88p., 97p., £1, £1·46, Worldwide postcard, Europe up to 20 grams, Worldwide up to 20 grams, Europe up to 40 grams, Worldwide up to 40 grams, 2nd Large, 1st Large, 1st Recorded Signed For, 1st Large Recorded Signed For (Nos. 1664, 1668, Y1667, Y1668, Y1670, Y1675, Y1676, Y1687, Y1727, Y1730, Y1735, Y1740, Y1742, Y1744, Y1745, 2357a/2359, 2652/2653 and U2981/U2982)	50·00

In 2002 a 'master' presentation pack entitled Royal Mail Definitive Stamps Collection was released, containing packs Nos. 43a, 53, 54, 55, 56 and 57 (Price £120).

1917

(Des Katja Thielan. Gravure De La Rue)

2006 (31 Aug). 70th Anniversary of the Year of Three Kings. Sheet 127×72 mm containing No. Y1748. Multicoloured. Two phosphor bands. Perf 15×14 (with one elliptical hole in each vertical side).

MS2658 **1917** £3 deep mauve	5·25	5·25
First Day Cover (Tallents House)		5·50
First Day Cover (Threekingham, Sleaford, Lincs)		5·50

Decimal Machin Index

(Stamps with elliptical perforations, including (N.V.Is)

Value	Process	Colour	Phosphor	Cat. No.	Source
2nd	litho Questa or Walsall	brt blue	1 centre band	1670	sheets (Questa), booklets of 4 (Walsall – HA6, Walsall HA9/11), booklets of 10 (Questa – HC11, HC13, HC16, HC18, HC20, Walsall – HC12), $7·15 'Pilot to Plane' booklet (Walsall – DX42)
2nd	photo/gravure Harrison/De La Rue), Enschedé, Questa or Walsall	brt blue	1 centre band	1664	sheets (Walsall, De La Rue), horizontal coil (Harrison/De La Rue), vertical coils (Harrison/De La Rue or Enschedé) booklets of 4 (Harrison – HA7/8, Walsall – HA12), booklets of 10 (Harrison/De La Rue – HC14/15, HC17, HC19, HC21), £1 booklet (Questa – FH44/a), £2 booklet (Questa – FW12), £7·29 'A Gracious Accession' booklet (Enschedé – DX28), £7·46 'A Perfect Coronation' booklet (Walsall – DX31), £7·43 The Brontë Sisters booklet (Walsall – DX34)
2nd	gravure Walsall (p 14)	brt blue	1 band at right	1665	£6·16 British Land Speed Record Holders booklet (DX21)
2nd	gravure Walsall (p 14)	brt blue	1 band at left	1665c	£6·16 British Land Speed Record Holders booklet (DX21)
2nd	gravure Questa (p 14)	brt blue	1 centre band	1664a	booklets of 10 (HC22)
1st	litho Enschedé, Questa or Walsall	brt orange-red	2 bands	1671	sheets (Questa), greetings card panes Questa – Y1671m/ma, Enschedé – Y1671mb), booklets of 4 (Walsall – HB6, HB8/13, HB15/16, Questa – HB7), booklets of 10 Walsall – HD10, HD12/19, HD22/3, HD25, HD28, HD34, HD36/8, HD40, Questa – HD11, HD21, HD26, HD50), £7·54 'Profile on Print' booklet (Questa – DX22)
1st	photo Harrison	brt orange-red	phos paper	1666	booklets of 4 (HB5), booklets of 10 (HD9, HD20)
1st	photo/gravure Harrison/De La Rue, Questa or Walsall/ISP Walsall	brt orange-red	2 bands	1667	sheets (Walsall), horizontal and vertical coils (Harrison, De La Rue), booklets of 4 (Walsall – HB14, HB17/18), booklets of 8 with 2 Millennium commems (Walsall – HBA1/2), booklets of 10 (Harrison/De La Rue – HD24, HD27, HD29/33, HD35, HD39, HD45/9, Walsall – HD44), £1 booklet (Questa – FH44/a), £2 booklet (Questa – FW12), £7·54 'Profile on Print' booklet (De La Rue – DX22), £15·14 '50th Anniversary of the Machin' booklet (ISP Walsall – DY21)
1st	gravure Questa (p 14)	brt orange-red	2 bands	1667a	booklets of 10 (HD51)
1st	gravure De La Rue, Enschedé, Harrison, Questa or Walsall/ISP Walsall	gold	2 bands	1668	sheets (Walsall, De La Rue), vertical coils (Enschedé, De La Rue), booklets of 10 (Harrison – HD41, HD43, Walsall – HD42), £6·15 B.B.C. booklet (Harrison – DX19), £6·83 'Across the Universe' booklet (Questa – DX29), £6·99 'Microcosmos' booklet (Enschedé – DX30), £7·46 'A Perfect Coronation' booklet (Walsall – DX31), £7·44 'Letters by Night' booklet (De La Rue – DX32), £7·23 'The Glory of the Garden' booklet (Enschedé – DX33), £7·26 Trafalgar booklet (Walsall – DX35), £7·40 Brunel booklet (Enschedé – DX36), £15·14 '50th Anniversary of the Machin' booklet (ISP Walsall – DY21)
1st	gravure ISP Walsall	brownish black	2 bands	1668s	£15·14 '50th Anniversary of the Machin' booklet (ISP Walsall – DY21)
1st	litho De La Rue or Walsall	gold	2 bands	1672	£7·40 Ian Fleming's James Bond booklet (De La Rue – DX41), £7·15 'Pilot to Plane' booklet (Walsall – DX42)
E	gravure De La Rue, Enschedé, Questa or Walsall	deep blue	2 bands	1669	sheets (De La Rue), booklets of 4 (Walsall – HF1), £7·29 'A Gracious Accession' booklet (Enschedé – DX28), £6·83 'Across the Universe' booklet (Questa – DX29), £6·99 'Microcosmos' booklet (Enschedé – DX30)
1p.	photo/gravure De La Rue, Enschedé, Harrison, Questa or ISP Walsall	crimson	2 bands	Y1667	sheets, £1 booklets (Questa – FH42/3), £6·91 World Changers booklet (Questa – DX23) , £7·66 British Army Uniforms booklet (Enschedé – DX40), £15·14 '50th Anniversary of the Machin' booklet (ISP Walsall – DY21)
1p.	litho Questa	lake	2 bands	Y1760	£1 booklet (FH41)
1p.	litho Cartor	reddish purple	2 bands	Y1761	£7·93 Royal Navy Uniforms booklet (DX47)
2p.	photo/gravure De La Rue, Enschedé, Harrison, Questa or Walsall/ISP Walsall	dp green	2 bands	Y1668	sheets, £1 booklet (Questa – FH43), £7·66 'The Machin' booklet (De La Rue – DX39), £11·47 Roald Dahl booklet (Walsall – DY3), £15·14 '50th Anniversary of the Machin' booklet (ISP Walsall – DY21)
4p.	photo/gravure De La Rue, Enschedé or Harrison	new blue	2 bands	Y1669	sheets
4p.	gravure De La Rue	new blue	phos paper	MS2146	Jeffery Matthews Colour Palette miniature sheet
5p.	photo/gravure De La Rue, Enschedé, Harrison or ISP Walsall	dull red-brown	2 bands	Y1670	sheets , £7·49 World of Invention booklet (De La Rue – DX38), £15·14 '50th Anniversary of the Machin' booklet (ISP Walsall – DY21)
5p.	gravure De La Rue	dull red-brown	phos paper	MS2146	Jeffery Matthews Colour Palette miniature sheet
5p.	litho De La Rue	chocolate	2 bands	Y1762	£7·75 Charles Darwin booklet (DX45)
5p.	litho Cartor	red-brown	2 bands	Y1763	£9·76 Great Britain Alone booklet (DX51), £9·97 Aerial Post Centenary booklet (DY2)
5p.	litho Cartor	lake-brown	2 bands	Y1764	£9·05 WWF booklet (DX52)

Decimal Machin Index (stamps with elliptical perforations, including (N.V.Is) MACHINS

Value	Process	Colour	Phosphor	Cat. No.	Source
5p.	litho Cartor	red-brown	2 bands	Y1765	Type III. £8·06 Classic Album Covers booklet (DX48)
6p.	photo/gravure Enschedé or Harrison	yellow-olive	2 bands	Y1671	sheets
6p.	litho Questa	yellow-olive	2 bands	Y1766	£6·04 Northern Ireland booklet (DX16)
6p.	gravure De La Rue	yellow-olive	phos paper	MS2146	Jeffery Matthews Colour Palette miniature sheet
7p.	gravure De La Rue	grey	2 bands	Y1672	sheets
7p.	gravure De La Rue	bright magenta	2 bands	Y1673	sheets
8p.	gravure De La Rue	yellow	2 bands	Y1674	sheets
9p.	gravure De La Rue	yellow-orange	2 bands	Y1675	sheets
10p.	photo/gravure De La Rue, Enschedé, Harrison or Walsall/ISP Walsall	dull orange	2 bands	Y1676	sheets, £11·47 Roald Dahl booklet (Walsall – DY3), £15·14 '50th Anniversary of the Machin' booklet (ISP Walsall – DY21)
10p.	litho Questa, De La Rue or Cartor	dull orange	2 bands	Y1767	£6 National Trust booklet (Questa - DX17), £7·75 Charles Darwin booklet (De La Rue - DX45), £9·76 'Britain Alone' booklet (Cartor - DX51), £9·05 WWF booklet (Cartor - DX52)
10p.	litho Cartor	pale brownish orange	2 bands	Y1768	£8·06 Classic Album Covers booklet (DX48)
10p.	gravure Walsall (p 14)	dull orange	2 bands	Y1676a	£6·16 British Land Speed Record Holders booklet (DX21)
10p.	gravure De La Rue	dull orange	phos paper	MS2146	Jeffery Matthews Colour Palette miniature sheet
12p.	gravure De La Rue	greenish blue	2 bands	Y1677	sheets
14p.	gravure De La Rue	rose-red	2 bands	Y1678	sheets
15p.	gravure De La Rue	bright magenta	2 bands	Y1679	sheets
16p.	gravure De La Rue	pale cerise	2 bands	Y1680	sheets
16p.	litho Cartor	pale cerise	2 bands	Y1769	£7·75 British Design Classics booklet (DX44)
17p.	gravure De La Rue	brown-olive	2 bands	Y1681	sheets
17p.	litho Cartor	bistre	2 bands	Y1770	£8·18 'Treasures of the Archive' booklet (DX46) and £7·93 Royal Navy Uniforms booklet (DX47)
19p.	photo/gravure Harrison or Questa	bistre	1 centre band	Y1682	sheets, vertical coils, £1 booklet (Questa – FH43), £2 booklet (Questa – FW11), £6·99 World Changers booklet (Questa – DX23)
19p.	litho Questa	bistre	1 band at left	Y1771	£6·04 Northern Ireland booklet (DX16), £6 National Trust booklet (DX17)
19p.	litho Questa	bistre	1 band at right	Y1771a	£6 National Trust booklet (DX17)
19p.	gravure Walsall (p 14)	bistre	1 band at right	Y1683	£7·50 'Special by Design' booklet (DX24)
20p.	gravure Enschedé	turquoise-green	2 bands	Y1684	sheets
20p.	photo/gravure Harrison or Questa	brt green	1 centre band	Y1685	sheets, £1 booklet (Questa – FH42), £2 booklet (Questa – FW10)
20p.	litho Questa	brt yellow-green	1 centre band	Y1772	£1 booklet (FH41), £2 booklet (FW9)
20p.	gravure Harrison	brt green	1 band at right	Y1686	£6·15 B.B.C. booklet (DX19)
20p.	gravure De La Rue or ISP Walsall	brt green	2 bands	Y1687	sheets, £15·14 '50th Anniversary of the Machin' booklet (ISP Walsall – DY21)
20p.	litho Cartor	light green	2 bands	Y1773	£8·06 Classic Album Covers booklet (DX48)
22p.	gravure De La Rue	drab	2 bands	Y1688	sheets
22p.	litho Cartor	olive-brown	2 bands	Y1774	£8·18 'Treasures of the Archive' booklet (DX46), £8·06 Classic Album Covers booklet (DX48) and £7·72 Royal Society booklet (DX49)
25p.	photo Harrison	rose-red	phos paper	Y1689	sheets, vertical coils, 50p booklets (FB67/73), £1 booklets (FH33/7), £2 booklets (FW1/5)
25p.	litho Walsall or Questa	red	2 bands	Y1775	£1 booklet (Walsall – FH31/2), (Questa – FH40), £2 booklet (Questa – FW8), £6·04 Northern Ireland booklet (Questa – DX16), £6 National Trust booklet (Questa – DX17), £6·84 European Football Championship (Questa – DX18)
25p.	photo/gravure Harrison or Enschedé	rose-red	2 bands	Y1690	sheets (Harrison or Enschedé), vertical coils (Harrison), 50p booklets (Harrison – FB74/5), £1 booklets (Harrison – FH38/9), £2 booklets (Harrison – FW6/7)
26p.	photo/gravure Harrison or Questa	red-brown	2 bands	Y1691	sheets, £1 booklets (Questa – FH42/3), £2 booklets (Questa – FW10/11), £6·15 B.B.C. booklet (Harrison – DX19), £6·99 World Changers booklet (Questa – DX23)
26p.	litho Questa	chestnut	2 bands	Y1776	£1 booklet (FH41), £2 booklet (FW9)
26p.	gravure Harrison	gold	2 bands	Y1692	sheets, £6·15 B B.C. booklet (Harrison – DX19)
29p.	gravure Enschedé	grey	2 bands	Y1693	sheets
30p.	photo/gravure Enschedé, Harrison or Walsall	dp olive-grey	2 bands	Y1694	sheets, £1·20 booklets (Walsall – GGAI/2)
30p.	litho Questa	olive-grey	2 bands	Y1777	£6 National Trust booklet (DX17)
31p.	photo/gravure Enschedé or Harrison	dp mauve	2 bands	Y1695	sheets
31p.	gravure De La Rue	dp mauve	phos paper	MS2146	Jeffery Matthews Colour Palette miniature sheet
33p.	gravure De La Rue	grey-green	2 bands	Y1696	sheets
34p.	gravure De La Rue	yellow-olive	2 bands	Y1697	sheets
35p.	gravure Enschedé	yellow	2 bands	Y1698	sheets
35p.	photo Harrison	yellow	phos paper	Y1699	vertical coils
35p.	litho Walsall or Questa	yellow	2 bands	Y1778	£1·40 booklets (Walsall – GK5/7), £6 National Trust booklet (Questa – DX17)
35p.	gravure De La Rue	sepia	2 bands	Y1700	sheets

MACHINS *Decimal Machin Index (stamps with elliptical perforations, including (N.V.Is)*

Value	Process	Colour	Phosphor	Cat. No.	Source
35p.	gravure Enschedé or De La Rue	yellow-olive	1 centre band	Y1701	sheets, £7·40 Brunel booklet (Enschedé – DX36)
36p.	gravure Enschedé	brt ultramarine	2 bands	Y1702	sheets
37p.	photo/gravure Enschedé, Harrison or Walsall	brt mauve	2 bands	Y1703	sheets (Enschedé or Harrison), vertical coils (Harrison), £1·48 booklets (Walsall – GL3/4)
37p.	litho Walsall	brt mauve	2 bands	Y1779	£1·48 booklets (GL1/2)
37p.	gravure De La Rue	grey-black	2 bands	Y1704	sheets, £7·44 'Letters by Night' booklet (De La Rue – DX32)
37p.	gravure De La Rue	brown-olive	1 centre band	Y1705	sheets
38p.	gravure Enschedé	rosine	2 bands	Y1706	sheets
38p.	gravure De La Rue or Walsall	ultramarine	2 bands	Y1707	sheets (D.L.R.), £1·52 booklet (Walsall – GLAI)
38p.	gravure Walsall (*p* 14)	ultramarine	2 bands	Y1707a	£7·50 'Special by Design' booklet (DX24)
39p.	photo/gravure Enschedé or Harrison	brt magenta	2 bands	Y1708	sheets
39p.	gravure De La Rue	brt magenta	phos paper	**MS**2146	Jeffery Matthews Colour Palette miniature sheet
39p.	gravure De La Rue or Walsall	grey	2 bands	Y1709	sheets (De La Rue), £7·43 The Brontë Sisters booklet (Walsall – DX34)
40p.	gravure De La Rue or Walsall	deep azure	2 bands	Y1710	sheets (D.L.R.), £1·60 booklet (Walsall – GMA1)
40p.	gravure De La Rue or Enschedé	turquoise-blue	2 bands	Y1711	sheets (D.L.R.), £7·40 Brunel booklet (Enschedé – DX36)
41p.	gravure Enschedé	grey-brown	2 bands	Y1712	sheets
41p.	photo Harrison	drab	phos paper	Y1713	vertical coils
41p.	gravure De La Rue	rosine	2 bands	Y1714	sheets
41p.	litho Walsall	drab	2 bands	Y1780	£1·64 booklets (GN1/3)
41p.	litho Questa	grey-brown	2 bands	Y1780a	£6 National Trust booklet (DX17)
42p.	gravure De La Rue, Enschedé or Walsall	dp olive-grey	2 bands	Y1715	sheets (De La Rue), £7·23 'The Glory of the Garden' booklet (Enschedé – DX33), £7·43 The Brontë Sisters booklet (Walsall – DX34)
43p.	gravure Enschedé	dp olive-brown	2 bands	Y1716	sheets
43p.	photo Harrison	sepia	2 bands	Y1717	sheets, vertical coils
43p.	gravure Walsall (*p* 14)	sepia	2 bands	Y1717a	£6·16 British Land Speed Record Holders booklet (DX21)
43p.	gravure De La Rue	emerald	2 bands	Y1718	sheets
44p.	gravure De La Rue	grey-brown	2 bands	Y1719	sheets
44p.	gravure De La Rue	bright blue	2 bands	Y1720	sheets
45p.	gravure De La Rue	brt mauve	2 bands	Y1721	sheets
46p.	gravure De La Rue or Enschedé	yellow	2 bands	Y1722	sheets (De La Rue), £7·66 'The Machin' booklet (De La Rue – DX39), £7·66 British Army Uniforms booklet (Enschedé – DX40)
47p.	gravure De La Rue or Enschedé	turquoise-green	2 bands	Y1723	sheets (De La Rue), £7·23 'The Glory of the Garden' booklet (Enschedé – DX33)
48p.	gravure De La Rue	bright mauve	2 bands	Y1724	sheets, £7·66 'The Machin' booklet (DX39)
48p.	litho De La Rue	bright mauve	2 bands	Y1781	£7·75 Charles Darwin booklet (DX45)
49p.	gravure De La Rue	red-brown	2 bands	Y1725	sheets
50p.	photo/gravure Enschedé, Harrison or Walsall	ochre	2 bands	Y1726	sheets (Enschedé or Harrison), £7·26 Trafalgar booklet (Walsall–DX35), £7·44 Victoria Cross booklet (Enschedé – DX37)
50p.	gravure De La Rue	grey	2 bands	Y1727	sheets
50p.	litho Cartor	grey	2 bands	Y1782	£7·68 British Design Classics Booklet (DX44)
54p.	gravure De La Rue or Enschedé	red-brown	2 bands	Y1728	sheets (D.L.R.), £7·66 British Army Uniforms booklet (Enschedé – DX40)
54p.	litho Cartor	chestnut	2 bands	Y1783	Type III. £8·06 Classic Album Covers booklet (DX48) and £7·72 Royal Society booklet (DX49)
56p.	gravure De La Rue	yellow-olive	2 bands	Y1729	sheets
60p.	litho Walsall	dull blue-grey	2 bands	Y1784	£2·40 booklets (GQ1/4)
60p.	gravure De La Rue	light emerald	2 bands	Y1730	sheets
60p.	litho Cartor	emerald	2 bands	Y1785	'Britain Alone' booklet (DX51)
62p.	gravure De La Rue	rosine	2 bands	Y1731	sheets
62p.	litho Cartor	rosine	2 bands	Y1786	£8·18 'Treasures of the Archive' booklet (DX46) and £8·06 Classic Album Covers booklet (DX48)
63p.	photo/gravure Enschedé, Harrison or Walsall	lt emerald	2 bands	Y1732	sheets (Enschedé or Harrison), vertical coils (Harrison), £2·52 booklets (Walsall – GR3/4)
63p.	litho Walsall	lt emerald	2 bands	Y1787	£2·52 booklets (GR1/2)
64p.	gravure De La Rue or Walsall	turquoise-green	2 bands	Y1733	sheets (D.L.R.), £2·56 booklet (Walsall – GS1)
64p.	gravure De La Rue	turquoise-green	phos paper	**MS**2146	Jeffery Matthews Colour Palette miniature sheet
65p.	gravure De La Rue or Walsall	greenish blue	2 bands	Y1734	sheets (D.L.R.), £2·60 booklet (Walsall – GT1)
67p.	gravure De La Rue	bright mauve	2 bands	Y1735	sheets
67p.	litho Cartor	bright mauve	2 bands	Y1788	£9·05 WWF booklet (DX52)
68p.	gravure De La Rue or Walsall	grey-brown	2 bands	Y1736	sheets (D.L.R.), £7·26 Trafalgar booklet (Walsall – DX35)
72p.	gravure De La Rue	rosine	2 bands	Y1737	sheets
78p.	gravure De La Rue	emerald	2 bands	Y1738	sheets
81p.	gravure De La Rue	turquoise-green	2 bands	Y1739	sheets
88p.	gravure De La Rue	bright magenta	2 bands	Y1740	sheets
90p.	gravure De La Rue	ultramarine	2 bands	Y1741	sheets

Decimal Machin Index (stamps with elliptical perforations, including (N.V.Is)) MACHINS

Value	Process	Colour	Phosphor	Cat. No.	Source
90p.	litho Cartor	bright blue	2 bands	Y1789	£7·93 Royal Navy Uniforms booklet (DX47)
97p.	gravure De La Rue	violet	2 bands	Y1742	sheets
97p.	litho Cartor	bluish violet	2 bands	Y1790	£9·05 WWF booklet (DX52)
£1	gravure Enschedé, Harrison or De la Rue	bluish violet	2 bands	Y1743	sheets, **MS**2743 (D.L.R.)
£1	gravure De La Rue	magenta	2 bands	Y1744	sheets, £7·66 'The Machin' booklet (DX39), **MS**2743
£1	gravure De La Rue	bluish violet	phos paper	**MS**2146	Jeffery Matthews Colour Palette miniature sheet
£1.46	gravure De La Rue	greenish blue	2 bands	Y1745	sheets
£1.50	recess	red	—	Y1800	sheets (Enschedé then D.L.R.)
£1.50	gravure De La Rue	brown-red	2 bands	Y1746	sheets
£2	recess	dull blue	—	Y1801	sheets (Enschedé then D.L.R.)
£2	gravure De La Rue	deep blue-green	2 bands	Y1747	sheets
£3	recess	dull violet	—	Y1802	sheets (Enschedé then D.L.R.)
£3	gravure De La Rue	deep mauve	2 bands	Y1748	sheets, **MS**2658
£5	recess	brown	—	Y1803	sheets (Enschedé then D.L.R.)
£5	gravure De La Rue	azure	2 bands	Y1749	sheets

Note. Harrison and Sons became De La Rue Security Print on 8 September 1997.
Photo/gravure stamps were printed from both photogravure and computor engraved (gravure) cylinders.

MACHINS *Decimal Machin Booklet Pane Guide (ordinary gum) ("Y" numbers)*

Decimal Machin Booklet Pane Guide (ordinary gum) ('Y' numbers) the shaded squares represent printed labels.

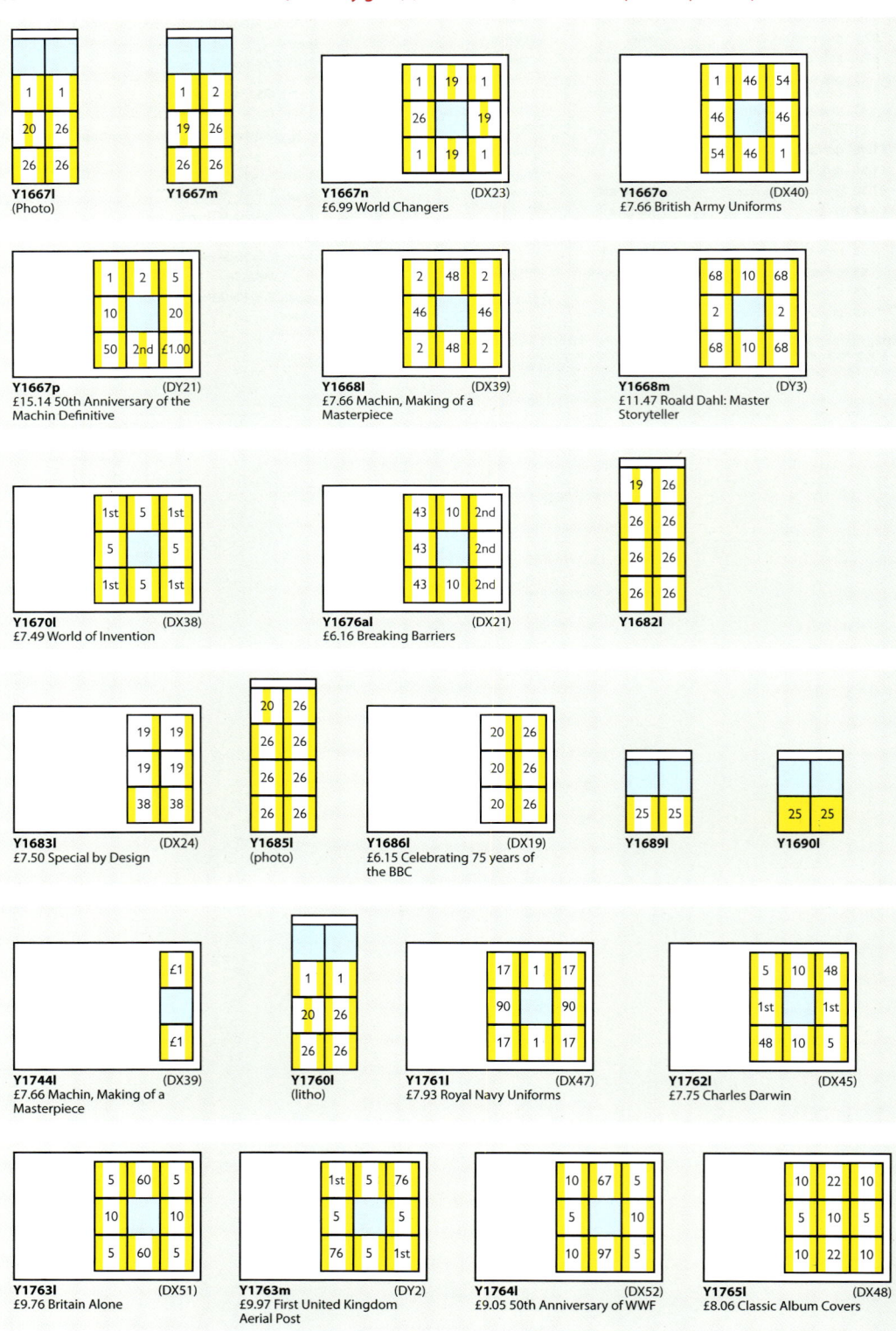

Y1667l (Photo)

Y1667m

Y1667n (DX23)
£6.99 World Changers

Y1667o (DX40)
£7.66 British Army Uniforms

Y1667p (DY21)
£15.14 50th Anniversary of the Machin Definitive

Y1668l (DX39)
£7.66 Machin, Making of a Masterpiece

Y1668m (DY3)
£11.47 Roald Dahl: Master Storyteller

Y1670l (DX38)
£7.49 World of Invention

Y1676al (DX21)
£6.16 Breaking Barriers

Y1682l

Y1683l (DX24)
£7.50 Special by Design

Y1685l (photo)

Y1686l (DX19)
£6.15 Celebrating 75 years of the BBC

Y1689l

Y1690l

Y1744l (DX39)
£7.66 Machin, Making of a Masterpiece

Y1760l (litho)

Y1761l (DX47)
£7.93 Royal Navy Uniforms

Y1762l (DX45)
£7.75 Charles Darwin

Y1763l (DX51)
£9.76 Britain Alone

Y1763m (DY2)
£9.97 First United Kingdom Aerial Post

Y1764l (DX52)
£9.05 50th Anniversary of WWF

Y1765l (DX48)
£8.06 Classic Album Covers

Decimal Machin Booklet Pane Guide (ordinary gum) ("Y" numbers) / Self-adhesive Machin Index **MACHINS**

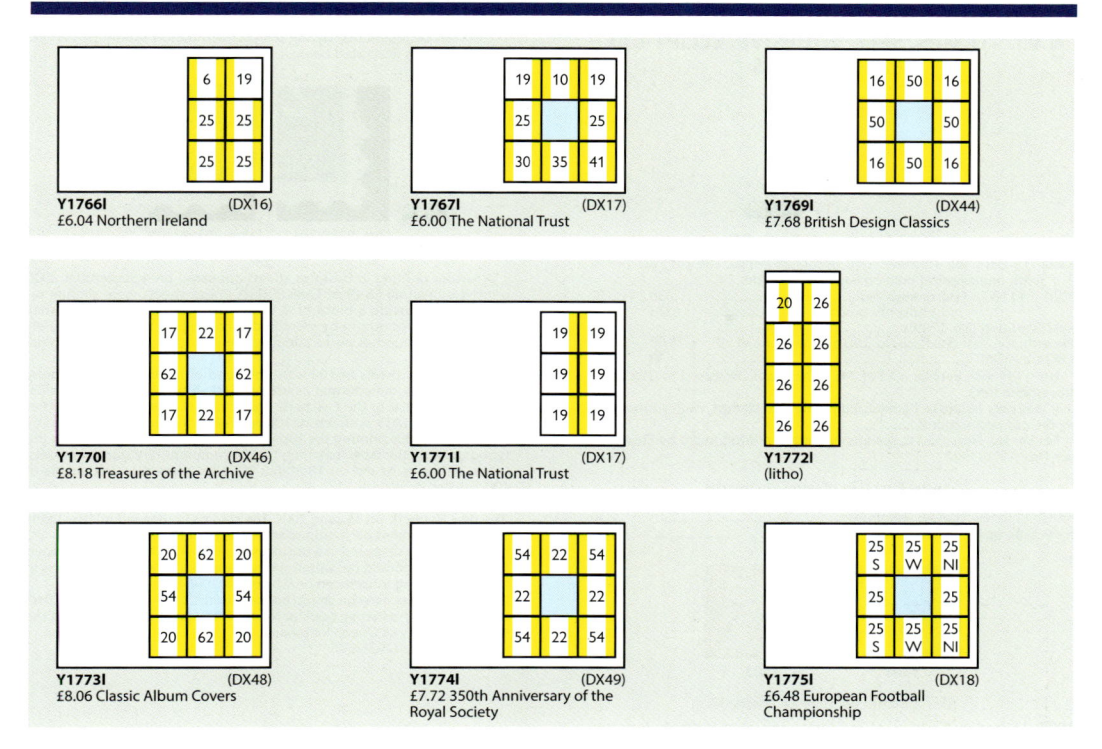

Y1766I (DX16)
£6.04 Northern Ireland

Y1767I (DX17)
£6.00 The National Trust

Y1769I (DX44)
£7.68 British Design Classics

Y1770I (DX46)
£8.18 Treasures of the Archive

Y1771I (DX17)
£6.00 The National Trust

Y1772I
(litho)

Y1773I (DX48)
£8.06 Classic Album Covers

Y1774I (DX49)
£7.72 350th Anniversary of the Royal Society

Y1775I (DX18)
£6.48 European Football Championship

355

N.V.I. STAMPS, SELF-ADHESIVE, ELLIPTICAL PERFORATIONS

1116

(Des J. Matthews. Litho Walsall)

1993 (19 Oct). Self-adhesive. Two phosphor bands. Die-cut Perf 14×15 (with one elliptical hole on each vertical side).

1789	**1116**	(1st) orange-red	1·50	1·50
		y. Phosphor omitted	£275	
First Day Cover (No. 1789)				2·50
Presentation Pack (PO Pack No. 29) (booklet pane of 20)			18·00	
PHQ Card (D6)			40	2·50

No. 1789 was initially sold at 24p. which was increased to 25p. from November 1993.

It was only issued in booklets containing 20 stamps, each surrounded by die-cut perforations.

For similar 2nd and 1st designs printed in photogravure by Enschedé see Nos. 1976/1977.

Special First Day of Issue Postmarks

British Philatelic Bureau, Edinburgh	2·50
Newcastle upon Tyne	2·50

1301 **1302**

(Des J. Matthews. Gravure Enschedé)

1997 (18 Mar). Self-adhesive. One centre phosphor band (2nd) or two phosphor bands (1st). Perf 14×15 die-cut (with one elliptical hole in each vertical side).

1976	**1301**	(2nd) bright blue	1·40	1·40
1977	**1302**	(1st) bright orange-red	1·40	1·40
Set of 2			2·75	2·75
First Day Cover				3·00
Presentation Pack (PO Pack No. 37)			3·50	

Nos. 1976/1977, which were sold at 20p. and 26p., were in rolls of 100 with the stamps separate on the backing paper.

No. 1976 exists with the printed image in two sizes; the normal stamp is 21.25 mm×17.25 mm, while the scarcer second version is 21.75×17.75 mm.

Special First Day of Issue Postmarks

British Philatelic Bureau, Edinburgh	2·75
Glasgow	2·75

(Gravure Enschedé, Questa or Walsall)

1998 (6 Apr)–**2006** (16 May). Self-adhesive. Designs as Types **913**/**914**. One centre phosphor band (2nd), or two phosphor bands (1st). Perf 15×14 die-cut (with one elliptical hole in each vertical side).

2039	(2nd) bright blue	1·00	1·00
	a. Imperf (pair, 6 mm gap) (1998)	£275	
	ab. Imperf (pair, 4 mm gap) (2000)	£100	
	b. Perf 14½×14 die-cut (22.6.98)	£300	
2040	(1st) bright orange-red	1·25	1·25
	a. Imperf (pair, 6 mm gap) (1998)	£275	
	ab. Imperf (pair, 4 mm gap) (2000)	£100	
	b. Perf 14½×14 die-cut (22.6.98)	£300	
	y. Phosphor omitted	£130	
	l. Booklet pane. No. 2040×6 plus commemorative label at left (29.1.2001)	11·50	

Nos. 2039/2040, initially sold for 20p. and 26p., were in rolls of 200 printed by Enschedé with the surplus self-adhesive paper removed.

2nd and 1st self-adhesive stamps as Nos. 2039/2040 were issued in sheets, printed in photogravure by Walsall Security Printers, on 22 June 1998. These are similar to the previous coil printings, but the sheets retain the surplus self-adhesive paper around each stamp. Stamps from these sheets have square perforation tips instead of the rounded versions to be found on the coils.

No. 2039 exists die-cut through the backing paper from Presentation Pack No. 71.

No. 2039 was issued in rolls of 10,000, printed by Enschedé on yellow backing paper with the surplus self-adhesive paper removed. A number appears on the back of every tenth stamp in the roll.

Nos. 2039a/2040a come from business sheets printed by Walsall and show a 6 mm space between the stamps.

Nos. 2039ab/2040ab come from business sheets printed by Walsall and Questa respectively and have a 4 mm space between stamps. 4 mm pairs also exist from booklets, but are much scarcer from this source.

Nos. 2039b and 2040b come from initial stocks of these Walsall sheet printings sent to the Philatelic Bureau and supplied to collectors requiring single stamps.

They can be indentified by the pointed perforation tips in the corners of the stamp, as illustrated below.

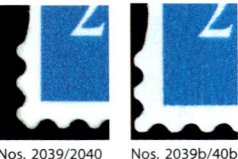

Nos. 2039/2040   Nos. 2039b/40b

A further printing in business sheets appeared on 4 September 2000 printed by Walsall (2nd) or Questa (1st). These sheets were slightly re-designed to provide a block of 4, rather than a strip, in the top panel. Individual stamps cannot be identified as coming from these new sheets as they have rounded perforation tips similar to those on the original coil printings.

The business sheets of 100 were re-issued on 9 May 2002 printed by Enschedé in the same format as used in September 2000. The individual stamps are similar to the Enschedé coil printings of April 1998. A further printing of No. 2039 in sheets of 100 appeared on 4 July 2002 printed by Enschedé. On this printing the top panel reverted to a strip of 4 with the typography on the label matching that of contemporary stamp booklets.

No. 2039 was issued on 18 March 2003 in stripped matrix sheets of 100, printed by Walsall.

The business sheets of 100 were again issued but without the strapline 'The Real Network' on 15 June 2004. The stamps in stripped matrix sheets of 100 had rounded perforations and were printed by Walsall.

No. 2039 was re-issued in a business sheet on 16 May 2006, in stripped matrix format, printed by Walsall, with an announcement about Pricing in Proportion being introduced on 21 August 2006 in the header.

Both values appeared in stamp booklets from 29 January 2001. No. 2040l comes from self-adhesive booklet No. MB2. The label commemorates the death centenary of Queen Victoria.

See also Nos. 2295/2298.

'MILLENNIUM' MACHINS

1437 Queen Elizabeth II

(Des A. Machin, adapted R. Scholey. Gravure De La Rue, Questa or Walsall/ISP Walsall (No. 2124), Walsall (Nos. 2124bl, 2124dl), Questa or Walsall (No. 2124d))

2000 (6 Jan–Aug). New Millennium. Two phosphor bands. Perf 15×14 (with one elliptical hole in each vertical side).

2124	**1437**	(1st) olive-brown	1·25	1·25
		a. Imperf (pair)	£600	
		l. Booklet pane. No. 2124×4 plus commemorative label at right (21.3.2000)	5·00	
		m. Booklet pane. No. 2124×9 with margins all round (4.8.2000)	8·50	
		y. Phosphor omitted	£500	
		d. Perf 14 (23.5.2000)	1·25	1·25
		dy. Phosphor omitted	20·00	
		dl. Booklet pane. No. 2124d×8 with central label and margins all round (15.2.2000)	8·00	
First Day Cover (Philatelic Bureau) (Type G, see Introduction) (No. 2124)				2·00
First Day Cover (Windsor) (Type G) (No. 2124)				2·00
First Day Cover (Philatelic Bureau) (No. 2124bm)				6·00
First Day Cover (London SW1) (No. 2124bm)				6·00
First Day Cover (Philatelic Bureau) (No. 2124dl)				6·00
First Day Cover (London SW5) (No. 2124dl)				6·00
Presentation Pack (PO Pack No. 48)			2·50	
PHQ Card (D16) (23.5.2000)			40	2·50

No. 2124d comes from stamp booklets printed by Questa. Similar booklets produced by Walsall have the same perforation as the sheet stamps.

Booklet pane No. 2124dl comes from Prestige Stamp booklet No. DX24.

The labels on booklet pane No. 2124l show either Postman Pat, publicising The Stamp Show 2000, or the National Botanic Garden of Wales.

1459

(Des J. Matthews. Gravure De La Rue)

2000 (22 May). Stamp Show 2000 International Stamp Exhibition, London. Jeffery Matthews Colour Palette. Sheet, 124×70 mm. Phosphorised paper. Perf 15×14 (with one elliptical hole in each vertical side).

MS2146 **1459** 4p. new blue; 5p. dull red-brown; 6p. yellow-olive; 10p. dull orange; 31p. deep mauve; 39p. bright magenta; 64p. turquoise-green; £1 bluish violet............ 15·00 15·00
First Day Cover (Philatelic Bureau)............ 15·00
First Day Cover (Earls Court, London SW5)............ 15·00
Exhibition Card (wallet, sold at £4·99, containing one mint sheet and one cancelled on postcard)............ 30·00

The £1 value is printed in Iriodin ink which gives a shiny effect to the solid part of the background behind the Queen's head.

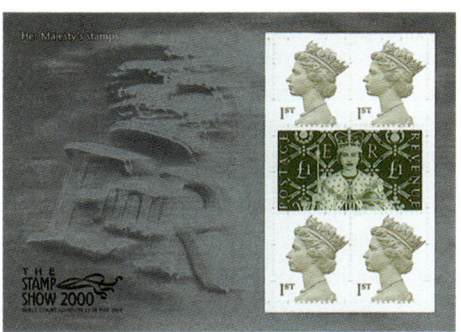

1459a

(Des Delaney Design Consultants. Gravure De La Rue)

2000 (23 May). Stamp Show 2000 International Stamp Exhibition, London. Her Majesty's Stamps. Sheet 121×89 mm. Phosphorised paper. Perf 15×14 (with one elliptical hole in each vertical side of stamps as T **1437**).

MS2147 **1459a** (1st) olive-brown (Type **1437**)×4; £1 slate-green (as Type **163**)............ 9·00 9·00
First Day Cover (Philatelic Bureau)............ 9·25
First Day Cover (City of Westminster, London SW1)............ 9·25
Presentation Pack (PO Pack No. M03)............ 40·00
PHQ Cards (set of 2) (PSM03)............ 80 15·00

The £1 value is an adaptation of the 1953 Coronation 1s.3d. stamp originally designed by Edmund Dulac. It is shown on one of the PHQ cards with the other depicting the complete miniature sheet.

N.V.I. AND DENOMINATED STAMPS, SELF-ADHESIVE GUM, ELLIPTICAL PERFORATIONS

(Gravure Questa, Walsall, Enschedé or De La Rue (1st), Walsall (others))

2002 (5 June–4 July). Self-adhesive. Two phosphor bands. Perf 15×14 die-cut (with one elliptical hole in each vertical side).

2295	914	(1st) gold............	1·25	1·25
		a. Imperf (pair)............	£850	
		y. Phosphor omitted............	£225	
2296	1093a	(E) deep blue (4.7.02)............	2·25	2·25
2297	367a	42p. deep olive-grey (4.7.02)............	5·00	5·00
2298		68p. grey-brown (4.7.02)............	5·75	5·75
Set of 4			13·00	13·00
PHQ Card (D22) (No. 2295) (Walsall) (27.3.03)............			40	1·10

No. 2295, sold for 27p., was initially only available in booklets of six or 12, printed by Questa or Walsall, with the surplus self-adhesive paper around each stamp removed. Later booklets were also printed by De La Rue.

No. 2295 exists die-cut through the backing paper from Presentation Pack No. 71

No. 2295 was issued in rolls of 10,000, printed by Enschedé on yellow backing paper with the surplus self-adhesive paper removed. A number appears on the back of every tenth stamp in the roll.

A further printing of No. 2295 in sheets of 100 appeared on 4 July 2002 produced by Enschedé and on 18 March 2003 in stripped matrix sheets of 100 printed by Walsall. The top panel shows a strip of four with the typography of the label matching that of booklet T **ME2**.

Nos. 2296/2298 were only issued in separate booklets, each containing six stamps with the surplus self-adhesive paper around each stamp removed.

POSTAL FORGERIES. A postal forgery of No. 2295 exists, produced in booklets of 12 with a varnish band printed across the centre of the stamps to mimic phosphor bands. A similar forgery is known with the wavy perforations, gauge 10.

OVERSEAS BOOKLET STAMPS

1655

(Des Sedley Place. Gravure Walsall)

2003 (27 Mar)–**10**. Overseas Booklet Stamps. Self-adhesive. As T **1655** Two phosphor bands. Perf 15×14 die-cut with one elliptical hole in each vertical side.

2357a	(Worldwide postcard) grey-black, rosine and ultramarine (1.4.04)............	1·90	1·90
2357b	(Europe up to 20 grams) deep blue-green, new blue and rosine (30.3.10)............	2·00	2·00
2358	(Europe up to 40 grams) new blue and rosine............	2·00	2·00
2358a	(Worldwide up to 20 grams) deep mauve, new blue and rosine (30.3.10)............	2·25	2·25
2359	(Worldwide up to 40 grams) rosine and new blue............	3·00	3·00
Set of 5		11·00	11·00
First Day Cover (Tallents House) (Type K, see Introduction) (Nos. 2358, 2359)............			5·00
First Day Cover (Windsor) (Type K) (Nos. 2358, 2359)............			5·00
Presentation Pack (PO Pack No. 60) (Nos. 2358, 2359)............		5·00	
PHQ Card (D23) (No. 2358)............		40	5·00

No. 2357a was intended to pay postcard rate to foreign destinations (43p.).

No. 2357a was available from philatelic outlets as a single stamp or in PO Packs Nos. 67 and 71 together with other definitive stamps. These single stamps were die-cut through the white backing paper.

Nos. 2358/2359 were intended to pay postage on mail up to 40 grams to either Europe (52p.) or to foreign destinations outside Europe (£1·12).

Nos. 2357b and 2358a were intended to pay postage on mail up to 20 grams to either Europe (initially 56p.) or to foreign destinations outside Europe (90p.).

They were only available in separate booklets of four (Nos. MI3 and MJ3) initially sold at £2·24 and £3·60, with the surplus self-adhesive paper around each stamp removed.

Operationally they were only available in separate booklets of 4 (Nos. MI1, MJ1 and MJA1), initially sold at £1·72, £2·08 and £4·48, with the surplus self-adhesive paper around each stamp removed.

For listings of first day covers (together with definitives issued on the same day) and presentation packs for Nos. 2357a/2357b and 2358a see after No. Y1803.

Single examples of Nos. 2358/2359 were available from philatelic outlets as sets of two or in PO Pack No. 60. These stamps were die-cut through the backing paper on the back and showed parts of the booklet covers. Nos. 2358a and 2358/2359 from PO Pack No. 67 (No. 2357a only), PO Packs Nos. 71 and 77 were die-cut through on plain white paper, while Nos. 2357b and 2358a in PO Pack No. 86 and all five values in PO Pack No. 88 were guillotined to show an area of margin surrounding the stamps.

> The purchase prices of NVI stamps are shown in the introduction of the catalogue.

PRICING IN PROPORTION

1915	1916

(Des J. Matthews)

2006 (1st Aug)–**07**. Pricing in Proportion. Perf 15×14 (with one elliptical hole in each vertical side).

(a) Ordinary gum. Gravure De La Rue, ISP Walsall or Enschedé (No. 2651).

(i) As T **1915***.*

2650	(2nd) bright blue (1 centre band)	1·00	1·00
	l. Booklet pane. Nos. 2650/2651, and Nos. 2652/2653 each×2, with central label and margins all round (5.6.07)	5·75	
2651	(1st) gold (2 bands)	1·25	1·25
	l. Booklet pane. Nos. 2651 and Y1726, each×4, with central label and margins all round (21.9.06)	5·50	

(ii) As T **1916***.*

| 2652 | (2nd Large) bright blue (2 bands) | 1·50 | 1·50 |
| 2653 | (1st Large) gold (2 bands) | 1·90 | 1·90 |

(b) Self-adhesive. Gravure Walsall or Enschedé. (No. 2654) or Walsall

(i) As T **1915***.*

2654	(2nd) bright blue (one centre band) (12.9.06)	1·00	1·00
	a. Imperf (pair)	£275	
2655	(1st) gold (2 bands) (12.9.06)	1·25	1·25
	y. Phosphor omitted	£150	

(ii) As T **1916***.*

| 2656 | (2nd Large) bright blue (2 bands) (15.8.06) | 1·50 | 1·50 |
| 2657 | (1st Large) gold (2 bands) (15.8.06) | 1·90 | 1·90 |

First Day Cover (Type K, see Introduction) (Nos. Y1677/Y1678, 2650/2653)		5·75
First Day Cover (Windsor) (Type K) (Nos. Y1677/Y1678, 2650/2653)		5·75
First Day Cover (Tallents House or Cuffley, Potters Bar, Herts) (Victoria Cross label pane 1st×4, 50p.×4 (No. 2651l))		5·75
Presentation Pack (PO Pack No. 74) (Nos. Y1677/Y1678, 2650/2653)		6·00

No. 2650 was issued in sheets (1 August) and coils of 500 (15 August).

No. 2654 was issued in rolls of 10,000, printed by Enschedé on yellow backing paper with the surplus self-adhesive paper removed. A number appears on the back of every tenth stamp in the roll.

Nos. 2654/2655 were available in separate booklets of six (No. RC1, *sold at* £1·92) or 12 (Nos. RD1 and RE1, *sold at* £2·76 or £3·84 respectively) and in business sheets of 100.

Nos. 2656/2657 were initially only available in separate booklets of four (Nos. RA1 and RB1), sold at £1·48 and £1·76.

All these booklets had the surplus self-adhesive paper around each stamp removed.

Nos. 2656/2657 were issued in sheets of 50, printed by Walsall, on 27 March 2007.

A postal forgery similar to No. 2651 exists with wavy perforations (gauge 10).

For PHQ cards for Nos. 2652/2653 see below No. Y1803.

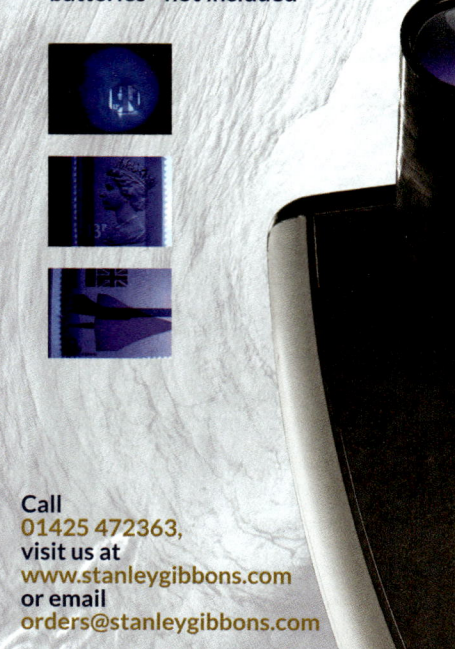

JOHN M. DEERING
INTERNATIONAL STAMP DEALERS IN FINE MODERN GB

The Definitive Specialists

offering a rare combination of comprehensive stocks & expert knowledge — for over 40 years

We only deal in Great Britain, mostly in material from 1967, and have become one of the world's leading dealers in specialised definitives (and Post & Go)...

... so, if you need help with mint GB since 1967 and would rather deal with an expert who truly understands Machins, Castles, Regionals and 'Post & Go' stamps (and all those tricky pictorial and commemorative printings from booklets and generic sheets), then you have come to the right place!

Mad About Machins! Passionate About Post & Go!

2nd Large on First
2nd Large up to 100g
Europe Large 100g
M21L Year Code

Our stock spans over 50 years of issues (Yes, **FIFTY** years!), is enormous and comprehensive, and includes cylinder & date blocks, coil strips, booklets & even specialised definitive covers. It doesn't stop with standard issues though, as we have a wide stock of varieties & errors.

- A modern firm but with a reputation for traditional values
- Anywhere in the world; make contact now

Get in touch today

World 100g Zone 1 & 3
Mail Rail
BDGB20 A012-1944-011

World 100g Zone 2
Mail Rail
BDGB20 A012-1944-012

£3
Missing gold Queen's head
Colour trial

Author of 'Machin Watch' in Gibbons Stamp Monthly

Machin Missing Phosphors
are standard stock items and all are thoroughly checked under ultra-violet; we are fussy!

Most credit cards accepted

We always maintain stocks of all date and source codes

Rare 3½p Colour Error

50x2ND
Valid for items up to: 240mm Long; 165mm Wide; 5mm Thick; 100g Weight

40+ YEARS

The Machin Specialists – for quality, service and expertise

Member of the Philatelic Traders' Society

The Machins • P O Box 2 • South Molton • Devon • EX36 4YZ • UK
Tel: 01398 341564 • Mob: 07421 456364 • E-mail: machins@johndeeringstamps.co.uk

SIMON HEELEY
SPECIALIST IN THE SECURITY MACHIN ISSUES

- ◊ **Extensive stocks of these Modern Classics.**
- ◊ **High degree of specialisation.**
- ◊ **Good range held including Singles, Cylinder and Date Blocks, Coils or Booklets.**
- ◊ **Post And Go Stamps including Inscriptions.**
- ◊ **Price lists available for specialised Security Machin Singles and Post And Go Stamps.**
- ◊ **Prompt service.**

Whether you are filling gaps in a printed album or require a certain year / source code, I would be pleased to help you build your collection.

LONG ESTABLISHED NEW ISSUE SERVICE AVAILABLE FOR ALL ASPECTS OF MODERN MINT G.B.

LET ME KEEP YOU UP TO DATE!

P.O. Box 7352, Kingswinford, West Midlands, DY6 6AZ

Tel 01384 293543.

simonheeleystamps@gmail.com

Simon Heeley
Fine Modern British Stamps

SECURITY MACHINS

> Please note that the 'U' numbers in this section are temporary and subject to change.

On 17 February 2009 a new form of Machin definitive appeared, incorporating additional security features to combat the re-use of uncancelled stamps.

The stamps no longer included a water-soluble layer of gum between the paper and the self-adhesive to prevent them being 'soaked off' envelope paper; in addition, four U-shaped slits were die-cut into the stamps to prevent them being peeled off paper and, to make forgery more difficult, an overall iridescent multiple 'ROYALMAIL' overprint was incorporated into the design.

In May 2010 2nd and 1st class stamps were issued in rolls with iridescent overprint but printed on paper with ordinary gum and without U-shaped slits. These are listed as U3065/U3066. Other values in this form subsequently appeared in prestige booklets.

> **USED STAMPS.** Because the self-adhesive stamps in this section do not include a water-soluble layer of gum, we recommend that used stamps are retained on their backing paper and trimmed with a uniform border of 1 mm–2 mm around all sides, taking care not to cut into the perforations.

Source Codes. In March 2009 stamps were issued with 'codes' incorporated into the iridescent overprint which allowed the source to be identified. The codes may be seen in the words 'ROYALMAIL', usually at the top right of the stamp, although some later Large Letter issues have it at the bottom right (marked 'BR' in the list below) or just to the front of the Queen's hair (marked 'FOH' in the list below).

The codes are:

2nd and 1st
MAIL		(ie without code letter) – counter sheets
MBIL	–	Business sheets
MCIL	–	'Custom' booklets, which include special stamps
MMIL	–	Miniature sheet (Nos. **MS**3222/**MS**3965) (not listed as individual stamps)
MPIL	–	Prestige booklet panes
MRIL	–	Rolls
MSIL	–	standard booklets of six
MTIL	–	booklets of 12

2nd and 1st Large
ROYALMAIL		(ie without code letter) – counter sheets
YBLM	–	Business sheets (2009)
MBI	–	Business sheets (2010)
BIL	–	Business sheets (2011–2013) (BR)
MBIL	–	Business sheets (from 2014) (FOH)
FOYAL	–	booklets of Four (2009)
MFI	–	booklets of Four (2010)
FIL	–	booklets of Four (2011–2013) (BR)
MFIL	–	booklets of Four (from 2014) (FOH)

For the Diamond Jubilee definitive with source codes, which are behind The Queen's head, the end of 'DIAMOND' is adjusted to:

MBND	–	Business sheets
MCND	–	'Custom' booklets of six
MMND	–	Miniature sheet (No. **MS**3272) (not listed as individual stamps)
MPND	–	Prestige booklet pane
MSND	–	standard booklet of six
MTND	–	booklets of 12

And for Large Letter stamps with source codes the end of 'JUBILEE' is adjusted to :

LBE	–	Business sheets
LFE	–	booklets of four

For the Long to Reign Over Us definitives with source codes, which are behind The Queen's neck, the end of 'REIGN' is adjusted to:

GC	–	'Custom' booklets of six
GM	–	Miniature sheet (No. **MS**3747) (not listed as individual stamp)
GP	–	Prestige booklet pane
GS	–	standard booklet of six

Year codes. From 2010 a year code (also sometimes referred to as a date code) was added to the iridescent overprint. Generally it appears in the upper left corner of the stamp, in front of the crown to The Queen's forehead or eye, but on later Large Letter stamps it appears lower down, above the 'ge' of 'Large'. Stamps are listed without or with year codes, and the different codes known are given in checklists at the end of this section. Note that year dates given within the listings are years of issue, not year codes.

> Note that, where stamps exist with more that one year code, the issue date given is for the first release, but prices are for the cheapest code.

U-shaped slits. The first issue featured U-shaped die-cut slits without a break in the middle of each 'U', but subsequent issues have incorporated a break to prevent the stamps tearing while being removed from the backing paper on which they were issued. We no longer list these as separate varieties but details are provided in the checklists at the end of this section.

A 1st gold stamp with U-slits but without iridescent overprint was supplied only to bulk mailing houses.

'ROYAL MAIL' printed backing paper. As an additional security measure, in early 2016 the backing paper on certain booklets appeared with a repeated undulating 'ROYALMAIL' background in two sizes of grey text printed upright on the front of the backing paper (Type PB-Up). This feature extended to business sheets and counter sheets during 2016 and 2017. In early 2017 the background was changed, so that alternate pairs of lines of the repeated 'ROYALMAIL' text were inverted in relation to each other. The pairs of lines can appear with the Large lettering above the small (Type PB-Ls), or with the small above the the Large (Type PB-sL). In October 2018 a fourth type appeared on some No. PM64 booklets. In this type the 'ROYALMAIL' background, in two sizes of grey text, is all inverted (Type PB-Inv). These differences are not listed in this catalogue, unless the stamps themselves are different. Their existence is, however, noted under the sections in which they occur, and in the checklists at the end of this section. For illustrations and further details please refer to the checklists. Booklets with 'ROYALMAIL' security text are listed in the relevant section of this catalogue.

> Details of known source and year-code combinations, and different year code changes, are provided in the series of tables following the listings. For the convenience of collectors, the printer of each combination is also given. We are grateful to John M. Deering for compiling these tables.

367

2009 (17 Feb)–**20**. Self-adhesive. Designs as T **367**. Two phosphor bands. U-shaped slits. Iridescent overprint. Die-cut Perf 14½×14 (with one elliptical hole in each vertical side).

(a) Without source or year codes, gravure De La Rue.
U2911	50p. brownish grey	2·00	1·50
U2912	£1 magenta	3·50	2·75
U2913	£1·50 brown-red	3·25	3·00
U2914	£2 deep blue-green	4·75	4·50
U2915	£3 deep mauve	5·75	5·50
U2916	£5 azure	9·50	9·25

(b) With source and year codes, gravure Walsall.
U2917	50p. brownish grey (MPIL) (8.5.10)	5·00	5·00
	l. Booklet pane Nos. U2917×2, U3011×2 and U3017×4, with central label and margins all round	16·00	

No. U2917 was first issued in £11·15 booklets, No. DX50 with 'MA10' year code. It was issued again in £9·99 premium booklet, No. DY1, with 'M11L' year code, (see also U3075l).

MACHINS Security Machins

(c) Without source code, with year code, gravure De La Rue (Nos. U2926/ U2927, U2929/U2930, U2932/U2933, U2935/U2937, U2939/U2940, U2941, U2945/U2946, U2948, U2950, U2954, U2956, U2958, U2961, U2968/U2969), De La Rue or Walsall/ISP Walsall (Nos. U2920/U2925, U2928, U2931, U2934, U2953, U2955, U2957, U2962) or ISP Walsall (others).

No.	Description		
U2920	1p. deep crimson (3.1.13)	40	35
U2921	2p. deep green (3.1.13)	40	35
U2922	5p. dull red-brown (3.1.13)	45	40
U2923	10p. dull orange (3.1.13)	60	50
U2924	20p. bright green (3.1.13)	70	60
U2925	50p. slate (3.1.13)	1·75	1·50
U2926	68p. deep turquoise-green (29.3.11)	2·25	2·00
U2927	76p. bright rose (29.3.11)	2·00	1·75
U2928	78p. bright mauve (27.3.13)	2·00	1·75
U2929	81p. emerald (26.3.14)	3·75	3·50
U2930	87p. yellow-orange (25.4.12)	4·25	4·00
U2931	88p. orange-yellow (27.3.13)	2·25	2·00
U2932	97p. bluish violet (26.3.14)	2·25	2·25
U2933	£1 magenta (10.10.11)	16·00	15·50
U2934	£1 bistre-brown (3.1.13)	3·00	2·75
U2935	£1·05 grey-olive (22.3.16)	2·75	2·50
U2936	£1·10 yellow-olive (29.3.11)	3·25	3·00
U2937	£1·17 orange-red (21.3.17)	3·00	2·75
U2938	£1·25 emerald (20.3.18)	2·75	2·50
U2939	£1·28 emerald (25.4.12)	4·00	3·75
U2940	£1·33 orange-yellow (24.3.15)	2·75	2·50
U2940a	£1·35 bright mauve (19.3.19)	3·00	2·75
U2941	£1·40 grey-green (21.3.17)	3·00	2·75
U2942	£1·42 deep rose-red (17.3.20)	3·00	2·75
U2943	£1·45 lavender-grey (20.3.18)	3·25	3·00
U2945	£1·47 lavender-grey (26.3.14)	3·50	3·25
U2946	£1·52 bright mauve (24.3.15)	3·00	2·75
U2947	£1·55 greenish blue (20.3.18)	3·00	2·75
U2948	£1·57 olive-brown (21.3.17)	3·25	3·00
U2949	£1·60 orange-yellow (19.3.19)	3·00	2·75
U2949a	£1·63 orange-red (17.3.20)	3·00	2·75
U2950	£1·65 grey-olive (29.3.11)	3·75	3·50
U2951	£1·68 yellow-olive (17.3.20)	3·50	3·25
U2952	£1·70 greenish blue (23.12.20)	3·50	3·25
U2953	£1·88 dull ultramarine (27.3.13)	3·75	3·50
U2954	£1·90 bright mauve (25.4.12)	4·00	3·75
U2955	£2 deep blue-green (4.13)	3·75	3·50
U2956	£2·15 greenish blue (26.3.14)	4·25	4·00
U2957	£2·25 deep violet (24.3.15)	3·75	3·50
U2958	£2·27 bistre (21.3.17)	4·00	3·75
U2959	£2·30 grey-olive (19.3.19)	3·50	3·25
U2960	£2·42 bluish violet (17.3.20)	3·75	3·75
U2961	£2·45 bluish green (24.3.15)	4·00	3·75
U2962	£2·55 deep rose-red (21.3.17)	5·00	4·75
U2963	£2·65 bluish violet (20.3.18)	4·50	4·25
U2964	£2·80 bluish green (19.3.19)	4·25	4·00
U2965	£2·97 bright magenta (17.3.20)	4·50	4·50
U2966	£3 deep mauve (11.9.19)	4·75	4·50
U2968	£3·15 turquoise-blue (24.3.15)	5·00	4·75
U2968a	£3·25 turquoise-green (23.12.20)	4·75	4·50
U2969	£3·30 bright magenta (24.3.15)	5·25	5·00
U2970	£3·45 grey-green (19.3.19)	5·00	4·75
U2971	£3·60 yellow-orange (19.3.19)	5·25	5·00
U2972	£3·66 pale ochre (17.3.20)	5·25	5·25
U2973	£3·82 emerald (17.3.20)	5·50	5·50
U2973a	£4·20 deep violet (23.12.20)	6·25	6·00
U2974	£5 azure (11.9.19)	8·00	7·75
Set of 57		£195	£185

No. U2936 and U2950 are with 'M11L' year code from stock officially issued/available over the post office counter, and are recorded in the tables following the main listings. A very few examples with an 'M12L' year code are known from a single sheet sent to a specialist catalogue publisher for research purposes. They were never officially issued and are therefore not recorded in the tables following the main listing.

Nos. U2911/U2917, U2926/U2933, U2935/U2936, U2939/U2940, U2945/U2946, U2950, U2953/U2954, U2956, U2961 and U2968/U2969 only exist on plain backing paper.

Nos. U2920/U2925, U2934, U2937, U2941, U2948, U2955, U2957/U2958 and U2962 were originally issued on plain backing paper, but later appeared on paper with repeating 'ROYALMAIL' text, with alternate pairs of lines inverted (Types PB-Ls/sL).

Nos. U2938, U2940a, U2942/U2943, U2947, U2949, U2949a, U2951/U2952, U2959/U2960, U2963/U2966, U2968a, U2970/U2974 only exist on backing paper with repeating 'ROYALMAIL' text, with alternate pairs of lines inverted (Types PB-Ls/sL).

Please note that the missing numbers in this and subsequent listings in this section have been left for future additions to this series.

2009 (17 Feb)–**17**. Self-adhesive. Designs as Types **913**/**914** or T **1916**. One centre band (Nos. U2975, U2979/U2981, U2995 and U3010/U3013) two bands (others). U-shaped slits. Iridescent overprint. Die-cut Perf 14½×14 (with one elliptical hole in each vertical side).

(a) Without source or year codes, gravure De La Rue.

No.	Description		
U2975	(2nd) bright blue	2·50	2·25
U2976	(1st) gold	2·75	2·50
U2977	(2nd Large) bright blue	3·00	2·75
U2978	(1st Large) gold	3·25	3·00

(b) With source code, without year code, gravure De La Rue (Nos. U2979/ U2980, U2982, U2984, U2987, U2989) or Walsall (others).

No.	Description		
U2979	(2nd) bright blue (MBIL) (31.3.09)	3·75	3·75
U2980	(2nd) bright blue (MRIL) (7.09)	4·50	4·50
U2981	(2nd) bright blue (MTIL) (31.3.09)	2·25	2·25
U2982	(1st) gold (MBIL) (31.3.09)	3·75	3·75
U2983	(1st) gold (MCIL) (10.3.09)	2·25	2·25
U2984	(1st) gold (MRIL) (7.09)	5·00	5·00
U2985	(1st) gold (MSIL) (31.3.09)	4·50	4·50
U2986	(1st) gold (MTIL) (31.3.09)	2·50	2·50
U2987	(2nd Large) bright blue (YBLM) (31.3.09)	3·75	3·75
U2988	(2nd Large) bright blue (FOYAL) (31.3.09)	3·75	3·75
U2989	(1st Large) gold (YBLM) (31.3.09)	3·75	3·75
U2990	(1st Large) gold (FOYAL) (31.3.09)	4·50	4·50

(c) Without source code, with year code, gravure De La Rue (Nos. U2996/ U2997 and U3001/U3002), De La Rue or Walsall/ISP Walsall (others).

No.	Description		
U2995	(2nd) bright blue (1.7.10)	1·60	1·25
U2996	(1st) gold (20.5.10)	3·50	3·50
U2997	(1st) vermilion (3.1.13)	2·00	1·75
U2998	(1st) bright scarlet (11.4.17)	1·70	1·40
U3000	(2nd Large) bright blue (26.1.11)	1·90	1·50
U3001	(1st Large) gold (3.11.10)	6·00	6·00
U3002	(1st Large) vermilion (3.1.13)	2·75	2·50
U3003	(1st Large) bright scarlet (11.4.17)	2·25	1·75

(d) With source and year codes, gravure De La Rue or Walsall/ISP Walsall (Nos. U3010 and U3031), De La Rue or Enschedé (No. U3018), De La Rue, Enschedé or Walsall (No. U3012), Enschedé or Walsall (No. U3023), De La Rue (Nos. U3015 and U3034) or Walsall/ISP Walsall (others).

No.	Description		
U3010	(2nd) bright blue (MBIL) (8.10)	2·00	1·75
U3011	(2nd) bright blue (MPIL) (8.5.10)	4·50	4·50
U3012	(2nd) bright blue (MRIL) (7.11)	4·25	4·25
U3013	(2nd) bright blue (MTIL) (2.10)	1·75	1·50
U3015	(1st) gold (MBIL) (6.10)	4·50	4·50
U3016	(1st) gold (MCIL) (25.2.10)	1·75	1·50
U3017	(1st) gold (MPIL) (8.5.10)	2·10	2·10
U3018	(1st) gold (MRIL) (15.7.11)	4·75	4·75
U3019	(1st) gold (MSIL) (26.1.10)	2·00	2·00
U3020	(1st) gold (MTIL) (2.10)	2·25	2·25
U3021	(1st) vermilion (MBIL) (3.1.13)	2·75	2·50
U3022	(1st) vermilion (MCIL) (9.1.13)	1·40	1·20
U3023	(1st) vermilion (MRIL) (3.1.13)	3·00	3·00
U3024	(1st) vermilion (MSIL) (3.1.13)	1·75	1·60
U3025	(1st) vermilion (MTIL) (3.1.13)	1·75	1·60
U3026	(1st) bright scarlet (MBIL) (20.10.16)	2·25	2·00
U3027	(1st) bright scarlet (MCIL) (20.10.16)	1·40	1·20
U3028	(1st) bright scarlet (MSIL) (20.10.16)	1·90	1·75
U3029	(1st) bright scarlet (MTIL) (20.10.16)	2·00	1·75
U3031	(2nd Large) bright blue (MBI/BIL/MBIL) (3.11)	2·75	2·50
U3032	(2nd Large) bright blue (MFI/FIL/MFIL) (8.5.10)	2·50	2·25
U3034	(1st Large) gold (MBI/BIL) (6.10)	4·50	4·50
U3035	(1st Large) gold (MFI/FIL) (8.5.10)	3·25	3·25
U3036	(1st Large) vermilion (BIL/MBIL) (3.1.13)	3·25	3·00
U3037	(1st Large) vermilion (FIL/MFIL) (3.1.13)	3·25	3·00
U3038	(1st Large) bright scarlet (MBIL) (20.10.16)	3·25	3·00
U3039	(1st Large) bright scarlet (MFIL) (20.10.16)	3·25	3·00

Nos. U2975/U2990, U2996/U2997, U3001/U3002, U3011/U3012, U3015/U3020, U3022/U3023 and U3034/U3035 only exist on plain backing paper.

Nos. U3021, U3024/U3025 and U3036/U3037 were originally issued on plain backing paper, but later appeared on paper with repeating 'ROYALMAIL' text the same way up (Type PB-Up).

Nos. U2995 and U3000 were originally issued on plain backing paper, but later appeared on paper with repeating 'ROYALMAIL' text, with alternate pairs of lines inverted (Types PB-Ls/sL).

Nos. U3010, U3013, U3031 and U3032 were originally issued on plain backing paper, but later appeared with repeating 'ROYALMAIL' text the same way up (Type PB-Up), and subsequently with alternate pairs of lines inverted (Types PB-Ls/sL).

Nos. U3026, U3028/U3029 and U3038/U3039 were originally issued on backing paper with repeating 'ROYALMAIL' text the same way up (Type PB-Up), but later appeared with alternate pairs of lines inverted (Types PB-Ls/sL).

No. U3027 was originally issued on backing paper with repeating 'ROYALMAIL' text the same way up (Type PB-Up), but later appeared with alternate pairs of lines inverted (Types PB-Ls/sL), and subsequently from some No. PM64 booklets with repeating 'ROYALMAIL' text the same way up but inverted (Type PB-Inv).

Nos. U2998 and U3003 only exist on backing paper with repeating 'ROYALMAIL' text, with alternate pairs of lines inverted (Types PB-Ls/sL).

For full details of which stamps and year codes exist on different backing papers, please see the checklists at the end of this section of the catalogue.

2132a **2132b**

2132c **2132d**

(Gravure De La Rue or from 2018 ISP Walsall)

2009 (17 Nov)–**13**. Self-adhesive. Designs as Types **2132a/2132d**. Two phosphor bands. U-shaped slits. Iridescent overprint. Die-cut Perf 14 (Nos. U3046, U3048, U3050) or 14½×14 (others) (all with one elliptical hole in each vertical side).

(a) Without source or year codes, gravure De La Rue.

U3045	(Recorded Signed for 1st) bright orange-red and lemon	4·25	3·75
U3046	(Recorded Signed for 1st Large) bright orange-red and lemon	4·75	4·00

(b) Without source code, with year code, gravure De La Rue (Nos. U3047/U3048), De La Rue or ISP Walsall (others).

U3047	(Recorded Signed for 1st) bright orange-red and lemon (11.4.11)	13·00	13·00
U3048	(Recorded Signed for 1st Large) bright orange-red and lemon (11.4.11)	23·00	23·00
U3049	(Royal Mail Signed for 1st) bright orange-red and lemon (27.3.13)	4·50	4·00
U3050	(Royal Mail Signed for 1st Large) bright orange-red and lemon (27.3.13)	5·00	4·50
U3051	(Special delivery up to 100g) blue and silver (26.10.10)........................	11·00	10·50
U3052	(Special delivery up to 500g) blue and silver (26.10.10)........................	12·00	11·50

No. U3045 was originally sold for £1·14 (£1·15 from 6 April 2010 and £1·23 from 4 April 2011).
No. U3046 was originally sold for £1·36 (£1·40 from 6 April 2010 and £1·52 from 4 April 2011).
No. U3047 was originally sold for £1·23 (£1·55 from 30 April 2012).
No. U3048 was originally sold for £1·52 (£1·85 from 30 April 2012).
No. U3049 was originally sold for £1·55 (£1·70 from 2 April 2013, £1·72 from 31 March 2014, £1·73 from 30 March 2015, £1·74 from 29 March 2016, £1·75 from 27 March 2017, £1·77 from 26 March 2018, £1·90 from 25 March 2019, £2·06 from 23 March 2020 and £2·25 from 1 January 2021).
No. U3050 was originally sold for £1·85 (£2 from 2 April 2013, £2·03 from 31 March 2014, £2·05 from 30 March 2015, £2·06 from 29 March 2016, £2·08 from 27 March 2017, £2·11 from 26 March 2018, £2·26 from 25 March 2019, £2·45 from 23 March 2020 and £2·69 from 1 January 2021).
No. U3051 was originally sold for £5·05 (£5·45 from 4 April 2011, £5·90 from 30 April 2012, £6·22 from 2 April 2013, £6·40 from 31 March 2014, £6·45 from 30 March 2015, £6·50 from 26 March 2018, £6·60 from 25 March 2019, £6·70 from 23 March 2020 and £6·85 from 1 January 2021).
No. U3052 was originally sold for £5·50 (£5·90 from 4 April 2011, £6·35 from 30 April 2012, £6·95 from 2 April 2013, £7·15 from 31 March 2014, £7·25 from 30 March 2015, £7·30 from 26 March 2018, £7·40 from 25 March 2019, £7·50 from 23 March 2020 and £7·65 from 1 January 2021).
Nos. U3045/U3048 only exist on plain backing paper.
Nos. U3049/U3052 were originally issued on plain backing paper, but later appeared on paper with repeating 'ROYALMAIL' text, with alternate pairs of lines inverted (Types PB-Ls/sL).

(Gravure De La Rue or Walsall (Nos. U3057/U3058) or De La Rue (others))

2011 (8 Mar–5 May). Self-adhesive. Designs as T **367**. Two phosphor bands. U-shaped slits. No iridescent overprint. Die-cut Perf 14½×14 (with one elliptical hole in each vertical side).

U3055	1p. crimson..	80	80
U3056	2p. deep green...................................	50	50
U3057	5p. dull red-brown.............................	60	60
	l. Booklet pane. Nos. U3057×4, U3058×2 and U2917×2 with central label and margins all round (5.5.11)............	10·50	
U3058	10p. dull orange...................................	70	70
U3059	20p. bright green.................................	1·00	1·00
Set of 5		3·25	3·25

Nos. U3055/U3059 were issued in counter sheets and do not have an iridescent overprint.
Nos. U3957/U3058 were issued again, but in £9·99 premium booklet, No. DY1.
No. 3057l combines stamps without and with iridescent overprint.

2010 (13 May)–**22**. Ordinary gum. Designs as Types **367** and **913/914**. Without source and year codes, gravure Walsall (U3060) or ISP Walsall (with one elliptical hole in each vertical side).

(a) With source and year codes, gravure Walsall (U3060) or ISP Walsall (U3061).

U3060	68p turquoise-green (MPIL) (10.1.12)	4·00	4·00
U3061	£1 magenta (MPIL) (5.6.17)	23·00	23·00

(b) NVIs with source and year codes, gravure De La Rue (Nos. U3065/U3066) or ISP Walsall (No. U3067).

U3065	(2nd) bright blue (MRIL) (13.5.10)	7·00	7·00
U3066	(1st) gold (MRIL) (13.5.10)............................	7·25	7·25
U3067	(1st) vermilion (MPIL) (5.6.17)	11·00	11·00

No. U3060 comes from booklet pane Y1668m in No. DY3 Roald Dahl's Children's Stories premium booklet, and has a 'M11L' year code.
No. U3061 comes from pane Y1667p in No. DY21 50th Anniversary of the Machin Definitive premium booklet, and has a 'M17L' year code.
Nos. U3065/U3066 were issued in separate coils of 500 or 1000, and have 'MA10' year codes.
No. U3066 also exists from Birth Centenary of Arnold Machin miniature sheet No. **MS**3222, from which it has source code 'MMIL' (and 'AM11' year code).
No. U3067 comes from booklet pane 1668ssl in No. DY21 50th Anniversary of the Machin Definitive premium booklet, and has a 'M17L' year code.
No. U3067 also exists printed gravure from 50th Anniversary of the Machin Definitive miniature sheet No. **MS**3965, from which it has source code 'MMIL' and year code 'M17L', but is not separately listed.
A 1st bright scarlet (similar to No. U3067) with 'M21L' year code but without a source code exists from a 95th Birthday of Her Majesty The Queen sheetlet (21.04.21), containing 1st bright scarlet×4, Nos. EN53, S160, W150, NI158 with central label and margins all round. The sheetlet printed by Walsall combines gravure (1st bright scarlet) and litho printing (others and phosphor bands). The sheetlet was commissioned by The Royal Mint for use on cover and was not available unused to the general public.

(c) With source and year codes, litho Enschedé (Nos. U3073, U3076), Cartor/ISP Cartor or Enschedé (Nos. U3071/U3075, U3082) or Cartor/ISP Cartor (others).

U3070	1p. crimson (MPIL) (14.3.19) .	75	75
	a. Source code without P (M IL) (14.3.19).	1·25	1·25
	l. Booklet pane. Nos. U3070×2, U3156×2, EN51, NI95, S158 and W148 with central label and margins all round (9.5.13)................	12·50	
	m. Booklet pane. Nos. U3070×2, U3071×3, U3079 and U3081×2 with central label and margins all round (19.2.15)................	14·50	
	n. Booklet pane. Nos. U3070, U3072a, U3094 and 3717, each×2 with central label and margins all round (14.5.15)....	14·00	
	o. Booklet pane. Nos. U3070, U3075, U3077a and U3089, each×2 with central label and margins all round (4.12.18)..................	12·50	
	p. Booklet pane. Nos. U3070a×2, U3075a×3, U3089a×2 and U3104, with central label and margins all round (14.3.19)................	11·75	
	q. Booklet pane. Nos. U3070×2, U3071×4 and U3096×2 with central label and margins all round (11.2.20)	10·00	
	r. Booklet pane. Nos. U3070 and 4403, each×4 with central label and margins all round (9.7.20)	7·50	
U3071	2p. deep green (MPIL) (9.5.13)	85	85
	a. Source code without P (M IL) (20.3.18).	1·00	1·00
	l. Booklet pane. Nos. U3071/U3072 and U3074, each×2 (9.5.13)...................	5·75	
	m. Booklet pane. Nos. U3071/U3072, each×2, and Nos. EN51a, NI95, S158a and W148 with central label and margins all round (20.2.14)	12·00	
	n. Booklet pane. Nos. U3071×2, U3074×2, U3157×3 and U3083 with central label and margins all round (15.2.17)...................	11·00	
	o. Booklet pane. Nos. U3071a×3, U3072b×3 and U3084a×2 with central label and margins all round (20.3.18)....	10·50	
	p. Booklet pane. Nos. U3071, U3077 and 3807, each×2 and Nos. 3808/3809 with central label and margins all round (24.5.19)	13·50	
	q. Booklet pane. Nos. U3071, U3150, 3786 and S159a, each×2, with central label and margins all round (17.3.20).....	8·00	
	r. Booklet pane. Nos. U3071×2, U3077×3 and U3150×3 with central label and margins all round (13.11.20).................	8·00	
	s. Booklet pane. Nos. U3071×2, U3074×2, U3077×2 and U3157×2 with central label and margins all round (28.5.21).................................	12·50	
	t. Booklet pane. Nos. U3071, U3074, U3077 and U3108, each×2, with central label and margins all round (4.2.22)...........................	14·50	
U3072	5p. red-brown (MPIL) (26.3.13)	90	90
	a. Deep brown-red (MPIL) (14.5.15)............	2·25	2·25
	b. Source code without P (M IL) (20.3.18).	1·25	1·25
	l. Booklet pane. Nos. U3072, U3074/U3075, U3080 and 3452×4 with central label and margins all round (26.3.13).....	16·00	
	m. Booklet pane. Nos. U3072, U3074, U3077 and U3082, each×2 with central label and margins all round (18.6.15).....	15·00	

MACHINS Security Machins

	n. Booklet pane. Nos. U3072×3, U3074×2 and U3083×3 with central label and margins all round (28.7.16)		9·75	
	o. Booklet pane. Nos. U3072×2, U3075, U3084, NI94×2 and 4049×2 with central label and margins all round (23.1.18)		10·50	
	p. Booklet pane. Nos. U3072×2, U3074×4 and U3109×2 with central label and margins all round (13.2.19)		30·00	
	q. Booklet pane. Nos. U3072×2 and U3084×2 and U3150×4, with central label and margins all round (26.11.19)		11·00	
	r. Booklet pane. Nos. U3072×2 and U3074×2 and EN53a, NI158, S160 and W150 with central label and margins all round (11.2.20)		8·00	
	s. Booklet pane. Nos. U3072×4, U3077×2 and U3110×2 with central label and margins all round (8.5.20)		15·00	
	t. Booklet pane. Nos. U3072×2, U3074×3, U3075×2 and U3116 with central label and margins all round (12.8.21)		18·00	
U3073	5p. red-brown (MPIL). Elliptical perforation near the top of sides of stamp (19.9.13)		2·00	2·00
	l. Booklet pane. Nos. U3073 and U3076, each×4, with central label and margins all round (19.9.13)		12·00	12·00
U3074	10p. dull orange (MPIL)		95	95
	l. Booklet pane. Nos. U3074×2, U3075×4 and U3082×2 with central label and margins all round (15.4.14)		10·00	
	m. Booklet pane. Nos. U3074×2, U3075×2, EN30, NI95, S131 and W122 with central label and margins all round (28.7.14)		9·50	
	n. Booklet pane. Nos. U3074, U3075, U3077 and U3082, each×2, with central label and margins all round (20.1.22)		13·50	
U3075	20p. bright green (MPIL) (26.3.13)		1·10	1·10
	a. Source code without P (M IL) (14.3.19)		1·75	1·75
	l. Booklet pane. Nos. U3075×3, U3150×2 and U3157×3 with central label and margins all round (16.2.21)		13·50	
	m. Booklet pane. Nos. U3075×3, U3150×3 and U3157×3 with central label and margins all round (17.9.21)		10·00	
U3076	50p. slate-blue (MPIL). Elliptical perforation near the top sides of stamp (19.9.13)		2·00	2·00
U3077	50p. slate (MPIL) (18.6.15)		1·60	1·60
	a. Grey (MPIL) (4.12.18)		2·00	2·00
U3078	76p. bright rose (MPIL) (9.9.11)		9·50	9·50
U3079	81p. deep turquoise-green (MPIL) (19.2.15)		8·00	8·00
U3080	87p. yellow-orange (MPIL) (26.3.13)		6·00	6·00
U3081	97p. bluish violet (MPIL) (19.2.15)		3·75	3·75
U3082	£1 sepia (MPIL) (15.4.14)		2·00	2·00
	l. Booklet pane. No. U3082 with eight reproduction King George V 1d. stamps all round (28.7.14)		4·00	
U3083	£1·05 grey-olive (MPIL) (28.7.16)		2·75	2·75
U3084	£1·17 bright orange (MPIL) (23.1.18)		4·00	4·00
	a. Source code without P (M IL) (20.3.18)		4·50	4·50
U3089	£1·25 emerald (MPIL) (4.12.18)		2·75	2·75
	a. Light green. Source code without P (M IL) (14.3.19)		2·75	2·75
U3094	£1·33 orange-yellow (MPIL) (14.5.15)		3·00	3·00
U3096	£1·35 bright purple (MPIL) (11.2.20)		4·00	4·00
U3099	£1·40 grey-green (MPIL) (14.12.17)		4·00	4·00
U3104	£1·45 lavender-grey source code without P (M IL) (14.3.19)		7·00	7·00
U3108	£1·50 brown-red (MPIL) (4.2.22)		8·50	8·50
U3109	£1·55 greenish blue (MPIL) (13.2.19)		15·00	15·00
U3115	£1·63 bright orange (MPIL) (8.5.20)		4·50	4·50
U3116	£1·70 greenish blue (MPIL) (12.8.21)		15·00	15·00
	(d) NVIs with source and year codes, litho Cartor/ISP Cartor.			
U3150	(2nd) bright blue (MPIL) (17.12.15)		1·90	1·90
	l. Booklet pane. Nos. U3150×2, and U3156×2 and 3786×4, with central label and margins all round (17.12.15)		12·50	
	m. Booklet pane. Nos. U3150×2, U3156×4 and U3099×2, with central label and margins all round (14.12.17)		13·50	
U3155	(1st) gold (MPIL) (9.9.11)		5·25	5·25
U3156	(1st) vermilion (MPIL) (9.5.13)		1·75	1·75
	l. Booklet pane. Nos. U3156×2, U3747×2, EN30b, NI95, S131a and W122, with central label and margins all round (21.4.16)		14·00	
	m. Booklet pane. Nos. U3156×4 and 3717×4 with central label and margins all round (13.9.18)		11·00	
U3157	(1st) bright scarlet (MPIL) (15.2.17)		2·10	2·10

Nos. U3070/U3157 were all issued in premium booklets.
No. U3070 comes from Nos. DY7, DY12, DY13, DY27, DY32 and DY35.
No. U3070a comes from No. DY29.
No. U3071 comes from Nos. DY7, DY9, DY12, DY20, DY30, DY32, DY33, DY36, DY38 and DY42.
No. U3071a comes from No. DY25.
No. U3072 comes from Nos. DY6, DY7 DY9, DY14, DY19, DY24, DY28, DY31, DY32, DY34 and DY39.
No. U3072a comes from No. DY13.
No. U3072b comes from No. DY25.
No. U3073 comes from No. DY8, and has the elliptical hole near the top of sides of stamp.
No. U3074 comes from Nos. DY6, DY7, DY9, DY10, DY11, DY14, DY19, DY20, DY28, DY32, DY38, DY39, DY41 and DY42.
No. U3075 comes from Nos. DY6, DY10, DY11, DY24, DY27, DY37, DY39, DY40 and DY41.
No. U3075a comes from No. DY29.
No. U3076 comes from No. DY8, and has the elliptical hole near the top of sides of stamp.
No. U3077 comes from Nos. DY14, DY30, DY34, DY36, DY38, DY41 and DY42.
No. U3077a comes from No. DY27.
No. U3078 comes from booklet pane Y1763m in No. DY2.
No. U3079 comes from No. DY12.
No. U3080 comes from No. DY6.
No. U3081 comes from No. DY12.
No. U3082 comes from Nos. DY10, DY11, DY14 and DY41.
No. U3082l comes from No. DY11 and contains one U3082 with year code M14L, and eight reproduction King George V 1d. stamps.
No. U3083 comes from Nos. DY19 and DY20.
No. U3084 comes from Nos. DY24 and DY31.
No. U3084a comes from No. DY25.
No. U3089 comes from No. DY27.
No. U3089a comes from No. DY29.
No. U3094 comes from No. DY13.
No. U3096 comes from No. DY32.
No. U3099 comes from No. DY23.
No. U3104 comes from No. DY29.
No. U3108 comes from No. DY42.
No. U3109 comes from No. DY28.
No. U3115 comes from No. DY34.
No. U3116 comes from No. DY39.
No. U3150 comes from Nos. DY15, DY23, DY31, DY33, DY36, DY37 and DY40.
No. U3155 comes from booklet pane Y1763m in No. DY2.
No. U3156 comes from Nos. DY7, DY15, DY17, DY23 and DY26.
No. U3157 comes from No. DY20, DY37, DY38 and DY40.
No. U3075, U3089 and U3104 with 'M19L' year code and source codes with P (MPIL) exist from a limited edition 'Marvel 80th Anniversary' premium booklet (sold at £39.99). The panes have a simulated pictorial cancellation 'CELEBRATING 80 YEARS OF MARVEL COMICS'.
No. U3075a, U3089a and U3104 from a standard Marvel premium booklet, No. DY29 have 'M18L' year and 'M IL' source codes.
For additional information see Security Machin source and year code tables at the end of this section.

First Day Covers

7.2.09	Nos. U2911/U2912 and U2975/U2978 (Type K, see introduction)	12·00
	Nos. U2911/U2912 and U2975/U2978 (Windsor, Type K)	12·00
	Nos. U2913/U2916 (Type K)	20·00
	Nos. U2913/U2916 (Windsor)	20·00
17.11.09	Nos. U3045/U3046 (Type K)	6·75
	Nos. U3045/U3046 (Windsor)	6·75
8.5.10	King George V Accession Centenary, se-tenant pane No. U2917l (Tallents House or London N1)	10·00
26.10.10	Nos. U3051/U3052 (Type K)	25·00
	Nos. U3051/U3052 (Windsor)	25·00
8.3.11	Nos. U3055/U3059 (Type K)	4·00
	Nos. U3055/U3059 (Windsor)	4·00
29.3.11	Nos. U2926/U2927, U2936, U2950 (Type K)	10·50
	Nos. U2926/U2927, U2936, U2950 (Windsor)	10·50
5.5.11	Morris & Co, se-tenant pane No. U3057l (Tallents House or Walthamstow)	6·50
25.4.12	Nos. U2930, U2939, U2954, U3271 and U3276 (Type K)	14·00
	Nos. U2930, U2939, U2954, U3271 and U3276 (Windsor)	14·00
3.1.13	Nos. U2920/U2925, U2934, U2997 and U3002 (Type K)	10·00
	Nos. U2920/U2925, U2934, U2997 and U3002 (Windsor)	10·00
26.3.13	Dr Who se-tenant pane No. U3072l (Tallents House or Cardiff)	11·00
27.3.13	Nos. U2928, U2931, U2953, U3049 and U3050 (Type K)	16·00
	Nos. U2928, U2931, U2953, U3049 and U3050 (Windsor)	16·00
9.5.13	Football Heroes se-tenant pane No. U3070l (Tallents House or Wembley, Middlesex)	10·50
19.9.13	Merchant Navy se-tenant pane No. U3073l (Tallents House or Clydebank)	8·00
20.2.14	Classic Locomotives se-tenant pane No. U3071m (Tallents House or Newcastle upon Tyne)	9·00
26.3.14	Nos. U2929, U2932, U2945 and U2956 (Type K)	14·00
	Nos. U2929, U2932, U2945 and U2956 (Windsor)	14·00

Date	Description	Price
15.4.14	Buckingham Palace *se-tenant* pane No. U3074l (Tallents House or London SW1)	9·00
28.7.14	First World War Centenary *se-tenant* pane No. U3074m (Tallents House or Newcastle upon Tyne)	10·00
19.2.15	Inventive Britain *se-tenant* pane No. U3070m (Tallents House or Harlow)	9·00
24.3.15	Nos. U2940, U2946, U2957, U2961 and U2968/U2969 (Type K)	25·00
	Nos. U2940, U2946, U2957, U2961 and U2968/U2969 (Windsor)	25·00
14.5.15	First World War Centenary (2nd issue) *se-tenant* pane No. U3070n (Tallents House or Winchester)	11·00
18.6.15	Battle of Waterloo Bicentenary *se-tenant* pane No. U3072m (Tallents House or Elstree, Borehamwood)	9·00
17.12.15	*Star Wars se-tenant* pane No. U3150l (Tallents House or Elstree, Borehamwood)	10·50
22.3.16	No. U2935 (Type K)	3·25
	No. U2935 (Windsor)	3·25
21.4.16	90th Birthday of Queen Elizabeth II *se-tenant* pane No. U3156l (Tallents House or Windsor)	12·50
28.7.16	150th Birth Anniversary of Beatrix Potter *se-tenant* pane No. U3072n (Tallents House or Near Sawrey, Ambleside)	10·00
15.2.17	Windsor Castle *se-tenant* pane No. U3071n (Tallents House or Windsor)	8·00
21.3.17	Nos. U2937, U2941, U2948, U2958 and U2962 (Type K)	17·00
	Nos. U2937, U2941, U2948, U2958 and U2962 (Windsor)	17·00
14.12.17	*Star Wars* (4th issue) Aliens and Droids *se-tenant* pane No. U3150m (Tallents House or Wookey, Wells)	12·00
23.1.18	*Game of Thrones se-tenant* pane No. U3072o (Tallents House or Belfast)	9·00
20.3.18	Nos. U2938, U2943, U2947 and U2963 (Type K)	14·00
	Nos. U2938, U2943, U2947 and U2963 (Windsor)	14·00
20.3.18	RAF Centenary *se-tenant* pane No. U3071o (Tallents House or Cranwell, Sleaford)	7·00
13.9.18	First World War Centenary (5th issue) *se-tenant* pane No. U3156m (Tallents House or London SW1)	10·50
4.12.18	Harry Potter *se-tenant* pane No. U3070o (Tallents House or Muggleswick, Consett)	8·75
13.2.19	Leonardo da Vinci *se-tenant* pane No. U3072p (Tallents House or Windsor)	8·50
14.3.19	Marvel *se-tenant* pane No. U3070p (Tallents House or Shield Row, Stanley)	9·50
19.3.19	Nos. U2940a, U2949, U2959, U2964, U2970 and U2971 (Type K)	23·00
	Nos. U2940a, U2949, U2959, U2964, U2970 and U2971 (Windsor)	23·00
24.5.19	Birth Bicentenary of Queen Victoria *se-tenant* pane No. U3071p (Tallents House or East Cowes)	8·50
26.11.19	*Star Wars* The Making of the Vehicles *se-tenant* pane No. U3072q (Tallents House or Maulder, Bedford)	10·00
11.2.20	Visions of the Universe. Bicentenary of the Royal Astronomical Society *se-tenant* pane No. U3070q (Tallents House or London W1)	7·25
17.3.20	James Bond *se-tenant* pane No. U3071q (Tallents House or Spy Post, Wellington)	8·50
17.3.20	Nos. U2942, U2949a, U2951, U2960, U2965, U2972 and U2973 (Type K)	28·00
	Nos. U2942, U2949a, U2951, U2960, U2965, U2972 and U2973 (Windsor)	28·00
8.5.20	75th Anniversary of the End of the Second World War *se-tenant* pane No. U3072s (Tallents House or London SW1)	8·50
9.7.20	Queen (rock band) *se-tenant* pane No. 3070r (Tallents House or Knebworth)	10·00
13.11.20	*Star Trek se-tenant* pane No. 3071r (Tallents House or Beambridge, Craven Arms)	8·50
23.12.20	Nos. U2952, U2968a, and U2973a (Type K)	16·00
	Nos. U2952, U2968a, and U2973a (Windsor)	16·00
16.2.21	Only Fools and Horses *se-tenant* pane No. U3075l (Tallents House or London SE15)	8·50
23.3.21	No. U4500 (Type K)	4·25
	No. U4500 (Windsor)	4·25

Presentation Packs

Date	Description	Price
17.2.09	Nos. U2911/U2912 and U2975/U2978 (PO Pack No. 82)	7·50
17.2.09	Nos. U2913/U2916 (PO Pack No. 83)	23·50
26.10.10	Nos. U3051/U3052 (PO Pack No. 89)	22·00
23.3.11	Nos. U2926/U2627, U2936, U2950 and U3055/U3059 (PO Pack No. 90)	15·00
25.4.12	Nos. U2930, U2939, U2954, U3271 and U3276 (PO Pack No. 94)	10·50
3.1.13	Nos. U2920/U2925, U2934, U2997 and U3002 (PO Pack No. 96)	7·50
27.3.13	Nos. U2928, U2931, U2953, U3048 and U3050 (PO Pack No. 97)	14·00
26.3.14	Nos. U2929, U2932, U2945 and U2956 (PO Pack No. 99)	10·00
24.3.15	Nos. U2940, U2946, U2957, U2961 and U2968/U2969 (PO Pack No. 101)	22·00
22.3.16	No. U2935 (PO Pack No. 103)	3·00
21.3.17	Nos. U2937, U2941, U2948, U2958 and U2962 (PO Pack No. 106)	17·00
20.3.18	Nos. U2938, U2943, U2947 and U2963 (PO Pack No. 108)	12·50
19.3.19	Nos. U2940a, U2949, U2959, U2964, U2970 and U2971 (PO Pack No. 110)	21·00
17.3.20	Nos. U2942, U2949a, U2951, U2960, U2965, U2972 and U2973 (PO Pack No. 112)	25·00
23.12.20	Nos. U2952, U2968a, and U2973a (PO Pack No. 114)	16·00

For presentation pack containing Nos. U3045/U3046 see after No. Y1803.

2268

(Litho Cartor)

2010 (8 May). London 2010 Festival of Stamps. Jeffery Matthews Colour Palette. Sheet 104×95 mm containing stamps as T **367** with a label. Two phosphor bands. Perf 15×14 (with one elliptical hole in each vertical side).

MS3073 **2268** 1p. reddish purple; 2p. deep grey-green; 5p. reddish-brown; 9p. bright orange; 10p. orange; 20p. light green; 60p. emerald; 67p. bright mauve; 88p. bright magenta; 97p. bluish violet; £1·46 turquoise-blue ... 50·00 50·00

For details of known source and year-code combinations, and the different year codes, please refer to the tables following these listings.

2408

(Gravure Walsall)

2011 (14 Sept). Birth Centenary of Arnold Machin (sculptor). Sheet 124×71 mm containing stamps as No. U3066×10 but with source code 'MMIL' and year code 'AM11'. Two phosphor bands. Perf 14½×14 (with one elliptical hole in each vertical side).

MS3222 **2408** (1st) gold×10 ... 13·00 13·50
First Day Cover (Stoke on Trent) ... 15·00
First Day Cover (Piccadilly, London W1) ... 15·00

914

2012 (6 Feb–1 Oct). Diamond Jubilee. (1st issue). Self-adhesive. Two phosphor bands. U-shaped slits. Iridescent overprint reading 'DIAMOND JUBILEE'. Die-cut perf 14½×14 (with one elliptical hole in each vertical side).

*(a) As T***914**.
(i) Without source code.
U3271 (1st) slate-blue ... 1·75 1·50

MACHINS Security Machins

	(ii) With source code.			
U3272	(1st) slate-blue (MTND)		1·75	1·75
U3273	(1st) slate-blue (MBND)		3·50	3·25
U3274	(1st) slate-blue (MCND) (31.5.12)		1·60	1·60
U3275	(1st) slate-blue (MSND) (1.10.12)		1·75	1·75
	*(b) As T **1916**.*			
	(i) Without source code.			
U3276	(1st Large) slate-blue (25.4.12)		2·50	2·25
	(ii) With source code.			
U3277	(1st Large) slate-blue (LFE) (25.4.12)		3·25	3·25
U3278	(1st Large) slate-blue (LBE) (25.4.12)		3·50	3·25
	(c) Ordinary gum. Without U-shaped slits. With source code.			
U3279	(1st Large) slate-blue (MPND)		3·75	3·75
	l. Booklet pane. Nos. U3279/3329, each×4, with central label and margins all round		14·00	

Nos. U3271 and U3276 are from counter sheets.
No. U3272 is from booklets of 12, No. MF6.
Nos. U3273 and U3278 are from business sheets.
No. U3274 is from booklets Nos. PM33 and PM34.
No. U3275 is from booklets of 6, No. MB11.
No. U3277 is from booklets of 4, No. RB3.
No. U3279 is from premium booklet No. DY4.
No. U3279 also exists from Diamond Jubilee miniature sheet No. **MS**3272, from which it has source code 'MMND', but is not separately listed.
For first day cover and presentation pack for Nos. U3271 and U3276 see under U3157.

914

(Gravure De La Rue (No. U3744) or ISP Walsall (Nos. U3745/U3746), or litho ISP Cartor (No. U3747))

2015 (9 Sept)–**16**. Long to Reign Over Us (1st issue). As T**914**. Self-adhesive. Two phosphor bands. U-shaped slits. Iridescent overprint reading 'LONG TO REIGN OVER US'. Die-cut perf 14½×14 (with one elliptical hole in each vertical side).

	(a) Without source code, with year code.			
U3744	(1st) bright lilac		1·75	1·75
	(b) With source and year codes.			
U3745	(1st) bright lilac (REIGS)		1·75	1·75
U3746	(1st) bright lilac (REIGC) (18.9.15)		1·60	1·60
	(c) Ordinary gum. Without U-shaped slits. With source and year codes.			
U3747	(1st) bright lilac (REIGP) (21.4.16)		3·50	3·50

No. U3744 comes from counter sheets printed by De La Rue and exists with both O15R and O16R year code.
No. U3745 comes from booklets of six, No. MB14, printed by ISP Walsall. Initial printings had a O15R year code and the front of the self-adhesive backing paper was unprinted. Later printings have repeating 'ROYALMAIL' wording printed on the front of the self-adhesive backing paper and exist with O15R and O16R year code.
No. U3746 comes from booklets Nos. PM49/PM53, printed by ISP Walsall, and has O15R (No. PM49) or O16R (Nos. PM50/PM53) year code.
No. U3747 comes from pane U3156l in £15·11 premium stamp booklet, No. DY17 and has O16R year code.
No. U3747 also exists printed gravure (by FNMT Spain) from Long to Reign Over Us miniature sheet No. **MS**3747, from which it has source code REIGM and year code O15R, but is not separately listed.

3041a

(Gravure ISP Walsall)

2017 (6 Feb). 65th Anniversary of Accession of Queen Elizabeth II. As T**3041a**. Two phosphor bands. Iridescent overprint reading '65TH ANNIVERSARY OF ACCESSION' with year code 'ACCE17ION'. Perf 14×14½.

U3920	£5 ultramarine		10·00	10·00
First Day Cover (Tallents House)				12·00
First Day Cover (Windsor)				12·00
Presentation Pack (PO Pack No. 105)			11·00	

No. U3920 does not have an elliptical perforation hole on each vertical side.

3085

(Des Atelier Works. Gravure and gold foil embossed. ISP Walsall)

2017 (5 June). 50th Anniversary of the Machin Definitive Two phosphor bands. Perf 14x14½ T**1116** and No. U3966 or 14½×14 (others).

MS3965 **3085**	No. X866; No. 1470; as No. 1789 (but ordinary gum); No. 2124; No. 2651; as No. U3067 (but MMIL source code); as No. U3966 (but gravure phosphor bands)		15·00	15·00
First Day Cover (Tallents House) (No. **MS**3965)				12·00
First Day Cover (High Wycombe) (No. **MS**3965)				12·00
Presentation Pack (PO Pack No. 541) (Nos. **MS**3964/ **MS**3865)			18·00	

On No. **MS**3965 only the £1 gold foil stamp is embossed.
The 5p, 20p and £1 stamps in No. **MS**3965 do not have an elliptical hole in each vertical side.

3086

(Litho and gold foil embossed. ISP)

2017 (5 June). 50th Anniversary of the Machin Definitive Two narrow phosphor bands. Perf 14×14½.

U3966 **3086**	£1 gold		4·50	5·50
	l. Booklet pane. Nos. U3966×4 with margins all round		16·00	

No. U3966 was embossed in gold foil, has the phosphor bands printed in litho and does not have an elliptical hole on each vertical side. It was issued in £15·59 booklet No. DY21 and No. **MS**3965.

Please note that for the convenience of collectors Nos. **MS**3965 and U3966/U3966l are listed additionally in the main section of this catalogue. This duplication is deliberate to ensure that both catalogue sections are complete and can be referenced to independently.

For the 20p. stamp as T**929** from the 50th Anniversary of the Machin booklet see No. 2133, booklet pane No. 1668ssl.

Please note that the 'U' numbers in this section are temporary and subject to change.

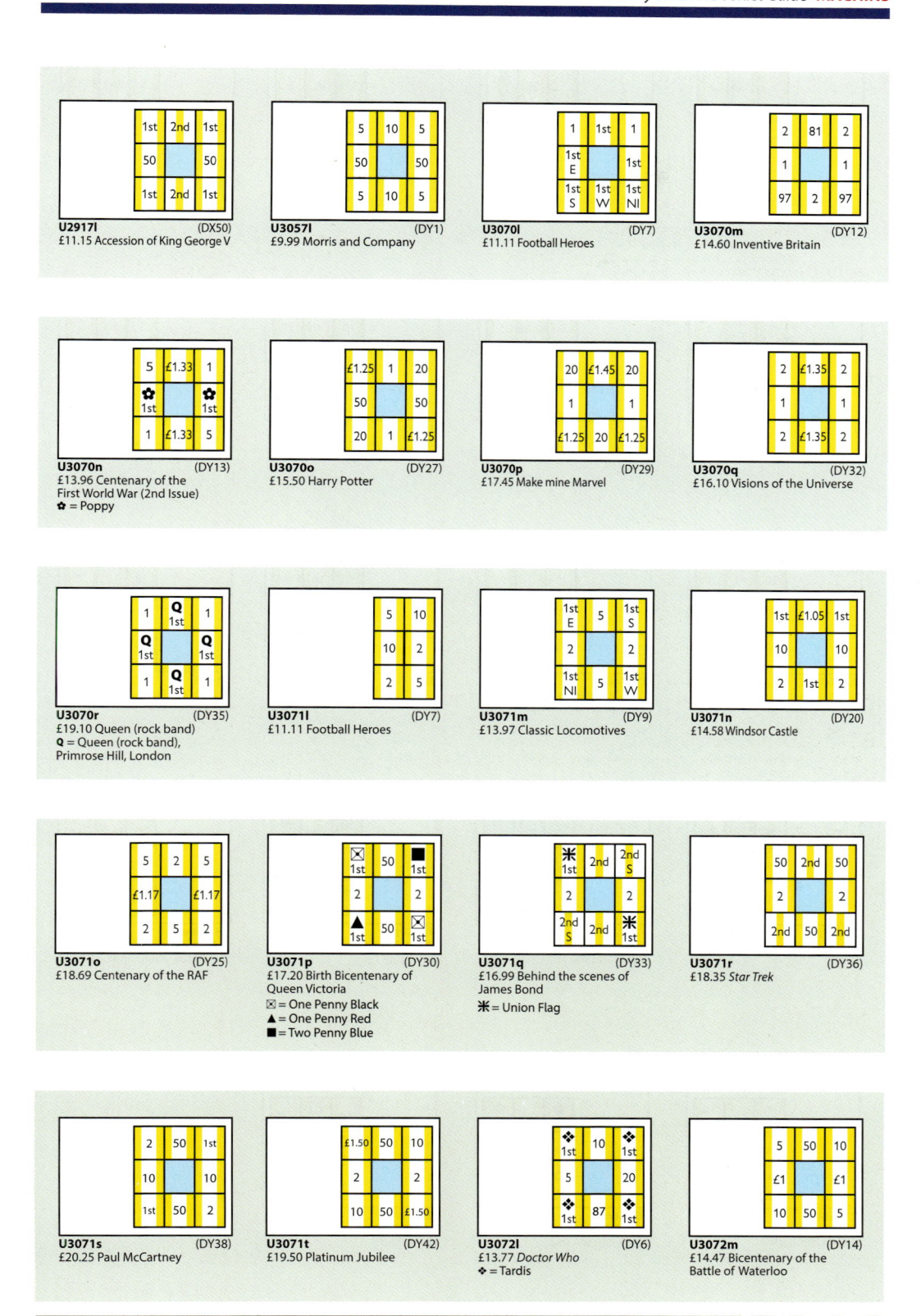

Security Machin Booklet Guide MACHINS

U2917l (DX50)
£11.15 Accession of King George V

U3057l (DY1)
£9.99 Morris and Company

U3070l (DY7)
£11.11 Football Heroes

U3070m (DY12)
£14.60 Inventive Britain

U3070n (DY13)
£13.96 Centenary of the First World War (2nd Issue)
✿ = Poppy

U3070o (DY27)
£15.50 Harry Potter

U3070p (DY29)
£17.45 Make mine Marvel

U3070q (DY32)
£16.10 Visions of the Universe

U3070r (DY35)
£19.10 Queen (rock band)
Q = Queen (rock band), Primrose Hill, London

U3071l (DY7)
£11.11 Football Heroes

U3071m (DY9)
£13.97 Classic Locomotives

U3071n (DY20)
£14.58 Windsor Castle

U3071o (DY25)
£18.69 Centenary of the RAF

U3071p (DY30)
£17.20 Birth Bicentenary of Queen Victoria
⊠ = One Penny Black
▲ = One Penny Red
■ = Two Penny Blue

U3071q (DY33)
£16.99 Behind the scenes of James Bond
✳ = Union Flag

U3071r (DY36)
£18.35 Star Trek

U3071s (DY38)
£20.25 Paul McCartney

U3071t (DY42)
£19.50 Platinum Jubilee

U3072l (DY6)
£13.77 *Doctor Who*
❖ = Tardis

U3072m (DY14)
£14.47 Bicentenary of the Battle of Waterloo

367

MACHINS — Security Machin Booklet Guide

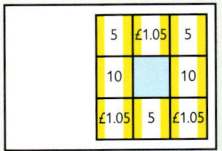

U3072n (DY19)
£15.37 The Tale of Beatrix Potter

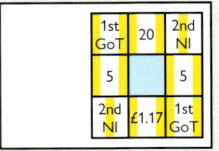

U3072o (DY24)
£13.95 Game of Thrones

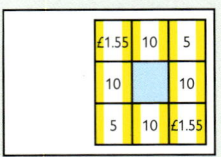

U3072p (DY28)
£13.10 Leonardo Da Vinci 500 Years

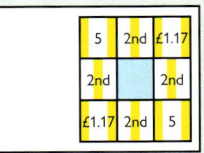

U3072q (DY31)
£17.65 Star Wars: The making of the Vehicles

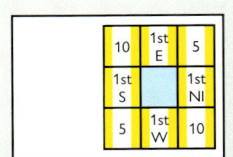

U3072r (DY32)
£16.10 Visions of the Universe

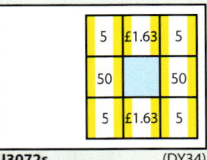

U3072s (DY34)
£19.80 75th Anniversary of the End of the Second World War

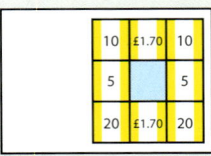

U3072t (DY39)
£18.03 Industrial Revolution

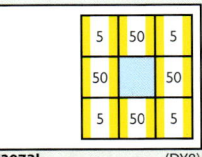

U3073l (DY8)
£11.19 Merchant Navy

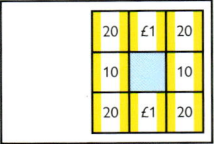

U3074l (DY10)
£11.39 Buckingham Palace

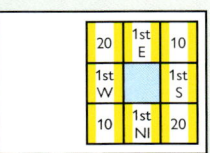

U3074m (DY11)
£11.30 Centenary of the First World War (1st Issue)

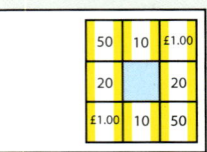

U3074n (DY41)
£20.85 Rolling Stones

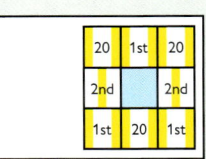

U3075l (DY37)
£21.70 Only Fools and Horses (TV sitcom, 1981-2003)

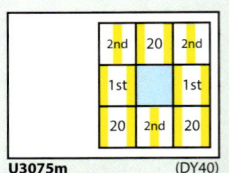

U3075m (DY40)
£21.20 DC Collection

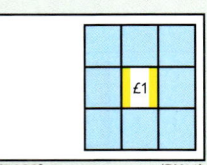

U3082l (DY11)
£11.30 Centenary of the First World War (1st Issue)

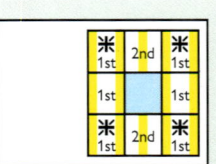

U3150l (DY15)
£16.99 The Making of Star Wars
✶ = Union Flag

U3150m (DY23)
£15.99 Star Wars: The making of the Droids, Aliens and Creatures

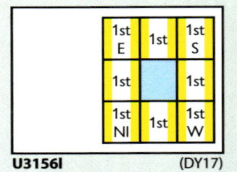

U3156l (DY17)
£15.11 90th Birthday of Queen Elizabeth II

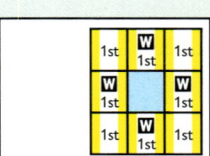

U3156m (DY26)
£15.65 The Great War 1918 (5th issue) ✿ = Poppy

U3279l (DY4)
£12.77 Diamond Jubilee
W = Wilding

368

Security Machins (Source and Year-code tables) MACHINS

The following series of tables gives details of all source and year-code combinations reported at the time of going to press. Each is related to its printer and variations in the U-shaped slits are also noted. These tables are copyright John M Deering and are reproduced with his permission.

'ROYALMAIL' printed backing paper: From early 2016 self-adhesive Security Machins appeared with a repeated undulating 'ROYALMAIL' background in two sizes of grey text printed on the front of the backing paper. Initially the two sizes of grey text were printed upright: Type PB-Up (Printed Backing Upright). In early 2017 the background was changed so that alternate pairs of lines of the repeated 'ROYALMAIL' text were inverted in relation to each other. The pairs of lines can appear with the Large lettering above the small (Type PB-Ls), or with the small above the Large (Type PB-sL). In October 2018 a fourth type appeared on some PM64 booklets. In this type the 'ROYALMAIL' background, in two sizes of grey text, is all inverted (Type PB-Inv). Where they exist these differences are noted in the following tables, and where a stamp is known with both Type PB-Ls and Type PB-sL the price noted is for the cheaper of the two, whichever that is. Type PB-Up and Type PB-Inv are noted and priced separately.

Type PB-Up

Type PB-Ls

Type PB-sL

Type PB-Inv

Denominated self-adhesive Security Machins, with source and year code (b).

(The source code is at top right, and the year code is to the left of the front of The Queen's forehead.)
(The 'U'-shaped slits are broken.)

SG No.	DESCRIPTION	
U2917	50p brownish grey, Walsall 'MPIL' ('U'-shaped slits with break at bottom only) 'MA10' (from DX50)	5·00
	50p brownish grey, Walsall 'MPIL' ('U'-shaped slits with break at top & bottom) 'MA10' (from DX50)	7·75
	50p brownish grey, Walsall 'MPIL' 'M11L' (from DY1 premium booklet)	5·25

Denominated self-adhesive Security Machins, no source code (as from counter sheets), with year code (c).

(Unless noted, front of self-adhesive backing is plain.)
(All have the year code to the left of the front of The Queen's crown.)
(The 'U'-shaped slits are broken.)

SG No.	DESCRIPTION	
U2920	1p DLR 'MAIL' (no source code) 'M12L'	50
	1p DLR 'MAIL' (no source code) 'M15L'	1·50
	1p DLR 'MAIL' (no source code) 'M16L'	50
	1p DLR 'MAIL' (no source code) 'M17L', Type PB-Ls/sL	1·50
	1p Walsall 'MAIL' (no source code) 'M18L', Type PB-sL	40
	1p Walsall 'MAIL' (no source code) 'M19L', Type PB-sL	45
	1p Walsall 'MAIL' (no source code) 'M20L', Type PB-Ls/sL	45
	1p Walsall 'MAIL' (no source code) 'M21L', Type PB-sL	45
U2921	2p DLR 'MAIL' (no source code) 'M12L'	60
	2p DLR 'MAIL' (no source code) 'M14L'	1·50
	2p DLR 'MAIL' (no source code) 'M15L'	60
	2p DLR 'MAIL' (no source code) 'M16L'	1·50
	2p DLR 'MAIL' (no source code) 'M17L'	1·50
	2p DLR 'MAIL' (no source code) 'M17L', Type PB-Ls/sL	60
	2p Walsall 'MAIL' (no source code) 'M18L', Type PB-Ls/sL	40
	2p Walsall 'MAIL' (no source code) 'M19L', Type PB-sL	45
	2p Walsall 'MAIL' (no source code) 'M20L', Type PB-Ls/sL	45
	2p Walsall 'MAIL' (no source code) 'M21L', Type PB-Ls/sL	45
U2922	5p DLR 'MAIL' (no source code) 'M12L'	60
	5p DLR 'MAIL' (no source code) 'M14L'	2·50
	5p DLR 'MAIL' (no source code) 'M15L'	2·50
	5p DLR 'MAIL' (no source code) 'M16L'	60
	5p DLR 'MAIL' (no source code) 'M17L', Type PB-Ls/sL	60
	5p Walsall 'MAIL' (no source code) 'M18L', Type PB-Ls/sL	45
	5p Walsall 'MAIL' (no source code) 'M19L', Type PB-Ls/sL	50
	5p Walsall 'MAIL' (no source code) 'M20L', Type PB-sL	50
	5p Walsall 'MAIL' (no source code) 'M21L', Type PB-Ls/sL	50
U2923	10p DLR 'MAIL' (no source code) 'M12L'	70
	10p DLR 'MAIL' (no source code) 'MA13'	1·00
	10p DLR 'MAIL' (no source code) 'M14L'	1·00
	10p DLR 'MAIL' (no source code) 'M15L'	1·25
	10p DLR 'MAIL' (no source code) 'M16L'	1·00
	10p DLR 'MAIL' (no source code) 'M17L'	4·00
	10p DLR 'MAIL' (no source code) 'M17L', Type PB-sL	70

MACHINS Security Machins (Source and Year-code tables)

SG No.	DESCRIPTION	
U2923 cont'd	10p Walsall 'MAIL' (no source code) 'M18L', Type PB-Ls/sL	65
	10p Walsall 'MAIL' (no source code) 'M19L', Type PB-Ls/sL	60
	10p Walsall 'MAIL' (no source code) 'M20L', Type PB-Ls/sL	60
	10p Walsall 'MAIL' (no source code) 'M21L', Type PB-sL	60
U2924	20p DLR 'MAIL' (no source code) 'M12L'	1·40
	20p DLR 'MAIL' (no source code) 'MA13'	1·60
	20p DLR 'MAIL' (no source code) 'M14L'	1·40
	20p DLR 'MAIL' (no source code) 'M15L'	1·25
	20p DLR 'MAIL' (no source code) 'M16L'	1·00
	20p DLR 'MAIL' (no source code) 'M17L', Type PB-Ls	80
	20p Walsall 'MAIL' (no source code) 'M18L', Type PB-Ls/sL	70
	20p Walsall 'MAIL' (no source code) 'M19L', Type PB-sL	75
	20p Walsall 'MAIL' (no source code) 'M20L', Type PB-Ls/sL	75
	20p Walsall 'MAIL' (no source code) 'M21L', Type PB-sL	75
U2925	50p slate DLR 'MAIL' (no source code) 'M12L'	2·25
	50p slate DLR 'MAIL' (no source code) 'M17L', Type PB-Ls	6·50
	50p slate Walsall 'MAIL' (no source code) 'M19L', Type PB-sL	1·75
U2926	68p DLR 'MAIL' (no source code) 'M11L'	2·25
	68p DLR 'MAIL' (no source code) 'M12L'	8·00
U2927	76p DLR 'MAIL' (no source code) 'M11L'	2·00
	76p DLR 'MAIL' (no source code) 'M12L'	7·75
U2928	78p Walsall 'MAIL' (no source code) 'M13L'	2·00
	78p DLR 'MAIL' (no source code) 'MA13'	4·00
U2929	81p DLR 'MAIL' (no source code) 'M14L'	3·75
U2930	87p DLR 'MAIL' (no source code) 'M12L'	4·25
U2931	88p Walsall 'MAIL' (no source code) 'M13L'	2·25
	88p DLR 'MAIL' (no source code) 'MA13'	4·25
U2932	97p DLR 'MAIL' (no source code) 'M14L'	2·50
U2933	£1·00 magenta, DLR 'MAIL' (no source code) 'M11L'	30·00
	£1·00 magenta, DLR 'MAIL' (no source code) 'M12L'	16·00
U2934	£1·00 bistre-brown, DLR 'MAIL' (no source code) 'M12L'	6·00
	£1·00 bistre-brown, DLR 'MAIL' (no source code) 'M14L'	4·00
	£1·00 bistre-brown, DLR 'MAIL' (no source code) 'M15L'	3·50
	£1·00 bistre-brown, DLR 'MAIL' (no source code) 'M16L'	3·25
	£1·00 bistre-brown, Walsall 'MAIL' (no source code) 'M18L' Type PB-Ls/sL	3·00
	£1·00 bistre-brown, Walsall 'MAIL' (no source code) 'M19L' Type PB-Ls/sL	3·00
	£1·00 bistre-brown, Walsall 'MAIL' (no source code) 'M21L' Type PB-sL	3·00
U2935	£1·05 DLR 'MAIL' (no source code) 'M16L'	2·75
U2936	£1·10 DLR 'MAIL' (no source code) 'M11L'	3·25
U2937	£1·17 DLR 'MAIL' (no source code) 'M17L'	3·00
	£1·17 DLR 'MAIL' (no source code) 'M17L', Type PB-Ls/sL	3·25
U2938	£1·25 Walsall 'MAIL' (no source code) 'M18L' Type PB-Ls/sL	2·75
U2939	£1·28 DLR 'MAIL' (no source code) 'M12L'	4·00
	£1·28 DLR 'MAIL' (no source code) 'MA13'	5·00
	£1·28 DLR 'MAIL' (no source code) 'M14L'	12·50
U2940	£1·33 DLR 'MAIL' (no source code) 'M15L'	2·75
	£1·33 DLR 'MAIL' (no source code) 'M16L'	4·50
U2940a	£1·35 Walsall 'MAIL' (no source code) 'M19L' Type PB-sL	3·00
U2941	£1·40 DLR 'MAIL' (no source code) 'M17L'	3·00
	£1·40 DLR 'MAIL' (no source code) 'M17L', Type PB-Ls	3·25
U2942	£1·42 Walsall 'MAIL' (no source code) 'M20L' Type PB-Ls/sL	3·00
U2943	£1·45 Walsall 'MAIL' (no source code) 'M18L' Type PB-Ls/sL	3·25

SG No.	DESCRIPTION	
U2945	£1·47 DLR 'MAIL' (no source code) 'M14L'	3·50
U2946	£1·52 DLR 'MAIL' (no source code) 'M15L'	3·00
U2947	£1·55 Walsall 'MAIL' (no source code) 'M18L' Type PB-Ls/sL	3·00
	£1·55 Walsall 'MAIL' (no source code) 'M19L' Type PB-Ls/sL	3·25
U2948	£1·57 DLR 'MAIL' (no source code) 'M17L'	3·25
	£1·57 DLR 'MAIL' (no source code) 'M17L' Type PB-Ls/sL	4·00
U2949	£1·60 Walsall 'MAIL' (no source code) 'M19L' Type PB-Ls/sL	3·00
U2949a	£1·63 Walsall 'MAIL' (no source code) 'M20L' Type PB-sL	3·00
U2950	£1·65 DLR 'MAIL' (no source code) 'M11L'	3·75
U2951	£1·68 Walsall 'MAIL' (no source code) 'M20L' Type PB-sL	3·50
U2952	£1·70 Walsall 'MAIL' (no source code) 'M21L' Type PB-Ls/sL	3·50
U2953	£1·88 Walsall 'MAIL' (no source code) 'M13L'	3·75
	£1·88 DLR 'MAIL' (no source code) 'MA13'	6·00
U2954	£1·90 DLR 'MAIL' (no source code) 'M12L'	4·00
U2955	£2·00 DLR 'MAIL' (no source code) 'MA13'	9·00
	£2·00 Walsall 'MAIL' (no source code) 'M19L' Type PB-Ls/sL	3·75
U2956	£2·15 DLR 'MAIL' (no source code) 'M14L'	4·25
U2957	£2·25 DLR 'MAIL' (no source code) 'M15L'	4·00
	£2·25 DLR 'MAIL' (no source code) 'M16L'	13·00
	£2·25 Walsall 'MAIL' (no source code) 'M18L' Type PB-Ls	3·75
U2958	£2·27 DLR 'MAIL' (no source code) 'M17L'	4·00
	£2·27 DLR 'MAIL' (no source code) 'M17L' Type PB-Ls/sL	5·25
U2959	£2·30 Walsall 'MAIL' (no source code) 'M19L' Type PB-sL	3·50
U2960	£2·42 Walsall 'MAIL' (no source code) 'M20L' Type PB-sL	3·75
U2961	£2·45 DLR 'MAIL' (no source code) 'M15L'	4·00
U2962	£2·55 DLR 'MAIL' (no source code) 'M17L'	5·00
	£2·55 DLR 'MAIL' (no source code) 'M17L' Type PB-Ls	5·75
	£2·55 Walsall 'MAIL' (no source code) 'M20L' Type PB-sL	5·00
	£2·55 Walsall 'MAIL' (no source code) 'M21L' Type PB-sL	5·00
U2963	£2·65 Walsall 'MAIL' (no source code) 'M18L' Type PB-Ls/sL	4·50
U2964	£2·80 Walsall 'MAIL' (no source code) 'M19L' Type PB-sL	4·25
U2965	£2·97 Walsall 'MAIL' (no source code) 'M20L' Type PB-sL	4·50
U2966	£3·00 Walsall 'MAIL' (no source code) 'M19L' Type PB-sL	4·75
U2968	£3·15 DLR 'MAIL' (no source code) 'M15L'	5·00
U2968a	£3·25 Walsall 'MAIL' (no source code) 'M21L' Type PB-Ls/sL	4·75
U2969	£3·30 DLR 'MAIL' (no source code) 'M15L'	5·25
U2970	£3·45 Walsall 'MAIL' (no source code) 'M19L' Type PB-sL	5·00
U2971	£3·60 Walsall 'MAIL' (no source code) 'M19L' Type PB-sL	5·25
U2972	£3·66 Walsall 'MAIL' (no source code) 'M20L' Type PB-sL	5·25
U2973	£3·82 Walsall 'MAIL' (no source code) 'M20L' Type PB-sL	5·50
U2973a	£4·20 Walsall 'MAIL' (no source code) 'M21L' Type PB-sL	6·25
U2974	£5·00 Walsall 'MAIL' (no source code) 'M19L' Type PB-sL	8·00

Security Machins (Source and Year-code tables) — MACHINS

SG No.	DESCRIPTION	
	2nd (bright blue) and 1st (as noted) self-adhesive Security Machins, no source code (as from counter sheets), with year code *(c)*.	
	(Unless noted, front of self-adhesive backing is plain.)	
	(All have the year code to the left of the front of The Queen's forehead or crown, or for the 'Large' issues from MA11 onwards it is above the 'ge' of 'Large'.)	
	(The 'U'-shaped slits are broken.)	
U2995	2nd DLR 'MAIL' (no source code) 'MA10'	6·50
	2nd DLR 'MAIL' (no source code) 'M11L'	4·50
	2nd DLR 'MAIL' (no source code) 'M12L'	2·50
	2nd DLR 'MAIL' (no source code) 'MA13'	2·50
	2nd DLR 'MAIL' (no source code) 'M14L'	2·50
	2nd DLR 'MAIL' (no source code) 'M15L'	2·50
	2nd DLR 'MAIL' (no source code) 'M16L'	2·50
	2nd DLR 'MAIL' (no source code) 'M17L'	3·00
	2nd DLR 'MAIL' (no source code) 'M17L', Type PB-Ls/sL	1·60
	2nd Walsall 'MAIL' (no source code) 'M18L', Type PB-sL	1·60
	2nd Walsall 'MAIL' (no source code) 'M19L', Type PB-sL	1·60
	2nd Walsall 'MAIL' (no source code) 'M20L', Type PB-sL	1·60
	2nd Walsall 'MAIL' (no source code) 'M21L', Type PB-Ls/sL	10·00
U2996	1st gold, DLR 'MAIL' (no source code) 'MA10'	3·75
	1st gold, DLR 'MAIL' (no source code) 'M11L'	3·50
U2997	1st vermilion, DLR 'MAIL' (no source code) 'M12L'	2·00
	1st vermilion, DLR 'MAIL' (no source code) 'MA13'	2·50
	1st vermilion, DLR 'MAIL' (no source code) 'M14L'	2·50
	1st vermilion, DLR 'MAIL' (no source code) 'M15L'	3·50
	1st vermilion, DLR 'MAIL' (no source code) 'M16L'	2·50
U2998	1st bright scarlet, DLR 'MAIL' (no source code) 'M16L', Type PB-sL	6·00
	1st bright scarlet, DLR 'MAIL' (no source code) 'M17L', Type PB-Ls/sL	1·70
	1st bright scarlet, Walsall 'MAIL' (no source code) 'M18L', Type PB-sL	2·00
	1st bright scarlet, Walsall 'MAIL' (no source code) 'M19L', Type PB-sL	2·00
	1st bright scarlet, Walsall 'MAIL' (no source code) 'M20L', Type PB-Ls/sL	2·00
	1st bright scarlet, Walsall 'MAIL' (no source code) 'M21L', Type PB-sL	2·25
U3000	2nd Large DLR 'ROYAL' (no source code) 'MA10'	9·50
	2nd Large DLR 'ROYAL' (no source code) 'MA11'	3·00
	2nd Large DLR 'ROYAL' (no source code) 'MA12'	3·00
	2nd Large DLR 'ROYAL' (no source code) 'MA13'	3·00
	2nd Large DLR 'ROYAL' (no source code) 'M14L'	2·75
	2nd Large DLR 'ROYAL' (no source code) 'M15L'	2·75
	2nd Large DLR 'ROYAL' (no source code) 'M16L'	1·90
	2nd Large DLR 'ROYAL' (no source code) 'M17L', Type PB-Ls/sL	2·75
	2nd Large Walsall 'ROYAL' (no source code) 'M18L', Type PB-sL	2·10
	2nd Large Walsall 'ROYAL' (no source code) 'M19L', Type PB-Ls/sL	2·10
	2nd Large Walsall 'ROYAL' (no source code) 'M20L', Type PB-Ls	2·10
	2nd Large Walsall 'ROYAL' (no source code) 'M21L', Type PB-Ls	2·25
U3001	1st Large, gold, DLR 'ROYAL' (no source code) 'MA10'	6·00
	1st Large, gold, DLR 'ROYAL' (no source code) 'MA11'	6·50
U3002	1st Large, vermilion, DLR 'ROYAL' (no source code) 'MA12'	3·00
	1st Large, vermilion, DLR 'ROYAL' (no source code) 'MA13'	3·50

SG No.	DESCRIPTION	
U3002 cont'd	1st Large, vermilion, DLR 'ROYAL' (no source code) 'M14L'	5·25
	1st Large, vermilion, DLR 'ROYAL' (no source code) 'M15L'	2·75
	1st Large, vermilion, DLR 'ROYAL' (no source code) 'M16L'	2·75
U3003	1st Large, bright scarlet, DLR 'ROYAL' (no source code) 'M17L', Type PB-Ls/sL	2·25
	1st Large, bright scarlet, Walsall 'ROYAL' (no source code) 'M18L', Type PB-sL	2·50
	1st Large, bright scarlet, Walsall 'ROYAL' (no source code) 'M19L', Type PB-Ls/sL	2·75
	1st Large, bright scarlet, Walsall 'ROYAL' (no source code) 'M20L', Type PB-Ls/sL	2·75
	1st Large, bright scarlet, Walsall 'ROYAL' (no source code) 'M21L', Type PB-Ls/sL	2·75

SG No.	DESCRIPTION	
	2nd (bright blue) and 1st (as noted) self-adhesive Security Machins, with source and year code *(d)*.	
	(Unless noted, the source code is at top right, the year code is to the left of the front of The Queen's forehead or crown, or for the 'Large' issues from MA11 onwards it is above the 'ge' of 'Large'.)	
	(The 'U'-shaped slits are broken.)	
U3010	2nd DLR 'MBIL' 'MA10'	6·75
	2nd DLR 'MBIL' 'M11L'	5·00
	2nd Walsall 'MBIL' 'M12L'	2·75
	2nd Walsall 'MBIL' 'M13L'	2·75
	2nd Walsall 'MBIL' 'M14L'	5·00
	2nd Walsall 'MBIL' 'M15L'	3·75
	2nd Walsall 'MBIL' 'M15L' Type PB-Up	3·75
	2nd Walsall 'MBIL' 'M16L' Type PB-Up	2·50
	2nd Walsall 'MBIL' 'M16L' Type PB-sL	2·50
	2nd Walsall 'MBIL' 'M17L' Type PB-Ls/sL	2·25
	2nd Walsall 'MBIL' 'M18L' Type PB-Ls/sL	2·00
	2nd Walsall 'MBIL' 'M19L' Type PB-Ls/sL	2·00
	2nd Walsall 'MBIL' 'M20L' Type PB-Ls/sL	2·00
	2nd Walsall 'MBIL' 'M21L' Type PB-Ls/sL	—
U3011	2nd Walsall 'MPIL' 'MA10' ('U'-shaped slits with break at bottom only) (from DX50)	4·50
	2nd Walsall 'MPIL' 'MA10' ('U'-shaped slits with break at top & bottom) (from DX50)	7·75
U3012	2nd DLR 'MRIL' 'MA10' only known USED from mail posted by bulk mailing houses. *Please note that the 2nd class stamp with these codes on ordinary gummed paper and without U-shaped slits is No. U3065.*	—
	2nd Enschedé 'MRIL' 'MA12'	5·25
	2nd Walsall 'MRIL' 'M12L'	5·25
	2nd Walsall 'MRIL' 'M15L'	4·25
U3013	2nd Walsall 'MTIL' 'MA10'	5·50
	2nd Walsall 'MTIL' 'M11L'	2·50
	2nd Walsall 'MTIL' 'M12L'	2·00
	2nd Walsall 'MTIL' 'M13L'	2·00
	2nd Walsall 'MTIL' 'M14L'	1·60
	2nd Walsall 'MTIL' 'M15L',	1·75
	2nd Walsall 'MTIL' 'M15L' Type PB-Up	8·50
	2nd Walsall 'MTIL' 'M16L' Type PB-Up	1·75

MACHINS Security Machins (Source and Year-code tables)

SG No.	DESCRIPTION	
U3013 cont'd	**2nd** Walsall 'MTIL' 'M16L', Type PB-sL	4·00
	2nd Walsall 'MTIL' 'M17L', Type PB-Ls/sL	2·00
	2nd Walsall 'MTIL' 'M18L', Type PB-Ls/sL	1·75
	2nd Walsall 'MTIL' 'M18L', Type PB-Up	5·00
	2nd Walsall 'MTIL' 'M19L', Type PB-Ls/sL	1·75
	2nd Walsall 'MTIL' 'M20L', Type PB-Ls/sL	1·75
	2nd Walsall 'MTIL' 'M21L', Type PB-Ls/sL	2·00
U3015	**1st** gold, DLR 'MBIL' 'MA10'	8·00
	1st gold, DLR 'MBIL' 'M11L'	4·50
U3016	**1st** gold, Walsall 'MCIL' 'MA10'	1·75
	1st gold, Walsall 'MCIL' 'M11L'	1·75
U3017	**1st** gold, Walsall 'MPIL' 'MA10' ('U'-shaped slits with break at bottom only) (from DX50)	2·10
	1st gold, Walsall 'MPIL' 'MA10' ('U'-shaped slits with break at top & bottom) (from DX50)	6·00
U3018	**1st** gold, DLR 'MRIL' 'MA10'	5·75
	1st gold, Enschedé 'MRIL' 'MA12'	4·75
U3019	**1st** gold, Walsall 'MSIL' 'MA10'	2·00
	1st gold, Walsall 'MSIL' 'M11L'	2·25
U3020	**1st** gold, Walsall 'MTIL' 'MA10'	4·00
	1st gold, Walsall 'MTIL' 'M11L'	2·25
	1st gold, Walsall 'MTIL' 'M12L'	6·75
U3021	**1st** vermilion, Walsall 'MBIL' 'M12L'	3·00
	1st vermilion, Walsall 'MBIL' 'M13L'	6·25
	1st vermilion, Walsall 'MBIL' 'M14L'	3·50
	1st vermilion, Walsall 'MBIL' 'M15L'	2·75
	1st vermilion, Walsall 'MBIL' 'M15L' Type PB-Up	3·75
	1st vermilion, Walsall 'MBIL' 'M16L' Type PB-Up	3·50
U3022	**1st** vermilion, Walsall 'MCIL' 'M12L'	1·90
	1st vermilion, Walsall 'MCIL' 'M13L'	1·40
	1st vermilion, Walsall 'MCIL' 'M14L'	1·40
	1st vermilion, Walsall 'MCIL' 'M15L'	1·40
U3023	**1st** vermilion, Enschedé 'MRIL' 'MA12'	3·95
	1st vermilion, 'MRIL' 'M13L'	3·00
U3024	**1st** vermilion, Walsall 'MSIL' 'M12L'	1·75
	1st vermilion, Walsall 'MSIL' 'M13L'	2·50
	1st vermilion, Walsall 'MSIL' 'M14L'	2·00
	1st vermilion, Walsall 'MSIL' 'M15L'	3·00
	1st vermilion, Walsall 'MSIL' 'M16L' Type PB-Up	2·00
U3025	**1st** vermilion, Walsall 'MTIL' 'M12L'	1·75
	1st vermilion, Walsall 'MTIL' 'M13L'	2·00
	1st vermilion, Walsall 'MTIL' 'M14L'	1·90
	1st vermilion, Walsall 'MTIL' 'M15L'	4·00
	1st vermilion, Walsall 'MTIL' 'M15L' Type PB-Up	9·00
	1st vermilion, Walsall 'MTIL' 'M16L' Type PB-Up	2·50
U3026	**1st** bright scarlet, Walsall 'MBIL' 'M16L' Type PB-Up	2·50
	1st bright scarlet, Walsall 'MBIL' 'M16L' Type PB-sL	3·50
	1st bright scarlet, Walsall 'MBIL' 'M17L' Type PB-Ls/sL	2·25
	1st bright scarlet, Walsall 'MBIL' 'M18L' Type PB-Ls/sL	2·25
	1st bright scarlet, Walsall 'MBIL' 'M19L' Type PB-Ls/sL	2·25
	1st bright scarlet, Walsall 'MBIL' 'M20L' Type PB-Ls/sL	2·25
	1st bright scarlet, Walsall 'MBIL' 'M21L' Type PB-Ls/sL	2·50
U3027	**1st** bright scarlet, Walsall 'MCIL' 'M16L' Type PB-Up	1·60
	1st bright scarlet, Walsall 'MCIL' 'M17L' Type PB-Up	1·60

SG No.	DESCRIPTION	
U3027 cont'd	**1st** bright scarlet, Walsall 'MCIL' 'M17L' Type PB-Ls/sL	1·60
	1st bright scarlet, Walsall 'MCIL' 'M18L' Type PB-Ls/sL	1·40
	1st bright scarlet, Walsall 'MCIL' 'M18L' Type PB-Inv	6·00
	1st bright scarlet, Walsall 'MCIL' 'M19L' Type PB-Ls/sL	1·40
	1st bright scarlet, Walsall 'MCIL' 'M20L' Type PB-Ls/sL	1·40
	1st bright scarlet, Walsall 'MCIL' 'M21L' Type P3-Ls/sL	1·40
U3028	**1st** bright scarlet, Walsall 'MSIL' 'M16L' Type PB-Up	2·00
	1st bright scarlet, Walsall 'MSIL' 'M16L' Type PB-Ls/sL	3·25
	1st bright scarlet, Walsall 'MSIL' 'M17L' Type PB-Up	1·90
	1st bright scarlet, Walsall 'MSIL' 'M17L' Type PB-Ls/sL	3·50
	1st bright scarlet, Walsall 'MSIL' 'M18L' Type PB-Ls/sL	2·00
	1st bright scarlet, Walsall 'MSIL' 'M18L' Type PB-Up	4·00
	1st bright scarlet, Walsall 'MSIL' 'M19L' Type PB-Ls/sL	2·00
	1st bright scarlet, Walsall 'MSIL' 'M20L' Type PB-Ls/sL	2·75
	1st bright scarlet, Walsall 'MSIL' 'M21L' Type PB-sL	4·00
U3029	**1st** bright scarlet, Walsall 'MTIL' 'M16L' Type PB-Up	2·00
	1st bright scarlet, Walsall 'MTIL' 'M16L' Type PB-Ls/sL	3·75
	1st bright scarlet, Walsall 'MTIL' 'M17L' Type PB-Ls/sL	2·00
	1st bright scarlet, Walsall 'MTIL' 'M18L' Type PB-Ls/sL	2·00
	1st bright scarlet, Walsall 'MTIL' 'M19L' Type PB-Ls/sL	2·00
	1st bright scarlet, Walsall 'MTIL' 'M20L' Type PB-Ls/sL	2·00
	1st bright scarlet, Walsall 'MTIL' 'M21L' Type PB-sL	2·25
U3031	**2nd** Large DLR 'MBI' 'MA10'	24·00
	2nd Large DLR 'BIL' 'MA11' (source code bottom right)	12·50
	2nd Large Walsall 'BIL' 'MA12' (source code bottom right) (The 'U' slits do not have breaks in them)	3·50
	2nd Large Walsall 'BIL' 'MA13' (source code bottom right)	4·25
	2nd Large Walsall 'BIL' 'MA13' (source code bottom right) (The 'U' slits do not have breaks in them)	5·00
	2nd Large Walsall 'MBIL' 'MA14' (source code in front of hair)	2·75
	2nd Large Walsall 'MBIL' 'MA15' (source code in front of hair)	4·75
	2nd Large Walsall 'MBIL' 'M16L' (not MA16) (source code in front of hair) Type PB-Up	3·25
	2nd Large Walsall 'MBIL' 'M17L' (source code in front of hair) Type PB-Ls/sL	3·00
	2nd Large Walsall 'MBIL' 'M18L' (source code in front of hair) Type PB-sL	2·75
	2nd Large Walsall 'MBIL' 'M19L' (source code in front of hair) Type PB-Ls/sL	2·75
	2nd Large Walsall 'MBIL' 'M20L' (source code in front of hair) Type PB-Ls/sL	2·75
	2nd Large Walsall 'MBIL' 'M21L' (source code in front of hair) Type PB-Ls/sL	3·00
U3032	**2nd** Large Walsall 'MFI' 'MA10'	38·00
	2nd Large Walsall 'FIL' 'MA11' (source code bottom right)	2·50
	2nd Large Walsall 'FIL' 'MA12' (source code bottom right)	3·25
	2nd Large Walsall 'FIL' 'MA13' (source code bottom right)	4·00

Security Machins (Source and Year-code tables) **MACHINS**

SG No.	DESCRIPTION	
U3032 cont'd	**2nd Large** Walsall 'MFIL' 'MA14' (source code in front of hair)	2·75
	2nd Large Walsall 'MFIL' 'MA15' (source code in front of hair)	4·75
	2nd Large Walsall 'MFIL' 'MA16L' (not MA16) (source code in front of hair) Type PB-Up	3·25
	2nd Large Walsall 'MFIL' 'MA17L' (source code in front of hair) Type PB-Ls	9·00
	2nd Large Walsall 'MFIL' 'MA18L' (source code in front of hair) Type PB-Ls/sL	8·00
	2nd Large Walsall 'MFIL' 'MA19L' (source code in front of hair) Type PB-Ls/sL	3·00
	2nd Large Walsall 'MFIL' 'MA20L' (source code in front of hair) Type PB-sL	3·00
	2nd Large Walsall 'MFIL' 'MA21L' (source code in front of hair) Type PB-sL	3·25
U3034	**1st Large**, gold, DLR 'MBI' 'MA10'	8·75
	1st Large, gold, DLR 'BIL' 'MA11' (source code bottom right)	4·50
U3035	**1st Large**, gold, Walsall 'MFI' 'MA10'	8·00
	1st Large, gold, Walsall 'FIL' 'MA11' (source code bottom right)	3·25
U3036	**1st Large**, vermilion, Walsall 'BIL' 'MA12' (source code bottom right) (The 'U' slits do not have breaks in them)	3·25
	1st Large, vermilion, Walsall 'BIL' 'MA13' (source code bottom right)	4·75
	1st Large, vermilion, Walsall 'BIL' 'MA13' (source code bottom right) (The 'U' slits do not have breaks in them)	4·75
	1st Large, vermilion, Walsall 'MBIL' 'MA14' (source code in front of hair)	3·25
	1st Large, vermilion, Walsall 'MBIL' 'MA15' (source code in front of hair)	5·00
	1st Large, vermilion, Walsall 'MBIL' 'MA15' (source code in front of hair) Type PB-Up	10·00
	1st Large, vermilion, Walsall 'MBIL' 'M16L' (not MA16) (source code in front of hair) Type PB-Up	4·00
U3037	**1st Large**, vermilion, Walsall 'FIL' 'MA12' (source code bottom right)	3·25
	1st Large, vermilion, Walsall 'FIL' 'MA13' (source code bottom right)	7·50
	1st Large, vermilion, Walsall 'MFIL' 'MA14' (source code in front of hair)	3·25
	1st Large, vermilion, Walsall 'MFIL' 'MA15' (source code in front of hair)	8·00
	1st Large, vermilion, Walsall 'MFIL' 'MA15' (source code in front of hair) Type PB-Up	8·00
	1st Large, vermilion, Walsall 'MFIL' 'M16L' (not MA16) (source code in front of hair) Type PB-Up	5·50
U3038	**1st Large**, bright scarlet, Walsall 'MBIL' 'M16L' (source code in front of hair) Type PB-Up	3·25
	1st Large, bright scarlet, Walsall 'MBIL' 'M17L' (source code in front of hair) Type PB-Ls/sL	9·00
	1st Large, bright scarlet, Walsall 'MBIL' 'M18L' (source code in front of hair) Type PB-Ls/sL	3·25
	1st Large, bright scarlet, Walsall 'MBIL' 'M19L' (source code in front of hair) Type PB-Ls/sL	3·25
	1st Large, bright scarlet, Walsall 'MBIL' 'M20L' (source code in front of hair) Type PB-Ls/sL	3·25
	1st Large, bright scarlet, Walsall 'MBIL' 'M21L' (source code in front of hair)	3·50
U3039	**1st Large**, bright scarlet, Walsall 'MFIL' 'M16L' (source code in front of hair) Type PB-Up	7·50
	1st Large, bright scarlet, Walsall 'MFIL' 'M17L' (source code in front of hair) Type PB-Ls/sL	5·25

SG No.	DESCRIPTION	
U3039 cont'd	**1st Large**, bright scarlet, Walsall 'MFIL' 'M18L' (source code in front of hair) Type PB-Ls/sL	3·25
	1st Large, bright scarlet, Walsall 'MFIL' 'M19L' (source code in front of hair) Type PB-Ls	3·25
	1st Large, bright scarlet, Walsall 'MFIL' 'M20L' (source code in front of hair) Type PB-sL	3·75
	1st Large, bright scarlet, Walsall 'MFIL' 'M21L' (source code in front of hair) Type PB-sL	3·75

Note. Where Walsall is stated as the printer, for later year codes the printer is more accurately ISP Walsall. However; being one and the same, later year codes are simply noted here as Walsall. ISP stands for 'International Security Printers' which encompasses both Cartor and Walsall.

SG No.	DESCRIPTION	

'Recorded Signed For', 'Royal Mail Signed For', and 'Special Delivery' self-adhesive Security Machins, no source code (as from counter sheets), with year code *(b)*.

(Unless noted, front of self-adhesive backing is plain.)

(Unless noted, the year code is to the left of the front of The Queen's forehead or crown.)

(The U-shaped slits are broken.)

U3047	**'Recorded Signed For' 1st** DLR 'MAIL' (no source code) 'MA10'	13·00
U3048	**'Recorded Signed For' 1st Large** DLR 'MAIL' (no source code) 'MA10'	23·00
U3049	**'Royal Mail Signed For' 1st** DLR (Note. The service name was revised in March 2013.) 'MAIL' (no source code) 'MA13'	4·50
	'Royal Mail Signed For' 1st DLR 'MAIL' (no source code) 'M15L' (not MA15)	6·00
	'Royal Mail Signed For' 1st DLR 'MAIL' (no source code) 'M16L'	6·00
	'Royal Mail Signed For' 1st DLR 'MAIL' (no source code) 'M17L' Type PB-Ls/sL	5·00
	'Royal Mail Signed For' 1st Walsall 'MAIL' (no source code) 'M19L' Type PB-sL	4·75
	'Royal Mail Signed For' 1st Walsall 'MAIL' (no source code) 'M20L' Type PB-sL	4·50
U3050	**'Royal Mail Signed For' 1st Large** DLR (Note. The service name was revised in March 2013.) 'MAIL' (no source code) 'MA13' (year code is above the 'ge' of 'Large')	5·00
	'Royal Mail Signed For' 1st Large DLR 'MAIL' (no source code) 'M15L' (not MA15) (year code is above the 'ge' of 'Large')	9·75
	'Royal Mail Signed For' 1st Large DLR 'MAIL' (no source code) 'M16L' (year code is above the 'ge' of 'Large')	9·00
	'Royal Mail Signed For' 1st Large DLR 'MAIL' (no source code) 'M17L' (year code is above the 'ge' of 'Large')	6·00
	'Royal Mail Signed For' 1st Large Walsall 'MAIL' (no source code) 'M18L' (year code is above the 'ge' of 'Large') Type PB-sL	5·00
	'Royal Mail Signed For' 1st Large Walsall 'MAIL' (no source code) 'M20L' (year code is above the 'ge' of 'Large') Type PB-Ls	5·00
U3051	**'Special Delivery up to 100g'** DLR 'MAIL' (no source code) 'MA10'	11·50
	'Special Delivery up to 100g' DLR 'MAIL' (no source code) 'M14L'	17·00
	'Special Delivery up to 100g' DLR 'MAIL' (no source code) 'M15L'	16·00
	'Special Delivery up to 100g' DLR 'MAIL' (no source code) 'M16L'	17·00
	'Special Delivery up to 100g' DLR 'MAIL' (no source code) 'M17L'	14·00

MACHINS *Security Machins (Source and Year-code tables)*

SG No.	DESCRIPTION	
U3051 *cont'd*	**'Special Delivery up to 100g'** DLR 'MAIL' (no source code) 'M17L' Type PB-Ls	15·00
	'Special Delivery up to 100g' Walsall 'MAIL' (no source code) 'M18L' Type PB-sL	15·00
	'Special Delivery up to 100g' Walsall 'MAIL' (no source code) 'M19L' Type PB-sL	15·00
	'Special Delivery up to 100g' Walsall 'MAIL' (no source code) 'M20L' Type PB-sL	11·00
U3052	**'Special Delivery up to 500g'** DLR 'MAIL' (no source code) 'MA10'	13·00
	'Special Delivery up to 500g' DLR 'MAIL' (no source code) 'M14L'	19·00
	'Special Delivery up to 500g' DLR 'MAIL' (no source code) 'M16L'	16·00
	'Special Delivery up to 500g' Walsall 'MAIL' (no source code) 'M18L' Type PB-sL	13·00
	'Special Delivery up to 500g' Walsall 'MAIL' (no source code) 'M20L' Type PB-sL	12·00

SG No.	DESCRIPTION	
	Denominated ordinary gummed (i.e. not self-adhesive) Security Machins, with source and year code *(a)*.	
	No 'U'-shaped slits. Printed gravure.	
U3060	68p Walsall 'MPIL' 'M11L' (from DY3 premium booklet)	4·00
U3061	£1·00 magenta, ISP Walsall 'MPIL' 'M17L' (from DY21 premium booklet)	23·00

Note. ISP stands for 'International Security Printers' which encompasses both Cartor and Walsall.

SG No.	DESCRIPTION	
	NVI ordinary gummed (i.e. not self-adhesive) Security Machins, with source and year code *(b)*.	
	No 'U'-shaped slits. Printed gravure.	
U3065	2nd DLR 'MRIL' 'MA10'	7·00
U3066	1st gold, DLR 'MRIL' 'MA10'	7·25
U3067	1st vermilion, ISP Walsall 'MPIL' 'M17L' (from DY21 premium booklet)	11·00

Note. ISP stands for 'International Security Printers' which encompasses both Cartor and Walsall. No. U3066 also exists from Birth Centenary of Arnold Machin miniature sheet **MS**3222, from which it has source code 'MMIL' (and 'AM11' year code), but is not separately listed. No. U3067 also exists from 50th Anniversary of the Machin Definitive miniature sheet **MS**3965, from which it has source code 'MMIL' and year code 'M17L', but is not separately listed.

SG No.	DESCRIPTION	
	Denominated ordinary gummed (i.e. not self-adhesive) Security Machins, with source and year code *(c)*.	
	No 'U'-shaped slits. Printed litho.	
U3070	1p Cartor 'MPIL' 'M13L' (from DY7 premium booklet)	1·00
	1p ISP Cartor 'MPIL' 'M14L' (from DY12 premium booklet)	1·00
	1p ISP Cartor 'MPIL' 'M15L' (from DY13 premium booklet)	1·00
	1p ISP Cartor 'MPIL' 'M18L' (from DY27 premium booket)	1·00

SG No.	DESCRIPTION	
U3070 *cont'd*	1p ISP Cartor 'MPIL' 'M19L' (from DY32 premium booklet)	1·00
	1p ISP Cartor 'MPIL' 'M20L' (from DY35 premium booklet)	75
U3070a	1p ISP Cartor 'M IL' 'M18L' i.e. source code without P (from DY29 premium booklet)	1·25
U3071	2p Cartor 'MPIL' 'M13L' (from DY7 premium booklet)	1·00
	2p Enschedé 'MPIL' 'M13L' (from DY9 premium booklet)	1·00
	2p ISP Cartor 'MPIL' 'M14L' (from DY12 premium booklet)	1·00
	2p ISP Cartor 'MPIL' 'M16L' (from DY20 premium booklet)	1·00
	2p ISP Cartor 'MPIL' 'M19L' (from DY30, DY32 and DY33 premium booklets)	1·00
	2p ISP Cartor 'MPIL' 'M20L' (from DY36 premium booklet)	85
	2p ISP Cartor 'MPIL' 'M21L' (from DY38 and DY42 premium booklets)	85
U3071a	2p ISP Cartor 'M IL' 'M18L' i.e. source code without P (from DY25 premium booklet)	1·00
U3072	5p Cartor 'MPIL' 'M12L' (from DY6 premium booklet)	1·50
	5p Cartor 'MPIL' 'M13L' (from DY7 premium booklet)	90
	5p Enschedé 'MPIL' 'M13L' (from DY9 premium booklet)	1·00
	5p ISP Cartor 'MPIL' 'M15L' (from DY14 premium booklet)	1·00
	5p ISP Cartor 'MPIL' 'M16L' (from DY19 premium booklet)	1·00
	5p ISP Cartor 'MPIL' 'M17L' (from DY24 premium booklet)	1·25
	5p ISP Cartor 'MPIL' 'M18L' (from DY28 premium booklet)	1·25
	5p ISP Cartor 'MPIL' 'M19L' (from DY31 and DY32 premium booklets)	1·00
	5p ISP Cartor 'MPIL' 'M20L' (from DY34 premium booklets)	1·10
	5p ISP Cartor 'MPIL' 'M21L' (from DY39 premium booklets)	1·10
U3072a	5p *deep red-brown*, ISP Cartor 'MPIL' 'M15L' (from DY13 premium booklet)	2·25
U3072b	5p ISP Cartor 'M IL' 'M18L' i.e. source code without P (from DY25 premium booklet)	1·25
U3073	5p Enschedé 'MPIL' 'M13L'; elliptical perforation near the top of sides of stamp (from DY8 premium booklet)	1·50
U3074	10p Cartor 'MPIL' 'M12L' (from DY6 premium booklet)	2·50
	10p Cartor 'MPIL' 'M13L' (from DY7 premium booklet)	1·25
	10p Enschedé 'MPIL' 'M14L' (from DY10 and DY11 premium booklets)	1·10
	10p ISP Cartor 'MPIL' 'M15L' (from DY14 premium booklet)	1·25
	10p ISP Cartor 'MPIL' 'M16L' (from DY19 and DY20 premium booklets)	1·10
	10p ISP Cartor 'MPIL' 'M18L' (from DY28 premium booklet)	1·25
	10p ISP Cartor 'MPIL' 'M19L' (from DY32 premium booklet)	1·25
	10p ISP Cartor 'MPIL' 'M21L' (from DY38, DY39, DY41 and DY42 premium booklets)	95
U3075	20p Cartor 'MPIL' 'M12L' (from DY6 premium booklet)	3·75
	20p Enschedé 'MPIL' 'M14L' (from DY10 and DY11 premium booklets)	1·10
	20p ISP Cartor 'MPIL' 'M17L' (from DY24 premium booklet)	2·00
	20p ISP Cartor 'MPIL' 'M18L' (from DY27 premium booklet)	1·75
	20p ISP Cartor 'MPIL' 'M20L' (from DY37 premium booklet)	1·50
	20p ISP Cartor 'MPIL' 'M21L' (from DY39, DY40 and DY41 premium bookets)	1·10
U3075a	20p ISP Cartor 'M IL' 'M18L' i.e. source code without P (from DY29 premium booklet)	1·75

Security Machins (Source and Year-code tables) — MACHINS

SG No.	DESCRIPTION	
U3076	50p slate, Enschedé 'MPIL' 'M13L'; elliptical perforation near the top of sides of stamp (from DY8 premium booklet)	2·00
U3077	50p slate, ISP Cartor 'MPIL' 'M15L' (from DY14 premium booklet)	2·00
	50p slate, ISP Cartor 'MPIL' 'M19L' (from DY30 premium booklet)	1·75
	50p slate, ISP Cartor 'MPIL' 'M20L' (from DY34 and DY36 premium booklets)	1·75
	50p slate, ISP Cartor 'MPIL' 'M21L' (from DY38, DY41 and DY42 premium booklets)	1·60
U3077a	50p grey, ISP Cartor 'MPIL' 'M18L' (from DY27 premium booklet)	2·00
U3078	76p Cartor 'MPIL' 'M11L' (from DY2 premium booklet)	9·50
U3079	81p ISP Cartor 'MPIL' 'M14L' (from DY12 premium booklet)	8·00
U3080	87p Cartor 'MPIL' 'M12L' (from DY6 premium booklet)	6·00
U3081	97p ISP Cartor 'MPIL' 'M14L' (from DY12 premium booklet)	3·75
U3082	£1·00 Enschedé 'MPIL' 'M14L' (from DY10 and DY11 premium booklets)	2·25
	£1·00 ISP Cartor 'MPIL' 'M15L' (from DY14 premium booklet)	2·25
	£1·00 ISP Cartor 'MPIL' 'M21L' (from DY41 premium booklet)	2·00
U3083	£1·05 ISP Cartor 'MPIL' 'M16L' (from DY19 and DY20 premium booklets)	2·75
U3084	£1·17 ISP Cartor 'MPIL' 'M17L' (from DY24 premium booklet)	15·00
	£1·17 ISP Cartor 'MPIL' 'M19L' (from DY31 premium booklet)	4·00
U3084a	£1·17 ISP Cartor 'M IL' 'M18L' i.e. source code without P (from DY25 premium booklet)	4·50
U3089	£1·25 ISP Cartor 'MPIL' 'M18L' (from DY27 premium booket)	2·75
U3089a	£1·25 ISP Cartor 'M IL' 'M18L' i.e. source code without P. *Light green* (from DY29 premium booklet)	2·75
U3094	£1·33 ISP Cartor 'MPIL' 'M15L' (from DY13 premium booklet)	3·00
U3096	£1·35 ISP Cartor 'MPIL' 'M19L' (from DY32 premium booklet)	4·00
U3099	£1·40 ISP Cartor 'MPIL' 'M17L' (from DY23 premium booklet)	4·00
U3104	£1·45 ISP Cartor 'M IL' 'M18L' i.e. source code without P (from DY29 premium booklet)	7·00
U3108	£1·50 ISP Cartor 'MPIL' 'M21L' (from DY42 premium booklet)	8·50
U3109	£1·55 ISP Cartor 'MPIL' 'M18L' (from DY28 premium booklet)	15·00
U3115	£1·63 ISP Cartor 'MPIL' 'M20L' (from DY34 premium booklet)	4·50
U3116	£1·70 ISP Cartor 'MPIL' 'M21L' (from DY39 premium booklet)	15·00

SG No.	DESCRIPTION	
U3156 cont'd	**1st** vermilion, ISP Cartor 'MPIL' 'M15L' (from DY15 premium booklet)	6·00
	1st vermilion, ISP Cartor 'MPIL' 'M16L' (from DY17 premium booklet)	2·50
	1st vermilion, ISP Cartor 'MPIL' 'M17L' (from DY23 premium booklet)	2·00
	1st vermilion, ISP Cartor 'MPIL' 'M18L' (from DY26 premium booklet)	2·00
U3157	**1st** bright scarlet, ISP Cartor 'MPIL' 'M16L' (from DY20 premium booklet)	2·25
	1st bright scarlet, ISP Cartor 'MPIL' 'M20L' (from DY37 premium booklet)	2·25
	1st bright scarlet, ISP Cartor 'MPIL' 'M21L' (from DY38 and DY40 premium booklets)	2·10

Note. ISP stands for 'International Security Printers' which encompasses both Cartor and Walsall.

SG No.	DESCRIPTION	

1st 'Long to Reign Over Us' self-adhesive Security Machins, no source code (as from counter sheets), with year code (a).

(All have the year code to the left of The Queen's neck, just above the front of the necklace.)

(The 'U'-shaped slits are broken.)

U3744	**1st** bright lilac, DLR 'REIGN' (no source code) 'O15R'	1·75
	1st bright lilac, DLR 'REIGN' (no source code) 'O16R'	7·25

SG No.	DESCRIPTION	

1st 'Long to Reign Over Us' self-adhesive Security Machins, with source and year code (b).

(Unless noted, front of self-adhesive backing is plain.)

(All have the source code behind the back of the Queen's hair at the bottom, the year code is to the left of The Queen's neck, just above the front of the necklace.)

(The 'U'-shaped slits are broken.)

U3745	**1st** bright lilac, ISP Walsall 'REIGS' 'O15R'	1·75
	1st bright lilac, ISP Walsall 'REIGS' 'O15R' Type PB-Up	35·00
	1st bright lilac, ISP Walsall 'REIGS' 'O16R' Type PB-Up	4·50
U3746	**1st** bright lilac, ISP Walsall 'REIGC' 'O15R'	1·60
	1st bright lilac, ISP Walsall 'REIGC' 'O16R' Type PB-Up	1·75

Note. ISP stands for 'International Security Printers' which encompasses both Cartor and Walsall.

SG No.	DESCRIPTION	

NVI ordinary gummed (i.e. not self-adhesive) Security Machins, with source and year code (d).

No 'U'-shaped slits. Printed litho.

U3150	**2nd** ISP Cartor 'MPIL' 'M15L' (from DY15 premium booklet)	4·25
	2nd ISP Cartor 'MPIL' 'M17L' (from DY23 premium booklet)	2·25
	2nd ISP Cartor 'MPIL' 'M19L' (from DY31 and DY33 premium booklets)	1·90
	2nd ISP Cartor 'MPIL' 'M20L' (from DY36 and DY37 premium booklets)	2·00
	2nd ISP Cartor 'MPIL' 'M21L' (from DY40 premium booklet)	2·00
U3155	**1st** gold, Cartor 'MPIL' 'M11L' (from DY2 premium booklet)	5·25
U3156	**1st** vermilion, Cartor 'MPIL' 'M13L' (from DY7 premium booklet)	1·75

SG No.	DESCRIPTION	

1st 'Long to Reign Over Us' ordinary gum (i.e. not self-adhesive) Security Machin, with source and year code (c).
No 'U'-shaped slits. Printed litho.

(Source code behind the back of the Queen's hair at the bottom, year code is to the left of The Queen's neck, just above the front of the necklace.)

U3747	**1st** bright lilac, ISP Cartor 'REIGP' 'O16R' (from DY17 premium booklet)	3·50

Note. ISP stands for 'International Security Printers' which encompasses both Cartor and Walsall. 1st bright lilac with ordinary gum but gravure (by FNMT Spain), with source code REIGM and year code O15R, exists from the Long to Reign Over Us miniature sheet **MS**3747, but is not separately listed.

BARCODED SECURITY MACHINS

> Please note that the 'V' numbers in this section are temporary and subject to change.

On 23 March 2021, Royal Mail piloted their first-ever barcoded postage stamp, in the form of a self-adhesive 2nd class Security Machin definitive, issued in 50×2nd class business sheets.

Replacing non-barcoded Security Machins, on 1 February 2022, 2nd and 1st class Security Machins in new colours with barcodes were introduced in retail booklets and counter sheets. The range was expanded on 28 February 2022 when business sheets of NVIs were issued. Then, barcoded versions of denominated Security Machins, some in a new design with The Queen's portrait set against a white background, with coloured borderline, were issued on 4 April 2022 in counter sheets.

Like non-barcoded Security Machins, the barcoded versions have the usual security features of U-shaped slits, an overall iridescent overprint, sometimes with source codes, year codes, and self-adhesive backing paper with 'ROYALMAIL' printed backing.

Barcoded Machins are nearly 50% larger than a traditional Machin definitive, partly due to the adjacent barcode. The main features, such as the value, iridescent overprint and U-shaped slits, are scaled up accordingly.

Unlike the non-barcoded versions, barcoded Large Letter stamps are the same size as standard letter stamps. They have the value instead placed at the top left, and at the lower left have the word Large printed sideways and reading upwards.

Each stamp's (2D) barcode (also known as a data matrix) is unique and printed alongside the stamp design's main body, and a simulated perforation line separates the two elements. The simulated perforation line and 2D barcode are printed in the same colour as the stamp. Barcode stamps are a two-process printing, the main design and simulated perforation in gravure, and each stamp's barcode is separately digitally printed. The barcode enables tracking and further helps combat counterfeiting.

> **USED STAMPS.** Because the self-adhesive stamps in this section do not include a water-soluable layer of gum, we recommend that used stamps are retained on their backing paper and trimmed with a uniform border of 1-2 mm around all sides, taking care not to cut into the perforations.

Source Codes: similarly to non-barcoded Security Machins, codes may be seen in the words 'ROYALMAIL' at the top right of the stamp.
The codes are:

2nd and 1st
MAIL		(ie without code letter) – counter sheets
MBIL	–	Business sheets
MEIL	–	standard booklets of eight
MFIL	–	standard booklets of four

2nd and 1st Large
MAIL		(ie without code letter) – counter sheets
MBIL	–	Business sheets
MFIL	–	standard booklets of four

> Note that, where stamps exist with more than one year code, the issue date given is for the first release, but prices are for the cheapest code.

'ROYALMAIL' printed backing paper. Barcoded stamps' self-adhesive backing paper has the repeating 'ROYALMAIL' wording, first introduced as an additional security measure in 2016. It is described at the beginning of the non-barcoded Security Machin section. Please refer to the Security Machin checklists for further details and illustrations of the pre-existing 'ROYALMAIL' backing Types.

Barcoded stamps from counter sheets have the 'ROYALMAIL' backing at 90 degrees to the stamp design, which brings about a new (fifth) backing Type. With the stamp design positioned upright (as a stamp is intended to be used), reading the backing from the left, the pairs of lines can appear with the Large lettering before (as opposed to over) the small (Type PB(L)-Ls), or with the small before the Large (Type PB(L)-sL). These differences are not listed in this catalogue unless the barcoded stamps themselves are different. However, their existence is noted under the sections in which they occur and in the checklists at the end of this section where the new Type is illustrated.

> Details of known source and year-code combinations, and different year code changes, are provided in the series of tables following the listings. For the convenience of collectors, the printer of each combination is also given. We are grateful to John M. Deering for compiling these tables.

3578  **3719**

(Gravure and digital ISP Walsall)

2021 (23 Mar)–**22**. Barcoded Security Machins. Design as T **3578** or T **3719**. Self-adhesive. One centre band (Nos. V4500/V4502, V4525) or two bands (others). U-shaped slits. Iridescent overprint. Die-cut perf 15×14½ with one elliptical hole in each vertical side.

(a) With source and year code.
V4500	(2nd) bright blue (MBIL) (23.3.21)	2·00	2·00
V4501	(2nd) emerald (MBIL) (28.2.22)	1·50	1·50
V4502	(2nd) emerald (MEIL) (1.2.22)	1·30	1·30
V4505	(1st) deep violet (MBIL) (28.2.22)	2·00	2·00
V4506	(1st) deep violet (MEIL) (1.2.22)	1·80	1·80
V4507	(1st) deep violet (MFIL) (1.2.22)	1·80	1·80
V4511	(2nd Large) grey-green (MBIL) (28.2.22)	2·25	2·25
V4512	(2nd Large) grey-green (MFIL) (1.2.22)	2·10	2·10
V4515	(1st Large) greenish blue (MBIL) (28.2.22)	3·00	3·00
V4516	(1st Large) greenish blue (MFIL) (1.2.22)	2·75	2·75

(b) Without source code, with yearcode.
V4525	(2nd) emerald (1.2.22)	1·10	1·10
V4526	(1st) deep violet (1.2.22)	1·60	1·60
V4527	(2nd Large) grey-green (1.2.22)	1·90	1·90
V4528	(1st Large) greenish blue (1.2.22)	2·50	2·50

No. V4500 came from business sheets of 50 stamps sold only through Royal Mail Philatelic Bureau, Edinburgh and through a volume retailer of business sheets. Philatelic customers could also purchase from the Philatelic Bureau, Edinburgh, a maximum of five loose single stamps.

Presentation packs were not made available for No. V4500.

Nos. V4500/V4502, V4505/V4507, V4511/V4512, and V4515/V4516 have backing paper with repeating 'ROYALMAIL' text, with alternate pairs of lines inverted (Type PB-Ls/sL).

Nos. V4525/V4528 have backing paper with repeating 'ROYALMAIL' text, with alternate pairs of lines inverted, at 90 degrees to the stamp design, (Type PB(L)-Ls/sL).

3720

(Gravure and digital ISP Walsall)

2022 (4 Apr). Barcoded Security Machins. Design as T **3720**. Self-adhesive. Two bands. U-shaped slits. Iridescent overprint. Die-cut perf 15×14½ (with one elliptical hole in each vertical side).

V4600	£1·85 grey-brown	2·50	2·50
V4610	£2·55 blue	3·50	3·50
V4620	£3·25 purple	4·50	4·50
V4630	£4·20 bright green	5·75	5·75

Nos. V4600, V4610, V4620, and V4630 have backing paper with repeating 'ROYALMAIL' text, with alternate pairs of lines inverted, at 90 degrees to the stamp design, (Type PB(L)-Ls/sL).

3721

(Gravure and digital ISP Walsall)

2022 (4 Apr). Barcoded Security Machins. Design as T **3721**. Self-adhesive. Two bands. U-shaped slits. Iridescent overprint. Die-cut perf 15×14½ (with one elliptical hole in each vertical side).

V4700	1p. blue	10	10
V4702	2p. deep green	10	10
V4705	5p. dull violet-blue	10	10
V4710	10p. turquoise-green	15	15

V4720	20p. bright green		30	30
V4750	50p. slate		90	90
V4780	£1 grey-brown		1·75	1·75
V4800	£2 new blue		3·00	3·00
V4820	£3 purple		4·25	4·25
V4840	£5 emerald		7·00	7·00

Nos. V4700, V4702, V4705, V4710, V4720, V4750, V4780, V4800, V4820, and V4840 have backing paper with repeating 'ROYALMAIL' text, with alternate pairs of lines inverted, at 90 degrees to the stamp design, (Type PB(L)-Ls/sL).

First Day Covers

23.3.21	No. V4500 (Type K)	4·25
23.3.21	No. V4500 (Windsor)	4·25
1.2.22	No. V4525/V4528 (Type K)	9·00
1.2.22	No. V4525/V4528 (Windsor)	9·00
4.4.22	Nos. V4600, V4610, V4620, V4630 (Type K)	17·00
4.4.22	Nos. V4600, V4610, V4620, V4630 (Windsor)	17·00
4.4.22	Nos. V4700, V4702, V4705, V4710, V4720, V4750, V4780 (Type K)	5·50
4.4.22	Nos. V4700, V4702, V4705, V4710, V4720, V4750, V4780 (Windsor)	5·50
4.4.22	Nos. V4800, V4820, V4840 (Type K)	16·00
4.4.22	Nos. V4800, V4820, V4840 (Windsor)	16·00

Presentation Packs

1.2.22	Nos. V4525/V4528 (PO Pack No. 116)	8·50
4.4.22	Nos. V4600, V4610, V4620, V4630 (PO Pack No. 117)	17·00
4.4.22	Nos. V4700, V4702, V4705, V4710, V4720, V4750, V4780 (PO Pack No. 118)	5·50
4.4.22	Nos. V4800, V4820, V4840 (PO Pack No. 119)	16·00

MACHINS Security Machins (Source and Year-code tables)

The following series of tables gives details of all source and year-code combinations reported at the time of going to press. Each is related to its printer and variations in the U-shaped slits are also noted. These tables are copyright John M Deering and are reproduced with his permission.

'ROYALMAIL' printed backing paper: Barcoded stamps from counter sheets have the 'ROYALMAIL' backing at 90 degrees to the stamp design, which brings about new backing Types. With the stamp design positioned upright (as a stamp is intended to be used), reading the backing from the left, the pairs of lines can appear with the Large lettering before (as opposed to over) the small (Type PB(L)-Ls), or with the small before the Large (Type PB(L)-sL). For further details and illustrations of the pre-existing 'ROYALMAIL' backing Types, please refer to the Security Machin checklists.

Type PB (L)-Ls

Type PB (L)-sL

SG No.	DESCRIPTION	
2nd and 1st self-adhesive Barcoded Security Machins, with source and year code (a).		
(Unless noted, the self-adhesive backing paper has repeating 'ROYALMAIL' text, with alternate pairs of lines inverted)		
(The source code is at top right, the year code is to the left of the front of The Queen's forehead or crown.)		
(The 'U'-shaped slits are broken.)		
V4500	**2nd** ISP Walsall 'MBIL' 'M21L', Type PB-Ls/sL	2·00
V4501	**2nd** ISP Walsall 'MBIL' 'M22L', Type PB-Ls/sL	1·50
V4502	**2nd** ISP Walsall 'MEIL' 'M22L', Type PB-sL	1·30
V4505	**1st** ISP Walsall 'MBIL' 'M22L', Type PB-sL	2·00
V4506	**1st** ISP Walsall 'MEIL' 'M22L', Type PB-sL	1·80
V4507	**1st** ISP Walsall 'MFIL' 'M22L', Type PB-Ls/sL	1·80
V4511	**2nd Large** ISP Walsall 'MBIL' 'M22L', Type PB-sL	2·25
V4512	**2nd Large** ISP Walsall 'MFIL' 'M22L', Type PB-Ls/sL	2·10
V4515	**1st Large** ISP Walsall 'MBIL' 'M22L', Type PB-Ls/sL	3·00
V4516	**1st Large** ISP Walsall 'MFIL' 'M22L', Type PB-sL	2·75

SG No.	DESCRIPTION	
2nd and 1st self-adhesive Barcoded Security Machins, no source code (as from counter sheets), with year code (b).		
(Unless noted, the self-adhesive backing paper has repeating 'ROYALMAIL' text, with alternate pairs of lines inverted, at 90 degrees to the stamp design.)		
(The year code is to the left of the front of The Queen's forehead or crown.)		
(The 'U'-shaped slits are broken.)		
V4525	**2nd** ISP Walsall 'MAIL' (no source code) 'M22L' Type PB(L)-Ls	1·10
V4526	**1st** ISP Walsall 'MAIL' (no source code) 'M22L' Type PB(L)-Ls/sL	1·60
V4527	**2nd Large** ISP Walsall 'MAIL' (no source code) 'M22L' Type PB(L)-Ls	1·90
V4528	**1st Large** ISP Walsall 'MAIL' (no source code) 'M22L' Type PB(L)-Ls	2·50

SG No.	DESCRIPTION	
Denominated self-adhesive Barcoded Security Machins, no source code (as from counter sheets), with year code.		
(Unless noted, the self-adhesive backing paper has repeating 'ROYALMAIL' text, with alternate pairs of lines inverted, at 90 degrees to the stamp design.)		
(The year code is to the left of the front of The Queen's forehead or crown.)		
(The 'U'-shaped slits are broken.)		
V4600	**£1.85** ISP Walsall 'MAIL' (no source code) 'M22L' Type PB(L)-Ls	2·50
V4610	**£2.55** ISP Walsall 'MAIL' (no source code) 'M22L' Type PB(L)-Ls	3·50
V4620	**£3.25** ISP Walsall 'MAIL' (no source code) 'M22L' Type PB(L)-Ls	4·50
V4630	**£3.40** ISP Walsall 'MAIL' (no source code) 'M22L' Type PB(L)-Ls	5·75

SG No.	DESCRIPTION	
Denominated self-adhesive Barcoded Security Machins, white background, no source code (as from counter sheets), with year code .		
(Unless noted, the self-adhesive backing paper has repeating 'ROYALMAIL' text, with alternate pairs of lines inverted, at 90 degrees to the stamp design.)		
(The year code is to the left of the front of The Queen's forehead or crown.)		
(The 'U'-shaped slits are broken.)		
V4700	**1p** ISP Walsall 'MAIL' (no source code) 'M22L' Type PB(L)-Ls	10
V4702	**2p** ISP Walsall 'MAIL' (no source code) 'M22L' Type PB(L)-Ls	10
V4705	**5p** ISP Walsall 'MAIL' (no source code) 'M22L' Type PB(L)-Ls	10
V4710	**10p** ISP Walsall 'MAIL' (no source code) 'M22L' Type PB(L)-Ls	15
V4720	**20p** ISP Walsall 'MAIL' (no source code) 'M22L' Type PB(L)-Ls	30
V4750	**50p** ISP Walsall 'MAIL' (no source code) 'M22L' Type PB(L)-Ls	90
V4780	**£1** ISP Walsall 'MAIL' (no source code) 'M22L' Type PB(L)-Ls	1·75
V4800	**£2** ISP Walsall 'MAIL' (no source code) 'M22L' Type PB(L)-Ls	3·00
V4820	**£3** ISP Walsall 'MAIL' (no source code) 'M22L' Type PB(L)-Ls	4·25
V4840	**£5** ISP Walsall 'MAIL' (no source code) 'M22L' Type PB(L)-Ls	7·00

ROYAL MAIL POSTAGE LABELS/ROYAL MAIL POST & GO STAMPS

ROYAL MAIL POSTAGE LABELS ('FRAMAS')

These imperforate labels were issued as an experiment by the Post Office. Special microprocessor-controlled machines were installed at post offices in Cambridge, London, Shirley (Southampton) and Windsor to provide an after-hours sales service to the public. The machines printed and dispensed the labels according to the coins inserted and the buttons operated by the customer. Values were initially available in ½p. steps to 16p. and in addition, the labels were sold at philatelic counters in two packs containing either three values (3½p., 12½p., 16p.) or 32 values (½p. to 16p.).

From 28 August 1984 the machines were adjusted to provide values up to 17p. After 31 December 1984 labels including ½p. values were withdrawn. The machines were taken out of service on 30 April 1985.

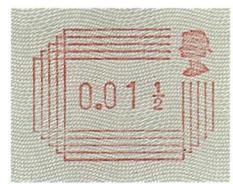

L1 *Machine postage-paid impression in red on phosphorised paper with grey-green background design. No watermark. Imperforate.*

1984 (1 May–28 Aug.)
Set of 32 (½p. to 16p.)	15·00	22·00
Set of 3 (3½p., 12½p., 16p.)	2·50	3·00
Set of 3 on First Day Cover (1.5.84)		6·50
Set of 2 (16½p., 17p.) (28.8.84)	4·00	3·00

ROYAL MAIL POST & GO STAMPS

Post & Go stamps were a new sort of postage stamp, introduced on 8 October 2008 at the Galleries post office in Bristol. The stamps are dispensed from self-service Post & Go machines which are stocked with rolls of partly-printed stamps which already have the design and background pre-printed in gravure. Once a transaction has completed the machine thermally prints a two-line service indicator (i.e. the value) and a four-part code into the stamp's background, and dispenses the finished ready-to-use stamp(s). The four-part code represents the branch in which the machine is sited, the machine number within the branch, and session and transaction numbers.

The Bristol installation followed trials of several self-service machines capable of dispensing postage labels. The Post & Go machine installed at Bristol was manufactured by Wincor Nixdorf, and dispensed postage labels as well as Post & Go stamps. Wincor Nixdorf machines were subsequently rolled out to other large post offices and remained in service until they were decommissioned in March 2015. A new series of machines, manufactured by NCR, made their appearance from 28 February 2014, dispensing Type IIA stamps (see below). From 28 February 2014 through to March 2015 both Wincor Nixdorf and NCR machines were in use within the network of post offices, but not at the same time in the same office.

In the interim, self-service on-demand Post & Go postage stamps have become commonplace, with some post offices having several machines.

Initially, and until autumn 2011 (see below, Tariff changes), five different tariff stamps were in the available range; 1st Class Up to 100g., 1st Large Up to 100g., Europe Up to 20g., Worldwide Up to 10g. and Worldwide Up to 20g.

Large and small typeface (Wincor): when the machines were first installed they were programmed to dispense five denominations and the service indicator lines were in a large size typeface (Type I), as T **FT1**. The large typeface remained current until September 2010 when the first pictorial Post & Go stamps, depicting British Birds, were released.

The larger pictorial element in the new design necessitated machines to be upgraded to print the service indicator both repositioned to the left and in a reduced size (Type II). The four-part code was also significantly reduced in size. Initially the pictorials were only available from 30 offices nationwide, and because the upgrading was phased over many months, the early pictorial issues had limited availability. The Machin design ran concurrently with the pictorials and started appearing with the smaller service indicator from 8 September 2010, when machines in London were the first to be upgraded in advance of the first pictorial issue. The smaller service indicator became the norm after all machines were upgraded.

Tariff changes: in the autumn of 2011 a new value, 'Worldwide up to 40g', was added to the range and began to appear whilst Birds (4th series) was current. The Machin design was the first to be seen with it though, having been trialled in one London office from 13 October.

Birds (4th series) appeared with 'Worldwide up to 40g' later in the year and due to the late use of earlier Birds issues they too are known with it, although it is not included in set prices for Birds, series 1 to 3.

Second class stamps were introduced to the range on 20 February 2013 but only in Special Packs, and from machines at Spring Stampex 2013. They were finally released at a postal location (a mobile 'pop-up' Christmas post shop in Newcastle-upon-Tyne) on 20 November 2013 (see below).

On 31 March 2014, the 'Worldwide up to 10g' and 'Worldwide up to 40g' stamps were withdrawn and replaced by new tariff stamps with 'Europe up to 60g' and 'Worldwide up to 60g' service indicators.

On 5 June 2014, the individual 'Europe up to 20g' and the 'Worldwide up to 10g' stamps were withdrawn and replaced with a combined tariff or 'dual value' stamp with the sevice indicator 'Euro 20g World 10g'.

On 30 March 2015 the 'Europe up to 60g' and 'Worldwide up to 60g' tariff stamps were withdrawn and replaced by 'Europe up to 100g' and 'Worldwide up to 100g' stamps.

On 1 September 2020, the 'Europe up to 100g' and 'Worldwide up to 20g' stamps were withdrawn and replaced by a second combined tariff stamp 'Euro 100g World 200g'. Simultaneously the 'Worldwide up to 100g' stamp was withdrawn and replaced by two new 'Zoned' worldwide tariff stamps: 'World up to 100g Zone 1-3' and 'World up to 100g Zone 2'.

On 1 January 2021 after a service life of only four months, both 'Zoned' stamps were withdrawn along with the original 'Euro 20g World 10g' stamp. They were replaced by the reintroduction of the 'Worldwide up to 100g' stamp and two lnew 'Large Letter' tariff stamps with service indicators 'Europe Large 100g' and 'Worldwide Large 100g'.

From 1 January 2021 following the numerous changes, the range of available values remained at six: 1st Class up to 100g, 1st Large up to 100g, Euro 100g World 20g, Worldwide up to 100g, Europe Large 100g and Worldwide Large 100g.

Worldwide up to 100g Zone 1-3: during the four months until superseded on 1 January 2021, machines sited in post offices generated the stamp 'Worldwide up to 100g Zone 1-3' using a hyphen between the 1 and the 3. The hyphen was far from satisfactory as the stamp could be misinterpreted to be also valid for Zone 2. However, post offices machines' could not be amended to replace the hyphen with anything more appropriate. Similar stamps from museums machines', which all bear inscriptions (see tables elsewhere in this listing), had the hyphen replaced by and ampersand from 18 September.

Following the introduction of the new values on 1 September 2020 and 1 January 2021 a miscellany of material is coming to light as post office stocks of older pictorial issues are gradually used up. This catalogue edition includes the material that we have verified to date, the editors welcome feedback from readers and listings will be expanded as appropriate in due course.

ROYAL MAIL POST & GO STAMPS

Special Packs: 1st stamps of the different 'Post & Go' pictorial designs are available in Special Packs from the Philatelic Bureau Edinburgh. For the Birds series these packs contained sheetlets of the six designs which were printed in gravure and had the two lines of the service indicator '1st Class' and 'up to 100g' printed much closer together (2 mm). From Farm Animals onwards the sheetlets were replaced by strips of six thermally printed from Hytech/Royal Mail Series I machines which also had the two lines of the service indicator printed closer together (3 mm). First day covers sold by the Philatelic Bureau Edinburgh use these types of stamps.

Year codes: codes first appeared on the 2012 Christmas Robin issue where there is an 'MA12' in the background to the left of the main pictorial design. The February 2013 2nd class stamps also have an MA12 year code and the year code became a standard feature from 2013.

For machin issue year code positions, see illustrations in the main listings.

Digitally-printed stamps: since November 2015 some stamp designs have been produced in single-design rolls, digitally printed instead of being printed by gravure. To date, these have been available from Post & Go machines sited at exhibitions and at The Postal Museum (see below), and at other locations that are outside the scope of this catalogue. Details may be found in the relevant tables.

Machines at exhibitions: from Spring Stampex 2011 through to and including Autumn Stampex 2017, Royal Mail sited Post & Go machines at stamp exhibitions. The machines were initially manufactured by Hytech International. Stamps from the early exhibition machines are easily identifiable from the (post offices') Wincor machine versions because the two lines of their service indicator are printed much closer together. Those from Wincor machines are spaced 4 mm apart. There are other minor differences.

Marking particular events (from autumn 2011 through to and including autumn 2017) machines at exhibitions have produced stamps with special inscriptions. Owing to their restricted availability stamps from exhibition machines with and without inscriptions are not listed separately. However, details are provided in tables following the Royal Mail Post & Go stamps listings. Machines for use at locations other than post offices have evolved. Following Hytech's version came a Royal Mail Series I machine, and from Spring Stampex 2014 the Royal Mail Series II machine was introduced.

Machines at The Postal Museum: The Postal Museum (previously The British Postal Museum & Archive, London), has two Post & Go machines permanently available. One machine is sited in the main gift shop area and the second is in the Mail Rail area. The purchase of a museum ticket is not necessary to use the machines. The machines are used by collectors to obtain material and also serve a local postal need for those preferring to buy their postage stamps there. Stamps from these machines always bear inscriptions of one sort or another. These are recorded in the tables at the end of this section.

Temporary pop-up Christmas post shops: in November 2012 a new type of post office, a temporary, pop-up, Christmas post shop, appeared in Camden, London. It had a Royal Mail Series I Post & Go machine that the public could use to buy postage stamps.

The availability of this type of machine at this sort of office resulted in the first publicly available versions from a Royal Mail Series I machine in a post office location. The olive-brown Machin and 2012 Christmas Robin designs were on sale at this post office. They differ from Wincor (Type II) versions through their code line, which consists of letters and numerals (Type III). Wincor-generated stamps have a code line entirely of numerals. Type III stamps also differ through their two service indicator lines which are printed much closer together (2.6 mm). See FS1b/FS3b, FS4b, FS5b, FS5eb, and FS51a/FS56a. The following year, in November/December 2013, the pop-up Christmas post shop evolved into a mobile version and went to several locations. It also had a Royal Mail Series I machine from which the 'new blue' (second class) Machin (FS93/FS94) and 2012 Christmas Robin designs were on sale.

Royal Mail Enquiry Offices: some Royal Mail enquiry offices had Royal Mail Series II machines installed from December 2014 through to October 2019. The machines dispensed stamps with a Type IIIA service indicator, and are given a full listing.

Unintentional use of large typeface: after upgrading machines to produce the smaller service indicator, some machines experienced software glitches resulting in the unintentional part reversion to the large typeface, or a semi corrupted version of it, and in some instances a mixture of both large and small on the same denomination. Machines at varying locations were affected and some went unchanged for several months, or were quickly amended and then simply reverted again. Such glitches seem to have continued on and off until December 2012 when all machines nationwide seemed to be functioning correctly.

There are two main types of part-reversion. The first type resulted in the 'Worldwide up to 10g' having the 'Up to 10g' in the larger typeface whilst 'Worldwide' was still in the smaller typeface (Fig. 1). At the same time and although still in the smaller typeface, the '1st Class', '1st Large' and 'Europe' were also affected by the glitch and had the service indicator lines positioned a little too far to the right. The 'Worldwide up to 20g' was similarly affected and results in the 'e' of Worldwide being printed on the pictorial design. Additionally, all five values show the (Type II) four-part code incorrectly spaced so that there is a large gap between the branch and machine number (see the four-part code on Fig. 1). The 'Worldwide up to 40g' had not been introduced at this point.

The second type of reversion is more significant and is of a complete return to the large typeface across the five original denominations, but with the 'Worldwide Up to 10g' stamp having the second line, 'Up to 10g', completely missing (Fig. 2). Note that the glitch has caused the (Type I) four-part code to be compressed.

The problems continued after the introduction of the 'Worldwide up to 40g' which when affected by the glitch caused the 'Worldwide' to be in the large typeface and the 'up to 40g' in the small typeface (Fig. 3). This is the opposite of the 'Worldwide up to 10g' from the first type of reversion.

Such reversions are outside the scope of this catalogue, but are footnoted for the interest of collectors.

Fig1 Figure 1

Figure 2

Figure 3

Incorrect design/service indicator combinations: following the introduction of 2nd Class units and stamps specifically designed for the use in them it was almost inevitable that 2nd Class designs would be found with 1st Class or International service indicators and vice-versa. These versions may have occurred because units were loaded by mistake with the wrong roll of designs. Sometimes a post office may have deemed it necessary to use an alternative design when the correct stock was not available. Irrespective of the reason for their existance, these stamps are outside the scope of this catalogue. However, for the interest of collectors, and where the provenance has been confirmed, some of them are footnoted.

Open value labels: In addition to Post & Go stamps, post offices' NCR machines dispense so-called 'Open Value' labels. Depending on the service purchased, these are generated either on non-stamp stock (a large self-adhesive label) or on the same pre-printed (Machin or pictorial) illustrated background stock as Post & Go stamps.

The labels have a thermally printed service indicator to specify the service selected, e.g. '1L' (1st Letter), '1LG' (1st Large Letter), '2SP' (2nd Small Parcel). Also printed on each label are the weight of the letter/parcel, the prevailing price of the service purchased, a VAT code and a four-part code.

Labels are generated by putting a single piece of mail onto the scales of the machine and selecting the destination and service. The labels are not designed to be taken away from the office, but are instead meant to be used straight away. With some services the process of generating the label automatically calls for the intervention of staff who apply the label and take the item away.

Such items are outside the scope of this catalogue. Note, however, that on 7 July 2014 Royal Mail released a special pack containing five 'Open Value' labels in the Machin Head design, as Types FT1 and FT14 (P&G 15) (Price £29).

Five Types of Post & Go service indicator, including subtypes of Types II and III:

FT1 (Type I)

Type I: As T **FT1**, with large, bold service indicator and four-part code consisting entirely of numerals (Wincor)

ROYAL MAIL POST & GO STAMPS

FT1a Type II

Type II: Smaller service indicator with lines 4 mm apart and code consisting entirely of numerals (Wincor)

Type IIA

Type IIA: Similar to Type II but with service indicator and code in changed typeface and ranged left with service indicator lines 3.3 mm apart and code consisting entirely of numerals (NCR)

FT1b Type III

Type III: Smaller service indicator with lines 2.6 mm apart and code consisting of letters and numerals (Royal Mail Series I).

Type IIIA

Type IIIA: As Type III, with the code being a mixture of letters and numerals and all wording ranged left. However, the top line of the service indicator is noticeably smaller and slightly further away from the second line, at 2.7 mm (Royal Mail Series II with revised typeface).

(Gravure Walsall, thermally printed service indicator)

2008 (8 Oct)–**20**. T **FT1**. Olive-brown background. Self-adhesive. Two phosphor bands. Multicoloured. Perf 14×14½.

FS1	(1st Class Up to 100g) (Type I)	9·00	9·00
	a. Type II (8.9.10)	3·25	3·25
	b. Type III (17.11.12)	10·50	10·50
	c. Type IIA (6.14)	6·50	6·50
	d. Type IIIA (3.6.15)	5·25	5·25
FS2	(1st Large Up to 100g) (Type I)	9·75	9·75
	a. Type II (8.9.10)	3·50	3·50
	b. Type III (17.11.12)	11·00	11·00
	c. Type IIA (6.14)	7·00	7·00
	d. Type IIIA (3.6.15)	5·50	5·50
FS3	(Europe Up to 20g)(Type I)	9·75	9·75
	a. Type II (8.9.10)	4·00	4·00
	b. Type III (17.11.12)	11·50	11·50
FS3c	(Euro 20g World 10g) (TIIA) (6.14)	7·00	7·00
	ca. Type II (20.10.14)	8·50	8·50
	cb. Type IIIA (3.6.15)	5·50	5·50
FS3d	(Europe up to 60g) (Type II) (31.3.14)	9·75	9·75
	dc. Type IIA (6.14)	8·50	8·50
FS3e	(Europe up to 100g) (Type IIA) (4.15)	9·75	9·75
	ea. Type IIIA (3.6.15)	8·50	8·50
FS3f	(Euro 100g World 20g) (Type IIA) (4.9.20)	13·00	13·00
FS4	(Worldwide Up to 10g) (Type I) (9.10.08)	11·00	11·00
	a. Type II (8.9.10)	6·00	6·00
	b. Type III (17.11.12)	11·50	11·50
FS5	(Worldwide Up to 20g) (Type I)	11·00	11·00
	a. Type II (8.9.10)	4·75	4·75
	b. Type III (17.11.12)	12·00	12·00
	c. Type IIA (6.14)	7·25	7·25
	d. Type IIIA (3.6.15)	6·00	6·00
FS5e	(Worldwide Up to 40g) (Type II) (13.10.11)	13·00	13·00
	eb. Type III (17.11.12)	14·00	14·00
FS5f	(Worldwide Up to 60g) (Type II) (31.3.14)	10·50	10·50
	fc. Type IIA (6.14)	9·25	9·25
FS5g	(Worldwide Up to 100g) (Type IIA) (4.15)	10·50	10·50
	ga. Type IIIA (3.6.15)	9·25	9·25
FS5h	(World 100g Zone 1-3) (Type IIA) (4.9.20)	14·00	14·00
FS5i	(World 100g Zone 2) (Type IIA) (4.9.20)	14·00	14·00
FS1/FS5	Set of 5 (Type I)	45·00	45·00
FS1a/FS3a, FS4a, FS5a, FS5e	Set of 6 (Type II)	32·00	32·00
FS1b/FS3b, FS4b, FS5b, FS5eeb	Set of 6 (Type III)	65·00	65·00
FS1c, FS2c, FS3c, FS3ddc, FS5c, FS5ffc	Set of 6 (Type IIA)	42·00	42·00
FS1d, FS2d, FS3ccb, FS3fa, FS5d, FS5gga	Set of 6 (Type IIIA)	35·00	35·00
Special Pack (As Nos. FS1/FS5 but service indicator and code lines in gravure) (Type I)		£100	

Although the very first Post & Go machines went live at the Galleries post office, Bristol, on 8 October 2008, one particular machine function had not been properly enabled and the Worldwide Up to 10g version was not available until 9 October.

The five stamps from the special pack and first day cover sold by the Philatelic Bureau, Edinburgh differ from machine-printed stamps in having the service indicator and branch code printed in gravure and have a narrow gap between the two lines of the service indicator. Also, they are easily identified through the code lines which are unique to the gravure printing: 020511 1-08445-01 (to -05).

Smaller service indicator versions similar to Type II were available from Hytech machines at Spring Stampex 2011. Subsequently, versions similar to Type II or Type III were available from exhibition machines, additionally with inscriptions. Details are provided in separate tables at the end of this section. Versions with various inscriptions have been available at the BPMA (now The Postal Museum) since December 2012.

Nos. FS1/FS5e are known printed unintentionally from Wincor machines with the typeface varieties resulting from software glitches causing a reversion to the large typeface; see notes to 'Unintentional use of large typeface'.

Nos. FS4a and FS5e were replaced on 31 March 2014 by Nos. FS3d and FS5f.

No. FS3a was replaced on 20 October 2014 by No. FS3cca.

Nos. FS3ddc and FS5ffc were replaced on in April 2015 by Nos. FS3e and FS5g.

No. FS5f was introduced on 1 September 2020 and replaced No. FS3e and FS5c. The substitution of two values by one was deliberate so as to accommodate FS5h.

Nos. FS5h and FS5i were introduced on 1 September 2020 to replace No. FS5g and to fill the space left by No. FS5c.

No. FS3c was available until 31 December 2020 (inclusive).

All Wincor machines, producing Type II stamps, were decommissioned before the 30 March 2015 tariff change.

T **FT1** (olive-brown) are known thermally printed with 2nd Class up to 100g and 2nd Large up to 100g, Type IIA, when put in a machine's second class unit. This may have occurred because it was mistakenly put in the wrong unit, or because standard second class (new blue Machin) T **FT14** stock were not available, and it was deemed necessary to use the other design instead.

No. FS3ccb exists with the 20g weight missing and is instead shown as Euro World 10g, and results from a software glitch. Only from Mount Pleasant Royal Mail enquiry office 29/31 March 2016.

> For full details of Post & Go stamps dispensed from machines at locations other than post offices and post shops, please refer to the tables following these listings.

FT2 Blue Tit

(Des Robert Gillmor and Kate Stephens. Gravure Walsall, thermally printed service indicator).

2010 (17 Sept)–**14**. Birds of Britain (1st series). Garden Birds. Self-adhesive. Two phosphor bands. Multicoloured Perf 14×14½.

FS6	(1st Class up to 100g) (Type II)	6·50	6·50
FS7	(1st Large up to 100g) (Type II)	7·00	7·00
FS8	(Europe up to 20g) (Type II)	8·50	8·50
FS8a	(Europe up to 60g) (Type II) (5.14)	80·00	80·00
FS9	(Worldwide up to 10g) (Type II)	14·00	14·00
FS10	(Worldwide up to 20g) (Type II)	10·00	10·00
FS10a	(Worldwide up to 40g) (Type II) (2.12)	40·00	40·00
FS10b	(Worldwide up to 60g) (5.14)		
	(Worldwide up to 60g) (Type II) (5.14)	80·00	80·00
FS6/FS8, FS9, FS10 Set of 5 (Type II)		40·00	40·00
First Day Cover (No. FS6 in 6 designs)			20·00
Special Pack (No. FS6 in sheetlet of 6 gravure designs) (Type II)		20·00	

381

ROYAL MAIL POST & GO STAMPS

Nos. FS6/FS10b were each available in six different designs: T **FT2**, Goldfinch, Wood Pigeon, Robin, House Sparrow and Starling.

Nos. FS6/FS10 were available from Post & Go terminals, initially in 30 post offices.

FS6/FS10 are known printed unintentionally from Wincor machines with both typeface varieties resulting from software glitches causing a reversion to the large typeface; see notes to 'Unintentional use of large typeface'.

Nos. FS8a, 10a, 10b resulted from the late use of old stock.

FT3 Blackbird

(Des Robert Gillmor and Kate Stephens. Gravure Walsall, thermally printed service indicator)

2011 (24 Jan)–**14**. Birds of Britain (2nd series). Garden Birds. Self-adhesive. Two phosphor bands. Multicoloured Perf 14×14½.

FS11	(1st class up to 100g) (Type II)	3·50	3·50
FS12	(1st Large up to 100g) (Type II)	3·75	3·75
FS13	(Europe up to 20g) (Type II)	4·25	4·25
FS13a	(Europe up to 60g) (Type II) (4.14)	20·00	20·00
FS14	(Worldwide up to 10g) (Type II)	8·50	8·50
FS15	(Worldwide up to 20g) (Type II)	4·25	4·25
FS15a	(Worldwide up to 40g) (Type II) (12.11)	20·00	20·00
FS15b	(Worldwide up to 60g) (Type II) (4.14)	20·00	20·00
FS11/FS13, FS14, FS15 Set of 5 (Type II)		20·00	20·00
First Day Cover (No. FS11 in 6 designs)			20·00
Special Pack (No. FS11 in sheetlet of 6 gravure designs) (Type II)			35·00

Nos. FS11/FS15b were each available in six different designs: T **FT3**, two Magpies, Long-tailed Tit, Chaffinch, Collared Dove and Greenfinch.

Nos. FS11/FS15a are known printed unintentionally from Wincor machines with the first type of software glitch causing a part reversion to the large typeface on Up to 10g. The issue is also known printed with the large typeface because a roll was supplied to an office yet to have its machine upgraded for the smaller service indicator. See notes to 'Unintentional use of large typeface'.

Nos. FS13a, FS15a, FS15b resulted from the late use of old stock.

FT4 Mallard

(Des Robert Gillmor and Kate Stephens. Gravure Walsall, thermally printed service indicator)

2011 (19 May)–**14**. Birds of Britain (3rd series). Water Birds. Self-adhesive. Two phosphor bands. Multicoloured. Perf 14×14½.

FS16	(1st Class up to 100g) (Type II)	2·50	2·50
FS17	(1st Large up to 100g) (Type II)	3·00	3·00
FS18	(Europe up to 20g) (Type II)	3·50	3·50
FS18a	(Europe up to 60g) (Type II) (4.14)	27·00	27·00
FS19	(Worldwide up to 10g) (Type II)	5·00	5·00
FS20	(Worldwide up to 20g) (Type II)	4·00	4·00
FS20a	(Worldwide up to 40g) (Type II) (12.11)	10·00	10·00
FS20b	(Worldwide up to 60g) (Type II) (4.14)	27·00	27·00
FS16/FS18, FS19, FS20 Set of 5 (Type II)		15·00	15·00
First Day Cover (No. FS16 in 6 designs)			8·75
Special Pack (No. FS16 in sheetlet of 6 gravure designs) (Type II)			8·00

Nos. FS16/FS20b were each available in six different designs: T **FT4**, Greylag Goose, Kingfisher, Moorhen, Mute Swan and Great Crested Grebe.

Nos. FS16/FS20 are known printed unintentionally from Wincor machines with both typeface varieties resulting from software glitches causing a reversion to the large typeface; see notes to 'Unintentional use of large typeface'.

Nos. FS18a, FS20a and FS20b resulted from the late use of old stock.

FT5 Puffin

(Des Robert Gillmor and Kate Stephens. Gravure Walsall, thermally printed service indicator)

2011 (16 Sept)–**14**. Birds of Britain (4th series). Sea Birds. Self-adhesive. Two phosphor bands. Multicoloured. Perf 14×14½.

FS21	(1st class up to 100g) (Type II)	2·25	2·25
FS22	(1st Large up to 100g) (Type II)	2·75	2·75
FS23	(Europe up to 20g) (Type II)	3·25	3·25
FS23a	(Europe up to 60g) (Type II) (31.3.14)	8·00	8·00
FS24	(Worldwide up to 10g) (Type II)	4·75	4·75
FS25	(Worldwide up to 20g) (Type II)	3·75	3·75
FS26	(Worldwide up to 40g) (Type II)	7·50	7·50
FS26a	(Worldwide up to 60g) (Type II) (31.3.14)	8·50	8·50
FS21/FS23, FS24/FS26 Set of 6 (Type II)		20·00	20·00
First Day Cover (No. FS21 in 6 designs)			7·25
Special Pack (No. FS21 in sheetlet of 6 gravure designs) (Type II)			9·00

Nos. FS21/FS26a were each available in six different designs: T **FT5**, Gannet, Oystercatcher, Ringed Plover, Cormorant and Arctic Tern.

Nos. FS21/FS25 are known printed unintentionally from Wincor machines with both typeface varieties resulting from software glitches causing a reversion to the large typeface. Additionally No. FS26 is known with the second type mixing both sizes of typeface; see notes to 'Unintentional use of large typeface'.

Nos. FS23a and FS26a resulted from the late use of old stock.

FT6 Welsh Mountain Badger Face

(Des Robert Gillmor and Kate Stephens. Gravure Walsall, thermally printed service indicator)

2012 (24 Feb)–**14**. British Farm Animals (1st series). Sheep. Self-adhesive. Two phosphor bands. Multicoloured. Perf 14×14½.

FS27	(1st Class up to 100g) (Type II)	2·75	2·75
FS28	(1st Large up to 100g) (Type II)	3·25	3·25
FS29	(Europe up to 20g) (Type II)	3·25	3·25
FS29a	(Euro 20g World 10g) (Type II) (10.14)	10·00	10·00
FS29b	(Europe up to 60g) (Type II) (31.3.14)	12·00	12·00
FS30	(Worldwide up to 10g) (Type II)	5·25	5·25
FS31	(Worldwide up to 20g) (Type II)	4·00	4·00
FS32	(Worldwide up to 40g) (Type II)	5·75	5·75
FS32b	(Worldwide up to 60g) (Type II) (31.3.14)	13·00	13·00
FS27/FS29, FS30/FS32 Set of 6 (Type II)		22·00	22·00
First Day Cover (No. FS27 in 6 designs)			8·75
Special Pack (P&G 6) (No. FS27 in strip of 6 designs) (Type II)			8·00

Nos. FS27/FS32b were each available in six different designs: T **FT6**, Dalesbred, Jacob, Suffolk, Soay, Leicester Longwool.

Nos. FS27/FS32 are known printed unintentionally from Wincor machines with the second typeface variety resulting from software glitches causing a reversion to the large typeface; see notes to 'Unintentional use of large typeface'.

Nos. FS29a, FS29b and FS32b resulted from the late use of old stock.

FT7 Berkshire

(Des Robert Gillmor and Kate Stephens. Gravure Walsall, thermally printed service indicator)

2012 (24 Apr)–**14**. British Farm Animals (2nd series). Pigs. Multicoloured. Self-adhesive. Two phosphor bands. Multicoloured. Perf 14×14½.

FS33	(1st class up to 100g) (Type II)	2·75	2·75
FS34	(1st Large up to 100g) (Type II)	3·25	3·25
FS35	(Europe up to 20g) (Type II)	3·25	3·25
FS35a	(Euro 20g World 10g) (Type II) (10.14)	8·75	8·75
FS35b	(Europe up to 60g) (Type II) (31.3.14)	13·00	13·00
FS36	(Worldwide up to 10g) (Type II)	5·25	5·25
FS37	(Worldwide up to 20g) (Type II)	4·00	4·00
FS38	(Worldwide up to 40g) (Type II)	5·75	5·75
FS38b	(Worldwide up to 60g) (Type II) (31.3.14)	13·00	13·00
FS33/FS35, FS36/FS38 Set of 6 (Type II)		22·00	22·00
First Day Cover (No. FS33 in 6 designs)			8·50
Special Pack (P&G 7) (No. FS33 in strip of 6 designs) (Type II)			8·00

Nos. FS33/FS38b were each available in six different designs: T **FT7**, Gloucestershire Old Spots, Oxford Sandy and Black, Welsh, Tamworth, British Saddleback.

ROYAL MAIL POST & GO STAMPS

Nos. FS33/FS38 are known in Type III and come from Post & Go machines used at exhibitions. Details are provided in separate tables at the end of this section.

Nos. FS33/FS38 are known printed unintentionally from Wincor machines with the second typeface variety resulting from software glitches causing a reversion to the large typeface; see notes to 'Unintentional use of large typeface'.

Nos. FS35a, FS35b and FS38b resulted from the late use of old stock.

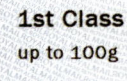

FT8 Union Flag

(Des Anton Morris and Dick Davies. Gravure Walsall, thermally printed service indicator)

2012 (21 May)–**20**. Union Flag T **FT8**. Self-adhesive. Two phosphor bands. Multicoloured Perf 14×14½.

FS39	(1st Class up to 100g) (Type II)	2·75	2·75
	a. Type IIA	3·00	3·00
FS40	(1st Large up to 100g) (Type II)	3·25	3·25
	a. Type IIA	3·25	3·25
FS41	(Europe up to 20g) (Type II)	3·50	3·50
FS41a	(Euro 20g World 10g) (Type IIA) (7.14)	3·50	3·50
	ab. Type II (10.14)	9·00	9·00
FS41b	(Europe up to 60g) (Type II) (31.3.14)	9·75	9·75
	ba. Type IIA (7.14)	11·50	11·50
FS41c	(Europe up to 100g) (Type IIA) (30.3.15)	9·50	9·50
FS41d	(Euro 100g World 20g) (Type IIA) (9.20)	13·00	13·00
FS42	(Worldwide up to 10g) (Type II)	5·25	5·25
FS43	(Worldwide up to 20g) (Type II)	4·50	4·50
	a. Type IIA (7.14)	4·50	4·50
FS44	(Worldwide up to 40g) (Type II)	6·00	6·00
FS44b	(Worldwide up to 60g) (Type II) (31.3.14)	10·50	10·50
	ba. Type IIA (7.14)	12·50	12·50
FS44c	(Worldwide up to 100g) (Type IIA) (30.3.15)	10·50	10·50
FS44d	(World 100g zone 1-3) (Type IIA) (9.20)	27·00	27·00
FS44e	(World 100g zone 2) (Type IIA) (9.20)	35·00	35·00
FS39/FS41, FS42/FS44 Set of 6 (Type II)		23·00	23·00
FS39a, FS40a, FS41a, FS41bba, FS43a, FS44bba Set of 6 (Type IIA)		35·00	35·00
First Day Cover (No. FS39 only)			2·50
Special Pack (P&G 8) (No. FS39 only) (Type IIA)			3·00

When first printed the Special Pack stamps had the upper service indicator line, 1st Class, in a slightly larger typeface and ranged left with the code line, and are therefore a Type II sub-type (Price £3·50). A reprint of the Special Packs has stamps in a smaller typeface, with all lines ranged left, and are therefore similar to Type IIA.

Nos. FS39/FS44 are known printed unintentionally from Wincor machines with the second typeface variety resulting from software glitches causing a reversion to the large typeface; see notes to 'Unintentional use of large typeface'.

T **FT8** is known thermally printed with 2nd Class up to 100g and 2nd Large up to 100g, Type IIA, when put in a machine's second class unit. This may have occurred because it was mistakenly put in the wrong unit, or because standard second class (new blue Machin) T **FT14** stock were not available, and it was deemed necessary to use the other design instead.

All Wincor machines, producing Type II stamps, were decommissioned before the 30 March 2015 tariff change.

FT9 Irish Moiled

(Des Robert Gillmor and Kate Stephens. Gravure Walsall, thermally printed service indicator)

2012 (28 Sept)–**14**. British Farm Animals (3rd series). Cattle. Self-adhesive. Two phosphor bands. Multicoloured Perf 14×14½.

FS45	(1st Class up to 100g) (Type II)	4·00	4·00
FS46	(1st Large up to 100g) (Type II)	4·75	4·75
FS47	(Europe up to 20g) (Type II)	5·00	5·00
FS47a	(Euro 20g World 10g) (Type IIA) (10.14)	10·00	10·00
FS47b	(Europe up to 60g) (Type II) (31.3.14)	12·00	12·00
FS48	(Worldwide up to 10g) (Type II)	6·00	6·00
FS49	(Worldwide up to 20g) (Type II)	5·25	5·25
FS50	(Worldwide up to 40g) (Type II)	7·00	7·00
FS50b	(Worldwide up to 60g) (Type II) (31.3.14)	13·00	13·00
FS45/FS47, FS48/FS50 Set of 6 (Type II)		29·00	29·00
First Day Cover (No. FS45 in 6 designs) (Type III)			8·50
Special Pack (P&G 9) (No. FS45 in strip of 6 designs) (Type III)			8·00

Nos. FS45/FS50b were each made available in six different designs: T **FT9**, Welsh Black, Highland, White Park, Red Poll, Aberdeen Angus.

Nos. FS45/FS50 are known in Type III and come from Post & Go machines used at exhibitions. Details are provided in separate tables at the end of this section.

Nos. FS45/FS50 are known printed unintentionally from Wincor machines with the second typeface variety resulting from software glitches causing a reversion to the large typeface; see notes to 'Unintentional use of large typeface'.

Nos. FS47a, FS47b and FS50b resulted from the late use of old stock.

FT10 Robin

(Des. Robert Gillmor and Kate Stephens. Gravure Walsall, thermally printed service indicator)

2012 (6 Nov)–**15**. Christmas Robin with year code in background. T **FT10**. Self-adhesive. Two phosphor bands. Multicoloured Perf 14×14½.

FS51	(1st Class up to 100g) (Type II)	2·75	2·75
	a. Type III (17.11.12)	4·25	4·25
	b. Type IIA (7.14)	4·50	4·50
FS52	(1st Large up to 100g) (Type II)	3·25	3·25
	a. Type III (17.11.12)	4·75	4·75
	b. Type IIA (7.14)	5·00	5·00
FS53	(Europe up to 20g) (Type II)	3·50	3·50
	a. Type III (17.11.12)	5·25	5·25
FS53c	(Euro 20g World 10g) (Type IIA) (7.14)	5·00	5·00
	ca. Type II (20.10.14)	9·00	9·00
FS53d	(Europe up to 60g) (Type II) (4.14)	10·00	10·00
	da. Type IIA (7.14)	9·00	9·00
FS53e	(Europe up to 100g) (Type IIA) (4.15)	13·00	13·00
FS54	(Worldwide up to 10g) (Type II)	4·00	4·00
	a. Type III (17.11.12)	5·25	5·25
FS55	(Worldwide up to 20g) (Type II)	4·50	4·50
	a. Type III (17.11.12)	5·50	5·50
	b. Type IIA (7.14)	5·25	5·25
FS56	(Worldwide up to 40g) (Type II)	5·75	5·75
	a. Type III (17.11.12)	6·50	6·50
FS56d	(Worldwide up to 60g) (Type II) (4.14)	11·00	11·00
	da. Type IIA (7.14)	9·75	9·75
FS56e	(Worldwide up to 100g) (Type IIA) (4.15)	14·00	14·00
FS51/FS53, FS54/FS56 Set of 6 (Type II)		22·00	22·00
FS51a/FS56a Set of 6 (Type III)		29·00	29·00
FS51b, FS52b, FS53c, FS53dda, FS55b, FS56dda Set of 6 (Type IIA)		35·00	35·00

Nos. FS51/FS56 are known printed unintentionally from Wincor machines with the second typeface variety resulting from software glitches causing a reversion to the large typeface; see notes to 'Unintentional use of large typeface'.

Nos. FS51, FS53, FS53cca, FS53d and FS56d exist with both MA12 and MA13 year codes (Type II).

Nos. FS51a/FS56a exist with both MA12 and MA13 year codes (Type III).

Nos. FS51b, FS52b, FS53c, FS53dda, FS53e, FS55b, FS56dda and FS56e exist with both MA12 and MA13 year codes (Type IIA).

Nos. FS53c, FS53d, FS56d resulted from the late use of old stock.

T **FT10** with year code MA12 and MA13 are known thermally printed with 2nd Class up to 100g and 2nd Large up to 100g, Type IIA, when put in a machine's second class unit. This may have occurred because it was mistakenly put in the wrong unit, or because standard second class (new blue Machin) T **FT14** stock was temporarily unavailable and it was deemed necessary to use alternative stock.

All Wincor machines, producing Type II stamps, were decommissioned before the 30 March 2015 tariff change.

T **FT10** was not made available in a Special Pack and was only available from Post & Go machines.

Nos. FS57 and FS58 are vacant.

FT11 Lesser Silver Water Beetle

ROYAL MAIL POST & GO STAMPS

(Des Kate Stephens. Illustrations by Chris Wormell. Gravure Walsall, thermally printed service indicator)

2013 (22 Feb)–**19**. Freshwater Life (1st series). Ponds. Self-adhesive. Two phosphor bands. Multicoloured. Perf 14×14½.

FS59	(1st Class up to 100g) (Type II)	2·25	2·25
	a. Type IIA (5.19)	4·75	3·75
FS60	(1st Large up to 100g) (Type II)	2·50	2·50
	a. Type IIA (5.19)	5·25	4·25
FS61	(Europe up to 20g) (Type II)	4·00	4·00
FS61a	(Euro 20g World 10g) (Type II) (10.14)	7·50	7·50
	ab. Type IIA (5.19)	7·50	7·50
FS61b	(Europe up to 60g) (Type II) (4.14)	9·00	9·00
FS61c	(Europe up to 100g) (Type IIA) (5.19)	30·00	30·00
FS62	(Worldwide up to 10g) (Type II)	4·00	4·00
FS63	(Worldwide up to 20g) (Type II)	4·00	4·00
	a. Type IIA (5.19)	6·00	4·75
FS64	(Worldwide up to 40g) (Type II)	5·00	5·00
FS64b	(Worldwide up to 60g) (Type II) (4.14)	9·50	9·50
FS64c	(Worldwide up to 100g) (Type IIA) (5.19)	30·00	30·00
FS59/FS61, FS62/FS64 Set of 6 (Type II)		20·00	20·00
FS59a/FS60a, FS61aab, FS61c, FS63a, FS64c Set of 6 (Type IIA)		70·00	70·00
First Day Cover (No. FS59 in 6 designs) (Type III)			9·50
Special Pack (P&G 11) (No. FS59 in strip of 6 designs) (Type III)			8·00

Nos. FS59/FS64c were each available in six different designs: T **FT11**, Three-spined Stickleback, Smooth Newt, Fairy Shrimp, Emperor Dragonfly and Glutinous Snail.

Nos. FS59/FS64 are known in Type III and come from Post & Go machines used at exhibitions. Details are provided in separate tables at the end of this section.

Nos. FS59a/FS60a, FS61aab, FS61c, FS63a, and FS64c resulted from the late use of old stock.

Nos. FS61a, FS61b, FS64b and FS64c resulted from the late use of old stock.

FT12 Perch

(Des Kate Stephens. Illustrations by Chris Wormell. Gravure Walsall, thermally printed service indicator)

2013 (25 June)–**19**. Freshwater Life (2nd series). Lakes. Self-adhesive. Two phosphor bands. Multicoloured. Perf 14×14½.

FS65	(1st Class up to 100g) (Type II)	2·75	2·75
	a. Type IIA (5.19)	3·50	3·50
FS66	(1st Large up to 100g) (Type II)	3·25	3·25
	a. Type IIA (5.19)	4·00	4·00
FS67	(Europe up to 20g) (Type II)	4·25	4·25
FS67a	(Euro 20g World 10g) (Type II) (10.14)	6·50	6·50
	ab. Type IIA (5.19)	6·50	6·50
FS67b	(Europe up to 60g) (Type II) (31.3.14)	8·25	8·25
FS67c	(Europe up to 100g) (Type IIA) (5.19)	24·00	24·00
FS68	(Worldwide up to 10g) (Type II)	4·25	4·25
FS69	(Worldwide up to 20g) (Type II)	4·25	£425
	a. Type IIA (5.19)	4·50	4·50
FS70	(Worldwide up to 40g) (Type II)	5·25	5·25
FS70b	(Worldwide up to 60g) (Type II) (31.3.14)	8·75	8·75
FS70c	(Worldwide up to 100g) (Type IIA) (5.19)	24·00	24·00
FS65/FS67, FS68/FS70 Set of 6 (Type II)		21·00	21·00
FS65a/FS66a, FS67aab, FS67c, FS69a, FS70c Set of 6 (Type IIA)		55·00	55·00
First Day Cover (No. FS65 in 6 designs) (Type III)			9·50
Special Pack (P&G 12) (No. FS65 in strip of 6 designs) (Type III)			8·00

Nos. FS65/FS70c were each available in six different designs: T **FT12**, European Eel, Crucian Carp, Caddis Fly Larva, Arctic Char and Common Toad.

Nos. FS65/FS70 are known in Type III and come from Post & Go machines used at exhibitions. Details are provided in separate tables at the end of this section.

Nos. FS65a/FS66a, FS67aab, FS67c, FS69a, and FS70c resulted from the late use of old stock.

Nos. FS67a, FS67b, and FS70b resulted from the late use of old stock.

FT13 Minnow

(Des Kate Stephens. Illustrations by Chris Wormell. Gravure Walsall, thermally printed service indicator)

2013 (20 Sept)–**19**. Freshwater Life (3rd series). Rivers. Self-adhesive. Two phosphor bands. Multicoloured. Perf 14×14½.

FS71	(1st Class up to 100g) (Type II)	2·25	2·25
	a. Type IIA (5.19)	3·50	3·50
FS72	(1st Large up to 100g) (Type II)	2·50	2·50
	a. Type IIA (5.19)	4·00	4·00
FS73	(Europe up to 20g) (Type II)	4·00	4·00
FS73a	(Euro 20g World 10g) (Type II) (10.14)	10·00	10·00
	ab. Type IIA (5.19)	6·50	6·50
FS73b	(Europe up to 60g) (Type II) (31.3.14)	7·50	7·50
FS73c	(Europe up to 100g) (Type IIA) (5.19)	24·00	24·00
FS74	(Worldwide up to 10g) (Type II)	4·00	4·00
FS75	(Worldwide up to 20g) (Type II)	4·00	4·00
	a. Type IIA (5.19)	4·50	4·50
FS76	(Worldwide up to 40g) (Type II)	5·00	5·00
FS76b	(Worldwide up to 60g) (Type II) (31.3.14)	8·00	8·00
FS76c	(Worldwide up to 100g) (Type IIA) (5.19)	24·00	24·00
FS71/FS73, FS74/FS76 Set of 6 (Type II)		20·00	20·00
FS71a/FS72a, FS73aab, FS73c, FS75a, FS76c Set of 6 (Type IIA)		55·00	55·00
First Day Cover (No. FS71 in 6 designs) (Type III)			9·50
Special Pack (P&G 13) (No. FS71 in strip of 6 designs) (Type III)			9·00

Nos. FS71/FS76c were each available in six different designs: T **FT13**, Atlantic Salmon, White-clawed Crayfish, River Lamprey, Blue-winged Olive Mayfly Larva, Brown Trout.

Nos. FS71/FS76 are known in Type III and come from Post & Go machines used at exhibitions. Details are provided in separate tables at the end of this section.

Nos. FS71a/FS72a, FS73aab, FS73c, FS75a, FS76b and FS76c resulted from the late use of old stock.

No. FS73a resulted from the late use of old stock.

(Gravure Walsall, thermally printed service indicator)

2013 (19 Nov)–**21**. T **FT1** with year code in background. Olive-brown background. Self-adhesive. Two phosphor bands. Perf 14×14½.

FS77	(1st Class up to 100g) (Type II)	3·50	3·50
	a. Type IIA (28.2.14)	2·25	2·25
	b. Type IIIA (30.3.15)	3·50	3·50

ROYAL MAIL POST & GO STAMPS

FS78	(1st Large up to 100g) (Type II)................	3·75	3·75
	a. Type IIA (28.2.14)................................	3·00	3·00
	b. Type IIIA (30.3.15)...............................	4·00	4·00
FS79	(Europe up to 20g) (Type II)......................	5·50	5·50
	a. Type IIA (28.2.14)................................	8·00	8·00
FS79b	(Euro 20g World 10g) (Type II) (20.10.14)...	8·00	8·00
	ba. Type IIA (5.6.14).................................	3·75	3·75
	bb. Type IIIA (30.3.15)..............................	4·25	4·25
FS80	(Europe up to 60g) (Type II) (31.3.14).......	6·50	6·50
	a. Type IIA (1.4.14)..................................	6·00	6·00
FS80c	(Europe up to 100g) (Type IIA) (30.3.15)...	4·00	4·00
	ca. Type IIIA (30.3.15)..............................	5·50	5·50
FS80d	(Euro 100g World 20g) (Type IIA) (1.9.20)...	3·75	3·75
FS80e	(Europe Large 100g) (Type IIA) (2.1.21).	9·50	9·50
FS81	(Worldwide up to 10g) (Type II)..............	—	—
	a. Type IIA (28.2.14)................................	—	—
FS82	(Worldwide up to 20g) (Type II)..............	5·00	5·00
	a. Type IIA (28.2.14)................................	3·75	3·75
	b. Type IIIA (30.3.15)...............................	4·75	4·75
FS83	(Worldwide up to 40g) (Type II)..............	—	—
	a. Type IIA (28.2.14)................................	—	—
FS84	(Worldwide up to 60g) (Type II) (31.3.14)...	7·50	7·50
	a. Type IIA (1.4.14)..................................	7·00	7·00
FS84c	(Worldwide up to 100g) (Type IIA) (30.3.15)...	4·75	4·75
	ca. Type IIIA (30.3.15)..............................	6·75	6·75
FS84d	(World 100g zone 1 & 3) (Type IIA) (1.9.20)...	9·75	9·75
FS84e	(World 100g zone 2) (Type IIA) (1.9.20).	9·75	9·75
FS84f	(Worldwide Large 100g) (Type IIA) (2.1.21)...	10·50	10·50
FS77/FS80, FS82, FS84 Set of 6 (Type II)..................		20·00	20·00
FS77a, FS78a, FS79ba, FS80c, FS82a, FS84c Set of 6 (Type IIA)...		20·00	20·00
FS77b, FS78b, FS79bbb, FS80cca, FS82b, FS84cca Set of 6 (Type IIIA)..		25·00	25·00

From FS77 onwards all Post & Go stamps incorporate a year code unless otherwise stated.

Year codes in the format of MA** are positioned to the left of the front of the Queen's forehead. Year codes in the format of R**Y are positioned further to the left of the design, approximately half way between the left edge of the stamp and the Queen's nose.

For full details of the different year codes, the values, the types and periods of use associated with these issues, please refer to the separate table at the end of this section.

Nos. FS81 and FS83 were replaced on 31 March 2014 by Nos. FS80 and FS84.
Nos. FS81a and FS83a were replaced on 1 April 2014 by Nos. FS80a and FS84a.
No. FS79a was replaced on 5 June 2014 by No. FS79bba.
No. FS79 was replaced on 20 October 2014 by No. FS79b.
Nos. FS80a and FS84a were replaced on 30 March 2015 by Nos. FS80c and FS84c.
No. FS80d was introduced on 1 September 2020 and replaced Nos. FS80c and FS82a. The substitution of the two values by one was deliberate so as to accommodate FS84d.
Nos. FS84d and FS84e were introduced on 1 September 2020 to replace No. FS84a and to fill the space left by No. FS82a.
No. FS79bba was available until 31 December 2020 (inclusive).
No. FS80c was reinstated on 1 January 2021, filling the space left by No. FS79bba.
Nos. FS80e and FS84f were introduced on 1 January 2021 to replace Nos. FS84d and FS84e.
All Wincor machines, producing Type II stamps, were decommissioned before the 30 March 2015 tariff change.
T **FT1** (olive-brown) with year code MA13, MA14, MA15, MA16, R17Y and R18Y are known thermally printed with 2nd Class up to 100g and 2nd Large up to 100g, Type IIA, when put in a machine's second class unit. Similarly, T **FT1** MA15, Type IIIA are known from Kingston enquiry office. This may have occurred because it was mistakenly put in the wrong unit, or because standard second class (new blue Machin) T **FT14** stock was temporarily unavailable and it was deemed necessary to use alternative stock.
No. FS79bbb exists with the 20g weight missing and is instead shown as Euro World 10g, and results from a software glitch. Only from Bradford Royal Mail enquiry office 29/31 March 2016.
T **FT1** (olive-brown) with year code was not made available in a Special Pack and is only available from Post & Go machines.

(Gravure Walsall, thermally printed service indicator)

2013 (17 Nov)–**16**. Union Flag T **FT8** with year code in background. Multicoloured. Self-adhesive. Two phosphor bands. Perf 14×14½.

FS85	(1st Class up to 100g) (Type II)................		
	a. Type IIA (10.8.16)................................	4·00	4·00
FS86	(1st Large up to 100g) (Type II)................		
	a. Type IIA (10.8.16)................................	4·25	4·25
FS87	(Europe up to 20g) (Type II)......................	—	—
FS87a	(Euro 20g World 10g) (Type IIA) (10.8.16)...	4·50	4·50
FS88	(Europe up to 60g) (Type II) (31.3.14).......	20·00	20·00
FS88a	(Europe up to 100g) (Type IIA) (10.8.16)...	5·50	5·50
FS89	(Worldwide up to 10g) (Type II)..............	—	—
FS90	(Worldwide up to 20g) (Type II)..............	—	—
	a. Type IIA (10.8.16)................................	4·75	4·75
FS91	(Worldwide up to 40g) (Type II)..............	—	—
FS92	(Worldwide up to 60g) (Type II) (31.3.14)...	21·00	21·00
FS92a	(Worldwide up to 100g) (Type IIA) (10.8.16)...	6·75	6·75
FS85/FS87, FS89/FS91 Set of 6 (Type II)..................		—	—
FS85a, FS86a, FS87a, FS88a, FS90a, FS92a Set of 6 (Type IIA)...		27·00	27·00

Nos. FS85/FS92a are MA13.
Nos. FS85, FS86, FS87, and FS90 are known from the Ludgate Circus post office in late 2013, and from Harrogate and Dorchester post offices following the 31 March 2014 tariff change.
Nos. FS89 and FS91 are only known from Ludgate Circus post office in late 2013.
(Worldwide up to 10g) and (Worldwide up to 40g) were replaced on 31 March 2014 by (Europe up to 60g) and (Worldwide up to 60g).
All Wincor machines, producing Type II stamps, were decommissioned before the 30 March 2015 tariff change.
T **FT8** with year code in background is known thermally printed with 2nd Class up to 100g and 2nd Large up to 100g, Type IIA, when put in a machine's second class unit. This may have occurred because it was mistakenly put in the wrong unit, or because standard second class (new blue Machin) T **FT14** stock was temporarily unavailable and it was deemed necessary to use alternative stock.
FT8 with year code was not made available in a Special Pack and was only available from Post & Go machines.

FT14

(Gravure Walsall, thermally printed service indicator)

2013 (20 Nov)–**15**. T **FT14** with background text reading 'ROYALMAIL' in alternate lines of large and small lettering with year code in background. New blue background. Self-adhesive. One phosphor band (over the Queen's head). Perf 14×14½.

FS93	(2nd Class up to 100g) (Type III).............	3·50	3·50
	a. Type IIA (2.14)....................................	2·50	2·50
	b. Type IIIA (30.3.15)...............................	3·50	3·50
FS94	(2nd Large up to 100g) (Type III)............	4·00	4·00
	a. Type IIA (2.14)....................................	2·75	2·75
	b. Type IIIA (30.3.15)...............................	3·75	3·75
Special Pack (P&G 10) (As Nos. FS93/FS94 but weight line inset at left) (Type III)..................................		10·00	

Post & Go stamps as T **FT14** were issued by the Philatelic Bureau, Edinburgh on 20 February 2013 in packs and on first day covers (price £7·00 per pack and £3·00 on first day cover). They were sold from Royal Mail Series I machines at Spring Stampex 2013 but were not made available through post offices until November 2013.
Nos. FS93/FS94 exist MA12 from Special Pack and Spring Stampex 2013, and MA12/MA13 from Christmas post shop.
Nos. FS93a/FS94a exist MA12, MA13, MA14 and MA15 (Type IIA)
Nos. FS93b/FS94b are MA12 and MA15 (Type IIIA)

ROYAL MAIL POST & GO STAMPS

T **FT14** with year code MA12 is known thermally printed with 1st Class up to 100g, 1st Class Large up to 100g, Euro 20g World 10g, Europe up to 60g, Worldwide up to 20g and Worldwide up to 60g, Type IIA, when mistakenly put in machine's first class unit.

T **FT14** with year code MA14 and MA15 are known thermally printed with 1st Class up to 100g, 1st Class Large up to 100g, Euro 20g World 10g, Europe up to 100g, Worldwide up to 20g and Worldwide up to 100g, Type IIA, when mistakenly put in machine's first class unit.

For the 2nd Class Machin design with the background text reading '2ndCLASS' in large lettering, alternating with 'ROYALMAIL' in small lettering, see Nos. FS157/FS158.

FT15 Primrose

(Des Kate Stephens. Illustrations by Julia Trickey. Gravure ISP Walsall, thermally printed service indicator)

2014 (19 Feb)–**15**. British Flora (1st series). Spring Blooms. Self-adhesive. Two phosphor bands. Multicoloured. Perf 14×14½.

FS95	(1st Class up to 100g) (Type II)	4·50	4·50
	a. Type IIA (5.14)	4·50	4·50
FS96	(1st Large up to 100g) (Type II)	5·25	5·25
	a. Type IIA (5.14)	5·25	5·25
FS97	(Europe up to 20g) (Type II)	5·50	5·50
	a. Type IIA (5.14)	15·00	15·00
FS97b	(Euro 20g World 10g) (Type IIA) (5.6.14)	6·00	6·00
	ba. Type II (10.14)	8·50	8·50
FS98	(Europe up to 60g) (Type II) (31.3.14)	10·00	10·00
	a. Type IIA (5.14)	7·50	7·50
FS98b	(Europe up to 100g) (Type IIA) (30.3.15)	11·50	11·50
FS99	(Worldwide up to 10g) (Type II)	6·50	6·50
FS100	(Worldwide up to 20g) (Type II)	5·75	5·75
	a. Type IIA (5.14)	5·75	5·75
FS101	(Worldwide up to 40g) (Type II)	7·50	7·50
FS102	(Worldwide up to 60g) (Type II) (31.3.14)	11·00	11·00
	a. Type IIA (5.14)	8·50	8·50
FS102b	(Worldwide up to 100g) (Type IIA) (30.3.15)	12·50	12·50
FS95/FS97 and FS99/FS101 Set of 6 (Type II)		32·00	32·00
FS95a, FS96a, FS97b, FS98a, FS100a, FS102a Set of 6 (Type IIA)		35·00	35·00
First Day Cover (No. FS95 in 6 designs) (Type II)			9·50
Special Pack (P&G 14) (No. FS95 in strip of 6 designs) (Type II)		8·00	

Nos. FS95/FS102b were each available in six different designs: T **FT15**, Snowdrop, Lesser Celandine, Dog Violet, Wild Daffodil, Blackthorn.

Nos. FS95/FS102b have year code MA14.

There was a late reprint of the Special Packs containing Type IIIA stamps (Price £20).

Nos. FS95/FS97, FS99/FS101 are known in Type III and come from Post & Go machines used at exhibitions. Details are provided in separate tables at the end of this section.

No. FS97a was replaced on 5 June 2014 by No. FS97b.

Nos. FS98b and FS102b resulted from the late use of old stock.

All Wincor machines, producing Type II stamps, were decommissioned before the 30 March 2015 tariff change.

FT16 Forget-me-not

(Des Kate Stephens. Illustrations by Julia Trickey. Gravure ISP Walsall, thermally printed service indicator)

2014 (17 Sept)–**21**. British Flora (2nd series). Symbolic Flowers. Self-adhesive. Two phosphor bands. Multicoloured Perf 14×14½.

FS103	(1st Class up to 100g) (Type IIA)	3·00	3·00
	a. Type II (17.9.14)	5·25	5·25
FS104	(1st Large up to 100g) (Type IIA)	3·25	3·25
	a. Type II (17.9.14)	5·50	5·50
FS104b	Europe up to 20g (Type II) (17.9.14)	25·00	25·00
FS105	(Euro 20g World 10g) (Type IIA)	3·50	3·50
	a. Type II (20.10.14)	9·25	9·25
FS106	(Europe up to 60g) (Type IIA)	6·75	6·75
	a. Type II (17.9.14)	6·75	6·75
FS106b	(Europe up to 100g) (Type IIA) (30.3.15)	10·00	10·00
FS106c	(Euro 100g World 20g) (Type IIA) (9.20)	4·50	4·50
FS106d	(Europe Large 100g) (Type IIA) (1.21)	10·00	10·00
FS107	(Worldwide up to 20g) (Type IIA)	4·50	4·50
	a. Type II (17.9.14)	6·00	6·00
FS108	(Worldwide up to 60g) (Type IIA)	7·25	7·25
	a. Type II (17.9.14)	7·25	7·25
FS108b	(Worldwide up to 100g) (Type IIA) (30.3.15)	11·00	11·00
FS108c	(World 100g zone 1 & 3) (Type IIA) (9.20)	14·50	14·50
FS108d	(World 100g zone 2) (Type IIA) (9.20)	17·50	17·50
FS108e	(Worldwide Large 100g) (Type IIA) (1.21)	11·00	11·00
FS103/FS104, FS105/FS106, FS107/FS108 Set of 6 (Type IIA)		26·00	26·00
FS103a/FS104a, FS104b, FS106a, FS107a, FS108a Set of 6 (Type II)		50·00	50·00
First Day Cover (No. FS103 in 6 designs) (Type IIIA)			9·50
Special Pack (P&G 16) (No. FS103 in strip of 6 designs) (Type IIIA)		8·00	

Nos. FS103/FS108e were each available in six different designs (all with year code MA14): T **FT16**, Common Poppy, Dog Rose, Spear Thistle, Heather and Cultivated Flax.

Nos. FS103/FS108 are known in Type IIIA and come from Post & Go machines used at exhibitions. Details are provided in separate tables at the end of this section.

No. FS104b was replaced on 20 October 2014 by No. FS105a.

Nos. FS106 and FS108 were replaced on 30 March 2015 by Nos. FS106b and FS108b.

Wincor machines, producing Type II stamps, were decommissioned before the 30 March 2015 tariff change.

In the run-up to Remembrance Sunday 2014, the Common Poppy design was made available on 21 October 2014 from single-design rolls for use in post offices and other locations for a limited period after that. When distributed to post offices in 2014 the single-design roll stock had year code MA14. Nos. FS103/FS108 (Type IIA) and Nos. FS103a/FS108a (Type II) exist in this form.

In subsequent years the Common Poppy from single-design rolls has been re-issued and usually only available for a limited period. It was available in post offices from 19 October 2015, 24 October 2016, 24 October 2017 and 23 October 2018. It does not appear that stock was automatically distributed in 2019/2020 with only some offices having it available from different day. The availability of Common Poppy is not limited to October/November as post offices may use it at any time of year.

The Common Poppy design in FS103/FS105, FS106b, FS07 and FS108b have year codes MA14, MA15, MA16, R17Y and R18Y.

There was a reprint of the Common Poppy in 2019 with R19Y, but this stock was not supplied to post offices but instead went to The National Museum Royal Navy for use in their machine, which only dispensed stamps with an inscription. Details are provided in tables at the end of this section. See also FS137/FS142 which are Type IIIA also for single-design rolls.

Nos. FS106c, FS106d, FS108c/FS108e only exist on Common Poppy from single-design rolls. They have year codes R17Y or R18Y.

T **FT16**, Common Poppy, Dog Rose, Spear Thistle, Heather and Cultivated Flax are each known thermally printed with 2nd Class up to 100g and 2nd Large up to 100g, Type IIA, when put in a machine's second class unit. This may have occurred because they were mistakenly put in the wrong unit, or because standard second class (new blue Machin) T **FT14** stock were not available, and it was deemed necessary to use the other design instead.

Single-design rolls of the Common Poppy, code MA14, MA15, MA16, R17Y, and R18Y are known thermally printed with 2nd Class up to 100g and 2nd Large up to 100g, Type IIA, when put in a machine's second class unit. This may have occurred because they were mistakenly put in the wrong unit, or because standard second class (new blue Machin) T **FT14** stock were not available, and it was deemed necessary to use the other design instead.

FT17 Common Ivy

(Des Kate Stephens. Illustrations by Julia Trickey. Gravure ISP Walsall, thermally printed service indicator)

2014 (13 Nov)–**15**. British Flora (3rd series). Winter Greenery. Blue background with one phosphor band at right (Nos. FS109/FS109b and FS110/FS110b) or olive-brown background with two phosphor bands (others). Self-adhesive. Multicoloured Perf 14×14½.

FS109	(2nd Class up to 100g) (Type IIA)	3·50	3·50
	b. Type IIIA (3.12.14)	4·50	4·50
FS110	(2nd Large up to 100g) (Type IIA)	4·00	4·00

FS111	b. Type IIIA (3.12.14)	5·00	5·00
	(1st Class up to 100g) (Type IIA)	3·50	3·50
	a. Type II (13.11.14)	7·25	7·25
FS112	b. Type IIIA (3.12.14)	4·75	4·75
	(1st Large up to 100g) (Type IIA)	4·00	4·00
	a. Type II (13.11.14)	7·50	7·50
FS113	b. Type IIIA (3.12.14)	5·25	5·25
	(Euro 20g World 10g) (Type IIA)	4·00	4·00
	a. Type II (13.11.14)	7·75	7·75
	b. Type IIIA (3.12.14)	5·50	5·50
FS113c	(Europe up to 20g) (Type II) (12.14)	25·00	25·00
FS114	(Europe up to 60g) (Type IIA)	4·50	4·50
	a. Type II (13.11.14)	8·25	8·25
	b. Type IIIA (3.12.14)	6·00	6·00
FS114c	(Europe up to 100g) (Type IIA) (5.15)	10·00	10·00
FS115	(Worldwide up to 20g) (Type IIA)	4·25	4·25
	a. Type II (13.11.14)	8·00	8·00
	b. Type IIIA (3.12.14)	5·75	5·75
FS116	(Worldwide up to 60g) (Type IIA)	5·75	5·75
	a. Type II (13.11.14)	9·00	9·00
	b. Type IIIA (3.12.14)	6·75	6·75
FS116c	(Worldwide up to 100g) (Type IIA) (5.15)	11·00	11·00
FS109/FS113, FS114, FS115, FS116 Set of 8 (Type IIA)		30·00	30·00
FS111a/FS113a, FS114a, FS115a, FS116a Set of 6 (Type II)		45·00	45·00
FS109b/FS113b, FS114b, FS115b, FS116b Set of 8 (Type IIIA)		40·00	40·00
First Day Cover (Nos. FS109b/FS112b; 4 designs) (Type IIIA)			9·50
Special Pack (P&G 17) (Nos. FS109b/FS112b; 4 designs as two pairs) (Type IIIA)			7·00

Nos. FS109/FS109b and FS110/FS110b were each available in two different designs: T **FT17** and Mistletoe.

Nos. FS111/FS111b through to No. FS116c were each available in two different designs: Butcher's Broom and Holly.

No. FS109 through to No. FS116c have year code MA14.

Defining their intended second class status, T **FT17** and Mistletoe have repeating background 'ROYALMAIL' wording in blue and a single phosphor band placed at the right-hand side.

The Special Pack stamps are Nos. FS109b T **FT17**; No. FS110b Mistletoe; No. FS111b Butcher's Broom, and No. FS112b Holly.

No. FS113c only came from a single Wincor machine in Keighley during December 2014.

Nos. FS109b/FS116b came from Royal Mail Series II machines situated at Royal Mail enquiry offices, and the stamps are easily identified by the code being a mixture of letters and numerals.

All Wincor machines, producing Type II stamps, were decommissioned before the 30 March 2015 tariff change.

T **FT17** and Mistletoe are also each known thermally printed with 1st Class up to 100g, 1st Class Large up to 100g, Euro 20g World 10g, Europe up to 60g, Worldwide up to 20g and Worldwide up to 60g, Type II, having been mistakenly sent to post offices using Wincor machines. Wincor machines did not dispense 2nd Class and 2nd Large.

Butcher's Broom and Holly are each known thermally printed with 2nd Class up to 100g and 2nd Large up to 100g, Type IIA, when put in a machine's second class unit. This may have occurred because they were mistakenly put in the wrong unit, or because T **FT17** and Mistletoe or standard second class (new blue Machin) T **FT14** stock were not available, and it was deemed necessary to use the other design instead.

For T **FT17** and the Mistletoe design with the blue background text reading '2ndCLASS' in large lettering, alternating with 'ROYALMAIL' in small lettering, see Nos. FS191/FS191a and FS192/FS192a.

For Butcher's Broom and Holly with the background text in greenish grey, see Nos. FS193/FS193a and FS198/FS198a.

FT18 Falcon

(Des Osborne Ross. Gravure ISP Walsall, thermally printed service indicator)

2015 (18 Feb–30 Mar). Working Sail. Self-adhesive. Two phosphor bands. Multicoloured. Perf 14×14½.

FS117	(1st Class up to 100g) (Type IIA)	3·75	3·75
FS118	(1st Large up to 100g) (Type IIA)	4·25	4·25
FS119	(Euro 20g World 10g) (Type IIA)	4·50	4·50
FS120	(Europe up to 60g) (Type IIA)	7·50	7·50
FS121	(Europe up to 100g) (Type IIA) (30.03.15)	14·00	14·00
FS122	(Worldwide up to 20g) (Type IIA)	5·25	5·25
FS123	(Worldwide up to 60g) (Type IIA)	8·25	8·25
FS124	(Worldwide up to 100g) (Type IIA) (30.03.15)	15·00	15·00
FS117/FS120, FS122, FS123 Set of 6 (Type IIA)		30·00	30·00
First Day Cover (No. FS117 in 6 designs) (Type IIIA)			9·50
Special Pack (P&G 18) (No. FS117 in strip of 6 designs) (Type IIIA)			8·00

Nos. FS117/FS124 were each available in six different designs: T **FT18**, Briar, Harry, Margaret, Stag, Nell Morgan.

Nos. FS117/FS124 have year code MA15.

Nos. FS117/FS120, FS122/FS123 are known in Type IIIA and come from Post & Go machines used at exhibitions. Details are provided in separate tables at the end of this section.

Nos. FS120 and FS123 were replaced on 30 March 2015 by Nos. FS121 and FS124.

T **FT18**, Briar, Harry, Margaret, Stag and Nell Morgan are each known thermally printed with 2nd Class up to 100g and 2nd Large up to 100g, Type IIA, when put in a machine's second class unit. This may have occurred because they were mistakenly put in the wrong unit, or because standard second class (new blue Machin) T **FT14** stock was temporarily unavailable and it was deemed necessary to use alternative stock.

FT19 Lion

(Des Osborne Ross. Illustrations by Chris Wormell, Gravure ISP Walsall, thermally printed service indicator)

2015 (13 May). Heraldic Beasts Self-adhesive. Two phosphor bands. Multicoloured Perf 14×14½.

FS125	(1st Class up to 100g) (Type IIA)	3·75	3·75
FS126	(1st Large up to 100g) (Type IIA)	4·25	4·25
FS127	(Euro 20g World 10g) (Type IIA)	4·50	4·50
FS128	(Europe up to 100g) (Type IIA)	5·50	5·50
FS129	(Worldwide up to 20g) (Type IIA)	5·25	5·25
FS130	(Worldwide up to 100g) (Type IIA)	6·75	6·75
FS125/FS130, Set of 6 (Type IIA)		27·00	27·00
First Day Cover (No. FS125 in 6 designs) (Type IIIA)			9·50
Special Pack (P&G 19) (No. FS125 in strip of 6 designs) (Type IIIA)			8·00

Nos. FS125/FS130 were each available in six different designs: T **FT19**, Unicorn, Yale, Dragon, Falcon and Griffin.

Nos. FS125/FS130 have year code MA15.

Nos. FS125/FS130 are known in Type IIIA and come from Post & Go machines used at exhibitions. Details are provided in separate tables at the end of this section.

T **FT19**, Unicorn, Yale, Dragon, Falcon and Griffin are each known thermally printed with 2nd Class up to 100g and 2nd Large up to 100g, Type IIA, when put in a machine's second class unit. This may have occurred because the issue was mistakenly put in the wrong unit, or because standard second class (new blue Machin) T **FT14** stock was temporarily unavailable and it was deemed necessary to use alternative stock.

FT20 Dover

(Des Osborne Ross. Illustrations by Andy Tuohy, Gravure ISP Walsall, thermally printed service indicator)

2015 (16 Sept). Sea Travel. Self-adhesive. Two phosphor bands. Multicoloured Perf 14×14½.

FS131	(1st Class up to 100g) (Type IIA)	3·75	3·75
FS132	(1st Large up to 100g) (Type IIA)	4·25	4·25
FS133	(Euro 20g World 10g) (Type IIA)	4·50	4·50
FS134	(Europe up to 100g) (Type IIA)	5·50	5·50
FS135	(Worldwide up to 20g) (Type IIA)	5·25	5·25
FS136	(Worldwide up to 100g) (Type IIA)	6·75	6·75
FS131/FS136, Set of 6		27·00	27·00
First Day Cover (No. FS131 in 6 designs) (Type IIIA)			9·50
Special Pack (P&G 20) (No. FS131 in strip of 6 designs) (Type IIIA)			8·00

Nos. FS131/FS136 were each available in six different designs: T **FT20**, Hong Kong, Sydney, Ha Long Bay, New York City and Venice.

Nos. FS131/FS136 have year code MA15.

T **FT20**, Hong Kong, Sydney, Ha Long Bay, New York City and Venice are each known thermally printed with 2nd Class up to 100g and 2nd Large up to 100g, Type IIA, when put in a machine's second class unit. This may have occurred because the issue was mistakenly put in the wrong unit, or because standard second class (new blue Machin) T **FT14** stock was temporarily unavailable and it was deemed necessary to use alternative stock.

Nos. FS131/FS136 are known in Type IIIA and come from Post & Go machines used at exhibitions. Details are provided in separate tables at the end of this section.

FT21 Common Poppy

(Des Kate Stephens. Illustrations by Julia Trickey. Gravure ISP Walsall, thermally printed service indicator)

2015 (19 Oct). Common Poppy in Type IIIA. Self-adhesive. Two phosphor bands. Multicoloured Perf 14×14½.

FS137	(1st Class up to 100g) (Type IIIA)	3·75	3·75
FS138	(1st Large up to 100g) (Type IIIA)	4·25	4·25
FS139	(Euro 20g World 10g) (Type IIIA)	4·50	4·50
FS140	(Europe up to 100g) (Type IIIA)	5·50	5·50
FS141	(Worldwide up to 20g) (Type IIIA)	5·25	5·25
FS142	(Worldwide up to 100g) (Type IIIA)	6·75	6·75
FS137/FS142 Set of 6 (Type IIIA)		27·00	27·00

Nos. FS137/FS142 came from Royal Mail Series II machines situated at Royal Mail enquiry offices, and the stamps are easily identified by the code being a mixture of letters and numerals.

In the run-up to Remembrance Sunday 2015 the Common Poppy design was for the first time offered through Royal Mail enquiry offices in single-design rolls. The annual tradition of re-issuing the Common Poppy in single-design rolls continued, with short-term availability from Royal Mail enquiry offices from 24 October 2016 and 24 October 2017. The Common Poppy design was not made available from Royal Mail enquiry offices in 2018 or 2019.

Nos. FS137/FS142 only exist with year code MA15.

T **FT21** was not made available in a Special Pack and was only available from Post & Go machines.

See also FS103/FS108b.

FT22 Mountain Hare

(Des Osborne Ross. Illustrations by Robert Gillmor. Gravure ISP Walsall, thermally printed service indicator)

2015 (16 Nov). Winter Fur and Feathers. Self-adhesive. One phosphor band at right (Nos. FS143/FS143a and FS144/FS144a) or two phosphor bands (others). Multicoloured Perf 14×14½.

FS143	(2nd Class up to 100g) (Type IIA)	2·25	2·25
	a. Type IIIA (16.11.15)	4·00	4·00
FS144	(2nd Large up to 100g) (Type IIA)	3·00	3·00
	a. Type IIIA (16.11.15)	4·25	4·25
FS145	(1st Class up to 100g) (Type IIA)	3·75	3·75
	a. Type IIIA (16.11.15)	4·25	4·25
FS146	(1st Large up to 100g) (Type IIA)	4·25	4·25
	a. Type IIIA (16.11.15)	4·50	4·50
FS147	(Euro 20g World 10g) (Type IIA)	4·50	4·50
	a. Type IIIA (16.11.15)	5·25	5·25
FS148	(Europe up to 100g) (Type IIA)	5·50	5·50
	a. Type IIIA (16.11.15)	6·50	6·50
FS149	(Worldwide up to 20g) (Type IIA)	5·25	5·25
	a. Type IIIA (16.11.15)	6·25	6·25
FS150	(Worldwide up to 100g) (Type IIA)	6·75	6·75
	a. Type IIIA (16.11.15)	7·50	7·50
FS143/FS150, Set of 8 (Type IIA)		28·00	28·00
FS143a/FS150a, Set of 8 (Type IIIA)		38·00	38·00
First Day Cover (Nos. FS143/FS146a; 4 designs) (Type IIIA)			8·00
Special Pack (P&G 21) (Nos. FS143a/FS146a; 4 designs as two pairs) (Type IIIA)			7·25

Nos. FS143/FS143a and FS144/FS144a were each available in two different designs: T **FT22** and Redwing.

Nos. FS145/FS145a through to FS150/FS150a were each available in two different designs: Red Fox and Squirrel.

Defining their intended second class status, T **FT22** and Redwing have repeated background text in blue, reading '2ndCLASS' (large typeface) and 'ROYALMAIL' (small typeface) in alternate lines and a single phosphor band placed at the right-hand side.

The Special Pack stamps are No. FS143a T **FT22**, No. FS144a Redwing, No. FS145a Red Fox, and No. FS146a Red Squirrel.

Nos. FS143/FS143a and FS144/FS144a have year code CL15S.

Nos. FS145/FS145a through to FS150/FS150a have year code MA15.

Nos. FS143a/FS150a came from Royal Mail Series II machines situated at Royal Mail enquiry offices, and the stamps are easily identified by the code being a mixture of letters and numerals.

No. FS147a in Red Fox and Squirrel exist with the 20g weight missing and is instead shown as Euro World 10g, and results from a software glitch. Only from Bradford Royal Mail enquiry office 29/31 March 2016.

T **FT22** and Redwing are also both known thermally printed with 1st Class up to 100g, 1st Class Large up to 100g, Euro 20g World 10g, Europe up to 100g, Worldwide up to 20g and Worldwide up to 100g, Type IIA, when mistakenly put in machine's first class unit. Similarly, in Type IIIA are known from Bradford enquiry office.

Red Fox and Squirrel are each known thermally printed with 2nd Class up to 100g and 2nd Large up to 100g, Type IIA, when put in a machine's second class unit. Similarly, in Type IIIA are known from Bradford enquiry office. This may have occurred because they were mistakenly put in the wrong unit, or because T **FT22** and Redwing or standard second class (new blue Machin) T **FT14** stock were not available, and it was deemed necessary to use the other design instead.

FT23 Post Boy, 1640s

(Des Howard Brown. Illustrations by Andrew Davidson. Gravure ISP Walsall, thermally printed service indicator)

2016 (17 Feb). Royal Mail Heritage. Transport. Self-adhesive. Two phosphor bands. Multicoloured Perf 14×14½.

FS151	(1st Class up to 100g) (Type IIA)	3·25	3·25
FS152	(1st Large up to 100g) (Type IIA)	3·50	3·50
FS153	(Euro 20g World 10g) (Type IIA)	3·75	3·75
FS154	(Europe up to 100g) (Type IIA)	4·50	4·50
FS155	(Worldwide up to 20g) (Type IIA)	4·25	4·25
FS156	(Worldwide up to 100g) (Type IIA)	6·25	6·25
FS151/156, Set of 6 (Type IIA)		23·00	23·00
First Day Cover (No. FS151 in 6 designs) (Type IIIA)			9·50
Special Pack (P&G 22) (No. FS151 in strip of 6 designs) (Type IIIA)			10·00

Nos. FS151/FS156 were each available in six different designs: T **FT23**; Mail coach, 1790s; Falmouth packet ship, 1820s; Travelling Post Office, 1890s; Airmail, 1930s and Royal Mail Minivan, 1970s.

Nos. FS151/FS156 have year code MA16.

T **FT23**; Mail coach, 1790s; Falmouth packet ship, 1820s; Travelling Post Office, 1890s; Airmail, 1930s and Royal Mail Minivan, 1970s are each known thermally printed with 2nd Class up to 100g and 2nd Large up to 100g, Type IIA, when put in a machine's second class unit. This may have occurred because the issue was mistakenly put in the wrong unit, or because standard second class (new blue Machin) T **FT14** stock was temporarily unavailable and it was deemed necessary to use alternative stock.

Nos. FS151/FS156 are known in Type IIIA and come from Post & Go machines used at exhibitions. Details are provided in separate tables at the end of this section.

Nos. FS151/FS156 in Type IIIA exist digitally printed in the Travelling Post Office, 1890s (Locomotive) design from single-design rolls used in Post & Go machines at exhibitions. Details are provided in separate tables at the end of this section.

Nos. FS151/FS156 in Type IIIA exist digitally printed in the Mail Coach, 1790s design from single-design rolls used in Post & Go machines at The Postal Museum. These stamps only exist with a museum inscription. Details are provided in separate tables at the end of this section.

The Mail Coach, 1790s design from digitally printed single-design rolls exists with Euro 100g World 20g, World up to 100g zone 1-3 and World up to 100g zone 2 values (Type IIIA). These stamps only exist from the Post & Go machine at The Postal Museum from 29 October 2020 and all bear a museum inscription. Details are provided in separate tables at the end of this section.

2016 (5 Aug). T **FT14** with background text reading, alternately, '2ndCLASS' in large lettering and 'ROYALMAIL' in small lettering, with year code. New blue background. Self-adhesive. One phosphor band (over the Queen's head). Perf 14×14½.

FS157	(2nd Class up to 100g) (Type IIA)	2·10	2·10
FS158	(2nd Large up to 100g) (Type IIA)	2·75	2·75

Nos. FS157/FS158 have year code CL16S, CL17S, CL18S or CL19S, with the code positioned half-way between the left edge of the stamp and the Queen's nose.

ROYAL MAIL POST & GO STAMPS

T **FT14** with background text reading, alternately, '2ndCLASS' in large lettering and 'ROYALMAIL' in small lettering, with year code CL16S and CL18S is known thermally printed with 1st Class up to 100g, 1st Class Large up to 100g, Euro 20g World 10g, Europe up to 100g, Worldwide up to 20g and Worldwide up to 100g, Type IIA, when mistakenly put in machine's first class unit.

Nos. FS157/FS158 were not made available in a Special Pack and are only available from Post & Go machines.

FT24 Seven-spot Ladybird

(Des Osborne Ross. Illustrations by Chris Wormell, Gravure ISP Walsall, thermally printed service indicator)

2016 (14 Sept). Ladybirds. Self-adhesive. Two phosphor bands. Multicoloured Perf 14×14½.

FS159	(1st Class up to 100g) (Type IIA)	2·50	2·50
	a. Type IIIA	4·25	4·25
FS160	(1st Large up to 100g) (Type IIA)	2·75	2·75
	a. Type IIIA	4·50	4·50
FS161	(Euro 20g World 10g) (Type IIA)	4·25	4·25
	a. Type IIIA	4·75	4·75
FS162	(Europe up to 100g) (Type IIA)	4·25	4·25
	a. Type IIIA	5·50	5·50
FS163	(Worldwide up to 20g) (Type IIA)	4·25	4·25
	a. Type IIIA	5·25	5·25
FS164	(Worldwide up to 100g) (Type IIA)	5·75	5·75
	a. Type IIIA	7·50	7·50
FS159/FS164, Set of 6 (Type IIA)		21·00	21·00
FS159a/FS164a, Set of 6 (Type IIIA)		29·00	29·00
First Day Cover (No. FS159a in 6 designs) (Type IIIA)			9·50
Special Pack (P&G 23) (No. FS159a in strip of 6 designs) (Type IIIA)			9·00

Nos. FS159/FS164a were each available in six different designs: T **FT24**, 14-spot Ladybird, Orange Ladybird, Heather Ladybird, Striped Ladybird and Water Ladybird.

No. FS159 through to No. FS164a have year code MA16.

T **FT24**, 14-spot Ladybird, Orange Ladybird, Heather Ladybird, Striped Ladybird and Water Ladybird are each known thermally printed with 2nd Class up to 100g and 2nd Large up to 100g, Type IIA, when put in a machine's second class unit. This may have occurred because the issue was mistakenly put in the wrong unit, or because standard second class (new blue Machin) T **FT14** stock was temporarily unavailable and it was deemed necessary to use alternative stock.

Nos. FS159a/FS164a (Type IIIA) come from Royal Mail Series II machines situated at Royal Mail enquiry offices. These may be identified by the code M00 at the beginning of the second group of data within the code line at the foot of the stamp. Stamps with codes other than M00 either come from machines at stamp exhibitions (see tables), or in the case of No. FS159a with code C00 come from special packs.

FT25 Hedgehog

(Des Osborne Ross. Illustrations by Chris Wormell, Gravure ISP Walsall, thermally printed service indicator)

2016 (14 Nov). Hibernating Animals. Self-adhesive. One phosphor band at right (Nos. FS165/FS165a and FS166/FS166a) or two phosphor bands (others). Multicoloured Perf 14×14½.

FS165	(2nd Class up to 100g) (Type IIA)	2·50	2·50
	a. Type IIIA	3·00	3·00
FS166	(2nd Large up to 100g) (Type IIA)	2·75	2·75
	a. Type IIIA	3·25	3·25
FS167	(1st Class up to 100g) (Type IIA)	2·75	2·75
	a. Type IIIA	4·25	4·25
FS168	(1st Large up to 100g) (Type IIA)	3·00	3·00
	a. Type IIIA	4·50	4·50
FS169	(Euro 20g World 10g) (Type IIA)	3·25	3·25
	a. Type IIIA	4·75	4·75
FS170	(Europe up to 100g) (Type IIA)	4·50	4·50
	a. Type IIIA	5·50	5·50
FS171	(Worldwide up to 20g) (Type IIA)	4·25	4·25
	a. Type IIIA	5·25	5·25
FS172	(Worldwide up to 100g) (Type IIA)	6·00	6·00
	a. Type IIIA	7·50	7·50
FS165/FS172, Set of 8 (Type IIA)		25·00	25·00
FS165a/FS172a, Set of 8 (Type IIIA)		32·00	32·00
First Day Cover (Nos. FS165a/FS168a in 4 designs) (Type IIIA)			8·00
Special Pack (P&G 24) (Nos. FS165a/FS168a; 4 designs as two pairs) (Type IIIA)			9·00

Nos. FS165/FS165a and FS166/FS166a were each available in two different designs: T **FT25** or Grass Snake.

Nos. FS167/FS167a through to Nos. FS172/FS172a were each available in two different designs: Dormouse or Brown Long-eared Bat.

Defining their intended second class status, T **FT25** and Grass Snake have repeated background text in blue, reading '2ndCLASS' (large typeface) and 'ROYALMAIL' (small typeface) in alternate lines and a single phosphor band placed at the right-hand side.

The Special Pack stamps are No. FS165a T **FT25**, No. FS166a Grass Snake, No. FS167a Dormouse, and No. FS168a Long-eared Bat.

Nos. FS165/FS165a and FS166/FS166a have year code CL16S.

Nos. FS167/FS167a through to Nos. FS172/FS172a have year code MA16.

Dormouse and Brown Long-eared Bat are each known thermally printed with 2nd Class up to 100g and 2nd Large up to 100g, Type IIA, when put in a machine's second class unit. This may have occurred because they were mistakenly put in the wrong unit, or because T **FT25** and Grass Snake or standard second class (new blue Machin) T **FT14** stock were not available, and it was deemed necessary to use the other design instead.

Nos. FS165a/FS172a (Type IIIA) come from Royal Mail Series II machines situated at Royal Mail enquiry offices. These may be identified by the code M00 at the beginning of the second group of data within the code line at the foot of the stamp.

No. FS165a with code C00 come from special packs.

FT26 Travelling Post Office: bag exchange

(Des Osborne Ross. Gravure ISP Walsall, thermally printed service indicator)

2017 (15 Feb). Royal Mail Heritage. Mail by Rail. Self-adhesive. Two phosphor bands. Multicoloured Perf 14×14½.

FS173	(1st Class up to 100g) (Type IIA)	2·50	2·50
	a. Type IIIA	4·25	4·25
FS174	(1st Large up to 100g) (Type IIA)	2·75	2·75
	a. Type IIIA	4·50	4·50
FS175	(Euro 20g World 10g) (Type IIA)	4·75	4·75
	a. Type IIIA	4·75	4·75
FS176	(Europe up to 100g) (Type IIA)	4·75	4·75
	a. Type IIIA	5·50	5·50
FS177	(Worldwide up to 20g) (Type IIA)	4·75	4·75
	a. Type IIIA	5·25	5·25
FS178	(Worldwide up to 100g) (Type IIA)	5·75	5·75
	a. Type IIIA	7·50	7·50
FS173/FS178, Set of 6 (Type IIA)		23·00	23·00
FS173a/FS178a, Set of 6 (Type IIIA)		27·00	27·00
First Day Cover (No. FS173a in 6 designs) (Type IIIA)			7·50
Special Pack (P&G 25) (No. FS173a in strip of 6 designs) (Type IIIA)			9·00

Nos. FS173/FS178a were each available in six different designs: T **FT26**; Post Office (London) Railway; Night Mail: poster; Travelling Post Office: loading; Travelling Post Office: sorting and Travelling Post Office: on the move.

Nos. FS173/FS178a have year code MA17.

T **FT26**; Post Office (London) Railway; Night Mail: poster; Travelling Post Office: loading; Travelling Post Office: sorting and Travelling Post Office: on the move are known thermally printed with 2nd Class up to 100g and 2nd Large up to 100g, Type IIA, when put in a machine's second class unit. This may have occurred because the issue was mistakenly put in the wrong unit, or because standard second class (new blue Machin) T **FT14** stock was temporarily unavailable and it was deemed necessary to use alternative stock.

Nos. FS173a/FS178a (Type IIIA) come from Royal Mail Series II machines situated at Royal Mail enquiry offices. These may be identified by the code M00 at the beginning of the second group of data within the code line at the foot of the stamp. Stamps with codes other than M00 either come from machines at stamp exhibitions (see tables), or in the case of No. FS173a with code C00 come from special packs.

FS173a/FS178a exist digitally printed in the Post Office (London) Railway design from single-design rolls used in the Post & Go machine at The Postal Museum. These stamps are known with an MA17, MA18 (FS173a/FS175a only) or R19Y year codes, and only exist with a museum inscription. Details are provided in separate tables at the end of this section.

The Post Office (London) Railway design from digitally printed single-design rolls exists with Euro 100g World 20g, World up to 100g zone 1-3 and World up to 100g zone 2 values (Type IIIA). These stamps are known with MA17, MA18 or R19Y year codes and only exist from the Post & Go machine at The Postal Museum from 29 October 2020, and all bear a museum inscription. Details are provided in separate tables at the end of this section.

ROYAL MAIL POST & GO STAMPS

FT27 Machin Commemorative Head

(Gravure ISP Walsall, thermally printed service indicator)

2017 (5 June)–**21**. Machin Anniversary 1967–2017. Self-adhesive. Two phosphor bands. Multicoloured. Perf 14×14½.

FS179	(1st Class up to 100g) (Type IIA)	3·00	3·00
	a. Type IIIA	3·00	3·00
FS180	(1st Large up to 100g) (Type IIA)	3·25	3·25
	a. Type IIIA	3·25	3·25
FS181	(Euro 20g World 10g) (Type IIA)	4·25	4·25
	a. Type IIIA	4·25	4·25
FS182	(Europe up to 100g) (Type IIA)	4·25	4·25
	a. Type IIIA	4·25	4·25
FS182*b*	(Euro 100g World 20g) (Type IIA) (9.20)	9·75	9·00
FS182*c*	(Europe Large 100g) (Type IIA) (1.21)	12·00	10·50
FS183	(Worldwide up to 20g) (Type IIA)	4·25	4·25
	a. Type IIIA	4·25	4·25
FS184	(Worldwide up to 100g) (Type IIA)	5·75	5·75
	a. Type IIIA	5·75	5·75
FS184*b*	(World 100g zone 1-3) (Type IIA) (9.20)	—	—
FS184*c*	(World 100g zone 2) (Type IIA) (9.20)	—	—
FS184*d*	(Worldwide Large 100g) (Type IIA) (1.21)	13·00	13·00
FS179/FS184, Set of 6 (Type IIA)		22·00	22·00
FS179a/FS184a, Set of 6 (Type IIIA)		22·00	22·00
First Day Cover (No. FS179a in 6 designs) (Type IIIA)			7·50
Special Pack (P&G 26) (No. FS179a in strip of 6 designs) (Type IIIA)		17·00	

Nos. FS179/FS184*d* were each available in six different colours: T **FT27**, light olive, violet, deep sepia, bright emerald and drab.

Nos. FS179/FS184*d* do not have a year code as such, but have repeated background text, reading MACHIN ANNIVERSARY, 1967 - 2017 (large typeface) and 'ROYALMAIL' (small typeface) in alternate lines.

T **FT27**, light olive, violet, deep sepia, bright emerald and drab are each known thermally printed with 2nd Class up to 100g and 2nd Large up to 100g, Type IIA, when put in a machine's second class unit. This may have occurred because the issue was mistakenly put in the wrong unit, or because standard second class (new blue Machin) T **FT14** stock was temporarily unavailable and it was deemed necessary to use alternative stock.

Nos. FS179a/FS184a (Type IIIA) come from Royal Mail Series II machines situated at Royal Mail enquiry offices. These may be identified by the code M00 at the beginning of the second group of data within the code line at the foot of the stamp. Stamps with codes other than M00 either come from machines at stamp exhibitions (see tables), or in the case of No. FS179a with code C00 come from special packs.

FT28 First UK Aerial Mail, 1911

Des Osborne Ross. Illustrations by Andrew Davidson. Gravure ISP Walsall, thermally printed service indicator)

2017 (13 Sept). Royal Mail Heritage. Mail by Air. Self-adhesive. Two phosphor bands. Multicoloured Perf 14×14½.

FS185	(1st Class up to 100g) (Type IIA)	2·25	2·25
	a. Type IIIA	3·25	3·25
FS186	(1st Large up to 100g) (Type IIA)	2·75	2·75
	a. Type IIIA	3·75	3·70
FS187	(Euro 20g World 10g) (Type IIA)	4·00	4·00
	a. Type IIIA	4·00	4·00
FS188	(Europe up to 100g) (Type IIA)	4·00	4·00
	a. Type IIIA	4·50	4·50
FS189	(Worldwide up to 20g) (Type IIA)	4·00	4·00
	a. Type IIIA	4·25	4·25
FS190	(Worldwide up to 100g) (Type IIA)	5·25	5·25
	a. Type IIIA	6·25	6·25
FS185/FS190, Set of 6 (Type IIA)		20·00	20·00
FS185a/FS190a, Set of 6 (Type IIIA)		22·00	22·00
First Day Cover (No. FS185a in 6 designs) (Type IIIA)			7·50
Special Pack (P&G 27) (No. FS185a in strip of 6 designs) (Type IIIA)		9·00	

Nos. FS185/FS190a were each available in six different designs: T **FT28**; Military Mail Flight, 1919; International Airmail, 1933; Domestic Airmail, 1934; Flying Boat Airmail, 1937 and Datapost Service, 1980s.

Nos. FS185/FS190a have year code R17Y.

T **FT28**; Military Mail Flight, 1919; International Airmail, 1933; Domestic Airmail, 1934; Flying Boat Airmail, 1937 and Datapost Service, 1980s are each known thermally printed with 2nd Class up to 100g and 2nd Large up to 100g, Type IIA, when put in a machine's second class unit. This may have occurred because the issue was mistakenly put in the wrong unit, or because standard second class (new blue Machin) T **FT14** stock was temporarily unavailable and it was deemed necessary to use alternative stock.

Nos. FS185a/FS190a (Type IIIA) come from Royal Mail Series II machines situated at Royal Mail enquiry offices. These may be identified by the code M00 at the beginning of the second group of data within the code line at the foot of the stamp. Stamps with codes other than M00 either come from machines at stamp exhibitions (see tables), or in the case of No. FS185a with code C00 come from special packs.

No. FS185a in all six designs exist from digitally printed rolls used in the Post & Go machine at The Postal Museum. These stamps have an R19Y year code and only exist with a museum inscription. Details are provided in separate tables at the end of this section.

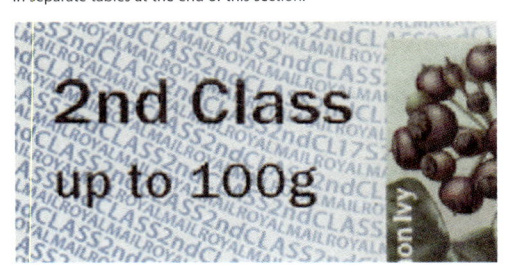

(Des Kate Stephens. Illustrations by Julia Trickey. Gravure ISP Walsall, thermally printed service indicator)

2017 (13 Nov)–**21**. British Flora (3rd series). Winter Greenery, 2017 re-issue. T **FT17** with blue background text reading, alternately, '2ndCLASS' in large lettering and 'ROYALMAIL' in small lettering, with one phosphor band at right (Nos. FS191/FS191a and Nos. FS192/FS192a), or greenish grey 'ROYALMAIL' background, with two phosphor bands (others). Self-adhesive. Multicoloured Perf 14×14½.

FS191	(2nd Class up to 100g) (Type IIA)	2·10	2·10
	a. Type IIIA	4·75	4·75
FS192	(2nd Large up to 100g) (Type IIA)	2·75	2·75
	a. Type IIIA	5·00	5·00
FS193	(1st Class up to 100g) (Type IIA)	2·25	2·25
	a. Type IIIA	4·75	4·75
FS194	(1st Large up to 100g) (Type IIA)	3·00	3·00
	a. Type IIIA	5·25	5·25
FS195	(Euro 20g World 10g) (Type IIA)	5·50	5·50
	a. Type IIIA	5·50	5·50
FS196	(Europe up to 100g) (Type IIA)	5·50	5·50
	a. Type IIIA	5·75	5·75
FS196*b*	(Euro 100g World 20g) (Type IIA) (3.11.20)	4·00	4·00
FS196*c*	(Europe Large 100g) (Type IIA) (2.1.21)	10·50	10·50
FS197	(Worldwide up to 20g) (Type IIA)	5·50	5·50
	a. Type IIIA	5·75	5·75
FS198	(Worldwide up to 100g) (Type IIA)	5·50	5·50
	a. Type IIIA	6·50	6·50
FS198*b*	(World 100g zone 1-3) (Type IIA) (3.11.20)	11·00	11·00
FS198*c*	(World 100g zone 2) (Type IIA) (3.22.20)	11·00	11·00
FS198*d*	(Worldwide Large 100g) (Type IIA) (2.1.21)	11·50	11·50
FS191/FS198, Set of 8 (Type IIA)		30·00	30·00
FS191a/FS198a, Set of 8 (Type IIIA)		40·00	40·00

Nos. FS191/FS191a and FS192/FS192a were each available in two different designs: T **FT17** and Mistletoe.

No. FS193 through to No. FS198*d* were each available in two different designs: Butcher's Broom and Holly.

No. FS191 through to No. FS198*d* are a re-issue of the 13 November 2014 designs, but with differences necessitating a separate listing.

For the 2014 issue see No. FS109 through to No. FS116*c*.

Nos. FS191/FS191a and FS192/FS192a may be differentiated from the 2014 issue through their repeated blue background text, reading '2ndCLASS' (large typeface) and 'ROYALMAIL' (small typeface) in alternate lines.

Nos. FS191/FS191a and FS192/FS192a may also be differentiated through the year code which is the CL**S format (the 2014 issue has year code MA14).

No. FS193 through to No. FS198*d* may be differentiated from the 2014 issue through their repeated greenish grey background text (the 2014 issue has olive-brown background text).

No. FS193 through to No. FS198*d* may also be differentiated through the year code which is in the R**Y format (the 2014 issue has year code MA14).

T **FT17** and Mistletoe, Butcher's Broom and Holly have been re-issued in November of each year since 2017. In each successive year there has been a reprint and new year codes.

Year codes for Nos. FS191/FS192 (Type IIA) are CL17S, CL18S, CL19S and CL20S.

ROYAL MAIL POST & GO STAMPS

Year codes for Nos. FS193/FS198 (Type IIA) are R17Y, R18Y and R19Y.
Year codes for Nos. FS196b, FS198b/FS198c are R17Y, R19Y and R20Y.
Year codes for Nos. FS196c and FS198d are R19Y and R19Y.
Nos. FS191a/FS198a (Type IIA) come from Royal Mail Series II machines situated at Royal Mail enquiry offices. These may be identified by the code M00 at the beginning of the second group of data within the code line at the foot of the stamp. Nos. FS191a/FS198a were available at Royal Mail enquiry offices in 2017 but were not made available in 2018 or 2019.
Year codes for Nos. FS191a/FS198a (Type IIA) are R17Y.

T **FT17** and Mistletoe with blue background text reading, alternately, '2ndCLASS' in large lettering and 'ROYALMAIL' in small lettering, with year code CL17 and CL18, are each known thermally printed with 1st Class up to 100g, 1st Class Large up to 100g, Euro 20g World 10g, Europe up to 100g, Worldwide up to 20g and Worldwide up to 100g, Type IIA, when mistakenly put in machine's first class unit.

Butcher's Broom and Holly with year code R17Y and R18Y are each known thermally printed with 2nd Class up to 100g and 2nd Large up to 100g, Type IIA, when put in a machine's second class unit. This may have occurred because they were mistakenly put in the wrong unit, or because T **FT17** and Mistletoe or standard second class (new blue Machin) T **FT14** stock were not available, and it was deemed necessary to use the other design instead.

Winter Greenery 2017 re-issue was not made available in a Special Pack and was only available from Post & Go machines.

FT29 The Iron Throne–Ice

(Design GBH. Illustrations by Rob Ball. Gravure ISP Walsall, thermally printed service indicator)

2018 (23 Jan)–**20**. Game of Thrones. Self-adhesive. One phosphor band at right (Nos. FS199/FS199a and FS200/FS200a) or two phosphor bands (others). Multicoloured Perf 14×14½.

FS199	(2nd Class up to 100g) (Type IIA)	7·75	7·75
	a. Type IIIA	5·25	5·25
FS200	(2nd Large up to 100g) (Type IIA)	8·00	8·00
	a. Type IIIA	5·50	5·50
FS201	(1st Class up to 100g) (Type IIA)	3·25	3·25
	a. Type IIIA	5·25	5·25
FS202	(1st Large up to 100g) (Type IIA)	3·75	3·75
	a. Type IIIA	5·75	5·75
FS203	(Euro 20g World 10g) (Type IIA)	12·00	12·00
	a. Type IIIA	9·00	9·00
FS204	(Europe up to 100g) (Type IIA)	27·00	27·00
	a. Type IIIA	9·00	9·00
FS204b	(Euro 100g World 20g) (Type IIA) (9.20)	16·00	16·00
FS205	(Worldwide up to 20g) (Type IIA)	27·00	27·00
	a. Type IIIA	9·00	9·00
FS206	(Worldwide up to 100g) (Type IIA)	16·00	16·00
	a. Type IIIA	9·00	9·00
FS206b	(World 100g zone 1-3) (Type IIA) (9.20)	19·00	19·00
FS206c	(World 100g zone 2) (Type IIA) (9.20)	23·00	23·00
FS199/FS206, Set of 8 (Type IIA)		95·00	95·00
FS199a/FS206a, Set of 8 (Type IIIA)		50·00	50·00
First Day Cover (Nos. FS199a and FS201a) (Type IIIA)			4·00
Special Pack (P&G 28) (Nos. FS199a and FS201a) (Type IIIA)			5·00

Nos. FS199/FS199a and FS200/FS200a were each available in one design: T **FT29** in blue (Ice).
No. FS201 through to No. FS206c were each available in one design: T **FT29** in yellow-orange (Fire).

Defining their intended second class status, T **FT29** has repeated background text in blue, reading '2ndCLASS' (large typeface) and 'ROYALMAIL' (small typeface) in alternate lines, and a single phosphor band placed at the right-hand side.

No. FS201 through to No. FS206c have repeated background text in yellow-orange with 'ROYALMAIL' in alternate lines of large and small typeface.

Nos. FS199/FS199a and FS200/FS200a have year code CL18S.
No. FS201 through to No. FS206c have year code R18Y.

The Iron Throne–Fire design is known thermally printed with 2nd Class up to 100g and 2nd Large up to 100g, Type IIA, when put in a machine's second class unit. This may have occurred because the issue was mistakenly put in the wrong unit, or because standard second class (new blue Machin) T **FT14** stock was temporarily unavailable and it was deemed necessary to use alternative stock.

T **FT29** The Iron Throne–Ice design is known thermally printed with 1st Class up to 100g, 1st Class Large up to 100g, Euro 20g World 10g, Europe up to 100g, Worldwide up to 20g and Worldwide up to 100g, Type IIA, when mistakenly put in machine's first class unit.

Nos. FS199a/FS206a (Type IIIA) come from Royal Mail Series II machines situated at Royal Mail enquiry offices. These may be identified by the code M00 at the beginning of the second group of data within the code line at the foot of the stamp.

Nos. FS199a and FS201a with code C00 come from special packs.

FT30 Packet *Antelope*, 1780

(Illustrations by Andrew Davidson. Gravure ISP Walsall, thermally printed service indicator)

2018 (14 Feb)–**20**. Royal Mail Heritage. Mail by Sea. Self-adhesive. Two phosphor bands. Multicoloured Perf 14×14½.

FS207	(1st Class up to 100g) (Type IIA)	2·25	2·25
	a. Type IIIA	3·25	3·25
FS208	(1st Large up to 100g) (Type IIA)	2·75	2·75
	a. Type IIIA	3·75	3·75
FS209	(Euro 20g World 10g) (Type IIA)	4·00	4·00
	a. Type IIIA	4·00	4·00
FS210	(Europe up to 100g) (Type IIA)	4·00	4·00
	a. Type IIIA	4·50	4·50
FS210b	(Euro 100g World 20g) (9.20)	13·50	13·50
FS211	(Worldwide up to 20g) (Type IIA)	4·00	4·00
	a. Type IIIA	4·25	4·25
FS212	(Worldwide up to 100g) (Type IIA)	5·25	5·25
	a. Type IIIA	6·25	6·25
FS212b	(World 100g zone 1-3) (Type IIA) (9.20)	14·50	14·50
FS212c	(World 100g zone 2) (Type IIA) (9.20)	16·50	16·50
FS207/FS212 Set of 6 (Type IIA)		20·00	20·00
FS207a/FS212a Set of 6 (Type IIIA)		23·00	23·00
First Day Cover (No. FS207a in 6 designs) (Type IIIA)			7·50
Special Pack (P&G 29) (No. FS207a in strip of 6 designs) (Type IIIA)			7·00

Nos. FS207/FS212c were each available in six different designs: T **FT30**; SS *Great Western*, 1838; SS *Britannia*, 1887; RMS *Olympic*, 1911; RMS *Queen Mary*, 1936; RMS *St Helena*, 1990.

Nos. FS207/FS212c have year code R18Y.

T **FT30**; SS *Great Western*, 1838; SS *Britannia*, 1887; RMS *Olympic*, 1911; RMS *Queen Mary*, 1936; RMS *St Helena*, 1990 are each known thermally printed with 2nd Class up to 100g and 2nd Large up to 100g, Type IIA, when put in a machine's second class unit. This may have occurred because the issue was mistakenly put in the wrong unit, or because standard second class (new blue Machin) T **FT14** stock was temporarily unavailable and it was deemed necessary to use alternative stock.

Nos. FS207a/FS212a (Type IIIA) come from Royal Mail Series II machines situated at Royal Mail enquiry offices. These may be identified by the code M00 at the beginning of the second group of data within the code line at the foot of the stamp.

No. FS207a with code C00 comes from special packs.

FT31 Pentacycle, 1882

(Illustrations by Andrew Davidson. Gravure ISP Walsall, thermally printed service indicator)

2018 (12 Sept)–**20**. Royal Mail Heritage. Mail by Bike. Self-adhesive. Two phosphor bands. Multicoloured Perf 14×14½.

FS213	(1st Class up to 100g) (Type IIA)	2·25	2·25
FS214	(1st Large up to 100g) (Type IIA)	2·75	2·75
FS215	(Euro 20g World 10g) (Type IIA)	4·00	4·00
FS216	(Europe up to 100g) (Type IIA)	4·00	4·00
FS216a	(Euro 100g World 20g) (Type IIA) (9.20)	12·50	16·00
FS217	(Worldwide up to 20g) (Type IIA)	4·00	4·00
FS218	(Worldwide up to 100g) (Type IIA)	5·25	5·25
FS218a	(World 100g zone 1-3) (Type IIA) (9.20)	13·50	19·00
FS218b	(World 100g zone 2) (Type IIA) (9.20)	13·50	23·00
FS213/FS218 Set of 6 (Type IIA)		20·00	20·00
First Day Cover (No. FS213 in 6 designs) (Type IIIA)			7·50
Special Pack (P&G 30) (No. FS213 in strip of 6 designs) (Type IIIA)			9·50

Nos. FS213/FS218b were each available in six different designs: T **FT31**; Motorcycle and trailer, 1902; Tricycle and basket, 1920; Bicycle, 1949; Motorcycle, 1965; Quad bike, 2002.

Nos. FS213/FS218b have year code R18Y.

T **FT31**; Motorcycle and trailer, 1902; Tricycle and basket, 1920; Bicycle, 1949; Motorcycle, 1965; Quad bike, 2002. are each known thermally printed with 2nd Class up to 100g and 2nd Large up to 100g, Type IIA, when put in a machine's second class unit. This may have occurred because the issue was mistakenly put in the wrong unit, or because standard second class (new blue Machin) T **FT14** stock was temporarily unavailable and it was deemed necessary to use alternative stock.

Nos. FS213/FS218 were not made available from the Royal Mail Series II machines (Type IIIA) situated at Royal Mail enquiry offices.

No. FS213 with code C00 comes from special packs.

ROYAL MAIL POST & GO STAMPS

Post & Go Machin design Type FT **1** but with year code in background. Olive-brown background. Self-adhesive. Two phosphor bands. Perf 14×14½. A simplified list of the different year codes, but shown listed in the range of six values/weights (and Types) available at the time (or current).

Service indicator	SG No.	Year code	Availability (inclusive)[1]
1st Class up to 100g, 1st Large up to 100g, Europe up to 20g, Worldwide up to 10g, Worldwide up to 20g, and Worldwide up to 40g:			
Type II	FS77, FS78, FS79, FS81, FS82, and FS83	MA13	19.11.13 – 30.3.14
Type IIA	FS77a, FS78a, FS79a, FS81a, FS82a, and FS83a	MA13	28.2.14 – 31.3.14
1st Class up to 100g, 1st Large up to 100g, Europe up to 20g, Europe up to 60g, Worldwide up to 20g, and Worldwide up to 60g:			
Type II	FS77, FS78, FS79, FS80, FS82, and FS84	MA13	31.3.14 – 19.10.14
Type IIA	FS77a, FS78a, FS79a, FS80a, FS82a, and FS84a	MA13	1.4.14 – 4.6.14
1st Class up to 100g, 1st Large up to 100g, Euro 20g World 10g, Europe up to 60g, Worldwide up to 20g, and Worldwide up to 60g:			
Type II	FS77, FS78, FS79*b*, FS80, FS82, and FS84	MA13	20.10.14 – 3.15
Type IIA	FS77a, FS78a, FS79ba, FS80a, FS82a, and FS84a	MA13	5.6.14 – 29.3.15
		MA14	
1st Class up to 100g, 1st Large up to 100g, Euro 20g World 10g, Europe up to 100g, Worldwide up to 20g, and Worldwide up to 100g:			
Type IIA	FS77a, FS78a, FS79ba, FS80*c*, FS82a, and FS84*c*	MA13	30.3.15 – 31.8.20
		MA14	
		MA15	
		MA16	
		R17Y	
		R18Y	
		R19Y	
		R20Y	
1st Class up to 100g, 1st Large up to 100g, Euro 20g World 10g, Euro 100g World 20g, World 100g Zone 1-3, and World 100g Zone 2:			
Type IIA	FS77a, FS78a, FS79ba, FS80*d*, FS84*d*, and FS84*e*	MA13	1.9.20 – 31.12.20
		MA14	
		MA15	
		MA16	
		R17Y	
		R18Y	
		R19Y	
		R20Y	
1st Class up to 100g, 1st Large up to 100g, Euro 100g World 20g, Worldwide up to 100g, Europe Large 100g, and Worldwide Large 100g:			
Type IIA	FS77a, FS78a, FS80*d*, FS84*c*, FS80*e*, and FS84*f*	MA14	from 1.1.21
		MA15	
		MA16	
		R17Y	
		R18Y	
		R19Y	
		R20Y	
1st Class up to 100g, 1st Large up to 100g, Euro 20g World 10g, Europe up to 100g, Worldwide up to 20g, and Worldwide up to 100g:			
Type IIIA	FS77b, FS78b, FS79bb, FS80ca, FS82b, and FS84ca	MA13	30.5.15 – 10.19
		MA15	

Note. When Machin Post & Go stamps first appeared with a year code it was in the format of MA** and positioned to the left of the front of The Queen's forehead (MA13 through to and including MA16). From 2017, the format and position changed simultaneously to R**Y and positioned further to the left of the design, approximately half way between the left edge and the Queen's forehead. The range of six values/weights noted are also the range that would appear in a collectors' strip of six (or, in the case of Type II, a pair of collectors' strips of three).

[1] Date of availability (inclusive) of the range of six values/weights (and Types). The dates do not take account of the availability of particular year codes which are randomly available and dependent on the stock that is available from a machine at the time.

Exhibitions simplified checklist **ROYAL MAIL POST & GO STAMPS**

Post & Go tables. The tables on the next few pages list Post & Go stamps with inscriptions from the following primary locations: UK and international stamp exhibitions, the UK's national Postal Museum (formerly The BPMA, and since 1 February 2016, The Postal Museum), Royal Mail Enquiry Offices and the Armed Forces' museums which have (or had) Post & Go machines. Inscriptions from other (secondary) locations are not within the scope of these tables. The final table lists Post & Go stamps from exhibitions and stamp fairs which were generated without inscriptions.

The tables have been compiled from information available at time of going to press. Note that the lists of dates of availability/duration are not exhaustive and are merely intended as a guide to the availability of the inscriptions. However, if you have additional relevant information (or spot any mistakes) please do get in touch in the usual way. The tables are intended to be a simplified record and do not attempt to list Post & Go stamps from the specified locations with errors, as such items are beyond the scope of this particular listing. Note that some of the catalogue numbers shown are provisional and may be subject to change.

In the 2018 catalogue these tables included prices for the first time. The prices shown are provided for the information of collectors and indicate what one might expect to pay for the said items in the retail market place. Unless noted to the contrary they are for Collectors' Strips (or for Collectors' Pairs of 2nd/2nd Large). If no price is given then at the time of publication the market price was not sufficiently established. (These tables are copyright John M Deering and for the convenience of collectors are reproduced in catalogue style with his permission.)

Post & Go stamps – the different exhibition issues with inscriptions to April 2021: A simplified checklist

Post and Go stamps – the inscriptions from UK and international stamp exhibitions, September 2011–September 2017: A simplified checklist of the Machin, Union Flag and pictorial issues

Stamp Design, Values, **Inscriptions** (see **bold** text) & Note(s)	Year Code	Availability (dates inclusive) & Note(s)	Cat. No. of Stamp Issue Without Inscription, or Closest Match	Collectors' Strip Price
Machin: 1st/1st L/E 20g/WW 10g/WW 20g/WW 40g				
Autumn Stampex 2011, 14–17 September 2011				
Arnold Machin 1911–1999	None	Available throughout exhibition	FS1a/3a, 4a, 5a & 5e (Type II)	17.00
Spring Stampex 2012, 22–25 February 2012				
Diamond Jubilee 1952–2012	None	Available throughout exhibition	FS1a/3a, 4a, 5a & 5e (Type II)	15.00
The National Philatelic Exhibition Perth 2012 (Scotland), 19–22 October 2012				
Perth 2012 **19–22 October**	None	Available to non-delegates only on 19–20 October	FS1b/3b, 4b, 5b & 5eb (Type III)	80.00
Spring Stampex 2013, 20–23 February 2013				
The Coronation **60th Anniversary**	None	Available throughout exhibition	FS1b/3b, 4b, 5b & 5eb (Type III)	15.00
The Coronation **60th Anniversary** First line slightly inset.	None	Only known from stock produced in advance of the exhibition for sale at Royal Mail exhibition stand. Available throughout exhibition	FS1b/3b, 4b, 5b & 5eb (Type III)	20.00
84th Annual Congress of Association of Scottish Philatelic Societies (Perth, Scotland), 19–20 April 2013				
84th Scottish **Congress 2013**	None	Available throughout exhibition	FS1b/3b, 4b, 5b & 5eb (Type III)	20.00
Australia 2013 World Stamp Exhibition (Melbourne, Australia), 10–15 May 2013				
Australia 2013 **World Stamp Expo** with '**GB**' code	None	Issued to coincide with the exhibition and only available from Royal Mail, Tallents House, Edinburgh	FS1b/3b, 4b, 5b & 5eb (Type III)	18.00
Australia 2013 **Stamp Expo** '**World**' missing, with '**AU**' code	None	Only available from machines at the exhibition	FS1b/3b, 4b, 5b & 5eb (Type III)	29.00
Spring Stampex 2014, 19–22 February 2014				
Stampex 2014 **19–22 February**	None	Available for the majority of the exhibition	FS1b/3b, 4b, 5b & 5eb (Type III)	23.00
	MA13	Sometimes available from the machine	FS77/79, 81/83 (but Type III)	25.00
Machin: 1st/1st L/E 20g/E 60g/WW 20g/WW 60g				
85th Annual Congress of Association of Scottish Philatelic Societies (Perth, Scotland), 11–12 April 2014				
85th Scottish **Congress 2014**	None	Available for the majority of the exhibition	FS1b/3b, 3d, 5b, 5f (but Type III)	30.00
	MA13	Sometimes available from the machine	FS77/80, 82 & 84 (but Type III)	28.00

ROYAL MAIL POST & GO STAMPS Exhibitions simplified checklist

Post and Go stamps – the inscriptions from UK and international stamp exhibitions, September 2011–September 2017: A simplified checklist of the Machin, Union Flag and pictorial issues

Stamp Design, Values, **Inscriptions** (see **bold** text) & Note(s)	Year Code	Availability (dates inclusive) & Note(s)	Cat. No. of Stamp Issue Without Inscription, or Closest Match	Collectors' Strip Price
Machin: 1st/1st L/E 20g WW 10g/E 60g/WW 20g/WW 60g				
PhilaKorea World Stamp Exhibition, Seoul, Korea 2014, 7–12 August 2014				
PhilaKorea 2014 World Stamp Expo	None	Available from Royal Mail, Tallents House, Edinburgh. Also available from machines throughout exhibition	FS1d, 2d, 3cb, 3d, 5d & 5f (Type IIIA)	18.00[1]
Issued to coincide with the exhibition and available from Royal Mail, Tallents House, Edinburgh, with '**GB**' code. Also available throughout exhibition, with '**KR**' code.	MA13	Available from Royal Mail, Tallents House, Edinburgh. Also available from machines throughout exhibition	FS77b, 78b, 79bb, 80, 82b & 84 (Type IIIA)	20.00[1]
Machin: 1st/1st L/E 20g WW 10g/E 100g/WW 20g/WW 100g				
86th Annual Congress of Association of Scottish Philatelic Societies (Perth, Scotland), 17–18 April 2015				
86th Scottish Congress 2015	MA13	Only available from machines at the exhibition	FS77b, 78b, 79bb, 80ca, 82b & 84ca (Type IIIA)	23.00
	None	Only available from machines at the exhibition	FS1d, 2d, 3cb, 3ea, 5d & 5ga (Type IIIA)	25.00
86th Scottish Congress '**2015**' missing after '**Congress**'.	MA13	Only available from stock produced in advance and for collection from the Post & Go stand at the exhibition	FS77b, 78b, 79bb, 80ca, 82b & 84ca (Type IIIA)	40.00
	None	Only available from stock produced in advance and for collection from the Post & Go stand at the exhibition (Only known from a very small part of this stock)	FS1d, 2d, 3cb, 3ea, 5d & 5ga (Type IIIA)	80.00
LONDON 2015 EUROPHILEX, 13–16 May 2015				
Europhilex London Penny Black 175	MA13	Available for the majority of the exhibition	FS77b, 78b, 79bb, 80ca, 82b & 84ca (Type IIIA)	15.00
	None	Sometimes available from the machine	FS1d, 2d, 3cb, 3ea, 5d & 5ga (Type IIIA)	19.00
SINGAPORE 2015 World Stamp Exhibition, 14–19 August 2015				
Singpex 2015 World Stamp Expo	None	Available from Royal Mail, Tallents House, Edinburgh.	FS1d, 2d, 3cb, 3ea, 5d & 5ga (Type IIIA)	18.00
Issued to coincide with the exhibition and available from Royal Mail, Tallents House, Edinburgh, with '**GB**' code. Also available throughout exhibition, with '**SG**' code.	MA13	Available from Royal Mail, Tallents House, Edinburgh. Also available from machines throughout exhibition	FS77b, 78b, 79bb, 80ca, 82b & 84ca (Type IIIA)	19.00[1]
Autumn Stampex 2015, 16–19 September 2015				
Queen Elizabeth II Longest Reign	None	Available for the majority of the exhibition	FS1d, 2d, 3cb, 3ea, 5d & 5ga (Type IIIA)	15.00
	MA13	Only available from a machine for a very short period on 18 September 2015. Apparently from one roll only	FS77b, 78b, 79bb, 80ca, 82b & 84ca (Type IIIA)	30.00
Spring Stampex 2016, 17–20 February 2016				
500 Years of Royal Mail	None	Available for the majority of the exhibition	FS1d, 2d, 3cb, 3ea, 5d & 5ga (Type IIIA)	15.00
	MA13	Sometimes available from the machine	FS77b, 78b, 79bb, 80ca, 82b & 84ca (Type IIIA)	22.00
87th Annual Congress of Association of Scottish Philatelic Societies (Perth, Scotland), 15–16 April 2016				
87th Scottish Congress 2016 Dual value correctly shown as '**Euro 20g World 10g**'.	MA13	Only available from machines at the exhibition	FS77b, 78b, 79bb, 80ca, 82b & 84ca (Type IIIA)	23.00
87th Scottish Congress 2016 Dual value with '**20g weight**' missing, and instead shown as '**Euro World 10g**'	None	Only available from stock produced in advance and for collection from the Post & Go stand at the exhibition (Stock without a year code is only known without the '**20g weight**' and is from the material produced in advance of the exhibition)	FS1d, 2d, 3cb, 3ea, 5d & 5ga (Type IIIA)	60.00

Exhibitions simplified checklist **ROYAL MAIL POST & GO STAMPS**

Post and Go stamps – the inscriptions from UK and international stamp exhibitions, September 2011–September 2017: A simplified checklist of the Machin, Union Flag and pictorial issues

Stamp Design, Values, **Inscriptions** (see **bold** text) & Note(s)	Year Code	Availability (dates inclusive) & Note(s)	Cat. No. of Stamp Issue Without Inscription, or Closest Match	Collectors' Strip Price
Machin: 1st/1st L/E 20g WW 10g/E 100g/WW 20g/WW 100g continued				
Spring Stampex 2017, 15–18 February 2017				
65th Anniversary of HM The Queen's Accession	MA14	Available for the majority of the exhibition	FS77b, 78b, 79bb, 80ca, 82b & 84ca (Type IIIA)	16.00
	MA13	Only known from a small part of the stock produced in advance of the exhibition for sale at Royal Mail exhibition stand	FS77b, 78b, 79bb, 80ca, 82b & 84ca (Type IIIA)	40.00
Machin Anniversary 1967–2017	MA14	Available for the majority of the exhibition	FS77b, 78b, 79bb, 80ca, 82b & 84ca (Type IIIA)	16.00
	None	Only available from a machine for a very short period on 16 February 2017. Apparently from one roll only	FS1d, 2d, 3cb, 3ea, 5d & 5ga (Type IIIA)	42.00
88th Annual Congress of Association of Scottish Philatelic Societies (Perth, Scotland), 21–22 April 2017				
88th Scottish Congress	MA15	Available from the machine for part of the exhibition	FS77b, 78b, 79bb, 80ca, 82b & 84ca (Type IIIA)	35.00
'**2017**' missing after '**Congress**' All stock dispensed from the exhibition's machine(s) was missing '2017'. (See also 50th Anniversary Machin design which has '2017').	None	Available from the machine for part of the exhibition	FS1d, 2d, 3cb, 3ea, 5d & 5ga (Type IIIA)	35.00
	MA13	Only available from the machine for a very short period. Apparently a part or single roll only	FS77b, 78b, 79bb, 80ca, 82b & 84ca (Type IIIA)	—
50th Anniversary Machin design in six different colours: 1st/1st L/E 20g WW 10g/E 100g/WW 20g/WW 100g				
88th Annual Congress of Association of Scottish Philatelic Societies (Perth, Scotland), 21–22 April 2017				
88th Scottish Congress 2017 Stock bearing '**2017**' only came from stock produced in advance of the exhibition.	n/a	The 50th Anniversary Machin design only came from stock produced in advance and for collection from the Post & Go stand at the exhibition. This design used was: i) Used by mistake (intended design was the standard Machin which was not used for stock produced in advance, instead could only be obtained from the exhibition's machine(s) [See elsewhere in this table]). ii) Had not been officially issued (it was pre-released – official issue date was the 5 June 2017)	FS179a/184a (Type IIIA)	95.00
50th Anniversary Machin design: 1st x 6 different colours				
Autumn Stampex 2017, 13–16 September 2017				
Autumn Stampex 2017	n/a	Available throughout exhibition	FS179a/184a (Type IIIA)	9.00
Union Flag: 1st/1st L/E 20g/WW 10g/WW 20g/WW 40g				
Autumn Stampex 2012, 26–29 September 2012				
Diamond Jubilee 1952–2012	None	Available throughout exhibition	FS39/44 (but Type III)	15.00
The National Philatelic Exhibition Perth 2012 (Scotland), 19–22 October 2012				
Perth 2012 19–22 October	None	Available to non-delegates only on 19–20 October	FS39/44 (but Type III)	80.00
84th Annual Congress of Association of Scottish Philatelic Societies (Perth, Scotland), 19–20 April 2013				
84th Scottish Congress 2013	None	Available throughout exhibition	FS39/44 (but Type III)	20.00
Australia 2013 World Stamp Exhibition (Melbourne, Australia), 10–15 May 2013				
Australia 2013 World Stamp Expo with '**GB**' code.	None	Issued to coincide with the exhibition and only available from Royal Mail, Tallents House, Edinburgh	FS39/44 (but Type III)	18.00
Australia 2013 Stamp Expo '**World**' missing, with '**AU**' code.	None	Only available from machines at the exhibition	FS39/44 (but Type III)	28.00
Autumn Stampex 2013, 18–21 September 2013				
The Coronation 60th Anniversary	MA13	Available throughout exhibition	FS85/7 & 89/91 (but Type III)	15.00

ROYAL MAIL POST & GO STAMPS *Exhibitions simplified checklist*

1st Class up to 100g — Arnold Machin 1911-1999 — 002011 94-000185-37	**1st Large** up to 100g — Diamond Jubilee 1952 - 2012 — 002012 23-000109-80	**Worldwide** up to 10g — Perth 2012 19-22 October — AOGB12 A2-000643-10
Worldwide up to 20g — The Coronation 60th Anniversary — A2GB13 B1-001689-77	**Worldwide** up to 20g — The Coronation 60th Anniversary — A2GB13 B1-003087-17	**Worldwide** up to 40g — 84th Scottish Congress 2013 — A4GB13 A4-001108-54
Worldwide up to 40g — Australia 2013 World Stamp Expo — A5GB13 B1-003875-42	**Worldwide** up to 40g — Australia 2013 Stamp Expo — A5AU13 A3-001510-12	**1st Large** up to 100g — Stampex 2014 19-22 February — B2GB14 A004-0405-236
Europe up to 20g — 85th Scottish Congress 2014 — B4GB14 B002-0135-141	**Europe** up to 60g — PhilaKorea 2014 World Stamp Expo — B8KR14 A003-1030-226	**Europe** up to 100g — 86th Scottish Congress 2015 — B4GB15 A006-0267-064
Europe up to 100g — 86th Scottish Congress — B4GB15 B001-2974-118	**Europe** up to 100g — Europhilex London Penny Black 175 — B5GB15 B001-2714-058	**Worldwide** up to 100g — Singpex 2015 World Stamp Expo — B8GB15 B001-1621-066
Worldwide up to 100g — Queen Elizabeth II Longest Reign — B9GB15 B001-1798-108	**Euro 20g** World 10g — 500 Years of Royal Mail — B2GB16 B001-4379-003	**Euro 20g** World 10g — 87th Scottish Congress 2016 — B4GB16 A011-2463-543
Euro World 10g — 87th Scottish Congress 2016 — B4GB16 B001-4624-087	**Europe** up to 100g — 65th Anniversary of HM The Queen's Accession — B2GB17 B001-8185-238	**Worldwide** up to 20g — Machin Anniversary 1967-2017 — B2GB17 B001-8163-215

The different inscriptions from exhibitions. Where the same inscription exists on more than one design only one may be pictured.

Exhibitions simplified checklist **ROYAL MAIL POST & GO STAMPS**

Post and Go stamps – the inscriptions from UK and international stamp exhibitions, September 2011–September 2017:
A simplified checklist of the Machin, Union Flag and pictorial issues

Stamp Design, Values, **Inscriptions** (see **bold** text) & Note(s)	Year Code	Availability (dates inclusive) & Note(s)	Cat. No. of Stamp Issue Without Inscription, or Closest Match	Collectors' Strip Price
Union Flag: 1st/1st L/E 20g/E 60g/WW 20g/WW 60g				
85th Annual Congress of Association of Scottish Philatelic Societies (Perth, Scotland), 11–12 April 2014				
85th Scottish Congress 2014	MA13	Available for the majority of the exhibition	FS85/8, 90 & 92 (but Type III)	30.00
	None	Sometimes available from the machine	FS39/41, 41b, 43 & 44b (but Type III)	27.00
Union Flag: 1st/1st L/E 20g WW 10g/E 60g/WW 20g/WW 60g				
PhilaKorea World Stamp Exhibition, Seoul, Korea 2014, 7–12 August 2014				
PhilaKorea 2014 World Stamp Expo Issued to coincide with the exhibition and available from Royal Mail, Tallents House, Edinburgh, with '**GB**' code. Also available throughout exhibition, with '**KR**' code.	None	Available from Royal Mail, Tallents House, Edinburgh. Also available from machines throughout exhibition	FS39, 40, 41a, 41b, 43 & 44b (but Type IIIA)	20.00[1]
	MA13	Only known from a very small part of the stock available from Royal Mail, Tallents House, Edinburgh	FS85/6, 87a, 88, 90 & 92 (but Type IIIA)	£125
Spring Stampex 2015, 18–21 February 2015				
Spring Stampex February 2015	None	Available throughout exhibition	FS39, 40, 41a, 41b, 43 & 44b (but Type IIIA)	15.00
Union Flag: 1st/1st L/E 20g WW 10g/E 100g/WW 20g/WW 100g				
86th Annual Congress of Association of Scottish Philatelic Societies (Perth, Scotland), 17–18 April 2015				
86th Scottish Congress 2015	None	Only available from machines at the exhibition	FS39, 40, 41a, 41c, 43 & 44c (but Type IIIA)	20.00
86th Scottish Congress '**2015**' missing after '**Congress**'.	None	Only available from stock produced in advance and for collection from the Post & Go stand at the exhibition	FS39, 40, 41a, 41c, 43 & 44c (but Type IIIA)	40.00
SINGAPORE 2015 World Stamp Exhibition, 14–19 August 2015				
Singpex 2015 World Stamp Expo Issued to coincide with the exhibition and available from Royal Mail, Tallents House, Edinburgh, with '**GB**' code. Also available throughout exhibition, with '**SG**' code.	None	Available from Royal Mail, Tallents House, Edinburgh. Also available from machines throughout exhibition	FS39, 40, 41a, 41c, 43 & 44c (but Type IIIA)	17.00[1]
HONG KONG 2015 (31st Asian International Stamp Exhibition), 20–23 November 2015				
Hong Kong November 2015 Issued to coincide with the exhibition and available from Royal Mail, Tallents House, Edinburgh, with '**GB**' code. Also available throughout exhibition, with '**HK**' code.	None	Available from Royal Mail, Tallents House, Edinburgh. Also available from machines throughout exhibition	FS39, 40, 41a, 41c, 43 & 44c (but Type IIIA)	16.00[1]
87th Annual Congress of Association of Scottish Philatelic Societies (Perth, Scotland), 15–16 April 2016				
87th Scottish Congress 2016 Dual value correctly shown as '**Euro 20g World 10g**'.	None	Only available from machines at the exhibition	FS39, 40, 41a, 41c, 43 & 44c (but Type IIIA)	20.00
87th Scottish Congress 2016 Dual value with '**20g weight**' missing, and instead shown as '**Euro World 10g**'.	None	Only available from stock produced in advance and for collection from the Post & Go stand at the exhibition	FS39, 40, 41a, 41c, 43 & 44c (but Type IIIA)	40.00

ROYAL MAIL POST & GO STAMPS — Exhibitions simplified checklist

Post and Go stamps – the inscriptions from UK and international stamp exhibitions, September 2011–September 2017: A simplified checklist of the Machin, Union Flag and pictorial issues

Stamp Design, Values, **Inscriptions** (see **bold** text) & Note(s)	Year Code	Availability (dates inclusive) & Note(s)	Cat. No. of Stamp Issue Without Inscription, or Closest Match	Collectors' Strip Price
Union Flag: 1st/1st L/E 20g WW 10g/E 100g/WW 20g/WW 100g continued				
World Stamp Show-NY 2016 (New York), 28 May–4 June 2016				
World Stamp Show NY2016 Issued to coincide with the exhibition and available from Royal Mail, Tallents House, Edinburgh, with '**GB**' code. Also available throughout exhibition, with '**US**' code.	None	Available from Royal Mail, Tallents House, Edinburgh. Also available from machines throughout exhibition	FS39, 40, 41a, 41c, 43 & 44c (but Type IIIA)	19.00[1]
Poppy: 1st/1st L/E 20g WW 10g/E 60g/WW 20g/WW 60g				
Autumn Stampex 2014, 17–20 September 2014				
First World War Centenary	MA14	Available throughout exhibition	FS103, 104, 105, 106, 107 & 108 (but Type IIIA)	18.00
Poppy: 1st/1st L/E 20g WW 10g/E 100g/WW 20g/WW 100g				
Autumn Stampex 2016, 14–17 September 2016				
The Battle of the Somme (+ tank logo)	MA15	Available throughout exhibition	FS137/142 (Type IIIA)	19.00
Autumn Stampex 2017, 13–16 September 2017				
WWI Battle of Passchendaele	MA15	Available throughout exhibition	FS137/142 (Type IIIA)	18.00
Hong Kong Sea Travel: 1st/1st L/E 20g WW 10g/E 100g/WW 20g/WW 100g				
HONG KONG 2015 (31st Asian International Stamp Exhibition), 20–23 November 2015				
Hong Kong November 2015 Issued to coincide with the exhibition and available from Royal Mail, Tallents House, Edinburgh, with '**GB**' code. Also available throughout exhibition, with '**HK**' code.	MA15	Available from Royal Mail, Tallents House, Edinburgh. Also available from machines throughout exhibition	FS131/136 (but Type IIIA & stamps digitally printed)	16.00[1]

The different inscriptions from exhibitions. Where the same inscription exists on more than one design only one may be pictured.

398

Exhibitions simplified checklist ROYAL MAIL POST & GO STAMPS

Post and Go stamps – the inscriptions from UK and international stamp exhibitions, September 2011–September 2017:
A simplified checklist of the Machin, Union Flag and pictorial issues

Stamp Design, Values, **Inscriptions** (see **bold** text) & Note(s)	Year Code	Availability (dates inclusive) & Note(s)	Cat. No. of Stamp Issue Without Inscription, or Closest Match	Collectors' Strip Price
New York Sea Travel: 1st/1st L/E 20g WW 10g/E 100g/WW 20g/WW 100g				
World Stamp Show-NY 2016 (New York), 28 May–4 June 2016				
World Stamp Show NY2016 Issued to coincide with the exhibition and available from Royal Mail, Tallents House, Edinburgh, with '**GB**' code. Also available throughout exhibition, with '**US**' code.	MA15	Available from Royal Mail, Tallents House, Edinburgh. Also available from machines throughout exhibition	FS131/136 (but Type IIIA & stamps digitally printed)	19.00[1]
Lion (Heraldic Beast): 1st/1st L/E 20g WW 10g/E 100g/WW 20g/WW 100g				
87th Annual Congress of Association of Scottish Philatelic Societies (Perth, Scotland), 5–16 April 2016				
87th Scottish Congress 2016 Dual value correctly shown as '**Euro 20g World 10g**'.	MA15	Only available from machines at the exhibition	FS125/130 (but Type IIIA)	20.00
87th Scottish Congress 2016 Dual value without '**20g weight**', and instead shown as '**Euro World 10g**'.	MA15	Only available from stock produced in advance and for collection from the Post & Go stand at the exhibition	FS125/130 (but Type IIIA)	36.00
88th Annual Congress of Association of Scottish Philatelic Societies (Perth, Scotland), 21–22 April 2017				
88th Scottish Congress '**2017**' missing after '**Congress**'.	MA15	Only available from machines at the exhibition, but different to stock produced in advance (see below) which was not fully appreciated until after exhibition had ended	FS125/130 (but Type IIIA)	—
88th Scottish Congress 2017	MA15	Stock bearing '**2017**' only came from stock produced in advance and for collection from the Post & Go stand at the exhibition	FS125/130 (but Type IIIA)	50.00
Thistle (Symbolic Flower): 1st/1st L/E 20g WW 10g/E 100g/WW 20g/WW 100g				
88th Annual Congress of Association of Scottish Philatelic Societies (Perth, Scotland), 21–22 April 2017				
88th Scottish Congress '**2017**' missing after '**Congress**'.	MA17	Only available from machines at the exhibition, but different to stock produced in advance (see below) which was not fully appreciated until after exhibition had ended	FS103, 104, 105, 106b, 107, 108b (but Type IIIA & stamps digitally printed)	—
88th Scottish Congress 2017	MA17	Stock bearing '**2017**' only came from stock produced in advance and for collection from the Post & Go stand at the exhibition	FS103, 104, 105, 106b, 107, 108b (but Type IIIA & stamps digitally printed)	50.00

[1] When a similar item is available from more than one location the price given is for the cheaper of the two.
Autumn Stampex 2017, 13–16 September 2017, was the last time Post & Go kiosks were at exhibitions.
Glitches affecting inscriptions and lasting only a very short time and/or which exist in small quantities are beyond the scope of these tables.

The different inscriptions from exhibitions. Where the same inscription exists on more than one design only one may be pictured.

ROYAL MAIL POST & GO STAMPS *The Postal Museum simplified checklist*

Post & Go stamps – the different issues and inscriptions from '*The Postal Museum*' (formerly 'The BPMA'), to April 2022: A simplified checklist

Post & Go stamps – the inscriptions from *The Postal Museum* (formerly 'The BPMA'), December 2012–April 2022: A simplified checklist of the Machin, Union Flag and pictorial issues

Stamp Design, Values, **Inscriptions** (see **bold** text) & Note(s)	Year Code	Availability (dates inclusive) & Note(s)	Cat. No. of Stamp Issue Without Inscription, or Closest Match	Collectors' Strip Price
Machin: 1st/1st L/E 20g/WW 10g/WW 20g/WW 40g				
The B.P.M.A. Low set; inscription is immediately above code line.	None	3 December 2012–18 February 2014	FS1b/3b, 4b, 5b & 5eb (Type III)	17.00
The B.P.M.A. Postage Due 1914	None	Sometimes available between 19 February–21 March 2014	FS1b/3b, 4b, 5b & 5eb (Type III)	23.00
An RMS II machine replaced existing machine from 24 March 2014. The stamps from it have a subtly different typeface.	MA13	Sometimes available between 19 February–21 March 2014 24–28 March 2014 (RMS II machine)	FS77/79, 81/83 (but Type III)	30.00[1]
Machin: 1st/1st L/E 20g/E 60g/WW 20g/WW 60g				
The B.P.M.A. Postage Due 1914	MA13	31 March–25 April 2014	FS77/80, 82 & 84 (but Type III)	25.00
Machin: 1st/1st L/E 20g WW 10g/E 60g/WW 20g/WW 60g				
The B.P.M.A. High set; inscription is immediately below service indicator. E 20g WW 10g in large typeface.	MA13	28 April–19 August 2014	FS77, 78, 79b, 80, 82 & 84 (but Type III)	30.00
The B.P.M.A. Inland Airmail 1934 + Airmail logo	None	Sometimes available between 20 August–20 October 2014	FS1d, 2d, 3cb, 3d, 5d & 5f (Type IIIA)	25.00
	MA13	Sometimes available between 20 August–20 October 2014	FS77b, 78b, 79bb, 80, 82b & 84 (Type IIIA)	20.00
The B.P.M.A. Low set; inscription is immediately above code line. All six values have a revised (smaller) typeface.	None	21 October 2014–17 February 2015	FS1d, 2d, 3cb, 3d, 5d & 5f (Type IIIA)	23.00
The B.P.M.A. Trollope 200 + Postbox logo	MA13	18 February–28 March 2015	FS77b, 78b, 79bb, 80, 82b & 84 (Type IIIA)	19.00

Europe up to 20g — The B.P.M.A. — ADGB12 A1-001063-69

Worldwide up to 40g — The B.P.M.A. Postage Due 1914 — A2GB14 A1-003615-96

Worldwide up to 60g — The B.P.M.A. Postage Due 1914 — B4GB14 A001-0247-210

Euro 20g World 10g — The B.P.M.A. — B6GB14 A001-0694-171

Europe up to 100g — The B.P.M.A. — B8GB15 A001-3598-136

Worldwide up to 100g — The B.P.M.A. Penny Black 175 — B5GB15 A001-3336-024

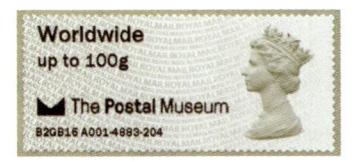

Worldwide up to 100g — The Postal Museum — B2GB16 A001-4893-204

1st Class up to 100g — The Postal Museum — B2GB16 A001-4571-343

Euro World 10g — The Postal Museum — B3GB16 A001-5079-226

Euro 20g World 10g — The Postal Museum — B7GB18 A001-0658-015

The different inscriptions from *The Postal Museum*. Where the same inscription exists on more than one design only one may be pictured.

The Postal Museum simplified checklist **ROYAL MAIL POST & GO STAMPS**

Post & Go stamps – the inscriptions from *The Postal Museum* (formerly 'The BPMA'), December 2012–April 2022:
A simplified checklist of the Machin, Union Flag and pictorial issues

Stamp Design, Values, **Inscriptions** (see **bold** text) & Note(s)	Year Code	Availability (dates inclusive) & Note(s)	Cat. No. of Stamp Issue Without Inscription, or Closest Match	Collectors' Strip Price
Machin: 1st/1st L/E 20g WW 10g/E 100g/WW 20g/WW 100g				
The B.P.M.A. **Trollope 200** + Postbox logo	MA13	30 March–30 April 2015	FS77b, 78b, 79bb, 80ca, 82b & 84ca (Type IIIA)	35.00
The B.P.M.A. Low set; inscription is immediately above code line. All six values have a revised (smaller) typeface.	MA13	1–5 May 2015 8 August 2015–29 January 2016	FS77b, 78b, 79bb, 80ca, 82b & 84ca (Type IIIA)	22.00
The B.P.M.A. **Penny Black 175** + Maltese Cross logo	MA13	6 May–7 August 2015	FS77b, 78b, 79bb, 80ca, 82b & 84ca (Type IIIA)	18.00
The Postal Museum + Museum's Envelope logo (small format) logo positioned before the wording. Envelope logo originally positioned inset from the left. From 17 February 2016 Envelope logo repositioned ranged left.	MA13	1 February–28 March 2016 1 April–19 August 2016 Late August–13 September 2016 Sometimes available between 14 November 2016–2 June 2017	FS77b, 78b, 79bb, 80ca, 82b & 84ca (Type IIIA)	20.00¹
	None	Available for a short time sometime between 19 August–late August 2016	FS1d, 2d, 3cb, 3ea, 5d & 5ga (Type IIIA)	—
	MA15	Sometimes available between 14 November 2016–2 June 2017	FS77b, 78b, 79bb, 80ca, 82b & 84ca (Type IIIA)	21.00
The Postal Museum + Museum's Envelope logo (small format) logo positioned before the wording. Dual value without '**20g weight**', and instead shown as '**Euro World 10g**'	MA13	29–31 March 2016	FS77b, 78b, 79bb *var*, 80ca, 82b & 84ca (Type IIIA) Single: i.e. Euro World 10g/FS79bb *var* (but TIIIA)	— 30.00
The Postal Museum **King Edward VIII 1936** + ERI VIII Cypher logo, + Museum's Envelope logo (small format) logo positioned before the wording.	None	14 September–24 October 2016	FS1d, 2d, 3cb, 3ea, 5d & 5ga (Type IIIA)	19.00
	MA13	Apparently available for a few hours only on 14 September 2016	FS77b, 78b, 79bb, 80ca, 82b & 84ca (Type IIIA)	
	MA15	24 October–11 November 2016	FS77b, 78b, 79bb, 80ca, 82b & 84ca (Type IIIA)	23.00
The Postal Museum Revised generic inscription without Envelope logo.	MA14	2 July–11 September 2018 Late autumn/winter 2019–18 March 2020 except when 'MA15' available	FS77b, 78b, 79bb, 80ca, 82b & 84ca (Type IIIA)	19.00
	None	Apparently available for a few hours only on 29 August 2018.	FS1d, 2d, 3cb, 3ea, 5d & 5ga (Type IIIA)	—
	MA15	1 January 2019–12 February 2019 Mid October–early 2020 except when 'MA14' available	FS77b, 78b, 79bb, 80ca, 82b & 84ca (Type IIIA)	19.00
The Postal Museum **'F' box 50** + Postbox logo	None	Apparently available for a few hours only on 12 September 2018	FS1d, 2d, 3cb, 3ea, 5d & 5ga (Type IIIA)	—
	MA14	12 September–22 October 2018	FS77b, 78b, 79bb, 80ca, 82b & 84ca (Type IIIA)	19.00
	MA15	22 October–7 November 2018	FS77b, 78b, 79bb, 80ca, 82b & 84ca (Type IIIA)	19.00
The Postal Museum **NPM 50** Unintentional issue when the Machin design was loaded into the machine and the return of the generic inscription (i.e. '**The Postal Museum**') was delayed due to a technical reason.	None	Apparently available for a few hours only on 11 October 2019	FS1d, 2d, 3cb, 3ea, 5d & 5ga (Type IIIA)	—
	MA14	Available for a few hours only on 11 October 2019	FS77b, 78b, 79bb, 80ca, 82b & 84ca (Type IIIA)	20.00
	MA15	11 October 2019–mid October 2019	FS77b, 78b, 79bb, 80ca, 82b & 84ca (Type IIIA)	22.00
Mail Rail	MA14	29 October–1 December 2019 except when 'MA15' available (see below) 1 January–18 March 2020	FS77b, 78b, 79bb, 80ca, 82b & 84ca (Type IIIA)	20.00
	MA15	Available for a few hours only on 9 November 2019	FS77b, 78b, 79bb, 80ca, 82b & 84ca (Type IIIA)	24.00

ROYAL MAIL POST & GO STAMPS — *The Postal Museum simplified checklist*

Post & Go stamps – the inscriptions from *The Postal Museum* (formerly 'The BPMA'), December 2012–April 2022: A simplified checklist of the Machin, Union Flag and pictorial issues

Stamp Design, Values, Inscriptions (see **bold** text) & Note(s)	Year Code	Availability (dates inclusive) & Note(s)	Cat. No. of Stamp Issue Without Inscription, or Closest Match	Collectors' Strip Price
Machin: 1st/1st L/E 20g WW 10g/E 100g WW 20g/WW 100g Zone 1 & 3/WW 100g Zone 2 *[Dual-zone value with ampersand i.e. 'World 100g Zone 1 & 3']*				
The Postal Museum Virtual Stampex 2020	MA14	Only available via mail order from The Postal Museum London online shop between 1–3 October 2020[2], i.e. duration Virtual Autumn Stampex 2020	FS77b, 78b, 79bb (Type IIIA), 80d, 84d var & 84e (but Type IIIA)	25.00
The Postal Museum	MA14	29 October–1 November 2020[2]	FS77b, 78b, 79bb (Type IIIA), 80d, 84d var & 84e (but Type IIIA)	25.00
Mail Rail	MA14	29 October–1 November 2020[2] 3 November 2020[2] 3–19 December 2020[2]	FS77b, 78b, 79bb (Type IIIA), 80d, 84d var & 84e (but Type IIIA)	25.00
Machin: 1st/1st Large/E 100g WW 20g/WW 100g/E Large 100g/WW Large 100g				
The Postal Museum Wish You Were Here + Postcard logo	MA13	20 May 2021–2 January 2022	FS77b, 78b, 80d (but Type IIIA), 84ca, 80e (but Type IIIA) and 84f (but Type IIIA)	30.00
The Postal Museum	MA14	5 January–18 February 2022	FS77b, 78b, 80d (but Type IIIA), 84ca, 80e (but Type IIIA) and 84f (but Type IIIA)	32.00
			Set of two singles: i.e. E Large 100g/FS80e & WW Large 100g/FS84f (but TIIIA)	20.00
	MA13	27 February–27 March 2022	FS77b, 78b, 80d (but Type IIIA), 84ca, 80e (but Type IIIA) and 84f (but Type IIIA)	32.00

Euro 100g / World 20g — The Postal Museum Virtual Stampex 2020 — B0GB20 A001-5337-304

Europe Large 100g — The Postal Museum Wish You Were Here — B5GB21 A001-5794-017

Worldwide Large 100g — The Postal Museum London 2022 — B2GB22 A001-7152-234

Worldwide Large 100g — The Postal Museum Sorting Britain — B3GB22 A001-7436-048

The different inscriptions from *The Postal Museum*. Where the same inscription exists on more than one design only one may be pictured.

The Postal Museum simplified checklist — ROYAL MAIL POST & GO STAMPS

Post & Go stamps – the inscriptions from *The Postal Museum* (formerly 'The BPMA'), December 2012–April 2022: A simplified checklist of the Machin, Union Flag and pictorial issues

Stamp Design, Values, **Inscriptions** (see bold text) & Note(s)	Year Code	Availability (dates inclusive) & Note(s)	Cat. No. of Stamp Issue Without Inscription, or Closest Match	Collectors' Strip Price
Machin: 1st/1st Large/E 100g WW 20g/WW 100g/E Large 100g/WW Large 100g				
The Postal Museum London 2022	MA13	19–26 February 2022	FS77b, 78b, 80*d* (but Type IIIA), 84ca, 80*e* (but Type IIIA) and 84*f* (but Type IIIA)	32.00
The Postal Museum Sorting Britain	MA13	30 March–22 April 2022	FS77b, 78b, 80*d* (but Type IIIA), 84ca, 80*e* (but Type IIIA) and 84*f* (but Type IIIA)	32.00
	R20Y	From 23 April 2022	FS77b, 78b, 80*d* (but Type IIIA), 84ca, 80*e* (but Type IIIA) and 84*f* (but Type IIIA)	32.00
Mail Rail	MA14	20 May–10 Novemeber 2021	FS77b, 78b, 80*d* (but Type IIIA), 84ca, 80*e* (but Type IIIA) and 84*f* (but Type IIIA) Set of two singles: i.e. E Large 100g/FS80e & WW Large 100g/FS84f (but TIIIA)	20.00
	MA13	From 8 December 2021	FS77b, 78b, 80*d* (but Type IIIA), 84ca, 80*e* (but Type IIIA) and 84*f* (but Type IIIA)	32.00
50th Anniversary Machin design: 1st x 6 different colours				
The Postal Museum + Museum's Envelope logo (small format) logo positioned before the wording.	n/a	5 June–12 July 2017	FS179a x 6 (Type IIIA)	9.50
The Postal Museum Official Opening 2017	n/a	25 July 2017 28 July–12 September 2017	FS179a x 6 (Type IIIA)	9.50
The Postal Museum Revised generic inscription without Envelope logo.	n/a	13 September–23 October 2017 2–22 January 2018 23 February–1 July 2018 For a brief time on 26 March 2018 Collectors' Strips of 1st WW 100g were dispensed in error	FS179a x 6 (Type IIIA)	9.00
The Postal Museum NPM 50	n/a	13 February 2019–10 October 2019	FS179a x 6 (Type IIIA)	9.00

The different inscriptions from *The Postal Museum*. Where the same inscription exists on more than one design only one may be pictured.

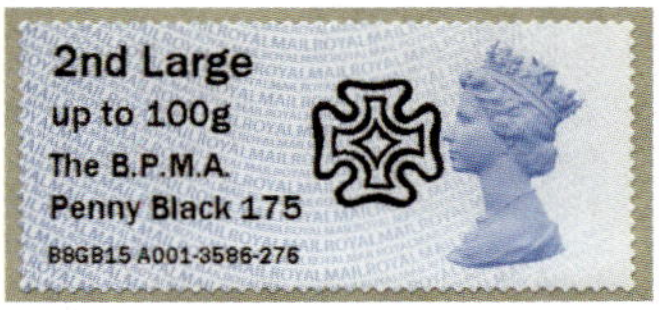

ROYAL MAIL POST & GO STAMPS *The Postal Museum simplified checklist*

Post & Go stamps – the inscriptions from *The Postal Museum* (formerly 'The BPMA'), December 2012–April 2022: A simplified checklist of the Machin, Union Flag and pictorial issues

Stamp Design, Values, Inscriptions (see **bold** text) & Note(s)	Year Code	Availability (dates inclusive) & Note(s)	Cat. No. of Stamp Issue Without Inscription, or Closest Match	Collectors' Strip Price
Machin: 2nd/2nd L				
The B.P.M.A. Inland Airmail 1934 + Airmail logo	MA12	20 August–20 October 2014	FS93b/94b (Type IIIA)	10.00
The B.P.M.A. Inland Airmail 1934 + Airmail logo in '**1st/1stL**' values. '**1st/1stL**' on (blue-coloured FT **14**) second class stock, due to a software glitch.	MA12	Available for a few hours only on 16 September 2014	FT **14** in 1st/1stL (Type IIIA) Set of two singles: i.e. 1st/1stL/FT 14 (TIIIA)	n/a 50.00
The B.P.M.A.	MA12	21 October–12 November 2014 29 December 2014–17 February 2015 1–5 May 2015 8 August–13 November 2015 4–29 January 2016	FS93b/94b (Type IIIA)	6.50
	MA13	Apparently available for a few hours only on 5 May 2015	FS93b/94b (Type IIIA)	—
The B.P.M.A. Trollope 200 + Postbox logo	MA12	18 February–30 April 2015	FS93b/94b (Type IIIA)	6.50
The B.P.M.A. Penny Black 175 + Maltese Cross logo	MA13	6 May–7 July 2015 10 July–(early) August 2015	FS93b/94b (Type IIIA)	6.50
The B.P.M.A. Penny Black 175 + Maltese Cross logo Maltese Cross logo set lower and to right (following a software upgrade).	MA12	Available (early) August–7 August 2015 (Repositioned Maltese Cross logo obscures 'MA12')	FS93b/94b (Type IIIA)	13.00
The Postal Museum + Museum's Envelope logo (small format) logo positioned before the wording. Envelope logo originally positioned inset from the left. From 17 February 2016 Envelope logo repositioned range left.	MA12	1 February–13 September 2016 3–24 January 2017 25 January–12 July 2017 except when 'CL16S' available (see below)	FS93b/94b (Type IIIA)	5.50[1]
	CL16S	Sometimes available between 25 January–12 July 2017	FS157/8 (but Type IIIA)	5.75
The Postal Museum King Edward VIII 1936 + ERI VIII Cypher logo, + Museum's Envelope logo (small format) logo positioned before the wording.	MA12	14 September–11 November 2016	FS93b/94b (Type IIIA)	6.00
The Postal Museum Official Opening 2017	CL16S	25 July 2017 28 July–12 September 2017	FS157/158 (but Type IIIA)	6.00
	MA15	(Early) September–12 September 2017	FS93b/94b (Type IIIA)	6.00
The Postal Museum Revised generic inscription without Envelope logo.	MA15	13 September–12 November 2017 2–22 January 2018 23 February–11 September 2018 1 January 2019–18 March 2020 29 October–1 November 2020[2]	FS93b/94b (Type IIIA)	6.00
The Postal Museum 'F' box 50 + Postbox logo	MA15	12 September–7 November 2018	FS93b/94b (Type IIIA)	6.00
The Postal Museum Wish You Were Here + Postcard logo	MA15	20 May–30 November 2022	FS93b/94b (Type IIIA)	5.00

The different inscriptions from *The Postal Museum*. Where the same inscription exists on more than one design only one may be pictured.

The Postal Museum simplified checklist **ROYAL MAIL POST & GO STAMPS**

Post & Go stamps – the inscriptions from *The Postal Museum* (formerly 'The BPMA'), December 2012–April 2022:
A simplified checklist of the Machin, Union Flag and pictorial issues

Stamp Design, Values, **Inscriptions** (see **bold text**) & Note(s)	Year Code	Availability (dates inclusive) & Note(s)	Cat. No. of Stamp Issue Without Inscription, or Closest Match	Collectors' Strip Price
Union Flag: 1st/1st L/E 20g/WW 10g/WW 20g/WW 40g				
The B.P.M.A. Low set; inscription is immediately above code line.	None	21 February–4 November 2013 / 30 December 2013–18 February 2014	FS39/44 (but Type III)	17.00
The B.P.M.A. Postage Due 1914 An RMS II machine replaced existing machine from 24 March 2014. The stamps from it have a subtly different typeface.	None	Sometimes available between 19–21 February 2014 / 22 February–21 March 2014 / 24–28 March 2014 (RMS II machine)	FS39/44 (but Type III)	23.00[1]
	MA13	Sometimes available between 19–21 February 2014	FS85/7 & 89/91 (but Type III)	55.00
Union Flag: 1st/1st L/E 20g/E 60g/WW 20g/WW 60g				
The B.P.M.A. Postage Due 1914	None	31 March–25 April 2014	FS39/41, 41b, 43 & 44b (but Type III)	20.00
Union Flag: 1st/1st L/E 20g WW 10g/E 60g/WW 20g/WW 60g				
The B.P.M.A. High set; inscription is immediately below service indicator. E 20g WW 10g in large typeface.	None	28 April–19 August 2014	FS39, 40, 41a, 41b, 43 & 44b (but Type III)	25.00
The B.P.M.A. Low set; inscription is immediately above code line. All six values have a revised (smaller) typeface.	None	21 October 2014–17 February 2015	FS39, 40, 41a, 41b, 43 & 44b (but Type IIIA)	25.00
The B.P.M.A. High set; inscription is immediately below service indicator. All six values have a revised (smaller) typeface.	None	18 February–28 March 2015	FS39, 40, 41a, 41b, 43 & 44b (but Type IIIA)	45.00
Union Flag: 1st/1st L/E 20g WW 10g/E 100g/WW 20g/WW 100g				
The B.P.M.A. Low set; inscription is immediately above code line. All six values have a revised (smaller) typeface.	None	30 March 2015–29 January 2016	FS39, 40, 41a, 41c, 43 & 44c (but Type IIIA)	25.00
The Postal Museum + Museum's large format Envelope logo positioned before wording.	None	1 February–28 March 2016 / 1 April 2016–12 July 2017	FS39, 40, 41a, 41c, 43 & 44c (but Type IIIA)	19.00
The Postal Museum + Museum's large format Envelope logo positioned before wording. Dual value without '**20g weight**', and instead shown as '**Euro World 10g**'	None	29–31 March 2016	FS39, 40, 41a var, 41c, 43 & 44c (but Type IIIA) / Single: i.e. Euro World 10g/FS41a var (but TIIIA)	— / 25.00
The Postal Museum Official Opening[3]	None	25 July 2017 / 28 July–12 September 2017	FS39, 40, 41a, 41c, 43 & 44c (but Type IIIA)	19.00
The Postal Museum Revised generic inscription without Envelope logo.	None	30 November 2018–10 September 2019	FS39, 40, 41a, 41c, 43 & 44c (but Type IIIA)	19.00

The different inscriptions from *The Postal Museum*. Where the same inscription exists on more than one design only one may be pictured.

ROYAL MAIL POST & GO STAMPS *The Postal Museum simplified checklist*

Post & Go stamps – the inscriptions from *The Postal Museum* (formerly 'The BPMA'), December 2012–April 2022:
A simplified checklist of the Machin, Union Flag and pictorial issues

Stamp Design, Values, Inscriptions (see **bold** text) & Note(s)	Year Code	Availability (dates inclusive) & Note(s)	Cat. No. of Stamp Issue Without Inscription, or Closest Match	Collectors' Strip Price
Union Flag: 1st/1st L/E 20g WW 10g/E 100g WW 20g/WW 100g Zone 1 & 3/WW 100g Zone 2 *[Dual-zone value with ampersand i.e. 'World 100g Zone 1 & 3']*				
The Postal Museum	None	29 October–1 November 2020[2] 3 November 2020[2] 3–19 December 2020[2]	FS39, 40, 41*a*, 41*d*, 44*d* & 44*e* (but Type IIIA)	25.00
Union Flag: 1st/1st Large/E 100g WW 20g/WW 100g/E Large 100g/WW Large 100g				
The Postal Museum	None	20 May–30 November 2021 05 January–27 March 2022	FS39, 40, 41*d*, 44*c*, 41 *var* & 44 *var* (but Type IIIA) Set of two singles: i.e. E Large 100g/FS41 *var* & WW Large 100g/FS44 *var* (but TIIIA)	32.00 20.00
The Postal Museum Sorting Britain	MA19	From 30 March 2022	FS85*a*, 86*a*, 87*a*, 88 *var*, 92 *var* & 92 *var* (but Type IIIA & stamps digitally printed)	30.00
Common Poppy: 1st/1st L/E 20g WW 10g/E 60g/WW 20g/WW 60g				
The B.P.M.A.	MA14	21 October–12 November 2014	FS103, 104, 105, 106, 107 & 108 (but Type IIIA)	20.00
Common Poppy: 1st/1st L/E 20g WW 10g/E 100g/WW 20g/WW 100g				
The B.P.M.A.	MA15	19 October–13 November 2015	FS137/142 (Type IIIA)	20.00
The Postal Museum + Museum's large format Envelope logo positioned before wording.	MA15	24 October–11 November 2016	FS137/142 (Type IIIA)	20.00
The Postal Museum Revised generic inscription without Envelope logo.	MA15	24 October–12 November 2017	FS137/142 (Type IIIA)	19.00
The Postal Museum WWI 1918-2018	MA15	23 October–29 November 2018	FS137/142 (Type IIIA)	20.00
Common Poppy: 1st/1st Large/E 100g WW 20g/WW 100g/E Large 100g/WW Large 100g				
Mail Rail	MA15	11 November–5 December 2021	FS137/142 (Type IIIA)	32.00
Lion (Heraldic Beast): 1st/1st L/E 20g WW 10g/E 100g/WW 20g/WW 100g				
The B.P.M.A.	MA15	16 September–16 October 2015 4–29 January 2016	FS125/130 (but Type IIIA)	20.00
The Postal Museum + Museum's large format Envelope logo positioned before wording.	MA15	1–16 February 2016	FS125/130 (but Type IIIA)	19.00
***Game of Thrones*: 2nd/2nd L, and 1st/1st L/E 20g WW 10g/E 100g/WW 20g/WW 100g**				
The Postal Museum[4]	CL18S/ R18Y	23 January–22 February 2018	FS199*a*/206*a* (Type IIIA) Set of 8:	 24.00

The different inscriptions from *The Postal Museum*. Where the same inscription exists on more than one design only one may be pictured.

The Postal Museum simplified checklist ROYAL MAIL POST & GO STAMPS

Post & Go stamps – the inscriptions from *The Postal Museum* (formerly 'The BPMA'), December 2012–April 2022:
A simplified checklist of the Machin, Union Flag and pictorial issues

Stamp Design, Values, **Inscriptions** (see **bold** text) & Note(s)	Year Code	Availability (dates inclusive) & Note(s)	Cat. No. of Stamp Issue Without Inscription, or Closest Match	Collectors' Strip Price
Royal Mail Heritage – Transport: 1st × 6 designs				
The Postal Museum + Museum's large format Envelope logo positioned before wording.	MA16	17 February–31 March 2016	FS151×6 (but Type IIIA)	9.00
Royal Mail Heritage – Mail Coach design: 1st/1st L/E 20g WW 10g/E 100g/WW 20g/WW 100g				
The Postal Museum + Museum's large format Envelope logo positioned before wording.	MA16	1 April 2016–12 July 2017	FS151/156 (but Type IIIA & stamps digitally printed)	19.00
The Postal Museum Official Opening[3]	MA16	25 July 2017 28 July–12 September 2017	FS151/156 (but Type IIIA & stamps digitally printed)	19.00
The Postal Museum Revised generic inscription without Envelope logo.	MA16	13 September 2017–11 September 2018 30 November 2018–12 February 2019	FS151/156 (but Type IIIA & stamps digitally printed)	20.00
The Postal Museum NPM 50	MA16	13 February–10 October 2019	FS151/156 (but Type IIIA & stamps digitally printed)	19.00
The Postal Museum New exhibit 2019	MA16	11 October 2019–18 March 2020	FS151/156 (but Type IIIA & stamps digitally printed)	19.00
Royal Mail Heritage – Mail Coach design: 1st/1st L/E 20g WW 10g/E 100g WW 20g/WW 100g Zone 1 & 3/WW 100g Zone 2 [Dual-zone value with ampersand i.e. 'World 100g Zone 1 & 3']				
The Postal Museum Postcards 150	MA16	29 October–1 November 2020[2] 3 November 2020[2] 3–19 December 2020[2]	FS151, 152, 153, 154 var, 156 var, 156 var (but Type IIIA & stamps digitally printed)	25.00
Royal Mail Heritage – Mail Coach design: 1st/1st Large/E 100g WW 20g/WW 100g/E Large 100g/WW Large 100g				
The Postal Museum Postcards 150	MA16	20 May–21 July 2021	FS151, 152, 154 var, 156, 156 var, 156 var (but Type IIIA & stamps digitally printed)	32.00
			Set of two singles: i.e. E Large 100g/FS156 var & WW Large 100g/FS156 var (TIIIA)	20.00
The Postal Museum	MA16	22 July 2021–27 March 2022	FS151, 152, 154 var, 156, 156 var (but Type IIIA & stamps digitally printed)	32.00
Royal Mail Heritage – Mail by Rail: 1st × 6 designs				
The Postal Museum + Museum's large format Envelope logo positioned before wording.	MA17	15 February–31 March 2017	FS173a x6 (Type IIIA)	8.75
Royal Mail Heritage – Mail by Rail: 1st/1st L/E 20g WW 10g/E 100g/WW 20g/WW 100g				
The Postal Museum Revised generic inscription without Envelope logo. Unintentional issue because machine was loaded with Royal Mail Heritage – Mail by Rail design, instead of Royal Mail Heritage – Post Office (London) Railway single-design issue.	MA17	Available for a few hours only on 4 October 2018	FS173a/178a (Type IIIA)	£125
The Postal Museum New exhibit 2019	MA17	Never available to the public via the museum's Post & Go kiosk. Only from a limited edition special pack entitled 'The Great Train Robbery: Crime & the Post' through the museum's gift shop	FS173a/178a (Type IIIA)	35.00

ROYAL MAIL POST & GO STAMPS — *The Postal Museum simplified checklist*

Post & Go stamps – the inscriptions from *The Postal Museum* (formerly 'The BPMA'), December 2012–April 2022:
A simplified checklist of the Machin, Union Flag and pictorial issues

Stamp Design, Values, **Inscriptions** (see **bold** text) & Note(s)	Year Code	Availability (dates inclusive) & Note(s)	Cat. No. of Stamp Issue Without Inscription, or Closest Match	Collectors' Strip Price
Royal Mail Heritage – Post Office (London) Railway design: 1st/1st L/E 20g WW 10g/E 100g/WW 20g/WW 100g				
The Postal Museum + Museum's large format Envelope logo positioned before wording.	MA17	3 April–12 July 2017	FS173a/178a (Type IIIA & stamps digitally printed)	19.00
The Postal Museum Official Opening[3]	MA17	25 July 2017 28 July–12 September 2017	FS173a/178a (Type IIIA & stamps digitally printed)	19.00
The Postal Museum Revised generic inscription without Envelope logo.	MA17	13 September 2017–18 March 2020	FS173a/178a (Type IIIA & stamps digitally printed)	19.00
Mail Rail	MA17	29 October 2019–18 March 2020 except when 'R19Y' available (see below)	FS173a/178a (Type IIIA & stamps digitally printed)	25.00
	R19Y	29 October 2019–18 March 2020 except when 'MA17' available (see above)	FS173a/178a (Type IIIA & stamps digitally printed)	19.00
Royal Mail Heritage – Post Office (London) Railway design: 1st/1st L/E 20g WW 10g/E 100g WW 20g/WW 100g Zone 1 & 3/WW 100g Zone 2 [Dual-zone value with ampersand i.e. '*World 100g Zone 1 & 3*']				
The Postal Museum	R19Y	29 October–1 November 2020[2] 3 November 2020[2]	FS173a, 174a, 175a, 175 *var*, 178 *var*, 178 *var* (Type IIIA & stamps digitally printed)	25.00
	MA18	Late on 3 November[2] 3–19 December 2020[2]	FS173a, 174a, 175a, 175 *var*, 178 *var*, 178 *var* (Type IIIA & stamps digitally printed)	39.00
Mail Rail	MA18	29 October–1 November 2020[2]	FS173a, 174a, 175a, 175 *var*, 178 *var*, 178 *var* (Type IIIA & stamps digitally printed)	25.00
	MA17	Late on 1 November 2020[2] 3 November 2020[2] 3–19 December 2020[2]	FS173a, 174a, 175a, 175 *var*, 178 *var*, 178 *var* (Type IIIA & stamps digitally printed)	39.00
Royal Mail Heritage – Post Office (London) Railway design: 1st/1st Large/E 100g WW 20g/WW 100g/E Large 100g/WW Large 100g				
The Postal Museum	MA18	20 May–September 2021	FS173a, 174a, FS176 *var*, 178a, 176 *var*, 178 *var* (Type IIIA & stamps digitally printed) Set of two singles: i.e. E Large 100g/FS176 *var* & WW Large 100g/FS178 *var* (TIIIA)	32.00 20.00
	R19Y	From September 2021	FS173a, 174a, FS176 *var*, 178a, 176 *var*, 178 *var* (Type IIIA & stamps digitally printed) Set of two singles: i.e. E Large 100g/FS176 *var* & WW Large 100g/FS178 *var* (TIIIA)	32.00 20.00

The different inscriptions from *The Postal Museum*. Where the same inscription exists on more than one design only one may be pictured.

The Postal Museum simplified checklist **ROYAL MAIL POST & GO STAMPS**

Post & Go stamps – the inscriptions from *The Postal Museum* (formerly 'The BPMA'), December 2012–April 2022:
A simplified checklist of the Machin, Union Flag and pictorial issues

Stamp Design, Values, **Inscriptions** (see **bold** text) & Note(s)	Year Code	Availability (dates inclusive) & Note(s)	Cat. No. of Stamp Issue Without Inscription, or Closest Match	Collectors' Strip Price
Mail Rail	MA17	20 May–July 2021 From 27 February 2022	FS173a, 174a, FS176 *var*, 178a, 176 *var*, 178 *var* (Type IIIA & stamps digitally printed)	32.00
			Set of two singles: i.e. E Large 100g/FS176 *var* & WW Large 100g/FS178 *var* (TIIIA)	20.00
	R19Y	Sometimes available between 22 July 2021–18 February 2022	FS173a, 174a, FS176 *var*, 178a, 176 *var*, 178 *var* (Type IIIA & stamps digitally printed)	32.00
	MA18	Sometimes available between 21 November 2021–18 February 2022	FS173a, 174a, FS176 *var*, 178a, 176 *var*, 178 *var* (Type IIIA & stamps digitally printed)	35.00
			Set of two singles: i.e. E Large 100g/FS176 *var* & WW Large 100g/FS178 *var* (TIIIA)	23.00
Mail Rail London 2022	R19Y	19–26 February 2022	FS173a, 174a, FS176 *var*, 178a (but Type IIIA), 176 *var*, 178 *var* (but Type IIIA & stamps digitally printed)	32.00
Royal Mail Heritage – Mail by Air: 1st × 6 designs				
The Postal Museum[4]	R17Y	13 September 2017–13 February 2018	FS185a x 6 (Type IIIA)	12.50
	R19Y	From 30 March	FS185a x 6 (Type IIIA but stamps digitally printed)	12.50
The Postal Museum Airmail 1919	R17Y	Available for a few hours only on 11 September 2019	FS185a x 6 (Type IIIA)	33.00
	R19Y	11 September 2019–18 March 2020	FS185a x 6 (but Type IIIA but stamps digitally printed)	12.50
Royal Mail Heritage – Mail by Air: 1st/1st Large/E 100g WW 20g/WW 100g/E Large 100g/WW Large 100g *[Six designs in six values as single value strips of six]*				
The Postal Museum Unintentionally, all six values could be dispensed after this issue was made available in place of Royal Mail Heritage – Mail Coach. Each value could be dispensed in single value strips of six. Collectors' strips could not be dispensed.	R19Y	30 March–22 April 2022	FS185a, 186a, 188 *var*, 190a, 188 *var*, 190 *var* (Type IIIA & stamps digitally printed)	
			Set of 36: i.e. six strips available in six issues	170.00
Royal Mail Heritage – Mail by Sea: 1st × 6 designs				
The Postal Museum[4]	R18Y	14 February–28 March 2018 12 September–22 October 2018	FS207a x6 (Type IIIA)	9.50
Voices from the Deep The Postal Museum	R18Y	29 March–11 September 2018	FS207a x6 (Type IIIA)	10.00
Royal Mail Heritage – Mail by Bike: 1st × 6 designs				
The Postal Museum[4]	R18Y	12 September–29 November 2018	FS213 x6 (but Type IIIA)	9.50

The different inscriptions from *The Postal Museum*. Where the same inscription exists on more than one design only one may be pictured.

ROYAL MAIL POST & GO STAMPS *The Postal Museum simplified checklist*

Post & Go stamps – the inscriptions from *The Postal Museum* (formerly 'The BPMA'), December 2012–April 2022:
A simplified checklist of the Machin, Union Flag and pictorial issues

Stamp Design, Values, Inscriptions (see bold text) & Note(s)	Year Code	Availability (dates inclusive) & Note(s)	Cat. No. of Stamp Issue Without Inscription, or Closest Match	Collectors' Strip Price
Robin: 1st/1st L/E 20g/WW 10g/WW 20g/WW 40g				
The B.P.M.A.	MA12	3 December 2012–20 February 2013	FS51a/56a (Type III)	20.00
	MA13	5 November–24 December 2013	FS51a/56a (Type III)	18.00
Fur & Feathers: 2nd/2nd L, and 1st/1st L/E 20g WW 10g/E 100g/WW 20g/WW 100g				
The B.P.M.A.	CL15S/ MA15	16 November–31 December 2015	FS143a/150a (Type IIIA) Set of 16: i.e. eight values in two designs	45.00
Hibernating Animals: 2nd/2nd L, and 1st/1st L/E 20g WW 10g/E 100g/WW 20g/WW 100g				
The Postal Museum + Museum's large format Envelope logo positioned before wording.	CL16S/ MA16	14 November–30 December 2016	FS165a/172a (Type IIIA) Set of 16: i.e. eight values in two designs	45.00
Winter Greenery: 2nd/2nd L, and 1st/1st L/E 20g WW 10g/E 60g/WW 20g/WW 60g				
The B.P.M.A.	MA14/ MA14	13 November–23 December 2014 29 October–1 November 2020[2]	FS109b/116b (Type IIIA) Set of 16: i.e. eight values in two designs	45.00
Winter Greenery 2017 issue: 2nd/2nd L, and 1st/1st L/E 20g WW 10g/E 100g/WW 20g/WW 100g				
The Postal Museum[4]	CL17S/ R17Y	13 November 2017–1 January 2018 8 November–31 December 2018 3 November 2020 (2nd/2nd L only)[2] 3–19 December 2020 (2nd/2nd L only)[2] 1 December 2021–2 January 2022 (2nd/2nd L only)	FS191a/198a (Type IIIA) Set of 16: i.e. eight values in two designs	48.00
Winter Greenery 2017 issue: 1st/1st L/E 20g WW 10g/E 100g/WW 20g/WW 100g				
Mail Rail	R17Y	2–31 December 2019	FS193a/198a (Type IIIA) Set of 16: i.e. eight values in two designs	40.00
Winter Greenery 2017 issue: 1st/1st L/E 20g WW 10g/E 100g WW 20g/WW 100g Zone 1 & 3/WW 100g Zone 2 *[Dual-zone value with ampersand i.e. 'World 100g Zone 1 & 3']*				
The Postal Museum	R17Y	3 November 2020[2] 3–19 December 2020[2]	FS193a/195a (Type IIIA), 196b, 198b/198c (but Type IIIA) Set of 16: i.e. eight values in two designs	48.00
Winter Greenery: 1st/1st Large/E 100g WW 20g/WW 100g/E Large 100g/WW Large 100g				
The Postal Museum	R17Y	1 December 2021–2 January 2022	FS193a, 194a, 196a (but Type IIIA), 198a, 196c (but Type IIIA), 198d (but Type IIIA) Set of 12: i.e. six values in two designs Set of 4: i.e. two values in two designs i.e. E Large 100g/FS196c & WW Large 100g/FS198d (TIIIA)	60.00 35.00

[1] When two similar items are available, the price given is for the cheaper of the two.

[2] Owing to COVID 19 restrictions, *The Postal Museum* closed its doors to the general public on 18 March 2020. It temporarily reopened between 29 October–4 November 2020 and 3–19 December 2020; both periods with a much-reduced Thursday to Sunday opening schedule. There was also a special one-day opening on Tuesday, 3 November 2020, for the museum's annual 'Winter Greenery' offering. *The Postal Museum* reopened on 20 May 2021.

[3] When used on the pictorial issues, the *The Postal Museum*'s official opening inscription deliberately omitted '2017'.

[4] Revised generic inscription without a large Envelope logo and the current norm.
Note: Issue does not exist with large Envelope logo.)

Glitches affecting inscriptions and lasting only a very short time and/or which exist in small quantities are beyond the scope of these tables.

Post & Go stamps – the inscriptions from Royal Mail Enquiry Offices, February 2015–March 2015: A simplified checklist of the Machin issues

Stamp Design, Values, **Inscriptions** (see **bold** text) & Note(s)	Year Code	Location of machine, Availability (dates inclusive) & Note(s)	Cat. No. of Stamp Issue Without Inscription, or Closest Match	Collectors' Strip Price
Machin: 1st/1st L/E 20g WW 10g/E 60g/WW 20g/WW 60g				
Bradford N This inscription was the result of a two office trial which ended very quickly, and Enquiry Office inscriptions ceased	MA13	Bradford North Royal Mail Enquiry Office 9 February–28 March 2015	FS77b, 78b, 79bb, 80*var*, 82b, & 84*var* (Type IIIA)	25.00
Crewe This inscription was the result of a two office trial which ended very quickly, and Enquiry Office inscriptions ceased	MA13	Crewe Royal Mail Enquiry Office 9 February–28 March 2015	FS77b, 78b, 79bb, 80*var*, 82b, & 84*var* (Type IIIA)	25.00
Machin: 2nd/2nd L				
Bradford N This inscription was the result of a two office trial which ended very quickly, and Enquiry Office inscriptions ceased	MA12	Bradford North Royal Mail Enquiry Office 9 February–28 March 2015	FS93b/94b (Type IIIA)	11.50
Crewe This inscription was the result of a two office trial which ended very quickly, and Enquiry Office inscriptions ceased	MA12	Crewe Royal Mail Enquiry Office 9 February–28 March 2015	FS93b/94b (Type IIIA)	11.50

The different inscriptions from exhibitions. Where the same inscription exists on more than one design only one may be pictured.

ROYAL MAIL POST & GO STAMPS *Armed Forces Museums simplified checklist*

Post & Go stamps – the different issues and inscriptions from *National Museum Royal Navy,* Portsmouth to April 2022: A simplified checklist

Post & Go stamps – the inscriptions from *The National Museum Royal Navy*, Portsmouth, July 2014–April 2022: A simplified checklist of the Machin, Union Flag and Common Poppy issues				
Stamp Design, Values, Inscriptions (see **bold text**) & Note(s)	Year Code	Location of dispensing machine, Availability (dates inclusive) & Note(s)	Cat. No. of Stamp Issue Without Inscription, or Closest Match	Collectors' Strip Price
Machin: 1st/1st L/E 20g WW 10g/E 60g/WW 20g/WW 60g				
The NMRN	None	*The National Museum of the Royal Navy,* Portsmouth[1] 28 July–20 October 2014 14 November 2014–29 March 2015	FS1d, 2d, 3cb, 3d, 5d & 5f (Type IIIA)	22.00
	MA13	*The National Museum of the Royal Navy,* Portsmouth[1] Apparently available for a few hours only on 8 May 2015 Only known on 8 May 2015 due to a reversion to the pre 30 March 2015 weight bands	FS77, 78, 79b, 80, 82 & 84 (but Type III) Set of two singles: i.e. E 60g/FS80 & WW 60g/FS84 (but TIII)	75.00 50.00
Machin: 1st/1st L/E 20g WW 10g/E 100g/WW 20g/WW 100g				
The NMRN	MA13	*The National Museum of the Royal Navy,* Portsmouth[1] 30 March–18 October 2015	FS77b, 78b, 79bb, 80ca, 82b & 84ca (Type IIIA)	20.00
	None	*The National Museum of the Royal Navy,* Portsmouth[1] Available for a few hours only on 30 March 2015	FS1d, 2d, 3cb, 3ea, 5d & 5ga (Type IIIA)	50.00
Royal Navy + large circle logo Generic inscription revised, i.e. '**Royal Navy**' replaces acronym, and large logo introduced.	MA13	*The National Museum of the Royal Navy,* Portsmouth[1] 16 November 2015–30 May 2016 1 July–15 August 2016 except when 'No year code' available (see below) 15 August 2016–18 August 2017 except when 'MA15' available (see below)	FS77b, 78b, 79bb, 80ca, 82b & 84ca (Type IIIA)	19.00
	None	*The National Museum of the Royal Navy,* Portsmouth[1] Sometimes available between 1 July 2016–18 August 2017 *Explosion Museum of Naval Firepower,* Gosport[4] 16 August 2016–18 May 2017 19 June–18 August 2017	FS1d, 2d, 3cb, 3ea, 5d and 5ga (Type IIIA)	20.00[5]
	MA15	*The National Museum of the Royal Navy,* Belfast[2] *HMS Caroline* 1 July 2016–spring/summer 2017 *The National Museum of the Royal Navy,* Hartlepool[3] *HMS Trincomalee* 1 July 2016–15 June 2017 *The National Museum of the Royal Navy,* Portsmouth[1] Sometimes available between 15 August 2016–18 August 2017	FS77b, 78b, 79bb, 80ca, 82b & 84ca (Type IIIA)	20.00[5]
Royal Navy Battle of Jutland + large circle logo	None	*The National Museum of the Royal Navy,* Portsmouth[1] 31 May–30 June 2016	FS1d 2d, 3cb, 3ea, 5d and 5ga (Type IIIA)	20.00
	MA13	*The National Museum of the Royal Navy,* Portsmouth[1] Apparently available for a few hours only on 31 May 2016	FS77b, 78b, 79bb, 80ca, 82b & 84ca (Type IIIA)	—
	MA15	*The National Museum of the Royal Navy,* Belfast[2] *HMS Caroline* *The National Museum of the Royal Navy,* Hartlepool[3] *HMS Trincomalee* 1–30 June 2016 (Note: Not 31 May)	FS77b, 78b, 79bb, 80ca, 82b & 4ca (Type IIIA)	20.00
Heligoland 'Big Bang' 1947 + large circle logo	MA15	*Explosion Museum of Naval Firepower,* Gosport[4] 19 May–18 June 2017	FS77b, 78b, 79bb, 80ca, 82b & 84ca (Type IIIA)	20.00
HMS Trincomalee 200 Years + large circle logo	MA15	*The National Museum of the Royal Navy,* Hartlepool[3] *HMS Trincomalee* 16 June–18 August 2017	FS77b, 78b, 79bb, 80ca, 82b & 84ca (Type IIIA)	20.00
Royal Navy Queen Elizabeth II Carrier + small circle logo	MA15	*The National Museum of the Royal Navy,* Portsmouth[1] 19–28 August 2017 The carrier is named *Queen Elizabeth* and not *Queen Elizabeth II* From 29 August 2017, the erroneous '**II**' was removed	FS77b, 78b, 79bb, 80ca, 82b & 84ca (Type IIIA)	23.00
Royal Navy Queen Elizabeth Carrier 2017 + small circle logo	MA15	*The National Museum of the Royal Navy,* Portsmouth[1] 29 August–17 September 2017 At the same time the erroneous '**II**' was removed from the inscription the date '**2017**' was added	FS77b, 78b, 79bb, 80ca, 82b & 84ca (Type IIIA)	24.00

Armed Forces Museums simplified checklist **ROYAL MAIL POST & GO STAMPS**

Post & Go stamps – the inscriptions from *The National Museum Royal Navy*, Portsmouth, July 2014–April 2022:
A simplified checklist of the Machin, Union Flag and Common Poppy issues

Stamp Design, Values, **Inscriptions** (see **bold** text) & Note(s)	Year Code	Location of dispensing machine, Availability (dates inclusive) & Note(s)	Cat. No. of Stamp Issue Without Inscription, or Closest Match	Collectors' Strip Price
Machin: 1st/1st L/E 20g WW 10g/E 100g/WW 20g/WW 100g continued				
HMS Trincomalee 200 Years + small circle logo	MA14	*The National Museum of the Royal Navy*, Hartlepool³ HMS Trincomalee 19 August–19 October 2017	FS77b, 78b, 79bb, 80ca, 82b & 84ca (Type IIIA)	22.00
	MA15	*The National Museum of the Royal Navy*, Hartlepool³ HMS Trincomalee Available for a few hours only on 19 August 2017	FS77b, 78b, 79bb, 80ca, 82b & 84ca (Type IIIA)	45.00
Royal Navy + small circle logo Small circle logo introduced in place of large version.	MA15	*Explosion Museum of Naval Firepower*, Gosport⁴ 19 August–19 October 2017 20 November 2017–31 October 2019 *The National Museum of the Royal Navy*, Portsmouth¹ 18 September–19 October 2017 20 November 2017–31 October 2019 1 December 2019–18 March 2020† 24 August–1 September 2020†	FS77b, 78b, 79bb, 80ca, 82b & 84ca (Type IIIA)	20.00⁵
	MA14	*The National Museum of the Royal Navy*, Hartlepool³ HMS Trincomalee 22 February 2018–31 October 2019 except when 'MA13' and 'No year code' available (see below) 3 December 2019–18 March 2020†	FS77b, 78b, 79bb, 80ca, 82b & 84ca (Type IIIA)	23.00
	MA13	*The National Museum of the Royal Navy*, Hartlepool³ HMS Trincomalee Available for a short time sometime between 17 September–late September 2018	FS77b, 78b, 79bb, 80ca, 82b & 84ca (Type IIIA)	40.00
	None	*The National Museum of the Royal Navy*, Hartlepool³ HMS Trincomalee Available for a short time sometime between 17 September–late September 2018 *Explosion Museum of Naval Firepower*, Gosport⁴ 7 December 2019–18 March 2020† 29 August–1 September 2020†	FS1d 2d, 3cb, 3ea, 5d and 5ga (Type IIIA)	40.00⁵
HMS Trincomalee 12th Oct 1817 + small circle logo	MA14	*The National Museum of the Royal Navy*, Hartlepool³ HMS Trincomalee 20 October–31 December 2017 except when 'MA15' available (see below)	FS77b, 78b, 79bb, 80ca, 82b & 84ca (Type IIIA)	20.00
	MA15	*The National Museum of the Royal Navy*, Hartlepool³ HMS Trincomalee Available for a short time sometime between 20 October–late October 2017	FS77b, 78b, 79bb, 80ca, 82b & 84ca (Type IIIA)	28.00
HMS Trincomalee 19th Oct 1817 + small circle logo '**19th Oct**' instead of '**12th Oct**' for less than one hour on the first day of the '**12th Oct 1817**' inscription.	MA14	*The National Museum of the Royal Navy*, Hartlepool³ HMS Trincomalee 20 October 2017	FS77b, 78b, 79bb, 80ca, 82b & 84ca (Type IIIA)	50.00
HMS Trincomalee + small circle logo	MA14	*The National Museum of the Royal Navy*, Hartlepool³ HMS Trincomalee 2–14 January 2018	FS77b, 78b, 79bb, 80ca, 82b & 84ca (Type IIIA)	20.00
Royal Navy Lest We Forget 100 Unintentional issue when the Machin design was loaded into the machine and the return of the generic inscription (i.e. '**Royal Navy**' + small circle logo) was delayed due to a technical reason.	MA13	*The National Museum of the Royal Navy*, Hartlepool³ HMS Trincomalee Available for a few hours only on 2 December 2019	FS77b, 78b, 79bb, 80ca, 82b & 84ca (Type IIIA)	40.00
	MA14	*The National Museum of the Royal Navy*, Hartlepool³ HMS Trincomalee Available for a few hours on 2 December and 3 December 2019	FS77b, 78b, 79bb, 80ca, 82b & 84ca (Type IIIA)	45.00

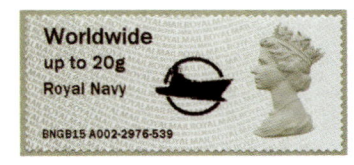

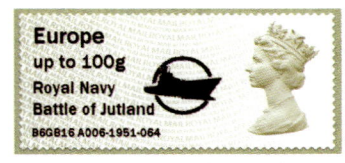

The different inscriptions from *National Museum Royal Navy*. Where the same inscription exists on more than one design only one may be pictured.

ROYAL MAIL POST & GO STAMPS *Armed Forces Museums simplified checklist*

Europe up to 100g
Heligoland
'Big Bang' 1947
B5GB17 A007-0125-004

Worldwide up to 100g
HMS Trincomalee
200 Years
B6GB17 A006-2152-006

Worldwide up to 20g
Royal Navy
Queen Elizabeth II Carrier
B8GB17 A002-3440-257

Euro 20g / World 10g
Royal Navy
Queen Elizabeth Carrier 2017
B9GB17 A002-3495-483

Worldwide up to 20g
HMS Trincomalee
200 Years
B8GB17 A006-2229-287

Worldwide up to 100g
Royal Navy
B9GB17 A007-0188-030

Euro 20g / World 10g
HMS Trincomalee
12th Oct 1817
B0GB17 A006-2309-411

Worldwide up to 100g
HMS Trincomalee
19th Oct 1817
B0GB17 A006-2284-060

Worldwide up to 20g
HMS Trincomalee
B1GB18 A006-2388-071

World 100g Zone 1-3
Royal Navy
B9GB20 A002-4106-329

World 100g Zone 1 & 3
Royal Navy
B9GB20 A006-2835-041

Worldwide Large 100g
Royal Navy
BNGB21 A006-3009-210

The different inscriptions from *National Museum Royal Navy*. Where the same inscription exists on more than one design only one may be pictured.

Post & Go stamps – the inscriptions from *The National Museum Royal Navy*, Portsmouth, July 2014–April 2022:
A simplified checklist of the Machin, Union Flag and Common Poppy issues

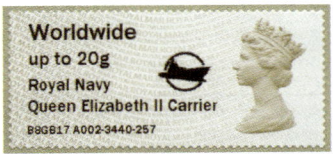

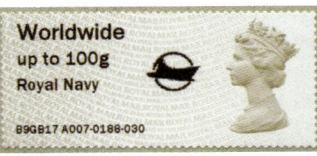

Stamp Design, Values, **Inscriptions** (see **bold** text) & Note(s)	Year Code	Location of dispensing machine, Availability (dates inclusive) & Note(s)	Cat. No. of Stamp Issue Without Inscription, or Closest Match	Collectors' Strip Price
Machin: 1st/1st L/E 20g WW 10g/E 100g WW 20g/WW 100g Zone 1-3/WW 100g Zone 2 [Dual value of E 100g WW 20g and two World Zoned stamps introduced on 1 September 2020]				
Royal Navy + small circle logo Dual-zone value with hyphen i.e. '**World 100g Zone 1-3**'	MA15	*The National Museum of the Royal Navy*, Portsmouth[1] 1–17 September 2020[†]	FS77b, 78b, 79bb (Type IIIA), 80*d*, 84*d* & 84*e* (but Type IIIA)	35.00[5]
		Explosion Museum of Naval Firepower, Gosport[4] 5–17 September 2020[†]		
	MA14	*The National Museum of the Royal Navy*, Hartlepool[3] HMS Trincomalee 4 September 2020[†]	FS77b, 78b, 79bb (Type IIIA), 80*d*, 84*d* & 84*e* (but Type IIIA)	45.00
	MA13	*The National Museum of the Royal Navy*, Hartlepool[3] HMS Trincomalee 4–17 September 2020[†]	FS77b, 78b, 79bb (Type IIIA), 80*d*, 84*d* & 84*e* (but Type IIIA)	40.00
	None	*Explosion Museum of Naval Firepower*, Gosport[4] 5 September 2020[†]	FS1*d*, 2*d*, 3*cb*, and 3*f*, 5*h*, 5*i* (but all Type IIIA)	45.00
Machin: 1st/1st L/E 20g WW 10g/E 100g WW 20g/WW 100g Zone 1 & 3/WW 100g Zone 2 [Service indicator for 'World Zones 1 and 3' revised on 18 September 2020]				
Royal Navy + small circle logo Dual-zone value with ampersand i.e. '**World 100g Zone 1 & 3**'	MA15	*The National Museum of the Royal Navy*, Portsmouth[1] 18 September–4 October 2020[†]	FS77b, 78b, 79bb (Type IIIA), 80*d*, 84*d* var & 84*e* (but Type IIIA)	35.00[5]
		Explosion Museum of Naval Firepower, Gosport[4] 20 September–4 November 2020[†] 3–19 December 2020[†]		
		The National Museum of the Royal Navy, Hartlepool[3] HMS Trincomalee 23 September–4 November 2020[†]	Single: i.e. Zone1 & 3/FS84*d* var	13.50[5]
	MA14	*The National Museum of the Royal Navy*, Hartlepool[3] HMS Trincomalee 23 September 2020[†]	FS77b, 78b, 79bb (Type IIIA), 80*d*, 84*d* var & 84*e* (but Type IIIA) Single: i.e. Zone1 & 3/FS84*d* var	— 20.00
	MA13	*The National Museum of the Royal Navy*, Hartlepool[3] HMS Trincomalee 23 September 2020[†]	FS77b, 78b, 79bb (Type IIIA), 80*d*, 84*d* var & 84*e* (but Type IIIA) Single: i.e. Zone1 & 3/FS84*d* var	45.00 17.00
	None	*The National Museum of the Royal Navy*, Portsmouth[1] 4 October–4 November 2020[†] 3–19 December 2020[†]	FS1*d*, 2*d*, 3*cb*, and 3*f*, 5*h* var, 5*i* (but all Type IIIA) Single: i.e. Zone1 & 3/FS5*h* var	45.00 15.00

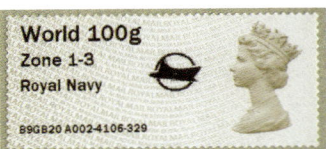

Armed Forces Museums simplified checklist **ROYAL MAIL POST & GO STAMPS**

Post & Go stamps – the inscriptions from *The National Museum Royal Navy*, Portsmouth, July 2014–April 2022:
A simplified checklist of the Machin, Union Flag and Common Poppy issues

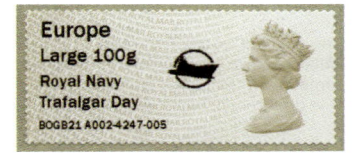

Stamp Design, Values, **Inscriptions** (see **bold** text) & Note(s)	Year Code	Location of dispensing machine, Availability (dates inclusive) & Note(s)	Cat. No. of Stamp Issue Without Inscription, or Closest Match	Collectors' Strip Price
Machin: 1st/1st Large/E 100g WW 20g/WW 100g/E Large 100g/WW Large 100g				
Royal Navy + small circle logo	None	*The National Museum of the Royal Navy*, Portsmouth[1] 17 May–30 July 2021	FS1d, 2d, 3f (but Type IIIA), 5ga, 3 var and 5 var (Type IIIA)	35.00
			Set of two singles: i.e. E Large 100g/FS3 var & WW Large 100g/FS5 var (but TIIIA)	23.00
	MA13	*The National Museum of the Royal Navy*, Hartlepool[3] *HMS Trincomalee* 17 May 2021 only	FS77b, 78b, 80d (but Type IIIA), 84ca, 80e (but Type IIIA) and 84f (but Type IIIA)	35.00[5]
		The National Museum of the Royal Navy, Portsmouth[1] 1 September–20 October 2021	Set of two singles: i.e. E Large 100g/FS80e & WW Large 100g/FS84f (but TIIIA)	23.00[5]
	MA14	*The National Museum of the Royal Navy*, Hartlepool[3] *HMS Trincomalee* 17 May 2021 1 September–10 November 2021	FS77b, 78b, 80d (but Type IIIA), 84ca, 80e (but Type IIIA) and 84f (but Type IIIA)	35.00[5]
		The National Museum of the Royal Navy, Portsmouth[1] 1 November 2021 only (2 November 2021 ♦♦)	Set of two singles: i.e. E Large 100g/FS80e & WW Large 100g/FS84f (but TIIIA)	23.00[5]
	MA15	*The National Museum of the Royal Navy*, Hartlepool[3] *HMS Trincomalee* 17 May–30 July 2021	FS77b, 78b, 80d (but Type IIIA), 84ca, 80e (but Type IIIA) and 84f (but Type IIIA)	35.00[5]
		Explosion Museum of Naval Firepower, Gosport[4] (19 May–15 June 2021 ♦) 16 June–30 July 2021 1 September–1 November 2021 (2 November 2021 ♦♦)	Set of two singles: i.e. E Large 100g/FS80e & WW Large 100g/FS84f (but TIIIA)	23.00[5]
	R20Y	*The National Museum of the Royal Navy*, Hartlepool[3] *HMS Trincomalee* 10–25 November 2021 11 December 2021–31 March 2022	FS77b, 78b, 80d (but Type IIIA), 84ca, 80e (but Type IIIA) and 84f (but Type IIIA)	32.00
Royal Navy Black Tot Day 31st July 1970 + circle logo	MA13	*The National Museum of the Royal Navy*, Portsmouth[1] 31 July–31 August 2021	FS77b, 78b, 80d (but Type IIIA), 84ca, 80e (but Type IIIA) and 84f (but TIIIA)	32.00
	MA15	*The National Museum of the Royal Navy*, Hartlepool[3] *HMS Trincomalee* 31 July–31 August 2021	FS77b, 78b, 80d (but Type IIIA), 84ca, 80e (but Type IIIA) and 84f (but Type IIIA)	32.00[5]
		Explosion Museum of Naval Firepower, Gosport[4] 31 July–31 August 2021		
	None	*The National Museum of the Royal Navy*, Hartlepool[3] *HMS Trincomalee* Sometimes available between 24–31 August 2021	FS1d, 2d, 3f (but Type IIIA), 5ga, 3 var and 5 var (Type IIIA)	—
	MA14	*The National Museum of the Royal Navy*, Hartlepool[3] *HMS Trincomalee* Sometimes available between 24–31 August 2021	FS77b, 78b, 80d (but Type IIIA), 84ca, 80e (but Type IIIA) and 84f (but Type IIIA)	—
Royal Navy Trafalgar Day + circle logo	MA14	*National Museum of the Royal Navy*, Portsmouth[1] 21–31 October 2021	FS77b, 78b, 80d (but Type IIIA), 84ca, 80e (but Type IIIA) and 84f (but Type IIIA)	35.00
Royal Navy Falklands 40th + circle logo	None	*The National Museum of the Royal Navy*, Hartlepool[3] *HMS Trincomalee* Sometimes available between 1–29 April 2022	FS1d, 2d, 3f (but Type IIIA), 5ga, 3 var and 5 var (Type IIIA)	—
	MA13	*The National Museum of the Royal Navy*, Hartlepool[3] *HMS Trincomalee* Apparently available for a few hours only on 1 April 2022 only	FS77b, 78b, 80d (but Type IIIA), 84ca, 80e (but Type IIIA) and 84f (but Type IIIA)	—
	R20Y	*The National Museum of the Royal Navy*, Hartlepool[3] *HMS Trincomalee* Sometimes available between 1–29 April 2022	FS77b, 78b, 80d (but Type IIIA), 84ca, 80e (but Type IIIA) and 84f (but Type IIIA)	35.00

The different inscriptions from *National Museum Royal Navy*. Where the same inscription exists on more than one design only one may be pictured.

ROYAL MAIL POST & GO STAMPS *Armed Forces Museums simplified checklist*

Post & Go stamps – the inscriptions from *The National Museum Royal Navy*, Portsmouth, July 2014–April 2022:
A simplified checklist of the Machin, Union Flag and Common Poppy issues

Stamp Design, Values, Inscriptions (see **bold** text) & Note(s)	Year Code	Location of dispensing machine, Availability (dates inclusive) & Note(s)	Cat. No. of Stamp Issue Without Inscription, or Closest Match	Collectors' Strip Price
Union Flag: 1st/1st L/E 20g WW 10g/E 60g/WW 20g/WW 60g				
The NMRN	None	*The National Museum of the Royal Navy*, Portsmouth[1] 28 July–20 October 2014 11 November 2014–29 March 2015	FS39, 40, 41*a*, 41*b*, 43 & 44*b* (but Type IIIA)	20.00
The NMRN Trafalgar Day	None	*The National Museum of the Royal Navy*, Portsmouth[1] 21 October–10 November 2014	FS39, 40, 41*a*, 41*b*, 43 & 44*b* (but Type IIIA)	35.00
The NMRN V.E. Day 70	None	*The National Museum of the Royal Navy*, Portsmouth[1] Apparently available for a few hours only on 8 May 2015. Only known on 8 May 2015 due to a reversion to the pre 30 March 2015 weight bands	FS39, 40, 41*a*, 41*b*, 43 & 44*b* (but Type IIIA) Set of two singles: i.e. E 60g/FS41*b* & WW 60g/FS44*b* (but TIII)	75.00 50.00

The different inscriptions from *National Museum Royal Navy*. Where the same inscription exists on more than one design only one may be pictured.

Armed Forces Museums simplified checklist **ROYAL MAIL POST & GO STAMPS**

Post & Go stamps – the inscriptions from *The National Museum Royal Navy*, Portsmouth, July 2014–April 2022:
A simplified checklist of the Machin, Union Flag and Common Poppy issues

Stamp Design, Values, **Inscriptions** (see **bold** text) & Note(s)	Year Code	Location of dispensing machine, Availability (dates inclusive) & Note(s)	Cat. No. of Stamp Issue Without Inscription, or Closest Match	Collectors' Strip Price
Union Flag: 1st/1st L/E 20g WW 10g/E 100g/WW 20g/WW 100g				
The NMRN	None	*The National Museum of the Royal Navy*, Portsmouth[1] 30 March–7 May 2015 30 May–18 October 2015	FS39, 40, 41a, 41c, 43 and 44c (but Type IIIA)	25.00
The NMRN V.E. Day 70	None	*The National Museum of the Royal Navy*, Portsmouth[1] 8–29 May 2015	FS39, 40, 41a, 41c, 43 and 44c (but Type IIIA)	20.00
Royal Navy Trafalgar Day Generic inscription revised, i.e. '**Royal Navy Trafalgar Day**' replaces acronym.	None	*The National Museum of the Royal Navy*, Portsmouth[1] 19 October–15 November 2015 23 September–23 October 2016 – all sites	FS39, 40, 41a, 41c, 43 and 44c (but Type IIIA)	20.00[5]
Royal Navy Generic inscription revised, i.e. '**Royal Navy**' replaces acronym.	None	*The National Museum of the Royal Navy*, Portsmouth[1] 16 November 2015–30 May 2016 14 November 2016–18 August 2017 18 September 2017–18 March 2020[†] 24 August–1 September 2020[†] *The National Museum of the Royal Navy*, Belfast[2] *HMS Caroline* 1 July 2016–spring/summer 2017 *The National Museum of the Royal Navy*, Hartlepool[3] *HMS Trincomalee* 1 July 2016–15 June 2017 22 February 2018–18 March 2020[†] *Explosion Museum of Naval Firepower*, Gosport[4] 16 August 2016–18 May 2017 19 June 2017–18 March 2020[†] 29 August–1 September 2020[†]	FS39, 40, 41a, 41c, 43 and 44c (but Type IIIA)	20.00[5]
Royal Navy Battle of Jutland	None	*The National Museum of the Royal Navy*, Portsmouth[1] 31 May–30 June 2016 1–30 June 2016 – all sites	FS39, 40, 41a, 41c, 43 and 44c (but Type IIIA)	20.00[5]
Heligoland 'Big Bang' 1947	None	*Explosion Museum of Naval Firepower*, Gosport[4] 19 May–18 June 2017	FS39, 40, 41a, 41c, 43 and 44c (but Type IIIA)	20.00
HMS Trincomalee 200 Years	None	*The National Museum of the Royal Navy*, Hartlepool[3] *HMS Trincomalee* 16 June–19 November 2017	FS39, 40, 41a, 41c, 43 and 44c (but Type IIIA)	20.00
Royal Navy QE II Carrier	None	*The National Museum of the Royal Navy*, Portsmouth[1] 19–28 August 2017 The Carrier is named *Queen Elizabeth* and not *Queen Elizabeth II*. From 29 August 2017 the erroneous 'II' was removed	FS39, 40, 41a, 41c, 43 and 44c (but Type IIIA)	23.00
Royal Navy QE Carrier 2017	None	*The National Museum of the Royal Navy*, Portsmouth[1] 29 August–17 September 2017 At the same time the erroneous 'II' was removed from the inscription the date '**2017**' was added	FS39, 40, 41a, 41c, 43 and 44c (but Type IIIA)	24.00
HMS Trincomalee 12th Oct 1817	None	*The National Museum of the Royal Navy*, Hartlepool[3] *HMS Trincomalee* 20 November–31 December 2017	FS39, 40, 41a, 41c, 43 and 44c (but Type IIIA)	20.00
HMS Trincomalee	None	*The National Museum of the Royal Navy*, Hartlepool[3] *HMS Trincomalee* 2–14 January 2018	FS39, 40, 41a, 41c, 43 and 44c (but Type IIIA)	20.00
Union Flag: 1st/1st L/E 20g WW 10g/E 100g WW 20g/WW 100g Zone 1-3/WW 100g Zone 2 [Dual value of E 100g WW 20g and two World Zoned stamps introduced on 1 September 2020]				
Royal Navy Dual-zone value with hyphen i.e. '**World 100g Zone 1-3**'	None	*The National Museum of the Royal Navy*, Portsmouth[1] 1–17 September 2020[†] *The National Museum of the Royal Navy*, Hartlepool[3] *HMS Trincomalee* 4–17 September 2020[†] *Explosion Museum of Naval Firepower*, Gosport[4] 5–17 September 2020[†]	FS39, 40, 41a, 41d, 44d & 44e (but Type IIIA)	35.00[5]

ROYAL MAIL POST & GO STAMPS *Armed Forces Museums simplified checklist*

Post & Go stamps – the inscriptions from *The National Museum Royal Navy*, Portsmouth, July 2014–April 2022:
A simplified checklist of the Machin, Union Flag and Common Poppy issues

Stamp Design, Values, Inscriptions (see **bold** text) & Note(s)	Year Code	Location of dispensing machine, Availability (dates inclusive) & Note(s)	Cat. No. of Stamp Issue Without Inscription, or Closest Match	Collectors' Strip Price
Union Flag: 1st/1st L/E 20g WW 10g/E 100g WW 20g/WW 100g Zone 1 & 3/WW 100g Zone 2 *[Service indicator for 'World Zones 1 and 3' revised on 18 September 2020]*				
Royal Navy Dual-zone value with ampersand i.e. '**World 100g Zone 1 & 3**'	None	*The National Museum of the Royal Navy*, Portsmouth¹ 18 September–4 November 2020† 3–19 December 2020†	FS39, 40, 41*a*, 41*d*, 44*d* var & 44*e* (but Type IIIA)	30.00⁵
		Explosion Museum of Naval Firepower, Gosport⁴ 20 September–4 November 2020† 3–19 December 2020†		
		The National Museum of the Royal Navy, Hartlepool³ HMS Trincomalee 23 September–4 November 2020†	Single: i.e. Zone1 & 3/FS44*d* var	12.00⁵
Union Flag: 1st/1st Large/E 100g WW 20g/WW 100g/E Large 100g/WW Large 100g				
Royal Navy	None	*The National Museum of the Royal Navy*, Portsmouth¹ 17 May–30 July 2021 1 September–20 October 2021 1 November 2021 only (2 November 2021 ♦♦)	FS39, 40, 41d, 41, 44c *var* & 44 *var* (but all Type IIIA)	32.00⁵
		National Museum of the Royal Navy, Hartlepool³ HMS Trincomalee 17 May–30 July 2021 1 September–25 November 2021 11 December 2021–31 March 2022		
		Explosion Museum of Naval Firepower, Gosport⁴ (19 May–15 June 2021♦) 16 June–30 July 2021 1 September–31 October 2021 (2 November 2021♦♦)	Set of two singles: i.e. E Large 100g/FS41 *var* & WW Large 100g/FS44 *var* (but TIIIA)	20.00⁵
Black Tot Day 31st July 1970 (Note: '**Royal Navy**' not included on this issue)	None	*The National Museum of the Royal Navy*, Portsmouth¹ 31 July–31 August 2021	FS39, 40, 41d, 44c, 41 *var* & 44 *var* (but all Type IIIA)	32.00⁵
		The National Museum of the Royal Navy, Hartlepool³ HMS Trincomalee 31 July–31 August 2021		
		Explosion Museum of Naval Firepower, Gosport⁴ 31 July–31 August 2021		
		Note: These stamps are identifiable only through their machine code i.e. National Museum of the Royal Navy, Portsmouth = 002 National Museum of the Royal Navy, Hartlepool = 006 Explosion Museum of Naval Firepower, Gosport = 007		
Royal Navy Trafalgar Day	None	*National Museum of the Royal Navy*, Portsmouth¹ 21–31 October 2021	FS39, 40, 41d, 44c, 41 *var* & 44 *var* (but all Type IIIA)	35.00
Royal Navy Lest We Forget	None	*The National Museum of the Royal Navy*, Hartlepool³ HMS Trincomalee 26 November–10 December 2021	FS39, 40, 41d, 44c, 41 *var* & 44 *var* (but all Type IIIA)	35.00
Royal Navy Falklands 40th	None	*The National Museum of the Royal Navy*, Hartlepool³ HMS Trincomalee 1–29 April 2022	FS39, 40, 41d, 44c, 41 *var* & 44 *var* (but all Type IIIA)	35.00
Common Poppy: 1st/1st L/E 20g WW 10g/E 60g/WW 20g/WW 60g				
The NMRN Remembrance	MA14	*The National Museum of the Royal Navy*, Portsmouth¹ 21 October–13 November 2014	FS103, 104, 105, 106, 107 & 108 (but Type IIIA)	35.00
Common Poppy: 1st/1st L/E 20g WW 10g/E 100g/WW 20g/WW 100g				
Royal Navy	MA15	*The National Museum of the Royal Navy*, Portsmouth¹ 19 October–15 November 2015 24 October–13 November 2016 – all sites apart from *The National Museum of the Royal Navy*, Belfast² – HMS Caroline which was closed at the time 20 October–19 November 2017 – all sites apart from *The National Museum of the Royal Navy*, Belfast² – HMS Caroline owing to the machine having been taken out of service spring/summer 2017	FS137, 138, 139, 140, 141 & 142 (Type IIIA)	20.00⁵

The different inscriptions from *National Museum Royal Navy*. Where the same inscription exists on more than one design only one may be pictured.

Armed Forces Museums simplified checklist — ROYAL MAIL POST & GO STAMPS

Post & Go stamps – the inscriptions from *The National Museum Royal Navy*, Portsmouth, July 2014–April 2022: A simplified checklist of the Machin, Union Flag and Common Poppy issues

Stamp Design, Values, **Inscriptions** (see **bold** text) & Note(s)	Year Code	Location of dispensing machine, Availability (dates inclusive) & Note(s)	Cat. No. of Stamp Issue Without Inscription, or Closest Match	Collectors' Strip Price
Common Poppy: 1st/1st L/E 20g WW 10g/E 100g/WW 20g/WW 100g: *continued*				
Royal Navy	MA15	*The National Museum of the Royal Navy*, Portsmouth[1] 19 October–15 November 2015 24 October–13 November 2016 – all sites apart from *The National Museum of the Royal Navy*, Belfast[2] – *HMS Caroline* which was closed at the time 20 October–19 November 2017 – all sites apart from *The National Museum of the Royal Navy*, Belfast[2] – *HMS Caroline* owing to the machine having been taken out of service spring/summer 2017	FS137, 138, 139, 140, 141 & 142 (Type IIIA)	20.00[5]
HMS Trincomalee 12th Oct 1817 With the introduction of this inscription, the Machin design should have replaced the *Common Poppy* design. Instead, the *Common Poppy* design was left in the machine resulting in an unintentional issue.	MA15	*The National Museum of the Royal Navy*, Hartlepool[3] *HMS Trincomalee* 20 November 2017	FS137, 138, 139, 140, 141 & 142 (Type IIIA)	45.00
Royal Navy Lest We Forget 100	MA15	*The National Museum of the Royal Navy*, Portsmouth[1] 1–30 November 2019 *The National Museum of the Royal Navy*, Hartlepool[3] *HMS Trincomalee* 1 November–2 December 2019	FS137, 138, 139, 140, 141 & 142 (Type IIIA)	20.00[5]
	MA16	*The National Museum of the Royal Navy*, Hartlepool[3] *HMS Trincomalee* Available for a few hours only on 27 November 2019	FS137, 138, 139, 140, 141 & 142 (Type IIIA)	30.00
	MA19	*The National Museum of the Royal Navy*, Hartlepool[3] *HMS Trincomalee* Available for a few hours only on 1 November 2019 *Explosion Museum of Naval Firepower*, Gosport[4] 1–30 November 2019	FS137, 138, 139, 140, 141 & 142 (Type IIIA)	21.00[5]
Common Poppy: 1st/1st Large/E 100g WW 20g/WW 100g/E Large 100g/WW Large 100g				
Royal Navy Lest We Forget	MA15	*The National Museum of the Royal Navy*, Hartlepool[3] *HMS Trincomalee* 26 November–10 December 2021	FS137, 138, 140 var, 142, 140 var, and 142 var (Type IIIA)	45.00
	MA19	*The National Museum of the Royal Navy*, Hartlepool[3] *HMS Trincomalee* Apparently available for a few hours only on 26 November 2021	FS137, 138, 140 var, 142, 140 var, and 142 var (Type IIIA)	38.00

Post & Go machines at Royal Navy Museums and the dates they were available from:

[1] *The National Museum of the Royal Navy* (NMRN), Portsmouth (machine code 002) – from 28 July 2014.

[2] *The National Museum of the Royal Navy*, Belfast – *HMS Caroline* (machine code 008) – from 1 June 2016–spring/summer 2017. Note: Machine taken out of service with no plans for it to be reinstated.

[3] *The National Museum of the Royal Navy*, Hartlepool – *HMS Trincomalee* (machine code 006) – from 1 June 2016.

[4] *Explosion Museum of Naval Firepower*, Gosport (machine code 007) – from 16 August 2016.

[5] When a similar item is available from more than one location the price given is for the cheaper version.

The machines at all the *National Museum Royal Navy* sites dispense stamps with the same generic inscription, although sometimes a particular site will mark a specific event through a unique inscription that is only available for a limited period.

[†] Owing to COVID 19 restrictions, the *Royal Navy* sites at Portsmouth, Hartlepool and *Explosion* at Gosport, closed their doors to the general public on 18 March 2020. The Portsmouth site reopened on 24 August 2020, Hartlepool on 4 September 2020, and Gosport on 29 August 2020. All sites closed again on 5 November 2020. The Portsmouth site temporarily reopened 3–19 December 2020 and Gosport 5–19 December 2020. Hartlepool remained closed. Portsmouth and Hartlepool sites reopened on 17 May 2021 and Gosport on 19 May 2021.

[♦] Post & Go machine out-of-service between 19 May–15 June 2021.

[♦♦] Post & Go machine out-of-service from 2 November 2021 up to, and including, the end date of this table i.e. April 2022.

Note: Each of *The Royal Navy Museum* sites has individual opening days outside the scope of this listing.

Glitches affecting inscriptions and lasting only a very short time and/or which exist in small quantities are beyond the scope of these tables.

The different inscriptions from *National Museum Royal Navy*. Where the same inscription exists on more than one design only one may be pictured.

ROYAL MAIL POST & GO STAMPS *Armed Forces Museums simplified checklist*

Post & Go stamps – the different issues and inscriptions from *The Royal Marines Museum*, Portsmouth to February 2017: A simplified checklist

Post & Go stamps – the inscriptions from *The Royal Marines Museum*, Southsea, January 2015–February 2017: A simplified checklist of the Machin, Union Flag and Common Poppy issues

Stamp Design, Values, Inscriptions (see bold text) & Note(s)	Year Code	Availability (dates inclusive) & Note(s)	Cat. No. of Stamp Issue Without Inscription, or Closest Match	Collectors' Strip Price
Machin: 1st/1st L/E 20g WW 10g/E 60g/WW 20g/WW 60g				
The RMM	MA13	13 January–29 March 2015	FS77b, 78b, 79bb, 80, 82b & 84 (Type IIIA)	19.00
	None	Apparently available for a few hours only on 13 January 2015	FS1d, 2d, 3cb, 3d, 5d & 5f (Type IIIA)	75.00
Machin: 1st/1st L/E 20g WW 10g/E 100g/WW 20g/WW 100g				
The RMM	MA13	30 March–18 October 2015	FS77b, 78b, 79bb, 80ca, 82b & 84ca (Type IIIA)	25.00
Royal Marines + circle logo Generic inscription revised, i.e. '**Royal Marines**' replaces acronym, and circle logo introduced.	MA13	16 November 2015–30 May 2016 1 July 2016–24 February 2017 after which the machine was relocated owing to the closure of the museum	FS77b, 78b, 79bb, 80ca, 82b & 84ca (Type IIIA)	19.00
Royal Marines Battle of Jutland + circle logo	MA13	31 May–30 June 2016	FS77b, 78b, 79bb, 80ca, 82b & 84ca (Type IIIA)	20.00
	MA15	Apparently available for a few hours only on 31 May 2016	FS77b, 78b, 79bb, 80ca, 82b & 84ca (Type IIIA)	—
Union Flag: 1st/1st L/E 20g WW 10g/E 60g/WW 20g/WW 60g				
The RMM	None	13 January–29 March 2015	FS39, 40, 41a, 41b, 43 & 44b (but Type IIIA)	19.00
Union Flag: 1st/1st L/E 20g WW 10g/E 100g/WW 20g/WW 100g				
The RMM	None	30 March–7 May 2015 1 June–18 October 2015	FS39, 40, 41a, 41c, 43 & 44c (but Type IIIA)	25.00
The RMM V.E. Day 70	None	8–31 May 2015	FS39, 40, 41a, 41c, 43 & 44c (but Type IIIA)	20.00
Royal Marines Trafalgar Day	None	19 October–15 November 2015 23 September–23 October 2016	FS39, 40, 41a, 41c, 43 & 44c (but Type IIIA)	20.00
Union Flag: 1st/1st L/E 20g WW 10g/E 100g/WW 20g/WW 100g				
Royal Marines Generic inscription revised, i.e. '**Royal Marines**' replaces acronym.	None	16 November 2015–30 May 2016 1 July–22 September 2016 14 November 2016–24 February 2017 after which the machine was relocated owing to the closure of the museum	FS39, 40, 41a, 41c, 43 & 44c (but Type IIIA)	19.00
Royal Marines Battle of Jutland	None	31 May–30 June 2016	FS39, 40, 41a, 41c, 43 & 44c (but Type IIIA)	20.00

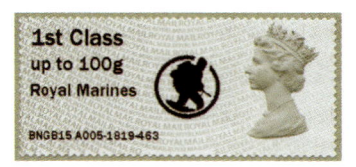

The different inscriptions from *The Royal Marines Museum*. Where the same inscription exists on more than one design only one may be pictured.

Armed Forces Museums simplified checklist **ROYAL MAIL POST & GO STAMPS**

Post & Go stamps – the inscriptions from *The Royal Marines Museum*, Southsea, January 2015–February 2017: A simplified checklist of the Machin, Union Flag and Common Poppy issues

Stamp Design, Values, Inscriptions (see bold text) & Note(s)	Year Code	Availability (dates inclusive) & Note(s)	Cat. No. of Stamp Issue Without Inscription, or Closest Match	Collectors' Strip Price
Common Poppy: **1st/1st L/E 20g WW 10g/E 100g/WW 20g/WW 100g**				
Royal Marines	MA15	19 October–15 November 2015 24 October–13 November 2016	FS137, 138, 139, 140, 141 & 142 (Type IIIA)	20.00

Glitches affecting inscriptions and lasting only a very short time and/or which exist in small quantities are beyond the scope of these tables.

Post & Go stamps – the different issues and inscriptions from *The Royal Navy Submarine Museum*, Gosport to April 2022: A simplified checklist

Post & Go stamps – the inscriptions from *The Royal Navy Submarine Museum*, July 2015–April 2022: A simplified checklist of the Machin, Union Flag and Common Poppy issues

Stamp Design, Values, Inscriptions (see bold text) & Note(s)	Year Code	Availability (dates inclusive) & Note(s)	Cat. No. of Stamp Issue Without Inscription, or Closest Match	Collectors' Strip Price
Machin: **1st/1st L/E 20g WW 10g/E 100g/WW 20g/WW 100g**				
The RNSM	MA13	28 July–18 October 2015	FS77b, 78b, 79bb, 80ca, 82b & 84ca (Type IIIA)	20.00
RN Submarine + circle logo Generic inscription revised, i.e. '**RN Submarine**' acronym, and logo introduced	MA13	16 November 2015–30 May 2016 1 July 2016–18 May 2017 except when 'MA15' available (see below) 19 June 2017–31 October 2019 5 December 2019–18 March 2020 26 August–1 September 2020	FS77b, 78b, 79bb, 80ca, 82b & 84ca (Type IIIA)	19.00
	MA15	Sometimes available between 1 July 2016–18 May 2017	FS77b, 78b, 79bb, 80ca, 82b & 84ca (Type IIIA)	20.00
RN Submarine **Battle of Jutland** + circle logo	MA15	31 May–30 June 2016	FS77b, 78b, 79bb, 80ca, 82b & 84ca (Type IIIA)	20.00
	MA13	Apparently available for a short time between 1–3 June 2016	FS77b, 78b, 79bb, 80ca, 82b & 84ca (Type IIIA)	—
HMS Alliance **14th May 1947** + circle logo	MA15	Only available for a short time on 19 May 2017	FS77b, 78b, 79bb, 80ca, 82b & 84ca (Type IIIA)	23.00
	MA13	19 May–18 June 2017	FS77b, 78b, 79bb, 80ca, 82b & 84ca (Type IIIA)	20.00
Machin: **1st/1st L/E 20g WW 10g/E 100g WW 20g/WW 100g Zone 1-3/WW 100g Zone 2** *[Dual value of E 100g WW 20g and two World Zoned stamps introduced on 1 September 2020]*				
RN Submarine + circle logo Dual-zone value with hyphen i.e. '**World 100g Zone 1-3**'	MA13	2–17 September 2020[1]	FS77b, 78b, 79bb (Type IIIA), 80*d*, 84*d* & 84*e* (but Type IIIA)	35.00
Machin: **1st/1st L/E 20g WW 10g/E 100g WW 20g/WW 100g Zone 1 & 3/WW 100g Zone 2** *[Service indicator for 'World Zones 1 and 3' revised on 18 September 2020]*				
RN Submarine + circle logo Dual-zone value with ampersand i.e. '**World 100g Zone 1 & 3**'	MA13	18 September–4 November 2020[1] 3–19 December 2020[1]	FS77b, 78b, 79bb (Type IIIA), 80*d*, 84*d* var & 84*e* (but Type IIIA) Single: i.e. Zone 1 & 3/FS84*d* var	— 15.00
Machin: **1st/1st Large/E 100g WW 20g/WW 100g/E Large 100g/WW Large 100g:** *continued*				
RN Submarine + circle logo	MA15	19 May–30 July 2021	FS77b, 78b, 80*d* (but Type IIIA), 84ca, 80*e* (but Type IIIA) and 84*f* (but Type IIIA)	35.00
	MA13	1 September–1 November 2021 (2–18 November 2021♦♦) 19–25 November 2021	FS77b, 78b, 80*d* (but Type IIIA), 84ca, 80*e* (but Type IIIA) and 84*f* (but Type IIIA) Set of two: i.e. E Large 100g/FS80*e* & WW Large 100g/FS84*f* (but TIIIA)	32.00 20.00
	R20Y	11 December 2021–31 March 2022	FS77b, 78b, 80*d* (but Type IIIA), 84ca, 80*e* (but Type IIIA) and 84*f* (but Type IIIA)	32.00
RN Submarine **Black Tot Day 31st July 1970** + circle logo	MA15	Available for a few hours only on 31 July 2021	FS77b, 78b, 80*d* (but Type IIIA), 84ca, 80*e* (but Type IIIA) and 84*f* (but Type IIIA)	—
	MA13	31 July–31 August 2021	FS77b, 78b, 80*d* (but Type IIIA), 84ca, 80*e* (but Type IIIA) and 84*f* (but Type IIIA)	32.00
RN Submarine **Falklands 40th** + circle logo	MA13	1–29 April 2022	FS77b, 78b, 80*d* (but Type IIIA), 84ca, 80*e* (but Type IIIA) and 84*f* (but Type IIIA)	35.00

ROYAL MAIL POST & GO STAMPS *Armed Forces Museums simplified checklist*

Post & Go stamps – the inscriptions from *The Royal Navy Submarine Museum*, July 2015–April 2022:
A simplified checklist of the Machin, Union Flag and Common Poppy issues

Stamp Design, Values, Inscriptions (see bold text) & Note(s)	Year Code	Availability (dates inclusive) & Note(s)	Cat. No. of Stamp Issue Without Inscription, or Closest Match	Collectors' Strip Price
Union Flag: 1st/1st L/E 20g WW 10g/E 100g/WW 20g/WW 100g				
The RNSM	None	28 July–18 October 2015	FS39, 40, 41*a*, 41*c*, 43 & 44*c* (but Type IIIA)	20.00
RN Submarine Generic inscription revised, i.e. '**RN Submarine**' replaces acronym.	None	19 October 2015–30 May 2016 1 July–23 October 2016 14 November 2016–18 May 2017 19 June–19 October 2017 20 November 2017–18 March 2020 26 August–1 September 2020	FS39, 40, 41*a*, 41*c*, 43 & 44*c* (but Type IIIA)	19.00
RN Submarine **Battle of Jutland**	None	31 May–30 June 2016	FS39, 40, 41*a*, 41*c*, 43 & 44*c* (but Type IIIA)	20.00
HMS Alliance **14th May 1947**	None	19 May–18 June 2017	FS39, 40, 41*a*, 41*c*, 43 & 44*c* (but Type IIIA)	20.00
Union Flag: 1st/1st L/E 20g WW 10g/E 100g WW 20g/WW 100g Zone 1-3/WW 100g Zone 2 *[Dual value of E 100g WW 20g and two World Zoned stamps introduced on 1 September 2020]*				
RN Submarine Dual-zone value with hyphen i.e. '**World 100g Zone 1-3**'	None	2–17 September 2020¹	FS39, 40, 41*a*, 41*d*, 44*d* & 44*e* (but Type IIIA)	35.00
Union Flag: 1st/1st L/E 20g WW 10g/E 100g WW 20g/WW 100g Zone 1 & 3/WW 100g Zone 2 *[Service indicator for 'World Zones 1 and 3' revised on 18 September 2020]*				
RN Submarine Dual-zone value with ampersand i.e. '**World 100g Zone 1 & 3**'	None	18 September–4 November 2020¹ 3–19 December 2020¹	FS39, 40, 41*a*, 41*d*, 44*d* var & 44*e* (but Type IIIA) Single: i.e. Zone 1 & 3/FS44*d* var	— 15.00

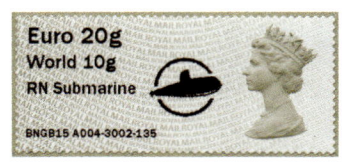

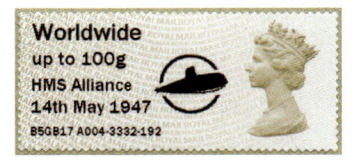

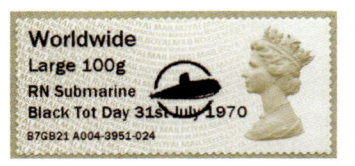

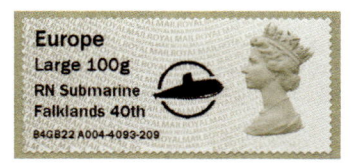

The different inscriptions from *The Royal Navy Submarine Museum*. Where the same inscription exists on more than one design only one may be pictured.

Armed Forces Museums simplified checklist — ROYAL MAIL POST & GO STAMPS

Post & Go stamps – the inscriptions from *The Royal Navy Submarine Museum*, July 2015–April 2022: A simplified checklist of the Machin, Union Flag and Common Poppy issues

Stamp Design, Values, Inscriptions (see bold text) & Note(s)	Year Code	Availability (dates inclusive) & Note(s)	Cat. No. of Stamp Issue Without Inscription, or Closest Match	Collectors' Strip Price
Union Flag: 1st/1st Large/E 100g WW 20g/WW 100g/E Large 100g/WW Large 100g				
RN Submarine	None	19 May–30 July 2021 1 September–1 November 2021 (2–18 November 2021 ♦♦) 19–25 November 2021	FS39, 40, 41d, 44c, 41 var & 44 var (but all Type IIIA) Set of two singles: i.e. E Large 100g/FS41 var & WW Large 100g/FS44 var (but TIIIA)	35.00 23.00
	MA19	11 December 2021–31 March 2022	FS85a, 86a, 87 var, 88 var, 92 var & 92 var (but all Type IIIA & stamps digitally printed)	32.00
Black Tot Day 31st July 1970 (Note: '**RN Submarine**' not included on this issue)	None	31 July–31 August 2021 (Note: These stamps from *The Royal Navy Submarine Museum*, identifiable only through their machine code, i.e. 004	FS39, 40, 41d, 44c, 41 var & 44 var (but all Type IIIA)	32.00
RN Submarine **Lest We Forget**	None	Available for a few hours only on 26 November 2021	FS39, 40, 41d, 44c, 41 var & 44 var (but all Type IIIA)	42.00
	MA19	26 November–10 December 2021	FS85a, 86a, 87 var, 88 var, 92 var & 92 var (but all Type IIIA & stamps digitally printed)	35.00
RN Submarine **Falklands 40th**	MA19	1–29 April 2022	FS85a, 86a, 87 var, 88 var, 92 var & 92 var (but all Type IIIA & stamps digitally printed)	35.00
Common Poppy: 1st/1st L/E 20g WW 10g/E 100g/WW 20g/WW 100g				
RN Submarine	MA15	19 October–15 November 2015 24 October–13 November 2016 20 October–19 November 2017	FS137, 138, 139, 140, 141 & 142 (Type IIIA)	20.00
RN Submarine **Lest We Forget 100**	MA15	1–30 November 2019	FS137, 138, 139, 140, 141 & 142 (Type IIIA)	20.00
RN Submarine + circle logo With the return of the generic inscription, the Machin design should have replaced the *Common Poppy* design. Instead, the *Common Poppy* was left in the machine resulting in an unintentional issue.	MA15	1–5 December 2019	FS137, 138, 139, 140, 141 & 142 (Type IIIA)	35.00
Common Poppy: 1st/1st Large/E 100g WW 20g/WW 100g/E Large 100g/WW Large 100g				
RN Submarine **Lest We Forget**	MA15	26 November–10 December 2021	FS137, 138, 140 var, 142, 140 var, and 142 var (Type IIIA)	35.00

[1] Owing to COVID 19 restrictions, *The Royal Navy Submarine Museum* closed its doors to the general public on 18 March 2020. It temporarily reopened between 26 August–4 November and 3–19 December 2020, both periods with a Wednesday to Sunday opening schedule, and remained closed until 19 May 2021.
♦♦ Post & Go machine out-of-service
Glitches affecting inscriptions and lasting only a very short time and/or which exist in small quantities are beyond the scope of these tables.

The different inscriptions from *The Royal Navy Submarine Museum*. Where the same inscription exists on more than one design only one may be pictured.

ROYAL MAIL POST & GO STAMPS *Armed Forces Museums simplified checklist*

Post & Go stamps – the different issues and inscriptions from *The Royal Navy Fleet Air Arm Museum*, RNAS Yeovilton to April 2022: A simplified checklist

Post & Go stamps – the inscriptions from *The Royal Navy Fleet Air Arm Museum*, RNAS Yeovilton, Ilchester, Yeovil, April 2015–April 2022: A simplified checklist of the Machin, Union Flag and Common Poppy issues

Stamp Design, Values, Inscriptions (see bold text) & Note(s)	Year Code	Availability (dates inclusive) & Note(s)	Cat. No. of Stamp Issue Without Inscription, or Closest Match	Collectors' Strip Price
Machin: 1st/1st L/E 20g WW 10g/E 100g/WW 20g/WW 100g				
The FAAM	MA13	14 April–18 October 2015	FS77b, 78b, 79bb, 80ca, 82b & 84ca (Type IIIA)	20.00
Fleet Air Arm + large circle logo Generic inscription revised, i.e. '**Fleet Air Arm**' replaces acronym, and large logo introduced.	MA13	16 November 2015–30 May 2016 1 July–2 December 2016 4 January–18 July 2017 except when 'MA15' available (see below) 22 August 2017–June 2018	FS77b, 78b, 79bb, 80ca, 82b & 84ca (Type IIIA)	19.00
	MA15	Available for a short time in early January 2017	FS77b, 78b, 79bb, 80ca, 82b & 84ca (Type IIIA)	20.00
	MA14	June 2018–5 November 2019	FS77b, 78b, 79bb, 80ca, 82b & 84ca (Type IIIA)	24.00
Fleet Air Arm Battle of Jutland + small circle logo	MA13	31 May–30 June 2016	FS77b, 78b, 79bb, 80ca, 82b & 84ca (Type IIIA)	20.00
Fleet Air Arm LZ551/G 1st Jet Carrier Landing	MA13	Only available for a short time on 3 December 2016	FS77b, 78b, 79bb, 80ca, 82b & 84ca (Type IIIA)	75.00
	MA15	3 December 2016–3 January 2017	FS77b, 78b, 79bb, 80ca, 82b & 84ca (Type IIIA)	20.00
Fleet Air Arm Sea King ZA298 Junglie + large circle logo	MA13	Only available for a short time on 19 July 2017	FS77b, 78b, 79bb, 80ca, 82b & 84ca (Type IIIA)	90.00
	MA15	19 July–21 August 2017	FS77b, 78b, 79bb, 80ca, 82b & 84ca (Type IIIA)	20.00
Fleet Air Arm Concorde 50 Years + Concorde 50 logo Due to poor thermal printing, the right-hand part of the Concorde logo is faintly printed, which is the norm for this issue. Conveniently, this allows the 'MA14' year code to be seen, which otherwise, would have been obscured.	MA14	6 November 2019–18 March 2020[1] 14 August–1 September 2020[1]	FS77b, 78b, 79bb, 80ca, 82b & 84ca (Type IIIA)	20.00

The different inscriptions from *The Royal Navy Fleet Air Arm Museum*. Where the same inscription exists on more than one design only one may be pictured.

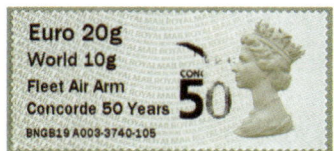

Armed Forces Museums simplified checklist — ROYAL MAIL POST & GO STAMPS

Post & Go stamps – the inscriptions from *The Royal Navy Fleet Air Arm Museum*, RNAS Yeovilton, Ilchester, Yeovil, April 2015–April 2022: A simplified checklist of the Machin, Union Flag and Common Poppy issues

Stamp Design, Values, Inscriptions (see bold text) & Note(s)	Year Code	Availability (dates inclusive) & Note(s)	Cat. No. of Stamp Issue Without Inscription, or Closest Match	Collectors' Strip Price
Machin: 1st/1st L/E 20g WW 10g/E 100g WW 20g/WW 100g Zone 1-3/WW 100g Zone 2 *[Dual value of E 100g WW 20g and two World Zoned stamps introduced on 1 September 2020]*				
Fleet Air Arm + large circle logo	MA14	1–2 September 2020[1]	FS77b, 78b, 79bb (Type IIIA), 80d, 84d & 84e (but Type IIIA)	—
Dual-zone value with hyphen i.e. **'World 100g Zone 1-3'**	MA13	2–17 September 2020[1]	FS77b, 78b, 79bb (Type IIIA), 80d, 84d & 84e (but Type IIIA)	35.00
Machin: 1st/1st L/E 20g WW 10g/E 100g WW 20g/WW 100g Zone 1 & 3/WW 100g Zone 2 *[Service indicator for 'World Zones 1 and 3' revised on 18 September 2020]*				
Fleet Air Arm + large circle logo Dual-zone value with ampersand i.e. **'World 100g Zone 1 & 3'**	MA13	18 September–6 October 2020[1] During this period, partly owing to a shortage of stock, the machine was rarely in service	FS77b, 78b, 79bb (Type IIIA), 80d, 84d var & 84e (but Type IIIA) Single: i.e. Zone 1 & 3/FS84d var	— —
Fleet Air Arm + small circle logo Small circle logo replaced large version Dual-zone value with ampersand i.e. **'World 100g Zone 1 & 3'**	MA13	7 October–4 November 2020[1] 3–11 December 2020[1] 18–20 December 2020[1]	FS77b, 78b, 79bb (Type IIIA), 80d, 84d var & 84e (but Type IIIA)	30.00
Machin: 1st/1st L/E 20g WW 10g/E 100g/WW 20g/WW 100g *(reversion to pre-September 2020 tariff stamps)*				
Fleet Air Arm + small circle logo Reversion to pre-September 2020 tariff stamp, but with small logo	MA13	12–17 December 2020[1]	FS77b, 78b, 79bb, 80ca, 82b & 84ca (Type IIIA)	38.00
Machin: 1st/1st Large/E 100g WW 20g/WW 100g/E Large 100g/WW Large 100g				
Fleet Air Arm + small circle logo	MA13	19 May–30 July 2021 1 September–1 November 2021 (2–18 November 2021 ♦♦) 19–25 November 2021 11 December 2021–31 March 2022	FS77b, 78b, 80d (but Type IIIA), 84ca, 80e (but Type IIIA) & 84f (but Type IIIA) Set of two singles: i.e. E Large 100g/FS80e & WW Large 100g/FS84f (but TIIIA)	32.00 20.00
Fleet Air Arm Black Tot Day 31st July 1970 + circle logo	MA13	31 July–31 August 2021	FS77b, 78b, 80d (but Type IIIA), 84ca, 80e (but Type IIIA) & 84f (but Type IIIA)	32.00
Fleet Air Arm Falklands 40th + circle logo	MA13	1–29 April 2022	FS77b, 78b, 80d (but Type IIIA), 84ca, 80e (but Type IIIA) & 84f (but Type IIIA)	35.00

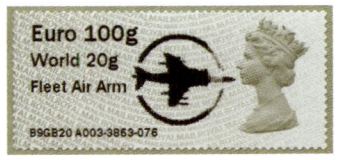

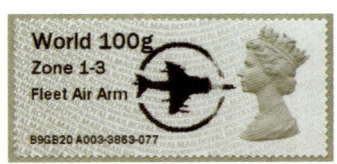

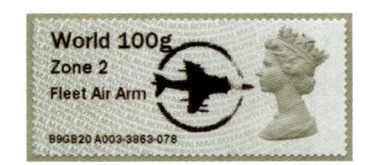

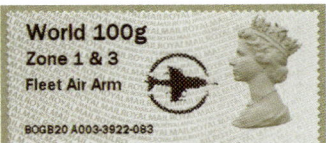

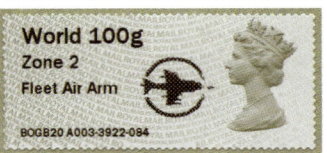

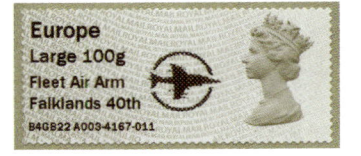

The different inscriptions from *The Royal Navy Fleet Air Arm Museum*. Where the same inscription exists on more than one design only one may be pictured.

ROYAL MAIL POST & GO STAMPS *Armed Forces Museums simplified checklist*

Post & Go stamps – the inscriptions from *The Royal Navy Fleet Air Arm Museum*, RNAS Yeovilton, Ilchester, Yeovil, April 2015–April 2022: A simplified checklist of the Machin, Union Flag and Common Poppy issues

Stamp Design, Values, Inscriptions (see bold text) & Note(s)	Year Code	Availability (dates inclusive) & Note(s)	Cat. No. of Stamp Issue Without Inscription, or Closest Match	Collectors' Strip Price
Union Flag: 1st/1st L/E 20g WW 10g/E 100g/WW 20g/WW 100g				
The FAAM	None	14 April–7 May 2015 30 May–18 October 2015	FS39, 40, 41a, 41c, 43 & 44c (but Type IIIA)	20.00
The FAAM **V.E. Day 70**	None	8–29 May 2015	FS39, 40, 41a, 41c, 43 & 44c (but Type IIIA)	20.00
Fleet Air Arm Generic inscription revised, i.e. '**Fleet Air Arm**' replaces acronym.	None	19 October 2015–30 May 2016 1 July–23 October 14 November–2 December 2016 4 January–18 July 2017 22 August–19 October 2017 20 November 2017–5 November 2019 12–17 December 2020¹ due to a temporary reversion to the pre-September 2020 tariff stamps	FS39, 40, 41a, 41c, 43 & 44c (but Type IIIA)	19.00
	MA19	Only available for a short time on 12 December 2020¹ due to a temporary reversion to the pre-September 2020 tariff stamps	FS85a, 86a, 87a, 88a, 90a & 92a (but Type IIIA & stamps digitally printed)	—
Union Flag: 1st/1st L/E 20g WW 10g/E 100g/WW 20g/WW 100g:				
Fleet Air Arm **Battle of Jutland**	None	31 May–30 June 2016	FS39, 40, 41a, 41c, 43 & 44c (but Type IIIA)	20.00
Fleet Air Arm **LZ551/G 03Dec45**	None	3 December 2016–3 January 2017	FS39, 40, 41a, 41c, 43 & 44c (but Type IIIA)	20.00
Fleet Air Arm **LZ551/G 03Dec45** Second line of inscription slightly inset	None	Only available for a short time on 3 December 2016 and then corrected	FS39, 40, 41a, 41c, 43 & 44c (but Type IIIA)	25.00
Fleet Air Arm **GR9A Harrier ZD433**	None	19 July–21 August 2017	FS39, 40, 41a, 41c, 43 & 44c (but Type IIIA)	19.00
Fleet Air Arm **Concorde 50 Years**	None	6 November 2019–18 March 2020¹ 14 August–1 September 2020¹	FS39, 40, 41a, 41c, 43 & 44c (but Type IIIA)	20.00
Union Flag: 1st/1st L/E 20g WW 10g/E 100g WW 20g/WW 100g Zone 1-3/WW 100g Zone 2 *[Dual value of E 100g WW 20g and two World Zoned stamps introduced on 1 September 2020]*				
Fleet Air Arm Dual-zone value with hyphen i.e. '**World 100g Zone 1-3**'	None	1–17 September 2020¹	FS39, 40, 41a, 41d, 44d & 44e (but Type IIIA)	35.00
Union Flag: 1st/1st L/E 20g WW 10g/E 100g WW 20g/WW 100g Zone 1 & 3/WW 100g Zone 2 *[Service indicator for 'World Zones 1 and 3' revised on 18 September 2020]*				
Fleet Air Arm Dual-zone value with ampersand i.e. '**World 100g Zone 1 & 3**'	None	18 September–6 October 2020¹ During this period, partly owing to a shortage of stock, the machine was rarely in service 18–20 December 2020¹	FS39, 40, 41a, 41d, 44d var & 44e (but Type IIIA) Single: i.e. Zone 1 & 3/FS44d var (but TIIIA)	— —
	MA19	7 October–4 November 2020¹ 3–12 December 2020¹	FS85a, 86a, 87a, 88 var, 92 var & 92 var (but Type IIIA & stamps digitally printed)	30.00
Union Flag: 1st/1st Large/E 100g WW 20g/WW 100g/E Large 100g/WW Large 100g				
Fleet Air Arm	None	19 May–30 July 2021 1 September–1 November 2021 (2–18 November 2021 ♦♦) 19–25 November 2021 11 December 2021–31 March 2022	FS39, 40, 41d, 44c, 41 var & 44 var (but all Type IIIA) Set of two singles: i.e. E Large 100g/FS41 var & WW Large 100g/FS44 var (but TIIIA)	35.00 23.00
Black Tot Day **31st July 1970** (Note: '**Fleet Air Arm**' not included on this issue)	None	31 July–31 August 2021 (Note: These stamps from *The Royal Navy Fleet Air Arm Museum* identifiable only through their machine code, i.e. 003	FS39, 40, 41d, 44c, 41 var & 44 var (but all Type IIIA)	32.00
Fleet Air Arm **Lest We Forget**	None	26 November–10 December 2021	FS39, 40, 41d, 44c, 41 var & 44 var (but all Type IIIA)	35.00
Fleet Air Arm **Falklands 40th**	None	Only available for a short time on 1 April 2022	FS39, 40, 41d, 44c, 41 var & 44 var (but all Type IIIA)	—
	MA19	1–29 April 2022	FS85a, 86a, 87 var, 88 var, 92 var & 92 var (but all Type IIIA & stamps digitally printed)	35.00

Armed Forces Museums simplified checklist ROYAL MAIL POST & GO STAMPS

Post & Go stamps – the inscriptions from *The Royal Navy Fleet Air Arm Museum*, **RNAS Yeovilton, Ilchester, Yeovil, April 2015–April 2022: A simplified checklist of the Machin, Union Flag and Common Poppy issues**

Stamp Design, Values, Inscriptions (see bold text) & Note(s)	Year Code	Availability (dates inclusive) & Note(s)	Cat. No. of Stamp Issue Without Inscription, or Closest Match	Collectors' Strip Price
Common Poppy: 1st/1st L/E 20g WW 10g/E 100g/WW 20g/WW 100g				
Fleet Air Arm	MA15	19 October–15 November 2015 24 October–13 November 2016 20 October–19 November 2017	FS137, 138, 139, 140, 141 & 142 (Type IIIA)	20.00
Common Poppy: 1st/1st Large/E 100g WW 20g/WW 100g/E Large 100g/WW Large 100g				
Fleet Air Arm **Lest We Forget**	MA15	26 November–10 December 2021	FS137, 138, 140 var, 142, 140 var, & 142 var (Type IIIA)	35.00

[1] Owing to COVID 19 restrictions, *The Royal Navy Fleet Air Arm Museum* closed its doors to the general public on 18 March 2020. It temporarily reopened between 14 August–4 November and 3–20 December 2020 (sometimes only opening Wednesday to Sunday), and remained closed until 19 May 2021.
♦♦ Post & Go machine out-of-service

Glitches affecting inscriptions and lasting only a very short time and/or which exist in small quantities are beyond the scope of these tables.

The different inscriptions from *The Royal Navy Fleet Air Arm Museum*. Where the same inscription exists on more than one design only one may be pictured.

ROYAL MAIL POST & GO STAMPS *Armed Forces Museums simplified checklist*

Post & Go stamps – the different issues and inscriptions from The Royal Signals Museum to April 2021: A simplified checklist

Post and Go stamps – the inscriptions from The Royal Signals Museum, Royal School of Signals, Blandford Camp, Blandford Forum, November 2016–April 2021: A simplified checklist of the Machin, Union Flag and Common Poppy issues				
Stamp Design, Values, Inscriptions (see bold text) & Note(s)	**Year Code**	**Availability (dates inclusive) & Note(s)**	**Cat. No. of Stamp Issue Without Inscription, or Closest Match**	**Collectors' Strip Price**
Machin: 1st/1st L/E 20g WW 10g/E 100g/WW 20g/WW 100g				
Royal Corps of Signals + Jimmy logo	None	From 3 November 2016[1]	FS1d, 2d, 3cb, 3ea, 5d & 5ga (Type IIIA)	20.00
	MA13	At different times, no year code and 'MA13' have been available	FS77b, 78b, 79bb, 80ca, 82b & 84ca (Type IIIA)	25.00
Union Flag: 1st/1st L/E 20g WW 10g/E 100g/WW 20g/WW 100g				
Royal Corps of Signals	None	3 November 2016–8 June 2017 From 20 November 2017[1]	FS39, 40, 41*a*, 41*c*, 43 & 44*c* (but Type IIIA)	20.00
Royal Signals White Helmets + Motorcycle logo	None	9 June–19 October 2017	FS39, 40, 41*a*, 41*c*, 43 & 44*c* (but Type IIIA)	20.00
Poppy: 1st/1st L/E 20g WW 10g/E 100g/WW 20g/WW 100g				
Royal Corps of Signals	MA15	20 October–19 November 2017	FS137, 138, 139, 140, 141 & 142 (Type IIIA)	20.00

[1] Owing to COVID 19 restrictions, The Royal Signals Museum closed its doors to the general public on 18 March 2020 and remains closed.

Glitches affecting inscriptions and lasting only a very short time and/or which exist in small quantities are beyond the scope of these tables.

The different inscriptions from The Royal Signals Museum. Where the same inscription exists on more than one design only one may be pictured.

Hytech & Royal Mail 'Series II' printings from exhibitions **ROYAL MAIL POST & GO STAMPS**

Post & Go stamps – the different printings from exhibitions and stamp fairs in the United Kingdom but without inscriptions (February 2011 – September 2017): a simplified checklist

Stamp Design, Values, Machine Type & Note(s)	Format produced CS	Format produced Set of 36	Event the stamps were available from, the date and duration (all the dates are inclusive)	Space between service indicator lines	Code string is numerals only (Type II)	Code string is letters & numerals (Type III)	Cat. No. of Stamp Issue Without Inscription, or Closest Match
Machin, 1st/1stL/E-20g/WW-10g/WW-20g without year code (N.B. five values only):-							
Hytech Postal Vision (trial machine) Weight line inset †	✓	n/a	Spring Stampex 2011 23–26 February: 4 days	3mm	yes		FS1a/5a
Machin, 1st/1stL/E-20g/WW-10g/WW-20g/WW-40g without year code:							
Royal Mail 'Series I' (sometimes known as Hytech 'next generation')	✓	n/a	York Stamp Fair 18–19 January 2013: 2 days Salisbury Stamp Fair 15–16 March 2013: 2 days Midpex Exhibition 6 July 2013: 1 day (N.B. similar stamps were first issued in November 2012 from a pop-up Christmas Post Shop in Camden, London)	2.6mm		yes	FS1b/3b, 4b, 5b & 5eb
Royal Mail 'Series II'	✓	n/a	Salisbury Stamp Fair 14–15 March 2014: 2 days	2.4mm		yes	FS1b/3b, 4b, 5b & 5eb
Machin, 1st/1stL/E-20g/WW-10g/WW-20g/WW-40g with MA13 year code:							
Royal Mail 'Series I' (sometimes known as Hytech 'next generation')	✓	n/a	York Stamp Fair 19–20 July 2013: 2 days Autumn Stampex 2013 18–21 September: 4 days Stafford Stamp Fair 8–9 November 2013: 2 days York Stamp Fair 17–18 January 2014: 2 days	2.6mm		yes	FS77/79, 81/83 (but Type III)
Royal Mail 'Series II'	✓	n/a	Salisbury Stamp Fair 14–15 March 2014: 2 days	2.4mm		yes	FS77/79, 81/83 (but Type III)
Machin, 1st/1stL/E-20g E-60g/WW-10g/WW-60g/WW-20g/WW-60g without year code:							
Royal Mail 'Series II' Euro 20g large typeface World 10g small typeface	✓	n/a	York Stamp Fair 18–19 July 2014: 2 days	2.4mm		yes	FS1b, 2b, 3c, 3d, 5b, & 5f
Royal Mail 'Series II' All values have a revised (smaller) typeface	✓	n/a	Autumn Stampex 2014 17–20 September: 4 days Stafford Stamp Fair 7–8 November 2014: 2 days Spring Stampex 2015 18–21 February: 4 days (N.B. limited availablilty and only known from stock produced in advance of the exhibition)	2.7mm		yes (Type IIIA)	FS1d, 2d, 3cb, 3d, 5d & 5f
Machin, 1st/1stL/E-20g WW-10g/E-60g/WW-20g/WW-60g with MA13 year code:							
Royal Mail 'Series II' Euro 20g large typeface World 10g small typeface	✓	n/a	York Stamp Fair 18–19 July 2014: 2 days	2.4mm		yes	FS77/78, 79b, 80, 82 & 84 (but Type III)
Royal Mail 'Series II' All values have a revised (smaller) typeface	✓	n/a	Autumn Stampex 2014 17–20 September: 4 days Stafford Stamp Fair 7–8 November 2014: 2 days Spring Stampex 2015 18–21 February: 4 days	2.7mm		yes (Type IIIA)	FS77b, 78b, 79bb, 80, 82b & 84
Machin, 1st/1stL/E-20g WW-10g/E-100g/WW-20g/WW-100g without year code:							
Royal Mail 'Series II' All values have a revised (smaller) typeface	✓	n/a	Midpex Exhibition 4 July 2015: 1 day (N.B. similar stamps were (officially) issued on 3 June 2015 from Royal Mail Enquiry offices	2.7mm		yes (Type IIIA)	FS1d, 2d, 3cb, 3ea, 5d & 5ga

ROYAL MAIL POST & GO STAMPS — Hytech & Royal Mail 'Series II' printings from exhibitions

Stamp Design, Values, Machine Type & Note(s)	Format produced CS	Format produced Set of 36	Event the stamps were available from, the date and duration (all the dates are inclusive)	Space between service indicator lines	Code string is numerals only (Type II)	Code string is letters & numerals (Type III)	Cat. No. of Stamp Issue Without Inscription, or Closest Match
Machin, 1st/1stL/E-20g WW-10g/E-100g/WW-20g/WW-100g with MA13 year code:							
Royal Mail 'Series II' All values have a revised (smaller) typeface	✓	n/a	Midpex Exhibition 4 July 2015: 1 day (N.B. similar stamps were (officially) issued on 30 March 2015 from Royal Mail Enquiry offices)	2.7mm		yes (Type IIIA)	FS77b, 78b, 79bb, 80ca, 82b & 84ca
Machin, 2nd/2ndL with MA12 year code:							
Royal Mail 'Series I' (sometimes known as Hytech 'next generation')	✓	n/a	Spring Stampex 2013 20–23 February: 4 days (N.B. similar stamps, but not identical, were (officially) issued in November 2013 from a travelling pop-up Christmas post office)	2.6mm		yes	FS93, 94
Union Flag, 1st/1stL/E-20g/WW-10g/WW-20g/WW-40g without year code:							
Royal Mail 'Series I' (sometimes known as Hytech 'next generation')	✓	n/a	Autumn Stampex 2012 26–29 September: 4 days York Stamp Fair 18–19 January 2013: 2 days Salisbury Stamp Fair 15–16 March 2013: 2 days Midpex Exhibition 6 July 2013: 1 day	2.6mm		yes	FS39/44 (but Type III)
Royal Mail 'Series II'	✓	n/a	Spring Stampex 2014 19–22 February: 4 days (N.B. This design only available on 21–22 February: 2 days) Salisbury Stamp Fair 14–15 March 2014: 2 days	2.4mm		yes	FS39/44 (but Type III)
Union Flag, 1st/1stL/E-20g/WW-10g/WW-20g/WW-40g with MA13 year code:							
Royal Mail 'Series I' (sometimes known as Hytech 'next generation')	✓	n/a	York Stamp Fair 19–20 July 2013: 2 days York Stamp Fair 17–18 January 2014: 2 days	2.6mm		yes	FS85/90 (but Type III)
Royal Mail 'Series II'	✓	n/a	Spring Stampex 2014 19–22 February: 4 days Salisbury Stamp Fair 14–15 March 2014: 2 days	2.4mm		yes	FS85/90 (but Type III)
Union Flag, 1st/1stL/E-20g/E-60g/WW-20g/WW-60g without year code:							
Royal Mail 'Series II'	✓	n/a	85th Annual Congress of Association of Scottish Philatelic Societies (Perth, Scotland) 11–12 April 2014: 2 days	2.4mm		yes	FS39/41, 41b, 43 & 44b (but Type III)
Union Flag, 1st/1stL/E-20g/E-60g/WW-20g/WW-60g with MA13 year code:							
Royal Mail 'Series II'	✓	n/a	85th Annual Congress of Association of Scottish Philatelic Societies (Perth, Scotland) 11–12 April 2014: 2 days	2.4mm		yes	FS85/91 (but Type III)
Union Flag, 1st/1stL/E-20g WW-10g/E-60g/WW-20g/WW-60g without year code :							
Royal Mail 'Series II' Euro 20g large typeface World 10g small typeface	✓	n/a	York Stamp Fair 18–19 July 2014: 2 days	2.4mm		yes	FS39, 40, 41a, 41b, 43, & 44b (but Type III)
Royal Mail 'Series II' All values have a revised (smaller) typeface	✓	n/a	Autumn Stampex 2014 17–20 September: 4 days Stafford Stamp Fair 7–8 November 2014: 2 days	2.7mm		yes (Type IIIA)	FS39, 40, 41a, 41b, 43, & 44b (but Type IIIA)
Union Flag, 1st/1stL/E-20g WW-10g/E-100g/WW-20g/WW-100g without year code :							
Royal Mail 'Series II' All values have a revised (smaller) typeface	✓	n/a	Europhilex 2015 13–16 May: 4 days Midpex Exhibition 4 July 2015: 1 day Autumn Stampex 2015 16–19 September: 4 days	2.7mm		yes (Type IIIA)	FS39, 40, 41a, 41c, 43 & 44c (but Type IIIA)

Hytech & Royal Mail 'Series II' printings from exhibitions **ROYAL MAIL POST & GO STAMPS**

Stamp Design, Values, Machine Type & Note(s)	Format produced CS	Format produced Set of 36	Event the stamps were available from, the date and duration (all the dates are inclusive)	Space between service indicator lines	Code string is numerals only (Type II)	Code string is letters & numerals (Type III)	Cat. No. of Stamp Issue Without Inscription, or Closest Match
Robin, 1st/1stL/E-20g/WW-10g/WW-20g/WW-40g with MA13 year code:							
Royal Mail 'Series I' (sometimes known as Hytech 'next generation')	✓	n/a	Stafford Stamp Fair 8–9 November 2013: 2 days (N.B. similar MA13 stamps were (officially) issued later in November 2013 from a travelling pop-up Christmas post office)	2.6mm		yes	FS51a/56a
Birds of Britain 3rd series, 1st/1stL/E-20g/WW-10g/WW-20g/1st (N.B. only produced in collectors' strips of six with additional '1st Class' value at bottom so all six designs represented):							
Royal Mail 'Series I' (sometimes known as Hytech 'next generation') Weight line inset †	✓	n/a	Autumn Stampex 2011 14–17 September: 4 days (N.B. This design only available on 14 September: 1 day)	3mm		yes	FS16/20
Birds of Britain 4th series, 1st/1stL/E-20g/WW-10g/WW-20g/WW-40g:							
Royal Mail 'Series I' (sometimes known as Hytech 'next generation') Weight line inset †	✓	✓	Autumn Stampex 2011 14–17 September: 4 days (N.B. This design only available on 16–17 September: 2 days) Spring Stampex 2012 22–25 February: 4 days (N.B. This design only available on 22–23 September: 2 days)	3mm		yes	FS21/26
Sheep (British Farm Animals 1st series), 1st/1stL/E-20g/WW-10g/WW-20g/WW-40g:							
Royal Mail 'Series I' (sometimes known as Hytech 'next generation') Weight line inset †	✓	✓	Spring Stampex 2012 22–25 February: 4 days (N.B. This design only available on 24–25 February: 2 days)	3mm		yes	FS27/32
Pigs (British Farm Animals 2nd series), 1st/1stL/E-20g/WW-10g/WW-20g/WW-40g:							
Royal Mail 'Series I' (sometimes known as Hytech 'next generation')	✓	✓	Autumn Stampex 2012 26–29 September: 4 days (N.B. This design only available on 26–27 September: 2 days)	2.6mm		yes	FS33/38 (but Type III)
Cattle (British Farm Animals 3rd series), 1st/1stL/E-20g/WW-10g/WW-20g/WW-40g:							
Royal Mail 'Series I' (sometimes known as Hytech 'next generation')	✓	✓	Autumn Stampex 2012 26–29 September: 4 days (N.B. This design only available on 28–29 September: 2 days)	2.6mm		yes	FS45/50 (but Type III)
Ponds (Freshwater Life 1st series), 1st/1stL/E-20g/WW-10g/WW-20g/WW-40g:							
Royal Mail 'Series I' (sometimes known as Hytech 'next generation')	✓	✓	Spring Stampex 2013 20–23 February: 4 days (N.B. This design only available on 22–23 February: 2 days)	2.6mm		yes	FS59/64 (but Type III)
Lakes (Freshwater Life 2nd series), 1st/1stL/E-20g/WW-10g/WW-20g/WW-40g:							
Royal Mail 'Series I' (sometimes known as Hytech 'next generation')	✓	✓	Midpex Exhibition 06 July 2013: 1 day York Stamp Fair 19–20 July 2013: 2 days	2.6mm		yes	FS65/70 (but Type III)
Rivers (Freshwater Life 3rd series), 1st/1stL/E-20g/WW-10g/WW-20g/WW-40g:							
Royal Mail 'Series I' (sometimes known as Hytech 'next generation')	✓	✓	Autumn Stampex 2013 18–21 September: 4 days (N.B. This design only available on 20–21 September: 2 days) Stafford Stamp Fair 8–9 November 2013: 2 days	2.6mm		yes	FS71/76 (but Type III)
Spring Blooms (British Flora 1st series), 1st/1stL/E-20g/WW-10g/WW-20g/WW-40g:							
Royal Mail 'Series II'	✓	✓	Spring Stampex 2014 19–22 February: 4 days	2.4mm		yes	FS95/97, 99/101 (but Type III)
Symbolic Flowers (British Flora 2nd series), 1st/1stL/E-20g WW-10g/E-60g/WW-20g/WW-60g:							
Royal Mail 'Series II'	✓	✓	Autumn Stampex 2014 17–20 September: 4 days	2.7mm		yes (Type IIIA)	FS103/108 (but Type IIIA)

431

ROYAL MAIL POST & GO STAMPS — Hytech & Royal Mail 'Series II' printings from exhibitions

Stamp Design, Values, Machine Type & Note(s)	Format produced CS	Format produced Set of 36	Event the stamps were available from, the date and duration (all the dates are inclusive)	Space between service indicator lines	Code string is numerals only (Type II)	Code string is letters & numerals (Type III)	Cat. No. of Stamp Issue Without Inscription, or Closest Match
Working Sail, 1st/1stL/E-20g WW-10g/E-60g/WW-20g/WW-60g:							
Royal Mail 'Series II'	✓	✓	Spring Stampex 2015 18–21 February: 4 days	2.7mm		yes (Type IIIA)	FS117/120, 122/123 (but Type IIIA)
Heraldic Beasts, 1st/1stL/E-20g WW-10g/E-100g/WW-20g/WW-100g:							
Royal Mail 'Series II'	✓	✓	Europhilex 2015 13–16 May: 4 days	2.7mm		yes (Type IIIA)	FS125/130 (but Type IIIA)
Lion design (from Heraldic Beasts issue) in single design rolls, 1st/1stL/E-20g WW-10g/E-100g/WW-20g/WW-100g:							
Royal Mail 'Series II'	✓	n/a	Autumn Stampex 2015 16–19 September: 4 days	2.7mm		yes (Type IIIA)	FS125/130 (but Type IIIA)
Sea Travel, 1st/1stL/E-20g WW-10g/E-100g/WW-20g/WW-100g:							
Royal Mail 'Series II'	✓	✓	Autumn Stampex 2015 16–19 September: 4 days	2.7mm		yes (Type IIIA)	FS131/136 (but Type IIIA)
Royal Mail Heritage: Transport, 1st/1stL/E-20g WW-10g/E-100g/WW-20g/WW-100g:							
Royal Mail 'Series II'	✓	✓	Spring Stampex 2016 17–20 February: 4 days	2.7mm		yes (Type IIIA)	FS151/156 (but Type IIIA)
Locomotive design (from Royal Mail Heritage: Transport issue) from single-design rolls, 1st/1stL/E-20g WW-10g/E-100g/WW-20g/WW-100g:							
Royal Mail 'Series II' Stamps digitally printed	✓	n/a	Spring Stampex 2016 17–20 February: 4 days Spring Stampex 2017 15–18 February: 4 days	2.7mm		yes (Type IIIA)	FS151/156 (but Type IIIA)
Ladybirds, 1st/1stL/E-20g WW-10g/E-100g/WW-20g/WW-100g:							
Royal Mail 'Series II'	✓	✓	Autumn Stampex 2016 14–17 September: 4 days	2.7mm		yes (Type IIIA)	FS159a/164a
Royal Mail Heritage: Mail by Rail, 1st/1stL/E-20g WW-10g/E-100g/WW-20g/WW-100g:							
Royal Mail 'Series II'	✓	✓	Spring Stampex 2017 15–18 February: 4 days	2.7mm		yes (Type IIIA)	FS173a/178a
Royal Mail Heritage: Mail by Air, 1st/1stL/E-20g WW-10g/E-100g/WW-20g/WW-100g:							
Royal Mail 'Series II'	✓	✓	Autumn Stampex 2017 13–16 September: 4 days	2.7mm		yes (Type IIIA)	FS185a/195a

Hytech Postal Vision was a trial machine introduced at Spring Stampex 2011. Machines referred to as Hytech version 1 were used at Autumn Stampex 2011 and Spring Stampex 2012. From Autumn Stampex 2012 modified machines were instead brought into use, sometimes referred to as Hytech 'next generation', Hytech version 2, and also Royal Mail Series I which is used in the above table. At Spring Stampex 2014 a new machine was brought into use and it is classified as a Royal Mail 'Series II' (although it is sometimes referred to as Royal Mail Series B).

† = Stamps generated from Hytech Postal Vision and Hytech version I machines have their weight lines inset, whereas stamps from Royal Mail 'Series I' and Royal Mail 'Series II' have their weight lines ranged left. From Autumn Stampex 2014, Royal Mail 'Series II' machines at exhibitions produced stamps with a smaller typeface. In place of gravure, digital printing is sometimes used for some single-design rolls. Stamps produced by this process are very shiny and have poor background definition, especially in the repeating 'ROYALMAIL' wording.

CS = Collectors' strips: the Machins from the Hytech Postal Vision trial machine are in strips of five, the Machin 2nds are in pairs, and all other collectors' strips are of six stamps. Sets of 36 (from and including Birds of Britain 4th series): all six denominations were available in all six designs making a complete set 36 stamps. Some of the catalogue numbers shown are provisional and may be subject to change

Regional Issues

PRINTERS (£.s.d. stamps of all regions): Photo Harrison & Sons. Portrait by Dorothy Wilding Ltd.

DATES OF ISSUE. Conflicting dates of issue have been announced for some of the regional issues, partly explained by the stamps being released on different dates by the Philatelic Bureau in Edinburgh or the Philatelic Counter in London and in the regions. We have adopted the practice of giving the earliest known dates, since once released the stamps could have been used anywhere in the United Kingdom.

I. ENGLAND

'Emblem' Regional colours. Where the Queen's head has been printed in a black screen, this appears as grey. Where stamps exist with either silver or grey heads, this is stated in the catalogue entries.

Head Types

Type I: Ribbon at back of the head appears as two separate and distinct strands
Type II: Ribbon solid and firmly joined to the head

EN1 Three Lions of England
EN2 Crowned Lion, Supporting the Shield of St George 
EN3 English Oak Tree 
EN4 English Tudor Rose 

(Des Sedley Place, from sculptures by David Dathan. Gravure Questa (No. EN1b) or De La Rue (others))

2001 (23 Apr)–**02.** One centre phosphor band (2nd) or two phosphor bands (others). Perf 15×14 (with one elliptical hole in each vertical side). All heads Type I.

EN1	**EN1**	(2nd) Three lions of England	1·25	1·00
		a. Imperf (pair)		
		l. Booklet pane. Nos. EN1/EN2, each×4, and No. S95, with margins all round (24.9.02)	8·50	
		la. Imperf pane	—	—
EN2	**EN2**	(1st) Lion and shield	1·50	1·00
		a. Imperf pair	£350	
EN3	**EN3**	(E) English oak tree	2·00	2·00
EN4	**EN4**	65p English Tudor rose	2·10	2·10
EN5		68p. English Tudor rose (4.7.02)	2·10	2·10
Presentation Pack (PO Pack No. 54) (Nos. EN1/EN4)			7·00	
PHQ Cards (set of 4) (D20) (Nos. EN1/EN4)			1·25	7·00

Nos. EN1/EN3 were initially sold at 19p., 27p. and 36p., the latter representing the basic European airmail rate.

First Day Covers

23.4.01	2nd, 1st, E, 65p. (Nos. EN1/EN4) Philatelic Bureau, (Type G, see Introduction)		2·50
	Windsor		2·00
4.7.02	68p. (No. EN5) Tallents House (Type K, see Introduction)		2·50
	London		1·50

Combined Presentation Pack for England, Northern Ireland, Scotland and Wales

4.7.02	PO Pack No. 59. 68p. (Nos. EN5, NI93, S99, W88)	8·50

2003 (14 Oct)–**17.** As Nos. EN1/EN3 and EN5, and new values, but with white borders. One centre phosphor band (2nd) or two phosphor bands (others). Type I heads unless otherwise stated. Perf 15×14 (with one elliptical hole in each vertical side).

(a) Gravure Walsall (No. EN6l) Walsall or De La Rue (No. EN10) or De La Rue (others).

EN6	**EN1**	(2nd) Three lions of England. Type II	1·25	1·00
		a. Imperf (pair)	£175	
		l. Booklet pane. Nos. EN6 and EN9, each×2, with central label and margins all round (24.2.05)	5·50	
		b. Type I (2006)	5·50	5·50
EN7	**EN2**	(1st) Lion and shield. Type II	1·50	1·25
		a. Imperf (pair)	£250	
		b. Type I (2006)	5·50	5·50
EN8	**EN3**	(E) English oak tree. Type II	2·00	2·00
EN9		40p. English oak tree Type II (11.5.04)	1·25	1·25
EN10		42p. English oak tree Type II (5.4.05)	1·75	1·75
EN11		44p. English oak tree Type II (28.3.06)	1·25	1·25
		a. Imperf (pair)	£1200	
		b. Type I (2006)	40·00	40·00
EN12		48p. English oak tree (27.3.07)	1·00	1·00
EN13		50p. English oak tree (1.4.08)	1·25	1·25
EN14		56p. English oak tree (31.3.09)	1·25	1·25
EN15		60p. English oak tree (30.3.10)	1·50	1·50
EN16	**EN4**	68p. English Tudor rose. Type II	1·75	1·75
EN17		72p. English Tudor rose Type II (28.3.06)	1·75	1·75
		a. Type I (2006)	25·00	25·00
EN18		78p. English Tudor rose (27.3.07)	2·00	2·00
EN19		81p. English Tudor rose (1.4.08)	2·00	2·00
EN20		90p. English Tudor rose (31.3.09)	2·25	2·25
EN21		97p. English Tudor rose (30.3.10)	2·50	2·50

(b) Litho Enschedé or ISP Cartor (No. EN30) or ISP Cartor (others). Queen's head in grey (Nos. EN29, EN30b and EN36) or silver (others).

EN29	**EN1**	(2nd) Three lions of England (3.1.13)	1·25	1·00
EN30	**EN2**	(1st) Lion and shield (Queen's head silver) (20.9.07)	1·50	1·50
		l. Booklet pane. Nos. EN30, NI95 S131 and W122 with five labels and margins all round	14·00	
EN30b		(1st) Lion and shield (Queen's head grey) (3.1.13)	2·00	1·75
EN31	**EN3**	68p. English oak tree (29.3.11)	1·75	1·75
EN32		87p. English oak tree (25.4.12)	2·25	2·25
EN33		88p. English oak tree (27.3.13)	2·25	2·25
EN34		97p. English oak tree (26.3.14)	2·40	2·40
EN35		£1 English oak tree (24.3.15)	2·40	2·40
EN36		£1·05 English oak tree (22.3.16)	2·75	2·75
EN41	**EN4**	£1·10 English Tudor rose (29.3.11)	2·50	2·50
EN43		£1·28 English Tudor rose (25.4.12)	2·60	2·60
EN44		£1·33 English Tudor rose (24.3.15)	2·75	2·75
Presentation Pack (PO Pack No. 63) (Nos. EN6/EN8, EN16)			6·00	
PHQ Cards (set of 4) (D24) (Nos. EN6/EN8, EN16)			1·25	6·50

The 72p. stamp from the 2006 Lest We Forget miniature sheet, No. **MS**2685, has the Type I head.

The price for No. EN17a is for the Type I stamp from counter sheets. Collectors should obtain this stamp from a reliable source.

No. EN6l comes from booklet No. DX34.

Stamps as Nos. EN18/EN19 but printed in lithography were only issued within No. **MS**2796 (No. EN18) or No. **MS**2886 (No. EN19).

No. EN30 was first issued for £7·66 stamp booklets, No. DX40, printed by Enschedé. No. EN30b was issued in sheets printed by ISP Cartor in January 2013.

REGIONAL ISSUES/England

A design as No. EN30 but self-adhesive was issued on 23 April 2007 in sheets of 20, each stamp accompanied by a *se-tenant* label showing an English scene (No. LS38). These sheets were printed in lithography by Cartor, perforated 15×14 without the elliptical holes, and sold at £7·35 each. They were also available with personalised photographs on the labels at £14·95 from the Royal Mail in Edinburgh.

Stamps as Nos. EN30, NI95, S131 and W122 but self-adhesive were issued on 29 September 2008 in sheets of 20 containing five of each design with *se-tenant* labels (No. LS49). These sheets were printed in lithography by Cartor and perforated 15×14 with one elliptical hole on each vertical side.

First Day Covers

14.10.03	2nd, 1st, E, 68p. (Nos. EN6/EN8, EN16) Tallents House (Type K, see Introduction).........	5·50
	London........	5·50
11.5.04	40p. (No. EN9) Tallents House (Type K).........	2·00
	London........	2·00
5.4.05	42p. (No. EN10) Tallents House (Type K).........	2·00
	London........	2·00
28.3.06	44p., 72p., (Nos. EN11, EN17) Tallents House (Type K) London........	3·50 3·50
27.3.07	48p., 78p., (Nos. EN12, EN18) Tallents House (Type K) London........	3·00 3·00
1.4.08	50p., 81p., (Nos. EN13, EN19) Tallents House (Type K) London........	3·00 3·00
31.3.09	56p., 90p. (Nos. EN14, EN20) Tallents House (Type K) London........	3·50 3·50
30.3.10	60p., 97p. (Nos. EN15, EN21) Tallents House (Type K). London........	4·00 4·00
29.3.11	68p., £1·10 (Nos. EN31, EN41) Tallents House (Type K)......... London........	4·50 4·50
25.4.12	87p., £1·28 (Nos. EN32, EN43) Tallents House (Type K)......... London........	4·75 4·75
27.3.13	88p. (No. EN33) Tallents House (Type K)......... London........	2·25 2·25
26.3.14	97p. (No. EN34) Tallents House (Type K)......... London........	2·25 2·25
24.3.15	£1, £1·33 (Nos. EN35, EN44) Tallents House (Type K).. London........	5·50 5·50
22.3.16	£1·05 (No. EN36) Tallents House (Type K)......... London........	2·50 2·50

Combination Presentation Packs for England, Northern Ireland, Scotland and Wales

11.5.04	PO Pack No. 68. 40p. (Nos. EN9, NI97, S112, W101)......	6·50
5.4.05	PO Pack No. 70. 42p. (Nos. EN10, NI98, S113, W102)...	6·25
28.3.06	PO Pack No. 73. 44p. and 72p. (Nos. EN11, EN17, NI99, NI102, S114, S120, W103, W109).........	10·00
27.3.07	PO Pack No. 76. 48p. and 78p. (Nos. EN12, EN18, NI124, NI128, S115, S121, W104, and W110).........	10·00
1.4.08	PO Pack. No. 79. 50p. and 81p. (Nos. EN13, EN19, NI125, NI129, S116, S122, W105, W111).........	10·00
29.9.08	PO Pack No. 81. 2nd, 1st, 50p. and 81p. (Nos. EN6/EN7, EN13, EN19, NI122/NI123, NI125, NI129, S109/S110, S116, S122, W98/W99, W105, W111).........	40·00
31.3.09	PO Pack No. 85. 56p. and 90p. (Nos. EN14, EN20, NI126, NI130, S117, S123, W106, W112).........	13·00
30.3.10	PO Pack No. 87. 60p. and 97p. (Nos. EN15, EN21, NI127, NI131, S118, S124, W107, W113).........	14·00
29.3.11	PO Pack No. 91. 68p. and £1·10 (Nos. EN31, EN41, NI101, NI111, S132, S138 W123, W129).........	15·00
25.4.12	PO Pack No. 95. 87p. and £1·28 (Nos. EN32, EN43, NI103, NI113, S133, S143, W124, W134).........	18·00
27.3.13	PO Pack No. 98. 88p. (Nos. EN33, NI104, S134, W125).	8·50
26.3.14	PO Pack No. 100. 97p. (Nos. EN34, NI105, S135, W126).........	8·50
24.3.15	PO Pack No. 102 £1 and £1·33 (Nos. EN35, EN44, NI106, NI114, S136, S144, W127, W135).........	18·00
22.3.16	PO Pack No. 104. £1·05 (Nos. EN36, NI 107, S137 and W128).........	10·00

EN5

(Des Peter Crowther, Clare Melinsky and Silk Pearce. Gravure De La Rue)

2007 (23 Apr). Celebrating England. Sheet 123×70 mm. Two phosphor bands. Perf 15×14 (with one elliptical hole in each vertical side) (1st) or 15×14½ (78p.).

MSEN50	**EN5**	(1st) No. EN7b; (1st) St George's flag; 78p. St George; 78p. Houses of Parliament, London.........	4·00	4·00
		First Day Cover (Tallents House).........		4·50
		First Day Cover (St Georges, Telford).........		4·50
		Presentation Pack (PO Pack No. M15).........	5·00	
		PHQ Cards (set of 5) (CGB2).........	2·00	8·00

No. **MS**EN50 was on sale at post offices throughout the UK.

Stamps as the 1st class St George's flag stamp within No. **MS**EN50 but self-adhesive were issued on 23 April 2009 in sheets of 20 with *se-tenant* labels showing English Castles, No. LS59.

These sheets were printed in lithography by Cartor and sold for £8·35 each.

The five PHQ cards show the four individual stamps and the complete miniature sheet.

EN6 St George's Flag

(Des Peter Crowther and Silk Pierce. Litho ISP Cartor (No. EN51) or Enschedé (No. EN51a))

2013 (9 May)–**14**. England Flag. Two phosphor bands. Perf 14½×14 (with one elliptical hole in each vertical side).

EN51	**EN6**	(1st) St George's Flag (Queen's head silver).........	4·50	4·50
		a. St George's Flag (Queen's head grey) (20.2.14).........	3·50	3·50

No. EN51 was issued in £11·11 Football Heroes booklets (No. DY7, booklet pane No. U3073l) and £16.49 Centenary of the First World War (3rd issue) booklets (No. DY18, booklet pane No. 3717a).

No. EN51a was issued in £13·97 Classic Locomotives booklets (No. DY9, booklet pane No. U3071m).

EN7 Three Lions of England

EN8 Crowned Lion, Supporting the Shield of St George

EN9 English Oak Tree

EN10 English Tudor Rose

(Des Sedley Place, from sculptures by David Dathan. Litho ISP Cartor)

2017 (21 Mar)–**20**. As previous set but with value indicated in revised typeface. One centre phosphor band (No. EN52) or two phosphor bands. Perf 15×14 (with one elliptical hole in each vertical side).

EN52	**EN7**	(2nd) Three Lions of England (20.3.18)...	1·00	75
EN53	**EN8**	(1st) Lion and shield (Indian red) (20.3.18).........	1·25	75
		a. Venetian red (11.2.20).........	1·50	1·50
EN54	**EN9**	£1·17 English Oak tree (21.3.17).........	2·75	2·75
EN55		£1·25 English Oak tree (20.3.18).........	2·75	2·75
EN56		£1·35 English Oak tree (19.3.19).........	3·00	3·00
EN60	**EN10**	£1·40 English Tudor Rose (21.3.17).........	3·00	3·00
EN60a	**EN9**	£1·42 English Oak tree (17.3.20).........	2·50	2·50
EN61	**EN9**	£1·42 English Oak tree (17.3.20).........	2·50	2·50
EN62	**EN10**	£1·45 English Tudor Rose (20.3.18).........	3·25	3·25
EN63		£1·55 English Tudor Rose (19.3.19).........	3·25	3·25
EN64		£1·63 English Tudor Rose (17.3.20).........	2·75	2·75
EN65	**EN9**	£1·70 English Oak tree (23.12.20).........	2·40	2·40

No. EN53a was issued in £16·10 Visions of the Universe booklet, No. DY32, booklet pane No. U3072r.

Numbers have been left for possible additions to the above definitive series.

First Day Covers

21.3.17	£1·17, £1·40. (Nos. EN54, EN60) Tallents House (Type K)	6·00
	London (as Windsor)	6·00
20.3.18	2nd, 1st, £1·25, £1·45. (Nos. EN52/EN53, EN55, EN61) Tallents House (Type K)	9·00
	London (as Windsor)	9·00
19.3.19	£1·35, £1·55 (Nos. EN56, EN62) Tallents House (Type K)	7·00
	London (as Windsor)	7·00
17.3.20	£1·42, £1·63 (Nos. EN60a, EN63) Tallents House (Type K)	7·00
	London	7·00
23.12.20	£1·70 (No. EN64) Tallents House (Type K)	3·75
	London	3·75

Combination Presentation Packs for England, Northern Ireland, Scotland and Wales

21.3.17	PO Pack No. 107. £1·17 and £1·40 (Nos. EN54, EN60, NI159, NI165, S161, S167, W151, W157)	22·00
20.3.18	PO Pack No. 109. 2nd, 1st, £1·25 and £1·45 (Nos. EN52/EN53, EN55, EN61, NI157/NI158, NI160, NI166, S159/S160, S162, S168, W149/W150, W152, W158)	25·00
19.3.19	PO Pack No. 111. £1·35, £1·55 (Nos. EN56, EN62, NI161, NI167, S163, S169, W153, W159a)	26·00
17.3.20	PO Pack No. 113. £1·42, £1·63 (Nos. EN60a, EN63, NI164a, NI168, S166a, S170, W156a, W160)	28·00
23.12.20	PO Pack No. 115. £1·70 (Nos. EN64, NI169, S171, W16 1)	11·00

II. NORTHERN IRELAND

N1

N2

N3

(Des W. Hollywood (3d., 4d., 5d.), L. Pilton (6d., 9d.), T. Collins (1s.3d., 1s.6d.))

1958–67. W **179**. Perf 15×14.

NI1	**N1**	3d. deep lilac (18.8.58)	15	15
		p. One centre phosphor band (9.6.67)	25	25
NI2		4d. ultramarine (7.2.66)	15	15
		a. Flower flaw	25·00	
		b. Two phosphor bands (10.67)	25·00	
		p. Two phosphor bands (10.67)	15	15
NI3	**N2**	6d. deep claret (29.9.58)	50	50
NI4		9d. bronze-green (2 phosphor bands) (1.3.67)	40	40
NI5	**N3**	1s.3d. green (29.9.58)	50	50
NI6		1s.6d. grey-blue (2 phosphor bands) (1.3.67)	40	40
		y. Phosphor omitted	£225	

First Day Covers

18.8.58	3d. (No. NI1)	30·00
29.9.58	6d., 1s.3d. (Nos. NI3, NI5)	35·00
7.2.66	4d. (No. NI2)	7·00
1.3.67	9d., 1s.6d. (Nos. NI4, NI6)	4·00

For Nos. NI1, NI3 and NI5 in Presentation Pack, see below Wales No. W6.

1968–69. No watermark. Chalk-surfaced paper. One centre phosphor band (Nos. NI8/NI9) or two phosphor bands (others). Gum arabic (No. NI7) or PVA gum (others). Perf 15×14.

NI7	**N1**	4d. deep bright blue (27.6.68)	25	25
		v. PVA gum* (23.10.68)	30·00	
NI8		4d. olive-sepia (4.9.68)	25	25
		y. Phosphor omitted		
NI9		4d. bright vermilion (26.2.69)	30	30
		y. Phosphor omitted	4·50	
NI10		5d. royal blue (4.9.68)	40	40
		y. Phosphor omitted	25·00	
NI11	**N3**	1s.6d. grey-blue (20.5.69)	1·50	1·50
		y. Phosphor omitted	£500	

First Day Cover (Nos. NI8, NI10) ... 3·00

Presentation Pack (PO Pack No. 25) (Nos. NI1p, NI4/NI6, NI8/NI10) ... 3·50

* No. NI7v was never issued in Northern Ireland. After No. NI7 (gum arabic) had been withdrawn from Northern Ireland but while still on sale at the philatelic counters elsewhere, about 50 sheets with PVA gum were sold over the London Philatelic counter on 23 October, 1968, and some were also on sale at the British Philatelic Exhibition Post Office.

There was no post office first day cover for No. NI9.

N4

I II

Redrawn design of T N4 (litho printings)

Two Types of Crown

Type I Crown with all pearls individually drawn.

Type II Crown with clear outlines, large pearls and strong white line below them. First 3 pearls at left are joined, except on Nos. NI39 and NI49.

The following stamps printed in lithography show a screened background behind and to the left of the emblem: 11½p., 12½p., 14p. (No. NI38), 15½p., 16p., 18p. (No. NI45), 19½p., 22p. (No. NI53) and 28p. (No. NI62). The 13p. and 17p. (No. NI43) also showed screened backgrounds in Type I, but changed to solid backgrounds for Type II. The 31p. had a solid background in Type I, but changed to a screened background for Type II. All other values printed in lithography have solid backgrounds.

(Des Jeffery Matthews after plaster cast by Arnold Machin)

1971 (7 July)–**93**. Decimal Currency. Chalk-surfaced paper. T **N4**.

(a) Photo Harrison. With phosphor bands. Perf 15×14.

NI12	2½p. bright magenta (1 centre band)	45	45
NI13	3p. ultramarine (2 bands)	30	30
	y. Phosphor omitted	50·00	
NI14	3p. ultramarine (1 centre band) (23.1.74)	20	20
NI15	3½p. olive-grey (2 bands) (23.1.74)	20	20
NI16	3½p. olive-grey (1 centre band) (6.11.74)	40	40
NI17	4½p. grey-blue (2 bands) (6.11.74)	30	30
NI18	5p. reddish violet (2 bands)	90	90
NI19	5½p. violet (2 bands) (23.1.74)	25	25
	y. Phosphor omitted	£250	
NI20	5½p. violet (1 centre band) (21.5.75)	25	25
NI21	6½p. greenish blue (1 centre band) (14.1.76)	20	20
NI22	7p. purple-brown (1 centre band) (18.1.78)	30	30
NI23	7½p. chestnut (2 bands)	1·25	1·25
	y. Phosphor omitted	£100	
NI24	8p. rosine (2 bands) (23.1.74)	40	40
	y. Phosphor omitted	75·00	
NI25	8½p. yellow-green (2 bands) (14.1.76)	40	40
NI26	9p. deep violet (2 bands) (18.1.78)	40	40
	y. Phosphor omitted	25·00	
NI27	10p. orange-brown (2 bands) (20.10.76)	40	40
NI28	10p. orange-brown (1 centre band) (23.7.80)	40	40
NI29	10½p. steel-blue (2 bands) (18.1.78)	50	50
NI30	11p. scarlet (2 bands) (20.10.76)	50	50
	y. Phosphor omitted	5·00	

(b) Photo Harrison. On phosphorised paper. Perf 15×14.

NI31	12p. yellowish green (23.7.80)	50	50
NI32	13½p. purple-brown (23.7.80)	60	60
NI33	15p. ultramarine (23.7.80)	60	60

(c) Litho Questa (Type II, unless otherwise stated). Perf 14 (11½p., 12½p., 14p. (No. NI38), 15½p., 16p., 18p. (No. NI45), 19½p., 20½p., 22p. (No. NI53), 26p. (No. NI60), 28p. (No. NI62)) or 15×14 (others).

NI34	11½p. drab (Type I) (1 side band) (8.4.81)	85	85
NI35	12p. bright emerald (1 side band) (7.1.86)	90	90
NI36	12½p. light emerald (Type I) (1 side band) (24.2.82)	50	50
	a. Perf 15×14 (28.2.84)	3·50	3·50
NI37	13p. light emerald (Type I) (1 side band) (24.2.82)	60	60
	a. Type II (28.11.86)	1·10	1·10
	y. Phosphor omitted (Type I)	£375	
NI38	14p. grey-blue (Type I) (phosphorised paper) (8.4.81)	60	60
NI39	14p. deep blue (1 centre band) (8.11.88)	50	50
NI40	15p. bright blue (1 centre band) (28.11.89)	60	60
NI41	15½p. pale violet (Type I) (phosphorised paper) (24.2.82)	80	80
NI42	16p. drab (Type I) (phosphorised paper) (27.4.83)	1·00	1·00
	a. Perf 15×14 (28.2.84)	5·00	5·00
NI43	17p. grey-blue (Type I) (phosphorised paper) (23.10.84)	80	80
	a. Type II (9.9.86)	£140	£140

REGIONAL ISSUES/Northern Ireland

NI44	17p. deep blue (1 centre band) (4.12.90)	60	60
NI45	18p. deep violet (Type I) (phosphorised paper) (8.4.81)	80	80
NI46	18p. deep olive-grey (phosphorised paper) (6.1.87)	80	80
NI47	18p. bright green (1 centre band) (3.12.91)	80	80
	a. Perf 14 (31.12.92*)	6·00	6·00
NI48	18p. bright green (1 side band) (10.8.93)	1·50	1·50
	l. Booklet pane. Nos. NI48, NI59, S61, S71, W49b and W60 with margins all round	8·00	
NI49	19p. bright orange-red (phosphorised paper) (8.11.88)	80	80
NI50	19½p. olive-grey (Type I) (phosphorised paper) (24.2.82)	1·50	1·50
NI51	20p. brownish black (phosphorised paper) (28.11.89)	80	80
NI52	20½p. ultramarine (Type I) (phosphorised paper) (27.4.83)	2·75	2·75
NI53	22p. blue (Type I) (phosphorised paper) (8.4.81)	80	80
NI54	22p. yellow-green (Type I) (phosphorised paper) (23.10.84)	80	80
NI55	22p. bright orange-red (phosphorised paper) (4.12.90)	80	80
NI56	23p. bright green (phosphorised paper) (8.11.88)	80	80
NI57	24p. Indian red (phosphorised paper) (28.11.89)	90	90
NI58	24p. chestnut (phosphorised paper) (3.12.91)	80	80
NI59	24p. chestnut (2 bands) (10.8.93)	1·50	1·50
NI60	26p. rosine (Type I) (phosphorised paper) (24.2.82)	90	90
	a. Perf 15×14 (Type II) (27.1.87)	2·00	2·00
NI61	26p. drab (phosphorised paper) (4.12.90)	1·10	1·10
NI62	28p. deep violet-blue (Type I) (phosphorised paper) (27.4.83)	1·00	1·00
	a. Perf 15×14 (Type II) (27.1.87)	1·40	1·40
NI63	28p. deep bluish grey (phosphorised paper) (3.12.91)	90	90
NI64	31p. bright purple (Type I) (phosphorised paper) (23.10.84)	1·40	1·40
	a. Type II (14.4.87)	1·75	1·75
NI65	32p. greenish blue (phosphorised paper) (8.11.88)	1·40	1·40
NI66	34p. deep bluish grey (phosphorised paper) (28.11.89)	1·40	1·40
NI67	37p. rosine (phosphorised paper) (4.12.90)	1·50	1·50
NI68	39p. bright mauve (phosphorised paper) (3.12.91)	1·50	1·50

* Earliest known date of issue.

No. NI47a was caused by the use of a reserve perforating machine for some printings in the second half of 1992.

Nos. NI48 and NI59 only come from booklets.

From 1972 printings were made on fluorescent white paper and from 1973 most printings had dextrin added to the PVA gum (see notes after 1971 Decimal Machin issue).

First Day Covers

7.7.71	2½p., 3p., 5p., 7½p. (Nos. NI12/NI13, NI18, NI23)	2·50
23.1.74	3p., 3½p., 5½p., 8p. (Nos. NI14/NI15, NI19, NI24)	2·00
6.11.74	4½p. (No. NI17)	80
14.1.76	6½p., 8½p. (Nos. NI21, NI25)	80
20.10.76	10p., 11p. (Nos. NI27, NI30)	90
18.1.78	7p., 9p., 10½p. (Nos. NI22, NI26, NI29)	90
23.7.80	12p., 13½p., 15p. (Nos. NI31/NI33)	1·50
8.4.81	11½p., 14p., 18p., 22p. (Nos. NI34, NI45, NI53)	1·25
24.2.82	12½p., 15½p., 19½p., 26p. (Nos. NI41, NI50, NI60)	2·00
27.4.83	16p., 20½p., 28p. (Nos. NI42, NI52, NI62)	2·00
23.10.84	13p., 17p., 22p., 31p. (Nos. NI37, NI43, NI54, NI64)	2·25
7.1.86	12p. (No. NI35)	90
6.1.87	18p. (No. NI46)	90
8.11.88	14p., 19p., 23p., 32p. (Nos. NI39, NI49, NI56, NI65)	2·50
28.11.89	15p., 20p., 24p., 34p. (Nos. NI40, NI51, NI57, NI66)	3·00
4.12.90	17p., 22p., 26p., 37p. (Nos. NI44, NI55, NI61, NI67)	3·00
3.12.91	18p., 24p., 28p., 39p. (Nos. NI47, NI58, NI63, NI68)	3·00

Presentation Packs

7.7.71	PO Pack No. 29. 2½p., 3p. (2 bands), 5p., 7½p. (Nos. NI12/NI13, NI18, NI23)	2·00
29.5.74	PO Pack No. 61. 3p. (1 centre band), 3½p. (2 bands) or (1 centre band), 5½p. (2 bands) or (1 centre band), 8p. (Nos. NI14, NI15 or NI16, NI19 or NI20, NI24). The 4½p. (No. NI17) was added later	3·00
20.10.76	PO Pack No. 84. 6½p., 8½p., 10p. (2 bands), 11p. (Nos. NI21, NI25, NI27, NI30)	1·50
28.10.81	PO Pack No. 129d. 7p., 9p., 10½p., 12p. (gravure), 13½p., 15p. (gravure), 11½p., 14p. grey-blue, 18p. deep violet, 22p. blue (Nos. NI22, NI26, NI29, NI31/NI34, NI38, NI45, NI53)	7·00
3.8.83	PO Pack No. 4. 10p. (1 centre band), 12½p., 16p., 20½p., 26p. rosine, 28p. deep violet-blue (Nos. NI28, NI36, NI42, NI52, NI60, NI62)	15·00
23.10.84	PO Pack No. 8. 10p. (1 centre band), 13p., 16p., 17p. grey-blue, 22p. yellow-green, 26p. rosine, 28p. deep violet-blue, 31p. (Nos. NI28, NI37, N142a, NI43, NI54, NI60, NI62, NI64)	12·50
3.3.87	PO Pack No. 12. 12p. (litho), 13p., 17p. grey-blue, 18p. deep olive-grey, 22p. yellow-green, 26p. rosine, 28p. deep violet-blue, 31p. (Nos. NI35, NI37, NI43, NI46, NI54, NI60a, NI62a, NI64)	16·00

Combined Presentation Packs for Northern Ireland, Scotland and Wales

8.11.88	PO Pack No. 17. 14p. deep blue, 19p., 23p., 32p. (Nos. NI39, NI49, NI56, NI65), 14p. (1 centre band), 19p. (phosphorised paper), 23p. (phosphorised paper), 32p. (Nos. S54, S62, S67, S77), 14p. deep blue, 19p., 23p., 32p. (Nos. W40, W50, W57, W66)	12·50
28.11.89	PO Pack No. 20. 15p. (litho), 20p., 24p. Indian red, 34p. (Nos. NI40, NI51, NI57, NI66), 15p. (litho), 20p., 24p. Indian red, 34p. (Nos. S56, S64, S69, S78), 15p. (litho), 20p., 24p. Indian red, 34p. (Nos. W41, W52, W58, W67)	12·00
4.12.90	PO Pack No. 23. 17p. deep blue, 22p. bright orange-red, 26p. drab, 37p., (Nos. NI44, NI55, NI61, NI67), 17p. deep blue, 22p. bright orange-red, 26p. drab, 37p., (Nos. S58, S66, S73, S79), 17p. deep blue, 22p. bright orange-red, 26p. drab, 37p. (Nos. W45, W56, W62, W68)	12·00
3.12.91	PO Pack No. 26. 18p. bright green, 24p. chestnut, 28p. deep bluish grey, 39p. (Nos. NI47, NI58, NI63, NI68), 18p. bright green, 24p. chestnut, 28p. deep bluish grey, 39p. (Nos. S60, S70, S75, S80), 18p. bright green, 24p. chestnut, 28p. deep bluish grey, 39p. (Nos. W48, W59, W64, W69)	12·00

(Des Jeffery Matthews after plaster cast by Arnold Machin)

1993 (7 Dec)–**2000**. Chalk-surfaced paper.

(a) Litho Questa. Perf 15×14 (with one elliptical hole in each vert side).

NI69	N4	19p. bistre (1 centre band)	80	80
NI70		19p. bistre (1 band at left) (26.7.94)	1·25	1·25
		y. Phosphor omitted	£500	
		l. Booklet pane. Nos. NI70×2, NI72×4, NI74 and NI76 and centre label with margins all round	4·50	
		m. Booklet pane. Nos. NI70, NI72, NI74 and NI76 with margins all round	3·50	
		my. Booklet pane. Phosphor omitted	£3000	
		c. Band at right (25.4.95)	1·75	1·75
		n. Booklet pane. Nos. NI70c, NI72, S82, S84, W71 and W73 with margins all round (25.4.95)	4·75	
		na. Part perf pane*	£3500	
NI71		20p. bright green (1 centre band) (23.7.96)	1·25	1·25
NI72		25p. red (2 bands)	75	75
		y. Phosphor omitted	£275	
NI73		26p. red-brown (2 bands) (23.7.96)	1·50	1·50
NI74		30p. deep olive-grey (2 bands)	1·10	1·10
		y. Phosphor omitted	£750	
NI75		37p. bright mauve (2 bands) (23.7.96)	2·25	2·25
NI76		41p. grey-brown (2 bands)	1·50	1·50
		y. Phosphor omitted	£750	
NI77		63p. light emerald (2 bands) (23.7.96)	3·50	3·50

(b) Gravure Walsall (19p., 20p., 26p. (No. NI81b), 38p., 40p., 63p., 64p., 65p.), Harrison or Walsall (26p. (No. NI81), 37p.). Perf 14 (No. NI80) or 15×14 (others) (both with one elliptical hole in each vertical side).

NI78	N4	19p. bistre (1 centre band) (8.6.99)	2·50	2·50
NI79		20p. bright green (1 centre band) (1.7.97)	2·50	2·50
NI80		20p. bright green (1 side band at right) (13.10.98)	3·00	3·00
		l. Booklet pane. Nos. NI80, S90a, W79a and Y1717a×3 with margins all round	7·00	
NI81		26p. chestnut (2 bands) (1.7.97)	1·60	1·60
		l. Booklet pane. Nos. NI81/NI82, S91/S92 and W80/W81 with margins all round (23.9.97)	6·00	
		b. Perf 14 (13.10.98)	3·00	3·00
NI82		37p. bright mauve (2 bands) (1.7.97)	1·90	1·90
NI83		38p. ultramarine (2 bands) (8.6.99)	5·50	5·50
NI84		40p. deep azure (2 bands) (25.4.2000)	3·50	3·50
NI85		63p. light emerald (2 bands) (1.7.97)	3·50	3·50
NI86		64p. turquoise-green (2 bands) (8.6.99)	6·50	6·50
NI87		65p. greenish blue (2 bands) (25.4.2000)	3·00	3·00

* No. NI70na, which comes from he 1995 National Trust £6 booklet, shows the top two values in the pane of six (Nos. S82, S84) completely imperforate and the two Wales values below partly imperforate.

Nos. NI70, NI80 and NI81b only come from booklets.

The listed booklet panes come from the following Sponsored Booklets:
Nos. NI70l/NI70m Booklet No. DX16
No. NI70n Booklet No. DX17
No. NI80l Booklet No. DX21
No. NI81l Booklet No. DX19

Northern Ireland/REGIONAL ISSUES

First Day Covers

7.12.93	19p., 25p., 30p., 41p. (Nos. NI69, NI72, NI74, NI76)	4·00
26.7.94	Northern Ireland *se-tenant* pane 19p., 25p., 30p., 41p. (No. NI70l)	5·00
23.7.96	20p., 26p., 37p., 63p. (Nos. NI71, NI73, NI75, NI77)	5·00
8.6.99	38p., 64p. (Nos.NI83, NI86)	10·00
25.4.00	1st, 40p., 65p. (Nos. NI84, NI87, NI88b)	12·50

Presentation Packs

8.6.99	PO Pack No. 47. 19p., 26p., 38p., 64p. (Nos. NI78, NI81, NI83, NI86)	15·00
25.4.00	PO Pack No. 52. 1st, 40p., 65p. (Nos. NI88b, NI84, NI87)	16·00

Combined Presentation Packs for Northern Ireland, Scotland and Wales

7.12.93	PO Pack No. 31. 19p., 25p., 30p., 41p., each×3 (Nos. NI69, NI72, NI74, NI76, S81, S84, S86, S88, W70, W73, W75, W77)	20·00
23.7.96	PO Pack No. 36. 20p., 26p., 37p., 63p., each×3 (Nos. NI71, NI73, NI75, NI77, S83, S85, S87, S89, W72, W74, W76, W78)	16·00
20.10.98	PO Pack No. 42. 20p. (1 centre band), 26p., 37p., 63p., each×3 (Nos. NI79, NI81/NI82, NI85, S90/S93, W79/W82)	18·00

N5

(Des Jeffery Matthews. Gravure Walsall)

2000 (15 Feb–25 Apr). T **N4** redrawn with '1st' face value as T **N5**. Two phosphor bands. Perf 14 (with one elliptical hole in each vertical side).

NI88	**N5**	(1st) bright orange-red	1·60	1·60
		l. Booklet pane. Nos. NI88, S108 and W97, each×3 with margins all round	12·00	
		b. Perf 15×14 (25.4.2000)	7·00	7·00

First Day Cover (Philatelic Bureau) (*se-tenant* pane No. NI88l) .... 7·00

First Day Cover (London SW5) (*se-tenant* pane No. NI88l) .... 7·00

No. NI88 was issued in £7·50 stamp booklet (No. DX24). No NI88b was issued in sheets.

N6 Basalt Columns, Giant's Causeway
N7 Aerial View of Patchwork Fields 
N8 Linen Pattern 
N9 Vase Pattern from Belleek 

(Des Rodney Miller Associates (Basalt columns), Richard Cooke (Aerial view of fields), David Pauley (Linen pattern), Tiff Hunter (Vase pattern). Litho Walsall or Enschedé (1st, 2nd), De La Rue or Walsall (E), Walsall (65p.), De La Rue (68p.))

2001 (6 Mar)–**03**. One centre phosphor band (2nd) or two phosphor bands (others). Perf 15×14 (with one elliptical hole in each vertical side).

NI89	**N6**	(2nd) Basalt columns, Giant's Causeway	1·25	1·25
		l. Booklet pane. No. NI89×5 and No. NI90×4 with margins all round (25.2.2003)	7·00	
		y. Phosphor omitted	£625	
NI90	**N7**	(1st) Aerial view of patchwork fields	1·50	1·50
		y. Phosphor omitted	35·00	
NI91	**N8**	(E) Linen pattern	2·25	2·25
NI92	**N9**	65p. Vase pattern from Belleek	2·25	2·25
NI93		68p. Vase pattern from Belleek (4.7.2002)	2·75	2·75

Presentation Pack (PO Pack No. 53) (Nos. NI89/NI92) .... 6·00

PHQ Cards (set of 4) (D19) (Nos. NI89/NI92) .... 1·25 7·50

Nos. NI89, NI90 and NI91 were initially sold at 19p., 27p. and 36p., the latter representing the basic European airmail rate.

A new printing of No. NI91, produced by De La Rue instead of Walsall, was issued on 15 October 2002. Stamps from this printing do not differ from those produced by Walsall.

Booklet pane No. NI89l was printed by Enschedé. For combined presentation pack for all four Regions, see under England.

First Day Covers

6.3.01	2nd, 1st, E, 65p. (Nos. NI89/NI92) Tallents House	2·75
	Belfast	3·00
4.7.02	68p. (NI93) Tallents House (Type K, see Introduction)	2·50
	Belfast	2·75

2003 (14 Oct)–**17**. As Nos. NI89/NI91 and NI93, and new values, but with white borders. One centre phosphor band (2nd) or two phosphor bands (others). Perf 15×14 (with one elliptical hole in each vertical side).

(a) (Litho Walsall (No. NI98), De La Rue or Enschedé (No. NI95), Cartor (Nos. NI101 and NI103/NI115) or De La Rue (others)).

NI94	**N6**	(2nd) Basalt columns, Giant's Causeway	1·25	1·25
NI95	**N7**	(1st) Aerial view of patchwork fields	1·50	1·50
		a. black omitted	£6000	
NI96	**N8**	(E) Linen pattern	2·25	2·25
NI97		40p. Linen pattern (11.5.04)	1·60	1·60
NI98		42p. Linen pattern bluish grey and black (5.4.05)	2·25	2·25
		a. Linen pattern *olive-grey and black* (26.7.05)	2·50	2·50
NI99		44p. Linen pattern (28.3.06)	1·40	1·40
NI100	**N9**	68p. Vase pattern from Belleek	2·50	2·50
NI101	**N8**	68p. Linen pattern (29.3.11)	2·00	2·00
NI102	**N9**	72p. Vase pattern from Belleek (28.3.06)	2·75	2·75
NI103	**N8**	87p. Linen pattern (25.4.12)	2·25	2·25
NI104		88p. Linen pattern (27.3.13)	2·25	2·25
NI105		97p. Linen pattern (25.3.14)	2·50	2·50
NI106		£1 Linen pattern (24.3.15)	2·50	2·50
NI107		£1·05 Linen pattern (22.3.16)	2·75	2·75
NI111	**N9**	£1·10 Vase pattern from Belleek (29.3.11)	2·50	2·50
NI113		£1·28 Vase pattern from Belleek (25.4.12)	2·75	2·75
NI114		£1·33 Vase pattern from Belleek (24.3.15)	2·75	2·75

(b) Gravure De La Rue.

NI122	**N6**	(2nd) Basalt columns, Giant's Causeway (20.9.07)	1·25	1·25
NI123	**N7**	(1st) Aerial view of patchwork fields (20.9.07)	1·50	1·50
NI124	**N8**	48p. Linen pattern (27.3.07)	1·25	1·25
NI125		50p. Linen pattern (1.4.08)	1·25	1·25
NI126		56p. Linen pattern (31.3.09)	1·25	1·25
NI127		60p. Linen pattern (30.3.10)	1·40	1·40
NI128	**N9**	78p. Vase pattern from Belleek (27.3.07)	1·60	1·60
NI129		81p. Vase pattern from Belleek (1.4.08)	2·00	2·00
NI130		90p. Vase pattern from Belleek (31.3.09)	2·25	2·25
NI131		97p. Vase pattern from Belleek (30.3.10)	2·50	2·50

Presentation Pack (PO Pack No. 66) (Nos. NI94/NI96, NI100) .... 7·50

PHQ Cards (set of 4) (D27) (Nos. NI94/NI96, NI100) .... 1·25 10·00

* The bright magenta used on the 68p. is fluorescent.

No. NI95 was printed in sheets and in £9·72 booklet, No. DX43 by De La Rue and was also issued in £7·66 booklet, No. DX40, printed by Enschedé and in premium booklets Nos. DY7 and DY18 (ISP Cartor) and Nos. DY9 and DY11 (Enschedé).

No. NI95a originates from an example of booklet pane NI154m with a progressive dry print of black.

No NI98 (Walsall printing) appears bluish grey and No. NI98a (De La Rue printing) appears olive-grey.

Nos. NI122/NI123 went on philatelic sale on 20 September 2007. They went on sale in Northern Ireland post offices as supplies of Nos. NI94/NI95 were used up.

A stamp as No. NI102 but printed in gravure was only issued within No. **MS**2685.

Stamps as Nos. NI128/NI129 but printed in lithography were only issued within No. **MS**2796 (No. NI128) or No. **MS**2886 (No. NI129).

A design as No. NI95 but self-adhesive was issued on 11 March 2008 in sheets of 20, each stamp accompanied by a *se-tenant* label showing a Northern Ireland scene (No. LS46). These sheets, perforated 15×14 without the elliptical holes, were printed in lithography by Cartor and sold at £7·35 each. They were also available with personalised photographs on the labels at £14·95 from the Royal Mail in Edinburgh.

Stamps as Nos. EN30, NI95, S131 and W122 but self-adhesive were issued on 29 September 2008 in sheets of 20 containing five of each design with *se-tenant* labels (No. LS49).

REGIONAL ISSUES/Northern Ireland

Stamps as No. NI95 but self-adhesive were issued again on 17 March 2009 in sheets of 20 with *se-tenant* labels showing Northern Ireland Castles, No. LS58. These sheets were printed in lithography by Cartor and originally sold at £7·74 each (£8·35 from 6 April 2009).

First Day Covers

Date	Description	Price
14.10.03	2nd, 1st, E, 68p. (Nos. NI94/NI96, NI100) Tallents House	3·25
	(Type K, see Introduction)	3·25
	Belfast	3·25
11.5.04	40p. (No. NI97) Tallents House (Type K)	1·75
	Belfast	1·75
5.4.05	42p. (No. NI98) Tallents House (Type K)	2·25
	Belfast	2·25
28.3.06	44p., 72p. (Nos. NI99, NI102) Tallents House (Type K)	3·50
	Belfast	3·50
27.3.07	48p., 78p. (Nos. NI124, NI128) Tallents House, (Type K)	2·50
	Belfast	2·50
1.4.08	50p., 81p. (Nos. NI125, NI129) Tallents House (Type K)	3·00
	Belfast	3·00
31.3.09	56p., 90p. (Nos. NI126, NI130) Tallents House (Type K)	3·50
	Belfast	3·50
30.3.10	60p., 97p. (Nos. NI127, NI131) Tallents House (Type K)	4·00
	Belfast	4·00
29.3.11	68p., £1·10 (Nos. NI101, NI111) Tallents House (Type K)	4·25
	Belfast	4·25
25.4.12	87p., £1·28 (Nos. NI103, NI113) Tallents House (Type K)	5·00
	Belfast	5·00
27.3.13	88p. (No. NI104) Tallents House (Type K)	2·25
	Belfast	2·25
26.3.14	97p. (No. NI105) Tallents House (Type K)	2·25
	Belfast	2·25
24.3.15	£1, £1·33 (Nos. NI106, NI114) Tallents House (Type K)	5·00
	Belfast	5·00
22.3.16	£1·05 (No. NI107) Tallents House (Type K)	2·50
	Belfast	2·50

N10

(Des David Lyons, Clare Melinsky, Ric Ergenhright and Silk Pearce. Litho De La Rue)

2008 (11 Mar). Celebrating Northern Ireland. Sheet 123×70 mm. Two phosphor bands. Perf 15×14½ (with one elliptical hole in each vertical side) (1st) or 15×14½ (78p).

MSNI152	**N10**	(1st) Carrickfergus Castle; (1st) Giant's Causeway; 78p. St Patrick; 78p. Queen's Bridge and Angel of Thanksgiving sculpture, Belfast	4·00 4·00
		First Day Cover (Tallents House)	4·75
		First Day Cover (Downpatrick, Co. Down)	4·75
		Presentation Pack (PO Pack No. 410)	5·00
		PHQ Cards (set of 5) (CGB3)	1·50 7·00

No. **MS**NI152 was on sale at post offices throughout the UK.
The five PHQ cards depict the complete miniature sheet and the four stamps within it.

N11

(Des Sedley Place. Gravure De La Rue)

2008 (29 Sept). 50th Anniversary of the Country Definitives. Sheet 124×70 mm, containing designs as Nos. NI1, NI3, NI5, S1, S3, S5, W1, W3 and W5 (regional definitives of 1958) but inscribed 1st and printed on pale cream. Two phosphor bands. Perf 15×14 (with one elliptical hole in each vertical side).

MSNI153	**N11**	(1st)×9 As No. W1; As No. S1; As No. W5; As No. S5; As No. NI1; As No. W3; As No. S3; As No. NI3; As No. NI5	7·00	7·00
		First Day Cover (Tallents House)		9·25
		First Day Cover (Gloucester)		9·25
		Presentation Pack (PO Pack No. 80)	10·00	
		PHQ Cards (set of 10)	3·00	12·50

No. **MS**NI153 was on sale at post offices throughout the UK.
The ten PHQ cards show the nine individual stamps and the complete sheet.

N11a    **N11b**    **N11c**

(Litho De La Rue)

2008 (29 Sept). 50th Anniversary of the Country Definitives (2nd issue). Two phosphor bands. Perf 15×14½ (with one elliptical hole in each vertical side).

NI154	**N11a**	(1st) deep lilac	1·60	1·60
		l. Booklet pane. Nos. NI154/NI156, S154/S156 and W144/W146	15·00	
		m. Booklet pane. Nos. NI154/NI156 and NI95×3	6·50	
NI155	**N11b**	(1st) deep claret	1·60	1·60
NI156	**N11c**	(1st) green	1·60	1·60
		First Day Cover (Tallents House) (No. NI154l)		6·00
		First Day Cover (Gloucester) (No. NI154l)		6·00

Nos. NI154/NI156 come from £9·72 booklet, No. DX43.

N12 Basalt Columns, Giant's Causeway    **N13** Aerial View of Patchwork Fields

N14 Linen Pattern    **N15** Vase Pattern from Belleek

(Des Rodney Miller Associates (Basalt columns), Richard Cooke (Aerial view of fields), David Pauley (Linen pattern), Tiff Hunter (Vase pattern). Litho ISP Cartor.)

2017 (21 Mar)–**20**. As previous set but with value indicated in revised typeface. One centre phosphor band (2nd) or two phosphor bands. Perf 15×14 (with one elliptical hole in each vertical side).

NI157	**N12**	(2nd) Basalt columns, Giant's Causeway (20.3.18)	1·00	75
NI158	**N13**	(1st) Aerial view of patchwork fields (20.3.18)	1·25	75
NI159	**N14**	£1·17 Linen pattern (21.3.17)	2·75	2·75
NI160		£1·25 Linen pattern (20.3.18)	2·75	2·75
NI161		£1·35 Linen pattern (19.3.19)	2·75	2·75
NI164	**N15**	£1·40 Vase pattern from Belleek (21.3.17)	3·00	3·00
NI165	**N14**	£1·42 Linen pattern (17.3.20)	2·50	2·50
NI166	**N15**	£1·45 Vase pattern from Belleek (20.3.18)	3·25	3·25
NI167		£1·55 Vase pattern from Belleek (19.3.19)	3·25	3·25
NI168		£1·63 Vase pattern from Belleek (17.3.20)	2·75	2·75
NI169	**N14**	£1·70 Linen pattern (23.12.20)	2·40	2·40

Numbers have been left for possible additions to the above definitive series.

Northern Ireland/Scotland/REGIONAL ISSUES

First Day Covers

21.3.17	£1·17, £1·40. (Nos. NI159, NI165) (Tallents House) (Type K)		6·00
	Belfast		6·00
20.3.18	2nd, 1st, £1·25, £1·45. (Nos. NI157/NI158, NI160, NI166) Tallents House (Type K)		9·00
	Belfast		9·00
13.9.19	2nd, 1st, £1·35, £1·55. (Nos. NI161/NI167) Tallents House (Type K)		7·00
	Belfast		7·00
17.3.20	£1·42, £1·63 (Nos. NI164a, NI168) Tallents House (Type K)		7·00
	Belfast		7·00
23.12.20	£1·70 (No. NI169) Tallents House (Type K)		3·75
	Belfast		3·75

III. SCOTLAND

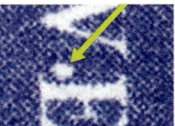

S1   S2   S3

Dot before second 'E' of 'REVENUE' (cyl. 2 dot, R.10/9)

Broken 'V' of 'REVENUE' (Cyl. 1 no dot, R. 11/2)

(Des G. Huntly (3d., 4d., 5d), J. Fleming (6d., 9d.), A. Imrie (1s.3d., 1s.6d.))

1958–67. W **179**. Perf 15×14.

S1	S1	3d. deep lilac (18.8.58)	15	15
		p. Two phosphor bands (29.1.63)	7·50	6·00
		pa. One phosphor band at right (30.4.65)	25	25
		pb. Band at left	25	25
		pc. Horizontal pair. Nos. S1pa/pb	60	75
		pd. One centre phosphor band (9.11.67)	15	15
S2		4d. ultramarine (7.2.66)	20	20
		a. dot before second 'E' of 'REVENUE'.	25·00	
		p. Two phosphor bands	20	20
		pa. dot before second 'E' of 'REVENUE'.	25·00	
S3	S2	6d. deep claret (29.9.58)	25	25
		p. Two phosphor bands (29.1.63)	25	25
S4		9d. bronze-green (2 phosphor bands) (1.3.67)	40	40
S5	S3	1s.3d. green (29.9.58)	40	40
		p. Two phosphor bands (29.1.63)	50	50
S6		1s.6d. grey-blue (2 phosphor bands) (1.3.67)	60	60

First Day Covers

18.8.58	3d. (No. S1)	17·00
29.9.58	6d., 1s.3d. (Nos. S3, S5)	25·00
7.2.66	4d. (No. S2)	7·00
1.3.67	9d., 1s.6d. (Nos. S4, S6)	6·00

The one phosphor band on No. S1pa was produced by printing broad phosphor bands across alternate vertical perforations. Individual stamps show the band at right or left (same prices either way).
For Nos. S1, S3 and S5 in Presentation Pac, see below Wales No. W6.

1967–70. No wmk. Chalk-surfaced paper. One centre phosphor band (Nos. S7, S9/S10) or two phosphor bands (others). Gum Arabic (Nos. S7, S8) or PVA gum (others). Perf 15×14.

S7	S1	3d. deep lilac (16.5.68)	15	15
S8		4d. deep bright blue (28.11.67)	30	30
S9		4d. olive-sepia (4.9.68)	15	15
S10		4d. bright vermilion (26.2.69)	15	15
S11		5d. royal blue (4.9.68)	25	25
S12	S2	9d. bronze-green (28.9.70)	4·00	4·00
		y. Phosphor omitted	£275	
S13	S3	1s.6d. grey-blue (12.12.68)	1·25	1·25
		y. Phosphor omitted	£125	
First Day Cover (Nos. S9, S11) (4.9.68)				3·00
Presentation Pack (PO Pack No. 23) (Nos. S3, S5p., S7, S9/S13) (9.12.70)				8·00

There was no Post Office first day cover for No. S10.

S4

I   II

Redrawn design of T S4 (litho printings.)

The introduction of the redrawn lion took place in 1983 when Waddington's had the contract and therefore the 13p., 17p., 22p. and 31p. exist in both types and perforated 14. The Questa printings, perforated 15×14, are all Type II.

The Types of Lion.
Type I: The eye and jaw appear larger and there is no line across the bridge of the nose.
Type II: The tongue is thick at the point of entry to the mouth and the eye is linked to the background by a solid line.
The following stamps printed in lithography show a screened background behind and to the left of the emblem: 12½p., 15½p., 16p., 19½p., 28p. (Nos. S50 and S74) and 31p. (Nos. S51 and S76). The 13p. and 17p. (No. S43) also showed screened backgrounds for both Type I and Type II of the John Waddington printings, but changed to solid backgrounds for the Questa Type II. All other values printed in lithography have solid backgrounds.

(Des Jeffery Matthews after plaster cast by Arnold Machin)

1971 (7 July)–**93**. Decimal Currency. Chalk-surfaced paper. T **S4**.

(a) Photo Harrison. With phosphor bands. Perf 15×14.

S14	2½p. bright magenta (1 centre band)	25	20
	y. Phosphor omitted	10·00	
	g. Gum arabic (22.9.72)	30	
	gy. Phosphor omitted	20·00	
S15	3p. ultramarine (2 bands)	25	15
	y. Phosphor omitted	17·00	
	g. Gum arabic (14.12.72)	30	
	ga. Imperf (pair)	£575	
	gy. Phosphor omitted	50·00	
S16	3p. ultramarine (1 centre band) (23.1.74)	15	15
S17	3½p. olive-grey (2 bands) (23.1.74)	20	20
	y. Phosphor omitted	50·00	
S18	3½p. olive-grey (1 centre band) (6.11.74)	20	20
S19	4½p. grey-blue (2 bands) (6.11.74)	25	25
S20	5p. reddish violet (2 bands)	90	90
S21	5½p. violet (2 bands) (23.1.74)	25	25
S22	5½p. violet (1 centre band) (21.5.75)	20	25
	a. Imperf (pair)	£450	
S23	6½p. greenish blue (1 centre band) (14.1.76)	20	25
S24	7p. purple-brown (1 centre band) (18.1.78)	25	25
S25	7½p. chestnut (2 bands)	90	90
	y. Phosphor omitted	7·00	
S26	8p. rosine (2 bands) (23.1.74)	35	35
S27	8½p. yellow-green (2 bands) (14.1.76)	35	35
S28	9p. deep violet (2 bands) (18.1.78)	35	35
S29	10p. orange-brown (2 bands) (20.10.76)	35	35
S30	10p. orange-brown (1 centre band) (23.7.80)	35	35
S31	10½p. steel-blue (2 bands) (18.1.78)	45	45
S32	11p. scarlet (2 bands) (20.10.76)	40	40
	y. Phosphor omitted	3·50	

(b) Photo Harrison. On phosphorised paper. Perf 15×14.

S33	12p. yellowish green (23.7.80)	45	45
S34	13½p. purple-brown (23.7.80)	60	60
S35	15p. ultramarine (23.7.80)	50	50

(c) Litho Waddington. (Type I unless otherwise stated). One side phosphor band (11½p., 12p., 12½p., 13p.) or phosphorised paper (others). Perf 14.

S36	11½p. drab (8.4.81)	55	55
	y. Phosphor omitted	£750	
S37	12p. bright emerald (Type II) (7.1.86)	1·25	1·25
S38	12½p. light emerald (24.2.82)	45	45
S39	13p. pale chestnut (Type I) (23.10.84)	75	75
	y. Phosphor omitted	£750	
	a. Type II (1.85)	8·00	8·00
	ay. Phosphor omitted	£750	
S40	14p. grey-blue (8.4.81)	45	45
S41	15½p. pale violet (24.2.82)	50	50
S42	16p. drab (27.4.83)	50	50
S43	17p. grey-blue (Type I) (23.10.84)	1·25	1·25
	a. Type II (1.85)	1·10	1·10

439

REGIONAL ISSUES/Scotland

S44		18p. deep violet (8.4.81)	70	70
S45		19½p. olive-grey (24.2.82)	1·25	1·25
S46		20½p. ultramarine (Type II) (27.4.83)	2·25	2·25
S47		22p. blue (8.4.81)	75	75
S48		22p. yellow-green (Type I) (23.10.84)	2·25	2·25
		a. Type II (1.86)	16·00	16·00
S49		26p. rosine (24.2.82)	70	70
S50		28p. deep violet-blue (Type II) (27.4.83)	70	70
S51		31p. bright purple (Type I) (23.10.84)	1·50	1·50
		a. Type II (11.85*)	£150	£150

(d) Litho Questa (Type II). Perf 15×14.

S52	**S4**	12p. bright emerald (1 side band) (29.4.86)	1·25	1·25
S53		13p. pale chestnut (1 side band) (4.11.86)	70	70
S54		14p. deep blue (1 centre band) (8.11.88)	45	45
		l. Booklet pane. No. S54×6 with margins all round (21.3.89)	1·50	
S55		14p. deep blue (1 side band) (21.3.89)	50	50
		l. Booklet pane. No. S55×5, S63×2, S68 and centre label with margins all round	9·00	
		la. Error. Booklet pane imperf	£1750	
S56		15p. bright blue (1 centre band) (28.11.89)	50	50
		a. Imperf (three sides) (block of four)	£275	
S57		17p. grey-blue (phosphorised paper) (29.4.86)	2·40	2·40
S58		17p. deep blue (1 centre band) (4.12.90)	70	70
S59		18p. deep olive-grey (phosphorised paper) (6.1.87)	70	70
S60		18p. bright green (1 centre band) (3.12.91)	60	60
		a. Perf 14 (26.9.92*)	1·00	1·00
		ay. Phosphor omitted	£900	
S61		18p. bright green (1 side band) (10.8.93)	1·40	1·40
S62		19p. bright orange-red (phosphorised paper) (8.11.88)	50	50
		l. Booklet pane. No. S62×9 with margins all round (21.3.89)	2·75	
		m. Booklet pane. No. S62×6 with margins all round (21.3.89)	2·25	
S63		19p. bright orange-red (2 bands) (21.3.89)	1·40	1·40
S64		20p. brownish black (phosphorised paper) (28.11.89)	70	70
S65		22p. yellow-green (phosphorised paper) (27.1.87)	1·10	1·10
S66		22p. bright orange-red (phosphorised paper) (4.12.90)	60	60
S67		23p. bright green (phosphorised paper) (8.11.88)	80	80
S68		23p. bright green (2 bands) (21.3.89)	9·00	9·00
S69		24p. Indian red (phosphorised paper) (28.11.89)	1·00	1·00
S70		24p. chestnut (phosphorised paper) (3.12.91)	75	75
		a. Perf 14 (10.92*)	6·00	6·00
S71		24p. chestnut (2 bands) (10.8.93)	1·40	1·40
S72		26p. rosine (phosphorised paper) (27.1.87)	2·25	2·25
S73		26p. drab (phosphorised paper) (4.12.90)	1·00	1·00
S74		28p. deep violet-blue (phosphorised paper) (27.1.87)	1·00	1·00
S75		28p. deep bluish grey (phosphorised paper) (3.12.91)	1·00	1·00
		a. Perf 14 (18.2.93*)	9·00	9·00
S76		31p. bright purple (phosphorised paper) (29.4.86)	1·50	1·50
S77		32p. greenish blue (phosphorised paper) (8.11.88)	1·00	1·00
S78		34p. deep bluish grey (phosphorised paper) (28.11.89)	1·25	1·75
S79		37p. rosine (phosphorised paper) (4.12.90)	1·25	1·25
S80		39p. bright mauve (phosphorised paper) (3.12.91)	1·50	1·50
		a. Perf 14 (11.92)	12·50	12·50

* Earliest known date of issue.

Nos. S55, S61, S63, S68 and S71 only come from booklets.

The listed booklet panes come from the Sponsored Booklet No. DX10; Nos. S54l, S55l, S62l/S62m.

No. S56a occured in the second vertical row of two sheets. It is best collected as a block of four including the left-hand vertical pair imperforate on three sides.

Nos. S60a, S70a, S75a and S80a were caused by the use of a reserve perforating machine for some printings in the second half of 1992.

From 1972 printings were on fluorescent white paper. From 1973 most printings had dextrin added to the PVA gum (see notes after the 1971 Decimal Machin issue).

First Day Covers

7.7.71	2½p., 3p., 5p., 7½p. (Nos. S14/S15, S20, S25)	1·50
23.1.74	3p., 3½p., 5½p., 8p. (Nos. S16/S17, S21, S26)	1·25
6.11.74	4½p. (No. S19)	1·00
14.1.76	6½p., 8½p. (Nos. S23, S27)	1·00
20.10.76	10p., 11p. (Nos. S29, S32)	1·00
18.1.78	7p., 9p., 10½p. (Nos. S24, S28, S31)	1·00
23.7.80	12p., 13½p., 15p. (Nos. S33/S35)	1·50
8.4.81	11½p., 14p., 18p., 22p. (Nos. S36, S40, S44, S47)	1·50
24.2.82	12½p., 15½p., 19½p., 26p. (Nos. S38, S41, S45, S49)	1·75
27.4.83	16p., 20½p., 28p. (Nos. S42, S46, S50)	2·00
23.10.84	13p., 17p., 22p., 31p. (Nos. S39, S43, S48, S51)	2·00
7.1.86	12p. (No. S37)	1·00
6.1.87	18p. (No. S59)	1·00
8.11.88	14p., 19p., 23p., 32p. (Nos. S54, S62, S67, S77)	2·00
21.3.89	Scots Connection se-tenant pane 14p., 19p., 23p. (No. S55l)	10·00
28.11.89	15p., 20p., 24p., 34p. (Nos. S56, S64, S69, S78)	2·50
4.12.90	17p., 22p., 26p., 37p. (Nos. S58, S66, S73, S79)	2·50
3.12.91	18p., 24p., 28p., 39p. (Nos. S60, S70, S75, S80)	2·50

Presentation Packs

7.7.71	PO Pack No. 27. 2½p., 3p. (2 bands), 5p., 7½p. (Nos. S14/S15, S20, S25)	2·00
29.5.74	PO Pack No. 62. 3p. (1 centre band), 3½p. (2 bands) or (1 centre band), 5½p. (2 bands) or (1 centre band), 8p. (Nos. S16, S17 or S18, S21 or S22, S26). The 4½p. (No. S19) was added later	2·00
20.10.76	PO Pack No. 85. 6½p., 8½p., 10p. (2 bands), 11p. (Nos. S23, S27, S29, S32)	1·50
28.10.81	PO Pack No. 129b. 7p., 9p., 10½p., 12p. (gravure), 13½p., 15p. (gravure), 11½p., 14p. grey-blue, 18p. deep violet, 22p. blue (Nos. S24, S28, S31, S33/S36, S40, S44, S47)	6·00
3.8.83	PO Pack No. 2. 10p. (1 centre band), 12½p., 16p., 20½p., 26p. (J.W.), 28p. (J.W.), (Nos. S30, S38, S42, S46, S49/S50)	14·00
23.10.84	PO Pack No. 6. 10p. (1 centre band), 13p. (J.W.), 16p., 17p. (J.W.), 22p. yellow-green, 26p. (J.W.), 28p. (J.W.), 31p. (J.W.), (Nos. S30, S39, S42/S43, S48/S51)	12·00
3.3.87	PO Pack No. 10. 12p. (litho), 13p. (Questa), 17p. grey-blue (Questa), 18p. deep olive-grey, 22p. yellow-green, 26p. rosine (Questa), 28p. deep violet-blue (Questa), 31p. (Questa) (Nos. S52/S53, S57, S59, S65, S72, S74, S76)	15·00

Presentation Packs containing stamps of Northern Ireland, Scotland and Wales are listed after those for Northern Ireland.

1977–1978 EXPERIMENTAL MACHINE PACKETS. These are small cartons containing loose stamps for sale in vending machines. The experiment was confined to the Scottish Postal Board area, where six vending machines were installed, the first becoming operational in Dundee about February 1977.

The cartons carry labels inscribed 'ROYAL MAIL STAMPS', their total face value (30p. or 60p.) and their contents.

At first the 30p. packet contained two 6½p. and two 8½p. Scottish Regional stamps and the 60p. packet had four of each. The stamps could be in pairs or blocks, but also in strips or singles.

With the change in postal rates on 13 June 1977 these packets were withdrawn on 11 June and on 13 June the contents were changed, giving three 7p. and one 9p. for the 30p. packet and double this for the 60p. packet. However, this time ordinary British Machin stamps were used. Moreover the Edinburgh machine, situated in an automatic sorting area, was supplied with 7p. stamps with two phosphor bands instead of the new centre band 7p. stamps, despite instructions having been given to withdraw the two band stamps. However, the demand for these packets was too great to be filled and by 27 June the machine was closed down. It was brought back into use on 16 August 1977, supplying 7p. stamps with the centre band.

The 6½p. and 8½p. Scottish Regional packets were put on sale at the Edinburgh Philatelic Bureau in June 1977 and withdrawn in April 1978. The packets with the 7p. and 9p. Machin stamps were put on sale at the Bureau in June 1977 and withdrawn in December 1978.

Such machine packets are outside the scope of this catalogue.

(Des Jeffery Matthews after plaster cast by Arnold Machin)

1993 (7 Dec)–**98**. Chalk-surfaced paper.

(a) Litho Questa. Perf 15×14 (with one elliptical hole in each vert side).

S81	**S4**	19p. bistre (1 centre band)	70	70
S82		19p. bistre (1 band at right) (25.4.95)	2·00	2·00
S83		20p. bright green (1 centre band) (23.7.96)	1·25	1·25
S84		25p. red (2 bands)	80	80
S85		26p. red-brown (2 bands) (23.7.96)	1·40	1·40
S86		30p. deep olive-grey (2 bands)	1·25	1·25
S87		37p. bright mauve (2 bands) (23.7.96)	1·75	1·75
S88		41p. grey-brown (2 bands)	1·25	1·25
		y. Phosphor omitted	£325	
S89		63p. light emerald (2 bands) (23.7.96)	2·50	2·50

Scotland / REGIONAL ISSUES

(b) Gravure Walsall (20p., 26p. (No. S91a), 63p.), Harrison or Walsall (26p. (No. S91), 37p.). Perf 14 (No. S90a) or 15×14 (others) (both with one elliptical hole in each vertical side).

S90	S4	20p. bright green (1 centre band) (1.7.97)	1·00	1·00
S90a		20p. bright green (1 side band at right) (13.10.98)	3·00	3·00
S91		26p. chestnut (2 bands) (1.7.97)	1·40	1·40
		a. Perf 14 (13.10.98)	3·00	3·00
S92		37p. bright mauve (2 bands) (1.7.97)	1·60	1·60
S93		63p. light emerald (2 bands) (1.7.97)	3·50	3·50

Nos. S82, S90a and S91a only come from booklets. The Harrison printings of Nos. S91/S92 come from booklet pane No. NI81l.

First Day Covers

7.12.93	19p., 25p., 30p., 41p. (Nos. S81, S84, S86, S88)	3·50
23.7.96	20p. 26p., 37p., 63p. (Nos. S83, S85, S87, S89)	4·00

For Presentation Pack containing stamps of Northern Ireland, Scotland and Wales see after No. NI87 of Northern Ireland.

S5 Saltire
S6 Lion Rampant of Scotland
S7 Thistle
S8 Tartan

(Des Anton Morris (Saltire), Frank Pottinger (Lion Rampant of Scotland), Tim Chalk (Thistle) and Tartan, supplied by Kinloch Anderson; adapted by Tayburn of Edinburgh. Gravure Questa (Nos. S94l, S95l), De La Rue (No. S99), De La Rue or Walsall (Nos. S94/S95), Walsall (others))

1999 (8 June)–**2002**. One centre phosphor band (2nd) or two phosphor bands (others). Perf 15×14 (with one elliptical hole in each vertical side).

S94	S5	(2nd) Saltire	1·25	1·25
		l. Booklet pane. Nos. S94×6 and S98×2 with centre label and margins all round (4.8.00)	6·00	
S95	S6	(1st) Lion Rampant of Scotland	1·50	1·50
		l. Booklet pane. Nos. S95/S96, each×4, with centre label and margins all round (22.10.01)	7·50	
S96	S7	(E) Thistle	2·25	2·25
S97	S8	64p. Tartan	5·50	5·50
S98		65p. Tartan (25.4.00)	2·00	2·00
S99		68p. Tartan (4.7.02)	2·25	2·25
Presentation Pack (PO Pack No. 45) (2nd, 1st, E, 64p.) (Nos. S94/S97)			9·50	
Presentation Pack (PO Pack No. 50) (65p.) (No. S98)			10·00	
Presentation Pack (PO Pack No. 55) (2nd, 1st, E, 65p.) (Nos. S94/S96, S98)			15·00	
PHQ Cards (set of 4) (D12) (Nos. S94/S97)			1·25	10·00

Nos. S94, S95 and S96 were initially sold at 19p., 26p. and 30p., the latter representing the basic European airmail rate.

New printings of Nos. S94/S95, produced by De La Rue instead of Walsall were issued on 5 June 2002. Stamps from this printing do not differ from those produced by Walsall.

No. S94l comes from booklet No. DX25.

No. S95l comes from booklet No. DX27.

For combined presentation pack for all four Regions, see under England.

First Day Covers

8.6.99	2nd, 1st, E, 64p. (Nos. S94/S97) Tallents House		3·50
	Edinburgh		4·00
25.4.00	65p. (No. S98) Tallents House		2·50
	Edinburgh		2·50
4.8.00	Queen Elizabeth the Queen Mother *se-tenant* pane 2nd, 65p. (No. S94l) Tallents House (as for Nos. 2160/2161)		4·75
	London SW1 (as for Nos. 2160/2161)		4·75
22.10.01	Unseen and Unheard *se-tenant* pane (1st), E, (No. S95l) Tallents House (as for No. **MS**2206)		7·00
	Rosyth, Dunfermline (as for No. **MS**2206)		7·00
4.7.02	68p. (No. S99) Tallents House (Type K) (see Introduction)		2·00
	Edinburgh		2·00

S9

(Des Jeffery Matthews. Gravure Walsall)

2000 (15 Feb). T **S4** redrawn with '1st' face value as T **S9**. Two phosphor bands. Perf 14 (with one elliptical hole in each vertical side).

S108	S9	(1st) bright orange-red	1·60	1·60

No. S108 was only issued in £7·50 stamp booklet (No. DX24).

2003 (14 Oct)–**17**. As Nos. S94/S96 and S99, and new values, but with white borders. One centre phosphor band (2nd) or two phosphor bands (others). Perf 15×14 (with one elliptical hole in each vertical side).

(a) *Gravure Walsall or De La Rue (42p.) or De La Rue (others).*

S109	S5	(2nd) Saltire	1·25	1·25
		l. Booklet pane. Nos. S109 and EN16, each×3, with margins all round (16.3.04)	5·50	
		m. Booklet pane. Nos. S109 and W103, each×3, with margins all round (1.3.07)	5·00	
S110	S6	(1st) Lion Rampant of Scotland	1·50	1·50
S111	S7	(E) Thistle	2·10	2·10
S112		40p. Thistle (11.5.04)	1·40	1·40
S113		42p. Thistle (5.4.05)	1·75	1·75
S114		44p. Thistle (28.3.06)	1·40	1·40
S115		48p. Thistle (27.3.07)	1·25	1·25
S116		50p. Thistle (1.4.08)	1·25	1·25
S117		56p. Thistle (31.3.09)	1·40	1·40
S118		60p. Thistle (30.3.10)	1·50	1·50
S119	S8	68p. Tartan	1·60	1·60
S120		72p. Tartan (28.3.06)	1·75	1·75
S121		78p. Tartan (27.3.07)	1·75	1·75
S122		81p. Tartan (1.4.08)	2·00	2·00
S123		90p. Tartan (31.3.09)	2·25	2·25
S124		97p. Tartan (30.3.10)	2·40	2·40

(b) *Litho Enschedé, De La Rue or ISP Cartor (1st) or ISP Cartor (others). Queen's head in grey (Nos. S130a and S131a) or silver (others).*

S130	S5	(2nd) Saltire (Queen's head silver) (27.6.12)	1·25	1·25
		a. Saltire (Queen's head grey) (5.16)	1·75	1·50
S131	S6	(1st) Lion Rampant of Scotland (Queen's head silver) (20.9.07)	1·50	1·50
		a. Lion Rampant of Scotland (Queen's head grey) (19.5.16)	2·00	2·00
S132	S7	68p. Thistle (29.3.11)	1·90	1·90
S133		87p Thistle (25.4.12)	2·25	2·25
S134		88p. Thistle (27.3.13)	2·25	2·25
S135		97p. Thistle (26.3.14)	2·40	2·40
S136		£1 Thistle (24.3.15)	2·40	2·40
S137		£1·05 Thistle (22.3.16)	2·60	2·60
S138	S8	£1·10 Tartan (29.3.11)	2·40	2·40
S143		£1·28 Tartan (25.4.12)	2·60	2·60
S144		£1·33 Tartan (24.3.15)	2·75	2·75
Presentation Pack (PO Pack No. 64) (Nos. S109/S111, S119)			6·00	
PHQ Cards (set of 4) (D25) (Nos. S109/S111, S119)			1·25	6·50

No. S109l comes from booklet No. DX32.

No. S109m from booklet No. DX38.

The Walsall printing of No. S113 was issued on 5 April 2005, and the De La Rue printing on 24 May 2005.

Stamps as No. S121/S122 but printed in lithography were only issued within No. **MS**2796 (No. S121) or No. **MS**2886 (No. S122).

No. S131 was issued on 20 September 2007 in £7·66 stamp booklets printed by Enschedé, No. DX40 and on 29 September 2008 in £9·72 booklets (No. DX43) printed by De La Rue. It was issued in sheets printed by ISP Cartor on 27 June 2012

A design as No. S131 but self-adhesive was issued on 30 November 2007 in sheets of 20, each stamp accompanied by a *se-tenant* label showing a Scottish scene. These sheets were printed in lithography by Cartor, perforated 15×14 without the elliptical holes, and sold at £7·35. They were also available with personalised photographs on the labels at £14·95 from the Royal Mail in Edinburgh.

Stamps as Nos. EN30, NI95, S131 and W122 but self-adhesive were issued on 29 September 2008 in sheets of 20 containing five of each design with *se-tenant* labels (No. LS49).

Numbers have been left for possible additions to this definitive series.

First Day Covers

14.10.03	2nd, 1st, E, 68p. (Nos. S109/S111, S119) Tallents House (Type K, see Introduction)		2·00
	Edinburgh		2·00
11.5.04	40p. (No. S112) Tallents House (Type K)		1·50
	Edinburgh		1·50
5.4.05	42p. (No. S113) Tallents House (Type K)		1·75
	Edinburgh		1·75
28.3.06	44p., 72p. (Nos. S114, S120) Tallents House (Type K)		3·00
	Edinburgh		3·00

REGIONAL ISSUES/Scotland

Date	Description	Price	
27.3.07	48p., 78p. (Nos. S115, S121) Tallents House (Type K)...	3·00	
	Edinburgh...	3·00	
1.4.08	50p., 81p. (Nos. S116, S122) Tallents House (Type K)...........	3·25	
	Edinburgh...	3·25	
31.3.09	56p., 90p. (Nos. S117, S123) Tallents House (Type K)..	3·50	
	Edinburgh...	3·50	
30.3.10	60p., 97p. (Nos. S118, S124) Tallents House (Type K)..	3·75	
	Edinburgh...	3·75	
29.3.11	68p., £1·10 (Nos. S132, S138) Tallents House (Type K)	4·25	
	Edinburgh...	4·25	
25.4.12	87p., £1·28 (Nos. S133, S143) Tallents House (Type K)	4·50	
	Edinburgh...	4·50	
27.3.13	88p. (No. S134) Tallents House (Type K)..........................	2·00	
	Edinburgh...	2·00	
26.3.14	97p. (No. S135) Tallents House (Type K)..........................	2·25	
	Edinburgh...	2·25	
24.3.15	£1, £1·33 (Nos. S136, S144) Tallents House (Type K)....	5·25	
	Edinburgh...	5·25	
22.3.16	£1·05 (No. S137) Tallents House (Type K)........................	2·50	
	Edinburgh...	2·50	

S9a

(Des Howard Brown. Gravure De La Rue)

2004 (5 Oct). Opening of New Scottish Parliament, Edinburgh. Sheet 123×70 mm. Printed in gravure by De La Rue. One centre phosphor band (2nd) or two phosphor bands (others). Perf 15×14 (with one elliptical hole on each vertical side).

MSS152	**S9a** Nos. S109, S110×2 and S112×2....................	5·00	5·00
First Day Cover (Tallents House)...			5·50
First Day Cover (Edinburgh)..			5·50

S10

(Des Peter Crowther, Clare Melinsky and Silk Pearce. Gravure De La Rue)

2006 (30 Nov). Celebrating Scotland. Sheet 124×71 mm. Two phosphor bands. Perf 15×14 (with one elliptical hole in each vertical side) (1st) or 14½×14 (72p).

MSS153	**S10** (1st) As No. S110; (1st) Saltire; 72p. St Andrew; 72p. Edinburgh Castle.....................	4·00	4·00
First Day Cover (Tallents House)..			4·25
First Day Cover (St Andrews, Fife)...			4·75
Presentation Pack (PO Pack No. M14)...................................		5·25	
PHQ Cards (set of 5) (CGB1)..		1·50	4·00

No. **MS**S153 was on sale at post offices throughout the UK.

Stamps as the 1st class Saltire stamp within No. **MS**S153 but self-adhesive were issued on 30 November 2009 in sheets of 20 with *se-tenant* labels showing Scottish Castles, No. LS68. These sheets were printed in lithography by Cartor and sold for £8·35 each.

The five PHQ cards depict the complete miniature sheet and the four stamps within it.

S10a    **S10b**    **S10c**

(Litho De La Rue)

2008 (29 Sept). 50th Anniversary of the Country Definitives. Two phosphor bands. Perf 15×14½ (with one elliptical hole in each vertical side).

S154	**S10a**	(1st) deep lilac..............................	1·60	1·60
		l. Booklet pane. Nos. S154/S156 and S131×3......................................	6·50	
S155	**S10b**	(1st) deep claret...........................	1·60	1·60
S156	**S10c**	(1st) green....................................	1·60	1·60

Nos. S154/S156 come from £9·72 booklets, No. DX43.

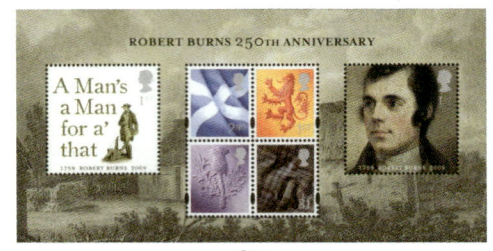

S11

(Des Tayburn. Gravure Enschedé)

2009 (22 Jan). 250th Birth Anniversary of Robert Burns (poet). Sheet 145×74 mm. One centre phosphor band (2nd) or two phosphor bands (others). Perf 14½ (size 34×34 mm) or 15×14 (with one elliptical hole in each vertical side) (others).

MSS157 **S11** (2nd) No. S109; (1st) 'A Man's a Man for a' that' and Burns ploughing (detail) (James Sargent Storer) (34×34 mm); (1st) No. S110; (1st) Portrait of Burns (Alexander Nasmyth) (34×34 mm); 50p. No. S116; 81p. S122..		5·00	5·00
First Day Cover (Tallents House)..			5·50
First Day Cover (Alloway, Ayr)..			5·50
Presentation Pack (PO Pack No. 422).....................................		6·00	
PHQ Cards (set of 3) (319)..		90	7·00

No. **MS**S157 was on sale at post offices throughout the UK.

The three PHQ cards show the two 34×34 mm Robert Burns stamps and the complete miniature sheet.

S12 Saltire

Des Peter Crowther (illustration) and Silk Pierce. Litho ISP Cartor or Enschedé)

2013 (9 May)–**14**. Scotland Flag. Two phosphor bands. Perf 14½×14 (with one elliptical hole in each vertical side).

S158	**S12**	(1st) Saltire (Queen's head silver).............	4·75	4·75
		a. Saltire (Queen's head grey) (20.2.14)..	3·50	3·50

No. S158 was issued in £11·11 Football Heroes booklet (No. DY7, booklet pane No. U3070l).

No. S158a was issued in £13·97 Classic Locomotives booklet (No. DY9, booklet pane No. U307lm) and £16·49 Centenary of the First World War (3rd issue) booklet (No. DY18, booklet pane 3717a).

S13 Saltire    **S14** Lion Rampant of Scotland

S15 Thistle    **S16** Tartan

Scotland/Wales / REGIONAL ISSUES

(Des Des Anton Morris (Saltire), Frank Pottinger (Lion Rampant of Scotland), Tim Chalk (Thistle) and Tartan, supplied by Kinloch Anderson; adapted by Tayburn of Edinburgh. Litho ISP Cartor)

2017 (21 Mar)–**2020**. As previous set but with value indicated in revised typeface. One centre phosphor band (2nd) or two phosphor bands (others). Perf 15×14 (with one elliptical hole in each vertical side).

S159	**S13**	(2nd) Saltire (silver-grey head) (20.3.18)..	1·00	75
		a. Saltire (Queens head dull grey) (17.3.20)...	1·50	1·50
S160	**S14**	(1st) Lion of Scotland (20.3.18)................	1·25	75
S161	**S15**	£1·17 Thistle (21.3.17)..............................	2·75	2·75
S162		£1·25 Thistle (20.3.18)..............................	2·75	2·75
S163		£1·35 Thistle (19.3.19)..............................	2·75	2·75
S166	**S16**	£1·40 Tartan (21.3.17)..............................	3·00	3·00
S166a	**S15**	£1·42 Thistle (17.3.20)..............................	2·50	2·50
S168	**S16**	£1·45 Tartan (20.3.18)..............................	3·25	3·25
S169		£1·55 Tartan (19.3.19)..............................	3·25	3·25
S170		£1·63 Tartan (17.3.20)..............................	2·75	2·75
S171		£1·70 Thistle (23.12.20)............................	2·40	2·40

S159 and S519a are both printed from black plates but owing to variations in the relative intensity, No. 159 gives a silver-grey effect while 159a is a duller grey.

No. S159a was issued in £16.99 James Bond booklet (No. DY33), booklet pane U3071q.

Numbers have been left for possible additions to the above definitive series.

First Day Covers

21.3.17	£1·17, £1·40. (Nos. S161, S166) Tallents House (Type K)...		5·00
	Edinburgh...		5·00
20.3.18	2nd, 1st, £1·25, £1·45. (S159/S160, S162, S168) Tallents House (Type K)...		9·00
	Edinburgh...		9·00
19.3.19	£1·35, £1·55. (Nos. S163/S169) Tallents House (Type K)...		7·00
	Edinburgh...		7·00
17.3.20	£1·42, £1·63 (Nos. S167, S166a) Tallents House (Type K)...		7·00
	Edinburgh...		7·00
23.12.20	£1·70 No. S171) Tallents House (Type K)............		3·75
	Edinburgh...		3·75

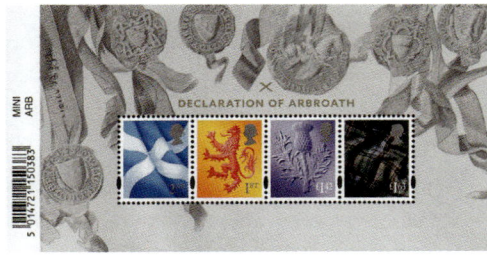

S17

(Des Tayburn. Litho ISP Cartor)

2020 (6 Apr). 700th Anniversary of the Declaration of Arbroath. Sheet 133×70 mm. Printed in lithography by ISP Cartor. One centre phosphor band (2nd) or two phosphor bands (others). Perf 15×14 (with one elliptical hole in each vertical side).

MSS180	**S17** Nos. S159/S160, S166a and S170..................		7·00
Commemorative Cover (Tallents House)............................			9·00
Commemorative Cover (Arbroath).......................................			9·00

IV. WALES

From the inception of the Regional stamps, the Welsh versions were tendered to members of the public at all Post Offices within the former County of Monmouthshire but the national alternatives were available on request. By August 1961 the policy of 'dual stocking' of definitive stamps was only maintained at Abergavenny, Chepstow, Newport and Pontypool. Offices with a Monmouthshire postal address but situated outside the County, namely Beachley, Brockweir, Redbrook, Sedbury, Tutshill, Welsh Newton and Woodcroft, were not supplied with the Welsh Regional stamps. With the re-formation of Counties, Monmouthshire became known as Gwent and was also declared to be part of Wales. From 1 July 1974, therefore, except for the offices mentioned above, only Welsh Regional stamps were available at the offices under the jurisdiction of Newport, Gwent.

W1 W2 W3

(Des Reynolds Stone)

1958–67. W **179**. Perf 15×14.

W1	**W1**	3d. deep lilac (18.8.58)............................	15	15
		p. One centre phosphor band (16.5.67)...	20	15
W2		4d. ultramarine (7.2.66)..........................	20	20
		p. Two phosphor bands (10.67).............	20	20
W3	**W2**	6d. deep claret (29.9.58).........................	35	35
W4		9d. bronze-green (2 phosphor bands) (1.3.67)...	35	35
		y. Phosphor omitted..............................	£375	
W5	**W3**	1s.3d. green (29.9.58).............................	40	40
W6		1s.6d. grey-blue (2 phosphor bands) (1.3.67)...	40	40
		y. Phosphor omitted..............................	50·00	
Presentation Pack*			£100	

* This was issued in 1960 and comprises Guernsey No. 7, Jersey No. 10, Isle of Man No. 2, Northern Ireland Nos. NI1, NI3 and NI5, Scotland Nos. S1, S3 and S5 and Wales Nos. W1, W3 and W5 together with a 6 page printed leaflet describing the stamps. There exist two forms: (a) inscribed '7s.3d.' for sale in the UK; and (b) inscribed '$1.20' for sale in the USA.

First Day Covers

18.8.58	3d. (W1)..	12·00
29.9.58	6d., 1s.3d. (W3, W5)...	25·00
7.2.66	4d. (W2)...	7·00
1.3.67	9d., 1s.6d. (W4, W6)..	4·00

White spot before 'E' of 'POSTAGE' (Cyl. 2 no dot, R. 17/12).

White spot above Dragon's hind leg (Cyl. 2 no dot, R. 20/1).

1967–69. No wmk. Chalk-surfaced paper. One centre phosphor band (Nos. W7, W9/W10) or two phosphor bands (others). Perf 15×14.

W7	**W1**	3d. deep lilac (6.12.67)............................	15	15
		y. Phosphor omitted..............................	70·00	
W8		4d. ultramarine (21.6.68).........................	15	15
		a. White spot before 'E' of 'POSTAGE'	25·00	
		b. White spot above dragon's hind leg..	25·00	
W9		4d. olive-sepia (4.9.68)............................	15	15
		a. White spot before 'E' of 'POSTAGE'	22·00	
		b. White spot above dragon's hind leg..	22·00	
W10		4d. bright vermilion (26.2.69)................	15	15
		y. Phosphor omitted..............................	2·00	
W11		5d. royal blue (4.9.68).............................	15	15
		y. Phosphor omitted..............................	3·00	
W12	**W3**	1s.6d. grey-blue (1.8.69).........................	2·75	2·75

The 3d. exists with gum arabic only; the remainder with PVA gum only. There was no Post Office first day cover for No. W10.

4.9.68	First Day Cover (Nos. W9, W11)............................	3·00
9.12.70	Presentation Pack (PO Pack No. 24) Nos. W4, W6/W7, W9/W11	5·50

W4 With 'p'

I II

Redrawn design of T W4 (litho ptgs.)

Two Types of Dragon

Type I: The eye is complete with white dot in the centre. Wing-tips, tail and tongue are thin.

Type II: The eye is joined to the nose by a solid line. Tail, wing-tips, claws and tongue are wider than in Type I.

REGIONAL ISSUES/Wales

The following stamps printed in lithography show a screened background behind and to the left of the emblem: 11½p., 12½p., 14p. (No. W39), 15½p., 16p., 18p. (No. W46), 19½p., 22p. (No. W54) and 28p. (No. W63). The 13p. and 17p. (No. W44) also show screened backgrounds in Type I, but changed to solid backgrounds for Type II. All other values printed in lithography have solid backgrounds.

Types of 5½p.

Cyl. 1 (W21) Cyl. 2 (W21b)

(Des Jeffery Matthews after plaster cast by Arnold Machin)

1971 (7 July)–93. Decimal Currency. Chalk-surfaced paper. T **W4**.

(a) Gravure Harrison. With phosphor bands. Perf 15×14.

W13	2½p. bright magenta (1 centre band)	20	20
	y. Phosphor omitted	7·50	
	g. Gum arabic (22.9.72)	20	
	ga. Imperf (pair)	£575	
W14	3p. ultramarine (2 bands)	25	20
	y. Phosphor omitted	30·00	
	g. Gum arabic (6.6.73)	25	
	gy. Phosphor omitted	12·00	
W15	3p. ultramarine (1 centre band) (23.1.74)	25	25
W16	3½p. olive-grey (2 bands) (23.1.74)	20	30
W17	3½p. olive-grey (1 centre band) (6.11.74)	20	20
W18	4½p. grey-blue (2 bands) (6.11.74)	25	25
W19	5p. reddish violet (2 bands)	80	80
	y. Phosphor omitted	20·00	
W20	5½p. violet (2 bands) (23.1.74)	25	25
	y. Phosphor omitted	£180	
W21	5½p. violet (1 centre band) (21.5.75)	25	25
	a. Imperf (pair)	£550	
	b. Low emblem and value (cyl. 2) (1977)	£180	£180
W22	6½p. greenish blue (1 centre band) (14.1.76)	20	20
W23	7p. purple-brown (1 centre band) (18.1.78)	25	25
W24	7½p. chestnut (2 bands)	1·25	1·25
	y. Phosphor omitted	75·00	
W25	8p. rosine (2 bands) (23.1.74)	30	30
	y. Phosphor omitted	£600	
W26	8½p. yellow-green (2 bands) (14.1.76)	35	35
W27	9p. deep violet (2 bands) (18.1.78)	35	35
W28	10p. orange-brown (2 bands) (20.10.76)	35	35
W29	10p. orange-brown (1 centre band) (23.7.80)	35	35
W30	10½p. steel-blue (2 bands) (18.1.78)	45	45
W31	11p. scarlet (2 bands) (20.10.76)	40	40

(b) Gravure Harrison. On phosphorised paper. Perf 15×14.

W32	12p. yellowish green (23.7.80)	45	45
W33	13½p. purple-brown (23.7.80)	55	55
W34	15p. ultramarine (23.7.80)	55	55

(c) Litho Questa (Type II unless otherwise stated). Perf 14 (11½p., 12½p., 14p. (No. W39), 15½p., 16p., 18p. (No. W46), 19½p., 20½p., 22p. (No. W54), 26p. (No. W61), 28p. (No. W63)) or 15×14 (others).

W35	11½p. drab (Type I) (1 side band) (8.4.81)	70	70
W36	12p. bright emerald (1 side band) (7.1.86)	1·00	1·00
W37	12½p. light emerald (Type I) (1 side band) (24.2.82)	50	50
	a. Perf 15×14 (Type I) (10.1.84)	2·75	2·75
W38	13p. pale chestnut (Type I) (1 side band) (23.10.84)	50	50
	a. Type II (1.87)	1·40	1·40
W39	14p. grey-blue (Type I) (phosphorised paper) (8.4.81)	55	55
W40	14p. deep blue (2 bands) (8.11.88)	55	55
W41	15p. bright blue (1 centre band) (28.11.89)	60	60
	y. Phosphor omitted	£125	
W42	15½p. pale violet (Type I) (phosphorised paper) (24.2.82)	70	70
W43	16p. drab (Type I) (phosphorised paper) (27.4.83)	1·10	1·10
	a. Perf 15×14 (Type I) (10.1.84)	1·10	1·10
W44	17p. grey-blue (Type I) (phosphorised paper) (23.10.84)	80	80
	a. Type II (18.8.87)	40·00	40·00
W45	17p. deep blue (1 centre band) (4.12.90)	60	60
	y. Phosphor omitted	18·00	
W46	18p. deep violet (Type I) (8.4.81)	80	80
W47	18p. deep olive-grey (phosphorised paper) (6.1.87)	80	80
W48	18p. bright green (1 centre band) (3.12.91)	55	55
	y. Phosphor omitted	£225	
	l. Booklet pane. No. W48×6 with margins all round (25.2.92)	1·75	
	ly. Phosphor omitted		
	b. Perf 14 (12.1.93*)	7·50	7·50
W49	18p. bright green (1 side band at right) (25.2.92)	1·75	1·75
	l. Booklet pane. No. X1020×2, 1451a, 1514a, W49×2, W60×2 and centre label with margins all round	8·50	
	ly. Phosphor omitted	£225	
	b. Band at left (10.8.93)	1·60	1·60
W50	19p. bright orange-red (phosphorised paper) (8.11.88)	70	70
W51	19½p. olive-grey (Type I) (phosphorised paper) (24.2.82)	1·25	1·25
W52	20p. brownish black (phosphorised paper) (28.11.89)	70	70
W53	20½p. ultramarine (Type I) (phosphorised paper) (27.4.83)	2·50	2·50
W54	22p. blue (Type I) (phosphorised paper) (8.4.81)	80	80
W55	22p. yellow-green (Type I) (phosphorised paper) (23.10.84)	80	80
W56	22p. bright orange-red (phosphorised paper) (4.12.90)	80	80
W57	23p. bright green (phosphorised paper) (8.11.88)	80	80
W58	24p. Indian red (phosphorised paper) (28.11.89)	90	90
W59	24p. chestnut (phosphorised paper) (3.12.91)	70	70
	l. Booklet pane. No. W59×6 with margins all round (25.2.92)	2·50	
	b. Perf 14 (14.9.92*)	6·00	6·00
W60	24p. chestnut (2 bands) (25.2.92)	90	90
W61	26p. rosine (Type I) (phosphorised paper) (24.2.82)	80	80
	a. Perf 15×14 (Type II) (27.1.87)	3·00	3·00
W62	26p. drab (phosphorised paper) (4.12.90)	1·25	1·25
W63	28p. deep violet-blue (Type I) (phosphorised paper) (27.4.83)	90	90
	a. Perf 15×14 (Type II) (27.1.87)	1·25	1·25
W64	28p. deep bluish grey (phosphorised paper) (3.12.91)	80	80
W65	31p. bright purple (Type I) (phosphorised paper) (23.10.84)	1·00	1·00
W66	32p. greenish blue (phosphorised paper) (8.11.88)	1·25	1·25
W67	34p. deep bluish grey (phosphorised paper) (28.11.89)	1·25	1·25
W68	37p. rosine (phosphorised paper) (4.12.90)	1·25	1·25
W69	39p. bright mauve (phosphorised paper) (3.12.91)	1·25	1·25

* Earliest known date of issue.

Nos. W48b and W59b were caused by the use of a reserve perforating machine for some printings in the second half of 1992.

Nos. W49, W49b and W60 only come from booklets.

The listed booklet panes come from the Sponsored Booklet No. DX13; Nos. W48l, W49l, W59l.

No. W60 exists with the phosphor omitted, but cannot be identified without the use of ultraviolet light (*Price* £300 *unused*).

From 1972 printings were on fluorescent white paper.

From 1973 most printings had dextrin added to the PVA gum (see notes after 1971 Decimal Machin issue).

First Day Covers

7.7.71	2½p., 3p., 5p., 7½p., (Nos. W13/W14, W19, W24)	2·00
23.1.74	3p., 3½p., 5½p., 8p. (Nos. W15/W16, W20, W25)	1·50
6.11.74	4½p. (No. W18)	80
14.1.76	6½p., 8½p. (Nos. W22, W26)	80
20.10.76	10p., 11p. (Nos. W28, W31)	80
18.1.78	7p., 9p., 10½p. (Nos. W23, W27, W30)	1·00
23.7.80	12p., 13½p., 15p. (Nos. W32/W34)	2·00
8.4.81	11½p., 14p., 18p., 22p. (Nos. W35, W39, W46, W54)	2·00
24.2.82	12½p., 15½p., 19½p., 26p. (Nos. W37, W42, W51, W61)	2·50
27.4.83	16p., 20½p., 28p. (Nos. W43, W53, W63)	2·50
23.10.84	13p., 17p., 22p., 31p. (Nos. W38, W44, W55, W65)	3·00
7.1.86	12p. (No. W36)	1·00
6.1.87	18p. (No. W47)	1·00
8.11.88	14p., 19p., 23p., 32p. (Nos. W40, W50, W57, W66)	3·00
28.11.89	15p., 20p., 24p., 34p. (Nos. W41, W50, W52, W58, W67)	4·00
4.12.90	17p., 22p., 26p., 37p. (Nos. W45, W56, W62, W68)	4·00
3.12.91	18p., 24p., 28p., 39p. (Nos. W48, W59, W64, W69)	4·25
25.2.92	Cymru-Wales *se-tenant* pane 18p. (2nd), 24p. (1st), 33p. (No. W49a)	8·50

Wales / REGIONAL ISSUES

Presentation Packs

Date	Description	Price
7.7.71	PO Pack No. 28. 2½p., 3p. (2 bands), 5p., 7½p. (Nos. W13/W14, W19, W24)	2·00
29.5.74	PO Pack No. 63. 3p. (1 centre band), 3½p. (2 bands) or (1 centre band), 5½p. (2 bands) or (1 centre band), 8p. (Nos. W15, W16 or W17, W20 or W21, W25). The 4½p. (No. W18) was added later	2·25
20.10.76	PO Pack No. 86. 6½p., 8½p., 10p. (2 bands), 11p. (Nos. W22, W26, W28, W31)	1·40
28.10.81	PO Pack No. 129c. 7p., 9p., 10½p., 12p. (photo), 13½p., 15p. (photo), 11½p., 14p. grey-blue, 18p. deep violet, 22p. blue (Nos. W23, W27, W30, W32/W35, W39, W46, W54)	6·00
3.8.83	PO Pack No. 3. 10p. (1 centre band), 12½p., 16p., 20½p., 26p. rosine, 28p. deep violet-blue (Nos. W29, W37, W43, W53, W61, W63)	14·00
23.10.84	PO Pack No. 7. 10p. (1 centre band), 13p., 16p., 17p. grey-blue, 22p. yellow-green, 26p. rosine, 28p. deep violet-blue, 31p. (Nos. W29, W38, W43a, W44, W55, W61, W63, W65)	12·00
3.3.87	PO Pack No. 11. 12p. (litho), 13p., 17p. grey-blue, 18p. deep olive-grey, 22p. yellow-green, 26p. rosine, 28p. deep violet-blue, 31p. (Nos. W36, W38, W44, W47, W55, W61a, W63a, W65)	15·00

Presentation Packs containing stamps of Northern Ireland, Scotland and Wales are listed after those for Northern Ireland.

(Des Jeffery Matthews after plaster cast by Arnold Machin. Litho Questa)

1993 (7 Dec)–**96**. Chalk-surfaced paper. Perf 15×14 (with one elliptical hole in each vertical side).

W70	**W4**	19p. bistre (1 centre band)	60	60
W71		19p. bistre (1 band at right) (25.4.95)	1·90	1·90
W72		20p. bright green (1 centre band) (23.7.96)	1·00	1·00
W73		25p. red (2 bands)	75	75
W74		26p. red-brown (2 bands) (23.7.96)	1·20	1·20
W75		30p. deep olive-grey (2 bands)	80	80
W76		37p. bright mauve (2 bands) (23.7.96)	1·60	1·60
W77		41p. grey-brown (2 bands)	1·40	1·40
W78		63p. light emerald (2 bands) (23.7.96)	3·50	3·50

No. W71 only comes from booklets.

First Day Covers

7.12.93	19p., 25p., 30p., 41p. (Nos. W70, W73, W75, W77)	3·75
23.7.96	20p., 26p., 37p., 63p. (Nos. W72, W74, W76, W78)	6·00

For Presentation Packs containing stamps of Northern Ireland, Scotland and Wales see after No. NI85 of Northern Ireland.

W5 Without 'p'

(Gravure Walsall (20p., 26p. (No. W80a), 63p.), Harrison or Walsall (26p. (No. W80), 37p.))

1997 (1 July)–**98**. Chalk-surfaced paper. Perf 14 (No. W79a) or 15×14 (others) (both with one elliptical hole in each vertical side).

W79	**W5**	20p. bright green (1 centre band)	80	80
W79a		20p. bright green (1 side band at right) (13.10.98)	3·25	3·25
W80		26p. chestnut (2 bands)	1·40	1·40
		a. Perf 14 (13.10.98)	3·25	3·25
W81		37p. bright mauve (2 bands)	1·75	1·75
W82		63p. light emerald (2 bands)	3·50	3·50

Nos. W79a and W80a were only issued in booklets.
The Harrison printings of Nos. W80/W81 come from booklet pane No. NI81l.

First Day Cover

1.7.97	20p., 26p., 37p., 63p. (Nos. W79, W80/W82)	6·00

Presentation Pack

1.7.97	PO Pack No. 39. 20p., 26p., 37p., 63p. (Nos. W79, W80/W82)	12·00

W6 Leek    **W7** Welsh Dragon

W8 Daffodil    **W9** Prince of Wales' Feathers

(Des David Petersen (Leek), Toby & Gideon Petersen (Welsh Dragon), Ieuan Rees (Daffodil), Rhiannon Evans (Prince of Wales' Feathers). Adapted Tutssels. Gravure De La Rue or Walsall (2nd, 1st), De La Rue (68p.), Walsall (others))

1999 (8 June)–**2002**. One phosphor band (2nd) or two phosphor bands (others). Perf 14 (No. W83a) or 15×14 (others) (both with one elliptical hole in each vertical side).

W83	**W6**	(2nd) Leek (1 centre band)	1·10	1·10
W83a		(2nd) Leek (1 band at right) (Perf 14) (18.9.2000)	2·25	2·25
		al. Booklet pane. No. 2124d and W83a, each×4, with centre label and margins all round	9·00	
W84	**W7**	(1st) Welsh dragon	1·75	1·75
W85	**W8**	(E) Daffodil	2·10	2·10
W86	**W9**	64p. Prince of Wales' Feathers	5·50	5·50
W87		65p. Prince of Wales' Feathers (25.4.2000)	2·50	2·50
W88		68p. Prince of Wales' Feathers (4.7.2002)	2·25	2·25

Presentation Pack (PO Pack No. 46) (2nd, 1st, E, 64p.) (Nos. W83, W84/W86)	9·00	
Presentation Pack (PO Pack No. 51) (65p.) (No. W87)	10·00	
Presentation Pack (PO Pack No. 56) (2nd, 1st, E, 65p.) (Nos. W83, W84/W85, W87)	16·00	
PHQ Cards (set of 4) (D13) (Nos. W83, W84/W86)	1·25	10·00

Nos. W83, W84 and W85 were initially sold at 19p., 26p. and 30p., the latter representing the basic European airmail rate.

New printings of Nos. W83 and W84, produced by De La Rue instead of Walsall, were issued on 28 May 2003 and 4 March 2003. Stamps from these printings do not differ from those produced by Walsall.

No. W83a comes from the £7 Treasury of Trees booklet (No. DX26).
For combined presentation pack for all four Regions, see under England.

First Day Covers

8.6.99	2nd (centre band), 1st, E, 64p. (Nos. W83, W84/W86) Philatelic Bureau	3·00
	Cardiff	3·25
25.4.00	65p. (No. W87) Philatelic Bureau	3·00
	Cardiff	3·50
18.9.00	Treasury of Trees *se-tenant* pane 1st (Millennium), 2nd (Nos. 2124d, W83a) Philatelic Bureau	5·00
	Llangernyw, Abergele	5·00
4.7.02	68p. (Nos. W88) Tallents House (Type K) (see Introduction)	2·50
	Cardiff	2·50

W10

(Des Jeffery Matthews. Gravure Walsall)

2000 (15 Feb). T **W4** redrawn with 1af/st face value as T **W10**. Two phosphor bands. Perf 14 (with one elliptical hole in each vertical side).

W97	**W10**	(1st) bright orange-red	1·60	1·60

No. W97 was only issued in £7·50 stamp booklet (No. DX24).

2003 (14 Oct)–**17**. As Nos. W83, W84/W85 and W88, and new values, but with white borders. One centre phosphor band (2nd) or two phosphor bands (others). Perf 15×14 (with one elliptical hole in each vertical side).

(a) (Gravure Walsall or De La Rue (42p.) or De La Rue (others)).

W98	**W6**	(2nd) Leek	1·10	1·10
W99	**W7**	(1st) Welsh Dragon	1·60	1·60
W100	**W8**	(E) Daffodil	2·25	2·25
W101		40p. Daffodil (11.5.04)	1·40	1·40
W102		42p. Daffodil (5.4.05)	2·00	2·00
W103		44p. Daffodil (28.3.06)	1·60	1·60
W104		48p. Daffodil (27.3.07)	1·10	1·10
W105		50p. Daffodil (1.4.08)	1·40	1·40
W106		56p. Daffodil (31.3.09)	1·50	1·50
W107		60p. Daffodil (30.3.10)	1·70	1·70
W108	**W9**	68p. Prince of Wales' Feathers	1·60	1·60
W109		72p. Prince of Wales' Feathers (28.3.06)	1·60	1·60
W110		78p. Prince of Wales' Feathers (27.3.07)	2·00	2·00
W111		81p. Prince of Wales' Feathers (1.4.08)	2·25	2·25

REGIONAL ISSUES/Wales

W112		90p. Prince of Wales Feathers (31.3.09)..	2·40	2·40
W113		97p. Prince of Wales Feathers (30.3.10)..	2·50	2·50

(b) Litho Enschedé, De La Rue or ISP Cartor (1st) or ISP Cartor (others).

W121	**W 6**	(2nd) Leek (1.13)...	1·40	1·40
W122	**W7**	(1st) Welsh Dragon (20.9.07).......................	1·60	1·60
W123	**W8**	68p. Daffodil (29.3.11)...................................	1·75	1·75
W124		87p Daffodil (25.4.12).....................................	2·25	2·25
W125		88p. Daffodil (27.3.13)...................................	2·25	2·25
W126		97p. Daffodil (26.3.14)...................................	2·50	2·50
W127		£1 Daffodil (24.3.15).......................................	2·50	2·50
W128		£1·05 Daffodil (22.3.16).................................	2·75	2·75
W129	**W9**	£1·10 Prince of Wales Feathers (29.3.11)..	2·50	2·50
W134		£1·28 Prince of Wales Feathers (25.4.12)..	2·75	2·75
W135		£1·33 Prince of Wales Feathers (24.3.15)..	2·75	2·75
Presentation Pack (PO Pack No. 65) (Nos. W98/W100, W108)..				5·00
PHQ Cards (set of 4) (D26) (Nos. W98/W100, W108)...........				5·00

The Walsall printing of No. W102 was issued on 5 April 2005 and the De La Rue on 24 May 2005.

Stamps as Nos. W110/W111 but printed in lithography were only issued within No. **MS**2796 (No. W110) or No. **MS**2886 (No. W111).

No. W122 was first issued in £7·66 stamp booklet, No. DX40 printed by Enschedé, then on 29 September 2008 in £9·72 booklet (No. DX43) printed by De La Rue and on 26 February 2009 in No. **MS**W147. It was issued in sheets printed by ISP Cartor in January 2013.

A design as No. W122 but self-adhesive was issued on 1 March 2007 in sheets of 20, each stamp accompanied by a *se-tenant* label showing a Welsh scene (No. LS37). These sheets were printed in lithography by Cartor, perforated 15×14 without the elliptical holes, and sold at £6·55 each. They were also available with personalised photographs on the labels at £14·95 from Royal Mail in Edinburgh.

Stamps as Nos. EN30, NI95, S131 and W122 but self-adhesive were issued on 29 September 2008 in sheets of 20 containing five of each design with *se-tenant* labels (No. LS49).

First Day Covers

14.10.03	2nd, 1st, E, 68p. (Nos. W98/W100, W108) Tallents House (Type K) (see Introduction).......................		3·25
	Cardiff...		3·25
11.5.04	40p. (No. W101) Tallents House (Type K)......................		1·75
	Cardiff...		1·75
5.4.05	42p. (No. W102) Tallents House (Type K)......................		2·00
	Cardiff...		2·00
28.3.06	44p., 72p. (Nos. W103, W109) Tallents House (Type K)		3·25
	Cardiff...		3·25
27.3.07	48p., 78p. (Nos. W104, W110) Tallents House (Type K)		3·50
	Cardiff...		3·50
1.4.08	50p., 81p. (Nos. W105, W111) Tallents House (Type K)		3·75
	Cardiff...		3·75
31.3.09	56p., 90p. (Nos. W106, W112) Tallents House (Type K)		4·00
	Cardiff...		4·00
30.3.10	60p., 97p. (Nos. W107, W113) Tallents House (Type K)		4·00
	Cardiff...		4·00
29.3.11	68p., £1·10 (Nos. W123, W129) Tallents House (Type K)		4·25
	Cardiff...		4·25
25.4.12	87p £1·28 (Nos. W124, W134) Tallents House (Type K)		5·00
	Cardiff...		5·00
27.3.13	88p. (No. W125) Tallents House (Type K)......................		2·25
	Cardiff...		2·25
26.3.14	97p. (No. W126) Tallents House (Type K)......................		2·50
	Cardiff...		2·50
24.3.15	£1, £1·33 (Nos. W127, W135) Tallents House (Type K).		5·25
	Cardiff...		5·25
22.3.16	£1·05 (No. W128) Tallents House (Type K)....................		2·75
	Cardiff...		2·75

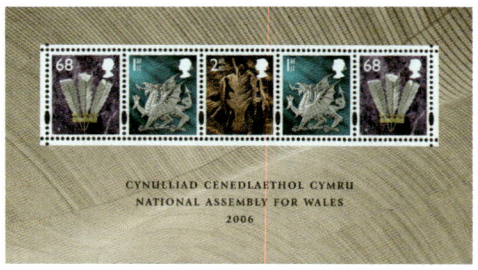

W10a

(Des Silk Pearce. Gravure De La Rue)

2006 (1 Mar). Opening of New Welsh Assembly Building, Cardiff. Sheet 123×70 mm. One centre phosphor band (2nd) or two phosphor bands (others). Perf 15×14 (with one elliptical hole in each vertical side).

MSW143	**W10a**	Nos. W98, W99×2 and W108×2................	4·50	4·50
First Day Cover (Tallents House)..				5·00
First Day Cover (Cardiff)..				5·00

W10b  **W10c**  **W10d**

(Litho De La Rue)

2008 (29 Sept). 50th Anniversary of the Country Definitives. Two phosphor bands. Perf 15×14½ (with one elliptical hole in each vertical side).

W144	**W10b**	(1st) deep lilac..	1·60	1·60
		l. Booklet pane. Nos. W144/W146 and W122×3	7·00	
W145	**W10c**	(1st) deep claret...	1·60	1·60
W146	**W10d**	(1st) green...	1·60	1·60

Nos. W144/W146 come from £9·72 booklet, No. DX43.

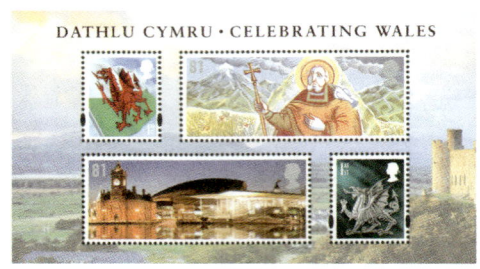

W11

(Des Clare Melinsky and Silk Pearce. Litho De La Rue)

2009 (26 Feb). Celebrating Wales. Sheet 123×70 mm. Two phosphor bands. Perf 15×14 (with one elliptical hole in each vertical side (1st) or 14½×14 (81p.).

MSW147 **W11**	(1st) Red Dragon; (1st) No. W122; 81p. St David; 81p. National Assembly for Wales, Cardiff......	4·25	4·25
First Day Cover (Tallents House)..			5·25
First Day Cover (St Davids)..			5·25
Presentation Pack (PO Pack No. 424)....................................		5·00	
PHQ Cards (set of 5) (CGB4)..		1·50	8·00

No. **MS**W147 was on sale at post offices throughout the UK.

Stamps as the 1st class Red Dragon stamp from No. **MS**W147 but self-adhesive were issued on 1 March 2010 in sheets of 20 with *se-tenant* labels showing Welsh Castles, No. LS71. These sheets were printed in lithography by ISP Cartor and sold for £8·35 each.

Miniature sheet collection containing Nos. **MS**EN50, **MS**NI152, **MS**S153 and **MS**W147 in a folder was available from 6 March 2009, sold at £31·95.

The five PHQ cards show the four individual stamps and the complete miniature sheet.

W12 Red Dragon

(Des Peter Crowther (illustrations) and Silk Pearce. Litho ISP Cartor or Enschedé)

2013 (9 May). Wales Flag. Two phosphor bands. Perf 14½×14 (with one elliptical hole in each vertical side).

W148	**W12**	(1st) Red Dragon..	4·00	4·00

No. W148 was issued in £11·11 Football Heroes booklet, No. DY7 (see booklet pane No. U3070l), £13·97 Classic Locomotives booklet, No. DY9 (see booklet pane No. U3071m) and £16·49 Centenary of the First World War (3rd issue), No. DY18 (booklet pane No. 3717a).

W13 Leek  **W14** Dragon  **W15** Daffodil  **W16** Prince of Wales' Feathers

Wales/Isle of Man/Channel Islands/Guernsey **REGIONAL ISSUES**

(Des David Petersen (Leek), Toby & Gideon Petersen (Welsh Dragon), Ieuan Rees (Daffodil), Rhiannon Evans (Prince of Wales' Feathers). Adapted Tussels. Litho Cartor)

2017 (21 Mar)–**20**. As previous set but with value indicated in revised typeface. One centre band (2nd) or two phosphor bands. Perf 15×14 (with one elliptical hole in each vertical side).

W149	**W13**	(2nd) Leek (20.3.18)	1·00	75
W150	**W14**	(1st) Dragon (20.3.18)	1·25	75
W151	**W15**	£1·17 Daffodil (21.3.17)	2·75	2·75
W152		£1·25 Daffodil (20.3.18)	2·75	2·75
W153		£1·35 Daffodil (19.3.19)	2·75	2·75
W156	**W16**	£1·40 Prince of Wales Feathers (21.3.17)	3·00	3·00
W157	**W15**	£1·42 Daffodil (17.3.20)	2·50	2·50
W158	**W16**	£1·45 Prince of Wales Feathers (20.3.18)	3·25	3·25
W159		£1·55 Prince of Wales' Feathers (19.3.19)	3·25	3·25
W160		£1·63 Prince of Wales Feathers (17.3.20)	2·75	2·75
W161		£1·70 Daffodil (23.12.20)	2·40	2·40

Numbers have been left for possible additions to the above definitive series.

First Day Covers

21.3.17	£1·17, £1·40 (Nos. W151, W156) Tallents House (Type K)	6·00
	Cardiff	6·00
20.3.18	2nd, 1st, £1·25, £1·45. (Nos. W149/W150, W152, W158) Tallents House (Type K)	9·00
	Cardiff	9·00
19.3.19	£1·35, £1·55. (Nos. W153, W159) Tallents House (Type K)	7·00
	Cardiff	7·00
17.3.20	£1·42, £1·63 (Nos. W157, W160) Tallents House (Type K)	7·00
	Cardiff	7·00
23.12.20	£1·70 (W61) Tallents House (Type K)	3·75
	Cardiff	3·75

V. Isle of Man

Although specifically issued for use in the Isle of Man, these issues were also valid for use throughout Great Britain.

(Des John Hobson Nicholson. Portrait by Dorothy Wilding Ltd. Photo Harrison)

1958 (18 Aug)–**68**. W **179**. Perf 15×14.

1	**1**	2½d. carmine-red (8.6.64)	70	70
2	**2**	3d. deep lilac (18.8.58)	50	50
		a. Chalk-surfaced paper (17.5.63)	6·50	6·50
		p. One centre phosphor band (27.6.68)	20	20
3		4d. ultramarine (7.2.66)	1·00	1·00
		p. Two phosphor bands (5.7.67)	30	30
Set of 3 (cheapest)			1·00	1·00
First Day Cover 3d. (18.8.58)				32·00
First Day Cover 2½d. (8.6.64)				45·00
First Day Cover 4d. (7.2.66)				15·00

No. 2a was released in London sometime after 17 May 1963, this being the date of issue in Douglas.
For No. 2 in Presentation Pack, see Regional issues below Wales No. W6.

Frame flaw (Cyl. 1 no dot, R. 20/1)

3

1968-69. No wmk, Chalk-surfaced paper. One centre phosphor band (Nos. 5/6) or two phosphor bands (others). P 15×14.

4	**2**	4d. blue (24.6.68)	25	25
5		4d. olive-sepia (4.9.68)	30	30
		y. Phosphor omitted	25·00	
6		4d. bright vermilion (26.2.69)	45	45
7		5d. royal blue (4.9.68)	45	45
		a. Frame flaw	25·00	
		y. Phosphor omitted	£175	
4/7 Set of 4			1·25	1·25
First Day Cover 4d., 5d. (4.9.68)				4·00

(Des J. Matthews. Portrait after plaster cast by Arnold Machin. Photo Harrison)

1971 (7 July). Decimal Currency. Chalk-surfaced paper. One centre phosphor band (2½p.) or two phosphor bands (others). Perf 15×14.

8	**3**	2½p. bright magenta	30	30
		y. Phosphor omitted	£1500	
9		3p. ultramarine	30	30
10		5p. reddish violet	70	70
		y. Phosphor omitted	£275	
11		7½p. chestnut	80	80
8/11 Set of 4			1·90	1·90
First Day Cover 2½p., 3p., 5p., 7p½. (7.7.71)				3·50
Presentation Pack			2·50	

All values were originally issued on ordinary cream paper, but the 2½p. and 3p. later appeared on white fluorescent paper.

Nos. 9/11 and current stamps of Great Britain were withdrawn from sale on the island from 5 July 1973 when the independent postal administration was established bt remained valid for use there for a time. They also remained on sale at the Philatelic Sales counters in the United Kingdom until 4 July 1974.

VI. Channel Islands

General Issues

C1 Gathering Vraic (seaweed) **C2** Islanders gathering Vraic

Broken Wheel (R.20/5)

(Des J. R. R. Stobie (1d.) or from drawing by Edmund Blampied (2½d.). Photo Harrison and Sons)

1948 (10 May). Third Anniversary of Liberation. W **127** of Great Britain. Perf 15×14.

C1	**C1**	1d. scarlet	25	55
C2	**C2**	2½d. ultramarine	25	60
		a. Broken wheel	75·00	
First Day Cover				35·00

VII. Guernsey

GERMAN OCCUPATION ISSUES, 1940-1945

BISECTS. On 24 December 1940 authority was given, by Post Office notice, that prepayment of penny postage could be effected by using half a British 2d. stamp, diagonally bisected. Such stamps were first used on 27 December 1940.

The 2d. stamps generally available were those of the Postal Centenary issue, 1940 (SG 482) and the first colour of the King George VI issue (SG 465). These are listed under Nos. 482a and 465b. A number of the 2d. King George V, 1912–22, and of the King George V photogravure stamp (SG 442) which were in the hands of philatelists, were also bisected and used.

1 Arms of Guernsey

1a Loops (half actual size)

REGIONAL ISSUES/Guernsey/Jersey

(Des E. W. Vaudin. Typo Guernsey Press Co Ltd)

1941–44. Rouletted.

(a) White paper. No wmk.

1	1	½d. light green (7.4.41)	6·00	3·50
		a. Emerald-green (6.41)	6·00	3·50
		b. Bluish green (11.41)	35·00	15·00
		c. Bright green (2.42)	25·00	12·00
		d. Dull green (9.42)	5·00	3·50
		e. Olive-green (2.43)	45·00	25·00
		f. Pale yellowish green (7.43 and later) (*shades*)	5·00	3·50
		g. Imperf (pair)	£250	
		h. Imperf between (horizontal pair)	£800	
		i. Imperf between (vertical pair)	£950	
2		1d. scarlet (18.2.41)	3·25	2·00
		a. Pale vermilion (7.43) (etc)	5·00	2·00
		b. Carmine (1943)	3·50	2·00
		c. Imperf (pair)	£200	90·00
		d. Imperf between (horizontal pair)	£800	
		da. Imperf vert (centre stamp of horizontal strip of 3)		
		e. Imperf between (vertical pair)	£950	
		f. Ptd double (scarlet shade)	£150	
3		2½d. ultramarine (12.4.44)	18·00	15·00
		a. Pale ultramarine (7.44)	15·00	10·00
		b. Imperf (pair)	£550	
		c. Imperf between (horizontal pair)	£1250	
1 First Day Cover				15·00
2 First Day Cover				20·00
3 First Day Cover				10·00

*(b) Bluish French banknote paper. W **1a** (sideways).*

4	1	½d. bright green (11.3.42)	32·00	25·00
5		1d. scarlet (9.4.42)	18·00	25·00
4 First Day Cover				£325
5 First Day Cover				£125

The dates given for the shades of Nos. 1/3 are the months in which they were printed as indicated on the printer's imprints. Others are issue dates.

REGIONAL ISSUES

2    **3** 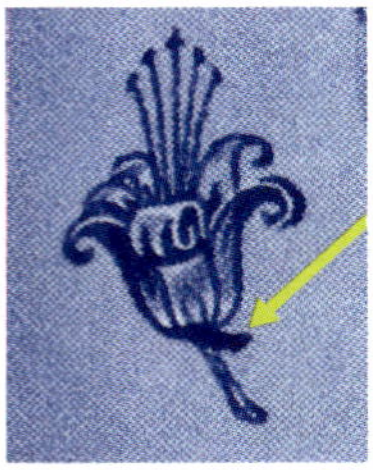   Stem flaw (Cyl. 1 no dot, R. 12/8)

(Des Eric A Piprell. Portrait by Dorothy Wilding Ltd. Photo Harrison & Sons)

1958 (18 Aug)–**67**. W **179** of Great Britain. Perf 15×14.

6	2	2½d. rose-red (8.6.64)	40	40
7	3	3d. deep lilac	30	30
		p. One centre phosphor band (24.5.67)	30	30
8		4d. ultramarine (7.2.66)	40	40
		a. Stem Flaw	25·00	
		p. Two phosphor bands (24.10.67)	20	20
		pa. Stem flaw	25·00	
6/8p Set of 3			1·00	1·00
6 First Day Cover				30·00
7 First Day Cover				20·00
8 First Day Cover				8·00

For No. 7 in Presentation Pack, see Regional Issues below Wales No. W6.

1968–69. No wmk. Chalk-surfaced paper. PVA gum*. One centre phosphor band (Nos. 10/11) or two phosphors bands (others). Perf 15×14.

9	3	4d. pale ultramarine (16.4.68)	20	20
		Ey. Phosphor omitted	50·00	
		a. Stem Flaw	25·00	
		y. Phosphor omitted	50·00	
10		4d. olive-sepia (4.9.68)	20	20
		Ey. Phosphor omitted	50·00	
		a. Stem Flaw	25·00	
		y. Phosphor omitted	50·00	
11		4d. bright vermilion (26.2.69)	20	20
12		5d. royal blue (4.9.68)	30	30
9/12 Set of 4			80	80
10, 12 First Day Cover				3·00

No. 9 was not issued in Guernsey until 22 April.
* PVA Gum. See note after No. 722 of Great Britain.

VIII. Jersey

GERMAN OCCUPATION ISSUES, 1940–1949

5 Arms of Jersey

(Des Major Norman Victor Lacey Rybot. Typo *Jersey Evening Post*)

1941–43. Stamps issued during the German Occupation White paper. No wmk. Perf 11 (line).

1	5	½d. bright green (29.1.42)	8·00	6·00
		a. Imperf between (vertical pair)	£900	
		b. Imperf between (horizontal pair)	£800	
		c. Imperf (pair)	£300	
		d. On greyish paper (1.43)	12·00	12·00
2		1d. scarlet (1.4.41)	8·00	5·00
		a. Imperf between (vertical pair)	£900	
		b. Imperf between (horizontal pair)	£800	
		c. Imperf (pair)	£325	
		d. On chalk-surfaced paper (9.41)	55·00	48·00
		e. On greyish paper (1.43)	14·00	14·00

First Day Covers

1.4.41	1d.		8·00
29.1.42	½d.		7·50

6 Old Jersey Farm    **7** Portelet Bay

8 Corbière Lighthouse    **9** Elizabeth Castle

10 Mont Orgueil Castle    **11** Gathering Vraic (seaweed)

(Des Edmund Blampied. Eng H. Cortot. Typo French Govt Ptg Works, Paris)

1943–44. No wmk. Perf 13½.

3	6	½d. Old Jersey Farm (1.6.43)	12·00	12·00
		a. Rough, grey paper (6.10.43)	15·00	14·00
4	7	1d. Portelet Bay (1.6.43)	3·00	50
		a. On newsprint (28.2.44)	3·50	75
5	8	1½d. Corbière Lighthouse (8.6.43)	8·00	5·75
6	9	2d. Elizabeth Castle (8.6.43)	7·50	2·00
7	10	2½d. Mont Orgueil Castle (29.6.43)	3·00	1·00
		a. On newsprint (25.2.44)	1·00	1·75
		ba. Thin paper (design shows through on reverse)	£225	
8	11	3d. Gathering Vraic (seaweed) (29.6.43)	3·00	2·75
3/8 Set of 6			30·00	21·00
Set of 6 Gutter Pairs			80·00	
First Day Covers (3)				36·00

* On No. 7ba the design shows clearly through the back of the stamp.

12    **13**

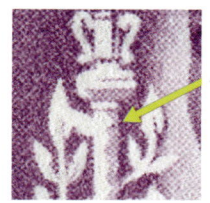

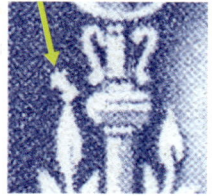

Halberd flaw (Cyl. 1 no dot, R. 20/23)

Leaf flaw (cyl. 1 no dot, R. 3/6)

(Des. Edmund Blampied (T **12**), W. Gardner (T **13**). Portrait by Dorothy Wilding Ltd. Photo Harrison & Sons)

1958 (18 Aug)–**67**. W **179** of Great Britain. Perf 15×14.

9	**12**	2½d. carmine-red (8.6.64)	45	45
		a. Imperf three sides (pair)	£3250	
10	**13**	3d. deep lilac (18.8.58)	30	30
		a. Halberd Flaw	25·00	
		p. One centre phosphor band (9.6.67)	20	20
11		4d. ultramarine (7.2.66)	25	25
		a. Leaf Flaw	25·00	
		p. Two phosphor bands (5.9.67)	25	25
9/11 Set of 3			80	80
18.5.58 3d. *First Day Cover*				20·00
8.6.64 2½d. *First Day Cover*				30·00
7.2.66 4d. *First Day Cover*				10·00

1968–69. No wmk. Chalk-surfaced paper. One centre phosphor band (4d. values) or two phosphor bands (5d.). Perf 15×14.

1968–69. No wmk. Chalk-surfaced paper. PVA gum*. One centre phosphor band (4d. values) or two phosphor bands (5d.). Perf 15×14.

12	**13**	4d. olive-sepia (4.9.68)	20	20
		Ey. Phosphor omitted	£1100	
13		4d. bright vermilion (26.2.69)	20	20
14		5d. royal blue (4.9.68)	20	20
12/14 Set of 3			50	50
Set of 3			50	50
4.9.68 4d., 5d. *First Day Cover*				3·00

* PVA Gum. See note after No. 722 of Great Britain.

POSTAL FISCAL STAMPS

POSTAL FISCAL STAMPS

PRICES. Prices in the used column are for stamps with genuine postal cancellations dated from the time when they were authorised for use as postage stamps. Beware of stamps with fiscal cancellations removed and fraudulent postmarks applied.

VALIDITY. The 1d. surface-printed stamps were authorised for postal use from 1 June 1881 and at the same time the 1d. postage issue, No. 166, was declared valid for fiscal purposes. The 3d. and 6d. values together with the embossed issues were declared valid for postal purposes by another Act effective from 1 January 1883.

SURFACE-PRINTED ISSUES

(Typo Thomas De La Rue & Co)

F1 Rectangular Buckle **F2**

F3 Octagonal Buckle **F4**

F5 Double-lined Anchor **F6** Single-lined Anchor

1853–57. Perf 15½×15.

(a) Wmk **F5** (inverted) (1853–1855).

			Unused	Used	Used on cover
F1	F1	1d. light blue (10.10.53)	50·00	65·00	£225
		Wi. Watermark upright	£180	—	
		Wj. Watermark reversed*	£180	—	
F2	F2	1d. ochre (10.53)	£130	£160	£600
		a. Tête-bêche (in block of four)	—	—	
		Wi. Watermark upright	—	—	
F3	F3	1d. pale turquoise-blue (12.53)	45·00	60·00	£350
F4		1d. light blue/*blue* (12.53)	90·00	95·00	£550
		Wi. Watermark upright	£160	£225	
F5	F4	1d. reddish lilac/*blue glazed paper* (25.3.55)	£130	£160	£450
		Wi. Watermark upright	£200	£300	

* Watermark reversed: with the stamp upright and viewed from the front, the cable finishes to the right of the base of the anchor shaft. Only one example is known of No. F2a outside The Postal Museum and the Royal Philatelic Collection.

(b) Wmk **F6** (1856–1857).

			Unused	Used	Used on cover
F6	F4	1d. reddish lilac (shades)	12·00	9·50	£180
		Wi. Watermark inverted	£160	—	
		Wj. Watermark reversed	£180	—	
		s. Optd 'SPECIMEN' (2)	£170		
F7		1d. reddish lilac/*bluish* (shades) (1857)	12·00	9·50	£180
		Wj. Watermark reversed	£180	—	

INLAND REVENUE

(**F7**)

1860 (3 Apr). No. F7 optd with T **F7**, in red

			Unused	Used	Used on cover
F8	F4	1d. dull reddish lilac/*blue*	£950	£725	£1500
		Wj. Wmk reversed	—	—	

BLUE PAPER. In the following issues we no longer distinguish between bluish and white paper. There is a range of papers from white or greyish to bluish.

F8 F9

F10

1860–67. Bluish to white Paper. Perf 15½×15.

(a) Wmk **F6** (1860).

			Unused	Used	Used on cover
F9	F8	1d. reddish lilac (5.60)	14·00	18·00	£180
		Wi. Watermark inverted	£130	—	
		s. Optd 'SPECIMEN' (2)	£180		
F10	F9	3d. reddish lilac (6.60)	£550	£340	£550
		s. Optd 'SPECIMEN' (2)	£240		
F11	F10	6d. reddish lilac (10.60)	£225	£225	£450
		Wi. Watermark inverted	£275	£225	
		Wj. Watermark reversed	£275	£225	
		s. Optd 'SPECIMEN' (2)	£225		

(b) W **40**. (Anchor 16 mm high) (1864).

			Unused	Used	Used on cover
F12	F8	1d. pale reddish lilac (11.64)	12·00	14·00	£180
		Wi. Watermark inverted	—	—	
F13	F9	3d. pale reddish lilac	£275	£200	£550
		s. Optd 'SPECIMEN' (9)	£225		
F14	F10	6d. pale reddish lilac	£250	£200	£550
		Wi. Watermark inverted	£350	—	

(c) W **40**. (Anchor 18 mm high) (1867).

			Unused	Used	Used on cover
F15	F8	1d. reddish lilac	25·00	27·00	£275
F16	F9	3d. reddish lilac	£120	£120	£450
		s. Optd 'SPECIMEN' (9, 10)	£190		
F17	F10	6d. reddish lilac	£110	95·00	£300
		s. Optd 'SPECIMEN' (9, 10)	£190		

For stamps perf 14, see Nos. F24/F27.

F11 F12

Nos. F19/F21 show 'O' of 'ONE' circular. No. F22 (Die 4) shows a horizontal oval

POSTAL FISCAL STAMPS

Four Dies of T **F12**

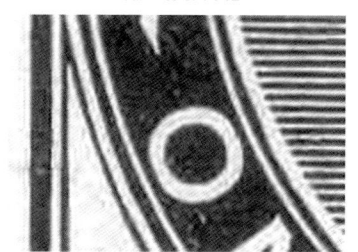

Round 'O' (Dies 1 to 3)

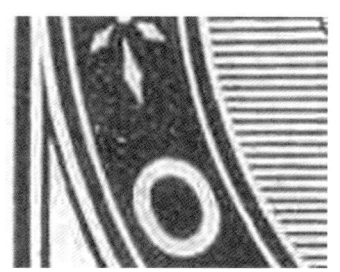

Oval 'O' (Die 4)

Small corner ornaments (Dies 1 and 2)

Medium corner ornaments (Die 3)

Large corner ornaments (Die 4)

Four lines of shading In left-hand ribbon (Die 1)

Two lines of shading in left-hand ribbon (Die 2)

Three lines of shading In left-hand ribbon (Die 3)

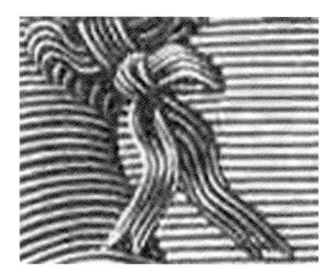

Heavy shading in both ribbons (Die 4)

Band of crown shaded (Dies 1 and 2)

POSTAL FISCAL STAMPS

F13   F14

F15

Band of crown unshaded (Die 3)

Band of crown unshaded at front only (Die 4)

Die 1: Round 'O' in 'ONE'. Small corner ornaments. Four lines of shading in left-hand ribbon. Band of crown shaded
Die 2: Round 'O' in 'ONE'. Small corner ornaments. Two lines of shading in left-hand ribbon. Band of crown shaded
Die 3: Round 'O' in 'ONE'. Medium corner ornaments. Three lines of shading in left-hand ribbon. Band of crown unshaded
Die 4: Oval 'O' in 'ONE'. Large corner ornaments. Heavy shading in both ribbons. Band of crown unshaded at front only

1867–81. White to bluish paper. Perf 14.

*(a) W **47** (Small Anchor).*

			Unsed	Used	Used on cover
F18	F11	1d. purple (1.9.67)	22·00	24·00	£140
		Wi. Watermark inverted	£130	—	
F19	F12	1d. purple (Die I) (6.68)	7·50	9·00	£140
		s. Optd 'SPECIMEN' (6, 9, 10)	60·00		
		Wi. Watermark inverted	90·00		
F20		1d. purple (Die 2) (6.76)	27·00	22·00	£300
		s. Optd 'SPECIMEN' (9)	£110		
F21		1d. purple (Die 3) (3.77)	14·00	18·00	£220
		s. Optd 'SPECIMEN' (9)	90·00		
F22		1d. purple (Die 4) (7.78)	8·50	10·00	£120

*(b) W **48** (Orb).*

F23	F12	1d. purple (Die 4) (1.81)	8·50	5·00	£110
		Wi. Watermark inverted	£130	—	

1881. White to bluish paper. Perf 14.

*(a) W **40** (Anchor 18 mm high) (January).*

			Unused	Used	Used on cover
F24	F9	3d. reddish lilac	£850	£525	£1000
F25	F10	6d. reddish lilac	£400	£225	£450

*(b) W **40** (Anchor 20 mm high) (May).*

F26	F9	3d. £625	£625	£425	£700
		s. Optd 'SPECIMEN' (9)	£350		
F27	F10	6d. £350	£350	£200	£450
		s. Optd 'SPECIMEN' (9)	£300		

ISSUES EMBOSSED IN COLOUR

(Made at Somerset House)

The embossed stamps were struck from dies not appropriated to any special purpose on paper which had the words 'INLAND REVENUE' previously printed, and thus became available for payment of any duties for which no special stamps had been provided.

The die letters are included in the embossed designs and holes were drilled for the insertion of plugs showing figures indicating dates of striking.

1860 (3 Apr)–**71**. Types **F13/F14** and similar types embossed on bluish paper. No wmk. Imperf.

F28	2d. pink (Die A) (1.1.71)	£775
	s. Optd 'SPECIMEN' (2, 9)	£200
F29	3d. pink (Die C)	£200
	a. Tête-bêche (vertical pair)	£1700
F30	3d. pink (Die D)	£775
F31	6d. pink (Die T)	
F32	6d. pink (Die U)	£400
	a. Tête-bêche (vertical pair)	
F33	9d. pink (Die C) (1.1.71)	£1000
	s. Optd 'SPECIMEN' (2, 9)	£200
F34	1s. pink (Die E) (28.6.61)	£775
	a. Tête-bêche (vertical pair)	
F35	1s. pink (Die F) (28.6.61)	£300
	a. Tête-bêche (vertical pair)	£1200
	s. Optd 'SPECIMEN' (2, 9)	£200
F36	2s. pink (Die K) (6.8.61)	£775
F37	2s.6d. pink (Die N) (28.6.61)	
F38	2s.6d. pink (Die O) (28.6.61)	£400
	s. Optd 'SPECIMEN' (2, 9)	£200

1871 (Aug). As last but perf 12½.

F39	2d. pink (Die A)	£500
	a. Tête-bêche (vertical pair)	
	s. Optd 'SPECIMEN' (9)	£120
F42	9d. pink (Die C)	£1200
	s. Optd 'SPECIMEN' (9)	£200
F43	1s. pink (Die E)	£775
F44	1s. pink (Die F)	£700
	s. Optd 'SPECIMEN' (9)	£200
F45	2s.6d. pink (Die O)	£400
	s. Optd 'SPECIMEN' (9)	£200

1874 (Nov). T **F15** embossed on white paper. Underprint in green. W **47** (Small Anchor). P 12½.

F48	1s. pink (Die F)	£775

1875 (Nov)–**80**. Types **F13/F15** and similar but colour changed and underprint as T **F15**. On white or bluish paper.

F50	2d. vermilion (Die A) (1880)	£600
	s. Optd 'SPECIMEN' (9)	£200
F51	9d. vermilion (Die C) (1876)	£775
	s. Optd 'SPECIMEN' (9, 10)	£200
F52	1s. vermilion (Die E)	£500
	s. Optd 'SPECIMEN' (9, 10)	£200
F53	1s. vermilion (Die F)	£1200
F54	2s.6d. vermilion (Die O) (1878)	£500
	s. Optd 'SPECIMEN' (9)	£200

1882 (Oct). As last but W **48** (Orbs).

F55	2d. vermilion (Die A)	†	
	s. Optd 'SPECIMEN' (9)	£225	
F56	9d. vermilion (Die C)	†	
	s. Optd 'SPECIMEN' (9)	£225	
F57	1s. vermilion (Die E)	†	
	s. Optd 'SPECIMEN' (9)	£225	
F58	2s.6d. vermilion (Die O)	£1000	£775
	s. Optd 'SPECIMEN' (9)	£225	

Although specimen overprints of Nos. F55/F57 are known there is some doubt if these values were issued.

The sale of Inland Revenue stamps up to the 2s. value ceased from 30 December 1882 and stocks were called in and destroyed. The 2s.6d. value remained on sale until 2 July 1883 when it was replaced by the 2s.6d. 'Postage & Revenue' stamp. Inland Revenue stamps still in the hands of the public continued to be accepted for revenue and postal purposes.

POSTAGE DUE STAMPS

PERFORATIONS. All postage due stamps to No. D101 are perf 14×15.

WATERMARK. The watermark always appears sideways and this is the "normal" listed in this Catalogue for Nos. D1/D68. Varieties occur as follows. The point of identification is which way the top of the crown points, but (where they occur) the disposition of the letters needs to be noted also. The meaning of the terms is given below: (1) as described and illustrated in the Catalogue, i.e. as read through the front of the stamp, and (2) what is seen during watermark detection when the stamp is face down and the back is under examination.

Watermark	Crown pointing (1) As described	Letters reading
Sideways	left	upwards
Sideways-inverted	right	downwards
Sideways and reversed	left	downwards, back to front
Sideways-inverted and reversed	right	upwards, back to front
	(2) As detected (stamp face down)	
Sideways	right	upwards, back to front
Sideways-inverted	left	downwards, back to front
Sideways and reversed	right	downwards
Sideways-inverted and reversed	left	upward

St Edward's Crown Watermark — **Multiple Crowns Watermark**

Sideways watermarks *as viewed from the back of the stamp*

St Edward's Crown Watermark — **Multiple Crowns Watermark**

Sideways inverted watermarks *as viewed from the back of the stamp*

D1 ½d. — **D2** 2/6

(Des G. Eve. Typo Somerset House (early trial printings of ½d., 1d., 2d. and 5d.; all printings of 1s.) or Harrison (later printings of all values except 1s.).

1914 (20 Apr)–**22**. W **100** (Simple Cypher) sideways.

			Unmtd mint	Mtd mint	Used
D1	D1	½d. emerald	1·50	50	25
		Wi. Watermark sideways-inverted	5·00	2·00	2·00
		Wj. Watermark sideways and reversed	30·00	18·00	20·00
		Wk. Watermark sideways-inverted and reversed			20·00
		s. Overprinted *'SPECIMEN'* (23)		45·00	
D2		1d. carmine	1·50	50	25
		a. Pale carmine	1·50	75	50
		Wi. Watermark sideways-inverted	5·00	2·00	2·00
		Wj. Watermark sideways and reversed			20·00
		Wk. Watermark sideways-inverted and reversed	30·00	18·00	20·00
		s. Overprinted *'SPECIMEN'* (23)		45·00	
D3		1½d. chestnut (1922)	£190	48·00	20·00
		Wi. Watermark sideways-inverted	£190	70·00	24·00
D4		2d. agate	1·50	50	25
		Wi. Watermark sideways-inverted	7·00	3·75	3·75
		Wk. Watermark sideways-inverted and reversed	28·00	18·00	18·00
		s. Overprinted *'SPECIMEN'* (23, 26)		40·00	
D5		3d. violet (1918)	28·00	9·00	75
		a. Bluish violet	28·00	10·00	2·75
		Wi. Watermark sideways-inverted	80·00	40·00	40·00
		Wk. Watermark sideways-inverted and reversed			
		s. Overprinted *'SPECIMEN'* (23, 26)		45·00	
D6		4d. dull grey-green (12.20)	£300	£150	50·00
		Wi. Watermark sideways-inverted	£150	40·00	5·00
		s. Overprinted *'SPECIMEN'* (23)		45·00	
D7		5d. brownish cinnamon	23·00	7·00	3·50
		Wi. Watermark sideways-inverted	45·00	20·00	20·00
		s. Overprinted *'SPECIMEN'* (23, 30)		45·00	
D8		1s. bright blue (1915)	£150	40·00	5·00
		a. Deep bright blue	£150	40·00	5·00
		Wi. Watermark sideways-inverted	£150	40·00	40·00
		Wk. Watermark sideways-inverted and reversed			
		s. Overprinted *'SPECIMEN'* (23, 26)		45·00	
Set of 8			£450	£130	32·00

Stamps from the above issue are known bisected and used for half their face value at the following sorting offices:

1d. Barrhead (1922), Bristol (1918), Cowes (1923), Elgin (1921), Kidlington (1922, 1923), Kilburn, London NW (1923), Malvern (1915), Palmers Green, London N (1922), Plaistow, London E (1916), River, Dover (1922), Rock Ferry, Birkenhead (1915, 1918), St Ouens, Jersey (1924), Salford, Manchester (1914), South Tottenham, London N (1921), Warminster (1922), Wavertree, Liverpool (1921), Whitchurch (1922), Winton, Bournemouth (1921), Wood Green, London N (1921)

2d. Anerley, London SE (1921), Bethnal Green, London E (1918), Christchurch (1921), Didcot (1919), Ealing, London W (1921), Hythe, Southampton (1923), Kirkwall (1922), Ledbury (1922), Malvern (1921, 1923), Sheffield (1921), Shipley (1922), Streatham, London SW (1921), Victoria Docks and North Woolwich (1921), West Kensington, London W (1921, 1922)

3d. Malvern (trisected and used for 1d.) (1921), Warminster (1922)

(Typo Waterlow)

1924. As 1914–1922, but on thick chalk-surfaced paper.

			Unmtd mint	Mtd mint	Used
D9	D1	1d. carmine	15·00	6·00	6·00
		Wi. Watermark sideways-inverted			

(Typo Waterlow and (from 1934) Harrison)

1924–31. W **111** (Block Cypher) sideways.

			Unmtd mint	Mtd mint	Used
D10	D1	½d. emerald (6.25)	2·50	1·25	75
		Wi. Watermark sideways-inverted	10·00	5·00	2·50
		s. Overprinted *'SPECIMEN'* (23, 26, 30)		45·00	
D11		1d. carmine (4.25)	2·50	60	25
		Wi. Watermark sideways-inverted	—	—	30·00
		s. Overprinted *'SPECIMEN'* (23, 26, 30)		55·00	
D12		1½d. chestnut (10.24)	£160	48·00	22·00
		Wi. Watermark sideways-inverted	—	—	75·00
		s. Overprinted *'SPECIMEN'* (23)		55·00	
D13		2d. agate (7.24)	9·00	1·00	25
		Wi. Watermark sideways-inverted	—	—	30·00
		s. Overprinted *'SPECIMEN'* (23, 30)		45·00	
D14		3d. dull violet (10.24)	15·00	1·50	25
		a. Printed on gummed side	£150	£125	†
		Wi. Wmk sideways-inverted	—	—	40·00
		s. Overprinted *'SPECIMEN'* (23)		55·00	

453

POSTAGE DUE STAMPS

			Unmtd mint	Mtd mint	Used
		c. Experimental paper W111a	£175	95·00	95·00
D15		4d. dull grey-green (10.24)	70·00	15·00	4·25
		Wi. Watermark sideways-inverted	£100	40·00	40·00
		s. Overprinted 'SPECIMEN' (23, 26)		55·00	
D16		5d. brownish cinnamon (1.31)	£175	65·00	45·00
D17		1s. deep blue (9.24)	60·00	8·50	50
		Wi. Watermark sideways-inverted			
		s. Overprinted 'SPECIMEN' (23)		55·00	
D18	D2	2s.6d. purple/yellow (5.24)	£275	85·00	1·75
		Wi. Watermark sideways-inverted	£750	—	90·00
		s. Overprinted 'SPECIMEN' (23, 30)	£450		55·00
Set of 9					

Stamps from the above issue are known bisected and used for half their face value at the following sorting offices:
1d. Ashton under Lyne (1932), Hastings (1930), Penryn, Cornwall (1928), Shenfield (1926), Wimbledon, London SW (1925)
2d. Perranwell Station (1932)

1936–37. W **125** (E 8 R) sideways.

D19	D1	½d. emerald (6.37)		15·00	10·50
D20		1d. carmine (5.37)		2·00	1·75
D21		2d. agate (5.37)		15·00	12·00
D22		3d. dull violet (3.37)		2·00	2·00
		s. Overprinted 'SPECIMEN' (30)			
D23		4d. dull grey-green (12.36)		65·00	35·00
		s. Overprinted 'SPECIMEN'			
D24		5d. brownish cinnamon (11.36)		90·00	30·00
		a. Yellow-brown (1937)		40·00	28·00
		s. Overprinted 'SPECIMEN' (30)			
D25		1s. deep blue (12.36)		25·00	8·50
		s. Overprinted 'SPECIMEN' (30)			
D26	D2	2s.6d. purple/yellow (5.37)		£325	12·00
Set of 8 (cheapest)				£450	£100

The 1d. of the above issue is known bisected and used for half its face value at the following sorting office:
1d. Solihull (1937)

1937–38. W **127** (G VI R) sideways.

D27	D1	½d. emerald (5.38)		13·00	3·75
		s. Overprinted 'SPECIMEN' (9, 30)			
D28		1d. carmine (5.38)		3·00	50
		Wi. Watermark sideways-inverted		£250	—
		s. Overprinted 'SPECIMEN' (9, 30)			
D29		2d. agate (5.38)		2·75	30
		Wi. Watermark sideways-inverted		£150	—
		s. Overprinted 'SPECIMEN' (9, 30)			
D30		3d. violet (12.37)		11·00	30
		Wi. Watermark sideways-inverted		£150	—
		s. Overprinted 'SPECIMEN' (9, 30)			
D31		4d. dull grey-green (9.37)		£110	10·00
		Wi. Watermark sideways-inverted		£300	—
		s. Overprinted 'SPECIMEN' (9, 30)			
D32		5d. yellow-brown (11.38)		17·00	75
		Wi. Watermark sideways-inverted		£150	—
		s. Overprinted 'SPECIMEN' (9, 30)			
D33		1s. deep blue (10.37)		80·00	75
		Wi. Watermark sideways-inverted		£150	—
		s. Overprinted 'SPECIMEN' (9, 30)			
D34	D2	2s.6d. purple/yellow (9.38)		85·00	1·25
Set of 8				£300	16·00

The 2d. from the above issue is known bisected and used for half its face value at the following sorting offices:
2d. Robin Hood's Bay Station, Yorks (1938), Boreham Wood (1951), Camberley (1951), Harpenden (1951, 1954), St Albans (1951)

> **DATES OF ISSUE.** The dates for Nos. D35/D39 are those on which stamps were first issued by the Supplies Department to postmasters.

1951–54. Colours changed and new value (1½d.). W **127** (G VI R) sideways.

D35	D1	½d. yellow-orange (18.9.51)		3·50	3·50
		a. Bright orange (5.54)		75·00	
D36		1d. violet-blue (6.6.51)		1·50	75
		Wi. Watermark sideways-inverted			
D37		1½d. green (11.2.52)		2·00	2·00
		Wi. Watermark sideways-inverted		£140	£140
D38		4d. blue (14.8.51)		50·00	22·00
		Wi. Watermark sideways inverted		†	£1000
D39		1s. ochre (6.12.51)		28·00	5·25
		Wi. Watermark sideways-inverted		£2800	—
Set of 5				75·00	30·00

The 1d. of the above issue is known bisected and used for half its face value at the following sorting offices:
1d. Camberley (1954), Capel, Dorking (1952)

1954–55. W **153** (Tudor Crown) sideways.

D40	D1	½d. bright orange (8.6.55)	7·00	5·25
		Wi. Watermark sideways-inverted	£150	£150
D41		2d. agate (28.7.55)	26·00	23·00
		Wi. Watermark sideways-inverted	—	—
D42		3d. violet (4.5.55)	75·00	60·00
D43		4d. blue (14.7.55)	26·00	32·00
		a. Imperf (pair)	£250	
D44		5d. yellow-brown (19.5.55)	20·00	20·00
D45	D2	2s.6d. purple/yellow (11.54)	£150	5·75
		Wi. Watermark sideways-inverted	—	—
Set of 6			£250	£130

1955–57. W **165** (St Edward's Crown) sideways.

D46	D1	½d. bright orange (16.7.56)	2·75	3·25
		Wi. Watermark sideways-inverted	£125	
D47		1d. violet-blue (7.6.56)	5·00	1·50
D48		1½d. green (13.2.56)	8·50	7·00
		Wi. Watermark sideways-inverted	85·00	—
D49		2d. agate (22.5.56)	45·00	3·50
D50		3d. violet (5.3.56)	6·00	1·50
		Wi. Watermark sideways-inverted	£100	
D51		4d. blue (24.4.56)	25·00	6·00
		Wi. Watermark sideways-inverted	£175	
D52		5d. brown-ochre (23.3.56)	26·00	20·00
D53		1s. ochre (22.11.55)	65·00	2·25
		Wi. Watermark sideways-inverted	—	—
D54	D2	2s.6d. purple/yellow (28.6.57)	£200	8·25
		Wi. Watermark sideways-inverted	—	—
D55		5s. scarlet/yellow (25.11.55)	£150	32·00
		Wi. Watermark sideways-inverted	—	£375
Set of 10			£475	75·00

Stamps from the above issue are known bisected and used for half their face value at the following sorting offices:
1d. Beswick, Manchester (1958), Huddersfield (1956), London SE (1957)
2d. Eynsham, Oxford (1956), Garelochhead, Helensburgh (1956), Harpenden (1956), Hull (1956), Kingston on Thames (1956), Leicester Square, London WC (1956), London WC (1956)
3d. London SE (1957)
4d. Poplar, London E (1958)

1959–63. W **179** (Multiple Crowns) sideways.

D56	D1	½d. bright orange (18.10.61)	15	1·25
		Wi. Watermark sideways-inverted	2·50	2·50
D57		1d. violet-blue (9.5.60)	15	50
		Wi. Watermark sideways-inverted	£125	—
D58		1½d. green (5.10.60)	2·50	2·50
D59		2d. agate (14.9.59)	1·10	50
		Wi. Watermark sideways-inverted	£200	—
D60		3d. violet (24.3.59)	30	30
		Wi. Watermark sideways-inverted	85·00	85·00
D61		4d. blue (17.12.59)	30	30
		Wi. Watermark sideways-inverted	£300	
D62		5d. yellow-brown (6.11.61)	45	60
		Wi. Watermark sideways-inverted	5·00	6·00
D63		6d. purple (29.3.62)	50	30
		Wi. Watermark sideways-inverted	£400	£400
D64		1s. ochre (11.4.60)	90	30
		Wi. Watermark sideways-inverted	75·00	75·00
D65	D2	2s.6d. purple/yellow (11.5.61)	3·00	50
		Wi. Watermark sideways-inverted	15·00	15·00
D66		5s. scarlet/yellow (8.5.61)	8·25	1·00
		Wi. Watermark sideways-inverted	25·00	25·00
D67		10s. blue/yellow (2.9.63)	11·50	5·75
		Wi. Watermark sideways-inverted	40·00	25·00
D68		£1 black/yellow (2.9.63)	45·00	8·25
Set of 13			65·00	20·00

Whiter paper. The note after No. 586 also applies to Postage Due stamps.
Stamps from the above issue are known bisected and used for half their face value at the following sorting offices:
1d. Chieveley, Newbury (1962, 1963), Henlan, Llandyssil (1961), Mayfield (1962), St Albans (1964)
2d. Doncaster (?)

1968–69. Typo. No wmk. Chalk-surfaced paper.

D69	D1	2d. agate (11.4.68)	75	1·00
		v. PVA gum (26.11.68)	75·00	
D70		3d. violet (9.9.68)	1·00	1·00
D71		4d. blue (6.5.68)	1·00	1·00
		v. PVA gum	£2250	
D72		5d. orange-brown (3.1.69)	8·00	11·00
D73		6d. purple (9.9.68)	2·25	1·75
D74		1s. ochre (19.11.68)	4·00	2·50
D69/D74 Set of 6			15·00	16·00

The 2d. and 4d. exist with gum arabic and PVA gum; the remainder with PVA gum only.
Stamps from the above issue are known bisected and used for half their face value at the following sorting offices:
4d. Northampton (1970)
6d. Kilburn, London NW (1968)

POSTAGE DUE STAMPS

1968–69. Photo. No wmk. Chalk-surfaced paper. PVA gum.
D75	**D1**	4d. blue (12.6.69)	7·00	6·75
D76		8d. red (3.10.68)	50	1·00

Nos. D75/D76 are smaller, 21½×17½ mm.
The 4d. is known bisected in April 1970 (Northampton).

Following changes in the method of collecting money due on unpaid or underpaid mail the use of postage due stamps was restricted from April 1995 to mail addressed to business customers and to Customs/VAT charges levied by the Royal Mail on behalf of the Customs and Excise. The use of postage due stamps ceased on 28 January 2000.

D3    **D4**

(Des Jeffery Matthews. Photo Harrison)

1970 (17 June)–**75**. Decimal Currency. Chalk-surfaced paper.
D77	**D3**	½p. turquoise-blue (15.2.71)	15	2·50
D78		1p. deep reddish purple (15.2.71)	15	15
D79		2p. myrtle-green (15.2.71)	20	15
D80		3p. ultramarine (15.2.71)	20	15
D81		4p. yellow-brown (15.2.71)	25	15
D82		5p. violet (15.2.71)	25	15
D83		7p. red-brown (21.8.74)	35	1·00
D84	**D4**	10p. carmine	30	30
D85		11p. slate-green (18.6.75)	50	1·00
D86		20p. olive-brown	60	25
D87		50p. ultramarine	2·00	1·25
D88		£1 black	4·00	1·00
D89		£5 orange-yellow and black (2.4.73)	25·00	1·50
Set of 13			30·00	7·75

Presentation Pack (PO Pack No. 36) (Nos. D77/D82, D84, D86/D88 (3.11.71)) .... 28·00
Presentation Pack (PO Pack No. 93) (Nos. D77/D88) (30.3.77) .... 9·00

Later printings were on fluorescent white paper, some with dextrin added to the PVA gum (see notes after X1058).
The 2p. from the above issue is known bisected and used for half its face value at Exeter (1977).

D5    **D6**

(Des Sedley Place Design Ltd. Photo Harrison)

1982 (9 June). Chalk-surfaced paper.
D90	**D5**	1p. lake	10	30
D91		2p. bright blue	30	30
D92		3p. deep mauve	15	30
D93		4p. deep blue	15	25
D94		5p. sepia	20	25
D95	**D6**	10p. light brown	30	40
D96		20p. olive-green	50	60
D97		25p. deep greenish blue	80	90
D98		50p. grey-black	1·75	1·75
D99		£1 red	3·00	1·25
D100		£2 turquoise-blue	5·00	4·25
D101		£5 dull orange	10·00	2·25
Set of 12			19·00	10·00
Set of 12 *Gutter Pairs*			38·00	
Presentation Pack (PO Pack No.135)			24·00	

D7

(Des Sedley Place Design Ltd. Litho Questa)

1994 (15 Feb). Perf 15×14 (with one elliptical hole in each vertical side).
D102	**D7**	1p. red, yellow and black	10	75
D103		2p. magenta, purple and black	10	75
D104		5p. yellow, red-brown and black	15	50
D105		10p. yellow, emerald and black	30	75
D106		20p. blue-green, violet and black	75	1·50
D107		25p. cerise, rosine and black	1·50	2·00
D108		£1 violet, magenta and black	7·00	7·00
D109		£1·20 greenish blue, blue-green and black	8·00	9·00
D110		£5 greenish black, blue-green and black	20·00	20·00
Set of 9			35·00	35·00
First Day Cover				45·00
Presentation Pack (PO Pack No.32)			38·00	

Special First Day of Issue Postmarks
London EC3 .... 45·00

JERWOOD PHILATELICS
(Established 2010)

Great Britain dealer specialising in:

* Stitched Booklets
* Folded Booklets
* Window Booklets
* Prestige Booklets
* Greetings & Christmas Booklets
* Machins, including Cylinder, Date Blocks etc.
* Smilers™ Sheets, inc. Business Customised Sheets
* Post & Go™ stamps
* Modern commemoratives, including varieties
* Royal Mail Year Books & Year Packs
* Accessories, including stockcards, mounts etc.
* Selected material from earlier reigns
* Regular auctions on Ebay of worldwide collections

Collections & quality single items bought

Detailed booklet listings using both the Stanley Gibbons and Modern British Philatelic Circle catalogues.

Website: www.jerwoodphilatelics.co.uk
Email: dave@jerwoodphilatelics.co.uk
Telephone: (0121) 249 5277

1103A Bristol Road South, Birmingham B31 2QP

Insert concise22 at checkout to receive a 10% discount on any order over £25. Free P&P on all UK orders.

MBPC catalogue numbers are used with kind permission. For more information on the Circle's activities and benefits of membership, please visit www.mbp-circle.co.uk

Member of the Philatelic Traders Society (Membership Number: 6026)

Post Office Stamp Booklets

The following listing covers all the booklets sold by post offices from 1904.

All major variations of contents and cover are included, but minor changes to the covers and differences on the interleaves have been ignored.

From 1913 each booklet carried an edition number, linked to an internal Post Office system of identification which divided the various booklets into series. In 1943 these edition numbers were replaced by edition dates. No attempt has been made to list separate edition numbers for booklets prior to 1943, although notes giving their extent are provided for each booklet.

Edition dates are listed separately and exist for all £.s.d. and most Decimal Stitched booklets (except for the 1s. booklets, the 2s. booklets (Nos. N1/N3), the 5s. Philympia booklets (No. HP34), the £1 Stamps for Cooks booklet (No. ZP1) and the Decimal Sponsored booklets). They are those found printed upon the booklets, either on the outer back cover or on the white leaves.

Note that the date of issue may not coincide with the edition date given on the booklet, thus No. DW1, issued on 13 November 1974 has an edition date of SEPT 1974.

ERRORS OF MAKE-UP of booklets exist but we do not list them here. More detailed listings can be found in the 2nd, 3rd and 4th volumes of the *Great Britain Specialised Catalogue*.

ILLUSTRATIONS. The illustrations of the covers are ¾ size except where otherwise stated. Those in Queen Elizabeth II Decimal Sections C to H are ⅔ size, except where otherwise stated.

PRICES quoted are for complete booklets containing stamps with average perforations (i.e. full perforations on two edges of the pane only). Booklets containing panes with complete perforations are worth more.

KING EDWARD VII

2s. Booklets

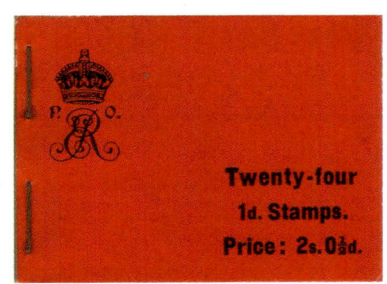

BA1

1904 (Mar). Red cover printed in black as T **BA1**. Panes of six stamps: 24×1d. Wmk Imperial Crown (No. 219).
BA1 .... £500

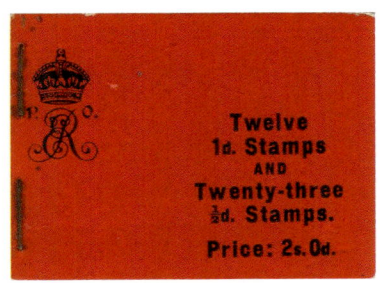

BA2

1906 (June). Red cover printed in black as T **BA2**. As before but make-up changed to include 12×1d. and 23×½d. and label showing one green cross (Nos. 217 and 219).
BA2 .... £2200

1907 (Aug). Red cover printed in black as T **BA2**. Make-up changed to include 18×1d. and 11×½d. and label showing one green cross (Nos. 217 and 219).
BA3 .... £3100

1908 (Aug). As before, but interleaves used for post office adverts printed in red.
BA4 .... £3400

1909 (Aug). As before, but interleaves used for trade advert printed in green.
BA5 .... £2700

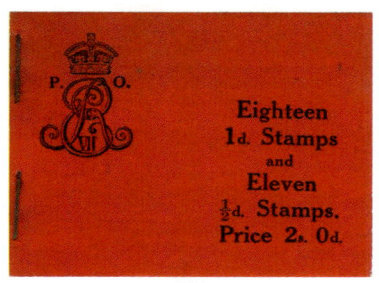

BA6

1911 (June). Red cover printed in black as T **BA6** showing a larger Post Office cypher on cover. As before, but containing stamps by Harrison & Sons (Nos. 267 and 272).
BA6 .... £2800

KING GEORGE V

2s. Booklets

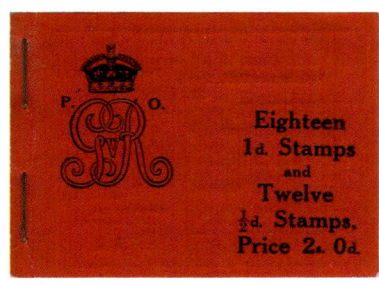

BB1

1911 (Aug). Red cover printed in black as T **BA2** showing King George V cypher. Panes of six stamps: 18×1d. and 12×½d. Wmk Crown (Nos. 325, 329) Die 1B.
BB1 .... £1600

BB2

1912 (Apr). As before, but red cover printed in black as T **BB2**.
BB2 .... £1900

1912 (Sept). As before, but wmk Simple Cypher (Nos. 334, 336) Die 1B.
BB3 .... £1300

457

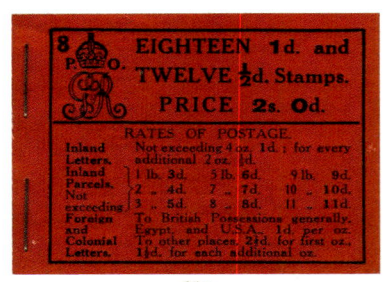

POST OFFICE STAMP BOOKLETS

BB5

1912 (Nov). As before, but red cover printed in black as T **BB5** but without edition number.
BB4 .... £1600

1913 (Jan). As before, but red cover printed in black as T **BB5**.
BB5 Edition numbers 8 or 9 .... £1300

1913 (Apr). As before, but 1912–1922 wmk Simple Cypher (Nos. 351, 357).
BB6 Edition numbers 10 to 35 .... £1300

1915 (Nov). As before, except lower panel of front cover which was changed to show New rates of postage.
BB7 Edition numbers 36 to 42 .... £1600

1916 (May). As before, but interleave adverts printed in black instead of green.
BB8 Edition numbers 43 to 45 .... £2000

1916 (July). As before, but orange cover printed in black as T **BB5**.
BB9 Edition numbers 46 to 64 .... £1500

BB10

1917 (Sept). As before, but orange cover printed in black as T **BB10**.
BB10 Edition numbers 65 to 81 .... £1350

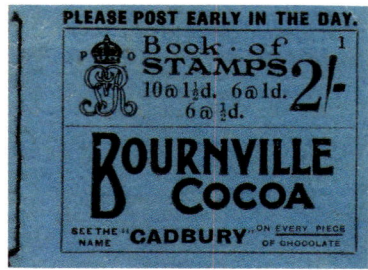

BB11

1924 (Feb). Blue cover printed in black as T **BB11**. Panes of six stamps: 10×1½d. (first completed by two perforated labels), 6×1d. and 6×½d. 1912–1922 wmk Simple Cypher (Nos. 351, 357, 362).
BB11 Edition numbers 1 or 2 .... £2600

1924 (Mar). As before, but 1924–1926 wmk Block Cypher (Nos. 418/420).
BB12 Edition numbers 3 to 102 and 108 to 254 .... £900

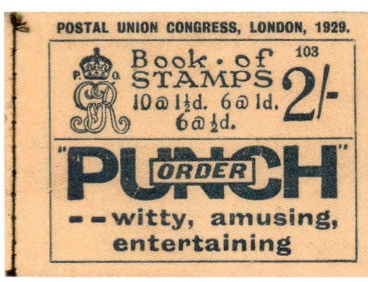

BB13

1929 (May). Postal Union Congress issue. Cover of special design as T **BB13** printed in blue on buff as before but containing stamps of the PUC issue (Nos. 434/436).
BB13 Edition numbers 103 to 107 .... £500

1934 (Feb). Blue cover printed in black as T **BB11**, but containing stamps with Block Cypher wmk printed by Harrison & Sons (Nos. 418/420).
BB14 Edition numbers 255 to 287 .... £1100

1935 (Jan). As before, but containing stamps of the photogravure issue (intermediate format) with the *se-tenant* advertisements printed in brown (Nos. 439/441).
BB15 Edition numbers 288 to 297 .... £2700

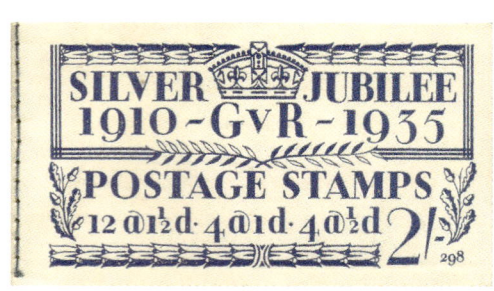

BB16

1935 (May). Silver Jubilee issue. Larger size cover printed in blue on buff as T **BB16** and containing pages of four stamps with no *se-tenant* advertisements: 12×1½d., 4×1d. and 4×½d. (Nos. 453/455).
BB16 Edition numbers 298 to 304 .... 90·00

1935 (July). As No. BB15, but containing stamps of the photogravure (small format) issue with *se-tenant* advertisements printed in black (Nos. 439/441).
BB17 Edition numbers 305 to 353 .... £600

3s. Booklets

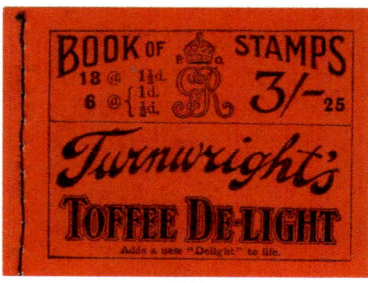

BB19

1918 (Oct). Orange cover printed in black as T **BB19**. Panes of six stamps: 12×1½d., 12×1d. and 12×½d. 1912–1922 wmk Simple Cypher (Nos. 351, 357, 362).
BB18 Edition numbers 1 to 11 .... £1850

1919 (July). As before, but make-up altered to contain 18×1½d., 6×1d. and 6×½d.
BB19 Edition numbers 12 to 26 .... £1850

POST OFFICE STAMP BOOKLETS

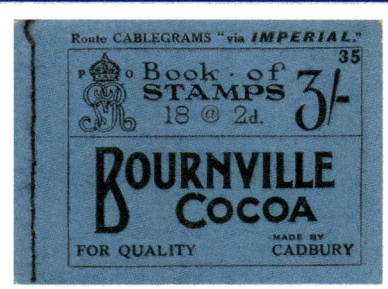

BB20

1921 (Apr). Experimental booklet bound in blue covers as T **BB20**, containing pages of six stamps: 18×2d. (Die I) (No. 368).
BB20   Edition numbers 35 and part 37 .... £2400

1921 (Dec). As before, but containing 2d. (Die II) (No. 370).
BB21   Edition numbers 12, 13 and part 37 ...... £2400

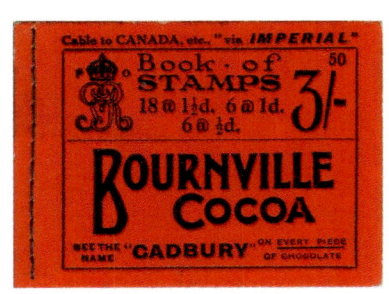

BB22

1922 (May). Scarlet cover printed in black as T **BB22**. Panes of six stamps: 18×1½d., 6×1d. and 6×½d. (Nos. 351, 357, 362).
BB22   Edition numbers 19, 20, 22, 23 and 25 to 54 .... £2400

BB23

1922 (June). Experimental booklet as Edition numbers 12 and 13 bound in blue covers as T **BB23**, containing panes of six stamps: 24×1½d. (No. 362).
BB23   Edition numbers 21 or 24 .... £2400

1924 (Feb). Scarlet cover printed in black as T **BB22**, but containing stamps with Block Cypher wmk, printed by Waterlow & Sons (Nos. 418/420).
BB24   Edition numbers 55 to 167 and 173 to 273 .... £550

1929 (May). Postal Union Congress issue. Cover of special design as T **BB13** printed in red on buff as before but containing stamps of the PUC issue (Nos. 434/436).
BB25   Edition numbers 168 to 172 .... £450

1934 (Mar). Scarlet cover printed in black as T **BB22**, but containing stamps with the Block Cypher wmk printed by Harrison & Sons (Nos. 418/420).
BB26   Edition numbers 274 to 288 .... £650

1935 (Jan). As No. BB29, but containing stamps of the photogravure issue (intermediate format).
BB27   Edition numbers 289 to 293 .... £2100

1935 (May). Silver Jubilee issue. Larger size cover printed in red on buff as T **BB16** and containing panes of four stamps: 20×1½d., 4×1d. and 4×½d. (Nos. 453/455).
BB28   Edition numbers 294 to 297 .... 90·00

1935 (July). As No. BB26, but containing stamps of the photogravure issue (small format) (Nos. 439/441).
BB29   Edition numbers 298 to 319 .... £550

3s.6d. Booklets

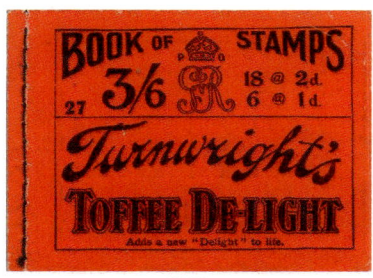

BB30

1920 (July). Orange cover printed in black as T **BB30**, containing panes of six stamps: 18×2d. and 6×1d. (Nos. 357, 368).
BB30   Edition numbers 27 to 32 .... £2200

BB31

1921 (Jan). Orange-red cover printed in black as T **BB31**, as before but make-up changed to include stamps of 1912–1922 issue with the Simple Cypher wmk: 12×2d. (Die I), 6×1½d., 6×1d. and 6×½d. (Nos. 351, 357, 362, 368).
BB31   Edition numbers 33, 34, 36 and 38.......... £2200

1921 (July). As No. BB31 including stamps of the 1912–1922 issue with Simple Cypher wmk: 12×2d. (Die I or Die II), 6×1½d., 6×1d. and 6×½d. (Nos. 351, 357, 362, 368 or 370).
BB32   Edition numbers 1 to 11, 14 to 18........... £2200

5s. Booklets

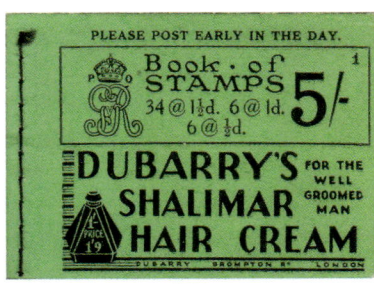

BB33

1931 (Aug). Green cover printed in black as T **BB33**. Panes of six stamps: 34×1½d., 6×1d. and 6×½d. The first 1½d. pane completed by two se-tenant advertisements. Printed by Waterlow & Sons on paper with Block Cypher wmk (Nos. 418/420).
BB33   Edition number 1 .... £6250

1932 (June). As before, but buff cover printed in black.
BB34   Edition numbers 2 to 6 .... £5250

POST OFFICE STAMP BOOKLETS

1934 (July). As before, but containing stamps with Block Cypher wmk printed by Harrison & Sons (Nos. 418/420).
BB35 Edition numbers 7 or 8 .... £2200

1935 (Feb). As before, but containing stamps of the photogravure issue (intermediate format) with *se-tenant* advertisements printed in brown (Nos. 439/441).
BB36 Edition number 9 .... £6250

1935 (July). As before, but containing stamps of the photogravure issue (small format) with *se-tenant* advertisements printed in black (Nos. 439/441).
BB37 Edition numbers 10 to 15 .... £650

KING EDWARD VIII

6d. Booklet

1936. Buff unglazed cover without inscription containing 4×1½d. stamps, in panes of two (No. 459).
BC1 Edition numbers 354 to 385 .... 65·00

2s. Booklet

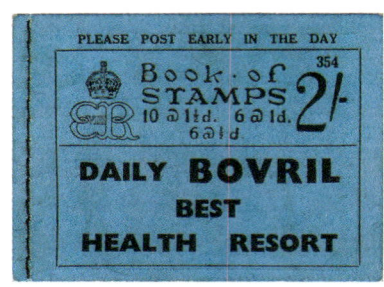

BC2

1936 (Oct). Blue cover printed in black as T **BC2**, containing pages of six stamps: 10×1½d., 6×1d. and 6×½d. (Nos. 457/459).
BC2 Edition numbers 354 to 385 .... £140

3s. Booklet

1936 (Nov). As No. BB29, except for the KEVIII cypher on the cover but without 'P' and 'O' on either side of the crown, and containing Nos. 457/459.
BC3 Edition numbers 320 to 332 .... £120

5s. Booklet

1937 (Mar). As No. BB37, but with the KEVIII cypher on the cover and containing Nos. 457/459.
BC4 Edition numbers 16 or 17 .... £275

KING GEORGE VI

6d. Booklets

1938 (Jan). As No. BC1, but containing stamps in the original dark colours. Buff cover without inscription (No. 464).
BD1 .... 75·00

1938 (Feb). As before, but pink unprinted cover and make-up changed to contain 2×1½d., 2×1d. and 2×½d. in the original dark colours (Nos. 462/164).
BD2 .... £300

1940 (June). Pale green unprinted cover and make-up changed to include two panes of four stamps with wmk sideways. Stamps in original dark colours with binding margin either at the top or bottom of the pane: 4×1d., 4×½d. (Nos. 462a/463a).
BD3 .... £150

1s. Booklets with Panes of 2

1947 (Dec). Cream cover, unglazed and without inscription containing panes of two stamps in pale shades, all with wmk normal. Panes of two stamps: 4×½d., 4×1d. and 4×1½d. (Nos. 485/487).
BD4 .... 28·00

1951 (May). As before, but containing stamps in changed colours (Nos. 503/505).
BD5 .... 28·00

1s. Booklets with Panes of 4

1948. Cream cover as before, but make-up changed to contain 4×1½d., 4×1d. and 4×½d. in panes of four of the pale shades with wmk normal (Nos. 485/487).
BD6 .... £9000

1951 (May). As before, but stamps in new colours all wmk normal, margins at either top or at the bottom. (Nos. 503/505).
BD7 .... 50·00

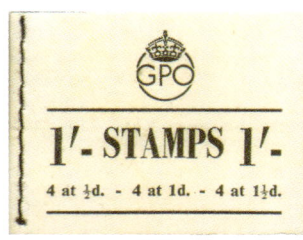

BD8

1952 (Dec). Cream cover printed in black as T **BD8**. Make-up as before but with wmk either upright or inverted and margins only at the top (Nos. 503/505).
BD8 .... 25·00

BD10

1954. As before but cover showing GPO emblem with St Edward's crown and oval frame as T **BD10** (Nos. 503/505).
BD10 .... 35·00

2s. Booklets

BD11

1937 (Aug). Blue cover printed in black as T **BB11**, but with KGVI cypher on the cover and containing stamps in the original dark colours. Panes of six stamps: 10×1½d., 6×1d. and 6×½d. The first 1½d. pane completed by two *se-tenant* advertisements.(Nos. 462/464).
BD11 Edition numbers 386 to 412 .... £1100

POST OFFICE STAMP BOOKLETS

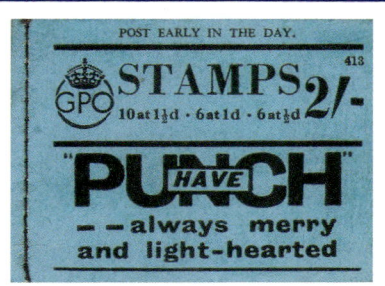

BD12

1938 (Mar). Blue cover printed in black as T **BD12** (Nos. 462/464).
BD12   Edition numbers 413 to 508 .... £1100

2s.6d. Booklets

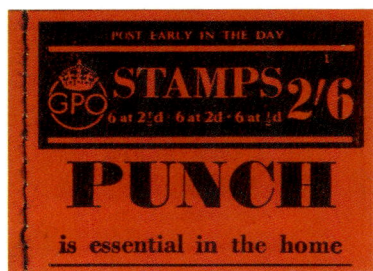

BD13

1940 (June). Scarlet cover printed in black as T **BD13**, containing panes of six stamps in original dark colours: 6×2½d., 6×2d. and 6×½d. (Nos. 462, 465/466).
BD13   Edition numbers 1 to 8 (part) £1700

1940 (Sept). As before, but blue cover printed in black as T **BD13**.
BD14   Edition numbers 8 (part) to 13 .... £1700

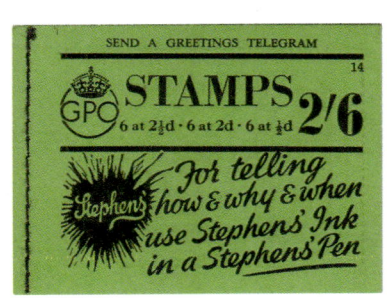

BD15

1940 (Oct). As before, but with green cover printed in black as T **BD15** (Nos. 462, 465/466).
BD15   Edition numbers 14 to 94 .... £975

1942 (Mar). As before, but containing stamps in pale shades (Nos. 485, 488/189).
BD16   Edition numbers 95 to 146 (Part) £975

1942 (Oct). Composition as before, but with unglazed green covers.
BD17   Edition numbers 146 (Part) to 214 .... £975

BD20 Type A Circular GPO Cypher

1943 (Aug). As before, but green cover printed in black as Type A, with different contents details (Nos. 485, 488/489).
BD18   Edition dates August 1943 to February 1951 .... 95·00

(1) AUG 1943 .... £110
(2) OCT 1943 .... £150
(3) NOV 1943 .... £180
(4) DEC 1943 .... £170
(5) JAN 1944 .... £160
(6) FEB 1944 .... £160
(7) MAR 1944 .... £160
(8) APR 1944 .... £160
(9) MAY 1944 .... £160
(10) JUNE 1944 .... £160
(11) JULY 1944 .... £160
(12) AUG 1944 .... £160
(13) SEPT 1944 .... £160
(14) OCT 1944 .... £160
(15) NOV 1944 .... £160
(16) DEC 1944 .... £160
(17) JAN 1945 .... £160
(18) FEB 1945 .... £160
(19) MAR 1945 .... £160
(20) APR 1945 .... £160
(21) MAY 1945 .... £160
(22) JUNE 1945 .... £160
(23) JULY 1945 .... £160
(24) AUG 1945 .... £160
(25) SEPT 1945 .... £160
(26) OCT 1945 .... £160
(27) NOV 1945 .... £160
(28) DEC 1945 .... £160
(29) JAN 1946 .... £150
(30) FEB 1946 .... £150
(31) MAR 1946 .... £150
(32) APR 1946 .... £150
(33) MAY 1946 .... £150
(34) JUNE 1946 .... £150
(35) JULY 1946 .... £150
(36) AUG 1946 .... £150
(37) SEPT 1946 .... £150
(38) OCT 1946 .... £400
(39) NOV 1946 .... £150
(40) DEC 1946 .... £150
(41) JAN 1947 .... £150
(42) FEB 1947 .... £150
(43) MAR 1947 .... £150
(44) APR 1947 .... £150
(45) MAY 1947 .... £150
(46) JUNE 1947 .... £150
(47) JULY 1947 .... £150
(48) AUG 1947 .... £150
(49) SEPT 1947 .... £150
(50) OCT 1947 .... £150
(51) NOV 1947 .... £150
(52) DEC 1947 .... £150
(53) JAN 1948 .... £180
(54) FEB 1948 .... £150
(55) MAR 1948 .... £150
(56) APR 1948 .... £150
(57) MAY 1948 .... £150
(58) JUNE 1948 .... £150
(59) JULY 1948 .... £150
(60) AUG 1948 .... £150
(61) OCT 1948 .... £140
(62) NOV 1948 .... £140
(63) DEC 1948 .... £140
(64) JAN 1949 .... £140
(65) FEB 1949 .... £150
(66) MAR 1949 .... £150
(67) APR 1949 .... £150
(68) MAY 1949 .... £150

(69) JUNE 1949	£150
(70) JULY 1949	£150
(71) AUG 1949	£150
(72) OCT 1949	£150
(73) NOV 1949	£150
(74) DEC 1949	£150
(75) JAN 1950	£120
(76) FEB 1950	£120
(77) MAR 1950	£120
(78) APR 1950	£120
(79) MAY 1950	£120
(80) JUNE 1950	£120
(81) JULY 1950	95·00
(82) AUG 1950	95·00
(83) SEPT 1950	95·00
(84) OCT 1950	95·00
(85) NOV 1950	95·00
(86) DEC 1950	95·00
(87) JAN 1951	95·00
(88) FEB 1951	95·00

1951 (May). As before, but containing stamps in the new colours (Nos. 503, 506/507).
BD19   Edition dates May 1951 to February 1952 .... 55·00

(1) MAY 1951	55·00
(2) JUNE 1951	75·00
(3) JULY 1951	£200
(4) AUG 1951	55·00
(5) SEPT 1951	£175
(6) OCT 1951	55·00
(7) NOV 1951	55·00
(8) DEC 1951	55·00
(9) JAN 1952	55·00
(10) FEB 1952	55·00

1952 (Mar). As before, but make-up changed to contain: 6×2½d., 6×1½d., 3×1d. and 6×½d. The 1d. pane was completed by three perforated labels in the lower row inscribed MINIMUM INLAND PRINTED PAPER RATE 1½d. (Nos. 503/505, 507).
BD20   Edition dates March 1952 to May 1953   50·00

(1) MAR 1952	50·00
(2) APR 1952	55·00
(3) MAY 1952	50·00
(4) JUNE 1952	50·00
(5) JULY 1952	55·00
(6) AUG 1952	50·00
(7) SEPT 1952	50·00
(8) OCT 1952	50·00
(9) NOV 1952	50·00
(10) DEC 1952	50·00
(11) JAN 1953	50·00
(12) FEB 1953	50·00
(13) MAR 1953	50·00
(14) APR 1953	50·00
(15) MAY 1953	55·00

3s. Booklets

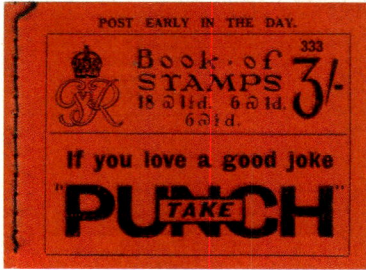

BD21

1937 (Aug). Scarlet cover printed black as T **BD21**, containing panes of six stamps: 18×1½d., 6×1d. and 6×½d. in the original dark colours (Nos. 462/464).
BD21   Edition numbers 333 to 343 .... £1900

BD22

1938 (Apr). As before, but scarlet cover printed in black as T **BD22** (Nos. 462/464).
BD22   Edition numbers 344 to 377 .... £1900

5s. Booklets

1937 (Aug). Buff cover printed in black as T **BB33**, containing stamps of the new reign in the original dark colours. Panes of six stamps: 34×1½d., 6×1d. and 6×½d. The first 1½d. pane completed by two *se-tenant* advertisements. (Nos. 462/464).
BD23   Edition numbers 18 to 20 .... £2000

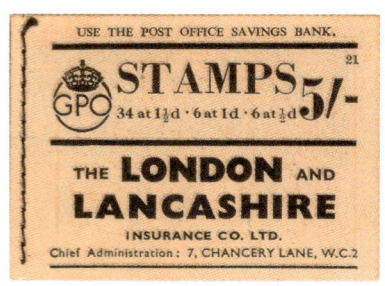

BD24

1938 (May). As before, but with redesigned front cover showing GPO emblem as T **BD24** instead of royal cypher.
BD24   Edition numbers 21 to 29 .... £2000

1940 (July). As before, but make-up changed to contain: 18×2½d., 6×2d. and 6×½d. in the original dark colours (Nos. 462, 465/466).
BD25   Edition numbers 1 to 16 (part)................ £2000

1942 (Mar). As before, but containing stamps in pale shades (Nos. 485, 488/489).
BD26   Edition numbers 16 (part) to 36 .... £2000

1943 (Sept). As before, but buff cover printed in black as Type A (see No. BD18, 2s.6d.) (Nos. 485, 488/489).
BD28   Edition dates September 1943 to December 1950................ £130

(1) SEPT 1943	£160
(2) OCT 1943	£225
(3) NOV 1943	£180
(4) DEC 1943	£225
(5) FEB 1944	£190
(6) MAR 1944	£190
(7) AUG 1944	£190
(8) OCT 1944	£190
(9) NOV 1944	£190
(10) JAN 1945	£190
(11) FEB 1945	£200
(12) APR 1945	£200
(13) JUNE 1945	£200
(14) AUG 1945	£200
(15) OCT 1945	£200
(16) DEC 1945	£200
(17) JAN 1946	£200
(18) MAR 1946	£180
(19) MAY 1946	£180
(20) JUNE 1946	£180
(21) AUG 1946	£180
(22) OCT 1946	£180
(23) DEC 1946	£180
(24) FEB 1947	£180
(25) APR 1947	£180
(26) JUNE 1947	£180

POST OFFICE STAMP BOOKLETS

(27) AUG 1947	£180
(28) OCT 1947	£180
(29) DEC 1947	£180
(30) FEB 1948	£180
(31) APR 1948	£180
(32) JUNE 1948	£180
(33) JULY 1948	£180
(34) AUG 1948	£180
(35) OCT 1948	£180
(36) DEC 1948	£200
(37) FEB 1949	£200
(38) APR 1949	£200
(39) JUNE 1949	£190
(40) AUG 1949	£190
(41) SEPT 1949	£190
(42) OCT 1949	£190
(43) DEC 1949	£190
(44) FEB 1950	£130
(45) APR 1950	£130
(46) JUNE 1950	£130
(47) AUG 1950	£130
(48) OCT 1950	£130
(49) DEC 1950	£130

BD29

1944 (Apr). As before, but buff cover printed in black as T **BD29** (Nos. 485, 488/489).
BD29 Edition dates April or June 1944 .... £5250

(1) APR 1944	£5250
(2) JUNE 1944	£5250

1951 (May). As before, but buff cover changed back to Type A (see No. BD18, 2s.6d.) and containing stamps in the new colours (Nos. 503, 506/507).
BD30 Edition dates May 1951 to January 1952 .... 65·00

(1) MAY 1951	65·00
(2) JULY 1951	65·00
(3) SEPT 1951	65·00
(4) NOV 1951	65·00
(5) JAN 1952	65·00

1952 (Mar). As before, make-up changed to contain: 18×2½d., 6×1½d., 3×1d. and 6×½d. The 1d. pane was completed by three perforated labels in the lower row inscribed MINIMUM INLAND PRINTED PAPER RATE 1½d. (Nos. 503/505, 507).
BD31 Edition dates March to November 1952 .... 55·00

(1) MAR 1952	55·00
(2) MAY 1952	55·00
(3) JULY 1952	55·00
(4) SEPT 1952	55·00
(5) NOV 1952	55·00

1953 (Jan). As before, but make-up changed again to include the 2d. value and containing: 12×2½d., 6×2d., 6×1½d., 6×1d. and 6×½d. (Nos. 503/507).
BD32 Edition dates January or March 1953 .... 65·00

(1) JAN 1953	65·00
(2) MAR 1953	65·00

QUEEN ELIZABETH II

I. £.s.d. BOOKLETS, 1953–1970.

TYPES OF BOOKLET COVER WITH GPO CYPHER

Type A Circular GPO Cypher

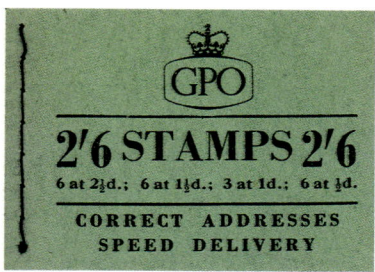

Type B Oval Type GPO Cypher

Type C New GPO Cypher (small)

Type D New GPO Cypher (large)

1s. Booklets

1953 (2 Sept)–**59**.
  I. White unprinted cover. Panes of two stamps: 4×1½d., 4×1d., 4×½d. For use in experimental 'D' machines.
  A. Wmk Tudor Crown (Nos. 515/517) EE.
E1 No date .... 5·00
  B. Wmk St Edward's Crown (Nos. 540/542).
E2 No date (11.57) .... 40·00

463

POST OFFICE STAMP BOOKLETS

II. White printed cover as Type B. Panes of four stamps: 4×1½d., 4×1d., 4×½d. For use in 'E' machines.
A. Wmk Tudor Crown (Nos. 515/517).
K1	No date (22.7.54)	8·00

B. Wmk St Edward's Crown (Nos. 540/542).
K2	No date (5.7.56)	5·00

C. Wmk Crowns (Nos. 570/572).
K3	No date (13.8.59)	5·00

2s. Booklets

1959 (22 Apr)–**65**. Panes of four stamps: 4×3d., 4×1½d., 4×1d., 4×½d.
I. Salmon cover as Type B. Wmk. St Edward's Crown (Nos. 540/542 and 545).
N1	No date	6·00

II. Salmon cover as Type C. Wmk Crowns (Nos. 570/572 and 575).
N2	No date (2.11.60)	6·50

III. Lemon cover as Type C. Wmk Crowns (Nos. 570/572 and 575).
N3	No date (2.61)	6·50

IV. Lemon cover as Type C. Wmk Crowns (sideways) (Nos. 570a, 571a, 572b, 575a) or phosphor (Nos. 610a, 611a, 612a, 615b).
N4	APR 1961	32·00
	p. With phosphor bands	55·00
N5	SEPT 1961	50·00
N6	JAN 1962	45·00
N7	APR 1962	55·00
N8	JULY 1962	50·00
	p. With phosphor bands	90·00
N9	NOV 1962	70·00
	p. With phosphor bands	90·00
N10	JAN 1963	55·00
	p. With phosphor bands	£180
N11	MAR 1963	55·00
N12	JUNE 1963	55·00
	p. With phosphor bands	75·00
N13	AUG 1963	55·00
	p. With phosphor bands	£100
N14	OCT 1963	55·00
	p. With phosphor bands	£140
N15	FEB 1964	55·00
	p. With phosphor bands	95·00
N16	JUNE 1964	55·00
	p. With phosphor bands	£120
N17	AUG 1964	80·00
	p. With phosphor bands	£120
N18	OCT 1964	55·00
	p. With phosphor bands	70·00
N19	DEC 1964	65·00
	p. With phosphor bands	70·00
N20	APR 1965	55·00
	p. With phosphor bands	65·00

1965 (16 Aug)–**67**. New Composition. Pages of four stamps: 4×4d. and pane of 2×1d. and 2×3d. arranged *se-tenant* horiz. Orange-yellow cover as Type C printed in black. Wmk Crowns (sideways) (Nos. 571a, 575a and 576ab) or phosphor (Nos. 611a, 615cd or 615cda (one side phosphor band) and 616ab).

N21	JULY 1965	3·50
	p. With phosphor bands	12·00
N22	OCT 1965	3·75
	p. With phosphor bands	12·00
N23	JAN 1966	6·25
	p. With phosphor bands	16·00
N24	APR 1966	6·25
	p. With phosphor bands	8·00
N25	JULY 1966	7·50
	p. With phosphor bands	£150
N26	OCT 1966	6·00
	p. With phosphor bands	10·00
N27	JAN 1967	8·00
	p. With phosphor bands	5·00
N28p	APR 1967. With phosphor bands	6·00
N29p	JULY 1967. With phosphor bands	4·00
N30p	OCT 1967. With phosphor bands	4·00

In the *se-tenant* pane the 3d. appears at left or right to facilitate the application of phosphor bands.

The following illustration shows how the *se-tenant* stamps with one phosphor band on 3d. were printed and the arrows indicate where the guillotine fell. The result gives 1d. stamps with two bands and the 3d. stamps with one band either at left or right.

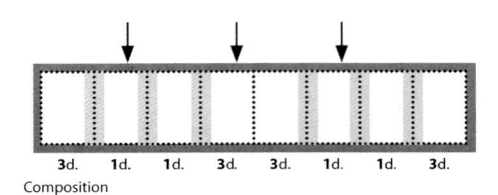

3d.	1d.	1d.	3d.	3d.	1d.	3d.

Composition

1967 (Nov)–**68**. Composition and cover as Nos. N21/N30. Wmk Crowns (sideways) (Nos. 611a, 615b (two phosphor bands) and 616ab).

N31p	JAN 1968	4·00
N32p	MAR 1968	4·50

2s. Booklets with Machin type stamps

1968 (6 Apr–Aug). Orange-yellow cover as Type C. Panes of four stamps: 4×4d. and pane of 2×1d. and 2×3d. arranged *se-tenant* horiz. PVA gum (Nos. 724, 730, 731v).

NP27	MAY 1968	1·20
NP28	JULY 1968	1·00
NP29	AUG 1968	3·75

1968 (16 Sept)–**70**. Grey cover as Type C. New Composition. 4d. stamps only comprising pane of 4×4d. with two phosphor bands (No. 731v) and pane of 2×4d. with one centre phosphor band (No. 732) *se-tenant* with two printed labels.

NP30	SEPT 1968	75
NP31	JAN 1969	£250

Same composition but all 6×4d. stamps have one centre phosphor band (No. 732).

NP31a	SEPT 1968	£600
NP32	NOV 1968	80
NP33	JAN 1969	75

Same composition but change to 4d. bright vermilion with one centre phosphor band (No. 733).

NP34	MAR 1969	1·10
NP35	MAY 1969	1·25
NP36	JULY 1969	1·75
NP37	SEPT 1969	1·50
NP38	NOV 1969	1·25
NP39	JAN 1970	2·00
NP40	MAR 1970	2·00
NP41	MAY 1970	2·00
NP42	JULY 1970	2·00
NP43	AUG 1970	2·00
NP44	OCT 1970	2·00
NP45	DEC 1970	2·00

2s. Booklets for Holiday Resorts

1963 (15 July)–**64**.

I. Lemon cover as Type C printed in red. New composition. Panes of four stamps: two of 4×2½d. and one of 3×½d. and 1×2½d. arranged se-tenant. Chalk-surfaced paper. Wmk Crowns (Nos. 570k and 574k).

NR1	No date, black stitching	4·00
	a. White stitching (3.9.63)	4·00

II. Lemon cover as Type C printed in red. Composition changed again. Panes of four stamps 2×½d. and 2×2½d. arranged sideways, vertically se-tenant. Wmk Crowns (sideways) (No. 570mn×4).

NR2	1964 (1.7.64)	1·50

2s. Booklet for Christmas Cards

1965 (6 Dec). Orange-yellow cover as Type C printed in red. Two panes of 4×3d. arranged sideways. Wmk Crowns (sideways) (No. 575a).

NX1	1965	1·00

2s.6d. Booklets

Green cover. Panes of six stamps: 6×2½d., 6×1½d., 3×1d. (page completed by three perforated labels), 6×½d.

LABELS. The wording printed on the labels differs as follows:

'PPR' = MINIMUM INLAND PRINTED PAPER RATE 1½d.

Two types exist:

A. Printed in photogravure, 17 mm high.

B. Typographed, 15 mm high.

'Shorthand' = SHORTHAND IN 1 WEEK (covering all three labels).

'Post Early' = PLEASE POST EARLY IN THE DAY.

'PAP' = PACK YOUR PARCELS SECURELY (1st label)
ADDRESS YOUR LETTERS CORRECTLY (2nd label),
AND POST EARLY IN THE DAY (3rd label).

1953–54. Composite booklets containing stamps of King George VI and Queen Elizabeth II.

A. KGVI ½d. and 1d. (Nos. 503/504) and QEII 1½d. and 2½d. (Nos. 517 and 519b). Cover as Type A. No interleaving pages.

F1	MAY 1953 (PPR 17 mm)	25·00
F2	JUNE 1953 (PPR 17 mm)	30·00
F3	JULY 1953 (PPR 17 mm)	35·00
F4	AUG 1953 (PPR 17 mm)	32·00

B. Same composition but with addition of two interleaving pages, one at each end. Cover as Type A.

F5	SEPT 1953 (PPR 17 mm)	£250
F6	SEPT 1953 (PPR 15 mm)	£130

C. Same composition and with interleaving pages but with cover as Type B.

F7	OCT 1953 (PPR 17 mm)	50·00
F8	OCT 1953 (PPR 15 mm)	£150
F9	NOV 1953 (PPR 17 mm)	60·00
F10	NOV 1953 (PPR 15 mm)	£250

F11	DEC 1953 (PPR 17 mm)	55·00
F12	JAN 1954 (Shorthand)	75·00
F13	FEB 1954 (Shorthand)	85·00

D. New composition: KGVI 1d. (No. 504) and QEII ½d., 1½d. and 2½d. (Nos. 515, 517 and 519b).

F14	MAR 1954 (PPR 17 mm)	£650
F14a	MAR 1954 (Shorthand)	

1954–57. Booklets containing only Queen Elizabeth II stamps. All covers as Type B.

A. Wmk Tudor Crown (Nos. 515/517 and 519b).

F15	MAR 1954 (PPR 15 mm)	£325
F16	APR 1954 (Post Early)	65·00
F17	MAY 1954 (Post Early)	65·00
F18	JUNE 1954 (Post Early)	65·00
F19	JULY 1954 (Post Early)	65·00
F20	AUG 1954 (Post Early)	65·00
F21	SEPT 1954 (Post Early)	65·00
F22	OCT 1954 (Post Early)	50·00
F23	NOV 1954 (Post Early)	50·00
F24	DEC 1954 (Post Early)	50·00

B. Same composition but with interleaving pages between each pane of stamps.

F25	JAN 1955 (Post Early)	75·00
F26	JAN 1955 (PAP)	£200
F27	FEB 1955 (PAP)	50·00
F28	MAR 1955 (PAP)	50·00
F29	APR 1955 (PAP)	50·00
F30	MAY 1955 (PAP)	65·00
F31	JUNE 1955 (PAP)	50·00
F32	JULY 1955 (PAP)	50·00
F33	AUG 1955 (PAP)	50·00

C. Mixed watermarks. Wmk Tudor Crown (Nos. 515/517 and 519b) and wmk St Edward's Crown (Nos. 540/542 and 544b) in various combinations.

F34	SEPT 1955 (PAP) from	60·00

2s.6d. booklets dated AUGUST, OCTOBER, NOVEMBER and DECEMBER 1955, JANUARY, MAY and JUNE 1956 exist both as listed and with the two watermarks mixed. There are so many different combinations that we do not list them separately, but when in stock selections can be submitted. The SEPTEMBER 1955 booklet (No. F34) only exists in composite form.

D. Wmk St Edward's Crown (Nos. 540/542 and 544b).

F35	OCT 1955 (PAP)	35·00
F36	NOV 1955 (PAP)	35·00
F37	DEC 1955 (PAP)	35·00
F38	JAN 1956 (PAP)	35·00
F39	FEB 1956 (PAP)	35·00
F40	MAR 1956 (PAP)	35·00
F41	APR 1956 (PAP)	45·00
F42	MAY 1956 (PAP)	35·00
F43	JUNE 1956 (PAP)	35·00
F44	JULY 1956 (PAP)	35·00
F45	AUG 1956 (PAP)	25·00
F46	SEPT 1956 (PAP)	45·00
F47	OCT 1956 (PAP)	35·00
F48	NOV 1956 (PAP)	35·00
F49	DEC 1956 (PAP)	35·00
F50	JAN 1957 (PAP)	35·00
F51	FEB 1957 (PAP)	35·00
F52	MAR 1957 (PAP)	35·00

E. Same wmk but new composition. Panes of six stamps: 6×2½d. (No. 544b), 6×2d. (No. 543b) and 6×½d. (No. 540).

F53	APR 1957	35·00
F54	MAY 1957	35·00
F55	JUNE 1957	30·00
F56	JULY 1957	30·00
F57	AUG 1957	30·00
F58	SEPT 1957	30·00
F59	OCT 1957	30·00
F60	NOV 1957	25·00
F61	DEC 1957	45·00

3s. Booklets

1958–65. Panes of six stamps: 6×3d., 6×1½d., 6×1d., 6×½d.

I. Red cover as Type B.

A. Wmk St Edward's Crown (Nos. 540/542 and 545).

M1	JAN 1958	28·00
M2	FEB 1958	38·00
M3	MAR 1958	30·00
M4	APR 1958	28·00
M5	MAY 1958	28·00
M6	JUNE 1958	28·00
M7	JULY 1958	30·00
M8	AUG 1958	32·00
M9	NOV 1958	32·00

The 3s. booklets dated NOVEMBER 1958, DECEMBER 1958 and JANUARY 1959 exist both as listed and with mixed St Edward's Crown and Crowns watermarks.

B. Wmk Crowns (Nos. 570/572 and 575) or graphite lines (Nos. 587/589 and 592).

M10	DEC 1958	35·00
M11	JAN 1959	35·00
M12	FEB 1959	35·00
M13	AUG 1959	40·00
	g. With graphite lines	£250
M14	SEPT 1959	40·00
	g. With graphite lines	£325

II. Brick-red cover as Type C. Wmk Crowns (Nos. 570/572 and 575), graphite lines (Nos. 587/589 and 592) or phosphor (Nos. 610/612 and 615).

M15	OCT 1959	35·00
	g. With graphite lines	£350
M16	NOV 1959	35·00
M17	DEC 1959	35·00
M18	JAN 1960	35·00
M19	FEB 1960	50·00
	g. With graphite lines	£325
M20	MAR 1960	50·00
	g. With graphite lines	£375
M21	APR 1960	45·00
	g. With graphite lines	£325
M22	MAY 1960	60·00
M23	JUNE 1960	60·00
M24	JULY 1960	50·00
M25	AUG 1960	45·00
	p. With phosphor bands	75·00
M26	SEPT 1960	50·00
M27	OCT 1960	50·00
M28	NOV 1960	38·00
	p. With phosphor bands	75·00

III. Brick-red cover as Type D. Wmk Crowns (Nos. 570/572 and 575) or phosphor (Nos. 610/612 and 615).

M29	DEC 1960	48·00
	p. With phosphor bands	75·00
M30	JAN 1961	60·00
M31	FEB 1961	60·00
M32	MAR 1961	60·00
M33	APR 1961	60·00
	p. With phosphor bands	75·00
M34	MAY 1961	60·00
M35	JUNE 1961	60·00
M36	JULY 1961	55·00
	p. With phosphor bands	75·00
M37	AUG 1961	60·00
	p. With phosphor bands	75·00
M38	SEPT 1961	60·00
	p. With phosphor bands	85·00
M39	OCT 1961	60·00
	p. With phosphor bands	£100
M40	NOV 1961	60·00
M41	DEC 1961	60·00
M42	JAN 1962	60·00
M43	FEB 1962	60·00
	p. With phosphor bands	£100
M44	MAR 1962	50·00
	p. With phosphor bands	£100
M45	APR 1962	60·00
	p. With phosphor bands	£100
M46	MAY 1962	60·00
	p. With phosphor bands	£100
M47	JUNE 1962	60·00
	p. With phosphor bands	£100
M48	JULY 1962	60·00
M49	AUG 1962	60·00
	p. With phosphor bands	90·00
M50	SEPT 1962	55·00
	p. With phosphor bands	£100
M51	OCT 1962	70·00
	p. With phosphor bands	£100
M52	NOV 1962	70·00
	p. With phosphor bands	£100
M53	DEC 1962	70·00
	p. With phosphor bands	£100
M54	JAN 1963	70·00
M55	FEB 1963	70·00
	p. With phosphor bands	£100
M56	MAR 1963	70·00
	p. With phosphor bands	£100
M57	APR 1963	70·00
	p. With phosphor bands	£100
M58	MAY 1963	70·00
	p. With phosphor bands	£500
M59	JUNE 1963	75·00
	p. With phosphor bands	70·00
M60	JULY 1963	60·00
	p. With phosphor bands	£100
M61	AUG 1963	70·00
	p. With phosphor bands	£100
M62	SEPT 1963	70·00
M63	OCT 1963	80·00
M64	NOV 1963	70·00
	p. With phosphor bands	£100
M65	DEC 1963	85·00
	p. With phosphor bands	£200
M66	JAN 1964	80·00
	p. With phosphor bands	75·00
M67	MAR 1964	80·00
	p. With phosphor bands	£100
M68	MAY 1964	80·00
	p. With phosphor bands	£120
M69	JULY 1964	60·00
	p. With phosphor bands	£100

POST OFFICE STAMP BOOKLETS

M70	SEPT 1964	60·00
	p. With phosphor bands	£100
M71	NOV 1964	45·00
	p. With phosphor bands	55·00
M72	JAN 1965	45·00
	p. With phosphor bands	70·00
M73	MAR 1965	35·00
	p. With phosphor bands	65·00
M74	MAY 1965	60·00
	p. With phosphor bands	£100

3s.9d. Booklets

1953–57. Red cover as Type B. Panes of six stamps: 18×2½d.
A. Wmk Tudor Crown (No. 519b).

G1	NOV 1953	40·00
G2	JAN 1954	60·00
G3	MAR 1954	40·00
G4	DEC 1954	40·00
G5	FEB 1955	40·00
G6	APR 1955	40·00
G7	JUNE 1955	40·00
G8	AUG 1955	40·00
G9	OCT 1955	40·00
G10	DEC 1955	40·00

3s.9d. booklets dated OCTOBER and DECEMBER 1955 exist both as listed and with the two watermarks mixed.

B. Wmk St Edward's Crown (No. 544b). Same composition but with interleaving pages between each pane of stamps.

G12	FEB 1956	30·00
G13	APR 1956	30·00
G14	JUNE 1956	30·00
G15	AUG 1956	30·00
G16	OCT 1956	30·00
G17	DEC 1956	30·00
G18	FEB 1957	30·00
G19	APR 1957	30·00
G20	JUNE 1957	17·00
G21	AUG 1957	40·00

4s.6d. Booklets

1957–65. Panes of six stamps: 18×3d.
I. Purple cover as Type B.
A. Wmk St Edward's Crown (No. 545).

L1	OCT 1957	30·00
L2	DEC 1957	30·00
L3	FEB 1958	35·00
L4	APR 1958	30·00
L5	JUNE 1958	32·00
L6	OCT 1958	30·00
L7	DEC 1958	30·00

B. Wmk Crowns (No. 575).

L8	DEC 1958	£130

II. Purple cover as Type C. Wmk Crowns (No. 575) or graphite lines (No. 592).

L9	FEB 1959	35·00
L10	JUNE 1959	40·00
L11	AUG 1959	30·00
	g. With graphite lines	45·00
L12	OCT 1959	45·00
L13	DEC 1959	35·00

III. Violet cover as Type C. Wmk Crowns (No. 575), graphite lines (No. 592) or phosphor (No. 615).

L14	FEB 1959	£100
L15	APR 1959	35·00
	g. With graphite lines	30·00
L16	JUNE 1959	60·00
	g. With graphite lines	30·00
L17	DEC 1959	60·00
L18	FEB 1960	35·00
	g. With graphite lines	60·00
L19	APR 1960	35·00
	g. With graphite lines	35·00
L20	JUNE 1960	40·00
L21	AUG 1960	40·00
	p. With phosphor bands	60·00
L22	OCT 1960	55·00

IV. Violet cover as Type D. Wmk Crowns (No. 575) or phosphor (No. 615).

L23	DEC 1960	75·00
L24	FEB 1961	75·00
	p. With phosphor bands	50·00
L25	APR 1961	50·00
	p. With phosphor bands	45·00
L26	JUNE 1961	75·00
L27	AUG 1961	70·00
	p. With phosphor bands	80·00
L28	OCT 1961	70·00
	p. With phosphor bands	60·00
L29	DEC 1961	70·00
L30	FEB 1962	65·00
	p. With phosphor bands	40·00
L31	APR 1962	75·00
	p. With phosphor bands	80·00
L32	JUNE 1962	80·00
	p. With phosphor bands	90·00
L33	AUG 1962	60·00
	p. With phosphor bands	90·00
L34	OCT 1962	60·00
	p. With phosphor bands	£275
L35	DEC 1962	70·00
	p. With phosphor bands	80·00
L36	FEB 1963	70·00
	p. With phosphor bands	80·00
L37	APR 1963	70·00
	p. With phosphor bands	55·00
L38	JUNE 1963	70·00
	p. With phosphor bands	55·00
L39	AUG 1963	80·00
	p. With phosphor bands	65·00
L40	OCT 1963	75·00
	p. With phosphor bands	£100
L41	NOV 1963	80·00
	p. With phosphor bands	65·00
L42	DEC 1963	75·00
	p. With phosphor bands	£300
L43	JAN 1964	£125
L44	FEB 1964	80·00
	p. With phosphor bands	55·00
L45	MAR 1964	£125
		£180
L46	APR 1964	£125
	p. With phosphor bands	65·00
L47	MAY 1964	80·00
	p. With phosphor bands	£100
L48	JUNE 1964	80·00
	p. With phosphor bands	£100
L49	JULY 1964	80·00
	p. With phosphor bands	65·00
L50	AUG 1964	80·00
	p. With phosphor bands	55·00
L51	SEPT 1964	80·00
	p. With phosphor bands	65·00
L52	OCT 1964	80·00
	p. With phosphor bands	£100
L53	NOV 1964	80·00
	p. With phosphor bands	65·00
L54	DEC 1964	80·00
	p. With phosphor bands	65·00
L55	JAN 1965	70·00
	p. With phosphor bands	60·00
L56	FEB 1965	60·00
	p. With phosphor bands	80·00
L57	MAR 1965	35·00
	p. With phosphor bands	£500
L58	APR 1965	55·00

1965 (26 July)–**67.** New composition. Panes of six stamps: 12×4d., 6×1d. Slate-blue cover as Type D. Wmk Crowns (Nos. 571 and 576a) or phosphor (Nos. 611 and 616a).

L59	JULY 1965	30·00
	p. With phosphor bands	32·00
L60	SEPT 1965	30·00
	p. With phosphor bands	32·00
L61	NOV 1965	30·00
	p. With phosphor bands	35·00
L62	JAN 1966	35·00
	p. With phosphor bands	32·00
L63	MAR 1966	30·00
	p. With phosphor bands	30·00
L64	JAN 1967	40·00
	p. With phosphor bands	30·00
L65	MAR 1967	70·00
	p. With phosphor bands	25·00
L66p	MAY 1967. With phosphor bands	15·00
L67p	JULY 1967. With phosphor bands	25·00
L68p	SEPT 1967. With phosphor bands	20·00
L69p	NOV 1967. With phosphor bands	15·00
L70p	JAN 1968. With phosphor bands	15·00
L71p	MAR 1968. With phosphor bands	10·00

4s.6d. Booklets with Machin type stamps

1968–70. Slate-blue cover as Type D. Panes of six stamps: 12×4d., 6×1d. PVA gum (Nos. 724, 731v).

LP45	MAY 1968	4·00

LP46 Ships series with GPO Cypher

POST OFFICE STAMP BOOKLETS

(Des S. Rose)
Blue cover as Type **LP46**. Ships series. Composition as last.
LP46	JULY 1968 (*Cutty Sark*)	70

Same composition but changed to 4d. with one centre phosphor band (No. 732).
LP47	SEPT 1968 (*Golden Hind*)	70
LP48	NOV 1968 (*Discovery*)	70

Same composition but changed to 4d. bright vermilion with one centre phosphor band (No. 733).
LP49	JAN 1969 (*Queen Elizabeth 2*)	90
LP50	MAR 1969 (*Sirius*)	2·00
LP51	MAY 1969 (*Sirius*)	1·25
LP52	JULY 1969 (*Dreadnought*)	1·25
LP53	SEPT 1969 (*Dreadnought*)	5·00
LP54	NOV 1969 (*Mauretania*)	1·50
LP55	JAN 1970 (*Mauretania*)	5·00
LP56	MAR 1970 (*Victory*)	1·50
LP57	MAY 1970 (*Victory*)	5·00

LP58 Ships Series with Post Office Corporation Crown Symbol

(Des S. Rose)
As last but cover changed to T **LP58**.
LP58	AUG 1970 (*Sovereign of the Seas*)	4·50
LP59	OCT 1970 (*Sovereign of the Seas*)	5·00

5s. Booklets

1953–57. Buff cover. Panes of six stamps. 12×2½d., 6×2d., 6×1½d., 6×1d., 6×½d.

I. Composite booklets containing stamps of King George VI and Queen Elizabeth II.

A. KGVI ½d., 1d. and 2d. (Nos. 503/504 and 506) and QEII 1½d. and 2½d. (Nos. 517 and 519b). Cover as Type A. No interleaving pages.
H1	MAY 1953	45·00
H2	JULY 1953	50·00

B. Same composition but with addition of two interleaving pages, one at each end. Cover as Type A.
H3	SEPT 1953	65·00

C. Same composition and with interleaving pages but cover as Type B.
H4	NOV 1953	50·00
H5	JAN 1954	65·00

D. New composition: KGVI 1d. and 2d. (Nos. 504 and 506) and QEII ½d., 1½d. and 2½d. (Nos. 515, 517 and 519b).
H6	MAR 1954	£1000

E. New composition: KGVI 2d. (No. 506) and QEII ½d. 1d., 1½d. and 2½d. (Nos. 515/517 and 519b).
H7	MAR 1954	£275

II. Booklets containing only Queen Elizabeth II stamps. Buff cover as Type B. Two interleaving panes as before.

A. Wmk Tudor Crown (Nos. 515/518 and 519b).
H8	MAR 1954	£225
H9	MAY 1954	£120
H10	JULY 1954	£130
H11	SEPT 1954	95·00
H12	NOV 1954	£120

B. Same composition but with interleaving pages between each pane of stamps.
H13	JAN 1955	95·00
H14	MAR 1955	75·00
H15	MAY 1955	80·00
H16	JULY 1955	£120

C. Wmk St Edward's Crown (Nos. 540/543 and 544b).
H17	SEPT 1955	40·00
H18	NOV 1955	42·00
H19	JAN 1956	45·00
H20	MAR 1956	55·00
H21	MAY 1956	48·00
H22	JULY 1956	45·00
H23	SEPT 1956	48·00
H24	NOV 1956	48·00
H25	JAN 1957	55·00

5s. booklets dated SEPTEMBER and NOVEMBER 1955 and JANUARY 1956 exist both as listed and with the two watermarks mixed. There are so many different combinations that we do not list them separately, but when in stock selections can be submitted.

D. Same watermark. Introduction of 2d. light red-brown (No. 543b) in place of No. 543.
H26	JAN 1957	48·00
H27	MAR 1957	65·00
H28	MAY 1957	50·00
H29	JULY 1957	40·00
H30	SEPT 1957	40·00
H31	NOV 1957	40·00

1958–65.

E. New composition. Panes of six stamps: 12×3d. (No. 545), 6×2½d. (No. 544b), 6×1d. (No. 541), 6×½d. (No. 540). Wmk St Edward's Crown.
H32	JAN 1958	40·00
H33	MAR 1958	40·00
H34	MAY 1958	42·00
H35	JULY 1958 (11.58)	28·00
H36	NOV 1958	28·00

5s. booklets dated JULY 1958, NOVEMBER 1958 and JANUARY 1959 exist with mixed watermarks.

F. Blue cover as Type C. Wmk Crowns (Nos. 570/571, 574/575), graphite lines (Nos. 587/588 and 591/592) or phosphor (Nos. 610/611, 614 and 615).
H37	JAN 1959	35·00
H38	MAR 1959	45·00
H39	JULY 1959	42·00
	g. With graphite lines	£130
H40	SEPT 1959	45·00
H41	NOV 1959	45·00
H42	JAN 1960	45·00
H43	MAR 1960	45·00
	g. With graphite lines	£170
H44	MAY 1960	50·00
H45	JULY 1960	55·00
H46	SEPT 1960	80·00
	g. With graphite lines	£170
	p. With phosphor bands	£120
H47	NOV 1960	60·00

G. As last but blue cover as Type D. Same composition.
I. Phosphor has two bands on 2½d. (No. 614).
H48	JAN 1961	60·00
H49	MAR 1961	60·00
	p. With phosphor bands	£160
H50	MAY 1961	60·00
H51	JULY 1961	95·00
	p. With phosphor bands	£170
H52	SEPT 1961	60·00
	p. With phosphor bands	£225
H53	NOV 1961	60·00
H54	JAN 1962	95·00
	p. With phosphor bands	£225

II. As last but phosphor has one band on 2½d. (No. 614a).
H55	MAR 1962	85·00
	p. With phosphor bands	£180
H56	MAY 1962	60·00
	p. With phosphor bands	£200
H57	JULY 1962	95·00
	p. With phosphor bands	£180
H58	SEPT 1962	90·00
	p. With phosphor bands	£250
H59	NOV 1962	90·00
	p. With phosphor bands	£250
H60	JAN 1963	60·00
	p. With phosphor bands	£600
H61	MAR 1963	60·00
	p. With phosphor bands	£250
H62	MAY 1963	80·00
	p. With phosphor bands	£250
H63	JULY 1963	95·00
	p. With phosphor bands	£170
H64	SEPT 1963	60·00
	p. With phosphor bands	£250
H65	NOV 1963	60·00
	p. With phosphor bands	£250
H66	JAN 1964	60·00
	p. With phosphor bands	£120
H67	MAR 1964	60·00
	p. With phosphor bands	£120
H68	MAY 1964	95·00
	p. With phosphor bands	£225
H69	JULY 1964	95·00
	p. With phosphor bands	£200
H70	SEPT 1964	60·00
	p. With phosphor bands	£200
H71	NOV 1964	85·00
	p. With phosphor bands	£120
H72	JAN 1965	50·00
	p. With phosphor bands	£120
H73	MAR 1965	48·00
	p. With phosphor bands	£225
H74	MAY 1965	45·00
	p. With phosphor bands	£140

POST OFFICE STAMP BOOKLETS

5s. Booklets with Machin type stamps

HP26 English Homes Series with GPO Cypher

(Des S. Rose)

1968 (27 Nov)–**70**. Cinnamon cover as T **HP26** (English Homes Series). Panes of six stamps: 12×5d. (No. 735).

HP26	DEC 1968 (Ightham Mote)	2·00
HP27	FEB 1969 (Little Moreton Hall)	2·00
HP28	APR 1969 (Long Melford Hall)	2·00
HP29	JUNE 1969 (Long Melford Hall)	2·00
HP30	AUG 1969 (Long Melford Hall)	5·00

HP31 English Homes Series with Post Office Corporation Crown Symbol

(Des S. Rose)

*As last but cover changed to T **HP31**.*

HP31	OCT 1969 (Mompesson House)	2·25
HP32	DEC 1969 (Mompesson House)	2·50
HP33	FEB 1970 (Cumberland Terrace)	2·25

HP34

(Des P. Gauld)

*As last but cover changed to T **HP34** (special edition to advertise Philympia International Philatelic Exhibition, London, September 1970).*

HP34	(no date) (3.3.70)	2·25

*As last but cover changed to T **HP31**.*

HP35	JUNE 1970 (The Vineyard, Saffron Walden)	2·50
HP36	AUG 1970 (The Vineyard, Saffron Walden)	3·25
HP37	OCT 1970 (Mereworth Castle)	3·25
HP38	DEC 1970 (Mereworth Castle)	3·25

6s. Booklets

1965 (21 June)–**67**. Claret cover as Type D. Wmk Crowns (No. 576a) or phosphor (No. 616a). Panes of six stamps: 18×4d.

Q1	JUNE 1965	45·00
	p. With phosphor bands	45·00
Q2	JULY 1965	45·00
	p. With phosphor bands	45·00
Q3	AUG 1965	80·00
	p. With phosphor bands	80·00
Q4	SEPT 1965	60·00
	p. With phosphor bands	60·00
Q5	OCT 1965	90·00
	p. With phosphor bands	90·00
Q6	NOV 1965	90·00
	p. With phosphor bands	90·00
Q7	DEC 1965	90·00
	p. With phosphor bands	£100
Q8	JAN 1966	90·00
	p. With phosphor bands	90·00
Q9	FEB 1966	90·00
	p. With phosphor bands	90·00
Q10	MAR 1966	90·00
	p. With phosphor bands	£100
Q11	APR 1966	90·00
	p. With phosphor bands	£200
Q12	MAY 1966	90·00
	p. With phosphor bands	£100
Q13	JUNE 1966	90·00
	p. With phosphor bands	90·00
Q14	JULY 1966	90·00
	p. With phosphor bands	90·00
Q15	AUG 1966	90·00
	p. With phosphor bands	£250
Q16	SEPT 1966	55·00
	p. With phosphor bands	55·00
Q17	OCT 1966	£100
	p. With phosphor bands	£170
Q18	NOV 1966	75·00
	p. With phosphor bands	45·00
Q19	DEC 1966	45·00
	p. With phosphor bands	80·00
Q20	JAN 1967	90·00
	p. With phosphor bands	90·00
Q21	FEB 1967	90·00
	p. With phosphor bands	50·00
Q22	MAR 1967	60·00
	p. With phosphor bands	50·00
Q23	APR 1967	45·00
	p. With phosphor bands	50·00
Q24p	MAY 1967. With phosphor bands	40·00
Q25p	JUNE 1967. With phosphor bands	40·00
Q26p	JULY 1967. With phosphor bands	£100
Q27p	AUG 1967. With phosphor bands	75·00

6s. Booklets with Machin type stamps

1967–70. Claret cover as Type D. Panes of six stamps: 18×4d. Two phosphor bands. Gum arabic (No. 731).

QP28	SEPT 1967	50·00
QP29	OCT 1967	60·00
QP30	NOV 1967	50·00
QP31	DEC 1967	50·00
QP32	JAN 1968	48·00
QP33	FEB 1968 (No. 731a)	48·00
QP34	MAR 1968 (No. 731a)	48·00
QP35	APR 1968 (No. 731a)	35·00
QP36	MAY 1968 (No. 731a)	18·00

Change to PVA gum (No. 731v).

QP37	MAY 1968	£450

QP38 Birds Series with GPO Cypher

(Des S. Rose)

*Orange-red cover as T **QP38** (Birds Series). Same composition. Two phosphor bands. PVA gum (No. 731v).*

QP38	JUNE 1968 (Kingfisher) (4.6.68)	2·00
QP39	JULY 1968 (Kingfisher)	10·00
QP40	AUG 1968 (Peregrine Falcon)	2·00

Change to one centre phosphor band (No. 732).

QP41	SEPT 1968 (Peregrine Falcon) (16.9.68)	1·40
QP42	OCT 1968 (Pied Woodpecker)	2·00
QP43	NOV 1968 (Pied Woodpecker)	1·50
QP44	DEC 1968 (Great Crested Grebe)	1·50
QP45	JAN 1969 (Barn Owl)	2·75

Change to 4d. bright vermilion with one centre phosphor band (No. 733).

QP46	FEB 1969 (Barn Owl) (20.2.69)	3·50
QP47	MAR 1969 (Jay)	2·50
QP48	MAY 1969 (Jay)	3·25
QP49	JULY 1969 (Puffin)	2·50
QP50	SEPT 1969 (Puffin)	5·00

POST OFFICE STAMP BOOKLETS

QP51 Birds Series with Post Office Corporation Crown Symbol

(Des S. Rose)

*As last but cover changed to T **QP51**.*
QP51	NOV 1969 (Cormorant)	3·25
QP52	JAN 1970 (Cormorant)	3·75
QP53	APR 1970 (Wren)	3·00
QP54	AUG 1970 (Golden Eagle)	3·00
QP55	OCT 1970 (Golden Eagle)	3·00

10s. Booklets

1961 (10 Apr–Oct). Green cover as Type D. Panes of six stamps: 30×3d., 6×2d., 6×1½d., 6×1d., 6×½d. Wmk Crowns (Nos. 570/573 and 575).
X1	No date	£150
X2	OCT 1961	£300

1962–64. New Composition. Panes of six stamps: 30×3d., 6×2½d., 6×1½d., 6×1d. (Nos. 571/572 and 574/575).
X3	APR 1962	£130
X4	AUG 1962	£180
X5	MAR 1963	£275
X6	JULY 1963	£180
X7	DEC 1963	£160
X8	JULY 1964	£130
X9	DEC 1964	£600

1965 (23 Aug)–**66**. Ochre cover as Type D. Panes of six stamps: 24×4d., 6×3d., 6×1d. Wmk Crowns (Nos. 571, 575, 576a).
X10	AUG 1965	40·00
X11	DEC 1965	80·00
X12	FEB 1966	65·00
X13	AUG 1966	40·00
X14	NOV 1966	38·00

1967–68. Ochre cover as Type D. Panes of six phosphor stamps: 24×4d., 6×3d., 6×1d. Wmk Crowns (Nos. 611, 615cca (one side phosphor band), 616a).
X15p	FEB 1967	10·00

Composition as No. X15p. Wmk Crowns (Nos. 611, 615e (one centre phosphor band), 616b).
X16p	AUG 1967	7·00
X17p	FEB 1968	8·00

10s. Booklets with Machin type stamps

XP4 Explorers Series with GPO Cypher

(Des S. Rose)

1968 (25 Mar–Aug). Bright purple cover as T **XP4** (Explorers Series). Pages of six stamps: 24×4d., 6×3d., 6×1d. PVA gum (Nos. 724, 729v, 731v).
XP4	MAY 1968 (Livingstone)	4·50
XP5	AUG 1968 (Livingstone)	4·50

1968 (16 Sept)–**70**. Yellow-green covers as T **XP4** (Explorers Series) New composition. Pages of six stamps: 12×5d. (with two phosphor bands), 12×4d. (with one centre phosphor band) and pane comprising 4×1d. *se-tenant* with vert pair of 4d. (each with one centre phosphor band). PVA gum (Nos. 725, 732 and 735).
XP6	SEPT 1968 (Scott)	3·00

Change to 4d. bright vermilion (one centre band) but se-tenant pane comprises 1d. with two phosphor bands and 4d. with one left side phosphor band (Nos. 724 and 733/734).
XP7	FEB 1969 (Mary Kingsley) (6.1.69)	2·50
XP8	MAY 1969 (Mary Kingsley)	3·25
XP9	AUG 1969 (Shackleton)	3·50
XP10	NOV 1969 (Shackleton)	5·00

XP11 Explorers Series with Post Office Corporation Crown Symbol

(Des S. Rose)

*As last but cover changed to T **XP11**.*
XP11	FEB 1970 (Frobisher)	5·00
XP12	NOV 1970 (Captain Cook)	6·00

£1 Booklet with Machin type stamps

ZP1

1969 (1 Dec). Stamps for Cooks. T **ZP1** (150×72 mm) with full colour pictorial cover showing Baked, Stuffed Haddock. Contains 12 recipes on interleaving pages and on *se-tenant* labels attached to booklet panes. PVA gum. Stapled.
ZP1	£1 containing panes of 15 stamps (5×3): 15×5d. (No. 735), 30×4d. (No. 733) and pane comprising 6×4d. (three each of Nos. 734 and 734b) *se-tenant* with 6×1d. (No. 724) and 3×5d. (No. 735)	£325
ZP1a	As last but booklet is sewn with thread instead of being stapled	6·50

II. DECIMAL BOOKLETS, 1971 ONWARDS.

A. Stitched Booklets.

The 25p, 30p, 35p, 45p. and 50p. booklets have pictorial covers (except for the 35p. and 45p.) without the design inscription. This was no longer necessary as the designs and background information were given on the inside of the front cover. Each series was numbered.

10p. Booklets

DN46 British Pillar Box Series

POST OFFICE STAMP BOOKLETS

(Des R. Maddox)

1971 (15 Feb–1 June). British Pillar Box Series. Orange-yellow cover as T **DN46**. Panes of four stamps: 2×2p. *se-tenant* vertically with 2×½p. and 2×1p. *se-tenant* vertically with 2×1½p. (Nos. X841l and X844l).

DN46	FEB 1971 (No. 1 1855 type)	1·25
DN47	APR 1971 (No. 1 1855 type) (19.3.71)	1·00
DN48	JUNE 1971 (No. 2 1856 type) (1.6.71)	1·75

In No. DN47 the pillar box is slightly reduced in size.

1971 (14 July)–**74**. British Pillar Box Series continued. Orange-yellow cover as T **DN46**. Contents unchanged but panes are *se-tenant* horizontally (Nos. X841la and X844m).

DN49	AUG 1971 (No. 2 1856 type) (14.7.71)	1·50
DN50	OCT 1971 (No. 3 1857–1859 type) (27.8.71)	1·50
DN51	DEC 1971 (No. 3 1857–1859 type) (6.10.71)	2·25
DN52	FEB 1972 (No. 4 1866–1879 type) (8.12.71)	2·25
DN53	APR 1972 (No. 4 1866–1879 type) (24.2.72)	1·75
DN54	JUNE 1972 (No. 5 1899 type) (12.4.72)	1·25
DN55	AUG 1972 (No. 5 1899 type) (8.6.72)	1·50
DN56	OCT 1972 (No. 6 1968 type) (2.8.72)	1·50
DN57	DEC 1972 (No. 6 1968 type) (30.10.72)	1·50
DN58	FEB 1973 (No. 7 1936 type) (5.1.73)	1·50
DN59	APR 1973 (No. 7 1936 type) (2.4.73)	5·00
DN60	JUNE 1973 (No. 8 1952 type) (18.4.73)	2·00
DN61	AUG 1973 (No. 8 1952 type) (4.7.73)	10·00
DN62	OCT 1973 (No. 9 1973 type) (16.8.73)	1·75
DN63	DEC 1973 (No. 9 1973 type) (12.11.73)	2·00
DN64	FEB 1974 (No. 9 1973 type) (17.12.73)	2·25
DN65	APR 1974 (No. 10 1974 type) (22.2.74)	1·50
DN66	JUNE 1974 (No. 10 1974 type) (23.4.74)	1·50

DN67 Postal Uniforms Series

(Des C. Abbott)

1974 (23 July)–**76**. Postal Uniforms Series. Orange-yellow cover as T **DN67**. Contents unchanged.

DN67	AUG 1974 (No. 1 1793 type)	1·00
DN68	OCT 1974 (No. 1 1793 type) (27.8.74)	1·00
DN69	DEC 1974 (No. 2 1837 type) (25.10.74)	1·00
DN70	FEB 1975 (No. 2 1837 type) (12.12.74)	1·00
DN71	APR 1975 (No. 3 1855 type) (26.3.75)	1·00
DN72	JUNE 1975 (No. 3 1855 type) (21.5.75)	1·00
DN73	AUG 1975 (No. 3 1855 type) (27.6.75)	1·00
DN74	OCT 1975 (No. 3 1855 type) (3.10.75)	50
DN75	JAN 1976 (No. 3 1855 type) (16.3.76)	50

25p. Booklets

DH39 Veteran Transport Series

(Des D. Gentleman)

1971 (15 Feb). Veteran Transport Series. Dull purple cover as T **DH39**. Panes of six stamps: 5×2½p. with one printed label, 4×2½p. with two printed labels, 5×½p. with one printed label (Nos. X841m and X851l/X851m).

DH39	FEB 1971 (No. 1 Knife-board omnibus)	3·00

DH40

1971 (19 Mar). Issued to publicise the National Postal Museum Exhibition of 80 Years of British Stamp Booklets. Dull purple cover as T **DH40**.

DH40	APR 1971	3·50

1971 (11 June)–**73**. Dull purple cover as T **DH39**. Veteran Transport Series continued.

DH41	JUNE 1971 (No. 2 B-type omnibus)	3·25
DH42	AUG 1971 (No. 2 B-type omnibus) (17.9.71)	8·00
DH43	OCT 1971 (No. 3 Showman's Engine) (22.11.71)	8·00
DH44	FEB 1972 (No. 4 Mail Van) (23.12.71)	4·50
DH45	APR 1972 (No. 4 Mail Van) (13.3.72)	5·50
DH46	JUNE 1972 (No. 5 Motor Wagonette) (24.4.72)	4·00
DH47	AUG 1972 (No. 5 Motor Wagonette) (14.6.72)	8·00
DH48	OCT 1972 (No. 6 Taxi Cab) (17.7.72)	6·00
DH49	DEC 1972 (No. 6 Taxi Cab) (19.10.72)	8·00
DH50	DEC 1972 Issue S (No. 6 Taxi Cab) (6.11.72)	4·50
DH51	FEB 1973 (No. 7 Electric Tramcar) (26.2.73)	6·00

Nos. DH42/DH51 contain panes showing the perforations omitted between the label and the binding margin.

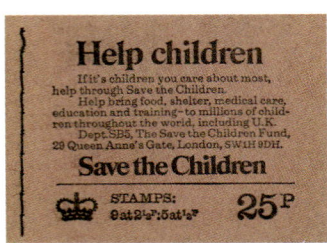

DH52

1973 (7 June). Dull mauve cover as T **DH52**.

DH52	JUNE 1973	6·00

No. DH52 contains panes showing the perforations omitted between the label and the binding margin.

30p. Booklets

DQ56 British Birds Series

(Des H. Titcombe)

1971 (15 Feb). British Birds Series. Bright purple cover as T **DQ56**. Panes of six stamps: 2 panes of 5×3p. with one printed label (No. X855l).

DQ56	FEB 1971 (No. 1 Curlew)	2·75

1971 (19 Mar). Bright purple cover as T **DH40**.

DQ57	APR 1971	3·75

POST OFFICE STAMP BOOKLETS

1971 (26 May)–**73**. Bright purple cover as T **DQ56**. British Birds Series continued.

DQ58	JUNE 1971 (No. 2 Lapwing)	3·75
DQ59	AUG 1971 (No. 2 Lapwing) (23.7.71)	3·75
DQ60	OCT 1971 (No. 3 Robin) (1.10.71)	3·75
DQ61	DEC 1971 (No. 3 Robin) (10.11.71)	4·50
DQ62	FEB 1972 (No. 4 Pied Wagtail) (21.12.71)	3·75
DQ63	APR 1972 (No. 4 Pied Wagtail) (9.2.72) .	3·75
DQ64	JUNE 1972 (No. 5 Kestrel) (12.4.72)	3·75
DQ65	AUG 1972 (No. 5 Kestrel) (8.6.72)	3·75
DQ66	OCT 1972 (No. 6 Black Grouse) (31.7.72)	4·25
DQ67	DEC 1972 (No. 6 Black Grouse) (30.10.72)	4·25
DQ68	DEC 1972 Issue S (No. 6 Black Grouse) (6.12.72)	4·25
DQ69	FEB 1973 (No. 7 Skylark) (29.1.73)	4·00
DQ70	APR 1973 (No. 7 Skylark) (2.4.73)	3·50
DQ71	JUNE 1973 (No. 8 Oystercatcher) (8.5.73)	4·00
DQ72	AUG 1973 (No. 8 Oystercatcher) (7.6.73)	5·50
DQ72a	As DQ72 but buff cover (10.8.73)*	4·50

* No. DQ72a was printed with a buff cover because of a shortage of the original purple coloured card.

Nos. DQ59/DQ72a contain panes showing the perforations omitted between the label and the binding margin.

1974 (30 Jan). Red cover similar to T **DH52**. Make-up as before but containing panes of 5×3p. (1 centre band) (No. X856) with blank label.

DQ73	SPRING 1974	3·00

1974 (2 June). Red cover similar to T **DT9**. Make-up as before.

DQ74	JUNE 1974	4·00

35p. Booklets

DP1 British Coins Series

(Des P Gauld)

1973 (12 Dec)–**74**. British Coins Series. Blue cover as T **DP1**. Panes of six stamps: 2 panes of 5×3½p. with one blank label (No. X858b).

DP1	AUTUMN 1973 (No. 1 Cuthred's Penny)	2·25
DP2	APR 1974 (No. 1 Cuthred's Penny) (10.4.74)	4·00
DP3	JUNE 1974 (No. 2 Silver Groat) (4.7.74)..	2·50

1974 (23 Oct). Blue cover as T **DT9**. Make-up as before but with No. X859.

DP4	SEPT 1974	2·50

45p. Booklets

1974 (9 Oct–26 Nov). British Coins Series continued. Yellow-brown cover as T **DP1**. Pages of six stamps: 2 panes of 5×4½p. (No. X865) with one blank label.

DS1	SEPT 1974 (No. 3 Elizabeth Gold Crown)	3·00
DS2	DEC 1974 (No. 3 Elizabeth Gold Crown) (1.11.74)	3·00
DS2a	As DS2 but orange-brown cover (26.11.74)*	20·00

* No. DS2a was printed with an orange-brown cover because of a shortage of the original yellow-brown card.

50p. Booklets

DT1

(Des Rosalie Southall)

1971 (15 Feb)–**72**. British Flowers Series. Turquoise-green cover as T **DT1**. Panes of six stamps: 6×3p., 4×3p. *se-tenant* horizontally with 2×2½p. (side band), 5×2½p. (centre band) with one printed label and 5×½p. with one printed label (Nos. X841m, X851l, X852l and X855×6).

DT1	FEB 1971 (No. 1 Large Bindweed)	5·00
DT2	MAY 1971 (No. 2 Primrose) (24.3.71)	6·00
DT3	AUG 1971 (No. 3 Honeysuckle) (28.6.71)	6·00
DT4	NOV 1971 (No. 4 Hop) (17.9.71)	6·25
DT5	FEB 1972 (No. 5 Common Violet) (23.12.71)*	6·25
DT6	MAY 1972 (No. 6 Lords-and-Ladies) (13.3.72)	6·25
DT7	AUG 1972 (No. 7 Wood Anemone) (31.5.72)	6·25
DT8	NOV 1972 (No. 8 Deadly Nightshade) (15.9.72)	5·25

* Although generally released on 24 December, this booklet was put on sale at the London EC1 Philatelic Counter and also at one other Philatelic Counter on 23 December.

Nos. DT4/DT8 contain panes showing the perforations omitted between the label and the binding margin.

DT9

1973 (19 Jan–June). Turquoise-green cover as T **DT9**.

DT9	FEB 1973	5·25
DT10	APR 1973 (26.2.73)	7·00
DT11	MAY 1973 (2.4.73)	6·75
DT12	AUG 1973 (14.6.73)	10·50

1973 (14 Nov)–**74**. Moss-green cover similar to T **DT9**. Pages of six stamps: 2 pages of 5×3½p. with one blank label (No. X858b) and 1 page of 5×3p. (centre band) and one blank label (No. X856).

DT13	AUTUMN 1973	4·50
DT14	MAR 1974 (18.2.74)	3·50

85p. Booklet

1974 (13 Nov). Purple cover similar to T **DT9**.

DW1	Containing 3 pages of 5×4½p. (No. X865) with one blank label and 1 page of 5×3½p. (No. X859) with one blank label	6·25

No. DW1 is dated SEPT 1974.

POST OFFICE STAMP BOOKLETS

SPONSORED AND PRESTIGE BOOKLETS

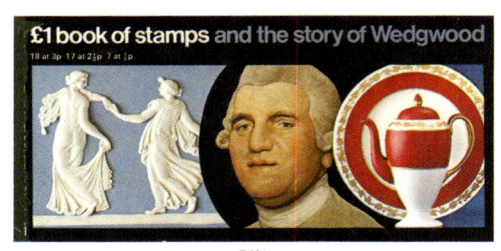

DX1

(Des J. Wallis)

1972 (24 May). The Story of Wedgwood. Full colour pictorial cover, T **DX1** (150×72 mm). Containing information and illustrations on interleaving panes and on *se-tenant* label attached to booklet panes.

DX1 £1 containing Nos. X841o/X841p, X851n and X855n booklet panes .... 60·00

Price quoted for No. DX1 is for examples showing the ½p. 1 side band, No. X842, (in pane No. X841p) with full perforations. Examples of the booklet with this ½p. value showing trimmed perforations are priced at £15.

ILLUSTRATIONS. Sponsored and Prestige booklet covers from No. DX2 are illustrated at one-third linear size unless otherwise stated.

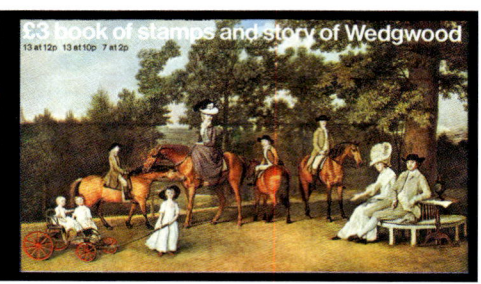

DX2

(Des J. Wallis)

1980 (16 Apr). The Story of Wedgwood. Multicoloured cover, T **DX2** (163×97 mm) showing painting Josiah Wedgwood and his Family by George Stubbs. Booklet contains text and illustrations on the labels attached to panes and on interleaving pages.

DX2 £3 containing booklet panes Nos. X849n, X849o, X888l and X895l............................. 3·75

No. DX2 is inscribed January 1980.

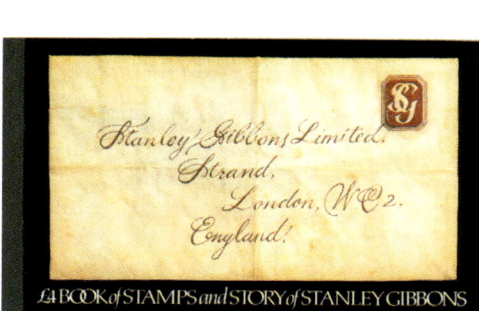

DX3

(Des B. Dedman)

1982 (19 May). Story of Stanley Gibbons. Multicoloured cover, T **DX3** (163×97 mm) showing early envelope design on front and stamp album with text on back. Booklet contains text and illustrations on labels attached to panes and on interleaving pages.

DX3 £4 containing booklet panes Nos. X849p, X899m and X907l/X907m......................... 5·00

No. DX3 is inscribed February 1982.

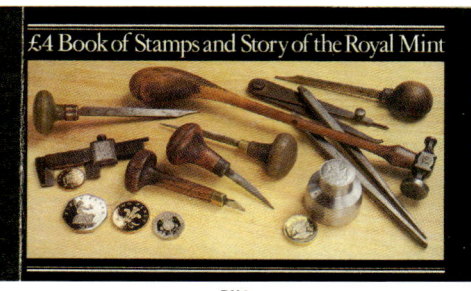

DX4

(Des B. West)

1983 (14 Sept). Story of the Royal Mint. Multicoloured cover, T **DX4** (163×97 mm) showing current coins, die and tools. Booklet contains text and illustrations on labels attached to panes and on interleaving pages.

DX4 £4 containing booklet panes Nos. X899m×2, X930l and X949l...................... 5·00

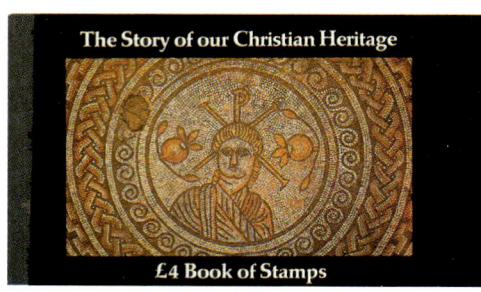

DX5

(Des P. Miles)

1984 (4 Sept). The Story of our Christian Heritage. Multicoloured cover, T **DX5** (163×97 mm) showing mosaic of Christ from Hinton St Mary Roman villa. Booklet contains text and illustrations on labels attached to panes and on interleaving pages.

DX5 £4 containing booklet panes Nos. X886bl, X901m×2 and X952l.................... 13·00

DX6

(Des D. Driver)

1985 (8 Jan). The Story of *The Times* (newspaper). Multicoloured cover, T **DX6** (163×95 mm) showing *Waiting for The Times* (painting by Haydon). Booklet contains text and illustrations on labels attached to panes and on interleaving pages.

DX6 £5 containing booklet panes Nos. X864l, X900l, X952l and X952m .... 8·50

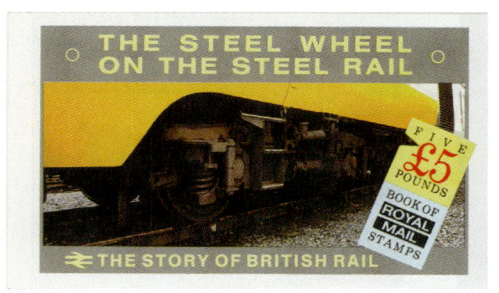

POST OFFICE STAMP BOOKLETS

DX7

(Des Trickett and Webb Ltd)

1986 (18 Mar). The Story of British Rail. Multicoloured cover, T **DX7** (162×95 mm) showing diesel locomotive. Booklet contains text and illustrations on labels attached to panes and on interleaving pages.
DX7 £5 containing booklet panes Nos. X896l, X897m, X952l and X952m .... 10·00

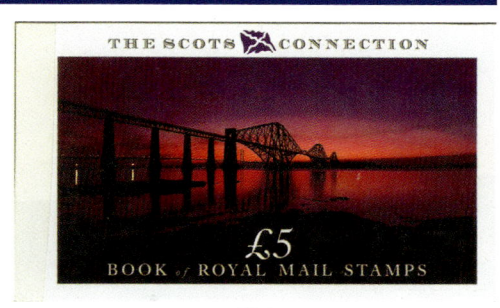

DX10

(Des Tayburn)

1989 (21 Mar). The Scots Connection. Multicoloured cover, T **DX10** (162×97 mm). Booklet contains text and illustrations on labels attached to the panes and on interleaving pages.
DX10 £5 containing booklet panes Nos. S54l, S55l, S62l and S62m .... 10·00

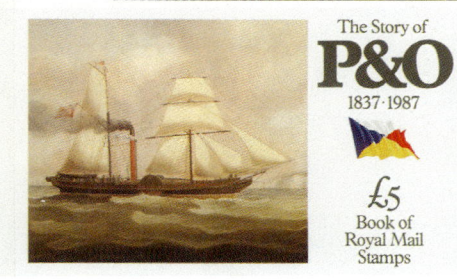

DX8

(Des Aitken Blakeley Designers)

1987 (3 Mar). The Story of P&O. Multicoloured cover, T **DX8** (162×95 mm) showing the *William Fawcett*. Booklet contains text and illustrations on labels attached to panes and on interleaving pages.
DX8 £5 containing booklet panes Nos. X847m, X900l, X900m and X955l .... 10·00

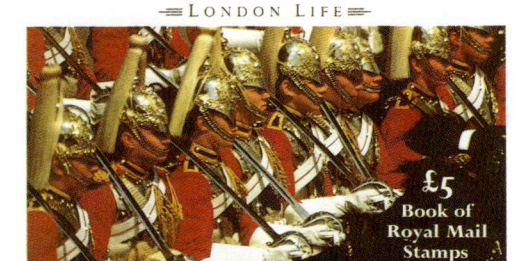

DX11

(Des D. Driver)

1990 (20 Mar). London Life. Multicoloured cover, T **DX11** (162×97 mm). Booklet contains text and illustrations on labels attached to the panes and on interleaving pages.
DX11 £5 containing booklet panes Nos. X906m, 1469n×2 and 1493a....................... 12·50

DX9

(Des The Partners)

1988 (9 Feb). The Story of the *Financial Times* (newspaper). Multicoloured cover, T **DX9** (162×97 mm). Booklet contains text and illustrations on labels attached to the panes and on interleaving pages.
DX9 £5 containing booklet panes Nos. X1005l, X1006l, X1009l and X1009m...................... 16·00

DX12

(Des Trickett and Webb Ltd)

1991 (19 Mar). Alias Agatha Christie. Multicoloured cover, T **DX12** (162×97 mm). Booklet contains text and illustrations on labels attached to the panes and on interleaving pages.
DX12 £6 containing booklet panes Nos. X1008l×2, X1016l and X1016m .... 9·00

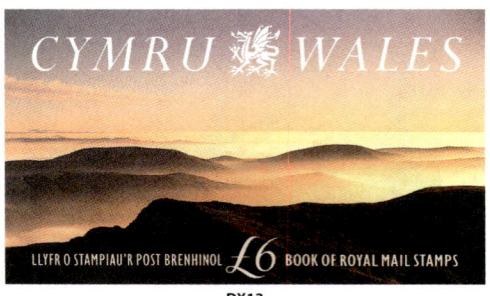

POST OFFICE STAMP BOOKLETS

DX13

(Des G. Evernden and J. Gibbs)

1992 (25 Feb). Cymru Wales. Multicoloured cover, T **DX13** (162×97 mm). Booklet contains text and illustrations on labels attached to the panes and on interleaving pages.
DX13 £6 containing booklet panes Nos. 1591a, W48l, W49l and W59l.................. 9·00

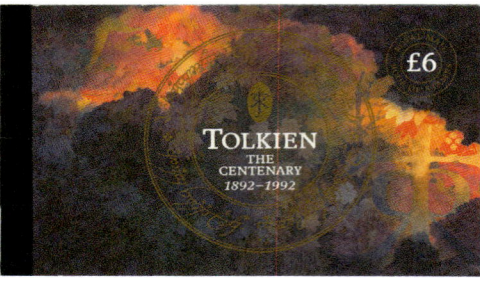

DX16

(Des Carroll, Dempsey and Thirkell Ltd)

1994 (26 July). Northern Ireland. Multicoloured cover, T **DX16** (162×97 mm). Booklet contains text and illustrations on labels attached to the panes and on interleaving pages.
DX16 £6·04 containing booklet panes Nos. Y1766l, 1812a and NI70l/NI70m, together with a 35p. postal stationery air card .... 12·00

DX14

(Des The Partners)

1992 (27 Oct). Birth Centenary of J. R. R. Tolkien (author). Multicoloured cover, T **DX14** (162×97 mm). Booklet contains text and illustrations on labels attached to the panes and on interleaving pages.
DX14 £6 containing booklet panes Nos. X1011/ X102l and X1017l×2 .... 9·00

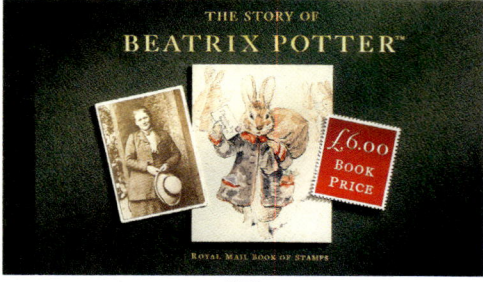

DX17

(Des The Partners)

1995 (25 Apr). Centenary of the National Trust. Multicoloured cover, T **DX17** (162×97 mm). Booklet contains text and illustrations on labels attached to the panes and on interleaving pages.
DX17 £6 containing booklet panes Nos. Y1767l, Y1771l, 1869a and NI70n .... 12·00

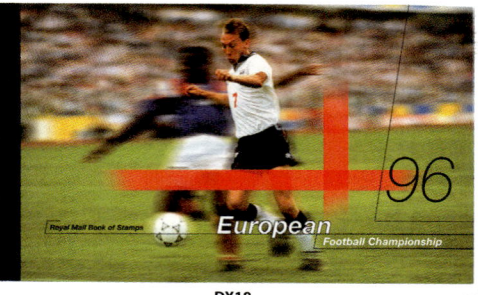

DX15

(Des The Partners)

1993 (10 Aug). The Story of Beatrix Potter. Multicoloured cover, T **DX15** (162×97 mm). Booklet contains text and illustrations on labels attached to the panes and on interleaving pages.
DX15 £5·64 containing booklet panes Nos. X1012m, 1451a1, 1649b and NI48l.......... 15·00
Although inscribed £6·00 No. DX15 was sold at the face value of its contents, £5·64.

DX18

(Des Why Not Associates)

1996 (14 May). European Football Championship. Multicoloured cover, T **DX18** (162×97 mm). Booklet contains text and illustrations on labels attached to the panes and on interleaving pages.
DX18 £6·48 containing booklet panes Nos. Y1775l, 1925a, 1926a and 1927a .... 9·00

POST OFFICE STAMP BOOKLETS

DX19

(Des H. Brown)

1997 (23 Sept). 75th Anniversary of the BBC. Multicoloured cover, T **DX19** (162×97 mm). Booklet contains text and illustrations on labels attached to the panes and on interleaving pages.
DX19 £6·15 containing booklet panes Nos. Y1686l, 1940ab, 1668l and NI81l.............................. 13·50

DX20

(Des Dew Gibbons Design Group)

1998 (10 Mar). The Wilding Definitives. Black and gold cover, T **DX20** (162×96 mm). Booklet contains text and illustrations on labels attached to the panes and on interleaving pages.
DX20 £7·49 containing booklet panes Nos. 2031b/2031c and 2032a/2032b.............. 11·00

Folder containing DX20, DX22, DX24 and **MS**2147 cancelled on presentation card... £150

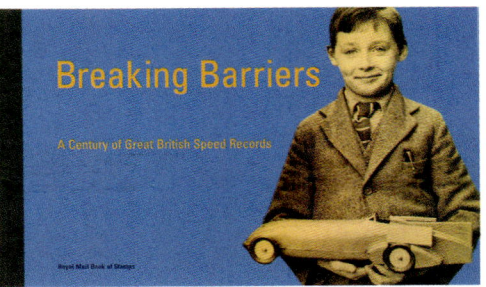

DX21

(Des Roundel Design Group)

1998 (13 Oct). Breaking Barriers. British Speed Record Holders. Multicoloured cover, T **DX21** (161×96 mm). Booklet contains text and illustrations on labels attached to the panes and on interleaving pages.
DX21 £6·16 containing booklet panes Nos. 1665l, Y1676al, 2059ac and NI80l......................... 18·00

(Des Dew Gibbons Design Group)

1999 (16 Feb). Profile on Print. Multicoloured cover as T **DX20** (162×96 mm). Booklet contains text and illustrations on labels attached to the panes and on interleaving pages.
DX22 £7·54 containing booklet panes Nos. 1667l, 1671n and 2077l/2079l................................. 25·00

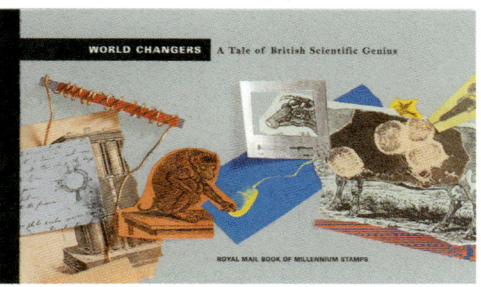

DX23

(Des Silk Pearce)

1999 (21 Sept). World Changers. Multicoloured cover as T **DX23** (163×96 mm). Booklet contains text and illustrations on labels attached to the panes and on interleaving pages.
DX23 £6·99 containing booklet panes Nos. Y1667n, 2072ab, 2080a, 2103ba and 2104ab... 17·00

(Des Dew Gibbons Design Group)

2000 (15 Feb). Special by Design. Multicoloured cover as T **DX20** (162×96 mm). Booklet contains text and illustrations on labels attached to the panes and on interleaving pages.
DX24 £7·50 containing booklet panes Nos. Y1683l, 2124dl, 2133al and NI88l .... 22·00

DX25

(Des J. Gibbs)

2000 (4 Aug). Queen Elizabeth the Queen Mother's 100th Birthday. Brownish grey and grey cover as T **DX25** (162×96 mm). Booklet contains text and illustrations on labels attached to the panes and on interleaving pages.
DX25 £7·03 containing booklet panes Nos. 2124m, 2160a, **MS**2161a and S94l .... 17·00

DX26

(Des Roundel Design Group)

2000 (18 Sept). A Treasury of Trees. Slate-green and bright green cover as T **DX26** (162×95 mm). Booklet contains text and illustrations on panes and interleaving pages.
DX26 £7 containing booklet panes Nos. 2155a, 2156a, 2158a, 2159a and W83al.............. 17·00

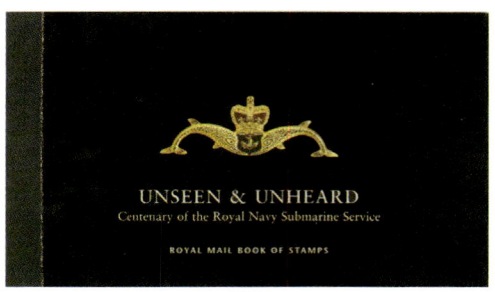

POST OFFICE STAMP BOOKLETS

DX27

(Des D. Davis)

2001 (22 Oct). Unseen and Unheard. Centenary of Royal Navy Submarine Service. Black, greenish yellow, new blue and red cover as T **DX27** (162×97 mm). Booklet contains text and illustrations on labels attached to the panes and on interleaving pages.

DX27 £6·76 containing booklet panes Nos.
2202ab, 2203ab, **MS**2206a and S95l...... 20·00

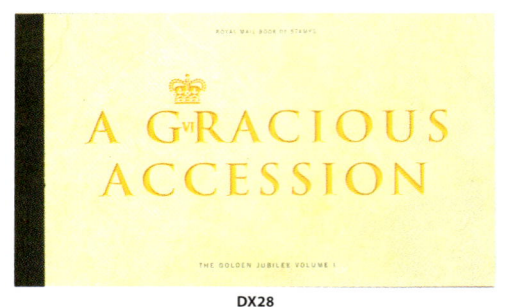

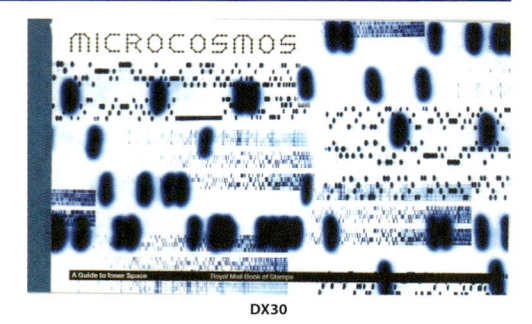

DX30

(Des CDT Design)

2003 (25 Feb). Microcosmos. 50th Anniversary of Discovery of DNA. Multicoloured cover as T **DX30** (164×95 mm). Booklet contains text and illustrations on labels attached to the panes and interleaving pages. Stitched.

DX30 £6·99 containing booklet panes Nos. 1668m,
2343a, 2345a and NI89l............................ 20·00

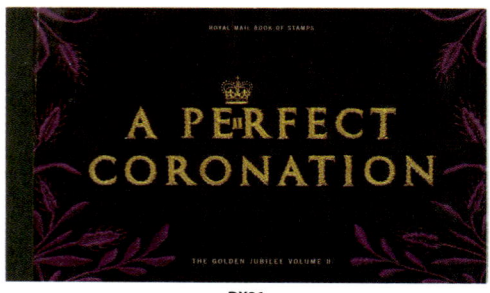

DX28

(Des GBH)

2002 (6 Feb). A Gracious Accession. Golden Jubilee of Queen Elizabeth II. Multicoloured cover as T **DX28** (161×96 mm). Booklet contains text and illustrations on labels attached to the panes and interleaving pages.

DX28 £7·29 containing booklet panes Nos. 1664n,
2253b/2254b and 2258b .... 22·50

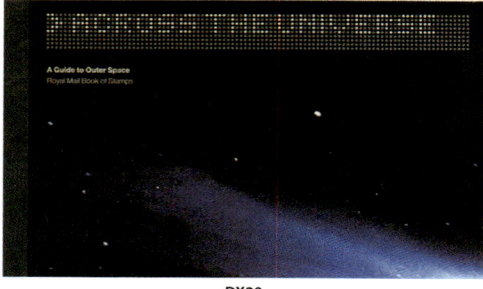

DX31

(Des GBH)

2003 (2 June). A Perfect Coronation. 50th Anniversary of Coronation. Multicoloured cover as T **DX31** (161×96 mm). Booklet contains text and illustrations on labels attached to the panes and on interleaving pages.

DX31 £7·46 containing booklet panes Nos. 1664o,
2368b/2369b and 2378a......................... 38·00

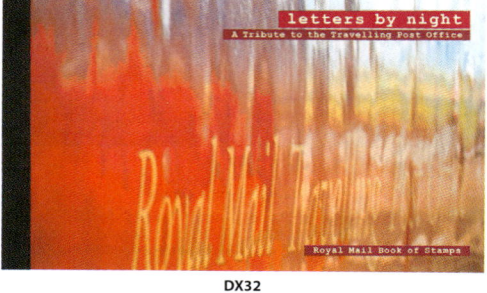

DX29

(Des CDT Design)

2002 (24 Sept). Across the Universe. Multicoloured cover as T **DX29** (164×95 mm). Booklet contains text and illustrations on labels attached to the panes and interleaving pages.

DX29 £6·83 containing booklet panes Nos. 1668m,
2126ac, **MS**2315a and EN1l .... 21·00

DX32

(Des Kate Stephens)

2004 (16 Mar). Letters by Night A Tribute to the Travelling Post Office. Multicoloured cover as T **DX32** (164×95 mm). Booklet contains text and illustrations on labels attached to the panes and interleaving pages. Stitched.

DX32 £7·44 containing booklet panes Nos. 1668o,
2392a, 2418a and S109l............................ 15·00

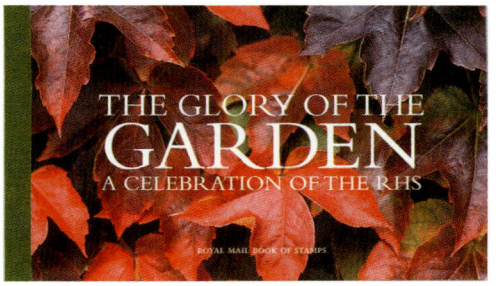

DX33

(Des John and Orna Designs)

2004 (25 May). The Glory of the Garden. Bicentenary of the Royal Horticultural Society. Multicoloured cover as T **DX33** (162×96 mm). Booklet contains text and illustrations on labels attached to the panes and interleaving pages. Stitched.

DX33 £7·23 containing booklet panes Nos. 1668p, 2456a, 2457a and 2463a .... 20·00

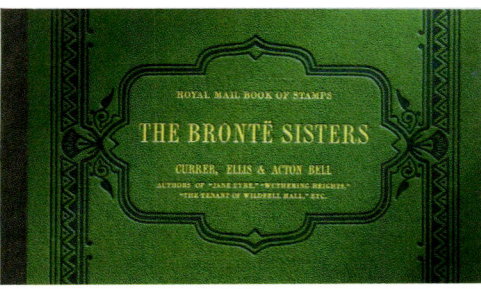

DX36 Plaque showing Clifton Suspension Bridge

(Des Hat-trick Design)

2006 (23 Feb). Birth Bicentenary of Isambard Kingdom Brunel. Grey and grey-black cover as T **DX36** (162×96 mm). Booklet contains text and illustrations on panes and interleaving pages. Stitched.

DX36 £7·40 containing booklet panes Nos. 1668r, 2607a/2608a and 2610a .... 15·00

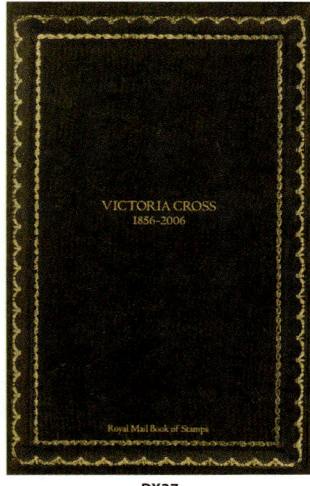

DX34

(Des Morgan Radcliffe)

2005 (24 Feb). The Brontë Sisters. 150th Death Anniversary of Charlotte Brontë. Multicoloured cover as T **DX34** (162×96 mm). Booklet contains text and illustrations on panes and interleaving pages. Stitched.

DX34 £7·43 containing booklet panes Nos. 1664p, EN6l, 2518a and 2520a .... 15·00

DX37

(Des Atelier Works)

2006 (21 Sept). 150th Anniversary of the Victoria Cross. Blackish-brown and gold cover as T **DX37** (162×96 mm). Booklet contains text and illustrations on panes and interleaving pages. Stitched.

DX37 £7·44 containing booklet panes Nos. 2651l, 2659b, 2660b and 2666a .... 15·00

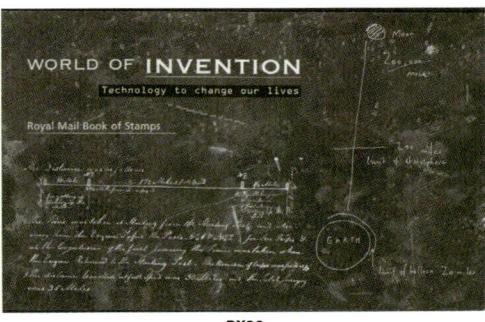

DX35 White Ensign

(Des Webb & Webb)

2005 (18 Oct). Bicentenary of the Battle of Trafalgar. Black, scarlet and ultramarine cover as T **DX35** (162×96 mm). Booklet contains text and illustrations on labels attached to the panes and interleaving pages. Stitched.

DX35 £7·26 containing booklet panes Nos. 1668q, 2574b/2575b and 2581a .... 16·00

DX38

(Des R. Warren-Fisher)

2007 (1 Mar). World of Invention. Black, olive-grey and grey cover as T **DX38** (162×95 mm). Booklet contains text and illustrations on panes and interleaving pages. Stitched.

DX38 £7·49 containing booklet panes Nos. S109m, Y1670l and 2721a/2721b .... 18·00

POST OFFICE STAMP BOOKLETS

DX39

(Des R. Warren-Fisher)

2007 (5 June). The Machin The Making of a Masterpiece. Multicoloured cover as T **DX39** (165×96 mm). Booklet contains text and illustrations on panes and interleaving pages. Stitched.

DX39 £7·66 containing booklet panes Nos. Y1668l, Y1744l, 2650l and 2741a .... 18·00

DX42 RAF Badge

(Des Silk Pearce)

2008 (18 Sept). Pilot to Plane. RAF Uniforms. Black on light blue cover as T **DX42** (162×96 mm). Booklet contains text and interleaving pages. Stitched.

DX42 £7·15 containing booklet panes Nos. 1670l, 2862b, 2865b and 2868a .... 15·00

DX40 Soldiers of 1854

(Des Atelier Works)

2007 (20 Sept). British Army Uniforms. Multicoloured cover as T **DX40** (164×96 mm). Booklet contains text and illustrations on panes and interleaving pages. Stitched.

DX40 £7·66 containing booklet panes Nos. Y1667o, 2774b, 2777b and EN30l .... 16·00

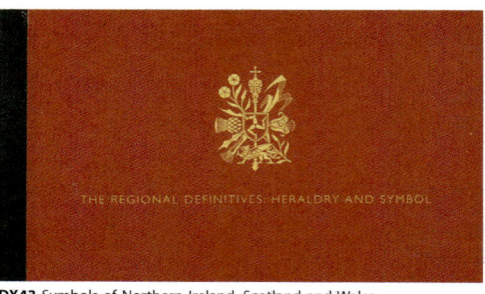

DX43 Symbols of Northern Ireland, Scotland and Wales

(Des Sedley Place)

2008 (29 Sept). 50th Anniversary of the Country Definitives. Multicoloured cover as T **DX43** (162×96 mm). Booklet contains text and illustrations on panes and interleaving pages. Stitched.

DX43 £9·72 containing booklet panes Nos. NI154l/ NI154m, S154l and W144l .... 24·00

DX41 Typewriter and Casino Royale

(Des GBH)

2008 (8 Jan). Ian Fleming's James Bond. Multicoloured cover as T **DX41** (164×96 mm). Booklet contains text and illustrations on panes and interleaving pages. Stitched.

DX41 £7·40 containing booklet panes Nos. 1672l, 2797a/2798a and 2805a .... 16·00

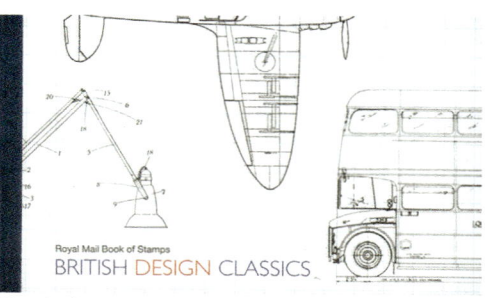

DX44 Graphic Drawings of Spitfire, Anglepoise Lamp and Routemaster Bus

(Des HGV)

2009 (13 Jan). British Design Classics. Multicoloured cover as T **DX44** (162×96 mm). Booklet contains text and illustrations on panes and interleaving pages. Stitched.

DX44 £7·68 containing booklet panes Nos. Y1769l, 2887b, 2888a and 2891a .... 24·00

DX45 Charles Darwin

(Des Howard Brown)

2009 (12 Feb). Birth Bicentenary of Charles Darwin. Multicoloured cover as T **DX45** (162×96 mm). Booklet contains text and illustrations on panes and interleaving pages. Stitched.
DX45 £7·75 containing booklet panes Nos. Y1762l,
         MS2904a, 2905a and 2906a...................... 40·00

DX48 Vinyl Disc

(Des True North)

2010 (7 Jan). Classic Album Covers. Black and pale blue cover as T **DX48** (162×96 mm). Booklet contains text and illustrations on panes and interleaving pages. Stitched.
DX48 £8·06 containing booklet panes Nos. Y1765l,
         Y1773l, 3009a and 3015a.......................... 35·00

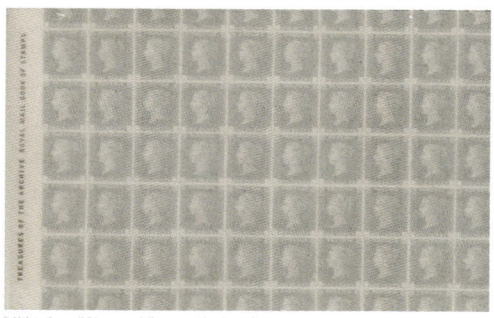

DX46 Proof Sheet of Penny Black Stamps

(Des Silk Pearce)

2009 (18 Aug). Treasures of the Archive. Clear cover showing illustrated pane as T **DX46** (162×96 mm). Booklet contains text and illustrations on panes and interleaving pages. Stitched.
DX46 £8·18 containing booklet panes Nos. Y1770l,
         2950a, 2955a and 2957a .... 22·00

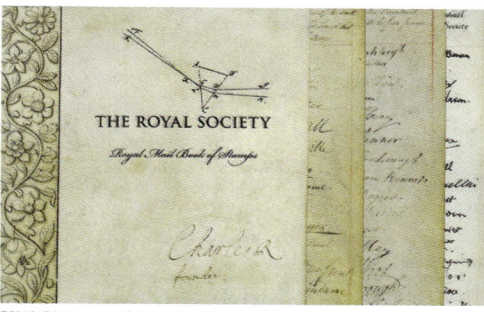

DX49 Diagram and Signatures

(Des Russell Warren-Fisher)

2010 (25 Feb). 350th Anniversary of the Royal Society. Multicoloured cover as T **DX49** (162×96 mm). Booklet contains text and illustrations on panes and interleaving pages. Stitched.
DX49 £7·72 containing booklet panes Nos. Y1774l,
         3026b, 3027a and 3029a............................ 17·00

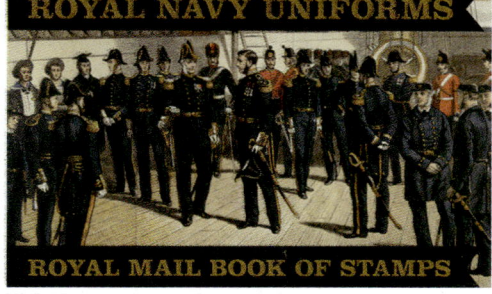

DX47 Officers, Marines and Seamen on Deck

(Des Webb and Webb Design Ltd)

2009 (17 Sept). Royal Navy Uniforms. Multicoloured cover as T **DX47** (163×96 mm). Booklet contains text and illustrations on panes and interleaving pages. Stitched.
DX47 £7·93 containing booklet panes Nos. Y1761l,
         2964b, 2967b and 2970a......................... 20·00

DX50

(Des Silk Pearce)

2010 (8 May). Centenary of Accession of King George V. Deep carmine and cream cover as T **DX50** (162×97 mm). Booklet contains text and illustrations on panes and interleaving pages. Stitched.
DX50 £11·15 containing booklet panes Nos. U2917l,
         3066a/3067a and 3070a............................. 28·00

POST OFFICE STAMP BOOKLETS

DX51

(Des Why Not Associates)

2010 (13 May). Britain Alone Grey, black and stone cover as T **DX51** (163×96 mm). Booklet contains text and illustrations on panes and interleaving pages. Stitched.

DX51 £9·76 containing booklet panes Nos. Y1763l, 3074a, 3076a and 3082a .... 20·00

DY2 Poster for First UK Aerial Mail, Hendon Aerodrome, 1911

(Des Robert Maude and Sarah Davies)

2011 (9 Sept). Centenary of the First United Kingdom Aerial Post. Black and grey cover as T **DY2** (161×96 mm). Booklet contains text and illustrations on panes and interleaving pages. Stitched.

DY2 £9·97 containing booklet panes Nos. Y1763m, 3216a, 3217a and 3221a.......... 40·00

The contents of No. DY2 have a face value of £9·02.

DX52 Wildlife

(Des Russell Warren-Fisher)

2011 (22 Mar). 50th Anniversary of the WWF. Multicoloured cover as T **DX52** (162×96 mm). Booklet contains text and illustrations on panes and interleaving pages. Stitched.

DX52 £9·05 containing booklet panes Nos. Y1764l, 3162b, 3164b and **MS**3172a..................... 25·00

DY3 Bookshelf

(Des Magpie Studio)

2012 (10 Jan). Roald Dahl's Children's Stories. Multicoloured cover as T **DY3** (163×96 mm). Booklet contains text and illustrations on panes and interleaving pages. Stitched.

DY3 £11·47 containing booklet panes Nos. Y1668m, 3254a, 3255a and 3260a.......... 20·00

The contents of No. DY3 have a face value of £10·52.

PREMIUM BOOKLETS: From the issue of the Morris and Co booklet, Royal Mail introduced an additional cost, over and above the face value of the stamps contained within them. They are separately numbered in a new series, commencing No. DY1.

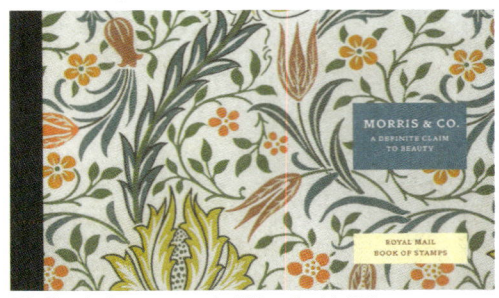

DY1 Flora (wallpaper pattern by William Morris), 1891

(Des Kate Stephens)

2011 (5 May). 150th Anniversary of Morris and Company (designers and manufacturers of textiles, wallpaper and furniture). Multicoloured cover as T **DY1** (162×96 mm). Booklet contains text and illustrations on panes and interleaving pages. Stitched.

DY1 £9·99 containing booklet panes Nos. U3057l, 3181a/3182a and 3186ab........................ 15·00

The contents of No. DY1 have a face value of £9·04.

DY4

(Des Russell Warren-Fisher)

2012 (31 May). Diamond Jubilee. Ultramarine, black and silver cover as T **DY4** (162×96 mm). Booklet contains text and illustrations on panes and interleaving pages. Stitched.

DY4 £12·77 containing booklet panes Nos. 3319Bb, 3320Bb, 3322Bb and U3279l... 20·00

The contents of No. DY4 have a face value of £11·84.

POST OFFICE STAMP BOOKLETS

DY5

(Des True North)

2012 (27 July). Olympic and Paralympic Games, London. Keeping the Flame Alive. Multicoloured cover as T **DY5** (162×96 mm). Booklet contains text and illustrations on panes and interleaving pages. Stitched.

DY5 £10·71 containing panes Nos. 2982b, 2983b, 2984b and 3337a.. 35·00

The contents of No. DY5 have a face value of £9·76.

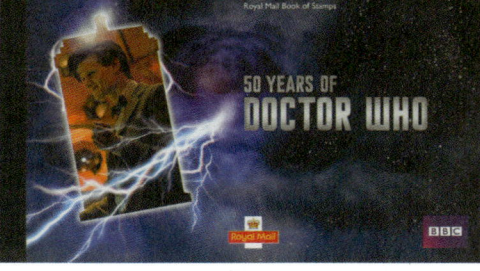

DY8 Merchant Ensign

(Des Russell Warren-Fisher)

2013 (19 Sept). Merchant Navy. Multicoloured cover, as T **DY8** (163×96 mm). Booklet contains text and illustrations on panes and interleaving pages. Stitched.

DY8 £11·19 containing panes Nos. U3073l, 3519a, 3522a and 3525a.. 18·00

The contents of No. DY8 have a face value of £10·24.

DY6

(Des GBH)

2013 (26 Mar). 50th Anniversary of *Doctor Who* (TV programme). Multicoloured cover as T **DY6** (163×96 mm). Booklet contains text and illustrations on panes and interleaving pages. Stitched.

DY6 £13·77 containing booklet panes Nos. U3072l, 3437b, 3440b, 3444b and **MS**3451a ...... 24·00

The contents of No. DY6 have a face value of £12·82.

DY9 Southern Railway Class M7 No. 53 on the Great Central Railway, 2012

(Des Delaney Design Consultants)

2014 (20 Feb). Classic Locomotives of the United Kingdom. Black, grey and gold cover as T **DY9** (163×96 mm). Booklet contains text and illustrations on panes and interleaving pages. Stitched.

DY9 £13·97 containing booklet panes Nos. U3071m, 3570a, 3571a, 3572a and 3573a.. 35·00

The contents of No. DY9 have a face value of £13·02.

DY7 Gordon Banks, John Barnes, Bobby Moore, Kevin Keegan and George Best

(Des True North)

2013 (9 May). Football Heroes. Multicoloured cover as T **DY7** (163×96 mm). Booklet contains text and illustrations on panes and interleaving pages. Stitched.

DY7 £11·11 containing booklet panes Nos. U3070l/U3071l, 3479a and 3484a........... 26·00

No. DY7 was issued in a souvenir foil wrapper.
The contents of No. DY7 have a face value of £10·56.

DY10

(Des So Design Consultants)

2014 (15 Apr). Buckingham Palace, London. Multicoloured cover as T **DY10** (162×96 mm). Booklet contains text and illustrations on panes and interleaving pages. Stitched.

DY10 £11·39 containing booklet panes Nos. U3074l, 3589ba, 3591ba and 3597a....................... 16·00

The contents of No. DY10 have a face value of £10·44.

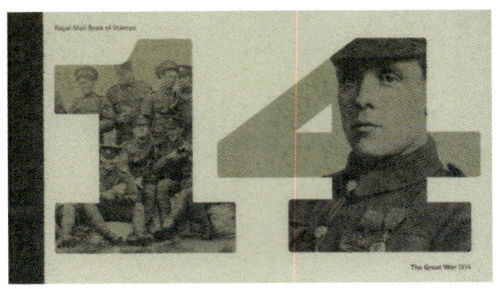

POST OFFICE STAMP BOOKLETS

DY11

(Des Hat-trick design)

2014 (28 July). Centenary of the First World War (1st issue). Multicoloured cover as T **DY11** (163×96 mm). Booklet contains text and illustrations on panes and interleaving pages. Stitched.

DY11 £11·30 containing panes Nos. U3074m, U3082l, 3626b and 3629b.......................... 16·00

The contents of No. DY11 have a face value of £10·35.

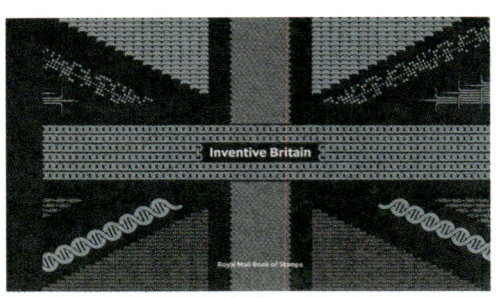

DY14 Arthur Wellesley, First Duke of Wellington, the Emperor Napoléon and Battle of Waterloo

(Des Webb & Webb Design Ltd)

2015 (18 June). Bicentenary of the Battle of Waterloo. Multicoloured cover as T **DY14** (161×96 mm). Booklet contains text and illustrations on panes and interleaving pages. Stitched.

DY14 £14·47 containing booklet panes Nos. U3072m, 3724a/37245a and 3730a....... 27·00

The contents of No. DY14 have a face value of £13·52.

DY12

(Des Supple Studio)

2015 (19 Feb). Inventive Britain. Black and silver cover as T **DY12** (162×96 mm). Booklet contains text and illustrations on panes and interleaving pages. Stitched.

DY12 £14·60 containing booklet panes Nos. U3070m, 3679b/3679c and 3681b......... 22·00

The contents of No. DY12 have a face value of £13·67.

DY15 Starfighters

(Des Interabang)

2015 (17 Dec). The Making of *Star Wars*. The British Story. Multicoloured cover as T **DY15** (163×95 mm). Booklet contains text and illustrations on panes and interleaving pages. Stitched.

DY15 £16·99 containing booklet panes Nos. U3150l, 3758b, 3759b, 3780a and 3783a .... 28·00

The contents of No. DY15 have a face value of £16·20.

No. DY15 was issued to coincide with the UK release of *Star Wars The Force Awakens*.

DY13 11th Battalion, 3rd Brigade, Australian Imperial Force on Great Pyramid of Khufu, 1915 and Worker at National Shell Filling Factory, Chilwell, Nottinghamshire

(Des Hat-trick design)

2015 (14 May). Centenary of the First World War (2nd issue). Multicoloured cover as T **DY13** (162×96 mm). Booklet contains text and illustrations on panes and interleaving pages. Stitched.

DY13 £13·96 containing panes Nos. 2776b, U3070n, 3711a and 3714a........................... 22·00

The contents of No. DY13 have a face value of £11·68.

DY16 Cancelled Penny Red

(Des Atelier Works)

2016 (18 Feb). 500 Years of Royal Mail. Multicoloured cover as T **DY16** (163×96 mm). Booklet contains text and illustrations on panes and interleaving pages. Stitched.

DY16 £16·36 containing booklet panes Nos. 3795a, 3796a, 3802a and 3807a .... 27·00

The contents of No. DY16 have a face value of £15·41.

POST OFFICE STAMP BOOKLETS

DY17 Queen Elizabeth II on State Visit to Germany, June 2015

(Des Kate Stephens)

2016 (21 Apr). 90th Birthday of Queen Elizabeth II. Multicoloured cover as T **DY17** (161×95 mm). Booklet contains text and illustrations on panes and interleaving pages. Stitched.
DY17   £15·11 containing booklet panes Nos. U3156l, 3826b, 3829b and MS3832b...................... 32·00

The contents of No. DY17 have a face value of £14·16.
A limited edition (1923) of this prestige stamp booklet was sold for £59·99. This special edition booklet had cover decorated with 22 carat gold foil filigree designs and the '90' pane also with 22 carat gold foil.

DY18 William Leefe Robinson (awarded Victoria Cross) and Infantry Attack, Battle of the Somme

(Des Hat-trick design)

2016 (21 June). Centenary of the First World War (3rd issue). Multicoloured cover as T **DY18** (161×95 mm). Booklet contains text and illustrations on panes and interleaving pages. Stitched.
DY18   £16·49 containing panes Nos. 3717a, 3838a, 3841a and 3844a............................ 25·00

The contents of No. DY18 have a face value of £15·54.

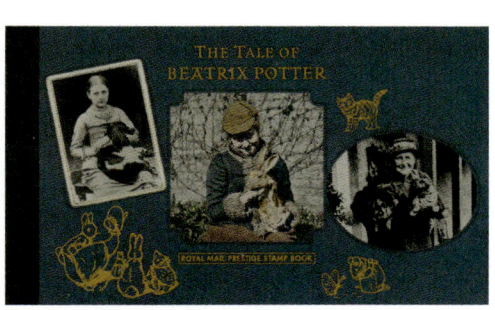

DY19 Beatrix Potter with Spaniel Spot, Rabbit Benjamin Bouncer and Two Pekingese Dogs

(Des Webb & Webb Design Ltd)

2016 (28 July). The Tale of Beatrix Potter. Multicoloured cover as T **DY19** (162×96 mm). Booklet contains text and illustrations on panes and interleaving pages. Stitched.
DY19   £15·37 containing booklet panes Nos. U3072n, 3856b, 3857b and 3864a.......... 24·00

The contents of No. DY19 have a face value of £14·42.
A limited edition (1866) of this prestige stamp booklet was sold for £59·99. This booklet contained two special end pages with sketches by Beatrix Potter and an extra central page with a Peter Rabbit illustration.

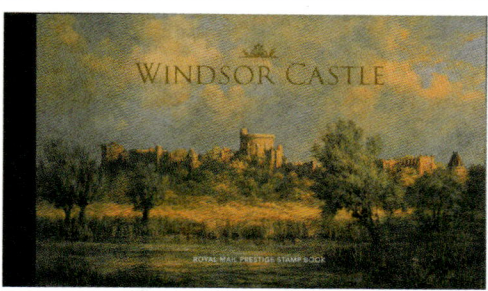

DY20 *Windsor Castle: from the River Thames* (Richard Willis)

(Des Silk Pearce)

2017 (15 Feb). Windsor Castle. Multicoloured cover as T **DY20** (162×96 mm). Booklet contains text and illustrations on panes and interleaving pages. Stitched.
DY20   £14·58 containing booklet panes Nos. U3071n, 3920b, 3921b and 3928a.......... 24·00

The contents of No. DY20 have a face value of £13·63.

DY21 Machin Definitives

(Des Godfrey Design)

2017 (5 June). 50th Anniversary of the Machin Definitive. Multicoloured cover as T **DY21** (162×96 mm). Booklet contains text and illustrations on panes and interleaving pages. Stitched.
DY21   £15·59 containing booklet panes Nos. 3958a, 3961a, U3966l, Y1667p and 1668sl......... 38·00

The contents of No. DY21 have a face value of £14·64.
A limited edition (500) of this stamp booklet with a duotone front cover with silver foil lettering was sold for £99·95. It was contained within a display case with a silver-plated Machin medallion.

DY22 Women's Land Army member competing in All England Girls' Farming Competition, Bishops Stortford, Hertfordshire, 1917 and Australian Troops crossing duckboard track through remains of Chateau Wood during Third Battle of Ypres (Passchendaele), 29 October 1917

(Des Hat-trick design)

2017 (31 July). Centenary of the First World War (4th issue). Grey and gold cover as T **DY22** (162×96 mm). Booklet contains text and illustrations on panes and interleaving pages. Stitched.
DY22   £15·41 containing booklet panes Nos. 2883b, 3717b, 3983a and 3986a........................... 25·00

The contents of No. DY22 have a face value of £14·46.

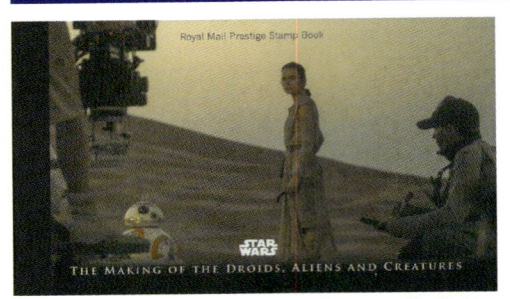

POST OFFICE STAMP BOOKLETS

DY23 Filming Rey (Daisy Ridley) and BB-8 in Desert near Abu Dhabi

(Des Interabang)

2017 (14 Dec). *Star Wars: The Making of Aliens, Creatures and Droids*. Multicoloured cover as T **DY23** (162×96 mm). Booklet contains text and illustrations on panes and interleaving pages. Stitched.
DY23 £15·99 containing booklet panes Nos.
U3150m, 3759c, 3762b and 4008a .... 25·00
The contents of No. DY23 have a face value of £14·32.
A limited edition (1977) of this prestige stamp booklet was sold for £75. It had silver foiling on the cover and was packaged in a silver metal clamshell..

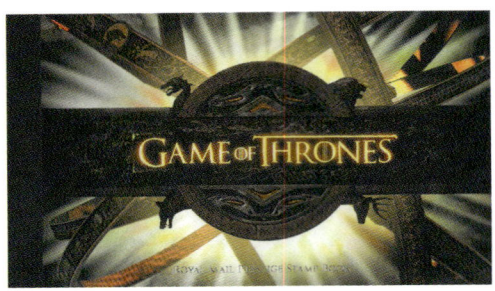

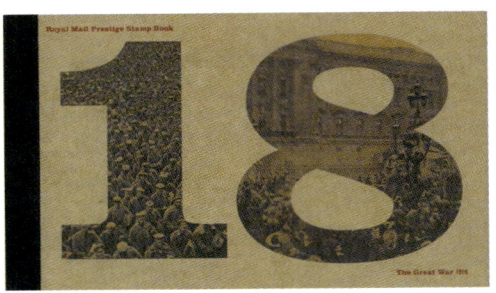

DY26 German Prisoners near Abbeville and Crowds outside Buckingham Palace

(Des Hat-trick design)

2018 (13 Sept). Centenary of the First World War (5th issue). Multicoloured cover, as T **DY26** (162×96 mm). Booklet contains text and illustrations on panes and interleaving pages. Stitched.
DY26 £15·65 containing panes Nos. 3627b,
U3156m, 4133a and 4136a .... 25·00
The contents of No. DY26 have a face value of £14·40.

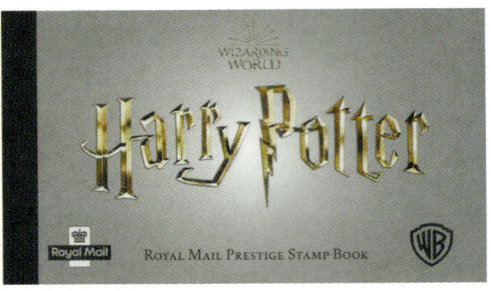

DY24 *Game of Thrones*

(Des GBH)

2018 (23 Jan). *Game of Thrones*. Multicoloured cover as T **DY24** (162×96 mm). Booklet contains text and illustrations on panes and interleaving pages. Stitched.
DY24 £13·95 containing booklet panes Nos. 4033b,
4036b, 4045a and U3072o .... 24·00
The contents of No. DY24 have a face value of £12·99.
A limited edition (2000) of this stamp booklet was issued in a leather folder and originally sold for £75.

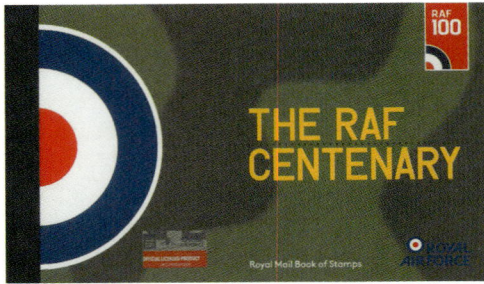

DY27 Harry Potter

(Des The Chase)

2018 (4 Dec). Harry Potter. Multicoloured cover as T **DY27** (162×96 mm). Booklet contains text and illustrations on panes and interleaving pages. Stitched.
DY27 £15·50 containing booklet panes Nos.
U3070o, 4141b, 4142b, 4164a and
4167a.. 25·00
The contents of No. DY27 have a face value of £13·97.
A limited edition prestige stamp booklet was originally sold for £45.

DY25 RAF Roundel and Centenary Emblem

(Des Common Curiosity)

2018 (20 Mar). Centenary of the RAF (Royal Air Force). Multicoloured cover as T **DY25** (163×96 mm). Booklet contains text and illustrations on panes and interleaving pages. Stitched.
DY25 £18·69 containing booklet panes Nos.
U3071o, 4058b, 4059b, 4067a and
4071a.. 30·00
The contents of No. DY25 have a face value of £18·54.
A limited edition (2018) of this stamp booklet with a yellow band at the left of the front cover was originally sold for £45.

DY28 The Head of the Madonna

(Des Kate Stephens)

2019 (13 Feb). 500th Death Anniversary of Leonardo da Vinci (1452–1519, artist). Multicoloured cover as T **DY28** (163×96 mm). Booklet contains text and illustrations on panes and interleaving pages. Stitched.
DY28 £13·10 containing booklet panes Nos.
U3072p, 4170b, 4171b and 4175b .... 32·00
The contents of No. DY28 have a face value of £11·64.

POST OFFICE STAMP BOOKLETS

DY29 Iron Man

(Des Interabang)

2019 (14 Mar). Marvel. Multicoloured cover as T **DY29** (162×96 mm). Booklet contains text and illustrations on panes and interleaving pages. Stitched.
DY29   £17.45 containing booklet panes Nos.
            U3070p, 4182b, 4185b, 4195a and
            4196a..   27·00

The contents of No. DY29 have a face value of £15·98.

A limited edition (4995) prestige stamp booklet was originally sold for £64·99. It had a Spider-man front cover and a Spider-man tin presentation case

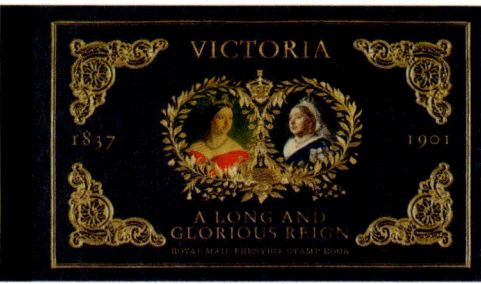

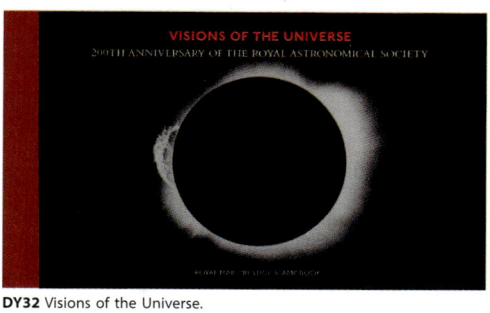

DY32 Visions of the Universe.

(Des True North)

2020 (11 Feb). Visions of the Universe. Bicentenary of the Royal Astronomical Society. Multicoloured cover as T **DY32** (162×96 mm). Booklet contains text and illustrations on panes and interleaving pages. Stitched.
DY32   £16·10 containing booklet panes Nos.
            U3070q, U3072r, 4323b and 4324b........   34·00

The contents of No. DY32 have a face value of £14·82.

DY30 Queen Victoria in 1856 (Franz Xavier Winterhalter) and 1890 (Heinrich von Angeli)

2019 (24 May). Birth Bicentenary of Queen Victoria. Multicoloured cover as T **DY30** (162×96 mm). Booklet contains text and illustrations on panes and interleaving pages. Stitched.
DY30   £17·20 containing booklet panes Nos.
            U3071p, 4219b, 4222b and 4226a............   50·00

The contents of No. DY30 have a face value of £15·64.

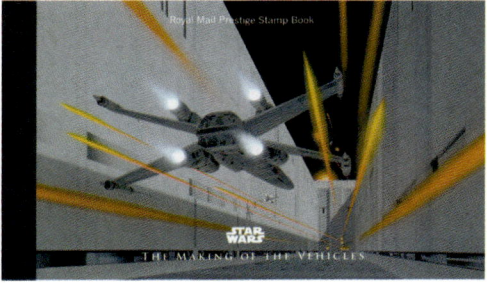

DY33 Filming of James Bond

(Des Interabang)

2020 (17 Mar). James Bond. Multicoloured cover as T **DY33** (163×96 mm). Booklet contains text and illustrations on panes and interleaving pages. Stitched.
DY33   £16·99 containing booklet panes Nos.
            U3071q, 4332b, 4336a and 4341a ....   25·00

The contents of No. DY33 had a face value of £15·28.

DY31 X-Wing Fighter

2019 (26 Nov). *Star Wars*. The Making of the Vehicles. Multicoloured cover as T **DY31** (162×96 mm). Booklet contains text and illustrations on panes and interleaving pages. Stitched.
DY31   £17·65 containing booklet panes Nos.
            U3072r, 4292b, 4293b, 4306a and
            4309a..   27·00

The contents of No. DY31 have a face value of £16·08.

DY34 Street Party, Manchester

(Des hat-trick design)

2020 (8 May). 75th Anniversary of the End of the Second World War. Multicoloured cover, 163×96 mm, as T **DY34**. Booklet contains text and illustrations on panes and interleaving pages. Stitched.
DY34   £19·80 containing booklet panes Nos.
            U3072s, 4356b, 4360b and 4365a...........   38·00

The contents of No. DY34 have a face value of £18·16.

POST OFFICE STAMP BOOKLETS

DY35 Queen Band Crest

(Des Baxter & Bailey)

2020 (9 Ju;ly). Queen (rock band). Gold and steel-blue cover, 163×96 mm, as T **DY35**. Booklet contains text and illustrations on panes and interleaving pages. Stitched
DY35   £19·10 containing booklet panes Nos. U3070r,
                4388b, 4392b and 4399a............................ 27·00
The contents of No. DY35 have a face value of £17·42.

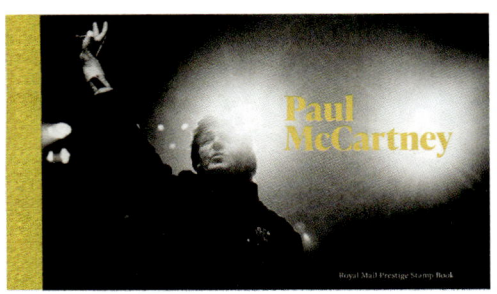

DY38 Onstage at the Ahoy, Rotterdam, Paul McCartney World Tour, 1989

(Des Baxter & Bailey)

2021 (28 May). Paul McCartney. Multicoloured cover, 162×96 mm, as Type **DY38**. Booklet contains text and illustrations on panes and interleaving pages. Stitched.
DY38   £20·25 containing booklet panes Nos.
                U3071s, 4517b, 4521b and 4528a........... 30·00
The contents of No. DY38 have a face value of £18·24.

A limited edition (1,970) prestige stamp booklet was originally sold for £49.99. It has a special edition front cover with a photograph of Paul McCartney taken in 2020 and comes in a matt black folder with a silver foil signature and a certificate of authenticity.

DY36 Starship USS *Enterprise* in Planetary Orbit, *Star Trek* Original Series

(Des Interabang)

2020 (13 Nov). *Star Trek*. Multicoloured cover, 162×96 mm, as T **DY36**. Booklet contains text and illustrations on panes and interleaving pages. Stitched.
DY36   £18·35 containing booklet panes Nos. U3071r,
                4443b, 4449b and 4458a............................ 26·00
The contents of No. DY36 have a face value of £17·17.

DY39 Black Country near Bilston, from engraving by John Alfred Langford, 1872

(Des Common Curiosity)

2021 (12 Aug). Industrial Revolutions. Multicoloured cover, 162×96 mm, as Type **DY39**. Booklet contains text and illustrations on panes and interleaving pages. Stitched.
DY39   £18·03 containing booklet panes Nos. U3072t,
                4555b, 4557b and 4562a............................ 35·00
The contents of No. DY39 have a face value of £16·38.

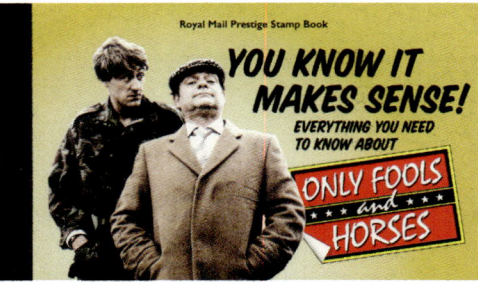

DY37 Only Fools and Horses

(Des (Des Interabang))

2021 (16 Feb). *Only Fools and Horses* (TV Sitcom, 1981–2003) Multicoloured cover as T **DY37** (162×96 mm). Booklet contains text and illustrations on panes and interleaving pages. Stitched.
DY37   £21·70 containing booklet panes Nos. U3075l,
                4477b, 4481b and 4488a............................ 30·00
The contents of No. DY37 have a face value of £19·77.

A limited edition (1981) prestige stamp booklet was originally sold for £54·99. It came packaged in Del Boy's briefcase style box and included a certificate of authenticity.

DY40 Batman, Wonder Woman and Superman

(Des Interabang)

2021 (17 Sept). DC Collection. Multicoloured cover, 162×95 mm, as Type **DY40**. Booklet contains text and illustrations on panes and interleaving pages. Stitched.
DY40   £21·20 containing booklet panes Nos.
                U3075m, 4575b, 4581b, 4591a and
                4593a............................ 32·00
The contents of No. DY40 have a face value of £19·58.

A limited edition (1,939) prestige stamp booklet was originally sold for £49.99. It has a special edition front cover and comes in a grey linen box embossed with the official DC logo with a certificate of authenticity.

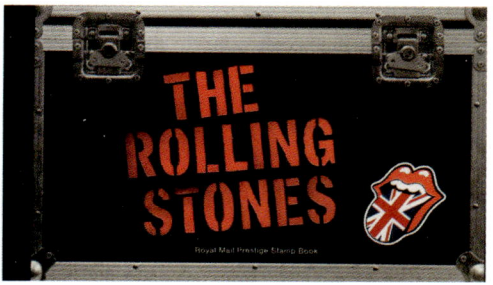

POST OFFICE STAMP BOOKLETS

DY41 The Rolling Stones

(Des Baxter & Bailey)

2022 (20 Jan). The Rolling Stones. Multicoloured cover, 161×95 mm, as Type **B41**.
DY41 £20·85 containing booklet panes Nos. U3074n, 4614b, 4616b and 4623a.......... 30·00

The contents of No. DY41 have a face value of £18·90.

A limited edition (5000) prestige stamp booklet was originally sold for £49.99. It had a special front cover showing the Rolling Stones tongue and lips logo and came in a flight case style presentation box with a certificate of authenticity.

DY42 Queen Elizabeth II leaving Fiji, February 1977

(Des Kate Stephens)

2022 (4 Feb). Platinum Jubilee. Multicoloured cover, 161×95 mm, as Type **DY42**. Booklet contains text and illustrations on panes and interleaving pages. Stitched.
DY42 £19·50 containing booklet panes Nos. U3071t, 3319c, 4627b and 4628b.......... 29·00

The contents of No. DY42 have a face value of £17·84.

B. Folded Booklets.

NOTE: All panes are attached to the covers by the selvedge. Inscribed dates are those shown with the printer's imprint.

Illustrations for 10p, 50p., £1 and £2 booklets are ¾ size; others are ⅔ size.

10p. Booklets

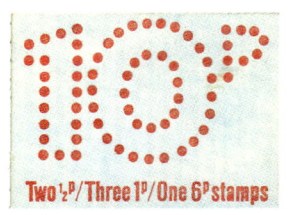

FA1

1976 (10 Mar)–**77**. Cover as T **FA1** printed in dull rose on very pale lavender. Containing booklet pane No. X841r.
FA1	NOV 1975..	45
FA2	MAR 1976 (9.6.76)...................................	60
FA3	JUNE 1977 (13.6.77)................................	40

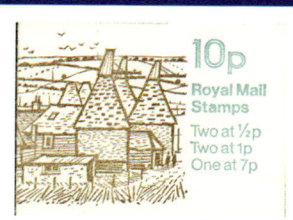

FA4

(Des N. Battershill)

1978 (8 Feb)–**79**. Farm Buildings Series. Bistre-brown and turquoise-blue covers as T **FA4**, containing booklet pane No. X843m.
FA4	Design No. 1, Oast Houses.....................	35
FA5	Design No. 2, Buildings in Ulster (3.5.78)..	40
FA6	Design No. 3, Buildings in Yorkshire (9.8.78)..	35
FA7	Design No. 4, Buildings in Wales (25.10.78)..	35
FA8	Design No. 5, Buildings in Scotland (10.1.79)..	35
FA9	Design No. 6, Buildings in Sussex (4.4.79)..	35

Nos. FA4/FA5 are inscribed January 1978, No. FA6 July 1978, No. FA7 October 1978, No. FA8 December 1978 and No. FA9 March 1979.

FA10

(Des Hamper and Purssell)

1979 (17 Oct)–**80**. London 1980 International Stamp Exhibition. Red and blue cover as T **FA10** showing Post Office exhibition stand and containing No. X845l.
| FA10 | Inscr August 1979.................................. | 30 |
| FA11 | Inscr January 1980 (12.1.80).................. | 35 |

50p. Booklets

All booklets were sold at the cover price of 50p. although some contain stamps to a greater value.

FB1

1977 (26 Jan). Cover as T **FB1** printed in maroon and pale blue.
| FB1A | containing booklet pane X841s............... | 1·50 |
| FB1B | containing booklet pane X841sa............. | 1·50 |

1977 (13 June). Cover as T **FB1**. Printed in chestnut and stone.
| FB2A | containing booklet pane X844n............... | 2·50 |
| FB2B | containing booklet pane X844na............. | 1·50 |

Nos. FB1A and FB1B are inscribed March 1976 and Nos. FB2A and FB2B June 1977.

FB3

POST OFFICE STAMP BOOKLETS

(Des J. Ireland)

1978 (8 Feb)–**79**. Commercial Vehicles Series. Olive-yellow and grey covers as T **FB3**. A. Containing booklet pane No. X844n. B. Containing booklet pane No. X844na.

		A	B
FB3	Design No. 1, Clement Talbot van..........	2·75	1·75
FB4	Design No. 2, Austin taxi (3.5.78)	2·75	1·50
FB5	Design No. 3, Morris Royal Mail van (9.8.78)	2·75	1·50
FB6	Design No. 4, Guy Electric dustcart (25.10.78)	3·75	1·50
FB7	Design No. 5, Albion van (10.1.79)........	4·00	3·75
FB8	Design No. 6, Leyland fire engine (4.4.79)	3·75	3·75

Nos. FB3/FB4 are inscribed January 1978, No. FB5 July 1978, No. FB6 October 1978, No. FB7 December 1978 and No. FB8 March 1979.

1979 (28 Aug). Contents changed. A. Containing booklet pane No. X849l. B. Containing booklet pane No. X849la.

		A	B
FB9	Design No. 6, Leyland fire engine	1·50	1·50

No. FB9 is inscribed August 1979.

FB10

(Des B. Smith)

1979 (3 Oct)–**81**. Veteran Cars Series. Orange-red and reddish lilac covers as T **FB10**. A. Containing booklet pane No. X849l. B. Containing booklet pane No. X849la.

		A	B
FB10	Design No. 1, 1907 Rolls-Royce Silver Ghost........................	1·50	1·50

No. FB10 is inscribed August 1979.

Contents changed. A. Containing booklet pane No. X849m. B. Containing booklet pane No. X849ma.

		A	B
FB11	Design No. 2, 1908 Grand Prix Austin (4.2.80)	1·50	1·50
FB12	Design No. 3, 1903–1905 Vauxhall (25.6.80)	1·50	1·50
FB13	Design No. 4, 1897–1900 Daimler (24.9.80)	1·50	1·50

No. FB11 is inscribed January 1980, No. FB 12 May 1980 and No. FB 13 July 1980.

Contents changed. A. Containing No. X841t. B. Containing No. X841ta.

FB14	Design No. 5, 1896 Lanchester (26.1.81)	1·50	1·50
FB15	Design No. 6, 1913 Bull-nose Morris (18.3.81)	1·75	1·75

Nos. FB14/FB15 are inscribed January 1981.

FB16

(Des R. Downer)

1981 (6 May)–**82**. Follies Series. Brown and orange-brown covers as T **FB16**. A. Containing No. X841t. B. Containing No. X841ta.

		A	B
FB16	Design No. 1, Mugdock Castle, Stirlingshire........................	1·50	1·50

No. FB16 is inscribed January 1981.

Contents changed. A. Containing No. X854l. B. Containing No. X854la.

FB17	Design No. 1, Mugdock Castle, Stirlingshire (26.8.81)...........	4·25	7·00
FB18	Design No. 2, Mow Cop Castle, Cheshire–Staffs border (30.9.81).............	4·25	4·25

Nos. FB17/FB18 are inscribed January 1981.

Contents changed. A. Containing No. X841u. B. Containing No. X841ua.

FB19	Design No. 3, Paxton's Tower, Llanarthney, Dyfed (1.2.82)	1·75	1·75
FB20	Design No. 4, Temple of the Winds, Mount Stewart, Northern Ireland (6.5.82)	1·75	1·75
FB21	Design No. 5, Temple of the Sun, Stourhead, Wilts (11.8.82)	1·00	1·75
FB22	Design No. 6, Water Garden, Cliveden, Bucks (6.10.82)	1·75	1·75

Nos. FB19/FB22 are inscribed February 1982.

FB23

(Des H. Titcombe)

1983 (16 Feb–26 Oct). Rare Farm Animals Series. Bright green and black covers as T **FB23**. A. Containing booklet pane No. X841u. B. Containing booklet pane No. X841ua.

		A	B
FB23	Design No. 1, Bagot Goat............................	1·75	2·00

Contents changed. Containing No. X845n.

FB24	Design No. 2, Gloucester Old Spot Pig (5.4.83)		3·50
	b. Corrected rate................................		12·00
FB25	Design No. 3, Toulouse Goose (27.7.83)		3·75
FB26	Design No. 4, Orkney Sheep (26.10.83)		3·75

No. FB23 is inscribed February 1982 and Nos. FB24/FB26 April 1983. The corrected rate reads, 36p. for 200g instead of 37p. for 200g.

FB27

(Des P. Morter)

1984 (3 Sept)–**85**. Orchids Series. Yellow-green and lilac covers as T **FB27**. Containing booklet pane No. X845p.

FB27	Design No. 1, *Dendrobium nobile* and *Miltonia* hybrid		2·50
FB28	Design No. 2, *Cypripedium calceolus* and *Ophrys apifera* (15.1.85)		2·50
FB29	Design No. 3, *Bifrenaria* and *Vanda tricolor* (23.4.85)		2·50
FB30	Design No. 4, *Cymbidium* and *Arpophyllum* (23.7.85)		2·50

Nos. FB27/FB30 are inscribed September 1984.

FB31

(Des M. Thierens Design)

1985 (4 Nov). Cover as T **FB31** printed in black and bright scarlet. Containing booklet pane No. X909l.

FB31	Pillar box design		2·75

No. FB 31 is inscribed November 1985.

FB32

(Des P. Morter)

1986 (20 May–12 Aug). Pond Life Series. Dull blue and emerald covers as T **FB32**. Containing booklet pane No. X909l.

FB32	Design No. 1, Emperor Dragonfly, Four spotted Libellula and Yellow Flag	1·75
FB33	Design No. 2, Common Frog, Fennel-leaved Pondweed and Long-stalked Pondweed (29.7.86)	2·25
	a. containing booklet pane No. X909Ela (12.8.86)	2·25

Nos. FB32/FB33a are inscribed November 1985.

FB34

(Des N. Battershill)

1986 (29 July). Roman Britain Series. Brown-ochre and Indian red cover as T **FB34**. Containing booklet pane No. X845q.

FB34	Design No. 1, Hadrian's Wall	6·50

No. FB34 is inscribed November 1985.

1986 (20 Oct)–**87**. Pond Life Series continued. Dull blue and emerald covers as T **FB32**. Containing booklet pane No. X845s.

FB35	Design No. 3, Moorhen and Little Grebe	3·50
FB36	Design No. 4, Giant Pond and Great Ramshorn Snails (27.1.87)	3·50

No. FB36 is inscribed October 1986.

1986 (20 Oct)–**87**. Roman Britain Series continued. Brown ochre and Indian red covers as T **FB34**. Containing booklet pane No. X847l.

FB37	Design No. 2, Roman Theatre of Verulamium, St Albans	2·25
FB38	Design No. 3, Portchester Castle, Hampshire (27.1.87)	2·40

No. FB38 is inscribed October 1986.

FB39

(Des Patricia Howes)

1987 (14 Apr)–**88**. Bicentenary of Marylebone Cricket Club Series Brown and dull ultramarine covers as T **FB39**. Containing booklet pane No. X847l.

FB39	Design No. 1, Father Time weather vane	1·75
FB40	Design No. 2, Ashes urn and embroidered velvet bag (14.7.87)	1·75
FB41	Design No. 3, Lord's Pavilion and wrought iron decoration on roof (29.9.87)	1·75
FB42	Design No. 4, England team badge and new stand at Lord's (26.1.88)	1·75

Nos. FB39/FB42 are inscribed October 1986.

FB43

(Des G. Evernden)

1987 (14 Apr)–**88**. Botanical Gardens Series. Covers as T **FB43**. Containing booklet panes No. X845s (Nos. FB43/FB44) or X845sa (Nos. FB45/FB46).

FB43	Design No. 1 (cover in ultramarine and rosered), Rhododendron, Elizabeth, Bodnant	3·25
FB44	Design No. 2 (cover in deep ultramarine and cobalt), Gentiana sino-ornata, Edinburgh (14.7.87)	3·25
FB45	Design No. 3 (cover in dull ultramarine and orange-yellow), Lilium auratum and Mount Stuart (incorrect inscr) (29.9.87)	1·75
	a. With corrected spelling Mount Stewart (30.10.87)	2·00
FB46	Design No. 4 (cover in dull ultramarine and yellow-orange), Strelitzia reginae, Kew (26.1.88)	2·00

Nos. FB43/FB46 are inscribed October 1986.
The panes from Nos. FB45/FB46 have imperforate vertical sides.

FB47

1988 (12 Apr–5 July). London Zoo. Children's Drawings Series. Covers as T **FB47**.

FB47	Pigs design (cover in black and rose) containing booklet pane No. X847l	2·00
FB48	Birds design (cover in black and yellow) containing booklet pane No. X845sa	2·00
FB49	Elephants design (cover in black and grey) containing booklet pane No. X847l (5.7.88)	2·00

Nos. FB47/FB49 are inscribed October 1986.
The pane from No. FB48 has imperforate vertical sides.

FB50

(Des P. Morter)

1988 (5 July). Marine Life Series. Blue and orange-brown cover as T **FB50**. Containing booklet pane No. X845sa.

FB50	Design No. 1, Parasitic Anemone on Common Whelk Shell and Umbrella Jellyfish	2·00

No. FB50 is inscribed October 1986 and has the vertical sides of the pane imperforate.

POST OFFICE STAMP BOOKLETS

FB51

(Des Lynda Gray)

1988 (5 Sept)–**89**. Gilbert and Sullivan Operas Series. Black and red covers as T **FB51**. Containing booklet pane No. X904l.

FB51	Design No. 1, *The Yeomen of the Guard* .	5·00
FB52	Design No. 2, *The Pirates of Penzance* (24.1.89)	5·00
FB53	Design No. 3, *The Mikado* (25.4.89)	5·00

1989 (18 July). Marine Life Series continued. Blue and orange brown cover as T **FB50**. Containing booklet pane No. X904l.

FB54	Design No. 2, Common Hermit Crab, Bladder Wrack and Laver Spire Shell	5·00

For Design No. 3, see £1 Booklet No. FH17.

FB55

(Des P. Hutton)

1989 (2 Oct)–**90**. Aircraft Series. Turquoise-green and light brown covers as T **FB55**. Containing booklet pane No. X906l.

FB55	Design No. 1, HP42, Armstrong Whitworth Atalanta and de Havilland Dragon Rapide	7·50

No. FB55 was incorrectly inscribed Atalanta.

As before, but containing Penny Black Anniversary booklet pane No. 1468l.

FB56	Design No. 2, Vickers Viscount 806 and de Havilland Comet 4 (30.1.90)	10·00

1990 (4 Sept)–**91**. Aircraft Series continued. Turquoise-green and light brown covers as T **FB55**. Containing booklet pane No. X911l.

FB57	Design No. 3, BAC 1-11 and VC10	10·00
FB58	Design No. 4, BAe ATP, BAe 146 and Aérospatiale–BAC Concorde (25.6.91)	10·00

FB59

(Des A. Drummond)

1991 (10 Sept)–**92**. Archaeology Series. Covers as T **FB59**. Containing booklet pane No. X925m.

FB59	Design No. 1 (cover in bright blue and lake brown), Sir Arthur Evans at Knossos, Crete	1·75
	a. Corrected rate (10.91)	2·00
FB60	Design No. 2 (cover in bright blue and yellow), Howard Carter in the Tomb of Tutankhamun (21.1.92)	1·75
FB61	Design No. 3 (cover in bright blue and yellow), Sir Austen Layard at Assyrian site (28.4.92)	1·50
FB62	Design No. 4 (cover in new blue and yellow), Sir Flinders Petrie surveying the Pyramids and temples of Giza (28.7.92)	1·75

On the inside front cover of No. FB59 the inland letter rates are shown as 1st class 24p., 35p., 43p., 51p. and 2nd class 18p., 28p., 33p., 39p. These were corrected on No. FB59a to read: 1st class 24p., 36p., 45p., 54p. and 2nd class 18p., 28p., 34p., 41p.

FB63

(Des J. Matthews)

1992 (22 Sept). 1000th Anniversary of Appointment of Sheriffs. Dull blue and scarlet cover as T **FB63**. Containing booklet pane No. X925m.

FB63	Design showing Crest, with Helm and Mantling, and Badge of The Shrievalty Association	1·60

FB64

(Des M. Newton)

1993 (9 Feb–6 July). Postal History Series. Covers as T **FB64**. Containing booklet pane No. X925m.

FB64	Design No. 1 (cover in grey-green and greyblack), Airmail postmarks	1·50
FB65	Design No. 2 (cover in dull orange and black), Ship mail postmarks (6.4.93)	1·50
FB66	Design No. 3 (cover in blue and grey-black), Registered mail postmarks (6.7.93)	1·50

1993 (1 Nov). Postal History Series continued. Rose-red and grey-black cover as T **FB64** containing booklet pane No. Y1689l.

FB67	Design No. 4, Paid postmarks	1·50

FB68

(Des A. Davidson)

1994 (25 Jan–6 Sept). Coaching Inns Series. Covers as T **FB68**. Containing booklet pane No. Y1689l.

FB68	Design No. 1 (cover in myrtle-green and pale myrtle-green), Swan with Two Necks	1·50
FB69	Design No. 2 (cover in sepia and buff), Bull and Mouth (26.4.94)	1·50
FB70	Design No. 3 (cover in reddish brown and cinnamon), Golden Cross (6.6.94)	1·50
FB71	Design No. 4 (cover in black and slate-blue), Pheasant Inn, Wiltshire (6.9.94)	1·50

POST OFFICE STAMP BOOKLETS

FB72

(Des D. Davis)

1995 (7 Feb–4 Apr). Sea Charts Series. Rosine and black covers as T **FB72**, containing booklet pane No. Y1689l.
FB72	Design No. 1, John o' Groats, 1800..........	1·50
FB73	Design No. 2, Land's End, 1808 (4.4.95)	1·50

1995 (6 June–4 Sept). Sea Charts Series continued. Rosine and black covers as T **FB72**, containing booklet pane No. Y1690l.
FB74	Design No. 3, St David's Head, 1812.......	2·00
FB75	Design No. 4, Giant's Causeway, 1828 (4.9.95)	2·00

65p. Booklet

1976 (14 July). Cover as T **FB1**, but larger (90×49 mm). Printed in turquoise-blue and pale buff. A. Selvedge at left. B. Selvedge at right.

		A	B
FC1	containing 10×6½p. (No. X872)	10·00	5·25

No. FC1 is inscribed March 1976.

70p. Booklets

1977 (13 June). Cover as T **FB1**, but larger (90×49 mm). Printed in purple-brown and dull rose. A. Selvedge at left. B. Selvedge at right.

		A	B
FD1	containing 10×7p. (No. X875)	4·00	4·00

No. FD1 is inscribed June 1977.

FD2

(Des E. Stemp)

1978 (8 Feb)–**79**. Country Crafts Series. Grey-green and red brown covers as T **FD2** (90×49 mm). Containing 10×7p. (No. X875). A. Selvedge at left. B. Selvedge at right.

		A	B
FD2	Design No. 1, Horse shoeing.....................	35·00	3·00
FD3	Design No. 2, Thatching (3.5.78).............	£175	3·00
FD4	Design No. 3, Dry stone walling (9.8.78)...	£165	3·00
FD5	Design No. 4, Wheel making (25.10.78)	5·75	4·00
FD6	Design No. 5, Wattle fence making (10.1.79)...	12·00	4·00

Nos. FD2/FD3 are inscribed January 1978, No. FD4 July 1978, No. FD5 October 1978 and No. FD6 December 1978.

FD7

(Des F. Wegner)

1979 (5 Feb). Official opening of Derby Mechanised Letter Office. Pale yellow-green and lilac cover as T **FD7** (90×49 mm). Containing 10×7p. (No. X875). A. Selvedge at left. B. Selvedge at right.

		A	B
FD7	Kedleston Hall.................................	5·50	5·50

No. FD7 is inscribed December 1978.
On sale only in the Derby Head Post Office area to promote postcode publicity and also at the Philatelic Bureau, Edinburgh and philatelic sales counters.

1979 (4 Apr). Country Crafts Series continued. Grey-green and red-brown covers as T **FD2** (90×49 mm). containing 10×7p. (No. 875) A. Selvedge at left. B. Selvedge at right.

		A	B
FD8	Design No. 6, Basket making....................	6·00	3·00

No. FD8 is inscribed March 1979.

80p. Booklet

FE1

(Des P. Hutton)

1979 (3 Oct). Military Aircraft Series. Blue and grey cover as T **FE1** (90×49 mm). Containing 10×8p. (No. X879) attached by the selvedge. A. Selvedge at left. B. Selvedge at right.

		A	B
FE1	Design No. 1, BE2B, 1914, and Vickers Gun Bus, 1915	2·25	2·25

No. FE1 is inscribed August 1979.

85p. Booklet

1976 (14 July). Cover as T **FB1** but larger (90×49 mm). Printed in light yellow-olive and brownish grey. A. Selvedge at left. B. Selvedge at right.

		A	B
FF1	containing 10×8½p. (No. X881)	5·50	7·50

No. FF1 is inscribed March 1976.

90p. Booklets

1977 (13 June). Cover as T **FB1**, but larger (90×49 mm). Printed in deep grey-blue and cobalt. A. Selvedge at left. B. Selvedge at right.

		A	B
FG1	containing 10×9p. (No. X883)	3·50	5·50

No. FG1 is inscribed June 1977.

FG2

(Des R. Maddox)

1978 (8 Feb)–**79**. British Canals Series. Yellow-olive and new blue covers as T **FG2** (90×49 mm). Containing 10×9p. (No. X883). A. Selvedge at left. B. Selvedge at right.

		A	B
FG2	Design No. 1, Grand Union........................	22·00	4·00
FG3	Design No. 2, Llangollen (3.5.78).............	3·00	£325
FG4	Design No. 3, Kennet & Avon (9.8.78)....	10·00	7·50
FG5	Design No. 4, Caledonian (25.10.78)......	4·25	3·50
FG6	Design No. 5, Regents (10.1.79)................	10·00	6·25

Nos. FG2/FG3 are inscribed January 1978, No. FG4 July 1978, No. FG5 October 1978 and No. FG6 December 1978.

POST OFFICE STAMP BOOKLETS

(Des F. Wegner)

1979 (5 Feb). Official Opening of Derby Mechanised Letter Office. Violet-blue and rose cover as T **FD7** (90×49 mm). Containing 10×9p. (No. X883). A. Selvedge at left. B. Selvedge at right.

		A	B
FG7	Tramway Museum, Crich	7·00	7·00

No. FG7 is inscribed December 1978.
On sale only in the Derby Head Post Office area to promote postcode publicity and also at the Philatelic Bureau, Edinburgh and philatelic sales counters.

1979 (4 Apr). British Canals Series continued. Yellow-olive and new blue cover as T **FG2** containing 10×9p. (No. X883). A. Selvedge at left. B. Selvedge at right.

		A	B
FG8	Design No. 6, Leeds & Liverpool	3·00	3·00

No. FG8 is inscribed March 1979.

£1 Booklets

All booklets were sold at the cover price of £1 although some contain stamps to a greater value.

FH1

(Des N. Battershill)

1979 (3 Oct). Industrial Archaeology Series. Red and green cover as T **FH1** (90×49 mm). Containing 10×10p. (No. X887). A. Selvedge at left. B. Selvedge at right.

		A	B
FH1	Design No. 1, Ironbridge, Telford, Salop	2·50	2·50

No. FH1 is inscribed August 1979.

1980 (4 Feb–24 Sept). Military Aircraft Series continued. Blue and grey covers as T **FE1** (90×49 mm). Containing 10×10p. (No. X888). A. Selvedge at left. B. Selvedge at right.

		A	B
FH2	Design No. 2, Sopwith Camel and Vickers Vimy	2·50	2·50
FH3	Design No. 3, Hawker Hart* and Handley Page Heyford (25.6.80)	3·50	3·50
FH4	Design No. 4, Hurricane ans Wellington (24.9.80)	2·50	2·50

* On the booklet cover the aircraft is wrongly identified as a Hawker Fury.

No FH2 is inscribed January 1980, No. FH3 May 1980 and No. FH4 July 1980.

FH5

(Des M. Newton and S. Paine)

1986 (29 July)–**87**. Musical Instruments Series. Scarlet and black covers as T **FH5**. Containing 6×17p. (No. X952).

FH5	Design No 1, Violin	3·00

No. FH5 is inscribed November 1985.

Contents changed. Containing No. X901n.

FH6	Design No. 2, French horn (20.10.86)	3·00
FH7	Design No. 3, Bass clarinet (27.1.87)	3·00

No. FH7 is inscribed October 1986.

FH8

(Des A. Davidson)

1987 (14 Apr)–**88**. Sherlock Holmes Series. Bright scarlet and grey-black covers as T **FH8**. Containing booklet pane No. X901n (Nos. FH8/FH9) or X901na (Nos. FH10/FH11).

FH8	Design No. 1, *A Study in Scarlet*	3·00
FH9	Design No. 2, *The Hound of the Baskervilles* (14.7.87)	3·00
FH10	Design No. 3, *The Adventure of the Speckled Band* (29.9.87)	3·00
FH11	Design No. 4, *The Final Problem* (26.1.88)	3·00

Nos. FH8/FH11 are inscribed October 1986.
The panes from Nos. FH10/FH11 have imperforate vertical sides.

1988 (12 Apr). London Zoo. Children's Drawings Series. Cover as T **FB47** in black and brown. Containing booklet pane No. X901na.

FH12	Bears design	3·00

No. FH12 is inscribed October 1986 and has the vertical sides of the pane imperforate.

FH13

(Des Liz Moyes)

1988 (5 July)–**89**. Charles Dickens Series Orange-red and maroon covers as T **FH13**.

FH13	Designs No. 1, *Oliver Twist*, containing booklet pane No. X901na	3·75
FH14	Design No. 2, *Nicholas Nickleby*, containing booklet pane No. X904m (5.9.88)	3·75
FH15	Design No. 3, *David Copperfield*, containing booklet pane No. X904m (24.1.89)	3·75
FH16	Design No. 4, *Great Expectations*, containing booklet pane No. X1051l (25.4.89)	8·50

No. FH13 is inscribed October 1986 and No. FH16 is inscribed September 1988.
Nos. FH13/FH16 have the vertical sides of the pane imperforate.

1989 (18 July). Marine Life Series continued. Cover as T **FB50** in turquoise-green and scarlet. Containing booklet pane No. X904m.

FH17	Design No. 3, Edible Sea Urchin, Common Starfish and Common Shore Crab	3·75

No. FH17 has the vertical edges of the pane imperforate.

FH18

(Des J. Sancha)

1989 (2 Oct)–**90**. Mills Series. Grey-black and grey-green matt card cover as T **FH18**.

FH18	Design No. 1, Wicken Fen, Ely containing booklet pane No. X960l	4·00

POST OFFICE STAMP BOOKLETS

As T **FH18** but glossy card cover containing Penny Black Anniversary booklet pane No. 1476l printed in litho by Walsall.
FH19   Design No. 1 (cover in bottle-green and pale green), Wicken Fen, Ely (30.1.90)......... 9·50

No. FH19 was an experimental printing to test a new cover material. This appears glossy when compared with Nos. FH18 and FH20.

As T **FH18** but changed to matt card cover containing Penny Black Anniversary booklet pane No. 1469l printed in photo by Harrison.
FH20   Design No. 2 (cover in grey-black and bright green), Click Mill, Dounby, Orkney (30.1.90)......... 6·00

1990 (4 Sept)–**91**. Mills Series continued. Covers as T **FH18**. Containing booklet pane No. X911m.
FH21   Design No. 3 (cover printed in light blue and buff) Jack and Jill Mills, Clayton, Sussex......... 3·00
FH22   Design No. 4 (cover printed in dull blue and bright yellow-green). Howell Mill, Llanddeusant, Anglesey (25.6.91)......... 3·00

Nos. FH18/FH22 have the vertical edges of the pane imperforate.

FH23

(Des J. Gibbs)

1991 (10 Sept)–**92**. 150th Anniversary of *Punch* Magazine. Magenta and grey-black covers as T **FH23** containing booklet pane No. X927l.
FH23   Design No. 1, Illustrations by Richard Doyle and Hoffnung......... 2·00
    a. Corrected rate (10.91)......... 2·00
FH24   Design No. 2, Illustrations by Sir John Tenniel and Eric Burgin (21.1.92)......... 2·00
FH25   Design No. 3, Illustrations by Sir John Tenniel and Anton (28.4.92)......... 2·00
FH26   Design No. 4, Illustrations by Sir John Tenniel and Hewison (28.7.92)......... 2·00

Nos. FH23/FH26 have the vertical edges of the pane imperforate.
No. FH23a has corrected letter rates as No. FB59a.

(Des J. Matthews)

1992 (22 Sept). 1000th Anniversary of Appointment of Sheriffs. Scarlet and dull blue cover as T **FB63** containing booklet pane No. X927l.
FH27   Design as Type **FB63** but elements in reverse order......... 2·00

No. FH27 has the vertical edges of the pane imperforate.

FH28

(Des J. Lawrence)

1993 (9 Feb–6 July). Educational Institutions Series. Covers as T **FH28** containing booklet pane No. X1050l printed in litho by Walsall.
FH28   Design No. 1 (cover in lake-brown and light blue), University of Wales......... 4·00
FH29   Design No. 2 (cover in deep dull green and lemon), St Hilda's College, Oxford (6.4.93)......... 4·00
FH30   Design No. 3 (cover in purple-brown and flesh), Marlborough College, Wiltshire (6.7.93)......... 4·00

1993 (1 Nov). Educational Institutions Series continued. Deep bluish green and lilac cover as T **FH28** containing 4×25p. (No. Y1775) printed in litho by Walsall.
FH31   Design No. 4, Free Church of Scotland College, Edinburgh......... 3·75

FH32

(Des H. Brockway)

1994 (25 Jan). 20th-century Prime Ministers Series. Brown and pale brown cover as T **FH32** containing 4×25p. (No. Y1775) printed in litho by Walsall.
FH32   Design No. 1, Herbert Asquith......... 1·75

(Des H. Brockway)

1994 (26 Apr–6 Sept). 20th-century Prime Ministers Series continued. Covers as T **FH32**. Containing 4×25p. (No. Y1689) printed in photo by Harrison.
FH33   Design No. 2 (cover in sepia and buff), David Lloyd-George......... 1·75
FH34   Design No. 3 (cover in greenish blue and pale blue), Winston Churchill (6.6.94)......... 1·75
FH35   Design No. 4 (cover in black and yellow-olive), Clement Attlee (6.9.94)......... 1·75

FH36

(Des L. Thomas)

1995 (7 Feb–4 Apr). 50th Anniversary of End of Second World War. Covers as T **FH36** containing 4×25p. (No. Y1689) printed in photo by Harrison.
FH36   Design No. 1 (cover in brown-olive and brownish black), Violette Szabo (SOE agent)......... 1·75
FH37   Design No. 2 (cover in red-brown and black), Dame Vera Lynn (entertainer) (4.4.95)......... 1·75

1995 (16 May–4 Sept). 50th Anniversary of End of Second World War Series continued. Covers as T **FH36** containing 4×25p. (No. Y1690) printed in photo by Harrison.
FH38   Design No. 3 (cover in black and steel-blue), R. J. Mitchell (designer of Spitfire)......... 1·75
FH39   Design No. 4 (cover in grey-green and black), Archibald McIndoe (plastic surgeon) (4.9.95)......... 2·00

FH40

1996 (16 Jan). Multicoloured laminated cover as T **FH40**. Stamps printed in litho by Questa.
FH40   containing 4×25p. stamps (No. Y1775)......... 4·00

For an initial test period No. FH40 was only available from machines at 12 post offices, five in London and seven in Scotland, in addition to philatelic outlets. Stocks were distributed nationally from May 1996.

POST OFFICE STAMP BOOKLETS

1996 (8 July)–**97**. Multicoloured laminated cover as T **FH40**. Stamps printed in litho by Questa.

FH41	containing booklet pane of No. Y1760l	3·75
	a. Corrected rate (4.2.97)	3·50
	b. Inland rate table at right	3·50

No. FH41 was reissued on 4 February 1997 showing the 200 gram second class rate on the inside cover altered from 47p. to 45p. A further printing issued 5 May 1998 was without the overseas postage rate table.

1998 (1 Dec). Multicoloured laminated cover as T **FH40**. Stamps printed in gravure by Questa.

FH42	containing booklet pane of No. Y1667l	20·00

1999 (26 Apr). Multicoloured laminated cover as T **FH40**. Stamps printed in gravure by Questa.

FH43	containing booklet pane of No. Y1667m	6·00

2000 (27 Apr)–**01**. Multicoloured laminated cover as T **FH40**. Stamps printed in gravure by Questa.

FH44	containing booklet pane of No. 1664l	6·75
	a. containing booklet pane No. 1664la (17.4.01)	7·00

£1·15 Booklets

1981 (26 Jan–18 Mar). Military Aircraft Series continued. Blue and grey covers as T **FE1** (90×49 mm). Containing 10×11½p. (No. X893). A. Selvedge at left. B. Selvedge at right.

		A	B
FI1	Design No. 5, Spitfire and Lancaster	3·00	3·00
FI2	Design No. 6, Lightning and Vulcan (18.3.81)	3·25	3·00

Nos. FI1/FI2 are inscribed January 1981.

FI3

(Des R. Maddox)

1981 (6 May–30 Sept). Museums Series. Blue and turquoise green covers as T **FI3** (90×49 mm). Containing 10×11½p. (No. X893). A. Selvedge at left. B. Selvedge at right.

		A	B
FI3	Design No. 1, Natural History Museum (British Museum), London	3·00	3·00
FI4	Design No. 2, National Museum of Antiquities of Scotland (30.9.81)	3·00	3·00

Nos. FI3/FI4 are inscribed January 1981.

£1·20 Booklets

1980 (4 Feb–24 Sept). Industrial Archaeology Series continued. Red and green covers as T **FH1** (90×49 mm). Containing 10×12p. (No. X943). A. Selvedge at left. B. Selvedge at right.

		A	B
FJ1	Design No. 2, Beetle Mill, Ireland	3·00	3·00
FJ2	Design No. 3, Tin Mines, Cornwall (25.6.80)	3·00	4·00
FJ3	Design No. 4, Bottle Kilns, Gladstone, Stoke-on-Trent (24.9.80)	3·00	3·25

No. FJ1 is inscribed January 1980, No. FJ2 May 1980 and No. FJ3 July 1980.

1986 (14 Jan). Pillar box Write Now. Yellow-green and pale red cover as T **FB31** (90×49 mm). Containing 10×12p. (No. X896). A. Selvedge at left. B. Selvedge at right.

		A	B
FJ4	Write Now (Pillar box design) (no imprint date)	4·50	4·50

FJ5

(Des R. Maddox)

1986 (29 Apr). National Gallery. Magenta and blue-green cover as T **FJ5** (90×49 mm). Containing 10×12p. (No. X896). A. Selvedge at left. B. Selvedge at right.

		A	B
FJ5	National Gallery design	4·25	4·25

No. FJ5 is inscribed November 1985.

FJ6

(Des Trickett and Webb Ltd)

1986 (29 July). Handwriting Bright orange and bright blue cover as T **FJ6** (90×49 mm). Containing 10×12p. (No. X896). A. Selvedge at left. B. Selvedge at right.

		A	B
FJ6	Maybe	4·25	4·25

No. FJ6 is inscribed November 1985.

£1·25 Booklets

1982 (1 Feb–6 Oct). Museums Series continued. Blue and turquoise-green covers as T **FI3** (90×49 mm). Containing 10×12½p. (No. X898). A. Selvedge at left. B. Selvedge at right.

		A	B
FK1	Design No. 3, Ashmolean Museum, Oxford	2·75	2·75
FK2	Design No. 4, National Museum of Wales, Cardiff (6.5.82)	2·75	2·75
FK3	Design No. 5, Ulster Museum, Belfast (11.8.82)	2·75	2·75
FK4	Design No. 6, Castle Museum, York (6.10.82)	2·75	2·75

Nos. FK1/FK4 are inscribed February 1982.

FK5

(Des S. Paine)

1983 (16 Feb–26 Oct). Railway Engines Series. Red and blue-green covers as T **FK5** (90×49 mm). Containing 10×12½p. (No. X898). A. Selvedge at left. B. Selvedge at right.

		A	B
FK5	Design No. 1, GWR *Isambard Kingdom Brunel*	4·00	4·00
FK6	Design No. 2, LMS Class 4P Passenger Tank Engine (5.4.83)	4·75	4·75
	a. Corrected rate	80·00	£125

POST OFFICE STAMP BOOKLETS

		A	B
FK7	Design No. 3, LNER *Mallard* (27.7.83).....	4·00	4·00
FK8	Design No. 4, SR/BR *Clan Line* (26.10.83)..	4·00	4·00

No. FK5 is inscribed February 1982 and Nos. FK6/FK8 April 1983. The corrected rate reads 36p. for 200 grams instead of 37p. for 200 grams.

£1·30 Booklets

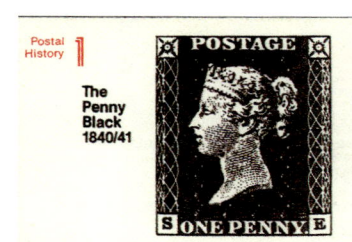

FL1

(Des J. Gibbs)

1981 (6 May–30 Sept). Postal History Series. Covers as T **FL1** (90×49 mm). Containing No. X894l. A. Selvedge at left. B. Selvedge at right.

		A	B
FL1	Design No. 1, Penny Black (red and black cover).................................	3·75	2·75
FL2	Design No. 2, The Downey Head, 1911 (red and green cover) (20.9.81)................	4·75	16·00

No. FL1 is inscribed April 1981 and No. FL2 September 1981.

FL3

(Des J. Thirsk)

1984 (3 Sept)–**85**. Trams Series. Yellow-orange and purple covers as T **FL3** (90×49 mm). Containing 10×13p. (No. X900). A. Selvedge at left. B. Selvedge at right.

		A	B
FL3	Design No. 1, Swansea/Mumbles Railway Car No. 3	2·75	2·75
FL4	Design No. 2, Glasgow Car No. 927 and Car No. 1194 (15.1.85)..........................	3·25	3·25
FL5	Design No. 3, Car No. 717, Blackpool (23.4.85)...	3·25	3·00
FL6	Design No. 4, Car No. 120 and D Class Car, London (23.7.85)............................	2·75	2·75

Nos. FL3/FL6 are inscribed September 1984.

FL27 FL7

(Des Anne Morrow)

1986 (20 Oct). Books for Children. Rose-red and lemon cover as T **FL7** (90×49 mm). Containing 10×13p. (No. X900). A. Selvedge at left. B. Selvedge at right.

		A	B
FL7	Teddy bears design	2·75	2·75

FL8

(Des Trickett and Webb Ltd)

1987 (27 Jan). Keep in Touch. Light green and bright blue cover as T **FL8** (90×49 mm). Containing 10×13p. (No. X900). A. Selvedge at left. B. Selvedge at right.

		A	B
FL8	Handclasp and envelope design............	2·75	2·75

No. FL8 is inscribed October 1986.

FL9

(Des Hannah Firmin)

1987 (14 Apr). Ideas for your Garden. Bistre and orange-brown cover as T **FL9** (90×49 mm). Containing 10×13p. stamps (No. X900). A. Selvedge at left. B. Selvedge at right.

		A	B
FL9	Conservatory design	2·75	2·75

No. FL9 is inscribed October 1986.

FL10

(Des Trickett and Webb Ltd)

1987 (14 July). Brighter Writer. Orange and bright reddish violet cover as T **FL10** (90×49 mm). Containing 10×13p. stamps (No. X900). A. Selvedge at left. B. Selvedge at right.

		A	B
FL10	Flower design...................................	2·75	2·75

No. FL10 is inscribed October 1986.

FL11

495

POST OFFICE STAMP BOOKLETS

(Des E. Stemp)

1987 (29 Sept). Jolly Postman. Pale blue and deep blue cover as T **FL11** (90×49 mm). Containing 10×13p. stamps (No. X900). A. Selvedge at left. B. Selvedge at right.

		A	B
FL11	Boy drawing design..........................	2·75	2·75

No. FL11 is inscribed October 1986.

FL12

(Des E. Hughes)

1988 (26 Jan). Bicentenary of Linnean Society. Blue and claret cover as T **FL12** (90×49 mm. Containing 10×13p. stamps (No. X900). A. Selvedge at left. B. Selvedge at right.

		A	B
FL12	Mermaid, fish and insect (from *Hortus Sanitatis*, 1497)................................	3·50	3·50

No. FL12 is inscribed October 1986.

FL13

1988 (12 Apr). Recipe Cards. Brown and green cover as T **FL13** (90×49 mm). Containing 10×13p. stamps (No. X900). A. Selvedge at left. B. Selvedge at right.

		A	B
FL13	Vegetables design.............................	2·75	2·75

No. FL13 is inscribed October 1986.

FL14

(Des Trickett and Webb Ltd)

1988 (5 July). Children's Parties. Blue-green and bright purple cover as T **FL14** (90×49 mm). Containing 10×13p. stamps (No. X900). A. Selvedge at left. B. Selvedge at right.

		A	B
FL14	Balloons and streamers design................	2·75	2·75

No. FL14 is inscribed October 1986.

£1·40 Booklets

1981 (26 Jan–18 Mar). Industrial Archaeology Series continued. Red and green covers as T **FH1** (90×49 mm). Containing 10×14p. (No. X946). A. Selvedge at left. B. Selvedge at right.

		A	B
FM1	Design No. 5, Preston Mill, Scotland	2·75	3·00
FM2	Design No. 6, Talyllyn Railway, Tywyn (18.3.81).....................................	3·00	2·75

Nos. FM1/FM2 are inscribed January 1981.

FM3

(Des E. Stemp)

1981 (6 May–30 Sept). 19th-century Women's Costume Series. Claret and blue covers as T **FM3** (90×49 mm). Containing 10×14p. (No. X946). A. Selvedge at left. B. Selvedge at right.

		A	B
FM3	Design No. 1, Costume, 1800–1815	2·75	2·75
FM4	Design No. 2, Costume, 1815–1830 (30.9.81).....................................	2·75	2·75

Nos. FM3/FM4 are inscribed January 1981.

FM5

(Des A. Drummond)

1988 (5 Sept). Pocket Planner. Grey-black and yellow cover as T **FM5** (90×49 mm). Containing 10×14p. stamps (No. X903). A. Selvedge at left. B. Selvedge at right.

		A	B
FM5	Legal Charge design...........................	2·75	2·75

FM6

(Des Debbie Cook)

1989 (24 Jan). 150th Anniversary of Fox Talbot's Report on the Photographic Process to Royal Society. Reddish orange and black cover as T **FM6** (90×49 mm). Containing 10×14p. stamps (No. X903). A. Selvedge at left. B. Selvedge at right.

		A	B
FM6	Photographs and darkroom equipment	2·80	2·80

No. FM6 is inscribed September 1988.

£1·43 Booklets

1982 (1 Feb–6 May). Postal History Series continued. Covers as T **FL1** (90×49 mm). Containing No. X899l. A. Selvedge at left. B. Selvedge at right.

		A	B
FN1	Design No. 3, James Chalmers (postal reformer) (orange and turquoise-blue cover)	3·00	3·00
FN2	Design No. 4, Edmund Dulac (stamp designer) (brown and red cover) (6.5.82).....................................	3·00	3·00

POST OFFICE STAMP BOOKLETS

FN3

(Des J. Gardner)

1982 (12 July). Holiday Postcard Stamp Book purple and turquoise-blue cover as T **FN3** (90×49 mm). Containing No. X899l. A. Selvedge at left. B. Selvedge at right.

		A	B
FN3	*Golden Hinde* on front, postcard voucher on back	3·00	3·00

1982 (21 July)–**83**. Postal History Series continued. Covers as T **FL1** (90×49 mm). Containing No. X899l. A. Selvedge at left. B. Selvedge at right.

		A	B
FN4	Design No. 5, Forces Postal Service (grey and violet cover)	3·00	3·00
FN5	Design No. 6, The £5 Orange (orange and black cover) (6.10.82)............	3·00	3·00
FN6	Design No. 7, Postmark History (bright scarlet and deep dull blue cover) (16.2.83)............................	3·00	3·00

No. FN1 is inscribed February 1982. Nos. FN2/FN3 May 1982, No. FN4 July 1982, No. FN5 October 1982, No. FN6 November 1982.

For booklet No. FS2 with cover price of £1·45, see £1·60 booklets.

£1·46 Booklets

1983 (5 Apr–26 Oct). Postal History Series continued. Covers as T **FL1** (90×49 mm). A. Containing No. X899n. B. Containing No. X899na.

		A	B
FO1	Design No. 8, Seahorse High Values (blue and green cover)	5·50	5·50
	a. Corrected rate	48·00	15·00
FO2	Design No. 9, Parcel Post Centenary (turquoise-blue and carmine cover) (27.7.83)	4·75	4·75
FO3	Design No. 10, Silver Jubilee of Regional Stamps (dull green and reddish violet cover) (26.10.83)	4·75	4·75

No. FO1 is inscribed March 1983, No. FO2 May 1983 and No. FO 3 June 1983.

The corrected rate reads 36p. for 200g instead of 37p. for 200g.

£1·50 Booklets

1986 (14 Jan). Pillar box Write Now. Ultramarine and red cover as T **FB31** (90×49 mm). A. Containing No. X897l. B. Containing No. X897la.

		A	B
FP1	Write Now (Pillar box design)	3·50	3·50

No. FP1 shows no imprint date.

1986 (29 Apr). National Gallery. Violet and vermilion cover as T **FJ5** (90×49 mm). A. Containing No. X897l. B. Containing No. X897la.

		A	B
FP2	National Gallery design	3·50	3·50

No. FP2 is inscribed November 1985.

1986 (29 July). Handwriting. Blue-green and bright blue cover as T **FJ6** (90×49 mm). A. Containing No. X897l. B. Containing No. X897la.

		A	B
FP3	No	3·50	3·50

No. FP3 is inscribed November 1985.

£1·54 Booklets

1984 (3 Sept)–**85**. Postal History Series continued. Covers as T **FL1** (90×49 mm). A. Containing No. X901l. B. Containing No. X901la.

		A	B
FQ1	Design No. 11, Old and new Postage Dues (reddish purple and pale blue cover)	3·00	3·00
FQ2	Design No. 12, Queen Victoria embossed stamps (yellow-green and blue cover) (15.1.85)	3·00	3·00
FQ3	Design No. 13, Queen Victoria surface printed stamps (blue-green and carmine cover) (23.4.85)	3·00	3·00
FQ4	Design No. 14, 17th-century mounted and foot messengers (deep brown and orange-red cover) (23.7.85)	3·00	3·00

No. FQ1 is inscribed July 1984 and Nos. FQ2/FQ4 are inscribed September 1984.

£1·55 Booklets

1982 (1 Feb–6 Oct). 19th-century Women's Costume Series continued. Claret and blue covers as **FM3** (90×49 mm). Containing 10×15½p. (No. X948). A. Selvedge at left. B. Selvedge at right.

		A	B
FR1	Design No. 3, Costume, 1830–1850	2·75	2·75
FR2	Design No. 4, Costume, 1850–1860 (6.5.82)	2·75	2·75
FR3	Design No. 5, Costume, 1860–1880 (11.8.82)	3·00	3·00
FR4	Design No. 6, Costume, 1880–1900 (6.10.82)	2·75	2·75

Nos. FR1/FR4 are inscribed February 1982.

£1·60 Booklets

FS1

(Des Carol Walklin)

1983 (5 Apr). Birthday Box Design. Magenta and red-orange cover as T **FS1** (90×49 mm). Depicting birthday cake and associated items. A. Selvedge at left. B. Selvedge at right.

		A	B
FS1	containing 10×16p. stamps (No. X949) (no imprint date)	3·50	3·50
	a. Rates altered and February 1983 imprint date	60·00	90·00

The converted rate reads 36p. for 200g. instead of 37p. for 200g.

FS2

(Des R. Maddox)

1983 (10 Aug). British Countryside Series. Special Discount Booklet (*sold at £1·45*). Greenish blue and ultramarine cover as T **FS2** (90×49 mm). Containing 10×16p. stamps (No. X949u). A. Selvedge at left. B. Selvedge at right.

		A	B
FS2	Design No. 1, Lyme Regis, Dorset	4·75	4·75

Stamps from No. FS2 show a double-lined D printed in blue on the reverse over the gum.

No. FS2 is inscribed April 1983.

1983 (21 Sept). British Countryside Series continued. Dull green on violet cover as T **FS2** (90×49 mm). Containing 10×16p. stamps (No. X949). A. Selvedge at left. B. Selvedge at right.

		A	B
FS3	Design No. 2, Arlington Row, Bibury, Gloucestershire	3·00	3·00

No. FS3 is inscribed April 1983.

POST OFFICE STAMP BOOKLETS

FS4

(Des M. Newton)

1984 (14 Feb). Write it Design. Vermilion and ultramarine cover as T **FS4** (90×49 mm). Containing 10×16p. stamps (No. X949). A. Selvedge at left. B. Selvedge at right.

		A	B
FS4	Fountain pen	3·50	3·50

No. FS4 is inscribed April 1983.

£1·70 Booklets

FT1

1984 (3 Sept). Social Letter Writing Series. Rose and deep claret cover as T **FT1** (90×49 mm). Containing 10×17p. (No. X952). A. Selvedge at left. B. Selvedge at right.

		A	B
FT1	Design No. 1, Love Letters	3·50	3·50

No. FT1 is inscribed September 1984.

1985 (5 Mar). Social Letter Writing continued. Special Discount Booklet (sold at £1.55). Turquoise-blue and deep claret cover as T **FT1** (90×49 mm). Containing 10×17p. (No. X952u). A. Selvedge at left. B. Selvedge at right.

		A	B
FT2	Design No. 2, Letters abroad	3·50	3·50

Stamps from No. FT2 show a double-lined D printed in blue on the reverse over the gum.
No. FT2 is inscribed September 1984.

1985 (9 Apr). Social Letter Writing Series continued. Bright blue and deep claret cover as T **FT1** (90×49 mm). Containing 10×17p. (No. X952). A. Selvedge at left. B. Selvedge at right.

		A	B
FT3	Design No. 3, Fan letters	3·25	3·25

No. FT3 is inscribed September 1984.

FT4

(Des B. Smith)

1985 (30 July). 350 Years of Royal Mail Public Postal Service Special Discount Booklet (sold at £1.53). Rosine and bright blue cover T **FT4** (90×60 mm). Containing 10×17p. (No. 1290u) with selvedge at top.

FT4	Datapost Service design	3·75

The stamps from this booklet show double-lined letters D printed on the reverse over the gum.
No. FT4 is inscribed September 1984.

1985 (8 Oct)–**86**. Social Letter Writing Series continued. Black and bright scarlet cover as T **FT1** (90×49 mm). Containing 10×17p. (No. X952). A. Selvedge at left. B. Selvedge at right.

		A	B
FT5	Design No. 4, Write Now (Pillar box)	3·25	3·25
	a. Revised rates (2nd class (60g) 12p.) (1.86)	24·00	16·00

1986 (29 Apr). National Gallery. Blue-green and blue cover as T **FJ5** (90×49 mm). Containing 10×17p. (No. X952). A. Selvedge at left. B. Selvedge at right.

		A	B
FT6	National Gallery design	3·50	3·50

No. FT6 is inscribed November 1985.

1986 (29 July). Handwriting. Red and bright blue cover as T **FJ6** (90×49 mm). Containing 10×17p. (No. X952). A. Selvedge at left. B. Selvedge at right.

		A	B
FT7	Yes	3·50	3·50

No. FT7 is inscribed November 1985.

£1·80 Booklets

1986 (20 Oct). Books for Children. New blue and orange-brown cover as T **FL7**. Containing 10×18p. (No. X955). A. Selvedge at left. B. Selvedge at right.

		A	B
FU1	Rabbits design	3·75	3·75

1987 (27 Jan). Keep in Touch. Magenta and bright blue cover as T **FL8**. Containing 10×18p. (No. X955). A. Selvedge at left. B. Selvedge at right.

		A	B
FU2	Handclasp and envelope design	3·75	3·75

No. FU2 is inscribed October 1986.

1987 (14 Apr). Ideas for your Garden Claret and brown-olive cover as T **FL9** (90×49 mm). Containing 10×18p. stamps (No. X955). A. Selvedge at left. B. Selvedge at right.

		A	B
FU3	Garden path design	3·75	5·00

No. FU3 is inscribed October 1986.

1987 (14 July). Brighter Writer. Turquoise-green and reddish orange cover as T **FL10** (90×49 mm). Containing 10×18p. stamps (No. X955). A. Selvedge at left. B. Selvedge at right.

		A	B
FU4	Berries and leaves design	3·75	3·75

No. FU4 is inscribed October 1986.

1987 (29 Sept). Jolly Postman. Deep blue and claret cover as T **FL11** (90×49 mm). Containing 10×18p. stamps (No. X955). A. Selvedge at left. B. Selvedge at right.

		A	B
FU5	Girl drawing design	3·75	3·75

No. FU5 is inscribed October 1986.

1988 (26 Jan). Bicentenary of Linnean Society. Dull yellow-green and dull claret cover as T **FL12** (90×49 mm). Containing 10×18p. stamps (No. X955). A. Selvedge at left. B. Selvedge at right.

		A	B
FU6	Wolf and birds (from *Hortus Sanitatis*, 1497)	3·75	3·75
	a. Inside cover text for FL12	95·00	95·00

No. FU6 is inscribed October 1986.
The inside cover text for FU6a has the special offer of the £1·30 booklet, No. FL12 (4×13p. stamps).

1988 (12 Apr). Recipe Cards. Claret and Indian red cover as T **FL13** (90×49 mm). Containing 10×18p. stamps (No. X955). A. Selvedge at left. B. Selvedge at right.

		A	B
FU7	Fruits, pudding and jam design	3·75	3·75

No. FU7 is inscribed October 1986.

1988 (5 July). Children's Parties. Violet and rosine cover as T **FL14** (90×49 mm). Containing 10×18p. stamps (No. X955). A. Selvedge at left. B. Selvedge at right.

		A	B
FU8	Balloons and party hats design	3·75	3·75

No. FU8 is inscribed October 1986.

POST OFFICE STAMP BOOKLETS

£1·90 Booklets

1988 (5 Sept). Pocket Planner. Yellow-green and magenta cover as T **FM5** (90×49 mm). Containing 10×19p. stamps (No. X956). A. Selvedge at left. B. Selvedge at right.

		A	B
FV1	Marriage Act design	4·50	4·50

1989 (24 Jan). 150th Anniversary of Fox Talbot's Report on the Photographic Process to Royal Society. Emerald and black cover as T **FM6** (90×49 mm). Containing 10×19p. stamps (No. X956). A. Selvedge at left. B. Selvedge at right.

		A	B
FV2	Fox Talbot with camera and Lacock Abbey	4·50	4·50

No. FV2 is inscribed September 1988.

£2 Booklets

FW1

(Des Debbie Cook)

1993 (1 Nov)–**94**. Postal Vehicles Series. Covers as T **FW1**. Containing 8×25p. (No. Y1689).

FW1	Design No. 1 (cover in dull vermilion and deep blue), Motorised cycle-carrier	3·25
FW2	Design No. 2 (cover in green and deep violet-blue), Experimental motor mail van (26.4.94)	3·25
FW3	Design No. 3 (cover in red and black), Experimental electric mail van, 1932 (6.9.94)	3·25

FW3

(Des The Four Hundred)

1995 (7 Feb–4 Apr). Birth Bicentenary of Sir Rowland Hill. Covers as T **FW3**. Containing 8×25p. (No. Y1689).

FW4	Design No. 1 (cover in purple and new blue), Rowland Hill as director of London and Brighton Railway Company	3·25
FW5	Design No. 2 (cover in deep mauve and greenish blue), Rowland Hill and Hazlewood School (4.4.95)	3·25

1995 (6 June–4 Sept). Birth Bicentenary of Sir Rowland Hill Series continued. Covers as T **FW3**. Containing 8×25p. (No. Y1690).

FW6	Design No. 3 (cover in deep blue-green and dull orange), Rowland Hill as Secretary to the Post Office	3·50
FW7	Design No. 4 (cover in red-brown and orange), Uniform Penny Postage petition and Mulready envelope (4.9.95)	3·50

1996 (16 Jan). Multicoloured laminated cover as T **FH40**. Stamps printed in litho by Questa.

FW8	containing 8×25p. stamps (No. Y1775).	3·75

For an initial test period No. FW8 was only available from machines at 12 post offices, five in London and seven in Scotland, in addition to philatelic outlets. Stocks were distributed nationally from May 1996.

1996 (8 July)–**97**. Multicoloured laminated cover as T **FH40**. Stamps printed in litho by Questa.

FW9	containing booklet pane of No. Y1772l	3·75
	a. Corrected rate (4.2.97)	3·75
	b. Inland rate table inside at right (5.5.98)	3·75

No. FW9 was reissued on 4 February 1997 showing the 200 gram second class rate on the inside cover altered from 47p. to 45p. A further printing issued 5 May 1998 was without the overseas postage rate table.

1998 (1 Dec). Multicoloured laminated cover as T **FH40**. Stamps printed in gravure by Questa.

FW10	containing booklet pane of No. Y1685l	20·00

1999 (26 Apr). Multicoloured laminated cover as T **FH40**. Stamps printed in gravure by Questa.

FW11	containing booklet pane of No. Y1682l	6·50

2000 (27 Apr). Multicoloured laminated cover as T **FH40**. Stamps printed in gravure by Questa.

FW12	containing booklet pane of No. 1664m	8·50

CHRISTMAS BOOKLETS

FX1

(Des J. Matthews)

1978 (15 Nov). Christmas Greetings. Rose-red and sage-green cover T **FX1** (90×49 mm).

FX1	£1·60 containing booklet pane No. X875l	2·50

No. FX1 is inscribed August 1978.

FX2

(Des P. Sharland)

1979 (14 Nov). Christmas Greetings. Red and green cover as T **FX2** (90×49 mm), showing Christmas cracker.

FX2	£1·80 containing booklet pane No. X879l	3·00

No. FX2 is inscribed October 1979.

FX3

(Des E. Fraser)

1980 (12 Nov). Christmas. Red and blue cover as T **FX3** (90×49 mm), showing Nativity scene.

FX3	£2·20 containing booklet pane No. X888m	3·25

No. FX3 is inscribed September 1980.

POST OFFICE STAMP BOOKLETS

FX4

(Des W. Sanderson)

1981 (11 Nov). Christmas. Red and blue cover as T **FX4**, (90×49 mm), showing skating scene.
FX4   £2·55 containing booklet pane No. X893l .... 4·25
No. FX4 is inscribed January 1981.

FX5

(Des A. Davidson)

1982 (10 Nov). Christmas. Red and green cover as T **FX5** (90×49 mm), showing Christmas Mummers.
FX5   £2·50 containing booklet pane No. X898l .... 5·00
No. FX5 is inscribed February 1982 and was sold at a discount of 30p. off the face value of the stamps.
Each stamp in the pane has a blue star printed on the reverse over the gum.

FX6

(Des Barbara Brown)

1983 (9 Nov). Christmas. Brown-lilac and yellow cover as T **FX6** (90×49 mm), showing pantomime scenes.
FX6   £2·20 containing 20×12½p. (No. X898v) .... 4·50
No. FX6 is inscribed April 1983 and was sold at a discount of 30p. off the face value of the stamps.
Each stamp in the pane has a double-lined blue star printed on the reverse over the gum.

FX7

(Des Yvonne Gilbert)

1984 (20 Nov). Christmas. Light brown and red-orange cover as T **FX7** (90×60 mm), showing Nativity scene.
FX7   £2·30 containing 20×13p. (No. 1267u) .... 5·00
No. FX7 is inscribed September 1984 and was sold at a discount of 30p. off the face value of the stamps.
The stamps from this booklet show double-lined blue stars printed on the reverse over the gum.

FX8

(Des A. George)

1985 (19 Nov). Christmas. Bright blue and rose cover as T **FX8** (90×60 mm), showing The Pantomime.
FX8   £2·40 containing 20×12p. (No. 1303u) .... 4·50
The stamps from this booklet show double-lined blue stars printed on the reverse over the gum.

FX9

(Des Lynda Gray)

1986 (2 Dec). Christmas. Red and dull blue-green cover as T **FX9** (90×49 mm), showing Shetland Yule cakes. A. Selvedge at left. B. Selvedge at right.
                                                        A   B
FX9   £1·20 containing 10×13p. (No. X900u) .... 4·50   8·00
No. FX9 is inscribed October 1986 and was sold at a discount of 10p. off the face value of the stamps.
Each stamp in the pane has a blue star printed on the reverse over the gum.

For 1990 and later Christmas stamps, see Barcode Booklets Section G.

£1·90 Greetings Booklet

FY1

POST OFFICE STAMP BOOKLETS

(Des L. Moberly)

1989 (31 Jan). Greetings Stamps. Multicoloured cover as T **FY1** (89×60 mm). Containing booklet pane No. 1423a, including 12 special greetings labels in a block (3×4) at right, attached by the selvedge.
FY1   Greetings design............................ 24·00
   No. FY1 is inscribed September 1988.
   The cover of No. FY 1 shows an overall pattern of elements taken from the stamp designs. Due to the method of production the position of these elements varies from cover to cover.

For Greetings stamps in Barcode booklets, see Barcode Booklets Section F.

III. BARCODE BOOKLETS

These booklets are listed in 11 sections:
SECTION C: G numbers containing Machin stamps with face value
SECTION D: H numbers containing Machin NVI stamps
SECTION E: J numers containing Machin Penny Black Anniversary stamps
SECTION F: KX numbers containing Greetings stampa
SECTION G: LX numbers containing Christmas stamps
SECTION H: M numbers containing self-adhesive NVI definitive stamps
SECTION I: N numbers containing self-adhesive definitive stamps with face value
SECTION J: PM numbers containing both special and definitive self-adhesive NVI stamps
SECTION K: Q numbers containing NVI 'Smiler' stamps in definitive size
SECTION L: R numbers containing stamps with value indicator at upper left
SECTION M: SA numbers containing NVI 'Smiler' stamps and definitive stamps
SECTION N: T numbers containing NVI barcode Machin stamps

These are produced for sale in both post offices and commercial outlets.
NOTE. All panes are attached to the covers by the selvedge. Barcode booklet covers are illustrated at two-thirds linear size, *unless otherwise stated*.

C. Barcode Booklets containing Machin stamps with values shown as Type 367.

COVERS. These are all printed in scarlet, lemon and black with the barcode on the reverse. Type **GA1** has a clear 'window' to view the contents, Type **GB3** is shorter and has a stamp illustration printed on the cover to replace the 'window'. These illustrations show an oblique white line across the bottom right-hand corner of the 'stamp'. Unless otherwise stated all covers were printed by Harrison.
   From early 1997 the printer of each booklet is identified by a small capital letter below the barcode on the outside back cover.

52p. Booklet

GA1

1987 (4 Aug). Laminated cover T **GA1** (75×60 mm).
GA1   containing booklet pane No. X900n...... 2·25
   No. GA1 is inscribed 20 October 1986.

56p. Booklets

1988 (23 Aug). Laminated cover as T **GA1** (75×56 mm).
GB1   containing booklet pane No. X903l....... 3·50

1988 (11 Oct). Laminated cover as T **GA1** (75×56 mm) printed by Walsall.
GB2   containing booklet pane No. X903l....... 5·25

GB3 Large Crown

1988 (11 Oct). Laminated cover as T **GB3** (75×48 mm) with stamp printed on the cover in deep blue.
GB3   containing booklet pane No. X903n...... 4·00
   No. GB3 is inscribed 5 September 1988 and has the horizontal edges of the pane imperforate.

1989 (24 Jan). Laminated cover as T **GB3** (75×48 mm) with stamp printed on the cover in deep blue by Walsall.
GB4   containing booklet pane No. X903q...... 20·00
   No. GB4 is inscribed 5 September 1988 and has the three edges of the pane imperforate.

72p. Booklet

1987 (4 Aug). Laminated cover as T **GA1** (75×60 mm).
GC1   containing booklet pane No. X955m ...... 2·25
   No. GC1 is inscribed 20 October 1986.

76p. Booklets

1988 (23 Aug). Laminated cover as T **GA1** (75×56 mm).
GD1   containing booklet pane No. X956l .... 4·00

1988 (11 Oct). Laminated cover as T **GA1** (75×56 mm) printed by Walsall.
GD2   containing booklet pane No. X956l .... 4·25

1988 (11 Oct). Laminated cover as T **GB3** (75×48 mm) with stamp printed on the cover in bright orange-red.
GD3   containing booklet pane No. X956n...... 5·00
   No. GD3 is inscribed 5 September 1988 and has the horizontal edges of the pane imperforate.

1989 (24 Jan). Laminated cover as T **GB3** (75×48 mm) with stamp printed on the cover in bright orange-red by Walsall.
GD4   containing booklet pane No. X956q...... 20·00
   No. GD4 is inscribed 5 September 1988 and has the three edges of the pane imperforate.

78p. Booklet

GD4a (As T **GM1** but without '4')

1992 (28 July). Multicoloured laminated cover as T **GD4a** (75×49 mm) with stamp printed on the cover in bright mauve by Walsall.
GD4a   containing 2×39p. stamps (No. X1058)
               (pane No. X1058l with right-hand vert
               pair removed) and pane of 4 airmail
               labels.. 4·00
   Stamps in No. GD4a have top or bottom edge imperforate.
   Booklet No. GD4a was produced in connection with a Kellogg's Bran Flakes promotion.

£1·04 Booklet

1987 (4 Aug). Laminated cover as T **GA1** (75×60 mm).
GE1   containing booklet pane No. X971bl .... 24·00
   No. GE1 is inscribed 20 October 1986.

POST OFFICE STAMP BOOKLETS

£1·08 Booklets

1988 (23 Aug). Laminated cover as T **GA1** (75×56 mm).
GF1   containing booklet pane No. X973l .... 8·00
   a. Postage rates omitted from inside
       back cover .... 20·00

1988 (11 Oct). Laminated cover as T **GB3** (75×48 mm) with stamp printed on the cover in chestnut.
GF2   containing booklet pane No. X973m .... 20·00
   No. GF2 is inscribed 5 September 1988 and has the horizontal edges of the pane imperforate.

£1·16 Booklets

GG1 Redrawn Crown

1989 (2 Oct). Laminated cover as T **GG1** (75×48 mm) with stamp printed on the cover in deep mauve by Walsall.
GG1   containing booklet pane No. X1054l..... 12·00
   No. GG1 has three edges of the pane imperforate.

1990 (17 Apr). Laminated cover as T **GG1** (75×48 mm) with stamp printed on the cover in deep mauve by Walsall.
GG2   containing booklet pane No. X1055l..... 12·00
   No. GG2 has three edges of the pane imperforate.

£1·20 Booklets

GGA1 (BY AIR MAIL par avion at bottom left)

1998 (5 May). Multicoloured laminated cover as T **GGA1** (75×50 mm) with stamps printed on cover in olive-grey by Walsall. Inscribed For items up to 20g on yellow tab at right.
GGA1   containing 4×30p. (gravure) (No.
       Y1694) and a pane of 4 airmail labels.... 2·25

GGA2 Create a card Design

1998 (3 Aug). Multicoloured laminated cover as T **GGA2** (75×50 mm) printed by Walsall. Inscribed See inside for offer details on yellow tab at right.
GGA2   containing 4×30p. (gravure) (No.
       Y1694) and a pane of 4 airmail labels.... 2·25
   This booklet was not placed on philatelic sale until 7 September 1998.

£1·24 Booklet

GH1 Crown on White

1990 (17 Sept). Multicoloured laminated cover as T **GH1** (75×49 mm) with stamp printed on the cover in ultramarine by Walsall.
GH1   containing booklet pane No. X1056l..... 4·00
   No. GH1 has the horizontal edges of the pane imperforate.

£1·30 Booklet

1987 (4 Aug). Laminated cover as T **GA1** (98×60 mm).
GI1   containing booklet pane No. X900o...... 3·50
   No. GI1 is inscribed 20 October 1986.

£1·32 Booklet

GJ1

1991 (16 Sept)–**92**. Multicoloured laminated cover as T **GJ1** (75×49 mm) with stamp printed on the cover in light emerald by Walsall. Inscr For letters up to 10g on yellow strip at right.
GJ1   containing booklet pane No. X1057l
       and a pane of 4 airmail labels .... 3·50
   a. Inscr For Worldwide Postcards on
       yellow strip (8.9.92) .... 7·00
   Nos. GJ1/GJ1a have the horizontal edges of the pane imperforate.

£1·40 Booklets

1988 (23 Aug). Laminated cover as T **GA1** (97×56 mm).
GK1   containing booklet pane No. X903m .... 8·50

1988 (11 Oct). Laminated cover as T **GA1** (97×56 mm) printed by Questa.
GK2   containing 10×14p. (No. X1007) .... 8·50

1988 (11 Oct). Laminated cover as T **GB3** (75×48 mm) with stamp printed on the cover in deep blue.
GK3   containing booklet pane No. X903p..... 5·50
   No. GK3 is inscribed 5 September 1988 and has horizontal edges of the pane imperforate.

1988 (11 Oct). Laminated cover as T **GB3** (75×48 mm) with stamp printed on the cover in deep blue by Questa.
GK4   containing 10×14p. (No. X1007) .... 10·00

1993 (1 Nov). Laminated cover as T **GJ1** (76×50 mm) with stamp printed on the cover in yellow by Walsall. Inscribed For Worldwide Postcards on yellow tab at right.
GK5   containing 4×35p. (No. Y1778) and a
       pane of 4 airmail labels............................. 3·25

POST OFFICE STAMP BOOKLETS

GK6

1995 (16 May). Multicoloured laminated cover as T **GK6** (75×48 mm) with stamps printed on the cover in yellow by Walsall.
GK6   containing 4×35p. (No. Y1778) and a pane of 4 airmail labels.............................. 3·25
T **GK6** (without diagonal white line across corners of stamps)

1996 (19 Mar). Multicoloured laminated cover as T **GK6** (75×48 mm) without International and showing Olympic symbols on the back. Stamps printed on the cover in yellow by Walsall.
GK7   containing 4×35p. (No. Y1778) and a pane of 4 airmail labels.............................. 3·50

£1·48 Booklets

GL1 (Worldwide Postcard Stamps ranged left without diagonal white lines across corner of stamps)

1996 (8 July). Multicoloured laminated cover as T **GL1** (75×48 mm) showing Olympic symbols on the back. Stamps printed on the cover in bright mauve by Walsall. Inscribed For Worldwide Postcards on yellow tab at right.
GL1   containing 4×37p. (No. Y1779) and a pane of 4 airmail labels.............................. 5·25

1997 (4 Feb). Multicoloured laminated cover as T **GL1** (75×48 mm) without Olympic symbols on the back. Stamps printed on the cover in bright mauve by Walsall. Inscribed For Worldwide Postcards on yellow tab at right.
GL2   containing 4×37p. (No. Y1779) and a pane of 4 airmail labels.............................. 5·25

GL3

1997 (26 Aug)–**98**. Multicoloured laminated cover as T **GL3** (75×48 mm) printed by Walsall. Inscribed For Worldwide Postcards on yellow tab at right.
GL3   containing 4×37p. (gravure) (No. Y1703) and a pane of 4 new design airmail labels .... 3·50
           a. Showing validity notice on inside back cover (5.5.98).................................. 3·50
No. GL3 has the postage rate table on the inside back cover.

1998 (3 Aug). Multicoloured laminated cover as T **GGA2** (Create a card design) (75×50 mm) printed by Walsall.
GL4   containing 4×37p. (gravure) (No. Y1703) and a pane of 4 airmail labels.... 5·00
This booklet was not placed on philatelic sale until 7 September 1998.

£1·52 Booklet

1999 (26 Apr). Multicoloured laminated cover as T **GGA1** (76×50 mm) with stamps printed on cover in ultramarine by Walsall. Inscribed For Worldwide Postcards on yellow tab at right.
GLA1   containing 4×38p. (gravure) (No. Y1707) and a pane of 4 airmail labels.... 3·25

£1·56 Booklet

GM1

1991 (16 Sept). Multicoloured laminated cover as T **GM1** (75×49 mm) with stamp printed on the cover in bright mauve by Walsall.
GM1   containing booklet pane No. X1058l and a pane of 4 airmail labels .... 5·75
No. GM1 has the horizontal edges of the pane imperforate.

£1·60 Booklet

2000 (27 Apr). Multicoloured laminated cover as T **GGA1** (76×50 mm) with stamps printed on cover in deep azure by Walsall. Inscribed For Worldwide Postcards on yellow tab at right.
GMA1   containing 4×40p. (gravure) (No. Y1710) and a pane of 4 airmail labels.... 4·00

£1·64 Worldwide Airmail Stamps Booklets

1993 (1 Nov). Laminated cover as T **GM1** (76×50 mm) with stamp printed on the cover in drab by Walsall. Inscribed For letters up to 10g on yellow tab at right.
GN1   containing 4×41p. (No. Y1780) and a pane of 4 airmail labels.............................. 3·00

1995 (16 May). Multicoloured laminated cover as T **GK6** (75×48 mm) with stamps printed on the cover in drab by Walsall. Inscribed For items up to 10g on yellow tab at right.
GN2   containing 4×41p. (No. Y1780) and a pane of 4 airmail labels.............................. 3·00

1996 (19 Mar). Multicoloured laminated cover as T **GK6** (75×48 mm) without International and showing Olympic symbols on the back. Stamps printed on the cover in drab by Walsall. Inscribed For items up to 10g on yellow tab at right.
GN3   containing 4×41p. (No. Y1780) and a pane of 4 airmail labels.............................. 3·00

£1·80 Booklet

1987 (4 Aug). Laminated cover as T **GA1** (98×60 mm).
GO1   containing booklet pane No. X955n...... 4·75
No. GO1 is inscribed 20 October 1986.

£1·90 Booklets

1988 (23 Aug). Laminated cover as T **GA1** (97×56 mm).
GP1   containing booklet pane No. X956m .... 6·50

1988 (11 Oct). Laminated cover as T **GA1** (97×56 mm) printed by Questa.
GP2   containing 10×19p. (No. X1013) .... 12·50

1988 (11 Oct). Laminated cover as T **GB3** (75×48 mm) with stamp printed on the cover in bright orange-red.
GP3   containing booklet pane No. X956o...... 6·50
No. GP3 is inscribed 5 September 1988 and has the horizontal edges of the pane imperforate.

1988 (11 Oct). Laminated cover as T **GB3** (75×48 mm) with stamp printed on the cover in bright orange-red by Questa.
GP4   containing 10×19p. (No. X1013) .... 12·50

£2·40 Booklets

1994 (9 Aug). Multicoloured laminated cover as T **GM1** (75×49 mm) with stamp printed on the cover in dull blue-grey by Walsall. Inscribed items up to 20g on yellow tab at right.
GQ1   containing 4×60p. (No. Y1784) and a pane of 4 airmail labels.............................. 4·50

POST OFFICE STAMP BOOKLETS

GQ2

1994 (4 Oct). Laminated cover as T **GQ2** (75×49 mm) with stamp printed on the cover in dull blue-grey by Walsall.
GQ2   containing 4×60p. (No. Y1784) and a pane of 4 airmail plus 4 Seasons Greetings labels... 4·75

1995 (16 May). Laminated cover as T **GK6** (75×48 mm) with stamps printed on the cover in dull blue-grey by Walsall. Inscribed For items up to 20g on yellow tab at right.
GQ3   containing 4×60p. (No. Y1784) and a pane of 4 airmail labels............................. 4·75

1996 (19 Mar). Multicoloured laminated cover as T **GK6** (75×48 mm) without International and showing Olympic symbols on the back. Stamps printed on the cover in dull grey blue by Walsall. Inscribed For items up to 20g on yellow tab at right.
GQ4   containing 4×60p. (No. Y1784) and a pane of 4 airmail labels............................. 4·75

£2·52 Booklets

1996 (8 July). Multicoloured laminated cover as T **GL1** (75×48 mm) but inscribed Worldwide Airmail Stamps and showing Olympic symbols on the back. Stamps printed on the cover in light emerald by Walsall. Inscribed For items up to 20g on yellow tab at right.
GR1   containing 4×63p. (No. Y1787) and a pane of 4 airmail labels............................. 8·00

1997 (4 Feb). Multicoloured laminated cover as T **GL1** (75×48 mm) without Olympic symbols on the back. Stamps printed on the cover in light emerald by Walsall. Inscribed For items up to 20g on yellow tab at right.
GR2   containing 4×63p. (No. Y1787) and a pane of 4 airmail labels............................. 8·00

1997 (26 Aug). Multicoloured laminated cover as T **GL1** (75×48 mm). Stamps printed on the cover in light emerald by Walsall. Inscribed For items up to 20g on yellow tab at right.
GR3   containing 4×63p. (gravure) (No. Y1732) and a pane of 4 airmail labels.... 5·00

1998 (5 May). Multicoloured laminated cover as T **GGA1** (75×50 mm). Stamps printed on the cover in light emerald by Walsall. Inscribed For items up to 20g on yellow tab at right.
GR4   containing 4×63p. (gravure) (No. Y1732) and a pane of 4 new design airmail labels .... 5·00

£2·56 Booklet

1999 (26 Apr). Multicoloured laminated cover as T **GGA1** (75×50 mm). Stamps printed on cover in turquoise-green by Walsall. Inscribed For items up to 20g on yellow tab at right.
GS1   containing 4×64p. (gravure) (No. Y1733) and a pane of 4 airmail labels.... 5·25

£2·60 Booklet

2000 (27 Apr). Multicoloured laminated cover as T **GGA1** (76×50 mm) with stamps printed on cover in greenish blue by Walsall. Inscr For items up to 20g on yellow tab at right.
GT1   containing 4×65p. (gravure) (No. Y1734) and a pane of 4 airmail labels.... 6·00

D. Barcode Booklets containing No Value Indicated stamps with barcodes on the back cover.

Panes of four 2nd Class stamps.

HA1 Redrawn Crown (small)

1989 (22 Aug). Laminated cover as T **HA1** (75×48 mm) with stamp printed on the cover in bright blue by Walsall.
HA1   (56p.) containing booklet pane No. 1449l .... 5·50
No. HA1 has three edges of the pane imperforate.

1989 (28 Nov). Laminated cover as T **HA1** (75×48 mm) with stamp printed on the cover in bright blue by Walsall containing stamps printed in gravure by Harrison.
HA2   (60p.) containing booklet pane No. 1445m..... 22·00
No. HA2 has three edges of the pane imperforate.

HA3 Crown on white

1990 (7 Aug). Multicoloured laminated cover as T **HA3** (75×48 mm) with stamp printed on the cover in bright blue by Walsall.
HA3   (60p.) containing booklet pane No. 1515l .... 5·00
No. HA3 has the horizontal edges of the pane imperforate.

1991 (6 Aug). Multicoloured laminated cover as T **HA3** (75×48 mm) with stamp printed on the cover in bright blue by Walsall (25.9.92). Barcode in black.
HA4   (68p.) containing booklet pane No. 1449m...... 5·00
    a. Barcode printed in blue............................ 5·00
No. HA4 has the horizontal edges of the pane imperforate and exists with the barcode printed in either black or blue.

HA5 Olympic Symbols

1992 (21 Jan). Multicoloured laminated cover as T **HA5** (75×48 mm) with stamp printed on the cover in bright blue by Walsall.
HA5   (72p.) containing booklet pane No. 1449m..... 5·50
No. HA5 has the horizontal edges of the pane imperforate.

> **PERFORATIONS.** Booklets from No. HA6 show perforations on all edges of the pane and contain stamps with one eilliptical hole on each vertical side.

1993 (6 Apr). Multicoloured laminated cover as T **HA3** (75×48 mm) with stamp printed on the cover in bright blue by Walsall.
HA6   (72p.) containing 4×2nd Class stamps (No. 1670) .... 5·50

POST OFFICE STAMP BOOKLETS

No. HA6 was re-issued on 6 December 1994 showing the inscriptions on the inside of the cover re-arranged.

1993 (7 Sept). Multicoloured laminated cover as T **HA3** (75×48 mm) with stamp printed on the cover in bright blue by Harrison.
HA7 (72p.) containing 4×2nd Class stamps (No. 1664) .... 5·00

HA8 (Second Class Stamps centred) (with diagonal white line across corners of stamps)

1995 (10 Jan). Multicoloured laminated cover as T **HA8** (75×48 mm) with stamps printed on the cover in bright blue by Harrison.
HA8 (76p) containing 4×2nd Class stamps (No. 1664) .... 5·00

1995 (12 Dec). Multicoloured laminated cover as T **HA8** (75×48 mm) with stamps printed on the cover in bright blue by Walsall, but without Pull Open inscription on yellow tab.
HA9 (76p.) containing 4×2nd Class stamps (No. 1670) .... 5·00
No. HA9 was initially sold at 76p, which was increased to 80p. from 8.7.96.

1996 (6 Feb). Multicoloured laminated cover as T **HA8** (75×48 mm) but without Pull Open inscription on yellow tab and showing Olympic symbols on the back. Stamps printed on the cover in bright blue by Walsall.
HA10 (76p.) containing 4×2nd Class stamps (No. 1670) .... 5·00

NOTE: From No. HA11 onwards, the printer of each booklet is identified by a small capital letter below the barcode on the outside back cover.

HA11 (Second Class Stamps ranged left) (without diagonal white line across corners of stamps)

1997 (4 Feb). Multicoloured laminated cover as T **HA11** (75×48 mm). Stamps printed on the cover in bright blue by Walsall.
HA11 (80p.) containing 4×2nd Class stamps (No. 1670) .... 5·00

1997 (26 Aug). Multicoloured laminated cover as T **HA11** (75×48 mm). Stamps printed on the cover in bright blue by Walsall.
HA12 (80p.) containing 4×2nd Class stamps (gravure) (No. 1664) .... 5·00
No. HA12 was re-issued on 5 May 1998 showing the positions of the imprint and the post code notice transposed, and again on 14 March 2000 with changed telephone number and added website address.

Panes of four 1st Class stamps

1989 (22 Aug). Laminated cover as T **HA1** (75×48 mm) with stamp printed on the cover in brownish black by Walsall.
HB1 (76p.) containing booklet pane No. 1450l .... 7·75
No. HB1 has three edges of the pane imperforate.
No. HB1 was initially sold at 76p, which was increased to 80p. from 2.10.89.

1989 (5 Dec). Laminated cover as T **HA1** (75×48 mm) with stamp printed on the cover in brownish black by Walsall containing stamps printed in photo by Harrison.
HB2 (80p.) containing booklet pane No. 1447m...... 22·00
No. HB2 has three edges of the pane imperforate.

1990 (7 Aug). Multicoloured laminated cover as T **HA3** (75×48 mm) with stamp printed on the cover in bright orange-red by Walsall (22.9.92). Barcode in black.
HB3 (80p.) containing booklet pane No. 1516l .... 6·00
  a. containing pane No. 1516cl..................... 12·00
  b. Barcode in blue... 6·00
No. HB3 has the horizontal edges of the pane imperforate.

1992 (21 Jan). Multicoloured laminated cover as T **HA5** (75×48 mm) with stamp printed on the cover in bright orange-red by Walsall.
HB4 (96p.) containing booklet pane No. 1516l .... 6·00
No. HB4 has the horizontal edges of the pane imperforate.

PERFORATIONS. Booklets from No. HB5 show perforations on all edges of the pane.

1993 (6 Apr). Multicoloured laminated cover as T **HA3** (75×48 mm) with stamp printed on the cover in bright orange-red by Harrison.
HB5 (96p.) containing 4×1st Class stamps (No. 1666) .... 6·00

1993 (17 Aug). Multicoloured laminated cover as T **HA3** (76×50 mm) with stamp printed on the cover in bright orange-red by Walsall.
HB6 (96p.) containing 4×1st Class stamps (No. 1671) .... 6·00
No. HB6 was re-issued on 1 November 1993 with changes to the inside cover text.

1994 (27 July). Multicoloured laminated cover as T **HA3** (76×50 mm) with stamp printed on the cover in bright orange-red by Questa.
HB7 (£1·00) containing booklet pane No. 1671l which includes a label commemorating the 300th anniversary of the Bank of England........ 6·00

1995 (10 Jan). Multicoloured laminated cover as T **HA8** (75×48 mm) with stamps printed on the cover in bright orange-red by Walsall.
HB8 (£1·00) containing 4×1st Class stamps (No. 1671) .... 6·00

1995 (16 May). Multicoloured laminated cover as T **HA8** (75×48 mm) with stamps printed on the cover in bright orange-red by Walsall.
HB9 (£1·00) containing booklet pane No. 1671la which includes a label commemorating the birth centenary of R. J. Mitchell (designer of Spitfire) ..... 6·00

1996 (6 Feb–Aug). Multicoloured laminated cover as T **HA8** (75×48 mm) showing Olympic symbols on the back. Stamps printed on the cover in bright orange-red by Walsall.
HB10 (£1·00) containing 4×1st Class stamps (No. 1671) .... 6·00
  a. Without diagonal white line across corners of stamps (8.96)............................ £125

1996 (16 Apr). Multicoloured laminated cover as T **HA11** (75×48 mm) with stamps printed on the cover in bright orange-red by Walsall. Inscribed Commemorative Label Inside on yellow tab at right.
HB11 (£1·00) containing booklet pane No. 1671la (includes label commemorating the 70th birthday of Queen Elizabeth II)...... 6·00

NOTE: From No. HB12 onwards, the printer of each booklet (with the exception of No. HB19) is identified by a small capital letter below the barcode on the outside back cover.

1997 (4 Feb). Multicoloured laminated cover as T **HA11** (75×48 mm). Stamps printed on the cover in bright orange-red by Walsall.
HB12 (£1·04) containing 4×1st Class stamps (No. 1671) .... 6·00

1997 (12 Feb). Multicoloured laminated cover as T **HA11** (75×48 mm). Stamps printed on the cover in bright orange-red by Walsall. Inscribed Special Label Inside on yellow tab at right.
HB13 (£1·04) containing booklet pane No. 1671la (includes label commemorating Hong Kong '97 international stamp exhibition)... 6·00

1997 (26 Aug). Multicoloured laminated cover as T **HA11** (75×48 mm). Stamps printed on the cover in bright orange-red by Walsall.
HB14 (£1·04) containing 4×1st Class stamps (gravure) (No. 1667)........................ 6·00
No. HB14 was re-issued on 5 May 1998 showing the positions of the imprint and the post code notice transposed, on 16 March 1999 with Please note that the First Class rate is no longer valid to Europe added to inside back cover and again on 14 March 2000 with changed telephone number and added website address.

POST OFFICE STAMP BOOKLETS

1997 (21 Oct). Multicoloured laminated cover as T **HA11** (75×48 mm). Stamps printed on the cover in bright orange-red by Walsall. Inscribed Commemorative Label Inside on yellow tab at right.
HB15 (£1·04) containing booklet pane No. 1671la (litho) (includes label commemorating Commonwealth Heads of Government Meeting, Edinburgh) .... 6·25

1998 (14 Nov). Multicoloured laminated cover as T **HA11** (75×48 mm). Stamps printed on the cover in bright orange-red by Walsall. Inscribed Commemorative Label Inside on yellow tab at right.
HB16 (£1·04) containing booklet pane No. 1671la (litho) (includes label commemorating 50th birthday of the Prince of Wales) .... 6·00

1999 (12 May). Multicoloured laminated cover as T **HA11** (75×48 mm). Stamps printed on the cover in bright orange-red by Walsall. Inscribed Commemorative Label Inside on yellow tab at right.
HB17 (£1·04) containing booklet pane No. 1667m (gravure) (includes label commemorating 50th anniversary of Berlin Airlift) .... 6·00

1999 (1 Oct). Multicoloured laminated cover as T **HA11** (76×50 mm). Stamps printed on the cover in bright orange-red by Walsall. Inscribed Commemorative Label Inside on yellow tab at right.
HB18 (£1·04) containing booklet pane No. 1667m (gravure) (includes label commemorating Rugby World Cup) ..... 6·00

2000 (21 Mar). Multicoloured laminated cover as T **HA11** (75×48 mm). Stamps printed on the cover in olive-brown by Walsall with Postman Pat. Inscribed Postman Pat Label Inside on yellow tab at right.
HB19 (£1·04) containing booklet pane No. 2124l (gravure) (includes label commemorating Stamp Show 2000, Earls Court) .... 6·00

2000 (4 Apr). Opening of National Botanic Garden of Wales. Multicoloured laminated cover as T **HA11** (75×48 mm). Stamps printed on the cover in olive-brown by Walsall. Inscribed Botanic Garden Label Inside on yellow tab at right.
HB20 (£1·04) containing booklet pane No. 2124l .... 6·00

Panes of eight 1st Class stamps plus pane of 2 Millennium commemoratives

HBA1

1999 (12 May). Multicoloured laminated cover as T **HBA1** (76×50 mm) showing Millennium and Machin stamps printed by Walsall.
HBA1 (£2·60) containing booklet pane No. 2085a and 8×1st Class stamps (gravure) (No. 1667) .... 13·50

1999 (21 Sept). Multicoloured laminated cover as T **HBA1** (76×50 mm) showing Millennium and Machin stamps printed by Walsall.
HBA2 (£2·60) containing booklet pane No. 2108a and 8×1st Class stamps (gravure) (No. 1667) .... 13·50

2000 (26 May). Multicoloured laminated cover as T **HBA1** (76×50 mm) showing Millennium and Machin stamps printed by Walsall.
HBA3 (£2·70) containing booklet pane No. 2126ab and 8×1st Class stamps (gravure) (No. 2124) .... 13·50

2000 (18 Sept). Multicoloured laminated cover as T **HBA1** (76×50 mm) showing Millennium and Machin stamps printed by Walsall.
HBA4 (£2·70) containing booklet pane No. 2153a and 8×1st Class stamps (gravure) (No. 2124) .... 13·50

Panes of ten 2nd Class stamps

1989 (22 Aug–2 Oct). Laminated cover as T **HA1** (75×48 mm) with stamp printed on the cover in bright blue by Harrison.
HC1 (£1·40) containing booklet pane No. 1445l .... 9·50
 a. Inside cover with new rates (2.10.89) .... 10·00

Nos. HC1/HC1a have the horizontal edges of the pane imperforate.

1989 (19 Sept). Laminated cover as T **HA1** (75×48 mm) with stamp printed on the cover in bright blue by Questa.
HC2 (£1·40) containing 10×2nd Class stamps (No. 1451) .... 9·50
No. HC2 has perforations on all edges of the pane.

1990 (7 Aug). Multicoloured laminated cover as T **HA3** (75×48 mm) with stamp printed on the cover in deep blue by Harrison.
HC3 (£1·50) containing booklet pane No. 1511l .... 10·00
No. HC3 has the horizontal edges of the pane imperforate.

1990 (7 Aug). Multicoloured laminated cover as T **HA3** (75×48 mm) with stamp printed on the cover in deep blue by Questa.
HC4 (£1·50) containing 10×2nd Class stamps (No. 1513) .... 10·50
No. HC4 has perforations on all edges of the pane.

1990 (7 Aug). Multicoloured laminated cover as T **HA3** (75×48 mm) with stamp printed on the cover in deep blue by Walsall.
HC5 (£1·50) containing booklet pane No. 1515m .... 9·50
No. HC5 has the horizontal edges of the pane imperforate.

1991 (6 Aug). Multicoloured laminated cover as T **HA3** (75×48 mm) with stamp printed on the cover in bright blue by Questa. Barcode in black.
HC6 (£1·70) containing 10×2nd Class stamps (No. 1451) .... 9·50
 a. Barcode printed in blue (22.9.92) .... 9·50
No. HC6 has perforations on all edges of the pane.
No. HC6a was sold at £1·80.

1991 (6 Aug). Multicoloured laminated cover as T **HA3** (75×48 mm) with stamp printed on the cover in bright blue by Walsall. Barcode in black.
HC7 (£1·70) containing booklet pane No. 1449n .... 9·50
 a. Barcode printed in blue (22.9.92) .... 9·50
No. HC7 has the horizontal edges of the pane imperforate.
No. HC7a was sold at £1·80.

1992 (21 Jan). Multicoloured laminated cover as T **HA5** (75×48 mm) with stamp printed on the cover in bright blue by Walsall.
HC8 (£1·80) containing booklet pane No. 1449n .... 9·50
No. HC8 has the horizontal edges of the pane imperforate.

1992 (31 Mar). Multicoloured laminated cover as T **HA5** (75×48 mm) with stamp printed on the cover in bright blue by Questa.
HC9 (£1·80) containing 10×2nd Class stamps (No. 1451) .... 9·50
No. HC9 has perforations on all edges of the pane.

1992 (22 Sept). Multicoloured laminated cover as T **HA3** (75×48 mm) with stamp printed on the cover in bright blue by Harrison.
HC10 (£1·80) containing booklet pane No. 1445l .... 9·50
No. HC10 has the horizontal edges of the pane imperforate.

PERFORATIONS. Nos. HC11/HC22 show perforations on all edges of the pane and contain stamps with one elliptical hole on each vertical side.

1993 (6 Apr). Multicoloured laminated cover as T **HA3** (75×48 mm) with stamp printed on the cover in bright blue by Questa.
HC11 (£1·80) containing 10×2nd Class stamps (No. 1670) .... 9·50
No. HC11 was re-issued on 17 August 1993 showing changes to the text on the inside of the cover and again on 6 September 1994 showing further changes.

1993 (1 Nov). Multicoloured laminated cover as T **HA3** (75×48 mm) with stamp printed on the cover in bright blue by Walsall.
HC12 (£1·90) containing 10×2nd Class stamps (No. 1670) .... 9·50

1995 (10 Jan). Multicoloured laminated cover as T **HA8** (75×48 mm) with stamps printed on the cover in bright blue by Questa.
HC13 (£1·90) containing 10×2nd Class stamps (No. 1670) .... 9·50

1995 (12 Dec). Multicoloured laminated cover as T **HA8** (75×48 mm) with stamps printed on cover in bright blue by Harrison.
HC14 (£1·90) containing 10×2nd Class stamps (No. 1664) .... 9·50

1996 (6 Feb). Multicoloured laminated cover as T **HA8** (75×48 mm) showing Olympic symbols on the back. Stamps printed on the cover in bright blue by Harrison.
HC15 (£1·90) containing 10×2nd Class stamps (No. 1664) .... 9·50

POST OFFICE STAMP BOOKLETS

1996 (6 Feb). Multicoloured laminated cover as T **HA8** (75×48 mm) showing Olympic symbols on the back. Stamps printed on the cover in bright blue by Questa.
HC16 (£1·90) containing 10×2nd Class stamps (No. 1670) .... 10·00

> **NOTE:** From No. HC17 onwards, the printer of each booklet is identified by a small capital letter below the barcode on the outside back cover.

1996 (6 Aug). Multicoloured laminated cover as T **HA8** (75×48 mm) but with diagonal white lines across corners of stamps, showing Olympic symbols on the back. Stamps printed on the cover in bright blue by Harrison.
HC17 (£2·00) containing 10×2nd Class stamps (No. 1664) .... 9·50

1996 (6 Aug). Multicoloured laminated cover as T **HA11** (75×48 mm) showing Olympic symbols on the back. Stamps printed on the cover in bright blue by Questa.
HC18 (£2·00) containing 10×2nd Class stamps (No. 1670) .... 10·00

1997 (4 Feb). Multicoloured laminated cover as T **HA11** (75×48 mm). Stamps printed on the cover in bright blue by Harrison.
HC19 (£2·00) containing 10×2nd Class stamps (No. 1664) .... 9·50

1997 (4 Feb). Multicoloured laminated cover as T **HA11** (75×48 mm). Stamps printed on the cover in bright blue by Questa.
HC20 (£2·00) containing 10×2nd Class stamps (No. 1670) .... 9·50
No. HC20 was re-issued on 5 May 1998 showing the positions of the imprint and the post code notice transposed.

1998 (5 May). Multicoloured laminated cover as T **HA11** (75×48 mm). Stamps printed on the cover in bright blue by De La Rue.
HC21 (£2·00) containing 10×2nd Class stamps (No. 1664) .... 9·50

1998 (1 Dec). Multicoloured laminated cover as T **HA11** (75×48 mm). Stamps printed on the cover in bright blue by Questa.
HC22 (£2·00) containing 10×2nd Class stamps (No. 1664a) (gravure) .... 10·00
No. HC22 was re-issued on 14 March 2000 with changed telephone number and added website address.

Panes of ten 1st Class stamps

1989 (22 Aug–2 Oct). Laminated cover as T **HA1** (75×48 mm) with stamp printed on the cover in brownish black by Harrison.
HD1 (£1·90) containing booklet pane No. 1447l .... 12·00
    a. Inside cover with new rates (2.10.89) .... 12·00
Nos. HD1/HD1a have the horizontal edges of the pane imperforate. No. HD1a was sold at £2.

1989 (19 Sept). Laminated cover as T **HA1** (75×48 mm) with stamp printed on the cover in brownish black by Questa.
HD2 (£1·90) containing 10×1st Class stamps (No. 1452) .... 12·00
No. HD2 has perforations on all edges of the pane.

1990 (7 Aug). Multicoloured laminated cover as T **HA3** (75×48 mm) with stamp printed on the cover in bright orange-red by Harrison. Barcode in black.
HD3 (£2·00) containing booklet pane No. 1512l .... 12·00
    b. Barcode printed in blue (22.9.92) .... 12·00
No. HD3 has the horizontal edges of the pane imperforate.

1990 (7 Aug). Multicoloured laminated cover as T **HA3** (75×48 mm) with stamp printed on the cover in bright orange-red by Questa. Barcode in black.
HD4 (£2·00) containing 10×1st Class stamps (No. 1514) .... 12·00
    b. Barcode printed in blue (22.9.92) .... 12·00
No. HD4 has perforations on all edges of the pane.

1990 (7 Aug). Multicoloured laminated cover as T **HA3** (75×48 mm) with stamp printed on the cover in bright orange-red by Walsall. Barcode in black.
HD5 (£2·00) containing booklet pane No. 1516m ..... 12·00
    c. Barcode printed in blue (22.9.92) .... 12·00
No. HD5 has the horizontal edges of the pane imperforate.

1992 (21 Jan). Multicoloured laminated cover as T **HA5** (75×48 mm) with stamp printed on the cover in bright orange-red by Harrison.
HD6 (£2·40) containing booklet pane No. 1512l .... 12·00
No. HD6 has the horizontal edges of the pane imperforate.

1992 (21 Jan). Multicoloured laminated cover as T **HA5** (75×48 mm) with stamp printed on the cover in bright orange-red by Walsall.
HD7 (£2·40) containing booklet pane No. 1516m ..... 12·00
No. HD7 has the horizontal edges of the pane imperforate.

1993 (9 Feb). Multicoloured laminated cover as T **HA3** (77×44 mm) with advertisement for Greetings Booklet on reverse showing Rupert Bear as in T **KX5**. Stamp printed on the cover in bright orange-red by Walsall.
HD8 (£2·40) containing booklet pane No. 1516m ..... 12·00
No. HD8 has the horizontal edges of the pane imperforate.

> **PERFORATIONS.** Nos. HD9/HD53 show perforations on all edges of the pane and contain stamps with one elliptical hole on each vertical side.

1993 (6 Apr). Multicoloured laminated cover as T **HA3** (75×48 mm) with stamp printed on the cover in bright orange-red by Harrison.
HD9 (£2·40) containing 10×1st Class stamps (No. 1666) .... 12·00
No. HD9 was re-issued on 17 August 1993 showing changes to the text on the inside of the covers.

1993 (6 Apr). Multicoloured laminated cover as T **HA3** (75×48 mm) with stamp printed on the cover in bright orange-red by Walsall.
HD10 (£2·40) containing 10×1st Class stamps (No. 1671) .... 12·00
No. HD10 was re-issued on 17 August 1993 showing changes to the text on the inside of the covers.

1993 (1 Nov). Laminated cover as T **HA3** (75×50 mm) with stamp printed on the cover in bright orange-red by Questa.
HD11 (£2·50) containing 10×1st Class stamps (No. 1671) .... 12·00
No. HD11 was re-issued on 4 October 1994 showing changes to the text on the inside of the cover.

1993 (1 Nov). Laminated cover as T **HA3** (75×50 mm) with advertisement for Greetings Booklet on reverse showing Rupert Bear as in T **KX5**. Stamp printed on the cover in bright orange-red by Walsall.
HD12 (£2·50) containing 10×1st Class stamps (No. 1671) .... 12·00

1994 (22 Feb). Multicoloured laminated cover as T **HA3** (75×48 mm) with stamp printed on the cover in bright orange-red by Walsall. Inscribed FREE POSTCARDS on yellow tab at right.
HD13 (£2·50) containing 10×1st Class stamps (No. 1671) and additional leaf giving details of Greetings Stamps postcard offer .... 12·00

1994 (1 July). Multicoloured laminated cover as T **HA3** (76×50 mm) with advertisement for Greetings Booklet on reverse showing Rupert Bear as in T **KX5**. Stamp printed on the cover in bright orange-red by Walsall. Inscribed OPEN NOW Chance to win a kite on yellow tab at right.
HD14 (£2·50) containing 10×1st Class stamps (No. 1671) with Better luck next time. etc on inside back cover .... 12·00
HD15 (£2·50) containing 10×1st Class stamps (No. 1671) with You've Won! etc on inside back cover .... 12·00
Nos. HD14/HD15 were initially only available from branches of W. H. Smith and Son. They were issued in connection with a competition in which the prizes were Paddington Bear kites.
The booklets were not available from Royal Mail philatelic outlets until 4 October 1994.

HD16

1994 (20 Sept). Multicoloured laminated covers as T **HD16** (76×50 mm) printed by Walsall. Inscribed ORDER YOURS INSIDE on yellow tab at right.
HD16 (£2·50) containing 10×1st Class stamps (No. 1671) with DO NOT OPEN UNTIL.... on front cover .... 12·00
HD17 (£2·50) containing 10×1st Class stamps (No. 1671) with KEEP IN TOUCH on front cover .... 12·00

POST OFFICE STAMP BOOKLETS

HD18 (£2·50) containing 10×1st Class stamps (No. 1671) with HAPPY BIRTHDAY on front cover .... 12·00
HD19 (£2·50) containing 10×1st Class stamps (No. 1671) with What's Happenin' Multicoloured on front cover .... 12·00

1995 (10 Jan). Multicoloured laminated cover as T **HA8** (75×48 mm) with stamps printed on the cover in bright orange-red by Harrison.
HD20 (£2·50) containing 10×1st Class stamps (No. 1666) .... 12·00

1995 (10 Jan). Multicoloured laminated cover as T **HA8** (75×48 mm) with stamps printed on the cover in bright orange-red by Questa.
HD21 (£2·50) containing 10×1st Class stamps (No. 1671) .... 12·00

1995 (10 Jan). Multicoloured laminated cover as T **HA8** (75×48 mm) with stamps printed on the cover in bright orange-red by Walsall.
HD22 (£2·50) containing 10×1st Class stamps (No. 1671) .... 12·00

HD23

1995 (14 Feb). Multicoloured laminated cover as T **HD23** (76×50 mm) showing card, Thorntons chocolates and box, printed by Walsall. Inscribed DETAILS INSIDE on yellow tab at right.
HD23 (£2·50) containing 10×1st Class stamps (No. 1671) .... 12·00

1995 (4 Apr). Multicoloured laminated cover as T **HA8** (76×48 mm) with stamps printed on cover in bright orange-red by Harrison.
HD24 (£2·50) containing 10×1st Class stamps (No. 1667) .... 12·00

1995 (24 Apr). Multicoloured laminated cover as T **HA8** (75×48 mm) with stamps printed on the cover in bright orange-red by Walsall. Inscribed W H Smith Special Offer on yellow tab at right.
HD25 (£2·50) containing 10×1st Class stamps (No. 1671) .... 12·00
No. HD25 was initially only available from W. H. Smith branches and offered 50p. off the purchase of own brand stationery.
The booklet was not placed on philatelic sale until 3 October 1995.

1995 (26 June). Multicoloured laminated cover as T **HA8** (76×48 mm) with stamps printed on the cover in bright orange red by Questa. Inscribed Sainsbury's Promotion on yellow tab at right.
HD26 (£2·50) containing 10×1st Class stamps (No. 1671) .... 12·00
No. HD26 was initially only available from Sainsbury's branches and offered the chance to win a year's free shopping.
The booklet was not placed on philatelic sale until 5 September 1995.

1995 (4 Sept). Multicoloured laminated cover as T **HD23** (76×48 mm) showing ceramic figures of Benjy Bear and Harry Hedgehog, printed by Harrison.
HD27 (£2·50) containing 10×1st Class stamps (No. 1667) .... 12·00

1996 (6 Feb). Multicoloured laminated cover as T **HA8** (76×48 mm) showing Olympic symbols on the back. Stamps printed on the cover in bright orange-red by Walsall.
HD28 (£2·50) containing 10×1st Class stamps (No. 1671) .... 12·00

1996 (19 Feb). Multicoloured laminated cover as T **HD23** (76×48 mm) showing Walt Disney World, printed by Harrison.
HD29 (£2·50) containing 10×1st Class stamps (No. 1667) .... 12·00

1996 (19 Mar). Multicoloured laminated cover as T **HA8** (76×48 mm) showing Olympic symbols on the back, printed by Harrison.
HD30 (£2·50) containing 10×1st Class stamps (No. 1667) .... 12·00

HD31

1996 (13 May). Multicoloured laminated covers as T **HD31** (76×48 mm) showing woman lighting Olympic torch, printed by Harrison, with each booklet showing a scratch card on the reverse based on different Olympic events.
HD31 (£2·50) containing 10×1st Class stamps (No. 1667) (Shot Put).. 12·00
HD32 (£2·50) containing 10×1st Class stamps (No. 1667) (Hurdles).. 12·00
HD33 (£2·50) containing 10×1st Class stamps (No. 1667) (Archery)... 12·00

NOTE: From No. HD34 onwards, the printer of each booklet is identified by a small capital letter below the barcode on the outside back cover.

1996 (15 July). Multicoloured laminated cover as T **HA11** (76×48 mm) showing Olympic symbols on the back. Stamps printed on the cover in bright orange-red by Walsall. Inscribed W. H. Smith Offer Inside on yellow tab at right.
HD34 (£2·60) containing 10×1st Class stamps (No. 1671) .... 12·00
No. HD34 was initially only available from branches of W. H. Smith and Sons. It was issued in connection with a special offer of AA/OS Leisure Guides.
The booklets were not available from Royal Mail philatelic outlets until 17 September 1996.

1996 (6 Aug). Multicoloured laminated cover as T **HA11** (76×48 mm), but with diagonal white line across corners of stamps and showing Olympic symbols on the back. Stamps printed on the cover in bright orange-red by Harrison.
HD35 (£2·60) containing 10×1st Class stamps (No. 1667) .... 12·00

1996 (6 Aug). Multicoloured laminated cover as T **HA11** (76×48 mm) showing Olympic symbols on the back. Stamps printed on the cover in bright orange-red by Walsall.
HD36 (£2·60) containing 10×1st Class stamps (No. 1671) .... 12·00

1996 (9 Sept). Multicoloured laminated cover as T **HD31** (76×48 mm) showing iced cakes on front and back, printed by Walsall. Inscribed OPEN FOR DETAILS on yellow tab at right.
HD37 (£2·60) containing 10×1st Class stamps (No. 1671) .... 12·00

1996 (7 Oct). Multicoloured laminated cover as T **HA11** (76×48 mm) showing Olympic symbols on the back. Stamps printed on cover in bright orange-red by Walsall. Inscribed Offer Inside on yellow tab at right.
HD38 (£2·60) containing 10×1st Class stamps (No. 1671) .... 12·00
No. HD38 was initially only available from ASDA stores and offered £1 off greetings cards. The booklet was not placed on philatelic sale until 13 January 1997.

1997 (4 Feb). Multicoloured laminated cover as T **HA11** (76×48 mm). Stamps printed on the cover in bright orange-red by Harrison.
HD39 (£2·60) containing 10×1st Class stamps (No. 1667) .... 12·00

1997 (4 Feb). Multicoloured laminated cover as T **HA11** (76×48 mm). Stamps printed on the cover in bright orange-red by Walsall.
HD40 (£2·60) containing 10×1st Class stamps (No. 1671) .... 12·00

1997 (21 Apr). Royal Golden Wedding. Multicoloured laminated cover as T **HA11** (76×48 mm). Stamps printed on the cover in gold by Harrison.
HD41 (£2·60) containing 10×1st Class stamps (No. 1668) .... 12·00

1997 (21 Apr). Royal Golden Wedding. Multicoloured laminated cover as T **HA11** (76×48 mm). Stamps printed on the cover in gold by Walsall.
HD42 (£2·60) containing 10×1st Class stamps (No. 1668) .... 12·00

1997 (15 Sept). Multicoloured laminated cover as T **HD31** (76×48 mm) showing a tropical beach scene printed by Harrison. Inscr FIRST CLASS TRAVEL on front, and OPEN FOR DETAILS on yellow tab at right.
HD43 (£2·60) containing 10×1st Class stamps (No. 1668) .... 12·00

1997 (8 Nov). Multicoloured laminated cover as T **HA11** (76×48 mm). Stamps printed on the cover in bright orange-red by Walsall.
HD44 (£2·60) containing 10×1st Class stamps (gravure) (No. 1667) .... 12·00
No. HD44 was re-issued on 5 May 1998 showing the positions of the imprint, which was now vertical, and the post code notice transposed and again on 16 March 1999 with Please note that the First Class rate is no longer valid to Europe added to inside back cover.

HD45

1998 (2 Feb). Multicoloured laminated cover as T **HD45** (76×48 mm) showing Disney illustration printed by De la Rue, with a scratch card on the reverse. Inscribed See reverse for Scratch and Win on yellow tab at right.
HD45 (£2·60) containing 10×1st Class stamps (gravure) (No. 1667) .... 12·00

HD46

1998 (27 Apr). Multicoloured laminated cover as T **HD46** (76×48 mm) showing Peugeot 106 printed by De La Rue. Inscribed WIN A PEUGEOT 106 on yellow tab at right.
HD46 (£2·60) containing 10×1st Class stamps (gravure) (No. 1667) .... 12·00
No. HD46 was not placed on philatelic sale until 23 June 1998.

1998 (5 May). Multicoloured laminated cover as T **HA11** (76×48 mm). Stamps printed on the cover in bright orange-red by De La Rue.
HD47 (£2·60) containing 10×1st Class stamps (gravure) (No. 1667) .... 12·00

1998 (1 July). Multicoloured laminated cover as T **HD46** (76×48 mm) showing JVC Camcorder printed by De La Rue. Inscribed WIN A JVC CAMCORDER on yellow tab at right.
HD48 (£2·60) containing 10×1st Class stamps (gravure) (No. 1667) .... 12·00
No. HD48 was not placed on philatelic sale until 27 August 1998.

1998 (3 Aug). Multicoloured laminated cover as T **GGA2** (76×48 mm) inscribed (Create a card design), printed by De La Rue.
HD49 (£2·60) containing 10×1st Class stamps (gravure) (No. 1667) .... 12·00
No. HD49 was not placed on philatelic sale until 7 September 1998.

1998 (7 Sept). Multicoloured laminated cover as T **HA11** (75×49 mm), with stamps printed on the cover in bright orange-red by Questa.
HD50 (£2·60) containing 10×1st Class stamps (litho) (No. 1671) .... 12·00

1998 (1 Dec). Multicoloured laminated cover as T **HA11** (75×48 mm). Stamps printed on the cover in bright orange-red by Questa.
HD51 (£2·60) containing 10×1st Class stamps (gravure) (No. 1667a)................. 12·00
No. HD51 was re-issued on 16 March 1999 with Please note that the First Class rate is no longer valid to Europe added to inside back cover.

2000 (6 Jan). Multicoloured laminated cover as T **HA11** (75×48 mm). Millennium definitives printed on the cover in olive-brown by Questa.
HD52 (£2·60) containing 10×1st Class stamps (gravure) (No. 2124d) .... 12·00
No. HD52 was re-issued on 14 March 2000 with a changed telephone number on the inside back cover.

2000 (6 Jan). Multicoloured laminated cover as T **HA11** (75×48 mm). Millennium definitives printed on the cover in olive-brown by Walsall.
HD53 (£2·60) containing 10×1st Class stamps (gravure) (No. 2124) .... 12·00
No. HD53 was was re-issued on 14 March 2000 with a changed telephone number on the inside back cover.

Panes of four European Airmail stamps

HF1

1999 (19 Jan). Multicoloured laminated cover as T **HF1** (75×50 mm). Stamps printed on the cover in deep blue by Walsall. Inscribed For items up to 20g on yellow tab at right.
HF1 (£1·20) containing 4×European Airmail stamps (No. 1669) and pane of four airmail labels .... 10·00
No. HF1 was re-issued on 27 April 2000 showing an amended Customer Services telephone number on the inside back cover.

E. Barcode Booklets containing Penny Black Anniversary stamps with barcodes on back cover.

60p. Booklet

JA1

1990 (30 Jan). Laminated cover as T **JA1** (75×48 mm) showing Penny Black Anniversary stamp in bright blue. Containing booklet pane No. 1475l, printed in litho by Walsall.
JA1 containing booklet pane No. 1475l .... 3·75
No. JA1 has three edges of the pane imperforate.

80p. Booklets

1990 (30 Jan). Laminated cover as T **JA1** (75×48 mm) showing Penny Black Anniversary stamp in brownish black and cream. Containing booklet pane No. 1476m, printed in litho by Walsall.
JB1 containing booklet pane No. 1476m..... 5·00
No. JB1 has three edges of the pane imperforate.

1990 (17 Apr). Laminated cover as T **JA1** (75×48 mm) showing Penny Black Anniversary stamp printed on the cover in brownish black by Walsall. Containing stamps printed in photo by Harrison.
JB2 containing booklet pane No. 1469r....... 4·50
No. JB2 has three edges of the pane imperforate.

£1·50 Booklets

1990 (30 Jan). Laminated cover as T **JA1** (75×48 mm) showing Penny Black Anniversary stamp in bright blue. Containing booklet pane No. 1467l printed in photo by Harrison.
JC1 containing booklet pane No. 1467l .... 5·50
No. JC1 has the horizontal edges of the pane imperforate.

POST OFFICE STAMP BOOKLETS

1990 (17 Apr). Laminated cover as T **JA1** (75×48 mm) showing Penny Black Anniversary stamp printed on the cover in bright blue, printed in litho by Questa.
JC2   containing 10×15p. (No. 1477) .... 10·00

1990 (12 June). Laminated cover as T **JA1** (75×48 mm) showing Penny Black Anniversary stamp in bright blue. Containing booklet pane No. 1475m, printed in litho by Walsall.
JC3   containing booklet pane No. 1475m..... 6·25
No. JC3 has three edges of the pane imperforate.

£2 Booklets

1990 (30 Jan). Laminated cover as T **JA1** (75×48 mm) showing Penny Black Anniversary stamp in brownish black and cream. Containing booklet pane. No. 1469m, printed in photo by Harrison.
JD1   containing booklet pane No. 1469m..... 6·25
No. JD1 has the horizontal edges of the pane imperforate.

1990 (17 Apr). Laminated cover as T **JA1** (75×48 mm) showing Penny Black Anniversary stamp printed on the cover in brownish black, printed in litho by Questa.
JD2   containing 10×20p. (No. 1478) .... 12·00

1990 (12 June). Laminated cover as T **JA1** (75×48 mm) showing Penny Black Anniversary stamp in brownish black and cream. Containing booklet pane No. 1476n, printed in litho by Walsall.
JD3   containing booklet pane No. 1476n..... 9·00
No. JD3 has three edges of the pane imperforate.

F. Barcode Booklets containing Greetings stamps with barcodes on the back cover.

For first greetings booklet, issued 31 January 1989, see No. FY1 in section B.

£2 Greetings Booklet

KX1 (*Illustration reduced. Actual size 135×85 mm*)

(Des Michael Peters and Partners)

1990 (6 Feb). Greetings Stamps. Scarlet, lemon and black cover as T **KX1** (135×85 mm) by Harrison. Containing booklet pane No. 1483a, and a separate sheet of 12 greetings labels.
KX1   (£2·00) Smile design cut-out showing stamps inside.. 13·50

Greetings Booklets containing No Value Indicated stamps

KX2

(Des T. Meeuwissen)

1991 (5 Feb). Greetings Stamps. Multicoloured laminated cover as T **KX2** (95×69 mm) by Harrison. Containing booklet pane No. 1536a, including 12 special greetings labels in a block (3×4) at right, attached by the selvedge.
KX2   (£2·20) Good Luck charms design.......................... 13·50

KX3

(Des Michael Peters and Partners)

1991 (26 Mar). Greetings Stamps. Multicoloured laminated cover as T **KX3** (95×69 mm) by Harrison. Containing booklet pane No. 1550a, including 12 special greetings labels in a block (3×4) at right, attached by the selvedge.
KX3   (£2·20) Laughing pillar box design .... 13·50
         a. Amended text to inside back cover (3.3.92)... 13·50
The note on the inside back cover of No. KX3 is headed Greetings Stamps.
In No. KX3a there is no heading but details of the validity of the stamps to European destinations have been added.

KX4

(Des Trickett and Webb)

1992 (28 Jan). Greetings Stamps. Multicoloured laminated cover as T **KX4** (95×69 mm) by Harrison. Containing booklet pane No. 1592a, including 12 special greetings labels in a block (3×4) at right, attached by selvedge.
KX4   (£2·40) Pressed Flowers design .... 13·50

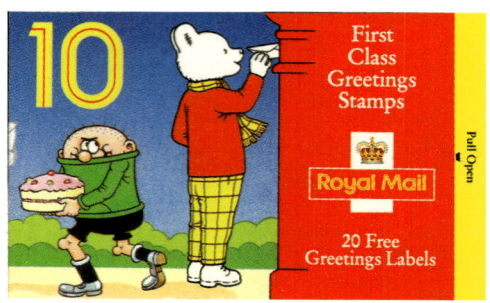

KX5

POST OFFICE STAMP BOOKLETS

(Des Newell and Sorrell)

1993 (2 Feb). Greetings Stamps. Multicoloured laminated cover as T **KX5** (96×60 mm) by Harrison. Containing booklet pane No. 1644a and pane of 20 special greetings labels in a block (5×4), both panes attached by a common gutter margin.

KX5 (£2·40) Children's Characters design .... 13·50

No. KX5 was re-issued on 15 June 1993 with 'Thompson' corrected to 'Thomson' (bottom line at left) and on 17 August 1993 with 'Sorell' corrected to 'Sorrell'.

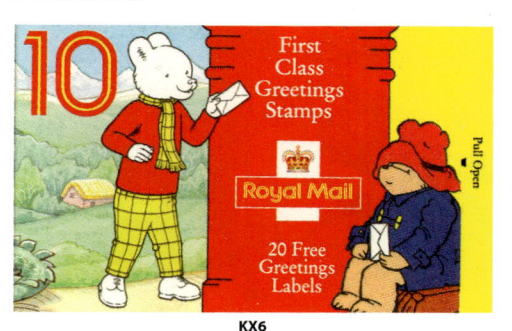

KX6

(Des Newell and Sorrell)

1994 (1 Feb). Greetings Stamps. Multicoloured cover as T **KX6** (96×60 mm) by Harrison. Containing booklet pane No. 1800a and pane of 20 special greetings labels in a block (5×4), both panes attached by a common gutter margin.

KX6 (£2·50) Children's Characters design .... 13·50

KX7

(Des Newell and Sorrell)

1995 (21 Mar)–96. Greetings Stamps. Multicoloured cover as T **KX7** (96×60 mm) by Walsall. Containing booklet pane No. 1858a and pane of 20 special greetings labels in a block (5×4), both panes attached by a common gutter margin. Inscribed Pull Open on yellow strip at right.

KX7 (£2·50) Clown design .... 13·50
    a. No inscription on yellow strip (5.2.96) .. 14·50

KX8

(Des M. Wolff)

1996 (26 Feb–11 Nov). Greetings Stamps. Multicoloured cover as T **KX8** (96×60 mm) by Walsall. Containing booklet pane No. 1905a and pane of 20 special greetings labels in a block (5×4), both panes attached by a common gutter margin.

KX8 (£2·50) MORE! LOVE design .... 13·50
    a. Containing pane No. 1905pa (11.11.96) 24·00

No. KX8a shows a redesigned inside front cover which omits references to 1996 dates.

KX9

(Des Tutssels)

1997 (6 Jan). Greetings Stamps. 19th-century Flower Paintings. Multicoloured cover as T **KX9** (96×61 mm) by Walsall. Containing booklet pane No. 1955a and pane of 20 special greetings labels in a block (5×4), both panes attached by a common gutter margin.

KX9 (£2·60) *Gentiana acaulis* design.............................. 13·50

No. KX9 was re-issued on 16 March 1999 with Please note that the First Class rate is no longer valid to Europe' added to inside front cover.

1997 (3 Feb). Greetings Stamps. 19th-century Flower Paintings. Multicoloured cover as T **KX9** (96×61 mm) by Walsall but with box inscribed WIN A BEAUTIFUL BOUQUET INSTANTLY Multicoloured printed in yellow on red over the flower on the front and with a scratch card on the inside back cover. Inscribed Open now – See if you've won on yellow tab at right. Containing booklet pane No. 1955a and pane of 20 special greetings labels in a block (5×4), both panes attached by a common gutter margin.

KX10 (£2·60) *Gentiana acaulis* design................................ 14·00

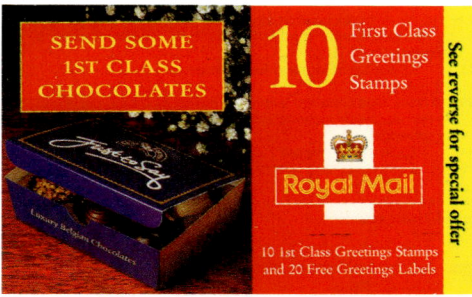

KX11

1998 (5 Jan). Greetings Stamps. 19th-century Flower Paintings. Multicoloured cover as T **KX11** (96×61 mm) by Walsall. Inscribed See reverse for special offer on yellow tab at right. Containing booklet pane No. 1955a and pane of 20 special greetings labels in a block (5×4), both attached by a common gutter margin.

KX11 (£2·60) Chocolate design.......................... 14·00

1998 (3 Aug). Greetings Stamps. 19th-century Flower Paintings. Multicoloured cover as T **GGA2** (88×61 mm) printed by Walsall. Containing booklet pane No. 1955a and pane of 20 special greetings labels in a block (5×4), both attached by a common gutter margin.

KX12 (£2·60) Create a card design .... 14·00

No. KX12 was not placed on philatelic sale until 7 September 1998.

POST OFFICE STAMP BOOKLETS

G. Barcode Booklets containing Christmas stamps with barcode on the back.

LX1

(Des A. Davidson)

1990 (13 Nov). Christmas. Multicoloured laminated cover as T **LX1** (96×60 mm) by Harrison. Containing booklet pane No. 1526b, attached by the selvedge.
LX1 £3·40 Snowman design.. 5·50

1991 (12 Nov). Multicoloured laminated cover as T **LX1**, but 95×70 mm by Harrison. Containing booklet pane No. 1582b attached by the selvedge.
LX2 £3·60 Holly design.. 5·75

LX3

(Des Karen Murray)

1992 (10 Nov). Multicoloured laminated cover as T **LX3** (95×70 mm) by Harrison. Containing booklet pane No. 1634a attached by the selvedge.
LX3 £3·60 Santa Claus and Reindeer design .... 5·75

1993 (9 Nov). Multicoloured laminated covers as T **LX3**, but 95×60 mm by Harrison, each showing Santa Claus and Reindeer. Panes attached by selvedge.
LX4 £2·50 containing ten 25p. stamps (No. 1791). 5·00
LX5 £3·80 containing twenty 19p. stamps (No. 1790) .... 6·00
No. LX4 was only available from Post Offices in the Central TV area and from philatelic outlets.

LX6

(Des Yvonne Gilbert)

1994 (1 Nov). Multicoloured laminated covers as T **LX6** (95×60 mm) by Harrison, showing different Nativity Play props. Panes attached by selvedge.
LX6 £2·50 containing ten 25p. stamps (No. 1844). 4·00
LX7 £3·80 containing twenty 19p. stamps (No. 1843) .... 5·50

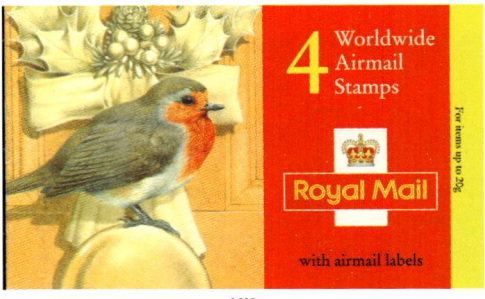

LX8

(Des K. Lilly)

1995 (30 Oct). Multicoloured laminated covers as T **LX8** (95×60 mm) by Harrison, showing Robins as depicted on the contents. Panes attached by selvedge.
LX8 £2·40 containing four 60p. stamps (No. 1900) plus 4 airmail labels .... 3·75
LX9 £2·50 containing ten 25p. stamps (No. 1897). 3·75
LX10 £3·80 containing twenty 19p. stamps (No. 1896) .... 6·00

LX11

1996 (28 Oct). Multicoloured laminated covers as T **LX11** (95×60 mm) by Harrison, showing scenes from the Nativity as depicted on the contents. Panes attached by selvedge.
LX11 (£2·60) containing ten 1st Class stamps (No. 1951) .... 13·50
LX12 (£4·00) containing twenty 2nd Class stamps (No. 1950) .... 19·00

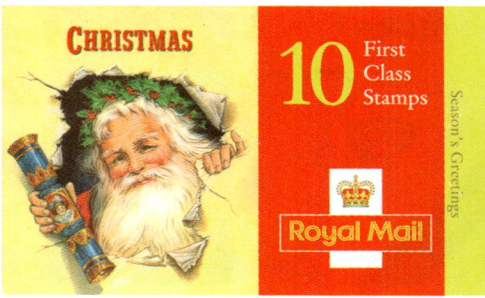

LX13

1997 (27 Oct). Multicoloured laminated covers as T **LX13** (95×60 mm) by Harrison, showing Father Christmas and crackers as depicted on the contents. Panes attached by selvedge.
LX13 (£2·60) containing ten 1st Class stamps (No. 2007) .... 13·50
LX14 (£4·00) containing twenty 2nd Class stamps (No. 2006) .... 19·00

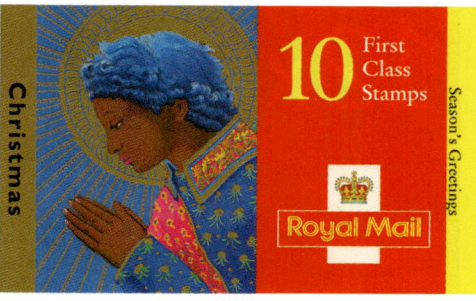

POST OFFICE STAMP BOOKLETS

LX15

1998 (2 Nov). Multicoloured laminated covers covers as T **LX15** (95×60 mm) by De La Rue, showing Angels as depicted on the contents. Panes attached by selvedge.
LX15	£2·60 containing ten 26p. stamps (No. 2065).	4·25
LX16	£4·00 containing twenty 20p. stamps (No. 2064)	6·25

LX17

1999 (2 Nov). Multicoloured laminated covers as T **LX17** (95×70 mm) by De La Rue, showing designs as depicted on the contents. Panes attached by selvedge.
LX17	£2·60 containing ten 26p. stamps (No. 2116).	4·25
LX18	£3·80 containing twenty 19p. stamps (No. 2115)	6·00

LX19

2000 (7 Nov). Multicoloured laminated covers as T **LX19** (96×70 mm) by De La Rue, showing designs as depicted on the contents. Inscribed Season's Greetings on yellow tab at right. Panes attached by selvedge.
LX19	£2·70 containing ten 1st Class stamps (No. 2171)	13·50
LX20	£3·80 containing twenty 2nd Class stamps (No. 2170)	19·00

2001 (6 Nov). Self-adhesive booklet containing Nos. 2238a and 2239a, each with a multicoloured header label showing barcode and Royal Mail emblem and further label at foot with telephone numbers, folded to form booklets 119×81 mm by De La Rue.
LX21	£3·24 containing twelve 1st Class stamps (No. 2239a)	16·00
LX22	£4·56 containing twenty four 2nd Class stamps (No. 2238a)	22·00

Nos. LX21/LX22 show the surplus self-adhesive paper around each stamp retained.

2002 (5 Nov). Self-adhesive booklet containing Nos. 2321a and 2322a, each with a multicoloured header label showing barcode and Royal Mail emblem and further label at foot with telephone numbers, folded to form booklets 105×72 mm by De La Rue.
LX23	£3·24 containing twelve 1st Class stamps (No. 2322a)	16·00
LX24	£4·56 containing twenty four 2nd Class stamps (No. 2321a)	22·00

No. LX23 was sealed into a cellophane packet which also contained a *Lord of the Rings* game card.
Nos. LX23/LX24 show the surplus self-adhesive paper around each stamp retained.

Notes. From No. LX25 all the booklets in this section have the surplus self-adhesive paper around each stamp removed, *unless otherwise stated.* All self-adhesive booklets containing 2nd Class Christmas stamps from No. LX31 onward have two small notches at the top right tab edge. All self-adhesive booklets containing 1st Class Christmas stamps from No. LX32 onward have a single small notch at the top right tab edge. From No. LX51 all booklets in this section have repeating undulating 'ROYALMAIL' background in two sizes of grey text printed on the front of the backing paper. On Nos. LX51/LX52 the text is upright (Type PB-Up); from LX53 onward alternate pairs of lines are inverted (i.e. Types PB-Ls and/or PB-sL, see footnotes) or as noted.

2003 (4 Nov). Self-adhesive booklet containing Nos. 2410a and 2411a, each with a multicoloured header label showing barcode and Royal Mail emblem and further label at foot with telephone numbers, folded to form booklets 106×71 mm by De La Rue.
LX25	£3·36 containing twelve 1st Class stamps (No. 2411a)	16·00
LX26	£4·80 containing twenty four 2nd Class stamps (No. 2410a)	22·00

2004 (2 Nov). Self-adhesive booklet containing Nos. 2495a and 2496a, each with a multicoloured header label showing barcode and Royal Mail emblem and further label at foot with contact information, folded to form booklets 105×71 mm by De La Rue.
LX27	£3·36 containing twelve 1st Class stamps (No. 2496a)	16·00
LX28	£5·04 containing twenty four 2nd Class stamps (No. 2495a)	22·00

2005 (1 Nov). Self-adhesive booklet containing Nos. 2582a and 2583a, each with a multicoloured header label showing barcode and Royal Mail emblem and further label at foot with contact information, folded to form booklets 106×71 mm by De La Rue.
LX29	£3·60 containing twelve 1st Class stamps (No. 2583a)	16·00
LX30	£5·04 containing twenty four 2nd Class stamps (No. 2582a)	22·00

LX31

2006 (7 Nov). Covers as T **LX31** (75×57 mm) by De La Rue. Self-adhesive.
LX31	£2·76 containing twelve 2nd Class stamps (No. 2678a)	13·50
LX32	£3·84 containing twelve 1st Class stamps (No. 2679a) (as Type **LX31** but red cover inscribed 12×1st)	16·00

POST OFFICE STAMP BOOKLETS

2007 (6 Nov). Covers as T **LX31** (75×57 mm) by De La Rue. Self-adhesive.
LX33	£2·88 containing twelve 2nd Class stamps (No. 2789a)..................................	13·50
LX34	£4·08 containing twelve 1st Class stamps (No. 2790a) (as Type **LX31** but red cover inscribed 12×1st)...............................	16·00

2008 (4 Nov). Covers as T **LX31** (75×57 mm) by De La Rue. Self-adhesive.
LX35	£3·24 containing twelve 2nd Class stamps (No. 2876a)..................................	13·50
	a. Oh YES it is! along right-hand edge of pane..	13·50
LX36	£4·32 containing twelve 1st Class stamps (No. 2877a) (as Type **LX31** but red cover inscribed 12×1st)...............................	16·00
	a. It's behind you! along right-hand edge of pane..	16·00

No. LX35 is inscribed Oh NO it isn't! and No. LX36 Abracadabra!, both along the right-hand edges of the booklet panes.

2009 (3 Nov). Covers as T **LX31** (75×57 mm) by De La Rue. Self-adhesive.
LX37	£3·60 containing twelve 2nd class stamps (No. 2991a)..................................	13·50
LX38	£4·68 containing twelve 1st class stamps (No. 2992a) (as Type **LX31** but red cover inscribed 12×1st)...............................	16·00

LX39 Wallace and Gromit posting Christmas Cards

2010 (2 Nov). Covers as T **LX39** (74×58 mm) by De La Rue. Self-adhesive.
LX39	£3·84 containing twelve 2nd class stamps (No. 3128a)..................................	13·50
LX40	£4·92 containing twelve 1st class stamps (No. 3129a) (as Type **LX39** but red cover inscribed 12×1st)...............................	16·00

2011 (8 Nov). Covers as T **LX31** (74×58 mm) by De La Rue. Self-adhesive.
LX41	£4·32 containing twelve 2nd class stamps (No. 3242a)..................................	13·50
LX42	£5·52 containing twelve 1st class stamps (No. 3243a) (as Type **LX31** but red cover inscribed 12×1st)...............................	16·00

2012 (6 Nov). Covers as T **LX31** (74×58 mm) by Walsall. Self-adhesive.
LX43	£6·00 containing twelve 2nd class stamps (No. 3415a)..................................	13·50
LX44	£7·20 containing twelve 1st class stamps (No. 3416a) (as Type **LX31** but red cover inscribed 12×1st)...............................	16·00

2013 (5 Nov). Covers as T **LX31** (89×66 mm) by Walsall. Self-adhesive.
LX45	£6·00 containing twelve 2nd class stamps (No. 3542a)..................................	13·50
LX46	£7·20 containing twelve 1st class stamps (No. 3543a) (as Type **LX31** but red cover inscribed 12×1st)...............................	16·00

2014 (4 Nov). Covers as T **LX31** (74×58 mm) by Walsall. Self-adhesive.
LX47	£6·36 containing twelve 2nd class stamps (No. 3650a)..................................	13·50
LX48	£7·44 containing twelve 1st class stamps (No. 3651a) (as Type **LX31** but red cover inscribed 12×1st)...............................	16·00

2015 (3 Nov). Covers as T **LX31** (89×65 mm) by ISP Walsall. Self-adhesive.
LX49	(£6·48) containing twelve 2nd class stamps (No. 3771a)..................................	13·50
LX50	(£7·56) containing twelve 1st class stamps (No. 3772a) (as Type **LX31** but red cover inscribed 12×1st)...............................	16·00

LX51

2016 (8 Nov). Covers as T **LX51** (89×65 mm) by ISP Walsall. Self-adhesive with repeating 'ROYALMAIL' wording (Type PB-Up) printed on the front of the self-adhesive backing paper.
LX51	(£6·60) containing twelve 2nd class stamp (No. 3903a)..................................	13·50
LX52	(£7·68) containing twelve 1st class stamps (No. 3904a) (as Type **LX51** but red cover inscribed 12×1st)...............................	16·00

2017 (7 Nov). Covers as T **LX51** (89×65 mm). Printed by ISP Walsall. Self-adhesive with repeating 'ROYALMAIL' wording printed on the front of the self-adhesive backing paper.
LX53	(£6·72) containing twelve 2nd class stamps (No. 4019a)..................................	13·50
LX54	(£6·72) containing twelve 2nd class stamps (No. 4019b)..................................	13·50
LX55	(£7·80) containing twelve 1st class stamps (No. 4020a) (as Type **LX51** but red cover inscribed 12×1st)...............................	16·00
LX56	(£7·80) containing twelve 1st class stamps (No. 4020b) (as Type **LX51** but red cover inscribed 12×1st)...............................	19·00

Nos. LX54 and LX56 were described by Royal Mail as Reserve stock and, initially, were only available from Philatelic Bureau, Edinburgh.
No. LX53 exists with the large 'ROYALMAIL' lettering above the small and with the small above the large in the alternate pairs of lines in the background text (Types PB-Ls/sL).
Nos. LX54, LX55 and LX56 exist with the large 'ROYALMAIL' lettering above the small in the alternate pairs of lines in the background text (Type PB-Ls).

2018 (1 Nov). Covers as T **LX51** (89×65 mm). Printed by ISP Walsall. Self-adhesive with repeating 'ROYALMAIL' wording printed on the front of the self-adhesive backing paper.
LX57	(£6·96) containing twelve 2nd class stamps (No. 4154a)..................................	17·00
LX58	(£8·04) containing twelve 1st class stamps (No. 4155a) (as Type **LX51** but red cover inscribed 12×1st)...............................	20·00

Nos. LX57 and LX58 exist with the large 'ROYALMAIL' lettering above the small in the alternate pairs of lines in the background text (Type PB-Ls).

2019 (5 Nov). Covers as T **LX51** (89×65 mm). Printed by ISP Walsall. Self-adhesive with repeating 'ROYALMAIL' wording printed on the front of the self-adhesive backing paper.
LX59	(£7·32) containing twelve 2nd class stamps (No. 4283a)..................................	12·50
LX60	(£8·40) containing twelve 1st class stamps (No. 4284a) (as Type **LX51** but red cover inscribed 12×1st)...............................	17·50

Nos. LX59 exists with the large 'ROYALMAIL' lettering above the small and with the small above the large in the alternate pairs of lines in the background text (Type PB-Ls/sL).
No. LX60 exists with the small 'ROYALMAIL' lettering above the large in the alternate pairs of lines in the background (Type PB-sL).

2020 (3 Nov). Covers as Type **LX51** (89×65 mm). Printed by ISP Walsall. Self-adhesive with repeating 'ROYALMAIL' wording printed on the front of the self-adhesive backing paper.
LX61	(£7·80) containing twelve 2nd class stamps (No. 4434a)..................................	12·50
LX62	(£9·12) containing twelve 1st class stamps (No. 4435a) (as Type **LX51** but red cover inscribed '12×1st')............................	17·50

No. LX61 exists with the large 'ROYALMAIL' lettering above the small and with the small above the large in the alternate pairs of lines in the background text (Type PB-Ls/sL).
No. LX62 exists with the small 'ROYALMAIL' lettering above the large in the alternate pairs of lines in the background text (Type PB-sL).

POST OFFICE STAMP BOOKLETS

2021 (2 Nov). Covers as T **LX51** (89×65 mm) by ISP Walsall. Self-adhesive with repeating 'ROYALMAIL' wording printed on the front of the self-adhesive backing paper.

LX63	(£7·92) containing twelve 2nd class stamps (No. 4606a)	12·50
LX64	(£10·20) containing twelve 1st class stamps (No. 4608a) (as Type LX51 but red cover inscr '12×1st'.........................	17·50

No. LX63 exists with the large 'ROYALMAIL' lettering above the small and with the small above the large in the alternate pairs of lines in the background text (Types PB-Ls/sL).

No. LX64 exists with the small 'ROYALMAIL' lettering above the large in the alternate pairs of lines in the background text (Type PB-sL).

H. Self-adhesive Barcode Booklets containing No Value Indicated stamps.

NOTES. All booklets in this section have the surplus self-adhesive paper around each stamp removed, *unless otherwise stated*. All 'MB' booklets from MB3 onward have a single small notch at the top right tab edge. All 'ME' booklets from ME2 onward have two small notches at the top right tab edge. All 'MF' booklets from MF3 onward have a single small notch at the top right tab edge.

Containing 6×2nd class stamps

MA1

2001 (29 Jan). Multicoloured cover as T **MA1** (74×56 mm). Stamps on the cover in bright blue printed by Walsall.

MA1	(£1·14) containing 6×2nd Class self-adhesive stamps (No. 2039)...........................	6·50
	a. Imperf (containing 2039ab).....................	—

No. MA1 has the surplus self-adhesive paper around each stamp retained.

No. MA1 was re-issued on 1 August 2001 showing Cod Post added to the Ffôn Testun inscription on the back cover.

Containing 6×1st Class stamps

2001 (29 Jan). Multicoloured cover as T **MA1** (74×56 mm). Stamps on the cover in bright orange-red printed by Walsall.

MB1	(£1·62) containing 6×1st Class self-adhesive stamps (No. 2040)...........................	7·50

No. MB1 has the surplus self-adhesive paper around each stamp retained.

No. MB1 was re-issued on 1 August 2001 showing Cod Post added to the Ffôn Testun inscription on the back cover.

MB2

2001 (29 Jan). Multicoloured cover as T **MB2** (74×56 mm). Stamps on the cover in bright orange-red with portrait of Queen Victoria printed by Walsall.

MB2	(£1·62) containing pane No. 2040l (includes label commemorating death centenary of Queen Victoria)	11·50

No. MB2 has the surplus self-adhesive paper around each stamp retained.

MB3

2002 (5 June). Gold cover as T **MB3** (74×56 mm) printed by Questa.

MB3	(£1·62) containing 6×1st Class self-adhesive stamps (No. 2295)..........................	7·50

2002 (5 June)–**08**. Gold cover as T **MB3** (74×56 mm) printed by Walsall.

MB4	(£1·62) containing 6×1st Class self-adhesive stamps (No. 2295)........................	7·50
	a. Inside cover with Smilers advertisement (27.1.05)	8·00
	b. Back cover with added text about new pricing structure (25.4.06)	8·50
	c. Inside cover with To find the correct postcodes for your mail notice (5.6.07)	7·50
	d. Inside cover with commemorative inscription for Machin Anniversary (5.6.07)..	7·50
	e. Inside cover with Harry Potter stamps advertisement (28.8.07)	7·50
	f. Inside cover with postcode text in English and Welsh (20.9.07)	8·00
	g. Inside cover with Carry On stamps advertisement (10.6.08)	7·50

No. MB4 was re-issued on 27 January 2005 (No. MB4a) with a Smilers advertisement (showing No. 2262 and photograph of baby) on the inside front cover. It was re-issued again on 26 July 2005 with a different Smilers advertisement (showing No. 2261 and photograph of bride).

No. MB4a was available from Philatelic Bureau, Edinburgh from 27 January 2005, and from general post offices from 22 March 2005.

No. MB4b does not have Smilers advertisement.

The added text on the back cover of No. MB4b reads 'Valid for items up to 60g before 21 August 2006. Under new pricing structure from 21 August 2006 – valid for postal items up to: 240 mm Long; 165 mm Wide; 5 mm Thick; 100g Weight'.

The text on the back cover of Nos. MB4c/MB4g reads 'Valid for items up to: 240 mm Long; 165 mm Wide; 5 mm Thick; 100g Weight'.

No. MB4d has Arnold Machin's signature along the right-hand edge of the booklet pane.

No. MB4g has characters from Carry On films illustrated along the right-hand edge of the booklet pane.

2002 (4 July). Multicoloured cover as T **MA1** (74×56 mm) with stamps on the cover in bright orange-red printed by Questa.

MB5	(£1·62) containing 6×1st Class self-adhesive stamps (No. 2040)...........................	7·50

No. MB5 was sold at £1·62.

POST OFFICE STAMP BOOKLETS

MB6 (The Real Network added below logo)

2003 (27 Mar). Gold cover with multicoloured emblem as T **MB6** (74×56 mm) printed by Walsall.
MB6 (£1·62) containing 6×1st Class self-adhesive stamps (No. 2295).................................. 7·50
 a. Imperf (containing 2295a).................. —

MB7 (Supporting London 2012)

2004 (15 June). London's bid to host Olympic Games, 2012. Gold cover with multicoloured emblem as T **MB7** (74×56 mm) printed by Walsall.
MB7 (£1·68) containing 6×1st Class self-adhesive stamps (No. 2295).................................. 8·50

Containing 6×1st Class 'Security' Machins

2009 (31 Mar)–11. Gold cover with multicoloured emblem as T **MB3** (74×57 mm) printed by Walsall.
MB8 (£2·16) containing 6×1st Class self-adhesive stamps (No. U2985) (code MSIL without year code)................................ 15·00
 a. Containing No. U3019 (code MSIL with year code) (26.1.10)..................... 10·00
 b. containing No. U3019 (code MSIL with year code). Inside cover with inscription and emblem for London 2010 Festival of Stamps (30.3.10)............ 8·75
 c. containing No. U3019 (code MSIL with year code) (19.8.10)........................ 7·50
 d. containing No. U3019 (code MSIL with year code). Inside front cover advertising the 2012 special stamp programme. Back cover with FSC logo (25.10.11).. 11·50

The e-mail address on the inside front cover of No. MB8 reads www.royalmail.com/Postcodes4free.

No. MB8a has a lower case 'p' in the email address www.royalmail.com/postcodes4free.

No. MB8b has LONDON 2010 FESTIVAL OF STAMPS along the right hand edge of the booklet pane.

Nos. MB8/MB8b are inscribed Walsall Security Printers, UK along the left hand edge of the back cover. This was removed for Nos. MB8c/MB8d.

No. MB8d was previously listed as MB8e.

Year codes for Nos. MB8a/MB8b are MA10, for No. MB8c MA10 or M11L and for No. MB8d M11L.

Containing 6×1st Class Olympic and Paralympic Games stamps

MB9

2012 (5 Jan). Olympic and Paralympic Games, London. Multicoloured cover (75×58 mm) as T **MB9** printed by Walsall.
MB9 (£2·76) containing self-adhesive pane No. 3250a with Paralympic Games stamp at top left.................................... 7·50
MB10 (£2·76) containing self-adhesive pane No. 3250a with Olympic Games stamp at top left.................................... 7·50

The inside cover of No. MB9 is inscribed London's vision is to reach young people all around the world, to connect them with the inspirational power of the Games, so that they are inspired to choose sport.

The inside cover of No. MB10 is inscribed Key dates for London 2012 and dates.

Containing 6×1st Class 'Security' Machins

MB11

2012 (1 Oct). Diamond Jubilee. Slate-blue cover with multicoloured emblem as T **MB11** (74×57 mm) printed by Walsall.
MB11 (£3·60) containing 6×1st Class self-adhesive stamps (No. U3275, code MSND)............ 8·00

MB12

2013 (3 Jan). Red cover with multicoloured emblem as T **MB12** (74×57 mm) printed by Walsall.
MB12 (£3·60) containing 6×1st Class vermilion self-adhesive stamps (No. U3024, code MSIL).. 8·00

POST OFFICE STAMP BOOKLETS

No. MB12 re-issued on 31 July 2014 with the Royal Mail telephone numbers on the back cover changed from 08457 740 740 and 08456 000 606 to 03457 740 740 and 03456 000 606.

The price shown for MB12 is with either the 08 or 03 telephone numbers. Year codes for MB12 are M12L, M13L or M14L, and with changed telephone numbers M14L or M15L.

Containing 6×1st Class 175th Anniversary of the Penny Black stamps

2015 (6 May). 175th Anniversary of the Penny Black. Red cover with multicoloured emblem as T **MB12** (75×57 mm) printed by ISP Walsall.
MB13 (£3·78) containing 6×1st Class self-adhesive stamps (No. 3709) .... 10·00

Containing 6×1st Class Long to Reign Over Us 'Security' Machins

MB14

2015 (9 Sept). Long to Reign Over Us. Lilac cover with multicoloured emblem as T **MB14** (74×58 mm) printed by ISP Walsall.
MB14 (£3·78) containing 6×1st Class self-adhesive stamps (No. U3745, code REIGS) .... 7·75
Year code for MB14 is O15R.

'ROYAL MAIL' printed backing paper. From early 2016, Barcode booklets appeared with a repeated undulating 'ROYALMAIL' background in two sizes of grey text printed on the front of the backing paper. Initially the two sizes of grey text were printed upright: Type PB-Up (Printed Backing Upright). In early 2017 the background was changed so that alternate pairs of lines of the repeated 'ROYALMAIL' text were inverted in relation to each other. The pairs of lines can appear with the Large lettering above the small (Type PB-Ls), or with the small above the Large (Type PB-sL). In October 2018 a fourth type appeared on some PM64 booklets. In this type the 'ROYALMAIL' background, in two sizes of grey text, is all inverted (Type PB-Inv).

2016. Long to Reign Over Us. Lilac cover with multicoloured emblem as T **MB14** (74×58 mm) printed ISP Walsall. Repeating 'ROYALMAIL' wording (Type PB-Up) printed on the front of the self-adhesive backing paper
MB15 (£3·78) Containing 6×1st Class self-adhesive stamps (No. U3745, code REIGS) .... 27·00
Year codes for MB15 are O15R or O16R.

Note that, where Security Machin booklets' stamps exist with more than one year code, the price shown is for the cheapest version. Where a booklet is known with both Type PB-Ls and Type PB-sL the price noted is for the cheaper of the two, whichever that is. For further details of Security Machin booklets with different year codes and/or different Types of 'ROYALMAIL' printed backing, please refer to the tables later in this listing.

Containing 6×1st Class 175th Anniversary of the Penny Red stamps

2016 (18 Feb). 175th Anniversary of the Penny Red. Red cover with multicoloured emblem as T **MB12** (74×57 mm) printed by ISP Walsall.
MB16 (£3·78) containing 6×1st Class self-adhesive stamps (No. 3806) .... 10·00

Containing 6×1st Class 'Security' Machins

MB17

2016 (28 July). Multicoloured cover as T **MB17** (74×57 mm) printed by ISP Walsall. Repeating 'ROYALMAIL' wording (Type PB-Up) printed on the front of the self-adhesive backing paper.
MB17 (£3·84) containing 6×1st Class vermilion self-adhesive stamps (No. U3024, code MSIL) .... 8·00
Year code for MB17 is M16L.

MB18

2016 (20 Oct). Multicoloured cover as T **MB18** (74×57 mm) printed by ISP Walsall. Repeating 'ROYALMAIL' wording printed on the front of the self-adhesive backing paper.
MB18 (£3·84) containing 6×1st Class bright scarlet self-adhesive stamps (No. U3028, code MSIL) (Type PB-Up) .... 9·50
   a. With alternate pairs of lines in background text inverted (Types PB-Ls/sL) .... 10·50

No. MB18a exists with the large 'ROYALMAIL' lettering above the small and with the small above the large in the alternate pairs of lines in the background text.
Year code for No. MB18 is M16L or M18L, and for No. MB18a is M16L, M17L, M18L, M19L or M20L (Types PB-Ls and sL), or M21L (Type PB-sL).

MB19

517

POST OFFICE STAMP BOOKLETS

2017 (5 June). The Machin Definitive. 50th Anniversary. Red cover with multicoloured emblem as T **MB19** (74×57 mm) printed by ISP Walsall. Repeating 'ROYALMAIL' wording (Type PB-Up) printed on the front of the self-adhesive backing paper.

MB19 (£3·90) containing 6×1st Class bright scarlet self-adhesive stamps (No. U3028, code MSIL).. 9·00

Year code for MB19 is M17L.

Containing 6×1st Class The Iron Throne stamps

2018 (23 Jan). *Game of Thrones*. Red cover with multicoloured emblem as T **MB19** (74×57 mm) printed by ISP Walsall. Repeating 'ROYALMAIL' wording printed on the front of the self-adhesive backing paper, with alternate pairs of lines inverted.

MB20 (£3·90) containing 6×1st Class self-adhesive stamps (No. 4044).. 7·50

No. MB20 has the large 'ROYALMAIL' lettering above the small (Type PB-Ls) in the alternate pairs of lines in the background text.

Containing 6×1st class (2×Penny Black, 2×Penny Red and 2×Two Pence Blue) stamps

2020 (10 Mar). London 2020 International World Stamp Exhibition. Red cover with multicoloured emblem as T **MB19** (74×57 mm) printed by ISP Walsall. Repeating 'ROYALMAIL' wording printed on the front of the self-adhesive backing paper, with alternate pairs of lines inverted.

MB21 (£4·20) containing self-adhesive pane No. 4331a of 2×Penny Black (No. 3709), 2×2 Pence Blue (No. 4331), and 2×Penny Red (No. 3806) stamps .... 10·00

No. MB21 exists with the large 'ROYALMAIL' lettering above the small and with the small above the large in the alternate pairs of lines in the background text (Type PB-Ls/sL).

Containing 6×1st class Queen (rock band) stamps

2021 (29 Mar). Queen (rock band). Red cover with Multicoloured emblem as Type **MB19** (74×57 mm) printed by ISP Walsall. Repeating 'ROYALMAIL' wording printed on the front of the self-adhesive backing paper, with alternate pairs of lines inverted.

MB22 (£5·10) containing six 1st class self-adhesive stamps (No. 4502).. 7·50

MB22 has the large 'ROYALMAIL' lettering above the small (Type PB-Ls) in the alternate pairs of lines in the background text.

Containing 10×2nd Class stamps

2001 (29 Jan). Multicoloured cover as T **MA1** (74×56 mm). Stamps on the cover in bright blue printed by Questa.

MC1 (£1·90) containing 10×2nd Class self-adhesive stamps (No. 2039).. 9·50

No. MC1 was intended for use in stamp machines.
No. MC1 has the surplus self-adhesive paper around each stamp retained.

Containing 10×1st Class stamps

2001 (29 Jan). Multicoloured cover as T **MA1** (74×56 mm). Stamps on the cover in bright orange-red printed by Questa.

MD1 (£2·70) containing 10×1st Class self-adhesive stamps (No. 2040).. 12·00

No. MD1 was intended for use in stamp machines.
No. MD1 has the surplus self-adhesive paper around each stamp retained.

Containing 12×2nd Class stamps

2001 (29 Jan). Multicoloured cover as T **MA1** (74×56 mm). Stamps on the cover in bright blue printed by Questa.

ME1 (£2·28) containing 12×2nd Class self-adhesive stamps (No. 2039).. 12·00

No. ME1 has the surplus self-adhesive paper around each stamp retained.
No. ME1 was re-issued on 1 August 2001 showing Cod Post added to the Ffôn Testun inscription on the back cover.

ME2

2002 (4 July). Blue cover with multicoloured emblem as T **ME2** (74×57 mm) printed by Questa.

ME2 (£2·28) containing 12×2nd Class self-adhesive stamps (No. 2039).. 12·00

ME3 (The Real Network added below logo)

2003 (27 Mar). Blue cover with multicoloured emblem as T **ME3** (74×57 mm) printed by Walsall.

ME3 (£2·28) containing 12×2nd Class self-adhesive stamps (No. 2039).. 12·00

2004 (15 June)–07. Blue cover with multicoloured emblem as T **ME2** (74×56 mm) printed by Walsall.

ME4 (£2·52) containing 12×2nd Class self-adhesive stamps (No. 2039).. 12·00
 a. Back cover with added text about new pricing structure (25.4.06) .... 12·00
 b. Back cover with text about validity (5.6.07) .... 12·00

The back cover of No. ME4a has added text as No. MB4b.
The back cover of No. ME4b has text as Nos. MB4c/MB4d.

Containing 12×2nd Class 'Security' Machins

2009 (31 Mar)–11. Blue cover with multicoloured emblem as T **ME2** (74×57 mm) printed by Walsall.

ME5 (£3·24) containing 12×2nd Class self-adhesive stamps (No. U2981, code MTIL without year code).. 13·00
 a. Ditto but containing No. U3013 (code MTIL with year code) (2.10) .... 60·00
 b. Ditto but with printer's imprint removed (19.8.10) .... 13·50
 c. Ditto but with FSC logo added (25.10.11)... 14·00

Nos. ME5/ME5a are inscribed Walsall Security Printers Limited, UK along the left-hand edge of the back cover. This was removed for Nos. MB5b/MB5c.

No. ME5c was re-issued on 31 July 2014 with the telephone numbers on the back cover charged from 08 to 03 numbers as for No. MB12.

The price shown for No. ME5c is with either the 08 or 03 telephone numbers.

Year code for No. ME5a is MA10, for No. ME5b MA10 or M11L, for No. ME5c M11L , M12L, M13L or M14L, and for No. ME5c with changed telephone numbers M14L or M15L.

2016. Blue cover with multicoloured emblem as T **ME2** (74×57 mm) printed by Walsall. Repeating 'ROYALMAIL' wording (Type PB-Up) printed on the front of the self-adhesive backing paper

ME6 (£6·48) containing 12×2nd Class self-adhesive stamps (No. U3013, code MTIL with year code).. 25·00

Year codes for No. ME6 are M15L or M16L.

ME7

POST OFFICE STAMP BOOKLETS

2016 (20 Oct). Blue cover with multicoloured emblem as T **ME7** (74×57 mm) printed by ISP Walsall. Repeating 'ROYALMAIL' wording printed on the front of the self-adhesive backing paper.

ME7	(£6·60) containing 12×2nd Class self-adhesive stamps (No. U3013 code MTIL) (Type PB-Up)	18·00
	a. With alternate pairs of lines in the background text inverted (Types PB-Ls/sL)	18·00

No. ME7a exists with the large 'ROYALMAIL' lettering above the small and with small above the large in the alternate pairs of lines in the background text.

Year code for No. ME7 is M16L and M18L, and for No. ME7a is M16L (Type PB-sL only), M17L, M18L, M19L, M20L or M21L (Types PB-Ls and sL).

Containing 12×1st Class stamps

2001 (29 Jan). Multicoloured covers as T **MA1** (74×56 mm). Stamps on the covers in bright orange-red printed by Questa (No. MF1) or Walsall (No. MF2).

MF1	(£3·24) containing 12×1st Class self-adhesive stamps (No. 2040) (Questa)	14·50
MF2	containing 12×1st Class self-adhesive stamps (No. 2040) (Walsall)	14·50

Nos. MF1/MF2 has the surplus self-adhesive paper around each stamp retained.

Nos. MF1/MF2 were re-issued on 1 August 2001 showing Cod Post added to the Ffôn Testun inscription on the back covers.

2002 (5 June)–**07**. Gold cover as T **MB3** (74×56 mm) printed by Walsall.

MF3	(£3·24) containing 12×1st Class self-adhesive stamps (No. 2295)	14·50
	a. Back cover with added text about new pricing structure (25.4.06)	15·00
	b. Back cover with text about validity (5.6.07)	14·50

The back cover of No. MF3a has added text as No. MB4b.
The back cover of No. MF3b has text as Nos. MB4c/MB4d.

2003 (27 Mar). Gold cover with multicoloured emblem as T **ME3** (74×57 mm) printed by Walsall.

MF4	(£3·24) containing 12×1st Class self-adhesive stamps (No. 2295)	14·50

> Note that, where Security Machin Booklets' stamps exist with more than one year code, the price shown is for the cheapest version. Where a booklet is known with both Type PB-Ls and Type PB-sL the price noted is for the cheaper of the two, whichever that is. For further details of Security Machin booklets with different year codes and/or different Types of 'ROYALMAIL' printed backing, please refer to the tables elsewhere in this listing.

Containing 12×1st Class 'Security' Machins

2009 (31 Mar)–**11**. Gold cover with multicoloured emblem as T **MB3** (74×57 mm) printed by Walsall.

MF5	(£4·32) containing 12×1st Class self-adhesive stamps (No. U2986, code MTIL without year code)	16·00
	a. Ditto but with printer's imprint removed (15.12.09)	17·00
	b. Ditto but containing No. U3020, code MTIL with year code (2.10)	26·00
	c. Ditto but with FSC logo added (25.10.11)	17·00

No. MF5 is inscribed Walsall Security Printers Limited, UK along the left hand edge of the back cover. This was removed for Nos. MF5a/MF5c.
Year codes for No. MF5b are MA10 or M11L and for No. MF5c M11L or M12L.

2012 (6 Feb). Diamond Jubilee. Slate-blue cover with multicoloured emblem as T **MB11** (74×57 mm) printed by Walsall.

MF6	(£5·52) containing 12×1st class self-adhesive stamps (No. U3272, code MTND)	14·00

2013 (3 Jan). Red cover with multicoloured emblem as T **MB12** (74×57 mm) printed by Walsall.

MF7	(£7·20) containing 12×1st Class vermilion self-adhesive stamps (No. U3025, code MTIL)	16·00

No. MF7 was re-issued on 31 July 2014 with the telephone numbers on the back cover charged from 08 to 03 numbers as for No. MB12.
The price shown for No. ME7 is with either the 08 or 03 telephone numbers.
Year codes for No. MF7 are M12L, M13L or M14L, and with changed telephone numbers M14L or M15L

2016. Red cover with multicoloured emblem as T **MB12** (74×57 mm) printed by Walsall. Repeating 'ROYALMAIL' wording (Type PB-Up) printed on the front of the self-adhesive backing paper

MF8	(£7·56) containing 12×1st Class vermilion self-adhesive stamps (No. U3025, code MTIL)	22·00

Year codes for No. MF8 are M15L or M16L.

2016 (20 Oct). Red cover with multicoloured emblem as T **ME7** (74×57 mm) printed by ISP Walsall. Repeating 'ROYALMAIL' wording printed on the front of the self-adhesive backing paper.

MF9	(£7·68) containing 12×1st Class bright scarlet self-adhesive stamps (No. U3029, code MTIL) (Type PB-Up)	19·00
	a. With alternate pairs of lines in the background text inverted (Types PB-Ls/sL)	19·00

No. MF9a exists with the large 'ROYALMAIL' lettering above the small and with the small above the large in the alternate pairs of lines in the background text

Year code for No. MF9 is M16L, and for No. MF9a is M16L, M17L, M18L, M19L or M20L (Type PB-Ls and sL), or M21L (Type PB-sL only).

Containing 20×1st Class stamps

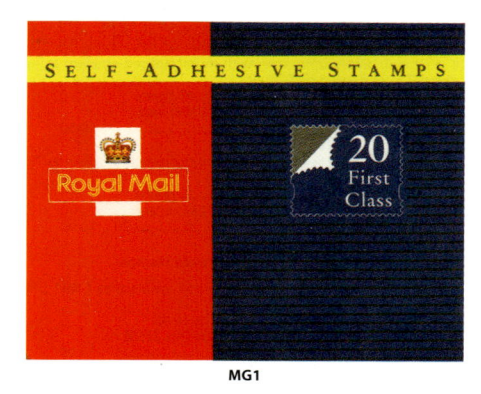

MG1

1993 (19 Oct). Multicoloured cover as T **MG1** (91×77 mm) printed by Walsall.

MG1	(£4·80) containing 20×1st Class No. 1789	20·00

No. MG1 has the surplus self-adhesive paper around each stamp retained.

Containing 6×E stamps

2002 (4 July). Multicoloured cover as T **ME2** (74×57 mm) printed by Walsall.

MH1	(£2·22) containing 6×E stamps (No. 2296) and six Airmail labels	14·00

The official issue of No. MH1 was without any notch on the tab edge. Some booklets with a single notch at the top right tab edge were manufactured and released in error.

2003 (28 May). Multicoloured cover as T **MB6** (74×57 mm) with The Real Network added below logo printed by Walsall

MH2	(£2·28) containing 6×E stamps (No. 2296) and six Airmail labels	14·00

Containing four Europe stamps

MI1 (The Real Network below logo)

2003 (27 Mar). Ultramarine cover with multicoloured emblem as T **MI1** (74×57 mm) printed by Walsall.

MI1	(£2·08) containing 4×Europe 40g self-adhesive stamps (No. 2358) and four Airmail labels	10·50

POST OFFICE STAMP BOOKLETS

MI2

2004 (15 June). Ultramarine cover with multicoloured emblem as T **MI2** (74×57 mm) printed by Walsall.
MI2 (£2·28) containing 4×Europe up to 40 grams self-adhesive stamps (No. 2358) and four Airmail labels .... 10·50

2010 (30 Mar). Deep green cover with multicoloured emblem as T **MI2** (74×57 mm) printed by Walsall.
MI3 (£2·24) containing 4×Europe up to 20 grams self-adhesive stamps (No. 2357b) and four Airmail labels .... 10·50

Containing four Worldwide stamps

2003 (27 Mar). Red cover with multicoloured emblem as T **MI1** (74×57 mm) printed by Walsall.
MJ1 (£4·48) containing 4×Worldwide up to 40 grams self-adhesive stamps (No. 2359) and four Airmail labels................................ 16·00

2004 (15 June). Red cover with multicoloured emblem as T **MI2** (74×57 mm) printed by Walsall.
MJ2 (£4·48) containing 4×Worldwide up to 40 grams self-adhesive stamps (No. 2359) and four Airmail labels................................ 16·00

2010 (30 Mar). Deep mauve cover with multicoloured emblem as T **MI2** (74×57 mm) printed by Walsall.
MJ3 (£3·60) containing 4×Worldwide up to 20 grams self-adhesive stamps (No. 2358a) and four Airmail labels .... 10·50

Containing four Worldwide postcard stamps

2004 (1 Apr). Grey-black cover with multicoloured emblem as T **MI2** (74×57 mm) printed by Walsall.
MJA1 (£1·72) containing 4×Worldwide postcard self-adhesive stamps (No. 2357a) and four Airmail labels .... 10·50

I. Self-adhesive. Barcode Booklets containing stamps with face values.

NOTE. All booklets in this section have the surplus self-adhesive paper around each stamp removed.

£2·52 Booklets

2002 (4 July). Multicoloured cover as T **ME2** (74×57 mm) printed by Walsall.
NA1 containing 6×42p. stamps (No. 2297) and six Airmail labels................................ 25·00
The official issue of No. NA1 was without any notch on the tab edge. Some booklets with a single notch at the top right tab edge were manufactured and released in error.

2003 (28 May). Multicoloured cover as T **MB6** (74×57 mm) with The Real Network added below logo printed by Walsall.
NA2 containing 6×42p. stamps (No. 2297) and six Airmail labels.................................... 23·00

£4·08 Booklets

2002 (4 July). Multicoloured cover as T **ME2** (74×57 mm) printed by Walsall with the surplus self-adhesive paper around each stamp removed.
NB1 containing 6×68p. stamps (No. 2298) and six Airmail labels.................................... 26·00
The official issue of No. NB1 was without any notch on the tab edge. Some booklets with a single notch at the top right tab edge were manufactured and released in error.

2003 (28 May). Multicoloured cover as T **MB6** (74×57 mm) with The Real Network added below logo printed by Walsall.
NB2 containing 6×68p. stamps (No. 2298) and six Airmail labels.................................... 26·00

J. Self-adhesive Barcode Booklets containing No Value Indicated Special or Occasions issues, with Definitive stamps.

NOTE. All booklets in this section have the surplus self-adhesive paper around each stamp removed, *unless otherwise stated*. From No. PM7 onwards the booklets have a single small notch at the top right tab edge.

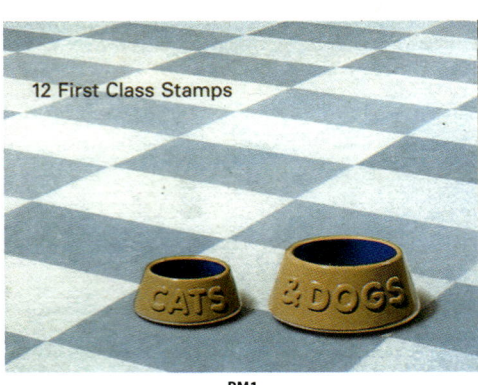

PM1

2001 (13 Feb). Cats and Dogs. Multicoloured cover as T **PM1** (84×64 mm). Printed by Walsall.
PM1 (£3·24) containing pane of 12×1st stamps (No. 2187b).. 25·00
No. PM1 has the surplus self-adhesive paper around each stamp retained.

PM2

2001 (17 Apr). Centenary of Royal Navy Submarine Service. Multicoloured cover as T **PM2** (75×57 mm). Printed by Questa.
PM2 (£1·62) containing pane No. 2207a........................ 70·00
No. PM2 has the surplus self-adhesive paper around each stamp retained.

2001 (4 Sept). Punch and Judy Show Puppets. Multicoloured cover as T **PM2** (74×57 mm). Printed by Questa.
PM3 (£1·62) containing pane No. 2230a........................ 15·00
No. PM3 has the surplus self-adhesive paper around each stamp retained.

2001 (22 Oct). Flags and Ensigns. Multicoloured cover as T **PM2** (74×57 mm). Printed by Questa.
PM4 (£1·62) containing pane No. 2208a........................ 15·00
No. PM4 has the surplus self-adhesive paper around each stamp retained.

2002 (2 May). 50th Anniversary of Passenger Jet Aviation. Airliners. Multicoloured cover as T **PM2** (74×57 mm). Printed by Questa.
PM5 (£1·62) containing pane No. 2290a........................ 7·50
No. PM5 has the surplus self-adhesive paper around each stamp retained.

2002 (21 May). World Cup Football Championship, Japan and Korea. Multicoloured cover as T **PM2** (74×57 mm). Printed by Walsall.
PM6 (£1·62) containing pane No. 2293a........................ 7·50
No. PM6 has the surplus self-adhesive paper around each stamp retained.

POST OFFICE STAMP BOOKLETS

PM7

2002 (10 Sept). Bridges of London. Gold cover with multicoloured emblem and stamp illustration as T **PM7** (74×57 mm). Printed by Questa.
PM7   (£1·62) containing pane No. 2314a......................   7·50

2003 (4 Mar). Occasions Greetings Stamps. Gold cover with multicoloured emblem and stamp illustration as T **PM7** (74×57 mm). Printed by Questa.
PM8   (£1·62) containing pane No. 2264ab....................   7·50

PM15

2008 (13 May). Beside the Seaside. Red cover with multicoloured emblem (74×57 mm) as T **PM15**. Printed by Walsall.
PM15   (£2·16) containing pane No. 2848a......................   7·50
No. PM15 has the self-adhesive paper removed from around the 1st class gold stamps only.

Booklets containing four 'Security' Machins* and two commemorative stamps

Unless otherwise stated Nos. PM16–PM32, PM35–PM48, and PM54–PM66 contain 1st Class Machin stamps with source code MCIL. Nos. PM33–PM34 contain 1st Class Diamond Jubilee Machin stamps with source code MCND. Nos. PM49/PM53 contain 1st Class Long to Reign Over Us Machin stamps with source code REIGC. Nos. PM16–PM21 are without a year code, and Nos. PM22–PM35, and PM37–PM83 are with year codes, which for the convenience of collectors are noted below along with the appropriate U-number. All have the self-adhesive paper removed from around the Machin stamps only.
*   No. PM36 contains four definitive-size Tardis stamps in place of the usual Machin design.

2009 (10 Mar). Design Classics 1. (Telephone Kiosk and Routemaster Bus). Red cover with multicoloured emblem as T **PM15** (74×57 mm). Printed by Walsall.
PM16   (£2·16) containing pane No. 2911a......................   7·50

2009 (21 Apr). Design Classics 2. (Mini). Red cover with multicoloured emblem as T **PM15** (74×57 mm). Printed by Walsall.
PM17   (£2·34) containing pane No. 2913a......................   7·50

2009 (21 May). 50th Anniversary of NAFAS (National Association of Flower Arrangement Societies). Red cover with multicoloured emblem as T **PM15** (74×57 mm). Printed by Walsall.
PM18   (£2·34) containing pane No. 2942a......................   10·00

2009 (18 Aug). Design Classics 3. (Concorde). Red cover with multicoloured emblem as T **PM15** (74×57 mm). Printed by Walsall.
PM19   (£2·34) containing pane No. 2914a......................   7·50

2009 (17 Sept). Design Classics 4. (Miniskirt). Red cover with multicoloured emblem as T **PM15** (74×57 mm). Printed by Walsall.
PM20   (£2·34) containing pane No. 2915a......................   7·50

2010 (7 Jan). Olympic and Paralympic Games, London (2012) 1 (Judo and Archery). Red cover with multicoloured emblem as T **PM15** (74×57 mm). Printed by Walsall.
PM21   (£2·34) containing pane No. 3020a......................   7·50

2010 (25 Feb). Olympic and Paralympic Games, London (2012) 2 (Track and Basketball). Red cover with multicoloured emblem as T **PM15** (74×57 mm). Printed by Walsall.
PM22   (£2·34) containing pane No. 3022a......................   7·50
Contains Security Machin No. U3016 with year code MA10.

2010 (15 June). Mammals. Red cover with multicoloured emblem as T **PM15** (74×57 mm). Printed by Walsall.
PM23   (£2·46) containing pane No. 3095a......................   11·00
Contains Security Machin No. U3016 with year code MA10.

2010 (27 July). Olympic and Paralympic Games, London (2012) 3 (Rowing and Tennis). Red cover with multicoloured emblem as T **PM15** (74×57 mm). Printed by Walsall.
PM24   (£2·46) containing pane No. 3107a......................   7·50
Contains Security Machin No. U3016 with year code MA10.

2010 (15 Sept). British Design Classics 5. (Spitfire). Red cover with multicoloured emblem as T **PM15** (74×57 mm). Printed by Walsall.
PM25   (£2·46) containing pane No. 2915ba....................   7·50
Contains Security Machin No. U3016 with year code MA10.

PM9 (The Real Network added below logo)

2003 (29 Apr). Extreme Endeavours. Gold cover with multicoloured emblem and stamp illustration as T **PM9** (74×57 mm). Printed by De La Rue.
PM9   (£1·62) containing pane No. 2366a......................   7·50

2003 (15 July). A British Journey. Scotland. Gold cover with multicoloured emblem and stamp illustration as T **PM9** (74×57 mm). Printed by De La Rue.
PM10   (£1·68) containing pane No. 2391a......................   7·50

2003 (18 Sept). Classic Transport Toys. Gold cover with multicoloured emblem and stamp illustration as T **PM7** (74×57 mm). Printed by De La Rue.
PM11   (£1·68) containing pane No. 2403a......................   7·50

2004 (16 Mar). A British Journey. Northern Ireland. Gold cover with multicoloured emblem and stamp illustration as T **PM7** (74×57 mm). Printed by De La Rue.
PM12   (£1·68) containing pane No. 2445a......................   7·50

2004 (13 Apr). Ocean Liners. Gold cover with multicoloured emblem and stamp illustration as T **PM7** (74×57 mm). Printed by De La Rue.
PM13   (£1·68) containing pane No. 2455a......................   7·50

2004 (15 June). A British Journey. Wales. Gold cover with multicoloured emblem and stamp illustration as T **PM7** (74×57 mm). Printed by De La Rue.
PM14   (£1·68) containing pane No. 2472a......................   7·50

POST OFFICE STAMP BOOKLETS

2010 (12 Oct). Olympic and Paralympic Games, London (2012) 4 (Football and Cycling). Red cover with multicoloured emblem as T **PM15** (74×57 mm). Printed by Walsall.
PM26 (£2·46) containing pane No. 3108ab .... 7·50
Contains Security Machin No. U3016 with year code MA10.

2011 (11 Jan). F.A.B. The Genius of Gerry Anderson. Red cover with multicoloured emblem as T **PM15** (74×57 mm). Printed by Walsall.
PM27 (£2·46) containing pane No. 3143a .... 7·50
Contains Security Machin No. U3016 with year code M11L.

2011 (24 Feb). 50th Anniversary of the British Heart Foundation. Red cover with multicoloured emblems as T **PM15** (74×57 mm). Printed by Walsall.
PM28 (£2·46) containing pane No. 3153a .... 7·50
Contains Security Machin No. U3016 with year code M11L.

2011 (14 June). Thomas the Tank Engine. Red cover with multicoloured emblem as T **PM15** (74×57 mm). Printed by Walsall.
PM29 (£2·76) containing pane No. 3194a .... 7·50
Contains Security Machin No. U3016 with year code M11L.

2011 (27 July). Olympic and Paralympic Games, London (2012) 5 (Wheelchair Rugby and Sailing). Red cover with multicoloured emblem as T **PM15** (74×57 mm). Printed by Walsall.
PM30 (£2·76) containing pane No. 3205a .... 7·50
Contains Security Machin No. U3016 with year code M11L.

2011 (23 Aug). Classic Locomotives of England. Red cover with multicoloured emblem as T **PM15** (74×57 mm). Printed by Walsall.
PM31 (£2·76) containing pane No. 3215a .... 7·50
Contains Security Machin No. U3016 with year code M11L.

2011 (15 Sept). Olympic and Paralympic Games, London (2012) 6 (Gymnastics and Fencing). Red cover with multicoloured emblem as T **PM15** (74×57 mm). Printed by Walsall.
PM32 (£2·76) containing pane No. 3206ab .... 7·50
Contains Security Machin No. U3016 with year code M11L.

2012 (31 May). Diamond Jubilee. Red cover with multicoloured emblem as T **PM15** (74×57 mm). Printed by Walsall.
PM33 (£3·60) containing pane No. 3327a .... 7·50
Contains slate-blue Machin No. U3274.

2012 (27 Sept). Classic Locomotives of Scotland. Red cover with multicoloured emblem as T **PM15** (74×57 mm). Printed by Walsall.
PM34 (£3·60) containing pane No. 3407a .... 7·50
Contains slate-blue Machin No. U3274.

2013 (9 Jan). 150th Anniversary of the London Underground. Red cover with multicoloured emblem as T **PM15** (74×57 mm). Printed by Walsall.
PM35 (£3·60) containing pane No. 3430a .... 7·50
Contains Security Machin No. U3022 with year code M12L.

2013 (26 Mar). 50th Anniversary of *Doctor Who* (TV programme). Red cover with multicoloured emblem as T **PM15** (74×57 mm). Printed by Walsall. Self-adhesive.
PM36 (£3·60) containing Tardis pane No. 3448a .... 14·00

2013 (9 May). Football Heroes. Red cover with multicoloured emblem as T **PM15** (74×57 mm). Printed by Walsall .
PM37 (£3·60) containing George Best and Bobby Moore pane No. 3475a .... 11·00
Contains Security Machin No. U3022 with year code M13L.

2013 (18 June). Classic Locomotives of Northern Ireland. Red cover with multicoloured emblem as T **PM15** (75×57 mm). Printed by Walsall.
PM38 (£3·60) containing pane No. 3497a .... 7·50
Contains Security Machin No. U3022 with year code M13L.

2013 (11 July). Butterflies. Red cover with Multicoloured emblem as T **PM15** (74×57 mm) Printed by Walsall.
PM39 (£3·60) containing pane No. 3509a .... 7·50
Contains Security Machin No. U3022 with year code M13L.

2013 (19 Sept). Royal Mail Transport. By Land and Sea. Red cover with multicoloured emblem as T **PM15** (74×57 mm). Printed by Walsall.
PM40 (£3·60) containing pane No. 3530a .... 14·00
Contains Security Machin No. U3022 with year code M13L.

2014 (20 Feb). Football Heroes. Red cover with multicoloured emblem as T **PM15** (74×57 mm). Printed by Walsall.
PM41 (£3·60) containing John Charles and Dave Mackay pane No. 3477a .... 11·00
Contains Security Machin No. U3022 with year code M13L.

2014 (15 Apr). Buckingham Palace, London. Red cover with multicoloured emblem as T **PM15** (74×57 mm). Printed by Walsall.
PM42 (£3·72) containing pane No. 3595a .... 7·50
Contains Security Machin No. U3022 with year code M14L.

2014 (17 July). Commonwealth Games, Glasgow. Red cover with multicoloured emblem as T **PM15** (74×57 mm). Printed by Walsall.
PM43 (£3·72) containing pane No. 3625a .... 7·50
Contains Security Machin No. U3022 with year code M14L.

2014 (18 Aug). Sustainable and Threatened Fish. Red cover with multicoloured emblem as T **PM15** (74×57 mm). Printed by Walsall.
PM44 (£3·72) containing pane No. 3632a .... 11·00
Contains Security Machin No. U3022 with year code M14L.

2014 (18 Sept). Classic Locomotives of Wales. Red cover with multicoloured emblem as T **PM15** (74×57 mm). Printed by Walsall.
PM45 (£3·72) containing pane No. 3634a .... 7·50
Contains Security Machin No. U3022 with year code M14L.

2015 (6 Jan). Alice in Wonderland. Red cover with multicoloured emblem as T **PM15** (74×57 mm). Printed by ISP Walsall.
PM46 (£3·72) containing pane No. 3668a .... 12·00
Contains Security Machin No. U3022 with year code M15L.

2015 (1 Apr). Comedy Greats. Red cover with multicoloured emblem as T **PM15** (74×57 mm). Printed by ISP Walsall.
PM47 (£3·78) containing pane No. 3707a .... 15·00
Contains Security Machin No. U3022 with year code M15L.

2015 (18 Aug). Bees. Red cover with multicoloured emblem as T **PM15** (74×57 mm). Printed by ISP Walsall.
PM48 (£3·78) containing pane No. 3743a .... 7·50
Contains Security Machin No. U3022 with year code M15L.

2015 (18 Sept). Rugby World Cup. Red cover with multicoloured emblem as T **PM15** (74×57 mm). Printed by ISP Walsall.
PM49 (£3·78) containing pane No. 3756a .... 12·00
Contains bright lilac Machin No. U3746 with year code O15R.

'ROYALMAIL' printed backing paper. From No. PM50 all booklets in this section have repeating undulating 'ROYALMAIL' background in two sizes of grey text printed on the front of the backing paper. On Nos. PM50/PM56 the text is upright (Type PB-Up). With the exception of PM64a where the text is all inverted (Type PB-Inv), from No. PM57 onward alternate pairs of lines are inverted (i.e. Type PB-Ls and/or Type PB-sL, see footnotes) or as noted. Where a booklet is known with both Type PB-Ls and Type PB-sL the price noted is for the cheaper of the two, whichever that is.

2016 (21 Apr). 90th Birthday of Queen Elizabeth II (Book I). Red covers with multicoloured emblem as T **PM15** (74×57 mm). Printed by ISP Walsall.
PM50 (£3·84) containing Prince Charles and Queen Elizabeth pane No. 3833a .... 15·00
Contains bright lilac Machin No. U3746 with year code O16R.

2016 (9 June). 90th Birthday of Queen Elizabeth II (Book II). Red covers with multicoloured emblem as T **PM15** (74×57 mm). Printed by ISP Walsall.
PM51 (£3·84) containing Prince George and Prince William pane No. 3835a .... 7·50
Contains bright lilac Machin No. U3746 with year code O16R.

2016 (28 July). 150th Birth Anniversary of Beatrix Potter. Red cover with multicoloured emblem as T **PM15** (74×57 mm). Printed by ISP Walsall.
PM52 (£3·84) containing pane No. 3862a .... 11·00
Contains bright lilac Machin No. U3746 with year code O16R.

2016 (16 Aug). Landscape Gardens. Red cover with multicoloured emblem as T **PM15** (74×57 mm). Printed by ISP Walsall.
PM53 (£3·84) containing pane No. 3877a .... 10·00
Contains bright lilac Machin No. U3746 with year code O16R.

PM54

2016 (20 Oct). Mr Men and Little Miss (children's books by Roger Hargreaves). Red cover with multicoloured emblem as T **PM54** (74×57 mm). Printed by ISP Walsall.
PM54 (£3·84) containing pane No. 3901a .... 7·50

Contains Security Machin No. U3027 with year code M16L.

2017 (15 Feb). Windsor Castle. Red cover with multicoloured emblem as T **PM54** (74×57 mm). Printed by ISP Walsall.
PM55 (£3·84) containing pane No. 3926a........................ 7·50
Contains Security Machin No. U3027 with year code M17L.

2017 (14 Mar). David Bowie (1947–2016, singer, songwriter and actor). Commemoration. Red cover with multicoloured emblem as T **PM54** (74×57 mm). Printed by ISP Walsall.
PM56 (£3·84) containing pane No. 3934a........................ 7·50
Contains Security Machin No. U3027 with year code M17L.

2017 (12 Oct). *Star Wars*. Red cover with multicoloured emblems as T **PM54** (74×57 mm). Printed by ISP Walsall.
PM57 (£3·90) containing Maz Kanata and Chewbacca pane No. 4015a .... 7·50
PM58 (£3·90) containing BB-8 and R2-D2 pane No. 4017a... 7·50
Nos. PM57/PM58 contain Security Machin No. U3027 with year code M17L.
No. PM57 exists with the large 'ROYALMAIL' lettering above the small and with the small above the large in the alternate pairs of lines in the background text (Types PB-Ls/sL).
No. PM58 exists with the small 'ROYALMAIL' lettering above the large in the alternate pairs of lines in the background text (Type PB-sL).

2018 (20 Mar). Centenary of the RAF (Royal Air Force). Red cover with multicoloured emblem as T **PM54** (74×57 mm). Printed by ISP Walsall.
PM59 (£3·90) containing Hurricane Mk I and Lightning F6 pane No. 4065a .... 7·50
Contains Security Machin No. U3027 with year code M18L.
No. PM59 exists with the large 'ROYALMAIL' lettering above the small and with the small above the large in the alternate pairs of lines in the background text (Types PB-Ls/sL).

2018 (11 May). Centenary of the RAF (Royal Air Force). Red cover with multicoloured emblem as T **PM54** (74×57 mm). Printed by ISP Walsall.
PM60 (£4·02) containing Red Arrows Flypast and Swan pane No. 4080a................................. 12·50
Contains Security Machin No. U3027 with year code M18L.
No. PM60 exists with the large 'ROYALMAIL' lettering above the small and with the small above the large in the alternate pairs of lines in the background text (Types PB-Ls). PM60 with small 'ROYALMAIL' lettering above large (sL) is also known to exist but appears to only be a tiny part of the overall printing.

2018 (26 June). 50th Anniversary of *Dad's Army* (BBC television sitcom 1968–1977). Red cover with multicoloured emblem as T **PM54** (74×57 mm). Printed by ISP Walsall.
PM61 (£4·02) containing pane No. 4107a........................ 13·00
Contains Security Machin No. U3027 with year code M18L.
No. PM61 exists with the small 'ROYALMAIL' lettering above the large in the alternate pairs of lines in the background text (Type PB-sL).

2018 (31 July). Hampton Court Palace. Red cover with multicoloured emblem as T **PM54** (74×57 mm). Printed by ISP Walsall.
PM62 (£4·02) containing pane No. 4116a........................ 25·00
Contains Security Machin No. U3027 with year code M18L.
No. PM62 exists with the large 'ROYALMAIL' lettering above the small in the alternate pairs of lines in the background text (Types PB-Ls). PM62 with small 'ROYALMAIL' lettering above large (sL) is also known to exist but appears to only be a small part of the overall printing.

2018 (13 Sept). Centenary of the First World War. Red cover with multicoloured emblem as T **PM54** (74×57 mm). Printed by ISP Walsall.
PM63 (£4·02) containing pane No. 4139a........................ 15·00
Contains Security Machin No. U3027 with year code M18L.
No. PM63 exists with the large 'ROYALMAIL' lettering above the small in the alternate pairs of lines in the background text (Type PB-Ls).

2018 (16 Oct). Harry Potter. Red cover with multicoloured emblem as T **PM54** (74×57 mm). Printed by ISP Walsall.
PM64 (£4·02) containing pane No. 4152a........................ 7·50
 a. With repeating 'ROYALMAIL' lettering the same way up but inverted (Type PB-Inv)... 20·00
Contains Security Machin No. U3027 with year code M18L.
No. PM64 exists with the small 'ROYALMAIL' lettering above the large in the alternate pairs of lines in the background text (Type PB-sL).
No. PM64a comes from a small part of the overall issue.

2019 (14 Mar). Marvel. Red cover with multicoloured emblem as T **PM54** (74×57 mm). Printed by ISP Walsall.
PM65 (£4·02) containing pane No. 4193a........................ 10·00
Contains Security Machin No. U3027 with year code M19L.
No. PM65 exists with the large 'ROYALMAIL' lettering above the small in the alternate pairs of lines in the background text (Type PB-Ls).

2019 (4 Apr). Birds of Prey. Red cover with multicoloured emblem as T **PM54** (74×57 mm). Printed by ISP Walsall.
PM66 (£4·20) containing pane No. 4210a........................ 50·00
Contains Security Machin No. U3027 with year code M19L.
No. PM66 exists with the large 'ROYALMAIL' lettering above the large in the alternate pairs of lines in the background text (Type PB-sL).

2019 (6 June). 75th Anniversary of D-Day. Red cover with multicoloured emblem as T **PM54** (74×57 mm). Printed by ISP Walsall.
PM67 (£4·20) containing pane No. 4237a........................ 10·00
Contains Security Machin No. U3027 with year code M19L.
No. PM67 exists with the large 'ROYALMAIL' lettering above the small in the alternate pairs of lines in the background text (Type PB-sL). PM67 with large 'ROYALMAIL' lettering above small (Ls) is also known to exist but appears to only be a small part of the overall printing.

2019 (3 Sept). Elton John. Red cover with multicoloured emblem as T **PM54** (74×57 mm). Printed by ISP Walsall.
PM68 (£4·20) containing pane No. 4262a........................ 12·95
Contains Security Machin No. U3027 with year code M19L.
No. PM68 exists with the large 'ROYALMAIL' lettering above the small and with the small above the large in the alternate pairs of lines in the background text (Types PB-Ls/sL).

2019 (19 Sept). Royal Navy Ships. Red cover with multicoloured emblem as T **PM54** (74×57 mm). Printed by ISP Walsall.
PM69 (£4·20) containing pane No. 4272a........................ 50·00
Contains Security Machin No. U3027 with year code M19L.
No. PM69 exists with the large 'ROYALMAIL' lettering above the small in the alternate pairs of lines in the background text (Type PB-Ls).

2019 (26 Nov). *Star Wars*. Red cover with multicoloured emblem as T **PM54** (74×57 mm). Printed by ISP Walsall.
PM70 (£4·20) containing Poe Dameron and Sith Trooper pane No. 4304a............................. 12·00
Contains Security Machin No. U3027 with year code M19L.
No. PM70 exists with the large 'ROYALMAIL' lettering above the small and with the small above the large in the alternate pairs of lines in the background text (Types PB-Ls/sL).

2020 (21 Jan). Video Games. Red cover with multicoloured emblem as T **PM54** (74×57 mm). Printed by ISP Walsall.
PM71 (£4·20) containing Tomb Raider pane No. 4321a.. 15·00
Contains Security Machin No. U3027 with year code M20L.
No. PM71 exists with the large 'ROYALMAIL' lettering above the small in the alternate pairs of lines in the background text (Type PB-Ls).

2020 (17 Mar). James Bond. Red cover with multicoloured emblem as T **PM54** (74×57 mm). Printed by ISP Walsall.
PM72 (£4·20) containing pane No. 4339a........................ 15·00
Contains Security Machin No. U3027 with year code M20L.
No. PM72 exists with the large 'ROYALMAIL' lettering above the small in the alternate pairs of lines in the background text (Type PB-Ls). PM72 with small 'ROYALMAIL' lettering above large (sL) is also known to exist but appears to only be a small part of the overall printing.

2020 (28 May). *Coronation Street*. Red cover with multicoloured emblems as T **PM54** (74×57 mm). Printed by ISP Walsall.
PM73 (£4·56) booklet containing pane No. 4378a ...... 7·50
Contains Security Machin No. U3027 with year code M20L.
No. PM73 exists with the small 'ROYALMAIL' lettering above the large in the alternate pairs of lines in the background text (Type PB-sL).

2020 (9 July). Queen (rock band). Red cover with multicoloured emblem as T **PM54** (74×57 mm). Printed by ISP Walsall.
PM74 (£4·56) booklet containing pane No. 4397a ...... 15·00
Contains Security Machin No. U3027 with year code M20L.
No. PM74 exists with the large 'ROYALMAIL' lettering above the small and with the small above the large in alternate pairs of lines in the background text (Types PB-Ls/sL).

2020 (18 Aug). Sherlock. Red cover with multicoloured emblem as T **PM54** (4×57 mm). Printed by ISP Walsall.
PM75 (£4·56) booklet containing pane No. 4418a ...... 10·00
Contains Security Machin No. U3027 with year code M20L.
No. PM75 exists with the small 'ROYALMAIL' lettering above the large in alternate pairs of lines in the background text (Type PB-sL).

2020 (13 Nov). *Star Trek*. Red cover with multicoloured emblem as T **PM54** (7×57 mm). Printed by ISP Walsall.
PM76 (£4·56) booklet containing pane No. 4456a ...... 7·50
Contains Security Machin No. U3027 with year code M20L.
No. PM76 exists with the large 'ROYALMAIL' lettering above the small and with the small above the large in the alternate pairs of lines in the background text (Types PB-Ls/sL).

2021 (14 Jan). National Parks. Red cover with multicoloured emblem as T **PM54** (74×57 mm). Printed by ISP Walsall
PM77 (£5·10) booklet containing pane No. 4474a ...... 7·50
Contains Security Machin No. U3027 with year code M21L.
No. PM77 exists with the small 'ROYALMAIL' lettering above the large in the alternate pairs of lines in the background text (Types PB-sL). PM77 with large 'ROYALMAIL' lettering above small (Ls) is also known to exist but appears to only be a tiny part of the overall printing

2021 (16 Feb). *Only Fools and Horses*. Red cover with multicoloured emblem as T **PM54** (74×57 mm). Printed by ISP Walsall
PM78 (£5·10) containing pane No. 4486a........................ 7·50
Contains Security Machin No. U3027 with year code M21L.

POST OFFICE STAMP BOOKLETS

No. PM78 exists with the small 'ROYALMAIL' lettering above the large in the alternate pairs of lines in the background text (Types PB-sL).

2021 (28 May). Paul McCartney. Red cover with multicoloured emblem as T **PM54** (74×57 mm). Printed by ISP Walsall.

PM79	(£5·10) booklet containing pane No. 4526a	7·50

Contains Security Machin No. U3027 with year code M21L.

No. PM79 exists with the small 'ROYALMAIL' lettering above the large in the alternate pairs of lines in the background text (Types PB-sL).

2021 (1 July). Dennis and Gnasher. Red cover with multicoloured emblem as T **PM54** (74×57 mm). Printed by ISP Walsall.

PM80	(£5·10) booklet containing pane No. 4540a	7·50

Contains Security Machin No. U3027 with year code M21L.

No. PM80 exists with the large 'ROYALMAIL' lettering above the small and with the small above the large in alternate pairs of lines in the background text (Types PB-Ls/sL).

2021 (22 July). Wild Coasts. Red cover with multicoloured emblem as T **PM54** (74×57 mm). Printed by ISP Walsall.

PM81	(£5·10) booklet containing pane No. 4553a	7·50

Contains Security Machin No. U3027 with year code M21L.

No. PM81 exists with the small 'ROYALMAIL' lettering above the large in the alternate pairs of lines in the background text (Types PB-sL).

2021 (17 Sept). DC Collection. Red covers with multicoloured emblems as T **PM54** (74×57 mm). Printed by ISP Walsall

PM82	(£5·10) booklet containing Batman and Robin pane No. 4588a.................................	7·50
PM83	(£5·10) booklet containing Wonder Woman pane No. 4590a.................................	7·50

Nos. PM81/PM82 contain Security Machin No. U3027 with year code M21L.

Nos. PM82/PM83 both exist with the large 'ROYALMAIL' lettering above the small and with the small above the large in alternate pairs of lines in the background text (Types PB-Ls/sL).

K. Self-adhesive Barcode Booklets containing No Value Indicated Smilers stamps in definitive size.

NOTE. Nos. QA1–QA4 and QB1 have the self-adhesive paper removed from around the stamps and have a single notch at the top right tab edge.

Containing six Smilers stamps

QA1

2005 (4 Oct). Gold cover with multicoloured emblem as T **QA1** (74×56 mm) by printed Walsall.

QA1	(£1·80) containing Smilers (1st series) Love pane No. 2567a.................................	9·00

QA2

2006 (17 July). Gold cover with multicoloured emblem as T **QA2** (74×56 mm) printed by Walsall.

QA2	(£1·92) containing Smilers (1st series) Love pane No. 2567a.................................	10·00

2006 (17 Oct). Gold cover with multicoloured emblem as T **QA1** (74×56 mm) printed by Walsall.

QA3	(£1·92) containing Smilers (2nd series) Thank You pane No. 2672a.................................	7·50

2008 (28 Feb). Gold cover with multicoloured emblem as T **QA2** (74×56 mm) printed by Walsall.

QA4	(£2·04) containing Smilers (3rd series) pane No. 2819a.................................	30·00

Containing 12 Smilers stamps

2015 (20 Jan). Red cover with multicoloured emblem as T **MB12** (74×57 mm) printed by ISP Walsall.

QB1	(£7·44) containing pane No. 3670a.................................	18·00

L. Self-adhesive Barcode Booklets containing stamps with value indicator at upper left.

NOTE. All booklets in this section have the surplus self-adhesive paper around each stamp removed, *unless otherwise stated*. All RA booklets have two large notches at the top right tab edge, while all RB booklets have a single large notch at the top right tab edge.

RA1

2006 (15 Aug). Blue cover with multicoloured emblem as T **RA1** (74×57 mm) printed by Walsall.

RA1	(£1·48) containing 4×2nd Class Large self-adhesive stamps (No. 2656)......................	6·00

Containing 4×2nd Class Large 'Security' stamps

2009 (31 Mar)–**11**. Blue cover with multicoloured emblem as T **RA1** (74×57 mm) printed by Walsall.

RA2	(£1·68) containing 4×2nd Class Large self-adhesive stamps (No. U2988 code FOYAL without year code).........................	7·50
	a. Ditto but containing No. U3032 (code MFIL with year code) (8.5.10)..................	£100
	b. Ditto but with printer's imprint removed (22.3.11)..	7·50
	c. Ditto but with FSC logo added (25.10.11)...	7·50

Nos. RA2/RA2a are inscribed Walsall Security Printers Limited, UK along the left-hand edge of the back cover. This was removed from Nos. RA2b/RA2c.

No. RA2c was re-issued on 31 July 2014 with the telephone numbers on the back cover changed from 08 to 03 numbers as for No. MB12.

The price shown for RA2c is with the 08 telephone number. With 03 telephone number £10·00.

Year code for No. RA2a is MA10, for No. RA2b MA11 and for No. RA2c MA11, MA12, MA13 or MA14, and with changed telephone numbers MA14 or MA15.

2016. Blue cover with multicoloured emblem as T **RA1** (74×57 mm) printed by ISP Walsall. Repeating 'ROYALMAIL' wording (Type PB-Up) printed on the front of the self-adhesive backing paper

RA3	(£3·00) containing 4×2nd Class Large self-adhesive stamps (No. U3032 code MFIL)..	22·00

Year code for RA3 is M16L.

2016 (20 Oct). Blue cover with multicoloured emblem as T **RA4** (74×56 mm) printed by ISP Walsall. Repeating 'ROYALMAIL' wording printed on the front of the self-adhesive backing paper

RA4	(£3·00) Containing 4×2nd Class Large self-adhesive stamps (No. U3032 code MFIL) (Type PB-Up)...........................	12·00
	a. With alternate pairs of lines in the background text inverted (Types PB-Ls/sL)...	11·00

No. RA4a exists with the large 'ROYALMAIL' lettering above the small and with the small above the large in the alternate pairs of lines in the background text.
Year code for No. RA4 is M16L, and for No. RA4a is M17L (Type PB-Ls only), M18L or M19L (Types PB-Ls and sL), M20L or M21L (Type PB-sL only).

> Note that, where Security Machin Booklets' stamps exist with more than one year code, the price shown is for the cheapest version. Where a booklet is known with both Type PB-Ls and Type PB-sL the price noted is for the cheaper of the two, whichever that is. For further details of Security Machin booklets with different year codes and/or different Types of 'ROYALMAIL' printed backing, please refer to the tables elsewhere in this listing.

Containing 4×1st Class Large stamps

RB1

2006 (15 Aug). Gold cover with multicoloured emblem as T **RB1** (74×57 mm) printed by Walsall.
RB1 (£1·76) containing 4×1st Class Large self-adhesive stamps (No. 2657) .... 7·50

Containing 4×1st Class Large 'Security' stamps

2009 (31 Mar)–**11** Gold cover with multicoloured emblem as T **RB1** (74×57 mm) printed by Walsall.
RB2 (£2·08) containing 4×1st Class Large self-adhesive stamps (No. U2990 code FOYAL without year code) .... 11·00
   a. Ditto but containing No. U3035 (code MFIL with year code) (8.5.10) .... 20·00
   b. Ditto but with printer's imprint removed (22.3.11) .... 8·50
   c. Ditto but with FSC logo added (25.10.11) .... 8·50
No. RB2/RB2a are inscribed Walsall Security Printers Limited, UK along the left-hand edge of the back cover. This was removed for Nos. RB2b/RB2c.
Year code for No. RB2a is MA10 and for Nos. RB2b/RB2c MA11.

2012 (25 Apr). Diamond Jubilee. Slate-blue cover with multicoloured emblem as T **RB1** (74×57 mm) printed by Walsall.
RB3 (£3·00) containing 4×1st Class Large self-adhesive stamps (No. U3277, code JUBILFE) .... 8·00

RB4

2013 (3 Jan). Red cover with multicoloured emblem as T **RB4** (74×57 mm) printed by Walsall.
RB4 (£3·60) containing 4×1st Class Large vermilion self-adhesive stamps (No. U3037, code MFIL) .... 8·50

POST OFFICE STAMP BOOKLETS

No. RB4 was re-issued on 31 July 2014 with the telephone numbers on the back cover changed from 08 to 03 numbers as for No. MB12. The price shown for No. RB4 is with either the 08 or 03 telephone numbers.
Year codes for No. RB4 are MA12, MA13 or MA14, and with changed telephone numbers MA14 or MA15.

2016. Red cover with multicoloured emblem as T **RB4** (74×57 mm) printed by ISP Walsall. Repeating 'ROYALMAIL' wording (Type PB-Up) printed on the front of the self-adhesive backing paper
RB5 (£3·80) containing 4×1st Class Large vermilion self-adhesive stamps (No. U3037, code MFIL) .... 13·00
Year code for No. RB5 is MA15 or M16L.

RB6

2016 (20 Oct). Red cover with multicoloured emblem as T **RB6** (74×57 mm). Printed by ISP Walsall. Repeating 'ROYALMAIL' wording printed on the front of the self-adhesive backing paper
RB6 (£3·84) containing 4×1st Class Large bright scarlet self-adhesive stamps (No. U3039, code MFIL) (Type PB-Up) .... 11·00
   a. With alternate pairs of lines in the background text inverted (Types PB-Ls/sL) .... 11·00
No. RB6a exists with the large 'ROYALMAIL' lettering above the small and with the small above the large in the alternate pairs of lines in the background text.
Year code for No. RB6 is M16L, and for No. RB6a is M17L, M18L (Types PB-Ls and PB-sL), M19L (Type PB-Ls only), M20L or M21L (Type PB-sL only).

Containing six Pricing in Proportion 1st class stamps

2006 (12 Sept)–**07**. Gold cover with multicoloured emblem as T **MB3** (74×57 mm) printed by Walsall.
RC1 (£1·92) containing 6×1st Class self-adhesive stamps (No. 2655) .... 7·50
   a. Inside cover with don't just send a stamp advertisement (2.10.06) .... 8·50
   b. Inside cover with To find the correct postcodes for your mail notice (1.2.07) ..... 8·00
Nos. RC1/RC1b has a single small notch at the top right tab edge.

Containing 12 Pricing in Proportion 2nd class stamps

2006 (12 Sept). Blue cover with multicoloured emblem as T **MB3** (74×57 mm) printed by Walsall.
RD1 (£2·76) containing 12×2nd Class self-adhesive stamps (No. 2654) .... 13·00
Nos. RD1 has two small notches at the top right tab edge.

Containing 12 Pricing in Proportion 1st class stamps

2006 (12 Sept). Gold cover with multicoloured emblem as T **MB3** (74×57 mm) printed by Walsall.
RE1 (£3·84) containing 12×1st Class self-adhesive stamps (No. 2655) .... 16·00
No. RE1 has a single small notch at the top right tab edge.

M. Self-adhesive Barcode Booklets containing No Value Indicated Smilers stamps in definitive size, with Definitive stamps.

NOTE. Nos. SA1 and SA2 have the surplus self-adhesive paper around each stamp removed and a single small notch at the top right tab edge.

2007 (16 Jan). Gold cover with multicoloured emblem as T **MB3** (74×57 mm) printed by Walsall.
SA1 (£1·92) containing 1st Class Pricing in Proportion Machin and Love stamps pane No. 2693a .... 18·00

2008 (15 Jan). Gold cover with multicoloured emblem as T **MB3** (74×57 mm) printed by Walsall.
SA2 (£2·04) containing 1st Class Love and Machin stamps with Be My Valentine label pane No. 2693b .... 16·00

POST OFFICE STAMP BOOKLETS

N. Self-adhesive Barcode Booklets containing NVI barcode Machin definitive stamps

Containing 4 × 1st Class Barcoded Security machins

TB1

2022 (1 Feb). Deep violet cover with multicoloured emblem as Type **TB1** (93×68 mm). Printed by ISP Walsall. Repeating 'ROYALMAIL' wording printed on the front of the self-adhesive backing paper.
TB1 (£3·40) Containing four 1st class deep violet self-adhesive barcoded stamps (No. V4507, code 'MFIL') .... 6·00

No. TB1 exists with the large ROYALMAIL lettering above the small and with the small above the large in the alternate pairs of lines in the background text (Type PB-Ls/sL).
Year code for No. TB1 is 'M22L'.
No. TB1 has a single small notch at the top right tab edge.

Containing 8 × 1st Class Barcoded Security machins

TD1

2022 (1 Feb). Deep violet cover with multicoloured emblem as Type **TD1** (93×68 mm). Printed by ISP Walsall. Repeating 'ROYALMAIL' wording printed on the front of the self-adhesive backing paper.
TD1 (£6·80) Containing eight 1st Class Barcoded Security Machin self-adhesive stamps (No. V4506, MEIL) .... 12·00

No. TD1 exists with the small ROYAL MAIL lettering above the large in the alternate pairs of lines in the background text (Type PB-sL).
Year code for No. TD1 is 'M22L'.
No. TD1 has a single small notch at the top right tab edge.

Containing 8 × 2nd Class Barcoded Security machins

TC1

2022 (1 Feb). Emerald cover with multicoloured emblem as Type **TC1** (94×68 mm). Printed by ISP Walsall. Repeating 'ROYALMAIL' wording printed on the front of the self-adhesive backing paper.
TC1 (£5·28) Containing eight 2nd class Barcoded Security machin self-adhesive stamps (No. V4502, code MEIL) .... 8·25

No. TC1 exists with the small ROYAL MAIL lettering above the large in the alternate pairs of lines in the background text (Type PB-sL).
Year code for No. TC1 is 'M22L'.
No. TC1 has two small notches at the top right tab edge.

Containing 4 × 2nd Large Barcoded Security Machin stamps

TE1

2022 (1 Feb). Grey-green cover with multicoloured emblem as Type **TE1** (93×68 mm). Printed by ISP Walsall. Repeating 'ROYALMAIL' wording printed on the front of the self-adhesive backing paper.
TE1 (£3·84) Containing four 2nd Large Barcoded Security machin self-adhesive stamps (No. V4512, MFIL) .... 6·50

No. TE1 exists with the large ROYALMAIL lettering above the small and with the small above the large in the alternate pairs of lines in the background text (Type PB-Ls/sL).
Year code for No. TE1 is 'M22L'.
No. TE1 has two large notches at the top right tab edge.

Containing 4 × 1st Large Barcoded Security Machin stamps

TF1

2022 (1 Feb). Greenish blue cover with multicoloured emblem as Type **TF1** (93×69 mm). Printed by ISP Walsall. Repeating 'ROYALMAIL' wording printed on the front of the self-adhesive backing paper.

TF1	(£5·16) Containing four 1st class Large self-adhesive Barcoded Security machins (No. V4516, code MFIL)	9·00

No. TF1 exists with the small ROYAL MAIL lettering above the large in the alternate pairs of lines in the background text (Type PB-sL).

Year code for No. TF1 is 'M22L'.

No. TF1 has a single large notch at the top right tab edge.

Where a booklet is known with both Type PB-Ls and Type PB-sL the price noted is for the cheaper of the two, whichever that is.

POST OFFICE STAMP BOOKLETS *Queen Elizabeth II / Barcode Booklets – Source and Year Code Tables*

Table A

6 × 1st Long to Reign Over Us retail booklets with self-adhesive Security Machins, with source code and year code.
Printed in gravure by ISP Walsall. With lilac covers as noted below.
Front of the self-adhesive backing paper plain, or with repeating 'ROYALMAIL' wording as noted.

Booklet	Stamp	Booklet description	Backing paper type	Source/year code	
MB14	U3745 1st bright lilac	Lilac cover (Type **MB14**)	Plain	'REIGS' 'O15R'	7·75
MB15	U3745 1st bright lilac	Lilac cover (Type **MB14**)	Type PB-Up Type PB-Up	'REIGS' 'O15R' 'REIGS' 'O16R'	£175 27·00

Table B

6 × 1st retail booklets with self-adhesive Security Machins, with source code (top right), with year code.
Printed in gravure by ISP Walsall. With covers as noted below.
Repeating 'ROYALMAIL' wording printed on the front of the self-adhesive backing paper.
Stamps vermilion or bright scarlet.

Booklet	Stamp	Booklet description	Backing paper type	Source/year code	
MB17	U3024 1st vermilion	Padlock cover, traditional style typeface on outside cover (sharp edges to value indicator) (Type **MB17**)	Type PB-Up	'MSIL' 'M16L'	8·00
MB18	U3028 1st bright scarlet	Padlock cover, new corporate style typeface on outside cover (rounded edges to value indicator) (Type **MB18**), as issued on 20 October 2016	Type PB-Up Type PB-Up	'MSIL' 'M16L' 'MSIL' 'M18L'	9·50 22·00
MB18a	U3028 1st bright scarlet	Cover as **MB18**	Type PB-Ls/sL 'MSIL' 'M16L' Type PB-Ls/sL 'MSIL' 'M17L' Type PB-Ls/sL 'MSIL' 'M18L' Type PB-Ls/sL 'MSIL' 'M19L' Type PB-Ls/sL 'MSIL' 'M20L' Type PB-sL 'MSIL' 'M21L'		18·00 19·00 11·00 12·00 12·00 24·00

Note. The repeating 'ROYALMAIL' wording that is printed on the front of the backing paper where alternate pairs of lines are inverted can exist in two versions, with Large lettering above small (Type PB-Ls), and with small lettering above Large (Type PB-sL). For further information see the notes to the tables listing source and year-code combinations which follow the Security Machin listing. Where a booklet is known with both Type PB-Ls and Type PB-sL the price quoted is for the cheaper of the two versions, whichever that is. Type PB-Up are noted and priced separately.

Table C

12 × 2nd retail booklets with self-adhesive Security Machins, with source code (top right), with year code.
Printed in gravure by ISP Walsall. With blue covers as noted below
Repeating 'ROYALMAIL' wording printed on the front of the self-adhesive backing paper.

Booklet	Stamp	Booklet description	Backing paper type	Source/year code	
ME6	U3013 2nd bright blue	Traditional style typeface on outside cover (sharp edges to value indicator) (Type **ME2**)	Type PB-Up Type PB-Up	'MTIL' 'M15L' 'MTIL' 'M16L'	£100 25·00
ME7	U3013 2nd bright blue	New corporate style typeface on outside cover (rounded edges to value indicator) (Type **ME7**), as issued on 20 October 2016	Type PB-Up Type PB-Up	'MTIL' 'M16L' 'MTIL' 'M18L'	18·00 40·00
ME7a	U3013 2nd bright blue	Cover as **ME7**	Type PB-sL 'MTIL' 'M16L' Type PB-Ls/sL 'MTIL' 'M17L' Type PB-Ls/sL 'MTIL' 'M18L' Type PB-Ls/sL 'MTIL' 'M19L' Type PB-Ls/sL 'MTIL' 'M20L' Type PB-Ls/sL 'MTIL' 'M21L'		40·00 23·00 18·00 18·00 18·00 18·00

Note. The repeating 'ROYALMAIL' wording that is printed on the front of the backing paper where alternate pairs of lines are inverted can exist in two versions, with Large lettering above small (Type PB-Ls), and with small lettering above Large (Type PB-sL). For further information see the notes to the tables listing source and year-code combinations which follow the Security Machin listing. Where a booklet is known with both Type PB-Ls and Type PB-sL the price quoted is for the cheaper of the two versions, whichever that is. Type PB-Up are noted and priced separately.

Table D

12 × 1st retail booklets with self-adhesive Security Machins, with source code (top right), with year code.
Printed in gravure by ISP Walsall. With red covers as noted below.
Repeating 'ROYALMAIL' wording printed on the front of the self-adhesive backing paper.
Stamps vermilion or bright scarlet.

Booklet	Stamp	Booklet description	Backing paper type	Source/year code	
MF8	U3025 1st vermilion	Traditional style typeface on outside cover (sharp edges to value indicator) (Type **MB12**)	Type PB-Up Type PB-Up	'MTIL' 'M15L' 'MTIL' 'M16L'	£100 22·00
MF9	U3029 1st bright scarlet	New corporate style typeface on outside cover (rounded edges to value indicator) (Type **ME7**), as issued on 20 October 2016	Type PB-Up	'MTIL' 'M16L'	19·00
MF9a	U3029 1st bright scarlet	Cover as **MF9**	Type PB-Ls/sL Type PB-Ls/sL Type PB-Ls/sL Type PB-Ls/sL Type PB-Ls/sL Type PB-sL	'MTIL' 'M16L' 'MTIL' 'M17L' 'MTIL' 'M18L' 'MTIL' 'M19L' 'MTIL' 'M20L' 'MTIL' 'M21L'	£110 20·00 19·00 19·00 19·00 19·00

Note. The repeating 'ROYALMAIL' wording that is printed on the front of the backing paper where alternate pairs of lines are inverted can exist in two versions, with Large lettering above small (Type PB-Ls), and with small lettering above Large (Type PB-sL). For further information see the notes to the tables listing source and year-code combinations which follow the Security Machin listing. Where a booklet is known with both Type PB-Ls and Type PB-sL the price quoted is for the cheaper of the two versions, whichever that is. Type PB-Up are noted and priced separately.

Table E

4 × 2nd Large retail booklets with self-adhesive Security Machins, with source code (in front of hair), with year code.
Printed in gravure by ISP Walsall. With blue covers as noted below.
Repeating 'ROYALMAIL' wording printed on the front of the self-adhesive backing paper.

Booklet	Stamp	Booklet description	Backing paper type	Source/year code	
RA3	U3032 2nd bright blue	Traditional style typeface on outside cover (sharp edges to value indicator) (Type **RA1**)	Type PB-Up	'MFIL' 'M16L'	22·00
RA4	U3032 2nd bright blue	New corporate style typeface on outside cover (rounded edges to value indicator) (Type **RA4**), as issued on 20 October 2016	Type PB-Up	'MFIL' 'M16L'	12·00
RA4a	U3032 2nd bright blue	Cover as **RA4**	Type PB-Ls Type PB-Ls/sL Type PB-Ls/sL Type PB-sL Type PB-sL	'MFIL' 'M17L' 'MFIL' 'M18L' 'MFIL' 'M19L' 'MFIL' 'M20L' 'MFIL' 'M21L'	30·00 27·00 11·00 11·00 11·00

Note. The repeating 'ROYALMAIL' wording that is printed on the front of the backing paper where alternate pairs of lines are inverted can exist in two versions, with Large lettering above small (Type PB-Ls), and with small lettering above Large (Type PB-sL). For further information see the notes to the tables listing source and year-code combinations which follow the Security Machin listing. Where a booklet is known with both Type PB-Ls and Type PB-sL the price quoted is for the cheaper of the two versions, whichever that is. Type PB-Up are noted and priced separately.

Table F

4 × 1st Large retail booklets with self-adhesive Security Machins, with source code (in front of hair), with year code.
Printed in gravure by ISP Walsall. With red covers as noted below.
Repeating 'ROYALMAIL' wording printed on the front of the self-adhesive backing paper.
Stamps vermilion or bright scarlet.

Booklet	Stamp	Booklet description	Backing paper type	Source/year code	
RB5	U3037 1st vermilion	Traditional style typeface on outside cover (sharp edges to value indicator) (Type **RB4**)	Type PB-Up Type PB-Up	'MFIL' 'MA15' 'MFIL' 'M16L'	25·00 15·00
RB6	U3039 1st bright scarlet	New corporate style typeface on outside cover (rounded edges to value indicator) (Type **RB6**), as issued on 20 October 2016	Type PB-Up	'MFIL' 'M16L'	35·00
RB6a	U3039 1st bright scarlet	Cover as **RB6**	Type PB-Ls/sL Type PB-Ls/sL Type PB-Ls Type PB-sL Type PB-sL	'MFIL' 'M17L' 'MFIL' 'M18L' 'MFIL' 'M19L' 'MFIL' 'M20L' 'MFIL' 'M21L'	18·00 11·00 11·00 11·00 11·00

Note. The repeating 'ROYALMAIL' wording that is printed on the front of the backing paper where alternate pairs of lines are inverted can exist in two versions, with Large lettering above small (Type PB-Ls), and with small lettering above Large (Type PB-sL). For further information see the notes to the tables listing source and year-code combinations which follow the Security Machin listing. Where a booklet is known with both Type PB-Ls and Type PB-sL the price quoted is for the cheaper of the two versions, whichever that is. Type PB-Up are noted and priced separately.

We may have a new look, but at the heart of everything we do it's still all about stamps.

Our dedicated shop team are here to help with all philatelic enquiries, from fulfilling everyday lists and new GB issues to recommending the best albums and stamp accessories to suit your collection.

Give them a call on +44 (0)20 7557 4436 or email them at shop@stanleygibbons.com they would love to hear from you.

STANLEY GIBBONS
THE HOME OF STAMP COLLEC

399 Strand
London

@StanleyGibbons
@StanleyGibbons
/StanleyGibbonsGroup

POST OFFICE LABEL SHEETS

POST OFFICE LABEL SHEETS

At the Stamp Show 2000 International Stamp exhibition visitors could purchase sheets of 10×1st class stamps in the Smiles designs (as Nos. 1550/15559), each stamp having a *se-tenant* label on which the exhibition visitor's picture was printed, the photographs being taken in a booth at the exhibition.

For those unable to visit the exhibition, the same sheet could be purchased from the Philatelic Bureau and from Post Office philatelic outlets with a Stamp Show 2000 label in place of the photograph.

For Christmas 2000, sheets of 20×19p. stamps in the Robin in Pillar Box design (as No. 1896) or 10×1st class Father Christmas with Cracker design (as No. 2007) were available through the Philatelic Bureau, with se-tenant labels as part of a customised service, purchasers supplying their own photographs for reproduction on the se-tenant label.

This service continued under the name Smilers, after the initial set of stamp designs employed, and was also made available at selected post offices. Corporate label panes, allowing commercial and charitable organisations to have their logo or message reproduced on the se-tenant labels were made available through the Bureau from 2000.

From 26 July 2018 it was announced that the Smilers service would be put on hold for an indefinite period.

Label sheets have continued to be offered with a standard greeting or message. These Generic Smilers have been available from the Philatelic Bureau or from philatelic outlets.

In 2015 a new style of sheet was released, entitled, Star Wars Heroes and Villains, comprising ten stamps and labels, this style has since become known as Collectors Sheets and are included in this listing.

As personalised, corporate and generic label sheets could only be purchased at a premium over the face value of the stamps within them, they are not given full listing in this catalogue; neither are individual stamps (with or without their se-tenant label), some of which are identifiable as having come from Label Sheets, due to perforation, phosphor or printing differences.

The list which follows comprises the generic sheets only. Differences between the stamp in the Label Sheets and those of the standard issues are given under the respective listings in this catalogue.

An asterisk (*) in the listing indicates a difference in process, phosphor of perforation from the original design.

LS1

2000 (22 May). The Stamp Show 2000. T **LS1**. Gravure Questa. Original selling price £2·95. Perf 15×14.
LS1 10×(1st) Smiles stamps, as Nos. 1550/1559 and attached labels............... 22·00

LS2

LS3

2000 (3 Oct)–**01**. Christmas. Types **LS2** and **LS3**. Gravure Questa. Original selling price £3·99 (Nos. LS2/LS2a) and £2·95 (Nos. LS3/LS3a). Perf 15×14.
LS2 20×19p. Robin in Pillar Box stamps, as No. 1896 and attached labels (Imprint Post Office 2000).............................. £125
  a. Imprint Consignia 2001 (9.10.01)............. £600
LS3 10×(1st) Father Christmas with Cracker stamps, as No. 2007 and attached labels (Imprint Post Office 2000)............. £125
  a. Imprint Consignia 2001 (9.10.01)............. £600

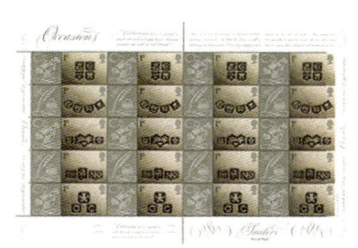

LS4

2001 (5 June). Occasions. T **LS4**. Litho* Questa. Original selling price £5·95. Perf 14×14½.
LS4 20×(1st) Occasions stamps as Nos. 2182/2186 in four vertical columns of five with attached labels............................ £120

2001 (3 July). Smiles As T **LS1** but with greetings shown in attached labels. Litho* Questa. Original selling price £2·95. Perf 14½×14*.
LS5 10×(1st) Smiles stamps, as Nos. 1550/1559 and attached labels............... £160

LS6

2001 (18 Dec). Greetings Cartoons T **LS6**. Litho Questa. Original selling price £2·95. Two phosphor bands. Perf 14½×14 (without* elliptical holes).
LS6 10×(1st) Greetings Cartoons, as Nos. 1905p/1914p and attached labels .... 28·00

LS7

2002 (23 Apr). Occasions Stamps. T **LS7**. Litho Questa. Original selling price £5·95. Perf 14*.
LS7 20×(1st) Occasions stamps as Nos. 2260/2264 in four vertical columns of five with attached labels............................ 60·00

POST OFFICE LABEL SHEETS

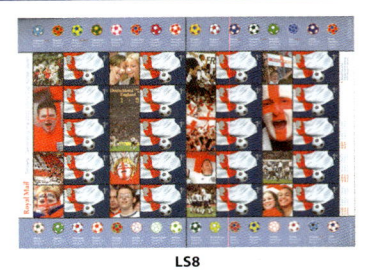

LS8

2002 (21 May). Football World Cup. T **LS8**. Litho* Questa. Original selling price £5·95. Perf 14½×14.
LS8   20×(1st) as bottom right quarter of flag stamp in No. **MS**2292 and attached labels .... 27·00

LS9

2002 (1 Oct). Smiles T **LS9**. Litho* Questa. Original selling price £5·95. Perf 15×14.
LS9   10×(1st) Teddy Bear and 10×(1st) Dennis the Menace, as Nos. 1550/1551, each with attached labels .. 28·00

LS10

2002 (1 Oct). Christmas. T **LS10**. Litho* Questa. Original selling price £5·95. Perf 14½×14*.
LS10   20×(1st) Father Christmas with Cracker, as No. 2007, with attached greetings labels .... 27·00

LS11

2003 (21 Jan). Flower Paintings. T **LS11**. Litho Questa. Original selling price £5·95. Perf 14½×14 (without* elliptical holes).
LS11   20×(1st) Flowers Greetings Stamps, as Nos. 1955/1964 (two of each design) with floral labels attached .... 27·00

LS12

2003 (4 Feb). Occasions. T **LS12**. Litho Questa. Original selling price £5·95. Perf 14½×14.
LS12   20×(1st) Tick box Occasions stamps, as Nos. 2337/2342 (four of Nos. 2338 and 2340 and 3 each of the others) with attached labels .... 27·00
         a. Multiple Choice in green............................
Multiple Choice at top left of sheet is generally in red.
No. LS12a is believed to have come from trial sheets which were put on sale in error.

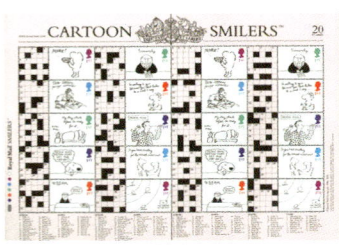

LS13

2003 (29 July). Crossword Cartoons. T **LS13**. Litho Questa. Original selling price £6·15. Two phosphor bands. Perf 14½×14 (without* elliptical holes).
LS13   20×(1st) Cartoons as Nos. 1905p/1914p with Crossword labels attached .... 27·00

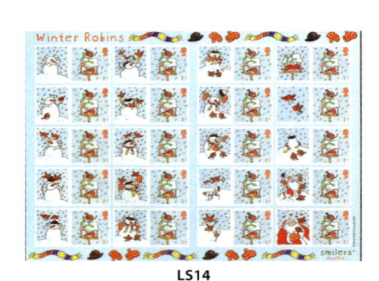

LS14

2003 (30 Sept). Christmas. Winter Robins. T **LS14**. Litho* De La Rue. Original selling price £6·15. Perf 14½.
LS14   20×(1st) Winter Robins, self-adhesive, as No. 2239 with labels alongside .... 27·00

LS15

POST OFFICE LABEL SHEETS

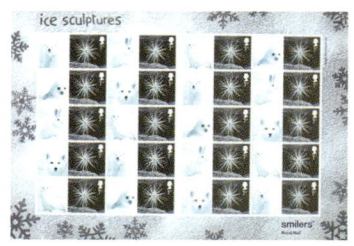

LS16

2003 (4 Nov). Christmas. Types **LS15** and **LS16**. Litho* De La Rue. Original selling prices £4·20 (2nd) and £6·15 (1st). Perf 14½×14.
LS15   20×(2nd) Ice Sculptures, self-adhesive, as No. 2410 with labels showing ice sculptures of polar fauna alongside ...... 20·00
LS16   20×(1st) Ice Sculptures, self-adhesive, as No. 2411 with labels showing photographs of polar fauna alongside. 27·00

LS17

2004 (30 Jan). Hong Kong Stamp Expo. T **LS17**. Litho Walsall. Original selling price £6·15. Perf 14.
LS17   20×(1st) Hello greetings stamps, as No. 2262 with labels alongside .... 27·00

LS18

2004 (3 Feb). Occasions Entertaining Envelopes T **LS18**. Litho De La Rue. Original selling price £6·15. Perf 14½×14.
LS18   20×(1st) Entertaining Envelopes greetings stamps, as Nos. 2424/2428 (four of each design) with attached labels .... 27·00

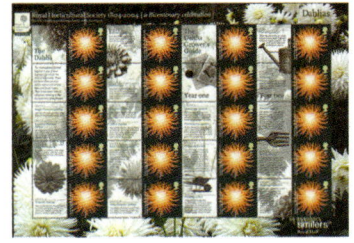

LS19

2004 (25 May). Royal Horticultural Society. T **LS19**. Litho* Walsall. Original selling price £6·15. Perf 14½.
LS19   20×(1st) Dahlia, as No. 2457 with attached labels .... 27·00

LS20

2004 (27 July). Rule Britannia. T **LS20**. Litho* Walsall. Original selling price £6·15. Perf 14½.
LS20   20×(1st) Union Flag, as T **1517** with attached labels .... 27·00

LS21

2004 (2 Nov). Christmas. T **LS21**. Litho* De La Rue. Original selling price £5·40. Perf 14½×14.
LS21   10×(2nd) and 10×(1st) Father Christmas, self-adhesive, as Nos. 2495/2496 with attached labels.............. 23·00

LS22

2005 (11 Jan). Farm Animals. T **LS22**. Litho* Walsall. Original selling price £6·15. Perf 14½.
LS22   20×(1st) Farm Animals, as Nos. 2502/2511 with attached labels.............. 27·00

LS23

2005 (15 Mar). Centenary of the Magic Circle. T **LS23**. Litho* Walsall. Original selling price £6·15. Perf 14½×14.
LS23   20×(1st) Spinning Coin, as No. 2525 with attached labels .... 27·00

POST OFFICE LABEL SHEETS

LS24

2005 (21 Apr). Pacific Explorer 2005 World Stamp Expo. T **LS24**. Litho Walsall. Original selling price £6·55. Perf 14*.
LS24   20×(1st) Hello greetings stamps, as No. 2262 with attached labels .... 27·00

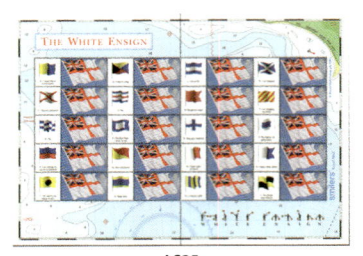

LS25

2005 (21 June). The White Ensign. T **LS25**. Litho* Cartor. Original selling price £6·55. Perf 14½.
LS25   20×(1st) White Ensign stamps, as T **1516** with attached labels.......................... 27·00

LS26

2005 (15 Sept). Classic ITV. T **LS26**. Litho Walsall. Original selling price £6·55. Perf 14½×14.
LS26   20×(1st) *Emmerdale* stamps, as No. 2562 with attached labels .... 27·00

The original printing of No. LS26 contained errors in some of the labels and was withdrawn prior to issue.

LS27

2005 (1 Nov). Christmas. Christmas Robins. T **LS27**. Litho* Cartor. Original selling price £5·60. Perf 14½.
LS27   10×(2nd) and 10×(1st) Robins, self-adhesive, as Nos. 2238/2239 with attached labels .... 23·00

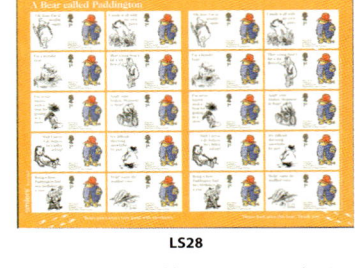

LS28

2006 (10 Jan). A Bear called Paddington. T **LS28**. Litho Cartor. Original selling price £6·55. Perf 14½.
LS28   20×(1st) Paddington Bear, self-adhesive*, as No. 2592 with attached labels.......................... 27·00

LS29

2006 (7 Mar). Fun Fruit and Veg. T **LS29**. Litho* Cartor. Original selling price £6·55. Perf 14½×14.
LS29   20×(1st) Fruit and Vegetables stamps, self-adhesive as Nos. 2348/2357 with attached labels .... 27·00

LS30

2006 (25 May). Washington 2006 International Stamp Exhibition. T **LS30**. Litho Cartor. Original selling price £6·95. Perf 14*.
LS30   20×(1st) Hello greetings stamps, as No. 2262 with attached labels .... 27·00

LS31

2006 (6 June). World Cup Football Championship, Germany. World Cup Winners T **LS31**. Litho Cartor. Original selling price £6·95. Perf 14½.
LS31   20×(1st) England footballer (1966) stamps, as No. 2628 with attached labels.......................... 27·00

POST OFFICE LABEL SHEETS

LS32

2006 (4 July). For Life's Special Moments. T **LS32**. Litho* Cartor. Original selling price £6·95. Perf 15×14.
LS32 20×(1st) Smilers stamps self-adhesive as Nos. 2567/2572 (four of Nos. 2568/2569 and three each of the others) with attached labels .... 27·00

LS33

2006 (17 Oct). Extra Special Moments. T **LS33**. Litho* Cartor. Original selling price £6·95. Perf 15×14.
LS33 20×(1st) Smilers stamps self-adhesive as Nos. 2672/2677 (four of Nos. 2672 and 2677, three each of the others) with attached labels .... 27·00

LS34

2006 (7 Nov). Christmas. T **LS34**. Litho* Cartor. Original selling price £6. Perf 15×14.
LS34 10×(2nd) and 10×(1st) Christmas self-adhesive as Nos. 2678/2679 with attached labels .... 23·00

LS35

2006 (9 Nov). We Will Remember Them. T **LS35**. Litho* Cartor. Original selling price £6·95. Perf 14½.
LS35 20×(1st) Poppies on barbed wire stems stamps as Type **1941** with attached labels .... 27·00

LS36

2006 (14 Nov). Belgica 2006 International Stamp Exhibition, Brussels. T **LS36**. Litho Cartor. Original selling price £6·95. Perf 14*.
LS36 20×(1st) Hello greetings stamps, No. 2262 with attached labels .... 27·00

LS37

2007 (1 Mar). Glorious Wales. T **LS37**. Litho Cartor. Original selling price £6·95. Perf 15×14 (without* elliptical holes).
LS37 20×(1st) Wales stamps, self-adhesive*, as No. W122 with attached labels .... 27·00

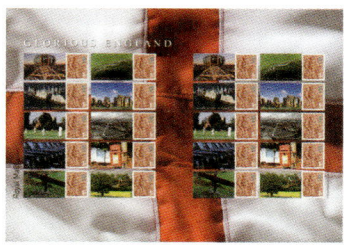

LS38

2007 (23 Apr). Glorious England. T **LS38**. Litho Cartor. Original selling price £7·35. Perf 15×14 (without* elliptical holes).
LS38 20×(1st) England stamps, self-adhesive* as No. EN30 with attached labels .... 27·00

On labels from the original printing Isle of Wight was incorrectly spelled Isle of White. These were recalled before issue but some were released in error. (*Price* £650)

LS39

2007 (17 May). Memories of Wembley Stadium. T **LS39**. Litho* Cartor. Original selling price £7·35. Perf 14½×14.
LS39 20×(1st) stamps as No. 2291 but without WORLD CUP 2002 inscription with attached labels .... 27·00

535

POST OFFICE LABEL SHEETS

LS40

2007 (5 June). 40th Anniversary of the First Machin Definitives. T **LS40**. Litho Cartor. Original selling price £7·35. Phosphor frame*. Perf 14½.
LS40   20×(1st) stamps as T **1984** with attached labels .... 27·00

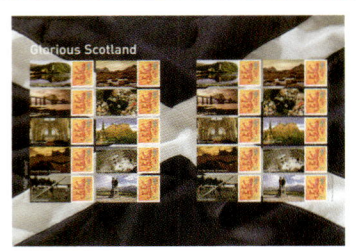

LS44

2007 (30 Nov). Glorious Scotland. T **LS44**. Litho Cartor. Original selling price £7·35. Perf 15×14 (without* elliptical holes).
LS44   20×(1st) Scotland stamps, self-adhesive*, as No. S131 with attached labels .... 27·00

LS41

2007 (17 July). Harry Potter. T **LS41**. Litho Walsall. Original selling price £7·35. Perf 15×14.
LS41   20×(1st) stamps as within No. **MS**2757 but self-adhesive*, four of each design with attached labels .... 27·00

LS45

2008 (15 Jan). I wrote to say. T **LS45**. Litho* Cartor. Original selling price £7·35. Perf 15×14 (with one elliptical hole in each vert side*).
LS45   20×(1st) Smilers stamps self-adhesive as Nos. 2568/2570 (eight of No. 2569, six each of Nos. 2568 and 2570) with attached circular labels............................ 27·00

LS42

2007 (6 Nov). Christmas. T **LS42**. Litho* Cartor. Original selling price £8·30. Perf 15×14.
LS42   8×(2nd), 8×(1st) and 4×78p. Christmas self-adhesive as Nos. 2789/2790 and 2793 with attached labels .... 23·00

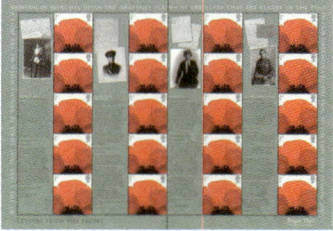

LS46

2008 (11 Mar). Glorious Northern Ireland. T **LS46**. Litho Cartor. Original selling price £7·35. Perf 15×14 (without* elliptical holes).
LS46   20×(1st) Northern Ireland stamps, self-adhesive*, as No. NI95 with attached labels .... 27·00

LS43

2007 (8 Nov). Letters from the Front. T **LS43**. Litho Cartor. Original selling price £7·35. Perf 14½.
LS43   20×(1st) Soldiers in poppy flower stamps as T **2038** with attached labels   27·00

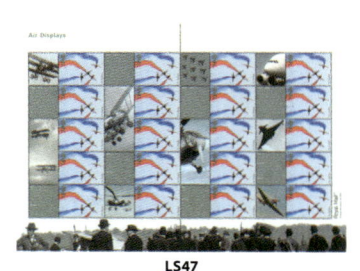

LS47

2008 (17 July). Air Displays. T **LS47**. Litho Cartor. Original selling price £7·75. Perf 14½×14.
LS47   20×(1st) Red Arrows stamps as No. 2855 with attached labels .... 27·00

POST OFFICE LABEL SHEETS

LS48

2008 (5 Aug). Beijing 2008 Olympic Expo. T **LS48**. Litho Cartor. Original selling price £7·75. Perf 14*.
LS48   20×(1st) Hello greetings stamps No. 2262 with attached labels .... 27·00

LS49

2008 (29 Sept). Glorious United Kingdom. T **LS49**. Litho Cartor. Original selling price £7·75. Perf 15×14 (with one elliptical hole in each vertical side).
LS49   5×1st England, 5×(1st) Northern Ireland, 5×(1st) Scotland and 5×(1st) Wales stamps, self-adhesive*, as Nos. EN30, NI95, S131 and W122 with attached labels .... 27·00

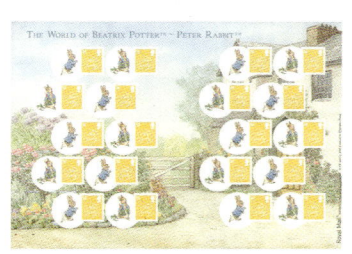

LS50

LS51

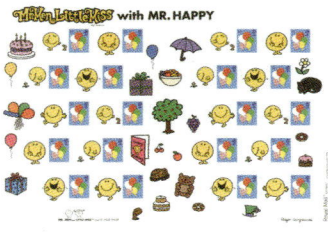

LS52

LS53

2008 (28 Oct). Smilers for Kids (1st series). Types **LS50**/**LS53**. Self-adhesive. Litho Cartor. Original selling price £7·95 each. Perf 15×14 (with one elliptical hole on each vertical side).
LS50   20×(1st) New Baby stamps as No. 2672* with attached circular Peter Rabbit labels.................................. 90·00
LS51   20×(1st) Sunflower stamps No. 2820 with attached circular Almond Blossom fairy labels .... 90·00
LS52   20×(1st) Balloons stamps No. 2822 with attached circular Mr Men labels.... 90·00
LS53   20×(1st) Balloons stamps No. 2822 with attached circular Noddy labels...... 90·00

No. LS50 contains stamps as No. 2672 but perforated with one elliptical hole on each vertical side.

Sheets as Nos. LS50/LS53 but containing ten stamps and ten labels were sold in packs at £7·95 per pack.

LS54

2008 (4 Nov). Christmas. T **LS54**. Litho* Cartor. Original selling price £8·85. Perf 15×14 (with one elliptical hole on each vertical side).
LS54   8×(2nd), 8×(1st) and 4×81p. Christmas self-adhesive as Nos. 2876/2877 and 2881 with attached labels .... 23·00

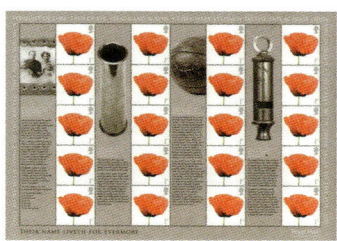

LS55

2008 (6 Nov). We Will Remember. T **LS55**. Litho Cartor. Original selling price £7·75. Perf 14½.
LS55   20×(1st) Soldier's face in poppy flower stamps as No. 2885 with attached labels .... 27·00

LS56

537

POST OFFICE LABEL SHEETS

2009 (13 Jan). Design Classics. T **LS56**. Litho Cartor. Original selling price £7·75. Perf 14×14½*.
LS56 20×(1st) Mini stamps as No. 2889 with attached labels .... 27·00

LS57

2009 (2 Mar). 40th Anniversary of the First Flight of Concorde. T **LS57**. Litho Cartor. Original selling price £7·75. Perf 14×14½*.
LS57 20×(1st) Concorde stamps as No. 2891   27·00

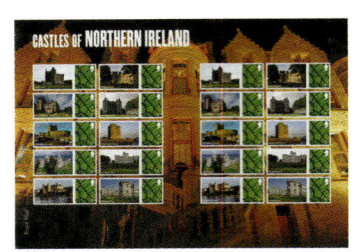

LS58

2009 (17 Mar). Castles of Northern Ireland. T **LS58**. Litho Cartor. Original selling price £7·75. Perf 15×14 (with one elliptical hole in each vertical side).
LS58 20×(1st) Northern Ireland stamps, self-adhesive*, as No. NI95 with attached labels .... 27·00

LS59

2009 (23 Apr). Castles of England. T **LS59**. Litho Cartor. Original selling price £8·35. Perf 15×14 (with one elliptical hole in each vertical side).
LS59 20×(1st) As St George's flag stamp from No. **MS**EN50 but self-adhesive* with attached labels .... 27·00

LS60

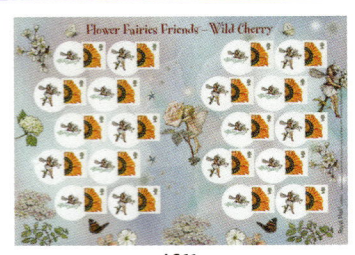

LS61

LS62

LS63

2009 (30 Apr). Smilers for Kids (2nd series). Types **LS60/LS63**. Self-adhesive. Litho* Cartor. Original selling price £8·50 each. Perf 15×14 (with one elliptical hole in each vertical side).
LS60 20×(1st) Hello stamps as No. 2819 with attached circular Jeremy Fisher labels .. 90·00
LS61 20×(1st) Sunflower stamps as No. 2820 with attached circular Wild Cherry fairy labels .... 90·00
LS62 20×(1st) Balloons stamps as No. 2822 with attached circular Little Miss Sunshine labels... 90·00
LS63 20×(1st) Balloons stamps as No. 2822 with attached circular Big Ears labels.... 90·00

Sheets as Nos. LS60/LS63 but containing ten stamps and ten labels were sold in packs at £7·95 per pack.

LS64

2009 (3 Aug). Thaipex 09 International Stamp Exhibition, Bangkok. T **LS64**. Litho Cartor. Original selling price £8·35. Perf 14*.
LS64 20×(1st) Hello greetings stamps as No. 2262 with attached labels .... 27·00

POST OFFICE LABEL SHEETS

LS65

2009 (18 Aug). Post Boxes. T **LS65**. Litho Cartor. Original selling price £8·35. Perf 14.
LS65   20×(1st) Letter box stamps as No. 2950 with attached labels .... 27·00

LS66

2009 (21 Oct). Italia 2009 International Stamp Exhibition, Rome. T **LS66**. Litho Cartor. Original selling price £8·35. Perf 14*.
LS66   20×(1st) Hello greetings stamps as No. 2262 with attached labels .... 27·00

LS67

2009 (3 Nov). Christmas. T **LS67**. Litho Cartor. Original selling price £9. Perf 14½×14 (with one elliptical hole in each vertical side).
LS67   8×(2nd), 8×(1st), 2×56p. and 2×90p. Christmas self-adhesive as Nos. 2991/2992, 2994 and 2996........................ 23·00

LS68

2009 (30 Nov). Castles of Scotland. T **LS68**. Litho Cartor. Original selling price £8·35. Perf 15×14 (with one elliptical hole in each vertical side).
LS68   20×(1st)As Scottish flag stamp from No. **MS**S153 but self-adhesive* with attached labels .... 27·00

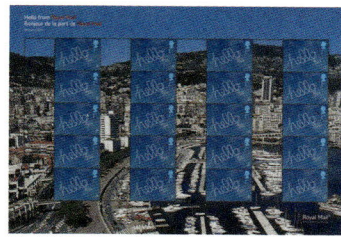

LS69

2009 (4 Dec). MonacoPhil 2009 International Stamp Exhibition, Monaco. T **LS69**. Litho Cartor. Original selling price £8·35. Perf 14*.
LS69   20×(1st) Hello greetings stamps as No. 2262 with attached labels .... 27·00

LS70

2010 (26 Jan). For all occasions T **LS70**. Litho Cartor. Original selling price £9·70. Perf 14½×14 (with one elliptical hole in each vertical side).
LS70   16×(1st), 2×(Europe up to 20 grams) and 2×(Worldwide up to 20 grams) stamps as within No. **MS**3024 but self-adhesive* two of each design with attached labels .... 30·00

LS71

2010 (1 Mar). Castles of Wales. T **LS71**. Litho Cartor. Original selling price £8. Perf 15×14 (with one elliptical hole in each vertical side).
LS71   20×(1st) As Red Dragon stamp from No. **MS**W147 but self-adhesive* with attached labels .... 27·00

LS72

2010 (8 May). London 2010 Festival of Stamps. T **LS72**. Self-adhesive Litho* Cartor. Original selling price £8·50. Die-cut Perf 15×14 (with one elliptical hole in each vertical side).
LS72   20×(1st) Hello greetings stamps as No. 2819 with attached labels .... 27·00

539

POST OFFICE LABEL SHEETS

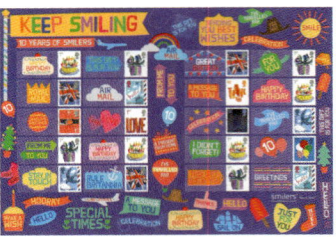

LS73

2010 (8 May). Keep Smiling Ten Years of Smilers T **LS73**. Self-adhesive. Litho Cartor. Original selling price £10. Die-cut Perf 15×14 (with one elliptical hole in each vertical side).
LS73   3×No. 2821 (1st) Union Jack, one each of Nos. 2572 (1st) Robin in pillar box, No. 2674 (1st) THANK YOU, No. 2693 (1st) LOVE, No. 2822 (1st) Balloons; No. 2823 (1st) Fireworks and also 4×(1st) Birthday cake, 4×(1st) Birthday present, 2×(Europe up to 20 grams) and 2×(Worldwide up to 20 grams) stamps as within No. **MS**3024 but self-adhesive* with attached labels .... 50·00

LS74

2010 (15 Sept). 70th Anniversary of the Battle of Britain. T **LS74**. Litho Cartor. Original selling price £8·50. Perf 14×14½*.
LS74   20×(1st) Spitfire stamps as No. 2887 with attached labels .... 27·00

LS75

2010 (2 Nov). Christmas. T **LS75**. Litho Cartor. Original selling price £9·30. Perf 14½×14 (with one elliptical hole in each vertical side).
LS75   8×(2nd), 8×(1st), 2×60p. and 2×97p. Christmas self-adhesive as Nos. 3128/3134 .... 23·00

LS76

2011 (12 Feb). Indipex International Stamp Exhibition, New Delhi. T **LS76**. Litho Cartor. Original selling price £8·50. Perf 15×14 (with one elliptical hole in each vertical side).
LS76   20×(1st) Union Jack self-adhesive stamps as No. 2821 with attached labels .... 27·00

LS77

2011 (28 July). Philanippon '11 World Stamp Exhibition, Yokohama. T **LS77**. Litho* Cartor. Original selling price £9·50. Die-cut perf 15×14 (with one elliptical hole in each vertical side)
LS77   20×(1st) Hello self-adhesive greetings stamps as No. 2819 with attached labels showing origami models .... 27·00

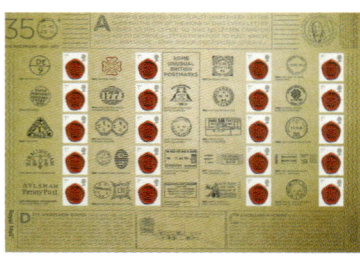

LS78

2011 (15 Sept). 350th Anniversary of the Postmark. T **LS78**. Litho Cartor. Original selling price £9·50. Die-cut perf 14½×14 (with one elliptical hole in each vertical side).
LS78   20×(1st) Recreation of Crown seal stamps as within No. **MS**3024 but self-adhesive with attached labels showing postmarks.. 27·00

LS79

2011 (8 Nov). Christmas. 400th Anniversary of the *King James Bible*. T **LS79**. Litho Cartor. Original selling price £10·45. Die-cut perf 14½×14 (with one elliptical hole in each vertical side).
LS79   8×(2nd), 8×(1st), 2×68p. and 2×£1·10 Christmas self-adhesive stamps as Nos. 3242/3248 with attached labels showing verses from the *King James Bible* .... 30·00

POST OFFICE LABEL SHEETS

LS80

2012 (20 Jan). Lunar New Year. Year of the Dragon. T **LS80**. Litho Cartor. Original selling price £9·50. Die-cut perf 15×14 (with one elliptical hole in each vertical side).
LS80   20×(1st) Fireworks self-adhesive greetings stamps as No. 2823 with attached labels .... 27·00

LS81

2012 (18 June). Indonesia 2012 International Stamp Exhibition, Jakarta. T **LS81**. Litho* Cartor. Original selling price £12·50. Die-cut perf 15×14 (with one elliptical hole in each vertical side).
LS81   20×(1st) Hello self-adhesive greetings stamps as No. 2819 with attached labels showing images of Indonesia ..... 27·00

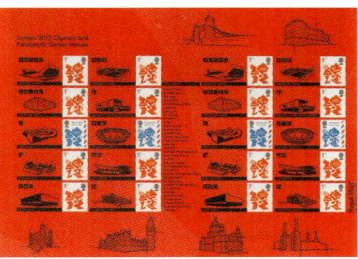

LS82

2012 (27 June). Olympic and Paralympic Games, London. Games Venues. T **LS82**. Self-adhesive. Litho Cartor. Die-cut perf 14½×14 (with one elliptical hole in each vertical side).
LS82   8×(1st) Olympic Games, 8×(1st) Paralympic Games, 2×Worldwide up to 20 grams Olympic Games and 2×Worldwide up to 20 grams Paralympic Games as Nos. 3250/3253 with attached labels showing Games venues .... 90·00

LS83

2012 (6 Nov). Christmas. Illustrations by Axel Scheffler. T **LS83**. Litho Cartor. Original selling price £13·10. Die-cut perf 14½×14 (with one elliptical hole in each vertical side).
LS83   8×(2nd), 8×(1st), 2×87p. and 2×£1·28 Christmas self-adhesive as Nos. 3415/3416, 3418 and 3420........................ 24·00

LS84

2013 (7 Feb). Lunar New Year. Year of the Snake. T **LS84**. Self-adhesive Litho Cartor. Original selling price £12·50. Die-cut perf 15×14 (with one elliptical hole in each vertical side).
LS84   20×(1st) Fireworks stamps as No. 2823 with attached labels showing Chinese decorations .... 27·00

LS85

2013 (26 Mar). 50th Anniversary of *Doctor Who* (TV programme). T **LS85**. Self-adhesive. Litho Cartor. Original selling price £12. Die-cut perf 14½×14 (with one elliptical hole in each vertical side).
LS85   20×(1st) TARDIS stamps as No. 3449 with attached labels showing Cybermen, Daleks, Silurians, Sontarans and The Master.. 27·00

LS86

2013 (10 May). Australia 2013 World Stamp Exhibition, Melbourne. T **LS86**. Self-adhesive. Litho* Cartor. Original selling price £12·50. Die-cut perf 15×14 (with one elliptical hole in each vertical side)
LS86   20×1st Hello self-adhesive greetings stamps as No. 2819 with attached labels showing images of Melbourne... 27·00

POST OFFICE LABEL SHEETS

LS87

2013 (2 Aug). Bangkok 2013 World Stamp Exhibition, Thailand. T **LS87**. Litho* Cartor. Original selling price £12·50. Die-cut perf 15×14 (with one elliptical hole in each vertical side).
LS87   20×1st Hello self-adhesive greetings stamps as No. 2819 with attached labels showing images of Thailand .... 27·00

LS88

2013 (5 Nov). Christmas. Madonna and Child Paintings. T **LS88**. Litho* ISP Cartor. Original selling price £13·62. Die-cut perf 14½×15 (with one elliptical hole in each vertical side*).
LS88   8×(2nd), 8×(1st), 2×88p. and one each of £1·28 and £1·88 Christmas self-adhesive as Nos. 3542/3543, 3545 and 3547/3548 with attached labels .... 40·00

LS89

2013 (10 Dec). Lunar New Year. Year of the Horse. T **LS89**. Self-adhesive. Litho* ISP Cartor. Original selling price £12·50. Die-cut perf 15×14 (with one elliptical hole in each vertical side).
LS89   20×1st Fireworks stamps as No. 2823 with attached labels .... 27·00

LS90

2014 (4 Nov). Christmas. Illustrations by Andrew Bannecker. T **LS90**. Litho* ISP Cartor. Original selling price £15·20. Die-cut perf 14½×15 (with one elliptical hole in each vertical side*).
LS90   8×(2nd), 8×(1st), 2×£1·28 and 2×£1·47 Christmas self-adhesive as Nos. 3650/3651 and 3654/3655 with attached labels .... 25·00

LS91

2014 (19 Nov). Lunar New Year. Year of the Ram. T **LS91**. Self-adhesive. Litho* ISP Cartor. Original selling price £12·90. Die-cut perf 15×14 (with one elliptical hole in each vertical side).
LS91   20×1st Fireworks stamps as No. 2823 with attached labels .... 27·00

LS92

2014 (1 Dec). Kuala Lumpur 2014 World Stamp Exhibition, Malaysia. T **LS92**. Litho* ISP Cartor. Original selling price £12·90. Die-cut perf 15×14 (with one elliptical hole in each vertical side).
LS92   20×1st Hello self-adhesive greetings stamps as No. 2819 with attached labels showing images of Malaysia .... 27·00

LS93

2015 (20 Jan). Smilers. T **LS93**. Litho* ISP Cartor. Original selling price £12·90. Die-cut perf 14½×14 (with one elliptical hole in each vertical side*).
LS93   20×1st Smilers stamps self-adhesive as Nos. 3670/3677 (3×Nos. 3670, 3672/3673 and 3675, 2×Nos. 3671, 3674 and 3676/3677) with attached labels £190

POST OFFICE LABEL SHEETS

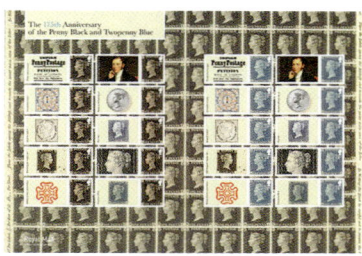

LS94

2015 (6 May). 175th Anniversary of the Penny Black. T **LS94**. Litho* ISP Cartor. Original selling price £13·10. Die-cut perf 14½×14 (with one elliptical hole in each vert side).

LS94   10×(1st) Penny Black and 10×(1st) Two Pence Blue (as within No. **MS**3710) self-adhesive* with attached labels .... 65·00

LS97

2015 (3 Nov). Christmas. T **LS97**. Litho* ISP Cartor. Original selling price £15·96. Die-cut perf 14½×15 (with one elliptical hole in each vert side*).

LS97   8×(2nd), 8×(1st) and one each of £1, £1·33, £1·52 and £2·25 Christmas self-adhesive as Nos. 3771/3772 and 3775/3778 with attached labels .... 28·00

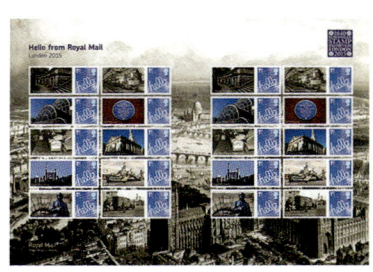

LS95

2015 (13 May). Europhilex London 2015 Exhibition. T **LS95**. Litho* ISP Cartor. Original selling price £13·10. Die-cut perf 15×14 (with one elliptical hole in each vert side).

LS95   20×(1st) Hello self-adhesive greetings stamps as No. 2819 with attached labels .... 27·00

LS98

2015 (9 Nov). Lunar New Year. Year of the Monkey. T **LS98**. Litho* ISP Cartor. Original selling price £13·10. Die-cut perf 15×14 (with one elliptical hole in each vert side).

LS98   20×(1st) Fireworks self-adhesive greetings stamps as No. 2823 with attached labels .... 27·00

LS99

2016 (18 Feb). 175th Anniversary of the Penny Red. T **LS99**. Litho ISP Cartor. Original selling price £13·10. Die-cut perf 14½×14 (with one elliptical hole in each vert side).

LS99   20×(1st) Penny Red self-adhesive stamps as No. 3806 with attached labels .... 27·00

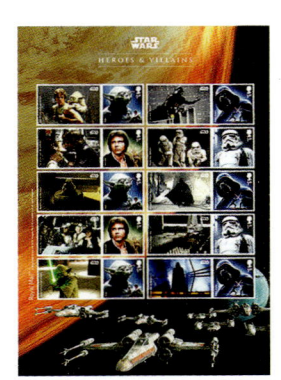

LS96

2015 (20 Oct). *Star Wars*. Heroes and Villains. T **LS96**. Litho ISP Cartor. Original selling price £6·80. Die-cut perf 14½.

LS96   10×(1st) *Star Wars* stamps as Nos. 3758/3759, each×3, and as Nos. 3761/3762, each×2, but self-adhesive* 15·00

LS100

543

POST OFFICE LABEL SHEETS

2016 (28 May). New York World Stamp Show. T **LS100**. Original selling price £13·30. Litho* ISP Cartor. Die-cut perf 15×14 (with one elliptical hole in each vert side).
LS100　　20×(1st) Hello self-adhesive greetings stamps as No. 2819 with attached labels .... 27·00

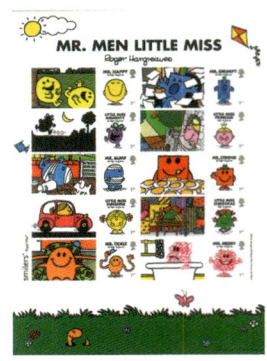

LS101

2016 (20 Oct). Mr Men and Little Miss (children's books by Roger Hargreaves). T **LS101**. Original selling price £6·90. Litho ISP Cartor. Die-cut perf 14½.
LS101　　10×(1st) Mr Men and Little Miss stamps as Nos. 3891/3900 but self-adhesive* .... 14·00

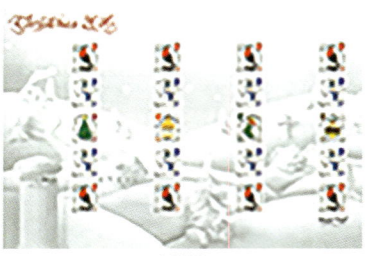

LS102

2016 (8 Nov). Christmas. T **LS102**. Original selling price £16·21. Litho ISP Cartor. Die-cut perf 14½×15 (with one elliptical hole in each vert side*).
LS102　　8×(2nd), 8×(1st) and one each of £1·05, £1·33, £1·52 and £2·25 Christmas self-adhesive as Nos. 3903/3904 and 3907/3910 with attached labels .... 25·00

LS103

2016 (8 Nov). Celebrating 50 Years of Christmas Stamps. T **LS103**. Original selling price £12·40. Litho ISP Cartor. Die-cut perf 14½×15 (with one elliptical hole in each vert side*).
LS103　　10×(2nd) and 10×(1st) Christmas self-adhesive stamps as Nos. 3903/3904 and 3907/3910 with attached labels ..... 23·00

LS104

2016 (15 Nov). Lunar New Year. Year of the Rooster. T **LS104**. Original selling price £13·30. Litho* ISP Cartor. Die-cut perf 15×14 (with one elliptical hole in each vert side).
LS104　　20×(1st) Fireworks self-adhesive greetings stamps as No. 2823 with attached labels .... 29·00

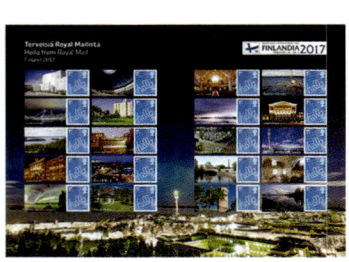

LS105

2017 (24 May). Finlandia 2017 European Stamp Exhibition, Tampere. T **LS105**. Original selling price £13·50. Litho* ISP Cartor. Die-cut perf 15×14 (with one elliptical hole in each vert side).
LS105　　20×(1st) Hello self-adhesive greetings stamps as No. 2819 with attached labels .... 27·00

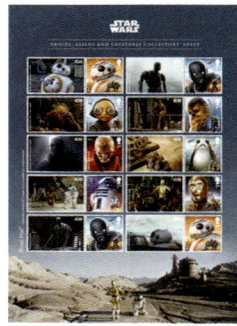

LS106

2017 (12 Oct). *Star Wars*. Droids, Aliens and Creatures. T **LS106**. Original selling price £7. Litho ISP Cartor. Die-cut perf 14½.
LS106　　10×(1st) As Nos. 4007/4010, 4011×2, 4012/4013 and 4014×2 with attached labels showing film stills. .... 14·00
For Ultimate Collector's Sheet see No. **MS**4014*a* in main section

LS107

POST OFFICE LABEL SHEETS

2017 (7 Nov). Christmas. T **LS107**. Original selling price £16·40. Litho ISP Cartor. Die-cut perf 14½×15 (with one elliptical hole in each vert side).

LS107   8×(2nd), 8×(1st) and one each of £1·17, £1·40, £1·57 and £2·27 Christmas self-adhesive stamps as Nos. 4019/4020 and 4023/4026 with attached labels .... 32·00

LS108

2017 (7 Nov). Christmas. T **LS108**. Original selling price £12·60. Litho ISP Cartor. Die-cut perf 14½×15 (with one elliptical hole in each vert side).

LS108   10×(2nd) and 10×(1st) Christmas self-adhesive stamps as Nos. 4028/4029 with attached labels .... 23·00

LS109

2017 (16 Nov). Lunar New Year. Year of the Dog. T **LS109**. Original selling price £13·50. Litho ISP Cartor. Die-cut perf 15×14 (with one elliptical hole in each vert side).

LS109   20×(1st) Fireworks self-adhesive greetings stamps as No. 2823 with attached labels .... 27·00

LS110

2018 (23 Jan). *Game of Thrones*. T **LS110**. Original selling price £7·50. Litho ISP Cartor. Die-cut perf 14×14½.

LS110   10×(1st) As Nos. 4033/4042 but self-adhesive* .... 14·00

LS111

2018 (26 June). 50th Anniversary of *Dad's Army* (BBC television sitcom 1968–1977). T **LS111**. Original selling price £7·50. Litho ISP Cartor. Die-cut perf 14×14½*.

LS111   10×(1st) *Dad's Army* stamps as Nos. 4101/4102, each×5, but self-adhesive* .... 30·00

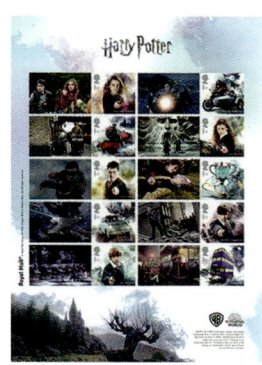

LS112

2018 (16 Oct) Harry Potter T **LS112**. Original selling price £7·70. Litho ISP Cartor. Die-cut perf 14×14½.

LS112   10×(1st) As Nos. 4141/4150 but self-adhesive* with ten labels .... 35·00

LS113

2018 (1 Nov). Christmas. T **LS113**. Original selling price £17·50. Litho* ISP Cartor. Die-cut perf 14½×15 (with one elliptical hole in each vert side).

LS113   8×(2nd), 8×(1st) and one each of £1·25, £1·45, £1·55 and £2·25 Christmas self-adhesive stamps as Nos. 4154/4155 and 4158/4161 with attached labels .... 24·00

545

POST OFFICE LABEL SHEETS

LS114

2018 (15 Nov). Lunar New Year. Year of the Pig. T **LS114**. Original selling price £14·40. Litho* ISP Cartor. Die-cut perf 15×14 (with one elliptical hole in each vert side).
LS114   20×(1st) Fireworks self-adhesive greetings stamps as No. 2823 with attached labels .... 27·00

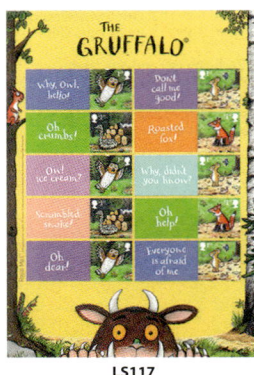

LS117

2019 (10 Oct). *The Gruffalo*. T **LS117**. Original selling price £11·50. Litho ISP Cartor. Die-cut perf 14*.
LS117   3×(1st) Owl, 3×(1st) Mouse, 2×£1·55 Snake, 2×£1·55 Fox (all as within No. **MS**4282 but self-adhesive*) with attached labels .... 25·00

LS115

2019 (14 Mar) Marvel. T **LS115**. Original selling price £7·70. Litho ISP *Cartor. Die-cut perf 14½.
LS115   10×(1st) As Nos. 4182/4191 but self-adhesive* with ten labels .... 14·00

LS118

2019 (5 Nov). Christmas. T **LS118**. Original selling price £18·40. Litho ISP Cartor. Die-cut perf 14½×15.
LS118   8×(2nd), 8×(1st) and one each of £1·35, £1·55, £1·60 and £2·30 Christmas self-adhesive stamps as Nos. 4283/4284 and 4287/4290 with attached labels .... 35·00

LS116

2019 (29 May). Stockholmia 2019 Exhibition. T **LS116**. Original selling price £15·10. Litho* ISP Cartor. Die-cut perf 15×14 (with one elliptical hole in each vert side).
LS116   20×(1st) Hello self-adhesive greetings stamps as No. 2819 with attached labels .... 27·00

LS119

2019 (18 Nov). Lunar New Year. Year of the Rat. T **LS119**. Original selling price £15·10. Litho* ISP Cartor. Die-cut perf 15×14 (with one elliptical hole in each vert side).
LS119   20×(1st) Fireworks self-adhesive greetings stamps as No. 2823 with attached labels .... 27·00

POST OFFICE LABEL SHEETS

LS120

2019 (26 Nov). *Star Wars*. T **LS120**. Original selling price £8·10. Litho ISP Cartor. Die-cut perf 14½.
LS120   10×(1st) As Nos. 4292/4301 but self-adhesive* with attached labels .... 15·00

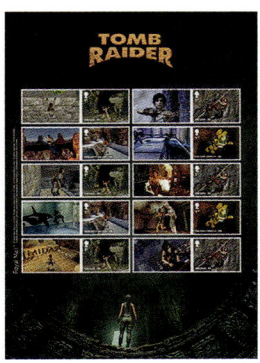

LS121

2020 (21 Jan). Video Games. T **LS121**. Original selling price £11·40. Litho ISP Cartor. Die-cut perf 14×14½.
LS121   3×(1st) *Tomb Raider*, 1996, 3×(1st) *Tomb Raider*, 2013, 2×£1·55 *Adventures of Lara Croft*, 1998, 2×£1·55 *Tomb Raider Chronicles*, 2000 (all as within No. **MS**4320 but self-adhesive*) with attached labels .... 25·00

LS122

2020 (17 Mar). James Bond. T **LS122**. Original selling price £12·60. Litho ISP Cartor. P 14.
LS122   5×(1st) and 5×£1·60 James Bond stamps Nos. 4332×3, 4333/4336 and 4337×3 with attached labels .... 35·00

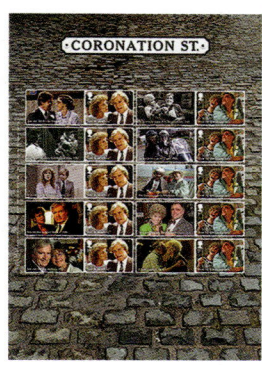

LS123

2020 (26 May). *Coronation Street*. T **LS123**. Original selling price £8·80. Litho ISP Cartor. Perf 14×14½*.
LS123   19×(1st) As Nos. 4371/4372, each×5, but self-adhesive* .... 25·00

LS124

2020 (9 July). Queen Album Covers. T **LS124**. Original selling price £13·15. Litho ISP Cartor. Die-cut perf 13 (with one elliptical hole in each vert side)*.
LS124   5×(1st) and 5×£1·63 Queen stamps as Nos. 4388/4389, 4390×2, 4391/4392, 4393×2 and 4394/4395 but self-adhesive* .... 25·00

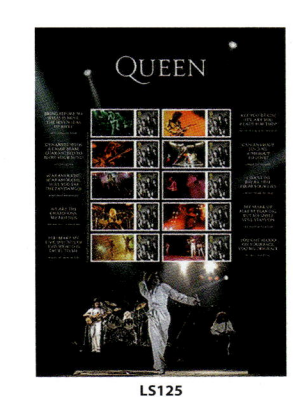

LS125

2020 (9 July). Queen Live. T **LS125**. Original selling price £8·80. Litho ISP Cartor. Die-cut perf 14½×14 (with one elliptical hole on each vert side)*
LS125   10×(1st) Queen stamp as No. 4403 but self-adhesive* .... 14·00

547

POST OFFICE LABEL SHEETS

LS126

2020 (18 Aug). *Sherlock* T **LS126**. Original selling price £11·95. Litho ISP Cartor. Perf 14*.
LS126   6×(1st), 2×£1·68 as Nos. 4411/4416 but self-adhesive* .... 55·00

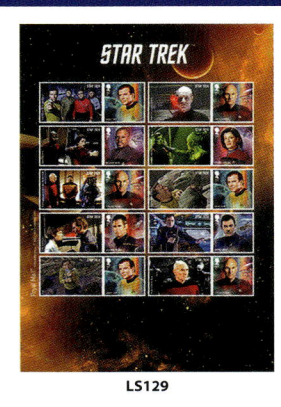

LS129

2020 (13 Nov). *Star Trek*. T **LS129**. Original selling price £8·70. Litho ISP Cartor. Die-cut perf 14½
LS129   10×(1st) Star Trek Captains stamps as Nos. 4443/4444×3 and 4445/4448 but self-adhesive*... 14·00

LS127

2020 (3 Nov). Christmas. Stained-glass Windows. T **LS127**. Original selling price £20·60. Litho ISP Cartor. Die-cut perf 14½×15.
LS127   8×(2nd), 8×(1st) and one each of £1·45, £1·70, £2·50 and £2·55 Christmas self-adhesive stamps as Nos. 4434/4435 and 4438/4441 with attached labels .... 75·00

LS130

2020 (8 Dec). Lunar New Year. Year of the Ox. T **LS129**. Original selling price £16·40. Litho* ISP Cartor. Die-cut perf 15×14 (with one elliptical hole in each vert side)
LS130   20×(1st) Fireworks self-adhesive greetings stamps as No. 2823 with attached labels .... 27·00

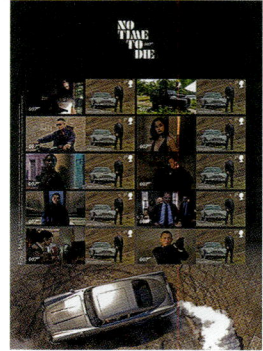

LS128

2020 (3 Nov). James Bond: *No Time to Die*. T **LS128**. Original selling price £8·80. Litho ISP Cartor. Die-cut perf 14×14½.
LS128   10×(1st) As Type **3430** with attached labels .... 14·00

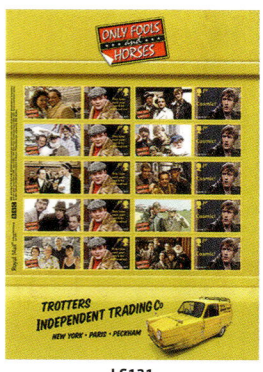

LS131

2021 (16 Feb). *Only Fools and Horses* (TV sitcom, 1981–2003). T **LS131**. Original selling price £9·60. Litho ISP Cartor. Die-cut perf 14×14½.
LS131   10×(1st) *Only Fools and Horses* self-adhesive* stamps as Types **3558/3559**, each×5..................................... 14·00

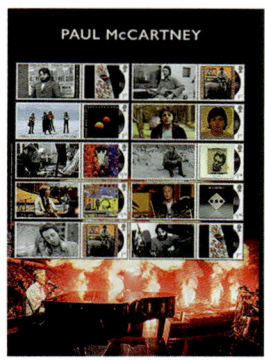

POST OFFICE LABEL SHEETS

LS132

2021 (28 May). Paul McCartney. Album Covers. T **LS132**. Original selling price £13. Litho ISP Cartor. P 14.
LS132   6x(1st) and 4x£1.70 Paul McCartney stamps as Nos. 4517/4518x2 and 4519/4524 with attached labels.............. 18·00

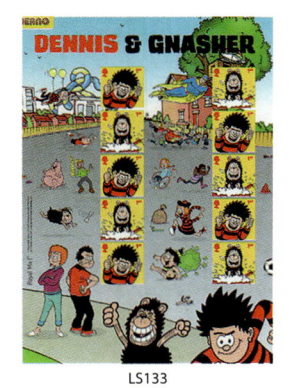

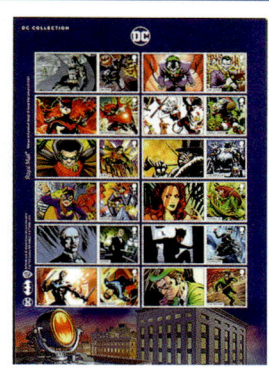

LS135

2021 (17 Sept). DC Collection. Batman. T **LS135**. Original selling price £11.40. Litho ISP Cartor. Die-cut perf 14½
LS135   12x(1st) DC Collection stamps as Nos. 4575/4586 with attached labels.............. 16·00

LS133

2021 (1 July). Dennis and Gnasher. T **LS133**. Original selling price £9.70. Litho ISP Cartor. Die-cut perf 14½.
LS133   10x(1st) Dennis and Gnasher self-adhesive stamps as Types **3614/3615**, each x5, with attached labels showing Beano characters .... 14·00

LS136

2021 (2 Nov). Christmas. Nativity Illustrations by Joseph Cocco. T **LS136**. Original selling price £21.75. Litho ISP Cartor. Die-cut perf 14½ x15 (with one elliptical hole in each vert side).
LS136   8x(2nd), 8x(1st) and two each of £1.70 and £2.55 Christmas self-adhesive stamps as Nos. 4606, 4608 and 4611/4612 with attached labels.............. 30·00

LS134

2021 (22 July). Wild Coasts. T **LS134**. Original selling price £9.70. Litho ISP Cartor. Die-cut perf 14½
LS134   10x(1st) Wild Coasts stamps as Nos. 4542/4551 but self-adhesive with attached labels showing coastal wildlife .... 14·00

LS137

2021 (8 Dec). Lunar New Year. Year of the Tiger. T **LS137**. Original selling price £18.20. Litho* ISP Cartor. Die-cut perf 14½x14 (with one elliptical hole in each vert side)
LS137   20x(1st) Fireworks self-adhesive greetings stamps as No. 2823 with attached labels .... 27·00

POST OFFICE LABEL SHEETS/ROYAL MAIL COMMEMORATIVE SHEETS

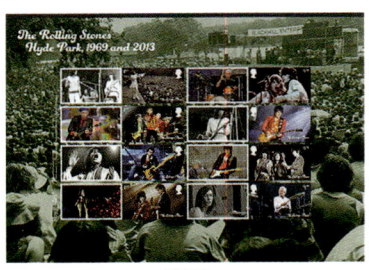

LS138

2022 (20 Jan). The Rolling Stones, Hyde Park 1969 and 2013. T **LS138**. Original selling price £11.50. Litho ISP Cartor. Die-cut perf 14
LS138   4x(1st) and 4x£1.70 Rolling Stones stamps as Nos. 4614/4621 with attached labels showing scenes from 1969 and 2013 concerts in Hyde Park...   17·00

LS139

2022 (20 Jan). The Rolling Stones on Tour. T **LS139**. Original selling price £11.50. Litho ISP Cartor. Die-cut perf 14
LS139   4x(1st) and 4x£1.70 Rolling Stones stamps as Nos. 4614/4621 with attached labels showing the band on tour ....   17·00

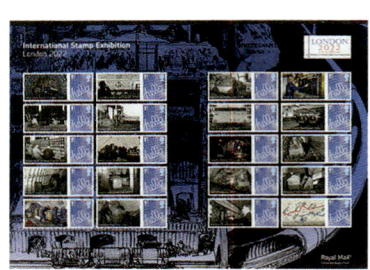

LS140

2022 (19 Feb). London 2022 International Stamp Exhibition. T **LS140**. Original selling price £18.20. Litho* ISP Cartor. Die-cut perf 15x14 (with one elliptical hole in each vert side)
LS140   20x(1st) Hello self-adhesive greetings stamps as No. 2819 with labels depicting the 'Mail Rail' subterranean railway system used to transport London mail from 1927 to 2003..............   27·00

ROYAL MAIL 'COMMEMORATIVE SHEETS'

The following Royal Mail commemorative sheets were sold at a significant premium over the face value of the stamps:

1.4.2008	100 Years of the Territorial Army. 10×1st Union Flag stamps with labels
24.7.2008	The London 1908 Olympic Games. 10×1st Union Flag stamps with labels
14.11.2008	60th Birthday of Prince Charles. 10×1st Wales self-adhesive stamps with labels
21.7.2009	40th Anniversary of Moon Landing. 10×1st Union Flag stamps with labels
18.9.2009	Big Ben 10×1st Union Flag stamps with labels
7.10.2009	800th Anniversary of the University of Cambridge. 10×1st Fireworks stamps (as Type **1993**) with labels
22.10.2009	Olympic and Paralympic Games (I). The Journey Begins 10×1st as Types **2192/2201** with labels
18.5.2010	Halley's Comet 10×1st Union Flag stamps with labels
8.7.2010	Grand Prix 10×1st Union Flag stamps with labels
27.7.2010	Olympic and Paralympic Games (II). One Aim 10×1st as Types **2290/2299** with labels
10.8.2010	Tenth Anniversary of the London Eye. 10×1st Union Flag stamps with labels
28.10.2010	Remembrance: The National Memorial Arboretum. 10×1st Poppies on Barbed Wire Stem stamps (as Type **2112**)
30.3.2011	50th Anniversary of the E Type Jaguar. 10×1st Union Flag stamps with labels
10.6.2011	90th Birthday of Prince Philip. 10×1st self-adhesive Union Flag stamps with labels
27.7.2011	Olympic and Paralympic Games (III). High Hopes. 10×1st as Types **2383/2392** with labels
10.4.2012	Centenary of the Sinking of the *Titanic*. 10×1st As Crown seal stamp from **MS**3024 with labels
1.5.2012	50th Anniversary of the First James Bond Film. 10×1st Union Flag stamps with labels
5.10.2012	40th Anniversary of the Last Goon Show. 10×1st Union Flag stamps with labels
8.11.2012	150th Anniversary of Notts County Football Club. 10×1st Fireworks stamps with labels
16.4.2013	60th Anniversary of Launch of Royal Yacht *Britannia*. 10×1st Union Flag stamps with labels
1.5.2013	Birth Bicentenary of David Livingstone (explorer and medical missionary) 10×1st Scottish Flag stamps (as within **MS**S153) and labels
19.9.2013	150th Birth Anniversary of Bertram Mackennal 10×1st As Crown Seal stamps from **MS**3024 with labels
25.2.2014	Middlesex County Cricket Club 10x1st Fireworks stamps with labels
25.3.2014	By Sea, By Land. 350th Anniversary of the Royal Marines 10x1st Union Flag stamps with labels
16.10.2014	50th Anniversary of Donald Campbell's Water and Land Speed Records. 10×1st Union Flag with labels
11.11.2014	Christmas Truce. 10×1st Poppies on Barbed Wire Stems stamps as Type **2588** with labels
18.3.2015	The Post Office Rifles during the Great War. 10×1st Union Flag stamps with labels
24.4.2015	Birth Bicentenary of Anthony Trollope. 10×1st Union Flag stamps with labels
20.8.2015	The Gurkhas Celebrating 200 Years of Service 1815-2015. 10×1st Union Flag stamps with labels
17.9.2015	Animals of the First World War 1914-1918. 10×1st Union Flag stamps with labels
12.1.2016	The Duke of Edinburgh's Award Diamond Anniversary 10×1st Union Flag stamps with labels
25.4.2016	ANZAC. 10×1st Poppies on Barbed Wire Stems stamps as Type **2588** with labels
14.10.2016	950th Anniversary of the Battle of Hastings. 10×1st England Flag stamps as Type **EN6** with labels
13.6.2017	HRH The Princess Royal Thirtieth Anniversary. 10×1st Union Flag stamps with labels
30.6.2017	Canada Celebrating 150 Years. 10×1st Fireworks stamps with labels
13.9.2017	Opening of The Postal Museum. 10×1st (4 Penny Black as T **2848**, 3 Two Pence Blue as T **2938**, 3 Penny Red as T **2937**) all with labels
1.6.2018	150th Anniversary of the Trades Union Congress. 10×1st Royalty Seal stamps with labels
10.10.2018	United for Wildlife. 10×1st Royalty seal stamps with labels

GSM Online & Archive

Ever since it was first launched as the *Stanley Gibbons Monthly Journal* in 1890, *Gibbons Stamp Monthly* has been informing and entertaining new and experienced collectors alike.

Now, thanks to the launch of the new *GSM Online & Archive* subscription, you can have access to every issue of *GSM*, from the first magazine right through to the very latest issue – that's over 130 years of philatelic knowledge to explore.

Covering every issue from 1890 to 2009, the new, long-awaited *GSM Archive* is a fully searchable online product that puts over 1650 issues of the most successful philatelic magazine on the market directly at your fingertips.

The *GSM Archive* allows you to browse through decades' worth of articles, reviews and contemporary news, or use the powerful inbuilt search function to precisely find the information you want. You can also save your searches for later reference and print any of the material for your own personal use.

Together with *GSM Online*, which is also included in your subscription, you can now read every issue of *GSM* in its various incarnations from 1890 to the present day.

With access to more than 40,000 pages of philatelic information, *GSM Online & Archive* is the perfect reference tool for collectors and philatelic researchers of all levels.

Available at www.stanleygibbons.com and through our customer services team on 01425 472 363

GIBBONS Stamp MONTHLY
First Choice for Stamp Collectors Since 1890

£79.99 ANNUAL SUBSCRIPTION

Stock Code: GSMOLA

COMMEMORATIVE / MINIATURE SHEET DESIGN INDEX

This index gives an easy reference to the inscriptions and designs of the Special Stamps 1953 to April 2021. Where a complete set shares an inscription or type of design, then only the catalogue number of the first stamp is given in addition to separate entries for stamps depicting popular thematic subjects. Paintings, inventions, etc., are indexed under the name of the artist or inventor, where this is shown on the stamp.

1. £.s.d. ISSUES 1953–70

Aberfeldy Bridge 764
Alcock, John (aviator) 791
Anniversaries 767, 791, 819
Antiseptic surgery, centenary 667
Antrim 690
Arbroath Declaration, 650th anniversary 819
Architecture
    Cathedrals 796
    Rural 815
Atlantic Flight, 50th anniversary 791
Auguries of Innocence (William Blake) 4347
Automatic sorting of mail 811

Battle of Britain, 25th anniversary 671
Battle of Hastings, 900th anniversary 705
Blake, William 4347
British birds
    Black-headed Gull (*Chroicocephalus ridibundus*) 696
    Blue Tit (*Cyanistes caeruleus*) 697
    Robin (*Erithacus rubecula*) 698
    Blackbird (*Turdus merula*) 699
British bridges 763
British discovery and invention 752
British paintings 748, 771
British ships 778
British technology 701
British wild flowers
    Hawthorn (*Crataegus*) 717
    Larger Bindweed (*Calystegia sepium*) 718
    Ox-eye Daisy (*Leucanthemum vulgare*) 719
    Bluebell (*Hyacinthoides non-scripta*) 720
    Dog Violet (*Viola riviniana*) 721
    Primrose (*Primula vulgaris*) 722
Brown, Arthur (aviator) 791
Burns, Robert commemoration 685

Cairngorms 692
Canterbury Cathedral 799
CEPT (European Conference of Postal and Telecommunications) 621, 626
Chichester, Sir Francis, World voyage 751
Christmas
    1966, Children's paintings 713
    1967, Paintings 756
    1968, Children's toys 775
    1969, Traditional Religious Themes 812
    1970, Robert de Lisle Psalter 838
Churchill, Sir Winston 661
Commonwealth Arts Festival 669
Commonwealth Cable 645
Commonwealth Games, Cardiff (1958) 567
Commonwealth Games, Edinburgh (1970) .. 832
Commonwealth Parliamentary Conference .. 629
Concorde, first flight 784
Constable, John (artist) 774
Cook's first voyage of discovery, 200th anniversary 770
Co-operative Alliance, 75th anniversary 821
Coronation 532
Cotswold Limestone 816
Cutty Sark (clipper ship) 781

De Montfort's Parliament, 700th anniversary 663
Dickens, Charles, death centenary 824
Durham Cathedral 796

East Indiaman (sailing ship) 780
EFTA (European Free Trade Association) ... 715
Elizabethan galleon 779
England Winners, World Cup Football Championship, 1966 700
Europa, CEPT, first anniversary 621
Europa, CEPT, tenth anniversary 792
European CEPT Conference, Torquay 626

Fife Harling (Scottish house) 815
First England–Australia flight, 50th anniversary . 795
Forth Road Bridge 659
Freedom from Hunger 634

Gandhi, Mahatma, birth centenary 807
General Letter Office, Tercentenary 619
Gipsy Moth IV (ketch) 751
SS *Great Britain* (passenger steamship) 782

Harlech Castle 691
Hovercraft (SR.N6 Winchester class) 703

International Botanical Congress, Tenth 655
International Geographical Congress, 20th . 651
International Labour Organisation, 50th anniversary 793
International Lifeboat Conference, ninth 639
International Telecommunications Union, centenary 683

Jet Engine 754
Jubilee Jamboree (1957) 557

Landscapes 689
Lawrence, Sir Thomas (artist) 748, 772
le Nain, Louis (artist) 758
Lister, Joseph 667
Literary anniversaries 824
Liverpool Metropolitan Cathedral 801
Lowry, L. S. (artist) 750

M4 Viaduct 766
Mauritania, (RMS, ocean liner) 783
Mayflower, 350th anniversary of voyage ... 822
Menai Bridge 765
Motor Cars (E-Type and Mini) 702
Murillo (artist) 757

NATO (North Atlantic Treaty Organisation), 20th anniversary 794
National Giro 808
National Nature Week 637
National Productivity Year 631
Nightingale, Florence, 150th birth anniversary .. 820
Nuclear Power (Windscale reactor) 704

Paris Postal Conference, centenary 636
Parliament, 700th anniversary 663
Parliamentary Conference, 46th 560
Penicillin 753
Philympia 1970 835
Pinkie (painting) 772
Piper, John (artist) 773
Post Office Savings Bank, centenary 623
Post Office technology commemoration 808
Post Office Tower, opening 679
Prince of Wales, Investiture 802

Queen Elizabeth 2 (RMS, ocean liner) 778
Queen Elizabeth I (painting) 771

Radar 752
Radio Telescope 701
Red Cross Centenary Congress 642
Royal Air Force, 50th anniversary 769
Royal Astronomical Society, 150th anniversary .. 823
Ruins of St Mary Le Port (painting) 773

St Giles, Edinburgh 798
St Paul's Cathedral 800
Salvation Army centenary 665
School of Seville (painting) 756
Shakespeare Festival 646
Stubbs, George (artist) 749
Sussex 689

Tarr Steps 763
Telecommunications, ISD 809
Television equipment 755
The Hay Wain (painting) 774
Trades Union Congress, centenary 767

Ulster Thatch 818
United Nations, 20th anniversary 681

Votes for Women, 50th anniversary 768

Welsh Stucco 817
Westminster Abbey, 900th anniversary 687
Windsor Castle 762
Wordsworth, William, 200th birth anniversary ... 828
World Cup Football Championship, 1966 ... 693
World Scout Jubilee Jamboree, 1957 557

York Minster 797

COMMEMORATIVE / MINIATURE SHEET DESIGN INDEX

2. DECIMAL CURRENCY 1971–2022

A Christmas Carol, 150th anniversary 1790
A Midsummer Night's Dream (Shakespeare) 3177
A Night at the Opera Tour, 1975 4401
A Star Shell (C. R. W. Nevinson) 3629
Abbotsbury Swannery 1639
Aberystwyth University College 890
Abolition of the Slave Trade, bicentenary
William Wilberforce and anti slavery poster 2728
Olaudah Equiano and map of trade routes 2729
Granville Sharp and slave ship 2730
Thomas Clarkson and plan of slave ship 2731
Hannah More and *The Sorrows of Yamba* 2732
Ignatius Sancho and trade/business card 2733
Accession of George V, centenary MS3065, 3066
Ackroyd, Norman (artist) 4095
Acrobatic dancers 2166
Action for Species.
Birds
White-tailed Eagle (*Haliaeetus albicilla*) 2764
Bearded Tit (*Panurus biarmicus*) 2765
Red Kite (*Milvus milvus*) 2766
Cirl Bunting (*Emberiza cirlus*) 2767
Marsh Harrier (*Circus aeruginosus*) 2768
Avocet (*Recurvirostra avosetta*) 2769
Bittern (*Botaurus stellaris*) 2770
Dartford Warbler (*Sylvia undata*) 2771
Corncrake (*Crex crex*) 2772
Peregrine Falcon (*Falco peregrinus*) 2773
Insects
Adonis Blue (*Polyommatus bellargus*) 2831
Southern Damselfly
(*Coenagrion mercuriale*) 2832
Red-barbed Ant (*Formica rufibarbis*) 2833
Barberry Carpet Moth
(*Pareulype berberata*) 2834
Stag Beetle (*Lucanus cervus*) 2835
Hazel Pot Beetle (*Cryptocephalus coryli*) 2836
Field Cricket (*Gryllus campestris*) 2837
Silver-spotted Skipper (*Hesperia comma*) 2838
Purbeck Mason Wasp
(*Pseudepipona herrichii*) 2839
Noble Chafer (*Gnorimus nobilis*) 2840
Mammals
Humpback Whale
(*Megaptera novaeangliae*) 3054
Wild Cat (*Felis silvestris*) 3055
Brown Long-eared Bat (*Plecotus auritus*) 3056
Polecat (*Mustela putorius*) 3057
Sperm Whale (*Physeter macrocephalus*) 3058
Water Vole (*Arvicola amphibius*) 3059
Greater Horseshoe Bat
(*Rhinolophus ferrumequinum*) 3060
Otter (*Lutra lutra*) 3061, 3095
Dormouse (*Muscardinus avellanarius*) 3062
Hedgehog (*Erinaceus europaeus*) 3063, 3096
Plants
Round-headed Leek
(*Allium sphaerocephalon*) 2931
Floating Water-plantain
(*Luronium natans*) 2932
Lady's Slipper Orchid (*Cypripedium calceolus*) 2933
Dwarf Milkwort (*Polygala amarella*) 2934
Marsh Saxifrage (*Saxifraga hirculus*) 2935
Downy Woundwort (*Stachys germanica*) 2936
Upright Spurge (*Euphorbia serrulata*) 2937
Plymouth Pear (*Pyrus cordata*) 2938
Sea Knotgrass (*Polygonum maritimum*) 2939
Deptford Pink (*Dianthus armeria*) 2940
Action Man Red Devil Parachutist 3997
Adventures of Lara Croft MS4320
African Elephant (*Loxodonta*) 3162
African Wild Dog (*Lycaon pictus*) 3170
Age of (British Royal dynasties)
Lancaster and York MS2818
Tudors MS2930
Stewarts MS3053
Stuarts MS3094
Hanoverians MS3229
Windsors MS3270
Age of Steam, railway photographs 1795
Air Displays
Red Arrows, Dartmouth Regatta 2855, 2869
RAF Falcons Parachute Team, Biggin Hill 2856
Red Arrows, Farnborough 2857
Vulcan and Avro 707s, Farnborough 2858
Avro 504 with parachutist on wing, 1933 2859
Air Race, Hendon, *c.* 1912 2860
Airliners
Airbus A340-600 2284
Concorde 2285, 2290
Trident 2286
VC10 2287
Comet 2288
Airmail-blue van and post box, 1930 956
Airy, Sir George, Transit Telescope 1257
Albert Memorial 1121
Album Covers 2686, 2999, 3849, 3933
with the beatles (The Beatles) 2686
Sgt Peppers Lonely Hearts Club Band
(The Beatles) 2687
Help! (The Beatles) 2688
Abbey Road (The Beatles) 2689
Revolver (The Beatles) 2690
Let It Be (The Beatles) 2691
The Division Bell (Pink Floyd) 2999
A Rush of Blood to the Head (Coldplay) 3000
Parklife (Blur) 3001
Power, Corruption and Lies (New Order) 3002
Let It Bleed (Rolling Stones) 3003
London Calling (The Clash) 3004
Tubular Bells (Mike Oldfield) 3005
IV (Led Zeppelin) 3006
Screamadelica (Primal Scream) 3007
The Rise and Fall of Ziggy Stardust and the
Spiders from Mars (David Bowie) 3008
The Piper at the Gates of Dawn (Pink Floyd) 3849
Atom Heart Mother (Pink Floyd) 3850
The Dark Side of the Moon (Pink Floyd) 3851
Animals (Pink Floyd) 3852
Wish You Were Here (Pink Floyd) 3853
The Endless River (Pink Floyd) 3854
Hunky Dory (David Bowie) 3933
Aladdin Sane (David Bowie) 3934
Heroes (David Bowie) 3935
Let's Dance (David Bowie) 3936
Earthling (David Bowie) 3937
Blackstar (David Bowie) 3938
Alexandra Palace 1493
Alice in Wonderland (Lewis Carroll)
The White Rabbit 3658
Down the Rabbit Hole 3659
Drink Me 3660
The White Rabbit's house 3661
The Cheshire-Cat 3662
A Mad Tea-party 3663
The Queen of Hearts 3664
The game of croquet 3665
Alice's evidence 3666
A pack of cards 3667
Alice's Adventures in Wonderland
(Lewis Carroll) 1094, 2594
Ali, Shachow 4644
All England Tennis Championships,
Wimbledon 1835
Allied POWs liberated, 1945 4362
Amateur Athletics Association, centenary 1134
Amateur Boxing Association, centenary 1136
Amazon rainforest, wildlife of MS3172
American Independence, bicentennial 1005
Amies, Hardy (dressmaker) 3309
Amphitheatre at Isca Fortress, Caerleon 4382
Amur Leopard (*Panthera pardus orientalis*) 3166
Ancient Britain
Battersea Shield, London 3912
Skara Brae village, Orkney Islands 3913
Star Carr headdress, Yorkshire 3914
Maiden Castle hill fort, Dorset 3915
Avebury stone circles, Wiltshire 3916
Drumbest horns, Co Antrim 3917
Grime's Graves flint mines, Norfolk 3918
Mold cape, Flintshire 3919
Angel of the North 3230
Angels 913, 993, 2064, 2789, 3550
Anglepoise lamp (George Carwardine) 2890
Animail MS3837
Animal Tales
The Tale of Mr. Jeremy Fisher (Beatrix Potter) 2589
Kipper (Mike Inkpen) 2590
The Enormous Crocodile (Roald Dahl) 2591
More About Paddington (Michael Bond) 2592
Comic Adventures of Boots
(Satoshi Kitamura) 2593
Alice's Adventures in Wonderland
(Lewis Carroll) 2594
The Very Hungry Caterpillar (Eric Carle) 2595
Maisy's ABC (Lucy Cousins) 2596
Animals, Species at Risk 1320
Anne, Queen 3093
Anne of Cleves (painting) 1969
Annigoni, Pietro Annigoni (painter) 3494
Anniversaries 887, 901
Anthem for Doomed Youth (poem) 4134
Antibiotic properties of Penicillin 3116
Archdruid 1010
Archer, John (politician) 3458
Archer, Jonathan (*Star Trek Enterprise*) 4447
Architecture
Modern University Buildings 890
Village Churches 904
Historic Buildings 1054
Modern European Architecture 1355
Armagh Observatory 1522
Modern Architecture 2634
Landmark Buildings 3973
Archive illustrations. Linnean Society
Bull-rout (Jonathan Couch) 1380
Yellow Water Lily (Major Joshua Swatkin) 1381
Beswick's Swan (Edward Lear) 1382
Morel (James Sowerbury) 1383
Arctic Skua (*Stercorarius parasiticus*) 4655
Arctic Tern (*Sterna paradisaea*) 4657
Armistice, World War I MS2886
Armourer re-arms Spitfire MS3735, 4073
Arthurian Legends
King Arthur and Merlin 1294
Lady of the Lake 1295
Queen Guinevere and Sir Lancelot 1296
Sir Galahad 1297
Arthur 4493
Arthur and Excalibur 4494
Arthur and Guinevere 4495
Arthur battles Mordred 4500
Artificial Lens Implant Surgery 3118
Aston Martin (car manufacturer) 3514
Aston Martin DB5, *Skyfall* 4340, 4342
Astronomy 1522, MS2315
Armagh Observatory 1522
Newton's moon and tide diagram 1523
Royal Observatory, Greenwich 1524
Stonehenge, Wiltshire 1525
Athletics 1134, 1328, 1564, 1925, 2983, 3022, 3196
Atlantic and Arctic Convoys MS3529
Atlantic Puffin (*Fratercula arctica*) 1419
Atmospheric Steam Engine 3277
Attlee, Clement (Prime Minister) 3644
Austen, Jane (author) 3431
Austen, Jane, birth centenary 989
Austin (car manufacturer) 1198, MS3518
Austin-Healey 100 (cars) 1947
Australian Settlement, bicentenary
Early settler and sailing clipper 1396
Queen Elizabeth II and
UK and Australian Parliament Buildings 1397
W. G. Grace (cricketer) and tennis racket 1398
Shakespeare, John Lennon and
Sydney Opera Houset 1399
Autumn 1779
Avro Lancaster I 1339, 1985

Babbage, Charles, birth bicentenary 1547, 3030
Badger (*Meles meles*) 1043, 2481
Badminton 1025, 2988
Bains, Ishan 4650
Ballerina 1183
Ballycopeland Windmill 3969
Ballyroney, County Down 2000
Balmoral Castle MS4225
Banks, Joseph (naturalist) 4118
Bankside Galleries, London 2143
Bannecker, Andrew (illustrator) 3650
Baran, Zafer and Barbara (artists) 4133
Barbirolli, Sir John (conductor) 1133
Barker, Ronnie (comedian) 3698
Barlow, Francis (Painter) 1090
Barn Owl (*Tyto alba*) 1320, 2125, 2327, 4082, 4087
Bashir, Julian (*Star Trek Deep Space Nine*) 4451
Basketball 1932, 2990, 3023
Bath Mail Coach, 1784 1258
Bath Spa Millennium project 2168
Bather 2168
Battersea Dogs and Cats Home,
150th anniversary 3036
Battle of Bannockburn 2111
Battle of Britain, 75th anniversary MS3735
Battle of Jutland commemorative medal 3843
Battle of Passchendaele, 90th anniversary MS2796
Battle of Somme, centenary MS2685
Battle of Waterloo, bicentenary
(paintings by Denis Dighton)
The Defence of Hougoumont 3724
The Scots Greys during the charge of the

COMMEMORATIVE / MINIATURE SHEET DESIGN INDEX

Union Brigade 3725
The French cavalry's assault on Allied defensive squares 3726
The defence of La Haye Sainte by the King's German Legion 3727
The capture of Plancenoit by the Prussians 3728
The French Imperial Guard's final assault 3729
Soldiers at Battle of Waterloo
   15th Infantry Regiment, IV Corps, Prussian Army 3730
   Light Infantry, King's German Legion, Anglo-Allied Army 3731
   92nd Gordon Highlanders, Anglo-Allied Army 3732
   Grenadiers, Imperial Guard, French Army 3733
BB8 (*Star Wars*) 4011, 4017
BBC, 50th anniversary
   Microphones, 1924-1969 909
   Horn loudspeaker 910
   TV camera, 1972 911
   Oscillator and spark transmitter, 1897 912
Be nice if every day I have left would be like this 4374
Beach pebbles 2134
Beachy Head lighthouse and charts 1287
Beck, Harry (London Underground map) 2895
Beddgelert, Gwynedd 1999
Beecham, Sir Thomas (conductor) 1131
Bees 3736
   Scabious Bee (*Andrena hattorfiana*) 3736
   Great Yellow Bumblebee
     (*Bombus distinguendus*) 3737
   Northern Colletes Bee (*Colletes floralis*) 3738
   Bilberry Bumblebee (*Bombus monticola*) 3739
   Large Mason Bee (*Osmia xanthomelana*) 3740
   Potter Flower Bee (*Anthophora retus*) 3741
Bell, Alexander Graham,
   First telephone call, centenary 997
Bell Textron Jet Pack, *Thunderball* 4339, 4341
Ben Arkle, Sutherland, Scotland (painting) 1811
Beside the Seaside
   Ice cream cone 2734, 2848
   Sandcastle 2735
   Carousel Horse 2736
   Beach huts 2737
   Deckchairs 2738
   Beach Donkeys 2739
Bicycle development 2074
Bicycles 1067
Biddulph Grange, Staffordshire 1224
Bignor Mosaic 4381
Binyon, Lawrence (poet) 3627
Bird Paintings
   Muscovy Duck 1915
   Lapwing 1916
   White-fronted Goose 1917
   Bittern 1918
   Whooper Swan 1919
Birds 1109, 1915, 2103, 2125, 2128, 2238, 2327, 2764, 3948
Birds of Prey
   White-tailed Eagle (*Haliaeetus albicilla*) 4200
   Merlin (*Falco columbarius*) 4201
   Hobby (*Falco subbuteo*) 4202
   Buzzard (*Buteo buteo*) 4203
   Golden Eagle (*Aquila chrysaetos*) 4204
   Kestrel (*Falco tinnunculus*) 4205
   Goshawk (*Accipiter gentilis*) 4206
   Sparrowhawk (*Accipiter nisus*) 4207
   Red Kite (*Milvus milvus*) 4208
   Peregrine Falcon (*Falco peregrinus*) 4209
Birds of prey, photographs
   Barn Owl (*Tyto alba*) 2327
   Kestrel (*Falco tinnunculus*) 2332
Birtwell, Celia (textile designer) 3312
Bishop, Ronald Eric (aircraft designer) 1986
Black, Sir James (pharmacologist) 3115, 3153
Black Holes 4326
Black Prince 961
Blackcap 3953
Black Rhinoceros (*Diceros bicornis*) 3169
Blackpool pleasure beach 3639
Blackpool Tower 3231
Blake, Admiral and *Triumph* (galleon) 1188
Blanchflower, Danny (footballer) 1929
Blenheim Palace 1225, 3869
Blind man with Guide Dog 1147
Bluebell wood 2155
Blues and Royals Drum Horse and drummer 1991
Blur (Rock band) 3001
Blyton, Enid (children's author), birth centenary
   Noddy 2001
   Famous Five 2002

Secret Seven 2003
Faraway Tree 2004
Malory Towers 2005
Boccia (paralympics sport) 2985
Bodleian Library, Oxford 1582
Bog Snorkelling, Llanwrtyd Wells, Wales 4246
Boleyn, Anne (painting) 1967
Bowie, David 3008, 3933
   The Rise and Fall of Ziggy Stardust and the Spiders from Mars 3008
   Hunky Dory 3933
   Aladdin Sane 3934
   Heroes 3935
   Let's Dance 3936
   Earthling 3937
   Blackstar 3938
Boxing 1136, 3106
Boy Scout movement 1181
Boyd Orr, John (humanitarian) 3812
Boys' Brigade 1179
Braemar Gathering (Highland games) 1838
Bridgeness distance slab 4384
Bridges
   Tarr Steps Clapper bridge, River Barle 3687
   Row Bridge, Mosedale Beck 3688
   Pulteney Bridge, River Avon 3689
   Craigellachie Bridge, River Spey 3690
   Menai Suspension Bridge, Menai Strait 3691
   High Level Bridge, River Tyne 3692
   Royal Border Bridge, River Tweed 3693
   Tees Transporter Bridge, River Tees 3694
   Humber Bridge, River Humber 3695
   Peace Bridge, River Foyle 3696
Bridges of London
   Millennium Bridge, 2001 2309
   Tower Bridge, 1894 .... 2310, 2314
   Westminster Bridge, 1864 2311
   Blackfriars Bridge, c. 1800 (William Marlow) ... 2312
   London Bridge, c. 1670 (Hollar) 2313
Brilliant Bugs
   Common Carder Bee (*Bombus pascuorum*) ... 4428
   Painted Lady Butterfly (*Vanessa cardui*) 4429
   Longhorn Beetle (*Rutpela maculata*) 4430
   Elephant Hawk-moth (*Deilephila elpenor*) .. 4431
   Marmalade Hoverfly (*Episyrphus balteatus*) .. 4432
   Ruby-tailed Wasp (*Chrysis ignita agg.*) 4433
Britain Alone
   Churchill inspecting troops 3074
   Land Girls 3075
   Home Guard 3076
   Evacuees 3077
   Air Raid Wardens 3078
   Women in Factories 3079
   Royal broadcast by Princesses 3080
   Fire Service 3081
   Evacuation of troops, Dunkirk 3082
   Upper Thames Patrol in
     Operation Little Ships 3083
   Rescued soldiers on board RN Destroyer ... 3084
   Trawler and boat loaded with troops 3085
Britain's entry into European Communities 919
British aircraft designers
   Reginald Mitchell 1984, 2868, 2887
   Roy Chadwick 1985
   Ronald Bishop 1986
   George Carter 1987
   Sir Sydney Camm 1988
British Amateur Gymnastics Association,
   centenary 1388
British Architects in Europe
   Willis, Faber and Dumas Building, Ipswich ... 1355
   Pompidou Centre, Paris 1356
   Staatsgallerie, Stuttgart 1357
   European Investment Bank, Luxembourg 1358
British Architecture
   University College of Wales, Aberystwyth 890
   Southampton University 891
   Leicester University 892
   Essex University 893
British Army uniforms
   Royal Scots, 1633 1218
   Royal Welch Fusiliers, mid 18th-centuary ... 1219
   95th Rifles (Royal Green Jackets), 1805 ... 1220
   Irish Guards, 1900 1221
   Parachute Regiment, 1983 1222
   Royal Military Police, 1999 2774
   5th Royal Tank Regiment, 1944 2775
   Royal Field Artillery, 1917 2776
   95th Rifles, 1813 2777
   Royal Regiment of Foot of Ireland, 1704 2778
   Earl of Oxford's Horse, 1661 2779
British Auto Legends

Jaguar E-Type, 1961 3512
Rolls-Royce Silver Shadow, 1965 3513
Aston Martin DB5, 1963 3514
MG MGB, 1962 3515
Morgan Plus 8, 1968 3516
Lotus Esprit, 1976 3517
Morris Minor Royal Mail van MS3518, 3530
British Coastlines
   Studland Bay, Dorset 2265
   Luskentyre, South Harris 2266
   Dover cliffs, Kent 2267
   Padstow Harbour, Cornwall 2268
   Broadstairs, Kent 2269
   St Abb's Head, Scottish Borders 2270
   Dunster beach, Somerset 2271
   Newquay beach, Cornwall 2272
   Portrush, County Antrim 2273
   Conwy, sand-spit 2274
British Composers
   George Frederick Handel 1282
   Gustuv Holst 1283
   Frederick Delius 1284
   Edward Elgar 1285
British Conductors
   Sir Henry Wood 1130
   Sir Thomas Beecham 1131
   Sir Malcolm Sargent 1132
   Sir John Barbirolli 1133
British Council, 50th anniversary
   Education for development 1263
   Promoting the arts 1264
   Technical training 1265
   Language and libraries 1266
   British Council Library, Middle East 1266
British Cultural Traditions
   Royal National Eisteddfod of Wales 1010
   Morris Dancing 1011
   Highland Gathering 1012
   Welsh harpist 1013
British Cycling Federation, centenary 1067
British Design Classics
   Supermarine Spitfire (R J Mitchell) 2887
   Mini skirt (Mary Quant) 2888
   Mini car (Sir Alec Issigonis) 2889
   Anglepoise lamp (George Carwardine) 2890
   Concorde (BAC/Aérospatiale) 2891
   K2 telephone kiosk (Sir Giles Gilbert Scott) ... 2892
   Polypropylene chair (Robin Day) 2893
   Penguin book cover (Edward Young) 2894
   London Underground map (Harry Beck) 2895
   Routemaster Bus (AAM Durrant designer) ... 2896
British Engineering
   Raspberry Pi microcomputer 4212
   The Falkirk Wheel rotating boat lift 4213
   Three-way catalytic converter 4214
   Crossrail 4215
   Superconducting magnet in MRI scanner 4216
   Synthetic bone-graft 4217
British Explorers
   David Livingstone 923
   Henry M Stanley 924
   Sir Francis Drake 925
   Walter Raleigh 926
   Charles Sturt 927
   Amy Johnson 2360
   Everest, British Team 2361, 2366
   Freya Stark 2362
   Ernest Shackleton 2363
   Sir Francis Chichester 2364
   Robert Falcon Scott 2365
British Fairs
   Merry-go-round 1227
   Big wheel, helter-skelter and animals 1228
   Side shows 1229
   Early produce fair 1230
British Film Year
   Peter Sellers 1298
   David Niven 1299
   Charlie Chaplin 1300
   Vivien Leigh 1301
   Alfred Hitchcock 1302
British Gardens
   Sissinghurst, Kent 1223
   Biddulph Grange, Staffordshire 1224
   Blenheim Palace 1225
   Pitmedden, Scotland 1226
British Horse Society, 50th anniversary
   Carriage Horse and coachman 1989
   Lifeguards' Horse and trooper 1990
   Blues and Royals Drum Horse and drummer 1991
   Duke of Edinburgh's Horse and groom 1992

COMMEMORATIVE / MINIATURE SHEET DESIGN INDEX

British Humanitarians
Sir Nicholas Winton 3810
Sue Ryder 3811
John Boyd Orr 3812
Eglantyne Jebb 3813
Joseph Rowntree 3814
Josephine Butler 3815
British Journey: England
Carding Mill Valley, Shropshire 2597
Beachy Head, Sussex Coast 2598
St Paul's Cathedral, London 2599
Brancaster, Norfolk Coast 2600
Derwent Edge, Peak District 2601
Robin Hood's Bay, Yorkshire coast 2602
Buttermere, Lake District 2603
Chipping Campden, Cotswolds 2604
St Boniface Down, Isle of Wight 2605
Chamberlain Square, Birmingham 2606
British Journey: Northern Ireland
Ely Island, Lower Lough Erne 2439
Giant's Causeway, Antrim Coast 2440
Slemish, Antrim Mountains 2441
Banns Road, Mourne Mountains 2442
Glenelly Valley, Sperrins 2443
Islandmore, Strangford Lough 2444
British Journey: Scotland
Loch Assynt, Sutherland 2385
Ben More, Isle of Mull 2386, 2391
Rothiemurchus, Cairngorms 2387
Dalveen Pass, Lowther Hills 2388
Glenfinnan Viaduct, Lochaber 2389
Papa Little, Shetland Islands 2390
British Journey: South West England
Old Harry Rocks, Studland Bay 2512
Wheal Coates, St Agnes 2513
Start Point, Start Bay 2514
Horton Down, Wiltshire 2515
Chiselcombe, Exmoor 2516
St James's Stone, Lundy 2517
British Journey: Wales
Barmouth Bridge 2466
Hyddgen Plynlimon 2467, 2472
Brecon Beacons 2468
Pen-pych, Rhondda Valley 2469
Rhewl, Dee Valley 2470
Marloes Sands 2471
British Land Speed record holders
Sir Malcolm Campbell (*Bluebird*) 2059
Sir Henry Segrave (*Sunbeam*) 2060
John G Parry Thomas (*Babs*) 2061
John R Cobb (*Railton Mobil Special*) 2062
Donald Campbell (*Bluebird CN7*) 2063
British Legion, 50th anniversary 887
British motor cars
Austin Seven and Metro 1198
Ford Model T and Escort 1199
Jaguar SS 1 and XJ6 1200
Rolls-Royce Silver Ghost and Silver Spirit 1201
British Museum, 250th anniversary
Coffin of Denytenamun, Egyptian 2404
Alexander the Great, Greek 2405
Sutton Hoo Helmet, Anglo-Saxon 2406
Sculpture of Parvati, South Indian 2407
Mask of Xiuhtecuhtli, Mixtec-Aztec 2408
Hoa Hakananai'a, Easter Island 2409
British Philatelic Bureau, Edinburgh 1495
British piers MS3641
British printing, 500th anniversary
The Canterbury Tales (woodcut) 1014
The Tretyse of Love (extract) 1015
The Game and Playe of Chesse (woodcut) 1016
Early printing press 1017
British pub signs
The Station 2392
Black Swan 2393
The Cross Keys 2394
The Mayflower 2395
The Barley Sheaf 2396
British Rail Inter-City Service HST 987
British Red Cross, 125th anniversary 1874
British river fish
Salmon (*Salmo salar*) 1207
Pike (*Esox lucius*) 1208
Trout (*Salmo trutta*) 1209
Perch (*Perca fluviatilis*) 1210
British textiles
Strawberry Thief (William Morris) 1192
Untitled (Steiner & Co) 1193
Cherry Orchard (Paul Nash) 1194
Chevron (Andrew Foster) 1195
British theatre
Ballerina 1183
Harlequin 1184
Hamlet (Shakespeare) 1185
Opera singer 1186
British trees 922, 949
British wildlife
Hedgehog (*Erinaceus europaeus*) 1039
Hare (*Lepus capensis*) 1040
Red Squirrel (*Sciurus vulgaris*) 1041
Otter (*Lutra lutra*) 1042
Badger (*Meles meles*) 1043
Britons of Distinction
Sir Basil Spence (architect) 3273
Frederick Delius (music composer) 3274
Mary 'May' Morris (textile designer) 3275
Odette Hallowes (SOE agent) 3276
Thomas Newcomen
(steam engine inventor) 3277
Kathleen Ferrier (opera singer) 3278
Augustus Pugin (Gothic architect) 3279
Montagu Rhodes James (author) 3280
Alan Turing (computer scientist) 3281
Joan Mary Fry
(campaigner for social reform) 3282
Brittain, Vera (feminist and pacifist) 3839
Britten, Benjamin (composer) 3459
Broads 4473
Broadstairs, Kent 2269
Brontë, Charlotte (authoress) 1125, 2518
Brontë, Charlotte, 150th death anniversary
Mr Rochester 2518
Come to Me 2519
In the Comfort of her Bonnet 2520
La Ligne des Rats 2521
Refectory 2522
Inspection 2523
Brontë, Emily (authoress) 1127
Brooks, Ernest (photographer) 3715
Bouguereau, William-Adolphe (painter) 3547
Brosnan, Pierce 4333
Brown, Capability (landscape architect) 3869
Brunel, Isambard Kingdom, birth bicentenary
Royal Albert Bridge, Plymouth-Saltash 2607
Box Tunnel 2608
Paddington Station 2609
PSS *Great Eastern* (paddle-steamer) 2610, 2614
Clifton Suspension Bridge design 2611
Maidenhead Bridge 2612
Buckingham Palace 1120, 3589, MS3601
Buckingham Palace, 1846–2014 3589-3591
Buckingham House, 1700–819 3592-3594
Grand Staircase 3595, 3598
Throne Room 3596, 3597
Blue Drawing Room 3599
Green Drawing Room 3600
Building project, Sri Lanka 1265
Bumble Bee (*Bombus terrestris*) 1277
Buoys 1289
Burne-Jones, Edward (artist and designer) 3186
Burnham, Michael (*Star Trek Discovery*) 4453
Burning the Clocks, Brighton 4239
Burns, Robert, death bicentenary
Opening lines of *To a Mouse* 1901
O my Luve's like a red, red rose 1902
Scots, wha hae wi Wallace bled 1903
Auld Lang Syne 1904
Busby, Sir Matt (footballer and manager) 2973
Buses 2210, 2896
Buses, 150th anniversary of
first double-decker 2210
Bush-cricket (*Decticus verrucivorus*) 1279
Bush House, Bristol 1247
Butler, Josephine (social reformer) 3815
Butterflies
Small Tortoiseshell (*Aglais urticae*) 1151
Large Blue (*Maculinea arion*) 1152
Peacock (*Aglais io*) 1153
Chequered Skipper
(*Carterocephalus palaemon*) 1154
Comma (*Polygonia c-album*) 3499, 3510
Orange-tip (*Anthocharis cardamines*) 3500
Small Copper (*Lycaena phlaeas*) 3501
Chalkhill Blue (*Polyommatus coridon*) 3502
Swallowtail (*Papilio machaon*) 3503
Purple Emperor (*Apatura iris*) 3504
Marsh Fritillary (*Euphydryas aurinia*) 3505
Brimstone (*Gonepteryx rhamni*) 3506
Red Admiral (*Vanessa atalanta*) 3507
Marbled White (*Melanargia galathea*) 3508
Buzzard 4203
Byron, Lord 4354

C-3PO (Star Wars) 4013
Caernarvon Castle 1056
Caerphilly Castle (railway loco) 986
Calrissian, Lando (*Star Trek*) 4293
Camm, Sir Sydney (aircraft designer) 1988
Campbell, Donald 2977
Campbell, Sir Malcolm,
50th death anniversary 2059
Canals
Grand Junction Canal, *Midland Maid* 1775
Stainforth and Keadby Canal,
Yorkshire Lass 1776
Brecknock and Abergavenny Canal,
Valley Princess 1777
Crinan Canal, *Pride of Scotland* 1778
Captain Cook and the *Endeavour* Voyage
Joseph Banks, Red-tailed Tropicbird and
Red Passion Flower 4118
Chief Mourner of Tahiti and a Scene with
a Canoe 4119
Captain James Cook and *Triumph of*
the Navigators 4120
Drawings of the Observations of a Transit
of Venus 4121
Scarlet Clianthus, and Portrait of a Maori
Chief 4122
Blue-Black Grassquit and Self-Portrait
of Sydney Parkinson 4123
Carnival, Notting Hill 2055
Carnoustie: 'Luckyslap' (golf) 1831
Carol singers 1071
Carols 943, 1202
Carr, Thomas James (painter) 882
Carriage Horse 1989, 3567
Carrick-a-Rede 3232
Carroll, Lewis (Author) 1094, 2054, 2594
Carry On and Hammer Horror Films
Carry On Sergeant 2849
Dracula 2850
Carry On Cleo 2851
The Curse of Frankenstein 2852
Carry On Screaming 2853
The Mummy 2854
Carter, George (aircraft designer) 1987
Carwardine, George (Anglepoise lamp) 2890
Casino Royale 4332
Castell Y Waun (Chirk Castle), Clwyd
(painting) 1810
Castles Definitives, 50th anniversary MS2530
Cathedrals
Lichfield Cathedral 2841
Belfast Cathedral 2842
Gloucester Cathedral 2843
St David's Cathedral, Haverfordwest 2844
Westminster Cathedral 2845
St Magnus Cathedral, Kirkwall, Orkney 2846
Catherine Morland (*Northanger Abbey*) 989
Catherine of Aragon (painting) 1966
Cats 1848, 3036
Sophie (black cat) 1848
Puskas (Siamese) and Tigger (tabby) 1849
Chloe (ginger cat) 1850
Kikko (tortoiseshell) and Rosie
(Abyssian) 1851
Fred (black and white cat) 1852
Cats and Dogs 2187, 3036
Cat's Eye Nebula 4323
Cattle 1240, 2505
Cavalier and Horse 2112
Caxton, William 1014
Centre for Life, Newcastle 2169
CEPT, 25th anniversary 1249
CERAMICA Museum, Stoke-on-Trent 2142
Cereal products 1431
Chadwick, Roy (aircraft design engineer) 1985
Chancellor Gorkon
(*Star Trek: The Undiscovered Country*) MS4455
Changing tastes in Britain
African woman eating Rice 2555
Indian woman drinking tea 2556
Boy eating sushi 2557
Woman eating pasta 2558
Woman eating chips 2559
Young man eating Apple 2560
Channel Tunnel, opening 1820
Chaplin, Charlie (film star) 1300, 2095
Charity issue 970
Charles I 3088
Charles II 3089
Charlotte Square, Edinburgh 975
Cheddleton Flint Mill 3970
Cheese Rolling, Cooper's Hill, Brockworth,
Gloucestershire 4243

COMMEMORATIVE / MINIATURE SHEET DESIGN INDEX

Chewbacca (*Star Wars*) 4008, 4016
Children's Christmas designs 3550, 4028
Children's fantasy novels
The Hobbit (J. R. R. Tolkein) 2050
The Lion, The Witch and the Wardrobe (C. S. Lewis) 2051
The Phoenix and the Carpet (E. Nesbit) 2052
The Borrowers (Mary Norton) 2053
Through the Looking Glass (Lewis Carroll) 2054
Children's paintings 1170, 1629, 3550, 4028
Children's Television, 50th anniversary
Muffin the Mule 1940
Sooty 1941
Stingray 1942
The Clangers 1943
Dangermouse 1944
Children's Toys and board games 1436
Chillingham Wild Bull 1241
Chisholm, Marie (nurse) 3985
Christie, Agatha 40th death anniversary
Murder on the Orient Express 3885
And Then There Were None 3886
The Mysterious Affair at Styles 3887
The Murder of Roger Ackroyd 3888
The Body in the Library 3889
A Murder is Announced 3890
Christmas
1971. Stained glass windows 894
1972. Angels 913
1973. Scenes depicting carol *Good King Wenceslas* 943
1974. Church roof bosses 966
1975. Angels 993
1976. English Medievel Embroideries 1018
1977. *The Twelve Days of Christmas* 1044
1978. Carol singers 1071
1979. Scenes depicting the Nativity 1104
1980. Christmas decorations 1138
1981. Children's paintings 1170
1982. Carols 1202
1983. Abstract scenes, with Birds 1231
1984. Scenes depicting the Nativity 1267
1985. Pantomime characters 1303
1986. Christmas legends 1341
1987. A Child's Christmas Day 1375
1988. Christmas cards 1414
1989. Ely Cathedral, 800th anniversary 1462
1990. Christmas scenes 1526
1991. Bodleian Library, Oxford Illuminated manuscripts 1582
1992. Stained glass windows 1634
1993. *A Christmas Carol* by Charles Dickens 150th anniversary 1790
1994. Children's Nativity plays 1843
1995. Christmas Robins 1896
1996. Biblical scenes 1950
1997. Christmas cracker,150th anniversary 2006
1998. Angels 2064
1999. Christians' tale 2115
2000. Spirit and faith 2170
2001. Robins 2238
2002. Christmas plants 2321
2003. Christmas ice sculptures 2410
2004. Father Christmas 2495
2005. Madonna and Child paintings 2582
2006. Christmas scenes 2678
2007. Paintings of Madonna and Child 2787
2007. Angels (*2nd issue*) 2789
2008. Pantomime characters 2876
2009. Stained glass windows 2991, 3186*a*
2010. Wallace and Gromit 3128
2011. *King James Bible*, 400th anniversary 3242
2012. Illustrations by Axel Scheffler 3415
2013. Madonna and Child paintings 3542
2014. Illustrations by Andrew Bannecker 3650
2015. Nativity scenes painted by David Holmes 3771
2016. Traditional images 3903
2017. Madonna and Child 4019
2018. Post Boxes 4154
2019. Nativity 4283
2020. Stained glass Windows 4434
Christmas plants
Blue Spruce Star (*Cupressaceae*) 2321
Holly (*Ilex aquifolium*) 2322
Ivy (*Hedera helix*) 2323
Misletoe (*Viscum album*) 2324
Pine cone 2325
Church bells 2174
Church Floodlighting Trust 2171
Churches 904
Churchill, Sir Winston (Prime Minister) 962, 2640, 3074, 3645
Cinema, centenary
Odeon, Harrogate 1920
Lady Hamilton (film) 1921
Old cinema ticket 1922
Pathé News 1923
Odeon, Machester 1924
Circus
Equestrienne 2279
Krazy Kar 2278
Lion Tamer 2276
Slack Wire Act 2275
Trick Tricyclists 2277
City of London, finance centre 2091
Civil Rights 2874
Clare, John 4345
Clark, Jim (racing driver) 2746
Classic Children's TV
Andy Pandy 3552
Ivor the Engine 3553
Dougal (*The Magic Roundabout*) 3554
Windy Miller (*Camberwick Green*) 3555
Mr Benn 3556
Great Uncle Bulgaria (*The Wombles*) 3557
Bagpuss 3558
Paddington Bear 3559
Postman Pat 3560
Bob the Builder 3561
Peppa Pig 3562
Shaun the Sheep 3563
Classic GPO Posters MS3801
Quickest way by air mail 3802
Address your letters plainly 3803
Stamps in books save time 3804
pack your parcels carefully 3805
Classic Locomotives
Dolgoch 0-4-0T 2417
CR Class 439 0-4-4T 2418
GCR Class 8K 2-8-0 2419
GWR Manor Class *Bradley Manor* 4-6-0 2420
SR West Country Class *Blackmoor Vale* 2421
BR Standard Class 2-6-4T 2422
Classic Locomotives of England
BR Dean Goods No. 2532 MS3144, 3215
Peckett R2 *Thor* MS3144
Lancashire & Yorkshire R 1093 No. 1100 MS3144
BR WD No. 90662 MS3144
Classic Locomotives of Northern Ireland MS3498
UTA W No. 103 *Thomas Somerset* 3497, 3572
UTA SG3 No. 35 3576
Classic Locomotives of Scotland
BR D34 Nos. 62471 & 62496 MS3283, 3407, 3571
BR D40 No. 62276 *Andrew Bain* MS3283, 3575
Andrew Barclay No. 807 *Bon Accord* MS3283
BR 4P No. 54767 *Clan Mackinnon* MS3283
Classic Locomotives of the United Kingdom
BR Dean Goods No. 2532 MS3144, 3215, 3570
BR D34 Nos. 62471 & 62496 MS3283, 3407, 3571
UTA W No. 103 *Thomas Somerset* 3497, 3572
LMS No. 7720 3573, MS3578, 3634
Peckett R2 *Thor* MS3144, 3574
BR D40 No. 62276 *Andrew Bain* MS3283, 3575
UTA SG3 No. 35 3576
Classic Locomotives of Wales MS3578, 3634
Hunslet No. 589 *Blanche* 3577, MS3578
LMS No. 7720 3573, MS3578, 3634
Classic Sports Cars
Triumph TR3 1945
MG TD 1946
Austin-Healey 100 1947
Jaguar XK120 1948
Morgan Plus 4 1949
Classic toys
The Merrythought Bear 3989
Sindy Weekender Doll 3990
Spirograph 3991
Stickle Bricks Super Set House 3992
Herald Trojan Warriors 3993
Spacehopper 3994
Fuzzy-Felt Farm Set 3995
Meccano Ferris Wheel 3996
Action Man Red Devil Parachutist 3997
Hornby Dublo Electric Train and TPO Mail Van 3998
Classic transport toys
Meccano, Constructor biplane 2397, 2403
Wells-Brimtoy, clockwork omnibus 2398
Hornby, M1 clockwork locomotive 2399
Dinky Toys, Ford Zephyr 2400
Mettoy, space ship *Eagle* 2401
Coal–modern pithead production platform 1051
Coastguard, 150th anniversary 902
Coccinelle (painting) 2447
Cockle-dredging from *Linsay II* 1166
Coed y Brenin 4250
Coldplay (Rock band) 3000
Coleridge, Samuel Taylor 4346
College of Arms, 500th anniversary 1236
Columbus, discovery of America 500th anniversary 1617
Comedians
Tommy Cooper 2041
Eric Morecambe 2042
Joyce Grenfell 2043
Les Dawson 2044
Peter Cook 2045
Comedy Greats
Spike Milligan 3697
The Two Ronnies 3698
Billy Connolly 3699
Morecambe and Wise 3700
Norman Wisdom 3701
Lenny Henry 3702
Peter Cook and Dudley Moore 3703
Monty Python 3704
French and Saunders 3705
Victoria Wood 3706
Comet 67P 4329
Comet orbiting Sun and planets 1315
Comics
The Dandy and Desperate Dan 3284
The Beano and Dennis the Menace 3285
Eagle and Dan Dare 3286
The Topper and Beryl the Peril 3287
Tiger and Roy of the Rovers 3288
Bunty and the Four Marys 3289
Buster and cartoon character Buster 3290
Valiant and the Steel Claw 3291
Twinkle and Nurse Nancy 3292
2000 AD and Judge Dredd 3293
Commercial Street development, Perth 1248
Common Carder Bee (*Bombus pascuorum*) 4428
Common Dormouse (*Muscardinus avellanarius*) 2015
Commonwealth Day 1211
Commonwealth Games, Brisbane, 1982 3326A
Commonwealth Games, Edinburgh, 1986
Athletics 1328
Rowing 1329
Weightlifting 1330
Shooting 1331
Hockey 1332
Commonwealth Games, Glasgow, 2014
Judo 3619
Swimming 3620
Marathon 3621
Squash 3622
Netball 3623
Para-athlete cycling 3624
Commonwealth Games, Manchester, 2002
Swimming 2299
Running 2300
Cycling 2301
Long jump 2302
Wheelchair Racing 2303
Commonwealth Heads of Government Meeting, 1977 1038
Commonwealth Parliamentary Conference, 19th 939
Commonwealth Parliamentary Association Conference, 32nd 1335
Communications satellite and dish aerials 1288
Computed tomography 3120
Computer science 1547, 2072
Conan Doyle, Sir Arthur (author) 2976
Concorde (BAC/Aérospatiale) 2285, 2891, 2897
Connery, Sean 4337
Connolly, Billy (comedian) 3699
Contemporary Art
Family Group (Henry Moore) 1767
Kew Gardens (Edward Bawden) 1768
St Francis and the Birds (Stanley Spencer) 1769
Still Life: Odyssey (Ben Nicholson) 1770
Conwy, sand-spit 2274
Cook, Captain James, voyages 2076, 4118
Cook, Peter (comedian) 3703
Cooper, Tommy (comedian) 2041
Corbett, Ronnie (comedian) 3698
Coronation, 25th anniversary 1059
Coronation, 50th anniversary 2368
Coronation, 60th anniversary (paintings)
Preliminary essay by Terence Cuneo, 1953 3491
Portrait by Nicky Philipps, 2012 3492
Portrait by Andrew Festing, 2012 3493

COMMEMORATIVE / MINIATURE SHEET DESIGN INDEX

Portrait by Pietro Annigoni, 1955 ... 3494
Portrait by Sergei Pavlenko, 2000 ... 3495
Portrait by Richard Stone, 1992 ... 3496
Coronation Street
'That woman's tongue...' ... 4369
'Woman, Stanley, woman' ... 4370
'Vera, my little swamp duck' ... 4371, 4378
'Ken! Do something!' ... 4372, 4379
'I can't abide to...' ... 4373
'Be nice if every day...' ... 4374
'I love you...' ... 4375
'I always thought ...' ... 4376
Couch, Jonathan (naturalist) ... 1380
Count Dooku (*Star Trek*) ... 4292
County Cricket, centenary ... 928
Court Masque Costumes ... 935
Court Masque Stage Scene ... 938
Coventry Cathedral ... 3273
Cowes Week (sailing) ... 1836
CR Class 439 (railway loco) ... 2418
Craddock, Alfie ... 4646
Craig, Daniel ... 4332
Cricket ... 1137
Crimean War, 150th anniversary
Private McNamara, 5th Dragoon Guards ... 2489
Piper Muir, 42nd Regiment of Foot ... 2490
Sgt Major Edwards, Scots Fusilier Guards ... 2491
Sgt Powell, 1st Regiment of Foot Guards ... 2492
Sgt Major Poole, Royal Sappers ... 2493
Sgt Glasgow, Royal Artillery ... 2494
Crown Jewels
Sovereign's Sceptre with Cross ... 3207
St Edward's Crown ... 3208
Rod and Sceptre with Doves ... 3209
Queen Mary's Crown ... 3210
Sovereign's Orb ... 3211
Jewelled Sword of Offering ... 3212
Imperial State Crown ... 3213
Coronation Spoon ... 3214
Crowned Lion with Shield of St George ... 2291, MS2740
Cuckoo ... 3956
Cuneo, Terence (painter) ... 1272, 3491
Cunningham, Viscount and HMS *Warspite* ... 1191
Curious Customs
Burning the Clocks, Brighton ... 4239
'Obby 'Oss, Padstow, Cornwall ... 4240
World Gurning Championships, Egremont, Cumbria ... 4241
Up Helly Aa, Lerwick, Shetland ... 4242
Cheese Rolling, Cooper's Hill, Brockworth, Gloucestershire ... 4243
Halloween, Londonderry ... 4244
Horn Dance, Abbots Bromley, Staffordshire ... 4245
Bog Snorkelling, Llanwrtyd Wells, Wales ... 4246
Cushing, Peter (actor) ... 3455
Cycle Network artworks ... 2144
Cycling ... 2301, 3101, 3108b, 3624
Cyclists 'Touring Club, centenary
Penny farthing and 1884 safety bicycle ... 1067
1920 touring bicycles ... 1068
Modern small-wheel bicycles ... 1069
1978 road-racers ... 1070
Cygnus A Galaxy ... 4330

D-Day, 50th anniversary ... 1824
D-Day, 75th anniversary
No. 4 Commando, 1st Special Service Brigade briefed by Commanding Officer Lt-Col R. Dawson before Embarkation ... 4230
HMS *Warspite* shelling German Gun Batteries in support of Landings on Sword Beach ... 4231
Paratroopers of British 6th Airborne Division synchronising Watches before take-off, 5 June 1944 ... 4232
Commandos of HQ 4th Special Service Brigade wade ashore on Juno Beach ... 4233
American A-20 Havoc Light Bomber ... 4234
East Yorkshire Regiment Troops take cover from Enemy Shell, 19 July 1944 ... 4235
Da Vinci, Leonardo, 500th death anniversary
The Skull Sectioned ... 4170
A Sprig of Guelder-Rose ... 4171
Studies of Cats ... 4172
A Star-of-Bethlehem and Other Plants ... 4173
The Anatomy of the Shoulder and Foot ... 4174
The Head of Leda ... 4175
The Head of a Bearded Man ... 4176
The Skeleton ... 4177
The Head of St Philip ... 4178
A Woman in a Landscape ... 4179
A Design for an Equestrian Monument ... 4180
The Fall of Light on a Face ... 4181
Dad's Army (TV programme), 50th Anniversary
Sergeant Wilson (John Le Mesurier) ('Do you think that's wise, sir?') ... 4099
Private Pike (Ian Lavender) ('I'll tell Mum!') ... 4100
Captain Mainwaring (Arthur Lowe) ('You stupid boy!') ... 4101, 4107
Lance Corporal Jones (Clive Dunn) ('Don't panic! Don't panic!') ... 4102, 4108
Private Walker (James Beck) ('It won't cost you much...') ... 4103
Private Frazer (John Laurie) ('We're doomed. Doomed!') ... 4104
Private Godfrey (Arnold Ridley) ('Do you think I might be excused?') ... 4105
Chief Warden Hodges (Bill Pertwee) ('Put that light out!') ... 4106
Dahl, Roald, children's stories
Charlie and the Chocolate Factory ... 3254
Fantastic Mr. Fox ... 3255
James and the Giant Peach ... 3256
Matilda ... 3257
The Twits ... 3258
The Witches ... 3259
The BFG carrying Sophie in his Hand ... 3260
The BFG wakes up the Giants ... 3261
Sophie sitting on Buckingham Palace window-sill ... 3262
The BFG and Sophie at Writing Desk ... 3263
Dairy products ... 1430
Daisies (*Bellis perennis*) ... 2150
Dalek from *Dr Who* TV programme ... 2094
Dalton, Timothy ... 4334
Dameron, Poe (*Star Wars*) ... 4300
Dangermouse (childrens TV) ... 1944
Darth Maul (*Star Wars*) ... 4297
Dartmoor ... 4464
Darwin, Charles (naturalist) ... 1175, 2649, 2898
Darwin, Charles (naturalist), birth bicentenary
Charles Darwin ... 2898
Marine Iguana (*Amblyrhynchus cristatus*) ... 2899
Finches (*Fringillidae*) ... 2900
Atoll ... 2901
Bee Orchid (*Ophrys apifera*) ... 2902
Orangutan (*Pongo abelii*) ... 2903
Darwin's Theory of evolution ... 2103
David, Elizabeth (cookery writer) ... 3457
David, Gerard (painter) ... 4019
David, Jacques-Louis (painter) ... 3545
Day, Robin (polypropylene chair designer) ... 2893
de Havilland DH9A ... 1338
de Havilland Mosquito ... 1340
de Havilland Mosquito B XVI ... 1986
de Morgan, William (tile designer) ... 3185
Del Boy ... 4486
Deacon, J. ... 4401
Dean, Dixie (footballer) ... 1925
Dead Man's Dump ... 3984
Dearle, John Henry (textile designer) ... 3183
Death of King Arthur ... 4501
Declaration of Arbroath, 700th anniversary ... MS180
Delius, Frederick (music composer) ... 3274
Delivery driver ... 4648
Demobilised servicemen, 1945 ... 4361
Derby, bicentenary ... 1087
Dersingham, Norfolk (painting) ... 1813
Derwentwater, England ... 1156
Devil's Bolete (*Rubroboletus satanas*) ... 2020
Diamond Jubilee, Queen Elizabeth II ... U3271 MS3272, A3319, 3327
Diana, Princess of Wales commemoration ... 2021
Dickens, Charles
A Christmas Carol, 150th anniversary
Bob Cratchit and Tiny Tim ... 1790
Mr and Mrs Fezziwig ... 1791
Scrooge ... 1792
The prize Turkey ... 1793
Mr Scrooge's nephew ... 1794
Dickens, Charles, birth bicentenary)
Mr Bumble (*Oliver Twist*) ... 3330
Mr Pickwick (*The Pickwick Papers*) ... 3331
The Marchioness (*The Old Curiosity Shop*) ... 3332
Mrs Gamp (*Martin Chuzzlewit*) ... 3333
Captain Cuttle (*Dombey and Son*) ... 3334
Mr Micawber (*David Copperfield*) ... 3335
Dighton, Denis (artist) ... 3724
Dimbleby, Richard (journalist) ... 3462
Dinosaurs
Iguanodon ... 1573
Stegosaurus ... 1574
Tyrannosaurus ... 1575
Protoceratops ... 1576
Triceratops ... 1577
Polacanthus ... 3532
Ichthyosaurus ... 3533
Iguanodon ... 3534
Ornithocheirus ... 3535
Baryonyx ... 3536
Dimorphodon ... 3537
Hypsilophodon ... 3538
Cetiosaurus ... 3539
Megalosaurus ... 3540
Plesiosaurus ... 3541
Dinosaurs' identification by Richard Owen, 150th anniversary ... 1573
Dipper (*Cinclus cinclus*) ... 1110
Disabled artist with foot painting ... 1150
Disabled man in wheelchair ... 1149
Diving ... 1566
Dizzy (video game), 1987 ... 4318
DNA, 50th anniversary of discovery ... 2343
DNA decoding ... 2102
DNA sequencing ... 3685
Doctors, nurses ... 4650
Dogs ... 1075, 1531, 2187, 2506, 2806, 3036
Doire Dach forest, Scotland ... 2159
Dolwyddelan, Gwynedd (painting) ... 1814
Domesday Book, 900th anniversary ... 1324
'Don't worry he's housetrained...' ... 4478
Dover cliffs, Kent ... 2267
Dover Lighthouse ... 4380
Dowding, Lord and Hawker Hurricane ... 1336
Downhill skiing ... 1389
Downing Street, London ... 3233
Doyle, Sir Arthur Conan (writer) ... 1784
Dr Who, 50th anniversary
11th Doctor (Matt Smith) ... 3437
Tenth Doctor (David Tennant) ... 3438
Ninth Doctor (Christopher Eccleston) ... 3439
Eighth Doctor (Paul McGann) ... 3440
Seventh Doctor (Sylvester McCoy) ... 3441
Sixth Doctor (Colin Baker) ... 3442
Fifth Doctor (Peter Davison) ... 3443
Fourth Doctor (Tom Baker) ... 3444
Third Doctor (Jon Pertwee) ... 3445
Second Doctor (Patrick Troughton) ... 3446
First Doctor (William Hartnell) ... 3447
TARDIS (Time And Relative Dimension In Space) ... 3448
Drake, Sir Francis (explorer) ... 925, MS2930
Dry Docked for Sealing and Painting ... 3986
du Maurier, Dame Daphne (novelist) ... 1938
Duckling ... 1481
Duke of Edinburgh Award Scheme 25th anniversary
Expeditions ... 1162
Skills ... 1163
Service ... 1164
Recreation ... 1165
Duke of Edinburgh's Horse ... 1992
Dunster beach, Somerset ... 2271
Dyce, William (artist) ... 2787, 4020
Dynamic Earth Centre, Edinburgh ... 2131

Earls Barton, Northants ... 905
Earth Centre, Doncaster ... 2140
Earth, view from *Apollo 11* ... 1254
Ecos Centre Nature Park, Ballymena ... 2138
Eden Project, St Austell ... 2157, 3979, 3979
Edinburgh Castle ... 3234
Edinburgh Mail snowbound, 1831 ... 1262
Edward IV ... 2815
Edward V ... 2816
Edward VI ... 2926
Edward VII ... 3265
Edward VIII ... 3267
Edwards, Duncan (footballer) ... 1927
Electricity–nuclear power station ... 1053
Elephant Hawk-moth (*Deilephila elpenor*) ... 4431
Eliot, George (authoress) ... 1126
Elite (video game), 1984 ... 4312
Elizabeth I ... 2929
Elizabeth II (paintings) ... 3269, 3491
Elton John
Honky Château ... 4253
Goodbye Yellow Brick Road ... 4254
Caribou ... 4255
Captain Fantastic and The Brown Dirt Cowboy ... 4256
Sleeping with The Past ... 4257

COMMEMORATIVE / MINIATURE SHEET DESIGN INDEX

The One....4258
Made in England....4259
Songs from The West Coast....4260
Emin, Tracey....4098
Eminent Britons
Fred Perry (lawn tennis champion)....2971
Henry Purcell (composer and musician)....2972
Sir Matt Busby (footballer and manager)....2973
William Gladstone (Prime Minister)....2974
Mary Wollstonecraft (pioneering feminist)....2975
Sir Arthur Conan Doyle (author)....2976
Donald Campbell....2977
Judy Fryd (campaigner)....2978
Samuel Johnson (lexicographer)....2979
Sir Martin Ryle (scientist)....2980
Emma and Mr Woodhouse (*Emma*)....990
Emperor dragonfly (*Anax imperator*)....1281
Enceladus....4324
Endangered Species
Common Dormouse (*Muscardinus avellanarius*)....2015
Lady's Dlipper Orchid (*Cypripedium calceolus*)....2016
Song Thrush (*Turdus philomelos*)....2017
Shining Ram's-horn Snail (*Segmentina nitida*)....2018
Mole Cricket (*Gryllotalpa gryllotalpa*)....2019
Devil's Bolete (*Rubroboletus satanas*)....2020
Endurance Expedition....3787
Energy resources
Oil–North Sea....1050
Coal–modern pithead production platform....1051
Natural Gas–flame rising from sea....1052
Electricity–nuclear power station....1053
Engineering Achievements
Humber Bridge....1215
Thames Flood Barrier....1216
Iolair (oilfield emergency support vessel)....1217
England-Australia Test Match, centenary....1137
English Channel, navigational chart....1255
English Civil War....2112
English Civil War, 350th anniversary
Pikeman....1620
Drummer....1621
Musketeer....1622
Standard bearer....1623
English Medieval embroidery
Virgin and Child....1018
Angel with Crown....1019
Angel appearing to shepherds....1020
The Three Kings....1021
Entente Cordiale, centenary....2446
Environment, protection. Children's paintings
Acid Rain Kills....1629
Ozone Layer....1630
Greenhouse Effect....1631
Bird of Hope....1632
Equal Pay Act....2875
Equestrian....2987
Essay of Coinage Head cropped and simplified, with only the denomination, October 1966....3961
Essay of the first plaster cast of the Diadem Head, without corsage, October 1966....3963
Essay with Coinage Head surrounded by Country symbols, April/May 1966....3960
Eurasian Beaver....4076
Europa (showing logo)
1993. Contemporary Art....1767
1994. Medical Discoveries....1839
1995. Peace and Freedom....1876/77
1996. Famous Women....1936/37
1997. Tales and Legends. Horror Stories....1980/81
1998. Festivals. Notting Hill Carnival....2055/56
1999. The Farmers' Tale....2107
2001. Pond Life....2220/21
2002. Circus....2276/77
2003. British Pub Signs....2392/93
2004. A British Journey: Wales....2467/68
2005. Gastronomy. Changing Tastes in Britain....2556/57
2006. Integration. Sounds of Britain....2667, 2669
2007. Centenary of Scouting and 21st World Scout Jamboree....2758/2760
2008. Working Dogs....2806
2009. Eminent Britons....2980
2010. Children's Books. *Winnie the Pooh* by A. A. Milne (1st)....3121
2011. 50th anniversary of the WWF (1st)....MS3172
2012. UK A-Z (2nd series)....3303
2013. Royal Mail Transport: By Land and Sea (1st)....3530
2014. Seaside Architecture (1st)....3635
Europa (showing symbol):
1982. British Theatre....1183
1983. Engineering Achievements....1215
1984. 25th anniversary of CEPT....1249
1985. European Music Year. British Composers....1282
1986. Nature Conservation–Endangered Species....1320
1987. British Architects in Europe....1355
1988. Transport and Mail Services in the 1930s....1392
1989. Games and Toys....1436
1990. Stamp World London 90 exhibition, British Philatelic Bureau....1493, 1495
1991. Europe in Space....1560
1992. International Events....1617/1618
Europe in Space....1560
European Architectural Heritage Year....975
European Assembly Elections, first direct....1083
European City of Culture, Glasgow, 1990....1494
European Communities....919
European Football Championship....1925
European Parliament, second Elections....1250
European Parliament, third direct Elections....1433
Evacuees return home, 1945....4359
Everyman Theatre, Liverpool....1380
Exeter Mail, attack on 1816....1259
Expo '92, Seville (British pavillion)....1619
Extreme Endeavours (British Explorers)....2360
Eye....2175

Face Paintings, children's
Nurture Children (Flower)....2178
Listen to Children (Tiger)....2179
Teach Children (Owl)....2180
Ensure Children's Freedom (Butterfly)....2181
FA Cup, 150 Years....4636
Fallow deer....1587
Family Allowance....2873
Family Planning....2872
Famous Authoresses....1125
Famous Women....1935
Faraday, Michael, birth bicentenary....1546
Faraday, Michael, work on electricity....2104
Farm Animals
British Saddleback Pigs....2502
Khaki Campbell Ducks....2503
Clydesdale Mare and foal....2504
Dairy Shorthorn Cattle....2505
Border Collie Dog....2506
Light Sussex Chicks....2507
Suffolk Sheep....2508
Bagot Goat....2509
Norfolk Black Turkeys....2510
Embden Geese....2511
Farman HF III biplane, 1911....955
Fashion
Hardy Amies skirt suit....3309
Norman Hartnell outfit....3310
John Pearce jacket for Granny Takes a Trip (boutique)....3311
Celia Birtwell print for outfit by Ossie Clarke....3312
Tommy Nutter suit for Ringo Starr....3313
Jean Muir outfit....3314
Zandra Rhodes 'Royal' dress....3315
Vivienne Westwood harlequin dress....3316
Paul Smith suit....3317
Alexander McQueen 'Black Raven'....3318
Father Christmas....2006
Faulkner, Kate (artist and designer)....3184
Felin Cochwillan Mill....3972
Fencing....1564, 3201, 3206b
Ferrier, Kathleen (opera singer)....3278
Festing, Andrew (painter)....3493
Fiennes, Ralph (actor) (as Lord Voldemort in Harry Potter)....3157
Films by GPO Film Unit....MS3068
Fire and Rescue services
Firefighting....2958
Chemical fire....2959
Emergency Rescue....2960
Flood Rescue....2961
Search and Rescue....2962
Fire Safety....2963
Fire Engines....950
Fire Prevention (Metropolis) Act, bicentenary....950
First Royal Christmas TV broadcast....A3322
First Cuckoo (Frederick Delius)....1284
First Mail Coach run, Bath and Bristol to London, bicentenary
Bath Mail Coach, 1784....1258
Exeter Mail, attack on 1816....1259
Norwich Mail in thunderstorm, 1827....1260
Holyhead and Liverpool Mails leaving London, 1828....1261
Edinburgh Mail snowbound, 1831....1262
First official airmail, Coronation 1911....955
First United Kingdom Aerial Post Centenary....3216, MS3220
Gustav Hamel....3216
Gustav Hamel in Cockpit....3217
Clement Greswell and Blériot monoplane....3218
Airmail delivered at Windsor....3219
First World War, centenary....3626, 3711, 3838, 3983, 4133
Poppy (Fiona Strickland)....3626, 4139
For the Fallen (Laurence Binyon)....3627
Private William Cecil Tickle, (kia 3 July 1916)....3628
A Star Shell (C. R. W. Nevinson)....3629
The Response (sculpture)....3630
Princess Mary's Gift Box Fund....3631
Poppies (Howard Hodgkin)....3711
All the Hills and Vales Along (C. H. Sorley)....3712
Rifleman Kulbir Thapa, VC (QAOGR)....3713
The Kensingtons at Laventie (Eric Kennington)....3714
A British soldier visits his comrade's grave near Cape Helles, Gallipoli (Ernest Brooks)....3715
London Irish Rifles' football from Loos....3716
Battlefield Poppy (Giles Revell)....3838
Your battle wounds are scars upon my heart (poem by Vera Brittain, *To My Brother*)....3839
Munitions Worker Lottie Meade....3840
Travoys arriving with wounded (Stanley Spencer)....3841
Thiepval Memorial, Somme, France....3842
Captain A. C. Green's Battle of Jutland commemorative medal....3843
Post Office Rifles....3844
Writing a letter from the Western Front....3845
Delivering the mail on the Home Front....3846
Home Depot at Regents Park, London....3847
Shattered Poppy (John Ross)....3983
Dead Man's Dump (Isaac Rosenberg)....3984
Nurses Elsie Knocker and Mairi Chisholm....3985
Dry Docked for Sealing and Painting (Edward Wadsworth)....3986
Tyne Cot Cemetery, Zonnebeke, Ypres Salient Battlefields, Belgium....3987
Private Lemuel Thomas Rees's life-saving Bible....3988
100 Poppies (Zafer and Barbara Baran)....4133, 4139
Anthem for Doomed Youth (poem by Wilfred Owen) (woodblock print by Andrew Davidson)....4134
Second Lieutenant Walter Tull (1888-1918)....4135
We Are Making a New World (Paul Nash)....4136
The Grave of the Unknown Warrior, Westminster Abbey, London....4137
Lieutenant Francis Hopgood's Goggles....4138
Fish....1207, 3609, 3632
Fisher, Lord and HMS *Dreadnought*....1190
Fishing industry....1166
Flags and Ensigns....MS2206, 2208
Flanagan, Terence Philip (painter)....881
Fleming, Ian (Author)....2797
Fleming, Sir Alexander, penicillin discovery....2082, 3116
Flower Paintings....1955, 2463
Flowers
Primrose (*Primula vulgaris*)....1079
Daffodil (*Narcissus pseudonarcissus*)....1080
Bluebell (*Endymion non-scriptus*)....1081
Snowdrop (*Galanthus nivalis*)....1082
Indian Blanket (*Gaillardia pulchella*)....1347
Globe Thistle (*Echinops bannaticus*)....1348
Echeveria....1349
Autumn Crocus (*Colchicum autumnale*)....1350
Flying Ford Anglia....4144
Folklore....1143
Fonteyn, Dame Margot (ballerina)....1936
Food and Farming Year, 1989....1428
Food imports....2109
Football....1391, 2093, 2167, 3104, 3108*a*
Football Heroes
Jimmy Greaves (England)....3463, 3479
John Charles (Wales)....3464, 3477, 3480
Gordon Banks (England)....3465, 3484
George Best, (Northern Ireland)....3466, 3475, 3485
John Barnes (England)....3467, 3486

COMMEMORATIVE / MINIATURE SHEET DESIGN INDEX

Kevin Keegan (England)....3468, 3481
Denis Law (Scotland)....3469, 3482
Bobby Moore (England)....3470, 3476, 3483
Bryan Robson (England)....3471, 3487
Dave Mackay (Scotland)....3472, 3478, 3488
Bobby Charlton (England)....3473, 3489
Football League, centenary....1391
For the Fallen (Laurence Binyon)....3627
Ford (car manufacturer)....1199
'Forest for Scotland' project....2159
Forests
Autumn at Glen Affric, Inverness-shire, Scotland....4247
Autumn in the Acer Glade, The National Arboretum, Westonbirt, Gloucestershire....4248
Sherwood Forest, Nottinghamshire....4249
Coed y Brenin, Gwynedd, Wales....4250
Waterfall in Glenariff, County Antrim, Northern Ireland....4251
Beech in Autumn, Sidwood, Kielder Forest, Northumberland....4252
Forth Railway Bridge....3235
Foster, Andrew (textile designer)....1195
Four Seasons
Winter....1587
Autumn....1779
Summer....1834
Spring....1853
Fox....1589, 2488
Fox-Talbot, Henry, photographic experiments....2071
Franklin, Benjamin (founding father, USA)....1005, 3028
French, Dawn (comedian)....3705
Frink, Dame Elizabeth (sculptress)....1937
Frobisher, Sir Martin (polar explorer)....898
Frost at Midnight (Samuel Taylor Coleridge)....4346
Fruit and Vegetables....1428, 2348
Strawberry....2348
Potato....2349
Apple....2350
Red Pepper....2351
Pear....2352
Orange....2353
Tomato....2354
Lemon....2355
Brussels Sprout....2356
Aubergine....2357
Fruits and leaves
Horse Chestnut (*Aesculus hippocastanum*)....1779
Blackberry (*Rubus fruitcosus*)....1780
Hazel (*Corylus maxima*)....1781
Rowan (*Sorbus aucuparia*)....1782
Pear (*Pyrus communis*)....1783
Fry, Elizabeth (social reformer)....1004
Fry, Joan Mary (campaigner for social reform)....3282
Fryd, Judy (campaigner)....2978
Fuzzy-Felt Farm Set....3995

Galápagos Finch (*Geospizinae*)....2103
Galápagos Islands, fauna and map....MS2904
Gallantry Awards
Victoria Cross....1517, 2666
George Cross....1518
Distinguished Service Cross and Medal....1519
Military Cross and Medal....1520
Distinguished Flying Cross and Medal....1521
Gambon, Michael (actor) (as Dumbledore in Harry Potter)....3156
Game of Thrones (TV programme)
Sansa Stark (Sophie Tucker)....4033
Jon Snow (Kit Harington)....4034
Eddard Stark (Sean Bean)....4035
Olenna Tyrell (Dianna Rigg)....4036
Tywin Lannister (Charles Dance)....4037
Tyrion Lannister (Peter Dinklage)....4038
Cersei Lannister (Lena Headey)....4039
Arya Stark (Maisie Williams)....4040
Jaime Lannister (Nicolaj Coster-Waldau)....4041
Daenerys Targaryen (Emilia Clarke)....4042
The Iron Throne....4044, 4049
The Night King and White Walkers....4045
Giants....4046
Direwolves....4047
Dragons....4048
Game of Thrones non-human characters....MS4043
Games, Abram (graphic designer)....3588
Gannets (*Morus bassanus*)....2128
Garratt Steam Locomotive No 143....2130
Garter Ceremony procession, 1997....3324A
Gaskell, Mrs Elizabeth (authoress)....1128
Gathering Water Lilies' (Peter Henry Emerson photograph)....2163
General Post, c. 1839....1096
Genius of Gerry Anderson (F.A.B.)
Joe 90....3136
Captain Scarlet....3137
Thunderbird 2 (*Thunderbirds*)....3138, 3143
Stingray....3139
Fireball XL5....3140
Supercar....3141
Genome....2343
Gentleman, David....MS4635
Geographical regions
Tropical island....1211
Desert....1212
Temperate farmland....1213
Mountain range....1214
George I....3223
George II....3224
George III....3225
George IV....3226
George V....3266
George V Accession centenary....MS3065, 3066
George VI....3268, 3826
Giant Tortoises and Darwin....1175
Giant's Causeway, Northern Ireland....1158
Giant's Causeway Visitor Centre....3977
Gifford, Colin (photographer)....1795
Gigantipos destructor (Ant)....2162
Gilbert and Sullivan Operas
The Yeoman of the Guard....1624
The Gondoliers....1625
The Mikado....1626
The Pirates of Penzance....1627
Iolanthe....1628
Gilbert Scott, Sir Giles (K2 telephone kiosk)....2892
Giotto spacecraft approaching comet....1313
Girlguiding, centenary....MS3025
Girls' Brigade....1180
Girls Guide movement....1182
Gladstone, William (Prime Minister)....2974, 3646
Glasgow, School of Art....1494
Glasgow tram No.1173....1394
Glastonbury Tor....3236
Glen Affric....4247
Glenarrif Forest....4251
Glenfinnan, Scotland....1155
Gloster Meteor F8....1987
Glyndwr, Owain....959
Goalball....3105
Gold (D-Day)....MS4236
Gold Medal Winners, Olympic Games
Rowing: women's pairs....3342
Cycling: road men's time trial....3343
Canoe slalom: men's canoe double (*C2*)....3344
Shooting: shotgun men's double trap....3345
Cycling: track men's team sprint....3346
Rowing: women's double skulls....3347
Cycling: track men's team pursuit....3348
Cycling: track women's keirin....3349
Rowing: men's fours....3350
Rowing: lightweight women's double skulls....3351
Cycling: track women's team pursuit....3352
Athletics: combined women's heptathlon....3353
Athletics: field men's long jump....3354
Athletics: track men's 10,000 m....3355
Sailing: Finn men's heavyweight dinghy....3356
Tennis: men's singles....3357
Equestrian: jumping team....3358
Cycling: track men's sprint....3359
Men's triathlon....3360
Equestrian: dressage team....3361
Cycling: track women's omnium....3362
Cycling: track men's keirin....3363
Equestrian: dressage individual....3364
Boxing: women's fly weight....3365
Taekwondo: women's under 57 kg....3366
Canoe sprint: men's kayak single (*K1*) 200 m....3367
Athletics: track men's 5000 m....3368
Boxing: men's bantam weight....3369
Boxing: men's super heavy weight....3370
Gold Medal Winners, Paralympic Games
Cycling: track women's C5 pursuit....3372
Swimming: men's 100m backstroke, S7....3373
Cycling: track men's C1 pursuit....3374
Athletics: track women's 100 m, T34....3375
Cycling: track men's B 1 km time trial....3376
Athletics: track men's 200 m, T42....3377
Equestrian: individual championship test, grade III....3378
Cycling: track women's C4-5 500 m time trial....3379
Swimming: women's 400 m freestyle, S6....3380
Rowing: mixed coxed four, LTAmix4+....3381
Athletics: field men's discus, F42....3382
Cycling: track men's B sprint....3383
Swimming: women's 200 m freestyle, S14....3384
Equestrian: individual championship test, grade 1a....3385
Athletics: track men's 5000 m, T54....3386
Equestrian: individual freestyle test, grade II....3387
Swimming: women's 200 m individual medley, SM6....3388
Athletics: track men's 100 m, T53....3389
Archery: women's individual compound open....3390
Swimming: women's 100 m backstroke, S8....3391
Equestrian: individual freestyle test, grade Ia....3392
Athletics: track men's 1500 m, T54....3393
Cycling: road women's C5 time trial....3394
Swimming: men's 200 m individual medley, SM8....3395
Equestrian: team open....3396
Sailing: single-person keelboat, 2.4 mR....3397
Cycling: road women's C4-5 road race....3398
Swimming: men's 400 m freestyle, S7....3399
Athletics: track women's 200 m, T34....3400
Athletics: track men's 800 m, T54....3401
Athletics: track men's 100 m, T44....3402
Athletics: field women's discus, F51/52/53....3403
Cycling: road edmix T1-2 road race....3404
Athletics: road men's marathon, T54....3405
Goldcrest....3951
Golden Eagle....4204
Goldeneye....4333
Golden Jubilee, of Queen's Accession....2253
Golden Lion Tamarin (*Leontopithecus rosalia*)....3171
Goldfinger....4337
Goldswothy, Andy (sculptor)....1853
Golf, Scottish Courses....1829
Gorgon's head, Bath....4386
Gorkon, Chancellor (*Star Trek: The Undiscovered Country*)....MS4455
Goshawk....4206
Grace, W. G. , (cricketer)....928
Grahame, Kenneth (Author)....1092
Granacci, Francesco (painter)....3542
Grandad....4491
Grandpa Dickson (rose)....1007
Grand Prix Racing Cars
Vanwell 2.5L, 1957....2744
BRM P57, 1962....2745
Lotus 25 Climax, 1963....2746
Tyrrell 006/2, 1973....2747
McLaren M23, 1976....2748
Williams FW11, 1986....2749
Granger, Hermione (Harry Potter)....4141, 4152
Gravitational Lensing....4328
Gray, Thomas, death bicentenary....885
Great British Fashion....3309
Great British Films
A Matter of Life and Death (1946)....3602
Lawrence of Arabia (1962)....3603
2001: A Space Odyssey (1968)....3604
Chariots of Fire (1981)....3605
Secrets and Lies (1996)....3606
Bend It Like Beckham (film)....3607
Love on the Wing (film)....MS3608
Spare Time (film)....MS3608
A Colour Box (film)....MS3608
A Night Mail (film)....MS3608
Great British Railways
LMS Coronation Class....3109
BR Class 9F *Evening Star*....3110
GWR King Class *King William IV*....3111
LNER Class A1 *Royal Lancer*....3112
SR King Arthur Class *Sir Mador de la Porte*....3113
LMS NCC Class WT No. 2....3114
Great Britons
Norman Parkinson....3453
Vivien Leigh....3454
Peter Cushing....3455
David Lloyd George....3456
Elizabeth David....3457
John Archer....3458
Benjamin Britten....3459
Mary Leakey....3460
Bill Shankly....3461
Richard Dimbleby....3462
Great Ormond Street Children's Hospital, 150th anniversary....2304
Great Tit....3948
Great Western Railway Castle Class....986

COMMEMORATIVE / MINIATURE SHEET DESIGN INDEX

Greensted-juxta-Ongar, Essex.....904
Greenwich Meridian, centenary.....1254
Greenwich Observatory.....1256
Greetings stamps
1989.....1423
1990, Smiles.....1483
1991, Good Luck.....1536
1991, Smiles.....1550
1992, Memories.....1592
1993, Gift giving.....1644
1994, Messages.....1800
1995, Greetings in Art.....1858
1996, Cartoons.....1905
1997, 19th-century flower paintings.....1955
2001, Occasions.....2182
2002, Occasions.....2260
2003, Occasions.....2337
2004, Occasions.....2424
Grey, Charles (Prime Minister).....3648
Grey, Lady Jane.....2927
Ground Finches and Darwin.....1177
Groundwork's Changing Places project.....2155
Grover, Isabella.....4648
Guinness, Sir Alec (actor).....3584
Gymnastics.....1388, 3202, 3206*a*

Hadrian's Wall.....4387
Hagrid's Motorbike.....4146
Halley, Dr Edmond as comet (cartoon).....1312
Halley's Comet, appearance of.....1312
Halloween, Londonderry.....4244
Hallowes, Odette (SOE agent).....3276
Hamlet (Shakespeare).....1185, 3173, 3816
Hampden Park, Glasgow.....2167
Hampton Court Palace.....1057, 1123, 4109
South Front.....4109
West Front.....4110
East Front.....4111
Pond Gardens.....4112
Maze.....4113
Great Fountain Garden.....4114
Great Hall.....MS4115, 4116
King's Great Bedchamber.....MS4115, 4117
Chapel Royal.....MS4115
King's Staircase.....MS4115
Hamstreet, Kent, OS maps.....1578
Hand spelling in sign language.....1148
Handball.....3204
Handley Page HP45 *Horatius* of Imperial Airways.....1395
Hardy, Thomas, 150th birth anniversary.....1506
Hare (*Lepus capensis*).....1040, 1588
Hargreaves, Roger (author, children's books).....3891
Hargreaves, Rosie (child painter).....3550
Hark the Herald Angels Sing (carol).....2115
Harlech Castle.....3237
Harlequin.....1184
Haroldswick, Shetland.....1997
Harp.....2176
Harrier Jump Jet, 50th Anniversary.....MS4218
Harris, Sir Arthur and Avro Lancaster.....1339
Harrison, John, 300th birth anniversary.....1654
Harrison, John, chronometer.....2069
Harry Potter (films)....3156, 3157, 4141, MS4151, 4164
Hermione Granger.....4141, 4152
Hogwarts Express.....4142
Harry Potter.....4143, 4153
Flying Ford Anglia.....4144
Ron Weasley.....4145
Hagrid's Motorbike.....4146
Ginny Weasley.....4147
Triwizard Cup.....4148
Neville Longbottom.....4149
Knight Bus.....4150
Pomona Sprout.....MS4151, 4164
Horace Slughorn.....MS4151, 4165
Sybill Trelawney.....MS4151, 4166
Remus Lupin.....MS4151, 4167
Severus Snape.....MS4151, 4168
Harry Potter, publication of final book
...and the Philosopher's Stone.....2750
...and the Chamber of Secrets.....2751
...and the Prisoner of Azkaban.....2752
...and the Goblet of Fire.....2753
...and the Order of the Phoenix.....2754
...and the Half-Blood Prince.....2755
...and the Deathly Hallows.....2756
Hartman, Dame Marea (sports administrator)..1939
Hartnell, Norman (fashion designer).....3310
Hauling in trawl net.....1167
Hats, Fashion
Toque Hat, by Pip Hackett.....2216
Butterfly Hat, by Dai Rees.....2217
Top Hat, by Stephen Jones.....2218
Spiral Hat, by Philip Treacy.....22198
Hawker Hurricane.....1336, 4059
Hawker Hunter FGA9.....1988
Hawker Typhoon.....1337
Health and Handicap charities.....970
Heart-regulating beta blockers.....3115, 3153
Hedgehog (*Erinaceus europaeus*)...1039, 3063, 3096
Helpringham, Lincolnshire.....907
Henry IV.....2812
Henry V.....960, 2813
Henry VI.....2814
Henry VI (Shakespeare).....3175
Henry VII.....2924
Henry VIII.....1187, 1965, 2925
Henry VIII, 450th death anniversary.....1965
Henry, Lenny (comedian).....3702
Hepburn, Thomas (social reformer).....1001
Herald Trojan Warriors.....3993
Heraldry.....1236, 1363, 2026
Arms of College of Arms.....1236
Arms of King Richard III.....1237
Arms of Earl Marshal of England.....1238
Arms of the City of London.....1239
Arms of the Lord Lyon King of Arms.....1363
Scottish Heraldic Banner of Prince Charles.....1364
Arms of the Royal Scottish Academy of.....1365
Arms of the Royal Society of Edinburgh.....1366
Lion of England and Griffin of Edward III.....2026
Falcon of Plantagent.....2027
Lion of Mortimer and Yale of Beaufort.....2028
Greyhound of Richmond.....2029
Unicorn of Scotland and Horse of Hanover...2029
Hereford Bull.....1242
Heroes of the Covid Pandemic
NHS Workers (Jessica Roberts).....4643
Captain Sir Tom Moore (Shachow Ali).....4644
NHS Hospital Cleaners (Raphael Valle Martin).....4645
NHS/My Mum (Alfie Craddock).....4646
Lab Technician (Logan Pearson).....4647
Delivery Driver (Isabella Grover).....4648
The NHS (Connie Stuart).....4649
Doctors, Nurses (Ishan Bains).....4650
High-Speed Train.....987
Highland Cow.....1240
Highland Gathering.....1012
Hill, Graham (racing driver).....2745
Hill, Sir Rowland.....1095, 1887
Hill, Sir Rowland, death centenary.....1095
Hitchcock, Alfred.....1302
HMS *Beagle*.....4271
HMS *Dreadnought*.....1190, 4267
HMS *Endeavour* (bark).....770
HMS *King George V*.....4270
HMS *Queen Elizabeth*.....4265
HMS *Victory*.....1189, 4266
HMS *Warrior*.....4268
HMS *Warspite*.....1191
Hobby (bird of prey).....4202
Hockey.....1332, 3103
Hockey Association, centenary.....1332
Hodgkin, Dorothy (scientist).....1935, 3034
Hodgkin, Howard (painter).....3711
Hogwarts Express.....4142
Hoisting seine net.....1169
Holmes, David (artist, illustrator).....3771
Holmes, Sherlock
The Reigate Squire.....1784
The Hound of the Baskervilles.....1785
The Six Napoleons.....1786
The Greek Interpreters.....1787
The Final Problem.....1788
Holyhead and Liverpool Mails leaving London, 1828.....1261
Holyroodhouse.....1055
Honey Bee.....MS3742
Hopgood, Lieutenant Francis.....4138
Horn Dance, Abbots Bromley, Staffordshire.....4245
Hornby Dublo Electric Train and TPO Mail Van.....3998
Horror Stories
Dracula.....1980
Dr Jekyll and Mr. Hyde.....1982
Frankenstein.....1981
The Hound of the Baskervilles.....1983
Horse-drawn rotary seed drill.....2108
Horse Chestnut (*Aesculus hippocastanum*).....949
Horse racing paintings
Saddling 'Mahmoud' for the Derby, 1936.....1087
The Liverpool Great National Steeple Chase, 1839.....1088
The First Spring Meeting, Newmarket, 1793.....1089
Racing at Dorsett Ferry, Windsor, 1684.....1090
Horses.....1063, 3564
Horse's hooves.....2153
House of Tudor
Henry VII.....2924
Henry VIII.....2925
Edward VI.....2926
Lady Jane Grey.....2927
Mary I.....2928
Elizabeth I.....2929
House of Stewart
James I.....3046
James II.....3047
James III.....3048
James IV.....3049
James V.....3050
Mary I.....3051
James VI.....3052
House of Stuart
James I.....3087
Charles I.....3088
Charles II.....3089
James II.....3090
William III.....3091
Mary II.....3092
Anne.....3093
House of Hanover
George I.....3223
George II.....3224
George III.....3225
George IV.....3226
William IV.....3227
Victoria.....3228
House of Windsor
Edward VII.....3265
George V.....3266
Edward VIII.....3267
George VI.....3268
Elizabeth II.....3269
Houses of Lancaster and York
Henry IV.....2812
Henry V.....2813
Henry VI.....2814
Edward IV.....2815
Edward V.....2816
Richard III.....2817
Howard, Catherine (painting).....1970
Howes, Captain Victor RN (painter).....3796
Hudson, Henry (polar explorer).....899
Huish Episcopi, Somerset.....908
Human Rights.....2101
Humber Bridge.....1215, 3695
Hummingbird, stylised.....2087
Hunslet No. 589
Blanche (railway loco).....3577, MS3578
Hunt, James (racing driver).....2748
Hurdling.....1565
Hurricane Mk I.....4059, 4066
Hyacinth Macaw.....MS3172
Hyde Park Concert, 1976.....4400
Hydroponic leaves.....2141

'I always thought...'.....4376
Iberian lynx (*Lynx pardinus*).....3167
'I can't abide...'.....4373
'I knew you was cheating...'.....4477
'I love you...'.....4375
ICC Cricket World Cup Winners.....MS4274
ICC Women's World Cup Winners.....MS4275
Ice Age Animals
Sabre-tooth Cat.....2615
Giant Deer.....2616
Woolly Rhino.....2617
Woolly Mammoth.....2618
Cave Bear.....2619
Imperial Airways flying boat, 1937.....957
Imperial State Crown.....1062, 3213
Inayat Khan, Noor (SOE operative).....3585
Independent Television, 50th anniversary
Inspector Morse.....2561
Emmerdale.....2562
Rising Damp.....2563
The Avengers.....2564
The South Bank Show.....2565
Who Wants to be a Millionaire.....2566
Industrial Archaeology.....1440, MS1444
Industrial Revolution, Pioneers
Matthew Boulton, (manufacturing).....2916
James Watt, (steam engineering).....2917

COMMEMORATIVE / MINIATURE SHEET DESIGN INDEX

Richard Arkwright, (textiles)....2918
Josiah Wedgwood, (ceramics)....2919
George Stephenson, (railways)....2920
Henry Maudslay, (machine making)....2921
James Brindley, (canal engineering)....2922
John McAdam, (road building)....2923
Industry Year 1986....1308
Information Technology....1196
Inland Waterways....1775
Insects....1277, 2831
Inter-Parliamentary Union conference....988, 1435
International air travel....2073
International Stamp Exhibition, London 1980..1118
International Year of the disabled....1147
Inventive Britain
Colossus (1st electronic digital computer)....3679
World Wide Web (communications)....3680
Catseyes (road safety)....3681
Fibre optics (rapid data transfer)....3682
Stainless steel (recyclable alloy)....3683
Carbon fibre (composite material)....3684
DNA sequencing (the Genome)....3685
i-Limb (power digits)....3686
Iolair (oilfield emergency support vessel)....1217
Irish Moiled Cow....1244
Irish Setter....1078
Ironbridge, Shropshire....1440, 3238
Issigonis, Sir Alec (Mini car designer)....2889
'It's a baby...'....4483
IWM North, Manchester....3981
Iwuji, Chuk (actor)....3175

Jaguar (car manufacturer)....1200, 3512
Jaguar XK120 (cars)....1948
James I....3046, 3087
James II....3047, 3090
James III....3048
James IV....3049
James V....3050
James VI....3052
James Bond
Casino Royale....4332
Goldeneye....4333
The Living Daylights....4334
Live and Let Die....4335
On Her Majesty's Secret Service....4336
Goldfinger....4337
Bell Texton Jet Pack, *Thunderball*....4339, 4341
Aston Martin DB5, *Skyfall*....4340, 4342
Little Nellie, *You Only Live Twice*....4343
Lotus Esprit Submarine, *The Spy Who Loved Me*....4344
James Bond book covers
Casino Royale....2797
Dr. No....2798
Goldfinger....2799
Diamonds are Forever....2800
For Your Eyes Only....2801
From Russia With Love....2802
James, Montagu Rhodes (author)....3280
Jane Eyre (Charlotte Brontë)....1125
Jannah (*Star Wars*)....4295
Janeway, Kathryn (*Star Wars Voyager*)....4446
Jebb, Eglantyne (social reformer)....3813
Jedi Starfighter (*Star Wars*)....4307
Jenner, Edward, smallpox vaccination....2080, 3029
Jet Engine - Sir Frank Whittle....1549
Jodrell Bank....3239
John, Sir William Goscombe (sculptor)....3630
Johnson, Samuel (lexicographer)....2979
Jones, Inigo, 400th birth anniversary....935
Jubilant public, 1945....4358
Judo....2986, 3020, 3619
Juno (D-Day)....MS4236
Jupiter's Auroras....4327

K2SO (*Star Wars*)....4014
K2 telephone kiosk (Sir Giles Gilbert Scott)....2892
Kaisei (Japanese cadet brigantine)....1618
Kanata, Maz (*Star Wars*)....4007, 4015
Keats, John, 150th death anniversary....884
Keats, John (*Ode on a Grecian Urn*)....4353
Kedleston Hall....MS3229
Kemp radio experiment 1897....912
Ken! Do something!....4372, 4379
Kennington, Eric (artist)....3714
Kensington Palace....1124
Kestelman, Sara (actor)....3177
Kestrel....2332, 4205
Kew Gardens, 150th anniversary....1502
Kielder Forest....4252
King Arthur and Merlin....1294, 4492
King George VI as Duke of York, with young Princess Elizabeth....3826
King James I Bible....2116, 3242
King Lear (Shakespeare)....3176
Kingdom of Fife Millennium Cycle Ways....2154
Kingfisher (*Alcedo atthis*)....1109
Kings and Queens
Houses of Lancaster and York....2812
House of Tudor....2924
House of Stewart....3046
House of Stuart....3087
House of Hanover....3223
House of Windsor....3265
Kipling, Rudyard, centenary of *Just So Stories*
How The Whale Got His Throat....2243
How The Camel Got His Hump....2244
How The Rhinoceros Got His Hump....2245
How The Leopard Got His Spots....2246
The Elephant's Child....2247
The Sing-Song of Old Man Kangaroo....2248
The Begining of the Armadillos....2249
The Crab that played with the Sea....2250
The Cat that Walked by Himself....2251
The Butterfly that Stamped....2252
Kirk, James T. (*Star Trek The Original Series*)....4443, 4456
Kitten....1479
Knight Bus....4150
Knights of the Round Table....4497
Knocker, Elsie (nurse)....3985
Krall (*Star Trek: Beyond*)....MS4455
Kursaal....3240

Lace 1 (trial proof) 1968 (painting)....2446
Lab technician....4647
Lady Hamilton (film)....1921
Lady of the Lake....1295
Lady's Slipper Orchid (*Cypripedium calceolus*)....2016
Ladybird (*Coccinella septempunctata*)....1278
Ladybird books
Adventures from History....3999
Well-loved Tales....4000
Key Words Reading Scheme....4001
Early Tales and Rhymes....4002
Hobbies and How it Works....4003
People at Work....4004
Nature and Conservation....4005
Achievements....4006
Lake District....4466
Lammastide....1145
Lammer, Alfred, flower photograhs....1347
Lancaster House....1253
Landon, Letitia Elizabeth....4352
Landmark Buildings
Aquatics Centre, Queen Elizabeth Olympic Park, London....3973
Library of Birmingham....3974
SEC Armadillo (formerly Clyde Auditorium), Glasgow....3975
Scottish Parliament, Edinburgh....3976
Giant's Causeway Visitor Centre, Co. Antrim....3977
National Assembly for Wales, Cardiff....3978
Eden Project, St Austell....3979
Everyman Theatre, Liverpool....3980
IWM (Imperial War Musuem) North, Manchester....3981
Switch House, Tate Modern, London....3982
Landscape Gardens
Blenheim Palace....3869
Longleat....3870
Compton Verney....3871
Highclere Castle....3872
Alnwick Castle....3873
Berrington Hall....3874
Stowe....3875
Croome Park....3876
Lannister, Cersei (*Game of Thrones*)....4039
Lannister, Jaime (*Game of Thrones*)....4041
Lannister, Tyrion (*Game of Thrones*)....4038
Lannister, Tywin (*Game of Thrones*)....4037
Large Blue Butterfly....4075
Latin Gradual manuscript....2172
Lawn tennis....1022, 1390
Lawn Tennis Association, centenary....1390
Lazenby, George....4336
Leakey, Mary (archeologist)....3460
Lear, Edward (author and poet)....1382
Lear, Edward, death centenary....1405
Led Zeppelin (Rock band)....3006
Leigh, Vivien (actress)....1301, 1921, 3454
Lemmings, 1991....4315
Lest We Forget....MS2685, MS2796, MS2886, 3414
Letheringsett, Norfolk....906
Lewis, C. S....2051, 3160
Library of Birmingham....3974
Lieutenant Francis Hopgood's goggles....4138
Lifeguards' Horse and trooper....1990
Lighthouses....2034, 3638
St John's Point, Co Down....2034
Smalls, Pembrokeshire....2035
Needles Rock, Isle of Wight....2036
Bell Rock, Arbroath....2037
Eddystone, Plymouth....2038
Southwold, Suffolk....3638
Lighting Croydon's skyline....2132
Lightning....2131
Lightning F6....4058, 4065
Lindisfarne Priory....3241
Linnean Society, bicentenary....1380
Lippo di Dalmasio (painter)....2788
Literary anniversaries....884
Little Nellie (*You Only Live Twice*)....4343
Little Owl....4083, 4088
Littlewood, Joan (theatre director)....3587
Live and Let Die....4335
Liverpool and Manchester Railway 1830....1113
Liverpool, Garden Festival Hall....1245
Livingstone, David (explorer)....923
Lloyd George, David (Prime Minister)....3456
LMS No. 7720 (railway loco)....3573, MS3578, 3634
Loading mail onto liner *Queen Elizabeth*....1393
Lobster potting....1168
Loch Lomond....4467
London 1980....1118
London 2012....MS2554
London 2010
Festival of Stamps....MS3065, 3066, 3073
London 2020....4331
London Aquatics Centre....3973
London Economic Summit Conference....1253
London Landmarks....1120
London Post, *c.* 1839....1097
London Underground, 150th anniversary....3423
Metropolitan Railway opens....3423
Tunnelling below London Streets....3424
Commute from the Suburbs (*poster*)....3425
Boston Manor Art Deco station....3426
Classic Rolling Stock....3427
Jubilee Line at Canary Wharf....3428
London Underground map (Harry Beck)....2895
Long-eared Owl....4086, 4091
Long jump....2302
Long to Reign Over Us....MS3747
Longbottom, Neville....4149
Longhorn Beetle (*Rutpela maculata*)....4430
Lorca, Gabriel (*Star Trek Discovery*)....4448
Lord Mayor's Show, London....1457, 2957
Lord of the Rings, 50th anniversary of publication of *Fellowship of the Rings* and *The Two Towers*
Map showing Middle Earth....2429
Forest of Lothlórien in spring....2430
Fellowship of the Rings dust-jacket....2431
Rivendell....2432
The Hall at Bag End....2433
Orthanc....2434
Doors of Durin....2435
Barad-dûr....2436
Minas Tirith....2437
Fangorn Forest....2438
Lotus (car manufacturer)....3517
Lotus Esprit Submarine, (*The Spy Who Loved Me*)....4344
Lowry Centre, Salford....2145
Lupin, Remus (Harry Potter)....MS4151
Luskentyre, South Harris....2266

Machin, Arnold....2741, MS2743, MS3222
Machin definitives, anniversaries....2741, 3958, MS3964, MS3965
Madonna and Child (William Dyce)....2787, 4020
Madonna and Child (paintings)
Madonna and Child....3542
Madonna of Humility (Lippo di Dalmasio)....2788
Virgin and Child with the young St John the Baptist (detail)....3543
St Roch praying to the Virgin for an end to the Plague (detail)....3545
La Vierge au Lys (*The Virgin of the Lilies*)....3547
Theotokos (*Mary, Mother of God*)....3548
Magic Circle, centenary
Spinning coin trick....2525

COMMEMORATIVE / MINIATURE SHEET DESIGN INDEX

Rabbit out of hat trick....2526
Knotted scarf trick....2527
Card trick....2528
Pyramid under fez trick....2529
Magic Tour, 1986....4399, 4402
Magical Realms
Rincewind (Terry Pratchett's Discworld)....3154
Nanny Ogg (Terry Pratchett's Discworld)....3155
Dumbledore (J. K. Rowling's Harry Potter)....3156
Lord Voldemort (J. K. Rowling's Harry Potter)..3157
Merlin (Arthurian Legend)....3158
Morgan Le Fay (Arthurian Legend)....3159
Aslan (C. S. Lewis' Narnia)....3160
The White Witch (C. S. Lewis' Narnia)....3161
Magna Carta....2101
Magna Carta, 800th anniversary
Magna Carta, 1215....3718
Simon de Montfort's Parliament, 1265....3719
Bill of Rights, 1689....3720
American Bill of Rights, 1791....3721
Universal Declaration of Human Rights....3722
Charter of the Commonwealth, 2013....3723
Magnetic Resonance Imaging....1841
Mail delivery services....1290
Malaria Parasite transmitted by mosquitoes....3119
Mallard and mailbags on pick-up arms....1392
Malory, Sir Thomas *Morte d'Arthur*....1294
Mansell, Nigel (racing driver)....2749
Marconi, Guglielmo, first wireless message....1889
Marconi radio experiment, 1897....912
Marcus, Carol (*Star Trek: Into Darkness*)....MS4455
Marine Iguanas and Darwin....1176
Marine Timekeeper No. 4....1654
Maritime Heritage
Henry VIII and *Mary Rose* (galleon)....1187
Admiral Blake and *Triumph* (galleon)....1188
Lord Nelson and HMS *Victory*....1189
Lord Fisher and HMS *Dreadnought*....1190
ViscountCunningham and HMS *Warspite*....1191
Marmalade Hoverfly (*Episyrphus balteatus*)....4432
Martin, Raphael Valle....4645
Marvel
Spider-Man....4182, 4193
Captain Marvel....4183
Hulk....4184, 4194
Doctor Strange....4185
Captain Britain....4186
Peggy Carter....4187
Iron Man....4188
Union Jack....4189
Black Panther....4190
Thor....4191
Thanos....MS4192, 4195
Thor, Doctor Strange and Iron Man
(*'He's strong'*)....MS4192, 4196
Hulk, Iron Man, Black Panther and
Spider-Man (*'but we're stronger'*)....MS4192, 4197
Captain Britain, Spider-Man, Iron Man,
Hulk, Thor and Black Panther
(*'together!'*)....MS4192, 4198
Captain Britain
(*'Fury, a portal is opening'*)....MS4192, 4199
Mary I....2928, 3051
Mary II....3092
Mary and Henry Crawford (*Mansfield Park*)....992
Mary Rose (galleon)....1187, MS2930, 4264
Massys, Quinten (painter)....4023
May, B....4402
Maybe twice in a lifetime (Halley's comet)....1314
McKellen, Ian and Annis, Francesca (actors)....3178
McQueen, Alexander (fashion designer)....3318
Meade, Lottie (munitions worker)....3840
Meat products....1429
Meccano Ferris Wheel....3996
Medals and Decorations....1517
Medical Breakthroughs
Beta blockers (Sir James Black)....3115, 3153
Penicillin (Sir Alexander Fleming)....3116
Hip replacement operation
(Sir John Charnley)....3117
Lens Implant Surgery (Sir Harold Ridley)....3118
Malaria Parasite transmission
(Sir Ronald Ross)....3119
Computed tomography scanner
(Sir Godfrey Houndfield)....3120
Medical Discoveries
Ultrasonic Imaging....1839
Scanning Electron Microscopy....1840
Magnetic Resonance Imaging....1841
Computed tomography....1842
Medieval migration to Scotland....2084
Medieval Mummers....1146
Medieval warriors
Robert the Bruce, 1274–329....958
Owain Glyndwr, 1354–1416....959
Henry the Fifth, 1387–1422....960
The Black Prince, 1330–1376....961
Memories of London 2012 (Olympics)....MS3406
Men's Singles Champion, Wimbledon....MS3511
Mercer, Joe (football player/manager)....3581
Merchant Navy....3519, 3525
East Indiaman *Atlas*....3519
Royal Mail Ship *Britannia*....3520, 3531
Tea Clipper *Cutty Sark*....3521
Cargo liner *Clan Matheson*....3522
Royal Mail Ship *Queen Elizabeth*....3523
Bulk carrier *Lord Hinton*....3524
Atlantic Convoy escorted by HMS *Vanoc*....3525
Merchant ship passing Thames Estuary
Naval Control Base....3526
HMS *King George V* in Arctic Waters....3527
Merchant Ships in North Sea convoy....3528
Mercury, Freddie....2092, 4399
Merlin (bird of prey)....4201
Metropolitan Police, 150th anniversary....1100
MG (car manufacturer)....3515
MG TD (cars)....1946
Micro Machines, 1991....4317
Middleton, Colin (painter)....883
Migration to Australia....2086
Migration to Great Britain....2087
Migratory Birds
Nightjar (*Caprimulgus europaeus*)....4651
Pied Flycatcher (*Ficedula hypoleuca*)....4652
Swift (*Apus apus*)....4653
Yellow Wagtail (*Motacilla flava*)....4654
Arctic Skua (*Stercorarius parasiticus*)....4655
Stone-curlew (*Burhinus oedicnemus*)....4656
Arctic Tern (*Sterna paradisaea*)....4657
Swallow (*Hirundo rustica*)....4658
Turtle Dove (*Streptopelia turtur*)....4659
Montagu's Harrier (*Circus pygargus*)....4660
Mikhail, Fadi (painter)....3548
Milburngate Centre, Durham....1246
Mile End Park, London....2150
Military Uniforms
Royal Military Police, 1999....2774
5th Royal Tank Regiment, 1944....2775
Royal Field Artillery, 1917....2776
95th Rifles, 1813....2777
Royal Regiment of Foot of Ireland, 1704....2778
Earl of Oxford's Horse, 1661....2779
Drum Major, RAF Central Band, 2007....2862
Helicopter rescue winchman, 1984....2863
Fighter pilot, Hawker Hunter, 1951....2864
Air Gunner, Lancaster, 1944....2865
Plotter, WAAF, 1940....2866
Pilot, 1918....2867
Flight Deck Officer, 2009....2964
Captain, 1941....2965
Second Officer, WRNS, 1918....2966
Able Seaman, 1880....2967
Royal Marine,1805....2968
Admiral, 1795....2969
Military units
Royal Scots....1218
Royal Welch Fusiliers....1219
Royal Green Jackets....1220
Irish Guards....1221
Parachute Regiment....1222
Mill towns, cloth industry....2089
Millennium beacon....2129
Millennium Bridge, Gateshead....2149
Millennium definitive....2124
Millennium Dome....2166
Millennium Greens project....2148
Millennium Point, Birmingham....2164
Millennium Projects Series
Above and Beyond....2125
Fire and Light....2129
Water and Coast....2134
Life and Earth....2138
Art and Craft....2142
People and Places....2148
Stone and Soil....2152
Tree and Leaf....2156
Mind and Matter....2162
Body and Bone....2166
Spirit and Faith....2170
Sound and Vision....2174
Millennium Seed Bank, Wakehurst Place,
Ardingly....2158, MS2941
Millennium Series
The Inventors' Tale....2069
The Travellers' Tale....2073
The Patients' Tale....2080
The Settlers' Tale....2084
The Workers' Tale....2088
The Entertainers' Tale....2092
The Citizens' Tale....2098
The Scientists' Tale....2102
The Farmers' Tale....2107
The Soldiers' Tale....2111
The Christians' Tale....2115
The Artists'Tale....2119
Millennium Timekeeper....MS2123
Milligan, Spike (comedian)....3697
Mills, New Lanark, Strathclyde....1442
Milne, Alan Alexander (Author)....1093
Mini car (Sir Alec Issigonis)....2889
Mini skirt (Mary Quant)....2888
Mitchell, Reginald J
(aeronautical engineer)....1984, 2868, 2887
Model Lodge, Kennington....MS4225
Modern Architecture
St Mary Axe, London....2634
Maggie's Centre, Dundee....2635
Selfridges, Birmingham....2636
Downland Gridshell, Chichester....2637
An Turas, Isle of Tiree....2638
The Deep, Hull....2639
Modern Pentathlon....3099
Mole Cricket (*Gryllotalpa gryllotalpa*)....2019
Montagu's Harrier (*Circus pygargus*)....4660
Moore, Captain Sir Tom....4644
Moore, Bobby
(footballer)....1926, 2093, 3470, 3476, 3483
Moore, Dudley (comedian)....3703
Moore, Roger....4335
Moorhen (*Gallinula chloropus*)....1111
More, Kenneth (actor)....3582
Morecambe, Eric (comedian)....2042, 3700
Morgan (car manufacturer)....3516
Morgan Plus 4 (cars)....1949
Morris and Co, 150th anniversary
Cray (fabric print), 1884....3181
Cherries (detail from panel), 1867....3182
Seaweed (wallpaper pattern), 1901....3183
Peony (ceramic tile), 1877....3184
Acanthus (ceramic tile), 1876....3185
The Merchant's daughter
(stained glass window)....3186
Morris Dancing....1011, 1144
Morris, Mary 'May' (textile designer)....3275
Morris, William (textile designer)....1192, 3181
Moss, Stirling (racing driver)....2744
Motorcycles
Norton F1(*1991*)....2548
BSA Rocket 3 (*1969*)....2549
Vincent Black Shadow (*1949*)....2550
Triumph Speed Twin (*1938*)....2551
Brough Superior (*1930*)....2552
Royal Enfield (*1914*)....2553
Mountain Gorilla (*Gorilla beringei beringei*)....3163
Mourne Mountains, Co Down
Northern Ireland (painting)....1812
Mr Darcy (*Pride and Prejudice*)....991
Mr. Men and Little Miss children's books
Mr Happy....3891
Little Miss Naughty....3892
Mr Bump....3893
Little Miss Sunshine....3894
Mr Tickle....3895
Mr Grumpy....3896
Little Miss Princess....3897
Mr Strong....3898
Little Miss Christmas....3899
Mr Messy....3900
Muffin the Mule (childrens TV)....1940
Muir, Jean (fashion designer)....3314
Muirfield: 18th Hole (golf)....1830
Munnings, Sir Alfred (Painter)....1087
Murray, Andy (tennis player)....MS3511
Music....1282, 2667
Musicals
Oliver!....3145
Blood Brothers....3146
We Will Rock You....3147
Monty Python's *Spamalot*....3148
Rocky Horror Show....3149
Me and My Girl....3150
Return to the Forbidden Planet....3151
Billy Elliot....3152
'My cuckoo's back again – hooray!'....4425
Mystery Plays, York Minster....2173
Mythical creatures

COMMEMORATIVE / MINIATURE SHEET DESIGN INDEX

Dragon 2944
Unicorn 2945
Giant 2946
Pixie 2947
Mermaid 2948
Fairies 2949

Nash, Paul
(artist and textile designer) 1194, 4136
National Assembly for Wales 3978
National Health Service, 50th anniversary 2046
National Pondlife Centre, Merseyside 2135
National Portrait Gallery
Sir Winston Churchill (Walter Sickert) 2640
Sir Joshua Reynolds (self-portrait) 2641
T. S. Eliot (Patrick Heron) 2642
Emmeline Pankhurst (G. A. Brackenbury) 2643
Virginia Woolf (George C. Beresford) 2644
Sir Walter Scott (Sir Francis L. Chantry) 2645
Mary Seacole (Albert Charles Challen) 2646
William Shakespeare (attrib to John Taylor) 2647
Dame Cicely Saunders
(Catherine Goodman) 2648
Charles Darwin (John Collier) 2649
National Space Science Centre, Leicester 2126
National Theatre, London 979
National Trust, centenary 1868
National Trust for Scotland, 50th anniversary 1155
Naval Flags and Ensigns
White Ensign 2208, 2581
'Jolly Roger', HMS *Proteus* 2209, 2970
National Parks
Broads 4473
Dartmoor 4464
Lake District 4466
Loch Lomond 4467
New Forest 4465
North York Moors 4469
Peak District 4471
Pembrokeshire Coast 4472
Snowdonia 4468
South Downs 4470
Nativity 2118
Natterjack Toad (*Bufo calamita*) 1323
Natural Gas - flame rising from sea 1052
Nature Conservation
Barn Owl (*Tyto alba*) 1320
Pine Marten (*Martes martes*) 1321
Wild Cat (*Felis silvestris*) 1322
Natterjack Toad (*Bufo calamita*) 1323
Nebulae 2709
Nelly O'Brien (painting) 933
Nelson, Lord and HMS *Victory* 1189
Nevinson, C. R. W. (war artist) 3629
New Abbey Corn Mill 3968
New Forest 4465
New Order (Rock band) 3002
New Wembley Stadium, London MS2740
New Worlds 2122
Newcomen, Thomas (steam engine inventor) .. 3277
Newquay beach, Cornwall 2272
Newton, Sir Isaac (physicist) 1351, 3027
The Principia Mathematica 1351
Ellipses (Motion of bodies) 1352
Optick Treatise 1353
The System of the World 1354
Newton's moon and tide diagram 1523
Newton/Hubble Telescope MS2106
NHS 2046
NHS hosital cleaners 4645
NHS workers 4643
NHS/My Mum 4646
Nigerian clinic 1263
Nightingale 3955
Nightjar (*Caprimulgus europaeus*) 4651
Nimrod MR2 4063
Niven, David (actor) 1299
Nobel Prizes, centenary
Chemistry (Carbon 60 molecule) 2232
Economic sciences (Globe) 2233
Peace (embossed Dove) 2234
Physiology of Medicine (green crosses) 2235
Literature (open book) 2236
Physics (Hologram of boron molecule) 2237
Norfolk and Norwich Millennium project 2163
North and South (Mrs Elizabeth Gaskell) 1128
North British Railway *Drummond*
(railway loco) 985
North York Moors 4469
Northern Gannet (*Sula bassana*) 1422
Norwich Mail in thunderstorm, 1827 1260

'Now brace yourself...' 4480
Nurses celebrate, 1945
Nursing care 2081
Nutter, Tommy (tailor) 3313
Nutley Windmill 3967

Oak (*Quercus robur*) 922
'Obby 'Oss, Padstow, Cornwall 4240
Ocean Liners (paintings)
RMS *Queen Mary 2* (Edward D. Walker) 2448
SS *Canberra* (David Cobb) 2449
RMS *Queen Mary* (Charles Pears) 2450
RMS *Mauretania* (Thomas Henry) 2451
SS *City of New York*
(Raphael Monleaon y Torres) 2452
PS *Great Western* (Joseph Walter) 2453, 2614
Ode on a Grecian Urn (John Keats) 4353
Ode to the Snowdrop (Mary Robinson) 4351
Odeon, Harrogate 1920
Odeon, Machester 1924
Oil - North Sea 1050
Old English Sheepdog 1075
Oldfield, Mike (musician) 3005
Olivier, Laurence 1921
Olympic and Paralympic Games
Canoe Slalom 2981
Athletics, Track 2983, 3022
Aquatics 2984
Judo 2986, 3020
Badminton 2988
Weightlifting 2989
Basketball 2990, 3023
Shooting 3098
Modern Pentathlon 3099
Taekwondo 3100
Cycling 3101, 3108*b*
Hockey 3103
Football 3104, 3108*a*
Boxing 3106
Athletics, Field 3196
Volleyball 3197
Wrestling 3199
Fencing 3201, 3206*b*
Gymnastics 3202, 3206*a*
Triathlon 3203
Handball 3204
Paralympic Games: Archery 2982, 3021
Paralympic Games: Boccia 2985
Paralympic Games: Equestrian 2987
Paralympic Games: Rowing 3097, 3107
Paralympic Games: Table tennis 3102, 3108
Paralympic Games: Goalball 3105
Paralympic Games: Sailing 3195, 3206
Paralympic Games: Wheelchair
Rugby 3198, 3205
Paralympic Games: Wheelchair Tennis 3200
Olympic and Paralympic Games, Atlanta
Athlete on starting blocks 1930
Throwing the javelin 1931
Basketball 1932
Swimming 1933
Athlete celebrating 1934
Olympic and Paralympic
Games, London MS2554, MS2861, 2981,
3020, 3097,3107, 3195, 3205,
3250, MS3341, 3342, MS3406
Olympic Games, Barcelona 1992 1615
Olympic Games emblem 3251, 3337
Omaha (D-Day) MS4236
On Her Majesty's Secret Service 4336
Only Fools and Horses
Del Boy 4486, 4488
'Don't worry he's housetrained...' 4478
'I knew you was cheating...' 4477
'It's a baby...' 4483
'Now brace yourself...' 4480
'Or coach has just blown up...' 4481
'Play it nice and cool...' 4479
Rodney 4486, 4489
'That's just over three million...' 4484
Uncle Albert 4490
'What have you been doing...' 4483
On the Meridien Line project 2151
Opera singer 1186
Operation Raleigh 1618
Orchids
Dendrobium hellwigianum 1659
Paphiopedilum Maudiae Magnificum 1660
Cymbidium lowianum 1661
Vanda Rothschildiana 1662
Dendrobium vexillarius var *albivride* 1663
Order of the Garter, 650th anniversary 2026

Order of the Thistle, 300th anniversary 1363
Ordnance Survey, 150th anniversary 1578
Osprey 4074
Otter (*Lutra lutra*) 1042, 3061, 3095
Ottery St Mary church, roof boss 968
'Our coach has just blown up!' 4481
Owen, Robert (social reformer) 1002
Owen, Wilfred (poet) 4134
Owls
Barn Owl (*Tyto alba*) 4082
Little Owl (*Athene noctua*) 4083
Tawny Owl (*Strix aluco*) 4084
Short-eared Owl (*Asio flammeus*) 4085
Long-eared Owl (*Asio otus*) 4086
Two Young Barn Owls (*Tyto alba*) 4087
Little Owl Chicks (*Athene noctua*) 4088
Tawny Owl Chick (*Strix aluco*) 4089
Short-eared Owl Chick (*Asio flammeus*) 4090
Long-eared Owl Chick (*Asio otus*) 4091
Oystercatcher (*Haematopus ostralegus*) 1421

Packet Ship, painting 3796
Padstow Harbour, Cornwall 2268
Painswick, Gloucestershire 1998
Painted Lady Butterfly (*Vanessa cardui*) 4429
Paintings of Dogs by George Stubbs
King Charles Spaniel 1531
A Pointer 1532
Two Hounds in a Landscape 1533
A Rough Dog 1534
Fino and Tiny 1535
P & O packet steamer Peninsular, 1888 954
Palace of Westminster
Palace of Westminster from Old
Palace Yard 4404
Palace of Westminster from River Thames 4405
Elizabeth Tower 4406
Commons Chamber 4407
Central Lobby 4408
Lords Chamber 4409
Palace of Westminster (19th Commonwealth
Parliamentary Conference) 939
Pantomime characters
Principal boy 1303
Genie 1304
Dame 1305
Good fairy 1306
Pantomime cat 1307
Ugly sister (*Cinderella*) 2876
Genie (*Aladdin*) 2877
Captain Hook (*Peter Pan*) 2879
Wicked Queen (*Snow White*) 2881
Paralympic Games emblem 3250, 3338
Paralympic Games, London 2982, 2985, 2987,
3021, 3097, 3102, 3105,
3107, 3108, 3195, 3198,
3200, 3205, 3206, 3250,
MS3371, 3372, MS3406
Paralympics, Barcelona 1992 1616
Parc Arfordirol, Llanelli Coast 2136
Parkinson, Norman (photographer) 3453
Parkinson, Sydney (natural history artist) 4123
Parr, Catherine (painting) 1971
Passenger jet aviation, 50th anniversary 2284
Pathé News 1923
Pavlenko, Sergei (painter) 3495
Peace–Burial at Sea (painting) 971
Peace and Freedom 1873
Peacekeeping 2114
Peak District 4471
Pearson, Logan 4647
Peckett R2 *Thor* (railway loco) MS3144, 3574
Peel, Robert (Prime Minister) 3647
Pembrokeshire Coast 4472
Penguin book cover (Edward Young) 2894
Penny Black, 150th anniversary 1467, MS1501
Penny Black, 175th anniversary 3709, 3807
Penny Black, 180th anniversary MS4355
Penny Red, 175th anniversary 3806, 3808
People of Salford (L. S. Lowry) 2145
Perch (*Perca fluviatilis*) 1210
Peregrine Falcon 4209
Perry, Fred (lawn tennis champion) 2971
Perry, Grayson (artist) 4093
Perutz, Max (molecular biologist). 3586
Peter Pan, Sir James Barrie
Tinkerbell 2304
Wendy, John and Michael Darling 2305
Crocodile and alarm clock 2306
Captain Hook 2307, 2879
Peter Pan 2308
Peter Rabbit 1805, 1649, 3856, 3862, MS3868

COMMEMORATIVE / MINIATURE SHEET DESIGN INDEX

Philipps, Nicola 'Nicky' Jane (artist) 3492
Photo by John Hedgecoe with
  Queen Elizabeth II wearing the Diadem,
  August 1966 3962
Photographs of Royal Family MS2786
Picard, Jean-Luc (*Star Trek*
  The Next Generation) 4444, 4457
Picture Postcards, centenary 1815
Pied Avocet (*Recurvirostra avosetta*) 1420, 2769
Pied Flycatcher (*Ficedula hypoleuca*) 4652
Pike (*Esox lucius*) 1208
Pilgrim Fathers, migration to Americas 2085
Pillar Boxes, 150th anniversary of first
  Green pillar box, 1857 2316
  Horizontal aperture box, 1874 2317
  Air Mail box, 1834 2318
  Double aperture box, 1939 2319
  Modern style box, 1980 2320
  Penfold Pillar Box 3797
Pilots scramble to their Hurricanes MS3735, 4071
Pine Marten (*Martes martes*) 1321, 2479
Pink Floyd (Rock band) 2999, 3849
  The Piper at the Gates of Dawn 3849
  Atom Heart Mother 3850
  The Dark Side of the Moon 3851
  Animals 3852
  Wish You Were Here 3853
  The Endless River (Pink Floyd) 3854
Pioneers of Communications 1887
Pitmedden, Scotland 1226
Pitt the Younger, William (Prime Minister) 3649
Plant Sculptures
  Dandelions 1853
  Chestnut leaves 1854
  Garlic leaves 1855
  Hazel leaves 1856
  Spring grass 1857
Platinum Jubilee
  Queen Elizabeth II at headquarters of MI5, ...
  London, February 2020 4627
  Queen Elizabeth II and Duke of Edinburgh,
  Washington, USA, October 1957 4628
  Queen Elizabeth II on walkabout in
  Worcester, April 1980 4629
  Trooping the Colour, London, June 1978 4630
  Leaving Provincial Museum of Alberta,
  Edmonton, Canada, May 2005 4631
  During Silver Jubilee celebrations,
  Camberwell, June 1977 4632
  At Victoria Park, St. Vincent, February 1966 4633
  Order of the Garter ceremony, Windsor,
  June 1999 4634
Planets Suite (Gustav Holst) 1283
'Play it nice and cool...' 4479
Plomley, Roy (radio broadcaster) 3579
Podracer (*Star Wars*) 4308
Poe's X-wing fighter (*Star Wars*) 4306
Poison Dart Frog MS3172
Polar Bear (*Ursus maritimus*) 3165
Polar Explorers 897
Police 1100
Police Dog 2808
Police Horses 3568
Polypropylene chair (Robin Day) 2893
Pond Life
  Common Frog (*Rana temporaria*) 2220
  Great Diving Beetle (*Dytiscus marginalis*) 2221
  Three-spined Stickleback
  (*Gasterosteus aculeatus*) 2222
  Southern Hawker Dragonfly (*Aeshna cyanea*) 2223
Pontcysyllte Aqueduct, Clwyd 1443
Pool Frog 4077
Poppies 2884, 3626, 3711, 3838, 3983, 4133
Poppies (seven on stem) 2883
Poppies (six on stem) MS3024, 3414, 3717
Populous (video game), 1989 4319
Porg (*Star Wars*) 4010
Portal, Lord and Mosquito 1340
Portrush, County Antrim 2273
Portsmouth Harbour development 2137
Postal Telegraph & Telephone,
  International World Congress, Brighton 1434
Post Boxes MS2954
  George V Type B Wall Box, 1933–1936 2950
  Edward VII Ludlow Wall Box,1901–1910 2951
  Victorian Lamp Box, 1896 2952
  Elizabeth II Type A Wall Box, 1962–1963 2953
Potter, Beatrix 150th birtday anniversary
  Peter Rabbit 3856
  Mrs. Tiggy-winkle 3857
  Squirrel Nutkin 3858
  Jemima Puddle-duck 3859
  Tom Kitten 3860
  Benjamin Bunny 3861
  Now run along, and don't get into mischief 3864
  And then, feeling rather sick, he went to
  look for some parsley. 3865
  But Peter, who was very naughty, ran
  straight away 3866
  He slipped underneath the gate, and was
  safe at last? 3867
Potter, Beatrix (author) 1091, 2589
Prehistoric skulls and Darwin 1178
Preliminary sketch by Arnold Machin
  based on the Penny Black,
  January 1966 3958
Preparatory work by Arnold Machin using
  photograph of his coin mould,
  February 1966 3959
Pride and Prejudice, Bicentenary of publication
  Sense and Sensibility 3431
  Pride and Prejudice 3432
  Mansfield Park 3433
  Emma 3434
  Northanger Abbey 3435
  Persuasion 3436
Primal Scream (Rock band) 3007
Prime Ministers
  Margaret Thatcher 3642
  Harold Wilson 3643
  Clement Attlee 3644
  Sir Winston Churchill 3645
  William Gladstone 3646
  Robert Peel 3647
  Charles Grey 3648
  William Pitt the Younger 3649
Prince Albert, Legacy MS4225
Prince Andrew and Miss Sarah Ferguson 1333
Prince Charles MS3832, 3833
Prince Charles and Lady Diana Spencer 1160
Prince Charles and Mrs Parker Bowles MS2530
Prince Edward and Miss Sophie
  Rhys-Jones 2096
Prince George MS3832, 3835
Prince Harry and Ms. Meghan Markle MS4092
Prince of Wales 70th Birthday MS4163
Prince of Wales Investiture, 25th anniversary
  Castell Y Waun (*Chirk Castle*), Clwyd 1810
  Ben Arkle, Sutherland, Scotland 1811
  Mourne Mountains,
  Co Down Northern Ireland 1812
  Dersingham, Norfolk 1813
Prince William MS3180, MS3832, 3836
Prince William, 21st birthday 2381
Prince William and Catherine Middleton MS3180
Prince's Lodging, Newmarket 937
Princess Anne and Captain Mark Phillips 941
Princess Elizabeth with Duke of Edinburgh 2011
Princess Elizabeth with her father,
  the Duke of York 3826
Princess Mary's Gift Box Fund 3631
Printing press, early 1017
Project SUZY, Teesside 2141
Public Education in England,
  150th anniversary 1432
Pugin, Augustus (Gothic architect) 3279
Pulsars 4325
Punch and Judy Show puppets
  Policeman 2224
  Clown 2225
  Mr Punch 2226, 2230
  Judy 2227, 2231
  Beadle 2228
  Crocodile 2229
Puppy 1482
Purcell, Henry (composer and musician) 2972

Q Branch (*James Bond*) MS4338
Quant, Mary (mini skirt designer) 2888
Queen (rock band)
  A Night at the Opera, 1975 4390, 4398
  Brian May 4402
  Freddie Mercury 4399
  Greatest Hits, 1981 4393
  Innuendo, 1991 4395
  John Deacon 4401
  News of the World, 1977 4391
  Queen 4403, 4502
  Queen II, 1974 4388, 4397
  Roger Taylor 4400
  Sheer Heart Attack, 1974 4389
  The Game, 1980 4392
  The Works, 1984 4394
Queen Amidala (*Star Wars*) 4301
Queen Elizabeth II, 60th Birthday 1316
Queen Elizabeth II, 80th Birthday 2620
Queen Elizabeth II, 90th Birthday 3826
Queen Elizabeth II Accession,
  40th anniversary 1602
Queen Elizabeth II addressing UN, 1957 3325A
Queen Elizabeth II and
  Prince Philip 916, 2012, 3830
Queen Elizabeth II
  Diamond Jubilee U3271 MS3272, 3319A, 3327
Queen Elizabeth II Diamond Wedding 2780
Queen Elizabeth II Golden Wedding 2780
Queen Elizabeth II, Platinum Jubilee 4627
Queen Elizabeth II with
  Prince Charles and Princess Anne 3828
Queen Guinevere and Sir Lancelot 1296
Queen Mother Commemoration 2280
Queen Mother's 80th Birthday 1129
Queen Mother's 90th Birthday 1507
Queen Mother's 100th Birthday 2160
Queen Victoria 1367, 3227, MS3229
Queen Victoria, Birth Bicentenary
  Queen Victoria (Heinrich von Angeli), 1890 4219
  Queen Victoria and Benjamin Disraeli, 1878 4220
  Queen Victoria with Servant John Brown,
  1876 4221
  Queen Victoria wearing her Robes of State,
  1859 4222
  Marriage of Queen Victoria and Prince
  Albert, 1840 4223
  Princess Victoria aged 11, 1830 4224
Queen Victoria's Accession,
  150th anniversary 1367
Queen's Award to Industry, 25th anniversary 1497
Queen's Beasts (heraldry) 2026

R2-D2 (*Star Wars*) 4012, 4018
Rabbit 1480
Racehorse Legends
  Frankel 3940
  Red Rum 3941
  Shergar 3942
  Kauto Star 3943
  Desert Orchid 3944
  Brigadier Gerard 3945
  Arkle 3946
  Estimate 3947
Racket Sports
  Lawn tennis 1022
  Table tennis 1023
  Squash 1024
  Badminton 1025
Radar–Robert Watson Watt 1548
Rae, Barbara 4096
Rae, Fiona 4094
Raeburn, Sir Henry, 150th death anniversary 932
Railway Locomotives 984, 1113, 1272, 1795,
  2417, 2716, 3109, 3215,
  MS3144, MS3283, 3497, 3570
Railway station, Victorian 2075
Raleigh, Walter (explorer) 926
Raphael (painter) 4024
Red Arrows MS4064, 4067, 4080
Red Kite 4208
Red Panda (*Ailurus fulgens*) 3168
Red Squirrel (*Sciurus vulgaris*) 1041, 2484
Redwing 1590
Reed beds, Braid River 2138
Reed, Malcolm (*Star Trek Enterprise*) 4452
Rees, Private Lemuel Thomas
  (South Wales Borderers) 3988
Reintroduced Species
  Osprey (*Pandion haliaetus*) 4074
  Large Blue Butterfly (*Maculinea arion*) 4075
  Eurasian Beaver (*Castor fiber*) 4076
  Pool Frog (*Pelophylax lessonae*) 4077
  Stinking Hawk's-beard (*Crepis foetida*) 4078
  Sand Lizard (*Lacerta agilis*) 4079
Religious anniversaries 1972
Remarkable Lives
  Roy Plomley 3579
  Barbara Ward 3580
  Joe Mercer 3581
  Kenneth More 3582
  Dylan Thomas 3583
  Sir Alec Guinness 3584
  Noor Inayat Khan 3585
  Max Perutz 3586
  Joan Littlewood 3587
  Abram Games 3588
Rescue at Sea
  Lifeboat, Barra 2825

COMMEMORATIVE / MINIATURE SHEET DESIGN INDEX

Lifeboat approaching dinghy, Appledore.......2826
Helicopter winchman, Portland.......2827
Inshore lifeboat, St Ives.......2828
Rescue helicopter, Lee-on-Solent.......2829
Lifeboat launch, Dinbych-y-Pysgod, Tenby.......2830
Rev R. Walker (*The Skater*) (painting).......934
Revell, Giles (photographer).......3838
Reynolds, Sir Joshua (painter).......931, 2641
Rhodes, Zandra (fashion designer).......3315
Ribchester helmet.......4383
Richard II (Shakespeare).......3825
Richard III.......2817
Right to Education.......2100
Right to Health.......2099
Rights of the Child.......2178
Ringing in the Millennium.......2174
RNLI lifeboat and signal flags.......1286
Road markings.......2144
Roberts, Jessica.......4643
Robert the Bruce.......958, 2111
Robin.......1896, 2238, 3904
Robinson, Mary.......4351
Robson, Molly (child painter).......3551
Rocket approaching Moorish Arch, Liverpool.......1113
Rodney.......4486
Rolling Stones (Rock band).......3003, 4014
Rolls-Royce (car manufacturer).......1201, 3513
Roman Britain.......1771
Roman Britain
Dover Lighthouse.......4380
Bignor mosaic.......4381
Amphitheatre at Isca Fortress, Caerleon.......4382
Ribchester helmet.......4383
Bridgeness distance slab.......4384
Copper-alloy figurine of warrior god.......4385
Gorgon's head from temple to Sulis Minerva.......4386
Hadrian's Wall.......4387
Roman Centurion.......888
Romano, Antoniazzo (painter).......3543
Romantic Poets
The Progress of Rhyme (John Clare).......4345
Frost at Midnight (Samuel Taylor Coleridge).......4346
Auguries of Innocence (William Blake).......4347
The Lady of the Lake (Walter Scott).......4348
To a Skylark (Percy Bysshe Shelley).......4349
The Rainbow (William Wordsworth).......4350
Ode to the Snowdrop (Mary Robinson).......4351
The Fate of Adelaide (Letitia Elizabeth Landon) 4352
Ode on a Grecian Urn (John Keats).......4353
She Walks in Beauty (Lord Byron).......4354
Romeo and Juliet (Shakespeare).......3178, 3818
Rosenberg, Isaac (poet and artist).......3984
Roses
Elizabeth of Glamis.......1006
Grandpa Dickson.......1007
Rosa Mundi.......1008
Sweet Briar.......1009
Silver Jubilee.......1568
Mme Alfred Carrière.......1569
Rosa moyesii.......1570
Harvest Fayre.......1571
Mutabilis.......1572
Ross, John (photographer).......3983
Ross, Sir James Clark (polar explorer).......897
Routemaster Bus (AAM Durrant designer).......2896
Rowing.......1329, 3097, 3107
Rowntree, Joseph (philanthropist).......3814
Royal Academy of Arts, 250th Anniversary
Summer Exhibition (Grayson Perry).......4093
Queen of the Sky (Fiona Rae).......4094
St Kilda: The Great Sea Stacs (Norman Ackroyd).......4095
Inverleith Allotments and Edinburgh Castle (Barbara Rae).......4096
Queuing at the RA (Yinka Shonibare).......4097
Saying Goodbye (Tracey Emin).......4098
Royal Air Force, Centenary
Lightning F6.......4058
Hurricane Mk.I.......4059
Vulcan B2.......4060
Typhoon FGR4.......4061
Camel F.1.......4062
Nimrod MR2.......4063
Red Arrows (Hawk T.1s) in formation.......MS4064
Red Arrows, Flypast.......4067, 4080
Red Arrows, Swan formation.......4068, 4081
Red Arrows, Syncro pair.......4069
Red Arrows, Python formation.......4070
Pilots scramble to their Hurricanes.......4071
Spitfires of 610 Squadron on patrol.......4072
Armourer Fred Roberts re-arms Spitfire.......4073
Royal Air Force, History of
Lord Dowding and Hawker Hurricane.......1336
Lord Tedder and Hawker Typhoon.......1337
Lord Trenchard and de Havilland DH9A.......1338
Sir Arthur Harris and Avro Lancaster.......1339
Royal Albert Hall.......MS4225
Royal Botanical Gardens, Kew, 250th anniversary.......MS2941
Royal Golden Wedding.......2011
Royal Horticultural Society, bicentenary
Dianthus Allwoodii Group.......2456
Dahlia, Garden Princess.......2457
Clematis, Arabella.......2458
Miltonia, French Lake.......2459
Lilium, Lemon Pixie.......2460
Delphinium, Clifford Sky.......2461
Gentiana acaulis (Georg Ehret).......2463
Tulipa (Georg Ehret).......2464
Iris latifolia (Georg Ehret).......2465
Royal Institute of Chemistry, centenary.......1029
Royal Mail 500.......3795, 3802
Tuke, Sir Brian.......3795
Mail Packet off Eastbourne (Capt Victor Howes, RN).......3796
Penfold Pillar Box.......3797
River Post.......3798
Mail Coach.......3799
Medway Mail Centre.......3800
Royal Mail Coach, 200th anniversary.......1258
Royal Mail public postal service, 350 Years.......1290
Royal Microscopical Society, 150th anniversary.......1453
Royal National Eisteddfod of Wales.......1010
Royal National Rose Society, centenary.......1006
Royal Navy Ships
Mary Rose, 1511 (Geoff Hunt).......4264
HMS *Queen Elizabeth*, 2014 (Robert G. Lloyd).......4265
HMS *Victory*, 1765 (Monamy Swaine).......4266
HMS *Dreadnought*, 1906 (H. J. Morgan).......4267
HMS *Warrior*, 1860 (Thomas Goldsworth Dutton).......4268
Sovereign of the Seas, 1637 (Paul Garnett).......4269
HMS *King George V*, 1939 (Robert G. Lloyd).......4270
HMS *Beagle*, 1820 (John Chancellor).......4271
Royal Navy Submarine Service, centenary.......2202, 2207
Royal Observatory, Greenwich.......977, 1524
Royal Opera House, London.......1122
Royal Platinum Wedding Anniversary of, Queen Elizabeth II and Prince Philip.......MS4032
Royal Shakespeare Company, 50th anniversary.......3173
Royal Silver Wedding.......916
Royal Society, 350th anniversary of the
Sir Robert Boyle (chemistry).......3026
Sir Isaac Newton (optics).......3027
Benjamic Franklin (electricity).......3028
Edward Jenner (smallpox vaccination).......3029
Charles Babbage (computing).......3030
Alfred Russell Wallace (theory of evolution).......3031
Joseph Lister (antiseptic surgery).......3032
Ernest Rutherford (atomic structure).......3033
Dorothy Hodgkin (crystallography).......3034
Sir Nicholas Shackleton (earth sciences).......3035
Royal Society of Arts, 250th anniversary
Sir Rowland Hill Award.......2473
William Shipley, founder of RSA.......2474
RSA as Typewriter keys and shorthand.......2475
Chimney sweep.......2476
Gill Typeface.......2477
Zero Waste.......2478
Royal Society for the Prevention of Cruelty to Animals, 100th anniversary.......1479
Royal Society for the Protection of Birds, centenary
Atlantic Puffin (*Fratercula arctica*).......1419
Pied Avocet (*Recurvirostra avosetta*).......1420
Oystercatcher (*Haematopus ostralegus*).......1421
Northern Gannet (*Sula bassana*).......1422
Royal Troon: The Postage Stamp (golf).......1832
Royal Wedding.......941, 1160, 1333, 2096, MS2531, MS3180, MS4092
Royal Welsh, 2nd Battalion with QEII.......A3321
Royal Welsh Show, Llanelwedd.......1834
RSC 50 Years.......3173
Ruby-tailed Wasp (*Chrysis ignita* agg.).......4433
Rugby Football Union, 100th anniversary.......889
Rugby League, centenary.......1891
Rugby Union.......1135, 1567
Rugby World Champions, 2003.......MS2416
Rugby World Cup 2015
Tackle.......3748
Scrum.......3749
Try.......3750
Conversion.......3751
Pass.......3752
Drop goal.......3753
Ruck.......3754
Line-out.......3755
Running.......2300, 3621
Rupert Bear
Then with a terrifying roar.......4420
The bath is rocked.......4421
Then Algy looks a trifle glum.......4422
The large bird says.......4423
'There's something puzzling.......'4424
'My cuckoo's back again.......4425
Though Rupert searches all around.......4426
The tree is such a lovely sight.......4427
Ryder, Sue.......3811
Ryle, Sir Martin (scientist).......2980

Safety at Sea
RNLI lifeboat and signal flags.......1286
Beachy Head lighthouse and charts.......1287
Communications satellite and dish aerials.......1288
Buoys.......1289
Sailing.......980, 3195
St Abb's Head, Scottish Borders.......2270
St Andrews Cathedral, Fife.......2117
St Andrews, The Old Course (golf).......1829
St Augustine, 1400th anniversary of arrival.......1974
St Columba, 1400th death anniversary.......1972
St Edmundsbury Cathedral, Suffolk.......2170
St Edward's Crown.......1060, 3208
St George's Chapel, Windsor.......978, MS3932
St Helen's Church, Norwich, roof boss.......967
St John Ambulance, centenary.......1359
St Kilda, Scotland.......1159
St Laurent (painting).......974
St Luke painting the Virgin (detail) (Eduard Jakob von Steinle).......4026
St Patrick Centre, Downpatrick.......2172
St Paul's Cathedral, London.......2599, MS2847
St Paul's, Covent Garden.......936
St Peter and St Paul, Overstowey.......2171
St Valentine's Day.......1143
Salmon (*Salmo salar*).......1207
Salt–crystallography.......1032
Sand Lizard.......4079
Santa (child's painting).......3551
Santa Claus on his sleigh on a starry night (Ted Lewis-Clark).......4029
Santa Maria (Columbus' flagship).......1617
Sargent, Sir Malcolm (conductor).......1132
Sartorius, John Nott (Painter).......1089
Sassoferrato, Giovanni Battista (painter).......4025
Satellite Agriculture.......2110
Saturn.......2105, MS2106, 3412
Saunders, Jennifer (comedian).......3705
Scanning Electron Microscopy.......1840
Scheffler, Axel (illustrator).......3415
Schofield, Paul (actor).......3176
Science Fiction
The Time Machine.......1878
The First Men in the Moon.......1879
The War of the Worlds.......1880
The Shape of things to Come.......1881
Scientific Achievements
Michael Faraday, birth bicentenary.......1546
Charles Babbage, birth bicentenary.......1547
Sir Robert Watson-Watt (Radar scientist).......1548
Sir Frank Whittle, 50th anniversary of first flight of jet engine in Gloster E28/39.......1549
Scott, Montgomery (*Star Trek* film).......MS4455
Scott, Robert Falcon (explorer).......900, 2365
Scott, Sir Walter.......886, 2645, 4348
Scottish Parliament.......3976
Scottish piper.......1012
Scouting, centenary and 21st World Scout Jamboree
Scout and campfire.......2758
Scouts rock climbing.......2759
Scout planting tree.......2760
Adult volunteer teaching Scout archery.......2761
Scout learning gliding.......2762
Scouts from many nations.......2763
SCRAN (Scottish Cultural Resources Access Network), Internet.......2165
Sea Life
Moon Jellyfish (*Aurelia aurita*).......2699
Common Starfish (*Asterias rubens*).......2700
Beadlet Anemone (*Actinia equina*).......2701
Bass (*Dicentrarchus labrax*).......2702
Thornback Rray (*Raja clavata*).......2703
Lesser Octopus (*Eledone cirrhosa*).......2704

COMMEMORATIVE / MINIATURE SHEET DESIGN INDEX

Common Mussels (*Mytilus edulis*)....2705
Grey Seal (*Halichoerus grypus*)....2706
Shore Crab (*Carcinus maenas*)....2707
Common Sun Star (*Crossaster papposus*)....2708
Sea Pictures (Edward Elgar)....1285
Seabird Centre, North Berwick....2128
Seaside Architecture
Eastbourne Bandstand....3635
Tinside Lido, Plymouth....3636
Bangor Pier....3637
Southwold Lighthouse....3638
Blackpool pleasure beach....3639
Bexhill-on-Sea shelter....3640
SEC Armadillo, Glasgow....3975
Sellers, Peter (actor)....1298
Sensible Soccer, 1992.... 4314
Serviceman welcomed home, 1945....4356
Servicemen and nurse of 1921.... 887
Seymour, Jane (painting)....1968
Shackleton and the *Endurance* Expedition
Entering the Antarctic Ice....3787
Endurance frozen in pack ice....3788
Striving to free *Endurance*....3789
Trapped in a pressure crack....3790
Patience Camp....3791
Safe arrival at Elephant Island....3792
Setting out for South Georgia....3793
Rescue of *Endurance* crew....3794
Shaftesbury, Lord (social reformer)....1003
Shakespeare, William, 400th death anniversary
to thine own self be true (*Hamlet*)....3816
Cowards die many times before their deaths. The valiant never taste of death but once (*Julius Caesar*)....3817
Love is a smoke made with the fume of sighs (*Romeo and Juliet*)....3818
The fool doth think he is wise, but the wise man knows himself to be a fool (*As You Like It*)....3819
There was a star danced, and under that was I born (*Much Ado About Nothing*)....3820
But if the while I think on thee, dear friend, all losses are restored and sorrows end (*Sonnet 30*)....3821
Love comforteth like sunshine after rain (*Venus and Adonis*)....3822
We are such stuff as dreams are made on; and our little life is rounded with a sleep (*The Tempest*)....3823
Life's but a walking shadow, a poor player That struts and frets his hour upon the stage (*Macbeth*)....3824
I wasted time, and now doth time waste me (*Richard II*)....3825
Shakespeare's Globe Theatre, reconstruction....1882
Shankly, Bill (football player/manager)....3461
Shattered Poppy....3983
She Walks in Beauty (Lord Byron)....4354
Sheep....1591, 2508
Shelley, Percy Bysshe....4349
Sher, Antony (actor)....3174
Sherlock
The Reichenbach Fall....4411
A Study in Pink....4412
The Great Game....4413
The Empty Hearse....4414
A Scandal in Belgravia....4415
The Final Problem....4416
The Red-Headed League....4418
The Adventure of the Speckled Band....4419
Sherwood Forest....4249
Shetland Pony....1064
Shining Ram's-horn Snail (*Segmentina nitida*)....2018
Shinzon (*Star Trek: Nemesis*)....MS4455
Shipbuilding....2090
Shire Horse....1063
Shonibare, Yinka....4097
Shooting....1331, 3098
Short-eared Owl....4085, 4090
Short S.21 flying boat *Maia*, 1937.... 957
Siberian Tiger (*Panthera tigris altaica*)....3164
Silver Jubilee of Queen's Reign....1033
Silver Jubilee walkabout, 1977....A3323
Sindy Weekender Doll....3990
Single European Market....1633
Sir Galahad....1297, 4499
Sir Gawain....4495
Sir Lancelot....4498
Sisko, Benjamin (*Star Trek Deep Space Nine*)....4445
Sissinghurst, Kent....1223
Sith Trooper (*Star Wars*)....4294
Ski Club of Great Britain, centenary....1389
Sky at Night, The, 50th anniversary
Saturn Nebula C55....2709
Eskimo Nebula C39....2710
Cat's Eye Nebula C6....2711
Helix Nebula C63....2712
Flaming Star Nebula C31....2713
The Spindle C53 (*nebula*)....2714
Skyfall....4340, 4342
Skylark....3952
Slave 1 (*Star Wars*)....4309
Slughorn, Horace (*Harry Potter*)....MS4151
Smilers booklet stamps
2567, 2672, 2693, 2819, 3670
Smith, Paul (fashion designer)....3317
Snape, Severus (Harry Potter)....MS4151
Snoke, Supreme Leader (*Star Wars*)....4009
Snowdonia....4468
Snow Family (Arwen Wilson)....4028
Snow, Jon (*Game of Thrones*)....4034
Snowstorm - Steamer off a Harbour's Mouth (painting).... 972
Social Reformers....1001
Solar eclipse....MS2106
Solar sensors....2140
Songbirds
Song Thrush (*Turdus philomelos*)....2017, 3954
Great Tit (*Parus major*)....3948
Wren (*Troglodytes troglodytes*)....3949
Willow Warbler (*Phylloscopus trochilus*)....3950
Goldcrest (*Regulus regulus*)....3951
Skylark (*Alauda arvensis*)....3952
Blackcap (*Sylvia atricapilla*)....3953
Nightingale (*Luscinia megarhynchos*)....3955
Cuckoo (*Cuculus canorus*)....3956
Yellowhammer (*Emberiza citrinella*)....3957
Sooty (childrens TV)....1941
Sopwith Camel F1....4062
Soran, Tolian (*Star Trek: Generations*)....MS4455
Sorley, Charles Hamilton (poet)....3712
Sounds of Britain
Sitar player and dancer....2667
Reggae guitarist and African drummer....2668
Fiddler and harpist....2669
Sax player and Blues guitarist....2670
Maraca player and Salsa dancers....2671
South American Leaf-cutter Ants....2139
South Downs....4470
Sovereign of the Seas....4269
Sovereign's Orb....1061
Sowerbury, James (naturalist, illustrator)....1381
Spacehopper....3994
Space Science
Sun seen from SOHO Observatory....3408
Venus seen from *Venus Express*....3409
Martian crater seen from *Mars Express*....3410
Asteroid Lutetia seen from *Rosetta* Probe....3411
Saturn seen from *Cassini* Satellite....3412
Titan seen from *Huygens* Probe....3413
Spanish Armada, 400th anniversary....1400
Sparrowhawk....4207
Speeder bikes (*Star Wars*)....4311
Spence, Sir Basil (architect)....3273
Spencer, Sir Stanley (painter)....1769, 3841
Spider Monkey....MS3172
Spirograph....3991
Spitfires of 610 Squadron on patrol....MS3735, 4072
Spock (*Star Trek The Original Series*)....4449
Sport centenaries....1134
Sports organisations
British Amateur Gymnastics Association....1388
Ski Club of Great Britain....1389
Lawn Tennis Association....1390
Football League....1391
Spring Flowers....1079
Sprout, Pomona (Harry Potter)....MS4151
Squash....1024, 3622
Stackpole Head, Wales....1157
Stag Beetle (*Lucanus cervus*)....1280, 2835
Stained glass windows....894, 1634, 2170, 2991, 3186
Stamp Classics....MS4169
Stanley, Henry M (explorer)....924
Starch - chromatography....1031
Stark, Arya (*Game of Thrones*)....4040
Stark, Eddard (*Game of Thrones*)....4035
Stark, Sansa (*Game of Thrones*)....4033
Star Trek
Captain James T. Kirk (William Shatner), *The Original Series*, 1966–9....4443, 4456
Captain Jean-Luc Picard (Patrick Stewart), *The Next Generation*, 1987–1994....4444, 4457
Captain Benjamin Sisko (Avery Brooks), *Deep Space Nine*, 1993–1999....4445
Captain Kathryn Janeway (Kate Mulgrew), *Voyager*, 1995–2001....4446
Captain Jonathan Archer (Scott Bakula), *Enterprise*, 2001–2005....4447
Captain Gabriel Lorca (Jason Isaacs), *Discovery*, 2017–....4448
Spock (Leonard Nimoy), *The Original Series*....4449
Deanna Troi (Marina Sirtis), *The Next Generation*....4450
Julian Bashir (Alexander Siddig), *Deep Space Nine*....4451
Malcolm Reed (Dominic Keating), *Enterprise*....4452
Burnham, Michael (Sonequa Martin-Greene), *Discovery*....4453
Ash Tyler/Voq (Shazad Latif), *Discovery*....4454
Star Wars....3758, 3780, 4007, 4292
Darth Vader....3758
Yoda....3759
Obi-Wan Kenobi....3760
Stormtrooper....3761
Han Solo....3762
Rey....3763
Princess Leia....3764
The Emperor....3765
Luke Skywalker....3766
Boba Fett....3767
Finn....3768
Kylo Ren....3769
X-Wing Starfighter....3780, 3784
At-At Walkers....3781
TIE Fighters....3782, 3783
Millennium Falcon....3785
Maz Kanata....4007, 4015
Chewbacca....4008
Supreme Leader Snoke....4009
Porg....4010
BB-8....4011
R2-D2....4012
C-3PO....4013
K-2SO....4014
Count Dooku....4292
Lando Calrissian....4293
Sith Trooper....4294
Jannah....4295
Grand Moff Tarkin....4296
Darth Maul....4297
Zorii....4298
Wicket W. Warrick....4299
Poe Dameron....4300
Queen Amidala....4301
Poe's X-wing fighter....4306
Jedi Starfighter....4307
Podracer....4308
Slave 1....4309
TIE silencer....4310
Speeder bikes....4311
State Coach....1059
Steam trains....2130, 3109
Steinle, Eduard Jakob von (painter)....4026
Stephenson's *Locomotion*, 1825.... 984
Steroids–conformational analysis....1029
Stewart, Jackie (racing driver)....2747
Stickle Bricks Super Set House....3992
Stingray (childrens TV)....1942, 3139
Stinking Hawk's-beard (plant)....4078
Stockton and Darlington Railway.... 984
Stone Curlew (*Burhinus oedicnemus*)....4656
Stone, Richard (portrait painter)....3496
Stonehenge, Wiltshire....1525
Strangford Stone, Killyleagh....2152
Strickland, Fiona....3626
Strip farming....2107
Stuart, Connie....4649
Stubbs, George (artist)....1531
Studio pottery....1371
Studland Bay, Dorset....2265
Sturt, Charles (explorer).... 927
Sub Post Offices
Haroldswick, Shetland....1997
Painswick, Gloucestershire....1998
Beddgelert, Gwynedd....1999
Ballyroney, County Down....2000
Submarines
Vanguard class, 1992....2202, 2207
Swiftsure class, 1973....2203
Unity class, 1939....2204
Holland type, 1901....2205
Sullivan, Sir Arthur, 150th birth anniversary....1624

COMMEMORATIVE / MINIATURE SHEET DESIGN INDEX

Summertime
Royal Welsh Show, Llanelwedd....1834
All English Tennis Championships, Wimbledon....1835
Cowes Week (sailing)....1836
Test Match, Lord's (cricket)....1837
Braemar Gathering (Highland games)....1838
Sunflower (*Helianthus annuus*)....2157
Supermarine Spitfire.... 1984, 2868, 2887, MS3735
Sustainable Fish
Herring (*Clupeidae*)....3609
Red gurnard (*Chelidonichthys cuculus*)....3610
Dab (*Limanda limanda*)....3611
Pouting (*Trisopterus luscus*)....3612
Cornish Sardine (*Sardina pilchardus*)....3613, 3633
Swallow (*Hirundo rustica*)....4658
Swans....1639
Swatkin, Major Joshua....1381
Swift (*Apus apus*)....4653
Swimming....2299, 3620
Swinton, Tilda (The White Witch Narnia)....3161
Switch House, Tate Modern....3982
Sword (D-Day)....MS4236

Table tennis.... 1023, 3102, 3108
Taekwondo....3100
Targaryen, Daenerys (*Game of Thrones*)....4042
Tarkin, Grand Moff (*Star Wars*)....4296
Tartan woollen ball, digitised....2165
Tate Modern, London....2143, 3982
Tawny Owl....4084, 4089
Taylor, R.....4400
Tedder, Lord and Hawker Typhoon....1337
Telephone, centenary
Housewife....997
Policeman....998
District nurse....999
Industrialist....1000
Templeton Carpet Factory, Glasgow....1496
Tennant, David (actor)....3173
Tennyson, Alfred, Lord, death centenary....1607
Test Match, Lord's (cricket)....1837
Test-tube baby, sculpture....2083
Thames Flood Barrier....1216
Thapa VC, Rifleman Kulbir (3 Gurkha Rifles)....3713
Thatcher, Margaret (Prime Minister)....3642
'That's just over three million...'....4484
'That woman's tongue. If it was a bit longer she could shave with it'....4369
The Adventure of the Dancing Men.... MS4417
The Adventure of the Second Stain.... MS4417
The Adventure of the Speckled Band.... MS4417, 4419
The Arsenal, Venice (painting)....973
The Ashes, England's victory (2005)....MS2573
The bath is rocked from side to side, And Pompey quite enjoys his ride....4421
The Beatles, Album covers
with the beatles....2686
Sgt Peppers Lonely Hearts Club Band....2687
Help!....2688
Abbey Road....2689
Revolver....2690
Let It Be....2691
The BFG (Roald Dahl)....3260, MS3264
The Cantebury Tales (woodcut)....1014
The Clangers (childrens TV)....1943
The Clash (Rock band)....3004
The *Endeavour* Voyage....4118
The FA Cup
Arsenal players Charlie George and Frank McLintock parading FA Cup, 1971....4636
Crowds on pitch at Wembley Stadium during 1923 Cup Final....4637
West Bromwich Albion supporters at 1968 Cup Final....4638
Keith Houchen equalises for Coventry City against Tottenham Hotspur, 1987 Final....4639
Lincoln City reach Quarter Finals, 2017 (FA Cup Upsets)....4640
King George VI and Queen Elizabeth present FA Cup to Sunderland Captain Raich Carter, 1937....4641
The Fate of Adelaide (Letitia Elizabeth Landon)....4352
The Final Problem, centenary of publication....1784
The Game and Playe of Chesse (woodcut)....1016
The Grave of the Unknown Warrior....4137
The Great Fire of London, 350th anniversary
Fire breaks out in bakery on Pudding Lane....3879
The fire spreads rapidly....3880
Houses are pulled down to create breaks....3881
As the fire reaches St Paul's....3882
The fire dies out....3883
Christopher Wren develops plans....3884
The Gruffalo
'Scrambled snake!'....4276
'Gruffalo crumble!'....4277
'All was quiet in the deep dark wood.'....4278
'A mouse took a stroll'....4279
'Roasted fox!'....4280
'Owl ice cream?'....4281
The Legend of King Arthur
Arthur....4493
Arthur and Excalibur....4494
Arthur and Guinevere....4495
Arthur battles Mordred....4500
Death of King Arthur....4501
Knights of the Round Table....4497
Merlin and Baby Arthur....4492
Sir Galahad....4499
Sir Gawain....4496
Sir Lancelot....4498
The Living Daylights....4334
The Lady of the Lake (Walter Scott)....4348
'The large bird says, Our king will know, Climb on my back and off we'll go'....4423
The Magic Roundabout....3554
The Merrythought Bear....3989
The Mill on the Floss (George Eliot)....1126
The New Crystal Palace, Sydenham....MS4225
The NHS....4649
The Old Vic, Bicentenary
Laurence Olivier in *The Dance of Death*....4125
Glenda Jackson in *King Lear*....4126
Albert Finney in *Hamlet*....4127
Maggie Smith in *Hedda Gabler*....4128
John Gielgud and Ralph Richardson in *No Man's Land*....4129
Sharon Benson in *Carmen Jones*....4130
Judi Dench and John Stride in *Romeo and Juliet*....4131
Richard Burton in *Henry V*....4132
The Post Office at War, 1914–1918....MS3848
The Principia Mathematica, 300th anniversary..1351
The Progress of Rhyme (John Clare)....4345
The Rainbow (William Wordsworth)....4350
The Red-Headed League.... MS4417, 4418
The Response (sculpture)....3630
The Rolling Stones
London, July 1969....4614
East Rutherford, New Jersey, USA, August 2019....4615
Rotterdam, Netherlands, August 1995....4616
Tokyo, Japan, March 1995....4617
New York, July 1972....4618
Oslo, Norway, May 2014....4619
Hertfordshire, August 1976....4620
Dusseldorf, Germany, October 2017....4621
Rolling Stones....4623
Rolling Stones....4624
Posters for Tour of Europe, 1974 and Tour of the Americas, 1975....4625
Posters for UK Tour, 1971 and American Tour, 1981....4626
The Rows, Chester....976
The Sleep of the Infant Jesus (Giovanni Battista Sassoferrato)....4025
The Small Cowper Madonna (Raphael)....4024
The Spy Who Loved Me....4344
The stamp designs of David Gentleman....MS4635
The Stamp Show 2000, Earls Court London.... MS2146, MS2147
The Tale of Peter Rabbit (Beatrix Potter)....1091
The Tempest (Shakespeare)....3174, 3823
The tree is such a lovely sight, That Rupert's chums gaze with delight....4427
The Tretyse of Love (extract)....1015
The Twelve Days of Christmas (carol)....1044
The Wind in the Willows (Kenneth Grahame)....1092
Then Algy looks a trifle glum, 'I'm going home', he tells his chum....4422
Then with a terrifying roar, The water bursts in through the door....4420
There's something puzzling all of you, says Rupert....4424
Thiepval Memorial, Somme, France....3842
Thomas, Dylan (poet)....3583
Thomas the Tank Engine (Rev Wilbert Awdry)
Thomas the Tank Engine....3187
James the Red Engine....3188
Percy the Small Engine....3189
Daisy (Diesel Railcar)....3190
Toby the Tram Engine....3191
Gordon the Big Engine....3192
'Goodbye, Bertie', called Thomas....3194
Thoroughbred....1066
Though Rupert searches all around.......4426
Threatened Fish
Common Skate (*Dipturus batis*)....3614, 3632
Spiny Dogfish (*Squalus acanthias*)....3615
Wolffish (*Anarhichas lupus*)....3616
Sturgeon (*Acipenseridae*)....3617
Conger Eel (*Conger erebennus*)....3618
Thunderbirds....3138, MS3142, 3143
Thunderball.... 4339, 4341
Tickle, Private William Cecil (Essex Regiment)....3628
TIE silencer (*Star Wars*)....4310
Tin mine, St Agnes, Cornwall....1441
Titanic (liner)....1890
To a Skylark (Percy Bysshe Shelley)....4349
Tolian Soran (*Star Trek: Generations*)....MS4455
Tolkien, J. R. R.....2050, 2429
Tomb Raider....MS4320
Torrs Walkway, New Mills....2127
Total Hip Replacement Operation....3117
Tower of London....1054
Trafalgar, Bicentenary of Battle
Entrepreante with dismasted HMS *Belle* Isle....2574
Nelson wounded on deck of *Victory*....2575
British Cutter *Entrepreante* attempting to rescue crew of burning French *Achille*....2576
Cutter and HMS *Pickle* (schooner)....2577
British Fleet attacking in two columns....2578
Franco/Spanish Fleet putting to sea from Cadiz....2579
Trains (paintings by Terence Cuneo)
Flying Scotsman....1272
Golden Arrow....1273
Cheltenham Flyer....1274
Royal Scot....1275
Cornish Riviera....1276
Trans Pennine Trail, Derbyshire....2153
Tree trunk and roots....2156
Trelawney, Sybill (Harry Potter)....MS4151
Trenchard, Lord and de Havilland DH9A....1338
Triathlon....3203
Triumph TR3 (cars)....1945
Triwizard Cup....4148
Troi, Deanna (*Star Trek The Next Generation*)....4450
Trooping the Colour....2540, A3320
Troops parade at end of war, 1945....4360
Ensign of the Scots Guards, 2002....2540
Queen taking the salute, 1983....2541
Household Cavalry trumpeter, 2004....2542
Welsh Guardsman, 1990s....2543
Queen riding side-saddle, 1972....2544
Queen and Duke in carriage, 2004....2545
Trout (*Salmo trutta*)....1209
TS2K Creative Enterprise Centre, London....2177
Tuke, Sir Brian (Master of the Posts)....3795
Tull, Second Lieutenant Walter....4135
Tunnicliffe, Charles F. (artist)....1915
Turing, Alan (computer scientist)....3281
Turing, Alan, work on computers....2072
Turnberry, 9th Hole (golf)....1833
Turner, Francis Calcraft (Painter)....1088
Turner, J. M. W. (Painter)....971
Turning the Tide, Durham Coast....2134
Turtle Dove (*Streptopelia turtur*)....4659
Tutankhamun discovery, 50th anniversary....901
Twopenny Blue, 175th anniversary....MS3710, 3809, 4331
Tyler, Ash (*Star Trek Discovery*)....4454
Tyne Cot Cemetery....3987
Typhoon FGR4....4061
Tyrell, Olenna (*Game of Thrones*)....4036

UK A–Z.... 3230, 3294
Angel of the North....3230
Blackpool Tower....3231
Carrick-a-Rede, Co Antrim....3232
Downing Street, London....3233
Edinburgh Castle....3234
Forth Railway Bridge....3235
Glastonbury Tor....3236
Harlech Castle....3237
Ironbridge, Shropshire....3238
Jodrell Bank....3239
Kursaal, Southend....3240
Lindisfarne Priory....3241
Manchester Town Hall....3294
Narrow Water Castle, Co Down....3295
Old Bailey, London....3296
Portmeirion....3297
The Queen's College, Oxford....3298

COMMEMORATIVE / MINIATURE SHEET DESIGN INDEX

Roman Baths, Bath 3299
Stirling Castle 3300
Tyne Bridge, Newcastle 3301
Urquhart Castle 3302
Victoria and Albert Museum, London 3303
White Cliffs of Dover 3304
Station X, Bletchley Park 3305
York Minster 3306
ZSL London Zoo 3307
Ulster '71 Paintings
A Mountain Road (painting) 881
Deer's Meadow (painting) 882
Slieve na brock (painting) 883
Uniform Postage, 1840 1098
Union Jack MS2206, 2570, 2805, 2821, 3786
United Kingdom: A Celebration MS4476
United Nations, 50th anniversary 1876
Universal Postal Union, centenary 954
University of Essex 893
University of Leicester 892
University of Southampton 891
Up Helly Aa, Lerwick, Shetland 4242
Urban Renewal 1245
Utah (D-Day) MS4236

Vaughan Williams, Ralph, birth centenary 903
Valle Martin, Raphael 4645
VE Day, 50th anniversary 1873, 1875
'Vera, my little swamp duck'. 4371, 4378
Victoria (Queen) 1367, 3227
Victoria Cross, 150th anniversary
Corporal Agansing Rai 2659
Boy Seaman Jack Cornwell 2660
Midshipman Charles Lucas 2661
Captain Noel Chavasse 2662
Captain Albert Ball 2663
Captain Charles Upham 2664
Victorian Britain 1367
Video Games
Elite, 1984 4312
Worms, 1995 4313
Sensible Soccer, 1992 4314
Lemmings, 1991 4315
Wipeout, 1995 4316
Micro Machines, 1991 4317
Dizzy, 1987 4318
Populous, 1989 4319
Tomb Raider, Lara Croft MS4320
Tomb Raider, 1996 4321
Tomb Raider, 2013 4322
Violinist and Acropolis, Athens 1264
Virgin and Child (attr. Gerard David) 4019
Virgin Mary with Child (attr. Quinten Massys) 4023
Visions of the Universe
Cat's Eye Nebula 4323
Enceladus 4324
Pulsars 4325
Black Holes 4326
Jupiter's Auroras 4327
Gravitational Lensing 4328
Comet 67P 4329
Cygnus A Galaxy 4330
Vitamin C - synthesis 1030
Volleyball 3197
Votes for Women 2098, 2870, 4050
The Lone Suffragette in Whitehall, *c.*1908 4050
The Great Pilgrimage of Suffragists, 1913 4051
Suffragette leaders at Earl's Court, 1908 4052
Women's Freedom League poster parade, *c.*1907 4053
Welsh Suffragettes, Coronation Procession, 1911 4054
Leigh and New released from prison, 1908 4055
Sophia Duleep Singh sells The Suffragette, 1913 4056
Suffragette Prisoners' Pageant, 1911 4057
Vulcan B2 4060

W&LLR No. 822 *The Earl* (railway loco) MS3578
Wadsworth, Edward (artist) 3986
Wales Millennium Centre (Canolfan Mileniwm), Cardiff 2176
Wallace and Gromit 3128
War Graves
Tyne Cot Cemetery, Zonnebeke, Belgium 3987
War Graves Cemetery, The Somme 2113
Ward, Barbara (economist) 3580
Warrick, Wicket W. (*Star Wars*) 4299
Warrior god, Cambridgeshire 4385
Water Music (George Frederick Handel) 1282
Waterloo, bicentenary of Battle 3724
Watt, James, discovery of steam power 2070
Waverley Class (railway loco) 985
We Are Making a New World (Paul Nash) 4136
Weasley, Ginny 4147
Weasley, Ron 4145
Weather
Rain 2197
Fair 2198
Stormy 2199
Very Dry 2200
Weaver's craft 2088
Webb, Philip (designer) 3182
Web of Life exhibition, London Zoo 2139
Weightlifting 1330, 2989
Welcome to the London
2012 Olympic Games MS3341
2012 Paralympic Games MS3371
Wells, H. G. (novelist) 1878
Welsh Bible, 400th anniversary 1384
Welsh Black Bull 1243
Welsh harpist 1013
Welsh Highland Railway, Rheilffordd Eryri 2130
Welsh Pony 1065
Welsh Rugby Union, centenary 1135
Welsh Springer Spaniel 1076
Wesley, John (theologian) 2115
West Highland Terrier 1077
Westminster Palace 988
Westonbirt, The National Arboretum 4248
Westwood, Vivienne (fashion designer) 3316
'What have you been doing...' 4483
Wheelchair Racing 2303
White-tailed Eagle 4200
Whittle, Sir Frank, 50th anniversary of first flight of jet engine in Gloster E28/39 1549
Wild Bird Protection Act, centenary 1109
Wild Cat (*Felis silvestris*) 1322, 2483, 3055
Wildfowl and Wetlands Trust, 50th anniversary 1915
Wilding definitive (decimal currency) 2031, 2258, 2378, 3329
Wildscreen at Bristol 2162
William III 3091
William IV 3227
Willow Warbler 3950
Wilson, Harold (Prime Minister) 3643
Windmills and Watermills
Nutley Windmill, East Sussex 3967
New Abbey Corn Mill, Dumfries and Galloway 3968
Ballycopeland Windmill, County Down 3969
Cheddleton Flint Mill, Staffordshire 3970
Woodchurch Windmill, Kent 3971
Felin Cochwillan Mill, Gwynedd 3972
Windsor Castle 3920, MS3932
The Long Walk 3920
The Round Tower 3921
The Norman Gate 3922
St George's Hall 3923
St Queen's Ballroom 3924
The Waterloo Chamber 3925
St George's Chapel Nave: roof boss 3926
St George's Chapel Nave: fan-vaulted roof 3927
St George's Chapel Quire: Garter banners 3930
St George's Chapel Quire: roof boss 3931
Winnie-the-Pooh (A. A. Milne) 1093, 3121
Winnie-the-Pooh and Christopher Robin 3121
Winnie-the-Pooh and Piglet 3122
Winnie-the-Pooh and Rabbit 3123
Winnie-the-Pooh and Eeyore 3124
Winnie-the-Pooh and friends 3125
Winnie-the-Pooh and Tigger 3126
Winton, Sir Nicholas (humanitarian) 3810
Wipeout (video game)1995 4316
Wireless, first message 1895 1889
Wisdom, Norman (actor) 3701
Wise, Ernie (comedian) 3700
Wollstonecraft, Mary (pioneering feminist) 2975
'Woman, Stanley, woman' 4370
Women of Distinction
Millicent Garrett Fawcett (suffragist) 2870
Elizabeth Garrett Anderson (physician) 2871
Marie Stopes (family planning pioneer) 2872
Eleanor Rathbone (campaigner) 2873
Claudia Jones (civil rights activist) 2874
Barbara Castle (politician) 2875
Women's Health 2871
Wood, Sir Henry (conductor) 1130
Wood, Victoria 3706
Woodchurch Windmill 3971
Woodland Animals
Pine Marten (*Martes martes*) 2479
Roe Deer (*Capreolus capreolus*) 2480
Badger (*Meles meles*) 2481
Yellow-necked Mouse (*Apodemus flavicollis*) 2482
Wild Cat (*Felis silvestris*) 2483
Red Squirrel (*Sciurus vulgaris*) 2484
Stoat (*Mustela erminea*) 2485
Natterer's Bat (*Myotis nattereri*) 2486
Mole (*Talpa europaea*) 2487
Fox (*Vulpes vulpes*) 2488
Worcester Cathedral, roof boss 969
Wordsworth, William 4350
Working Dogs
Assistance Dog (Retreiver) 2806
Mountain Rescue Dog (Cross-bred) 2807
Police Dog (German Shephard) 2808
Customs Dog (Springer Spaniel) 2809
Sheepdog (Border Collie) 2810
Guide Dog (Labrador) 2811
Working Horses
Riding for the Disabled Association 3564
The King's Troop ceremonial Horse 3565
Dray Horses 3566
Royal Mews carriage Horses 3567
Police Horses 3568
Forestry Horse 3569
World Congress of Roses, Belfast 1568
World Cup (football) 2093, 2291, 2628
World Cup Football Championship, Germany
England (1966) 2628
Italy (1934, 1938, 1982) 2629
Argentina (1978, 1986) 2630
Germany (1954, 1974, 1990) 2631
France (1998) 2632
Brazil (1958, 1962, 1970, 1994, 2002) 2633
World Cup Rugby Championship, London 1567
World Gurning Championships, Egremont, Cumbria 4241
World Heritage Sites
Hadrian's Wall, England 2532
Uluru-Kata Tjuta National Park, Australia 2533
Stonehenge, England 2534
Wet Tropics of Queensland, Australia 2535
Blenheim Palace, England 2536
Greater Blue Mountains Area, Australia 2537
Heart of Neolithic Orkney, Scotland 2538
Purnululu National Park, Australia 2539
World Hockey Cup for men, London 1986 1332
World of Invention
The Iron Bridge (Thomas Telford) 2715
Steam locomotive and railway tracks 2716
Map of British Isles and Australia 2717
TV camera and television set (John Logie Baird) 2718
Globe as Web (email and internet) 2719
Couple with luggage on Moon (space travel) 2720
World of Literature 2121
World of Music 2120
World of the Stage 2119
World Orchid conference, Glasgow 1659
World Owl Trust, Muncaster 2125
World Student Games, Sheffield 1991 1564
World War One 2113, 3626, 3711, 3838, 3983, 4133
World War Two, 60th anniversary of end MS2547
World War Two, 75th anniversary of end
Serviceman returning 4356
Nurses celebrating 4357
Crowds celebrating 4358
Evacuee children returning home 4359
Troops march along Oxford Street 4360
Soldiers and sailors leaving demobilisation centre 4361
Liberated prisoners 4362
Navy personnel i 4363
Hall of Names, Holocaust History Museum, Yad Vashem, Jerusalem 4365
Runnymede Memorial 4366
Plymouth Naval Memorial 4367
Rangoon Memorial, Myanmar 4368
World War Two, Atlantic & Arctic convoys MS3529
Worms, 1995 4313
Wren 3949
Wrestling 3199
Wright, Billy (footballer) 1928
Wuthering Heights (Emily Brontë) 1127
WWF (Worldwide Fund for Nature), 50th anniversary
African Elephant (*Loxodonta*) 3162
Mountain Gorilla (*Gorilla beringei beringei*) 3163
Siberian Tiger (*Panthera tigris altaica*) 3164
Polar Bear (*Ursus maritimus*) 3165
Amur Leopard (*Panthera pardus orientalis*) 3166

COMMEMORATIVE / MINIATURE SHEET DESIGN INDEX

Iberian Lynx (*Lynx pardinus*) 3167
Red Panda (*Ailurus fulgens*) 3168
Black Rhinoceros (*Diceros bicornis*) 3169
African Wild Dog (*Lycaon pictus*) 3170
Golden Lion Tamarin
(*Leontopithecus rosalia*) 3171

X-ray of hand and computer mouse 2164

Yachts 980
Year of the Artist 2175
Year of the Child, International 1091
Year of Three Kings, 70th anniversary ms2658
Yellowhammer (*Motacilla flava*) 1112, 3957
Yews For The Millennium project 2156
York, 1900th anniversary 888
York Minster, Chapter House ceiling 2173
York Minster, roof boss 966
Young, Edward (Penguin book cover) 2894
You Only Live Twice 4343
Youth Organisations
  Boys' Brigade 1179
  Girls' Brigade 1180
  Boy Scout movement 1181
  Girls Guide movement 1182

Zorii (*Star Wars*) 4298

Miniature Sheet Design Index

Stanley Gibbons receives, on a regular basis, enquiries concerning the allocation of SG Numbers to some of individual stamps included in Miniature Sheets. Stamps which are available from more than one source, usually from counter sheets in addition to the Miniature sheet, are allocated numbers.

From this flow of enquiries a decision was made, as part of the review of the design index, to include a new section identifying all the Miniature Sheets issued for GB. These are listed numerically by SG Number, alphabetically by title of sheet and finally (alphabetically) by the individual stamps printed within the MS.

Numerically by SG Number

ms1058 British Architecture (4th series) Historic Buildings
ms1099 Death centenary of Sir Rowland Hill
ms1119 London 1980 International Stamp Exhibition
ms1409 Death centenary of Edward Lear (artist and author)
ms1444 Industrial Archaeology
ms1501 Stamp World London '90 International Stamp Exhibition
ms2106 Solar Eclipse
ms2123 Millennium Series Millennium Timekeeper
ms2146 Stamp Show 2000 International Stamp Exhibition, London Jeffery Matthews Colour Palette
ms2147 Stamp Show 2000 International Stamp Exhibition, London Her Majesty's Stamps
ms2161 Queen Elizabeth the Queen Mother's 100th Birthday
ms2201 The Weather
ms2206 Centenary of Royal Navy Submarine Service
ms2215 150th anniversary of first Double-decker Bus
ms2289 50th anniversary of passenger Jet Aviation Airliners
ms2292 World Cup Football Championship, Japan and Korea
ms2315 Astronomy
ms2326 50th anniversary of Wilding Definitives (1st issue)
ms2367 50th anniversary of Wilding Definitives (2nd issue)
ms2402 Classic Transport Toys
ms2416 England's Victory in Rugby World Cup Championship, Australia
ms2423 Classic Locomotives
ms2454 Ocean Liners
ms2462 Bicentenary of the Royal Horticultural Society (1st issue)
ms2501 Christmas Father Christmas by Raymond Briggs
ms2524 150th death anniversary of Charlotte Brontë Illustrations of scenes from *Jane Eyre* by Paula Rego
ms2530 50th anniversary of first Castles Definitives
ms2531 Royal Wedding Prince Charles and Mrs Camilla Parker Bowles
ms2546 Trooping the Colour
ms2547 60th anniversary of end of the Second World War
ms2554 London's successful bid for Olympic Games, 2012
ms2573 England's Ashes Victory
ms2580 Bicentenary of the Battle of Trafalgar Scenes from Panorama of the Battle of Trafalgar by William Heath
ms2588 Christmas Madonna and Child Paintings
ms2613 Birth bicentenary of Isambard Kingdom Brunel (engineer)
ms2658 70th anniversary of the Year of Three Kings
ms2665 150th anniversary of the Victoria Cross (1st issue)
ms2684 Christmas Traditional Secular
ms2685 Lest We Forget (1st issue) 90th anniversary of the Battle of the Somme
ms2692 The Beatles. Beatles Memorabilia
ms2727 World of Invention (2nd issue)
ms2740 New Wembley Stadium, London
ms2743 40th anniversary of the first Machin Definitives
ms2757 Publication of final book in the Harry Potter series Crests of Hogwarts School and its Four Houses
ms2786 Diamond Wedding of Queen Elizabeth II and Duke of Edinburgh
ms2795 Christmas (2nd issue) Angels
ms2796 Lest We Forget (2nd issue) 90th anniversary of the Battle of Passchendaele
ms2803 Birth centenary of Ian Fleming (Author of James Bond books) Book Covers
ms2818 Kings and Queens (1st issue) Houses of Lancaster and York
ms2847 Cathedrals 300th anniversary of St Paul's Cathedral
ms2861 Handover of Olympic Flag from Beijing to London
ms2882 Christmas Scenes from Pantomimes
ms2886 Lest We Forget (3rd issue) 90th anniversary of the Armistice
ms2904 Birth bicentenary of Charles Darwin (naturalist and evolutionary theorist) Fauna and Map of the Galapagos Islands
ms2930 Kings and Queens (2nd issue) House of Tudor
ms2941 Action for Species (3rd series) 250th anniversary of Royal Botanic Gardens, Kew
ms2954 Post Boxes
ms2998 Christmas Stained glass windows
ms3019 Classic Album Covers (2nd issue)
ms3024 Business and Consumer Smilers
ms3025 Centenary of Girlguiding
ms3053 Kings and Queens (3rd issue) House of Stewart
ms3065 London 2010 Festival of Stamps and centenary of Accession of King George V (1st issue)
ms3072 London 2010 Festival of Stamps and centenary of Accession of King George V (2nd issue)
ms3073 London 2010 Festival of Stamps Jeffery Matthews Colour Palette
ms3086 Britain Alone (2nd issue) Evacuation of British Troops from Dunkirk, 1940
ms3094 Kings and Queens (4th issue) House of Stuart
ms3127 Europa. Children's books *Winnie the Pooh* by A. A. Milne. Book Illustrations by E. H. Shepard
ms3135 Christmas with Wallace and Gromit
ms3142 F.A.B. The Genius of Gerry Anderson (producer of TV programmes)
ms3144 Classic Locomotives (1st series). England Classic Locomotives of England
ms3172 50th anniversary of the WWF Wildlife of the Amazon Rainforest
ms3179 50th anniversary of the Royal Shakespeare Company The four Theatres of the Royal Shakespeare Company, Stratford-upon-Avon
ms3180 Royal Wedding. Official Engagement portraits by Mario Testino Prince William and Miss Catherine Middleton
ms3193 Thomas the Tank Engine Book Illustrations from The Railway Series
ms3204a Olympic and Paralympic Games, London (2012) (5th issue)
ms3220 First United Kingdom Aerial Post, centenary (1st issue) First United Kingdom Aerial Post, 9 September 1911
ms3222 Birth centenary of Arnold Machin
ms3229 Kings and Queens (5th issue) House of Hanover
ms3249 Christmas. 400th anniversary of the *King James Bible*.
ms3264 Roald Dahl's Children's Stories (2nd issue) 30th anniversary of the publication of *The BFG*
ms3270 Kings and Queens (6th issue) House of Windsor
ms3272 Diamond Jubilee. (2nd issue) Queen Elizabeth II
ms3283 Classic Locomotives (2nd series). Scotland Classic Locomotives of Scotland
ms3308 UK A–Z (2nd series)
ms3336 Birth bicentenary of Charles Dickens Scenes from *Nicholas Nickleby, Bleak House, Little Dorrit* and *A Tale of Two Cities*

569

COMMEMORATIVE / MINIATURE SHEET DESIGN INDEX

MS3341	Welcome to London, Olympic Games Sports and London Landmarks	
MS3371	Welcome to London, Paralympic Games Paralympic Sports and London Landmarks	
MS3406	Memories of London 2012 Olympic and Paralympic Games Scenes from Olympic and Paralympic Games	
MS3422	Christmas. Illustrations by Axel Scheffler	
MS3429	150th anniversary of the London Underground Classic London Underground Posters	
MS3451	50th anniversary of *Doctor Who* (TV programme) (1st issue) *Dr. Who* 1963–2013	
MS3474	Football Heroes (1st issue)	
MS3498	Classic Locomotives (3rd series). Northern Ireland Classic Locomotives of Northern Ireland	
MS3511	Andy Murray, Men's singles champion, Wimbledon Andy Murray's Wimbledon Victory	
MS3518	British Auto Legends The Workhorses	
MS3529	Merchant Navy (2nd issue) Second World War Atlantic and Arctic convoys	
MS3549	Christmas. Madonna and Child paintings	
MS3578	Classic Locomotives (4th series). Wales Classic Locomotives of Wales	
MS3601	Buckingham Palace, London (2nd issue) Buckingham Palace	
MS3608	Great British Films. Films by GPO Film Unit	
MS3641	Seaside Architecture British piers	
MS3657	Christmas. Illustrations by Andrew Bannecker	
MS3678	Smilers (5th series)	
MS3710	175th anniversary of the Penny Black Penny Black and 1840 2d. blue	
MS3734	Bicentenary of the Battle of Waterloo Soldiers and Battle of Waterloo map	
MS3735	75th anniversary of the Battle of Britain Battle of Britain	
MS3742	Bees The Honey Bee	
MS3747	Long to Reign Over Us (2nd issue) Long to Reign Over Us	
MS3770	*Star Wars* (1st issue). *Star Wars*	
MS3779	Christmas Meditations on the imagery of Christmas	
MS3801	Royal Mail 500 (1st issue) Classic GPO Posters	
MS3832	90th birthday of Queen Elizabeth	
MS3837	Animail	
MS3848	Centenary of the First World War (3rd issue) The Post Office at War, 1914–1918	
MS3855	Pink Floyd on Stage	
MS3868	150th Birth anniversary of Beatrix Potter (writer, illustrator and conservationist) Illustrations from *The Tale of Peter Rabbit*	
MS3911	Christmas Celebrating 50 years of Christmas stamps	
MS3932	Windsor Castle (2nd issue) St George's Chapel	
MS3939	David Bowie (1947–2016, singer, songwriter and actor) Commemoration David Bowie Live	
MS3964	50th Anniversary of the Machin Definitive	
MS3965	50th Anniversary of the Machin Definitive	
MS4027	Christmas. Madonna and Child	
MS4032	Royal Platinum Wedding Anniversary of Queen Elizabeth II and Duke of Edinburgh	
MS4043	*Game of Thrones* non-human characters	
MS4064	RAF Centenary	
MS4092	Royal Wedding Prince Harry and Ms. Meghan Markle	
MS4115	Hampton Court Palace	
MS4124	Captain Cook and the *Endeavour* Voyage	
MS4151	Harry Potter	
MS4162	Christmas	
MS4169	Stamp Classics	
MS4192	Marvel Marvel Heroes UK	
MS4218	British Engineering 50th Anniversary of Harrier Jump Jet	
MS4225	Birth Bicentenary of Queen Victoria (1st issue) The Legacy of Prince Albert	
MS4236	75th Anniversary of D-Day	
MS4261	Elton John Elton John Live	
MS4274	ICC Cricket World Cup Winners (men)	
MS4275	ICC Cricket World Cup Winners (women)	
MS4282	*The Gruffalo*	
MS4291	Christmas. Nativity	
MS4303	*Star Trek* (5th issue)	
MS4320	Video Games *Tomb Raider*	
MS4338	James Bond Q Branch	
MS4355	180th Anniversary of the Penny Black	
MS4364	75th Anniversary of the End of the Second World War Memorials	
MS4377	*Coronation Street* Rovers Return Barmaids	
MS4396	Queen (rock band) Queen Live	
MS4417	*Sherlock* Sherlock Holmes Mysteries by Sir Arthur Conan Doyle	
MS4442	Christmas. Stained glass Windows	
MS4455	*Star Trek* *Star Trek* The Movies	
MS4476	United Kingdom: A Celebration	
MS4485	*Only Fools and Horses*	
MS4622	The Rolling Stones	
MS4635	The stamp designs of David Gentleman	
MS4642	The FA Cup	

REGIONALS

MSEN50	Celebrating England	
MSNI152	Celebrating Northern Ireland	
MSNI153	50th anniversary of the Country Definitives	
MSS152	Opening of new Scottish Parliament building, Edinburgh	
MSS153	Celebrating Scotland	
MSS157	250th birth anniversary of Robert Burns (Scottish poet)	
MSS180	700th Anniversary of the Declaration of Arbroath	
MSW143	Opening of New Welsh Assembly building, Cardiff	
MSW147	Celebrating Wales	

Alphabetically by title of sheet

40th anniversary of the first Machin definitives	MS2743
50th anniversary of *Doctor Who* (TV programme) *Dr. Who* 1963–2013	MS3451
50th anniversary of first Castles definitives	MS2530
50th anniversary of the Machin definitive	MS3965, MS3966
50th anniversary of passenger Jet Aviation Airliners	MS2289
50th anniversary of the Royal Shakespeare Company The four Theatres of the Royal Shakespeare Company, Stratford-upon-Avon	MS3179
50th anniversary of the WWF Wildlife of the Amazon Rainforest	MS3172
50th anniversary of Wilding definitives (1st issue)	MS2326
50th anniversary of Wilding definitives (2nd issue)	MS2367
60th anniversary of end of the Second World War	MS2547
70th anniversary of the Year of Three Kings	MS2658
75th Anniversary of D-Day	MS4236
75th anniversary of the Battle of Britain Battle of Britain	MS3735
75th Anniversary of the End of the Second World War Memorials	MS4364
90th birthday of Queen Elizabeth II	MS3832
150th anniversary of first Double-decker Bus	MS2215
150th anniversary of the London Underground Classic London Underground Posters	MS3429
150th anniversary of the Victoria Cross	MS2665
150th birth anniversary of Beatrix Potter (writer, illustrator and conservationist) (2nd issue) Illustrations from *The Tale of Peter Rabbit*	MS3868
150th death anniversary of Charlotte Brontë Illustrations of scenes from *Jane Eyre* by Paula Rego	MS2524
175th anniversary of the Penny Black Penny Black and 1840 2d. blue	MS3710
180th Anniversary of the Penny Black Penny Black	MS4355
Action for Species (3rd series) 250th anniversary of Royal Botanic Gardens, Kew	MS2941

Andy Murray, Men's singles champion, Murray's Wimbledon Victory	MS3511
Animail	MS3837
Astronomy	MS2315
Bees The Honey Bee	MS3742
Bicentenary of the Battle of Trafalgar Scenes from *Panorama of the Battle of Trafalgar* by William Heath	MS2580
Bicentenary of the Battle of Waterloo Soldiers and Battle of Waterloo map	MS3734
Bicentenary of the Royal Horticultural Society	MS2462
Birth bicentenary of Charles Darwin (naturalist and evolutionary theorist) Fauna and Map of the Galápagos Islands	MS2904
Birth bicentenary of Charles Dickens Scenes from *Nicholas Nickleby*, *Bleak House*, *Little Dorrit* and *A Tale of Two Cities*	MS3336
Birth bicentenary of Isambard Kingdom Brunel (engineer)	MS2613
Birth bicentenary of Queen Victoria. The Legacy of Prince Albert	MS4225
Birth centenary of Arnold Machin	MS3222
Birth centenary of Ian Fleming (Author of James Bond books) Book Covers	MS2803
Britain Alone Evacuation of British Troops from Dunkirk, 1940	MS3086
British Architecture (4th series) Historic Buildings	MS1058
British Auto Legends The Workhorses	MS3518
British Engineering 50th Anniversary of Harrier Jump Jet	MS4218
Buckingham Palace, London Buckingham Palace	MS3601
Business and Consumer Smilers	MS3024
Cathedrals 300th anniversary of St Paul's Cathedral	MS2847
Captain Cook and the *Endeavour* Voyage	MS4124
Centenary of Girlguiding	MS3025
Centenary of Royal Navy Submarine Service	MS2206
Centenary of the First World War (3rd issue) The Post Office at War, 1914–1918	MS3848
Christmas. 400th anniversary of the *King James Bible*	MS3249
Christmas. Angels	MS2795
Christmas. Celebrating 50 years of Christmas stamps	MS3911
Christmas. Father Christmas by Raymond Briggs	MS2501
Christmas. Illustrations by Andrew Bannecker	MS3657
Christmas. Illustrations by Axel Scheffler	MS3422
Christmas. Madonna and Child paintings	MS2588
Christmas. Madonna and Child paintings	MS3549
Christmas. Madonna and Child paintings	MS4027
Christmas. Meditations on the imagery of Christmas	MS3779
Christmas. Nativity	MS4291
Christmas. Post Boxes	MS4162
Christmas. Scenes from Pantomimes	MS2882
Christmas. Stained glass windows	MS2998
Christmas. Stained glass windows	MS4442
Christmas. Traditional Secular	MS2684
Christmas with Wallace and Gromit	MS3135
Classic Album Covers (2nd issue)	MS3019
Classic Locomotives	MS2423
Classic Locomotives (1st series). England Classic Locomotives of England	MS3144
Classic Locomotives (2nd series). Scotland Classic Locomotives of Scotland	MS3283
Classic Locomotives (3rd series). Northern Ireland Classic Locomotives of Northern Ireland	MS3498
Classic Locomotives (4th series). Wales Classic Locomotives of Wales	MS3578
Classic Transport Toys	MS2402
Coronation Street Rovers Return Barmaids	MS4377
David Bowie Live	MS3939
Death centenary of Edward Lear (artist and author)	MS1409
Death centenary of Sir Rowland Hill	MS1099
Diamond Jubilee. (2nd issue) Queen Elizabeth II	MS3272
Diamond Wedding of Queen Elizabeth II and Duke of Edinburgh	MS2786
Elton John	MS4261
England's Ashes Victory	MS2573

570

COMMEMORATIVE / MINIATURE SHEET DESIGN INDEX

England's Victory in Rugby World Cup
    Championship, Australia MS2416
Europa. Children's books
    Winnie the Pooh by A. A. Milne.
    Book Illustrations by E. H. Shepard.... MS3127
F.A.B. The Genius of Gerry Anderson
    (producer of TV programmes) MS3142
First United Kingdom Aerial
    Post, centenary (1st issue) First
    United Kingdom Aerial Post,
    9 September 1911 .... MS3220
Football Heroes MS3474
Game of Thrones,
    Non-human characters MS4043
Great British Films. Films by GPO Film Unit ... MS3608
Hampton Court Palace MS4115
Handover of Olympic Flag
    from Beijing to London MS2861
Harry Potter MS4151
ICC Cricket World Cup Winners MS4274
ICC Cricket World Cup Winners (women) ... MS4275
Industrial Archaeology MS1444
James Bond. Q Branch MS4338
Kings and Queens (1st issue)
    Houses of Lancaster and York MS2818
Kings and Queens (2nd issue)
    House of Tudor MS2930
Kings and Queens (3rd issue)
    House of Stewart MS3053
Kings and Queens (4th issue)
    House of Stuart MS3094
Kings and Queens (5th issue)
    House of Hanover MS3229
Kings and Queens (6th issue)
    House of Windsor MS3270
Lest We Forget (1st issue) 90th anniversary
    of the Battle of the Somme MS2685
Lest We Forget (2nd issue)
    90th anniversary of
    the Battle of Passchendaele MS2796
Lest We Forget (3rd issue)
    90th anniversary of the Armistice.... MS2886
London 1980 International
    Stamp Exhibition MS1119
London 2010 Festival of Stamps
    Jeffery Matthews Colour Palette........ MS3073
London 2010 Festival of Stamps and
    centenary of Accession of King George V
    (1st issue) MS3065
London 2010 Festival of Stamps and
    centenary of Accession of King George V
    (2nd issue) MS3072
London's successful bid
    for Olympic Games, 2012 .... MS2554
Long to Reign Over Us (2nd issue)
    Long to Reign Over Us MS3747
Marvel Heroes UK MS4192
Memories of London 2012 Olympic and
    Paralympic Games Scenes from Olympic
    and Paralympic Games.................... MS3406
Merchant Navy (2nd issue) Second World War
    Atlantic and Arctic convoys.............. MS3529
Millennium Series Millennium Timekeeper ... MS2123
New Wembley Stadium, London........ MS2740
Ocean Liners MS2454
Olympic and Paralympic Games,
    London (2012) (5th issue).............. MS3204a
Only Fools and Horses MS4485
Pink Floyd Pink Floyd on Stage MS3855
Post Boxes... MS2954
Publication of final book in the Harry Potter
    series Crests of Hogwarts School and its
    Four Houses MS2757
Queen Elizabeth the Queen Mother's
    100th Birthday MS2161
Queen (rock band) MS4396
RAF Centenary MS4067
Roald Dahl's Children's Stories (2nd issue)
    30th anniversary of the publication of
    The BFG MS3264
Royal Mail 500 (1st issue)
    Classic GPO Posters MS3801
Royal Platinum Wedding anniversary
    of Queen Elizabeth II and Duke
    of Edinburgh MS4032
Royal Wedding. Official Engagement
    portraits by Mario Testino
    Prince William and Miss Catherine
    Middleton MS3180
Royal Wedding Prince Charles and
    Mrs Camilla Parker Bowles.............. MS2531
Royal Wedding Prince Harry and
    Ms. Meghan Markle MS4092

Seaside Architecture British piers MS3641
Sherlock
    Sherlock Holmes Mysteries by Sir Arthur
    Conan Doyle MS4417
Smilers (5th series) MS3678
Solar Eclipse MS2106
Stamp Classics MS4169
Stamp Show 2000 International Stamp
    Exhibition, London
    Her Majesty's Stamps..................... MS2147
Stamp Show 2000 International Stamp
    Exhibition, London
    Jeffery Matthews Colour Palette....... MS2146
Stamp World London '90
    International Stamp Exhibition MS1501
Star Trek
    The Movies MS4455
Star Wars (1st issue) *Star Wars* MS3770
Star Wars (5th issue) *Star Wars* MS4303
The Beatles Beatles Memorabilia MS2692
The Gruffalo MS4282
The FA Cup MS4642
The Rolling Stones MS4622
The stamp designs of David Gentleman.... MS4635
The Weather MS2201
Thomas the Tank Engine Book
    Illustrations from The Railway Series MS3193
Trooping the Colour MS2546
UK A–Z (2nd series) MS3308
United Kingdom: A Celebration MS4476
Video Games. *Tomb Raider* MS4320
Welcome to London, Olympic Games
    Sports and London Landmarks....... MS3341
Welcome to London, Paralympic Games
    Paralympic Sports and London
    Landmarks MS3371
Windsor Castle (2nd issue)
    St George's Chapel MS3932
World Cup Football Championship,
    Japan and Korea MS2292
World of Invention (2nd issue) MS2727

REGIONALS

50th anniversary of the Country
    definitives....................................... MSNI153
250th birth anniversary of Robert Burns
    (Scottish poet)................................. MSS157
700th anniversary of the Declaration
    of Arbroath...................................... MSS180
Celebrating England MSEN50
Celebrating Northern Ireland MSNI152
Celebrating Scotland MSS153
Celebrating Wales MSW147
Opening of new Scottish Parliament
    building, Edinburgh........................ MSS152
Opening of New Welsh Assembly building,
    Cardiff... MSW143

Alphabetically by the individual stamps printed within the MS.

MS2147   £1 slate-green
    (1953 Coronation 1s. 3d. design)
    Her Majesty's Stamps..................... 2380
MS3734   15th Infantry Regiment, IV Corps,
    Prussian Army Soldiers and
    Battle of Waterloo Map 3730
MS3272   1953 Coinage portrait by
    Mary Gillick Diamond Jubilee of QEII
MS3272   1960 £1 Banknote portrait by
    Robert Austin Diamond Jubilee of QEII
MS4635   1962 3d. National Productivity Year
    The Stamp Designs of David Gentleman
MS4635   1965 4d. 25th Anniversary of the
    Battle of Britain The Stamp Designs
    of David Gentleman
MS4635   1966 6d. 900th Anniversary of the
    Battle of Hastings The Stamp
    Designs of David Gentleman
MS4635   1969 9d. British Ships The Stamp
    Designs of David Gentleman
MS3272   1971 £5 Banknote portrait by
    Harry Eccleston Diamond Jubilee of QEII
MS3272   1971 decimal coin portrait by
    Arnold Machin Diamond Jubilee of QEII
MS4635   1973 9p. British Trees The Stamp
    Designs of David Gentleman
MS4635   1976 8½p. Social Reformers The
    Stamp Designs of David Gentleman

MS3734   92nd Gordon Highlanders,
    Anglo-Allied Army
    Soldiers and Battle of Waterloo Map. 3732
MS3608   *A Colour Box* (1935) directed by
    Len Lye Films by GPO Film Unit
MS3939   *A Reality Tour*, 2004 David Bowie Live
MS3019   *A Rush of Blood to the Head*
    (Coldplay) Classic Album Covers......... 3010
MS3336   *A Tale of Two Cities*
    Charles Dickens, birth bicentenary
MS3429   A train every 90 seconds (Abram
    Games), 1937, Thanks to the
    Underground (Zero (Hans Schleger),
    1935 and Cut travelling time, Victoria
    Line (Tom Eckersley), 1969 Classic
    London Underground Posters
MS3429   Abram Games, poster designer
    Classic London Underground Posters
MS3801   Address your letters Plainly
    Classic GPO Posters 3803
MS4442   Adoration of the Magi, St. Andrew's
    Church, East Lexham
    Christmas 2020. Stained glass
    Windows 4434, 4436
MS4320   *Adventures of Lara Croft*
    Video Games
MS2215   AEC Regent 1, Daimler COG5,
    First Double-decker bus,
    150th anniversary 2211
MS2215   AEC Regent III RT Type,
    First Double-decker bus,
    150th anniversary 2212
MS2289   Airbus A340-600 (2002)
    Passenger Jet aviation,
    50th anniversary 2284
MS2904   *Amblyrhynchus cristatus* (Marine Iguana)
    Charles Darwin, birth bicentenary
MS3336   Amy Dorrit introduces Maggy to
    Arthur Clennam (*Little Dorrit*)
    Charles Dickens, birth bicentenary
MS3283   Andrew Barclay No. 807 *Bon Accord*
    propelling wagons along Miller Street,
    Aberdeen, June 1962
    Classic Locomotives of Scotland
MS3868   'And then, feeling rather sick, he
    went to look for some parsley.'
    Illustrations from *The Tale of
    Peter Rabbit* 3865
MS3511   Andy Murray
    kissing Wimbledon Trophy
    Men's Singles Champion, 2013
MS3511   Andy Murray serving
    Men's Singles Champion, 2013
MS4291   Angel and Shepherd Christmas. Nativity
MS3308   Angel of the North UK A–Z 3230
MS2795   Angel playing Flute (JOY)
    Christmas, 2007 2793
MS2795   Angel playing Lute (GOODWILL)
    Christmas, 2007 2790
MS2998   Angel playing Lute Church of
    St James, Staveley, Kendal, Cumbria
    (William Morris) Christmas
    Stained glass windows............. 2991, 2993
MS2795   Angel playing Tambourine (GLORY)
    Christmas, 2007 2794
MS2795   Angel playing Trumpet (PEACE)
    Christmas, 2007 2789
MS3549   Antoniazzo Romano, Artist
    Madonna and Child paintings .. 3543, 3546
MS3735   Armourer Fred Roberts replaces
    ammunition boxes on
    Supermarine Spitfire
    Battle of Britain, 75th anniversary
MS3222   Arnold Machin, Birth Centenary U3002
MS4338   Aston Martin DB5, *Skyfall* James Bond
MS3770   AT-AT Walkers *Star Wars*
MS2554   Athlete celebrating
    London's successful bid for Olympic
    Games, 2012 1934
MS2554   Athlete on starting blocks
    London's successful bid for Olympic
    Games, 2012 1930
MS3371   Athlete wearing running blades
    Paralympic Sports and
    London Landmarks
MS3371   Athlete wearing running blades
    and Olympic Stadium
    Paralympic Sports and
    London Landmarks
MS3341   Athletes in race
    Sports and London Landmarks
MS3341   Athletes in race and
    Olympic Stadium
    Sports and London Landmarks

COMMEMORATIVE / MINIATURE SHEET DESIGN INDEX

MS3518	Austin FX4 (1958–1997) London taxi British Auto Legends The Workhorses	
MS4291	Baby Jesus in Manger Christmas. Nativity	
MS3249	Baby Jesus in the Manger (Luke 2:7) *King James Bible*, 400th anniversary.... 3246	
MS3747	Badge of the House of Windsor Long to Reign Over Us	
MS3747	Badge of the House of Windsor depicting Round Tower of Windsor Castle Long to Reign Over Us	
MS2289	BAe/Aerospatiale Concorde (1976) Passenger Jet aviation, 50th anniversary 2285	
MS2786	Balmoral, 1972 Diamond Wedding of Queen Elizabeth II	
MS4225	Balmoral Castle, Scotland...................... 4227 The Royal Legacy of Prince Albert	
MS2201	Barometer dial The Weather 2197–2200	
MS3837	Bat Animail	
MS2818	Battle of Agincourt, 1415 Houses of Lancaster and York	
MS2796	Battle of Passchendaele, 90th anniversary ....As 2884	
MS2685	Battle of the Somme, 90th anniversary ....As 2883	
MS2692	Beatles tea tray and badges Beatles memorabilia	
MS4338	Bell-Textron Jet Pack, *Thunderball* James Bond	
MS4377	Bet Lynch (Julie Goodyear) *Coronation Street* Rovers Return Barmaids	
MS3249	Biblical quote; Luke 2:7 *King James Bible*, 400th anniversary.... 3246	
MS3249	Biblical quote; Luke 2:10 *King James Bible*, 400th anniversary.... 3247	
MS3249	Biblical quote; Matthew 1:21 *King James Bible*, 400th anniversary...........................3242, 3244	
MS3249	Biblical quote; Matthew 1:23 *King James Bible*, 400th anniversary...........................3243, 3245	
MS3249	Biblical quote; Matthew 2:10 *King James Bible*, 400th anniversary.... 3248	
MS4476	Binary code (Industry and Innovation)	
MS3024	Bird carrying envelope (Lucy Davey) Business and Consumer Smilers	
MS3024	Birthday cake (Annabel Wright) Business and Consumer Smilers	
MS2588	Black Madonna and Child from Haiti Madonna and Child paintings 2582	
MS3308	Blackpool Tower UK A–Z.......................... 3231	
MS3336	*Bleak House* Charles Dickens, birth bicentenary	
MS3220	Blériot Monoplane First United Kingdom Aerial Post........ 3218	
MS3019	Blur Classic Album Covers.................... 3011	
MS3474	Bobby Charlton (England), footballer Football Heroes...................................... 3473	
MS3474	Bobby Moore (England), footballer Football Heroes 3470	
MS2613	Box Tunnel Isambard Kingdom Brunel, birth bicentenary 2608	
MS2665	Boy Seaman Jack Cornwell, RN Victoria Cross, 150th anniversary........ 2660	
MS3578	BR 5600 No. 5652 Classic Locomotives of Wales	
MS3283	BR Class 4P No. 54767 *Clan Mackinnon* pulling fish train, Kyle of Lochalsh, October 1948 Classic Locomotives of Scotland	
MS3283	BR Class D34 Nos. 62471 *Glen Falloch* and 62496 *Glen Loy* at Ardlui, 9 May 1959 Classic Locomotives of Scotland	
MS3283	BR Class D40 No. 62276 *Andrew Bain* at Macduff, July 1950 Classic Locomotives of Scotland	
MS3144	BR Dean Goods No. 2532 Classic Locomotives of England	
MS2423	BR Standard Class, Keighley and Worth Valley Railway, Yorkshire Classic Locomotives 2422	
MS3144	BR WD No. 90662 Classic Locomotives of England	
MS4396	Brian May, Magic Tour, Nepstadion, Budapest, 1986 Queen Live 4402	
MS3641	Brighton Pier British Piers	
MS2215	Bristol Lodekka FSF6G First Double-decker bus, 150th anniversary........... 2213	
MS4236	British 3rd Division landing at Sword Beach... 4238 75th Anniversary of D-Day	
MS4236	British 50th Division landing on Gold Beach .... 4237 75th Anniversary of D-Day
MS2580	British Cutter *Entreprenante* attempting to rescue crew of burning French *Achille* Battle of Trafalgar, Bicentenary 2576
MS3072	British Empire Exhibition 1924, 1½d. brown stamp London 2010 Festival of Stamps......... 3067
MS3072	British Empire Exhibition 1924, 1d. red stamp London 2010 Festival of Stamps......... 3068
MS2580	British Fleet attacking in two columns Battle of Trafalgar, Bicentenary 2578
MS3025	Brownies Girlguiding UK
MS3474	Bryan Robson (England), Footballer Football Heroes...................................... 3471
MS3601	Buckingham Palace, London Buckingham Palace 3597-3600
MS2786	Buckingham Palace, London Diamond Wedding of Queen Elizabeth II
MS3657	Building a Snowman Christmas Illustrations by Andrew Bannecker....... 3654
MS3868	'But Peter, who was very naughty, ran straight away....' Illustrations from *The Tale of Peter Rabbit*................. 3866
MS4192	'But we're stronger' (Hulk, Iron Man, Black Panther and Spider-Man)........... 4197 Marvel Heroes UK
MS1058	Caernarvon Castle British Architecture (4th series) 1056
MS2530	Caernarfon Castle; £1 dull vermilion First Castles Definitives, 50th anniversary
MS2727	Camera and Television (John Logie Baird) World of Invention 2724
MS4236	Canadian 3rd Division landing at Juno Beach 75th Anniversary of D-Day
MS3204a	Canoe Slalom Olympic and Paralympic Games, London (2012) 2981
MS2665	Captain Albert Ball, RFC Victoria Cross, 150th anniversary........ 2663
MS2665	Captain Charles Upham, New Zealand Military Forces Victoria Cross, 150th anniversary........ 2664
MS2882	Captain Hook from *Peter Pan* Christmas. Pantomimes 2879
MS2665	Captain Noel Chavasse, RAMC Victoria Cross, 150th anniversary........ 2662
MS4455	Carol Marcus (Alice Eve), *Star Trek Into Darkness* *Star Trek.* The Movies
MS3657	Carol Singing Christmas Illustrations by Andrew Bannecker....... 3655
MS3308	Carrick-a-Rede, Co. Antrim UK A–Z 3232
MS2530	Carrickfergus Castle 50p. brownish-black First Castles Definitives, 50th anniversary
MS2803	*Casino Royale* (book covers) Ian Fleming, birth centenary 2797
MS3094	Castle Howard (John Vanbrugh, 1712) House of Stuart
MS1409	*Cat* (from alphabet book) Edward Lear, death centenary 1407
MS1409	'Cat' (from alphabet book) Edward Lear, death centenary 1409
MS3422	Cat and Mouse decorating Christmas Tree Christmas. Illustrations by Axel Scheffler 3421
MS2847	Cathedral Gallery–St Paul's, left side St Paul's Cathedral
MS2847	Cathedral Gallery–St Paul's, right side St Paul's Cathedral
MS2847	Cathedral Nave–St Paul's, left side St Paul's Cathedral
MS2847	Cathedral Nave–St Paul's, right side St Paul's Cathedral
MS3498	CDRJC Class 5 No. 4 Classic Locomotives of Northern Ireland
MS3229	Ceiling by Robert Adam, Kedleston Hall, 1763 House of Hanover
MS2501	Celebrating the Sunrise Father Christmas, Raymond Briggs..... 2496
MS4455	Chancellor Gorkon (David Warner), *Star Trek The Undiscovered Country* *Star Trek.* The Movies
MS3270	Channel Tunnel, 1996 House of Windsor
MS4115	Chapel Royal Hampton Court Palace
MS3336	Charles Darnay arrested by French revolutionaries (*A Tale of Two Cities*) Charles Dickens, birth bicentenary
MS3429	Charles Paine, poster designer Classic London Underground Posters
MS4124	Charting a new course: New Zealand and Australia Captain Cook and the *Endeavour* Voyage
MS3837	Chimpanzee Animail
MS2588	Choctaw Virgin Mother and Child (Fr. John Giuliani) Madonna and Child paintings 2585
MS3911	Christmas Pudding Celebrating 50 years of Christmas stamps 3910
MS2684	Christmas Tree Christmas, 2006 2683
MS3911	Christmas Tree Celebrating 50 years of Christmas stamps 3907
MS3127	Christopher Robin (putting on wellingtons) and Pooh (from *Winnie the Pooh*) Winnie the Pooh by A. A. Milne
MS3127	Christopher Robin reads to *Winnie the Pooh* (from Winnie the Pooh) *Winnie the Pooh* by A. A. Milne
MS2998	Church of Ormesby St Michael, Great Yarmouth, Norfolk Christmas Stained glass windows................. 2992, 2995
MS2998	Church of St James, Staveley, Kendal, Cumbria Christmas Stained glass windows................. 2991, 2993
MS2998	Church of St Mary the Virgin, Rye, East Sussex Christmas. Stained glass windows 2996
MS3094	Civil War Battle of Naseby, 1645 House of Stuart
MS2786	Clarence House Diamond Wedding of Queen Elizabeth II
MS3498	Classic Locomotives of Northern Ireland.. 3497
MS3578	Classic Locomotives of Wales ... 3573, 3577
MS2462	Clematis Arabella RHS, bicentenary of 2458
MS3220	Clement Greswell (pilot) and Blériot Monoplane First United Kingdom Aerial Post 3218
MS2613	Clifton Suspension Bridge Design Isambard Kingdom Brunel, birth bicentenary 2611
MS2123	Clock face and map of Asia Millennium Timekeeper
MS2123	Clock face and map of Europe Millennium Timekeeper
MS2123	Clock face and map of Middle East Millennium Timekeeper
MS2123	Clock face and map of North America Millennium Timekeeper
MS3518	Coastguard Land Rover British Auto Legends The Workhorses
MS3518	Coastguard Land Rover Defender 110 (from 1990) British Auto Legends The Workhorses
MS3019	Coldplay Classic Album Covers................................ 3010
MS3657	Collecting the Christmas Tree Christmas. Illustrations by Andrew Bannecker.....................3650, 3652
MS2588	Come let us adore Him (Dianne Tchumut) Madonna and Child paintings 2587
MS2524	Come to Me Charlotte Brontë, 150th death anniversary 2519
MS2861	Corner Tower of the Forbidden City, Beijing Handover of Olympic Flag from Beijing to London
MS2665	Corporal Agansing Rai, Ghurka Victoria Cross, 150th anniversary........ 2659
MS1444	Cotton Mills, New Lanark, Strathclyde Industrial Archaeology ... 1442
MS2727	Couple with Suitcases on Moon (space travel) World of Invention........ 2726
MS2423	CR Class 439, Bo'ness and Kinneil Railway, West Lothian Classic Locomotives 2418
MS2740	Crowned Lion with Shield of St George New Wembley Stadium, London...As 2291
MS2292	Crowned Lion with Shield of St George World Cup Football Championship, Japan & Korea............ 2291
MS4642	Cup Final souvenirs The FA Cup
MS2580	Cutter and HMS *Pickle* (schooner) Battle of Trafalgar, Bicentenary 2577
MS3451	Cyberman *Dr. Who* 1963–2013
MS3371	Cyclist and London Eye Paralympic Sports and London Landmarks

572

COMMEMORATIVE / MINIATURE SHEET DESIGN INDEX

MS3341 Cyclist and London Eye Sports and London Landmarks
MS3678 Dad (Webb & Webb Design Ltd) Smilers, 2015...3677
MS2462 Dahlia, Garden Princess RHS, bicentenary of 2457
MS2215 Daimler Fleetline CRG6LX-33, First Double-decker bus, 150th anniversary.................................. 2214
MS3451 Dalek *Dr. Who* 1963–2013
MS3474 Dave Mackay (Scotland), Footballer Football Heroes 3472
MS3429 David Booth, poster designer Classic London Underground Posters
MS3019 David Bowie Classic Album Covers................................ 3018
MS3939 David Bowie (1947–2016, singer, songwriter and actor) Commemoration David Bowie Live
MS2289 de Havilland Comet (1952) Passenger Jet aviation, 50th anniversary 2288
MS4485 Del Boy (*Only Fools and Horses*) 4486
MS3848 Delivering the mail on the Home Front The Post Office at War, 1914–1918 3846
MS3220 Delivery of first Airmail to Post Master General First United Kingdom Aerial Post......... 3219
MS2462 Delphinium Clifford Sky RHS, bicentenary of 2461
MS3474 Denis Law (Scotland), footballer Football Heroes 3469
MS3747 Depiction of Round Tower of Windsor Castle Long to Reign Over Us
MS3678 Designer–Caroline Gardner Ltd Smilers, 2015................................... 3672
MS3678 Designer–NB Studio Smilers, 2015......................3670, 3675, 3676
MS3678 Designer–Rebecca Sutherland Smilers, 2015................................... 3673
MS3678 Designer–The Chase Smilers, 2015................................... 3674
MS3678 Designer–Webb & Webb Design Ltd Smilers, 2015.......................... 3671, 3677
MS3024 Designer Andrew Davidson Business and Consumer Smilers
MS3024 Designer Annabel Wright Business and Consumer Smilers
MS2685 Designer Gareth Howat Battle of the Somme, 90th anniversary 2883
MS2796 Designer Gareth Howat Battle of Passchendaele, 90th anniversary 2884
MS3429 Designer Mary Koop Classic London Underground Posters
MS3429 Designer Maxwell Armfield Classic London Underground Posters
MS3024 Designer Neil Oliver Business and Consumer Smilers
MS2501 Designer Raymond Briggs Father Christmas Raymond Briggs... 2495-2500
MS3529 Destroyer HMS *Vanoc* escorting Atlantic Convoy Atlantic and Arctic Convoys, Second World War 3525
MS2106 Development of astronomical telescopes Solar eclipse 2105
MS3747 Device from The Queen's Personal Flag Long to Reign Over Us
MS3272 Diamond Jubilee of QEII Diamond Jubilee of QEII U3273
MS2803 *Diamonds are Forever* (book covers) Ian Fleming, birth centenary 2800
MS2462 *Dianthus Allwoodii* Group RHS, bicentenary of 2456
MS2402 Dinky Toys Ford Zephyr, *c.*1956 Classic Transport toys......................... 2400
MS3608 Directed by Harry Watt and Basil Wright Films by GPO Film Unit
MS3608 Directed by Humphrey Jennings Films by GPO Film Unit
MS3608 Directed by Len Lye Films by GPO Film Unit
MS3608 Directed by Norman McLaren Films by GPO Film Unit
MS4124 Disaster avoided: repairs on the Endeavour River Captain Cook and the *Endeavour* Voyage
MS3341 Diver and Tate Modern Sports and London Landmarks
MS4261 Dodger Stadium, 1975 Elton John Live

MS2423 *Dolgoch*, Rheilffordd Talyllyn Railway, Gwynedd Classic Locomotives 2417
MS3308 Downing Street UK A–Z....................... 3233
MS2803 *Dr. No* (book covers) Ian Fleming, birth centenary 2798
MS3451 *Dr. Who* TV programme 1963–2013 *Dr. Who* 1963–2013................................ 3449
MS3641 Dunoon Pier British Piers
MS2530 Edinburgh Castle; £1 royal blue First Castles Definitives, 50th anniversary
MS3308 Edinburgh Castle UK A–Z....................... 3234
MS2954 Edward VII Ludlow Letter Box, 1901–1910 Post Boxes................................ 2951
MS3801 Edward McKnight Kauffer, 1936 poster designer Classic GPO Posters 3802
MS3429 Edward McKnight Kauffer, poster designer Classic London Underground Posters
MS2954 Elizabeth II Type A Wall Letter Box, 1962–1963 Post Boxes................................ 2953
MS1409 *Edward Lear as a Bird* (self-portrait) Edward Lear, death centenary 1406
MS2727 Email and internet World of Invention 2725
MS2547 End of the Second World War, 60th anniversary End of the Second World War, 60th anniversary 1668, 1875
MS4274 England Captain Eoin Morgan lifting Cricket World Cup Trophy ICC Cricket World Cup Winners
MS4275 England Captain Heather Knight and teammates celebrating ICC Cricket World Cup Winners (women)
MS2416 England flags and fans England's victory in Rugby World Cup
MS4274 England players celebrating ICC Cricket World Cup Winners
MS4275 England players congratulating Anya Shrubsole ICC Cricket World Cup Winners (women)
MS4274 England players congratulating Ben Stokes ICC Cricket World Cup Winners
MS4275 England team after their victory ('CHAMPIONS') ICC Cricket World Cup Winners (women)
MS4275 England team celebrating on balcony at Lord's Cricket Ground ICC Cricket World Cup (women)
MS2416 England team standing in circle before match England's victory in Rugby World Cup
MS2573 England team with Ashes trophy England's Ashes victory, 2005
MS3270 England's winning World Cup football team, 1966 House of Windsor
MS2740 English definitive, (2nd) New Wembley Stadium, London....... EN6a
MS2685 English definitive, 72p Battle of the Somme, 90th anniversary EN17
MS2796 English definitive, 78p. Battle of Passchendaele, 90th anniversary EN18
MS2740 English definitive, 78p. New Wembley Stadium, London........EN18
MS2886 English definitive, 81p. Armistice, 90th anniversary.................EN19
MS2292 English Flag World Cup Football Championship, Japan & Korea
MS2292 English Flag–bottom left quarter, and football World Cup Football Championship, Japan & Korea 2293
MS2292 English Flag - bottom right quarter, and football World Cup Football Championship, Japan & Korea 2294
MS2546 Ensign of the Scots Guards, 2002 Trooping the Colour 2540
MS2580 *Entreprenante* with dismasted British *Belle Isle* Battle of Trafalgar, Bicentenary 2574
MS4274 Eoin Morgan (with trophy) and England team ICC Cricket World Cup Winners
MS3964 Essay of Coinage Head cropped and simplified, with only the Denomination, October 1966.............. 3961
MS3964 Essay of the First Plaster Cast of the Diadem Head, without Corsage, October 1966.. 3963
MS3964 Essay with Coinage Head surrounded by Country Symbols, April/May 1966 3960

MS3549 Fadi Mikhail, Artist Madonna and Child paintings 3548
MS2201 FAIR The Weather............................... 2198
MS2684 Father Christmas Christmas, 2006..............................2679, 2681
MS2501 Father Christmas on Snowy Roof Father Christmas, Raymond Briggs..... 2495
MS3341 Fencer Sports and London Landmarks
MS3341 Fencer and Tower Bridge Sports and London Landmarks
MS2930 Field of Cloth of Gold Royal Conference, 1520 The House of Tudor
MS3608 Film–A Colour Box (1935) Films by GPO Film Unit
MS3608 Film–Love on the Wing (1938) Films by GPO Film Unit
MS3608 Film–Night Mail (1936) Films by GPO Film Unit
MS3608 Film–Spare Time (1939) Films by GPO Film Unit
MS2743 First Machin definitives, 40th anniversary Machin, £1 bluish violet........................Y1743
MS2743 First Machin definitives, 40th anniversary Machin, £1 magenta Y1744
MS2685 First World War Battle of the Somme, 90th anniversary 2883
MS2796 First World War Battle of Passchendaele, 90th anniversary 2884
MS2886 First World War Armistice, 90th anniversary.................. 2885
MS2206 Flag of Chief of Defence Staff RN Submarine Service, 100th anniversary
MS2904 Flightless Cormorant (*Phalacrocorax harrisi*) Charles Darwin, birth bicentenary
MS2904 Floreana Mockingbird (*Mimus trifasciatus*) Charles Darwin, birth bicentenary
MS2292 Football World Cup Football Championship, Japan & Korea.......................2293, 2294
MS3204a Football Olympic and Paralympic Games, London (2012)....................................... 3104
MS2740 Football New Wembley Stadium, London
MS3429 For the Zoo (Charles Paine), 1921, Power (Edward McKnight-Kauffer), 1931 and The Seen (James Fitton), 1948 Classic London Underground Posters
MS2803 *For Your Eyes Only* (book covers) Ian Fleming, birth centenary 2801
MS3518 Ford Anglia 105E (1959–1967) police car British Auto Legends The Workhorses
MS3518 Ford Anglia police car British Auto Legends The Workhorses
MS3180 Formal portrait of Prince William and Miss Catherine Middleton in Council Chamber, St James's Palace Royal Wedding. Prince William and Catherine Middleton
MS3308 Forth Railway Bridge UK A–Z................. 3235
MS3053 Foundation of Court of Session, 1532 House of Stewart
MS3053 Foundation of the College of Surgeons, Edinburgh, 1505 House of Stewart
MS3053 Foundation of the University of St Andrews, 1413 House of Stewart
MS4282 Fox *The Gruffalo*
MS3549 Francesco Granacci, Artist Madonna and Child paintings 3542
MS2930 Francis Drake (circumnavigation), 1580 The House of Tudor
MS2580 Franco/Spanish Fleet putting to sea from Cadiz Battle of Trafalgar, Bicentenary 2579
MS4396 Freddie Mercury, Magic Tour, Wembley Stadium, 1986 Queen Live.. 4399
MS3127 From *Now we are Six* Winnie the Pooh by A. A. Milne
MS2803 *From Russia with Love* (book covers) Ian Fleming, birth centenary 2802
MS3193 From *The Eight Famous Engines* Thomas the Tank Engine
MS3193 From *The Three Railway Engines* Thomas the Tank Engine
MS3193 From *Toby the Tram Engine* Thomas the Tank Engine

573

COMMEMORATIVE / MINIATURE SHEET DESIGN INDEX

MS	Description	Ref
MS3127	From *Winnie the Pooh* Winnie the Pooh by A. A. Milne	
MS4192	'Fury, a portal is opening' (Captain Britain) Marvel Heroes UK	4199
MS4043	*Game of Thrones* non-human characters	
MS3406	Games makers Scenes from Olympic and Paralympic Games	
MS3406	Games makers and Olympic Stadium Scenes from Olympic and Paralympic Games	
MS2423	GCR Class 8K, *Leicestershire* Classic Locomotives	2419
MS4377	Gemma Winter (Dolly-Rose Campbell) *Coronation Street* Rovers Return Barmaids	
MS2882	Genie from *Aladdin* Christmas. Pantomimes	2877
MS3179	Geoffrey Streatfield in *Henry V*, 2007, The Courtyard Theatre Royal Shakespeare Company, The Four Theatres	
MS2954	George Type B Wall Letter Box, 1933–1936 Post Boxes	2950
MS3474	George Best (Northern Ireland), footballer Football Heroes	3466
MS2904	Giant tortoise (*Nannopterum harrisi*) and Cactus Finch (*Geospiza scandens*) Charles Darwin, birth bicentenary	
MS4476	Glass facade, microphone stand (Creativity)	
MS3308	Glastonbury Tor UK A–Z	3236
MS2727	Globe as Web (email and internet) World of Invention	2725
MS3429	Golders Green, 1908, By Underground to fresh air (Maxwell Armfield), 1915 and Summer Sales (Mary Koop), 1925 Classic London Underground Posters	
MS2803	*Goldfinger* (book covers) Ian Fleming, birth centenary	2799
MS3193	'Goodbye, Bertie', called Thomas Thomas the Tank Engine	
MS3474	Gordon Banks (England), footballer Football Heroes	3465
MS4485	Grandad (*Only Fools and Horses*)	4491
MS3678	Grandparent (NB Studio) Smilers, 2015	3676
MS4115	Great Hall Hampton Court Palace	4116
MS3734	Grenadiers, Imperial Guard French Army Soldiers and Battle of Waterloo Map	3733
MS3135	Gromit carrying Christmas Pudding Christmas with Wallace and Gromit	3133
MS3135	Gromit posting Christmas Cards Christmas with Wallace and Gromit	3129, 3132
MS3135	Gromit wearing Oversized Sweater Christmas with Wallace and Gromit	3134
MS2757	Gryffindor Harry Potter. Crests of Hogwarts School	
MS3025	Guides Girlguiding UK	
MS2692	Guitar Beatles memorabilia	
MS3220	Gustav Hamel in Cockpit First United Kingdom Aerial Post	3217
MS3220	Gustav Hamel (pilot) First United Kingdom Aerial Post	3217
MS3220	Gustav Hamel receiving mailbag First United Kingdom Aerial Post	3216
MS2423	GWR Manor Class *Bradley Manor*, Severn Valley Railway, Worcestershire Classic Locomotives	2420
MS2588	Haitian painting Madonna and Child paintings	2582
MS4364	Hall of Names, Holocaust History Museum, Yad Vashem, Jerusalem	4365
MS4261	Hammersmith Odeon, 1973 Elton John Live	
MS1058	Hampton Court Palace British Architecture (4th series)	1057
MS2861	Handover of Olympic Flag from Beijing to London Handover of Olympic Flag from Beijing to London	4365
MS4476	Hands forming heart (Community)	
MS3801	Hans Schleger, 1942 Classic GPO Posters	3803
MS3801	Hans Unger, 1951 Classic GPO Posters	3805
MS3678	Happy Birthday (NB Studio) Smilers, 2015	3670
MS3308	Harlech Castle UK A–Z	3237
MS4218	Harrier GR3 50th Anniversary of Harrier Jump Jet	
MS3801	Harry Stevens, 1960 Classic GPO Posters	3804
MS3735	Hawker Hurricanes Battle of Britain, 75th anniversary	
MS2289	Hawker Siddley Trident (1964) Passenger Jet aviation, 50th anniversary	2286
MS3024	*Hello* in plane vapour trail (Lucy Davey)	
MS2818	Henry V's triumph at Battle of Agincourt, 1415 Houses of Lancaster and York	
MS2998	Henry Holiday Christmas. Stained-glass windows	2992, 2994, 2995, 2997
MS3868	'He slipped underneath the gate, and was safe at last…'. Illustrations from *The Tale of Peter Rabbit*	3867
MS2147	Her Majesty's Stamps	2124, 2380
MS4192	'He's strong' (Thor, Doctor Strange and Iron Man) Marvel Heroes UK	4196
MS3529	HMS *King George V* in Arctic Waters Atlantic and Arctic Convoys, Second World War	3527
MS3529	HMS *Vanoc* escorting Atlantic Convoy Atlantic and Arctic Convoys, Second World War	3525
MS2757	Hogwarts Harry Potter. Crests of Hogwarts School	
MS3511	Holding Trophy (Andy Murray) Men's Singles Champion, 2013	
MS1058	Holyroodhouse British Architecture (4th series)	1055
MS3848	Home Depot at Regent's Park, London The Post Office at War, 1914–1918	3847
MS4151	Horace Slughorn Harry Potter	
MS2402	Hornby M1 Clockwork Locomotive and Tender, c.1948 Classic Transport toys	2399
MS2757	Hufflepuff Harry Potter. Crests of Hogwarts School	
MS3578	Hunslet No. 589 *Blanche* Classic Locomotives of Wales	3577
MS3172	Hyacinth Macaw (*Anodorhynchus hyacinthinus*) Wildlife of the Amazon Rainforest	
MS3657	Ice Skating Christmas Illustrations by Andrew Bannecker	3656
MS3511	In action (Andy Murray) Men's Singles Champion, 2013	
MS2524	In the Comfort of her Bonnet Charlotte Brontë, 150th death anniversary	2520
MS2524	Inspection Charlotte Brontë, 150th death anniversary	2523
MS2727	Iron Bridge (Thomas Telford) World of Invention	2721
MS1444	Ironbridge, Shropshire Industrial Archaeology	1440
MS3308	Ironbridge UK A–Z	3238
MS3019	IV (Led Zeppelin) Classic Album Covers	3016
MS2757	J. K. Rowling Harry Potter. Crests of Hogwarts School	
MS3549	Jacques-Louis David, Artist Madonna and Child paintings	3545
MS3172	Jaguar (*Panthera onca*) Wildlife of the Amazon Rainforest	
MS3429	James Fitton, poster designer Classic London Underground Posters	
MS3193	James was more dirty than hurt (from Toby the Tram Engine) Thomas the Tank Engine	
MS3179	Janet Suzman as Ophelia, *Hamlet*, 1965 Royal Shakespeare Company, The Four Theatres	
MS4303	Jedi Starfighter *Star Wars*	4307
MS3474	Jimmy Greaves (England), footballer Football Heroes	3463
MS3308	Jodrell Bank UK A–Z	3239
MS3474	John Barnes (England), footballer Football Heroes	3467
MS3474	John Charles (Wales), footballer Football Heroes	3464
MS4396	John Deacon, A Night at the Opera Tour, Hammersmith Odeon, 1975 Queen Live	4396
MS3053	John Knox (Reformation, 1559) House of Stewart	
MS2727	John Logie Baird World of Invention	2724
MS3094	John Milton (*Paradise Lost*, 1667) House of Stuart	
MS2206	Jolly Roger flown by HMS *Proteus* (submarine) RN Submarine Service, 100th anniversary	2209
MS4291	Joseph Christmas. Nativity	
MS3249	Joseph visited by the Angel (Matthew 1:21) *King James Bible*, 400th anniversary	3242, 3244
MS2998	Joseph, Parish Church of St Michael, Minehead, Somerset (Henry Holiday) Christmas. Stained glass windows	2994
MS3179	Judy Dench as Lady Macbeth, 1976, The Other Place Royal Shakespeare Company, The Four Theatres	
MS3229	Kedleston Hall, 1763 House of Hanover	
MS3474	Kevin Keegan (England), footballer Football Heroes	3468
MS2573	Kevin Pietersen, Michael Vaughan and Andrew Flintoff on opening day of first Test, Lords England's Ashes victory, 2005	
MS2941	Kew Gardens Royal Botanic Gardens, Kew	
MS4169	King Edward VII 1910 2d. Tyrian plum stamp Stamp Classics	
MS4169	King Edward VIII 1936 1½d. red-brown stamp Stamp Classics	
MS4169	King George V 1913 Seahorse' 2s. 6d. brown stamp Stamp Classics	
MS3065	King George V and Queen Elizabeth II Accession of King George V, Centenary Stamp Classics	
MS4169	King George VI 1940 Penny Black Centenary ½d. green stamp	
MS4115	King's Great Bedchamber Hampton Court Palace	4117
MS4115	King's Staircase Hampton Court Palace	
MS3837	Koala Animail	
MS4455	Krall (Idris Elba), *Star Trek Beyond Star Trek*. The Movies	
MS3308	Kursaal, Southend, Essex UK A–Z	3240
MS2524	La Ligne des Rats Charlotte Brontë, 50th death anniversary	2521
MS3549	*La Vierge au Lys* (William-Adolphe Bouguereau) Madonna and Child paintings	3547
MS3144	Lancashire and Yorkshire Railway 1093 No. 1100 Classic Locomotives of England	
MS3911	Lantern Celebrating 50 years of Christmas stamps	3908
MS3019	Led Zeppelin Classic Album Covers	3016
MS3019	*Let It Bleed* (Rolling Stones) Classic Album Covers	3013
MS2215	Leyland X2 Open-top, First Double-decker bus, 50th anniversary	2210
MS4124	Life on Raiatea: boathouse and canoes Captain Cook and the *Endeavour* Voyage	
MS3734	Light Infantry, King's German Legion, Anglo-Allied Army Soldiers and Battle of Waterloo Map	3731
MS2462	Lilium, Lemon Pixie RHS, bicentenary of	2460
MS3308	Lindisfarne Priory UK A–Z	3241
MS3336	*Little Dorrit* Charles Dickens, birth bicentenary	
MS4338	Little Nellie, *You Only Live Twice* James Bond	
MS4377	Liz McDonald (Beverley Callard) *Coronation Street* Rovers Return Barmaids	
MS3641	Llandudno Pier British Piers	
MS3578	LMS No. 7720 Classic Locomotives of Wales	3573
MS3578	LMS No. 7720 Classic Locomotives of Wales	As 3573
MS3283	Locomotive No. 54767 *Clan Mackinnon* Classic Locomotives of Scotland	
MS3283	Locomotive No. 807 *Bon Accord* Classic Locomotives of Scotland	
MS3498	Locomotives Classic Locomotives of Northern Ireland	3497
MS3578	Locomotives Classic Locomotives of Wales	3573
MS3578	Locomotives Classic Locomotives of Wales	3577
MS3283	Locomotives 62276 *Andrew Bain* at Macduff, July 1950 Classic Locomotives of Scotland	

COMMEMORATIVE / MINIATURE SHEET DESIGN INDEX

MS3283 Locomotives, 62471 *Glen Falloch* and 62496 *Glen Loy* Classic Locomotives of Scotland
MS1119 London 1980, International Stamp Exhibition London 1980, Int Stamp Exhibition... 1118
MS3019 *London Calling* (The Clash) Classic Album Covers 3014
MS2861 London Eye Handover of Olympic Flag from Beijing to London
MS3341 London Eye Sports and London Landmarks
MS3371 London Eye Paralympic Sports and London Landmarks
MS1099 London Postman, *circa* 1839 Sir Rowland Hill, death centenary 1097
MS3518 London taxi British Auto Legends. The Workhorses
MS3308 London Zoo UK A–Z................................ 3307
MS2554 London's successful bid for Olympic Games, 2012 London's successful bid for Olympic Games, 2012 As 1930–1934
MS4338 Lotus Esprit Submarine, *The Spy Who Loved Me* James Bond
MS3678 Love (Rebecca Sutherland) Smilers, 2015... 3673
MS3608 *Love on the Wing* (1938) directed by Norman McLaren Films by GPO Film Unit
MS2147 Machin, (1st) olive-brown Her Majesty's Stamps.............................. 2124
MS2547 Machin, (1st) gold End of the Second World War, 60th anniversary 1668
MS3222 Machin, (1st) gold Arnold Machin, Birth Centenary U3002
MS3272 Machin, (1st) slate-blue Diamond Jubilee of QEII .... As U3271
MS2743 Machin 1967 4d. brown First Machin definitives, 40th anniversary
MS3073 Machin, 1p. reddish purple Jeffery Matthews colour palette, 2010
MS3073 Machin, 2p. deep grey-green Jeffery Matthews colour palette, 2010
MS2146 Machin, 4p. new blue Jeffery Matthews colour palette, 2000
MS2146 Machin, 5p. dull red-brown Jeffery Matthews colour palette, 2000
MS3073 Machin, 5p. reddish-brown Jeffery Matthews colour palette, 2010
MS2146 Machin, 6p. yellow-olive Jeffery Matthews colour palette, 2000
MS3073 Machin, 9p. bright orange Jeffery Matthews colour palette, 2010
MS2146 Machin, 10p. dull orange Jeffery Matthews colour palette, 2001
MS3073 Machin, 10p. orange Jeffery Matthews colour palette, 2010
MS3073 Machin, 20p. light green Jeffery Matthews colour palette, 2010
MS2146 Machin, 31p. deep mauve Jeffery Matthews colour palette, 2000
MS2146 Machin, 39p. bright magenta Jeffery Matthews colour palette, 2000
MS3073 Machin, 60p. emerald Jeffery Matthews colour palette, 2010
MS2146 Machin, 64p. turquoise-green Jeffery Matthews colour palette, 2000
MS3073 Machin, 67p. bright mauve Jeffery Matthews colour palette, 2010
MS3073 Machin, 88p. bright magenta Jeffery Matthews colour palette, 2010
MS3073 Machin, 97p. bluish violet Jeffery Matthews colour palette, 2010
MS2743 Machin, £1 bluish violet First Machin definitives, 40th anniversary Y1743
MS2146 Machin, £1 bluish violet Jeffery Matthews colour palette, 2000
MS2743 Machin, £1 magenta First Machin definitives, 40th anniversary Y1744
MS3073 Machin, £1·46 turquoise-blue Jeffery Matthews colour palette, 2010
MS2658 Machin, £3 deep mauve Year of Three Kings, 70th anniversary Y1748
MS4261 Madison Square Garden, 2018 Elton John Live
MS3549 *Madonna and Child* (Francesco Granacci) Madonna and Child paintings . 3542, 3544
MS2588 *Madonna and Child* (Marianne Stokes) Madonna and Child paintings 2583

MS3249 Madonna and Child (Matthew 1:23) King James Bible, 400th anniversary.................. 3243, 3245
MS2588 Madonna and Child paintings Madonna and Child paintings 2582–2587
MS3549 Madonna and Child paintings Madonna and Child paintings 3542–3548
MS2998 Madonna and Child, Church of Ormesby St Michael, Great Yarmouth, Norfolk (Henry Holiday) Christmas. Stained glass windows................ 2992, 2995
MS2588 Madonna and the Infant Jesus (from India) Madonna and Child paintings 2586
MS2613 Maidenhead Bridge Isambard Kingdom Brunel, birth bicentenary........................... 2612
MS3742 Making honey The Honey Bee
MS4162 Man and Boy approaching Rural Pillar Box Christmas 4158
MS4162 Man approaching Pillar Box Christmas 4159
MS4162 Man and Girl posting Letters in Wall-mounted Postbox Christmas 4154
MS3308 Manchester Town Hall UK A–Z............. 3294
MS2727 Map of British Isles and Australia (telephone) World of Invention........... 2723
MS4124 Mapping New Zealand: a Maori clifftop fort Captain Cook and the *Endeavour* Voyage
MS2904 Marine Iguana (*Amblyrhynchus cristatus*) Charles Darwin, birth bicentenary
MS4291 Mary and Baby Jesus Christmas. Nativity
MS2930 *Mary Rose* (galleon), 1510 The House of Tudor
MS2402 Meccano Constructor Biplane, *c.*1931 Classic Transport toys............................ 2397
MS3529 Merchant Ship passing the Naval Control Base in the Thames Estuary Atlantic and Arctic Convoys, Second World War 3526
MS3529 Merchant Ships in North Sea convoy Atlantic and Arctic Convoys, Second World War 3526
MS2402 Mettoy Friction Drive Space Ship Eagle, *c.*1960 Classic Transport toys... 2401
MS2573 Michael Vaughan, Third Test, Old Trafford England's Ashes victory, 2005
MS2665 Midshipman Charles Lucas, RN Victoria Cross, 150th anniversary......... 2661
MS3019 Mike Oldfield Classic Album Covers .. 3015
MS2206 Military RN Submarine Service, 100th anniversary........................... 2208-2209
MS3086 Military Evacuation of British troops from Dunkirk, 1940 3082-3085
MS3734 Military–15th Infantry Regiment, IV Corps, Prussian Army Soldiers and Battle of Waterloo Map. 3730
MS3734 Military–92nd Gordon Highlanders, Anglo–Allied Army Soldiers and Battle of Waterloo Map 3732
MS3735 Military–Fighter pilots of 32 Squadron, RAF Hawkinge, Kent Battle of Britain, 75th anniversary
MS3734 Military–Grenadiers, Imperial Guard, French Army Soldiers and Battle of Waterloo Map 3733
MS3734 Military–Light Infantry, King's German Legion, Anglo-Allied Army Soldiers and Battle of Waterloo Map... 3731
MS3735 Military–Operations Room at Bentley Priory Battle of Britain, 75th anniversary
MS3735 Military–Spotters of the Auxiliary Territorial Service Battle of Britain, 75th anniversary
MS2546 Military, Ceremonial Trooping the Colour 2540–2545
MS3529 Military, Naval Atlantic and Arctic Convoys, Second World War 3525–3528
MS2580 Military, Sea battles Battle of Trafalgar, Bicentenary 2574–2579
MS2665 Military, VC recipients Victoria Cross, 150th anniversary 2659–2664
MS3371 Millennium Bridge and St Paul's Cathedral Paralympic Sports and London Landmarks
MS3770 *Millennium Falcon Star Wars*
MS2941 Millennium Seed Bank, Wakehurst Place Royal Botanic Gardens, Kew

MS2462 Miltonia, French Lake RHS, bicentenary of 2459
MS2904 *Mimus trifasciatus* (Floreana Mockingbird) Charles Darwin, birth bicentenary
MS4225 Model Lodge, Kennington..................... 4226 The Legacy of Prince Albert
MS3204a Modern Pentathlon Olympic and Paralympic Games, London (2012)... 3099
MS4455 Montgomery Scott (Simon Pegg), new *Star Trek* Movie *Star Trek*. The Movies
MS1119 Montage of London Buildings London 1980, Int Stamp Exhibition... 1118
MS3518 Morris Minor Royal Mail van (1953–1971) British Auto Legends The Workhorses
MS4282 Mouse *The Gruffalo*
MS2524 Mr Rochester Charlotte Brontë, 150th death anniversary 2518
MS3336 Mrs. Bagnet is charmed with Mr. Bucket (*Bleak House*) Charles Dickens, birth bicentenary
MS2588 Mughal painting of 1620-1630 Madonna and Child paintings 2586
MS3678 Mum (The Chase) Smilers, 2015... 3674
MS2904 *Nannopterum harrisi* (Giant Tortoise) and *Geospiza scandens* (Cactus Finch) Charles Darwin, birth bicentenary
MS3308 Narrow Water Castle, Co. Down UK A–Z... 3295
MS2861 National Stadium, Beijing Handover of Olympic Flag from Beijing to London
MS3529 Naval Convoy in the North Sea Atlantic and Arctic Convoys, Second World War 3528
MS2580 Nelson wounded on deck of HMS *Victory* Battle of Trafalgar, Bicentenary 2575
MS3678 New Baby (NB Studio) Smilers, 2015... 3675
MS3019 New Order Classic Album Covers 3012
MS3336 *Nicholas Nickleby* caning headmaster Wackford Squeers (*Nicholas Nickleby*) Charles Dickens, birth bicentenary
MS3608 *Night Mail* (1936) directed by Harry Watt and Basil Wright Films by GPO Film Unit
MS3498 No. 103 *Thomas Somerset* with Belfast Express Classic Locomotives of Northern Ireland 3497
MS3578 No. 589 *Blanche* Classic Locomotives of Wales 3577
MS3868 'Now run along, and don't get into mischief'. Illustrations from *The Tale of Peter Rabbit* 3864
MS3024 Ocean liner (Andrew Davidson) Business and Consumer Smilers
MS4642 Official match-day items The FA Cup
MS3308 Old Bailey, London UK A–Z.................. 3296
MS3406 Olympic Games closing ceremony and handover to Rio Scenes from Olympic and Paralympic Games
MS3341 Olympic Stadium Sports and London Landmarks
MS3371 Olympic Stadium Paralympic Sports and London Landmarks
MS3406 Olympic Stadium Scenes from Olympic and Paralympic Games
MS2554 Olympics London's successful bid for Olympic Games, 2012 As 1930–1934
MS2861 Olympics Handover of Olympic Flag from Beijing to London
MS2501 On Edge of Roof with Torch Father Christmas, Raymond Briggs..... 2499
MS2501 On Roof in Gale Father Christmas, Raymond Briggs..... 2497
MS3710 One Penny Black, 175th anniversary One Penny Black, 175th anniversary... 3709
MS3406 Opening ceremony of Paralympic Games Scenes from Olympic and Paralympic Games
MS2573 Opening day of first Test, Lords England's Ashes victory, 2005
MS3735 Operations Room at RAF Bentley Priory Battle of Britain, 75th anniversary
MS3179 Ophelia, *Hamlet* Royal Shakespeare Company, The Four Theatres
MS3837 Orangutan Animail

575

COMMEMORATIVE / MINIATURE SHEET DESIGN INDEX

MS	Title	Ref
MS2818	Owain Glyn Dwr (Parliament), 1404 Houses of Lancaster and York	
MS4282	Owl *The Gruffalo*	
MS3801	'pack your parcels carefully' Classic GPO Posters	3805
MS2613	Paddington Station Isambard Kingdom Brunel, birth bicentenary	2609
MS2941	Pagoda, Kew Gardens Royal Botanic Gardens, Kew	
MS2454	Painting by Charles Pears Ocean Liners	2450
MS2454	Painting by David Cobb Ocean Liners	2449
MS2588	Painting by Dianne Tchumut Madonna and Child paintings	2587
MS2454	Painting by Edward D Walker Ocean Liners	2448
MS2588	Painting by Fr. John Giuliani Madonna and Child paintings	2585
MS2454	Painting by Joseph Walter Ocean Liners	2453
MS2588	Painting by Marianne Stokes Madonna and Child paintings	2583
MS2454	Painting by Raphael Monleaon y Torres Ocean Liners	2452
MS2454	Painting by Thomas M. M. Hemy Ocean Liners	2451
MS3549	Paintings–*La Vierge au Lys* Madonna and Child paintings	3547
MS3549	Paintings–*Madonna and Child* Madonna and Child paintings	3542
MS3549	Paintings–*St Roch Praying to the Virgin for an end to the Plague* (detail) Madonna and Child paintings	3545
MS3549	Paintings–Theotokos, Mother of God Madonna and Child paintings	3548
MS3549	Paintings–*Virgin and Child with the Young St John the Baptist* (detail) Madonna and Child paintings	3543, 3546
MS3371	Palace of Westminster Paralympic Sports and London Landmarks	
MS2941	Palm House, Kew Gardens Royal Botanic Gardens, Kew	
MS3406	Paralympic Games Scenes from Olympic and Paralympic Games	
MS3204a	Paralympic Games: Archery Olympic and Paralympic Games, London (2012)	2982
MS3204a	Paralympic Games: Boccia Olympic and Paralympic Games, London (2012)	2985
MS3204a	Paralympic Games: Dressage Olympic and Paralympic Games, London (2012)	2987
MS3204a	Paralympic Games: Goalball Olympic and Paralympic Games, London (2012)	3105
MS3204a	Paralympic Games: Rowing Olympic and Paralympic Games, London (2012)	3097
MS3204a	Paralympic Games: Sailing Olympic and Paralympic Games, London (2012)	3195
MS3204a	Paralympic Games: Table Tennis Olympic and Paralympic Games, London (2012)	3102
MS3371	Paralympic Sports Paralympic Sports and London Landmarks	
MS2998	Parish Church of St Michael, Minehead, Somerset Christmas. Stained glass windows	2994
MS3019	*Parklife* (Blur) Classic Album Covers	3011
MS3179	Patrick Stewart in *Antony and Cleopatra*, 2006, Swan Theatre Royal Shakespeare Company, The Four Theatres	
MS3498	Peckett No.2 Classic Locomotives of Northern Ireland	
MS3144	Peckett R2 *Thor* Classic Locomotives of England	
MS3710	Penny Black One Penny Black, 175th anniversary	3709
MS4355	Penny Black One Penny Black, 180th anniversary	
MS3229	Penny Black (uniform postage) 1840 House of Hanover	
MS2904	*Phalacrocorax harrisi* (Flightless Cormorant) Charles Darwin, birth bicentenary	
MS3964	Photo by John Hedgecoe with Queen Elizabeth II wearing the Diadem, August 1966	3962
MS3272	Photograph by Dorothy Wilding Diamond Jubilee of QEII	
MS4162	Pillar Box near Church Christmas	4161
MS3735	Pilots of 32 Squadron await orders, RAF Hawkinge, Kent Battle of Britain, 75th anniversary	
MS3735	Pilots scramble to their Hurricanes Battle of Britain, 75th anniversary	
MS3019	Pink Floyd Classic Album Covers	3009
MS3855	Pink Floyd Pink Floyd on Stage	
MS2315	Planetary nebula in Aquila Astronomy	
MS2315	Planetary nebula in Norma Astronomy	
MS4364	Plymouth Naval Memorial	4367
MS4303	Podracers	4308
	Star Wars	
MS4303	Poe's X-wing fighter	4306
	Star Wars	
MS3172	Poison Dart Frog (*Ranitomeya amazonica*) Wildlife of the Amazon Rainforest	
MS3742	Pollination The Honey Bee	
MS4151	Pomona Sprout Harry Potter	
MS1444	Pontcysyllte Aqueduct, Clwyd Industrial Archaeology	1443
MS2685	Poppies on barbed wire stems (Seven) Battle of the Somme, 90th anniversary	2883
MS3024	Poppies on Barbed Wire Stem (Six) Business and Consumer Smilers	
MS3308	Portmeirion, Wales UK A–Z	3297
MS3272	Portrait by Arnold Machin Diamond Jubilee of QEII	
MS3272	Portrait by Harry Eccleston Diamond Jubilee of QEII	
MS3180	Portrait by Mario Testino Royal Wedding. Prince William and Catherine	
MS3272	Portrait by Mary Gillick Diamond Jubilee of QEII	
MS3272	Portrait by Robert Austin Diamond Jubilee of QEII	
MS3272	Portrait from photograph by Dorothy Wilding Diamond Jubilee of QEII	
MS3747	Portrait of Queen Elizabeth II from photograph by Dorothy Wilding Long to Reign Over Us	
MS3657	Post Box Christmas. Illustrations by Andrew Bannecker	3651, 3633
MS3657	Posting Christmas cards Christmas. Illustrations by Andrew Bannecker	3651, 3653
MS4622	Posters for Tour of Europe, 1974 and Tour of the Americas, 1975	4625
MS4622	Posters for UK Tour, 1971 and American Tour, 1981	4626, 4624
MS1099	Postman, *circa* 1839 Sir Rowland Hill, death centenary	1096
MS4162	Postal worker emptying Post box Christmas	4155, 4157
MS3220	Postmaster General 1911, Herbert Louis Samuel First United Kingdom Aerial Post	3219
MS3019	*Power, Corruption and Lies* (New Order) Classic Album Covers	3012
MS3371	Powerlifter Paralympic Sports and London Landmarks	
MS3371	Powerlifter, Millennium Bridge and St Paul's Cathedral Paralympic Sports and London Landmarks	
MS3964	Preliminary sketch by Arnold Machin based on the Penny Black, January 1966	3958
MS3964	Preparatory work by Arnold Machin using photograph of his coin mould, February 1966	3959
MS3019	Primal Scream Classic Album Covers	3017
MS2161	Prince Charles Queen Mother's 100th birthday	
MS3832	Prince Charles 90th birthday of Queen Elizabeth...As 3833	
MS2531	Prince Charles and Mrs Camilla Parker Bowles laughing Royal Wedding, Charles & Camilla	
MS2531	Prince Charles and Mrs Camilla Parker Bowles smiling to camera Royal Wedding, Charles & Camilla	
MS3832	Prince George 90th birthday of Queen Elizabeth...As 3835	
MS4092	Prince Harry and Ms. Meghan Markle Royal Wedding, Prince Harry & Meghan	
MS3832	Prince William 90th birthday of Queen Elizabeth...As 3836	
MS2161	Prince William Queen Mother's 100th birthday	
MS3180	Prince William and Miss Catherine Middleton embracing Royal Wedding. Prince William and Miss Catherine Middleton	
MS2786	Princess Elizabeth, Prince Philip, Prince Charles and Princess Anne, Clarence House, 1951 Diamond Wedding of Queen Elizabeth II	
MS3406	Procession of athletes Scenes from Olympic and Paralympic Games	
MS3406	Procession of athletes, Paralympic GamesScenes from Olympic and Paralympic Games	
MS3024	Propeller driven aircraft (Andrew Davidson) Business and Consumer Smilers	
MS2613	PSS *Great Eastern* (paddle steamer) Isambard Kingdom Brunel, birth bicentenary	2610
MS3832	Queen Elizabeth II 90th birthday of Queen Elizabeth...As 3834	
MS4169	Queen Elizabeth II 1953 Coronation 2½d. carmine-red stamp Stamp Classics	
MS2161	Queen Elizabeth II Queen Mother's 100th birthday	
MS2161	Queen Elizabeth the Queen Mother Queen Mother's 100th birthday	2160
MS2546	Queen and Duke of Edinburgh in carriage, 2004 Trooping the Colour	2545
MS2786	Queen and Prince Philip, Buckingham Palace, 2007 Diamond Wedding of Queen Elizabeth II	
MS3270	Queen Elizabeth the Queen Mother and King George VI in bomb damaged street, *c.* 1940 House of Windsor	
MS2161	Queen Mother's 100th birthday Queen Mother's 100th birthday	2160
MS4396	Queen, Primrose Hill, London, 1974 Queen Live	4403
MS2546	Queen riding side-saddle, 1972 Trooping the Colour	2544
MS2546	Queen taking the salute as Colonel-in-Chief of the Grenadier Guards, 1983 Trooping the Colour	2541
MS4169	Queen Victoria 1891 £1 green stamp Stamp Classics	
MS3747	Queen Victoria 'Long to Reign Over Us	
MS3229	Queen Victoria (Diamond Jubilee), 1897 House of Hanover	
MS3710	Queen Victoria 2d. Blue One Penny Black, 175th anniversary	
MS1501	Queen Victoria and Queen Elizabeth II, 20p brownish brown & cream Stamp World London Int Stamp	1469
MS3801	'Quickest Way by Air Mail' Classic GPO Posters	3802
MS2727	Railways World of Invention	2722
MS3025	Rainbows Girlguiding UK	
MS4364	Rangoon Memorial, Myanmar	4368
MS4377	Raquel Watts (Sarah Lancashire) *Coronation Street* Rovers Return Barmaids	
MS2757	Ravenclaw Harry Potter Crests of Hogwarts School	
MS2692	Record *Love Me Do* Beatles memorabilia	
MS3024	Recreation of crown seal (Neil Oliver) Business and Consumer Smilers	
MS2524	Refectory Charlotte Brontë, 150th death anniversary	2522
MS2684	Reindeer Christmas, 2006	2682
MS3422	Reindeer with Decorated Antlers Christmas. Illustrations by Axel Scheffler	3415, 3417
MS4151	Remus Lupin Harry Potter	
MS3086	Rescued soldiers on board Royal Navy Destroyer, Dover Evacuation of British troops from Dunkirk, 1940	3084
MS2206	RN Submarine Service, 100th anniversary RN Submarine Service, 100th anniversary	2208, 2209
MS3270	Robert Falcon Scott House of Windsor	
MS3229	Robert Walpole (first Prime Minister), 1721 House of Hanover	
MS3911	Robin Celebrating 50 years of Christmas stamps	3904, 3906

576

COMMEMORATIVE / MINIATURE SHEET DESIGN INDEX

MS	Description	Ref
MS3422	Robin with Star Decoration in Beak Christmas. Illustrations by Axel Scheffler	3420
MS4485	Rodney (*Only Fools and Horses*)	4486
MS4396	Roger Taylor, Hyde Park Concert, 1976 Queen Live	4400
MS3019	Rolling Stones Classic Album Covers	3013
MS3308	Roman Baths, Bath UK A–Z	3299
MS2613	Royal Albert Bridge Isambard Kingdom Brunel, birth bicentenary	2607
MS4225	Royal Albert Hall, London The Legacy of Prince Albert	4229
MS2930	Royal Exchange (centre of commerce), The House of Tudor	1565
MS2786	Royal family, Balmoral, 1972 Diamond Wedding of Queen Elizabeth II	
MS2786	Royal family, Windsor Castle, 1965 Diamond Wedding of Queen Elizabeth II	
MS3518	Royal Mail van British Auto Legends The Workhorses	
MS3179	Royal Shakespeare Company, Swan Theatre Royal Shakespeare Company, The Four Theatres	
MS3179	Royal Shakespeare Company, The Courtyard Theatre Royal Shakespeare Company, The Four Theatres	
MS3179	Royal Shakespeare Company, The Other Place Royal Shakespeare Company, The Four Theatres	
MS3179	Royal Shakespeare Theatre Royal Shakespeare Company, The Four Theatres	
MS2531	Royal Wedding, Charles & Camilla Royal Wedding, Charles & Camilla	
MS2416	Rugby England's victory in Rugby World Cup	
MS4364	Runnymede Memorial	4366
MS2941	Sackler Crossing, Kew Gardens Royal Botanic Gardens, Kew	
MS3529	Sailors clearing ice from the decks of HMS *King George V* in Arctic Waters Atlantic and Arctic Convoys, Second World War	3527
MS3932	St George's Chapel Quire: Garter Banners St George's Chapel	3930
MS3932	St George's Chapel Quire: St George's Cross Roof Boss St George's Chapel	3931
MS4027	*St Luke painting the Virgin* (detail) (Eduard Jakob von Steinle) Madonna and Child	4026
MS2998	St Mary's Church, Upavon, Wiltshire Christmas. Stained glass windows	2997
MS2547	St Paul's Cathedral and Searchlights End of the Second World War, 60th anniversary	1875
MS2547	St Paul's Cathedral, Architecture End of the Second World War, 60th anniversary	1875
MS2847	St Paul's Cathedral, Architecture St Paul's Cathedral	
MS3549	*St Roch Praying to the Virgin for an end to the Plague* (detail) (Jacques-Louis David) Madonna and Child paintings	3545
MS3422	Santa with Robin Christmas. Illustrations by Axel Scheffler	3416, 3419
MS2106	Saturn (development of astronomical telescopes) Solar eclipse	2105
MS3270	Scott Expedition to South Pole, 1912 House of Windsor	
MS2685	Scottish definitive, 72p Battle of the Somme, 90th anniversary	S120
MS2796	Scottish definitive, 78p. Battle of Passchendaele, 90th anniversary	S121
MS2886	Scottish definitive, 81p. Armistice, 90th anniversary	S122
MS3019	*Screamadelica* (Primal Scream) Classic Album Covers	3017
MS3072	Sea Horses design stamp, 1913 10s. blue London 2010 Festival of Stamps	3071
MS3072	Sea Horses design stamp, 1913 £1 green London 2010 Festival of Stamps	3070
MS2573	Second Test cricket, Edgbaston England's Ashes victory, 2005	
MS3025	Senior Section members, Girl Guides Girlguiding UK	
MS4151	Severus Snape Harry Potter	
MS2315	Seyfert 2 galaxy in Circinus Astronomy	
MS2315	Seyfert 2 galaxy in Pegasus Astronomy	
MS2501	Sheltering behind Chimney Father Christmas, Raymond Briggs	2500
MS4291	Shepherds and Star Christmas. Nativity	
MS2998	Shepherd, St Mary's Church, Upavon, Wiltshire (Henry Holiday) Christmas. Stained glass windows	2997
MS3249	Shepherds visited by the Angel (Luke 2:10) *King James Bible*, 400th anniversary	3247
MS4455	Shinzon (Tom Hardy), *Star Trek: Nemesis Star Trek. The Movies*	
MS4303	Slave 1 *Star Wars*	4309
MS2757	Slytherin Harry Potter Crests of Hogwarts School	
MS3837	Snake Animail	
MS4282	Snake *The Gruffalo*	
MS2684	Snowman Christmas, 2006	2678, 2680
MS2684	Snowman Celebrating 50 years of Christmas stamps	3903, 3905, MS3911
MS3422	Snowman and Penguin Christmas Illustrations by Axel Scheffler	3418
MS2106	Solar eclipse Solar eclipse	2105
MS2886	Soldier's Face in Poppy Flower Armistice, 90th anniversary	2885
MS2796	Soldiers in Poppy flower Battle of Passchendaele, 90th anniversary	2884
MS3264	Sophie sitting on Buckingham Palace window-sill Roald Dahl's *The BFG*	3262
MS2727	Space travel World of Invention	2726
MS3608	*Spare Time* (1939) directed by Humphrey Jennings Films by GPO Film Unit	
MS4303	Speeder bikes *Star Wars*	4311
MS3172	Spider Monkey (*genus Ateles*) Wildlife of the Amazon Rainforest	
MS3657	Sport – Ice Skating Christmas. Illustrations by Andrew Bannecker	3656
MS3204a	Sport: Athletics, Track Olympic and Paralympic Games, London (2012)	2983
MS3204a	Sport: Athletics, Field Olympic and Paralympic Games, London (2012)	3196
MS3204a	Sport: Badminton Olympic and Paralympic Games, London (2012)	2988
MS2554	Sport: Basketball London's successful bid for Olympic Games, 2012	1932
MS3204a	Sport: Basketball Olympic and Paralympic Games, London (2012)	2990
MS3204a	Sport: Boxing Olympic and Paralympic Games, London (2012)	3106
MS2573	Sport: Cricket England's Ashes victory, 2005	
MS3204a	Sport: Cycling Olympic and Paralympic Games, London (2012)	3101
MS3341	Sport: Cyclist Sports and London Landmarks	
MS3371	Sport: Cyclist Paralympic Sports and London Landmarks	
MS3341	Sport: Diver Sports and London Landmarks	
MS3204a	Sport: Diving Olympic and Paralympic Games, London (2012)	2984
MS3204a	Sport: Fencing Olympic and Paralympic Games, London (2012)	3201
MS3204a	Sport: Gymnastics Olympic and Paralympic Games, London (2012)	3202
MS3204a	Sport: Handball Olympic and Paralympic Games, London (2012)	3204
MS3204a	Sport: Judo Olympic and Paralympic Games, London (2012)	2986
MS3204a	Sport: Shooting Olympic and Paralympic Games, London (2012)	3098
MS2554	Sport: Swimming London's successful bid for Olympic Games, 2012	1933
MS3204a	Sport: Taekwondo Olympic and Paralympic Games, London (2012)	3100
MS2554	Sport: Throwing the javelin London's successful bid for Olympic Games, 2012	1931
MS3204a	Sport: Wheelchair Rugby Olympic and Paralympic Games, London (2012)	3198
MS3204a	Sport: Wheelchair Tennis Olympic and Paralympic Games, London (2012)	3200
MS3204a	Sport: Wrestling Olympic and Paralympic Games, London (2012)	3199
MS3204a	Sports: Hockey Olympic and Paralympic Games, London (2012)	3103
MS3735	Spotters of the Auxiliary Territorial Service looking for enemy aircraft Battle of Britain, 75th anniversary	
MS2423	SR West Country Class *Blackmoor Vale*, Bluebell Railway, East Sussex Classic Locomotives	2421
MS3932	St George's Chapel Nave: Fan-vaulted Roof St George's Chapel	3929
MS3932	St George's Chapel Nave: Sir Reginald Bray Roof Boss St George's Chapel	3928, MS3932
MS3801	'Stamps in Books save Time' Classic GPO Posters	3804
MS1501	Stamp World London International Stamp Exhibition Stamp World London Int Stamp	1469
MS3770	*Star Wars Star Wars*	
MS3308	Station X, Bletchley Park, Bucks UK A–Z	3305
MS3024	Steam locomotive (Andrew Davidson) Business and Consumer Smilers	
MS2727	Steam Locomotive and Railway Tracks World of Invention	2722
MS3086	Steamship and other boat loaded with troops Evacuation of British troops from Dunkirk, 1940	3085
MS3308	Stirling Castle, Scotland UK A–Z	3300
MS3911	Stocking Celebrating 50 years of Christmas stamps	3909
MS3735	Supermarine Spitfires Battle of Britain, 75th anniversary	
MS3735	Supermarine Spitfires of 610 Squadron, Biggin Hill, on patrol Battle of Britain, 75th anniversary	
MS4642	Supporters' memorabilia The FA Cup	
MS4151	Sybill Trelawney Harry Potter	
MS3193	Tank Engine Thomas Again Thomas the Tank Engine	
MS3451	TARDIS *Dr. Who* 1963–2013	3449
MS3341	Tate Modern Sports and London Landmarks	
MS2727	Telephone World of Invention	2723
MS3742	Tending young The Honey Bee	
MS4192	Thanos Marvel Heroes UK	4195
MS4417	*The Adventure of the Dancing Men* Sherlock Holmes Mysteries by Sir Arthur Conan Doyle	
MS4417	*The Adventure of the Second Stain* Sherlock Holmes Mysteries by Sir Arthur Conan Doyle	
MS4417	*The Adventure of the Speckled Band* Sherlock Holmes Mysteries by Sir Arthur Conan Doyle	4419
MS3779	The Animals of the Nativity Christmas. 2015	3775
MS3779	The Annunciation Christmas. 2015	3778
MS3264	The BFG and Sophie at Writing Desk Roald Dahl's *The BFG*	3263
MS3264	The BFG carrying Sophie in his Hand Roald Dahl's *The BFG*	3260
MS3264	The BFG wakes up the Giants Roald Dahl's *The BFG*	3261
MS3601	The Blue Drawing Room Buckingham Palace	3599
MS2588	The Bridgeman Art Gallery Madonna and Child paintings	2584
MS3019	The Clash Classic Album Covers	3014
MS3855	The Dark Side of the Moon Tour, 1973 Pink Floyd on Stage	
MS3019	*The Division Bell* (Pink Floyd) Classic Album Covers	3009
MS3855	The Division Bell Tour, 1994 Pink Floyd on Stage	

577

COMMEMORATIVE / MINIATURE SHEET DESIGN INDEX

MS	Title	Ref
MS3142	The genius of Gerry Anderson *Thunderbirds*	
MS3601	The Grand Staircase Buckingham Palace	3598
MS3601	The Green Drawing Room Buckingham Palace	3600
MS4442	The Holy Family, St Columba's Church, Topcliffe Christmas 2020. Stained glass Windows	4440
MS3779	The Journey to Bethlehem Christmas. 2015	3771
MS3429	The London Transport Collection (Tom Eckersley), 1975, London Zoo (Abram Games), 1976 and The Tate Gallery by Tube (David Booth), 1987Classic London Underground Posters	
MS4027	*The Madonna and Child* (William Dyce) Madonna and Child	4020
MS3779	The Nativity Christmas. 2015	3772
MS4225	The New Crystal Palace, Sydenham...	4228
	The Legacy of Prince Albert	
MS3451	The Ood *Dr. Who* 1963–2013	
MS3848	The Post Office Rifles The Post Office at War, 1914–1918	3844
MS3308	The Queen's College, Oxford UK A–Z	3298
MS3747	The Queen's Personal Flag Long to Reign Over Us	
MS4417	The Red-Headed League Sherlock Holmes Mysteries by Sir Arthur Conan Doyle	4418
MS3019	*The Rise and Fall of Ziggy Stardust and the Spiders from Mars* (David Bowie) Classic Album Covers	3018
MS4622	The Rolling Stones	4623, 4624
MS3939	The Serious Moonlight Tour, 1983 David Bowie Live	
MS3779	The Shepherds Christmas. 2015	3776
MS4027	*The Sleep of the Infant Jesus* (Giovanni Battista Sassoferrato) Madonna and Child	4025
MS4027	*The Small Cowper Madonna* (Raphael) Madonna and Child	4024
MS3939	The Isolar II Tour, 1978 David Bowie Live	
MS3779	The Three Wise Men Christmas. 2015	3777
MS3601	The Throne Room Buckingham Palace	3597
MS1058	The Tower of London British Architecture (4th series)	1054
MS2588	The Virgin Mary with the Infant Christ Madonna and Child paintings	2584
MS3855	The Wall Tour, 1981 Pink Floyd on Stage	
MS3939	The Ziggy Stardust Tour, 1973 David Bowie Live	
MS3549	Theotokos, Mother of God (Fadi Mikhail) Madonna and Child paintings	3548
MS3193	They told Henry, 'We shall leave you there for always' (from The Three Railway Engines) Thomas the Tank Engine	
MS2727	Thomas Telford World of Invention	2721
MS4291	Three Wise Men Christmas. Nativity	
MS3142	Thunderbird 1 *Thunderbirds*	
MS3142	Thunderbird 2 *Thunderbirds*	
MS3142	Thunderbird 3 *Thunderbirds*	
MS3142	Thunderbird 4 *Thunderbirds*	
MS3770	TIE fighters (original) *Star Wars*	
MS4303	TIE silencer	4310
	Star Wars	
MS1444	Tin Mine, St Agnes Head, Cornwall Industrial Archaeology	1441
MS4192	'together!' (Captain Britain, Spider-Man, Iron Man, Hulk, Thor, Black Panther)	4197
	Marvel Heroes UK	
MS4455	Tolian Soran (Malcolm McDowell), *Star Trek Generations*	
	Star Trek. The Movies	
MS4320	*Tomb Raider*, 1996	4321
	Video Games	
MS4320	*Tomb Raider*, 2013	4322
	Video Games	
MS4320	*Tomb Raider Chronicles, 2000*	
	Video Games	
MS3429	Tom Eckersley, poster designer Classic London Underground Posters	
MS2292	Top Right Quarter of English Flag, and Football World Cup Football Championship, Japan & Korea	2294
MS2292	Top Left Quarter of English Flag, and Football World Cup Football Championship, Japan & Korea	2293
MS3341	Tower Bridge Sports and London Landmarks	
MS2861	Tower of London Handover of Olympic Flag from Beijing to London	
MS2402	Toys Classic Transport toys	2397
MS2613	Transport, Ships Isambard Kingdom Brunel, birth bicentenary	2610
MS3204a	Triathlon Olympic and Paralympic Games, London (2012)	3203
MS2546	Trumpeter of the Household Cavalry, 2004 Trooping the Colour	2542
MS3019	*Tubular Bells* (Mike Oldfield) Classic Album Covers	3015
MS3065	Two portraits of King George V Accession of King George V, centenary	
MS3308	Tyne Bridge, Newcastle UK A–Z	3301
MS3855	UFO Club, 1966 Pink Floyd on Stage	
MS2882	Ugly Sisters from *Cinderella* Christmas. Pantomimes	2876
MS2685	Ulster definitive, 72p Battle of the Somme, 90th anniversary	NI102
MS2796	Ulster definitive, 78p. Battle of Passchendaele, 90th anniversary	NI128
MS2886	Ulster definitive, 81p. Armistice, 90th anniversary	NI129
MS4236	Uncle Albert (*Only Fools and Horses*)	4490
MS2206	Union Jack RN Submarine Service, 100th anniversary	
MS3308	Urquhart Castle, Scotland UK A–Z	3302
MS4236	US 4th Infantry Division, Utah Beach 75th Anniversary of D-Day	
MS4236	US troops going ashore at Omaha Beach 75th Anniversary of D-Day	
MS3498	UTA Class W No. 103 Thomas Somerset with *Belfast Express*, Downhill, near Castlerock, *c.*1950 Classic Locomotives of Northern Ireland	3497
MS3498	UTA SG3 No. 35 Classic Locomotives of Northern Ireland	
MS3086	Vessels from Upper Thames Patrol in Operation Little Ships Evacuation of British troops from Dunkirk, 1940	3083
MS2289	Vickers VC10 (1964) Passenger Jet aviation, 50th anniversary	2287
MS3308	Victoria and Albert Museum, London UK A–Z	3303
MS2954	Victorian Lamp Letter Box, 1896 Post Boxes	2952
MS2416	Victorious England players after match England's victory in Rugby World Cup	
MS3024	Vintage sports roadster (Andrew Davidson) Business and Consumer Smilers	
MS4442	Virgin and Child, All Saints' Church, Otley Christmas 2020. Stained glass Windows	4439
MS4027	*Virgin and Child* (attr. Gerard David) Madonna and Child	4023
MS4442	Virgin and Child, Christ Church, Coalville Christmas 2020. Stained glass Windows	4441
MS4442	Virgin and Child, Church of St. James, Hollowell Christmas 2020. Stained glass Windows	4438
MS4442	Virgin and Child, St. Andrew's Church, Coln Rogers Christmas 2020. Stained glass Windows	4435, 4437
MS3549	*Virgin and Child with the Young St John the Baptist* (detail) (Antoniazzo Romano) Madonna and Child paintings	3543, 3546
MS4027	*Virgin Mary with Child* (attr. Quinten Massys) Madonna and Child	4019
MS3204a	Volleyball Olympic and Paralympic Games, London (2012)	3197
MS3578	W&LLR No. 822 *The Earl* Classic Locomotives of Wales	
MS3742	Waggle dance The Honey Bee	
MS2941	Wakehurst Place Royal Botanic Gardens, Kew	
MS3135	Wallace and Gromit decorating Christmas Tree Christmas with Wallace and Gromit	3131
MS3678	Wedding (Caroline Gardner Ltd) Smilers, 2015	3672
MS3451	Weeping Angel *Dr. Who* 1963–2013	
MS3204a	Weightlifting Olympic and Paralympic Games, London (2012)	2989
MS3678	Well Done (Webb & Webb Design Ltd) Smilers, 2015	3671
MS2402	Wells-Brimtoy Clockwork Double-decker Omnibus, *c.*1938 Classic Transport toys	2398
MS2685	Welsh definitive, 72p, Battle of the Somme, 90th anniversary	W109
MS2796	Welsh definitive, 78p Battle of Passchendaele, 90th anniversary	W110
MS2886	Welsh definitive, 81p Armistice, 90th anniversary	W114
MS2546	Welsh Guardsman, 1990s Trooping the Colour	2543
MS4476	Wheelchair athlete (Sport)	
MS3371	Wheelchair basketball player and Palace of Westminster Paralympic Sports and London Landmarks	
MS3308	White Cliffs of Dover UK A–Z	3304
MS2206	White Ensign RN Submarine Service, 100th anniversary	2208
MS2882	Wicked Queen from *Snow White* Christmas. Pantomimes	2881
MS2326	Wilding Definitive, (2nd) carmine-red Wilding definitives, 50th anniversary	
MS2326	Wilding Definitive, (1st) green Wilding definitives, 50th anniversary	
MS2367	Wilding Definitive, (E) chestnut Wilding definitives, 50th anniversary (2nd)	
MS2326	Wilding Definitive, 1p orange-red Wilding definitives, 50th anniversary	
MS2326	Wilding Definitive, 2p ultramarine Wilding definitives, 50th anniversary	
MS2367	Wilding Definitive, 4p deep lilac Wilding definitives, 50th anniversary (2nd)	
MS2326	Wilding Definitive, 5p red-brown Wilding definitives, 50th anniversary	
MS2367	Wilding Definitive, 8p ultramarine Wilding definitives, 50th anniversary (2nd)	
MS2367	Wilding Definitive, 10p reddish purple Wilding definitives, 50th anniversary (2nd)	
MS2367	Wilding Definitive, 20p bright green Wilding definitives, 50th anniversary (2nd)	
MS2367	Wilding Definitive, 28p bronze-green Wilding definitives, 50th anniversary (2nd)	
MS2326	Wilding Definitive, 33p brown Wilding definitives, 50th anniversary	
MS2367	Wilding Definitive, 34p brown-purple Wilding definitives, 50th anniversary (2nd)	
MS2326	Wilding Definitive, 37p magenta Wilding definitives, 50th anniversary	
MS2367	Wilding Definitive, 42p Prussian blue Wilding definitives, 50th anniversary (2nd)	
MS2326	Wilding Definitive, 47p bistre-brown Wilding definitives, 50th anniversary	2378
MS2326	Wilding Definitive, 50p green Wilding definitives, 50th anniversary	
MS2367	Wilding Definitive, 68p grey-blue Wilding definitives, 50th anniversary (2nd)	2379
MS3172	Wildlife of the Amazon Rainforest	
MS2818	William Caxton, first English printer, 1477 Houses of Lancaster and York	
MS3094	William Harvey (discovery of blood circulation, 1628) House of Stuart	
MS2998	William Morris Christmas. Stained glass windows	2991, 2993
MS3747	William Wyon's City Medal Long to Reign Over Us	
MS3747	William Wyon's City Medal depicting Queen Victoria Long to Reign Over Us	
MS3549	William-Adolphe Bouguereau, Artist Madonna and Child paintings	3547
MS2786	Windsor Castle Diamond Wedding of Queen Elizabeth II	

COMMEMORATIVE / MINIATURE SHEET DESIGN INDEX

MS2530 Windsor Castle; 50p.
  Black First Castles Definitives,
  50th anniversary
MS3932 Windsor Castle St George's Chapel
MS4642 Winners' medal and trophy The FA Cup
MS3127 Winnie the Pooh and
  Christopher Robin (from *Now we are Six*)
  Winnie the Pooh by A. A. Milne
MS3127 Winnie the Pooh and
  Christopher Robin sailing in
  umbrella (from *Winnie the Pooh*)
  Winnie the Pooh by A. A. Milne
MS2998 Wise Man, Church of St Mary the
  Virgin, Rye, East Sussex
  (Sir Edward Burne-Jones)
  Christmas. Stained glass windows 2996
MS3249 Wise Men and Star (Matthew 2:10)
  King James Bible, 400th anniversary .. 3248
MS2501 With Umbrella in Rain
  Father Christmas, Raymond Briggs.... 2498
MS1099 Woman and Young Girl with Letters,
  1840 Sir Rowland Hill,
  death centenary 1098
MS4162 Woman with Dog posting Letters
  Christmas 4160
MS3837 Woodpecker Animail
MS2292 World Cup Football
  Championship,
  Japan & Korea 2291, 2293
MS2292 World Cup Football Championship,
  Japan & Korea World Cup Football
  Championship, Japan & Korea 2294
MS2416 World Cup trophy
  England's victory in Rugby World Cup
MS3172 World Wildlife Fund (WWF),
  50th anniversary
  Wildlife of the Amazon Rainforest
MS3641 Worthing Pier British Piers
MS3848 Writing a letter from the
  Western Front The Post Office at War,
  1914–1918 3845
MS3770 X-wing Starfighter *Star Wars*
MS3770 X-wing Starfighters *Star Wars*
MS2658 Year of Three Kings,
  70th anniversary Year of Three Kings,
  70th anniversary Y1748
MS2692 Yellow Submarine lunch-box and
  key-rings Beatles memorabilia
MS3193 'Yes, Sir', Percy shivered miserably
  (from The Eight Famous Engines)
  Thomas the Tank Engine
MS3308 York Minster UK A–Z 3306
MS2818 Yorkist victory at Battle of Tewkesbury,
  1471 Houses of Lancaster and York
MS3025 Youth organisations Girlguiding UK
MS3429 Zero (Hans Schleger), poster designer
  Classic London Underground Posters

REGIONALS

MSS57 A Man's a Man for a' that and Burns
  ploughing (detail)
  (James Sargent Storer)
MSNI152 Carrickfergus Castle
MSEN50 Celebrating England
MSNI152 Celebrating Northern Ireland
MSS153 Celebrating Scotland
MSW147 Celebrating Wales
MSS153 Edinburgh Castle
MSEN50 English definitive, (1st) Crowned lion
  supporting shield, Type I.................. *As* EN7b
MSNI152 Giant's Causeway
MSEN50 Houses of Parliament, London
MSW143 Leek, (2nd) W98
MSS152 Lion Rampant of Scotland, (1st) S110
MSS153 Lion Rampant of Scotland, (1st) S110
MSS157 Lion Rampant of Scotland, (1st) S110
MSS180 Lion Rampant of Scotland (1st) S160
MSW147 National Assembly for Wales, Cardiff
MSS152 Opening of new Scottish Parliament
  building, Edinburgh
MSW143 Opening of New Welsh Assembly
  building, Cardiff
MSS157 Portrait of Burns (Alexander Nasmyth)
MSW143 Prince of Wales' Feathers, 68p. W108
MSNI152 Queen's Bridge and
  'Angel of Thanksgiving' sculpture, Belfast
MSW147 Red dragon .... *As* W148
MSS153 St Andrew
MSW147 St David
MSEN50 St George
MSEN50 St George's flag .... *As* EN51
MSNI152 St Patrick
MSS152 Saltire, (2nd) S109
MSS157 Saltire, (2nd) S109
MSS153 Saltire.. *As* S158

MSS180 Saltire (2nd)
MSNI153 Scottish definitive, (1st) deep claret.....*As* S3
MSNI153 Scottish definitive, (1st) deep lilac ......*As* S1
MSNI153 Scottish definitive, (1st) green.............*As* S5
MSS157 Tartan, 81p..S122
MSS180 Tartan, £1·63..S170
MSS152 Thistle, 40p..S112
MSS157 Thistle, 50p..S116
MSS180 Thistle £1·42..S166a
MSNI153 Ulster definitive, (1st) deep claret ....*As* NI3
MSNI153 Ulster definitive, (1st) deep lilac.........*As* NI1
MSNI153 Ulster definitive, (1st) green ....*As* NI5
MSNI153 Welsh definitive, (1st) deep claret...... *As* W3
MSNI153 Welsh definitive, (1st) deep lilac .... *As* W1
MSNI153 Welsh definitive, (1st) green................ *As* W5
MSW143 Welsh dragon, (1st) W99
MSW147 Welsh dragon, (1st)....................................W122
MSNI153 50th anniversary of the Country
  definitives
MSS157 250th birth anniversary of Robert Burns
  (Scottish poet)

Stanley Gibbons Auctions
operating philatelic auctions since 1901.

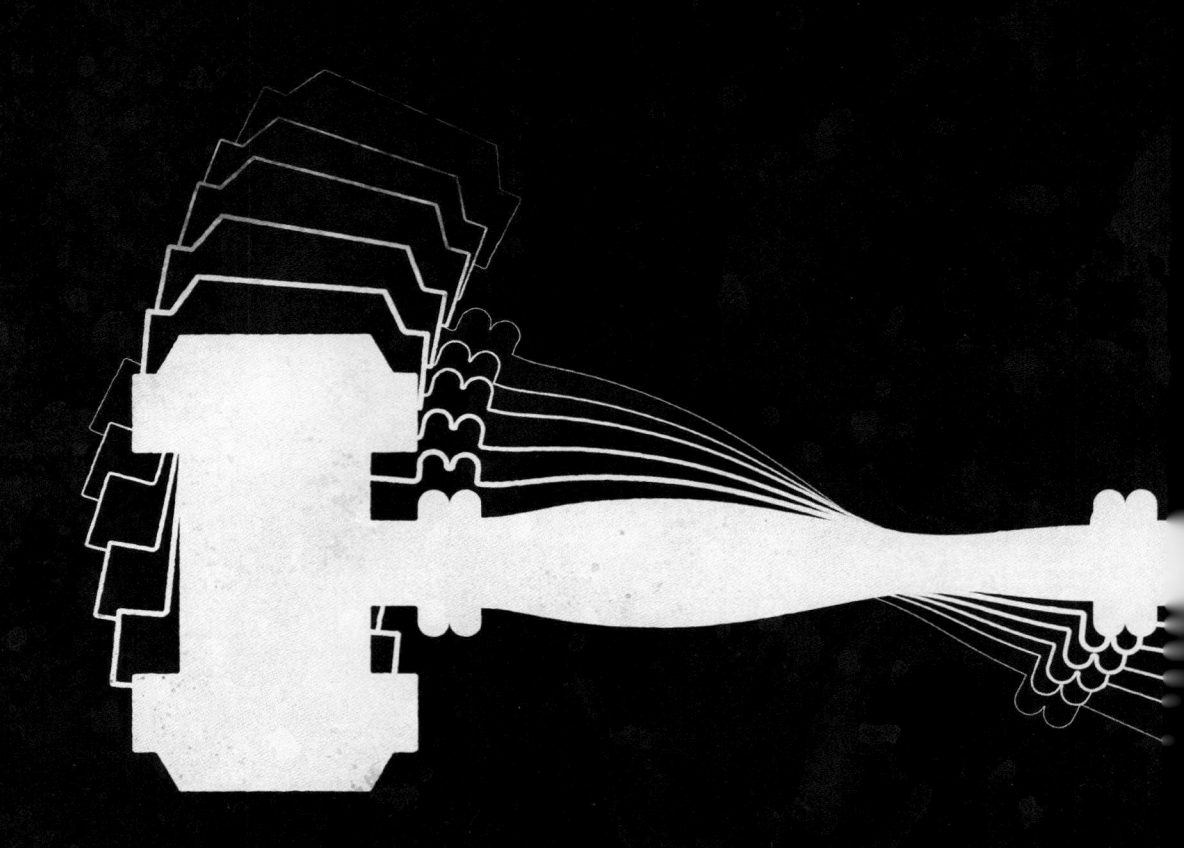

Speak to our experts about consigning your material.

Entrust your collection to a company with integrity, unrivalled expertise and regular public and online auctions.

To receive our catalogues or to discuss the sale of your stamps contact

020 7836 8444
auctions@stanleygibbons.com

STANLEY GIBBONS AUCTIONS

@StanleyGibbons   /StanleyGibbonsGroup   @StanleyGe

Stanley Gibbons Stamp Catalogues

Commonwealth & British Empire Stamps 1840–1970 (124th edition, 2022)

King George VI (9th edition, 2018)

Commonwealth Country Catalogues

Australia & Dependencies (11th Edition, 2018)
Bangladesh, Pakistan & Sri Lanka (3rd edition, 2015)
Brunei, Malaysia & Singapore (5th edition, 2017)
Canada (7th edition, 2020)
Cyprus, Gibraltar & Malta (5th edition, 2019)
East Africa with Egypt & Sudan (4th edition, 2018)
Eastern Pacific (3rd edition, 2015)
Falkland Islands (8th edition, 2019)
Hong Kong (6th edition, 2018)
India (including Convention & Feudatory States) (5th edition, 2018)
Indian Ocean (4th edition, 2022)
Ireland (7th edition, 2019)
Leeward Islands (3rd edition, 2017)
New Zealand (6th edition, 2016)
Northern Caribbean, Bahamas & Bermuda (4th edition, 2016)
St Helena & Dependencies (6th edition, 2017)
West Africa (2nd edition, 2012)
Western Pacific (4th edition, 2017)
Windward Islands & Barbados (3rd edition, 2015)

Stamps of the World 2022

Volume 1	Abu Dhabi – Charkhari
Volume 2	Chile – Georgia
Volume 3	German Commands – Jasdan
Volume 4	Jersey – New Republic
Volume 5	New South Wales – Singapore
Volume 6	Sirmoor – Zululand

Great Britain Catalogues

2022 Collect British Stamps (73rd edition, 2022)
2022 Channel Islands & Isle of Man (31st edition, 2022)
2022 GB Concise (37th edition, 2022)

Great Britain Specialised

Volume 1	Queen Victoria, Part 1 Line-engraved and Embossed Issues (1st edition, 2020)
Volume 2	King Edward VII to King George VI (14th edition, 2015)
Volume 3	Queen Elizabeth II Pre-decimal issues (13th edition, 2019)
Volume 4	Queen Elizabeth II Decimal Definitive Issues – Part 1 (10th edition, 2008)
	Queen Elizabeth II Decimal Definitive Issues – Part 2 (10th edition, 2010)

Foreign Countries

Arabia (1st edition, 2016)
Austria and Hungary (8th Edition 2014)
Belgium & Luxembourg (1st edition, 2015)
China (12th edition, 2018)
Czech Republic and Slovakia (1st edition, 2017)
Denmark and Norway (1st edition, 2018)
Finland and Sweden (1st edition, 2017)
France, Andorra and Monaco (1st edition, 2015)
French Colonies (1st edition, 2016)
Germany (12th edition, 2018)
Italy and Colonies (1st edition, 2022)
Middle East (1st Edition, 2018)
Netherlands & Colonies (1st edition, 2017)
North East Africa (2nd edition 2017)
Poland (1st edition, 2015)
Portugal (1st edition, 2020)
Southern Balkans (1st edition, 2019)
Spain and Colonies (1st edition, 2019)
Switzerland (1st edition, 2019)
United States of America (8th edition, 2015)

We have catalogues to suit every aspect of stamp collecting

Our catalogues cover stamps issued from across the globe - from the Penny Black to the latest issues. Whether you're a specialist in a certain reign or a thematic collector, we should have something to suit your needs. All catalogues include the famous SG numbering system, making it as easy as possible to find the stamp you're looking for.

STANLEY GIBBONS
THE HOME OF STAMP COLLECTING

STANLEY GIBBONS | 399 Strand | London | WC2R 0LX
www.stanleygibbons.com

@StanleyGibbons   /StanleyGibbonsGroup   @StanleyGibbons

MAGNIFIERS

LEFT TO RIGHT

2x Dome LED Magnifier
RDLM2X
£32.95

10x Jewellers Loupe
RJLM10X
£17.45

8x LED Inspection Stand Magnifier
RISM8X
£34.95

6x Linen Tester
RLTM6X
£17.45

Digital Catalogues

Access generations of philatelic expertise at the touch of a finger when using Stanley Gibbons digital catalogues.

We now produce a large selection of catalogues, catering to the wide spectrum of collectors, and covering all levels of philatelic knowledge. We also produce digital versions of many of our catalogues, which can be purchased and accessed anywhere in the world using our web and mobile apps, available on Apple and Android devices.

Why Go Digital?

- Access your favourite Stanley Gibbons catalogues, instantly, wherever you go, online via your desktop computer or offline using our app on your tablet or mobile phone.
- Make large savings compared to the price of hard copies.
- Navigate quickly with hyperlinked contents pages.
- Search for information easily using the search bar.
- Bookmark your favourite pages.
- Use the zoom magnifier to get a closer look.
- All your digital catalogue titles can be accessed from the Digital Catalogues tab when logged into My Account.

Please note, you must register an account in order to access digital catalogues.

The app can be downloaded from the Apple and Android stores.

Why not buy a digital copy?
2022 Great Britain Concise, 37th Edition

2022
Italy and Colonies
1st Edition

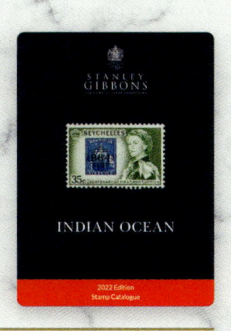

2022
Indian Ocean
4th Edition

Available at www.stanleygibbons.com/publishing/digital-catalogues.

ATTENTION OWNERS OF LARGE/ VALUABLE COLLECTIONS –

from / respond to: **Andrew McGavin**

Are You THINKING of SELLING?

This is How The Stamp Trade Works

Philatelic Expert Lets You into his *Selling Secrets* so you can benefit from a *totally different* (and New) Selling Experience

1 **If You want to learn** how the stamp trade works, please read on… When I was 15, I did. I wondered if there was some secret source of supply? So, I bought my 1st stamp mixture, (wholesale I thought), broke it into 50 smaller units, advertised it in Stamp Magazine 'Classifieds', and waited for the orders to roll in… I'm still waiting, 51 years later !...

Wrong Offer ✗   *Wrong Price* ✗   *Wrong Place* ✗
(naïve seller) ✓ = ☹ *me but I was only 15 at the time!*

ANDREW PROMOTING PHILATELY ON THE ALAN TITCHMARSH SHOW ITV

About The Author ▶ Andrew found his Father's stamps at the age of 10. A year later at Senior School he immediately joined the School Stamp Club. He 'specialised'(!) in British, but soon was interested in Queen Victoria which he could not afford. The 2nd to last boy wearing short trousers in his school year, he religiously bought Post Office New Issues on Tuesdays with his pocket money. He soon found that he enjoyed swapping / trading stamps as much as collecting them. Aged 19, eschewing University he quickly found a philatelic career in London, leading to creating his own companies in stamps. Andrew has authored many internationally published Stamp 'Tips' articles, appearing on Local Radio and National TV promoting Philately with Alan Titchmarsh. Andrew's area of expertise is unusual – in so far as his grounding in collecting and wide philatelic knowledge has given him a deep understanding of Philately. He has studied Philately for the past 51 years, in combination with Commerce and Marketing Expertise, enabling him to create synergies in 'lifetime' interlinked Stamp Selling Systems, selling unit-priced stamps through to handling collections & Rarities up to £700,000 each. Today Andrew is fortunate to be co-owner with his Wife, of Universal Philatelic Auctions (aka UPA) – the Largest No Buyer's Premium Reducing-Estimate System Stamp Auction in the World, creating records selling stamps to 2,261 different bidders from 54 different countries 'in his international auctions. Andrew stopped collecting stamps aged 18 reasoning that his enjoyment of stamps would be in handling them and selling them… He loves working in stamps and looks forward to each philatelic day

REQUEST MY 'TOP TIPS OF THE TRADE' FREE BOOKLET

2 **Three years later,** attending my first public stamp auctions I wondered how some bidders seemed to buy everything, paying the highest price? It didn't occur to me that they were probably Auction Bidding Agents, paid by absent (dealer) bidders to represent them. I wondered why two collectors sitting side by side muttered to each other **"he's a dealer"** as if that justified him paying the highest price…

…but did it really? What was the real reason? How could a Dealer pay a higher price than a Collector? It doesn't make sense, does it? Collectors are customers. Customers usually pay the highest price, unless… for a Collector, this was…

Wrong Presentation ✗   *Wrong Place* ✗
therefore Wrong Price ✗

3 **Fast-forward 48 years later** to a British Empire collection, lot #1 in an International Stamp Auction – Estimated at £3,000, but we were the highest bidder at £21,000 – **YES** – some 7×higher. Including Buyer's Premium in the extraordinary sum of £4,788 we actually paid GBP£25,788= upon a £3,000 estimate… **however,** we broke it down into sets, singles, mini-collections etc. We made a profit. Some might say it found its price. Others may say:

Wrong Estimate ✗ *Wrong Presentation* ✗
Wrong Structure ✗ *Wrong Protection of Price* ✗

– Lucky for the seller that 2 well-heeled bidders saw the potential value that day or it could have been given away… the seller could easily have lost out couldn't he? or she?

So, by un-peeling the layers of obfuscation, hopefully we can all agree:
**The Secret is Simple –
it's ALL ABOUT : TIMING**

Plus the 3 Philatelic 'P's –
Presentation ✔ Place ✔ and Price ✔

4 **Understanding the problem…** always remember the car trade ha their own little 'bible' – *Glass's Guide* I've no idea, I've not even looked – i this internet-dominated world, it ma even have disappeared. Well, ther was an insider Stamp Trade publicatio for Stamp Dealers called *"The Stam Wholesaler"*. There was nothing tha special about it – and you would not hav learnt much or found massively reduce prices by subscribing then – **BUT** – was a forum, a paper focal point, a las 'bastion' in this on-line transparent wor that we inhabit… whereby dealers (an auctioneers) can try and communicat with each other. I published my ow articles there…

More recently in print, I di cussed the outcome of my 10 year simple research, asking dealers an auctioneers 'what is your bigge problem?'

To a man, (why are we almost men), they replied – **"my bigge problem is stock, if I can get mo of the right stock I can sell it easily**

Strange that, nobody ever asked the same question back – because answer would have been entirely diffe ent (and I don't treat it as a problem) **I seek to satisfy more collector c ents than any other stamp auctio**

This is the reason why my comp ny has such massive advertising. Thi the reason why we spend up to 8% turnover – up to £200,000 per annu in marketing costs. (Most dealers do even sell £200K per annum).

5 **Why is that?** Because, as t world revolved **the Stan Market, imperceptibly Chang and incrementally – Massively**

So, although few will tell you th

it's clearly evident that the problem for most Sellers of Stamps today is no longer absent stock – but <u>absent collectors in the place they choose to sell their stamps in.</u> Simply put, other Dealers, Auctions, Stamp Fairs have not invested in marketing to have a strong Customer-core. To be fair, this is not true of all – but it is true of most – so that a former competitor had 800 bidders in a recent auction. In my most recent 18,933 lots UPA 80th Auction we had 1,893 different bidders from 51 different countries, 95% of whom were Collectors. Some other well-advertised auctions only have 200 bidders (a high percentage of whom are dealers – so that, essentially they are Dealer-dominated auctions) – so that when you sell through them – you're paying up to 18% (including VAT) seller's commission and the buyer is paying up to 25% **and** more in Buyer's Premium, credit card fees, on-line bidding fee, delivery and insurance etc… <u>AND all of that so that your stamps may be sold, wait for it – TO DEALERS and some collectors),</u> but Dealers, that naturally must make a profit to survive…

6 **Now, let's examine the cost implications – Example:** Your stamp collection sells in public auction for £800. Upon a 25% buyer's premium, the dealer pays £1,000 and could be more. He breaks it into £2,000+ selling price (much lower and he'll go out of business). The auction charges you a seller's commission of up to 18% (VAT included) upon the £800 sale price. This is GBP£144. Therefore you receive approaching £656 – which is approximately 33% of the dealer's £2,000+/- retail selling price - **BUT…** now that we have identified the problem…

Isn't the Solution Staring us Right in The Face ?

7 **Why Pay an Auction to Sell to Dealers: <u>Sell to Collectors</u> instead?** In our example with buyer's premium, sellers commission, lotting fees, extra credit card charges, VAT and even insurance - you're already being charged in different ways up to 40% of the selling price to sell, possibly or probably, <u>to the wrong person.</u>

Why not direct that 40% cost you're paying to sell to Collectors instead? <u>Sounds good</u>, so why hasn't is been done before ?

WE CAN SAFELY COLLECT YOUR STAMPS NOW

Contact UPA: 01451 861 111

UNSOLICITED TESTIMONIAL:

Dear Folk at UPA,

I've dealt with the public for 37 + years, and as both a consumer, and a businessman, I have created huge numbers of orders from all over the world from a complete range of suppliers from all aspects of our daily lives.

But I don't believe I have ever encountered such sensitivity, such kind thought, such understanding as I have with you in our initial meeting, our subsequent successful transaction, and now this.

I recall well the item you highlight, and realise that this one item has such colossal personal value, I could never part with it.

It has been an absolute pleasure dealing with yourself, and I am more than willing for you to use this e-mail as commendation to others who may be thinking of disposing of their collection.

Many, many thanks for a memorable experience, and I will try to emulate your thought and care in my own business sphere.

Yours sincerely
D. E. B. Bath, UK

8 **Truth is,** it Has been done before…Sometimes the 'old' ways are the best ways aren't they? But in today's enthusiasm to obscure the obvious so that money may be taken, almost surreptitiously, in numerous different ways, (without us apparently noticing until we see the cheque in our pocket) – the transparent 'seller pays' has been deliberately 'obscured' – so much so that, **amazingly,** the latest 2017 European Auction Selling Legislation just introduced – now requires auctions that charge 'buyer's premiums' <u>to warn the buyer in advance.</u> Just imagine going into the petrol station, and being warned that the price you're paying to put fuel in you tank is not the real price, you have to pay a premium! Obviously, there would be an uproar…

9 **How can you cut out the middleman and sell to Collectors instead?** Well, I can think of two ways. 1). **DIY** - Do It Yourself selling on eBay. That may be fine for lower grade material – but, would you risk auctioning relatively unprotected rare material on eBay ? We don't and we're professionals, so we should know what we're doing. Or 2). Cut out the extra middle-man. **Use my company UPA, which reaches collectors instead.** Here's how it works: Continuing from our previous **Example**:

The auction sold your stamps to a dealer for £1,000 – but You received circa £656

UPA sells them to collectors for you for up to £2,000 – even after 40% commission you receive up to £1,200. Up to £544 more. Now that's amazing, isn't it?

10 **Sounds Good Andrew, but Can You 'Deliver'?** Obviously, nothing is as simple as that, and as we auction stamps to collectors some collections may 'break' to the example £2,000+/- but the stamps may be sold for more or less – especially as we reserve all lots at 20% below, (Estimate £2,000 = £1,600 reserve) and not everything sells first or even 2nd time so prices may come down… Naturally, it's not that straightforward for a dealer either – he may sell at a discount to 'move' stock **OR**, like many dealers he may be sitting on the same unsold stamps, that you see time and time again, in dealer's stocks years later and still at the same unattractive prices… So, I think it is more reasonable for you to expect up to 36% to 50% more, indirectly or directly via my **Collector's Secret Weapon:** Universal Philatelic Auctions, which moves material more quickly, by incrementally reducing estimate (and reserve) price in a structured selling system…

Request Your Next FREE Catalogue NOW

UNIVERSAL PHILATELIC AUCTIONS
4 The Old Coalyard, West End, Northleach, Glos. GL54 3HE UK
Tel: 01451 861111 • Fax: 01451 861297
www.upastampauctions.co.uk • info@upastampauctions.co.uk

ATTENTION OWNERS OF LARGE/ VALUABLE COLLECTIONS

11 **Q.) What is the Collector's 'Secret Weapon'?**

A.) It's called the Unique UPA Reducing Estimate System...

This is a rather long explanation, I don't want to bore you, but 20 years ago, when my wife and I set up Universal Philatelic Auctions I detected that the stamp trade's biggest problem then was not what sold – **but what didn't sell**... So, because I didn't want to try to keep on offering the same either unsaleable or overpriced stock I created the unique UPA Reducing Estimate (and reserve) Selling System. Simply put, if a lot doesn't sell in the 1st auction we reduce the estimate (and reserve) by 11% and unlike other dealers and auctions **WE TELL YOU – 'US'** = once unsold. If unsold after the following auction we **reduce by a further 12%** and **WE TELL YOU 'US2'**, if unsold after a 3rd UPA auction we reduce by a further 13% and **WE TELL YOU 'US3'** and so on till the lot finds its price, is sold or virtually given away...

12 Any Scientist will tell you that combinations of ingredients can produce powerful results. So we created the unique combination of my UPA Reducing Estimate System, married (in stone), with UPA's fair 'NO BUYER'S Premium' policy, PLUS each lot carries my total 'no quibble' guarantee – this formula is the reason why within the span of 4 auctions (one year)... 90%-95% of lots broken from a collection have sold. This Unique Philatelic Selling System **Formula** is the reason why we are the largest stamp auction in the UK today with more than 2,250 different regular bidders.

In Hindsight Dealers warned me 20 years ago that my idea wouldn't work. 20 years later I think I've proven that it does. (Reader: Please Request a complimentary UPA catalogue – using the contact details further below)

13 **OK, Cut to the Chase Andrew, what's the offer?** All of my Selling Systems are based upon **selling to Collectors Globally**, so that 95% of stamps sold by UPA are sold directly to Collectors. If you wish to benefit by up to 50% or more, depending upon your circumstance and type of material, by cutting out the middleman – then this offer may be for you. Generally 'time' is the enemy in our lives, and for most dealers not being able to sell stock. Now is the time to let 'time' do the 'heavy-lifting' and consider making 'time' work for you, so that at UPA you can make time your friend.

14 **AND the SMALL PRINT?** Some lots are too small in value for us to offer this system. Other lots may not be suited to selling in this manner (e.g. surplus mint British decimal stamps best used for postage) – especially if the market is heavily compromised by stock overhang in specific areas. Some Collectors will not wish to use time and systems to leverage price, others will want to agree a specific price and know that they are paid precisely this amount. No client is treated like a number and no client is forced like a square peg into a round hole.

15 **OK, What Do I Do Next?**

a). You contact UPA to discuss with Andrew or a highly-qualified Auction Valuer/Describer what you have to dispose of and your options bearing in mind your specific interests / requirements

b). If you wish, get a 2nd opinion, but investigate what type of auction / dealer you are dealing with. Is it a Dealer's auction with relatively few collectors? Can you see where / how the Dealer sells? If you can't easily see any pricelists or high quality selling catalogues – that Dealer may sell your stamps to other dealers...

c). Finally you ask U P A to collect your stamps, insure in transit for an estimated replacement retail value...

16 **What Happens then?** A member of my Team telephones/e-mails you to confirm safe receipt. 'Overnight' valuations, unless simple, are rare. Valuing stamp collections that have taken tens of years to create takes time. Depending upon your priorities / timescale I, or an experienced member of my Team will contact you to discuss your requirements and the options available to you for the sale of your collection. Provided only that you feel well-informed and comfortable do we agree strategy

17 **How Strong is the Stamp and Cover Market?** Everybody knows that the strongest areas are GB and British Empire. Post-Independence / QEII material sells but if hinged at considerable discount. Mint hinged material pre 1952 is regarded as the industry 'norm' and therefore desirable – but genuine never-hinged commands a premium. Europe sells but at reduced levels, Americas is good, as generally is Asia but the 'heat' has come off China which is still good – and Russia which can still be good. East Europe is weaker. Overall, Rarities throughout can command their own price levels and real Postal History has good demand.

18 **What Should I Do Next?** Discuss your collection with U P A. Contact Andrew or an experienced member of his Team now...

19 **Guarantee: I want You to be absolutely Sure** So if You're not sure we'll transport and return your stamps for FREE up to £200 in actual shipping cost at our expense. It sounds generous (and it is) but it's far less than the cost of driving 100+ miles each way and 3 to 6 hours in your home valuing your stamps

20 **My Double Cast Iron Guarantee:** We can do better job valuing your stamps in our office than in your home. If you don't agree I'll pay you an extra £50 for you to pay somebody trusted to open the boxes and put your albums back in the same place, on the shelf they came from.

21 **Act NOW: Contact Andrew**

or an experienced member of his Team using the on-line selling form at our website, by fax, telephone or by mail. We'll work harder for you not to regret the decision to sell all or part of your collection...

Andrew

Andrew McGavin, Philatelic Expert,
Author, Managing Director
Universal Philatelic Auctions UPA

UNIVERSAL PHILATELIC AUCTIONS GBCon22
4 The Old Coalyard, West End, Northleach, Glos. GL54 3HE UK
Tel: 01451 861111 • Fax: 01451 861297
www.upastampauctions.co.uk • info@upastampauctions.co.uk